Putty

From Tel-el-Kebir to Cambrai:
The Life and Letters of Lieutenant General Sir William Pulteney
1861-1941

Anthony Leask

Helion & Company Limited

Helion & Company Limited
26 Willow Road
Solihull
West Midlands
B91 1UE
England
Tel. 0121 705 3393
Fax 0121 711 4075
Email: info@helion.co.uk
Website: www.helion.co.uk
Twitter: @helionbooks
Visit our blog http://blog.helion.co.uk/

Published by Helion & Company 2015

Designed and typeset by Bookcraft Ltd, Stroud, Gloucestershire
Cover designed by Paul Hewitt, Battlefield Design (www.battlefield-design.co.uk)
Printed by Gutenberg Press Limited, Tarxien, Malta

Cover: 12th Division attacking at the Battle of Cambrai 20 November 1917 by
David Pentland. Inset on front cover: Sir William Pulteney Pulteney by
Philip Alexius de Laszlo oil on canvas, 1917. (© National Portrait Gallery, London)

ISBN 978-1-910294-95-6

British Library Cataloguing-in-Publication Data.
A catalogue record for this book is available from the British Library.

For details of other military history titles published by Helion & Company Limited contact
the above address, or visit our website: http://www.helion.co.uk.

We always welcome receiving book proposals from prospective authors.

Contents

List of Illustrations

List of Maps

Foreword

Most Australians, and many beyond Australia, have heard of Sir John Monash. In June 1918, having headed a brigade at Gallipoli and a division in France, Monash was appointed to command the Australian Corps in the last stages of the war. By the time the fighting ended in November, this civil engineer of German-Jewish descent had exercised active corps command for just five months. By contrast, few Britons, possibly even few British military historians, have heard of Sir William Pulteney. An Etonian, he was commissioned into the Scots Guards in 1881 and for much of his career led the socially distinguished and exclusive existence of a late Victorian officer serving close to the crown. In September 1914 he took command of III British Corps on its formation. He led it on the western front for the next 42 months, through the battles of the Somme in 1916 and Cambrai in 1917. By the time he gave up the corps, in February 1918, he had become the longest serving corps commander of the British Expeditionary Force. Yet almost uniquely among the senior British officers of the First World War (certainly of his length of service) there has been no proper account of his life until now.

No doubt that deficit might have been put right if 'Putty' had left a readily accessible and unified collection of papers. He did not. In their absence, innuendo, second-hand reports and isolated comments have had to do duty for rigorous archival research. Anthony Leask has at last put Pulteney centre stage. His diligence has been exemplary; he has discovered letters in others' archives, and rigorously prioritised primary sources over later judgements and anecdotal evidence. Above all, he has placed those three and a half years in France in the context of the man's life as a whole, so putting Pulteney's moment of greatest responsibility in the context of his entire career, and of his other interests and preoccupations.

This book is neither a defence nor an attack on British generalship. Through scrupulous objectivity, Anthony Leask invites his readers to make up their own minds. Pulteney, because he had secured his commission via the militia, did not attend the Royal Military College at Sandhurst, and he was selected for corps command despite never having passed through the Staff College at Camberley. That lack of formal professional training, characteristic of a twentieth-century commander, precludes him from being an archetypical First World War general. In his excoriating attacks on British high command penned in the 1930s Basil Liddell Hart argued that the British army had gone wrong because it had tried to be like that of the Germans. The problem was not one of too little attention to the creation of a general staff, but too much.

Pulteney was not a trained staff officer, but nor was the original commander of the British Expeditionary Force, Sir John French, and nor were almost all the successful commanders of the nineteenth century reaching back to Wellington. Furthermore, when the First World War broke out, Britain, uniquely of the original belligerents, had no properly established corps headquarters. For other armies, the corps was the level at which the joint command of all three arms, cavalry, infantry and artillery, might be exercised, and the units allocated to each corps in peace time were the basis of its expansion and maintenance in war time. Before the war the British army had formed two corps headquarters for the purposes of exercises and manoeuvres, and the officers who had had that experience staffed the two original corps which made up the British Expeditionary Force sent to France. Sir Douglas Haig led I Corps, and Sir James Grierson II Corps. Grierson's premature death meant that he was replaced by Sir Horace Smith-Dorrien, who went on to become for many the hero of the retreat from Mons. However, it is worth recalling that Pulteney was chosen to lead III Corps before Smith-Dorrien was selected for II Corps, and that in May 1915 Smith-Dorrien was dismissed from what was by then an army command and never held operational authority again.

In 1914 the staff of III Corps, unlike those of the first two, had to be improvised. While French and his successor, Douglas Haig, sacked other generals, they retained Pulteney. Part of the problem with assessing corps commanders in the British army is that the onset of trench warfare drove the exercise of senior unit command at the tactical and operational level down to the division, leaving the corps, according to Aylmer Haldane, who was himself to exercise corps command, as a kind of post office. Divisions established firm identities, but they were rotated in and out of corps. As a result the latter were in some respects distanced from those under their authority and struggled to establish close relationships.

On 4 December 1917, after the German counter-attack at Cambrai, Haig saw Pulteney. He thought he looked tired and anxious. And so might anybody who had been as long at the front in senior command as Putty had by then. Pulteney was sent home ten weeks later, on 16 February 1918. Pulteney may have been exhausted, but there is another possible dimension to his departure. Two other corps commanders, Sir Thomas Snow and Sir Charles Woollcombe, were removed either side of Pulteney. After the 3rd battle of Ypres had ended in the mud of Passchendaele, Haig's own position was itself under threat. He survived but his Director of Military Intelligence, Sir John Charteris, and the British Expeditionary Force's Chief of Staff, Sir Launcelot Kiggell, were ousted that same winter. Haig's powers were being cut down to size, not least by the departure of those, like Pulteney, with whom he had served longest.

Anthony Leask leaves both judgement and speculation to his readers, but does so by giving them the evidence on which to found those opinions. Himself both a general and the son of a general, he puts the case for reconsidering Pulteney's career and his reputation with circumspection and without special pleading. He rigorously rejects the immediate and superficial, refusing to take things at their face value without proper consideration. We are all in his debt, and so too should be the shade of 'Putty' himself.

Professor Sir Hew Strachan

Acknowledgements

Allen, Lady Allen
Annick, Madame Henry Annick, Madame le Maire Templeux-la-Fosse
Bailey, Frances Bailey, Curator National Trust NI
Bailey, Matthew Bailey, Assistant Manager Rights and Images, National Portrait Gallery
Baker, Lieutenant Colonel Mark Baker and Carol Mason (Archivist) RH Chelsea
Balfour, Hew Balfour
Barker-McCardle, Jim Barker-McCardle previously Chief Constable of Essex
Barne, Colonel NML Barne (Miles Barne's diary)
Barnes, Colonel Ian Barnes, LSH
Beauvais, Jean-Louis de Beauvais, Secretaire de Maire Templeux-la-Fosse
Beckett, Ian Beckett, Professor of Military History University of Kent
Bellevue, Le Bellevue Bailleul
Boileau, Colonel John Boileau, LSH
Bourke, Lorraine Bourke PRONI
Bourne, Dr John Bourne, Hon Professor of First World War Studies, University of Wolverhampton
Bowden, Richard Bowden, Archivist Portman Estate
Bowles, Mr and Mrs Bowles, Ashley Court
Brooke, Sir Francis Brooke Bt
Bush, Jacky Bush, Netherbury Church
Campbell, Dr David Campbell
Carter, Robin Carter in Canada
Cator, Alby Cator
Cator, Kit Cator
Chamberlain, Max Chamberlain, VMR
Chamberlain, Oliver Chamberlain, descendant of Alice Pulteney
Churchill, Michael Churchill, Cheam School
Clark, Miss Pamela Clark, Royal Archives
Clarke, Mrs Laura, Collections Administrator Eton College
Cornet, Mr Patrick Cornet, Historian Hénencourt
Courcy, Anne de Courcy
Cross, Reverend Cross, St Martin's Church Ryarsh
Crossley, Colonel Gordon Crossley, FGH
Curthoys, Judith Curthoys, Archivist Christ Church College Oxford
Cuthbert, Mr and Mrs Aidan Cuthbert

Denison-Smith, Lieutenant General Sir Anthony Denison-Smith
Dennison-Smith, Dr David Dennison-Smith
Dillard, Peggy L Dillard Director Woodrow Wilson Presidential Library
Durham, Earl of Durham (and archivist Hester Borron)
Durieux, Francois Durieux, Maire Beauquesne
Evans, Paul Evans, Librarian and Archivist Royal Artillery Museum
Fergusson, Sir Charles Fergusson Bt, grandson of GOC 5th Division
Fergusson, Mr Adam Fergusson, grandson of GOC 5th Division
Fletcher, David Fletcher, and Stuart Wheeler Historians Tank Museum
Fothringham, Thomas Steuart Fothringham
Gallant, Ros Gallant, Ashley
Gorman, LSgt Kevin Gorman, Scots Guards Archives
Gorczynski, Philippe Gorczynski, Tank Deborah
Gordon, Tom Gordon, Royal Scots Museum
Graham, Lieutenant General Sir Peter Graham
Grange, Henry-Louis de La Grange
Hayley, Aidan Hayley assistant archivist Chatsworth
Hamilton, Lord Hamilton of Dalzell, descendant of ADC
Harrison, Reverend Rodney and Mrs Jenny Harrison
Hatfield, Mrs Penny Hatfield, Archivist Eton College
Henderson, Dr Diana Henderson, Director Scots at War Trust
Heneage, Christopher Heneage, Hainton Hall
Hindlip, Lord Hindlip
Hopkins, Clare Hopkins, Archivist Trinity College Oxford
Hudson, Julia Hudson
Hughes Rev Sally Hughes, St Mary the Virgin Ashley
Jacobs, Roger Jacobs (Victorian Carriages)
Jameson, Kristin Jameson, Tourin Co Waterford
Jenkins, Stanley Jenkins, Soldiers of Oxfordshire Trust
Jones, Simon Jones, Historian La Boiselle Project
Kennedy, Comdt Padraic Kennedy OIC Military Archives ROI
Kinsella-Bevan, Colonel and Mrs Kinsella-Bevan (grand-niece of Jessie)
Lascelles, Mr Rupert Lascelles, grandson of Beatrice Pulteney/Lascelles
Lauritzen, Lady Rose
Leakey, Lieutenant General David Leakey, Black Rod
Lee, Pamela Lee, Churchwarden Birchanger
Linlithgow, Marquess of Linlithgow, grandson of ADC
Lloyd, Janine Lloyd, Household Cavalry Museum and Archives
McIntosh, Rob McIntosh Curator Archives and Library Army Medical Services Museum
McMicking, Mrs Belinda McMicking (grand-daughter of Alice Pulteney/Boyle)
McNorgan, Major Mike McNorgan, FGH
Massie, Dr Alastair Massie, NAM
Milne, Lord George Milne, grandson of Field Marshal
Molyneux, Mr Ted Molyneux, Curator National Rifle Assocation Museum
Montgomery, Ian Montgomery, PRONI

Morris, Martin Morris, Archivist Co Longford
Motum, Lieutenant Colonel Mike Motum and Debbie Young, The Rifles (Taunton)
Napier, Colonel Gerald Napier late Royal Engineers
Newton, Fr Barrie Newton, Church of the Annunciation Bryanston Street
Nowlan, General Paddy Nowlan, President Irish Military History Society
Orgill, Andrew, Librarian RMA Sandhurst
Patterson, Kerry Patterson and Barrie Duncan, Asst Mus Offrs S Lanarkshire
Platt, Lance Sergeant Platt, Scots Guards Archives
Porter, Lauren Porter, Print Room, Royal Collection
Prior, David Prior Assistant Keeper to Records Parliamentary Archives
Pulteney, Mr Clive Pulteney
Rhodes, Mrs Elizabeth Rhodes, Lord Lyon's Office
Richold, Margaret Richold, Ashley
Riordan, Michael Riordan Archivist Queen's College Oxford
Roberts, Andrew Roberts in Uganda
Rowe, Dr Michael Rowe, Bath
Ruggles-Brise, Sir Timothy Ruggles-Brise Bt
Scott, Brough Scott, grandson of Seely Comd Canadian Cavalry Brigade
Screene, Lorraine Screene, Archivist QMUL
Shutlak, Garry Shutlak Nova Scotia Archives
Siller, Mrs Brenda Siller (photograph of male staff at Ashley Court c1871)
Spencer, Lieutenant Colonel Richard Spencer
Steinhart, Edward I Steinhart, author
Stevenson, Val Stevenson
Strachan, Professor Sir Hew Strachan, All Souls College Oxford
Sturgis, Miss Ann Sturgis (grand-daughter of Captain HR Sturgis Rifle Brigade)
Swaney, Mrs Ros Swaney, Ashley
Taylor, Simon Taylor RMA Sandhurst
Tearle, Suzanne Tearle
Thomson, Major Bill Thomson, Secretary AFA
Trevorrow, Mrs Eve Trevorrow, great-niece of Jessie
Tubby, Carol Tubby, Manager Hargrave House
Tumusiime, James Tumusiime, Fountain Publishers Uganda
Viggers, Lieutenant General Sir Freddie Viggers, Black Rod
Warren, Sir David Warren, previously HMA Tokyo
Wilson, Christopher Wilson in Uganda
Winn, Nigel Winn, Crowborough Historical Society
Woolmore, Bill Woolmore, VMR
Wright, Colonel Peter Wright, Defence Advisor Kampala
Yaxley, David Yaxley, Archivist Houghton Hall

My thanks to them and many others who have helped with the research and production of this book

Author's Note

Pulteney's letters have been included without significant editing; any lack of punctuation is his.

Spellings sometimes vary with different sources; in Uganda this may well be because the words are spelled phonetically and/or are from different languages.

After the name of each person is a footnote about them so that the reader can judge their significance in Pulteney's life ie. same age, school, regiment etc. This is repeated, although sometimes shortened, if the name has not occurred for some time.

Grid references are included only where absolutely necessary. However, the place should be identifiable without a map from the other information.

List of Abbreviations

General

AAG	Assistant Adjutant General
ADC	Aide de Camp
ADOS	Assistant Director Ordnance Services
ADS	Advanced Dressing Station
ADVS	Assistant Director Veterinary Services
AFA	Army Football Association
AG	Adjutant General
AQMG	Assistant Quarter Master General
APS	Assistant Private Secretary
Bde	Brigade
BEF	British Expeditionary Force
BGGS	Brigadier General, General Staff
BM	Brigade Major
Bn	Battalion
Bty	Battery
CB	Counter Battery/Bombardment
CCS	Casualty Clearing Station
CE	Chief Engineer
CGS	Chief of the General Staff
CIGS	Chief of the Imperial General Staff
CinC	Commander in Chief
Comd	Commander
CO	Commanding Officer
Coy	Company
CRA	Commander Royal Artillery
CRS	Corps Rest Station
DA&QMG	Deputy Adjutant and Quartermaster General
DAA&QMG	Deputy Assistant Adjutant and Quartermaster General
DDIWT	Deputy Director Internal Water Transport
DDMS	Deputy Director Medical Services
Det	Detachment
DR	Despatch Rider

Fd	Field
FGCM	Field General Court Martial
Flt	Flight
Gen Hosp	General Hospital
GHQ	General Headquarters
GHR	General Headquarters Rear
GOC	General Officer Commanding
GS	General Staff
GSO	General Staff Officer
HAG	Heavy Artillery Group
HE	High Explosive
How	Howitzer
Hy	Heavy
IG	Inspector General/Irish Guards
IO	Intelligence Officer
Intsum	Intelligence Summary
KB	Kite Balloon
LO	Liaison Officer
LP	Listening Post
LVG	Luftverkehrsgesellschaft (aeroplane)
MAC	Motor Ambulance Convoy
MDS	Main Dressing Station
MG	Machine-Gun
MGO	Master General of the Ordnance
MI	Mounted Infantry
MMG	Motor Machine-Gun
MO	Medical Officer
MS	Military Secretary
OKH	Oberste Heeresleitung (German Supreme HQ)
OpO	Operation Order
Opsum	Operational Summary
OR	Other Rank
OTC	Officer Training Corps
Pdr/pr	Pounder
POW	Prisoner of War
psc	Passed Staff College
QAIMNS	Queen Alexandra's Imperial Military Nursing Service
QMG	Quartermaster General
RAMC	Royal Army Medical Corps
RE	Royal Engineers
RFA	Royal Field Artillery
RFC	Royal Flying Corps
RGA	Royal Garrison Artillery
Sadr	Sadler
SB	Stretcher Bearer

SC	Staff Captain
SMTO	Senior Mechanical Transport Officer
Sqn	Squadron
TM	Trench Mortar
WO	War Office

Regiments

A&SH	Argyll and Sutherland Highlanders
Bedford	Bedfordshire Regiment
Berks	Berkshire Regiment
Border	Border Regiment
Buffs	East Kent Regiment (see also E Kent)
BW	Black Watch
Cameron(s)	Cameron Highlanders
Cameronians	Cameronians (Scottish Rifles)
Cheshire	Cheshire Regiment
CofG	Corps of Guides
Coldm Gds	Coldstream Guards
CY	Cheshire Yeomanry
Devon(s)	Devonshire Regiment
DCLI	Duke of Cornwall's Light Infantry
DLI	Durham Light Infantry
DLOY	Duke of Lancaster's Own Yeomanry
Dorset	Dorset Regiment
DOW	Duke of Wellington's Regiment
E Kent(s)	East Kent Regiment (Buffs)
E Lancs	East Lancashire Regiment
E Surrey(s)	East Surrey Regiment
E Yorks	East Yorkshire Regiment
Essex	Essex Regiment
FGH	Fort Garry Horse
GH	Green Howards (Yorkshire Regiment)
Glos	Gloucestershire Regiment
Gren Gds	Grenadier Guards
Hamps	Hampshire Regiment
HLI	Highland Light Infantry
IG	Irish Guards
IH	Irish Horse
ILH	Imperial Light Horse
Innis Fus	Inniskilling Fusiliers
IY	Imperial Yeomanry
KDG	King's Dragoon Guards
Kings	King's Liverpool Regiment
KOL	King's Own Lancashire Regiment

KOSB	King's Own Scottish Borderers
KOYLI	King's Own Yorkshire Light Infantry (see also YLI)
KRRC	King's Royal Rifle Corps
KSLI	King's Shropshire Light Infantry (see also SLI)
Leics	Leicestershire Regiment
Leinster	Leinster Regiment
Lincoln(s)	Lincolnshire Regiment
LF	Lancashire Fusiliers
LG	Life Guards
London	London Regiment
LSH	Lord Strathcona's Horse
Manchester(s)	Manchester Regiment
Middx	Middlesex Regiment
Monmouth	Monmouthshire Regiment
NF	Northumberland Fusiliers
NH	Northumberland Hussars
NIH	North Irish Horse
N Lancs	North Lancashire Regiment (Loyals)
Norfolk(s)	Norfolk Regiment
N Staffs	North Staffordshire Regiment
Northants	Northamptonshire Regiment
Notts & Derby	Nottinghamshire and Derbyshire Regiment (see also Sher For)
Ox H	Oxfordshire Hussars
Ox LI	Oxfordshire Light Infantry
Ox & Bucks	Oxfordshire and Buckinghamshire Light Infantry
Queens	Royal West Surrey Regiment
QWR	Queens Westminster Rifles
RB	Rifle Brigade
RDF	Royal Dublin Fusiliers
RF	Royal Fusiliers
RHG	Royal Horse Guards
R Irish Fus	Royal Irish Fusiliers
R Irish	Royal Irish Regiment
RIR	Royal Irish Rifles
RLR	Royal Lancaster Regiment (King's Own)
RMA	Royal Marine Artillery
RMF	Royal Munster Fusiliers
RS	Royal Scots
RSG	Royal Scots Greys
RSF	Royal Scots Fusiliers
RWF	Royal Welsh Fusiliers
RWK	Royal West Kents (see also W Kent)
Seaforth	Seaforth Highlanders
SG	Scots Guards
Sher For	Sherwood Foresters (see also Notts & Derby)

SLI	Shropshire Light Infantry
Som LI	Somerset Light Infantry
S Staffs	South Staffordshire Regiment
Suffolk	Suffolk Regiment
Sussex	Royal Sussex Regiment
SWB	South Wales Borderers
SY	Surrey Yeomanry
VCR	Natal Volunteer Composite Regiment
VMR	Victorian Mounted Rifles
WAMI	Western Australia Mounted Infantry
Warwick(s)	Warwickshire Regiment
Welch	Welch Regiment
W Kent(s)	West Kent Regiment (see also RWK)
W Surrey	Royal West Surrey Regiment (see also Queens)
WG	Welsh Guards
Wilts	Wiltshire Regiment
Worcs	Worcestershire Regiment
W Yorks	West Yorkshire Regiment
Y&L	York and Lancaster Regiment
6 DG	6th Dragoon Guards
3 H	3rd Hussars
4 H	4th Hussars
6 D	6th Dragoons
7 H	7th Hussars
8 H	8th Hussars
10 H	10th Hussars
12 L	12th Lancers
16 L	16th Lancers
19 H	19th Hussars
20 H	20th Hussars

Introduction

Lieutenant General Sir William Pulteney Pulteney (Putty)
GCVO KCB KCMG DSO

It is now one hundred years since the First World War, the Great War, the war that cost the United Kingdom alone nearly one million dead. Few families escaped losing a loved one, and many of those fathers, brothers, husbands who did return were different people, scarred physically and or mentally forever by the horrors that few could describe and most did not want to share.

The British Army had only six regular divisions at the outbreak of war: by the time it ended the army had expanded to over sixty front-line divisions, a tenfold increase. Only two men commanded the army in France during the war. Field Marshal Sir John French was Commander in Chief until 1915 when he was succeeded by Field Marshal Sir Douglas Haig. Between them and the divisions were two intermediate levels of command. The corps commanded a number of divisions, additional heavy artillery and other corps troops. Initially there were three corps but as the number of divisions increased the army level of command was introduced between GHQ and the corps.

Collectively the army and corps commanders have had a bad press, often focussed on the appalling loss of life, particularly in certain major battles of the war. Much has been written about them including many individual biographies. The essence of their responsibility was and still is very simple. A commander tells his subordinates what he wants them to do, gives them additional resources, and coordinates their actions if necessary. Coordination will always be needed if more than one organisation is involved in a task but this should not be seen as an opportunity for a commander to place unnecessary or unacceptable constraints on how his objective is to be achieved. Once given his orders, it was then up to each subordinate to plan his part and order his subordinates in a similar way. Orders could and were questioned either as to their feasibility or the allocation of resources. Failure to challenge unreasonable or impossible orders was a failure of leadership just as much then as it is today. Failure to consider such challenges is an equal failure. If an objective has to be taken or held within a wider mission and the operation has been well planned and executed, casualties and indeed significant numbers of casualties may still be inevitable. Of course major casualties may also be a consequence of an ill-conceived or unnecessary mission or one that is under-resourced, badly planned or badly executed but failure should not be assumed a consequence of incompetence.

This is the story of Lieutenant General Sir William Pulteney, one that has not been told before. This is remarkable if for no other reason than that he commanded III Corps in France for three and a half years without respite between 1914 and 1918. During this time his corps played a significant part in the major battles of the Marne, Aisne, Ypres, Somme and Cambrai. Other corps commanders were promoted, rested by a home posting, or sacked, but not him. It is not one story because to understand Pulteney, the corps commander, it is necessary to understand the man. This includes his origins and early life (1861 to 1881), his military service from 1881 to 1914, and his personal life. Each one of these could be the subject of a separate book. Most of the corps and army commanders were long married, fathers or grandfathers. Pulteney, however, married in 1917 just before the Battle of Cambrai, in which he was to play a major part, to a girl fifteen years younger than him.

Although little has been written about him, Pulteney has not escaped the criticisms of history. Some have argued that he was ignorant and uneducated because he left school early and received no formal military training. Furthermore they would say that he achieved what he did through the misuse of patronage. Then he has not escaped the criticisms of all generals, especially those in the First World War, in that he lived in comfort, well behind the lines, and out of touch. Finally, there are his perceived errors of judgement, that on occasions he was too cautious or too rash, and that he was responsible for tactical mistakes that resulted in failure and very high casualties. You the Reader will be able to judge.

This will not be easy because criticism is negative and pervasive, unless it is carefully scrutinised. Only by understanding the people and the circumstances can a criticism be considered fair or false. An understanding of Pulteney and the decisions he took or did not take will inevitably bring with it a wider understanding of those who had the responsibility to command large numbers of men in this war. My interest began with a visit to the Somme battlefield. Looking back from Ovillers you can see at a glance the task faced by 8th Division on 1 July 1916 and, in the cemetery, the heavy price they paid. Pulteney was the corps commander and a Scots Guardsman.

1

Reflection

The Story of my life, from year to year – the battles, sieges, fortunes that I have passed
Wm Shakespeare *Othello* Act 1 Sc 3

It was before six o'clock and still dark when Private George Hogbin woke Lieutenant General Sir William Pulteney, General Officer Commanding III Corps, widely known from his early school days and in the army as 'Putty'. Hogbin, the son of a Ramsgate butcher, had been his orderly since they came back from South Africa fourteen years earlier. The mug of tea that he brought that morning of 20 November 1917 was Putty's cue; it was one hour to Zero.

The last hours before every Zero hour are a time when a commander is alone, and the more senior the commander the more alone he is. Unable to influence events further, the temptation to seek out others has to be resisted since all have their own preparations to make. His plan is made and waits to be put to the test. Success or failure will be measured not just in the achievement of the mission given to him but in lives lost, of friend and enemy, and there is little more that he can do for several hours. It is time to put his trust in those under him; all he can do is wait, alone with his thoughts.

HQ III Corps was in Templeux-la-Fosse, before the war a prosperous farming village of more than 600 inhabitants but now a shattered waste land. Partly hidden in woods and below the ridge line the headquarters was well sited close to the Péronne to Cambrai road, the axis of their attack. Late the previous evening Putty would have had his last meeting with his principal staff officers, though there would have been little to discuss; then a quick word with his two ADCs about the arrangements for the morning before retiring to his own room. Sleep there might well have been but there would also be plenty of time for reflection.

He may well have reflected on the many previous Zero hours that he and his III Corps had faced together. In 1914, after the retreat, III Corps had fought on the left flank of the BEF in the battles of the Marne and Aisne. Then came relief by the French and the great left hook attacking the German right flank with the corps advancing to take Armentières.

For all of 1915 it held the line south of Armentières, in the flooded plain of the River Lys, while, at the same time, helping to build a new army by absorbing and training territorial and new army divisions. There were still many Zeros as III Corps played a part on the flanks of the offensives to the north at Ypres and to the south at Neuve Chapelle and Loos. Then, in 1916, it went south to play a key role in the battles of the Somme, battles of attrition against the enemy's fortress defences fought over four months and at a very high price; there had been many Zeros on the Somme. After it was over III Corps was moved further south in 1917, only to have to re-cross the River Somme and its canal to take Péronne and advance to the Hindenburg Line. By now it was becoming a different war, one of manoeuvre, mobility, initiative, and above all one that depended on the close and flexible integration of all the components of the corps – infantry, artillery, air and now tanks.

It had been a long and bloody road for III Corps and the job was still not done. Putty might well have pondered on those he had served under and their very different styles of leadership, styles that were often handicapped by the vastly expanded and still very inexperienced staffs that supported them. Static trench warfare encouraged such staffs to senseless bureaucracy. At one time 2nd Army required so many reports and returns on a myriad of subjects that its' staff was in danger of becoming the greater enemy. In 4th Army the very frequent conferences merely encouraged changes in the plan and the later changes often gave those who had to implement it insufficient time to make their own arrangements. Now was the test of 3rd Army's methods and practices. Tomorrow would tell.

He might well have reflected on those who had died in the three years. 6th Division was back in the corps for tomorrow's Zero, a very different division to the one he had commanded and got to know so well in the three years before the war. Both Scots Guards battalions, and he had commanded both, had lost so many officers and men that he had known personally that there had been few familiar faces when he presented the prizes at the 2nd Battalion's recent athletics meeting at Cartigny. Yet, as for so many soldiers, such thoughts could have been only fleeting. More likely he would have thought about his own Zero just a month earlier when he married Jessie Arnott, the woman he first met and fell in love with six years ago. It had taken a long time, perhaps too long, but at the Church of the Annunciation in Bryanston Square behind Marble Arch his brother, Arthur, had conducted the service, still the rector of Ashley where their father had been rector when they were born. Time, and tomorrow's Zero, would have prevented them marrying in Ireland, Jessie's home, or in Ashley. A quick visit to London, basing himself as usual at the Ritz, was all that could be arranged. It had been, of necessity, a small affair with just a few family and close friends.

For the last 22 years, since handing over as Adjutant 2nd Battalion Scots Guards and going on active service to Uganda in 1895, he had been in command of soldiers; company, battalion, brigade, division and now corps. Unlike many of his contemporaries there had been no spells on the staff or of training. Putty was comparatively well-off, enjoyed life, and his ability to relate to people of all backgrounds made him well-liked by those who knew him. But his close friends were in the main officers of the Scots Guards with whom he had served before 1895. Now, married, Jessie had become the most important person in his life and this night must have dominated all his thoughts. Maybe he wrote to her in the hours before Zero.

There would have been much to dwell on. The task itself could be stated very simply: to smash a hole in the German Hindenburg Line through which the Cavalry Corps could pass into the Cambrai plain, create havoc and roll up the German positions. And yet, as on the Somme, such a simple statement obscured the difficulties; there was much that could go wrong. Putty might have thought about the Hindenburg Line itself, not in fact a single line at all but a series of forti-fied lines in depth that drew heavily on all the German experience of defensive warfare gained over the past three years. An extra layer of defence was the St Quentin Canal, in itself a major obstacle. On III Corps front there were 1½ divisions facing the four of III Corps. Too often the German enemy had been underestimated. There would have been a passing temptation to dwell on the difficulties that lay ahead but Putty's experience would have resisted such doubts creeping in at this stage. Now was the time to demonstrate confidence that the job could be done.

He would have thought about his own men out there in the darkness waiting for their Zero. On a frontage of 4 miles and stretching back for many miles behind the front line, men of III Corps were making their last minute preparations, alone in the night with their own thoughts. The four divisions of the corps, 6th, 12th, 20th and 29th, the Corps Heavy Artillery and all the corps troops numbered over 100,000 men. Every house, wood and field was packed with men, horses and the materiel of war. Every road and track was alive with men and wagons moving slowly and patiently in both directions, but in the main forward. The complexity of this task alone, of assembling the corps for the battle, was a daunting one since it was being done in darkness and using three winding and narrow roads which were already beginning to break up under the heavy traffic.

This was a very different III Corps to that of 1914. Each division now had many more machine-guns as well as trench mortars of varying calibres to supplement its own artillery. But the greatest difference was the corps troops, now numbering as much as another division. The Corps Heavy Artillery with 171 guns had as its primary task counter-battery and the bombardment of headquarters and reserve positions; it now had the much improved technology to locate the enemy's guns which hitherto had been so difficult. In total III Corps now had 500 guns manned by 10,000 gunners for the battle ahead. They were to fire 150,000 rounds next day, compared with 70,000 on the first day of the Somme and this was a major logistical challenge.

Then there were the tanks; no longer a novelty but a capability whose potential had still to be fully realised and exploited. 256 were supporting III Corps, out there in its assembly positions. Getting them forward had posed numerous problems, as had maintaining them.

All were dependent on the numerous tasks to be carried out by the engineers: required to repair and operate the railways and tramways, to repair and keep open the roads, to bridge the St Quentin Canal, to lay smoke, to provide camouflaged assembly positions, and for a myriad of construction tasks not least the provision of water for men and horses.

The medical plan required particular attention, one in which Putty always took a special interest. Evacuation of the wounded had to be done against the logistical flow forward, mainly of ammunition, but engineer stores for consolidation and forage for horses both placed major demands on the few inadequate roads. The treatment and indeed survival of the wounded depended on the effective positioning of the various medical units, collecting sections and dressing stations, so that the wounded were correctly assessed and then treated at the most appropriate place.

More than one hundred corps troops units competed for the very small amount of real estate and space behind the divisions on the roads and tracks. Including the Cavalry Corps which was to be passed through III Corps more than one hundred thousand horses required hay and feed, water, and veterinary services. In such a confined space this was a planning exercise of mammoth proportions. Executing it in darkness over a short period of time required a level of attention to detail and a flexible approach to the unexpected rarely seen so far in this war. Further back on their airfields, the squadrons of the Royal Flying Corps that were to support III Corps that day also waited. Fully integrated into the planning, they would play a key role once daylight came. Reconnaissance sorties would provide vital information on the deployment of the enemy's reserves; artillery cooperation sorties provided the eyes of the artillery especially seeking out the enemy batteries not previously located, and close air support would help the attacking divisions forward by bombing and machine-gunning enemy strong points.

For all of this and probably throughout the night Putty would have spent much of the time, albeit possibly unconsciously, listening rather than in thought. This was to be the application of the principle of war 'surprise' on a grand scale. On previous occasions the preliminary bombardment, often sustained over several days, gave the enemy ample warning that an attack was imminent. His air reconnaissance would have provided confirmation of forward movement and assembly. This time all the preparations had been made covertly with most movement in darkness, camouflage had been used extensively, and the extra attacking divisions screened from enemy patrols. There would be no preliminary bombardment; total reliance was to be placed on the one avalanche of steel erupting at the given time – Zero. But the risk was high and it would have been in Putty's mind that, despite all the planning and all the careful preparation, it could be the Germans who provided the surprise. If their artillery caught the attacking divisions of III Corps concentrated in their assembly positions, his plans would be in disarray and the losses catastrophic. Such attacks as were still possible would fall easy prey to alerted machine-gun and mortar teams. The closer to Zero the greater would be the impact of a loss of surprise. As the hours and then the minutes passed Putty would not have been alone in listening and praying; all of III Corps would have been collectively holding their breath.

Looking out into the darkness of that November morning it seemed that fortune was already on their side. The dark and moonless night was compounded by a thick early ground mist which, although hindering observation, reporting and engagement of targets, would greatly increase the chance of surprise being achieved. The wind too would play its part in masking the noise, especially of the tanks. All was still silent. As Putty pulled on his breeches, then his highly polished leather boots, before finally putting on his jacket and sam browne, he would have been only too well aware the price of again underestimating the enemy; yet great was the prize for success.

With just a few minutes to go, much as an actor going on stage, he would have joined his staff. At precisely 6.20 am first the darkness was penetrated by the flashes of the guns of the corps and others to the north and south, then the ground shook as if struck by an earthquake. Surprise had been achieved and the III Corps' attack had begun. As darkness gave way to the first light of the morning Putty could now only await for the first reports to come. It was time for breakfast.

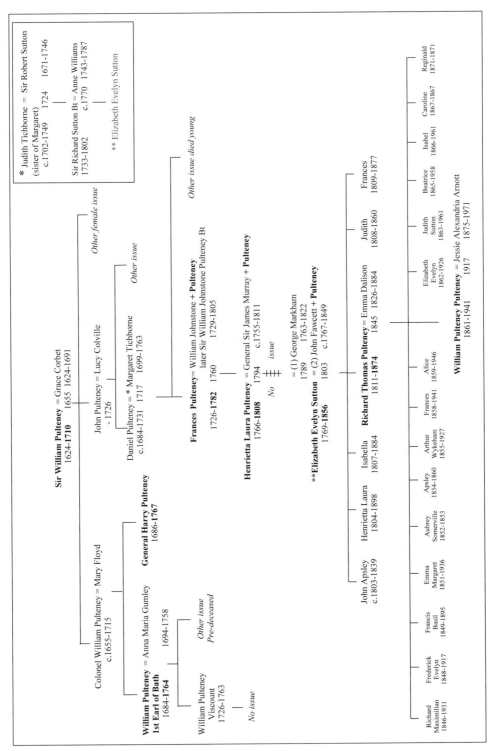

Putty's Pulteney inheritance.

2

The Pulteneys

The story of William Pulteney Pulteney or Putty really begins seven generations earlier with Sir William Pulteney (1624-1710) a descendant of the Pulteneys of Misterton in Leicestershire, a wealthy lawyer, married to Grace Corbet, and for some years MP for Westminster. They had two sons and one daughter – William (c1655-1715), John (died 1726) and Anne (1663-1746).[1] Colonel William was the older and married Mary Floyd; they also had two sons, William (1684-1764) created 1st Earl of Bath and Harry (1686-1767). The younger brother, John, was MP for Hastings; he married Lucy Colville and they had a son, Daniel.

The Earl of Bath, Secretary for War (1714-1717) and the Prime Minister for less than forty-eight hours in 1746, inherited considerable wealth and added to it substantially in his life time. He had two children both of whom predeceased him and when he died in 1764 his fortune passed under his will to his brother General Harry Pulteney, a bachelor. Harry had been commissioned into the Coldm Gds in 1703 and served with them until appointed to the Colonelcy of the 13th (Pulteney) Regiment in 1739. He was also an MP on three occasions. When he died, three years after William Earl of Bath, his fortune passed to Frances Johnstone, the daughter of his cousin Daniel Pulteney.

Daniel Pulteney (c1684-1731), himself a MP, married Margaret Tichborne but William Pulteney Pulteney, the subject of this story, was also descended from Judith Tichborne, Margaret's sister. Judith married first the Earl of Sunderland and then Sir Robert Sutton MP (1671-1746); his son, Sir Richard Sutton Bt MP (1733-1802), would have a daughter, Elizabeth Evelyn, and she would be William Pulteney Pulteney's paternal grandmother.

Meanwhile Daniel and Margaret Pulteney had four children, three sons all of whom died in early life and the one daughter, Frances (1726-1782). In 1760, at the age of thirty-four, she married William Johnstone (1729-1805)[2] who later inherited a baronetcy on the death of his brother in 1794. Before he inherited the baronetcy he had changed his name to Pulteney. But before this they had produced a daughter Henrietta Laura, known as Laura. So she was born a Johnstone although her name was changed to Pulteney when her father changed his name and they did not revert back when he inherited the baronetcy. Frances had inherited the Earl of Bath's fortune when he died in 1764 and the retention of the family name may have been

---

1   Married 2nd Duke of Cleveland.
2   Scottish lawyer and MP.

Lady Francis Pulteney, 1726-1782. (Lady Allen)

Sir William Johnstone Pulteney 5th Bt,
1729-1805. (Gainsborough Yale)

a condition of that inheritance. Johnstone used his wife's fortune and his business acumen to become one of the wealthiest people in England at that time.

Thus Laura Pulteney (1766-1808) was born the only child of parents with extraordinary wealth and influence; she inherited both and added to them substantially in her lifetime. On 26 July 1794 at Bath House in Piccadilly, her London home, she married her cousin General Sir James Murray (c1755-1811).[3] Murray later entered Parliament and was Secretary at War 1807-1809 in the 3rd Duke of Portland's Government. He too changed his name to Pulteney. Murray died as a result of an accident in 1811: he was out shooting on his Norfolk estate when he was blinded in one eye by a bursting powder flask and died of resulting complications. They had no children. Her father's influence and her great wealth were responsible for Laura receiving the titles of Baroness Bath in 1792 and later Countess of Bath in 1803, both in her own right. In her will she left her personal and disposable fortune to 'my friend and relation Elizabeth Evelyn Markham, eldest daughter of Sir Richard Sutton Bart of Norwood Park in the County of Nottingham, and the wife of the Reverend George Markham (1763-1822)[4] third son of William Markham, Archbishop of York'.

3   7th Bt; late R Irish.
4   Dean of York 1802-1822.

Henrietta Laura Pulteney Countess of Bath, 1766-1808. (Lady Allen)

General Sir James Murray Pulteney 7th Bt, c. 1755-1811. (Scottish National Portrait Gallery)

Elizabeth Evelyn Sutton (1769-1856), William Pulteney Pulteney's grandmother, had married Reverend George Markham in 1789 but in 1802/3 they were the subject of a much publicised divorce. An abstract from the Annual Register for 4 May 1802 states: 'A most affecting trial took place before the Sheriff of Middlesex and a special jury. It was brought by the Reverend Markham son of the Archbishop of York against a man of the name of Fawcett for criminal conversation with his wife. The plaintiff had been married to this lady in 1789 and at the period of the discovery of this adulterous intercourse had become the mother of 9 children. The defendant was a school fellow of the plaintiff who introduced him to his family as a friend. Some of the most respectable characters gave evidence to the harmony which had always subsisted between plaintiff and his wife. The damages were laid at £20,000 and the jury returned a verdict of £7,000. The most afflicting part of this melancholy event is that the adulterous intercourse existed upwards of 5 years before it was discovered. The defendant has fled to the Continent'. Although the abstract refers only to nine children this may be because Sarah, the tenth child, was born after 4 May 1802 and that Elizabeth Evelyn was pregnant with her at the time of the hearing. Apparently no-one questioned who the father was of the children born in 1802 and the five years before it.

Sometime afterwards Elizabeth Evelyn married her lover John Fawcett (1767-1849), William Pulteney Pulteney's grandfather. They had six children together after the divorce. Any child born before they married was not able to inherit under the terms of Laura's will, so a significant part of her fortune passed to their son Richard Thomas Pulteney, William Pulteney Pulteney's father. Elizabeth Evelyn lived with Henrietta Laura at Bath House while the divorce was going

Elizabeth Evelyn Pulteney, 1769-1856 (William's grandmother). (Sir William Beachey & J. R. Boyle)

John Fawcett Pulteney, c. 1767-1849. (William's grandfather). (Clive Pulteney)

through so it seems unlikely that Laura had overlooked any complication this might have caused when she made her will in 1794 and then later. However, it does seem strange that the older and only other son, John Apsley, did not also inherit directly under Laura's will: he died in 1839, aged 33, seventeen years before his mother, which may well have complicated matters further.

For the first few years after the divorce and certainly until Elizabeth Evelyn inherited under Laura's will in 1811 the Fawcetts lived in Lancashire where most of the remaining children were born. Sometime after 1813 Elizabeth Evelyn brought Northerwood House in Lyndhurst, Hampshire: the estate included farms and properties in Lyndhurst, Boldre, Milford and other parts of the county. Elizabeth Evelyn and John Fawcett and all the Fawcett children assumed the surname and arms of Pulteney by Royal Licence on 9 August 1813, a requirement under Laura's will. John died in 1849 and Elizabeth Evelyn remained at Northerwood House until she too died on 18 March 1856.

Richard Thomas Pulteney, William Pulteney Pulteney's father, was born on 30 June 1811 at Ulveston in Lancashire. For the first two years of his life he would have been a Fawcett, then along with his parents and all the other children his name was changed to Pulteney. Eighty years had passed since Daniel Pulteney's death, and during that time the name had twice passed through the female line, through Frances and Laura, and then through Laura's close friend and distant relative, Elizabeth Evelyn. The name and the ancestry it bestowed were of major significance to all the family. Richard graduated from Trinity College Oxford in 1829 at the age of 18. He was ordained deacon in Buckdean Parish, Lincoln and licensed in 1835, after which he was the stipendiary curate of Algakirk in Lincolnshire. At this time many rectors

Reverend Richard Thomas Pulteney, 1811-1874
(William's father) by Camille Silvy albumen
print, 31 January 1862.
(© National Portrait Gallery, London)

Emma Pulteney (née Dalison), 1826-1884
(William's mother) by Camille Silvy albumen
print, 31 January 1862.
(© National Portrait Gallery, London)

possessed the living of a parish, with all its income, but chose to live elsewhere and employ a curate, normally on a pittance. From 1841 Richard was the curate of Ryarsh in Kent where the vicar was Reverend Lambert B Larking the translator of the Doomsday Book. It was probably here that he met Emma Dalison (1826-1884), the third daughter of Maximilian Dudley Digges Dalison (1793-1870) of Tonbridge; he married her on 13 May 1845 in Malling, Kent.

The family moved to Netherbury in Dorset where Richard was also curate some time before 1848. Then in 1853 he was appointed the Rector of Ashley in Northamptonshire and the family moved into the rectory there. The living had been purchased by his father 15 years earlier, when Richard was ordained, for £4,000 and the advowson was transferred in 1837 although the incumbent remained in post until he died. It may be that Ashley was chosen because of its close proximity to Misterton in Leicestershire where Daniel Pulteney's grandfather, Sir William Pulteney, had lived in the seventeenth century.

The way the name had passed down the generations and its consequent importance to the family would inevitably have been an influence on William Pulteney Pulteney's life. That he had inherited no Pulteney genes and was a Fawcett biologically must also have been in his mind from time to time.

Pulteney wealth

Laura was a very wealthy woman having inherited the Pulteney fortune from her mother in 1782. Her father also became a very wealthy man; it was said that he was the greatest American stockholder ever known, and that he owned almost a million acres in New York State. How great was this wealth, where was it held, and how much of it was passed to Elizabeth Evelyn are the key questions. Some sources give this wealth as £12 billion in today's values: on the face of it the last question should easily be answered by examination of Laura's will but this only sets out the specific bequests and gives no detail on the size of the residuary bequests nor what they comprised. To complicate matters further it, of course, makes no mention of any gifts made in her lifetime. Finally, Elizabeth Evelyn came from a family that too possessed considerable wealth, even more so when Laura died. For all these reasons it may only be possible to estimate Elizabeth Evelyn's inheritance. But this is only the first of three steps in the process. The next step is to assess Richard's inheritance, and this has the added complication of Elizabeth Evelyn's divorce. Once this has been done, then and only then can William Pulteney Pulteney's inheritance be considered. There is a further difficulty, that of assessing values to give meaning both in 1882, when William Pulteney Pulteney was 21, and at the beginning of the 21st Century. To do this for cash will not be easy; to do it, for example, in respect of a sugar plantation in Tobago will be infinitely more challenging. Inflation and taxation complicate an already complex analysis. At the same time estimates will again suffice since the primary objective is to assess William's inherited wealth and any advantage that it might have given him in life.

Laura had inherited five sources of wealth. From her mother, Frances, came the Pulteney estates in London, in Soho and Piccadilly. From her father came estates in Scotland and America, and sugar plantations in the West Indies. She inherited at least two substantial sums of cash, one of which was sufficient to buy and develop the Bath estates. Finally she inherited that part of the Bradford estates which included 25,000 acres in Shropshire, 14,000 acres in Montgomeryshire, and more in Northamptonshire, Staffordshire, and Cheshire. Most of the estates were entailed and passed back to other families or relations when she died without issue. The Suttons, through their relationship to Daniel Pulteney, received most of the Pulteney estate in London and the descendants of the long dead Anne Pulteney most of the estates outside London. Effectively Laura had received the income from these estates in her lifetime but these incomes were substantial and would have allowed her to make significant further investments in her own name. Also some of the inheritance from her father was not entailed, such as some sugar plantations which he bought in his lifetime. All that is known for certain is that Laura on her death in 1808 left Elizabeth Evelyn £800,000 in cash (more than £100 million today) and her magnificent jewellery. Of the latter nothing was ever heard again.

Elizabeth Evelyn lived until 1856. Her will of 1849 made specific bequests totalling no more than £300,000. To Richard Pulteney she bequeathed by a separate deed dated 2 July 1849 plantations in the West Indies, and he was also the residuary beneficiary of her remaining cash, property and other assets. So three years after becoming the Rector of Ashley in 1853, Richard inherited from his mother. He also inherited large sums of money which were invested in the United States, bonds and other securities. These had arisen from the sale of estates owned by Laura in the United States: on her death, legal title was initially held by trustees acting for Elizabeth Evelyn and they had gradually sold the estates. Then, by indenture dated 10 September

1862, the trustees conveyed the title to the remaining lands to Reverend Richard Pulteney but it seems likely that fraud and incompetence had caused the loss of much of their value.

So much is known but there are at least three other possible sources of residuary inheritance under Elizabeth Evelyn's will. She could and probably did inherit under her father Sir John Sutton's will; she owned Northerwood and considerable estates in Hampshire; and it may be that not all the estates owned by Laura were entailed. One property, at least, 97 Piccadilly in London, was still owned by Reverend Richard Pulteney in 1875.

It is very difficult to determine how much Reverend Richard did inherit from his mother because nearly 50 years had passed since Laura's death. In his lifetime he transformed the village of Ashley. Hardly a building escaped his attention: the church, school, rectory, farms, cottages even an inn all were renovated with little thought to cost. He bought two farms in and around the village, supported the school, provided a reading room and a cricket pitch, and it is likely that he supported the village and those who lived in it in many other ways. Nevertheless it is difficult to assess this expenditure at more than £20 million at 2010 values. He did have 16 children, two went to Harrow and two to Eton, and three of these four went to Cambridge; perhaps education including tutors and governesses could have added £3 million. Then there are his additional family living costs for the years from 1856 until his death in 1874, although there is no evidence of extravagance. Finally, he bought the Hargrave estate for his family after his death.

Reverend Richard Pulteney's will proved 16 July 1874 listed his effects as under £500,000 in the United Kingdom. Specific bequests included £70,000 to his wife, Emma, and £20,000 to each of the surviving children; they totalled £381,200 (somewhere between £50 and £100 million in 2010). The residuary estate would therefore not have exceeded £120,000. In his will he mentioned Hargrave Lodge with cottages and lands near there and then simply refers to all other lands which he owned in the Parish of Stansted Mountfitchet or elsewhere in the County of Essex. There is no mention of Northerwood or any properties or lands in Hampshire, or any of the lands and properties in Ashley. His wife, Emma, left only £20,000 when she died in 1884.

Under his father's will, William Pulteney Pulteney received a specific bequest of £20,000 and one twelfth of the residuary estate adding no more than a further £10,000, perhaps less than £3 million in total today. This does not, of course, include any gifts made by his father in his lifetime. William could not have afforded to serve in the Scots Guards in London without a private income; he had three guns made by Stephen Grant in 1886 which in 2010 would have cost £200,000, and he leased a house in Central London for much of his life. Against this he left only £4,000 to his wife Jessie when he died in 1941.

Any conclusion is difficult. However, what is inescapable is the conclusion that Reverend Richard Pulteney's inherited wealth, at least £20 million today, was sufficient to lead a very comfortable life as the Rector of Ashley, to invest substantially in the village, and to provide for his wife and children.

Brothers and sisters

William Pulteney Pulteney was one of sixteen children. For his mother to have that number, between the ages of 20 and 45, was not unusual in Victorian times, or that some should die at a very young age. Birth control would not have occurred to Reverend Richard Pulteney; even if it had it would have been contrary to his religious beliefs which were at the high end of the

Richard Maximilian Pulteney,
1846-1931 (William's oldest
brother) Malta, 1871.

Anglican faith. The influence of his brothers and sisters was profound in shaping William's character and his destiny, and most were to play a part in his life.

Four of the children died in childhood. Aubrey Somerville was born at Netherbury in Dorset where his father was the curate. He was the fourth child and lived just nine months before he died from whooping cough and convulsions, not uncommon in young children at this time. In January that year the family moved to Ashley so the upheaval with four young children and Aubrey just five months old may well have been a contributing factor. It was also the start of the Crimean War. The next child was Apsley born in 1854 at the rectory in Ashley. He lived for five years before dying of a malignant sore throat and scarlet fever. Aubrey and Apsley were buried side by side in the Ashley churchyard.

Caroline was the fifteenth child born in 1867 at the rectory in Ashley when her mother was 41 years old. She lived for only a few months and the cause of her death was given as atrophy, wasting from lack of nourishment, perhaps caused by a premature or complicated birth. The last child was Reginald born in 1871 with his mother now 45 years old. He too only lived a few months before his death caused by convulsions, most likely as a result of a high fever brought on by an infection. Caroline and Reginald are also buried in the Ashley churchyard.

William therefore had four brothers and seven sisters who were to play a part in his life. All four brothers were older than him. Richard Maximilian was the oldest, born in 1846 at Northerwood, the home of his paternal grand-parents. His parents had married the year before and because he was the first child it was perhaps not surprising that his parents decided he should be born at Northerwood where no expense would be spared in ensuring the best possible care. After school Richard was commissioned by purchase into the 52nd Regiment, Oxfordshire Light Infantry and served with them in Ireland, Malta and Gibraltar: he was the Adjutant from 1869-1874. On the regiment's return from Gibraltar in 1876 he was appointed Adjutant of the

Oxfordshire Militia, an appointment that was held by a regular officer for four years. In 1881, on completion of his four years, Richard retired but continued to serve as a militia officer in the Oxfordshire Militia retiring in the rank of Major. Some time before 1871 he must have married because it was in that year that his son, also called Richard, was born. Richard Maximilian and his family lived in Oxford where he was to greatly influence his brother, William; indeed it is likely that he had done so from a very early age. He died in France at the age of 85.

The second son was Frederick Evelyn, born two years after Richard in 1848 when the family was still living in Netherbury. He went to prep school at Elstree and then in 1861 to Harrow before going up to Trinity College, Cambridge. Most of his later life was spent as a tea and coffee planter in Ceylon, possibly working on plantations that were Pulteney investments. At some stage he returned to live in London (12 Stanhope Street) and died in Gloucester on 29 November 1917, midway through the Battle of Cambrai, and is buried at Ashley. There is no evidence that he ever married.

The third child and third son, Francis Basil, was born just over a year later in 1849, with the family still in Netherbury. He went to prep school at Cheam, perhaps to separate him from Frederick Evelyn. However, he also went to Harrow and the two boys then went on together to Trinity College, Cambridge. On graduation, Francis became a lawyer working in the Chancery Registrar's office. In 1881 he married Harriet Jane Osborn the daughter of Sir George Robert Osborn Bt and Lady Charlotte Kerr; Harriet died the following year shortly after giving birth to their son, Reginald. Emma Pulteney had moved to Hargrave House, Stansted in 1876 two years after her husband's death, and she lived there until she died in 1884. For the unmarried children this became their home and it may be that Francis lived there with his son when not in London. In 1886 Francis married again, to Dorothy, and she too was living at Hargrave at that time. Francis died in 1895 and was buried at Ashley, and Hargrave House was then sold in 1898 by which time the rest of the family had returned to Ashley or moved elsewhere. William gave Francis as his next of kin until 1895 because Francis was effectively the head of the family, and a lawyer, and Hargrave House was William's home too.

Six years then passed before the next son, Arthur Wykeham, was born in 1855. In the intervening years a sister, Emma Margaret, was born in 1851, of whom more later, and the two boys who had died in childhood in 1852 and 1854. Arthur went to Eton and like his two older brothers on to Trinity College, Cambridge. He was ordained in 1880 and curate of Cranford, Northamptonshire 1880-1882 before returning to Ashley as its rector eight years after his father's death, a position he was to hold for over forty years until his death in 1927. Arthur never married and when Hargrave House was sold the rectory became both his home and again the family home. In 1919 Arthur obtained permission from the Bishop of Peterborough to bequeath the house to his sister Beatrice, on condition that he built a modern replacement. So, on his death, Beatrice inherited the property now Ashley Court, and she and her family moved there in 1928. Arthur is also buried in Ashley. Although very different in character to his brother, William was only six years younger than Arthur, and they were both at Eton. In the period 1903 to 1908 when William was stationed in London the rectory was his home too.

Emma Margaret was born at Netherbury in 1851 so was ten years old when William was born and likely that she played an important role in his early life, especially as his mother was to produce five more children, all of them daughters, in the six years before he went to prep school. Emma married in 1877, three years after her father's death and one year after the family moved to Hargrave. The next daughter, Frances, was born in 1858. She never married and died in 1941 ten days before William, and within a few miles of him. Frances ran the household for much of the family's time at Hargrave and when this was sold she bought Sion House in Birchanger nearby, and lived there for over forty years.

Alice was born in 1859 and was two years older than William. She married Lieutenant Colonel Richard Cavendish Boyle (1851-1920) in 1883 and they had four children. Her son, Richard, was brought up by her bachelor uncle Arthur at Ashley until he went to Dartmouth. Two of Alice's daughters were staying with her sister Frances at the time of the 1901 census suggesting that the family was a close one. Alice died in 1946.

A year after William was born in 1861, Elizabeth Evelyn, named after her grandmother, was born in 1862. She too would have been brought up initially with William and her older sisters, Frances and Alice. Elizabeth Evelyn married Major Gerald Arthur Boyle (1865-1912), a cousin of Alice's husband, in 1890 when the family was at Hargrave: she died in 1926. Judith Sutton was born a year later in 1863 and she too would have been brought up with William and her sisters. She never married and for many years lived at Hargrave where she was a keen supporter of the Essex Foxhounds. Later she lived in London and died in 1961 at the age of 97.

Beatrice was born in 1865; she married Lieutenant Colonel Reginald Lascelles (1864-1939) in 1895 and they had three children. The Lascelles family lived in the rectory with Arthur during the First World War, and Beatrice inherited the house in 1927. She died in 1958 at the age of 93 and was buried with her husband at Ashley, the ninth and last of the children to be buried in the Ashley churchyard. Isabel was born a year after Beatrice in 1866, and was one of the first women to qualify as a doctor doing so in 1909. She never married and died in 1961, the same year as her sister Judith, aged 95.

In such a large family it would have been inevitable that the love and attention given to each child individually was cursory and much was left to nursemaids and governesses. William, as the youngest son, would have looked to his oldest brother as a role model, even more so since all his other brothers and his father had more of an academic and intellectual leaning. Brought up with six of his sisters in his early years must have made William more independent, more inclined to be a boy, more interested in outdoor activities, more inclined to talk to the male servants and the boys in the village, and more inclined towards a man's world.

Ashley

Ashley lies on the very edge of Northamptonshire close to the River Welland, the nearest town being Market Harborough about five miles away. The village is referred to in the Doomsday Survey of 1086 under its original spelling of Ascele, meaning ash tree clearing. At that time there were 73 houses and a population of 320; today there are about 120 houses, while the population has gradually declined to just over 200. In every respect it was and still is a typical small English village. Reminiscing on his father's arrival in the village, Arthur noted:

> It seemed to him very desolate, the church, the cottages and the farmhouses were all dilapidated, and the poor were herded together in squalid dwellings. Little wonder his spirits sank as low within him as did the wheels of the chaise (which brought him from the station) in the mire. Mountsorrel granite was unknown on the roads in those days; the usual method employed to patch them was a limestone from Cottingham, which formed a deep slough in winter and thick white dust in summer.

Although Ashley was small the villagers had access to most of the services they required and the railway came when Ashley Station was opened in 1850. A wide range of craft and tradesmen lived in the village and a large number of men and women were employed on the farms and in service at the manor, rectory and perhaps elsewhere. It was not the absence of work but the low level of wages that caused the poverty, and all that was about to change with coming of the industrial revolution. The head of the Palmer family of Carlton Curlieu, descendant of the first Attorney General, was the non-resident Lord of the Manor at the time of the Pulteney arrival, an event to which they would have given only passing interest. They could not have anticipated the impact the family, and particularly Reverend Richard, would have on the village. He set about a programme of improvement that would transform it. His investment in it went way beyond the simple charity of a wealthy benefactor; there was a religious passion and self-indulgence that drove him to make his mark on this piece of Victorian England, very much in the Pulteney tradition of property and land ownership and development.

One of the first places he gave his attention to was the church with its 13th Century features. At his own expense, he brought in the architect, Sir George Gilbert Scott, for a major re-build and the addition of a sumptuous interior which started in 1863. The result must have been in marked contrast to the lives of those who lived in the village, but it would also have encouraged them to come and worship in the church and make it a focal point in all that they did. Reverend Richard later endowed an organ fund 'for the more seemly Praise to God ... and to be applied to the repairing and tuning of the said organ and also defraying the cost of the organist and purchase of music'. In 1869 he presented a clock for the church tower and then invested an endowment for its repair and maintenance. He also presented the pink marble octagonal font, said to have cost £2000. Finally, he made an endowment for the provision of fuel to heat the church, and all this benevolence is recorded on the brass plaques that abound.

Ashley Church, c. 1930. (Ashley Village Archive)

In 1858 he started on the school which he rebuilt and endowed for boys and girls, together with a schoolmaster's house opposite, all at an estimated building cost of £2000, the same as the cost of the font. This was also designed by Sir George Gilbert Scott and like all his buildings in the village was built of local stone with mullioned windows. Many of the buildings have the Pulteney crest, the three leopard heads, carved in stone on their front. The school became 'fully operational' in 1872 just two years before Reverend Richard died although it continued to function in the meantime. That year he provided a harmonium for the school and had all the children to tea in the Rectory. In 1873 he examined the First (top) class in Arithmetic. The whole family took an interest in the school and Emma Pulteney, his wife, and their younger children visited most weeks.

The education of the older villagers was not neglected because he bought and converted a building in the centre of the village into a reading room where newspapers and other publications were made available. The original square for the cricket field next to the church was laid with Cumberland turf under his instructions and matches were played there until the start of the Second World War. In 1856 Reverend Richard bought the George Inn opposite the rectory, then one of several pubs in the village.

Opposite the church was one of the two farms that he bought at some time, to add to the land owned by the church in the village. This farm he demolished and rebuilt at the end of the village and called it Northerwood Grange after the family home in Lyndhurst. It is said that he did this because the smell of the farm offended visitors on their way to and from the church. In its place he built a terrace of cottages, of which he had several built in the village designed by a protégé of Sir George Gilbert Scott, and built of ironstone from local quarries. Many of the cottages were occupied by those who worked at the rectory but did not live in, such as the gardeners, grooms and coachmen.

Reverend Richard's extension and modernisation of the rectory reflected his wealth and the position it gave him in Victorian society. The three large downstairs rooms were the drawing room, dining room and study, overlooking the formal gardens, with the kitchen, butler's pantry, housekeeper's parlour, sculleries and other offices behind. The study was also the library and probably where the younger children were taught by their father until they went to prep school or in the case of the girls were taught by the governess. Upstairs were the main bedrooms with a children's wing, perhaps no more than 7 bedrooms in all, and the playroom and nursery. Finally there were the staff quarters on the top floor, about 6 or 7 rooms accommodating the 11 staff who lived in, the senior ones with their own rooms and the junior ones sharing. Outside were the stables and housing for the carriages, greatly extended by Reverend Richard. He was also keen to incorporate the new technologies installing inside-plumbing, electricity from a generator in the yard, and central heating at an early stage. The house had very large and beautiful greenhouses as well as substantial vegetable and fruit gardens, and orchards, all of which would have fed the entire household. Apart from the eight year gap the family lived in the house for a hundred years, becoming the owner in 1919. When it was eventually sold in 1954 the property consisted of the main house, the two farms – Northerwood of 116 and Westhope of 12 acres, 11 other properties, allotments, the whole totalling 142 acres.

At the time of William's birth in 1861 many of his father's projects were just starting or about to start and for much of his first six years Ashley would have been a large building site with many outside people brought in and employed alongside the villagers. All the projects would

Ashley Rectory, now Ashley Court, 2012.

have required Reverend Richard's attention on working days, and the wages he paid would have fed back into the pubs and shops, increasing the general prosperity of the village. Ashley and its inhabitants of note are recorded in a poem 'Our Village Celebrities' of about 1871: this verse on Reverend Richard paints the picture:

> The Rector, we children looked on in great awe,
> And we bowed and we curtseyed whenever we saw
> The great man approaching, with sharp swinging gait,
> With silk kerchief wiping the sweat from his pate.

Early Life in Ashley 1861-1867

William Pulteney Pulteney was born on 18 May 1861, probably in the rectory at Ashley. Whether this bold statement of being twice named Pulteney sufficed to mask the fact that he had inherited no Pulteney blood or that his grandmother, under her previous names of Sutton, Markham and Fawcett, had been involved in one of the scandals of the previous century is difficult to know. The likelihood is that he would have had to deal with these issues from time to time, and probably as early as prep school. From the beginning William would have realised that he was privileged both in his family's wealth and their position. The latter would have been greatly exaggerated in his young mind by his father's situation in the village as the leader of the

Staff at Ashley Rectory, c. 1871. (Ashley Village Archive)

community: again this would have been brought home to him at prep school where he would meet, perhaps for the first time, the sons of men of much greater wealth and influence.

On 9 August 1861, at the age of three months, William was baptised by his father in Ashley Church, yet to receive the attention of Sir George Gilbert Scott. From an early age he would have worshipped there with the rest of the family and all those who worked for them. For the first three years of his life he would have been in the hands of the two nursery maids under the supervision of his mother, when she was able to give the time, and seeing his father at certain times of the day only, perhaps only once. Since the nursery maids had at least two girls to look after in the nursery at the same time, it is unlikely that he received much individual attention or love, and would have been treated in the same way as his sisters.

At some time around the age of three William would have started being educated by his father. This may have been in addition to education received from the governess who was employed mainly to teach the girls, or it maybe that Reverend Richard did it all himself. The four main subjects would have been reading, writing, arithmetic and religion. Interestingly his handwriting was to be particularly good which suggests that he was well taught at an early age.

Horses would have been part of his life from the very beginning and it is likely that he would have been taught to ride by one of the grooms as soon as he was old enough to sit on a horse. He would have also learnt to shoot and fish at a young age. The River Welland passed close to the house and it is probably here that he learnt to fish, and all the children learnt to swim in the river. William developed into an excellent athlete, excelling at running and football. Football was not a sport that would have been given any priority at his schools which suggests that he learnt the basics and developed his skills in Ashley before he went to prep school, perhaps with the village boys. It may also be that his ability in later life to relate to people from all backgrounds was a consequence of growing up with girls at home and therefore playing more with the other boys in the village than he might otherwise have done.

A trip out of Ashley would have been a special occasion. From time to time he would have gone to Market Harborough by carriage with his father or both parents. Even more exciting would have been the train journeys. Indeed the train was still a novelty in Ashley and it would be surprising if the railway station was not a draw for all the young boys of the village. Longer journeys would have been likely from time to time, to London and further afield. His cousin, John Granville Beaumont Pulteney, was living at Northerwood at this time with at least two of his and William's aunts so the occasional visit to Lyndhurst by train would have been a big occasion.

Overall it is difficult to decide how much advantage William was born with; some undoubtedly. What seems certain is that his family and early life at Ashley provided strong and positive influences.

3

Cheam, Eton and the Oxfordshire Militia 1869-1881

Cheam

The first day at prep school is a daunting experience for most boys; away from home for the first time, few are not homesick, but all are determined not to show it. The degree to which the stiff upper lip is required depends on the individual – character, background and ability.

William went to Cheam, the prep school near Newbury in Berkshire, where his brother Francis had been twelve years earlier. Francis had gone on to Harrow and was now at Trinity College, Cambridge; and it may well have been he who influenced their father's choice of Cheam for Putty, rather than Elstree where two of his other brothers went. Exactly when William acquired the nickname of 'Putty' is not known but it was probably at Cheam that the other boys found the pronunciation of 'Pulteney' troublesome. Throughout his life he was known as Putty in an affectionate rather than a derogatory way, even by himself, so that is how he will now be known.

When Putty arrived at Cheam Reverend Robert Stammers Tabor (1819-1909) was the headmaster and had been since 1856, and he continued to be the headmaster throughout Putty's time at the school, retiring in 1890. He was married to Mary Dolman, a parson's daughter; they had seven sons, two of whom died in infancy, and five daughters. Both the headmaster and his father being clergymen and both having large families may well have made Putty's start at Cheam a little easier, but he was also a natural all-round athlete and this too would have helped. Balanced against this were two significant disadvantages that Putty had to cope with. Despite the changes of name there would be few clergymen who were not aware of his grandmother's affair and divorce, and the boys may well have known too. To add to his difficulties, he had been brought up almost entirely with girls and this could have made it more difficult for him to relate to the other boys. Bullying was rife at this time and it may have been a tough start for Putty. Peel's 'History of Cheam since 1645' includes Tabor's recollections of this time, as well as those of some of the boys who were there in the same period.

It was Tabor who decided to turn Cheam into a purely preparatory school and, while it was not the first such school to be established, it was in the forefront of this development. It quickly prospered: the previous headmaster had expected about 20 boys to carry on under Tabor but by 1864 the numbers reached 100 for the first time, and for the next few years including Putty's time at the school were generally just under that number. Cheam was regarded as an expensive school of its type but Tabor found no difficulty in filling it. In 1863 the fees were raised to 150 guineas a year but there was no subsequent rise. Inevitably there were extras, including two guineas each term for washing. Medicines were charged for as were vaccinations. Pocket money was provided by parents, never more than ten shillings a term.

Tabor's building programme was an extensive one and included a chapel dedicated in 1869 and an asphalt-covered playground that the boys could use to play dry shod.

As the school grew, the highest class was still always called the First Class and the lowest the Sixth, and the number of masters reflected the number of classes. Tabor himself taught the First Class; there were French and German masters, and a music master.

There were two matrons – Mrs Scrivener and Mrs Allwright. Charles Hardinge[1] wrote of the latter 'We all love her' and another old boy wrote 'the resourceful matron, one of our best friends at all times'. The scourge of epidemics fell heavily on Cheam; in 1869 measles struck, not for the first time, started by Ivo Bligh,[2] in the middle of the summer term.

The Cheam day, described by Tabor, started at 6 am:

> We rise. A master is with the elder boys when they rise in the mornings and takes them from the dormitories into the school rooms. The matron and her assistant attend to the younger boys. At 6.40 am the class bell rings and I and the chaplain then give religious instruction. The bible is read and the boys are questioned. There is an examination in what has been read at the end of the term. From 7-7.45 am the boys work in the various class rooms, followed by family prayers at 7.45 am and then breakfast at 8 am. 8.30-9 am is play and then return to classrooms until 12 noon. The bell rings at the end of each hour for the classes to change. The subject of instruction varies from hour to hour and the classes as a rule change their master and their room every hour. 12-1 pm play and those who wish learn to swim. Dinner is 1-1.50 pm after which some of the boys are drilled by a Sergeant for an hour (on Thursday afternoon and Saturday evening they are taught to sing). On whole school days we work again 3-5 pm. On Wednesday and Saturday no work is done between 12 and 7 pm, but the boys play in the fields or take a walk with a master. 5.30-6 pm is hand washing and 7-8 pm preparation for the next day: the younger boys prepare with a master. At 8 pm the junior boys went up to bed and at 9 pm the 27th or 30th Bell was the sign for the seniors to go up.

Sunday was slightly more relaxed with Tabor noting: 'My object was to make it a happy day'. There was no work but in its place were three services, two in the chapel and a short evening service, and much time between devoted to learning scripture or catechism. During the afternoon the boys were encouraged to write letters home.

It must have been Tabor who from the start settled to three terms in the year. To begin with the boys still called them halves, as they had been hitherto. Officially they were known as quarters, but this was as much a misnomer as halves, and later they were called terms. The Christmas holidays seem generally to have lasted about five weeks, the Easter holidays about three which later became four, and the summer holidays seven.

---

1   Later 1st Baron Hardinge (1858-1944) Cheam (1868-1872) Viceroy of India 1910-1916.
2   Ivo Francis Walter Bligh 8th Earl of Darnley (1859-1927) Eton Captain England 1st Ashes Test series in Australia.

In 1870 the Pulteneys went on a family holiday to Llandudno, at the end of August. They travelled by train with at least nine of the children ranging from Isabel, then aged 4, to Emma, then aged 19. In his letters to his Land Agent, Reverend Richard Pulteney refers to his family as his 'tribe'. They took adjoining houses; Reverend Richard gives an idea of the holiday in this letter to his Land Agent on 6 September 1870:

> Barring colds which threaten to run through the home in an [epidemic] the younger pack of the [family] circle at all events are enjoying themselves – we had counted upon my sister and Mr Bridge[3] yesterday but they will not turn up till tomorrow – I am afraid he is not quite first rate and if he will find the … cold. We have made two or three interesting excursions. Yesterday some of the family went up Snowdon but I am happy to say that I was not one of their number as they became enveloped in cloud the last half hour of their ascent and wet through to the skin – the wind too was fearful. We have a poor home compared with what we used to inhabit at Worthing and find everything in a … small way – suited to parties of three or four but not for anything on our … colossal scale. Next door we have the … Therpey and the … Bookes which makes it very pleasant as there is perpetual intercourse going on between us … of the boys are lodged where John Bright[4] hangs out and I occasionally catch sight of that distinguished functionary, he is … for … having boxes and brackets of game sent to him which I envy. What wonderful events [reference to Franco-Prussian War?] have taken place since I saw you last.

In a further letter on 3 October, Reverend Richard wrote: 'We had a tuneful journey back from Llandudno on Monday'. From these letters it is clear that a family holiday at the sea was a regular summer event and that the Pulteney family was very much a team: just imagine all the family singing on the train back from Llandudno; this is not a stiff, rather formal clergyman of the Victorian age but rather the opposite.

The Cheam history noted that parents often went down to the school, especially on Saturdays, to visit their boys since it was within easy distance of London. There was no regular half-term but parents appear sometimes to have taken their boys away for a night or two. Reverend Richard would have found this difficult both because of the time it would have taken to get to and from Ashley and the preparation for Sunday. Maybe his family at Northerwood visited Putty or took him out from time to time, or he went out with a friend; some of the boys would not see their parents in term time.

Speech Day was the big event of the year – a 'gala day'. Villiers[5] says 'it was a day worth living for' and tells how the boys' sisters used to bring them ices from the big tent while the parents were eating and listening to speeches, and 'then came the fireworks, done by the Crystal Palace men, after dark'.

Creature comforts at Cheam were few. The living standard was judged spartan in the extreme, but certainly no worse and probably a great deal better than in most other boarding schools of those days. There were many different opinions about the food. Hamilton,[6] used to porridge,

---

3   Probably Judith and her husband Reverend Basil Beridge.
4   John Bright (1811-1889) Liberal politician and reformer.
5   Possibly Edward Hyde Villiers 5th Earl of Clarendon (1846-1914). Liberal politician.
6   Ian Standish Monteith Hamilton (1853-1947). Later General Sir Ian.

spoke disparagingly of the breakfast, which consisted of a fair-sized slice of bread, a smallish pat of butter, a very thin shaving of beef and a cup of tea. Hardinge described it as 'nothing but chunks of bread smothered with salt butter and tea ready mixed from hot-water cans'. Evidently the dinners were good. Hamilton described the dinners as always beef or mutton with vegetables, followed by open tarts or apple dumplings and milk puddings or roly-poly. His recollection of tea was 'lots of bread and butter, with jam once a week for ordinary mortals, and as many cups of tea as they liked'. It sounds as if the food was at least adequate, though it may not have seemed so to boys used to the gargantuan meals served in most upper-class Victorian homes.

Tabor's detractors spoke of him as a snob. A more serious accusation against him is that of cruelty. That he was a strict disciplinarian is not open to question, and it seems likely that at times he overstepped the bounds of what was reasonable punishment in those less squeamish days. Lord Aberdeen[7] spoke of 'that well-known and excellent preparatory school' and ended the account of his time there with 'From Mr Tabor I parted with regret, having always felt he was a true friend'. Lord Randolph Churchill (1849-1895), according to the biography written by his famous son, was most kindly treated and quite content. Bullying was endemic in English schools, and inevitably Cheam had its Flashmans. Only Ian Hamilton found the bullying 'systematic and cruel'; scant mention of it in most records suggests that there was in reality a minimum of it at Cheam.

Only from the Tabor age can games in the modern sense have been regularly played or organised. In the 1860s many of the staff were active players of cricket, but in the 1860s and 1870s it is likely that most cricket was confined to games inside the school, often with masters taking part. Yet an astonishing stream of distinguished cricketers poured out of Cheam in those days. It is doubtful if any of the winter games were played at all regularly under Robert Tabor except football, fives and athletics. So much for Peel's history of Cheam at this time; it provides a very clear picture of what life would have been like for Putty.

The great majority of Cheam boys went on to Eton, with a large minority going to Harrow. Putty would meet many of them again over the years. Two of those not already mentioned are John Philip Du Cane[8] who was to be Putty's first BGGS III Corps in 1914, and Edward Gleichen[9] who commanded 15 Bde 5th Division in Belfast when Putty commanded 6th Division in Cork before the war. Gleichen would certainly have been at Cheam at the same time as Putty.

Much of Putty's character was formed during his time at Cheam. The academic side seems to have been neglected either because of lack of ability or lack of application. To balance this he was beginning to excel at all sports. Even more important Cheam allowed him to develop from someone used to the company of girls to someone who was now also at ease in the company of boys of all abilities. For Putty, Cheam was to end on a sad note when his father died on 22 June 1874, at the end of the summer term. It must have been a difficult time for him as the only 'man' of the house dealing with his mother and sisters grieving; and then he had to return to his last term at Cheam.

---

7   Probably John Campbell Hamilton-Gordon 7th Earl of Aberdeen (1847-1934).
8   Later General Sir John Du Cane (1865-1950).
9   Later Major General Lord Edward Gleichen (1863-1947).

Eton

Putty arrived at Eton at the beginning of the Lent term 1875 and was in Evans House; here he was following in the footsteps of his brother, Arthur, who had left the previous year. Henry Dundas'[10] memoirs has this description of Eton:

> The new world of Eton has often been compared to a university rather than a school. The spacious dignity of its buildings and of its grounds, its chapel, its traditions of liberty and independence of its members, all give that impression. Its vast numbers make the various houses in which the boys are lodged more like little colleges, each with its own individuality and traditions, and the members of each keeping very much together. In the supervision of these houses an Eton master has three advantages not always enjoyed at other schools. In the first place, his numbers are not too large or too small; no house has less than thirty-six or more than forty-two. In the second place, the boys are put down for a house master (often soon after they are born), and not for the building in which he happens to reside; and the house master has absolute control over his own list. In the third place, each boy has a separate room; and there is an excellent custom at Eton whereby house masters wander round their houses during the hour between evening prayers and lights out, when every boy has to be in his room, and the house master thus has the opportunity of seeing a boy by himself and without formality.

Continuing, he noted:

> An Eton boy fulfils the condition of Aristotle that he should learn to obey before he begins to govern. On his arrival he has to 'fag' so long as he is a Lower Boy. The duration of his existence as a Lower Boy depends on his intellect; it may be a year, or two years, or even nearly three years. The governing body of the house is 'the Library' of some four to seven members. The official members of the Library are the Captain of the House (appointed by the house master and responsible for the welfare of the House), the Captain of Games (appointed by the outgoing Captain), and the President of the Library (elected by the Debating Society). Other members of the Library were co-opted. Below the Library was the Debating Society (elected by ballot) of some fourteen members, including the Library.

Dundas was at Eton a long time after Putty but this sets the scene. Gambier Parry[11] in his 'Annals of an Eton House' described Evans House at the time of the Pulteneys: 'Evans House was founded in 1839 with William Evans (1798-1877) being the Dame. However, it was his sister, Jane Evans (c1826-1906), who ran the house during the time William Pulteney was at Eton. The years 1872-1876 were the *Anni Mirabiles* of the house in its sporting history – football, cricket and rowing. When Jane Evans took over in 1871 she is described as a woman of forty-five, tall, dark, and strongly built. Those who might meet her for the first time would have

---

10　Captain Henry Lancaster Neville Dundas (1897-1918) SG 1915-1918 killed in action.
11　Major Ernest Gambier Parry (1853-1936) late RWF, artist and writer.

Jane Evans, 1826-1906,
William's Dame at
Eton by John Singer
Sargent. (Reproduced
by permission of the
Provost and Fellows of
Eton College)

Evans House, 1881. (Reproduced by permission of
the Provost and Fellows of Eton College)

said she looked extremely capable, and that behind the fun that sparkled in her eyes and played the corners of her mouth there was immense strength of character, a deep seriousness, and unlimited power of loving. She was never down-hearted for long'.

Writing of Arthur Wykeham Pulteney's time in Evans House, Gambier Parry noted:

Arthur Wykeham Pulteney was in the House XI that won the football cup in 1872 and reached the final in 1873. He played in the House Cricket XI in 1873, when the House won the cup. The Bishop of Winchester[12] recalled him as always capable and level-headed.

Charles Abraham[13] recalled the joys of passage football: 'I can see Pulteney's beaming face emerging from a bully which had lasted an unconscionable time and during the whole of which he had been under an appalling mass of humanity'. Arthur left in 1874 aged 19: Putty arrived the following year.

Others wrote to Gambier Parry about Jane Evans. Kenyon-Slaney[14] recalled:

Hers was a splendid character; an unusual compound of the best of feminine and the best of masculine characteristics. A thorough judge of boy nature, she knew unerringly who to trust and how to trust, and she was seldom, if ever, deceived. She loved her boys with her whole heart, she gave them her entire confidence, she was unflinchingly loyal to them in their difficulties and their scrapes, so long as they were frank and honest with her, although she never hesitated in her approval of a flogging when a flogging was deserved; and so she set up in the house an atmosphere of truth and honour which pervaded it throughout.

12   Herbert Edward Ryle (1856-1925).
13   Charles Thomas Abraham (1857-1945); later Bishop of Derby.
14   Colonel William Slaney Kenyon-Slaney (1847-1908) late Gren Gds MP for Newport.

Edward Lyttelton[15] wrote:

> Her methods were simplicity itself. She would mark, unobserved, the younger boys who were destined to be influential in the house, and, as they became old enough to understand, she would imbue them with the conviction that things really did depend on them; that they must rise above their inclinations to selfishness and folly, or they would be false to a great trust.

His brother, Alfred Lyttelton's[16] description was just as fulsome:

> Profound in her affections, anything like a display of them she regarded as not altogether wholesome. She held reticence in high esteem, and had a healthy distrust of gush, and this combination in her of deep feelings and reserve were very congenial to boys who unconsciously admired the former and most conspicuously appreciated the latter. In general, her humour was of the sunniest and most genial quality, being sometimes with difficulty suppressed on occasions of lighter breaches of discipline. Thus, throughout all her relations with us, a true sense of proportion guided her thought and action, and fussiness never invaded the spacious and serene balance and good sense of her rule. Jane Evans' influence permeated everywhere and in all spheres of activity in the house. She did not pretend to learning, but she upheld its promoters, and gloried in the scholarly successes of her boys; she watched our football matches in the worst weather, stimulated us by her mild valour, and displayed a quiet but strong pride when our efforts brought the old house to the front. In time of disaster her tact was of the finest, and nothing could be more healing than the robust sympathy with which, like a good nurse who purposely infuses a little humdrum into her consolations, she minimised, though she never ignored, the poignancy of defeat. The boys' library reflected the broad and tolerant aspects of her influence. There, no doubt, much athletic shop was discussed, but not a little talk of books and politics was encouraged and boys whose interests were not mainly in games were there received with respect and recognition.

Another to write to Gambier Parry with his thoughts was Lord Farrer:[17]

> Again, I remember, her courage when she was very ill in 1876. I was Captain of the House, and Absence was called by myself only at prayers, she having a dislike to any master coming into the house. After this had gone on for a long period the Headmaster sent for me and said that he thought it most necessary that a master should come in to superintend the house. I said that, of course, in that case it must be done; but I hoped he would allow me to mention it to her before the step was finally decided upon. I went back and sent in to her the best message I could, and her answer was that I was to go back and tell the Headmaster that, sooner than have a master in her house, she would get up herself to superintend call-over.

15   Reverend Hon Edward Lyttelton (1855-1942) played football for England and cricket for Middlesex, later Headmaster 1905-1916.
16   Alfred Lyttelton (1857-1913) played football and cricket for England, later Colonial Secretary in Arthur Balfour's Government 1903-1905.
17   Thomas Cecil Farrer (1859-1940) later 2nd Baron Farrer.

This was a somewhat difficult message for a boy to convey; but I did my best, and the Head was very kind in postponing action. From that very day Jane Evans began to recover, and lived, and I am glad to say, for many years, though her life had been despaired of. I think she disliked more than anything else the growing tendency to luxury and display, which she always maintained would be destructive of the best Eton tradition, and everyone knows she exercised a process of the most careful selection for the boys in her house, shipping off undesirables with complete ruthlessness. The tradition of Eton was more to her than any aristocratic prejudices. It was part of Jane Evans' plan never to appeal to the authorities of the school if she could avoid it, and if the rules of the house were broken and she could not influence the boy by other means, she would appeal to the parents.

1876 was Putty's second year at Eton and Jane Evans' illness must have affected him. It came at a time when her guiding hand was much needed.

Several wrote on the character of the house including Herbert Gladstone[18]:

We were somewhat exclusive, and this is an unpopular characteristic the world over. In other words, we hung together very much. The large majority of the boys in the House had their intimate friends in the house.

Edward Hamilton[19] wrote:

It was the first house, and the only one in my day, that had a library. If I recollect rightly, the books most in demand were those by Harrison Ainsworth;[20] Dickens' and Thackeray's works were also much in request.

Gambier Parry continued:

A house debating society was founded by Lord Grimthorpe[21] in 1872. The matter of female suffrage came up from time to time and on one occasion was vetoed by 11 to 1. The opener opposed to the motion said: 'Women in this respect are placed on an equal footing with minors, idiots, lunatics and criminals'.

Two other extracts add to the picture of Putty's life in Evans House:

Breakfasts as they became known, attended by the leading boys of the house, did not become an established custom until 1872. Then the Captain and Second Captain usually breakfasted with the family every morning, the meal being held in the Hall. But for the rest of the house there was no regular breakfast, each boy having his 'orders' of three Eton rolls, butter, tea, milk and sugar, in his own room or joint mess.

18   Herbert Gladstone (1854-1930) later Home Secretary and afterwards Viscount Gladstone, Governor General of South Africa.
19   Edward Hamilton (1847-1908) later Sir Edward Hamilton Permanent Secretary to the Treasury.
20   William Harrison Ainsworth (1805-1832) historical novelist and close friend of Dickens.
21   Ernest William Beckett (1856-1917) later 2nd Baron Grimthorpe.

Sir Edward Hamilton wrote:

> It might be supposed that we Lower-boys of the sixties would have welcomed a free break-
> fast such as our sons enjoyed in later times, for our lot was not an easy one. We came out of
> early school at 8.30 am. At 9.10 am we had to be in chapel. In those forty minutes we had
> to get back from school, do our fagging, and run to chapel. Needless to say, breakfast was
> always gobbled in a few minutes, and the occasions by no means rare when we went without
> altogether, or bolted a hot bun with butter in it and a cup of coffee at Brown's on our way to
> chapel, had we the four pence to pay for it. Dinners were then at 2 pm.

He continued:

> Until some years after Jane Evans' period had begun there was only one bath in the house,
> and this occupied a large portion of the boys' kitchen. As soon as the cooking there was
> over, the woman in charge folded back the wooden partition, and the bath was open for use
> by any boy fortunate enough to obtain it. First come first served was the rule. Thus, in a
> house of fifty boys our ablutions in winter were certainly few and far between.

Of Putty in Evans House at Eton Gambier Parry wrote: 'William Pulteney was in the House
XI that year [1877] when they again reached the final'. Lowther[22] wrote: 'Putty was a keen and
good football player from his earliest days at Eton'. Drummond[23] was an exact contemporary of
Putty in Evans House and many years later wrote his obituary. Two extracts from it are relevant
to these times: 'In those early days keen for a lark of any sort, though not vicious. Probably classed
in Miss Evans' mind as one of the naughty boys' and 'an instance of Miss Evans' occasional lack
of appreciation, greatly wise as she was, of fine dormant qualities in these youngsters was illustrated by her remark when, in 1896, she was told that Putty had been awarded the DSO for his
services in Central Africa. "What!" she said "Pulteney Minor? I never should have believed it!"'

Tim Card, in his recent book 'Eton Renewed', provides a stark summary of life in Evans
House at Eton during Putty's time:

> The early 1870s were marked by what Edward Lyttlelton, a boy in the school then and later
> Headmaster, called a 'hideous amount of vice'. No preventive measures were taken; new
> boys were never warned; and then if detection came, expulsion followed. Boys' opinion was
> often on the side of those convicted. In 1871 a club called the Hallelujah Club was organ-
> ized – the conditions of its membership are not fit for publication. It was a time of internal
> conflict between the classics masters who acted as the boys' tutors in almost every respect,
> and the other masters who were considered inferior; even in a house where the housemaster
> was not a classics master it was the latter that had control of boy's time, and responsibility
> for discipline. There were also conflicts between athletes and intellectuals.

22   Henry Cecil Lowther (1869-1940) SG and best man at Putty's wedding.
23   Laurence George Drummond (1861-1946) SG.

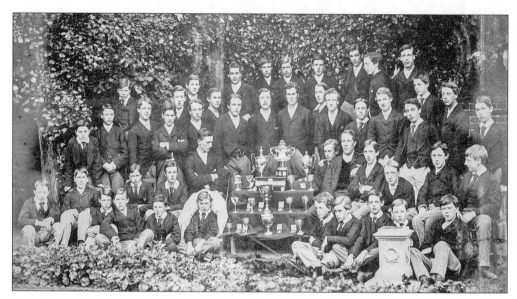

Evans House Eton, 1875. William on extreme left.
(Reproduced by permission of the Provost and Fellows of Eton College)

It was in Evans's House that the new pattern for running a house appeared. William Evans had always encouraged his boys to take responsibility; he had also provided his house with a library. When his daughters assumed control of the house, the managing committee of the library gradually grew in importance, and came to be called 'The Library'. When Annie Evans died in 1871 and Jane Evans took sole charge of the house, she developed the institution – having the Library to breakfast with her every morning. Although the Library was self-electing, Miss Evans would influence their choice. A system of self-government had developed, which, even though it retained elements of barbarism, allowed the house to be one of the best run in the school, and bred a tremendous esprit de corps. In 1876, when Jane Evans was very ill, the house conducted itself with a success that astonished some of the masters.

Putty left Eton at the end of the winter term 1877 and was commissioned into the Oxfordshire Militia the following year at the age of 17. However, there is evidence of him serving as an officer in that Militia in 1876 when he was still at Eton: presumably this arrangement was unofficial and mainly in the school holidays, and possible because his brother, Richard, was the Adjutant. It is not known why Putty left Eton at 16½; his full participation in old Etonian activities for the rest of his life seems to rule out the obvious negative reasons such as discipline, inability to pay, or academic failure. By his own admission he did not apply himself academically and it may be that leaving to join the army via the militia was preferable to continuing with his education and entering via Sandhurst. Jane Evans might well have influenced him differently but she was very ill in 1876, a critical time for Putty; his father had just died and with that the family left their home in Ashley and moved in 1876 to Hargrave; it was also the year that Richard became Adjutant of the Oxfordshire Militia and rented a house in Oxford.

Oxfordshire Militia 1876-1881

His older brother Richard's influence may have played a significant part in Putty's decision to leave Eton and join the Oxfordshire Militia. Fifteen years older than him Richard had been commissioned into the 52nd Regiment (Oxfordshire Light Infantry) in 1867, when Putty was only six years old and still at home. This and his subsequent promotions to the rank of captain were by purchase. As has been previously outlined, much of his service was spent with his regiment in Ireland, Malta and Gibraltar where there was little opportunity to distinguish himself but for five years he was the adjutant, suggesting an officer of some intelligence and ability. Then he was appointed Adjutant of the Oxfordshire Militia, an appointment he held for a further five years until he retired in 1880: he then continued to serve in the Oxfordshire Militia, as a Militia officer. Sometime before 1871 he must have married because it was in that year that his son, also Richard, was born and this may well have been the cause of his lack of advancement. Not only was he under 25 years in age but he was also the adjutant, so he may have married without the permission of his commanding officer. If that was so his father would not have approved either, and the inheritance when he received it several years later would have been too late to make any difference. Much of this is speculation but it does provide a possible explanation for the re-entry of his brother into Putty's life just when he was badly in need of some guidance.

The Soldiers of Oxfordshire Trust have a photograph of the Oxfordshire Militia at annual camp in 1876 with Lieutenant W Pulteney and Captain and Adjutant RM Pulteney both in it. Putty was then only 15 years old so a number of rules must have been broken. In any event it seems that he attended the training that summer which is well described in the history of the Oxfordshire Militia: 'Mobilisation/Training started on 3 July. 5th Corps[24] consisted of three infantry divisions. 3rd Division, under Prince Edward of Saxe-Weimar, being allotted to Gloucestershire and stationed on Minchinhampton Common. This was divided into two brigades, the first consisting of the two Gloucestershire Militia Battalions and the Oxfordshire, under Major-General Fordyce. Mobilisation was the term adopted, but the division at Minchinhampton could not move, as it had no transport, and the whole affair proved to be a pleasant picnic. Each field officer had a bell tent instead of the usual marquee, and the captain and subaltern of each company were allowed a tent between them. The recruits had been called up for preliminary drill in the spring and dismissed, so the battalion proceeded to Minchinhampton only about 450 strong. The new adjutant was Richard Pulteney, late adjutant of the 52nd, and right well was he appreciated by all ranks'.

The history also gives an outline programme:

15 July. The Duke of Cambridge came down to see the division, and appeared well satisfied.
20 July. The people round Minchinhampton had been very civil to the troops, and they organised some athletic sports for the officers and men, with liberal prizes.
21 July. Prince Edward had the whole division out for a short drill.
25 July. There was a great burning of powder for the entertainment of the neighbourhood, the two brigades fighting a mighty battle on the slopes towards Brinscomb.

---

24   The United Kingdom was divided into eight Army Corps; 2nd and 5th were mobilised in July 1876.

26 July. The regular inspection took place under Prince Edward, and was satisfactory enough.

27 July. On returning to Oxford, the men were for two days in billets, the last time this most objectionable method of housing troops was resorted to.

29 July. Training/Mobilisation ended. The battalion marched up to Cowley Barracks in a storm and there deposited the arms (probably Snider rifles) in the Keep, where in future all stores and equipment were to be housed, the old armoury in Oxford being handed over to the County Police.

Putty returned to Eton for the autumn term 1876: whether he had any contact with the militia again until 1878 is not known but it is most likely that he did, as well as seeing his brother Richard from time to time. The annual camp in 1877 took place in May and June and the history records: 'The camp that year was in the enclosed space behind Cowley Barracks and was most unsatisfactory. With the exception of one march to Oxford the battalion was never out of the enclosure'. It seems unlikely that Putty was with them but he was now able to concentrate on his aim of getting a commission in the army via the militia.

The militia of the county of Oxford dates back from a time little after the Norman Conquest. At first it was liable to be marched to any part of the kingdom, but, in the reign of Edward III it was enacted by statute that no militia man should be sent out of his county, except in times of public danger. Upon Charles II ascending the throne, the militia was re-established on its former footing. The Lord Lieutenant was made immediately subordinate to the Sovereign, and granted commissions (subject to the King's approval) to the field and regimental officers. The Oxfordshire Militia served in Ireland 1813-14 and it was called out again during the Crimean War in 1854 (773 strong) and served for eleven months in Corfu (and consequently carried 'Mediterranean' on its colours). This was the regiment that Putty was about to join, this time officially.

Calwell in his book *Wilson: His Life and Diaries* explains:

At this time there was another possible route into the army though the militia; what in those days used to be called the back door. A militia officer could gain a regular commission by successfully taking a competitive exam after undergoing two periods of training. This was not an unusual means of by-passing Woolwich or Sandhurst. Sir John French[25] and Sir Henry Wilson[26] entered the Army this way.

On 9 March 1878 the *Oxford Journal* contained this notice:

The recruits who have joined the regiment since the last training are summoned by an order, signed by Captain and Adjutant Pulteney, to assemble at the Barracks at Temple Cowley at 10 am on Monday 8 April for 83 days' training; and the remainder of the regiment are warned to be present at 8 am on Monday 3 June, at the same place, for 27 days' training.

25   Later Field Marshal Earl of Ypres (1852-1925).
26   Later Field Marshal Sir Henry Hughes Wilson Bt (1864-1922).

Putty probably attended both periods of training, and the regimental history gives the programme:

1 June. The recruits proceeded to Aldershot to pitch the camp on Redan Hill, ready for the arrival of the battalion.

3 June. The remainder of the battalion assembled at Cowley Barracks and returned there on 29 June. This was the first occasion on which it had assembled and left Oxford on the same day, the return and paying off of the men also being accomplished on the last day of training.

4 June. The battalion was attached to 1 Bde, Aldershot Division [Bde Comd: Major General Pakenham]. This officer went through the form of inspection the day after arrival, but was afterwards seen no more.

The line battalions of the Bde were 31st and 49th, 4th Middlesex Militia being also attached.

There had been a scare of war with Russia and the reserve or a portion of it had been called to the colours. All the battalions were therefore very strong, some mustering nearly 1200.

There were three big field days during the training, one in the neighbourhood of Long Valley and the others over the Fox Hills towards Pirbright, the last fight happening on an extremely sultry day. The Oxfordshire lads stuck gamely to their work and very few fell out, but it was not so with the line battalions, the road home being lined on both sides by dozens of men who had fallen out.

27 June. Colonel Baynes [Comd 43rd Bde Depot] came from Oxford to make the formal inspection, which passed off very well.

During the last two years while at Minchinhampton and Cowley the men had received no musketry instruction, but this year this essential portion of their training was resumed. A new system of attack in loose order was introduced into the drill book and practised this year. One other innovation must be noted, a new head dress. A modification of the German Pickelhaube, in the form of a spiked helmet, was introduced for officers and staff sergeants, but militia NCOs and men still wore only glengarries.

On 2 October 1878 Putty was commissioned into the Oxfordshire Militia; he was 17 years old. His commissioned service was to span 42 years, but his was not yet a regular commission; for that he had to fulfil the requirements of two years training and pass the competitive examination. His brother Richard would undoubtedly have helped him with both, and Putty may well have lived with him and his family in Oxford during this time.

The history says of the training in 1879:

The training this year was perhaps the least satisfactory that the battalion has ever experienced. As in 1877 the camp was at Cowley, one or two companies being in the barracks. From motives of economy on the part of the Government, the training that started on 2 June only lasted three weeks. The weather was singularly wet. On 19 June, as in the previous year, the inspection by Colonel Baynes took place. Two days later, on 21 June, the training ended. The battalion had only been outside the barrack-field once, on the occasion of a march through Oxford.

Oxfordshire Militia, 1880. Pulteney at back right. (The Soldiers of Oxfordshire Museum)

In 1880 the Oxfordshire Militia was embodied for training and Putty's attendance is recorded in a photograph of the officers. The history again gives an outline of the programme:

> 31 May. The battalion again assembled for training at Aldershot. It was encamped on Church Plateau on the North Camp, and attached to 3 Bde (Comd Major General Peyton). The line battalions of the brigade were 52nd and 1 RB, with the Edmonton Militia attached. The weather was again very wet.
>
> 15 June. There was only one big field day when the whole division engaged in a big fight upon the Fox Hills.
>
> 24 June. The inspection under Major General Peyton came off.
> The strength of the battalion on dismissal, including all ranks, was 753.

The history of the regiment continues: 'After this training two officers joined the regular army, 2nd Lieutenant W Pulteney being appointed to the Scots Guards in April 1881'. In this decision Putty would have been influenced by Laurence Drummond who was his exact contemporary in Evans House at Eton and who would also join the Scots Guards. Two other officers of the Oxfordshire Militia deserve mention: one is Sir George Dashwood Bt who will be mentioned again in the next chapter; the other is Charles Rivers Bulkeley who had two sons – Thomas Henry Rivers Bulkeley[27] and Charles Ivor Rivers Bulkeley.[28] It may be only coincidence that Thomas was born during the time that Putty was in the battalion but it is difficult to believe that it was only coincidence that both sons should have joined the Scots Guards, since their father had not served in the regiment.

27   Thomas Henry Rivers Bulkeley (1879-1914) SG killed in action.
28   Charles Ivor Rivers Bulkeley (1885-1915) SG killed in action.

4

Regimental soldiering at home and abroad 1881-1895

Ireland 1881

Putty was commissioned into the Scots Guards from the Oxfordshire Militia on 23 April 1881, just short of his 20th birthday. Sometime before then he would have been accepted for the regiment by the Lieutenant Colonel Commanding, Colonel Reginald Gipps.[1] He may well have been influenced by George Dashwood[2] who had served in the Scots Guards prior to joining the Oxfordshire Militia, and had been in the militia with Putty and his brother. Another influence on Putty and possibly Gipps may have been Maximilian Dudley Digges Dalison[3], the son of Putty's mother's brother and his cousin.

Putty was at Hargrave at the beginning of April and would have spent a day or two that month at Headquarters Scots Guards having his uniform inspected by the Regimental Adjutant and various items of kit issued; then, on 26 April, he was posted to 1 SG stationed at Ship Street Barracks, Dublin, located on the south side of Dublin Castle. The battalion had been suddenly ordered there on 20 December 1880 because serious disturbances had developed in the Country and the Dublin garrison was considerably reinforced, including two Foot Guards battalions. Gipps was promoted to Major General in July 1881 to command the troops in Dublin: 1 SG was commanded by Lieutenant Colonel Knox[4] who had also served in the Crimea.

Joining the battalion was likely to have been a daunting experience but Laurence Drummond[5] wrote many years later: 'In those early years in the Regiment Putty found himself amongst numerous brother-officers of gay, convivial spirit, out to enjoy life in every way, sporting or other, and with his cheery, happy nature and keen sense of humour he quickly and easily fitted in, and was popular with all'. Scots Guards records show that Putty was 5' 9" tall and had 'ability' in French: on 1 July 1881 he was promoted to Lieutenant. He was almost a year in Dublin being put through every aspect of young officer training; because he had not been to

---

1   Later General Sir Reginald Ramsay Gipps (1831-1908) Eton SG 1849-1881 MS 1892. Gipps fought with 1 SG at the Alma (wounded), Balaclava, Inkerman (wounded), and Sebastopol.
2   Sir George Dashwood 6th Bt (1851-1933) SG 1870-1875.
3   Maximilian Dudley Digges Dalison (1852-1885) SG 1871-1885 killed in action 2 SG Nile Expedition.
4   George William Knox (1838-1894) SG 1855-1885.
5   Laurence George Drummond (1861-1946) Eton SG 1879-1908.

Sandhurst this training would have been especially rigorous. There were numerous garrison and battalion duties to be carried out but still more than enough opportunity to enjoy Dublin's social life and Putty was in the thick of it. However, the year in Dublin came to an end on 18 March 1882 when the battalion returned to Wellington Barracks.

Ensign Pulteney Scots Guards, 1881.
(Chamberlain)

Officers 1 SG Dublin, 1882. (RHQ Scots Guards Archives)

Egypt 1882

In early 1882 a group of Egyptian Army officers under Orabi (or Arabi) overthrew the Khedive and seized power in the Country. The British and French Governments were determined to restore the situation and a combined fleet arrived off Alexandria on 20 May. Meanwhile Egyptian troops were reinforcing the coastal defences in anticipation of an attack; these events heightened tension in Alexandria, and triggered riots in the city, with Egyptians turning on foreigners, and many were killed and much property destroyed. An ultimatum was sent to Orabi's officers in Alexandria to dismantle their coastal batteries which they refused: the French had not supported the ultimatum, and decided against participation in the armed intervention. At 7 am on 11 July the British fleet bombarded the Egyptian gun emplacements; damage was considerable and the response minimal. Then, on 13 July, a large naval force was landed in the city and, despite some heavy resistance for several hours, succeeded in forcing the Egyptian troops to withdraw.

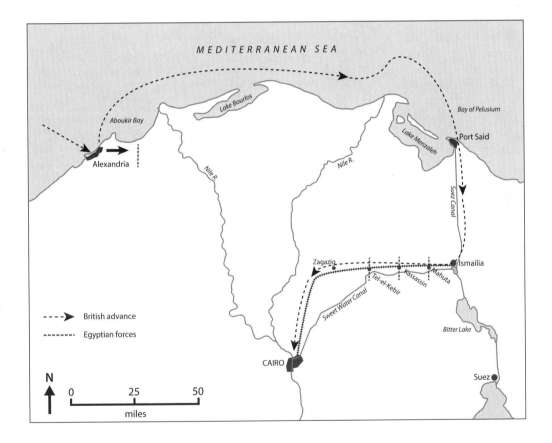

Map 1 Egypt 1882.

Lieutenant General Garnet Wolseley was given the task of destroying Orabi's regime, taking Cairo, and restoring the nominal authority of the Khedive Tawfiq; to do it he was given a force of about 31,000. 24,000 British troops were concentrated in Malta and Cyprus and a further 7,000 Indian troops brought via Aden. Wolseley first tried to reach Cairo by advancing from Alexandria but it soon became apparent that Orabi had prepared very strong defences covering this approach; the terrain also made it particularly difficult. Therefore he decided to secure the Suez Canal, assemble his force at Ismailia, and advance through the desert following the line of the railway. For this to succeed he would have to deceive Orabi as to his intentions for as long as possible.

Lieutenant Pulteney was to play a very small part in Orabi's defeat. For him it all started at 7 am on 29 July when 1 SG paraded at Wellington Barracks. Lieutenant Balfour,[6] who had been at Eton with Putty and joined the regiment the same year, kept a record and his observations and experiences would have been very similar to Putty's. He wrote of this battalion parade:

> Parade marching order, officers in patrol jackets with helmets greatcoat rolled and water bottles. They don't expect us to wear our goggles yet then. Every man has been supplied with a veil and a pair of blue tinted goggles for this expedition. Imagine the British guardsman in a loose serge frock, green veil and blue goggles. I don't fancy the older men like this kit much: my old Sergeant Devereux[7] was delighted when there was a prospect of the clothing not being ready to start in 'We shall march out of London in our best tunics and bearskins like Guardsmen Sir'.

The men's serges were red and the officers' patrol jackets blue; all ranks wore white pith helmets.

The next day (30 July) Balfour recorded:

> 6 am. Battalion fell in. Curly[8] reads a letter from the Queen: 'The Queen regrets that she is unable to bid goodbye to the Scots Guards before their departure but she knows that the Scots Guards will do their duty as they have always done'. At last we reformed column and marched off or rather forced our way through the mass of humanity which barred us all the way to Westminster Bridge. Embarked on penny steamers [Thames riverboat service] to the tune of Hieland Laddie and Auld Lang Syne with of course God Save the Queen. The crowd lined the embankment right down to the City and waved hats and handkerchiefs energetically occasionally cheering.
>
> 10 pm. Embarked satisfactorily on the *Orient*, a fine four-masted ship and at 12 Midnight sailed out of harbour. Just after leaving the docks the Duke of Connaught[9] came on board with the Duchess, the Prince[10] and Princess of Wales and three girls, the Dukes

6   Charles Barrington Balfour (1862-1921) SG 1881-1890 & 1900-1901.
7   1302 Sergeant later Colour Sergeant Thomas Devereux (1845-1922) SG 1864-1885.
8   Colonel George William Knox CO 1 SG.
9   Major General HRH The Duke of Connaught (1850-1942) 3rd son of Queen Victoria Comd Gds Bde later Colonel SG.
10   Later King Edward VII.

of Edinburgh[11] and Cambridge.[12] They went over the ship shook hands and said goodbye to us all and departed amidst great cheering, the Duchess wept exceedingly. Some of the men climbed up into the rigging to see them off, and the pipe major in descending caught his kilt in the rigging and hung suspended.

SS *Orient* of 5,386 tons usually operated on the UK to Australia route. She had accommodation for 22 Saloon Class, 130 1st Class and 300 3rd Class passengers. Embarked was HQ 1st Division, HQ Gds Bde and 1 SG. The battalion strength was 31 officers and 765 other ranks in eight companies. There had been some trepidation amongst the young officers of the battalion at the Duke of Connaught's presence in the Mess. Balfour noted: 'The Duke was very pleasant we were afraid before starting of constant ceremony getting out of the way taking off caps in the saloon etc. He was very genial though and watched Topps[13] and Pulteney and all of us bear-fighting after dinner with great amusement'.

Gibraltar was the briefest stop on 4 August, then it was on to Malta which the *Orient* reached on 7 August. Balfour described this visit:

> Great excitement as to what orders might be. Appearance of a boat with staff officer with our letters and intelligence that they had telegraphed to England to know what to do with us, as they not expecting us so soon had sent no orders. After some confabulation we may go on shore, be on board by 10 pm.
>
> We therefore made for a boat and about eight of us got in but as all persisted in sitting on one side, I had hardly set my foot in her before she turned over. Eight officers in full uniform in the water! Coke,[14] Jack,[15] Topps, Dundas,[16] Hare.[17] Pulteney and the Oyster[18] stuck to the boat and pulled Topps out. All emerged alright and went and changed and then with greatest caution started afresh. After a hasty dinner at the club (Naval and Military) with champagne as a farewell to Malta we started for the ship.

The next day, 8 August, the *Orient* sailed at 1 pm with much speculation as to their destination. Balfour noted: 'At sea again with the usual round of watches and meals with the days and nights getting hotter and hotter'. Two days later (10 August) a low lying coast of sand with windmills was sighted: Egypt at last; and the SS *Orient* came to anchor outside the harbour of Alexandria. There she sat until the following night when, with pipers playing, she steamed into the inner harbour.

---

11   Prince Alfred 2nd son of Queen Victoria.
12   Prince George grandson of King George III CinC British Army.
13   Lieutenant Charles Edward Hartopp (1858-1929) SG 1879-1888 later 5th Bt.
14   Captain Viscount Thomas William Coke (1848-1941) SG 1868-1894 later 3rd Earl of Leicester.
15   Lieutenant John Bourchier Stracey (1853-1931) SG 1872-1899.
16   Lieutenant Robert Dundas (1857-1910) SG 1879-1893 later 2nd Bt.
17   Lieutenant Thomas Leigh Hare (1859-1941) SG 1880-1885 later 1st Bt.
18   Lieutenant Everard Ernest Hanbury (1862-1923) SG 1882-1902.

1 SG disembarking at Alexandria, 1882.
(Royal Collection Trust/© Her Majesty Queen Elizabeth II, 2014)

Balfour continued on 12 August:

The first thing I saw was the *Batavia* with the 2nd Grenadiers steaming in, great cheering from the men as they pass. Coming into the harbour too we see the *Iberia* with the Coldstream, so all the Brigade of Guards has now arrived. By about 3 pm we have disembarked. We are drawn up in line and salute the Duke. We then marched to the railway station through the town, and arrived at Ramleh just before dark. On getting out at the station we had a trudge of about ½ mile through deep sand to our camping ground, a simple plain of sand as far as one could see sloping upwards. Tents were pitched just before dark, some of them in the dark. Ramleh is the fashionable watering place of Alexandria, and our camp is surrounded with deserted villas many looted by the arabs, figs in the gardens however in plenty; except for the gardens the whole place is sand. On 13 August we have a look through a telescope at Arabi's *(sic)* lines. They seem strong works, his soldiers working like anything on them.

Rations very good when stewed, plenty of them. Bread good, fruit plentiful and delicious. Subsequently however some of us have our doubts on the agreeableness of the fruit in its ulterior consequences. Water supply not very good at first, so took a fatigue party down to deserted villas and utilised a well the Bedouins had not broken. Too hot to move about in the sun. The sun is a factor we do not sufficiently reckon on at first; result is that many of us get prickly heat.

For Putty and the other young officers of 1 SG it must have been a great adventure, one not dissimilar to the start of a novel by GA Henty. But now they were beginning to realise the three great challenges that faced them: the heat and hostile terrain; the inadequate equipment; and the appalling staff work which affected everything they did. Although they did not know it, all three were to be greater enemies than Arabi's Army.

After five days at Ramleh the Gds Bde was ordered to re-embark, and in the early morning of 19 August 1 SG marched back to Alexandria along the line of the railway. That evening the loaded transports steamed out to where the fleet lay at anchor outside the harbour. Balfour noted: 'Quite exciting'. Then the fleet and transports sailed for Aboukir Bay and prepared as if to force a landing next day. But directly it was dark, and covered by fire of the gunboats, they slipped quietly away to Port Said arriving off the entrance to the Suez Canal at sunrise on 20 August.

SS *Orient* passed down the Canal next day and at 4 pm on 22 August arrived off Ismailia. At 4.30 am next morning 1 SG landed, as Balfour recalled:

> We go on shore in two large horse boats tugged by two pinnaces. Boats have a will of their own however and turn round and round in a hopeless manner. The engineer on the pinnace is just getting matters all right, when up comes a fiery Captain RN very hoarse shouting contradictory orders at the top of what voice he has and muddles matters more thoroughly than before, keeping us turning now this way now that for some time. At last he lets the engineer have his own way, who lashes the two horse boats together, with a steam pinnace outside each, and so we get in all right. We form up along a road under acacia trees in blossom; very sweet smell they have, place cool and shady too in the early morning, and march to our bivouac.

Wolseley intended to advance on Cairo by the Sweet-Water Canal which joined the Suez Canal at Ismailia and passed through Tel-el-Kebir and the railway junction at Zagazig. A small force under Major General Graham (Comd 2 Bde) was pushed forward to protect the locks of the Sweet-Water Canal but found a superior force of Egyptians nearby at Tel-el-Mahuta, and so Wolseley ordered up the Gds Bde in support. Balfour recalled that day:

> Suddenly, while I was taking great interest in the preparation of some lentile [sic] soup, an order comes: 'Battalion to parade in marching order at 12.45 pm'. About 1 pm the brigade marches out of Ismailia, Grenadiers leading, then us, then the Coldstream, each band playing different tunes, but this does not much matter, as one's own band is not heard much beyond the centre of the battalion. First part of march through soft sand. Glare of sand tremendous, however goggles relieve that, pebble in one's mouth a good thing to keep off thirst. Another halt on the line, and rush into a swamp to fill water bottles, water tastes good, think it is a spring, but a little brandy will make it safe. Fall in and on, men getting roused by prospect of a fight, and marching briskly. See a few shells bursting in front and at last turn off the railroad. Deploy in line F Coy outlying picquet, G Coy inlying picquet. Pile arms – lie down – confound it – whole line has to get up and move about ½ mile to the left.

By now it was 6.45 pm and the sun had set; they had only covered about nine miles. Private Macaulay[19] of 1 SG recalled that the march was 'across a long stretch of shifting sand on which our feet slipped backwards at every step. The hot wind that was blowing made us terribly thirsty, and soon the pint and a half which each of our water bottles held was exhausted'.

Balfour again:

> At dawn we fall in. After marching two miles over hard sand see guns firing at something in front. Are we going to fight anybody? At last reach the top of ridge and extend for attack. Don't see anyone to attack. Enemy's position must have been in those sand hills in front, brute must have bolted in the night. Guns firing at the last of them. We see his camp, now deserted, and march through pretty strongly entrenched, dammed the railway too with a huge sand bank and the canal. Up the other side of the canal. Arab village, mosque, palms, shade hurrah at last. Halt and pile arms. Very glad march over don't think I could go any further. Tardy arrival of tinned beef at 5 pm seized and eaten voraciously, many however seem too done up to eat. The village mosque is just above us the oasis lying in a hollow and has a good well but canal water is better and am afraid the men have been drinking some beastly swamp water from a ditch. Move for the night into the sand outside for fear of mosquitos and malaria. The men lie in their ranks, we most of us all together a little below them. Men cheering up and singing now something has come to eat.

So much for Putty's first action at Mahuta: Arabi had indeed retired and Major General Graham pushed on to Kassassin. The Gds Bde remained at Mahuta where they had the unpleasant but vital task of repairing the railway and cleaning out the canal. The work was interrupted on 28 August for Arabi made an attempt to drive General Graham out of Kassassin, and the Gds Bde was again ordered up in support; they were not required and after sunset returned to Mahuta. Balfour is more descriptive:

> After dinner in the middle of the second tune from the pipes a sudden order comes to fall in. Men fall in at once hoping that something has turned up at last. And soon the whole of the troops in camp were in motion, the brigade in echelon of battalions, the cavalry and artillery on the left.
>
> Marching by moonlight very pleasant and cool everyone in great spirits, after marching about 4 miles we made a long halt, and gradually everybody dropped off to sleep. Curious sight to see the whole brigade sleeping in the ranks just as they had halted. Enjoyed a sound sleep of an hour or two when the word came to fall in. Hallo the Grenadiers are retreating, 'Scots Guards right about turn, Quick March'. What is the meaning of this? Marked difference in the marching, all tramp along in a sullen indifferent way. 8 miles march for nothing. It turns out in the morning that the enemy had attacked Graham in great force and most of the firing we had heard was theirs but he had stood his ground and when their advance was checked the Household Cavalry and 7 DG swept down on their flank and utterly routed them.

19 Possibly 3985 Private Alexander McAulay (1858-NK) SG 1877-1889.

And back at Mahuta:

The typical guardsman would look curious in Pall Mall. Bristly beards (some have grown very well) hair cropped as if he had been undergoing 14 days, as brown as a Spaniard stained serge frock of an uncertain colour, trousers and boots somewhere underneath a thick coating of dust. The men get very hard work again digging out the block on the canal and railway: while at it they work tremendously hard, as the RE all say no ordinary infantry of the line could do the work they do. 29 August tents at last! Brought up by boat on the canal and now not only tents but kit bags and beds turn up. Here's luxury! Instantaneous rush on baths, general cleaning of teeth and brushing of hair. The tents look like a ship fully dressed all the clothes we have worn for the last week hung out to air and a change of clothes adopted, quite a curious sensation to feel thoroughly clean.

The Gds Bde was to spend over a week at Mahuta. Balfour wrote: 'One knows certainly that the medical stores are in a disgraceful state, the most ordinary remedies being conspicuous by their absence: what has a damping effect on one's ardour is to hear there is no chloroform, don't fancy my leg being sawn off without it. Hear that an unfortunate Life Guards man had his arm taken out at the shoulder and his yells were something awful to hear. Getting accustomed to heat now, so issue forth to explore surrounding country. Find that there is an Egyptian antiquity near here. The Villain,[20] Pulteney, Squire and I go and inspect it. It is close by the village three figures cut in red granite rather smaller than life size in the usual Egyptian style, guide books say it is a statue of Ramses II. At last we heard we were to move on the night of 9 September'.
    But then on 9 September:

Get lazily out of bed and hear we are to start at once. The old story of an attack at the front, hear that the enemy is within 2 miles, hope so, don't believe it. Advance a mile and a half and halt, no signs of the enemy. I thought not. On again, sand feels like London pavement in the hottest part of the season only soft, reflects the glare of the sun, like the heat of an oven, feel as if I was being fried when I lie down to rest at the halts. Arrive Kassissin.

Arabi had made another attempt to drive the British from Kassassin, but this was easily repulsed and he then withdrew into the lines he had prepared at Tel-el-Kebir. These lines were extensive covering a front of some 6,000 yards, which could only be approached over open sand. General Wolseley therefore decided to make an attack upon them at dawn on 13 September, which entailed an advance at night when it was cooler. For a force the size of Wolseley's Army this would be a novel operation requiring very careful preparation: in the event it was to be completely successful.
    Back with 1 SG at Kassissin, Balfour recalled:

Our tents and baggage arrived with laudable quickness this morning. Better camp this than Mahuta, no dust though the flies are worse. But we are well to the front now before everyone else, with a tent of Arabi's visible in front of us. Tel-el-Kebir can be seen from a

20   Lieutenant Charles Edward Hartpole Bowen (1862-1884) SG 1881-1884.

ridge near: at last the Guards are in their proper place. Here they stayed while the army assembled in and around Kassissin.

At 11 am on 12 September the army deployed. On the right was the Cavalry Division, echeloned slightly back; then came 1st Division with Major General Graham's Bde leading and the Gds Bde in the second line. On its left was 2nd Division with the Highland Bde leading, its left flank being parallel with the railway and Sweet-Water Canal, beyond which was the Indian Contingent. The forty-two guns were in the centre between 1st and 2nd Divisions. At 1.30 am the advance began at a steady pace. The Egyptian 1st Line swung back on the right, thus it was the Highland Bde who were closest when the first gleam of light appeared. They at once charged and carried the enemy's defences. Major General Graham's Bde assaulted a little later and by the time the Guards reached the enemy's parapet the battle was virtually over. In effect this was a flanking movement which proved unnecessary because the enemy did not stand and fight: the Egyptian Army was completely routed and lost all its guns.

Balfour recorded his experience:

At last the day began to break, we must be getting near now. 'Brigade halt, lie down'. 'The Coldstream and Grenadiers will extend, Scots Guards reserve'. Hallo is that a shot, crack – crack crack – crackle crackle bang – it was with a feeling of delight I heard this so afraid was I that our old friend would again give us the slip. In a moment what seemed to be the whole horizon was lit all along with flashes like summer lightning or a flickering fire. The first bang was followed by a swish and a shell came whizzing over us, one after the other they plunged into the same place, and then we rose up and deployed to the left in rear of the Coldstream. All our men were perfectly indifferent to the firing, deployed and lay down as if they were at drill. It struck me as strange we heard no bullets over our heads but soon I observed they were dropping about kicking up a little dust every here and there. Shells are getting a bit closer. Time to move I think. We soon do. 'Rise up and advance'. A short 50 mins; the firing began at 5.30 am and by 6.20 am the trenches were only occupied by dead and dying arabs. We scrambled through the ditch into his lines which look as if they ought to have stood him in better stead. Our men are marching the deuce of a pace about 4 miles an hour I should think, which makes one feel very hot now the sun is getting up in the sky. Press on up the ridge in front of us. Here we are! Palms, green fields, village, canal, railway, and there just below us the whole of Arabi's camp. Tents, camels, horses, everything left. Increased pace downhill. Fall out by half companies for water and then disperse to loot. We fall in and march to the top of the hill and bivouac. In the evening tremendous enthusiasm was evoked by the bands of the brigade playing massed. Three cheers for the Queen. Three cheers for the Duke of Connaught, Three cheers for Sir Garnet Wolseley, and we retired to bed.

The next day, 14 September, 1 SG marched down to the station for the journey to Cairo. Balfour again:

Suddenly the bugles sounded, the train has arrived, and we start at once. We get our things on and fall in, and march down to the station. Very tired; train pretty crammed; sleep out of the question; jolting is a mild expression to apply to this train. It resembles the transit of the modest kind of country cart over gigantic boulders of rock. At intervals stop and chat with

Officers 1 SG at Citadel Cairo, 1882. (RHQ Scots Guards Archives)

regiments bivouaced on the line: at length we reach Zagazig where we have to wait an hour or two. The pyramids in sight and at last Cairo about 11.30 am (15 September). All the available male population swarm out to see us. Quite an unexpected surprise to wait only half an hour or so before starting. The pipes struck up 'Hieland Laddie' and we marched into the streets. The women make a most extraordinary shrill screaming noise from the top storied windows of the houses to express joy, and certainly they treated us to a full dose of it. At the time we did not know whether it was pain, pleasure or surprise at the pipes; it was as curious a noise as I ever heard. The streets seemed interminable and together with the heat it being just about midday, the dust and the narrow streets, and the hill at the end leading up to the Citadel we all felt pretty beat when we arrived there.

1 SG spent the next six weeks in the Citadel. A last word from Balfour:

At first we could not all of us go out, one a company staying in barracks but in a day or two when the town was full of troops and no disorder had ensued only the field officer and picquet officer remained in. Cairo not the place we had hoped, nights beastly hot. One wakes up feeling languid and tired and utterly indifferent as to how one is to spend the day. Cold tub even doesn't set one up much and then comes the ordeal of breakfast. Ordeal, because if we had not had a good training in the desert, I don't think we could stand the way the flies swarm over everything. On the 25th Khedive arrives from Alexandria, battalion has to help line the streets. Men very much smartened up, belts and helmets being pipeclayed again and serges very much cleaned.

On 31 October the battalion left Cairo and embarked at Alexandria by half-battalions, arriving in London between 14 and 16 November. It lost 15 men: one died of wounds at the battle of Tel-el-Kebir, the remainder died of enteric fever. Putty will have learnt much about himself in this brief and successful campaign, and emerged from it a much stronger man both physically and mentally. Unlike many of the other officers he does not appear to have suffered from the effects of the sun or other illness; so, either had a very strong constitution or took care of himself, or both. His greatest experience would have been the time he spent living and working with his soldiers.

1st Battalion Scots Guards at Home 1883-1888

Putty was to spend the next five years with 1 SG following the rotation of all Guards battalions at home. After the winter of 1882 spent at Wellington Barracks recovering from the Egyptian Campaign, the battalion moved to Windsor in March 1883. Here life for a young officer would have been a mix of public duties at Windsor Castle, administrative duties in barracks, low level training especially musketry, and some sport. Five months later, in August 1883, the battalion moved to the Tower where the mix would have been much the same.

The following year, 1884, the battalion again moved twice. In April it moved to Aldershot where the focus was on training and preparation for the intense public duties that were to come; then, in July, the battalion moved to Chelsea where it was to remain until September 1885. During that time Putty did duties at Buckingham Palace, St James Palace (Queen's Guard) and the Bank of England (Bank Picquet). He is also recorded as having been picquet officer on numerous occasions, a member of a court of inquiry and of a district court martial. Remembering that the numbers involved in all duties were considerably larger than those today, and the time required for practices and rehearsals, there would have been little time for any other military activities. However, for a young officer, there would have been more than enough time to enjoy London, and the evidence suggests Putty did just that.

Sixteen months later, September 1885, 1 SG moved back to Dublin where they stayed for almost exactly a year. Here there were public duties to be done at Dublin Castle with some training at the Curragh, as well as time to pick up the social contacts of four years earlier. It may be on this tour in Ireland that he met the Marquess and Marchioness of Londonderry with whom he was to have a particularly close relationship: the 6th Marquess was the Lord Lieutenant of Ireland 1886-1889. Then it was back to Chelsea Barracks in September 1886 for another twelve months of intense public duties. The only differences of note from the previous time were Putty's duties on Tylt Yard Guard, then the entrance to Horse Guards as well as Buckingham Palace and mounted for the last time in 1898, and on St George's Detachment which was probably a guard at St George's Barracks in Charing Cross; the Barracks existed until 1889 and may well have been empty pending disposal. In 1887 the Major General inspected 1 SG for the first time in Putty's service and it was also noticeable that there was more training fitted in with the public duties during this tour at Chelsea.

Whenever he had the opportunity Putty got away shooting or fishing which, over the years, brought him into contact with many people of influence. Towards the end of September he was shooting partridges at Fotheringam in Angus, at the invitation of Walter Fothringham.[21] Then at the end of 1887 1 SG moved from Chelsea to Windsor and was replaced by 2 SG. Putty did not go to Windsor and was posted to 2 SG.

21   Walter Thomas James Fothringham (1862-1936) Eton SG 1883-1891.

2nd Battalion Scots Guards at Home 1888-1890

Putty had done little to distinguish himself during his first seven years in the 1st Battalion but now, in the 2nd Battalion, that was about to change. One reason for this was the increase in sporting activity at all levels in the army. Putty was an excellent all-round athlete and a very keen and effective organiser of sport; in due course he was to become responsible for the development of football in the army, and serve on the Football Association. However, his two representative matches in 1888 give little indication of what was to come. On 29 February he represented the Household Brigade against Old Etonians at Queen's Club, a match they lost 2-9. Then, on 8 March, he represented 2 SG against 3 Gren Gds at Battersea Park, and again they lost 1-2.

On the military side there was better progress when in July he passed his promotion exam to Captain with a distinction in tactics. Two months later the battalion moved to Richmond Barracks, Dublin for another year. The *Brigade of Guards Magazine* noted in October:

> The 2 SG cricket season terminated with the return match against the Vice-Regal team when they avenged their defeat in the first match. An excellent photograph was taken of the combined teams. A copy of this, elegantly mounted, has been presented to the Sergeants Mess by Mr Pulteney, the captain of the team.

It also recorded that he was a member of the committee for the 2 SG Athletics Meeting held at Richmond Barracks, Dublin on 12 June 1889: perhaps less noteworthy was his own performance – winning the Menagerie Race (with a guinea pig) and coming third in the 100 yards handicap for officers. Later that month the battalion went to the Curragh for annual musketry and other military training. The tour ended on 7 September when 2 SG travelled from the Curragh by train to Kingsdown and embarked on HMS *Assistance*, arriving at Woolwich on 11 September; from there they travelled by train to Chelsea.

The 2 SG football team had been preparing for the season while they were in Ireland and on 12 November they played the 1st round of the Army Cup against the Northumberland Fusiliers winning 7-1. *The Harborough Advertiser & Midland Mail*, local to Putty's home at Ashley, has two articles from this period:

> As an Eton boy, Pulteney naturally became imbued with a love of athletic games and while at school he played football regularly, but from lack of opportunity he was unable to do so from 1879 to 1889, when 2nd Battalion Scots Guards formed their first football team. This long interval doubtless prevented him taking the rank as a player to which his ability entitled him. From 1889 he was centre forward of his battalion team.

And

> In 1889 he proved that his powers of endurance were equal to his energy, for having undertaken the feat of walking eighty miles, straight away, on the Great North road in twenty-four hours, he succeeded in covering the distance in twenty-one and a half hours (including three hours rest) – a very smart performance.

These articles may well have originated from the battalion or from his family but nevertheless give an idea of his sporting and physical abilities.

In 1890 Putty passed his Musketry Course at Hythe achieving 1st Class grade; this was another subject in which he took great interest. But it was as a football player that he would probably best remember that year. On 25 January he represented 2 SG against 1 SG in the 3rd round of the Army Cup at Burton's Court, a game they won. He played for the battalion again in the quarter-final against the Cameronians at Chester, and they won this game 4-0. Putty, playing centre forward, scored all four goals. Later that month the battalion played the Somerset Light Infantry in the semi-final at Richmond, London; again they won 5-4, and again Putty scored four of their goals. The Army Football Association record of the match says:

> Lieutenant Pulteney (centre forward) kicking off, the Scots Guards attacked on the left and centre, but being repulsed were compelled to act on the defensive. A good run by Chadwick[22] enabled Pulteney to kick the first goal for the Scots.

The final of the Army Cup was played against the Royal Highlanders at Kennington Oval on 31 March: 2 SG lost 1-3. The Army Football Association recorded:

> Two officers, Lieutenant Erskine [23] and Lieutenant Pulteney played for the Scots Guards, and the latter specially distinguished himself during the engagement. Led by Lieutenant Pulteney, the Scots Guards executed some brilliant charges, amid furious cheering from the redcoats (Gate: 2,000) that circled the ground, and at one time it looked as if the comparatively under-sized Highlanders were certain to get the worst of it.

Putty's time in 2 SG came to an end in May when he was posted to Caterham as Adjutant of the Guards Depot, an appointment he was to hold for just nine months.

Adjutant Guards Depot 1890-1891

On 28 May the Guards Depot held its athletics meeting with the *Brigade of Guards Magazine* recording:

> There were some 50 or 60 events and these were worked off, as may be expected, with clock-like precision and military smartness which reflected great credit on the committee, Lieutenant and Adjutant WP Pulteney, and Captain and Quartermaster TW Gunton [Gren Gds], who also looked after well the comfort of visitors.

Two days later, on 30 May, Putty represented the Guards Depot in the Household Brigade and Garrison Sports at Burton's Court, coming third in the 400 yards for officers.

By now elected to the 3rd Guards Club he attended his first dinner at the Metropole Hotel on 3 June when the Duke of Athlone was in the chair; and he continued to support the club for the

---

22   8008 Private James Chadwick (1868-NK) SG 1888-1901.
23   Lord Walter John Francis Erskine (1865-1955) Eton SG 1888-1892 later Earl of Mar and Kellie.

rest of his life, rarely missing its annual dinner except when prevented from attending by war. On 25 July he would have been on parade when Field Marshal HRH The Duke of Connaught, Commander in Chief, reviewed the Scots Guards in Hyde Park.

Football was not neglected: in September he refereed a 6-a-side football match at 2 SG's 'Annual Athletics Sport' at Pirbright Camp. The following month the Guards Depot Football Club report in the *Brigade of Guards Magazine* said: 'Mr Pulteney, our Adjutant, has intro-duced something new at the Depot in the shape of colours'. A later edition noted that, on 15 November, Putty had represented Guards Depot Football Club in the first round of the Surrey Cup (Junior Competition) against Barnes, a match they won 3-1.

At the end of the year (27 December) he was invited to shoot at Panshanger, at the invitation of Earl Cowper (Francis Thomas de Grey Cowper 7th Earl Cowper 1834-1905, Ettie Grenfell's uncle). The other guns included William Grenfell[24], Balfour[25] and Walter Fothringham. It may well have been then that he met Ettie Grenfell[26] for the first time. She had married Willie Grenfell three years earlier on 17 February 1887. It is possible that he met Ettie before the Grenfells were married, but there is no evidence to support this other than her relationship with the Earls of Cowper; the 6th Earl was her grandfather and her uncle, the 7th Earl, was Lord Lieutenant of Ireland 1880-1882. Perhaps this was where their relationship started but it is never mentioned in any of his many letters to her, and it seems highly unlikely given her age at that time.

It is clear that Putty played a full part in the activities of the Guards Depot but he must also have been an effective adjutant because he returned to 2 SG in February 1891 to take up the appointment of adjutant in the battalion, an appointment that he was to hold for four years. The Commandant Guards Depot in 1890 was Major Henry Edward Colville[27] who Putty was to serve under again in Uganda and South Africa. Colville kept a record of his officers and Putty's record includes a summary: 'Success – Good. Fit for DAAG or Brigade Major'. This is remark-able considering the short time he was at the Depot; Colville must have thought very highly of him.

Adjutant 2nd Battalion Scots Guards 1891-1895

The adjutant is the principal staff officer in a battalion, responsible to the commanding officer for its day to day running. For all of Putty's time as adjutant, the commanding officer was Lieutenant Colonel Campbell.[28] Campbell, 'Bar', had served in 1 SG during the Egyptian Campaign of 1882; after command of 2 SG he went on to command the Regiment, and was afterwards 3rd Baron Blythswood. The battalion's military programme will give an idea of what Putty did in these four years and the sporting records, particularly football, are also helpful. But there are also, for the first time, a number of Putty's letters to Ettie Grenfell and others which give a more detailed account, as well as providing an insight to the character of the man.

24   William Henry Grenfell later 1st Lord Desborough (1855-1945) and Ettie Grenfell's husband.
25   Possibly Arthur Balfour (1848-1930) Eton then Chief Secretary for Ireland.
26   Ethel Anne Priscilla Grenfell née Fane (1867-1952).
27   Major Henry Edward Colville Gren Gds (1852-1907) Eton.
28   Lieutenant Colonel Barrington Bulkley Douglas Campbell (1845-1918) SG 1864-1898 and CO 2 SG 1891-1896.

2 SG was at Windsor when Putty became its adjutant. It moved to Wellington Barracks in August 1892, to the Tower of London in September 1893, and to Chelsea Barracks in July 1894. From the outset it is clear from the Orders Book that Putty got a firm grip on the battalion with battalion parades held, at least to begin with, almost every day for drill, route marches or fatigues. The barracks were regularly inspected and divine services held every week; in every area Putty seems to have been determined to drive up standards. On 3 March 1891 he was elected as a member of the committee of the Army Football Association on which he was to then to serve, except when overseas, for the next thirty years.

On 21 June Putty wrote to Ettie Grenfell from Victoria Barracks, Windsor:

> My dear Mrs Grenfell, Am so sorry, that your telegram was not replied to until this morning but was away acting on a committee at the Athletic Sports in London going up by the 10.25 train so did not get your telegram in time to answer it last night. Am so sorry, really, that I could not come but was booked this Sunday to go to the Raincliffes[29] if I went anywhere but owing to the 'Blue Seal' dinner in the town of Greenwich this evening am afraid I don't see my way to the river at all. Are you going to be at Taplow all this week if so will come over if I may someday. Believe me. Yours sincerely WP Pulteney.

Ettie became a woman of extraordinary influence at the highest levels of the Country. Putty may well have been in love with her but she had many other admirers and confidantes. His letters to her are open and often indiscreet; they carry an implicit trust on how the information was to be used. What her feelings were for him and how far the relationship developed can only be matters for speculation because the reader will only see his letters, but she did keep more than one hundred of them for the rest of her life.

Soon after the Grenfells' wedding in 1887 a group of like-minded friends began to form around them, and especially Ettie: in due course they became known as the 'Souls'. The group acted on an intellectual plane with men and women discussing a wide range of subjects on the basis of equality, including the arts, politics, and more abstract issues; it was also about relationships between the sexes, friendships expressed in romantic and affectionate language. One observer put it simply: 'They shot, and ate, and drank, and flirted, and talked. The only unforgivable sin was to be dull or stupid'. They considered themselves superior in wit, originality and charm to any other social set. Ettie had a central role in the Souls and in many ways it was her charm and intelligence that provided a focus. However, Arthur Balfour (Prime Minister 1902-1905) and Mary Elcho[30] were two of the early principals. The gatherings were invariably at weekends and in the summer at Panshanger and Wrest, Ettie's uncle's homes, but then often at Taplow. Other Souls at that time were Margot Tennant[31], Alfred Lyttelton who had been

---

29   Probably William Henry Forester Denison Viscount Raincliffe 1st Earl of Londesborough (1834-1900) Eton.

30   Lady Mary Constance Elcho née Wyndham – her daughter Lady Cynthia married Herbert Henry Asquith's son.

31   Margot Tennant (1864-1945) married Herbert Henry Asquith (1852-1928) Prime Minister 1908-1916).

in Evans House at Eton and married Margot Tennant's sister Laura, and George Curzon[32]. Pembroke (10th Earl), whose nephew was to be Pulteney's ADC in 1914, and Harry Cust[33] were also Souls. Charles Harbord[34] may well have been one as also Winston Churchill. Kitchener had been a friend of Willie Grenfell since 1885 and Ettie was said to be the only women he was at ease with, but he does not appear to have been a Soul. Putty would have been an unlikely Soul but it is possible that he was one.

Putty wrote to her again on 25 July:

> My dear Mrs Grenfell, If this will suit for next Friday talk it over with Mrs Drummond. Come down to Windsor so as to get there about 4. I will have boats for us ready to go on the river and return for dinner in Barracks at 8.30 dine and return by the 10.45. There will be you and Mrs L and Willie and Lawrence [Laurence Drummond SG] now you must get another young man for yourself and two more ladies one for William and the other for Lawrence. Pleasant morning to you am off to Windsor. Yours sincerely WP Pulteney.

The letters are reproduced verbatim because there is sometimes more than one meaning, and to allow the reader to get into the character of the man. Putty's use of a formal signature seems to have been an affectation at this stage in his life. He wrote again to Ettie on 29 July from Victoria Barracks, Windsor:

> Dear Mrs Willie, Just my luck I am obliged to go down into Essex today to my sister's place, it looks like being a horrible day down anywhere, am 'awfully sorry' as should have enjoyed the pleasure of your society much more; but I got a telegram last night which left me no option as to my plans today. Return last train tonight so if you don't go to London tomorrow send me a wire and we will river if you feel inclined. Believe me. Yours sincerely WP Pulteney.

He had also sent her a telegram at 9.52 am that morning:

> Cannot come over today am obliged to go to Essex if you don't go to London tomorrow will come over if I may. Pulteney.

There may well be innuendo in his new way of addressing Ettie but that can only be conjecture. He wrote to her again the following day (30 July) from Victoria Barracks, Windsor:

> Dear Mrs Willie, Oh, you best of chaperons, keep the chaff about 'the tallest' I could not get my gallant Colonel [probably Lieutenant Colonel Campbell CO 2 SG] to leave me, suggested going to call on you while he went for his coat but the previous recollections

---

32 George Nathaniel Curzon (1859-1925) Eton Viceroy of India 1899-1905 and Lord Privy Seal in Asquith's Government 1915.

33 Henry 'Harry' John Cockayne-Cust (1861-1917) Eton politician, renowned conversationalist and womaniser.

34 Hon Charles Harbord (1855-1924) SG 1873-1904 Deputy Chief Whip in Lords, Asquith and Lloyd George's Governments, later 6th Baron Suffield – one of Ettie's suitors.

(rather dire on your side they appeared to be) of your charms were too much for the Colonel so he insisted on coming too. Yes, all the others know about coming in the afternoon, we ought to have good fun if the weather is fine and everybody in good spirits. Had a dreadful journey to get wet through and was dreadfully envious of Max when I heard of him from you this morning. What is the meaning of the little crescent you so often make in your writing? Yours very sincerely WP Pulteney.

Again from Victoria Barracks, Windsor on 2 August:

My dear Mrs Willie, Can you give me a brief description of the waterproof left behind on Friday night as cannot find it at present anywhere, many thanks for the return of my coat, did you find out that there was no lining in the sleeves it was a coat which would not bear being worn by such a fair lady in daylight but it has been honoured by you now in the dark. Am not going into Essex after all on Tuesday so if you are going to be at Taplow and want a slave to row you about send a wire any time, from 2 o'clock am at your command, go down to Essex on the Wednesday morning for the day. How did the 'Wrest' part go off. Yours very sincerely WP Pulteney.

On 26 August he wrote:

My dear Mrs Willie, Shall be delighted to come over tomorrow only wire me in the morning what time you expect me, can get away from here by the 1 o'clock train, train arriving Taplow 1.30 or would come after lunch by the train arriving at 3.12 just according to what you expect me to do. Started up from here in a punt yesterday afternoon against that fearful wind but only got just beyond the Duke of Sutherland's place when the pole smashed in half and we had to send down to the lock for a man to tow us up. Two of us then walked back here from the Club in an hour and twenty minutes the third party arriving a quarter of an hour afterwards, nice sociable thing to do wasn't it? Yours sincerely WP Pulteney.

The letters were becoming longer and more informative. On 5 September, from Victoria Barracks, Putty wrote:

Dear Mrs Willie, Have been wanting to write to you all the week but the reason for the delay was waiting for a definite answer about going to Walter Fotheringham but up to the present none has come, though it was faithfully promised at the end of this week from Blair,[35] am very down in my luck and unhappy for several reasons though the grounds for my trouble I cannot entrust to paper. What a world it is, one of the ladies on the other side of the water wrote calling me I don't know what because of going to see you once or twice, was stupid enough to mention the fact that you have been so nice to the banished officer at Windsor, so you were, have just told her to keep those little accusations to herself otherwise there will be troubles in days to come. Took my first holiday down to Alton Towers Lord

---

35   Blair Castle, home of John James Hugh Henry Stewart-Murray 7th Duke of Atholl (1840-1917) SG 1859-1866.

Shrewsbury's place,[36] such a lovely place, if you have never seen it you must go there, there was one Earl of Shrewsbury who did all the landscape gardening of an enormous glen (very nearly wrote the wrong word, not a christian name?!) there is an epitaph put up to the good man, the epitaph being 'He made the desert smile' it amused me, have been promised it for my honeymoon as earthly paradise to take the lady of my choice to <u>when</u> that event comes off. I shot all three days the remainder except the noble Lord S all went to the Derby races, it was rather a funny party, and there was a good rough and tumble after dinner one night. There was a splendid stream last Sunday and I punted Lord Calthorpe [6th Baron 1829-1910] and Lady Randolph Churchill[37] from the Guards Club to the Hatch in an hour and some funny thoughts passed through my mind touching the people I was punting. Am dining with that party tonight, but have not fallen in love with Lady S yet though she is very nice, am taking my warning from you or rather your words of advice. Do write and tell me any news, love to Willie. Believe me. Yours sincerely WP Pulteney (crescent).

This letter gives an indication of the circles in which Putty was now moving. He wrote again to Ettie Grenfell from Victoria Barracks on 16 September; she was staying at Gobernuisgach Reay Forest, Lairg which the Grenfells had rented for the shooting:

My dear Mrs Willie, You must write again when you have time your letter quite freshened me up just at a time when I wanted it most, things are down in the world have got the (mumps), want change of air me thinks. Glad from your letter to hear 'you are getting quite good on the hill' always thought you were 'quite good' before you got to the hill ha-ha. Poor little trouts you seem to be catching heaps but the big ones seem to beat you but still they would not be (refined) if they were big, would they? Was under solemn promise not to tell anyone otherwise nearly let out that Lady Sarah Churchill was engaged to the soldier Wilson,[38] I wormed it out of Lady Randolph Churchill when she was down here, don't think it is much of a match but they say they are very happy which is the great thing isn't it? Thus far have I got without letting out that the (Masterly) plan has all fallen through as the Ls go to Langwell (Scotland) the same time as you only found it out on Monday, had chanced it being all right the week before and written to say would go up, but shan't now as don't think they have got any pals going to be at Murtly [probably Murthly Castle home of Walter Fothringham] at that time and as it costs so much £ s d, have written to Walter Fothringham to say that I can't go on that account which is the very truth indeed. No, have not played any more picquet, have you? Am reduced to playing whist with the Duchess of Marlborough[39] she plays extraordinary well for her age, bye the bye was taught besique by

---

36   Major Charles Henry John Chetwynd-Talbot 20th Earl of Shrewsbury (1860-1921). Shrewsbury had two sisters: Lady Gertrude who married 13th Earl of Pembroke and Lady Theresa who married 6th Marquess of Londonderry. 15th Earl of Pembroke and 7th Marquess of Londonderry were to be Putty's ADCs in 1914.
37   Lady Randolph Churchill (1854-1921) Lord Randolph Churchill died 1895 and she then married George Cornwallis-West (1874-1951) SG 1895-1901 and 1917-1920 whom she later divorced.
38   Captain Gordon Chesney Wilson RHG (1865-1914) later Lieutenant Colonel killed in action 6 November 1914.
39   Probably Francis Anne Emily Vane (1822-1899) wife of 7th Duke of Marlborough and mother of Lord Randolph Churchill.

Lady Randolph, forgot to mention that in my last letter, think I must have created a good impression as was asked down to Newmarket next Saturday but it is the day we move to London so could not accept. Am quite sorry to leave this place, my room looks quite naked as my servant has packed all the photos and pictures, shan't see them again until Sunday I suppose isn't sad? Went down to Caterham on Monday to look at the young lambs went with the General and Colonel of the Regiment[40] so felt a little bit of a swell more especially as I laid down the law the whole time if you don't have 'cheek' when one is young one never will have it. How I envy your life up there one would be so fit something delightful to think of why you have your breakfast the same time as the Adjutant. We have got a farewell dinner here tonight, partly to finish off all the wine in the Mess and partly to commemorate that my little friend (Wm Herey)[41] has forwarded his papers resigning his commission to me, you bet I didn't forget to send them on, poor little fellow the whole of his case has been most sad, am sorry for him really now between ourselves. Do write again Mrs Willie and Believe me. Yours very sincerely WP Pulteney.

Putty stayed with Walter Fothringham at Murthly Castle for the first half of October. The other guests included Lord Carnegie[42], Captain Menzies,[43] Captain Scott Murray,[44] and LJ Benson (Walter's brother in law). They shot partridges at the beginning, fished the Tay for the next five days, and on the last two days they were again shooting.

Later that month Putty was at Cotterstock Hall, Oundle[45] from where he wrote to Ettie on 25 October:

My dear Mrs Willie, The general does thank you with all his polished official manners for again gracing him with a view of your hand writing, most kind of you, your letter like yourself quite charming in all its references. Thanks am in the best of health, things going better all round, the (mumps) is on the wane just at present may it take its departure altogether together with the leaves. But this is sad to think that you are really seriously off abroad to Indian climes so soon and for such a long time, but we must have a shake of the hand before you go, have got lots of things I want to have a chat about, several things which the cool head with the dark hair can give the humble and obedient servant her opinion, an opinion valued for its soundness even by the half past seven breakfasty adjutant with all his nasty nagging ways, formal letters etc. I go up to London on Tuesday afternoon late, am playing a football match in the afternoon at Burtons Court Chelsea from 3.30-5 pm after which if alive shall go to the Turkish Baths to be cleaned from the mud, have bruises rubbed, wounds washed etc. Will you by chance be in London that morning or if staying in London that night do lets dine and do a play after that shall not be in the village until the 31st. Dear dog Fred went with his master to Murtly Castle NB[46] for a fortnight they

40   Field Marshal HRH Arthur Duke of Connaught and Strathearn Colonel SG 1883-1904.
41   Possibly John Eustace Hercy (1887-1891) SG.
42   Lord Charles Noel Carnegie later 10th Earl of Southesk (1854-1941) a relative of Fothringham.
43   Captain Neil James Menzies (1855-1910) SG 1874-1892 later 8th Bt.
44   Captain Basil Henry Scott-Murray (1858-1927) SG 1880-1899.
45   Home of Henry Wickham Wickham (1855-1933) SG 1874-1887.
46   Probably Murthly Castle North Britain home of Walter Fothringham.

both enjoyed themselves immensely, though the river was in bad order, no ladies in the house except Mrs Balfour for three days and Lady Carnegie[47] for two so gave myself up entirely to sports as they are termed three salmon were foolish enough to take my fly and be landed they weighed 20, 21 and 28 lbs, so they all had been alive quite long enough to know better. The weather was bad, rain etc, the same as everywhere else. Got a splendid rise of a person who is a mutual friend will tell you when we meet, diplomacy was brought into play with the most satisfactory results. Now tell me did you ever fathom the Lady C difficulty or was there nothing to it, am sure your intelligence has found that out by now. Am stiff after first days hunting yesterday, we had a very nice run indeed with (Wm) Mackenzie's though we thought the hounds hunted better than the master who tried to hunt them, such a delightful warm day, the nerve in good order, quiet horse felt like competing all over for anything or anybody, isn't that a nice feeling after all the best thing in life is to feel really well, as am on leave won't let them forward me any unpleasant things about the lambs, the consequence was on return from NB the other day was met in Barracks by everyone with a brass hat on, each with a little complaint about the other, all full of the glorious deeds that they severally one by one had performed in my absence for the glory of the regiment and of course last but not least in serving their adjutant. Met Judge Lord Morris[48] on the Queen's Guard, St James the night previous to his departure for Wynyard[49] he was full of eulogies on behalf of your host, told me he liked you on which point we were in common though it was not about a person who ought to be classed with such a word as common. Am utterly and entirely ruining myself by firing cartridges, have shot away over 500 this week, the week after next it will be a matter of treble that amount must go without dinner during the winter months to recruit the poor purse. Do write again when you have the time the Club or Wellington Barracks always finds me in London and a telegram is always redirected from either so if I am by chance in 'the village' the same day you fix upon let's have a talk and Believe me. Yours sincerely WP Pulteney.

And then from Wellington Barracks on 4 November:

My dear Mrs Willie, Have been trying to see if I could get out of a shooting engagement to accept your most inviting invitation (alas!) I have no horses either at Windsor or London except my 17 hands charger and it would be a shame to take him out of the Barrack Square as his poor old fore legs would never stand it, but apart from that have been engaged for a week to shoot where I am going tomorrow so don't think that I can throw them over now at the last moment, though I should have liked to have driven about with you more than anything in this world, expect you will find Mrs Ellis also following on wheels with one or two others at her heels. I hear all sorts of stories about Newmarket, terrible rows etc. Am worked to death have no peace of mind of any sort when I once show my face in these Barracks. Went to see Adolphus Tempest act in the Pantomime Rehearsal last night he is no good. The night before I went to see 'Jessica' at the Criterion, don't go to see that. Shall

---

47   Lady Ethel Mary Elizabeth Carnegie née Bannerman (1868-1947) wife of Lord Carnegie.
48   Michael Morris (1826-1901) previously Lord Chief Justice for Ireland and now Lord of Appeal.
49   Home of Marquess of Londonderry in Co Durham.

be back next Saturday the 7th and am playing football at Windsor that day against the Windsor Phoenise we shall be beaten. Yours very sincerely WP Pulteney.

Again after Christmas, on 3 January 1892, he wrote:

My dear Mrs Willie, The best of health, happiness, appetite, with success to the crushers, to you for this good year, which we have just entered into, right glad I was for one to see the last of 91, was very tired of it, don't know why but a New Year seems to put fresh life into one whether it is the good resolutions or the speedy breaking of them gives one the extra fillip can't tell – well am more than anxious to know how you have got on, am afraid you had bad weather in the Mediterranean if it was anything approaching to what we had here – a charmingly bound little book arrived at the beginning of Xmas week, no name, no compliments, all hearsay evidence to give one the clue to the donor, delightful book, so many thanks to you trust you remember on your travels 'all hurry is worse than useless'; think on the adage 'Tis pace that kills' etc 'Ye wearie wayfarer' – Thankful for one thing we in London are that Xmas is a thing of the past the lambs all overeat them-selves, but they were too sleepy to get out of the Barracks luckily, otherwise they would all have overdrunk themselves as well – they behaved in the most exemplary manner so well in fact that it seemed impossible to last, but the most severe trial for the Scotchman viz the New Year is over with even less (exhilarance) of spirits – a mutual friend not far from here saw a lot of one another during Xmas, became quite good at besique after a few lessons, shall be able to compete with you when you come back if lessons continue to be taken, looking very well she is now though she had a bad time in bed the begin-ning of last month – Not the tallest but very nearly the tallest has also been in London during Xmas also looking very well and full of nice ideas, then again another friend in Upper Grosvenor Street has also been laid up for the last fortnight with bronchitis, more besique has been played there, altogether there have been several friends to wile away the evenings after the soldier's long hard fought days which has given your humble servant a little needed relaxation, fancy have not been out of the Metropolis since 1 December for an hour except to pay a visit to my old friend Caterham where I had to go to make myself most disagreeable which purpose me thinks I effected pretty well as Dick Somerset[50]the adjutant there said, had no idea you could be so nasty, but the brow was knit and it was business with the lambs that morning, came away in my own mind covered with glory which was all right wasn't it. I am doing Laurence's work for him for a week while he is away, he is our new Regimental Adjutant but alas not for long as in April am afraid he is going on General Methuen's Staff in the Home District, it is a great pity in some ways and a very good thing for him in others, have advised him to take General Methuen's Staff myself as am sure it will lead to something else afterwards – give my love to all my friends in India especially Charlie Harbord, tell him he is forgiven notwithstanding the fact that he cut his own brother officers when he was over here, the last accounts of Lord Suffolk are very satisfactory, the influenza is flying about all over the place people are dropping from its effects at every house, it seems coming worse with the New Year which

50   Captain Hon Richard Fitzroy Somerset (1865-1899) Gren Gds son of 2nd Baron Raglan.

is very unpleasant of it – The pearl case is now at an end except there have been some very naughty little stories based on it – Mrs Manton had a dinner and baccarat after, the good lady and Mari lost 3000 between them, a baronet from Mount St a friend of yours won most of it, he wanted it badly, me too have been having rather fun lately, he is still firm to his purpose and has since been in love with two ladies, one of which received a lovely dog which we never cease to chaff him about, but it is no good for she loves another – give my love to Willie and do write you must excuse this very dull letter and Believe me. Yours very sincerely WP Pulteney (with crescent).

On 1 February 1892 Putty was elected Honorary Secretary of the Army Football Association, an appointment that was to take much of his time over the next three years. It was probably no coincidence that this happened at the same time as an ankle injury which forced his retirement as a player. In the meantime he received a letter from Ettie in India because he wrote to her from Wellington Barracks on 3 March:

Dear Mrs Willie, Heaps of thanks for a charming letter dated 17 January from Madras, as there is nothing I should like better than to give you a diamond tiara, here goes in the shape of a letter, trust the contents will continue to shine and be brilliant without being sent out to the jeweller to be shined up, do forgive the word shine occurring twice but it is only another and on to my poor leg – well here we are enjoying the most horrible weather, constant changes from snow to rain more fickle than your humble servant. You shall not accuse me of having forgotten the Anglo Indian when she returns if the former will deign to recognise the humble adjutant. Thanks the glorious phalanx of sixteen are all well; have been only fairly happy but with 16 on the tapis one is lucky not to be miserable – I will certainly come to be your Military Secretary when you want me though whether the letters will be able to be read I cannot tell – You say you will be back on the 29th of this month so this letter ought to catch you about Suez or wherever you have directed them to send you the little epistles. Have been to two mask balls which have been given at Covent Garden, there my behaviour was not of the best, though fits of devilry carried the stern mind of the adjutant away he enjoyed himself the more, the first ball there was none escaped detection but the 2nd ok what a failure, could detect none was looking for a tall lady who does not live far from here who told me she was going in a crimson domino but weak creature that I am it never struck me that woman must tell the untruth, so now no more faith in tall women of course she went in something quite another colour so now have got the ump in that quarter, the tall no longer give me medium height, for all that one of the 16 who is down in the country wrote to me upbraiding me for not having been to call on her called me a little brute but added she could not help liking me because I was so straight we thought the Orderly Room ceiling would have come down upon my head the truth was so unexpected!! There are only three regiments left in the Army Cup or rather should say only two as two of them are the 1st and 2nd Scots Guards which fact is most satisfactory to me but am afraid the 71st will beat us both this year, the lambs are mad with excitement, they play in the Barrack Square from morning to night, they kicked the ball into a ladies face driving by, about a month ago, such a furious letter it took the adjutant all his time to pacify the poor thing but his polished manners told in the long run and she now loves the lambs because of the courteous adjutant, what a world of humbug London has got over the

Alington[51] marriage it brought on many tales which were amusing to the readers of the *Sporting Times* etc, but for a person really in love give me my Lord of Chelsea[52] the young lady is fairly master of that situation, future father mother and all the rest in law included. Your life of travel must have been very jolly one only think that I have not been out of London since the 1st December for one single night you will find a poor creature to look at – our mutual friend who lived not very far from Taplow Court last year in a house by the mill is shortly going to have an addition to her family, poor thing how I pity her. Will you come and spend Easter in Paris with me am under a sort of compact to go and gallop at the manoeuvres at Dover but want a rest together with hilarity so am thinking of giving the volunteers the church, between ourselves they do not interest me very much – What is one to do? The clergyman here is very angry because only three of the lambs attended his church on Ash Wednesday, he taxes me with not working them up in that line more, but the blame rests with him as that is his department not mine, a regiment at the Curragh used to order so many a company to attend but don't agree with those principles. How was my friend Charlie Harbord, well I trust he ought to have been very nice to you if he obeyed my instruction which as a good soldier of course he did do. Speedy return to you both. Believe me. Yours sincerely WP Pulteney.

This letter was to be his last, at least the last that is known to exist, until their correspondence resumed seventeen years later. They must have seen each other from time to time during that period but perhaps Ettie decided to cool it or maybe he did; by then she had two children (Julian aged 4 and Billy aged 2) and may well have been pregnant with Monica. Whatever the reason Putty was as busy as ever over the next two years (1892-1894) with his job as adjutant, his numerous sporting and social engagements, and the organisation of football in the army. On 4 May 1892 he was promoted to Captain.

At that time officers did not usually mix with the soldiers except when required to do so by their military duties. For an officer to play football, let alone be very good at it, would have been unusual: for the same officer, a comparatively junior one, to have devoted an enormous amount of time and energy to its organisation was remarkable. The sport was at an embryonic stage and a very considerable amount of detailed staff work would have been required to ensure its efficient organisation, administration and development.

Putty was also very busy fishing and shooting at every opportunity. In October he again stayed at Murthly Castle with Walter Fothringham and, fishing on the Tay, caught six fish – grilse and salmon. Several of the party from the previous year were there, also Laurence Drummond. Putty returned to London for a meeting of the AFA at the end of the month but in early November was at Philforth Castle in Aberdeenshire as a guest of Lord Saltoun.[53] Other guns included Earl of Mar,[54] Lord Carnegie, The Mackintosh,[55] and Walter Fothringham. Nearly 3000 rabbits and 1200 pheasants were shot.

51   Henry Gerard Sturt 1st Baron Allington (1825-1904) m2 10 February 1892.
52   Henry Arthur Cadogan Viscount Chelsea (1868-1908) m1 30 April 1892.
53   Alexander William Frederick Fraser 19th Lord Saltoun (1851-1933).
54   John Francis Erskine Goodeve-Erskine 27th Earl of Mar (1836-1930).
55   Alfred Donald Mackintosh 28th Chief (1851-1938).

Meetings of the AFA were now being held quarterly; at the meeting on 27 February 1893 it was recorded: 'Pulteney (as Hon Sec) proposed that in the event of a draw an extra half hour should be played and the timing of matches planned accordingly'. Writing in 1893 the *Market Harborough Advertiser & Midland Mail* noted: 'The extraordinary progress which Army football has made during the last few years is, in great measure, due to the untiring energy of the honorary secretary of the Army Association. Succeeding H McCalmont, the founder of the Army Cup competition, when but a few regiments boasted a football team, the present secretary has seen the entry grow rapidly. To Captain Pulteney is also due the arrangement of the first match in which a representative Army team took part viz that with the Corinthians at the Oval last year. This season the engagements have been increased, and besides the Corinthians, Surrey and London have also been met. But these are not all the advantages in connection with football which Captain Pulteney has obtained for soldiers, for he has pleaded with great success for their free admission, when in uniform, to all the principal grounds'. The article went on: 'His soldierly qualities are highly spoken of by his comrades, and he is very popular in his regiment, both among the rank and file and with his brother officers. He has done all in his power to encourage every kind of sport among his men. His efforts in this respect have met with more than ordinary success, as the records of the battalion team will show. Besides being well known as a footballer, Captain Pulteney is a good cricketer and a first-class shot, and he plays a very fair game of lawn tennis'.

Perhaps too much weight should not be given to this article but it is another piece of evidence on Putty's ability and achievements. On 15 January 1894 the AFA decided to apply for membership of the Football Association and Putty was nominated as its representative. That year seven meetings of the AFA were held; the agenda usually covered planning of the Army Cup,

Captain Pulteney Adjutant 2 SG, 1893.
(Ashley Village Archive)

development of the rules, and disciplinary matters. The meeting on 13 February focussed on the eligibility of professional players and transfers between units during the season. It involved much detailed staff work as one exchange of correspondence demonstrates. A letter was sent to Captain Pulteney, Hon Sec AFA from 15 Company SDRA Football Club, RA Mess, Fort Fareham, Hants on 9 November 1893:

> Will you kindly give me an explanation of the word 'corps' in Rule 24 AFA. There seems to be some doubt as to whether three of our men, who have been posted to us from other batteries and our depots, are eligible to play for us for the AFA Challenge Cup. They have all got the required three months service mentioned in Rule 11. I am sorry to trouble you, but I should like to get this cleared up before we play 'The Kings Own' on 21st inst. Yours truly, (AC Rothery).

Putty replied:

> Dear Sir, In reply to your letter of 9th inst the word corps means with you Royal Artillery. Men transferred to you from other batteries are eligible to play provided that they do not come from an Artillery Station that has entered in Army Cup this season 1894-1895 since 1st October 1894. Yours truly WP. 11 November 94. Chelsea. Approved Committee Meeting 21 January 1895.

By now he had become an efficient and effective staff officer.

At the beginning of 1895 everything changed. Putty resigned as Honorary Secretary of the AFA and handed over to Lowther[56] although he remained on the committee and attended its meeting on 11 February. Then, on 14 February, he handed over as adjutant to Cuthbert (Gerald James Cuthbert 1861-1931 SG 1882-1906 & 1909-1913).

Uganda 1895-1897

A letter was sent on 14 February 1895 from the Foreign Office to Colonel Colville,[57] Commissioner in Uganda:

> I am directed by the Earl of Kimberley[58] that his Lordship has selected Captain William Pulteney Pulteney 2nd Battalion Scots Guards as military officer for service with Soudanese troops in the room of Captain Thruston who has resigned. Captain Pulteney will leave England by the mail of 15th inst travelling via Brindisi.

It is difficult to be certain why Putty volunteered for this overseas service: his time as adjutant was coming to an end and the alternatives could have been an appointment as a company commander in one of the battalions or possibly attendance at the Staff College. Uganda would have been a much more exciting prospect; he had served under Colonel Colville at the Guards

56   Henry Cecil Lowther (1869-1940) SG 1888-1917.
57   Henry Edward Colville (1852-1907) late Gren Gds.
58   John Wodehouse 1st Earl of Kimberley (1826-1902) Secretary of State for Foreign Affairs.

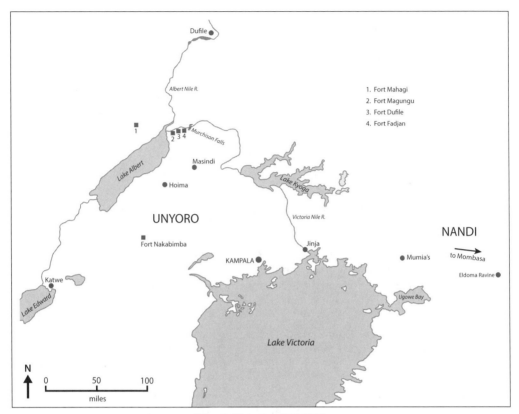

Map 2 Uganda 1895-1897.

Depot five years earlier and this may well have influenced his decision. It is also possible that his relationship with Ettie was a factor, but that seems improbable. More likely was his financial situation; even though comparatively wealthy it must have been expensive living in London and with his level of social and sporting activities; indeed there had been hints of this in his letters to Ettie. Writing many years later, Laurence Drummond says much the same: 'Before very long, however, he (Putty) found that this gay life was too expensive for his original means; swiftly he resolved to take his soldiering more seriously and devote himself to it'. Whatever the reason, the decision was to take him on active service at a critical time in his career and in British history.

Three sources provide an insight to Putty's time in Uganda: the official reports; the narratives of another Scots Guards officer, Lieutenant Vandeleur;[59] and a few letters to Gerald Cuthbert who replaced him as adjutant. The editor of the *Brigade of Guards Magazine* wrote in the March 1895 edition:

---

59   Cecil Foster Seymour Vandeleur (1869-1901) SG 1889-1900, killed in action.

Captain Pulteney, Scots Guards, has been selected for service under Colonel Colville in Uganda. It may be said, without exaggeration, that the whole army will follow his career with interest, for it is to him, in a large measure, that it owes the initiation of the movement which has established football as a winter sport in every garrison in the United Kingdom.

When Putty arrived in Uganda British rule was by no means secure. There were internal problems with some of the tribes, especially the Unyoro in the west, into whose area he was heading, and the Nandi in the east. In addition there were external threats from other European powers and, of much more immediacy, from arab slave traders operating from the coast. The forces available to Major Cunningham,[60] who was the Assistant Commissioner and Commandant of Troops, consisted of a very small number of British officers, companies of Sudanese mercenaries each about 100 strong, and a few machine-guns. In total it did not amount to more than a battalion. He was also able to co-opt a much larger number of poorly-armed irregulars, essentially friendly tribes acting for revenge or booty, who were invaluable in the advance or pursuit.

The Sudanese made excellent fighting soldiers, and could be trained to a high standard of musketry and discipline. They responded less well to the loneliness of garrison work in remote areas, especially frequent re-assignment, and when this was compounded by low pay, poor food and bad officers, problems could and did occur. Putty was fortunate in that much of his time was to be spent on operations. Major Cunningham began the second expedition against the Unyoro in April 1895 with a force consisting of 6 companies of Sudanese (500 men), 20,000 Walanda or Baganda, 2 Hotchkiss guns and 2 Maxim guns. The force crossed the Nile and defeated the rebel chief Kabarega's army. But by the time of Putty's arrival at his command in Unyoro, in June, there was still much to be done by way of consolidation and the establishment of British rule over a vast area.

First though Putty had to get to his command, a journey on foot of almost one thousand miles which would take him nearly three months. His first letter to Gerald Cuthbert was written from the Mogoleni River on 4 April:

My dear Cupid, Here I am within 9 miles of Kibwezi at which place I shall have finished 200 miles of tramp; as you can imagine one's experiences are multitudinous as regards variety in a job of this sort, to start with you are landed at Zanzibar and told to report yourself to the consul, who entertains you royally but tells you nothing. I had to make up my own mind when to return to Mombasa and Berkeley the Vice Consul told me I had better go to Smith Mackenzie to manage my caravan, beyond which point I have had no orders, nor were any given me however I went back to Mombasa in the same ship that brought me out arriving on the 16th and starting on the 18th March, I was foolish enough to study the Intelligence Department book dated 93 and to my surprise I find it very inaccurate a lot of the information misleading and fully two years behind the times in fact I wish I never had seen it as the path made by Mackinnon up to Kibwezi is so good that the sooner the official book is altered as regards its information about the various camps the better as they must be in possession of the facts from the railway survey. Had a touch of fever at (Magi Chuwi) but am now stronger and well again and gradually being acclimatised. I never saw such a

60   George Glencairn Cunningham (1862-NK) DCLI.

blackguard as I look, a beard ¼ grown hair never parted the first week it looked awful but now that I have become bronzed I look a bit better, trudge along in a helmet (Elwood's Patent) a very good one Kharkee jacket, jaager shirt flannel trousers, shooting boots and a red flannel belt round what was my tummy, my ablutions entirely depend on the class of water I camp near if it is mud holes I go without it if good water they are very laborious and take place after the march when the flannels are washed by 'the Boy' in the bath, at Tsavo there was a swift muddy river up above the waist so I stripped and swum about in it until they found me a towel. I have got 80 men in my caravan which consists as follows: Headman and man for his tent, 2nd Headman, 5 Askaris, 4 Boys (3 of whom are impedi-ments), 68 Porters. I had four men deserted me at (Magi Chuwi) and 3 at the (Pines) Voi among the latter being my cook whom I had given such refreshment the night before for bagging oatmeal and watering my soup that he cried enough, the blackguard took his rifle with him and the only satisfaction I had with him was 3 days previous when he came to me with an enormous belly of wind and asked to be doctored, I gave him such a dose of Eno that Boreas had no chance, the other man he took with him was an old deserter who would have been arrested the next day, one man I sent back from Taru with terrible venereal. Each man carries 65 lbs on his head as a load besides which he carries his food (10 days to start with) a large water bottle and his clothes they are all registered and numbered you would scarcely believe it possible to carry the weight, you get hold of 70 lbs and see and on last Tuesday I got 19 miles out of them, the average pace is 2¼ miles an hour, if they can swill themselves with water they will go for miles like blazes but it is very different when there is none, however now that I have got them fit I do not anticipate any great difficul-ties the great trouble is the start, they are all blind drunk and have committed every excess possible during the last week, they each receive 2 months' pay in advance and like a good many soldiers I know buzz the lot before they start, in cunning and devilry they take a lot of beating. Get me some (6) bits of medal ribbons (Egyptian campaign medal and Khedive Star 1882) made by the master tailor ready to sew on and send them me in an envelope. I envy you your spring drills and the manoeuvres, but not the fitting clothing, mind the Battn are the best at the Queen's Birthday, first at shooting and everything else. Expect to be at Kampala the first week in June. Remember me to the CO and all the boys. Yours ever, WP Pulteney.

Putty's affectation of using a nickname to address his correspondent but a formal signature for himself was a source of some amusement; it was some years before he used his own nick-name. This letter also makes evident his pride in 2 SG; that and his close interest in all regi-mental matters is a recurring theme in his letters to Gerald Cuthbert.

While Putty was on the march, Cunningham was operating against Kabarega in the north of Unyoro. Meanwhile disturbances had broken out in southern Unyoro owing to arab caravans bringing arms and gunpowder into the country in exchange for slaves and ivory. Vandeleur had been sent into this area, which was completely unmapped, with two companies Sudanese to operate against the slavers. Reporting to the Earl of Kimberley the Commissioner wrote: 'Summary of Proceedings against arabs carrying on illicit trade in gunpowder and slaves: On receipt of intelligence it was evident Mr Foaker (50 Soudanese and 100 Waganda) should be reinforced at once, and, therefore, despatched a letter to Captain Pulteney who was on his way to join Major Cunningham in Unyoro, and instructed him to proceed at once to Nakabimba and

Site of Fort Nakabimba, 2012.

take over command of the Soudanese and Waganda irregulars from Mr Foaker. At the same time more Soudanese and armed Waganda in all about 120 were sent from Kampala with all possible despatch to overtake Captain Pulteney'.

Putty arrived at Nakabimba and took over command on 16 June; he had left Mombasa on 18 March so had been on the march for three months. The Estimates for 96/97 show there were 7 British officers in the Country including Colville, Cunningham, Vandeleur and Putty. They also show that the force at Nakabimba consisted of one British officer, 3 Soudanese native officers, and 103 rank and file. It does not need much imagination to appreciate the challenges Putty now faced in a Country that was virtually unknown, under threat from both hostile natives and arab slavers, and in command of native troops about whom he knew very little.

Another report from the Commissioner to the Earl of Kimberley noted:

> Captain Pulteney writing from Nakabimba the day after his arrival at that place reports that the Waganda scouts on 15th inst had fallen in with a small caravan of Waziba, natives from the district of Bukoba, who were proceeding from Unyoro with a small quantity of ivory and 16 slave women and children. The Waziba offering resistance a fight ensued, resulting in 6 of them being killed, the remainder effecting their escape. Sixteen slaves, several of whom were Waganda women and two from Toru, who had been kidnapped by Wanyoro, have since been returned to their homes.

Seen today the site of Fort Nakabimba is high up and there is usually a breeze, so heat may not have been an issue for Putty. It is 100 yards from the track that winds up from the River Uzuzi, and so is astride a main N-S route from where it could control the Unyoro and especially prevent them from attacking their neighbours and slave trading. There are eucalyptus trees now, introduced in late 19th C. The ground is rocky and water would have to have been brought up from the river. On 23 June 1895 Vandeleur wrote:

We could see the Nakabimba fort, which had just been built by Mr Foaker, on a high hill south of the Msisi, but it took us a long time to descend into the narrow gorge and cross the river. As we ascended the steep and stony path up the opposite hillside the discordant blasts of the Sudanese buglers re-echoed through the mountains and gave notice of our approach. It was, indeed, a surprise, for the garrison of the fort, but not equal to that which I experienced when, to my delight and astonishment, I saw my former adjutant and brother officer, Captain Pulteney coming down with Mr Foaker to meet me in this wild and mountainous part of Central Africa, the last place in which I should have expected to see him. Our mails and news from home had been very few and far between, so it will be imagined with what joy I met a brother officer who had just come out. It is said that we talked for two days consecutively, during which Foaker learnt something about the Brigade of Guards. The fort is in Latitude 38' 24" north, and is 4582 feet above the sea, so that the climate there was naturally much colder and fresher than in other parts of Unyoro. It is a wild and rugged country, but there are a good many Wanyoro living in the valleys among the hills. Not far from here lie the far-famed Mountains of the Moon, the snow-covered Ruwenzori range which so seldom deigns to reveal its splendour to the human eye.

Vandeleur was also a very keen explorer; he continued on 25 June:

After a day's rest at Nakabimba I started with Pulteney, who intended to come with me as far as Mwenda's, on my return journey by a different route for the purpose of surveying. Marching along the river for three hours we reached the crossing known as Ruantomara, which is made by heaping bundles of papyrus one over the other to form a causeway. It was in very bad order, some of the papyrus having been washed away, so that from only being in 2 ft of water one suddenly subsided into a hole almost up to one's neck. Many loads were dropped into the water, including my tent and bed, and some of Pulteney's tin boxes. It took one and a half hours for the small column to get across the river, which was not more than 30 yards broad. On the second day we left the granite hills and descended into the plain again. Now it so happened that two arabs named Mse and Juma bin Fakir, with a large caravan, had selected this very route to leave the country by, thinking to avoid me by making a detour to the west, as they considered that I was certain to return by my old road. Scouts in front reported that a caravan of some sort was coming along the road (a native track one foot wide, buried in elephant grass 10 feet high), so we halted to allow it to approach. Strolling leisurely along at its head who should walk into our arms as we lay concealed in the grass but the two arab leaders. In a moment all was confusion – arabs, Zanzibaris, Wanyamwezi porters with food and tusks of ivory on their heads, and slaves, all dived into the grass as our men rushed out with a wild hurroosh. Some were pulled out by their legs, others by their arms, but a great many escaped, as the attempt to find them in the long grass was just like looking for a needle in a bundle of hay. This mattered little, however, as we had secured the leaders. I do not think I ever remember seeing men so utterly flabbergasted as Messrs Mse and Juma bin Fakir, as they stood trembling in the hands of the delighted Sudanese soldiers who, with their customary lightening-like léger-de-main, were appropriating any little articles of value they could lay their hands on, to keep as a souvenir of the occasion. The rout was complete, and the road onwards for miles was strewn with debris of gourds, bits of cloth, potatoes, Indian corn, and pots and pans dropped by the flying remnants of the caravan, hotly pursued by the irregulars. We reached Mwenda's on the fourth day, and found all well. Here Pulteney left me to return to Nakabimba, where he became a terror to arab slavers and a good friend to the Wanyoro.

Putty's letter to the Commissioner from Nakabimba on 1 July included:

Capture of arab caravan under Mzee bin Suliman and Juma bin Fakir. It would appear desirable to stop caravans coming through Ntale's country as one and all the prisoners admit the fact that they paid tribute to be allowed to pass though his country, which means that he has been encouraging this illicit trade in powder, the arab Mzee saying that he paid him a great deal and other prisoners stating that he took as much as 1/7 of the trade goods. My opinion is that the roads and river Msisi will want careful watching and patrolling until Muhenda and Kikukuli [Wanyoro military leaders] have come in or been caught.

In his report of the incident to the Earl of Kimberley the Commissioner noted:

From the evidence of the prisoners and slaves besides several arabic documents found by Lieutenant Vandeleur, the head of the traders in contraband is an arab called Khalfan, and as he was known to have escaped from Mwanda's when the camp was surprised, Captain Pulteney kept a sharp look out for him on his return south.

Putty wrote again to the Commissioner on 18 July from Nakabimba: 'Successful repulse of caravan under Khalfan on 14 July. On my return I found a patrol from Hoima which had been vigorously attacked by Kikukuli's men en route. Lwekula has also just reported a raid on the part of Kikukuli' and on 19 July 'Kikukuli, Mwenda and Buengo (chief of Kissubi) have just sent saying they wish to come in'. It seems unlikely that they did come in because Kikukuli was defeated and surrendered in October 1895 and it was not until January 1896 that Muhenda was finally captured.

The Commissioner's reports to the Earl of Kimberley give more information. On 19 July he wrote: 'Captain Pulteney again writes that having received news that Khalfan had crossed the Insisi River 35 miles from Nakabimba on his way south, he started in pursuit with the utmost despatch' and covering the period 24-26 July 'Overtaking the caravan on the night of 24 July, Khalfan's men immediately opened fire on the Soudanese who returned it and completely routed the caravan which fled in every direction, four men being killed and a few wounded. Fourteen slave women and children were taken and 22 loads of ivory. Captain Pulteney had one man wounded. Khalfan unfortunately escaped, though Captain Pulteney pursued him until dark and again the whole of the next day.'

When the pursuit ended, and with what result, and when Putty returned to Nakabimba are unknown, but he was back at Nakabimba again on 14 September for he wrote from there that day to Gerald Cuthbert; and he forwarded it to the editor of the *Brigade of Guards Magazine* in which it was published:

Your letter of last April 25th, reached me here the end of August, just before I went away north after some hostile Unyoro. The chief, however, as is his way, took to his heels the day we left here, leaving his subjects to fight the battle, therefore beyond catching about sixty wretched prisoners, your humble servant was jolly well sold, as he expects to be often again. It is a bad time of year to be on the war path, as the rains are on, and won't finish until the first week in November, which means no joke in this land of swamps. Well, here I am all by myself, with 120 faithful Soudanese followers. I have travelled through most of Uganda, Unyoro, and Ankole, since my arrival in May, my ten toes have stood me well, as I have never been off them. The curse of this part of the world, the 'jigger', luckily is not very partial to me, anyway only three have entered my feet up to the present, which to judge by the Nubians and most other Europeans, is a very low average; truly they are little fiends, no bigger than a pin's head, they burrow in under one's nails, where they lay a little black bag, full of eggs, one has to watch one's feet morning and evening, as if left in long they make terrible holes. The ravages they make on these natives is beyond belief, however, they don't seem to mind losing a toe or two. I find it difficult not to drift into untidy and unpunctual habits among all this mass of filth, the more especially being all alone. I have tried to impress the necessity of water on my lambs, but much to my regret with little success. I am very glad I came, as I certainly have learned something of Africa, the geography of which was almost unknown to me, I am ashamed to say. There is one great disappointment which rankles a bit, that there is no more chance of an expedition from this end down the Nile until the railway reaches Lake Victoria, than there is of flying. Of course we could be used to divert a few of the Mahdi's followers while an attack from the south was made, but my dreams of trotting down to Khartoum are very distant. The rail could not reach there much before the end of '98, by which time, with good luck I shall be doing sentry go in London town. My period of engagement was nominally supposed to be two years from the coast, which would mean starting back about January 1897. However, by that time I think one will have every opportunity of judging whether it will be of any use trying to stay any longer. I have been more than fortunate in my health up to the present, but I expect on my return to be nothing but an enormous quinine tabloid!! I don't think it does me much harm, though it does affect the memory without doubt, also with me my eyes. Mr Vandeleur is doing A1 up here, he is a credit to the regiment in every way, he says it is rather rough being pursued by his adjutant whom he ran away from! I do not expect to see any more of the Brigade up here unless they can speak arabic, there is no doubt it is a great handicap having to learn it, more especially as you must teach yourself. I am getting on slowly with it, but find it so difficult not to mix Swahili, Unyoro, and Waganda, all of which one gets to know a few words of. If a London doctor saw as many patients in a day as I do, he would be making at least five thousand a year. Yours sincerely WP Pulteney.

This letter has been edited by the editor of the *Brigade of Guards Magazine*, hence the numerous commas and a few inaccuracies. It concludes Putty's first four months during which, even from this fragmentary information, he showed considerable energy, initiative and determination. Sometime later in September Putty was summoned to Kampala with forty-two of his men to take part in the first expedition against the Nandi across the eastern border of the Country. Nakabimba was left in charge of a Sudanese officer with sixty men. Lieutenant Vandeleur was also summoned from his post at Hoima where similar arrangements were made.

The main route to the coast passed through the Nandi country and they had been making frequent attacks on British caravans and mails. On 1 October the Commissioner wrote to the Earl of Kimberley outlining his plans for the expedition:

> The Force will leave Kampala on 14th inst and proceed to the Guaso Masa, where it will be reinforced by Captain Sitwell and Mr Grant with one hundred and forty more Soudanese. It had been contemplated to enter the Nandi country simultaneously from the Mau side and from the Lake [Ugowe Bay], but various circumstances have rendered this plan impractical and the expedition will therefore operate from the land side only, using the new station at the Guaso Masa as a base of operations or point of departure.

The expedition started from Kampala on 14 October and marched round the lake, crossing the Victoria Nile at Jinja, and reached Mumia's on the 29 October. The diary of the Nandi Field Force noted:

> The Force consisted of Major Cunningham (Devons), Captain Pulteney and Lieutenant Vandeleur (Scots Guards), a doctor (Dr Mackinnon), a civilian officer (Mr Foaker), 7 native officers, 15 native sergeants and 354 rank and file (Nos 1, 4, 5 and 9 Companies Soudanese). In addition there were about 500 Soudanese followers and 200 other natives. The Force had one Maxim gun. Five days rations were issued to every man.

It left Mumia's on 3 November and on 8 November ascended the Nandi plateau. Commenting on the Force, Vandeleur's chronicler says:

> Such a force proved inadequate to the task imposed on it, as the country was mountainous and it was impossible to ascertain anything concerning it, for the surrounding natives held the Nandi in such dread that they refused to act as guides.

Vandeleur described events that day:

> We marched along the escarpment the next day, and discovered some small huts and patches of mtama cultivation, the first signs of the Wa-Nandi. We saw a few natives, and discovered in one of the huts a cup and other articles which had belonged to West (previously killed by the Nandi). After several ineffectual attempts to ascend, we found a very steep path, which led to an open grass-covered space close to the top, and we camped here at 6332 feet. A section of No 4 Company went out from here into the dense forest behind, captured sixteen cattle and a few goats, and killed 2 Nandi. Our column used to pack into a thorn zariba, about 80 to 90 yards square, as the Wa-Nandi were known to be fond of night attacks. The

officers' tents were together in the middle, and the men used to build small grass huts all round. The smoke from the fires at night was unbearable, and it was difficult to pick one's way through the fires and the sleeping forms round them, as one went the rounds at night. I happened to be visiting the sentries in this camp at midnight, when a fire suddenly broke out among the huts of No 9 Company, and spread with the greatest rapidity, fanned by the strong wind that was blowing. Each man was carrying eighty rounds of ammunition in his belt, and many of these were left on the ground as the men, roused from sleep, rushed to get out of the way. The confusion was increased by the sound of the cartridges exploding, which gave the impression at first that we were being attacked. The line of flames was advancing straight for the tents, so Pulteney's and Mackinnon's tents, which were nearest to the danger, were taken down, and their effects strewn about all over the zariba, being with difficulty collected again in the morning. By this time a line of men had collected, and succeeded in beating out the flames just before they reached the tents, but not before much damage had been done.

Next day the official diary recorded:

Marched 6 am. Obliged to retrace our steps in order to find a road through the forest. Climbed up to crest of range 6850 feet and then east through a belt of thick forest for 2 hours after which the country became open and undulating. Nandi lurking about the forests, some shots being fired at them, while they wounded a Sudanese follower with an arrow. Camped at noon at Samwite 6627 feet. Patrols captured 45 cattle, 31 sheep and goats and killed 4 Nandi. Latter using rifles hit the snider belonging to an irregular.

It was impossible to carry all the food the Force needed because of shortage of porters, so it was entirely dependent on the country for supplies. Vandeleur wrote of this day:

The wind increased to a gale, and when morning broke it was intensely cold, and we sat shivering over a hurried breakfast. The Zanzibaris and Lendu porters were stiff with cold, and could with difficulty carry their loads. Fortunately they are the most light-hearted people, and soon became good-humoured, and began to chaff each other. It was found impossible to get through the thick forest in front of us, and we had with disgust to retrace our steps, and make our way right down to the bottom of the steep hills by the same rocky and stony path by which we had ascended. Two miles to the north we found another track, which led up to the high ridge and through the forest.

The following day (10 November), the official diary recorded:

The Force marched 6 am. Road leading through short belts of forest, open glades with short grass and across three swamps where Nandi bowmen lay in wait. At 10 am a party of Nandi were dispersed by Maxim gun, 1 being killed. Camped at 12.20 about 7 miles west of Mount Alagabit. A patrol sent north failed to discover any signs of Nandi or any trace of Captain Sitwell's column (Claude George Henry Sitwell 1858-1900 Manchesters). All around Mount Alagabit uninhabited the Masai guides saying that since the post at

Guaso Masa the Wa Nandi living around have moved SW. The march times each day were dictated by the length and slow movement of the column.

Next day Cunningham wrote:

Camped on west slope of Mount Alagabit, where I had directed Captain Sitwell to meet me with his column. A patrol returned without having seen any signs of this column.

Vandeleur noted of 11 November:

We had not seen many of the natives as yet, though poisoned arrows had been shot at us in the forest, two or three of the followers being picked off from behind the trees. Camp is 7126 feet above the sea, and from the top one has a very good view over the valley of the Guaso Masa River, and across a very open country to the eastward, which is uninhabited, and where hartebeest, water-buck, and oribi are to be found.

Vandeleur gives a good narrative of the next two days:

The second column did not arrive and on 12 November a section (about twenty-five men) was sent to the Guaso Masa Fort to see what had happened. Covering the distance of 32 miles in the day, they reported that the force had marched off three days before led in the wrong direction by the Masai guides. It was an unfortunate thing, as every man available was required for this expedition, in which so many had to be employed in guarding the followers and the baggage. By 13 November food was running short, and all idea of meeting the second column had to be given up. The country south of Alagabiet is very swampy, a characteristic caused by the streams running down this way from the forest, and we had to retrace our steps along our old road to Samwiti. It was more like being in Scotland than in Africa at this height, and the days were cold, with very often rain in the afternoon. From Samwiti we steered straight for a high bluff called Usun, to the right of which there appeared to be a gap in the long line of hills in the distance. One of the principal objects to be obtained by the expedition was to try and find a shorter route for the Mombasa-Uganda road, which at present made such a detour to the northward. After leaving Samwiti, villages became more numerous, and there were cattle tracks in all directions. There was still a good deal of forest, belts of which run out from the main forest to the south-west. Many natives were hanging about the line of march, and attempted to interfere with the somewhat difficult passage of a swampy stream, but these were held in check by the Maxim, whilst the leading company crossed, and camp was formed on some rising ground on the farther side after only a short march. Patrols were sent out, and it soon became apparent that large bodies of the enemy were in the vicinity, and intended to try conclusions with us. A thorn zariba was made, in which the women followers and baggage were left, with a portion of the force to guard them, whilst the remainder of the Sudanese and Waganda irregulars went out to cover the return of one of the patrols across the Kimonde River, which it was feared, from the heavy firing in the direction, had got into difficulties. The river, down to which the ground sloped steeply, was about 6 feet deep, and was crossed by a native bridge. To the east of it, open grassy undulations were here and there varied by patches of forest.

He went on to describe the action on 14 November:

Only a few natives could be seen on the ridge and it was with astonishment we suddenly saw a crowd of about 500 coming over the top of the hill at great speed, apparently excellently organised, and formed in three sides of a square, above which a dense thicket of long-bladed spears flashed in the sunlight. Wheeling to the left as if by some common impulse, on they came in spite of a Maxim gun posted behind the river, and charged down with tremendous dash on to the force which was some way up the slope on the east bank, and which closed up as well as it could to face the impending attack. It was a critical moment but luckily the Sudanese stood firm, and as the great mass of natives approached closer the heavy fire began to tell. Nearer and nearer they came, and it almost seemed that they would overwhelm No 4 Company, which had to bear the brunt of the attack; but at last, wavering before this leaden hail, which they had never before experienced, their ranks broke and they scattered in all directions, leaving many of their number on the ground. Half a company left at the bridge had, on the first alarm, advanced to the support of their comrades, and the flying natives had now to run the gauntlet of the fire from these men as they retired over the hill, leaving the ground strewn with their big shields and spears. It was a splendid charge, and if continued for 30 yards or so more would have been a successful one. Fourteen of our men, including the sergeant of the Waganda contingent, were cut off and killed. The charge was a revelation to us, after fighting the cautious Wanyoro and arabs towards Lake Albert, and at once accounted for the warlike reputation and prestige amongst other East African tribes which the Wa-Nandi possessed. Such an onslaught would have annihilated any smaller force without firearms, or a weekly guarded caravan travelling in single file along the Uganda road, and it was providential that the natives should have selected this occasion, instead of waiting until we were in column of route, hampered by carriers, followers, and women.

In his report Cunningham said that more than 100 Nandi were killed and that darkness prevented any follow-up.

Putty's version of events that day was contained in a letter he wrote on 14 November to Gerald Cuthbert published in the *Brigade of Guards Magazine*:

Your letter of the 27th August reached me a little over a week ago, just as we left the main road in Kabras to fight these Nandi people. Have come a long way for this expedition, all the way from Unyoro. It will mean a thousand miles on my ten toes by the time we get back there. The Nandi have murdered an English trader named West, besides attacking four caravans, two of them successfully, hence this punitive expedition. White man has never entered the country before, and no allies would come with us, such is their fear of these people. We have now got them in front of us in great numbers, which means we shall have a big fight, or more likely have to resist a powerful night attack; that being their usual mode of fighting. It is rather nasty fighting, as they secrete themselves in the long grass and then shoot a poisoned arrow at you, it being almost impossible to see to shoot them. There is a chance of finding a much shorter route to the Lake Victoria through this country, so beyond being a grand chance for me it is very interesting in many ways. Just as I was writing a message came in for the Maxim, and a splendid fight ensued, the enemy charging in square on to No. 4 Company, just like dervishes; for two or three minutes, which seemed hours, the position seemed very critical. However, at last they fled in every direction, having lost about a hundred killed. Now we understand why no allies would come with us, and thoroughly recognise what a powerful lot of savages we have taken on, very different to Unyoro fighting. We have lost nine Waganda and three Soudanese, all speared. The spears and shields are of beautiful make. The sight of the enormous blade coming at one makes one's blood run cold! I don't think you would admire my beard, which is about as white as my moustache would be if it ever grew, but alas, grows much quicker than the hair on the top, where the helmet is finishing what the forage cap began! I am very glad I came out here, as I have certainly learnt a great deal, besides seeing the centre of Africa at other peoples' expense. Mind you write and tell me all the interesting gossip from home, you can't tell how it amuses one out here, it does not matter if it is true or not, as there is no one to repeat it to. I will keep this letter open until this campaign is finished just to put in the result as a PS. Yours very sincerely WP Pulteney PS 22 November 1895. Chance of sending a mail (with Vandeleur), have had some hard fighting, but all well, expect to get back to Mumia's about 5 December.

Cunningham reported:

On the morning of 15 November reconnoitred south with 4 and 9 Companies but saw very few of the enemy about. Chose a site for camp at Kabobis about 7 miles SE of last camp and sent a company back to escort the baggage. One follower was speared close to old camp whilst out foraging against orders. We halted here for a day. Parties out reconnoitring killed a Nandi and procured a quantity of grain. At 3.45 am on 17 November while pitch dark the Nandi attacked the camp. The company occupying the face attacked at once opened fire and the enemy retired leaving 1 dead (and evidence of many more).

About this time Putty wrote to Lowther:

We got into Nandi country three weeks ago, since which we have been fighting on and off all the time. On the 15th [should be 14 November] they attacked us in great force, charging in square like dervishes, but the rifles told their tale. On the 17th they made their night attack about an hour before daylight, but the sentries spotted them and they left quicker than they came. Since then it has been a case of bolt with them, except for attempting to reach the cattle-boma at night and the usual poisoned arrows at stragglers or in the forest. We have failed up to the present to find a route for the railway from Lake Nakuro to Ugowe Bay (Lake Victoria) and tomorrow we start to the south-west to have another try; but, personally, I do not consider it feasible for the railway.

Reverting to Vandeleur's narrative:

On 18 November we continued our march to the south-east, and crossed two channels of the river Kaimin by means of native bridges. The latter are made with big trees, and are quite the best I have seen constructed by natives. Several bodies of armed natives showed in front and on the flanks as we left the valley of the Kaimin River and gradually ascended the opposite slope. The Maxim came into action at about 800 yards range, and the column closed up and advanced very carefully to prevent the large crowd of porters and Sudanese followers, which are such an encumbrance, from being charged. These were all massed together like a flock of sheep, and guarded on each side, whilst No 9 Company skirmished in front and cleared a way for the advance. At several points along the ridge in front spears waving on the sky-line, or a Nandi warrior peering over the top, revealed the fact that they were only waiting for a favourable opportunity to charge down. After their losses on 14 November they had, however, become cautious, and had learnt to respect the Martini rifles. At 10 am we crossed another small valley, and, marching for two hours more camped on a high hill called Teito, 7119 feet above the sea, from the top of which we had the most lovely view. We had been gradually ascending until we had come to the end of the high plateau, marked by a precipitous drop of 1000 feet into the valley beneath. Away to the south-west stretched the great plain watered by the Nyando River, which runs down to Ugowe Bay, and far away in the distance could be seen the blue waters of Lake Victoria. To the south, again, on the farther side of the plain, the country towards Sotik and Lumbwa appeared hilly and mountainous. We were now in the heart of Nandi country, and the sides of the numerous hills around were dotted with clusters of little huts and marked by patches of cultivation; but a few miles beyond this to the north-east there extended a bare and open plain, uninhabited, and with hardly a tree on it.

Inevitably there are variations in the narratives particularly in directions and the spelling of place names, hardly surprising with the absence of maps and the different languages. Vandeleur was the geographer and explorer and took great trouble with accuracy, so in this respect his account should be given prominence. During the last ten days of the month the force continued to advance through Nandi country with daily skirmishes and casualties on both sides. Cunningham recorded that on 23 November Vandeleur and 50 men left for Eldoma Ravine Station taking two sick soldiers unable to walk to be sent on to Mumia's: he also noted the intense cold and drenching mist. Vandeleur returned on 26 November. On 25 November Cunningham wrote:

OC with Captain Pulteney and one company Sudanese ascended Tindereit Range on the south side of the River Lagame [Sagame]; about 200 Nandi visible on a high hill 3 miles south of range. A large quantity of food found in the houses. Two irregulars and one follower speared having gone off looting by themselves against orders.

Writing on 1 December Vandeleur continued:

There were a few people living on the mountains in the vicinity, but this is about their limit, and there were no houses in the plain to the south or towards the lake. It is 59 miles from here to Lake Nakuru, and the Masai with us said that there was a fairly good track over the mountains, and that it was open until the descent through the forest on the farther side. This track would probably bring one out close to the Guaso Masa River, and if it could be used for road and railway would shorten the route from the East Coast to Lake Victoria very considerably, as there is no difficulty in going along the Nyando Valley to Ugowe

Bay, where there is a harbour. We marched in a westerly direction from here into the big plain, 4000 feet above the sea, which is covered with short grass and a few thorn bushes and small trees. There are no inhabitants until one approaches the lake, where there are several villages belonging to chief called Kitoto. A few antelope, hartebeest, water-buck, and some small gazelles were seen, and Pulteney shot a large python coiled round the branches of a small tree. Towering over the plain to the north-west rises the great Nandi escarpment, which runs right down to Ugowe Bay and then round by the Wa-Tiriki and Maragolia Hills. It was very hot and steamy in the plain, and there were thunderstorms in the evening and night. After four weeks spent on the high ground and the mountains we felt the change in the climate very much, and were glad to leave the hot plain. We crossed the River Enolgotwe, flowing between steep banks, and 4 miles farther on reached the base of the hills, where we found a very well-marked road, evidently used by the Wa-Nandi for driving their cattle and flocks down to graze. It was too late to commence the ascent, and we camped here almost at the foot of the escarpment.

Next day he wrote:

On 2 December we climbed to the top of the plateau again along a small water-course, and on arriving there found the hills covered with boulders of granite and very bare. There was a dense mist most of the day, and it was very cold and damp. The country reminded me exactly of Mr Rider Haggard's description of the unknown country in his book 'Children of the Mist', excepting that we failed to find the beautiful Princess, and were received with poisoned arrows instead. The poison did not have much effect when the arrows were taken out at once, and under the skilful treatment of Dr Mackinnon the patients nearly all recovered. We were now heading straight for Mumia's, and 9 miles from the edge of the plateau reached the forest. We travelled along its edge for some distance before entering it, which we did by a very bad path, frightfully muddy and steep in places. Every now and then an arrow whizzed across the track, and the men halting and turning outwards fired a volley into the bush, in order to put to flight our unseen enemies.

In his official diary Cunningham tells of the six days march back to Mumia's over bad tracks faced with heavy rain and the cold. Skirmishes and casualties were a daily occurrence with 5 Nandi killed on 4 December. The force arrived back at Mumia's on 9 December as Vandeleur describes:

We came down to the Lusomo River, a swollen torrent about 20 yards broad, which we crossed by means of a capital native bridge made of creepers. The cattle and donkeys managed to swim across farther up, with the exception of one of the latter, which was swept past us down to the rapids below the bridge. The river swarmed with crocodiles, and one of the people from the fort was carried off in the act of drawing water at the crossing, the last seen of him being his arm above water in a strong stream. About 5 miles beyond the river we reached Mumia's where we remained till 14 December.

It was considered that the Wa-Nandi had not been sufficiently quelled so that, on 14 December, the force consisting of Cunningham, Pulteney, Vandeleur and Dr Mackinnon, 410 Sudanese, a few Masai guides, and crowd of porters and followers, marched in to the country again. Presumably this was Cunningham's decision but it seems a strange one, especially as the operation was to last only two weeks. Again it was well described by Vandeleur:

> We had a long march through the forest on 17 December, eventually camping not far from our old camp at Samwiti. On 19 December we travelled along our former road, we camped at Kiture; Cunningham parleyed with some natives on a hill, without much result. With the usual native diplomacy, they wanted us to go all the way to the Eldoma Ravine, when they said their leaders would then come in and make peace. Even while this conversation was going on, a Sudanese and a Wanyamwezi porter were speared close to the camp. On 22 December, after a running fight with the natives, during which a few men were wounded by arrows, we captured a large number of cattle in an enormous ravine leading up from the plain, 1000 feet deep and about a mile broad at the top. Turning in a westerly direction, we now kept along the edge of the plateau, through what proved to be a densely populated country. We halted near Moraba Peak on Christmas Day 1895, which we celebrated as best we could. Sure enough we were not allowed to rest in peace after our Christmas dinner, but were turned out about midnight by the sentries firing on natives round the zariba. No organised attack took place owing to the bright moonlight. Next day (26 December) we continued our march, and the head of the column was attacked whilst entering a narrow gorge. A few friendly irregulars, who were in front, were seized with panic, and throwing down their shields and spears, ran back among the soldiers, who, advancing into the rocks, commenced firing wildly in all directions, and it was some time before order could be restored. The enemy was soon dispersed, and we eventually camped under Kevillat Peak, at the edge of the Nandi country. On 27 December we returned to Mumia's, having traversed the Nandi country in every direction, and reached it on 31 December just in time to spend New Year's Day there.

The force left Mumia's on 5 January 1896 and started on its return march reaching Jinja on 17 January and Kampala two days later. Vandeleur's assessment of the campaign was very positive:

> The results of the expedition have been most important. Not only have all attacks on caravans ceased, but the main road from the east coast has been carried straight through this hitherto unknown country. At a point on the escarpment the ground slopes gradually down towards the Rukus Valley, forming an open, slightly undulating plain, until the Nandi villages are reached. A belt of thick forest, from 8 to 10 miles in width, forms rather an obstacle, but after this Kavirondo and a fine open country is attained. Instead of passing through an uninhabited desert as before, the road now very soon reaches an extremely fertile country, and there is a great saving in distance.

The Field Force never took the Nandi by surprise, and their scouts manning the hilltop outposts kept the column under observation throughout. It rarely held any more ground than that on which it stood, and to that extent it failed to defeat and subjugate the Nandi. Nevertheless, the government hoped that Vandeleur's optimistic assessment would in the end prove correct, control would be gradually established through a garrisoned post, and that friendly relations would follow as Nandi suspicions were allayed by the presence of a government officer in the centre of the country. Vandeleur returned to the coast and home, and Putty returned to Unyoro and initially Nakabimba. For the rest of his time in Uganda he was responsible for pacification in Unyoro, which was to prove a complex and difficult task.

Putty wrote to the Commissioner on 29 February about control of Bujiro in Bugangaizi by a sub-chief of Luwekula's who ousted a Unyoro named Baliegulu in mid-1895. The removal of Kabarega had been accomplished by driving him and many of his territorial chiefs from Unyoro. Much of the S and SW areas of Unyoro (including Nakabimba) were annexed to Buganda; Buganda chiefs were appointed to rule over Unyoro and the replacement of Wanyoro sub-chiefs by Baganda appointees began. Masindi became the Government HQ in Unyoro.

He wrote again to the Commissioner on 11 March from Kamwarumba (a Ganda village on Kruli road). 'Visited by a Nyoro chief placed by Ternan named Wakatama who had been told by Ganda to turn all ivory over to Mwanga, Chief of Kusimbo; from the look of the country it would appear more merciful to pay it a tribute instead of exacting one'. This is a poor agricultural area near the Nile and Putty must have seen the unfairness of these Ganda claims to tribute from impoverished Unyoro. His next letter to the Commissioner was from Masindi on 23 March and included:

The following principal Wanyoro chiefs will now be under Rwabandongo:

1. Mugema (formerly chief of Bugangaizi county)
2. Muhengo (chief of Buyaga)
3. Carto (chief of Kisimbi)
4. Muhenda (chief of Muhenda)
5. Kikukule (chief of Kijamba) Bugangaizi to be split at the Msisi R. Recommends Lwekula as chief over South Bugangaizi.

Now based at Masindi, Putty was heavily involved in Baganda/Wanyoro politics.

He wrote to Gerald Cuthbert (at Richmond Barracks, Dublin where 2 SG was now stationed) from Masindi on 4 April:

The English mail came in yesterday bringing letters and papers up to January 10th and telegrams up to the 22nd. Many thanks for your letter of Dec 7th giving me some battalion news. The Ashanti business seems to have been a bit of a (shunt) but see from the Zanzibar telegrams there has been no fighting, they have had a good walk with much talking for nothing. Glad to hear you have got up a Boxing Club in Dublin it is a great thing having Sergeant Philip[61] over there that brute Dering[62] was always trying to collar him. Old Jack Stracey[63] seems to be trying on an old game though how A.P.[64] can be furious is beyond me he had better try to reorganise Jameson Rhodes & Co the old Boers seem to have bested them to rights. It seems funny to think of Ned Milner[65] volunteering for Caterham the

61   4992 Sergeant James Lindley Philip SG 1880-1901.
62   Possibly Henry Edward Dering (1866-1931) SG 1886-1906 Inspector of Gymnasia 1893-1896 later 10th Bt.
63   John Bourchier Stracey (1853-1931) SG 1872-1899 took part in Jameson raid.
64   Arthur Henry Fitzroy Paget (1851-1928) SG 1869-1900.
65   Edward Milner (1858-1932) SG 1881-1903 ADC to Governor of South Australia 1892-1895.

dinner parties down there won't suit him even though he does forget to ask the Governor as the tale goes of him in Hong Kong. So glad to hear Jock Dalrymple[66] is much better was afraid he would have to go on ½ pay for a year at least from the November account I got of him. Am becoming a rare good judge of tea and coffee the mess president won't be able to humbug me with any inferior qualities on my return. This seems to be an unhealthy spot all the Europeans who have been out have had to chuck it up on account of fever the troops also seem to suffer a good deal. Am building the biggest cow house you ever saw the present one having been built in the wettest spot they could find the cattle dying accordingly. Yours ever, WP Pulteney.

Putty continued to write frequently to the Commissioner during the year, reporting on his administration. On 10 April from Masindi he wrote about an attack by askaris on some friendly Nyoro killing two – 'to be regretted as the Wanyoro had begun to settle peaceably'. In his next letter, again from Masindi, on 12 April, he advised 'the establishment of a fort near Kirota near Nile to prevent Kaba (Kabarega) raiding for food and force inhabitants of N Bun(yoro) on one side of the front or the other. Patrols don't work as inhabitants run away or if friendly must profess allegiance to Kaba out of fear'.
On 19 May he wrote to the Commissioner from Masindi a letter setting out his:

Gross objections to Cervale's supposed speech in baraza which ceded S Bunyoro to the Ganda as prizes of war 1. Because the territory was in no way conquered by the Ganda and was still unsubmitted in 6.95 when he arrived at Nakabimba. 2. Lwekula's attempts to wrest control were resisted after submission to British by Chief Balielugulu of Bujiro 'I would point out that the chiefs Muhenda, Muhengo, Lugoi, Kalego, Carto are in their own districts … certainly they will object in a Cath… District practically under Lwekula and I sincerely hope that it will never be said of me that they were removed from their property for making such objection, their submission having been accepted with no such provision'. He will resign his civil post if that happens.

It is evident from this fragment that Putty was determined to act with integrity in his deal-ings with the Wanyoro, recognising that without trust there would be no peace. However, the situation was immensely complex as Putty's next letter to the Commissioner on 25 June reporting the arrival of Rwabadongo shows:

Will settle him at Kitanwa. The districts of Bugoma, Kibero and Magungu I have placed under him. Presents him with 26 cattle apprecoated [?] boundaries – N Nile, S R Ngussi, W Lake Albert, E Hoima-Masindi-Murchison Falls Road.

A week later, on 1 July, he reported to the Commissioner that Bikamba the chief of Masindi was suspected of arms trading by Rwabadongo and himself.

---

66   Hon North de Coigny Dalrymple (1853-1906) SG 1871-1904.

Letters to and from Gerald Cuthbert were taking up to four months each way and Putty wrote again from Masindi on 25 July:

My dear Cupid, Very many thanks for yours of the 1st April which reached me last week don't apologise any more for not having written enough, there is no doubt plenty of the letters sent off from England never reach one chiefly from the envelopes breaking they get most unmercifully knocked about both coming up and going down. Have been here since I got back from Dufile last month but am off again on 1st August across Lake Albert to Mahagi where the poor wretches are owed seven months' pay however the cloth has just arrived so now can face them, if it was not that (Ternan) has written to say he is so seedy he is obliged to go to the coast should have gone on a bit of a shooting expedition up at the N end of the Lake but they may give me the command of the troops in which case I shall have to go to Port Alice [Entebbe] in fact it may alter my plans of returning altogether, it might mean my staying on until this time next year at which period I should be entitled to 6 months leave from the Foreign Office besides having the command of an expedition should one come off, it is always worth hanging on in the hopes of an advance down the Nile being ordered but as no orders have come up to the present am inclined to think the advance of British troops is not going to take place until the autumn of 97, entre nous it would be soundest not to attempt an advance from this end until the English were actually in possession of Khartoum, to do any good these troops want a couple of years training though the improvement the last few months of peace has enabled us to make in them is truly marvellous, when the most senior officer quietly informs you that sights are no good in this country it shows the material one has got to work on, have just put the three companies here through a practice course of musketry, with Remington rifles, the ammunition was so old and bad that the results of the scoring was little criterion but it has doubtless done them no end of good anyway the fire discipline is very different. Am engaged in taking in the grain crops, (mahindi), (mitarma) etc these I sowed at the beginning of April and have got a pretty good crop, quite enough to last until January when the next crop should be ready, have induced these Nubians to make enormous pieces of cultivation which if they will only continue the motion will enable them to live pretty well without looting the country for thousands of miles. The Wanyoro chiefs are almost impossible to deal with on account of it being beyond the wit of man to extract the truth, the men are naturally such an indolent race that I doubt any good being ever got out of them, the women till the ground and the men eat it, the only thing they do is to build houses otherwise they sit in the sun all day drinking beer. You seem to have had a bad time of it with the battalion with scarlet fever and typhoid, here we have just started smallpox so you ain't alone in your maladies, have done my best to isolate the cases but when they live like bees it is very difficult, in fact really out of the question. We nearly had a flare up with the Belgians the other day, they came and built a fort at Katwe on Lake Albert Edward within ½ mile of ours also quietly ordered our native officer to haul down our flag. They have apologised though so all is at an end, the place in question is a nicish point, as there is a salt bed there it leads to competition. Well good luck my dear Cupid. Yours ever, WP Pulteney PS. The enclosed letter is more in the subaltern's line than your humble servant's. WPP.

By now Putty was becoming concerned about the military situation. In a letter to the Commissioner from Masindi on 31 July, he wrote:

The Wanyoro chief Muhenda has left his country south of the Ngussi Burahya and is at present in the Magungu District (Magungu is the north western part of Unyoro on the Nile and Lake Albert). Rwabadongo informs me that Muhenda sent to him to say he was coming to live under him but that he now intends crossing the river Nile and going into the Shuli Ach ... country to join Kabarega's people. Muhenda is reported to have 70 guns with him. I have not thought it desirable to follow him up into the Magungu district because he would immediately cross the river whereas if he remains this side of the river no doubt many of his followers will desert back to Rwabadongo.

On 30 August Putty, now at Mruli, wrote to Ternan (Commandant Uganda Rifles):

Intelligence received that Mahdists and Kaba[rega] are joining forces, supported by Madi, Langri and Bakedi to invade Magungu in October. Muhenda has joined him and a quantity of arms and powder have recently been obtained through Rwabadongo.

Writing again to Ternan from Mruli on 7 September covering the diary of a patrol, Putty noted:

Patrol to shell Jasi's HQ at Tochi on E bank from where they collected food on W Side. Muhenda was attacked by Langi and lost 50 men and all but 7 of his guns. Kabarega seized the guns and told Muhenda he wasn't wanted. Rujumba, a son of Rionga would settle at Powara and be joined by his people from Lango if there were troops there.

Jasi was Kabarega's oldest son and fought with him until 1899 when Kabarega was captured and he was killed. Tochi is probably N of Mruli where the Kafu joins the Nile coming out of Lake Kioga. Back at Masindi on 15 September, Putty wrote to the Commissioner:

Capture of sword being sent to chiefs all round Unyoro by Kabarega, purpose unknown. Messenger a man named Sardi. Rwabadongo says it was sent to buy Jembes and arouses suspicion.

The following day he wrote to Gerald Cuthbert:

My dear Cupid, Many thanks for your letter of 1st June which reached me the beginning of this month having come up very quick. This day two months I should be leaving on my way to the coast but just at present there are rumours of attacks by dervishes impending, so unless it all turns out all bunkum shall probably have to remain a bit longer, personally don't believe in the scare but it never does to chance things so have made as many preparations as possible, the worst of it is that most probably it means another journey to Dufile to see if there is any move on the part of the dervishes, three weeks in a steel boat oh such a pleasant trip!!! The rains are on now which makes things unpleasant besides touching one up with fever, but only very slightly, just fancy your humble servant only weighing 11 st 5 lbs very nearly a stone lighter than when I left Eton, all one's muscle has gone don't want to lose any more weight there is that bally trudge to the coast before me. This should reach you about New Year's day so wish you and the Battalion every luck for 97. The first Battn seem to have been in a bad way with their Sergt Majors, it is a pity that they did not take Wilson[67] as Sergt Major a change would have done good although W was never a Drill his voice being hopeless. Steele[68] should make a good drill the men understand him but I never did. Glad little Barne[69] is a success with the signallers but those two Coldstream battalions always take a lot of beating. Hope you got on all right at the Irish military tournament the Grenadiers seem to have run up well at the Hall, where are the Munster Fusiliers now they used to win everything at one time? Have done a pretty good record in house building this week as in the 6 days have pulled down two houses and built two new ones, on a different principle, this place would be a good example to the Engineers at home, it was very uncomfortable before as the roofs were so flat the water came in by the buckets, besides they were all in one if a fellow turned round in his bed he was heard by the next fellow, this when one had a fever was a great nuisance, besides if one house caught fire nothing could save the whole show. These Nubians would suit you they are rare good fellows and do an immense amount of work without a grumble as long as they get plenty to drink and have as many women as can get into one house they are content, they are pretty good plucked fellows, but will blaze away into the grass if there is an enemy about whether they see anyone or not, their idea being that it is the noise not the bullet that frightens the enemy, with the Wanyoro this surmise is correct but it won't work with the dervishes. An Armenian clerk arrived two days ago foresee he will be a bloody nuisance in a place like this, however have got plenty of work to hand over to him, also some Indian artisans have arrived which are indeed a blessing they look the most fearful scoundrels that ever were seen, do not think their looks are any libel on them either. Must finish now Cupid with best luck to all. Yours ever, WP Pulteney.

On 3 November Putty was awarded the DSO. The citation states: 'William Pulteney Pulteney. Capt, The Scots Guards. In recognition of services in the recent operations against slave-trading Arabs in the Uganda Protectorate'.

His last letter to Gerald Cuthbert was written on 7 November from Murchison Falls, Unyoro:

My dear Cupid, Your letter of the 8th August reached me here two days ago which is very good going. Put my name down for the battn or regimental present to Frank Erskine[70] if it comes off at the altar before I return. I was to have left here today for the coast but there is no one to relieve me but hope to get away the 1st January from Kampala anyway. Am sending a telegram to the regimental orderly room to say when I am starting when you hear of my arrival at Mombasa do you mind sending Wilson[71] over a fortnight after you hear that interesting piece of news, tell him to go down to Ashley my brother's place

---

67   5359 DSgt John Wilson SG 1881-1896 DSgt 2 SG 1893-1896 transferred to 1 SWB.
68   6546 DSgt John Steele SG 1883-1899.
69   Possibly Miles Barne (1874-1917) SG 1893-1904 & 1915-1917 died of wounds.
70   James Francis Erskine (1862-1936) SG 1883-1910.
71   Probably 9513 Private James Wilson.

and get my kit ready for swaggering about London in, my uniform can wait a bit tell him my brother will tell him what to do; if he wants to stay with his present master he can do so but I have no doubt he can be spared for a month just to put me straight but hope to God he don't want to leave me because he knows my ways. There seems to be quite a run of promotion going on in the regiment just a present, it looks like my being a major before 1900. Am building a zariba here, it is a lovely place about ½ mile below the falls but nothing but rocks anywhere so can't get on very well, we are now in touch with the natives right down to Wadelai so that we get any information about any dervish movement south pretty quick. We had some heavy shooting at (Kabarega) last month from (Foreira) and bolted him off to (Fatiko) there is no doubt that I ought to have been a gunner am a nailer with the Hotchkiss. The truth of it is that they want a great many more soldiers and English officers up here they will be having a repetition of the Italians if they don't. You should be coming over to London about the time I am getting there so we will have a jolly though shall probably have to go a bit easy at first. The mail is going off from here tomorrow so am pretty busy you must excuse more. Hope to find you well in the Army Football Cup on my return. Tell Jamieson to stop the *Sportsman* being sent any longer to me I think he ordered it for me from Scripps in South Molton St if he didn't just drop them a line to tell them not to send it any longer. Yours ever, WP Pulteney PS. Send all letters to Guards Club to await my arrival after you get this.

Putty did not write to the Commissioner again until 3 January when, from Masindi, he reported that Rwabadongo wanted to move to Butuku near the Semliki, outside Pulteney's jurisdiction. His last letter to Ternan, then Acting Commissioner, was on 1 February:

I also am strongly of the opinion that it would be greatly to the advantage of the Protectorate if Rwabadongo resided in Kampala and not in Unyoro for many reasons – Rwabadongo has absolutely failed to administer Western Unyoro; although I had given him his choice of situation in Bugoma Kibero or Magungu, on my return from Fadjan [Fort at Murchison Falls] at the beginning of this year he had not settled anywhere. The district over which he was to preside was much too large for him for many reasons. In the first place Rwabadongo has not nearly as much authority with the Wanyoro which from his former position I was led to expect he had. Again for some reason or another he is very unpopular with the Wanyoro. Whenever asked to do anything he states he has no power and that the people will do nothing for him. My opinion being that his friendship is not real to us but on the contrary he is an agent to Kabarega. Amara, Aberswezi and Rajumba all confidently assert that Rwabadongo does everything he can to help Kabarega and lately I have come to the same conclusion. I am of the opinion that Aberswezi should be chief of the Hoima and Bugoma District. Further that Melindwa should be chief of the Kibero District and Bikamba the Masindi District. Amara chief of Magungu N and inclusive of Mount Sessi. Mugeni chief of Ampino. Rajumba chief of Foweira Mashudi and Mruli. Rwabadongo left 5.2 for Kampala.

It seems likely that Putty left Uganda in February 1897, returning to England sometime in April or May. On 1 May he was promoted to the rank of Major; and on 9 July Putty was presented with the DSO by Queen Victoria at Windsor Castle.

For most of the rest the year Putty was on leave, his employment under the Foreign Office in Uganda officially ending on 22 September. His health had suffered in Uganda as Laurence Drummond indicated when writing many years later:

> Pulteney suffered a severe attack of black-water fever whilst in Uganda which left its marks on him for a considerable time, but certainly never quenched his spirits nor his perpetual sense of humour, for, on coming to see us shortly after his return home, he assured our small children that his temperature during his fever in Africa had been so high that the crumbs in his bed had turned to toast! This yarn was naturally received with shrieks of delight by the children, who only wished to emulate the performance of their much-loved 'Mr Putty' in their own beds.

Blackwater fever is a complication of malaria with the possibility of kidney failure, and getting himself fit again would have taken some time. Putty spent the whole of August 1897 on leave in France, probably in the south which was to become a favourite of his.

Towards the end of 1897 Putty was appointed to command R Coy SG, one of two new companies formed at that time to give each battalion nine companies. The reason for this is obscure but it may have been a preliminary step to the formation of 3 SG. In November of that year Putty became a member of the Committee of the Brigade of Guards Employment Society, helping men returning to civilian life; this activity he was to continue for the rest of his regimental soldiering. Very little else is known about his next twelve months.

Congo 1898-1899

From 31 December 1898 to 17 June 1899 Putty was the Vice Consul of Boma in the Congo Free State: the port town of Boma was the capital of the Congo from 1886 to 1926 when it moved to Leopoldville (now Kinshasa). On 4 January 1899 a letter was sent from HBM Envoy Brussels[72] to Congo State/Department des Affaires Étrangers:

> HBM Government has had for some time under consideration the question of appointing a resident consular officer in the Independent State of the Congo but it has been found difficult to come to any conclusion as to the character of the Post, or the best site for a Consulate. The completion of the railway to Leopoldville now affords an opportunity of studying the question on the spot, and HBM's Government have therefore decided to send Major Pulteney an officer of considerable African experience to visit the Congo State and report both on the best site and on other points of which it may be desirable in the interest of British commerce to station Vice Consuls. When employed on the mission he will hold HBM Commission as Vice Consul in the Independent State of the Congo, and I have the honour in compliance with instructions received from the Marquess of Salisbury to notify this appointment to the Government of the Independent State of the Congo, and beg to request that instructions may be sent to the Governor (or Government) and their officials to give Major Pulteney, who hopes to start by the steamer

72   Sir Francis Plunkett (1835-1907).

leaving Antwerp on the 6th Inst, all the assistance which he may desire in moving from place to place within the State in pursuance of his instructions, and to recognise him in his capacity as Vice Consul of HBM.

On 6 January the Foreign Office sent a telegram to Brussels:

Major Pulteney DSO Scots Guards HM Vice Consul in the Congo State leaves Antwerp on the 6th Inst. He is going out to report specifically where the Chief Consulate post in the Congo State should be and would be glad if facilities for his baggage could be obtained along the way.

Sir Francis Plunkett, HBM Envoy Brussels, wrote again to the Department des Affaires Étrangers on 17 January:

With reference to the note I had the honour of addressing … on the … inst respecting Major WP Pulteney I beg now to forward herewith the Commission of the Queen, my gracious Sovereign, appointing Major Pulteney to be HBM's Vice Consul for the Territories of the Independent State of the Congo, and, in compliance with instructions received from the Marquess of Salisbury, I have to request that you will kindly obtain the … of the Sovereign of the Independent State to enable Major Pulteney to … on the discharge of his official duties.

Putty was well on his way when this was written and arrived in Boma towards the end of January 1899. The only evidence of what he then did is his letter from HBM Consulate Boma on 10 May 1899 to Her Majesty's Principal Secretary of State for Foreign Affairs (Marquess of Salisbury)

My Lord, I have the honour to acknowledge Mr Bertie's[73] despatch of 21st January 99 calling attention to the proceedings of the Congolese local authorities on the upper river as criticised by a correspondent of the *Petit Belge*, copy returned, and referred to in Sir F Plunkett's despatch [Brussels No 9 Africa 14 Jan 1899]. In my opinion the statements made by Mr Paul Coureur are substantially correct, there were four whites killed by the Bungas, their deaths were avenged by a victory of Major Lothaire's[74] in which I am told no fewer than 1500 shields [Bunga] were counted on the ground after the battle. It is apparent that Major Lothaire's Campaign possesses practically unlimited powers of action. The Company's [Antwerp Trade Company] headquarters at Mobeka I visited, they are well arranged and exceptionally favoured as regards position and called at by all the State steamers either ascending or descending the river. Judging by the number of loads of goods taken up monthly by the State boats and the amount of rubber brought down it is evident that Major Lothaire's Company enjoys exceptional advantages from the State. The reason of the Bunga revolt was undoubtedly the result of the means employed for the collection

73   Francis Leveson Bertie (1844-1919) Asst PUS FO later Ambassador in Paris 1905-1918.
74   Major Hubert Lothaire.

of rubber; from all the information I could gather there does not appear to be any material difference between the methods employed by Major Lothaire's Company in the collection of rubber and those employed by the State. There were several (Clira) and Elmina men in Major Lothaire's employ at Mobeka, they stated they were well treated and appeared contented. From what I saw personally at Mobeka there must be between 30 and 40 tons of rubber coming in a month; even if it is one of the richest districts in the Congo it is evident that the collection of such an enormous quantity would be a strain on organised labour but far greater with a forced labour market. I have the honour to be My Lord, Your obedient and humble servant William Pulteney Pulteney.

From this letter it is evident that Putty's brief was considerably wider than that declared to the Belgians or to the Government of the Congo. He must have returned to England soon after making this report because in October 1899 Putty was Second in Command 1 SG en route for South Africa.

5

South Africa 1899-1902

Second in Command 1st Battalion Scots Guards 1899

On 21 October 1 SG marched from Chelsea Barracks to Nine Elms Station through cheering crowds and entrained for Southampton. Colonel Paget[1] was in command and Putty, now Lieutenant Colonel, was with him as Second in Command. Once at Southampton the battalion embarked in the SS *Nubia* owned by the Anchor Line, a small ship of 3,551 tons, for South Africa. Lowther (now Adjutant 1 SG 1899-1901) described the voyage:

> In due course we collected our necessaries and sailed in HMT *Nubia*; we were packed like herrings, and underwent the usual maritime discomforts of those unaccustomed to troopships. I do not refer to the uneasiness due to the motion and dear to the elementary humourist of the weekly comic Press, but to the tiresome crowding, indifferent food, endless parades, and futile endeavours to keep eighteen hundred men fit on two exiguous promenade decks.

Cuthbert[2] D Coy 1 SG described arriving at St Vincent in the Cape Verde Islands and the twenty-three hours it took to coal, and the crossing of the equator on 3 November when 'Neptuning' was carried out by the ship's officers. Cator,[3] also D Coy 1 SG, recalled that on 10 November in the South Atlantic it was very rough with waves breaking over the forecastle. These three officers clearly did not enjoy the voyage: for the soldiers it must have been dreadful.

The CinC, Sir Redvers Buller,[4] had decided that the situation in Natal was so critical that he must go there himself and had diverted to Durban the first troops which reached Cape Town. If it was of the first importance to save Natal and to relieve Ladysmith, the relief of Kimberley came second and that task was entrusted to Lord Methuen[5] GOC 1st Division and the Guards

---

1 Arthur Henry Fitzroy Paget (1851-1928) SG 1869-1900.
2 Captain James Harold Cuthbert (1876-1915) SG 1896-1905 & 1914-1915 killed in action.
3 Captain Albermarle Bertie Edward Cator (1877-1932) SG 1897-1923.
4 General Sir Redvers Henry Buller (1839-1908) late KRRC.
5 Major General Hon Paul Sandford Methuen (1845-1932) Eton SG 1864-1888 and 1904-1932 later Field Marshal 3rd Baron Methuen.

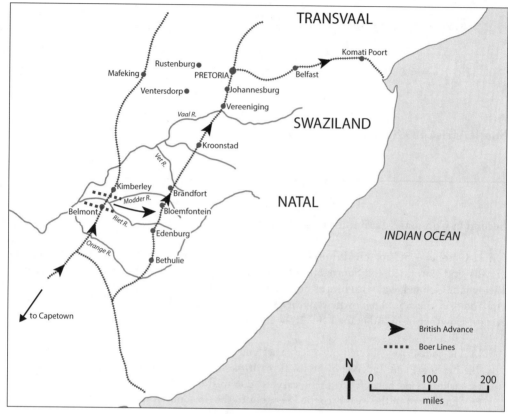

Map 3 South Africa 1899-1900.

Brigade[6] was sent north to Orange River Station as soon as it arrived. From there the line of advance to Kimberley would follow the single railway line that ran north to Rhodesia.

On 13 November the *Nubia* arrived in Table Bay and those onboard heard for the first time that Ladysmith was surrounded by the Boers. The sea was at first too rough for the ship to enter the docks, but it quieted down during the night. On board with Putty was his horse George, his groom 1644 Private Robert Harrison,[7] and his orderly 2202 Private Henry Thomas Rendle.[8] All three were to be with him throughout the three years of the war. The *Nubia* entered Cape Town Docks on 14 November and at 10.30 am the first five companies of 1 SG were disembarked; an hour later they had entrained and started north. The remaining three companies followed later with the light baggage. It was to be a long journey because they did not arrive at the Orange

6   Comd Major General Sir Henry Colville (1852-1907) late Gren Gds previously Commissioner in Uganda.
7   Private Robert Harrison (1877-NK) SG 1897-1916 on transfer.
8   Private Thomas Rendle (1880-NK) SG 1898-1910.

River until after midday on 16 November; and it was here that the four battalions of the Guards Brigade were assembled.

Methuen's 1st Division struck camp on the night of 20 November: 1 SG left camp at dawn and marched the twelve miles to Witte Putts. Next day was spent in reconnaissance of the enemy positions near Belmont, and later that day the force made a short approach march. The Boers were holding three ranges of hills east and south-east of Belmont Station. Of these, the one nearest to the railway was named Gunhill, the next north-east of Gunhill was called Table Mountain, and the third and most important ran east of Table Mountain and was called Mont Blanc. Methuen's plan was that 9 Bde, moving with its left just south of Belmont Station should attack Table Mountain while the Guards carried Gunhill. When Table Mountain was taken 9 Bde was to come down on Mont Blanc from the north, while the Guards held the Boers in front. The mounted troops were to cover both flanks. General Colville ordered the Guards Brigade to advance against Gunhill in two lines, the Grenadiers and Scots Guards in the first line and the two Coldstream battalions in support.

They paraded at 2 am on 23 November and at 3.15 am advanced; the objective of 1 SG being the nearest point to be attacked the battalion was the first to become engaged. After scrambling through some wire fences the battalion, about 4 am, got to within about 150 yards of the spur, when the enemy opened a hot fire. Bayonets had been fixed and Colonel Paget ordered the charge to be sounded. The spur was carried with a ringing cheer and with little loss, but on getting to the crest the battalion was exposed to frontal fire from Mont Blanc and to enfilade fire from both flanks. The regimental history describes what happened next: 'The fire from the right ceased as the Grenadiers charged and carried the next spur of Gunhill to the south, and that coming from the left was stopped by the prompt action of Lieutenant Colonel Pulteney, in command of the left company. He at once attacked the Boers on the spur to the north of that captured by the battalion, drove them off, and captured thirty of their ponies, on which he mounted a party of his men and started with them in pursuit of the flying enemy, who he followed up to the southern spur of Table Mountain, where he was stopped by fire from the Boers hidden behind the boulders'.

Cator who was with D Coy commanded by Gerald Cuthbert (Cupid) described this part of the battle in rather more detail:

> As soon as we got near Gun Hill we could just distinguish the enemy in the dawn against the skyline. They opened a heavy fire on us, keeping under cover, and till sunrise we were exposed to heavy cross fire without being able to see our enemy. As daylight appeared we kept a heavy fire on them and eventually turned them out. I myself thought the fight all over, so went down to bind up some wounded with some bandages I had brought with me. I had just finished binding up a man's foot when a bullet whistled straight into the ground six inches off. I then saw that the enemy had only fallen back on to a high ridge behind their first position. I was told that Cuthbert had gone on, so followed him with six men. We climbed up the Boers' first position and found a flat valley behind it covered with things they had left: dead horses, blankets, carts and wounded besides a drove of horses which we mounted. Putty and Cupid and some of their men mounted them, but some left them as our artillery burst amongst them, thinking they were Boers. I and my men had lost touch with the company, so we assailed the next ridge. After plugging away we got up without a casualty. We were joined by all sorts of men – Grenadiers, Coldstream, Fusiliers,

Northamptons. Our ground was simply swept by a hail of bullets and directly one popped one's head up it was received with a volley. Putty tried sticking his helmet up and then told off his best shots to get to a flank under cover and as soon as the enemy shot at the hat two men popped up and took a shot. This was quite successful. After remaining here for two hours firing hard, we were relieved to hear Elwes[9] with a maxim gun popping away on our left front. This was too much for them and they scattered. We then advanced with fixed bayonets and suddenly came on another party to which we gave a very heavy fire and they bolted down a water course the other side of the kopje. In another half-hour's time the charge was sounded and we all doubled forward with a hearty cheer. The Boers opposite to us hoisted the white flag and we took them prisoners.

So much for 1 SG's first action 'The Battle of Belmont' and Putty's part in it. The battalion lost 10 other ranks killed, 3 officers and 35 other ranks wounded = 48. In his despatch for the day General Methuen wrote: 'I note with pleasure the valuable services rendered by Lieutenant Colonel Pulteney'.

That afternoon, still 23 November, half 1 SG was sent under Putty to occupy Belmont Station. Next day (24 November) the whole battalion was ordered to guard the station while the remainder of the force advanced towards Graspan, the next Boer position on the road north. They caught up on 25 November while the action was in progress, and again the Boers were driven from their positions. 1 SG was divisional reserve and did not fire a shot.

The regimental history takes up the story on 27 November:

The force advanced towards the Modder River, a trying march of some fourteen miles in great heat, while water was bad and scarce. The Boers had occupied a position near the junction of the Riet and Modder Rivers and it was Methuen's intention to mask this position and to move on to Jacobsdal, about nine miles to the east. But during the night he received information that the Boers were entrenching a position about half-way between the Modder River and Kimberley. He conceived the Boers at Modder River village to be an advanced post and decided to turn them out, before starting on his turning movement to Jacobsdal, to prevent them from making attacks against his communications. Methuen did not believe that there were more than about 400 Boers opposed to him on the river, while actually a considerable force had taken up a skilfully entrenched position on a wide front on the north bank of the Riet. Owing to this change of plan 1 SG was turned out about 4.30 am 28 November and marched without breakfasts. Methuen directed Colville to advance with his left on the railway and his right on a group of high poplars about a mile up the Riet while 9 Bde attacked with its right on the railway. The ground over which the Gds Bde was to advance was flat and open, while the enemy position on the bank was concealed by trees and bushes. Both the Riet and the Modder flow through deep channels and these afforded the Boers covered ways by which they could move to any part of the position. The Gds Bde began to deploy a little before 7 am – 1 SG on the right, Gren Gds in the centre and 2 Coldm Gds on the left nearest the railway. 1 Coldm Gds were in the second line.

---

9   Henry Cecil Elwes (1874-1950) SG 1895-1904 & 1916-1918.

Major Baden-Powell[10] OC F Coy, described the advance of 1 SG:

> We were going steadily forward believing that we should meet with no opposition, when suddenly a very hot fire opened all along our front, not more than two or three hundred yards off. We lay flat down at once, the front line keeping up a steady fire though there was nothing to be seen in front but bushes. After a bit I advanced the second line up to the first by short rushes and ordered the men to dig shelter pits with their bayonets as they lay; this was easy in the soft sandy ground. If the Boers had kept up a steady well-aimed fire on us we must have been annihilated, but most of their bullets went over our heads. This went on for a long time under a very hot sun. Then we got orders to fall back, and retired bit by bit to a big reservoir which made a good natural fort.

The history recorded:

> The retirement was ordered by General Colville about 9 am, when he saw that an advance across the open was impossible. There was no knowledge how far the left of the enemy's line extended, and about an hour before this retirement was ordered Lieutenant Colonel Pulteney, with two companies and the machine-gun under Lieutenant Elwes, was moved to the right with the object of getting round the enemy's flank. But this movement was also stopped: all the machine-gun detachment being killed or wounded. Colonel Paget then reinforced Colonel Pulteney with four companies from his second line, but even with this reinforcement no progress was made.

The Boers later withdrew and next day (29 November) Cator wrote:

> Crossed Modder River and took the town. No opposition. Found lots of dead and wounded by the water. The whole town riddled by bullets. The last forty-eight hours the most terrible I have ever passed in my life. No sleep and no food, dog tired and all ones friends getting killed and wounded.

So far the Boer Commander in the Transvaal, De la Rey, had had the best of the encounters on the Modder River. 1 SG remained there for nearly two weeks: by then the Boers had been reinforced and prepared a defensive position centred on Magersfontein Hill about six miles to the north-east. Methuen decided to attack this on 11 December. The Gds Bde assembled at 1 am with 1 SG being in the rear of the brigade. It was an intensely dark night and soon after the start there was a heavy thunderstorm. Great difficulty was experienced in keeping direction and connection, and the difficulties were greatest in the rear of the column. Colonel Paget decided to halt the battalion until the first streak of light came, and it was then moved to the left to act as escort to the guns where it remained until late in the afternoon.

Meantime the difficulties of the night march of the Highland Bde had been as great as the Gds Bde. It did not reach its position just south of the Magersfontein ridge until 4 am, and it was just about to deploy when a heavy fire was opened on it from its front and right flank.

---

10   Fletcher Smyth Baden Baden-Powell (1860-1937) SG 1882-1904 & 1915-1917.

General Wauchope[11] fell at once, and the brigade never had a chance of taking the ridge. At 3 pm 1 SG was ordered forward to assist in covering its retirement and that night was spent on outpost duty. Cator recalled:

> The night was fearfully cold and our stomachs empty. At 1 am Gerry Ruthven brought up rum, bully beef and biscuits and he made a capital meal.

Next day (12 December) Cator continued:

> Not a shot fired until 9 am, when the enemy began shelling us. The ground in front of us was littered with dead and wounded, some of whom we buried. At 11.30 am we got orders that we were to cover the withdrawal of the guns and then retire ourselves. The guns limbered up and moved off, shells bursting all round them; their men were simply splendid and took no more notice of the shells than if they had been flies. As soon as the guns retired about a mile our brigade rose and followed. At 4 pm all firing ceased and we returned to Modder River. 1 SG had hardly been engaged and only lost two men wounded.

The battalion spent the next two months at Modder River. The temperature recorded on 24 December in Cator's tent was 120 degrees. Apart from occasional spells of outpost duty and strengthening the defensive line, the period was mainly uneventful. An exception was on 6 January when, as told by Cator:

> 1 SG paraded at 3.30 pm for reconnaissance in force towards Maggerfontein. We advanced to within 1500 yards of their trenches, scouts pushed out at 5 pm. Boers thought they were going to be attacked and were seen galloping down to their position. Our object had been achieved – to see if their trenches were still occupied in force, which they certainly were. At 7.45 pm we retired to camp, our wire entanglements causing great havoc in the dark.

He also noted on 7 February: 'Putty, Par, Dick and I went out shooting in the evening. Shot 24 pigeon and 4 plover'.

Major Maude,[12] reconnoitring the Boer position at Magersfontein early on 16 February, discovered that the Boers had moved off, and that afternoon 1 SG and 1 Coldm Gds occupied the enemy's lines, which they had been watching for so many weeks. The trenches, which were admirably sited, were found to be full of arms, ammunition, clothing and food; the Boers had evidently left in a great hurry.

On the night of 18 February 1 SG marched the 21 miles to Klip Drift and then the 6 miles to Klip Kraal Drift where it remained until 5 March, when it joined the remainder of Roberts' army at Osfontein, near Paardeberg. Cator described this time: 'We are on half rations here and hunger is rather a common complaint. Incessant rain and camp one pool of water, the wretched men no place to lie down, ground so wet'.

---

11   Andrew Gilbert Wauchope late BW (1846-1899) Comd 3 Highland Bde.
12   Frederick Stanley Maude Coldm Gds (1864-1917) Eton BM Gds Bde Putty's GSO 1 in III Corps 1914.

Pulteney (left) with Paget CO 1 SG Modder River, 31 January 1900. (RHQ Scots Guards Archives)

Officers 1 SG in front of mess hut, 31 January 1900. (RHQ Scots Guards Archives)

Considerable Boer forces, many of them drawn from Natal, had taken up a position at Poplar Grove to bar the way to Bloemfontein, and Roberts advanced against this position on 7 March. The Gds Bde advanced in the centre of the force, 1 SG leading, but as soon as French's[13] mounted troops got round the Boer left the enemy decamped and the brigade never fired a shot. On 10 March the army began the advance on Bloemfontein in three columns, the Gds Bde in the centre column. That day the left column, 6th Division and the bulk of the mounted troops, defeated a Boer force at Dreifontein. This proved to be the last stand of the Boers before Bloemfontein, and on the evening of 13 March the brigade entered the capital of the Free State; they had covered the last forty miles in twenty-six hours in very hot weather on half rations.

The battalion was moved by train to Edenburg on 15 March with companies dropped off at bridges en route, to secure the railway communications with the Cape Colony. At Edenburg

13   Major General John Denton Pinkstone French late 8 H (1852-1925) GOC Cavalry Division.

and surrounding area the rest of battalion spent the next fortnight collecting arms and administering an oath of allegiance to Free Staters, who poured in. While there Colonel Paget left the battalion on promotion to command 20 Bde, and Putty took command. It was almost six months since they had left London.

Commanding Officer 1st Battalion Scots Guards 1900

Putty was to command 1 SG for nearly nine months. At Bloemfontein, at the beginning of April, the battalion received new boots and clothing of which it was in sore need. However, it was fortunate in being away from Bloemfontein during most of the period since its occupation, as it escaped the worst effects of the great epidemic of enteric fever, caused by men having drunk the water of the Modder, poisoned by dead Boers and dead animals at Paardeburg. This epidemic caused more loss than any battle in the war.

At the end of March the Boers had captured the waterworks east of Bloemfontein, and in consequence of this renewed activity, the Gds Bde was sent down the line on 7 April, 1 SG being dropped off at Ferreira Siding. The rest of the month can be summarised as much marching and no action. There was, however, a lot of rain and it was very cold up in the mountains. By the end of the month the battalion was back in Bloemfontein where Gerald Cuthbert takes up the story of the march to Pretoria:

> We hoped for a little rest, but almost immediately on arrival news spread through the camp that the advance on Pretoria was to commence on the following Tuesday. We had practically no preparations to make as everything was already cut down to the lowest limits. The Bn 1st Line transport consisted of 1 machine-gun (old pattern wheeled maxim), 2 water carts, 4 SAA carts and a Scotch cart which carried some entrenching tools, and also the medical and signalling equipment. For the whole battalion ten mule wagons were allowed. One was allotted to each company to carry the greatcoats and one blanket per man, also reserve rations and forage. One wagon was detailed as cooks' wagon, and carried cooking utensils, fuel, and the day's rations, unless there was any prospect of companies being detached; in which case the rations were put on the company wagons. It was found very convenient keeping this cooks' wagon distinct, as it was always pushed ahead, sometimes even with the 1st Line transport, and often arrived in camp soon after the arrival of the Bn, and enabled the men's dinners to be ready several hours sooner than would otherwise have been the case. The tenth wagon was divided between the officers' baggage, and headquarters stores. Each officer was allowed one bundle only; no kitbag, bullock trunk, camp bed etc. was allowed. Of course there were no tents, and we always bivouacked until after our return from Komati Poort. The troops carried (in addition to their ammunition and equipment) a rolled blanket and waterproof sheet.

The advance began on 1 May. Roberts' method was to advance on a wide front with large bodies of mounted troops on each flank. The Boers did not stand when their flanks were threatened, and the result for the infantry was a great deal of hard marching, deploying, and reforming in column of march, but very little fighting. Gerald Cuthbert's detailed account gives a good idea of Putty's actions:

We marched off at 6 am through the town of Bloemfontein. Once clear of the town, the column spread out on a broader front, the brigades moving in column of battalions, with advance guard and flanking parties far out. About 4 miles north of Bloemfontein the Gds Bde diverged slightly to the westward and moved through a very pretty wooded valley called Glen Lyon, down the long slopes towards the Modder River, the banks of which we reached at 1.30 pm and, after crossing it, the brigade halted and the men's teas were prepared. After a good rest, the battalion marched again at 3.45 pm, and after a long toil-some climb reached Karee Siding at 7 pm and bivouacked. This had been a 23 miles march, but the men were very fit, and made light of it. From Karee, just before sunset, we had a fine view to the north; below us in the plain ran a branch of the Modder, with thickly wooded banks where the Boers had their advanced posts, then a bare flat plain 5 or 6 miles broad, beyond which was the town of Brandfort flanked by rocky kopjes and wooded hills, making a strong position.

On the morning of 2 May we rested, while the Boer position was reconnoitred. Our line of advance was on the west side of the railway, and the road led down from the heights we occupied into the plain, passing between two long low stony kopjes, and then, about half a mile north of them, crossing a thickly wooded spruit, with a stone house near the drift. These were all held by the Boers, but whether in strength, or only by outposts, we had not been able to ascertain. About midday orders came that 1 SG and 1 Coldm Gds were to move forward after dark, and take these kopjes, which were about 5 miles to our front, and at daylight were to clear the wooded line of the spruit. 1 SG was to take the eastern-most kopje and the railway culvert, while the Coldstream were to move on our left, and take the western-most kopje. At 4.20 pm we paraded, and moved slowly forward keeping well out of sight till darkness set in. It was a very dark quiet night, but the men moved noiselessly, though the usual difficulties were experienced of keeping touch and direction in the inky blackness.

The advance was very slow, and it was midnight before we got close to the kopjes. Scouts were pushed round their base and flanks, and they were found to be unoccupied. There was nothing now to do but wait for dawn, as it was no use entering the thick bush by the spruit in the darkness, so after occupying the kopje and the bridge we lay down in shelter behind them. At the first streaks of dawn [3 May] the Coldstream and ourselves advanced to clear the line of the spruit when a spattering fire from the further bank showed the bush was held by the enemy. However, they proved only to be a weak picquet, and retired at once. On reaching the northern edge of the bush we sent back to report all clear, and having sent out patrols etc, waited for the arrival of the division. Soon after 6 am they appeared, and a very pretty sight it was to watch it streaming down from the Karee Heights and spreading out in the plain below. Meantime the battalion cooked their breakfasts, and marched again at 10.40 am acting as reserve to the brigade. We pressed on across the open plain in long scattered lines, marching on a high clump of poplars in the town of Brandfort. Soon news came that the Boer right was turned, and simultaneously their guns were withdrawn, and we heard that they were falling back on the Vet River where they meant to make a stand. At 2.45 pm we entered Brandfort, and marching through the town, took up a position on some stony kopjes NE covering the bivouac of the army. Brandfort was full of Boer women, who were most spiteful and loudly prophesied our total annihilation within a few days.

Writing of the orders given by Maude (BM Gds Bde) on 2 May, Putty recalled:

Among the lasting impressions made upon me by Joe Maude was on the advance from Bloemfontein. The Boers were reported to be holding Brandfort in strength, and Pole-Carew,[14] preceded by Pilkington's [CO 2 WAMI] mounted detachments, was the central column marching on that place. Orders for the attack were issued and dictated to us commanding officers by Maude. They were the most lucid orders that we had had up to that time. Perhaps his orders sometimes had a little too much detail, but I well remember they were far in front of anything we had before.

Gerald Cuthbert's narrative continues on 4 May:

A day of rest for us, as the engineers were hard at work trying to repair the railway; they worked splendidly, and it was marvellous how soon trains began to follow us up the line. Almost every culvert had been blown up, every bridge was destroyed, and sometimes for miles dynamite had been placed under the rails and then exploded, and the rails were consequently twisted and distorted into the most curious shapes. We marched at 6.30 am 5 May to force the passage of the Vet River; it was a long, hot, and dusty march, and at Eensgevonden Station we halted to give the men a rest, and refill water-bottles.

The enemy apparently were holding the drift over the Vet River strongly: our cavalry and mounted infantry could not get on, had moved off to the flanks, and were trying to work round the Boers. The railway here crosses the river on a high iron bridge with stone piers; these had been destroyed by dynamite, and the iron girders lay in a confused mass in the river bed. Covering the drift on the south side was a long rocky kopje with a long glacis slope down to it, the former was strongly held by the Boers, who kept up a heavy fire whenever anything showed within range. There is a good deal of rough rocky ground here, covered with bush, this gave the enemy excellent cover, and they maintained a heavy fire. Their guns were placed singly well back on the northern slope, and were most difficult to locate as they were all using smokeless powder. Our guns came into action by batteries, and it was very pretty seeing them galloped up, unlimbered, and their teams galloped back under cover. The Boer guns out-ranged ours, so our artillery had to move close in to try and reach them. Lord Roberts came down and watched the firing, standing right out in front of our firing line, much to the delight of the men, as, though he was heavily shelled, being so near our batteries, which of course drew the Boers' fire, he never took the least notice of it, or attempted to get under cover. Evening was coming on fast, the artillery on both sides stopped firing, as it became too dark to see, and the rifle fire all along the river gradually died away; and we bivouacked on the ground we held. Soon after we got orders that 1 SG was to attack the long kopje at daybreak, and hold it until the division arrived.

This we did, going cautiously down in the dusk, in skirmishing order, and rushing the kopjes as day [6 May] broke only to find the Boers had abandoned the position (again their flank had been turned)! We found an enormous quantity of spare ammunition on

14   Major General Reginald Pole-Carew late Coldm Gds (1849-1924) GOC 11th Division.

the kopjes we occupied; every Boer must have had three or four hundred rounds beside him, and there were little scharzes built all along the kopje with piles of ammunition in each. Behind, under shelter of rocks, were numbers of boxes, all full of ammunition, so the enemy had evidently expected to be able to hold on to their position. The battalion breakfasted on the kopje, and at 9 am the rest of the division advanced, and crossed the Vet River by the drift we were covering. There was very little water in the river, but the banks were steep, and very sandy, and the transport had a hard pull to get through. The battalion was told off to assist the wagons over, and hard job it was, but the men worked well, and everything got safely across. After a hot tiring march, the ground rising all the way, we reached Smaldeel Junction, and bivouacked in the angle between the main line to Kroonstad, and the Winburg branch. This was a most uncomfortable camp. We were jammed in between the two lines of railway, which here ran upon high embankments. The bivouac was according to the standing order, which was always very strictly adhered to 'line of quarter-columns of battalions at 15 paces interval', so we were all huddled together, and, owing to the confined space, the latrines were dug 50 paces away, and the smell was insupportable.

Here the Army halted for two days, as the engineers were having a very hard job trying to repair the old deviation over the Vet River; the bridge was so completely destroyed that it would (and did) take months to renew. Here we also got a mail; the first since leaving Bloemfontein. The advance commenced again on 9 May; along the west side of the railway passing Theron Siding, and halting for a rest about midday at a charming farm called Leeuwfontein. There was a good spring here, and a nice old Dutch farm house, with a good garden and orchard, and quite big shady trees. There was also a prickly pear fence, covered with fruit, and officers and men very soon were trying to get the fine spines out of their fingers. The prickly pear, though a poor fruit at most times, has got a pleasant acid flavour which makes it acceptable after a long thirsty march. After three-quarters of an hour, the brigade marched again, bivouacking eventually at Welgelegen Siding, where it arrived at 2.45 pm. On arrival we were told that the Boers were holding the Zand River strongly, and that we should have to fight for the drift. The railway bridge of course had been blown up.

The brigade paraded at 6.15 am next day [10 May], 1 SG forming the advanced guard. The mounted troops soon got touch of the Boers, and a running fight ensued. We, as advanced guard, had a good view of all that went on, though we had practically no fighting. We got down to the Zand River about 11.30 am and crossed it without opposition, the Boers having fallen back to some rising ground to the north. The battalion had advanced about a mile and a half, and was lying down hidden in the standing mealies, of which a great quantity is grown in the rich ground along the banks of the Zand River. The whole battalion was deployed in long lines at 10 paces interval, with about 400 yards between lines, on account of the artillery fire which was intermittent. The Boers had been holding on to a high rocky, wooded kopje about 2 miles to our right, but now Tucker's division,[15] which had crossed about 6 miles to the eastward, was coming up and consequently turning them. His guns commenced shelling the kopje, and soon the Boers abandoned it, and came streaming out across the plain on their ponies, straight towards us. They had not seen us,

15   Major General Charles Tucker (1838-1935) late S Staffs GOC 7th Division.

on account of the high standing corn, and having been fully occupied watching Tucker. Unluckily, a small party of mounted infantry on our right began to fire too soon and at the same time our horse artillery batteries opened at about 2500 yards: the galloping Boers who had been coming west, swerved off to the northward, spreading out like a fan. We fired at long range, and the horse artillery shells burst apparently right among them, but it was extraordinary how little damage seemed to be done. The battalion was on outpost that night; and I remember it as one of the few occasions during the war on which I saw the Boer camp-fires in any number.

Before dawn they had cleared, and we heard that they had fallen back on a prepared position at Boschplaats, just south of Kroonstad. Having been outposts, we became rear-guard the following day and did not move until 7.30 am. We had a long hot march, and bivouacked at Dispoort, near Geneva Siding at 5 pm, just as it was getting dusk. This camp I remember as typical of the close formation always adopted, and so different from the loose camps later in the war. The bivouac was on the reverse slope of a long rolling hill. The whole of the infantry division, 2 bdes of 4 bns each, was bivouacked in line, each bde being in line of bn quarter-columns with 15 paces between bns, and 30 paces between bdes. Officers bivouacked in line with their companies in the space between bns. The place was like an ant-heap – hardly room to move, and in the darkness, if one had occasion to go anywhere, it was impossible to avoid stepping on slumbering forms.

We paraded at 5.50 am 12 May to march the eighteen miles to Kroonstad. News had come that the Boers had abandoned their position at Boschplaats, and that De Wet had tried to prevent their retreat by sjamboking them at the drift, just outside the town. We had an uneventful march, and, having marched past Lord Roberts in the market place, camped on the north-east side of the town at 2.50 pm. During the march I inspected the trenches the Boers had dug at Boschplaats; they were of the deep narrow type, in short lengths, as at Magersfontein, and beautifully arranged. They were generally in two lines, the first more or less make-believe, and intended to catch the eye, and draw the fire of our artillery, while the 2nd and real line was about 400 yards back, and so placed that the holders could easily slip away and reach their horses.

Here at Kroonstad we stayed 13-21 May. The big railway bridge had been completely destroyed by the Boers, and the whole Army was employed, in working parties of battalions, in digging out, and laying rails on, the old deviation. This was very hard, but most important work. The men worked admirably, and both Lord Roberts and Lord Kitchener gave the brigade high praise; they constantly came to see how the work progressed. On 19 May we got the news that Mafeking was relieved, and we dined at the Central Hotel to celebrate the event. The nights here were bitterly cold, three or four degrees of frost every night, and on the night of 19 May the thermometer went down to 25 degrees (F). However there was never a cloud in the sky, and the sun warmed one up during the day.

We paraded at 7 am on 22 May and marched the eighteen miles to Honingspruit where we arrived at 5 pm, very tired. The following days were uneventful, just hard marching, with the usual advanced and flank guards, and, worst of all, when the battalion's turn came, the rearguard. This always meant getting into camp very late, sometimes long after dark, in addition to the extra labour entailed by off-loading and re-loading broken-down wagons, helping them over drifts etc; and the minor discomforts of dinners at midnight. The Boers kept steadily falling back before us: they had prepared a position at Rhenoster Spruit which

Colonel Pulteney, 25 May 1900. (RHQ Scots Guards Archives)

we reached on 23 May; it was a strong one, and if they had held it, might have given us a good deal of trouble. But Lord Roberts' system of advancing in 3 columns each six or eight miles apart, effectively took the fight out of the Boers; we could always outflank them in any position they took up.

On the morning of 24 May the proclamation came out annexing the Orange Free State to the British Empire and on 27 May we reached Viljoen's Drift on the Vaal River, and crossing it at 10.30 am, made our first bivouac in the Transvaal one mile north of Vereeniging. The Vaal here is a large and deep river; all the infantry came across on the pont, a large flat float working on a wire cable, which took 200 men each trip. The crossing was well managed, and it was wonderful how quickly the large force and its transport were transferred to the northern bank. The railway bridge, to our surprise, had only one span destroyed, and the large stone piers were left intact. The Boers had been so much hurried by our rapid advance, that they had not had time to carry out the work thoroughly.

The Gds Bde paraded at 6.45 am 28 May and marched the twenty miles to Klip River Station where we arrived at 3.30 pm, a long tiring march, and camped in a mealie field. It was bitterly cold, that night was the coldest we had had as yet; we were at an altitude of just over 5000 feet above the sea, and my thermometer showed ten degrees of frost at dawn. The ground and all our blankets were white with the hoar-frost, and I remember well my admiration for our Sergeant-Major Ross,[16] who was hard at work shaving, and I think was the only man in the brigade who did that morning. When the sun rose, the whole brigade, who had been stamping about to try and warm themselves, gave a great cheer.

We paraded at 7 am that day (29 May) and marched north; this was a most exciting day, as we were momentarily expecting to find the Boers in position. It was a hard march, the ground rising all the way, we were really climbing up the great ridge of the Rand itself, and constant reports came in of the enemy occupying the line Johannesburg – Germiston – Boksburg in force; also that Hutton (Comd 1 MI Bde) was having a hard fight at Florida,

16   8322 Sergeant-Major Thomas Ross (1871-1938) SG 1889-1919.

some miles to the west of Johannesburg. After we reached Natal Spruit, we could hear guns in front, and here we deployed into attack formation. Out on the veldt, 3 or 4 miles east of us, we could see a dense mass of cavalry halted, this was Broadwood's Cavalry Brigade[17] waiting for us to move on Germiston. The brigade moved on by Elsburg Station and then turned north-west, our point being Germiston Station. Everything seemed quiet, but one could see through the glasses that the huge tailing-heaps of the Swimmer and Jack, and Robinson deep gold mines were covered with natives, evidently looking out for something. As the Grenadiers, who were leading, came within rifle-shot of the station, a brisk fire broke out from the houses, station, and railway embankment. 1 SG moved up on the right of the Grenadiers and we were soon among the houses. This was the only place where I saw anything that could be called street-fighting during the war; and for about ten minutes we doubled from house to house firing down the street, but it was quickly over, the Boers galloping over the rocky Elandsfontein ridge in the direction of Zuurfontein. We held the ridge till dark, and then got orders to fall back 4 miles to camp on the high ground south of Germiston. It was a trying march, as the men were very tired, having been on the move (and covered 24 miles) since 7 am: but we reached our bivouac at 7.30 pm having some difficulty to find it in the dark, and as fortunately the cooks wagon had arrived, we got the dinner ready by 10 pm.

The brigade received orders to march to Johannesburg on 30 May, but these were subsequently cancelled and 1 SG was ordered to find the outposts on the east and south sides of the camp. At 9.30 am next day the outposts were withdrawn and we marched along the high road to Johannesburg where the whole force defiled past Lord Roberts in the great square, which was thronged with the inhabitants. Wheeling round the square, we left it by the NE corner and followed the Pretoria road down the steep hill past Orange Grove, and camped about 7 miles out.

On 1 and 2 June we rested: and most of both officers and men explored Johannesburg. The final advance on Pretoria commenced on 3 June. 1 SG formed the advanced guard (infantry) to the division; and paraded at 6.35 am moving over very pretty country, crossing the Yokeskei River en route, to Leeuwkop, where we arrived at 12 noon. The battalion was on outpost on the NE side of the camp. The veldt grass here was very long, and dry as tinder; somehow it became ignited, the fire rolling down on the bivouac at great speed, and it was only by great exertions on the part of the brigade that it was got under before damage was done. Next day (4 June) the battalion marched at 6 am forming the infantry rearguard of 11th Division. There was good deal of artillery and rifle fire all day long, and the high hills south of Pretoria about Zwartkop looked a strong position, but the Boers never really stood. By nightfall we had climbed the steep ascent to the west of Zwartkop, and in the moonlight moved to a position west of the great Schartzkop Fort which overlooks Pretoria. Here we lay down, ready to attack early next morning.

5 June was a great day for us, as receiving orders to stand fast at dawn, and not attack, we guessed something had happened, and soon after news came that the Boers had surrendered Pretoria. How the men cheered! They, and indeed all of us, thought that this means the end of the war; and little did we imagine that we had still more than 2 years to spend in

17   Major General Robert Broadwood late 12 L (1862-1917) died of wounds.

the country. At 7 am we marched into Pretoria, and proceeded to the railway station which we occupied, seizing a great quantity of rolling stock, though the Boers had removed all they had time to. The town was divided into districts, and all houses were searched for arms and ammunition; and we soon had a large heap from our district collected on the platform. At 3 pm that same afternoon, the Gds Bde marched past Lord Roberts in the Market Square, and then filed out at the west end of the town to our camp near the race-course.

Since leaving Bloemfontein 1 SG had marched 307 miles, much of the time with the advancing army. Throughout, Putty and the battalion would have been subject to constant scrutiny and comparison by Roberts and many others who were or would be in positions of influence. They did not stay in Pretoria for very long. The occupation of their capital had at first made the Transvaalers despondent, but the news which reached them of the successes of De Wet, who had cut the railway in the Orange River Colony in a number of places, cheered them up and Botha was able to assemble 8,000 men for another stand in the hills about 15 miles east of Pretoria, astride the railway to Delagoa Bay. Therefore on 7 June 11th Division was moved out to Silverton Station seven miles from Pretoria on this railway. The next three days were spent closing up to the Boer position and late on 11 June Roberts issued orders that it, known as Diamond Hill, was to be captured next day. The Gds Bde took part in this action (12 June) but 1 SG was left behind initially to act as escort to the guns. Cator takes up the story:

> Marched off last in the brigade and went southwards along the bottom of the kopjes and remained two or three hours behind the two 5 inch guns, then we got orders to advance half a battalion in support of the Grenadiers and leave the other half as baggage guard. Went on with right half under Putty. All round most terrible heavy firing, have not heard such heavy firing since Modder and Magersfontein. We didn't get up to their position till nearly dark and the firing was still very heavy. The two Coldstream battalions had taken the Boers first position. We and the Grenadiers bivouacked underneath. No blankets and the most piercing gale blowing, never so cold in my life.

Early on 13 June it was found that the Boers had gone and the Gds Bde returned to Pretoria until 23 June when it was ordered back to Donkerhoek, near Diamond Hill, to relieve the mounted troops. There it remained until 23 July, when Roberts was ready for his advance up the Delagoa Bay railway. The outpost duties during the stay at Donkerhoek were heavy and there was constant scrapping with Boer patrols. However, as railway communication improved supplies became plentiful and regular issues of pay, which had not been possible for a long time, were resumed. At Donkerhoek the battalion was issued with new clothing and boots, and a felt hat with turned-up brim took the place of the helmet. There 1 SG got ready for the advance to the frontier with Portuguese East Africa.

1 SG received orders to resume the advance along the Delagoa Bay railway on 23 July; the Boer Government, with what remained of Botha's army, having established a moving head-quarters on this line. This advance was very similar to that from Bloemfontein to Pretoria, the Boers falling back before the turning movement of the mounted troops. On 4 August 1 SG entered Middelburg without having fired a shot where it remained until 15 August when it moved forward to Pan Station, about ten miles farther east. On 24 August the advance began

Colonel Pulteney taking a siesta, August 1900. (RHQ Scots Guards Archives)

on Belfast and the Gds Bde occupied the high ground south of the town without opposition; the enemy was found to be in a strong position east of it. The brigade was waiting for French to effect his turning movement, being freely sniped by the Boers, when in the afternoon of 26 August it received orders to move northwards to support the mounted troops. This is Cator's account: 'The mounted infantry and horse artillery went out in most dashing style and got engaged with the Boers on a kopje about 4 miles out on our left front and about 3 pm (later according to some accounts) we got orders to advance and support them. We had only gone about half a mile when we came under such heavy fire that we had to right form and attack the Boers on our right flank. The attack was made by 1 SG with 1 Coldm Gds in support. The men were all as keen as mustard and went for the Boers in a splendid way, the enemy's fire getting hotter and hotter, but, thank God, the Boers shot very badly. As we came up they quitted and took to long range fire from a second position, but as it was getting dark we did not push on after them but entrenched ourselves for the night'. The casualties in 1 SG in this action were three killed and seventeen wounded.

The brigade reached the Watervaal Onder on 30 August where it remained until 12 September. In the last thirteen days it had covered one hundred and forty-six miles over country very different from the veldt of the Orange River Colony. It consisted of an intricate mass of mountains, and the weather was very hot and steamy, so the marches, short as the crow flies, entailed real hard work. Cator described one day (29 August):

If anyone had told me a year ago that a cavalry division, an infantry division, heavy guns and ammunition columns could cross country we came over today I would have thought him mad. At 4 am I was woke by reveille. It seemed as if I had only just gone to sleep. I poked my nose out of the blanket and found it pitch dark and raining a horrible drizzle. We marched off at 5 am and climbed straight up a mountain, 7,500 feet above sea level. Meantime the rain had turned into a scotch mist, so thick that we had to rest for an hour till it cleared. On the fog lifting I saw the grandest scenery I have ever seen in my life. We were bang on the edge of a precipice, a thousand feet below was a delightful valley and we could see French's troops winding their way down it and ascending another enormous hill the other side. Coming into the valley was like coming into a new land. A spruit was rushing down over the rocks and on its banks were growing great tree ferns and masses of maidenhair fern. We then had another steep hill to climb and then a long run down into Helvetia. Here we arrived to see the tail end of the Boers leaving cover for all they were worth.

1 SG arrived at Komati Poort on 12 September where an immense mass of railway stores, some guns and a quantity of ammunition were captured, but no Boers. They had all fled. The rest of the month was uneventful although every day until 25 September the battalion was on the march. Cator described two of these days:

Parade 4.30 am 16 September. Started off the road leading round the hill down a ledge with a sheer drop of 2000 feet into the valley below. A half mile down the road took a sharp turn to the right, very nervous work getting the wagons round the corner, the men having to hang on to hold them back and prevent them from running over the side. Seven miles on the road became fearfully steep and took us a long time to get everything safely down. Here we halted for two hours as the heat was almost unbearable, then again marched until 8.30 pm.

And

23 September marched to Dorsprong Station and here we stopped hot and tired no water to be had. Had been in camp about an hour when we got order to fall in and march on another five miles to Tenbosch Spruit. Dear me will this marching never end my feet so sore and feel fearfully tired from short nights and long days and oh the thirst of this beastly country, twenty more miles with no water, the wretched men in a very bad way, as they have never trained themselves for going without water, I myself have always avoided drinking in the day time unless I could possibly avoid it.

The battalion returned to Pretoria on 29 September, arriving on 3 October. Here they found camp pitched for them, the first tents they had had since April in Bloemfontein: they had marched another 310 miles in that time. The battalion remained at Pretoria until 21 October when it was ordered off to join Paget's column at Pinaar's River station, forty miles north of Pretoria. This marked the breakup of a large part of the army into small columns able to operate effectively against what was now becoming a well-mounted guerrilla enemy. Paget's Column operated in the Rustenberg district west of Pretoria. Cator described this period under their previous CO:

Most fearfully tired and we had no water since yesterday. Rained all day (25 October). Hardest two days we have had for some time. Long marches all very well in the cold weather but in this heat it is killing work. On 28 October we march to Sein Kop 6 miles, here we halt for the day. Cavalry leave us and with them the General. Putty left in command of the force which now consists of: 1 SG, ½ bn Munsters, section of field artillery, ½ co sappers, 2 cow guns and 80 ox wagons with supplies. We hadn't a mounted mare with us so consequently

Colonel Pulteney's horse 'George' which he rode throughout the South African War, 10 October 1900.
(RHQ Scots Guards Archives)

were rather badly off for scouts and any moment the force might have been ambushed in the thick bush. Marched off again 4 pm and pushed on till 8 pm when it came on to pour with rain; it became too dark to pursue our way any further and dossed down where we stood. Next day (29 October) we paraded at 3.30 am and marched to the Crocodile River which we crossed at a drift, river very swollen and deep. On arrival we sighted two armed Boers who bolted as we approached, one dropped his pass permitting him to remain on his farm. I was sent off with my half company to burn his farm and collect his stock. Went off and found the farm with five or six women who all began weeping and assured me that their husbands were only out for exercise and they hadn't any rifles or ammunition. On lighting the houses the roofs were full chocked with ammunition and went off like a miniature arsenal alight. Marched again till we got to Bethanie, a large native town, here we were overtaken by the most fearful storm so we had to halt. The heaviest rain we have had out here and fearfully strong wind behind it, everyone soaked through and through. Paraded at 5 am 30 October and marched to Beersheba, another native town; heat fearful and the going very heavy, wagons going in up to their axles.

The battalion reached Rustenberg next day (31 October) where Cator recalled: 'Town beginning to starve as the rain has delayed the weekly convoy coming from Pretoria, consequently

General Cunningham[18] has wired to Pretoria to send us off at once as our men have to be fed and are doing nothing so he is anxious to be rid of us'.

The regimental history noted: 'General Paget had received a wire from Lord Roberts to say that 1 SG were under orders for home and must be sent back to Pretoria'. They reached Pretoria on 8 November to find that Roberts was himself leaving for England and Kitchener taking his place, but 1 SG's hopes for home were soon dashed. The end of the war, so confidently predicted, was still far off, with a general stirring of the Boers in the Transvaal, Orange River Colony and in the north of Cape Colony. That day 1 SG started south by train and reach Springfontein on 19 November. The anniversary of Belmont was celebrated on 23 November with a double ration of rum and a sing-song.

Putty was made a Brevet Colonel on 29 November, and on 3 December orders were received for a move south next day: the battalion was to reinforce the defence of the Orange River line between Bethulie and Norval's Pont. Cator described the move:

> Hang around all day in pouring rain waiting for train to take half bn of us to Norval's Pont and half to Albert Junction Cape Colony, everything flooded out, cattle dying and dead from exposure. Wade down to the station to get dinner and sleep in railway truck.

Bn HQ was established at Norval's Pont on 5 December with detachments up and down the river, and here they remained until 13 December.

Cator again:

> We have had a nice peaceful time here, no Boers about at all. De Wet has gone north again having managed to cross the Caledon River. Alas! Our nice time is drawing to a close a telegram has arrived saying 'Lord Kitchener wants the Scots Guards to be ready to start for Pretoria at five minutes notice, a train is being arranged to convey us.' One wonders what on earth can be up to send us back nearly 500 miles, when will this everlasting job end? Our train was the first to travel all night since June. When we got to Elandsfontein we got orders to go to Krugersdorp and proceeded there via Johannesburg arriving at our destination at 4.30 pm.

On 13 December Clements[19] had suffered a reverse in the Megaliesberg at Noitgedacht, at the hands of De la Rey, and the Boers were expected to attack Krugersdorp. The attack did not take place and on 19 December 1 SG moved out in a column under Gordon,[20] one of a several columns under French that moved to the assistance of Clements. Cator described this operation:

> Marched off about 3.30 am the cavalry being late. March twelve miles in a north-westerly direction towards Megaliesberg Rand. Heard tremendously heavy firing all the morning from Clements direction at Vlakfontein. General French turned north and held the hills above; no sooner there than we saw the whole of De la Rey's force about 2000 Boers

18   Possibly Brigadier General George Glencairn Cunningham under whom Putty had served in Uganda.
19   Major General Ralph Arthur Penrhyn Clements late SWB (1855-1909) Comd 12 Bde.
20   Possibly Brigadier General JR Gordon late 15 H.

retreating past our front in the valley below. We at once saw that French had missed a tremendous chance of jugging the lot. Anyway it wasn't altogether a failure as 60 dead Boers were picked up.

The regimental history recorded that on 21 December: 'Colonel Pulteney was detached with a column of his own consisting of 1 SG, the Dublin Fusiliers, two field guns and a howitzer, and was employed in conjunction with other columns in a sweep of the country between the Potchefstroom railway and the Megaliesberg. On this work the battalion spent the second Christmas of the war very uncomfortably'. Cator wrote on 22 December: 'Another short day though early starts are the fashion and make one just as tired as longer days rising later. 1.30 am is an awful time for breakfast' and on 27 December:

> We took 7 prisoners today. Parade 2 am and march to the source of the Mooi River. We are one of four columns converging on Byers who has some 2000 men and 2 guns. Up to present time of writing beyond being in a most filthy temper from want of sleep and dog tired from continual trekking, nothing extraordinary has happened. I have only managed to put in five hours sleep the last two nights my feet are blistered, and am hungry as a vulture.

Pulteney's Column

By the end of December French had established a line of columns from Olifant's Nek through Ventersdorp to Klerksdorp, thus covering the railway effectively. Putty's Column was part of the central group of columns in the Ventersdorp district. At the beginning of 1901 he was formerly appointed to command it and Gerald Cuthbert succeeded him as CO 1 SG. From 17 January Putty's own staff diary provides a record of the column's activities and is the primary source although the contributions of several SG officers are also included to give important detail.

On 3 January Putty's Column was at Rietfontein in the Witwatersrand, about twenty-five miles north of Ventersdorp, being one of four columns under the general direction of Babington.[21] The general object was to drive De la Rey and Beyers west, but it was found that Beyers had got through to the east and was near Hekpoort, and next day Babington's, Gordon's and Putty's columns moved against him. Putty's column had their first scrap with the Boers on 5 January: there was thick fog and in this a Boer patrol got between two forces. Both fired at it and when it disappeared continued to fire at each other. Fortunately the mistake was discovered before any serious harm was done and when the fog lifted the Boers were found in position on a ridge of the Witwatersrand. The mounted troops and guns turned them out of their first position but could make no headway against the second. Three companies of 1 SG then advanced and turned the enemy out at a cost of two men wounded. Cator noted:

> We would have done the Boers a great deal more damage than we did had not the General (Gordon) withdrawn his guns from the position we captured, the result being the Boers who were bolting in hundreds had nothing but long range rifle fire shot at them.

---

21   Brigadier General James Melville Babington late 16 L (1854-1936) Comd 1 Cav Bde.

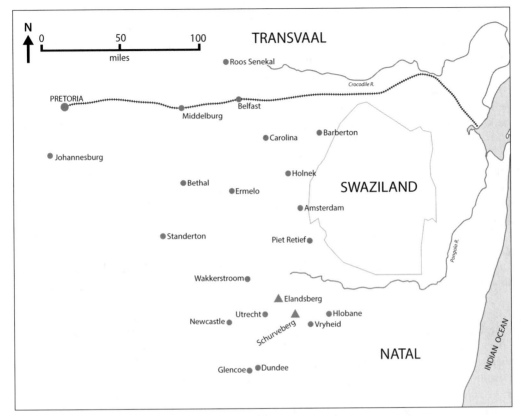

Map 4 South Africa 1900-1902.

Putty's Column then moved down to the Krugersdorp-Mafeking road to help a convoy arriving from Krugersdorp. The escort consisted of B Coy 1 SG, two squadrons of the Greys, and two guns of O Bty, under Major McGrigor,[22] and it was heavily engaged with a considerable force of Boers about seven miles west of Krugersdorp. On the approach of the column the Boers withdrew; B Coy had three men wounded in the action.

After more than a week's trekking, the column reached Johannesburg on 15 January. During the next ten days French prepared for his eastern drive and ten columns were formed, including Putty's. Lowther, Cuthbert[23] and Stephen[24] joined Putty's staff as intelligence, signalling officer and provost marshal respectively. Putty's Column on 17 January consisted of two squadrons Carabiniers, Inniskillings (6 D), 500 Scots Guards, T Bty RHA, J Sect Pompoms, sect fd tp RE, 9 Bearer Coy, elements 11 Fd Hosp and 13 Coy ASC. The total strength was 63 officers and 1,485 men = 1,548 all ranks, 826 horses and 10 guns. The column was now an all-arms

22   William Colquhon Grant McGrigor (1861-1924) SG 1883-1912 & 1914 OC B Coy.
23   James Harold Cuthbert (1876-1915) SG 1896-1905 & 1914-1915 killed in action.
24   Albert Alexander Leslie Stephen (1879-1914) SG 1899-1914 killed in action.

brigade: its mounted troops gave it the ability to operate against the Boers over a wide area while its infantry ensured a secure mobile base, especially for its artillery and logistics. The coordinated operations of several columns could contain and destroy the enemy forces or, as later in the war, drive the enemy into a stop line.

On 22 January two squadrons 12 L replaced those of the Carabiniers and 1 SG was now complete in the column. A further change was made on 25 January with two squadrons 14 H replacing those of 12 L. The column now consisted of 64 officers and 1,993 men = 2,057 all ranks, 1,045 horses, 6 × 12 pdr, 1 × pompom and 3 × maxims. As Putty noted, 6 D were armed with rifles, allowing them to fight dismounted as infantry.

The column left Johannesburg on 26 January and marched to Boksburg. Cator noted: 'Mosquitoes maddening. Altogether there are 11 columns converging on the Ermelo district'. This drive through the eastern Transvaal, whither Beyers had escaped, was under the general direction of French. They left Boksburg at 5.30 am 27 January and arrived at Springs 9 am. One squadron 14 H reconnoitred south but saw no signs of Boers. Putty noted that one howitzer, 87 Bty RFA joined him that day. On 28 January they marched to Droogefontein where they were in communication with Allenby's Column at Strypan, Knox's Column at Middlebuilt, and Dartnell's Column at Leeuwfontein. According to Cator, French joined Putty's Column that day.

The column left Droogefontein at 4 am and proceeded towards Nooitgedacht, in touch with Allenby who was moving on Gruisfontein and Knox moving on Steenkuilspruit. On arriving near Boschmanskop Allenby became engaged with the enemy and Putty's force was ordered up to take over Allenby's position, while he moved round towards the left. The Boers were then seen to be leaving their positions in large numbers and Putty's Column was ordered up to Boschmanskop where a halt was made and the horses and mules watered. The column moved on at 11.30 am towards Nooitgedacht arriving there at 2.30 pm. The enemy had a long range gun on a position E of the town and it shelled the baggage but did no damage: the cavalry and horse artillery made the enemy withdraw this gun and retreat east, shelling it as they did so.

On 31 January the column moved to Wintershoek where that evening the convoy arrived with 3 days supplies. At 4.30 am next day they left Wintershoek; the road was very bad and the ox wagons had great difficulty in moving, especially the wagons that had arrived the night before, 5 spans being required at times to drag the wagons out of bad ground. They crossed the Waterval without opposition and moved eastwards towards Zondagskraal. On moving to Grootlaagte they found Allenby engaged on their right, so a turning movement was made by the cavalry under Rimington,[25] which caused the enemy to retire. The column bivouacked at Winkelhoek at 4 pm but the baggage did not arrive until 8 pm.

Putty noted on 2 February that they arrived at Syferfontein without much opposition; when they got there, Cator wrote, they found 1500 Boers on the ridge beyond where they were going to camp, so they had to go on with the guns and shell them out. The advance continued to Frisgewaagd (3 February) and then to Bethal on 4 February; French was still with the column when it entered Bethal unopposed. The chain of columns then extended roughly from the Delagoa Bay railway near Middelburg in the north, with Smith-Dorrien's column well forward near Carolina, through Bethal to the Vaal east of Standerton. Putty's Column continued to

25   Lieutenant Colonel Michael Frederic Rimington (1858-1928) CO 6 D.

Remhoogte (5 February) and on 6 February entered Ermelo. Smith-Dorrien had a stiff fight with Botha about twenty-five miles NE of Ermelo, but Putty's column entered it in very heavy rain without opposition, to find it full of abandoned Boer wagons. At Ermelo the column halted for supplies: the Boers had apparently retired E and SE towards Amsterdam and Piet Retief.

The column left Ermelo at 3 pm 11 February and arrived at Damascus that evening where it bivouacked. Events on 12 February are described by Cator:

> Reveille 3.30 am and march in thick fog which did not lift till 8 am. Crossed Vaal River and then went over some hills and came on Tobias Smuts the Boer General's farm, behind which was a long line of very formidable hills on whose tops we could see the Boers plainly holding a position for five or six miles. Halting here till our scouts reconnoitred the positions to our surprise we saw the Boers one and all get up and gallop away without so much as firing a shot. We went on over the hill, here we found another line of hills, the Boers meant hanging on to those and our guns were soon in action. We came up alongside them and awaited developments watching a very pretty engagement with our advanced guard they having gained the summit alright, but the Boers (about 600 of them) had cunningly placed their trenches on the reverse slope so that directly anyone peered over the crest line he came in for a hot reception. After waiting for a couple of hours two companies of us (D & E Coys 1 SG) were sent to support the advanced guard, B & C Coys to support 6 D who had gone on down the valley to turn the Boers' left. On arrival at the top we heard tremendously heavy firing from Rimington's direction and the Boers in front of us decamped. Rimington we heard afterwards had engaged the Boers' front with one squadron, while he with the two remaining squadrons had gone round turned their left flank and charged them as they bolted getting well home. He then dismounted his men brought a very heavy fire to bear on them his maxim doing very good work, he picked up 4 dead, 12 wounded and took 8 prisoners, the result of his charge, while for the rest of the evening the Boer ambulances were very busy on the ground in front of his maxim. He also captured their laager and 2,000 head of cattle.

Next morning (13 February) they left bivouac at 5 am. One squadron 14 H, one squadron 6 D and two guns were sent by the Geelhoutbloom road towards Brereton's Store, while the main body and transport went by the Lydon road. This demonstrated the value of mounted infantry or, as in this case, cavalry that could dismount and fight as infantry. Cator recalled:

> Endeavoured to bring along with us 30,000 sheep which we found hidden but it was slow work and we could not wait for them. About 11 am the road got very bad and we had a long halt while all the wagons were descending into the plain, however we passed the time killing sheep and cooking mutton chops. All along the road we kept finding Boer wagons which we burnt, the oxen belonging to them we brought along. Early in the day General French had passed me and asked how the men were, and said he was afraid that they had been having some very long days and what splendid chaps he thought them. All the infantry on the neighbouring column have chucked it and refuse to march with the cavalry and have to be carried in wagons.

They arrived at the Assegai River on 16 February and found it in flood. The mounted troops and artillery were sent over, and later on the infantry by means of the ferry. At 8 am the river having dropped 6 inches, the baggage was sent over; the column arrived at Piet Retief at 11 am, met up with Knox's Column, and camped south of the town. Putty then sent Rimington with the 6 D, one squadron 14 H, one section RHA, and a pompom towards Anhalt to watch the country between Marienthal and Piet Retief, and to get in touch with Dartnell. Harold Cuthbert (Column Signals Officer) recalled: At Piet Retief it scarcely stopped raining once for eight days and nights, rendering the rivers impassable'. Lowther (Column IO) wrote:

> Our stay at Piet Retief was the most miserable the battalion had to go through during the whole war. Supplies ran out and we were reduced to three quarters of a pound of mealie a day, with as much meat as was required, but as there was no salt the men could not eat much of it. There were no groceries of any kind, no lights, no rum and no lime juice. There was no fighting to cheer the men up and no occupation for them. We dug up a lot of small arms ammunition in the vicinity. The gaoler's house provided a roof for Putty's staff; the troops lived on the veld outside. They had an awful time of it, for the ground was muddy and rain constant.

Farms in the neighbourhood were cleared of supplies and constant work was required on the roads. 32 Boers gave themselves up on 20 February. Cator noted (23 February):

> The idea of getting the convoy for some time out of the question. Short rations making one very hungry, I miss the sugar more than anything. The convoy has now got as far as the Intombi River which is 300 yards broad and a raging torrent. The Assegai River is also impassable save for the pont and we are sending some wagons over empty so as to go on and come back quickly with some sugar, salt and biscuits as soon as they can get a pont or raft to cross the Intombi.

It was not until the last days of the month that the weather improved and supplies arrived. During February the column had killed and wounded 40 Boers and captured 10; a further 55 had surrendered. They also captured 204 weapons, 15,000 rounds of ammunition, 112 horses (for remounts), 1,034 other horses, 28 mules, 539 trek oxen, 2,000 cattle, 50,000 sheep and 290 wagons/carts.

It rained all day on 2 March. Cator wrote: '75 Boers came in here and give themselves up' and on 5 March: 'Still raining in torrents, men looking wretched and miserable, not only are they wet-through day after day, night after night, but they are half starved as well'. Supplies were beginning to get through but it was slow work as the convoys had to be unloaded and the supplies carried across the pont. Matters evidently came to a head on 6 March for, as Cator recorded:

> Pouring rain, Cupid (Gerald Cuthbert CO 1 SG) went down and applied to the Brigadier for the men's tents, the Brigadier said he was all against the men having tents, this answer having much the same effect on Cupid as a match in a powder cask, and he fairly tongue lashed old Putty and told him to practice what he preached and come out of his beastly

Pulteney's Column crossing the Swartwater, 22 March 1901. (RHQ Scots Guards Archives)

house and try a night on the veldt in the rain, ended by Brigadier saying he would think it over.

Putty was not a Brigadier at this time; and there were to be no tents. The column at last left Piet Retief on 15 March, and moved south to Vryheid. Lowther wrote that day:

> One of our great joys was Jimmy, a dog-faced baboon. We found him tied up in a deserted farm west of Ermelo, and brought him along. A friendly beast, following most of us like a dog, he was particularly attached to Colonel Pulteney, who was far from reciprocating this affection. His unfortunate habit of jumping on that distinguished officer's shoulders earned him many a clout.

They arrived at Vryheid on 25 March where Rimington rejoined the column. French's plan was that, while three columns held a blocking line from Piet Retief to the River Dongola (or Pongola), he, with four columns including Putty's, would make a last drive eastwards up to the Swaziland border. This produced little result beyond the capture of more wagons and cattle, and by 31 March the column was back in Vryheid. According to Smith-Dorrien, French spent some time with Putty during this drive.

Putty's Column was now to leave French and move by train to Pretoria. On 1 April French inspected 1 SG and, according to Cator, 'spoke very warmly on the marching powers and good discipline of the battalion, and thanked the troops for the way they had borne their recent hardships'. When Putty arrived in Pretoria on 8 April he was ordered to proceed with his column by rail to Belfast. On route he saw Blood,[26] who commanded the 35,000 troops in eastern Transvaal, at his HQ in Middelburg. Blood had six columns to take part in a new drive divided into two groups under Kitchener[27] and Fetherstonhaugh.[28] Initially Putty would be under the latter.

The column was assembled at Belfast by 16 April with Putty noting that the ox transport was in very bad condition. The Royals had replaced 14 H in the column and 1 SG still had not arrived when the column set off at 9 am. Putty recorded in his staff diary: 'Start delayed owing to the mist. A little sniping, one man Royals wounded. One squadron 6 D was left at Belfast

---

26   Lieutenant General Sir Bindon Blood late RE (1842-1940).
27   Major General Frederick Walter Kitchener late W Yorks (1858-1912) brother of Earl Kitchener.
28   Major General Richard Steele Fetherstonhaugh late KRRC (1845-1932) Comd 9 Bde.

to act as scouts for the Scots Guards when they arrived. In the evening a helio message was received reporting their arrival at Belfast'. Cator recalled: 'Being now 7000 feet up we all felt the cold at night fearfully'.

Rimington with two squadrons 6 D, two squadrons Royals, one squadron 19 H temporarily attached, and a section T Bty cleared the hills east of Belfast on 18 April. 1 SG rejoined the column next day (19 April) with Cator noting: 'Very pretty country and very mountainous. Our column set out in NW direction across fearful range of hills. Boers who were there in great numbers yesterday were not to be found'. The ox convoy was still in very bad condition; the oxen were in such a weak state that it could not be got into camp that evening and had to be parked about 2 miles out. Organising the movement of the column each day required meticulous planning. Apart from the ox convoy there were 1,200 horses and over 1,000 mules to be moved on very poor roads through mountainous country. Organising it without leaving an opportunity for the Boers to attack was difficult enough, but Putty would have wanted to keep his fighting troops for offensive operations and only have the absolute minimum committed to protection of wagons, carts and guns.

As the column moved north (21 April) Putty noted: 'Slight opposition. 4 burghers captured and 5 surrendered'. On 22 April he wrote:

> Moved to Roos Senekal at 6.30 am, the road passing through a difficult defile and dropping into the valley; the latter part of the road very bad, and ox transport did not get in till 5 pm. 60 Boers, mostly of the Boksburg Commando, surrendered.

They were at Roos Senekal for a week (until 29 April) during which Putty sent out detachments, mainly of Royals and 6 D, to clear the surrounding countryside. A few Boers were captured and many more surrendered. On 29 April the column marched to Blinkwater: then on 1 May Putty doubled-back to Roos Senekal with part of the column to catch some Boers who were reported to have gone back there. Putty described this action:

> A clear moonlight night. Halted at De Lager's Drift after midnight and moved on at 1.30 am, and arrived in close vicinity of Roos Senekal just after the moon had set and before daylight. The Royals with one gun were sent to the west and north of the town, 6 D (one and a half sqns) to the east. 1 SG (four coys) blocked the south. Soon after daylight a small laager was seen just south of the town, and the Boers discovering our presence fled to the hills, losing 3 killed, 1 wounded, and 9 prisoners. 7 wagons, 12,000 rounds SA ammunition, and about 100 cattle were taken.

After a halt at Klipspruit on 4 May where Blood was camped, and Kitchener rode in and saw Putty, the column moved on to Bankfontein. It rested here until 11 May and this concluded Blood's drive to the north: 4 Boers had been killed by the column and 164 had been captured or surrendered. While at Bankfontein the officers of 1 SG and those of the Royals had a game of Eton football, all the players being old Etonians. 1 SG won by four goals and a rouge to two rouges. The photographs show Putty in the thick of it.

On 11 May Putty rode into Middelburg and saw General Blood. The record shows that all the tents were sent into Middelburg that day: Putty was not adverse to tents being brought forward when the column was stationary and secure for a few days or more but was not prepared for them to be used when maximum alertness was required. Blood's next plan was a drive south of the Delagoa Bay railway to clear the valleys of the Klien Oliphant and Koomati Rivers. This brought the columns through the mountainous country SW of Barberton, which had not till then been entered by British troops. Putty's Column left Barberton at 6 am 12 May and moved to Rockdale; Blood rode over to Rockdale and saw Putty that day. T Bty RHA and J Sect Pompoms had left the column and four guns 66 Bty (15 pdr), a naval 12 pdr and P Sect Pompoms joined it; its strength, noted for the first time as a brigade on 13 May, was 74 officers and 2,082 men = 2,156, 1,156 horses, 4 × 15 pdr, 1 × 12 pdr, 1 × how, 1 × pompom and 4 × maxims.

On 14 May the column was at Boschmansfontein where Cator wrote: 'Never felt anything like the cold on my watch 3 am till 6 am – 16 degrees of frost'. On 15 May they were at De Witte's Kranz where 7 Boers were captured with 4 wagons and about 200 oxen. There was slight sniping at the rearguard and one man of 6 D was wounded. The column continued next day (16 May) to Haartebeestspruit, then to Botha's rust (17 May), Simonsdale (18 May), and reached Bothwell on 19 May. Here they received a convoy with 6 days supplies; so far there had been little opposition. On 20 May they reached Lilleburn where a few Boers were seen in the distance, and next day they moved to Holnek where again there was sniping and another man of 6 D was wounded.

Putty noted on 22 May:

> Empty ox wagons, sufficient to carry 3 days' supplies, were sent to Weltevreden with one squadron Royals as escort. Boer families and stock were also sent. The column moved to east of Holnek and camped at Pitsville, no opposition. 6 D reconnoitred south of Pitsville but found nothing: in communication with General Kitchener. Works were made for a post consisting of two companies 1 SG, one squadron cavalry and one 15 pdr gun which it was proposed to leave at Holnek.

This entry summarises Putty's conflicting priorities: keeping his column supplied, clearing the land and dealing with captures, securing his column while pushing forward, and keeping in contact with neighbouring columns. They left the detachment at Holnek and pushed on; the column reached Zonstraal on 23 May where the convoy reached it the following day. A reconnaissance was made on 25 May with two squadrons Royals, two squadrons 6 D, one section 66 Bty and a pompom towards Amsterdam. 3 Boers, 30 cattle and 1,400 sheep were captured.

From Zonstraal the column marched on 26 May to Tyger Kloof: it left another detachment at Brandybal consisting of one squadron 6 D, two companies 1 SG and one 15 pdr 66 Bty. Having established picquets on both flanks, Putty left the remaining 4 companies 1 SG and the howitzer at Tyger Kloof to search the neighbouring farms for ammunition and stores, which they did with some success. Meanwhile he went on with his remaining mounted troops into the Koomati Valley reaching Steynsdorp on 27 May and Kranskop next day. Three days supplies reached Tyger Kloof on 30 May; also that day a squadron of Royals moving towards Roodewal surprised and captured 12 Boers.

Putty's command was now very spread out: he was at Brandybal with the rest of his column until 11 June with much of his time spent organising the resupply of his detachments and with reconnaissance; he also had frequent meetings with Kitchener. Then, on 12 June, he moved to Redhill picking up all but the Tyger Kloof detachment; this rejoined next day. The column then crossed the Umpilusi River and advanced on Amsterdam arriving there at 4 pm 15 June. There was little opposition, just the usual sniping at the rearguard. The march had taken them along the border with Swaziland and all along it parties of Swazis were seen sitting with their hide shields and assegais waiting for any Boers who might attempt to break into their country.

The column left Amsterdam and marched to Glen Eland where 4 Boers surrendered. Putty was then in communication with Kitchener and received orders to move to Carolina. The march back began on 17 June: 6 D were detached via Spitzkop and came across several small parties of Boers; a good deal of firing took place but they had no casualties. The horses of the column were now losing condition rapidly owing to constant work, the cold, and the absence of good grazing. The return was unopposed except for the sniping of the rearguard: one man of the Royals was killed. They arrived in Carolina on 21 June where orders were received from Blood to proceed to Grobler's Rect and prevent movement of the enemy east. This was reached on 24 June and by the end of the month the column was at Vaalbank. This drive had been relatively unproductive with just 9 Boers captured or surrendered in June; the Boers were getting much cleverer in avoiding the columns and hiding their weapons and supplies.

On 1 July orders came from Blood for Putty's Column to move to Roodepoort; as the column was out of supplies Putty decided to move to Middelburg and there refill. Next day the column reached Aaronsfontein: one man 6 D was killed. On 3 July they moved to Rockdale where orders were received from Pretoria for the mounted troops to move to Pretoria by road, and 1 SG by train. The force moved into Middelburg on 6 July and 1 SG entrained for Pretoria. The mounted troops were handed over to Beatson.[29] Putty himself had become ill and had to go into hospital but was in Pretoria when the column was finally broken up on 16 July. He had served three months under Generals French and Babington, then three months under Generals Blood, Kitchener and Fetherstonhaugh, all in the Transvaal. During this time it had participated in four major drives. Its casualties from enemy action during this time were two men killed and eight wounded.

August 1901-March 1902

When he had recovered from his illness Putty was given command of a newly formed column. The Boers had been pushed across the Natal frontier: Putty's Column was to operate in northern Natal, west of the Schurveberg, under the orders of Burn-Murdoch[30] GOC Newcastle SD.

Burn-Murdoch noted in his diary on 10 August: '200 8 H and 600 Australians are being sent to this district. I understand that they are coming here (Newcastle). Pulteney who was on his way to Pretoria from Maritzburg has been stopped to command them'. Next day (11 August) he continued: 'I have been ordered to organise and equip Pulteney's Column here. Pulteney came to lunch to talk over matters'. On 12 August he wrote: 'On my way back (from the station) I went to see Pulteney at the Bridge Hotel. The first train of Pulteney's Australians (Victorians) arrived at 6.30 and nearly 700 arrived during the night so we have more than we calculated on'. Next day (13 August): 'Pulteney has now got most of his people but they are desperately short of transport' and on 14 August: 'Orders came from General Hildyard[31] to move Pulteney's

---

29   Major General SB Beatson late Bengal Lancers.
30   Brigadier General John Francis Burn-Murdoch late 1 D (1859-1931) Comd 1 Cav Bde.
31   Major General Henry John Thoroton Hildyard (1846-1916) late Som LI GOC 5th Division.

Column to Utrecht, I have made all the arrangements, they will march as far as Umbana this afternoon. Pulteney's Column marched at 3.30 pm. They number in all 1,066. Not a bad little force'. By the time the column left Utrecht on 17 August it consisted of HQ (4 officers + 18 men), 14 H (9 + 156), 5th Victorian Mounted Rifles (VMR – 42 + 683), RDFMI (1 + 85), 20 Bty RFA (1 + 34 with two guns), L Sect Pompom (1 + 12), 37 Coy RE (0 + 4) and Det 14 Gen Hosp (2 + 15). 4 officers and 103 men from Utrecht were also temporarily attached to the column.

Burn-Murdoch noted in his diary on 16 August:

> Wire came from General Hildyard saying that as Colonel Bloomfield[32] move has been delayed Pulteney is to operate beyond the Elandsberg and Pivaan Poorte under my orders. I have wired Pulteney to move out tonight leaving his baggage at One Tree Hill on Spitzkop under escort of Utrecht troops. Much to my surprise I found that his column was still at Utrecht and had not moved up the hill. We have information of three laagers near Zackiels Nek. Pulteney who did not get my wire until late in the afternoon says that he cannot move tonight. I have therefore arranged for him to move tomorrow to Knights Farm then to make a night march to surprise the laagers near Zackiels Nek. He will leave his baggage at One Tree Hill under Utrecht troops.

Continuing the next day (17 August) he wrote:

> Pulteney came to see me at 8 am. He is prepared to move up to Knights Farm today and on to One Tree Hill tomorrow. I told him that I thought the original plan should be carried out as I had communicated with Wakkerstroom and because no surprise could take place by marching from Knights Farm to One Tree Hill during the day. Pulteney left for Knights Farm at 1 pm and started for his night march at 9 pm. I talked to Pulteney on the telephone at 6 pm.

When they reached Zackiel's Nek in the morning they saw no sign of a laager; a few Boers sniped the rearguard on their return having marched 30 miles since the previous night. Burn-Murdoch recorded on 18 August:

> I heard from Pulteney that he had arrived at Zackiels Nek at dawn – no laager and no cattle were to be seen and he returned to his baggage at One Tree Hill. I signalled to him that unless he had, from his information, a better objective I would like him to clear the country beyond Pivaan Poorte and the Elandsberg informing me when he would be at Watervaal and letting me know his intention. Late in the evening I heard from him that he did not intend to do much tomorrow.

The column rested on 19 August and Putty sent his plans for operations up to 24 August to Burn-Murdoch: he was not entirely happy with them, as he noted:

> He proposes (he intends to rest today) to move to the eastern Elandsberg tomorrow returning to One Tree Hill for the night. On the 21 August he proposes again to move out

---

32   Probably Colonel Charles Blomfield LF (1855-1928).

to clear the Pivaan Poorte country meeting his baggage at Spitzkop. On the 22 August he marches to Klipfontein going on up the Schurveberg the same night. He will send back the Utrecht troops to Knights Farm on the 22nd. He sent in for provisions to Knights Farm today. I do not quite like these short journeys out from the same camp but he is to have a free hand and I can but wire my approval.

Next day, 20 August, they marched to Elandsberg Nek and Putty wrote:

This road is very bad and would be practically impassable in wet weather. Got on to Elandsberg Nek with slight opposition and cleared country on S side and to E. Saw about 90 Boers on N side of Elandsberg in two parties; left proclamations on Nek and at farms. On returning, rearguard was attacked by about 30 Boers from the direction of Pivaan's Poort. These were driven off and the retirement through Pivaan's Poort effected, the guns covering the same. Casualties: Lieutenant (Sydney) Selman LW (Left Wing) VMR and 1615 Pte (John Cameron) Matheson LW VMR severely wounded. Two Boers were seen to fall.

Burn-Murdoch received this report at about 9 pm and replied: 'Your 35 received. Do your plans as detailed in your p32 now hold good country should be thoroughly cleared your baggage moving up to you if necessary'.

He also noted: 'I had arranged to go to Beacon Hill tomorrow but I must now delay until I hear from Pulteney'.

The attached details were sent back to Utrecht on 22 August and the column continued to three miles west of the Schurveberg. Putty described next day:

Sent an advanced party up the Schurveberg, leaving camp at 4.30 am. Main body followed at 6 am. Advanced party, RW VMR and RDFMI, met with opposition at eastern end of Schurveberg at daylight from about 30 Boers, who retired towards Pivaan's Poort. Main body got to top of hill at 7.15 am and supported advanced party with guns. Boers were under John Potgeiter and John De Jager; the latter's horse was shot and 5 Boers were seen to fall. Outspanned and watered at Trek Drift over Pivaan River on main road to Vryheid 11 am, went on at 12.30 pm and camped at Kambuladraai 2.30 pm. Got into communication by helio with Colonel Blomfield's column from Vryheid at 8 am who was on Kambuladraai and had left Vryheid at 3 am to cooperate with this column. He returned to Vryheid 11.30 am. No cattle to be seen. Casualties: 1101 Private John James Lawrence VMR and 795 Private [Frederick George] Dow VMR killed; Major AC Daly W Yorks, OC RW VMR, 3355 Private [J] Breheny RDFMI and 1040 Private [John] Supple VMR dangerously wounded; 1155 Private [Herbert Foster] Brunet VMR and 1694 Saddler [Harold Victor] Cook VMR severely wounded. 2 Boers were seen to fall.

The account of Lieutenant JH Patterson MO 5 VMR is more descriptive:

Reveille at 3 am and the right wing VMR and one company Dublin Fusiliers under our CO Major Daly started soon afterwards. We were to hold some hills a few miles away. Just as dawn was breaking one company VMR was left on a ridge, the rest advanced, then another company deployed to the left. Just at this time the road became very bad and only single file could pass. I was riding with Major Daly but went back to place my Tonga Ambulance under cover of some rocks and leave it there. This just saved me from being in a very hot corner. Just as they were going down this very rough piece Daly spotted some Boers trying to take a hill 300 yards away – this distance being level and open. He ordered the advance at the gallop but only about 10 men were ready – the others toiling down the narrow pass. At this juncture I arrived and saw Daly and his men galloping for all they were worth and a heavy fire opened. By the time I got down I saw a man galloping back and heard him call for me. It was Anderson and he said 'For God's sake come. Daly is badly hit', and away I went. Our men had the hill and the Boers were in retreat not 200 yards away when I got there. I passed Daly, not seeing him the first time, and first found poor Lawrence. He was just breathing his last and back I went to Daly to find him badly hit through the pelvis. Whilst attending to him the rest of the men got going and let the Boers have it. Afterwards I went on to find a Dublin shot in two places and one of our men, Supple, shot through the abdomen. At the same time our company on the left had one man killed, Dow, and one wounded.

Putty's Column marched to Vryheid on 24 August and came under Colonel Blomfield's command. It stayed in the town until 27 August, filling up with 4 days' supplies; Stewart's (probably Lieutenant Colonel HK Stewart) column also joined them there. At 7.30 am 27 August the columns marched due east along the road to Waterval, Putty's Column finding the advanced and left flank guards of the force. A few Boers sniped at the left flank guard from the farm of Hlobani; two companies LW VMR were sent out to try and catch them, covered by the guns. The Boers got on to the top of Hlobani Mountain. The left flank guard and two companies VMR withdrew at dusk, bringing in one prisoner of the Vryheid Commando. The farm Hlobani was burnt and the son of the owner reported to be killed. Casualties in the action were: Lieutenant SR Coulter VMR killed; 1403 Private Ellis VMR wounded dangerously; 781 Private Barry VMR wounded severely; and three other men VMR wounded slightly.

Captain Clarence Wilson Johannesberg Mounted Rifles observed the action:

The steady calm onward sweep of the Victorians – all dismounted – was equal to an attack by our incomparable Tommies themselves. The feat they carried out this time was a foolish and unnecessary thing in itself, but it showed a watching army what the men were made of. The position they were ordered to take was a position that half a dozen determined men could hold against 500, and then retire without loss to themselves. On this occasion the Boers had sent their horses round a kopje by some of their number, and climbed up on foot.

Lieutenant JH Patterson MO VMR also saw the action:

LW VMR under cover of a big gun and a pompom advanced on Hlobani. On reaching the foot of the hill they dismounted and advanced; all the way they were exposed to the enemy's fire, the enemy being in a cosy position high up on the hill. It was a terrible climb as I know when my turn came later on.

Finally, 1649 Private Edmund Sheldrick Johnson VMR took part in the action and described it in a letter to his mother:

> We dismounted about 1200 yards from the foot of the hill and charged on foot under fire of the big guns, got half way up and could not get any further for a big cliff of rocks a rabbit couldn't get up. We got the order to crawl; if we showed a head there would be a dozen bullets at it in quick time. I got down to it like as if I was sneaking up on a mob of ducks but one found me and I got it through the heel.

Mist in the morning of 28 August delayed the march until 10 am when Putty's Column found the rear and left guard. They cleared the farms on Veelgeluk and then camped above Waterval, Louis Botha's home, with a two mile avenue of wattle and blue gums; it was burnt and blown down on 30 August, and the following day the column returned to Vryheid. Summarising the month Putty wrote:

> The country through which the column has been operating since its formation on 14 August was hard on the horses and mules. The young grass just appearing afforded a little grazing and hay was drawn at Vryheid. The health of the troops was good; the rations were also good. The small amount of food-stuffs, taken or destroyed, is accounted for by the fact that other columns have been through every part recently visited by the column. The Boers met with showed every inclination to fight, and are living on the N side of the Elandsberg and Hlobani. They appear to be badly off for food except mealies and fresh meat.

Having filled up again with supplies at Vryheid on 1 September the column marched south next day, clearing farms, and reached Nqutu in Zululand on 6 September. Here the main problem was an epidemic of measles with Patterson himself succumbing; he wrote: 'The morning parade totalled 390 men out of a normal strength of 1,080'. When the column arrived at Dundee on 8 September Putty was ordered to proceed to Glencoe and then by train to Volksrust as soon as possible. The situation was that Botha had marched on 7 September south from Blaauwkop for Piet Retief. The blockhouse line from Wakkerstroom was still not complete and Kitchener (CinC) sent columns in pursuit. Writing of these days, Burn-Murdoch noted:

> Pulteney entrains at Dundee this evening and should get to Volksrust during the night; (9 September) During the night one wing of Pulteney's people passed through Volksrust I went down to meet the mail train both Stewart and Pulteney came by it. Pulteney lunched with us and (10 September) Pulteney's Column is at Volksrust.

The column had refitted and was ready to move from Volksrust on 11 September: two guns 13 Bty RFA joined them that day. Putty's orders were to cooperate with Garratt's (Lieutenant Colonel FS Garratt 6 DG) column from Wakkerstroom, and Stewart and Gough's[33] from Vryheid, and clear up the Piet Retief district. He, therefore, marched to Wakkerstroom on

---

33   Lieutenant Colonel Hubert de la Poer Gough 16 L (1870-1963) Eton.

14 September and camped on high ground north of the bridge; one squadron 8 H joined the column there. Burn-Murdoch recorded on 15 September:

> Still very wet. We got a wire from Garratt dated 5 am 14 September. He said that L Botha with 1,500 men was moving on Utrecht. I extracted General Lyttelton [probably then GOC Natal] from church. An order was sent to Pulteney to move at once towards Utrecht via Beacon Hill.

It was very cold with heavy rain on 15 September: the roads were very bad and many wagons got stuck. Progress was slow and Putty wrote on 16 September: 'All information points to Boers being in large number in Pongola Bush'. They set off again at 7 am on 17 September with Putty noting: 'The rain during night made the roads more slippery and heavy than ever. Marched on towards Utrecht down very bad hill with help of drag ropes, and camped at 6 pm, a few wagons not getting in till 9 pm'. At 6.30 am Putty received orders from DAG Natal to march towards Staels Drift as quickly as possible. Putty noted that day:

> Marched 7 am with 14 wagons only and 1st line transport, one day's supplies on man and horse, and one on wagons. The remainder of the baggage followed the column into Utrecht. Arrived Utrecht 11 am, outspanned, and went on towards Staels Drift 12.30 pm; sect 20 Bty RFA joined the column at Utrecht, also Major Graham [District Commissioner Utrecht]. Major King's column consisting of one squadron 14 H and two Coys RDFMI joined the column at Staels Drift, also det Fd Hosp.

Putty sent an escort half way to Utrecht early on 19 September to meet the wagons which had been left there, and they arrived Staels Drift at 11.30 am. Putty continued:

> Am watching drifts day and night from Dicks Drift to Inchanga. Information points to Boers in large numbers being at Blood River Poort. Very cold, and rain all the afternoon. Received orders 4.45 pm from DAG Natal to go to Cattle Drift but, owing to bad weather and late hour, decided to go there at daylight tomorrow.

Judging by his staff diary, Putty received only the briefest of orders, and they were often contradictory or unrealistic: also his superiors seemed to have no understanding of the conditions – terrain and weather. Later, a more flexible approach was adopted with a senior column commander being given a broad directive and he in turn coordinating the operations of two or more columns.

It rained all night and was still raining when the column marched at 5.30 am 20 September to Cattle Drift. Putty noted: 'Men suffering from exposure, having no blankets' and at Cattle Drift next day: 'River has risen 2' 6" during night. All drifts impassable; rain during morning. Wagons from Utrecht left there 2 pm yesterday and stuck in a drift 3 miles out. Sent a message to the wagons by a native who swam the river to turn them off to Umbana. Patrols report all clear. 7 pm river still rising one inch an hour. Came under orders of Gen Spens.[34]

---

34   Brigadier General James Spens late Som LI (1853-1934).

Sent 29 wagons to Newcastle for supplies'. He was still at Cattle Drift on 22 September when he noted:

> River risen 2 ft during night [ie was now more than 4'6" above normal]. Came under orders of Gen Bruce Hamilton;[35] 29 wagons with supplies left Newcastle 9 am. Wagons with kits from Utrecht arrived Umbana 5 pm. Received orders 2.30 pm to proceed Dundee leaving Major King's column here. Wagons with 3 days' supplies from Newcastle arrived 6 pm.

Next day (23 September) at 6.30 am Putty's Column marched to Dundee, and Putty wrote:

> Wagons all being lightly loaded with 2 days' supplies and no kits, were able to do a long march of 28 miles over an indifferent road. Engineers did a lot of repairs to drifts. Came under orders Gen Clements.[36]

They stayed at Dundee for three days and while there the baggage arrived and 109 remounts were drawn for VMR. Three companies Scottish Rifles (later 2 Cameronians) also joined the column. So they were stronger and replenished when they set off next day (27 September) in very hot weather to De Jager's Drift and camped on the Transvaal side of the Buffalo River which was 3'6" deep at the drift.

Putty wrote that day:

> Received orders overnight to march as advanced guard to Rooikop and Bemba's Kop leaving 8.30 am. Owing to information received that main body of Boers had gone S, these orders were changed, and at 7 am orders were received to go to Vant's Drift to join Gen Bruce Hamilton. Started crossing Buffalo to Natal side 8.30 am and filled up at Supply Depot with 9 days' groceries at full rate and 9 days' biscuit at ¾ rate. Could not carry any more corn so took one day's corn on 3 ox wagons from the rail-head, and took a fourth ox wagon from there to assist the infantry ox wagons which had very poor spans. Gough's column accompanied me.

Next day they reached Vant's Drift where Putty received orders: 'To follow Gen Bruce Hamilton without transport by forced marches via Isandhlwana, Fort Louis and Babanange to Itala'. By the end of the day they had crossed the nek of Isandhlwana and camped 3 miles further E of it. Meanwhile the transport followed on escorted by the Scottish Rifles and two coys VMR.

They set off again on 29 September only to receive orders that there was no urgency for reinforcements, the Boers having retired NE from Itala and to wait in neighbourhood Fort Louis for the transport. This done the column with its transport reached Latking's Store where it camped: it remained there until 1 October.

35 Major General Bruce Meade Hamilton late E Yorks (1857-1936).
36 Major General Ralph Arthur Penrhyn Clements late SWB (1855-1909) Comd 12 Bde.

Pulteney's Column at Isandhlwana, September 1901. (RHQ Scots Guards Archives)

Summarising a month at the mercy of uncertainty, indecision and incompetence, Putty wrote:

During the month of September the column has covered a lot of ground, principally through country that other columns have been over. The different moves being for the most part strategical, it has not met with much opposition. The trek from Wakkerstroom to Utrecht (15-18 September) was over a road that no column had attempted to go by before, and was extremely hard on the transport. Drag ropes had to be used continually. The grazing now is very good and hay was drawn whenever possible. There have been about 20 cases of measles in RW VMR of a very mild form and occurring at intervals of a day or two, otherwise the health of the troops has been good, notwithstanding the exposure to the men without blankets in heavy rain 18-23 September. I was unable to get a Field Hospital at Volksrust, and it was only at Dundee when 330 Scottish Rifles joined the column without a MO that I got the nucleus of one, viz: a MO, 4 tents, 2 orderlies – no ambulances. I have one ambulance with each unit, making 3 – and 2 tongas. There has been a little difficulty with the natives employed with the transport owing to 40 boys being time expired and wanting to go to their homes. The rations have been good. The column has marched 300 miles during the month.

The hunting down of the Boers and the scorched earth policy continued. On 1 October orders were received to march at once to Nqutu; meanwhile the Scottish Rifles were temporarily detached. The column reached Nqutu on 3 October and Clements arrived there next day with a supply convoy. Putty completed to 5 days' supplies on regimental wagons, leaving the supply column at Nqutu, and marched with General Hamilton's Column,[37] finding advanced and right flank guards, to Nondweni. They marched again on 5 October finding the left flank, rear and baggage guards, along the direct road to Vryheid, reaching Spitzkop that evening and Bethal on 6 October. Here they spent three days with the usual supply problems as noted by Putty on 7 October: 'Sent all wagons at 5.30 am to meet convoy at Scheepers Nek or Vryheid and fill up with 5 days' supplies; all kits and supplies in hand remaining on the ground. Two companies VMR with one gun and all Scotch and Cape Carts went to the Bethal Mission House to get mealies. Rations for everything put on half scale except meat which was increased to 1½ lbs.

37   Brigadier General Gilbert HC Hamilton late 14 H.

Got 6,000 lbs mealies from the Mission'. The convoy with supplies from Vryheid arrived on 9 October and rations and forage were put back on full scale again.

Next day (10 October) the column continued its march towards Vryheid which they reached at 9.30 am next day. The intention had been to complete to 5 days' supplies and go N but Putty noted: 'Owing to a change in the orders only one day's supplies were drawn, and the column marched independently to Scheeper's Nek which they did in heavy rain. Received orders at Vryheid to go to Glencoe Junction en route to Orange River Colony'. When Putty and his column reached Rooikop on the morning of 12 October he again came under the orders of Gilbert Hamilton, and his orders were again changed; instead of going on to De Jagers the column marched to Utrecht via Grootvlei arriving there in the afternoon of 13 October.

All the dismounted men, sick horses and mules were left at Utrecht to go to Newcastle; the column then set off on 14 October, having drawn two days' supplies, and met up again with Gilbert Hamilton's Column. Next morning they provided the baggage and left flank guards when the two columns took the road via Grootvlei and the Pivaans Waterval, and camped at Elands Nek on the high ground between Elandsberg and Zackiels Nek. Putty described the searching of the high ground next day (16 October):

Detached from Gen Hamilton and marched at 7 am towards Zackiel's Nek. Sent two companies Scottish Rifles on to the high hill E of the Nek and reached the Nek with the mounted troops at 10.30 am. The infantry searched the hill and Kloofs E of the Nek and found a wagon, Cape cart and 3 bags of grain. Another company of infantry drove through the bush on the slopes of the hill west of the Nek and found some clothing and bivouacs. Some of the VMR reconnoitred 4 miles to the NW, N and NE; they also found bivouacs in the bush and drove in 66 cattle, 500 sheep and 60 ponies. One of the VMR, 974 Private Houghton, was shot through the heart at close range with a revolver while clearing the bush. Got into helio communication with General Plumer[38] at Naauwgevonden. Infantry held the Nek and high ground E of the Nek and the remainder of the column camped at Gelukwater.

Three columns participated in events described by Putty on 17 October:

Marched at 6.30 am with 1st line transport only and mounted troops. 2nd line transport with three companies VMR and Scottish Rifles marched to General G Hamilton's camp at Eland Nek. The road over Zackiels Nek is impassable for 2nd line transport owing to a bad bog on S side and the road being very much out of repair. Column marched over Nek on to the Pongola River. As the column was marching E along the right bank of the Pongola, it was suddenly fired on from the other side of the river at 1200 yds range, and was thus prevented from going along the road close to the river near Uitvlucht, while the high hills to the S prevented the guns and vehicles going any other way. Communication had been established with Gen Plumer at Geluk, and he sent out some troops along the left bank of the river. The advanced guard crossed the hills to the S, then the river and seized the kopjes on either side of Uitvlucht under cover of the guns. The column then continued its march,

38   Brigadier General Herbert Charles Onslow Plumer late Y&L (1857-1932) Eton later Field Marshal.

the advanced guard now forming a left flank guard. Although the Boers opened fire at only 1200 yds range the only casualty was 4197 Gunner Jeffries, 20 Bty RFA GSW slight, and 2 Artillery horses hit.

The Scottish Rifles marched with Hamilton's Column on 18 October with the intention of clearing the bush on the southern slope of the Pongola Hill. This had to be abandoned owing to heavy fog. Putty's Column marched across the Pondaan River to the high ground S of the Ekombela Mission Station where it camped holding the drifts. The operation again had to be abandoned next day owing to fog: 5,000 sheep were taken by 12 men of VMR who crossed a stream to get them under heavy fire. On 20 October they started clearing the Pongola Bush when orders came from W Kitchener to abandon the operation: no explanation seems to have been given but the column set off over a very bad road towards Paardeplaats. 20 empty wagons were sent to collect supplies but meanwhile the column was reduced to half rations. Further orders were received from Kitchener on the night 21/22 October to march to Goldgewonden to work in conjunction with Garratt in clearing Buffels Bosch (near Zourbron). Burn-Murdoch noted in his diary on 22 October 'I understand that Plumer's, Pulteney's and Garratt's Columns remain to operate to the E of Natal'.

The column marched towards Goldgewonden next day (23 October) but on arrival at La Belle Esperance received orders from Kitchener not to come any further. Putty noted: 'Camped at La Belle Esperance and sent out to clear Kloofs on the N side of Pongola Hill. Burnt some wagons and found 2 rifles hidden. Drew one day's corn from convoy which arrived today: troops put on full rations again. Four coys RWK attached to the column from Col Garratt's column'. On 25 October Putty's Column marched to Wolbedacht where the convoy from Utrecht rejoined them. That day Putty's and Garratt's Columns cleared the bush at the eastern end of the hill above the Ekombela Mission Station. The infantry found several ways down into the bush from the top, but the bush was very thick and thorny and impossible to move about in except where paths existed; 2000 sheep were captured. Putty wrote: '4 officers and 165 men VMR with 200 horses, and 2 officers and 91 men Scottish Rifles joined the column', a reminder that the reinforcement system continued to operate even in the most difficult circumstances.

They continued to clear the bush next day (26 October) as Putty recorded:

> Took out four coys Scottish Rifles and most of the mounted troops: cooperated with Gen Plumer from Geluk and Col Garratt from N on top of the hill. Cleared the whole of the bush from E and S, carrying out the programme which was abandoned on 20 October. Burnt a quantity of furniture, clothing, wagons, wool, skins and bivouacs, destroyed a tannery, several mealie grinders and strippers, a crop of young potatoes, pigs, fowls, yokes and saddlery. Several caves were found in which various articles were hidden, and there were 2 wired-in cattle Kraals in the middle of the bush. Over 10,000 lbs of mealies were destroyed, one prisoner taken, a family of 2 women and 9 children brought in, and a wounded Boer. 3 Boers found dead. There was evidence of a number of Boers having lived in the bush.

The operation continued next day with Putty's Column bringing in 10 families consisting of 10 women and 16 children, 4,000 sheep and a few cattle and horses. A patrol also brought one

Boer with his rifle. Putty concluded that day: 'The whole country between the Elandsberg and the Slangapies is clear of all stock and Boers'.

Putty sent out 100 men RW VMR under Major Vallentin at 10 pm 28 October to Pivaan's Poort, supported by 100 men LW VMR under Major Frazer that left at 11 pm. Plumer's and Garratt's Columns also deployed detachments so that the operations covered the whole of the Elandsberg from Zacknil's Nek to Pivaan's Poort. Putty noted:

> Major Vallentin successfully surprised 3 farms in Pivaan's Poort, and took 10 prisoners all with rifles and bandoliers. In addition 38 horses were brought in, 15 of which were fit for remounts; two wagons and 2 carts were destroyed as well as 26,880 lbs mealies. Heavy rain and fog in the afternoon greatly hampered the operations round Zacknil's Nek. I went on to Pragh Kop in the morning and established a signalling station in communication with the different parties out and with Gen Plumer.

The rain continued the next two days, with fog in the mornings; as a consequence the columns were unable to move.

In his summary for October Putty wrote:

> The column has been on the move during the whole month and has not been into the line once. The health of the troops has been good and only 4 cases of measles have occurred. The weather has been very trying, being generally fine for a few days and then wet for a like number. The rations have been good, but several boxes of biscuits have been bad. The troops were on half rations 5-8 October and 20-23 October, and horses and mules since 23 October have been on a reduced scale of forage viz: 7 lbs per horse and 5 lbs per mule, owing to some of the corn which arrived on 25 October being issued to other columns. There has been plenty of fresh meat, both mutton and beef. The column was frequently used as a stop and thus drove a good number of Boers and cattle into other columns. The bush work was very hard on the infantry and dismounted men, and the fog and mist greatly interfered with operations, while the rain made the roads very bad for transport. Total captures for October: 3 Boers killed and 12 taken prisoner, 18 rifles and 1,355 rounds of ammunition, 61 horses fit for remount and 111 others, 3 mules, 368 cattle, 116 trek oxen, 12,400 sheep, 27 wagons and 9 carts, and 47,000 lbs mealies. 33 women and 85 children were brought in.

Putty spent 1 November arranging the resupply of his column and then (2 November) marched with Garratt's Column to the Schurveberg, with Garratt camping on the top and Putty at the bottom. Next morning Putty left his camp standing and went with most of the mounted troops, one gun and pompom towards Blood River Poort while Garratt went S along the top of the Schurveberg. Putty's Column found a good stock of mealies and eight rifles hidden in the rocks. He noted: 'A good deal of cultivation had been going on round the farms. Some of the farms appear to have never been visited before, and the natives are very reluctant to give any information'. Operations continued in this area on 4 November with Putty noting: 'Cleared the whole of the N end of the Schurveberg, getting a few sheep and a good number of horses. Several farms here also were not cleared, but will be cleared tomorrow together with those by Pivaans Poort'.

Events of 5 November are described in outline by Putty in his staff diary:

150 men LW VMR under Major Frazer made a night march to Nooitgedacht leaving camp at 10 pm last night. Major Vallentin with 100 men RW VMR left at 1 am and went to Mooihoek. 40 men 8 H got to high ground on Nooitgedacht by daylight and the remainder of 8 H with one gun and pompom left at 4 am. Colonel Garratt's troops made a night march to the N end of the Schurveberg. The night operations therefore covered the country between Elandsberg and Pivaan River Bridge. Major Frazer surprised a laager at Bedrog where there were about 70 Boers sleeping in and about the farm house. Two Boers were killed and 12 taken prisoner. 76 good Boer horses were captured, also some cattle and a quantity of Boer saddles, blankets, rifles and ammunition was burnt in the farm houses. Boers tried to prevent party returning with prisoners but Col Garratt sent part of his force to cover their retirement; he killed 2 Boers and captured one making total Boer casualties for day 17. Both columns brought in a lot of families, 19 in all, and some wagons. Our casualties were: Lieutenant JG Chrisp, 1570 Private [Robert Glenn] Harrison and 1576 Private [FH] Caughey killed; 1011 Private [James] Clarke and 1533 Private [Thomas] McCallum severely wounded; two other men were slightly wounded, and all were of LW VMR.

From the various accounts of the action it appears that LW VMR was passing a large farm about two miles short of their objective when they heard the sound of horses. Not suspecting that there would be more than six to eight Boers in the farm, Major Frazer ordered Lieutenant Chrisp with his F Coy which numbered 35 (25 fighting men, the remainder being horse-holders) to surround the farm and search through it. The fighting in the darkness was intense; outnumbered three to one by the enemy who knew the ground F Coy nevertheless prevailed before reinforcements arrived, but paid a high price for this success. Before they came under Putty's command VMR had, on one occasion, been surprised by the Boers; this in the minds of some cast doubt on their fighting ability. The night of 5 November removed any such doubt.

Lieutenant Chrisp VMR funeral at Vryheid, November 1901. (Australian War Memorial)

The column marched to Vryheid on 6 November and spent several days in the town. A convoy arrived there on 7 November bringing ordnance stores and some stores for the Field Force Canteen, the latter were much wanted as the troops had had no chance of buying extras for a long time.

1282 Bugler Jack Carolin VMR wrote to his father from Vryheid on 8 November. Referring to the poor opinion that some had of the VMR up to now he wrote: 'I am satisfied his (Kitchener's) opinion is entirely different or he would not have put us under Colonel Pulteney and our Major Frazer, two of the best men and regiments Britain's army can produce. The former belongs to the Scots Guards and the latter to the Bengal Lancers'. This is of interest because it gives an indication of what the VMR thought of Putty. Major Frazer Bengal Lancers[39] commanded LW VMR on occasions but there is also a suggestion that he acted as BM of the column.

The column was still in Vryheid on 10 November awaiting orders; that day a church parade was held in the Dutch church. On the night 12/13 November RW VMR with two coys Scottish Rifles were sent out to surprise Vaalkop and farms in the vicinity but found no Boers. At noon 13 November Putty received orders from DAG Natal to march to Wakkerstroom Block House line with 10 days' supplies as soon as possible and cooperate with General Plumer there. The VMR history relates:

> In November Kitchener (CinC) assembled 15,000 men, including Plumer's and Pulteney's at Wakkerstroom, to deal with Botha. Night raids were preferred but it was decided to conduct another sweeping movement to force the commandos eastwards through Bethal, Ermelo and Carolina, and up against the Swazi border. This time the troops were not to carry out deportation and devastation and had help from the blockhouse line. The drive began on 15 November.

The ox wagons started up the hill out of Vryheid followed by the remainder of the transport on 15 November, with all the ox wagons having to be double spanned. Lieutenant Ballantyne ASC joined the column as transport officer before they left which must have been a great relief to Putty; the logistic support of the column was often a greater challenge than the Boers. The rest of the column marched at 4 am 16 November and outspanned on N side of Pivaan Bridge. Putty noted:

> From heights NW of bridge about 10 am 400 Boers with about 3,000 head of cattle were seen moving towards junction of Pongola and Pivaan. Natives stated their horses were very tired. This party was still seen moving in the same direction later in the day. Advanced guard exchanged shots with their rear guard – no casualties.

On night 22/23 November, Putty crossed the Assegai in fine moonlight and marched to Rooikop. The action on 23 November is described by him:

> From Rooikop at 12.30 am RW VMR went on to the high ground towards Geelhoutboom; the farm on Rooikop was surprised and also a small laager with 14 women on the high

---

39   Possibly Major Walter Fraser Bengal L NK-1929.

ground. About 200 Boers were seen with cattle. 400 cattle were captured, 4 wagons burnt and about 2,000 sheep captured. The Boers followed up the force bringing away the cattle but were driven off. 8 H saw 100 Boers going NW a long way off. Guns and LW VMR took up a position on high ground W of Rooikop. On Geelhoutboom 4 Boers were seen to fall. Casualties: 1634 Shoeing Smith James Rankin severely wounded [died of wounds 28 November], 1096 Sergeant Robert Carlisle slightly wounded, both LW VMR.

Lieutenant Patterson MO VMR noted:

Unfortunately the distance of our destination was again underestimated and after climbing rocky hills and passing through dreadful country day broke and we were on a high hill a mile and a half from the laager. We are right on Botha's commando and it's a long time since I saw so many Boers.

Lieutenant Maygar[40] won the Victoria Cross that day. Putty's citation said:

At Geelhoutboom, 23 November 1901, Lieutenant Maygar galloped out and ordered the men of a detached post, which was being outflanked, to retire. The horse of one of them being shot under him, when the enemy were within 200 yards, Lieutenant Maygar dismounted and lifted him on to his own horse, which bolted into boggy ground, causing both of them to dismount. On extricating the horse and finding that it could not carry both, Lieutenant Maygar again put the man on its back, and told him to gallop for cover at once, he himself proceeding on foot. All of this took place under a very heavy fire.

The whole force advanced north towards Amsterdam to attempt to catch Botha and the Transvaal government at a conference. On 24 November Putty wrote: 'Had greatest difficulty with transport at drifts which was increased by rain falling'. It was drier on 25 November at the end of which they camped at Grootfontein with Plumer. Putty noted: 'Saw some Boers on high ground on Glenfillon on our right flank. Native scouts reported a large commando on Glenfillon last night'. Next day (26 November) Putty left the Scottish Rifles and all dismounted men under Major Fell[41] and pushed on, operating on Plumer's right: the two columns camped together at the end of the day. Putty again: 'Had about 50 Boers in front of column and a few on the right flank on Glenfillon. Cleared several farms and captured at least 6,000 sheep'. Continuing on 27 November, working with Plumer's Column, Putty's Column drove all the sheep along with it and captured 4,000 more. In the afternoon they thoroughly searched Geelhoutboom and cleared the farms; four Boers were captured in the bush, one of whom was severely wounded. They then met up with Major Fell at Brereton's Store, and stayed there until 3 December.
    Summarising the month of November, Putty wrote:

The column operated in the Utrecht, Vryheid, Piet Retief and Wakkerstroom districts, and has not been in to the line at all. The health of the troops has been good, and they have been

40   Leslie Cecil Maygar (1872-1917) killed in action.
41   Robert Black Fell 2IC 2 Scottish Rifles later Brigadier General.

on full rations all the month. The rations have been good as usual, with the exception of some bad boxes of biscuits and sometimes, even at Vryheid, bad mealies. There has been an abundant supply of fresh meat – both mutton and beef. The mules now all are seasoned and very few casualties occur with them. There have hardly been any cases of horse sickness yet, but the remounts which are sent to the column are most inferior. The night marches, which are necessary to catch Boers, are trying on the troops and horses. The families were cleared from the Randberg which is a regular stronghold for the Boers. The weather has been very hot and there were some very heavy thunderstorms at Vryheid. The block house line greatly facilitates supplies coming out to columns. 2 Boers had been killed and 16 taken prisoner during the month; 34 rifles, 2,150 rounds of ammunition, 102 horses fit for remounts and 184 others, 9 mules, 134 trek oxen, 303 cattle, 17,100 sheep, 16 wagons and 1 cart, and 23,740 lbs mealies had been captured.

They had been ordered to march at 5 am 2 December but the heavy rain which fell the day before made the spruits so full that this was impossible. Eventually they marched on 3 December with Plumer's force: rain fell nearly all day. The VMR history records that on 3 December: 'Botha broke through the line and reached a point 20 miles E of Ermelo, where he was surprised in a night raid on the 4 December which caused him to head SE across the Vaal, clashing with Plumer's and Pulteney's forces. Pulteney forced the Boers north while Hamilton drove eastward'. If Putty saw events so clearly this is not apparent from his staff diary.

They reached Donkerhoek and next day (5 December) Putty sent the ox convoy, dismounted men, worn out horses and sick, with an escort to Wakkerstroom. He noted:

Scottish Rifles with 2 guns Plumer's Force and 25 mounted men of Plumer's and same number from this column formed a camp on Beelzebub with all the baggage. Mounted troops with two days' supplies and first line transport marched 7 pm.

Putty recorded events on 6 December:

Part of Plumer's Force went to Kalkoenskraal and the RW VMR of the column with half the 8 H went to Wilhelm Hendriksvlei and Goodehoop, while the main body marched to the N end of Uitgezocht, halting at 12.30 am and going on at 5 am. Plumer's troops met with great opposition from about 500 Boers and all the other troops went to their support.

Lieutenant Patterson MO VMR provides more detail:

It's now daylight and we soon hear very heavy firing on our left front where the Queenslanders (Plumer's column) are and word comes back to support their right. On we go at the trot and soon see many Boers, so many that at first we mistake them for another British column. On and on and we are in action after a hard ride and the Boers in retreat. By 11 am horses ridden to almost a standstill and men worn out after 17 hours and no food or sleep. We see a wonderful sight about 6 miles ahead, Louis Botha's commando and laager. We are done so we sit down and glare at each other.

On 7 December the column camped at Mooipoort where Putty noted: 'Convoy with 7 days' supplies arrived from Wakkerstroom. Major Daly W Yorks arrived and was attached to the staff for intelligence duties. Lieutenant McDermott ASC arrived as supply officer in succession to Lieutenant Hutchinson ASC. 160 mounted men and 180 horses arrived from the Depot (VMR) in Newcastle'. They remained in the Mooipoort area until 10 December: the two columns then set off again with Putty's Column going via Amersfort to Goedetrouw where it camped with Plumer on the night 11 December. Putty never claimed any success that was not directly attributable to his column but the columns were acting together as the VMR history makes clear: 'On 13 December they chased Botha from 5.30 am until 7 pm, returning by midnight with prisoners, cattle, Cape carts and wagons. They cooperated with General Hamilton, rounding Boers up against other columns and the blockhouse line'.

After a day recovering and re-supplying, the column marched to Grootvallei where Putty wrote on 15 December:

> After getting though Kleinfontein Nek, two coys VMR moved in the direction of Zoetfontein, where some cattle were reported to be. These they were unable to capture as a considerable body of Boers were holding a line from Grootfontein to Zoetfontein. Ox convoy arrived from Wakkerstroom bringing in 4 days' supplies; 2 Boers surrendered.

And next day:

> Sent in mule wagons to Wakkerstroom to draw 3 days' supplies and 6 days' groceries, escorted by two coys Scottish Rifles and 20 men VMR under Major Fell. Major Lawrence,[42] Bde Major left the column with this convoy en route to England to join Staff College. RW VMR under Major Vallentin went out in direction of Winterskraal, captured 65 cattle and 2,000 sheep. They were sniped by small parties of Boers in the kloofs whom it was impossible to dislodge. They had the following casualties: 944 Private J Whelan killed; 1038 Private T W Jenkinson slightly wounded.

885 Sergeant Major George Fullarton VMR in a letter to his brother gave more detail:

> We are now more than three months out from the railway line, and we have only halted at a town once during that time viz Vryheid. The Boers left in the field now must be very few, and we scarcely ever see them in daylight at all, for as soon as they know there's a column about they make a bolt for it, often leaving their cattle, sheep and ponies (unbroken) behind. We do a good deal of night-work now. I suppose we do two night marches a week. They are not very pleasant, but we never mind so long as we do good work, as we nearly always do, for we generally get in these night marches about 20 Boers, and their horses, cattle, and sheep at the cost of a casualty or two on our side. A few nights ago we rushed a farmhouse just at dawn, where it was known there were eight Boers. We completely surprised them and captured the lot. Some distance further on we could see cattle grazing so we galloped on and surprised 200 Boers, but were just as much surprised ourselves. However, we got their

---

42   Freeling Ross Lawrence (c1873-1914) 14 H psc1903.

stock. I suppose there were about 700 cattle, 1000 sheep and 200 ponies. Unfortunately we can never form an accurate idea of their casualties, but we must have killed and wounded a good many Boers, as we were at close range. The Boers who are still in the field are the very pick of the Boer army and very desperate, and when we take their stock from under their noses they let us know it. When we are retiring we catch it, and this day we had three chaps wounded (one died of his wounds and another was shot by accident). We have been chasing Botha about these last three months, and have twice had him in a tight corner, but he has managed to get away. Everything favours the Boers. One must see the country to understand what it is. We are still having a great deal of rain, and we still have a great many fogs, which are very dense and sometimes last till midday, thereby hampering our movements.

The column moved to Zoetfontein on 17 December where the mule convoy arrived from Wakkerstroom bringing 3 days' supplies and 6 days' groceries; the combined columns then marched to Kalkoenskraal on 18 December. Putty wrote:

> Colonel Jervis' Corps advanced guard, Colonel Colvin's Corps (both Plumer's) operating on the left via the Elandsberg, and 8 H and LW VMR on right via Kalkbank and Uitgezocht. RW VMR formed the rearguard. A little sniping took place.

The tactics were different next day: the mounted troops and guns of Putty's Column marched at 1 am, and occupied high ground E of Dronkvleispruit where a halt was made till the baggage of both columns, under Major Fell, arrived. 8 H who formed the advanced guard were heavily sniped from a ridge about 2 miles N of camp at Lyden. A gun was sent out and the Boers withdrew. Putty was to march again at 9 pm but a heavy storm burst over the camp just before and this was postponed till 11 pm. For the first two hours the weather was quite clear then, as Putty described:

> Another heavy storm broke over us and it became necessary to halt till daylight [20 December], owing to the intense darkness; then pushed on to high ground above Rotterdam. Owing to a mistake on the part of the guide we went too far in the direction of Klipfontein instead of turning off right handed towards Spitzkop. When the mistake was discovered, we retraced our steps but it was too late, and we saw 70 or 80 Boers leave the western slopes of Spitzkop and make off in NE direction. Another party of 300 were reported to leave the neighbourhood of Manerfestad also going NE. Gen Plumer's mounted troops were unable to cooperate owing to his horses stampeding in a heavy hailstorm at Vaalbank Spruit the night before. Camped on plateau above Rotterdam; rained all night.

Both columns marched on 21 December to Spitzkop, Putty's column leading, but they had no contact with the enemy. Next day they marched back to the high ground above Rotterdam and camped on the eastern slope. The action at Glenfillan on 23 December is described by Putty in his staff diary:

> Information received that large commando in vicinity of Glenfillan. Both columns [Plumer and Putty] paraded 1.30 am, Pulteney's Column leading. Marched SE to point just E of Lijden, which was reached at dawn and a short halt made. B and C Coys VMR under

Captain Hutton were then sent to seize high ground E of Geelhoutboom. As these coys approached a heavy fire was opened by a Boer picquet about 30 strong. They however pushed forward with great dash and drove the Boers from the position, killing one Boer and taking 6 prisoners. They had one man, 1032 Private John Fawcett Daff, severely wounded. Large bodies of the enemy (500 to 600) were then seen making W for Glenfillan. Enemy fought a rearguard action being driven from ridge to ridge by our men. All our guns came into action, getting good targets as the enemy shewed in large bodies. Men and horses were seen to fall but it was impossible to estimate their casualties as wounded men were removed by their comrades. From Glenfillan enemy retired in a southerly direction and were finally seen making SW near Waterval. Pursuit was abandoned about 2 pm; the horses, especially artillery, being much distressed. Both columns camped at Fosskop.

Lieutenant JF Stebbins VMR in letters to his mother wrote:

We had a great engagement lasting all day [23 December]. We left our camp at 1 am and fell across the Boers' camp just as daylight was breaking. We got so close we captured their lookout post, and then the game started in earnest, fighting through about 9 miles of exceedingly rough country, the Boers fighting a rear guard action all the way, which they can do to perfection and are second to none. After the day's fighting night comes on and they all break up into small parties and scatter in all directions through the hills meeting 15 or 20 miles off the following morning, which of course knocks our troops out altogether.

Lieutenant Patterson MO VMR wrote:

Day was breaking and we saw a wonderful sight: hundreds and hundreds of Boers fairly surprised and in retreat and we kept them going, the guns kicking up an infernal din over our heads. We kept on for hours, wounded Boers telling us that both Louis and Chris Botha were there and had 1000 men.

Both columns marched again at 4 am 24 December but a very dense mist came down soon afterwards and lasted on and off till 10 am: this gave the enemy time to get away. About 30 Boers attacked the rearguard of the convoy as it was going through Mooipoort Nek. The column camped at Naauwpoort where orders were received that 20 Fd Bty RA was to proceed to Newcastle. On Christmas Day a church parade was held at 9.30 am then the column moved camp about 1½ miles further S to a better defensive position. Putty noted:

Sent in ox convoy and sufficient mule wagons to draw 8 days' supplies into Wakkerstroom. Section 20 Fd Bty RA went in with convoy, also all sick and following details – 8 H (5 dismounted men, 10 sick horses), RW VMR (83 dismounted men, 51 sick horses) and LW VMR (21 dismounted men, 36 sick horses). Mule wagons arrived from Wakkerstroom at 12 noon bringing Xmas Dinners (including plum puddings) and gifts and one pint of beer per man. Heavy mist most of the day.

The force remained in the same position for the next two days. On 26 December the convoy arrived from Wakkerstroom with 8 days' supplies; section 53 Fd Bty RA under Major Gordon and reinforcements for 8 H and VMR also arrived to join the column. Next day Major Vallentin handed over command of RW VMR and took over Jervis' Corps in Plumer's Column. The columns marched to Vlakplaats on 28 December with only mule transport and 4 days' rations. The ox convoy under Major Fell escorted by all infantry and 50 mounted men moved in towards Wakkerstroom their orders being to form a post near Hurricane Hill and send the wagons in for a further 6 days' supplies.

The action on 29 December was recorded by Putty:

> Marched 1.30 am with Plumer's Column, baggage left in camp to march 4 am. Reached a point about 1 mile E of Strydkraal at dawn when a very heavy mist came on; this necessitated a lengthy halt till about 9 am. It was then decided to camp at Strydkraal and the baggage and escort was accordingly left at that place. The remainder of the mounted troops and guns pushed on at once in a NW direction to high ground at Potfontein. Here the advanced scouts reported a party of Boers, numbers uncertain, crossing our front from right to left. A message was also received from General Spens by helio to say he was in pursuit of these men and asking us to cooperate. All the mounted troops, except those escorting guns, immediately pushed forward at a gallop and seized a line Badenhorst Goodenough to second N in Leuwfontein. This move headed the Boers who were trying to break round our left. They turned sharp back and ran into General Spens' men who captured 24; 2 Boers who were pressed by a coy of Colvin's [Plumer's] were driven on to the railway line and surrendered there. The troops then returned to camp at Strydkraal the last man arriving about 9 pm; a very hard day on the horses, who were on the go from 1.30 am to (in some cases) 9 pm. All the horses covered quite 40 miles and a great many at least 50 miles. A lot of fast work had to be put in the middle of the day when it was extremely hot, and no water could be got till late in the afternoon.

On 30 December both columns marched to Wydgelegen, a long march of 24 miles, and everyone was very tired after the hard work of the previous day. All available mule wagons were sent to Hurricane Hill on 31 December and returned with 9 days' supplies; also the three coys Scottish Rifles rejoined the column. Putty noted: 'Rinderpest raging in Wakkerstroom – 20 of our oxen died'.

Summarising December Putty wrote:

> Owing to large bodies of the enemy being concentrated in the neighbourhood of the Elandsberg and Randberg, this column has operated during the month practically entirely in conjunction with Plumer's column. The operations towards Amsterdam in the early part of the month were much hampered by rain. Unless the Elandsberg is held with a line of blockhouses it is practically impossible to prevent the enemy breaking backwards and forwards between there and the Randberg. To the W in the Amersfort district, a large portion of the country has been thoroughly well cleared and good work done. The weather has been indifferent during the month, heavy rain in the earlier part and later both rain and heavy mist. These mists have been a great impediment to operations, especially to night marches, springing up as they do at dawn and lasting till 9 or 10 am. There is no doubt that the operation of the combined columns has had a very good effect in the Western District and has been the cause of numerous surrenders to the Blockhouse

Line. There has been practically no horse sickness, and the horses have on the whole done well, considering the enormous amount of work they have done and the frequency of night marches. The abundance of good grazing has been most beneficial to them. The class of remounts sent to the column has been distinctly better. The mules are beginning to feel the strain of the hard work and many require rest. The health of the troops has been good. The rations have been good with the exception of mealies issued at Volksrust on 14 December, over 2,000 lbs of which were bad, another 1,000 lbs commencing to go mouldy. I reported this to Director of Supplies, Natal by wire on 25 December. A new supply officer Lieutenant McDermott ASC joined the column on 7 December in relief of Lieutenant Hutchinson. Major Lawrence BM left the column on 16 December having been nominated to the Staff College. Major Daly 2 W Yorks attached VMR performed the duties of BM 16-31 December. The sect 20 Bty RFA under Lieutenant Dobson left the column on 25 December and was replaced by a sect 53 Bty RFA under Major Gordon on 26 December. The sect 20 Bty did very good work while under my command. The detachment VCR under Lieutenant Montgomery left the column on 31 December being ordered to rejoin the headquarters of their regiment at Dundee. I was extremely sorry to lose this detachment as they were of the greatest assistance, as besides being excellent men in the field, they could speak both Kaffir and Dutch.

Eight Boers were captured by the column in December and two more surrendered to it. 10 rifles, 39 horses fit for remounts and 268 others, 49 trek oxen and 57 cattle, 13,500 sheep, 27 wagons and 21 carts, and 30,160 lbs mealies were also captured. On 1 January 1902 the force was still at Welgelegen but they set off again at 12.30 am to Spitzkop reaching there at 5 am; but the fog became so thick it was impossible to move again till 8 am. The column camped at Balmoral and moved N next day to Rotterdam where it was in communication with Ermelo and Spens' Column.

The next action on 4 January is described by Putty:

Major Fell was left in command of camp on Rotterdam. The mounted force and guns left at 5 am and moved NE. 8 H were sent to hold Spitzkop on Alkmaa; the remainder, Vallentin's Corps (Plumer's) in advance, worked towards Bankkop driving some Boers in front of them. The force then moved forwards over the hills on Bankkop and the 8 H were withdrawn from Spitzkop. The last ridge was strongly held by the enemy and Vallentin's Corps getting to close quarters, the Boers opened fire; Vallentin's Corps being checked and lost considerably. LW VMR went out on the right flank and RW VMR on the left, and the 15 pdrs came into action. The Boers were driven from their position with some loss, 5 being picked up. The two 15 pdrs with 8 H as escort were taken to a kopje on the right and the VMR advanced along the hill to find the end and some kopjes beyond held by the enemy. Colonel Jenner (Plumer's) came up on our left and eventually the Boers were driven off and retired in a NW direction. During the action the pompom came under rifle fire at about 1,000 yards. The 15 pdr guns shelled the Boers retiring eastward. Total loss of the force: 2 officers (1 died of wounds) and 18 men killed, 2 officers and 36 men wounded. Casualties in Pulteney's Column: Lieutenant GJ Bell OC D Coy VMR and 773 Private HF Dillon VMR wounded. Major Fell reported having captured one Boer with rifle and bandolier.

Sergeant WW Judd's (VMR) letter to his relatives gives more detail:

On 4 January we moved before daylight on a two days' reconnaissance in force. Pulteney's Column was on the left of the range and the 5th Queensland Bushmen under Lieutenant Colonel Vallentin, our late leader, on the ridge of the hill. While we were awaiting intelligence from the scouts, word came that Botha had attacked Vallentin and cut his force up. We galloped to the ridge and got the 15 pdrs into action, shelling the hills and forcing the Boers to retire. Then we advanced over the valley, and when we reached the flank found that the news was only too true. Colonel Vallentin and twenty four Queenslanders were lying dead, while thirty six were wounded. Some of the bodies were gashed horribly with heavy explosive ball. They had 1,000 veterans in position and we had only 300 RW VMR. Word came in that the pompom (Plumer's) was in danger on the left flank, and we galloped up to save it. We heard the thunder of hoofs as the Imperial Yeomanry came flying from the gun which they had deserted under the awful attack of the burghers. Then the maligned Fifth Victorians came on the scene. The enemy was already virtually in possession of the gun, but D Coy charged into the storm of bullets. Lieutenant Bell fell at the head of his men, wounded in the stomach. The enemy retreated before the charge and the gun was saved. Botha was forced back to the cover of a high flat hill, rising precipitately from the valley. The Boer casualties were 47 killed and 68 wounded.

The column left Bankkop on 5 January and marched back to Rotterdam. Putty wrote:

Major Fell reported having sent out a patrol and killed one Boer, also 60 cattle and 4 mules captured, a ton of mealies destroyed, and two boxes of correspondence the property of General Smuts found in a cave.

Next day they marched to Grootfontein: a few Boers were seen and one captured. Then, on 7 January, Putty wrote:

Marched at 5.30 am towards the Assegai River and Derdehoek where 60 to 70 Boers were seen with a good many cattle and sheep, some of which were taken. RW VMR pushed forward into the valley and the Boers were shelled in retiring but without much effect.

They camped at Klipfontein and on 8 January marched in under Hurricane Hill camping about three miles from Wakkerstroom. The column spent two weeks in this position evacuating the sick and receiving supplies and reinforcements. Rinderpest had broken out badly amongst the transport oxen and they had to be sent to Volksrust for inoculation.

Little was achieved 22-24 January because of heavy rain and thick mist. Putty described the action on 25 January:

Pulteney's column left camp at 12 midnight on a combined movement in which troops from Wakkerstroom, Castrol's Nek blockhouse line, Plumer's and Colville's Column were utilised. Objective was a rough tract of country lying N of Castrol's Nek range E of Sterkfontein and Johnstons Hoek S of Spitzkop and W of Kromhoek and Molegat. The rendezvous for Pulteney's Column was at Vryheid and all positions were to be occupied before dawn. Pulteney's orders were to drive the country within this area up to the cordon. Shortly after daybreak the column began to advance: RW VMR under Major Daly was sent across the ravine on to Winterskraal to work southwards. Part of LW VMR went forward detaching one company to search kloofs to the east. The 15 pdr guns with 8 H moved south to Deepdale, on the south edge of which a small party of Boers were seen and shelled. From this point one company of LW VMR was detached and with a pompom sent to assist RW VMR. Meantime the Boers began to move and attempted the road up the valley from S Botha's farm. This they found blocked and they turned and rode eastwards. Then the mist more or less cleared and helios began to work. During this RW VMR was clearing the country southwards and eventually worked round to Johnstonshoek and Waaihoek. The 15 pdrs and 8 H were pushed forward and the former commanded the valley on either side of Dromhoek on to which a company of LW VMR was sent. Mounted troops from both Colvin's and Colville's forces now worked into the valley from the E. Six Boers were taken by RW VMR and the remainder seeing it was hopeless surrendered, 36 in all. The country covered by RW VMR was very rough and several horses were damaged, two had to be destroyed. Our casualties were nil; Boer loss unknown.

Mist prevented operations for the next few days, then Putty recorded the action on 31 January: 'The mounted force, Viall's Corps leading, Pulteney's in support and Colvin's in rear, left camp at midnight in thick mist and marched via Balmoral on to Rotterdam, reaching it in rain and fog soon after 7 am. About 8 am the fog lifted and several lots of cattle were seen. 8 H were sent to get them and a 15 pdr was brought up to cover them and shelled some small parties of Boers as they bolted. 8 H got one lot of 170 head and a few ponies and mules'.

Summarising the month, Putty wrote:

Owing to the concentration of the enemy the column worked throughout the month in conjunction with General Plumer's force. Rain and fog have continually hampered and delayed operations. The health of the horses on the whole has been good, few died from sickness. The total loss during the month was 98 – 60 of which occurred due to the action on 4 January. Of the 50 remounts sent on 9 January to RW VMR 13 had to be returned on 16 January as useless. Rinderpest appeared on 9 January, but broke out badly on 11 and 12 January, all the oxen were sent into Volksrust for inoculation. Oxen to replace them were sent out on 21 January and taking them all round were a very small and poor lot. The health of the men has been very fair, but in the latter part of the month there has been an increase in the number of fever cases; the majority of these are probably enteric and are nearly all amongst men who recently joined from Newcastle.

Putty's Column stayed near Rotterdam until 8.30 pm 2 February when the mounted force left camp with Colvin's force in advance, Viall's in support and Putty's with all guns in reserve. Putty tells the story of the action on 3 February:

Marched throughout night and arrived at Vaalbank Spruit about daybreak and moved on to Mooifontein. The advanced parties on moving westward met with a certain amount of opposition especially on the right flank, round which a party of 100 Boers moved heading for the Vaal, and across which they retired. RW VMR were detached and took the guns of

Colvin's and Viall's Corps up to the front; they then worked with Plumer's Corps for the remainder of the day. This force made a wide left-handed turning movement towards the Elandsberg, upon which positions had been taken by Colville's Column. While the turning movement was going on Pulteney's Column moved up to Vermaaks Kraal. The Boers tried the Elandsberg and finding it occupied slipped away left-handed driving their cattle. 8 H were sent back to find the convoy and if possible to bring supplies to Rolfontein, but did not find them till 8.30 pm. Plumer's and Pulteney's Columns bivouacked at Rolfontein without baggage. In the early morning Plumer took 5 prisoners, Pulteney and Colville one each: it was very unlucky all the Boers were not rounded up. Horses must have covered between 50 and 60 miles during these operations.

On 8 February the whole force, complete with its transport and supplies, was at Rolfontein where Putty takes up the story on 10 February:

Mounted troops left at 7.30 am [probably 7.30 pm] and after passing through Amersfoort, Viall's Corps went westward, the remainder turning NW marching all night. The main force passing through Hartebeestfontein reached the high ground on Weltwreden shortly after daybreak; Viall's Corps was seen on the high ground on Strydkraal. A small party of Boers were seen on our right, but the information of a large gathering at Grootvlie was incorrect. Two Boers were taken by LW VMR. The force returned to Rolfontein by 7 pm.

On 12 February the mounted force left at 7.45 pm in two columns (Plumer No 1 Column and Putty with Major Wiggin's Column No 2); the remainder of the troops were left under Major Fell. Putty wrote of the action on 13 February: 'No 2 Column reached Goldehoop just before daybreak, and then moved across the Mabusa River on to Welgelegen. No 1 Column worked on the right of No 2 and General Spens on the left. The latter killed one Boer and took 7 prisoners'. They set off again at 8 am 14 February via Beltresna and Glenfillan to Vosskop searching kloofs en route. A thick fog came on in the afternoon; there was also a thick mist early next morning which delayed the start. On 16 February Putty recorded: 'Left camp at 6.30 am and went to Reitspruit. LW VMR supporting on the left worked up to a kloof on the Elandsberg and took 3 prisoners. Two more Boers were reported to be hiding in the kloof; a patrol was sent out and found them'. They stayed in this position until 23 February and patrols were sent out daily. 60 mounted men VMR took 12 prisoners on Derdehoek on 20 February; a patrol LW VMR took 2 prisoners on Sterkfontein on 22 February; another patrol LW VMR took one prisoner the same day on Goedgemoed.

Putty's staff diary noted on 19 February: 'Lieutenant Cuthbert SG rejoined column. Lieutenant Macdonald took over the duties of supply officer'. The diary is an outline of events and mentions of his staff are few. Two of the three SG officers, Cuthbert and Stephen who served in his first column, had joined his second column in August 1901: in addition he had a BM, intelligence officer and supply officer, a total of 5 officers.

On 24 February the whole force, having marched all night, reached Rotterdam and camped at Goodehoek. Next day they left for Rolfontein: two coys LW VMR sighted two Boers on Kromhoek who they captured after a long chase. The force remained at Rolfontein until the evening of 27 February when they set off again. Putty wrote (28 February):

Marched through Amersfort to Wydgelegen where 2 men were captured in a farmhouse; thence to Tweepoort which was searched before daybreak. From here the 8 H and two coys LW VMR were sent southwards to hold high ground of Strydkraal. At daybreak the whole force moved westward, the left being connected to the railway by some MI from Platrand, the right in touch with Colonel Viall's Corps (Plumer). The coy VMR working in touch with Viall's Corps assisted in the capture of 13 Boers.

Putty summarised February:

The continuous operations carried out in conjunction with other columns no doubt caused the concentration of the enemy and their break through the Piet Retief blockhouse line. After this several small parties and single men were captured and a large amount of food-stuffs destroyed. All the families stated they were very hard up for food and the majority asked to be sent into the line. With the exception of 14 and 15 February, operations were not delayed by the weather. The loss of horses during the month (131) compares unfavourably with last month, and occurred chiefly amongst the last remounts which were not fit for hard work. Rinderpest and lung sickness killed a good many oxen during the month; the total loss being 226. The inoculated oxen were not immune from rinderpest and suffered more than the captured and non-inoculated stock. The general health of the column has been good. There has been a considerable increase in the number sent to hospital, chiefly owing to the number of fever cases, but during the last 2 weeks they have increased 50%. Number sent in January: 58. February: 70.

Putty's Column was at Kromdraai on 1 March where Lieutenant Patterson MO VMR wrote: 'Yesterday in a combined drive 75 Boers were taken and best of all K (Kitchener) directing operations got 600. So things are looking up'. Next day they moved to Darling about 2½ miles N of Standerton and camped close to Plumer. On 3 March the VMR history records:

Plumer got word from Kitchener that Botha, Steyn and De Wet were going to meet in conference with 600 burghers near Vrede in the Orange River Colony, and marched with Wing's Western Australians and 18 H in the lead, followed by the Victorians (probably all Pulteney's mounted troops), then Viall and Colvin.

Putty wrote on 3 and 4 March:

Detachment Scottish Rifles under Major Fell left for Platrand. Mounted troops left camp at 5.30 pm [3 March]. Colonel Wing's Column joined and took the advance. Marched via Roberts' Drift to Hartebeestfontein where a wounded Boer was picked up, and on to Uitzicht. From here some Boers were seen in a SE direction and the whole force swung round left-handed. An attempt was made to cut them off, but they cleared and were pursued by two coys RW VMR who chased them as far as Tweefontein. Camped on S side of Vaal close to Roberts' Drift about 7 pm [4 March]; the distance covered by the mounted force was over 60 miles – 14 horses had to be destroyed.

Lieutenant Patterson MO VMR wrote of this:

> We marched through Standerton, a grand force of mounted men. It was a very cold night and I nearly froze to death. We kept on until dawn [4 March] and then halted for half an hour. No word could be got of the enemy and it appeared certain that none of the Generals were there. We moved on and soon 60 Boers were reported and the Victorians (RW VMR) were ordered to advance rapidly. Bell with his company took the advance, then O'Reilly, then the Major's staff, then Chomley and Hutton. We soon spotted them and they started to gallop: so did we. It was a great gallop especially for Bell and O'Reilly. Horses were dropping out everywhere and eventually Bell who went further than anyone else was left with only six men and had to give it up. We eventually got there at 8.45 pm after being continuously on the move for 27¾ hours with the exception of the halt mentioned.

Putty's Column remained there until 7 March when it crossed the drift to the N bank of the Vaal, back into the Transvaal. On 8 March the column marched to Standerton camping N of Standerton Kop; it was then broken up. The Scottish Rifles had already left on 3 March; VMR handed in their horses, ordnance and transport on 9 March and departed for Cape Town en route for Australia on 10 March; and it seems likely that the rest of the column left about this time. The war itself continued until May when the last of the Boers surrendered.

In a letter to his wife from Newcastle on 10 March General Lyttelton[43] then probably GOC Natal wrote: 'I also saw in Pulteney's diary that most of the families they find out in the veldt asked to be brought in to our lines'. Putty's report must have been written after 1 March and it is of interest that Lyttelton should have seen it so quickly.

There is no record of how Putty spent the next three months or indeed where he spent it. A photograph taken on 2 July is of 17 SG officers at Bloemfontein. A week later (9 July) he was onboard SS *Britain* when she left Cape Town for Southampton. During the war Putty had been mentioned three times in despatches: LG 26 January 1900 (Despatch of Lieutenant General Lord Methuen), LG 10 September 1901 (Despatch of Field Marshal Earl Roberts CinC South Africa) and LG 29 July 1902 (General Lord Kitchener CinC South Africa). He was also appointed CB for his service in the war.

Putty served nearly three years in South Africa, almost continually in the field on operational service. The evidence of Putty's athleticism and toughness was already there but his performance in South Africa takes this to an even higher level. Almost continually in the saddle for 12 months, in all weathers, covering large distances by day and night, and often sleeping in bivouac, suggests a man of very considerable physical strength, stamina and determination. Apart from a spell in hospital between his two column commands, probably with fever and more than likely a recurrence of something from Uganda, he did not have a break. This physical robustness must have been backed with a similar mental strength. At the end of a very demanding day he had to deal with the administration of his column, plan the next day, and issue the necessary orders. The evidence points to this being done meticulously, and that every man knew what he

---

43   General Neville Lyttelton (1845-1931) late RB Eton Evans House CinC South Africa 1902-1904 later CGS 1904-1908 CinC Ireland 1908-1912.

In camp at Bloemfontein, July 1902. (Cuthbert)

was required to do, every day. There is no evidence of criticism in the numerous letters home by officers and soldiers, and most notably those of VMR.

By the time of his second column Putty was showing considerable skill in manoeuvring and applying his units together against the enemy. All the time he had to balance the conflicting operational priorities – resupplying his column and protecting the convoys from attack, the movement of his camp including baggage and supplies so that it was always protected and in the right place, and offensive action against the enemy. There were also the problems of dealing with the large numbers of captured cattle, sheep, oxen, mules and horses, and of communication and coordination with the other columns. He had a small staff but there were many decisions for him to take at the end of each day.

Each of the four main elements of the column required separate consideration; each had its strengths and weaknesses. The artillery was good for turning the enemy out of prepared positions but needed protection at all times. The infantry was good for protecting the convoys and camps but was restricted to marching pace and their daily movement had to be planned with great care. The cavalry was good for reconnaissance and escort duties but their use in offensive operations was limited. The mounted infantry, or cavalry that could dismount with the rifle, combined the speed of movement of the cavalry and the firepower of the infantry. All four capabilities were complementary and each had to be used to best advantage. The evidence suggests that Putty understood this and achieved it most if not all of the time.

The very small number of casualties (9 killed and 22 wounded) in his second column indicates that Putty achieved a high level of operational security. All the evidence suggests a leader of considerable boldness and initiative, and one who led by example. The spat with Gerald Cuthbert shows that he had the moral courage to make difficult and unpopular decisions, and in this case the balance of argument supports him. There are examples of Putty being prepared to take risks but not when the lives of those under him might be sacrificed needlessly. There is no evidence of inflexibility or pig-headedness in a war where the ability to respond flexibly and rapidly to changing circumstances was an essential requirement. There can have been few officers who left South Africa having served such a hard hands-on apprenticeship at this level as Putty.

His superiors were the key judges of Putty's performance and many got to know him very well. In 1 SG Putty served under Paget: later as CO 1 SG his bde comd was Colville under whom he had served at the Depot and in Uganda. GOC 1st Division was Methuen. If they could be considered biased in his favour this could not have been so when he commanded his columns. In his first column his superiors were French and Blood. French spent some time with Putty's Column and they got to know each other very well. In his second column he served under and alongside numerous general officers and, most significantly, Plumer who he also got to know very well. Furthermore he also came to the attention of Roberts, Kitchener and Lyttelton at various times during the war. All the evidence suggests that he was highly regarded as a field commander.

His relationship with General Burn-Murdoch requires examination: Burn-Murdoch was GOC Newcastle and Putty's 2nd Column was under his command for several months. Initially Burn-Murdoch wanted to assert his authority but Putty had been given a free hand; some tension to start with was perhaps inevitable. However, Burn-Murdoch's criticism of Putty's tactics in the first few days seems unreasonable and unjustified. His column had only just been formed and the VMR came with low morale and a poor reputation, having been earlier surprised by the Boers and suffered casualties as a result. He needed time to get everyone settled and begin to work together: significantly, after a week in the field the problems ceased.

Some last words go to Private Drysdale VMR in his letter published in the *Yea Chronicle* on 16 February: 'It is a great pity that we have not had him [Putty] over us from the start. There is not a man in the contingent who would not swear by him'.

6

Command in England and Ireland

2nd Battalion Scots Guards 1904-1908

Putty had been overseas on operational service for nearly seven years, latterly in command of an all arms brigade. Once back, he had a spell of leave during which he met Edith Castlereagh at a house party at Lowther Castle.[1] Charley Castlereagh was shooting grouse in Northumberland so Edith was on her own and it was perhaps here that their friendship began.

On 5 October 1902 he was present at Windsor station when HRH The Duke of Connaught met 1 SG on their return from South Africa. He then re-joined 1 SG for just over a year; it was commanded by Lieutenant Colonel Harbord, and Putty was once again the Second in Command. One of his first priorities was to resume his involvement with Army Football and very quickly he was appointed Chairman of the Army Football Association. For him the main events in 1903 were being invited to a dinner party given by the King and Queen at Windsor Castle, commanding the battalion at Victoria Barracks Windsor when General Lord Methuen presented King's South Africa Medals, and being invited to Buckingham Palace for a dance on the occasion of the King and Queen's 40th Wedding Anniversary.

On 31 March 1904 Putty took over as CO 2 SG from Lieutenant Colonel Romilly,[2] 2 SG was then stationed at Wellington Barracks in London; during his nearly four years in command it moved four times – to Aldershot in September 1904, to Chelsea Barracks in October 1905, to the Tower of London in October 1906, and back to Aldershot in October 1907. For much of his time in command Putty lived in London at 3 Lower Berkeley Street (later renamed 3 Fitzhardinge Street). This was leased to his sister, Isabel, from the Portman Estate and was to be his home for more than 50 years; Isabel moved out and the lease was transferred when he married in 1917. The Georgian house was on five floors and at the back in the mews there was a coach house and stabling with accommodation above where Putty's orderly and groom lived.

Commanding a battalion of Foot Guards in London then was little different to now. The three main tasks were administration of the men, barracks and equipment; training, especially shooting and fitness, and sport; and public duties. In June 1904 Putty took the battalion to Pirbright for the completion of its annual course of musketry. Amongst his many social and

---

1   Home of 5th Lord Lonsdale (1857-1944) Eton.
2   Frederick William Romilly (1854-1935) SG 1873-1909.

1 SG, April 1903. (Hew Balfour)   CO 2 SG, June 1905. (Hew Balfour)

sporting activities was a visit to Walter Fothringham at Murthly Castle 17-21 September; at that time train was by far the quickest and most comfortable means of travel, and Putty used it on this occasion and frequently over the next ten years. In November 2 SG took part in the State Visit of the King and Queen of Portugal. In addition to running Army Football, he was now President of the Household Brigade Football Challenge Cup Competition with the Household Cavalry, 10 battalions of Foot Guards and the Guards Depot competing. Whenever he could, Putty competed in battalion sports and other events.

At the beginning of 1905 he was invited to shoot at Houghton Hall[3] with the Prince of Wales.[4] The year that followed was much the same as the previous one: in March Putty attended the King's Levée at St James Palace; in May 2 SG paraded for field operations before HM The King at Frensham; and then in June it took part in a Royal Review on Laffain's Plain, part of the State Visit of the King of Spain. At that time the Sovereign (Edward VII) saw the commanding officer of a Foot Guards battalion regularly, and a personal friendship was also growing between Putty and the Prince of Wales. The King presented Putty with the CB for his service in South Africa at an investiture in Buckingham Palace on 24 July. Then, in November, the battalion provided a guard of honour and street liners for the State Visit of the King of Greece.

3   Owned by George Henry Hugh Cholmondeley 4th Marquess of Cholmondeley (1858-1923) Eton Lord Great Chamberlain.
4   Later King George V, 1910.

One other significant event during the year was the battalion's annual sports competition on 3 July. Putty ran in the officers' race, and there was nothing unusual about this, but the *Guards Magazine* also reported that Lady French attended, and she may well have presented the prizes. By this time Putty could be considered a friend of General French, now GOC Aldershot Command, under whom he was again serving.

In early 1906 2 SG was issued with the new short rifle and conversion training had to be fitted in to the programme, leading up to the annual training at Pirbright in May. Public duties continued, the main events for the battalion that year being the State Opening of Parliament by HM The King in February and the State Visit of the King and Queen of Norway in November. In August Putty ran the London District Rifle Meeting; the number of entries was so unprecedently large that year that the Committee, of which Putty was the Chairman, decided to start the meeting a day earlier than usual.

His friend, Gerald Cuthbert, had commanded 1 SG since 1904, and was then posted to be AAG in Cairo. Their correspondence resumed, mainly on regimental matters; Putty wrote to him from 3 Lower Berkeley Street on 14 August:

> My dear Cupid, As it is only a penny postage will write you another line. Was very glad to hear you give such a good account of yourself, it must be piping hot out there now I remember well the August in 1882, Arthur Hay[5] used to sweat champagne neat. We have had a frightful row over change of quarters as my battalion should have gone to Windsor and they have shunted the 3rd Battn Grenadiers there instead. Chang[6] and self were nearly put under arrest, we got beat over it, a case where 'might' was wrong, Paul[7] would not interfere and is a poor fighter for our interests. Yarde[8] is hiding in Paris, staying with old Meat [Henry Cecil Lowther Military Attaché in Paris] as long as he keeps out of the way I think he will be alright, as the lady I understand is taking up another young man already. Freddy Stopford[9] took over yesterday and a good job too. Meat is over here for a couple of days, he is going to the French manoeuvres in charge of French, Grierson,[10] young Brett and another. I am going to do duty in London until change of quarters when the hard worked Pa[11] comes back; I am Field Officer next month. Luck to you. Yours ever, WP Pulteney.

He wrote to him again on 3 September:

> My dear Cupid, Thanks for yours of the 26 August – you complain of 97 degrees in the shade but we poor blighters are at 93 degrees at the present moment and houses not built to be cool in but just the opposite. The men are going away by the score, all the best men in

---

5   Lieutenant Hon Arthur Hay (1855-1932) SG 1878-1886.
6   Colonel Frederick William Romilly (1854-1935) SG 1873-1909 now Lieutenant Colonel Commanding SG.
7   Lieutenant General Paul Sandford 3rd Baron Methuen Colonel SG GOC Eastern Command.
8   Hon John Reginald Lopes Yarde-Buller (1873-1930) SG 1896-1907 & 1914-1919 later 3rd Baron Churston.
9   Major General Frederick William Stopford (1854-1917) late Gren Gds Commanding Brigade of Guards and GOC London District.
10 Major General James Moncrieff Grierson (1859-1914) late RA GOC 1st Division 1906 vice Paget.
11 Frederic James Heyworth (1863-1916) SG 1883-1914 2IC 2 SG.

each of the three battalions, they don't seem to have the very smallest difficulty in getting employment the good ones refer to us for characters I suppose the indifferent ones write their own, I shall have fifty gone by the 14th of this month and another fifty by 1 October, the 1st Battn about the same, and the 3rd Battn an extra fifty so we can calculate on a reduction of 350 men by 1 October, we are at the present moment 105 under strength and no reservists coming in. Young Romeo[12] is back and takes over the adjutancy today and I believe Giggles Gordon[13] wants to get the adjutancy of the Depot but they had much better send young Hamilton[14] there. We move to that cursed Tower on 5 October, shall have a nice time with all the blackguards at the East End – Pa is away!!!! I take my leave 9 October till 9 November. Yours ever, WP Pulteney.

The letters give a good idea of Putty's life at this time and his interest in the officers and soldiers under his command. He wrote again on 24 September:

My dear Cupid, Many thanks for your letter, your account of the night marches was capital if the columns lose their way in a desert, what would they be in thick woods. I hear the Coldstream lost theirs at manoeuvres but luckily the 1st Battn had Esmé[15] to lead them and they arrived all right. Jerry Ruthven[16] went down umpiring he says the telephone was an enormous success and very well run, so it must have altered since last year. The Coldstream are off on Saturday, they are all going to the Covent Garden the previous night headed by Towney Butler. I reckon that 220 men altogether have or will have converted their service by 1 October in the regiment, each of the other two Battns will be about 820 strong on 1 October and by 1 April we shall be very little above our present rotten establishment and we are going to have a detachment at either Caterham or Windsor about 130 men from each Battn. Practically no recruits are coming in at the present moment we get about 3 a week. I saw Arthur Paget (GOC 1st Division) yesterday he is busy saying good bye to the Brigade and other generals, he tells me that he is to get another billet [GOC Eastern Command] but I don't know what. Yours ever, WP Pulteney.

Putty had to deal with the inevitable discipline problems in his battalion. On 27 September SG Records show that Private Bernard Keenan[17] was charged with being drunk and disorderly in Borough Road with the witnesses being PC175M Carpenter and Lance Sergeant Calvert. Drink was but one such problem and on this occasion Putty admonished him: the full story is likely to have been much more colourful.

The battalion moved to the Tower on 5 October after which Putty went on leave. He was at Harehope Hall, Alnwick on 28 October from where he again wrote to Cuthbert in Cairo:

12   Bertram Henry Samuel Romilly (1878-1940) SG 1898-1924 Adjt 1 SG 1906-1907.
13   Possibly Granville Cecil Douglas Gordon (1883-1930) SG 1901-1915.
14   Possibly Cecil Fife Pryce Hamilton (1879-1914) SG 1901-1914 died of wounds.
15   Lord Esmé Charles Gordon-Lennox (1875-1949) SG 1896-1920.
16   Hon Walter Patrick Ruthven (1870-1956) SG 1891-1919 later 2nd Baron Ruthven.
17   5060 Private Bernard Keenan (1884-NK) SG 1903-1906 from Newton Stewart Co Tyrone.

My dear Cupid, Many thanks for your letter of the 14th. We have finished with the 3rd Battn and nobody will remember that it ever existed from its fighting records, any amount of men went to the reserve on conversion of service who took the first job offered to them and now are looking out for others which I trust they will find difficult to get and make the future generation more careful, it would be a good thing to send a circular at the end of six months to the employers to see if they are still in their employ. Chang [Lieutenant Colonel Commanding Scots Guards] is busy putting out a recruiting poster with many photos in it but with Maclean[18] as Regt Adjt to hurry him up I doubt it being ready before 1907. No I have not heard that A. P. [General Sir Arthur Paget] has got the Irish Command he told me he was getting something but as he did not volunteer to say what I didn't question him [Paget went to Eastern Command vice Methuen then to Irish Command in 1911]. I am going from here tomorrow to shoot with Harold [Harold Cuthber] at Beaufront the weather has at last broken up and we may expect a good deal of rain. I think they are certain to keep you on in Egypt as they get you cheaper than a brigadier and that is everything in the present day. I am trying to establish post offices in all the London barracks to encourage thrift and eventually put reservists in charge of. Am very broke just now and don't see my way to soldiering at home much longer as soon as I have finished my three years with substantive rank next April I shall be on the lookout for something else to do I think or anyway not to soldier in England. Cresswell[19] has taken to hunting again and the religious fever is now past and he has become human again. Best of luck to the old Coldstream. Yours ever, WP Pulteney.

On 30 October he arrived at Beaufront Castle, Hexham to shoot with Harold Cuthbert. Other guests were Cator and Lowther, both to become Major Generals in due course. 247 pheasants were shot.

There was an interesting remark in Colonel Romilly's letter written on 4 December to Gerald Cuthbert, Harold's uncle, in Egypt: 'Frankey Lloyd[20] I believe has another year and a half to run; his successor will probably be either Fergusson[21] or Pulteney, probably the latter if French is allowed his say'.

Putty next wrote to Gerald Cuthbert from the Tower on 21 December:

My dear Cupid, I owe you a letter in response to yours of 7 Nov and although it is the shortest day of the year here goes. We will begin with a riddle 'Why is Love like Ice' ans 'Try a block' not bad for this festive season is it? Paul Methuen[22] has got the flue also Chang so that cursed disease is doing its very 'damndest' I suppose we shall all get it in our turn. Chips[23] has got hold of the Regimental Orderley Room with the result that a recruiting poster has already been issued, with Maclean it would have arrived next autumn, what

18   Major Hector Fitzroy Maclean (1873-1932) SG 1896-1919.
19   Addison Francis Baker Cresswell (1874-1921) SG 1893-1895 owner of Harehope Hall, Hexham.
20   Brigadier General Francis Lloyd (1853-1926) late Gren Gds Comd 1 Gds Bde.
21   Lieutenant Colonel Charles Fergusson (1865-1951) Eton CO 3 Gren Gds 1904-1907 later 7th Bt.
22   Lieutenant General Paul Sandford 3rd Baron Methuen Colonel SG and GOC Eastern Command.
23   Captain John Trefusis Carpenter-Garnier (1874-1914) SG 1896-1914 killed in action Adjt 2 SG 1903-1905.

the regiment want to look to now more than anything is their recruiting my battalion is overrun with frauds and the authorities are frightened to say anything because all that happens is that district won't send us any more recruits. Permanent passes for all night leave are going to be done away with and leave only given up to 1 am except for married men, a very good thing too. Yarde goes off with the Duke of Connaught on the 11th of next month, if the lady does not turn up on the ship he is all right as I hear that she has another man in tow already (the 2nd since Yarde). Lady Cowley is going to have a baby which cast reflections on Topps'[24] powers, he had better be called 'Unders' in future. The drag is going pretty well at Windsor and several of our boys are going pretty well especially Norman and young Nugent.[25] The result of the probationers' exam has not yet been divulged but I expect they will let most of them through. Love to all in Cairo. Yours ever, WP Pulteney.

A month later, on 18 January 1907, he wrote again from 3 Lower Berkeley Street:

My dear Cupid, Many thanks for your letter of 30 Dec, you seem to be getting on all right, am glad to see that they are ranking you as a substantive Colonel I have got a billet to qualify as one, otherwise by the warrant am not qualified for a General and with any luck I shall be one almost within a year if they don't pass me over and if they do I shall chuck it as am qualified for my pension on the 1st April and shall look out for a civilian job. McNeil's[26] papers are in, he has got a civilian billet in Edinburgh he will be a loss to the regiment in many ways especially his old pipes, Willie Holbeck[27] will be gazetted out any time now so the vacancies keep being made, we have no one ready at Sandhurst at present but we ought to watch it that we don't get too low again, we don't want any more probationers – Gladwin[28] and Trafford[29] of my lot passed and will be gazetted next month. I wish you would say a word to Wingate[30] if you get the chance for Norman Orr-Ewing,[31] his name is down for the Egyptian Army, he would do very well indeed out there and is a very good boy full of dash and very broke. Very sad about Fergusson's father[32] I had a letter from Charles this morning he has little hope of recovering his body. Coddy[33] is soon to be made a General and Arthur Henniker[34] gets the Coldstream. Yes, I know Macfarlane who commands the KOSB a good fellow – any amount of flue about the boys get it in turn at the Tower. Have you heard about the Suffragette lady who complained to the magistrate about being turned out of the House that she had been pinned to the floor by a rising but

24 Charles Edward Hartopp (1858-1929) SG 1879-1889 later 5th Bt.
25 2nd Lieutenant Richard Francis Robert Nugent (1884-1914) SG 1905-1911 & 1914 killed in action.
26 Major Neil Archibald McNeill (1878-1963) SG 1899-1908 & 1914-1918.
27 Lieutenant William Hugh Holbeck (1882-1914) SG 1902-1907 & 1914 killed in action.
28 2nd Lieutenant Ralph Hamilton Fane Gladwin (1887-1914) SG 1905-1914 killed in action.
29 2nd Lieutenant Edward Bernard Trafford (1885-NK) SG 1905-1922.
30 Major General Francis Reginald Wingate (1861-1953) late RA Sirdar of Egyptian Army.
31 Norman Archibald Orr-Ewing (1880-1960) SG 1900-1919 seconded Egyptian Army 1907 later 4th Bt.
32 Sir James Fergusson 6th Bt (1832-1907) late Gren Gds killed in a Jamaican earthquake.
33 Alfred Edward Codrington (1854-1945) late Coldm Gds GOC 1st London Division TF 1908.
34 Probably Arthur Henry Henniker-Major (1855-1912) Coldm Gds.

unruly member. We have got to get rid of some more men out of the regiment before 1st April. Best of luck to you. Yours ever, WP Pulteney.

As he entered his third year in command of 2 SG he was beginning to think of his future but the day to day problems of managing his officers and men continued to dominate his thoughts. In February Putty commanded the troops on parade for the opening of the new Central Criminal Court by the King and Queen; then, on 8 March, he wrote again to Gerald Cuthbert:

My dear Cupid, Many thanks for your letter of the 24 February, very good of you to collect some stamps they will be much appreciated. Fergusson [CO 3 Gren Gds] and myself had an awful blow over the substantive rank as they said in the letter from the War Office that we should not get it until we had completed our full period of command but I have heard privately that if we are selected for promotion to Maj Gen we shall be asked to go on half pay before that happens so if I don't hear within the next four months I shall know they are not going to promote me a Maj Gen and shall bid them adieu. As you say fancy Maxse[35] getting the Coldstream I should have lost some money over it five years ago. I think the Malta billet is in readiness for Lyttelton[36] I cannot think of anyone else. Alston[37] is going to be married at the end of May, have told him he must chuck the adjutancy and must look out for another, but shall take young Jack Balfour[38] in all probability he is a capital boy and works uncommonly hard. The recruits are going down to Pirbright on the 19th of this month which is very early indeed, the General is going to have a standing camp down there and means to go down two days a week and ride about to look at the training and the musketry which is of course far the best way to inspect, instead of coming down one day with a liver as Bully used to. Moncur[39] is turning out a great success as Sergt Maj, he is very solid and ... but quite straight which is something and the men trust him. We go to Pirbright by ½ Battns on the 1st May and finishing the end of August. Remember me to Granville and all the Coldstream. Yours ever, WP Pulteney.

For the next few weeks the battalion was preparing for the inspection by the Major General Commanding London District (Major General Stopford) which took place at the Tower on 30 April. Next day the left half of the battalion left for Pirbright; Putty went with them and it was from there that he wrote his next letter to Cuthbert on 1 May:

My dear Cupid, Thanks for your letter of 14 April. Here I am down at this old spot again, of course having come down in the coldest and wettest weather possible with all the boys labelling the place with the usual epithets, am in command of the camp here until the end of August when I return to the Tower until October when Aldershot takes me once again

35   Lieutenant Colonel Frederick Ivor Maxse (1862-1958).
36   General Sir Neville Lyttelton. Putty was wrong; he did not go to Malta but was CinC Ireland 1908-1912.
37   Francis George Alston (1878-1961) SG 1900-1931 Adjt 2 SG 1906-1907.
38   Robert Frederick Balfour (1883-1914) Adjt 2 SG 1907; later Putty's ADC killed in action.
39   8966 Regimental Sergeant Major James Moncur (1873-1923) SG 1891-1921 from Edinburgh Garrison Sergeant Major.

under their fold. Yes I should like to get Bullreth's place very much indeed it would suit me down to the ground and it is quite time one got into the field again against a Turk or Senoussi. I want to put another campaign in before I am 50 and time is running on as am 46 on the 18th of this month. Harry Trefusis[40] is leaving he has come into a large place and some money on the death of his uncle Rolle, it is a good thing as he would never have done to command a Battn. Yarde has sent in his papers as also has young Bewicke,[41] the last named is no great loss – I hear also that Stanley Clarke[42] is coming back from Macedonia he did very well out there – Remember me to Eldon Gorst[43] we used to be at Eton together, what a start he has made for himself in life. Alston gives up the adjutancy on the 1 June and I intend to make young Jack Balfour, have not decided yet but am inclined to make Victor Mackenzie[44] my assistant adjt. He is a smart fellow and keen. Have left Pa in command at the Tower it is quite time he did some duty too – Love to the Coldstream. Yours ever, WP Pulteney.

In May Prince Fushimi Hiroyasu[45] of Japan visited 2 SG and had lunch with the officers. HRH The Duke of Connaught was also there, although no longer Colonel of the Regiment. Putty was to visit Japan with the Duke's son, Prince Arthur, many years later and thereafter maintained a close interest in Japanese affairs: perhaps this is where it all started. 2 SG provided street liners for the State Visit of the King and Queen of Denmark in June, and the following month the half battalions changed over with the right half going to Pirbright where Putty spent much of his time: not all the time because he was reported at a dinner and ball given by Lord and Lady Nunburnholme (Charles Wilson 1st Baron Nunburnholme 1833-1907 died 27 Oct) at their residence in Grosvenor Square on 8 July.

Putty wrote to Gerald Cuthbert again from Pirbright on 4 June:

My dear Cupid, Thanks for your letter of 12th May which found me here in the most damnable weather I have ever known down at this place, there has been nothing but rain and the temperature savours of the Arctic Region. I attacked the War Office in person last week as regards my own position they insist on my taking up some appointment before they make me a general so am now on the lookout for one, Fergusson goes to Ireland in August and is also sent there to qualify in a billet. Have got some experiments on here on Friday night in night firing hope we shall not shoot anybody but some fool generally gets in the way at these sort of hours, I believe the Japanese got some good work in outside Port Arthur at night firing towards the end of the show. Fushimi presented us with a cup in memory of his luncheon at The Tower, have not seen it yet but believe it is quite a nice one. The Duke of Connaught told me all sorts of tales about how well things were done in Egypt and other things which should have made your ears tingle. One squadron of the KDGs

40   Major Hon Henry Walter Trefusis (1864-1948) SG 1887-1907.
41   Calverley Bewicke (1883-1963) SG 1905-1907 and 1915-1920.
42   Lieutenant Colonel Albert Edward Stanley Clarke (1879-1926) SG 1898-1910 Macedonian Gendarme 1904.
43   Sir Eldon Gorst (1861-1911) Eton Consul-General Egypt 1907-1911.
44   Victor Audley Falconer Mackenzie (1882-1944) SG 1902-1928 later 3rd Bt.
45   Prince Fushimi Hiroyasu (1875-1946) studied in Great Britain 1907-1910.

averaged marksmen here I say they ought to give them buttsmen badges to wear, the 1st Grenadiers made a big score of 212 we only went 204 but everything was quite absolutely fair. McNeill is trying to get a job in Edinburgh I hope he will as it means a good addition to his income which at present is nil. [Minirner] Brodie is going to be married in fact myself Pa and George Paynter are the only ones that are not among the captains. Stiffen writes to me to say that matters are very unsettled out Macedonia way so expect the old Turk will have to keep his eye on the Bulgarians for a bit. Am here until end of August. Yours ever WP Pulteney.

In a letter from Carpenter-Garnier to Gerald Cuthbert, back on leave in England, on 13 September is this note: 'The 2nd Bn Sports were held yesterday and Putty scored a triumph in the officers' race, which shows the state of discipline is satisfactory!' In October the battalion changed quarters again, moving from the Tower to Ramillies Barracks, Aldershot. Putty wrote to Gerald Cuthbert on 11 October from Quidenham, Attleborough;[46]

My dear Cupid, Thanks for your letter send the photo to me at Lower Berkeley St before you go. No, I finish my time up to 1st April, though they have told me privately they are giving me a brigade very likely the Guards Brigade I imagine though I know nothing definite only a good many hangers on have congratulated me on getting it, it really is better than being made a General and being on the shelf for two years like Coddy and Pilcher are at present. Give my love to Walter [Fothringham], I wish I could have been there this week but was booked here. We got 90 brace on Wednesday, stopped by rain at 3pm. 120 brace yesterday and I expect the same today if the weather holds up. Yours ever WP Pulteney.

Then on 26 October he was again shooting with the Prince of Wales at Houghton Hall. The battalion was still required to do public duties and in November provided street liners for the State Visit of the Emperor of Germany. That day Putty was on leave at Heveningham Hall, Suffolk;[47] it was from there that he wrote to Gerald Cuthbert, back now in Cairo:

My dear Cupid, Thanks for your letter of the 2nd which reached me yesterday. Am staying with old Jos, he is just the same as he used to be and has not altered a day. Gipps is here but is unable to shoot, his leg is mending gradually but it is a long job with a man that age – Ralph Vivian[48] is here too and Ralph Blois,[49] the latter looking more like a lizard looking over a wall than ever – Have not heard whether Connie Maxwell[50] goes to Egypt he told me six weeks ago he was going to stay with the Duke of Connaught but I expect it is about time he moved on. Arthur Hennicker I believe has got the Guards Brigade at Aldershot after Lloyd and I believe they are going to offer me Belfast (15 Bde) it is a

46   Home of Arnold Allen Cecil Keppel 8th Earl of Albermarle (1858-1942) Eton SG 1878-1883.
47   Home of Colonel Joshua Charles Vanneck 4th Baron Huntingfield (1842-1915) SG 1863-1892 and who he had served with in Egypt 1882.
48   Lieutenant Colonel Ralph Vivian (1845-1924) SG 1864-1883.
49   Captain Ralph Barrett Macnaghten Blois (1866-1950) SG 1886-1896, 1900-1901, 1914-1919 later 9th Bt.
50   John Grenfell Maxwell (1859-1961) BW Staff of Duke of Connaught GOC Egypt 1908-1912.

damnable place but one must take what is going. The sea journey must have done you a lot of good and prepared you for a good dinner in Cairo. Give my love to Topps if you see him out there. The German Emperor is over here, the little boys in the streets shout out at him 'How's your anus Sir'. Stayed last Sunday with Arthur Paget [no longer GOC 1st Division, GOC Eastern Command 1908] he is very pleased at being made a KCB. Yours ever, WP Pulteney.

Putty was in London on 16 November for the wedding of his nephew, son of his brother Richard Maximilian, and was a regular attendee at such family events. Later that month, 2 SG was inspected by Brigadier General Lloyd Comd 1 Gds Bde, and on 30 November Putty wrote to Gerald Cuthbert from the Guards Club:

My dear Cupid, Many thanks for your letter of the 25 Nov. I think you can dismiss the rumour re Malta for I believe there is no doubt the Duke of Connaught is going there, if anybody is made CinC of the British Army it will be Kitchener but it is not likely to happen for a couple of years. I go to Fermoy to command the 16th Brigade there on the 7 February should have liked to have the Aldershot Brigade but was obliged to take what they offered me. It was a terrible thing about poor Odger Colvile [sic] and too tragic for words his being killed by Rawley[51] but poor fellow he had only himself to blame, after all he never cared about any recreation that he didn't risk his life at. Have got a lot of bother over one of my young fellows who wants to marry a lady on the stage, young Basil Loder,[52] am off this afternoon to interview the mother and am not looking forward to it. I leave the Battn the end of the year and I suppose Little John[53] succeeds me though they talk of Laurence[54] being made to finish up his time – should laugh if he did. Am rotting Tubby Granard[55] in here he sends you his love. Yours ever, WP Pulteney.

Throughout his time in command of the battalion Putty continued as Chairman of the Committee of the Army Football Association with two meetings being held in December. On 29 December he wrote again to Gerald Cuthbert:

My dear Cupid, Thanks for your letter of 22 December. I do not know who the man masquerading as Orr can be as Orr[56] himself is safe doing duty at Aldershot until the end of this month. Little John takes over from me on Tuesday and I make my bow on Wed 7th morning after nearly 27 years' service in the old corps. Have nearly got my leaving present together out of 41 Colonels who have commanded the Battn since 1843 I have got

51   Major General Sir Henry Edward Colville, Putty's superior in Uganda and South Africa now retired, died after his motor cycle collided with Brigadier General Henry Seymour Rawlinson (1864-1925) Eton late Coldm Gds Comd 2 Bde's car at Bisley.
52   2nd Lieutenant Basil Charles Robert Loder (1885-1934) SG 1905-08.
53   Lieutenant Colonel William Colquhon Grant McGrigor (1861-1924) SG 1883-1912 & 1914.
54   CO 3 SG 1904-1906 on disbandment.
55   Captain Bernard Arthur William Patrick Hastings 8th Earl of Granard (1874-1948) SG 1899-1911.
56   Possibly Arthur Roxburgh Orr (1884-1915) SG 1904-1915 killed in action.

the photos of 39 in six frames, Eden and Hamilton[57] are the only two I haven't got. Am afraid young Loder means to be an ass and marry that girl when I release him from duty on 1 June, encouraged by his mother and helped by Eustace Loder. Hope you saw Addie Cresswell and gave him some tips about Khartoum. Best of luck for 1908. Yours ever, WP Pulteney.

At the beginning of January 1908 Putty handed over to Lieutenant Colonel McGrigor after nearly four years in command of 2 SG. His departure is best described by him in his letter to Gerald Cuthbert written on 7 January from 3 Lower Berkeley Street:

My dear Cupid, Glad you found Addie all right, bad luck about Mrs Cresswell's clothes after all it pays to stick to the old P & O. I hope Addie will get a bit of shooting it will do him good. Am in the Gazette tonight I believe, Laurence Drummond has been posted to the 2nd Battn until his time is up on the 7 March but I imagine he will shirk going down to Aldershot from what I know of him, I go over to Ireland on 6 February. We had a hard frost up till yesterday and now it is as muggy and wet as it can be. The boys gave me a great dinner on Saturday night, the Beetle and George Paynter[58] were in their very best form and why they were not run in I can't imagine, Chang [Lieutenant Colonel Commanding SG] for a wonder made quite a decent speech. The men gave me a tremendous jolly when I left last Wednesday, rushed the cab, took the horse out and ran me down the Alexandra Road it gave one a bit of a lump in the throat. Yours ever, WP Pulteney.

On 20 January Putty sent an article to the editor of the *Brigade of Guards Magazine* on 'Technical Instruction'. He had resumed his involvement in the Brigade of Guards Employment Society on his return from South Africa and latterly been the Chairman of its Technical Training Committee; the article reflects his continuing interest in preparing men for civilian life: 'I have acceded to your request and written some remarks on Technical Instruction for the Brigade Magazine. It is not a very lively subject to write upon, but I trust it will bring the matter to the notice of the serving soldier in a manner which will arouse his interest and bring to his notice both the object of Technical Instruction and the opportunities it opens to him'. The article then covers what the soldier has to offer a civilian employer and the various schemes that had been set up to help him find employment in due course: driving a motor vehicle, London knowledge for motor-cabmen, shoemaking and typewriting being some of them.

16 Infantry Brigade Fermoy 1908-1909

On 6 February 1908 Putty set off to Fermoy in Ireland to take over command of 16 Infantry Brigade (16 Bde), part of 6th Division whose headquarters was in Cork. Two of its battalions were stationed in Fermoy, one was in Tipperary, and one in Bullevant. Over the next six years Putty was to be a frequent traveller between Fermoy/Cork and London. A fast service was inaugurated in 1906, departing London at 8.45 am and 8.45 pm daily, and arriving in Cork at 9.20

---

57   George Morton Eden (1806-1862) SG 1839-1854; Charles John James Hamilton (1810-1892) SG 1827-1854 later 3rd Bt.
58   Major George Camborne Beauclerk Paynter (1880-1950) SG 1899-1927.

pm and 9.20 am. The services from Cork to London departed fifteen minutes earlier. Although it was a long rail and boat journey, a full sleeper and dining service was provided; overall the comfort, speed and reliability of the service was vastly different to that today, and reflected the importance of Cork to the prosperity and power of the Country.

At that time Fermoy had a population of approximately 7,000 and was reputed to have the largest military establishment in Ireland. East Barracks had been built in 1806 and included a 130 bed hospital; West Barracks was built in 1809 and had a 42 bed hospital. Between them the two barracks had accommodation for 183 officers, 2,816 men and 152 horses. Overall the military garrison represented nearly half the population of the town. Major Cecil Lothian Nicholson Worcs[59] was his BM for most if not all of Putty's time in command. Lieutenant Colonel Henry Sinclair Horne RA[60] commanded 33 Bde RFA in Fermoy, just overlapping with Putty.

He wrote to Gerald Cuthbert in Cairo from the Royal Hotel Fermoy on 30 March:

> My dear Cupid, Thanks for your letter of the 20th. Things going along all right here, have quite settled down and mastered the ropes, the crab of this brigade is that the regiments were constantly changing, one no sooner gets to know the people than they are off however no more will change until September when the Dublin Fusiliers [2 RDF] go. I wonder they have come to no conclusion yet about the Coldstream the rumour in London is that they are doomed in favour of another Battn of Irish Guards but doubt the truth of it. Have done very well fishing the people about are most kind and give me as much as I can do, being so close I get on the water by 2 pm after my work and fish till I can't see or am beat, the best one I have got has been 25 lbs. Believe Little John is getting on all alright, the Battn won the Grierson Football Cup and is very well up in the Evelyn Wood Cup, Jerry Ruthven[61] has gone to the Territorial Army and Charlie Willoughby[62] talks of leaving which is a loss of two very good officers to him. I hope to get over for a week about the Regtl dinner and shall see you then with any luck. Plenty of riding and fishing is improving my figure, besides one does not overeat oneself with hotel food here. Generally manage to put in a Saturday to Monday with friends in fact have only spent one Sunday here so far. The 1st Battn are still in the Army football Cup I do wish they would get into the final but am much afraid the Lancashire Fusiliers will beat them. Yours ever, WP Pulteney.

As the letter indicates Putty lived at the Royal Hotel in Fermoy, and was to remain there throughout his time in command of 16 Bde. The Bde HQ would have been too small to have a mess of its own and Putty would not have wanted to live in the Officers Mess of one of his battalions.

He was back in England to chair a meeting of the Army Football Association (AFA) in April; in May he was in London to attend the King's Levée at St James Palace on appointment to command a brigade, and was introduced by General Sir John French, Inspector General of the Forces. In June he was again back in London to attend the Third Guards Club Dinner.

---

59   Major Cecil Lothian Nicholson Worcs (1865-1933) later Major General.
60   Lieutenant Colonel Henry Sinclair Horne (1861-1929) later GOC XV Corps and 1st Army.
61   Gerald Ruthven DAA&QMG 2nd London Division TF.
62   Major Hon Charles Strathven Heathcote-Drummond-Willoughby (1870-1956) SG 1890-1908.

Royal Hotel Fermoy c. 1904, Pulteney's home when Comd 16 Bde.

Camp Aglish, 1910. (County Waterford Image Archive)

On 15 September Putty wrote again to Gerald Cuthbert back on sick leave at Beaufront Castle, this time from Camp Aglish, Cappoquin:

> My dear Cupid, Very sorry to hear from Chipps [Carpenter-Garnier] that you are not quite fit again yet, whatever you do mind you get absolutely right before you return to Egypt or you will very likely never get right. Sir John French comes on to the scene here early tomorrow morning and leaves us again on Thursday so we may expect two strenuous days, have got my brigade into good order but they have got too many young soldiers among them, The Sherwood Foresters [2 Sher For] have had no less than 370 recruits joined them since the 1st January this year. I return to Fermoy on Friday after not having slept out of a tent since 2nd August for a single night, nice hard looking bit of stuff I look now too. Rain we have had in buckets and the glass has begun to go down again which means being wet to the skin for 48 hours. Have got to go to the Curragh on the 28th to run a tactical fitness exam under General Parsons[63] it does seem rather ridiculous when General Plumer [now GOC 5th Division 1907-1911] and all those fellows are stationed there. Expect to be in London on Oct 5th and go up that night to Scotland to fish on the Spey with Ralph Vivian. Poor old Gipps I shall miss him dreadfully. Write me your news. Yours ever, WP Pulteney.

Sometime in 1908 Putty was appointed a Vice President of the AFA alongside General Sir John French and Lieutenant General Sir Horace Smith-Dorrien GOC Aldershot Command, but he continued to serve on the committee, renamed council, and chair it as often as he could.

A letter written by Gladys Heneage from Hainton Hall (home of Lord and Lady Heneage) to Gerald Cuthbert in Cairo on 22 December noted: 'I have seen General Pulteney once or twice over in Ireland, he was at Convamore (home of Earl of Countess of Listowel, Gladys Heneage's mother-in-law's parents) when we were there, he is a most charming person'. Gladys Heneage née Cuthbert was Harold Cuthbert's sister and Gerald Cuthbert was her uncle; the Heneages and Harold Cuthbert were to play a part in the relationship that developed between Putty and Jessie Arnott who eventually became his wife.

Putty wrote to Gerald Cuthbert, now back in Cairo, on 27 December:

> My dear Cupid, A line to wish you luck for 1909 also to tell you to write me the news from your part of the world. Not much doing over here this time of the year but in a couple of months' time we shall begin to worry them again. It has been a very good year for wood-cock over here you would enjoy going after them, there is practically nothing else in the coverts but you have to keep at attention the whole time as they are nippy. I complete my year here on 8 February and expect to be promoted in May in which case shall get away in July after the 3 months grace they give one, a bad time to change a brigadier just as the brigade training commences but that is no affair of mine. The rain lately over here has been practically incessant, combined with the short days it means getting through a lot of reading especially all alone in the evenings. Suppose the question of the regiment will soon crop up conclude Frank Erskine[64] will get it as they will be too narrow minded to offer

---

63   Major General Lawrence Worthington Parsons (1850-1923) late RA GOC 6th Division 1907-1909.
64   Lieutenant Colonel James Francis Erskine (1862-1936) SG 1883-1910 CO 1 SG 1906-1910.

it to you, an admission they are not likely to make [Colonel Cuthbert did command the Regiment 1909-1913]. Have got a draft of the Dublin Fusiliers leaving for your country on 6 January very good lot of men they are too but singularly out of place in the heat it seems to be the only thing that knocks the Irishman out rain and cold they revel in. Write me your news. Yours ever, WP Pulteney.

Putty was promoted to Major General on 1 January 1909 and three months later his time in command of 16 Bde was at an end. Thereafter he concentrated on the AFA and chaired meetings in his house (3 Lower Berkeley Street) on 8 and 29 April, and in Aldershot on 12 April. On 11 April he wrote to Ettie Desborough from Warren House, Coombe Wood, Kingston Hill:[65]

My dear Chief, A line to offer you my very best congratulations for having bred the winner of the Newcastle Scholarship.[66] Splendid work. Remember me in London a poor general on ½ pay who will be at a loose end all the summer. Am staying here with Arthur Paget, burglars got into the house last week and relieved the drawing room of many of what he calls Minnie's trifles, not heirlooms my dear boy he says merely things that can be replaced at a dealers for a few hundred pounds. Yours ever, WP Pulteney.

Putty's only recorded military activities during the rest of the year are the regular meetings of the AFA. However, a letter from General Sir Neville Lyttelton (previously CGS and now CinC Ireland 1908-1912) to his wife from Tourin, Cappoquin, Co Waterford on 11 September is intriguing:

Yesterday was very fine and we had a good days work. Pulteney had a scheme set him which was very well carried out by him and his brigadiers and the battalions were very well handled. Had a similar dinner party as on the previous night, except that Pulteney and two others came over from the camp [probably Camp Aglish].

It seems that Putty was already acting as GOC 6th Division, at least for this training, although he did not take command of the division officially until 1910. The division was commanded by Major General Charles Theophilus Evelyn Metcalfe,[67] but he was unwell and was to leave prematurely. Tourin was the home of Sir Richard John Musgrave:[68] Lyttelton stayed there occasionally, perhaps because it was close to Camp Aglish; Putty stayed there on 12 and 19 September and on many other occasions over the next four years; and the Musgraves were close friends of the Arnotts. Putty may well have met Jessie for the first time at Tourin and they often stayed there at the same time.

The first six months of 1910 were again dominated by the frequent meetings of the AFA. *The Times* recorded on 4 February:

---

65   Home of General Sir Arthur Paget GOC Eastern Command 1908-1911.
66   Her son Billy Grenfell won the Newcastle prize for classics: killed in action 30 July 1915.
67   Major General Charles Theophilus Evelyn Metcalfe (1856-1912) late RB Eton.
68   Sir John Musgrave (1850-1930) 5th Bt.

A command order issued yesterday by Lieutenant General Sir HL Smith-Dorrien, CinC Aldershot Command contains the following appeal to spectators at Army football matches: It has been brought to the attention of the GOCinC by Major General WP Pulteney, President of the Committee of the AFA, that a very undesirable habit is gradually coming into fashion amongst the spectators. The habit referred to consists of shouting remarks to the players such as 'knock him down' or some similar such advice which, besides being bad form, is apt to incite the players to forget themselves.

On 13 May the proclamation of 'King George V' was read in the town square of Fermoy with 2 Sher For and 2 DLI of 16 Bde on parade: it is possible that Putty was also there.

6th Division Cork 1910-1914

Putty took over command of 6th Division on 16 July 1910 from Major General Metcalfe and was to command it for four years, almost to the outbreak of war. The HQ of the division was in Cork and Putty lived in Government House. The division consisted of 16, 17 and 18 Infantry Brigades and the divisional troops. 16 Bde in Fermoy he would have known well; 17 Bde in Cork less so but, inevitably, he would have seen a lot of it; 18 Bde was stationed in Lichfield and he would have only seen it on annual training. The divisional troops were stationed all over the south of Ireland and beyond, and consisted of: one squadron of divisional cavalry; one cyclist company; the divisional artillery of three field artillery brigades each of three field batteries and a brigade ammunition column, a howitzer brigade of three howitzer batteries and a brigade ammunition column, a heavy battery, and the divisional ammunition column; the divisional engineers made up of two field companies and the divisional signal company; and three field ambulances.

Putty's GSO1 for most of the first three years was Colonel Milne RA.[69] His first ADC was Captain Sturgis RB.[70] Sturgis had been Metcalfe's ADC and came on the recommendation of General Lyttelton: one consequence of this was that the CinC was more up to date on Cork gossip than he might otherwise have been. The appointment was a great success, and Putty was to become godfather to Sturgis' son in due course. Lyttelton writing to his wife on 25 July noted:

We got here about 7.30 after a (prosperous) journey with a two hours break at Cork where we had luncheon with Pulteney and a talk about things. Sturgis told me he had heard from Metcalfe who said he was physically stronger, and he had gone to his mother in Bournemouth. Pulteney and Sturgis are very pleased with one another and perhaps he will keep him on.

The 1910 annual manoeuvres were first reported in the *Irish Times* on 27 August:

The military manoeuvres which will be carried out in the Irish Command in September will be on an unusually large scale. With the exception of the few men who will be left in garrison to carry on the necessary duties there, the whole of the troops in Ireland will be engaged.

---

69   George Francis Milne (1866-1948) later Field Marshal 1st Baron Milne.
70   Henry Russell Sturgis (1879-1967) Eton.

Government House Cork, Pulteney's home when GOC 6th Division. (Image courtesy of the National Library of Ireland)

Roughly speaking the 5th Division, of which Major General W Pitcairn Campbell[71] is the GOC will be pitted against the 6th Division which embraces the troops in the south of Ireland, and of which Major General WP Pulteney has lately taken over command.

General Lyttelton was running the manoeuvres and reporting to his wife, to whom he wrote on 5 September from the Royal Hotel in Fermoy:

Pulteney told me Sturgis was doing him very (well) and I hope he will keep him over the years. 18 Bde from England is very good under Gorringe,[72] a very capable man. I had a talk today with Pulteney about pooling the charities and he is to talk to his two brigadiers. I gave him a paper which I had drawn up and I shall have another consultation with them.

The *Irish Times* correspondent reporting from Fermoy on 9 September noted:

This morning the encampment at Moorepark and Kilworth presented a busy spectacle when the force of the 6th Division under command of Major General WP Pulteney struck camp, and prepared for marching to the scene of war.

On 12 September the *Irish Times* reported the start of the manoeuvres and an account of the action is in General Lyttelton's letters to his wife on 14 and 15 September:

So far we have been very lucky with the weather except for a short fall of rain yesterday morning, but it was not general. Pulteney up to date has distinctly got the better of Johnny Campbell. There was a considerable fracas with the cavalry of both sides yesterday [13

71   William Pitcairn Campbell (1856-1933) late KRRC.
72   Brigadier General George Frederick Gorringe (1868-1945) late RE.

September] but the results were much worse for Johnny. Both (measured) their cavalry, but whereas Pulteney got plenty of information from his cyclists though none from his cavalry Johnny got none from either. The marching has been very good so that they got on too fast and I had to put on the (drag) for fear of finishing too soon.

And next day: 'Another fine day but dull. Very brisk fighting in which Pulteney (again) got the better of Campbell'.

In late January 1911 Putty was at the Marquess and Marchioness of Londonderry's house party at Mount Stewart: he may well have met them and the Castlereaghs earlier but it must have been about this time that Putty's friendship with Theresa Londonderry and Edith Castlereagh developed. Sometime in February he attended a Fancy Dress Ball in aid of Queenstown Hospital: on the list of those who attended were the Musgraves and close to Putty on that list is a Miss Arnott. On 2 March, at Victoria Barracks Cork, Putty presented Royal Life-Saving Society Awards for proficiency, assisted by Brigadier General Bewicke-Copley Comd 17 Bde.[73] The *Cork Examiner* reported: 'Major General Pulteney, in a very able speech, congratulated the candidates on their success, and stated that he was pleased to present the various awards. As soldiers they ought to be prepared to go to the assistance of any person in distress'. Later that month he was at the Army Point to Point at Knocklong as Steward, according to the *Irish Times*, or as Patron, according to the *Cork Examiner*. A week later he presented the 6th Division Cup at the Black and Tan Point to Point Races held between Knocklong and Emly (4 miles, 48 fences).

On 17 March General Lyttelton wrote to his wife:

This morning began with family prayers, Lady A[74] playing the harmonium indifferently and singing a hymn with very slight support from the minute congregation. Pulteney, who is said to be deeply in love with a youthful Miss Arnott from Cork, told me that Lady Paget made about £60 by the sale of work.

This is the first evidence of Putty's love which was to have its ups and downs over the next six years; it is more than likely that Lyttelton heard of it directly or indirectly from Sturgis. Putty stayed with the Musgraves at Tourin five times in 1911, on each occasion for several days; Jessie Arnott stayed three times, each coinciding with Putty.

In April Putty was at a house party given by General Lyttelton and his wife at the Royal Hospital in Dublin for the races in Punchestown. The Coronation of King George V took place in June and the *Irish Times* reported on the events in Cork on 11 June: in the morning there was a Special Coronation Service in the military church at which Putty and the staff of HQ 6th Division were present; at noon there was a full dress parade of troops taken by Putty; and in the afternoon a Coronation Service was held in St Finn Barre's Cathedral with Putty again present.

On 14 June he attended the Lord Mayor of Cork's Reception and two days later was at the High Sherriff's Garden Party; the guest lists suggest that Jessie Arnott and other members of her family were at both. With so many commitments in Ireland his visits to England became less frequent, especially his attendance at meetings of the AFA, but he was back in London on 4

73 Brigadier General Bewicke-Copley Comd 17 Bde (1855-1923) late KRRC.
74 Probably Lady Aberdeen – Ishbel Hamilton-Gordon wife of 7th Earl Lord Lieutenant of Ireland 1905-1915.

July for the baptism of the son of Major Lord Esmé[75] and Lady Gordon-Lennox at the Guards Chapel. Putty was to be a godfather; he had numerous god-children, perhaps ten or more.

King George V visited Ireland in July: Putty attended Lord and Lady Powerscourt's[76] house party at Powerscourt for the Royal Visit and a few days later was presented at the King's Levée by General Lyttelton. On 24 July he was back in Cork with General Lyttelton staying with him, and the following month he had lunch with the Lytteltons in Dublin. The Irish Command manoeuvres were held as usual in September with Putty commanding 6th Division in the field. Lyttelton wrote to his wife on 16 September, the day after the manoeuvres ended: 'I don't see how I can have Sturgis as extra ADC. Pulteney does not at all like losing him'. There is no obvious explanation for the change of ADCs about to happen in 1912 other than it was time for Sturgis to move on. It was in September that year, and partly when 6th Division was in the Field, that Putty 'incurred the grave displeasure of the Army Council' over its selection of Colonel Milne for an appointment in the War Office. Following a number of letters and telegrams, Putty was deemed to have over-stepped the mark on Milne's behalf (with his agreement) in objecting to the appointment because he considered Milne should be promoted. This was to have little, if any, impact on Putty's career: Sir John French became CIGS in early 1912.

On 22 November Putty was shooting at Castle Forbes in Aberdeenshire.[77] The other guns were the Earl of Rosse,[78] Viscount Powerscourt (with whom Putty had stayed in July), Lord Hamilton of Dalzell,[79] Earl of Granard (SG) and Lord Herschell.[80]

1912 was a similar year. In January Putty attended the Marchioness of Ormonde's[81] house party at Kilkenny Castle for the Kilkenny Hunt Ball; in March he was back in London for the King's Levée at St James Palace. Captain Balfour[82] became his ADC on 1 April and was to continue in the appointment until the outbreak of war when he returned to 1 SG.

On 15 June Putty must have been at Government House, Cork because it was from there that he wrote to Gerald Cuthbert (now Lieutenant Colonel Commanding SG): 'My best congratulations on your well-deserved CB. Shall hope to see you at the Regtl Dinner'. He did get back for the dinner at the Ritz Hotel on 24 June, an occasion he rarely missed; Field Marshal Lord Methuen presided. In July Putty was again in England, attending the King and Queen's State Ball at Buckingham Palace.

He was at Leopardstown Races in August as a guest of General Paget (late SG previously GOC Eastern Command) in the Royal Pavilion on the course. Paget had taken over as CinC Ireland from Lyttelton, and Putty was fortunate to have another CinC that he knew very well. However, Major General Fergusson's[83] biographer describes Paget: 'His carefree attitude to his army career might have brought it to an early end but for good fortune and the support of King Edward VII' and 'Physically too he was extremely fit and active. None the less, this old

75 Major Lord Esmé Gordon-Lennox (1875-1949) SG 1896-1920.
76 Mervyn Wingfield 8th Viscount Powerscourt (1880-1947).
77 Home of Horace Courtenay Gammell Forbes 19th Lord Forbes (1823-1914).
78 William Parsons 5th Earl (1873-1918) IG died of wounds.
79 Lord Hamilton of Dalzell SG and Putty's ADC in 1915.
80 Richard Farrer Herschell 2nd Baron (1878-1929) PS to Earl of Aberdeen Lord Lieutenant of Ireland 1905-1907 Government Whip in Lords 1907-1915.
81 Wife of John Arthur Wellington Foley Butler 4th Marquess of Ormonde (1849-1943).
82 Robert Frederick Balfour (1883-1914) SG 1903-1914 Putty's Adjt in 2 SG killed in action.
83 Late Gren Gds now GOC 5th Division.

war-horse should have been put out to grass years ago. He was too out of date, too casual and intellectually too shallow'. If this view reflects that of Fergusson, it is hardly surprising in the light of what was to come.

In March 1913 Putty went on leave for Easter to the Continental Hotel, Cannes: the south of France was a favourite spot whenever he had the opportunity, especially in later life. He was back by 4 April because he wrote that day to Ettie Desborough (Lady in Waiting to Queen Mary since 1911):

> My dear Chief, A line to say how sorry I am about poor Lady Cowper.[84] I realise how much you will feel her death, she was often so kind to me at Panshanger. I shall never forget her besides the first time I ever saw you was at a shooting party at Brocket, a nice fluffy haired girl with a twinkle in her eye who has grown nicer ever since. Wish you could have seen a Bridge tournament I gave here yesterday in aid of the Cork Industrial Society, 16 Corkites came to luncheon and 14 tables full of various arrivals competed we cleared £14 which was very good I felt to entertain with an object did more good than the usual garden party, one lady came with practically no clothes on, even Lady Castletown[85] blind as she is came and asked if she would not catch cold! Had a good out at Cannes the change and rest set me up after this relaxing place besides getting into gossip woke me up I never heard such a place for scandal, they all thought that Lord Warwick[86] was going to die and that Lady W[87] would marry Aster,[88] so I said she would be a Michaelmas Daisy then! Not bad for me. Launcelot Lowther's[89] French lady was out here but she puts so much powder on her cheeks it must take him a long time to get through. Shall not be over in England until beginning of May. Yours ever, Putty.

His reported activities in the next five months were mainly social. In April he attended the Pagets' house party at the Royal Hospital, Dublin for Punchestown week; he was a guest at the King and Queen's State Ball at Buckingham Palace in July; and at the Pagets' house party for the Dublin Horse Show week in August. Later that month he was at a dance given by the Earl and Countess of Aberdeen at Vice Regal Lodge in Dublin.

The annual manoeuvres took place in September. Reporting the previous divisional training, the *Irish Times* wrote on 12 September:

> The 6th Division under command of Major General WP Pulteney carried out some excellent manoeuvres today in the district north-west of Limerick Junction, notwithstanding that the troops had a very trying time owing to the inclemency of the weather. It rained

84   Wife of 7th Earl Cowper one of the wealthiest landowners in the country. He had no children and virtually adopted his niece Ethel and left Panshanger to her.
85   Possibly Emily Ursula Clare St Leger (1853-1927) wife of 2nd Baron Castletown (1848-1937) Eton LG.
86   Francis Greville 5th Earl of Warwick (1853-1924) Eton.
87   Frances Evelyn 'Daisy' Greville Countess of Warwick (1861-1938).
88   Probably William Waldorf Astor 1st Viscount Astor (1848-1919) whose first wife died 1894.
89   Probably Lancelot Edward Lowther later 6th Earl of Lonsdale (1867-1953).

incessantly all day, and from an early hour the soldiers were drenched through. Heavy roads made the marching very tiresome.

However, it was *The Times* that reported on the main manoeuvres that started on 15 September in considerable detail. Again there must have been a preliminary phase as these extracts from a report on 16 September from Nenagh and later indicate:

> The struggle for the pass between Nenagh and Thurles was continued today by the forces under Sir Charles Fergusson and General Pulteney, and a very interesting battle took place. Last night each commander held one half of the pass with his advanced troops, while the bulk of his command was camped near his end of the defile. The outposts of the two forces within the pass were from half a mile to a mile apart. No movements in advance of this line of outposts were permitted till 7.30 am today. The objective of General Fergusson's 5th Division was the flank of the main White Army to the eastward. A chain of commanding heights runs eastward from a point near the northern entrance to the pass to Knockanora Hill, 1,429 ft high, some three miles distant. If the 5th Division could occupy these heights in time it seemed likely that it might fend off any attack by General Pulteney and then remain in a good position to carry out its original mission.
>
> Sir Charles Fergusson issued orders to resume the offensive this morning. He directed Brigadier General Capper[90] to move at 4.30 am with his 13 Bde and 15 Bde RFA to occupy Knockanora. Brigadier General Rolt's[91] 14 Bde was given for its first objective some spurs which run down from the mountains towards the pass, while Count Gleichen's[92] 15 Bde was at first retained in general reserve near the northern end of the pass. 8, 24 and 28 Bdes RFA were directed to occupy positions of readiness on the spurs allotted to 14 Bde. The cavalry were sent off to the right, while the transport was packed in readiness for movement.
>
> General Pulteney's orders were equally business-like. His advanced guard was ordered to move forward to make the enemy disclose his dispositions, and his remaining troops were held ready to operate as required. His cavalry were ordered to act against the enemy's left flank, and trains were packed in readiness for movement. As the advanced guard moved forward it quickly accomplished its object of causing the enemy to reveal his dispositions. General Fergusson's orders had been carried out to the letter. From the dominating heights artillery opened, and in combination with General Rolt's well-handled brigade, made things lively for Brigadier General Ingouville-Williams[93] 16 Bde, which formed the advanced guard. General Pulteney brought the whole of his artillery into action in good positions, but was unable to make further headway. He therefore brought up Brigadier General Congreve's[94] 18 Bde, which prolonged the line to the right, and in particular occupied Monamaddra Hill, 1,013 ft high, a little more than a mile south of Knockanora. General Congreve found a massive bank, which gave his firing line excellent cover.

90 Thompson Capper (1863-1915) late E Lancs killed in action.
91 Stuart Peter Rolt (1862-1933) late Y&L.
92 Lord Edward Gleichen (1863-1937) late Gren Gds.
93 Edward Charles Ingouville-Williams (1861-1916) late E Kent killed in action.
94 Walter Norris Congreve VC (1862-1927) late RB later General.

General Pulteney's position was now improved, and he awaited the developments which were not long in coming. General Capper had occupied the long crest of Knockanora as ordered, but the length of the front was excessive for his command, and the extreme eastern end of the hill, was only lightly occupied. Colonel Hogg 4 H was quick to seize the opportunity that now offered itself. Dismounting his regiment, he attacked the height on foot, carried it, and brought up his horse battery, which enfiladed and harassed the Brown troops in occupation of the crest line. General Capper could no longer conceal his position. He sent two companies to retake the hill, but they were repulsed, and from this time forward 4 H and the horse guns monopolised the attention of a whole battalion. General Capper was already short of a battalion, left in Dublin, and when eventually General Fergusson ordered an advance 13 Bde could only use two battalions for attack. 4 H thus proved most valuable to General Pulteney and showed what cavalry can do when closely co-operating with its sister arms.

General Pulteney was in no hurry to advance. He was in a good position to resist an attack and if his enemy marched away eastward he could be pursued. Sir Charles Fergusson was bound to dispose of General Pulteney in order to obtain freedom of manoeuvre for prosecuting his mission, and he consequently determined to bring up all his available troops and to make a simultaneous attack upon General Pulteney's centre and right. The attack was very well executed. General Capper's two battalions, admirably led, crept down from the heights and made use of every inch of cover to close with General Congreve on Monamaddra, but numbers and ground were against them and the attack failed. General Rolt's Brigade, reinforced by part of Count Gleichen's Brigade and supported by a heavy fire from the guns and maxims, made a furious attack upon General Pulteney's centre. This attack also was conducted in good style, but it was adjudged to have failed mainly because 3 RB lining the rough ground at the western end of Monamaddra brought a severe enfilading fire to bear upon his attack, and must have caused it serious losses. Both attacks, nevertheless, came near to success and proved, once more, how well the troops in Ireland have been trained. Most commanders in General Pulteney's position would now have thrown their reserves into the fight for a vigorous counter-stroke in order to profit by the enemy's repulse. General Pulteney, however, judged otherwise. He had been successful and carried out the mission entrusted to him. Had he led his men against the steep slopes of Knockanora he would certainly have suffered heavy losses from Sir Charles Fergusson's well posted artillery, and the tables might easily have been turned upon him. He therefore did well to be content with his success and not to compromise his position by an act of imprudence. On learning General Pulteney's decision General Sir Arthur Paget promptly stopped the operations and sent the troops back to their camps in preparation for the command manoeuvres, which begin tomorrow.

The Times reports continued on 18 September with the 'Battle of Dunkerrin':

When my last report was sent off the 3rd Brown Army, under the command of General Sir Arthur Paget CinC Ireland, was on the march to attack a White Army which was reported to be in position two miles south-east of Dunkerrin. In order to strike at his enemy effectively General Paget had first to march north and then wheel to the right. This operation afforded a useful test of the staff work in the command and the march discipline of the troops. General Pulteney's 6th Division formed the right column on the inside or eastern flank. It marched from Toomyvara by Barna towards Dunkerrin, halting about three miles short of this place, covered by an advanced guard. Sir Charles Fergusson's 5th Division moved by a parallel road to the westward and halted at Kilcomin. General Gough's[95] Cavalry Brigade, which formed the outer column, moved from Nenagh upon Shinrone. The march was well regulated and well executed. Units were well closed up, the hired and other transport preserved its distances, and few checks occurred. Reporting centres were established first at Cloghjordan and then near Kilcomin.

As General Paget reached these centres the airmen of the RFC came back from the front to report. General Capper (White commander) had taken up a position about three miles long: 16 Bde of General Pulteney's division was the first in action, and after a brisk skirmish occupied Dunkerrin as an advanced post. General Fergusson similarly pushed forward his advanced guard to Brooklawn and drove in the White outposts. General Gough, on the left, was opposed by a force of cavalry stronger than his own and was unable to make headway. The afternoon was spent in reconnaissance of the position by 2nd Aeroplane Squadron and the divisions. When all the reports had been received Sir Arthur Paget collected his commanders and issued his orders for the attack. These orders first described the White position so far as it was known. The objectives of the two divisions were assigned, and the front of attack was divided between them. They were ordered to be deployed on the Dunkerrin-Roscrea road, about two miles north of the position, by 4.30 this morning, and they were directed to advance at that hour to the attack of the enemy's main position. The cavalry was ordered to cooperate on the left. The divisional and brigade commanders issued their orders conformably with these instructions. Column routes were reconnoitred and assigned, while positions for the guns were carefully selected.

General Capper's position was a fairly strong one with a command of about 300 ft over the ground in front. From Castleroan eastward he occupied four tactical points which were entrenched and given a suitable garrison, the guns were well placed, and the reserve was massed in the rear of the centre. Below and along the whole front of his position was a maze of small fields with steep, high banks topped by thick, untrimmed hedges, which gave an assailant cover indeed, but offered a serious obstacle to movement. The Brown columns deployed at the appointed hour with the utmost regularity and began their advance. General Pulteney was first in contact on the Brown right against Castleroan, whence a spiteful fire broke out at 5 am. By this hour it was dawn, and as the mists cleared away the artillery of the two sides came into action and fighting became general. 16 Bde of General Pulteney's division led the attack on Castleroan. It was supported by 17 Bde while 18 Bde was at first in reserve. A long struggle took place for the two tactical positions in this part of the field, and it was not until after two hours of fighting that the resistance of the enemy and the difficulties of the ground were overcome.

As the Brown divisions, their order slightly disturbed by the resistance encountered, offered ragged edges on the points attacked, General Capper's reserve came out and had a cut at them. The attack failed for lack of numbers and eventually, pressed and harried, White withdrew towards the river Nore. The lie of the ground, the scarcity of roads, and

95   Hubert de la Poer Gough (1870-1963) late 16 L Eton.

the almost inaccessible character of these Irish fields prevented the Brown artillery from harassing White in his retreat. Commanders and staffs gave proof of competence and the troops of vigour and high training. There was little to criticise, and Sir Arthur Paget has only reason to be satisfied with the forces in Ireland.

This article, although somewhat complacent, does give an indication of the preparedness of the army for war, and particularly 6th Division and Putty. The official inspection report is also complimentary: it is dated 12 September which suggests that it took place just before the start of the Command manoeuvres: Report of the Inspection of the 6th Division in the field by the Inspector-General of the Home Forces (submitted to the Army Council in his Annual Report 1914). The report includes orders given to GOC, his orders to the division, and various opinions of the IG. He concluded:

> I was of the opinion that the GOC 6th Division trusted too much to his cavalry to obtain his information. The Divisional Cavalry was weak and unable to compel the enemy to disclose his dispositions. The march discipline of the division was somewhat disappointing, which I am afraid was not entirely attributable to the bad weather. Speaking generally, the work of the division was excellent, in spite of the trying conditions under which the operations were carried out. CW Douglas General.[96]

The issue of forcing Ulster into Home Rule with the rest of Ireland had been simmering for some time but it was only towards the end of the year that the position of the army became a matter of intense and open debate. If the army was to be used to enforce Home Rule 'would it fight' was a hypothetical question that became very emotive; it led to debates on whether officers could and should resign before any order was given, whether officers with an interest in Ulster could resign, and the implications of refusing to serve there. The officers most involved in what became known as the 'Curragh Incident' were mainly in 3 Cav Bde, including Gough, and in units of 5th Division also stationed at the Curragh. Contingency planning was not directly about enforcement but more organising a show of force to deter any breakdown of law and order; security of arms and ammunition held in armouries throughout Ulster was one of the greatest concerns.

An extract from Lieutenant General Sir John Spencer Ewart's[97] diary on 14 November summarises the issue:

> Meeting of the Selection Board. Afterwards Sir Arthur Paget came to see me about Ireland. He told me that both his divisional Generals thought that 25 per cent of the officers in Ireland would resign if there was any question of coercing Ulster. He himself put it at 15 per cent. He said it was impossible to forecast what the men would do.

In January 1914 Putty was a guest of Sir Charles and Lady Barrington[98] for the woodcock shoot at Glenstal, and it was generally a quieter winter, the last before the storm. But before that

---

96   Charles Whittingham Douglas (1850-1914) late Gordons Inspector General Home Forces 1912-1914 CIGS 1914.
97   Lieutenant General Sir John Spencer Ewart (1861-1930) late Camerons AG 1910-1914.
98   Charles Burton Barrington 5th Bt (1848-1943).

broke there was the problem of Ulster to be addressed. On the afternoon of 20 March Paget held his second conference of the day in the Royal Hospital, Dublin. It started at 2 pm with Putty and his two bde comds, Ingouville-Williams Comd 16 Bde and Doran (late R Irish) Comd 17 Bde, amongst those present. According to Major General Fergusson, who was also there:

> The Commander of the Forces (Paget) said that he believed we had all read his speech at the Corinthian Club, which gave his views. Were all officers prepared to accept them? Those present notified that they were prepared to do so, General Doran stating his repugnance to the situation. I understood that should there be any disturbance in the north, the 5th Division supplemented by 11 Bde from Colchester would move probably to the line of the Boyne. It would be reinforced by the 1st Division from Aldershot. The 6th Division, less necessary garrisons for the south which were subsequently worked out by Generals Pulteney and Friend[99] would move to Dublin reinforced by its 18 Bde from England. It was explained that there would be no act of aggression: that a big demonstration would, it was hoped, meet the case. At 2.45 pm the 6th Division brigadiers left to return to their commands.

Meanwhile Brigadier General Gough and officers 3 Cav Bde had threatened resignation rather than be used in the apparently planned military coercion of Ulster into accepting Irish Home Rule. Gough secured a guarantee from Secretary of State for War (Seely) that the army would not be so employed. Seely, French (now CIGS) and Ewart (AG) later all resigned when that guarantee was repudiated by Asquith's Cabinet.

On 22 March Brigadier General Forestier-Walker[100] issued a memorandum confirming the contingency plans for 6th Division: 18 Bde to move from Lichfield to Dublin; HQ 6th Division and three battalions to move from Cork to Dublin; battalions to Curragh, Cork, Kinsale and Fermoy (with two batteries); half battalions to Limerick and Tipperary.

Two letters written on 23 March indicate where some people thought blame and responsibility lay for the 'Curragh Incident'. Congreve Comd 18 Bde wrote to Gough Comd 3 Cav Bde:

> News travels slowly here and I have only just got my paper telling me how you have been making history. I write a line to tell you how much I sympathise with you and how rightly I think you have acted. I had made up my mind long ago to do the same – but it is dreadful that we should be driven to such action by this d...d Government and men like Paget who I feel convinced has been bought body and soul. Good luck to you – and am sure you will be no loser for your action in this.

The other letter of interest that day was from Theodore Riversdale Walrond (1860-1917) to Lord Milner.[101] An extract is:

> Paget who could and perhaps should have treated the matter as a military operation in support of the civil power (ie under the law) to maintain law and order in Ulster, instead

---

99   Lovick Bransby Friend (1856-1944) late RE Major General Administration Irish Command.
100 George Townshend Forestier-Walker (1866-1939) late RA BGGS Irish Command.
101 Alfred Milner 1st Viscount Milner (1854-1925) businessman and politician.

gave the officers under his command (starting with 3 Cav Bde) the choice before they started of shooting down Ulstermen or being dismissed without a pension.

Putty's only recorded views were in a letter from Government House, Cork on 19 April to Paget in the first instance and presumably in response to one seeking his views:

> My opinion of the general state of feeling existing in the 6th Division, as regards Ulster, is as follows:
> 1. They can be relied on to support law and order.
> 2. They would not enforce home rule on an actively reluctant Ulster.
> 3. There is little chance of this feeling altering unless HM the King proclaims the Ulster Volunteers as rebels.
> 4. In fact the Troops would move for the King.

A few days later the *Irish Times* reported:

> A very fine spectacle was witnessed at Killusty, near Fethard, Co Tipperary when 43 Bty RFA (Fethard) and 86 Bty RFA (Clomei) fired on targets on the northern slope of Slievenamon Mountain. Each battery had six guns. General Pulteney superintended the operations. The marksmanship of both batteries, especially the 86th, was exceptionally good.

Putty was probably visiting but it is interesting that events in Ulster were not allowed to interfere with training.

Contingency planning continued but otherwise life returned to normal. In May Putty attended the opening of the annual exhibition of the County Cork Industrial Association in County Hall. Then, in June, he was a guest at a State Dinner given by the Lord Lieutenant at Vice Regal Lodge to celebrate the King's birthday, before travelling to London for the Third Guards Club dinner at the Ritz Hotel the next night: it was the last until after the war and Putty was in the Chair.

He was dragged back in to the aftermath of the 'Curragh Incident' in June as Paget tried to explain, to the King's Private Secretary and others, his use of the King's name. Putty wrote to Paget from Government House, Cork on 29 June:

> My dear General, General Friend has told me about Lord Stamfordham's letter to you with reference to your using the King's name at the conferences on the 20th March. What happened at the conference either in the morning before luncheon or the one after either General Fergusson or General Doran asked you if they were the King's orders, you replied all orders are from the King, the manner in which you said it left me perfectly certain that you personally had had no instructions from the King himself about the scheme or possible action, so much was this conveyed to my mind that I never used the King's name in the conference with my brigadiers, nor do I believe for one second that if any of us had thought you had had personal instructions from the King that any officer or man would have failed to answer the call whatever they were bidden to do. You will find this borne out by my letter to General Forestier-Walker when asked for my views of the feelings of the troops in the

matter after the crisis when I said that I did not think the officers would go unless it was the King's personal wish. Yours ever WP Pulteney.

After four years Putty's time in command of 6th Division was now at an end and he handed over to Major General Keir[102] in July. In the ten years since South Africa he had again commanded a battalion (for 4 years), then a brigade, and lastly a division (also for 4 years). He was 53 years old and there can have been few of his contemporaries with more experience in command. 6th Division performed well both in barracks and in the field under his command. The British Army only had six regular divisions and any weakness or transgression would have been quickly noted, yet none were.

The evidence of the Irish Command manoeuvres in 1913 reveals a little of Putty's character. His decision to consolidate rather than exploit his success against 5th Division shows close attention to the orders that he had been given: this was repeated on numerous occasions in the years ahead. Arguably it demonstrated undue caution even lack of initiative but equally this prudence and sense of purpose was one of the attributes that earned him the trust of his superiors. They knew that if they ordered him to do something he would do it, no more, no less, to the very best of his ability.

Three senior officers may well have contributed to the rise of Putty's star during these years. French had got to know Putty very well in South Africa; Putty served briefly under him when he was GOC Aldershot Command 1905-1907; and then French would have seen him from time to time when he was IG 1907-1912. French was President of the Selection Board 1907-1912 and probably when Putty was appointed to 16 Bde and 6th Division; finally, as CIGS 1912-1914, General French no doubt would have watched Putty's progress closely. The other two were his CinCs in Ireland. Lyttelton had been in the same house as Putty at Eton, although many years earlier, and Putty served under him in South Africa. Before becoming CinC Ireland he had been CGS (later renamed CIGS) 1904-1908. He saw Putty in command of 16 Bde and, initially, 6th Division. His successor, Paget, knew him exceptionally well both being Scots Guardsmen, and having served together in South Africa. Luck is always a factor in advancement and in having these three 'friends' as his superiors Putty was indeed fortunate; at the same time there is no evidence that any of them showed unjustified favouritism or that he sought it. He seems to have done well at each level of command and justified his advancement.

Putty got to know the King and the Prince of Wales well while he was CO 2 SG and, in King George V's later words, were friends. However, there is nothing to suggest this extended beyond shooting in the same party from time to time, and being invited to Buckingham Palace or Windsor Castle.

Some have expressed surprise that Paget did not get command of III Corps: even if he was not ruled out on age, the events at the Curragh would have hardly endeared him to French. Edmonds writing in 1937 claimed that Paget was the best choice to command III Corps in 1914, but was passed over because he had a row with French on manoeuvres in 1913. Few would have shared Edmonds' view: there seems little doubt that Putty was French's choice.

The 'grave displeasure of the Army Council' was to be forgotten, at least for the time being.

102 John Lindsay Keir (1856-1937) late RA.

7

III Corps Command 1914

War was declared on 4 August 1914: Putty was promoted to temporary Lieutenant General the following day. The day after (6 August), at Kitchener's meeting, the decisions taken included the appointment of French as CinC BEF, the appointment of three corps commanders (Haig I, Grierson II and Pulteney III), and the concentration of the BEF at Amiens. Putty was probably given some warning by French but it all happened very quickly. Unlike I and II Corps, the headquarters of III Corps did not exist; staff and equipment had to be assembled. Expeditionary Force Tables November 1912 set out in detail where each unit was located in peace time, where it was to mobilise and where its mobilisation equipment was held. Under army troops were the three echelons of GHQ and the HQs of two 'armies' all to mobilise at Southampton. There was no provision for a third 'army' – III Corps. A biographer of Henry Wilson[1] noted: 'The intention at the outset had been to call the forces under the three subordinate commanders, Haig, Grierson and Pulteney; but on the 11th was very sensibly altered to Army Corps'.

Just one example of the adhoc arrangements for III Corps was the setting up of the Corps Signal Company. Their war diary for 5 August states:

> First day of mobilisation. HQ 3rd Army Signal Company is to be formed by conversion of an airline section after its arrival in the area of concentration. Following additional personnel are to be provided: 1 Major, 1 Captain, 1 CSM, 1 CQMS, 1 Sergt, 2 batmen, 4 lorry drivers. These are to be obtained from Army Signal School (including Major Newbigging OC), RE Depot Chatham and RE Training Depot. The above with motor cyclists (1 Sergt, 1 artificer, and 10 Corporals) provided by RE Records will mobilise at Southampton by the 10th day. Two 30 cwt motor lorries and 4 lorry drivers will be sent by WO to Southampton on the 9th day.

To compound Putty's difficulties there was no established doctrine on what a corps should consist of or how it should operate. Since he had not been to the Staff College it is unlikely that he gave these matters much thought although the Irish Command manoeuvres would have given him some guidance. There was little time for the headquarters to do any training; they would have to learn on the job. The *Staff Manual (War) Provisional 1912* pointed out that 'the

---

1   Major General Henry Wilson (1864-1922) late RB Sub COS HQ BEF.

efficient performance of staff duties is far more difficult in a new organisation than in one which has existed for some time, and in which commanders and staff know each other well and are accustomed to work together'. It was not to be. However, a very capable if rather top heavy team of staff officers was appointed over the next few days; remember that the headquarters would have to function 24 hours a day, indefinitely.

The Brigadier General, General Staff (BGGS), the chief of staff, was Brigadier General John Du Cane late RA, an officer known to be 'laid back'. Under him there was a GSO1 Lieutenant Colonel Maude Coldm Gds, two GSO2s Major Harington King's Liverpool and Major Davidson KRRC, and a GSO3 Captain Pitt-Taylor RB. The Deputy Adjutant and Quartermaster General (DA&QMG), the personnel and logistics officer, was Brigadier General Charles McGrigor late KRRC who had been at Eton with Putty and was a year older than him. Under him was an AA&QMG Colonel Chichester late Dorset, AQMG Colonel Du Boulay late RA and DAA&QMG Major Wingfield RB.

The BGRA was Brigadier General Phipps-Hornby VC and the CE was Brigadier General Glubb. Their roles developed during the war to command of the artillery and engineers in the corps but at this stage they had no staff and their role was purely advisory. There were four other specialist officers: DDMS' role was also more one of coordination and advice, and he also acted as MO to the headquarters; the Supply Officer supported the headquarters – supply and ordnance matters in the corps were the responsibility of the Q Staff; the APM's two main responsibilities were traffic control and enforcement of discipline; an officer responsible for postal services completed the team. Further information on the staff and their successors is in Appendix B.

Lieutenant Robert Balfour had been Putty's ADC before the war but he rejoined 1 SG on mobilisation and was killed in action at Ypres on 27 October. The Scots Guards could not provide ADCs until later in the war when officers who had been wounded or were unfit for front line service became available; until then RHG provided his two ADCs. Captain Viscount Castlereagh (Charlie, sometimes Charley), to be Marquess of Londonderry when his father died in 1915, was 35 years old and had been at Eton and Sandhurst. He did not serve in South Africa but was appointed adjutant of RHG in London at the young age of 22. In 1901 he was Field Marshal Lord Wolseley's ADC when he was tasked by King Edward VII with formally announcing his succession to the Courts of Europe and beyond. Then, in the General Election of 1906, he was elected MP for Maidstone. In Parliament he became involved in Haldane's Territorial and Reserve Forces Bill, coal mining issues (he was the owner of several mines in Co Durham), tariff reforms, women's suffrage (in which his wife, Edith, was very interested), 1911 Parliament Bill, and 3rd Irish Home Rule Bill. He had contacts at the highest level including both the King and Prime Minister; he was very wealthy, considered to be among the wealthiest men in the Country; and was reported to be self-opinionated bordering on arrogant. It is diffi-cult to imagine someone less suitable to be Putty's ADC at such a demanding time: Putty's friendship with Castlereagh's mother and his wife played a major part in the appointment. He wrote to Edith in early August:

> Dear Lady C. I have done it for you at the War Office and will take Charley. What are you doing tonight! If not dining out let us dine together. I willingly take Charley but did not mean to answer his own request unless I had been sure you wished him to go, you are a brave and (best) woman. Yours ever, Putty.

His relationship with Edith was a very close one as this and the many subsequent letters reveal.

It started well. On 24 August Castlereagh wrote to his wife: 'I hate the separation from you but it was bound to come in some form or other, and this for me is very pleasant, to be going with Putty'. He wrote to Ettie Desborough at about the same time: 'Putty has been more than charming and makes everything so easy'.

His other ADC was Captain Reginald Earl of Pembroke and Montgomery RHG, also an Etonian, although a year younger than Castlereagh. Before the war Pembroke had been ADC to General Paget CinC Ireland, so Putty would have known him well, and this choice was an obvious and sensible one. Not to be forgotten was 2590 Private George Charles Hogbin SG, Putty's orderly, who had been with him since South Africa and was to remain with him for the rest of his life. Another key member of the team was the Camp Commandant, Lieutenant Colonel Rose BW, responsible for the administration of the headquarters. Rose was a regular officer and had commanded 1 BW. He served as Camp Commandant HQ III Corps for all of the time Putty commanded the corps and, since they were of similar age, their relationship would have been a close one.

On 20 August Putty, Du Cane and Maude went to Harrow to see 4th Division (Major General Snow) which was to begin moving to France the next day. By 26 August HQ III Corps was assembled at the Polygon Hotel in Southampton: in addition to the 19 officers there were 2 warrant officers, 8 sergeants, 4 corporals and 73 privates, a total of 106 all ranks. The other ranks included clerks, orderlies, grooms, drivers, cooks and signallers. It would take time for them to learn their respective jobs in the field, and it is very doubtful if any of them thought they might have to face the enemy. Harington (GSO 2 HQ III Corps) wrote:

> There was only one man who was glad when Joe Maude left us and that was our head clerk. He had been in the War Office before the war and was used to putting on his hat at 5 pm and going home. He did not understand war. Colonel Maude was a man so full of energy that when he dictated an order he expected it to be typed and issued in a moment. This was always too much for the head clerk.

With the headquarters were 51 horses, 6 motor cars and 3 motor lorries (one for the electric light equipment). That they were able to assemble all the equipment they required in a very short time owed much to the mobilisation officer, Major Wingfield, but they would have had very little time to learn how to use it all. Nevertheless all the arrangements worked smoothly and at 10 pm 26 August they embarked on SS *Braemar Castle* and sailed for Le Havre, arriving at noon the following day, and disembarked to set up the headquarters for the first time on French soil at the Hotel de Normandie. Before they left Putty had said his farewells to family and friends; he sent this telegram to Edith Castlereagh: 'Very sorry to have not seen you at station au revoir and all blessings. Putty'.

Next day, 28 August, Putty went to Rouen to see the Inter-Governmental Commission: on the morning of 29 August he motored round the vicinity of Le Havre in connection with the scheme for its defence, an indication perhaps that Sir John French was contemplating withdrawal of the BEF to its base. But during the day he received orders to report to GHQ at Compiègne and set off by car with Du Cane via Paris, with the rest of the staff following either by road later in the evening or by train the next day. They had had little idea what was happening and rumours were rife.

HQ III Corps was established operationally for the first time in the school at Villeneuve sur Verberie on 30 August; much of that day was spent by Putty and his staff visiting GHQ, being briefed on the situation, and preparing to take over command of its first units (4th Division and independent 19 Bde) the following day. Considering what was happening during these days, with the BEF in full retreat, this must have been extremely difficult. 6th Division had been held back by Kitchener in England, and was to join it later.

Analysis of Putty's performance in the Great War requires a detailed understanding of III Corps' actions; most will be as a consequence, direct or indirect, of a decision made by Putty. The III Corps' story that follows draws heavily on official sources but is supplemented where appropriate by the recollections of individuals. Any correspondence of Putty's, both official and private, has been included, to try and give an insight to the man behind the decisions. Inevitably the story includes a mass of detail about units and individuals but this provides important background. The organisation of III Corps in 1914 is included to provide a start point for what follows; thereafter organisational changes are only mentioned if they are especially relevant. Three groups of people would have seen Putty at close hand during the three and a half years that he commanded III Corps, his superior commanders (Appendix A), his subordinate commanders (Appendix D), and his own staff (Appendix B). Their views are included whenever possible.

The order of battle of III Corps at the outset was:

HQ III Corps
Corps Troops: Two troops Irish Horse (IH) – Sep 1914

4th Division

B Squadron 19th Hussars (B Sqn 19 H)

10th Infantry Brigade (10 Bde)
1st Battalion Royal Warwickshire Regiment (1 Warwicks)
2nd Battalion Seaforth Highlanders (2 Seaforth)
1st Battalion Royal Irish Fusiliers (1 R Irish Fus)
2nd Battalion Royal Dublin Fusiliers (2 RDF)

11th Infantry Brigade (11 Bde)
1st Battalion Somerset Light Infantry (1 Som LI)
1st Battalion East Lancashire Regiment (1 E Lancs)
1st Battalion Hampshire Regiment (1 Hamps)
1st Battalion Rifle Brigade (1 RB)

12th Infantry Brigade (12 Bde)
1st Battalion Royal Lancaster Regiment (King's Own) (1 RLR)
2nd Battalion Lancashire Fusiliers (2 LF)
2nd Battalion Royal Inniskilling Fusiliers (2 Innis Fus)
2nd Battalion Essex Regiment (2 Essex)

14th Brigade Royal Field Artillery (14 Bde RFA) with 39, 68 and 88 Batteries (Btys)
29th Brigade Royal Field Artillery (29 Bde RFA) with 125, 126 and 127 Batteries (Btys)
32nd Brigade Royal Field Artillery (32 Bde RFA) with 27, 134 and 135 Batteries (Btys)
37th (Howitzer) Brigade Royal Field Artillery (37 Bde RFA) with 31, 35 and 55 Batteries
(Btys) – 4.5"
31st Heavy Battery Royal Garrison Artillery (31 Hy Bty RGA) – 60 pounders

7th Field Company Royal Engineers (7 Fd Coy RE)
9th Field Company Royal Engineers (9 Fd Coy RE)

6th Division

C Squadron 19th Hussars (C Sqn 19 H)

16th Infantry Brigade (16 Bde)
1st Battalion East Kent Regiment (Buffs) (1 E Kent)
1st Battalion Leicestershire Regiment (1 Leics)
1st Battalion Shropshire Light Infantry (1 SLI)
2nd Battalion York and Lancaster Regiment (2 Y&L)

17th Infantry Brigade (17 Bde)
1st Battalion Royal Fusiliers (1 RF)
1st Battalion North Staffordshire Regiment (1 N Staffs)
2nd Battalion Leinster Regiment (2 Leinster)
3rd Battalion Rifle Brigade (3 RB)

18th Infantry Brigade (18 Bde)
1st Battalion West Yorkshire Regiment (1 W Yorks)
1st Battalion East Yorkshire Regiment (1 E Yorks)
2nd Battalion Sherwood Foresters (2 Sher For)
2nd Battalion Durham Light Infantry (2 DLI)

2nd Brigade Royal Field Artillery (2 Bde RFA) with 21, 42 and 53 Batteries (Btys)
12th (Howitzer) Brigade Royal Field Artillery (12 Bde RFA) with 43, 86 and 87 Batteries
(Btys) – 4.5"
24th Brigade Royal Field Artillery (24 Bde RFA) with 110, 111 and 112 Batteries (Btys)
38th Brigade Royal Field Artillery (38 Bde RFA) with 24, 34 and 72 Batteries (Btys)
24th Heavy Battery Royal Garrison Artillery (24 Hy Bty RGA) – 60 pounders

12th Field Company Royal Engineers (12 Fd Coy RE)
38th Field Company Royal Engineers (38 Fd Coy RE)

Note: Both divisions also had a Signal Company, a Cyclist Company, three Field Ambulances
(Fd Ambs), and a Divisional Ammunition Column (DAC).

19th Infantry Brigade (19 Bde)
1st Battalion The Middlesex Regiment (1 Middx)
1st Battalion Cameronians (1 Cameronians)
2nd Battalion Royal Welch Fusiliers (2 RWF)
2nd Battalion Argyll and Sutherland Highlanders (2 A&SH)

The III Corps sign was an equilateral triangle, the base being black, the left side red, and the third side white. This sign was devised by Putty, the colours being his racing colours.

The Corps

Organisations, equipment, tactics and procedures were to evolve during the course of the war and Putty had to adapt to this constant change. Indeed, as will become apparent, he took a great interest in every aspect of his corps and every opportunity to influence its evolution. A short explanation of the corps will help to set the scene.

As already mentioned, the corps as such did not exist before 1914 and is not specifically mentioned in FSR (I and II) and the *Staff Manual (War) Provisional 1912* that provided the doctrine for the army's operations in 1914. This is often the cause of some surprise but the doctrine established principles and the corps could and did operate on an extrapolation of these principles without difficulty. Aldershot Command and Irish Command, both of which had two divisions, exercised as a corps on an annual basis; indeed Aldershot Command provided HQ I Corps on mobilisation.

The role of the corps was to provide effective command, control, communication and support for the conduct of operations in order to achieve the objectives given to it. Essential to this effectiveness was its ability to influence the battle at the critical place and time. Put more simply, perhaps, the corps had to have the capability to be more than the sum of the divisions under its command. One way of doing this was the creation of a corps reserve: a corps of three divisions or more might have one division in reserve but in 1914 a corps only had two divisions, so its reserve was normally a brigade. The CinC also gave each corps a cavalry brigade from time to time, to increase its capability to manoeuvre and to enable it to deal quickly with the unexpected.

The capability of the corps was to be greatly enhanced during the war by three major developments. In 1914 it had no artillery of its own, other than that brought into corps reserve. Gradually the allocation of heavy artillery, with guns up to 15", gave it the capability to influence the battle. Aeroplanes, with RFC squadrons attached to the corps, further enhanced this capability. Finally, the arrival of tanks, and their use in cooperation with artillery and air, developed it even further. In every other area, engineers, medical, logistics and administration, the corps also developed. Doctrine tried to keep pace with this rapid change but sometimes failed to do so; initiative, common-sense and leadership were then the keys to success.

HQ III Corps went to war with 19 officers: of these 5 were in the General Staff with the main functions of operations and intelligence and 4 in the AQ Staff responsible for personnel and logistics. That this small number was inadequate soon became apparent but the additional high calibre staff officers did not exist in an army that was expanding so rapidly. Corps HQ have been often criticised for being too far back and out of touch. Allocation of real estate was extremely difficult with so many conflicting demands for every building, field, wood and road. Putty was well aware of the problems and sought to minimise them; the Advanced Report Centre, a forward communication facility, became the corps tactical headquarters when the operational situation required. In the early years HQ III Corps was able to operate from a substantial building such as the chateau but by 1917 there were few such buildings standing and the HQ was forced into temporary huts hidden within the village ruins.

The HQ operated to a routine. At its centre was a minimum of a GSO, a clerk and a signaller. The Camp Commandant was responsible for security and administration; initially security was provided by those off duty from their primary task but this improved with the addition of a defence platoon and expansion of the corps cavalry. There were 3 messes, 2 for officers and one for other ranks. A Mess had the five general officers and their ADCs, B Mess all the other officers. As the size of the HQ increased a C Mess was later added. The daily ration, which was pooled in each mess, consisted of: meat (fresh, frozen or preserved) 1.2 lb, reduced to 1 and then 0.75; bread 1.25 lb reduced to 0.75 (or biscuit or flour); bacon 4 oz; cheese 3 oz, reduced to 2; vegetables fresh 8 oz or dried 2 oz; tea 5/8 oz; jam 4 oz reduced to 3; sugar 3 oz; salt 0.5 oz; mustard 0.05 oz reduced to 0.02; pepper 1/36 oz; milk condensed 1/16 tin increased to 1/12 tin; pickles weekly 1 oz; oatmeal thrice weekly as an extra; butter as an extra until July 1917. To this would be added local purchase, especially out of the front line, of eggs, fresh milk, vegetables, fruit, butter, wine and game. Additionally there would be parcels from home of preserved foods of all type. Rationing and feeding was only a problem in the front line because the rations dictated centralised cooking and this had to be done in the rear; keeping the food hot while it was carried forward often at night and under shell fire was very difficult.

Putty too worked to a routine. The morning reports came in at 5 am each morning and the next few hours were the BGGS' time to consider them and hold his morning staff meetings. Putty would keep out of the way and have time to deal with his military correspondence; how much depended on the methods of his superior and the number of his subordinates. About 8 am he would be briefed on events overnight, plans and key issues; then he would see staff officers individually as required. Putty invariably saw his DDMS at 9 am each day to discuss casualties, medical and health matters. The evening reports came in at 5 pm each day and the routine was repeated as necessary.

Most days were spent visiting those under his command, especially on their arrival to explain what he expected of them and on departure to thank them. Without PA equipment it was very difficult to get a message across effectively to more than a battalion size group. Putty knew that he was not good at this but did not shirk from the task: sometimes it worked, on occasions it did not. Inspections were equally important and just as difficult to get right; talk to too many individually, particularly in the rain, they became too protracted; talk to too few and they were seen by some as a formality. It was a difficult balance to get right.

Putty visited his divisions frequently to get to know them and assess their effectiveness. This was easiest done when a unit was out of the line and Putty could ride round several units in one day. If a division was in the line he would visit its HQ for an update with its commander, visit brigade HQs, and perhaps one or more battalions of its reserve brigade. If he visited a battalion in the front line it would take much of the day, and when he got there a large proportion of the officers and men would be under cover and resting. For most of the day, especially in the mornings, the forward lines would be almost deserted except for a few sentries leaning against the parapet with their periscopes in constant use, and for a sniper here and there. Apart from the obvious morale factor of the corps commander being seen in the front line, it could be a wasted day since he would be actually seen by very few. So these visits would be chosen with great care, combining them with a reconnaissance or escorting a visitor. Personal knowledge of the front line was important all the time – the state of the trenches, wire, morale, enemy activity – but depriving men of essential sleep was to be avoided. After dark a whole population would suddenly appear out of the earth and work would begin: if he tried to visit then he would not be seen and would disrupt this essential activity.

He had to attend conferences and meetings, both his own and those at the higher headquarters. These occurred routinely and also when an operation was being planned; they usually lasted a full day, including lunch, allowing time for informal and one to one discussions. HQ III Corps received numerous visitors; many required Putty's personal attention and had to be carefully briefed then taken by him to visit units or parts of the line to reinforce any message that needed to be put over. Such visits were important both to III Corps and to the wider prosecution of the war but they took up much time. Visitors often stayed the night and dinner was an opportunity for more relaxed and informal discussion.

Putty would get about by car or by horse; car was quicker but the roads in the corps area were so congested that riding was often preferred for shorter journeys. Not only was it a means of taking exercise but it also avoided marching columns or other traffic having to clear passage for him, always unpopular. He had little spare time and most of it was spent either eating or sleeping. His personal administration and correspondence was dealt with either in the early morning or in the late evening after dinner; considering the number of letters that he is known to have written and received this must have taken at least one hour each day.

Fighting battles, or more correctly the conduct of operations, over-rode everything else. Their planning and execution would have taken a considerable amount of his time; then he had to exercise leadership to ensure his mission was achieved. This may seem obvious in an attack but it applied equally and just as importantly to holding the line. Strong leadership and supervision were necessary to ensure there was no complacency, that the defence never became passive and allowed the enemy the initiative. Men worked to strengthen the defences, every hour of every day; the defences could never be strong enough. As many men as could be spared were in the rear training to improve their individual and collective skills; those in the front line had to be alert all the time. None of this would retain the initiative and defence had to be aggressive; patrols had to be out attacking the enemy's working parties, raiding and taking prisoners to provide valuable information; artillery, machine-guns and snipers used to cause attrition and lower morale; communication trenches, supply dumps and routes, and artillery positions engaged when an opportunity was presented such as information from a prisoner on the timing of a relief.

There could be no weakness that the enemy might sense and exploit. Relief in the line was constant at all levels; these were complex high risk operations with many men on the move in a confined area at night, very vulnerable to enemy artillery fire if detected. Careful planning and good security were essential. Divisional artillery was usually relieved at a different time to the rest of the division, so the incoming division had to ensure effective coordination with the outgoing division's artillery from the outset, and this was difficult. In many ways greater leadership was required to hold the line because there were so many conflicting priorities and risks to be balanced.

These were some of the challenges that Putty faced, and they had to be faced immediately; 4th Division and 19 Bde were falling back, much reduced after the battles of Mons and Le Cateau.

Retreat to Paris 30 August-6 September 1914

Just 15 minutes after HQ III Corps set up at Villeneuve sur Verberie GHQ issued orders for a further retreat to the south with III Corps, identified in the orders for the first time, instructed to move on the route St Sauveur-Verberie. It would be difficult to imagine a more testing situation for the new corps commander on his first day, with his untrained and untried HQ. 4th Division was commanded by Snow who had been at Eton but was three years older than him. It had fought at Le Cateau on 26 August and been retreating southwards ever since; in the four days the division had marched 100 miles. It was now severely reduced in strength, few men still had their packs and equipment, most had bleeding feet, and all were very tired. 19 Bde was in an even worse state since it had also fought at Mons on 23 August. Comd 19 Bde, Laurence Drummond, was a close friend of Putty's; they were exact contemporaries in the same house at Eton and in the Scots Guards, but he had been injured at Le Cateau and the brigade was now commanded by Ward, CO 1 Middx. 19 Bde had no supporting or administrative units and had to rely on those of 4th Division, an added difficulty for Snow and Putty. When McGrigor (DA&QMG III Corps) told Putty that two of the commanding officers in 4th Division had been responsible for signing a document of surrender in St Quentin four days earlier, a document that was being held as evidence for a FGCM, this news could not have come at a worse time.

The following day Putty issued his first operation order (III Corps OpO No.1). 31 August was a very hot day and the corps had to make a long flank march through the Forest of Compiègne. Many units did not reach their destinations until very late, and with the heat, dust and consequent thirst adding to their long march, they were exhausted. There were also constant concerns about being cut off, especially by German cavalry infiltrating through the forest; a 5 mile gap existed on their right flank to II Corps at Crépy, and, although on the left they were in contact with the French via the Cavalry Division, and the River Oise was an obstacle, it was not secure.

At 8.50 pm that evening GHQ ordered III Corps to move back to the line Nanteuil-Baron and its rearguard to reach a line running E-W through Néry by 6 pm. Owing to the lateness of the hour that many units arrived, some as late as 10.15 pm, Putty represented that this was impossible. However, he reported that the transport of the corps would move off at 1 am. This was not challenged: it must have been clear to French, if he did not already know it, that Putty would balance his duty to obey orders with his responsibility to those under him. It would have been an uneasy night with constant alarms, the passage of orders, and essential administration; few would have had more than 3 hours sleep.

With the transport well ahead of them, the fighting units of III Corps joined the retreat at 5 am on 1 September; this proceeded in an orderly way with brigades moving in bounds from one ridge line to the next. German cavalry surprised part of the Cavalry Division near Néry which made the withdrawal of III Corps difficult. On hearing the firing about Néry Lieutenant Colonel Ward, acting Comd 19 Bde protecting III Corps right, immediately marched his brigade to the sound of the guns; his prompt action surprised the enemy cavalry, and they withdrew leaving the guns of L Bty RHA which they had captured and eight of their own.

Meanwhile 11 Bde 4th Division, the rearguard, began to withdraw from St Sauveur, 12 Bde already at 9.30 am being in position 6 miles to the S between Mount Cornon and Chamicy. At 10 am the Germans attacked 1 Som LI and 1 RB (11 Bde) covering the retirement of the other two battalions, and were beaten off with considerable loss. 10 Bde, in the west, moved over open

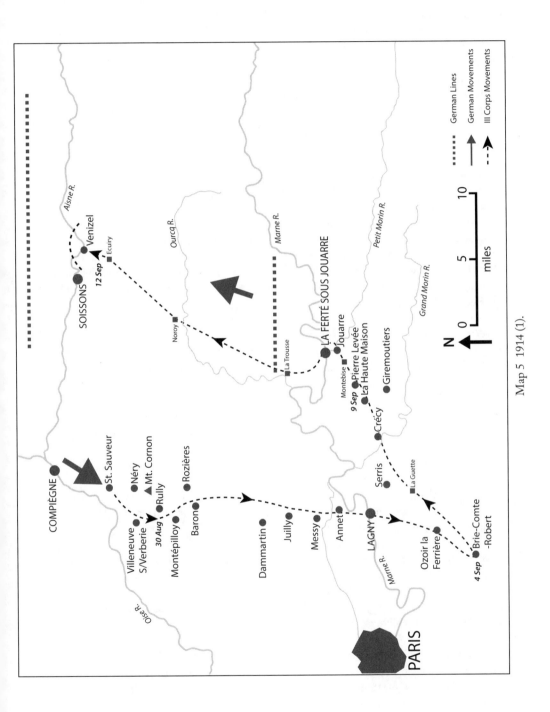

Map 5 1914 (1).

country to Rully and there half the brigade halted for water, the remainder moved onto the ridge to the S. It was here that Putty met Haldane (Comd 10 Bde) and told him 'that to his south there was some German cavalry, which had apparently worked round the eastern flank and was hanging around the villages of Baron and Versigny, and directed him to drive it off'. When 1 RB 11 Bde entered Rozières at 7 pm they found 300 Uhlans from 4th German Cavalry Division had just pulled out of the village in great haste.

With the Germans attacking their rearguard, working their way between II and III Corps to attack their right flank, and on occasions getting behind them to cut the retreat, it must have been a confusing picture at HQ III Corps; they also came close to attack and capture that day as Harington related:

> Our BGRA and I were sent on, he to reconnoitre a gun position, I to select a HQ. We rode a long way and then he left me. I found what I thought would be a suitable HQ location at a farm, and there I waited for the HQ to arrive. I had a most uncanny and lonely feeling, just my groom and myself. At long last the corps commander and staff arrived, and they had hardly got out of their cars when we saw a party of Uhlans within a few hundred yards. I shall never forget the ADCs, the present Lords Londonderry and Pembroke, myself and the chauffeurs, who had rifles but had probably never fired them before, all lying in the cabbages firing at the Uhlans. We learned afterwards that a German cavalry division had passed within a mile.

Nevertheless by nightfall III Corps was to large extent secure holding the Montépilloy-Rozières Ridge with its HQ at Baron. The successful actions on 1 September seemed to have had an effect on the German advance for III Corps' march next day S to Dammartin and Longperrier was unmolested. Haldane recalled:

> We moved off, and as dawn broke reached a wood about 1 mile south of Baron. After passing through it, we arrived in open country, and marched along a dusty road bordered by corn and beetroot fields. Our route took us through the villages of Montagny and Ève, whence the little town of Dammartin en Goele, which is situated on an isolated hill, came in view. At 11 am we entered its narrow streets, and quarters for the night were speedily arranged in that part of it which was allotted to my brigade. The sun was blazing hot, and the troops were weary and not a few suffering from the effects of trying to assuage their thirst by eating unripe pears and apples.

So smoothly had the move S gone that HQ III Corps was able to issue its orders for the following day (3 September) at 3.15 pm. It spent the night at the Chateau des Julieres, as usual the only building of any size in the village.

Once again it was an early start on 3 September as III Corps marched S across the River Marne. Haldane's 10 Bde was rearguard and he wrote:

> 1.10 am. My staff and I were afoot, while the rumbling of vehicles over cobbled street announced that 4th Division was again moving rearwards. The rearguard was not to march from its starting point, three quarters of a mile S of Dammartin, till 4.30 am. By the time my troops were underway it was almost daylight, and as the sun rose above the horizon it

was plain that the march, as on the previous day, would be a thirsty one. The enemy proved to be again at a distance, and we tramped unmolested through St Mard, Juilly, St Mesmes, Messy, Claye, Souilly, Annet, Thorigny and over the River Marne to Lagny. We marched to bivouacs near the Bois de Chigny arriving there at 3.15 pm. Shortly after my arrival I was bidden to report myself at Corps HQ at Lagny.

Haldane makes no mention of the reason for this summons, but it seems likely that it had to do with the incident at St Quentin and the impending court martial.

HQ III Corps was established at the mairie in Lagny and, once the rearguard had crossed the Marne, the bridge over it at Annet and the two bridges at Lagny were destroyed. The remaining bridges were destroyed later that night on French's orders (GHQ OpO 15) when the decision was made to continue the retreat next day. Initially it was hoped to offer stubborn resistance above the Serris Plateau but the movement of the corps on right and left prevented this: at 11.45 am HQ III Corps issued OpO No.5 for a further withdrawal to a line Jossigny-Conches facing NE, just beside what is now Euro Disney. HQ III Corps made its last rearward move to Brie Comte Robert.

Putty had time to write to Ettie Desborough that day:

> My dear Chief, I took over at a disadvantage, finding a retiring army in the field, however I have a day's rest so write to tell you that all is well with me, long hours have tried us all, men's eyes have a peculiar stare after the strain and they talk as in a dream but otherwise their spirit is quite marvellous and by God the British officer is the grandest man in the world. You wanted to know how to help, the greatest necessity is the Voluntary Aid Society to collect the wounded on a retirement out of the villages in which they have been left, you could not do this without an agreement with the Germans and I do not know if that would be possible, if the inhabitants had not left the villages there would be no bother as they are accustomed to look after such things in this Country but in cases where everyone has disappeared it is difficult to hope for their welfare with the Germans unable to deal with their own numbers. The heat is very trying. Bless you. Write me a line addressed Headquarters 3rd Army Expeditionary Force. I always get letters that come out by the despatch carriers to Sir John French, Hindlip, Cyril Hankey etc. Yours ever Putty.

That evening, at 6.35 pm, GHQ ordered a move SW the following day (5 September) which took III Corps to a line facing E, touching the defences of Paris, from Brie Comte Robert to Ozoir la Ferrière. By nightfall this had been completed and the retreat was over. Since he had taken command six days earlier Putty's III Corps had marched 100 miles, to add to the 100 miles that many had already marched, often in close contact with the enemy. Maude (GSO1) recorded that he did not average three hours sleep out of twenty-four. For the AQ Staff there was no let up with stragglers re-joining, reinforcements beginning to arrive, and equipment losses to be made good. French visited HQ III Corps to explain the situation, with confirmatory orders issued by GHQ at 5.15 pm. Von Kluck in his headlong rush SE had, it appeared, ignored not only the fortress of Paris, but also 6th French Army and the BEF now in position to fall upon his right flank and rear.

III Corps OpO No.7 issued at Brie Comte Robert was simple and clear:

1. The bulk of the German forces which have been following British troops in their retreat has moved SE against the left of the 5th French Army around St Barthelemy. The British Force is about to assume the offensive to the NE against the German right flank, in conjunction with 6th French Army.
2. III Corps will advance tomorrow (6 Sep) towards Serris, acting in conjunction with II Corps on its right.
3. Starting Point: Railway crossing 1.5 miles east of Ozoir la Ferrière. Time: 5 am. Route: Pontcarré-Ferrières-Jossigny-Serris. 4th Division will furnish the advanced guard of one infantry brigade and attached troops. On reaching Ferrières a flank guard of 2 battalions and 1 battery will be provided by 4th Division. 19 Bde will follow 4th Division.
4. Trains (baggage) are to be parked in the vicinity of Ozoir la Ferrière by 11 am.
5. Railhead for supplies tomorrow, 6 Sep, Brunoy.
   RV for ammunition parks tomorrow, 6 Sep, Brie Comte Robert at 10 am.
6. Comd 19 Bde will detail half a battalion to proceed to Ozoir la Ferrière to provide security for the train, and half a battalion to proceed to Brie Comte Robert to provide security of the ammunition parks.
7. Report Centre – Brie Comte Robert up to 6 am, after that hour Ferrières.

Thus III Corps with minimum fuss changed gear and advanced to attack the German right flank. The transformation in the morale of the corps, inevitably affected by such a long and debilitating retreat, was almost instantaneous. There was, however, one unpleasant duty for Putty that day; at 11.30 am HQ III Corps ordered 4th Division to convene a FGCM to try Lieutenant Colonel Mainwaring CO 2 RDF and Lieutenant Colonel Elkington CO 1 Warwicks for their conduct in St Quentin ten days earlier.

At 5 am on 6 September the advance started. The ground to be traversed forms part of the great plateau E and NE of Paris and is cut by the deep valleys, almost ravines, of several rivers including the Marne and Aisne. These rivers were passable only at the bridges or by bridging, and formed ideal lines on which to fight delaying actions. When considering the rate of advance of III Corps it is worth remembering that a division on the march occupied 15 miles of road, so III Corps about 20 miles. The marching speed of the column, assuming no interference from the enemy, would not have exceeded 2.5 miles an hour so that the time to pass a point would have been at least 8 hours. Marching on heavily cambered cobbled roads in leather soled boots was extremely tiring, and unpaved minor roads had their own problems of dust or mud depending on the weather. The organisation of the advance so that the corps could react to any enemy attack or attempt to impose delay required meticulous planning and traffic control. Ensuring that the trains could be got forward when they were required was but one challenge; the expectation at the end of the day's advance would be to receive food, fodder and the many other requirements without delay, a rather different situation to the retreat when the fighting troops were withdrawing on to their trains.

Advance to the Aisne 6 September-7 October 1914

III Corps' advance that day was not opposed, though hostile patrols were encountered from time to time in the Forêt de Crécy. The final position taken up for the night was on the Grand Morin from Villers sur Morin southward, with HQ III Corps at Chateau La Guette. Everyone got what they needed most, a good night's rest. The following morning (7 September), III Corps' cyclist patrols reported that the area on the far side of the Grand Morin was clear, the corps then crossed the river E of Crécy, and the advance continued. Although it was a hot and tiring day the men looked better daily. All the indications pointed to the Germans retiring and 10 Bde, the advance guard, was unopposed except for snipers. After orders had been given to go into bivouac, from Giremoutiers to La Haute Maison, gun and rifle fire was opened on 2 Innis Fus (12 Bde) on their way to take up an outpost position. One officer was killed and 21 other ranks were wounded, and such was the concern about a possible counter-attack that even HQ III Corps stood to.

The River Marne that lay ahead was also an obstacle to the German retirement northwards with congestion reported at the bridge of La Ferté sous Jouarre. It was also reported, however, that a considerable enemy force (according to a later German report, four Jäger battalions and a cavalry brigade) was at Pierre Levée 5 miles SW of the bridge to cover it; it may have been elements of this force that caused the alarms the previous night. French ordered Putty to continue his advance on 8 September towards Jouarre.

By 4 am next morning 4th Division had discovered that the enemy had evacuated Pierre Levée and within two hours III Corps was beginning to close on the river: 12 Bde 4th Division advancing on Jouarre and 19 Bde on its left upon Signy Signets. Aerial reconnaissance reported a great number of the enemy massed about La Ferté sous Jouarre waiting their turn to cross the river, while the passage of infantry over the bridge was unceasing; according to a later German report the whole of 5th German Division passed through La Ferté sous Jouarre that day.

When the leading battalion of 19 Bde reached the ridge overlooking the Marne, it was caught by artillery fire from the heights just NW of La Ferté sous Jouarre. No great damage was done but the brushing away of the enemy's advanced troops revealed their main force holding the N bank of the Marne in strength, with a bridgehead well provided with machine-guns at La Ferté sous Jouarre (according to Von Kluck, the town was defended by 2nd German Cavalry Division). The Marne could not be easily forced, and there was nothing for the moment that could be done but bring the artillery forward to knock out the machine-guns and to seek a way round. This was exasperating, for heavy columns of the enemy were still crossing the river at La Ferté, and masses of men in sight on the northern bank, but out of range.

At 2 pm orders were issued for a right flanking attack: 11 Bde 4th Division and 19 Bde to cross the Petit Morin close to the town and 12 Bde 4th Division to cross it at Courcelles about a mile and a half to the E. The Germans in the houses resisted, but by dark the part of the town that lies S of the Marne had been cleared of the enemy and 12 Bde had taken Courcelles and the high ground above it; HQ III Corps had moved forward to Montebise Chateau.

French visited Putty that day (about 4.30 pm 3 miles S of Jouarre); he recalled:

> I found III Corps on the left advancing well at all points, driving the enemy before them and inflicting considerable loss all along the line. Pulteney was in touch with 8th French Division on his left. There appeared to be a considerable force of the enemy in the woods

lying to the S of Lizy, N of the Marne, and later reports stated that some 90 German guns were deployed there against the right of 6th French Army. I impressed on Pulteney the necessity for pushing on to the utmost of his ability in aid of 6th Army. It looked as if he would have considerable opposition at Changis and La Ferté sous Jouarre. The Germans retiring over the Marne at the latter place occupied the town in strength and blew up the bridge. Although III Corps were not able to pass the Marne till daybreak on 10 September, there could be no doubt that the vigour of Pulteney's attack took considerable pressure off the right of 6th French Army. The British troops fought all day all along the line with splendid spirit, energy and determination, and were skilfully handled and led.

III Corps' task on 9 September was to establish a bridgehead over the Marne. The river itself was a major obstacle being 70 to 90 yards wide at La Ferté sous Jouarre and its N bank was held by the enemy in strength, with a division in the town. It was the greatest challenge that Putty and his corps had faced so far. At 4.45 am, pursuant to Putty's orders, 11 and 12 Bdes advanced in two columns with the intention of repairing the bridges in front of them, crossing the river and establishing a bridgehead. They seized the high ground E of La Ferté, so that the artillery could be brought up to engage the German guns and the part of the town S of the river. The broken bridges were found by 11 Bde (left) to be unapproachable because of snipers and machine-guns; and the greater part of the morning was spent engaging suspect buildings with artillery. Meanwhile, 12 Bde (right) pushed two battalions into the loop of the river between Chamigny and Luzancy; they drove the enemy from the weir W of Luzancy, crossed the Marne by the weir, and climbed to the road from La Ferté to Montreuil, which was the line of the German retreat, but reached it too late to intercept any German troops.

Shortly before noon the artillery bombarded the town, as a result of which the Germans abandoned the approaches to the bridges. The RE were then able to reconnoitre, but the repair work was not started until 4 pm. However, 1 RB (11 Bde) followed the two battalions of 12 Bde across the weir and 2 Innis Fus (12 Bde) crossed the river higher up by the railway viaduct which was still intact. 1 E Lancs and 1 Hamps (11 Bde) were ferried across in boats below La Ferté; this operation was not completed until 9 pm, by which time the engineers had sufficient material ready at the site to supplement the pontoons and begun the construction of a floating bridge.

When darkness fell on 9 September three battalions of 11 Bde (left) and three of 12 Bde (right) were across the river and each had one on the home bank. 10 Bde was at Grand Mont Menard and 19 Bde between Jouarre and Signy Signets. French visited Putty early in the morning; as he related in his book '1914':

> I found Pulteney S of La Ferté early in the morning, and heavy fighting going on to gain passage of the river which the enemy was still vigorously disputing. It was a remarkable scene. The banks of the Marne at this point are somewhat steep, and there is high commanding ground on either side of the river. The old town of La Ferté, so famous in Napoleon's campaign of 1814, presented a picturesque appearance with its ancient church and buildings. Surrounded and held by the enemy, it seemed to frown down on the broken bridge, forbidding all approach. The enemy was vigorously defending the passage, strongly supported by artillery from high ground N of the town. 4th Division in two columns attempted to advance on the bridge with a view to repairing it and then establishing a bridgehead on the northern bank, but all their attempts were frustrated by the German

Passage of the Marne: D Coy 1 Cameronians 19 Bde crossing a pontoon bridge at La Ferté sous Jouarre, 10 September 1914. (© IWM Q56721)

guns. Just after dark Hunter-Weston's 11 Bde[2] was able to reach the southern bank, where a number of boats were seized. In these the brigade was pushed across, and by 10 pm had established an effective footing on the northern bank, under cover of which a pontoon bridge was constructed by the RE of 4th Division under very heavy fire. It was a very fine piece of work, to which GOC III Corps particularly drew my attention. During this operation CO 1 E Lancs (11 Bde) was killed.

The CinC's recollection is not entirely accurate and he does not give credit to the four battalions (mainly 12 Bde) that crossed the river higher up by the weir and railway bridge earlier in the day, effectively turning the defence of La Ferté.

Putty somehow found the time to send his first letter to Edith Castlereagh on 9 September:

Dear Lady C, I only just had time to scribble a line in the car yesterday, Jack Seely[3] was talking such nonsense I could not level my brain to give you any news. Charlie is very well indeed and has put on so much flesh he can scarcely get his belt on. Reggie had a birthday yesterday he ought to be older if talking makes one for he seldom stops. All our spirits have been much better since we began to advance, the depression of the retirement was very trying. Took good care to take the sheets off the bed the last two nights as Germans had

2   Brigadier General Aylmer Gould Hunter-Weston (1864-1940) late RE.
3   Colonel Jack Edward Bernard Seely (1868-1947) late Hamps Yeo S of S for War 1912-1914.

slept there the previous nights, the brutes had drunk all the champagne. Have been rather depressed over an attack of gout the last two days but I hope from the signs that it is passing off, I do not know what I should do if I was incapacitated. The weather has been desperately hot, the men have felt the sun in the middle of the day a great deal, yesterday we had the first shower of rain and pretty heavy it was too but now it is just as hot again. Must stop. Best love Yours ever Putty.

It was to be the first of many letters he wrote to her as the relationship developed from that of a friend and the wife of his ADC to something closer.

During the night the pontoon bridge was completed and on 10 September III Corps crossed the Marne. Maude (GSO1 HQ III Corps) noted in his diary: 'RE did excellently and the greater part of III Corps passed over the bridge at a very early hour'. When the corps resumed its advance it became clear that the Germans were in full retreat. Many prisoners were taken, about 500 that day; wounded were discovered in houses, and roads were littered with abandoned vehicles of all kinds. 10 Bde led on the right through Dhuisy to Coulombs with 19 Bde on a parallel road to the W. HQ III Corps also crossed at Ferté behind 19 Bde and was established that night at La Trousse Chateau.

III Corps' casualties since the advance began on 6 September were amazingly low, just 133, a tribute perhaps to the way these operations were conducted. Putty used his four brigades so that Snow usually had two on the main axis, 19 Bde was on the secondary axis, and the fourth brigade was in corps reserve. This achieved a degree of operational balance while taking due regard for any sensitivity Snow might have felt, although there is no evidence of any friction between him and Putty. In any event Snow was injured in a riding accident near Ferté and Wilson[4] acted as divisional commander until 21 September.

As the Germans fell back ahead of them on their lines of communication, often in some haste but rarely in total disarray, resistance inevitably hardened and the River Aisne ahead of them was another major obstacle. The march N on 11 September was unopposed; the problems were congestion on the roads caused by an encroaching French column, and by the rain which started at midday and made the roads muddy and slippery. That night the corps reached the line Noroy-Chouy with HQ III Corps at Noroy. At 6 pm the FGCM of the two commanding officers assembled; both officers were cashiered.

At 5.30 am 12 September III Corps continued its advance N, having received orders to seize the crossing over the River Aisne at Venizel. When the advanced guard, 10 Bde, reached Tigny, 45th French Division on its left became engaged with the enemy holding a position covering Soissons. III Corps pressed on and 10 Bde reached the ridge above Septmonts at 3 pm: at about this time the divisional cavalry reported that the bridge at Venizel had been damaged but was still passable both by infantry and cavalry, the ground to the N of it had been entrenched for defence, and a large column (III German Corps) was moving NE from Soissons over the plateau on the N side of the river. With great difficulty the guns of 31 Hy Bty were hauled up to the top of the ridge of Septmonts to fire on this column, and 29 Bde RFA also unlimbered to support an advance on Venizel. All of this took time and darkness came before any result was achieved. Wilding CO 2 Innis Fus (12 Bde), however, had sent down two companies to

---

4   Brigadier General Henry Fuller Maitland Wilson (1859-1941) late RB Eton Comd 12 Bde.

the Venizel Bridge and when they appeared the Germans attempted its demolition. Of the four charges only one exploded, the girders were cut, but the reinforced concrete of the roadway was still sound enough to carry light loads; the enemy holding the bridge were driven off and the rest of the charges removed.

That night III Corps closed up to the river with HQ III Corps in the Chateau de Crise at Ecuiry where it was to remain until 7 October. It was now clear that the main enemy position was on the ridge to the N of the river; spurs ran down to the Aisne from it and the entire country between the ridge and the river, a mixture of fields, woods and copses, was completely overlooked. French noted: 'Early in the day I joined Pulteney at some cross-roads two miles S of Buzancy. The enemy was opposing the passage of the Aisne to 6th French Army and 4th Division held a position on the bridges SE of Soissons to assist it'.

At 7.45 pm GHQ ordered: 'The Army will continue the pursuit tomorrow (13 September) at 7 am and directed Corps to reach a line 5 miles beyond the Aisne on the plateau'. The left route of III Corps (inclusive) ran almost due N to Coucy le Chateau. During the night 11 Bde crossed the bridge at Venizel and advanced on Bucy le Long seizing the high ground before daybreak at the point of the bayonet. The enemy was unprepared, abandoned their trenches, and fell back to their main line. It was a most satisfactory end to a march of some thirty miles in pouring rain and temperatures more appropriate to November.

On 13 September the French on the left of III Corps began to cross at Soissons and II Corps on its right at Missy. The Germans shelled Venizel to prevent III Corps crossing but a pontoon bridge was completed by 5.30 pm. About the same time they counterattacked 12 Bde at St Marguerite; the attack was repulsed although 12 Bde had 200 casualties. During the evening the rest of 4th Division crossed, leaving 19 Bde, the hy bty and two fd btys on the S side.

That evening Putty wrote to Theresa Londonderry:

> Dear Lady Londonderry, Many thanks for your letter of 10 Sep. You are quite right machine-guns are very necessary but they should be of the light portable type and supplemented by automatic rifles. Alas have met no French ladies since we landed that were outside the peasant class but expect they will turn up to go hand in hand with us in to Berlin. We have had great quantities of rain the last few days which we could do without as far as transport is concerned but at the same time it has cooled the air at a time the men were feeling the effects of the sun. My God if you could see what the British soldier is doing led by the most splendid officers in the world it would make every mother in England envious to think she had not a son a sailor or soldier. Charlie very fit and well and doing capitally, he has a much larger head than I gave him credit for. Love to all. Yours very sincerely, WP Pulteney.

He also wrote to Ettie Desborough:

> My dear Chief, Thanks for your letter of 31 August which reached me yesterday if you want to get a letter through quick send it by one of the messengers Cyril Hankey, Dalmeny or Hindlip. You will have got my letter about the International Red Cross Field Ambulance, everywhere we go advancing we see the necessity of providing for the wounded of the other side in the way of lying down cases that cannot be moved, the French people however are very good at the work but their supplies have been absolutely denuded by the retiring

Germans. The heroic work of the British soldier and the bravery of its officers is the most wonderful thing in the world, their parents must be swelling with pride, every day one asks them to do the utmost tasks and never do they fail one we have indeed pulled our weight in this struggle and won the everlasting gratitude of France. Oh the joy of the attack instead of the defence, every yard of ground regained is balm. Bless you dear. Yours ever Putty.

It had been hoped that the Germans would withdraw during the night but they did not. At 8 am 14 September III Corps was holding on to the spurs N of Bucy le Long; on its left 45th French Division was trying to cross at Soissons; on its right, across the Aisne at Missy, 5th Division was attacking Chivres. During the day repeated efforts were made to gain ground, but without success, and the enemy guns shelled continuously. At 7.30 pm Putty went to see French and it was decided that II Corps would make a fresh attack on Chivres at 5 am on 15 September, and that I Corps, on the extreme right, would turn westwards to attempt to relieve the pressure on II and III Corps. Information was also that the French were advancing on both flanks, and would soon relieve the pressure on the BEF, so the CinC ordered a strong defence to be maintained for the time being.

III Corps' situation at dark was that 12 Bde, on the right, was holding the St Marguerite Spur with 11 Bde on its left, reinforced by two battalions of 10 Bde, holding the spurs E and W of Bucy le Long. The remaining two battalions of 10 Bde were in reserve at Bucy le Long and 19 Bde in support near Venizel. It was extremely difficult to get observation for the artillery N of the river so some of it was withdrawn to the S side. During the night another pontoon bridge was put across the river, giving the corps two, in addition to the road bridge at Venizel which had now been repaired. Although the German strength in front did not appear to be very great, the whole of II German Corps and 5th Division III German Corps were facing them. All the approaches to the enemy's position, which was of great natural strength and entrenched, were swept by artillery and machine-guns. At 11 pm GHQ OpO issued for 15 September only contained information on the situation, but French saw Putty and ordered him to entrench the positions he occupied; it was the same message.

III Corps was to spend three weeks on the Aisne; this introduction to static warfare provided a foretaste of what was to come. There were few who by now had not appreciated the importance of artillery but heavy artillery, with its longer range and greater weight of shell, would be the key to success; and the German superiority in numbers came as an unpleasant surprise. Of equal concern was the German supremacy in numbers of machine-guns and the advantage this gave to the defender. Winter was approaching for which the BEF was ill-prepared; the cold and the wet with the consequent mud affected everyone and everything they did. One other aspect of static warfare was to bedevil higher level decision making and that was the reluctance to give up ground which had been hard-won even when that ground was of no tactical importance and difficult to hold, and further forward movement improbable. This inflexibility was a serious handicap in every respect, and led to unnecessary casualties.

On 15 September Putty decided to withdraw the rest of his artillery to the S of the river where it could better support the defensive positions of the corps. But he had another problem; the corps was very vulnerable to attack from the air, particularly the bridges, and it had just one anti-aircraft gun, deployed to Bucy le Long. Throughout the day the corps worked to improve its trenches, but the enemy's shell fire was heavy and caused considerable losses. No wire or other engineer stores were yet available, except what the field companies carried, so many men spent the day collecting wire from the fences of nearby farms and houses which was then converted into entanglements during the night. During the day III Corps used up its remaining stock of 60 pounder and 4.5" howitzer ammunition, and no more was available for three days; little now could be done to counter the enemy's artillery. That evening, at 8.30 pm, GHQ issued OpO 26: 'CinC wishes the line now held to be strongly entrenched, and it is his intention to assume a general offensive at the first opportunity'. Since further forward movement was impossible until the French had advanced sufficiently to threaten the German positions ahead, it was strange that the CinC did not contemplate pulling back behind the Aisne. The one encouragement Putty received was the arrival of Keir (GOC 6th Division) with his BGRA, and the knowledge that the division was only a day's march away.

The following day (16 September) was not much better. The French on III Corps' left requested artillery support for their advance, further reducing what little support could be given to its own troops. 6th Division arrived but was put into GHQ Reserve and its brigades used to give temporary relief to the tired divisions of I and II Corps. Worse still Putty received orders to transfer 19 Bde to II Corps, again temporarily, to replace 14 Bde (5th Division). The CinC twice visited HQ III Corps at Ecuiry that day with encouraging news of the French advance on the left, and orders from GHQ were yet again to 'hang on to its present position and assume the offensive if the opportunity occurs'. 10 Bde's patrols the previous night reported that the enemy was constructing further wire entanglements, and the weather was making many of the roads very bad, so the pressures on Putty and his staff, faced with conflicting priorities and lack of resources, continued to grow.

That evening he wrote to Ettie Desborough:

> My dear Chief, Many thanks for the soap which arrived quite safely, how clever of you violet is my favourite scent. The fighting has been very severe for the last four days, but we have given a good account of ourselves, the Guards Brigade on Monday did splendidly. We want heavy howitzers with high explosive shell. The aeroplanes on both sides do wonderful work, indicating the positions of batteries by means of dropping coloured lights, what a science war is becoming. The expenditure of ammunition is incredible you would not believe it possible for the Germans to have had so much available they must have been manufacturing for years while our ordnance people have been economising. Every blessing Yours ever Putty.

As III Corps strengthened its defences, under constant shell fire, its eyes were first on the French on its left; there after a promising start the advance was not making much progress. Hopes were then focussed on the French operating on the BEF's right flank where some success was reported. The CinC had allowed Putty to retain 6th Divisional Artillery but the shortage of ammunition made this of limited value. He visited Putty again on 18 September to be told that the road bridge at Venizel was now able to carry all traffic except motor lorries and heavy artillery: the possibility of withdrawal behind the Aisne was also discussed because the next day instructions were received to 'make arrangements of a precautionary nature in case it should be found necessary to give up our position N of the River Aisne'. Glubb (CE) and Harington (GSO2) carried out a reconnaissance on 19 September to select a main position on the Belleu-Acy Plateau. Meanwhile the situation on the left had become confused with a report that 7th French Corps had been attacked and the enemy had got six or seven battalions across the river. Later Du Cane (BGGS) visited the French HQ and discovered that they had regained the lost ground, but there was little cause for the earlier optimism.

Putty wrote to Edith Castlereagh on 19 September:

> Dear Lady C, You are splendid, your letters are worth their weight in gold, what a pig you are never to have written such good ones before. We have done nothing since we last wrote and am very bored with our present position which merely consists of issuing orders to units that are in the trenches all of whom are shot at while we are in little danger except for an odd shell on top of the hill, however one never knows what is going to happen the next minute so one has to endure it. The men are quite splendid, have been to the hospital to see the wounded twice this week, one fellow told me he felt much better since his leg was cut off, all except the lying down cases we can get away to the base hospitals all right and a good woman from Paris sent motor ambulances and took away all the lying down cases except five that were too bad to move. Companies of maxims of the light kind and heavy howitzers are what our army wants most. Several of the prisoners we get seem to have had enough of it and want to go back to Germany. Yes if I had been Quartermaster General and you wanted to send clothes out to the Blues it would only have been on one condition. The gout has gone, I was a poor thing while it lasted but showed it as little as I could. Yours ever Putty.

Most of Putty's letters contain comments on the prosecution of the war on other fronts and at home; they are not included in the interests of brevity and because they are not directly relevant to Putty's own responsibilities.

The weather was very bad with heavy storms and the river rising, and signs of worse to come. The AQ Staff were still wrestling with many shortages caused by the retreat; there were, for example, a large number of men who did not have a greatcoat or a pack. Meanwhile the new main position S of the river having been marked out every available unit was put to work, and civilian labour gathered from the villages to assist with the digging. A second anti-aircraft gun arrived and was deployed to Septmonts to provide some protection to the work. The rise of the river made it necessary to move the pontoon bridges because the approaches were becoming impassable. That day French decided to put Rawlinson in command of 4th Division: it is not clear why he did this because Rawlinson was to be moved again two weeks later, or if he consulted Putty. They knew each other well although Rawlinson was three years younger. Haig's (then GOC I Corps) views of Rawlinson are interesting; writing in 1915 he said 'Rawlinson is unsatisfactory in this respect, loyalty to his subordinates' and 'Though not a sincere man, Rawlinson has brains and experience'. Such qualities would not have been helpful at this difficult time.

On 23 September the Battle of the Aisne was effectively over; in it III Corps' casualties were 35 officers and 1,220 other ranks. Nevertheless, that day Putty and Smith Dorrien (GOC II Corps) met with their respective divisional commanders to consider an attack on the Chivres Plateau. Rawlinson noted:

> by no means an easy matter for the Germans have now had time to dig themselves in and construct barbed wire entanglements along most of their front; the village of Vregny which will be my first objective is not an easy place to take as the approach along the valley through the woods is directly commanded by enemy guns on the Condé ridge to the E.

Putty wrote to Ettie Desborough on 23 September:

> My dear Chief, Ever so many thanks for the pair of socks and Boracic ointment (antiseptic for boils and other skin problems), both the most useful of things. We have got a lovely fine day at last after continuous rain it will be a blessing to the men in the trenches. The artillery duel has been increasing ever since we arrived here; we call the German big shells portmanteaus they are a prodigious weight just over 200 lbs. The owner of the house I am living in came down from Paris to see it yesterday he was delighted to find it in such good order, there must be quite good partridge shooting here judging from the number we put up while riding it is a pity neither of my ADCs have got a gun to help vary the menu. The postal arrangements are bad and letters take much too long to come out and to get home they ought to have a motor service from the base and not be dependent on the trains. Write me news and send me interesting cuttings. Saw Maurice Baring[5] the other afternoon. All blessings. Yours ever Putty.

He wrote to her again next day about Jessie Arnott; it and everything else about Jessie and his relationship with her are included in a later chapter.

The following week saw little change in the tactical situation. The entrenchments grew stronger daily and some ground was gained at night but this had little significance other than to keep the pressure off III Corps. The main problems were logistical and administrative, as the AQ diary noted: 'All units of the Corps were still very deficient in ordnance stores and equipment. The only stores received by 2 A&SH (19 Bde) since the retreat from Mons are 20 greatcoats. There are no cooking pots in the battalion and a large number of mess tins deficient. Some of the men have no socks and the soles of their boots are nearly through'. It was perhaps not surprising that McGrigor (DA&QMG) was taken sick and sent to a hospital in Paris. He was replaced by Brigadier General Walter Campbell late Gordons.

Rawlinson (GOC 4th Division) wrote in his diary on 26 September: 'Putty came over'. It was an interesting choice of words.

Putty wrote again to Ettie Desborough on 29 September:

> My dear Chief, Have got two letters from you in the last three days for which my most heartful thanks. I sent into Army Headquarters to ask about John Manners,[6] George Cecil[7] and Ivan Hay[8] but they have no news, there is a rumour that the first named is dead the other two are wounded they believe and probably in the hands of the Germans but nothing definite is known. Operations here have come to a dead lock immediately in front of my Corps, we are both dug in so that neither side dare attack the other; a continuous artillery duel goes on but neither side does much damage to the other as our aeroplanes locate the batteries. We want a big Howitzer with a range of Ten Thousand yards for this work, the great thing is it shows the great German impetus is a thing of the past and gradually their attacks are becoming weaker, the class of soldier in the firing line very different and much

---

5   Maurice Baring (1874-1945) Eton RFC.
6   Lieutenant Hon John Neville Manners Gren Gds killed in action 1 September 1914.
7   2nd Lieutenant George Edward Cecil Gren Gds killed in action 1 September 1914.
8   Probably Lord Arthur Vincent Hay IG killed in action 14 September 1914.

deteriorated from the splendid material they began the war with, all this is good and means ultimate victory to us who still have many reserves to call on. Laurence Drummond had much better stay and train troops at home for he is an excellent trainer and has not the constitution to stand the strain out here. I lost a good friend yesterday, Major Green of the Worcesters,[9] BM 17 Bde. Best loved blessings Yours ever Putty.

On 30 September the CinC held a conference of his corps commanders at Fère en Tardenois. In his despatch for September 1914 French wrote:

Lieutenant General WP Pulteney took over command of III Corps before the commencement of the Battle of the Marne. Throughout the subsequent operations he showed himself to be a most capable field commander and has rendered very valuable services.

At the end of that month the strength of the corps was – Corps Troops: 690 men and 523 horses; 4th Division: 18,131 men and 4,406 horses; 19 Bde: 4,700 men and 430 horses; a total of 23,521 men and 5,359 horses. The 4th Division strength includes its first significant reinforcement of 1,200 men who arrived in Septmonts on 20 September. After a month in the field HQ III Corps had begun to settle into its routine. Putty was out most days accompanied by an ADC, a groom and an escort of the corps cavalry; the other ADC and Private Hogbin remained at the HQ to plan the next day, to prepare for Putty's return in the evening, to move his office and possessions if the headquarters was moving, and to be ready to react to unexpected events such as the arrival of new orders. The process of assessing information and producing orders was at times too slow, but it improved with experience, and in periods of static warfare it was often unnecessary to produce new orders on a daily basis.

On 1 October 4th Division reported that its brigades had nearly completed their advanced trenches; Rawlinson was thinking that when this line was completed he would be able to keep two battalions out of each brigade in reserve. Meanwhile GHQ was issuing secret orders to II Corps for its withdrawal, as the first move of the BEF to the left flank, sometimes called the 'Race to the Sea'. III Corps was to take over the positions held by 5th Division in Missy. 6th Division was beginning to concentrate S of the river in the area of Serches but this meant that 4th Division became more rather than less stretched. For Putty all of this was made more difficult by Rawlinson being relieved and once again Wilson (Comd 12 Bde) being put in command of 4th Division. On 2 October French met the corps commanders and GOC Cavalry Division at HQ 3rd Division to discuss 'probable move to the left flank'. The next few days were devoted to planning a very complex operation to start on the night of 6/7 October. 69th French Division was to relieve 4th Division in the trenches; meanwhile III Corps was to set off with 19 Bde leading, followed by 6th Division (less 16 Bde still with I Corps) and then 4th Division. The march to the entraining station was a long one, first S to Oucy la Ville then E through Villers Cotteret and Crépy en Valois to Verberie; it crossed both III Corps' line of advance to the Aisne and, further W, the line of its retreat to Paris, and the French lines of communication. It was made at night keeping under cover of woods and villages by day, thus concealing the direction of march from the enemy. The operation, which was executed most successfully and without the

9   Arthur Dawson Green (1874-1914) killed in action 28 September.

Germans learning for some time what was happening, threw much additional work on Putty's Staff.

On 8 October HQ III Corps moved to a chateau W of Verberie where it could supervise the entrainment of the corps. Before they moved Putty wrote to Theresa Londonderry:

> Dear Lady Londonderry, Many thanks for your letter of 30 Sep which Charlie gave me this morning. Yes am quite fit and have had no return of the gout; it frightened me a good deal at the time as the medicine to arrest it is so lowering and came just at the time that the strain was on me. We expect to be moving from here shortly so don't be surprised if you are not able to follow our movement after a bit; shall be glad to get away myself, am tired of the River Aisne. How splendid about your Ulster Volunteers, they ought to be the very best material. Have just got two troops of the Irish Horse arrived to do my escort under Lord Massarene;[10] the horses stampeded this morning and have not heard whether they have collected them all again or not. Charlie very fit and well, he is getting fatter every day and his moustache quite military. Yours very sincerely WP Pulteney.

And to Ettie Desborough: 'My dear Chief, My Corps has had very little fighting this last few days, endless shell fire on both sides which we have got the best of. You dear thing sending me those socks it is too kind of you to think of it. Yours ever Putty'.

It would wrong to assume the letters that survive, and are quoted, are the only ones Putty wrote during the war. The frequency of these letters suggests that he was an avid letter-writer and would also have written to his brothers and sisters, Arthur Wykeham and Isabel in particular, to Jessie Arnott the girl he had fallen in love with, and to many friends both military and civilian. He stopped writing to his close friend, Gerald Cuthbert, with whom he had regularly corresponded before the war, probably because Cuthbert had commanded 13 Bde in 5th Division at the Curragh before the war and was still doing so. This does not explain why the correspondence did not restart later, but that did not happen. Putty's letters, often frank and sometimes indiscreet, cover topics from the progress of the war to trivial and often amusing anecdotes; they give an insight to the man and his feelings at the time a letter was written.

Left Hook to Armentières October 1914

III Corps, now more than 45,000 strong, moved by rail to the neighbourhood of St Omer over the three days of 9, 10 and 11 October. Haldane wrote of 10 Bde's experience: 'The arrangements for the train journey were not at all satisfactory for the men had to travel in trucks that had recently carried cattle and horses, and it was now too late to procure straw. We left at midnight (10 October) in two long trains, which moved at intervals of four hours, and at 10.30 am (11 October) reached Hesdigneul, which is about four miles SE of Boulogne'. It was to be a long journey.

HQ III Corps moved by road to St Omer with Harington (GSO2) again sent ahead; he noted:

---

10   Algernon William John Clotworthy Skeffington 12th Viscount Massarene (1873-1952) IH.

I was sent up N [8 October] to arrange for the arrival of III Corps. I went in the Rolls Royce of Jimmy Rothschild.[11] It was a good long journey and all went well till I arrived at a little railway crossing short of St Omer, where I was told that the Germans were in and around the town. I found the inhabitants in a state bordering on panic. The Germans were only a few miles off. I stayed in a convent or hospital, I forget which, but I had the engine running all night in case of trouble. I sat up with the old French Territorial Commandant most of the night and he kept saying 'Will the English be here in the morning?' I hoped as much as he that they would be. Much to my relief, the trains bringing III Corps started to arrive in the morning (10 October). The HQ which I selected for the Corps in Rue de Bleuets St Omer subsequently became Sir John French's HQ.

The presence of Jimmy Rothschild as one of Putty's ADCs is not easily explained; at this stage of the war he was a private in the French Army. One explanation is that he joined because he knew Castlereagh or Pembroke, or when HQ III Corps was quartered at one of his chateaux.

1 Cameronians 19 Bde, the first battalion to arrive, moved out 5 miles E to Renescure to cover the arrival of the corps; by 6 pm the brigade was complete with one battery of artillery. By 7.30 pm 6th Division mounted troops (19 H) and cyclists had arrived and were sent forward to the line St Venant-Hazebrouck-Cassel as a screen and to report on the situation when GOC 6th Division arrived. There were, however, serious delays on the railway. HQ III Corps reached St Omer late in the evening and 6th Division by 6 am next day (11 October). At 9.30 am (11 October) these orders were issued by HQ III Corps:

> 6th Division will carry out the following movements today so as to be suitably disposed to advance in the direction of Aire, Hazebrouck or Cassel as the situation may demand. Advanced guard consisting of divisional mounted troops, one artillery battery and an infantry brigade with attached troops to Ebblinghem with outposts on the line Blaringhem-Lynde-Le Nieppe. Main body in area Wardrecques-Campagne-Arques-Blendecques. Strong posts to consist of one battalion with cyclists about F de Lysel E of St Omer watching the front with detachments at cross roads at Clairmarais and connecting up with the French who are holding the northern and eastern edges of the Forêt de Clairmarais and Momelin. Advanced guard to push on reconnaissance to Hazebrouck and explore the northern parts of the Forest de Nieppe about La Motte au Bois and another reconnaissance to Cassel.

The corps was very vulnerable and these orders achieved a difficult balance, guarding against a surprise attack from NE, E or SE, and pushing forward without delay so that the enemy could not prepare strong defensive positions. At 7 pm (11 October) III Corps OpO No.22 was issued: 'Intention of CinC to advance in a NE direction, prolonging the French left and cooperating with them in enveloping the enemy's right flank. 6th Division will move at 5.30 am tomorrow on Hazebrouck with the object of covering the detrainment of the rear units of III Corps at Hazebrouck Station. Units of 4th Division which have detrained W of Hazebrouck will be suitably disposed by tomorrow evening along the St Omer-Clairmarais-Le Nieppe-Staple road

---

11   Baron James 'Jimmy' Armond Edmond de Rothschild (1878-1957) extra ADC.

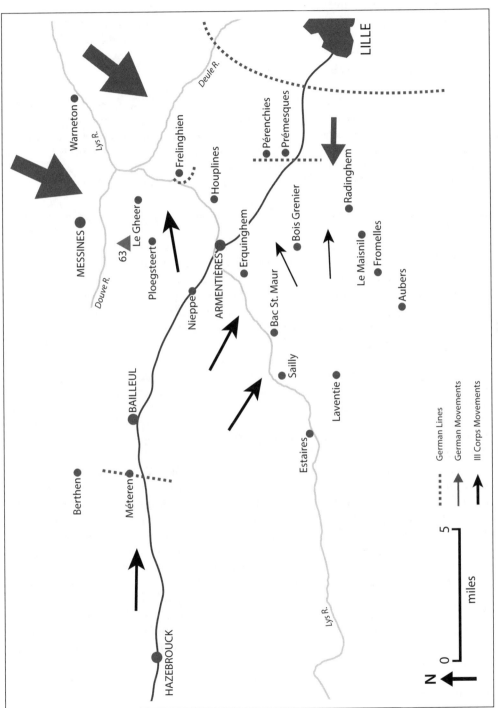

Map 6 1914 (2).

with their head at Staple'. This statement of the CinC's intention was later to be the cause of some friction between Putty and Smith-Dorrien whose II Corps would be to his S.

Putty's intention was to get forward E of Hazebrouck as quickly as possible with 4th Division coming up on the left of 6th Division. The French provided buses to assist the move forward but they arrived very late and until Hazebrouck Station was secured no firm plans could be made to run trains to it; these transport problems delayed the deployment.

Two descriptions of the ground give an idea of what lay ahead:

> One of the most remarkable features of Flanders is the sub-surface water which, always high, rises as autumn progresses; any excavation or depression soon fills with water and its sides fall in, while the surface of the ground is rapidly churned by traffic into the consistency of cream cheese. Except in heavy frost troops are confined to the roads: it was bad for infantry, almost impossible for mounted action and very difficult for artillery.

Such was the terrain over which III Corps had to advance and high ground assumed an even greater tactical importance:

> On the left lay the 130 metre range of steep-sided hills running down from the Mont de Cats. Quite apart from the physical difficulty they presented to any assault, and they lay in the path of Allenby's Cav Corps, these hills offered superb artillery observation over the area of III Corps' proposed advance. The series of steep ridges projecting S from the main line of hills also provided the enemy with a perfect set of defensive positions and plenty of dead ground for the deployment of artillery.

So, with a compelling need for haste, III Corps began its advance to the River Lys. Cav Corps, on its left, took Mont des Cats on the evening of 12 October with little opposition; it appeared that the enemy had not yet had time to occupy these positions in strength. Putty was determined to push on before the enemy did so, and ordered his corps to advance on Bailleul. However, the delays in the rear continued. The buses did not begin to arrive until midday (12 October), and meantime the artillery and transport had started. There was in consequence much congestion of traffic in the streets of St Omer and its suburb Arques, and many buses lost their way; it was considered that the troops would have reached their destinations many hours earlier and suffered less fatigue had they marched. 12 Bde, the last to arrive, was railed right up to Hazebrouck but, as a result of all the delays, III Corps was not ready to advance until 10.30 am 13 October. Meanwhile, when the advanced guard reached a point five miles beyond Hazebrouck about 9 am, they found the enemy entrenched on the far side of a small stream, the Méterenbecque. Their position was on the long ridge on which is situated Méteren, a well-built village with a prominent church tower, and surrounded by cultivated fields. They seemed determined to stand and the RFC reported two batteries of artillery and about 500 infantry moving westward to Méteren. Cav Corps also met opposition and was unable to turn the Méteren position from the N. Although 10 Bde, the advanced guard of 4th Division, was making good progress at Flêtre, Putty decided to halt and arrange to attack with the whole of III Corps on a five mile front Merris-Méteren.

He may well have been reluctant to risk an attack by 6th Division alone because he did not know the enemy's strength. In fact in front of III Corps were two cavalry divisions (from IV and VII Cavalry Corps), 4 Jäger battalions and 3 batteries of artillery; there was also part of one division XIX Corps. Another factor could have been the difficult conditions especially for artillery: the country was close, flat and dotted with farms each of which was a potential strong point; the only observation points were on the German side; and the weather was wet and misty.

At 7 am on 13 October HQ III Corps moved forward to Hazebrouck and at 11.15 am issued these orders (G.67):

1. The enemy is reported to be holding a line extending from Neuf Berquin through Bleu-Outtersteene-Bailleul S.O.-Méteren-Berthen.
2. III Corps will attack this line as soon as it can be assembled and deployed. 4th Division will attack Méteren and the ridge running due N from the village. 6th Division, less 19 Bde, will attack Bailleul S.O. and Outtersteene.
3. 19 Bde will remain as Corps Reserve between Strazeele and Pradelles.
4. Cav Corps has been asked to cooperate by attacking Berthen.
5. The attack will be timed by the movements of 4th Division which will probably be in a position to advance from Flêtre at 1 pm. CH Harington Major GS

Before describing this action, part of the Battle of Armentières 13 October-2 November, Sir John French's account gives an overview:

On this day GHQ were moved to St Omer. On the way there I went to Hazebrouck to see GOC III Corps. Pulteney is a very old friend and comrade of mine, to whom I should like to devote a few lines of this story. The keenest of soldiers from his early youth, he was the adjutant of his battalion of the Scots Guards. Thence he sought service in Africa, where he did excellent work, although he suffered severely from the climate. I was delighted to find him with me as one of the three corps commanders who fought with the first expeditionary force sent to France. Throughout my period as CinC he wholly justified the estimate which I had formed of his capacity and capability in the field. He enjoyed the full confidence of the officers and men who served under him. Possessed of an iron nerve and indomitable courage, he remained imperturbable and unmoved in the face of the most difficult and precarious situations. No matter how hard the task imposed upon him he never made difficulties, but always carried out the role assigned to him with energy and skill. It had been my hope to see him in command of an army [see 1915], for which I feel sure he was thoroughly qualified; but my withdrawal from France prevented my carrying out my intentions with regard to him. His conduct of the operations which I am just about to describe was characterised by his customary skill, boldness and decision. The great results which occurred from the First Battle of Ypres may be fairly traced back to his initial leading of III Corps in the series of successful advances which were the most prominent and important amongst the opening phases of that great combat.

I got back as quickly as possible to HQ at St Omer, where reports were awaiting me. I learnt that the town had been heavily bombed during the day. Much damage had been done to buildings; and several soldiers and civilians had been killed and wounded. It was a somewhat unpleasant welcome for us, but the effect of it was completely wiped out by the news I received from Pulteney of the victory he had attained. He found the enemy in a strong position covering Bailleul, with their left resting on Bleu (close to Vieux Berquin) and their right on Berthen. The attack opened at 1.30 pm and by nightfall 6th Division had captured Bailleul, while 4th Division captured and occupied a strong position facing E one mile to the N. This was an excellent day's work performed by III Corps.

In that close country the advance developed into an infantry battle, to which artillery observers, in hop and other small fields on a wet and misty day, could give very little assistance. Progress was slow and costly; the enemy trenches, mostly occupied by dismounted cavalry, were well sited and barely visible and they had good artillery observation from the church tower at Méteren. When III Corps finally rushed the main position that evening the enemy quickly disengaged and faded away into the dark. III Corps casualties were 708 and the German losses were estimated at around one thousand.

But the line Bailleul-St Jans Cappel was reported strongly held and Putty, therefore, decided to resume the offensive on the morning of 14 October before the German cavalry could be supported by more of XIX German Corps from Lille only 20 miles from Méteren.

About 10 pm that evening reports from II Corps indicated that they had lost Givenchy, and were with difficulty holding on to their positions. Smith-Dorrien asked Putty for one of III Corps' divisions to be directed to his assistance. Part of the problem was the widening gap between the two corps which was held by Conneau's French Cav Corps. Smith-Dorrien did not believe that the gap could be held by cavalry alone, and also thought that Putty had agreed to cover it; the exchange of correspondence shows a degree of ill-feeling on Smith-Dorrien's part. Putty's orders were to keep closed up to the Cav Corps on his left and move NE, outflanking the German right. He believed that he could best assist Smith-Dorrien by keeping III Corps concentrated and continuing his advance as ordered; GHQ agreed with him. It is difficult to assess if Smith-Dorrien's ill-feeling was to result in lasting resentment but the relationship, never much more than professional, seemed to deteriorate further when Smith-Dorrien later commanded 2nd Army and in which III Corps served. It may all be a consequence of the friction between French and Smith-Dorrien after Le Cateau; Smith-Dorrien thinking that Putty was more trusted than he was, as seemed to be the case. Smith-Dorrien makes no mention of this in his diary of these days or that he raised the matter with the CinC. It is difficult to fault Putty in all of this; pulled in two directions he decided on a course of action for his corps that was both tactically sound, by keeping it concentrated, and complied with his orders.

Reconnaissance on the morning of 14 October established, after much difficulty and considerable delay due to heavy mist and rain, the Germans had withdrawn from Bailleul and its vicinity and retired behind the Lys: the town was occupied at 10 am. Progress was still slow, owing to the opposition by rear-guard of cavalry and machine-guns, the difficulty of reconnaissance, and the impossibility of artillery support in such bad weather and in such close country. By the evening 4th Division was in and E of Bailleul and 6th Division extended the line southward and was in touch with the French cavalry. In difficult circumstances III Corps had pushed back from a strong defensive position a German force at least equal to it in size, and this had been done without any significant use of artillery. Some of the credit for this must go to Putty and his decision to mount an attack with the full corps at the outset; this fixed the enemy to their front and turned both flanks. Had they stayed to fight at least 15,000 of the enemy might have been caught on the W bank of the Lys.

French met his corps commanders at HQ III Corps at 12 noon on 15 October: his orders to Putty were to press on to the River Lys, occupy Armentières, repair the bridges, and be ready to advance NE astride the river and clear of Lille, taking its defenders in the flank. He noted that he also instructed Putty 'to endeavour to gain touch with II Corps'. It is difficult to see how Putty could have done this given the distance and the French Cav Corps between them, and with his right directed on Fleurbaix. The confusion is made greater by the order to II Corps (GHQ OpO No.37 issued 8.30 pm): 'As soon as opposition is sufficiently overcome to permit it, the corps will close to its left and lessen the gap between itself and III Corps'.

III Corps issued orders at 2.45 pm for 6th Division to secure the bridges at Sailly and Bac St Maur and 4th Division those at Erquinghem and Pont de Nieppe. During the day 16 Bde returned to 6th Division and 19 Bde was taken into GHQ Reserve. Although it was foggy and the ground had not been reconnoitred, three of the four bridges were captured during the evening before III Corps ordered a halt because of the unfavourable weather. 18 Bde found Sailly deserted and the bridge partly destroyed, but 38 Fd Coy RE repaired it by the light of the burning church. At Bac St Maur, men of 12 Fd Coy RE crossed the river on a raft, swung back the bridge, and the village was occupied. On the left, 11 Bde in the early morning found the bridge at Erquinghem undamaged; but the one at Pont de Nieppe barricaded and defended; in accordance with III Corps' instructions 4th Division waited until 6th Division had crossed the Lys, swung NE, and was ready to assist it.

All seemed to be going well. French noted:

> I am free to confess, however, 15 October, the day on which I date the opening of the Battle of Ypres, I believed the danger was past. I believed that the enemy had exhausted his strength in the great bid he had made to smash our armies on the Marne, and to capture Paris. The fine successes of our Cav and III Corps did much to confirm these impressions in my mind.

On 16 October both divisions of III Corps consolidated their gains. On the right 6th Division moved forward to a position across the river forward of a line Sailly-Erquinghem, its right being in touch with Conneau's French Cav Corps; the division was about to begin the difficult manoeuvre of swinging N. On its left, 11 Bde 4th Division sent 1 Som LI across the bridge at Erquinghem, as 6th Division was approaching it from the S, and they took it without loss. At 4 pm 1 Hamps 11 Bde seized the bridge at Pont de Nieppe, under covering artillery fire: on their left 12 Bde occupied Ploegsteert and placed guns on Hill (sometimes called Point) 63, a commanding height N of the village. 4th Division mounted troops covering the corps' left flank reached Neuve Église where they were in touch with the Cav Corps. French wrote: 'On my way back (from visiting Allenby) I came to HQ III Corps (and saw Pulteney). They were getting on fairly well and had made some progress, but they had not yet taken Armentières'. Capturing French towns brought numerous administrative problems for Putty and HQ III Corps AQ Staff; for example, several cases of rape in Bailleul said to have been committed by the Germans had to be investigated.

III Corps ordered both divisions to move E at 7.30 am 17 October with 6th Division getting forward on a line Bois Grenier-Chapelle d'Armentières and 4th Division pushing one brigade into Armentières. If this operation proved successful, Putty intended to move NE bringing the rest of 4th Division across the Lys. 6th Division met little opposition and at noon had secured its objective with all three brigades in line; 10 Bde 4th Division passed through 11 Bde and entered Armentières. This place, a large town with wide streets, was full of refugees from Lille.

Hotel de Ville Bailleul, 1914. HQ III Corps 1914-15

Small parties of Germans had remained behind, firing from the houses; but they were dislodged without great difficulty, and 10 Bde moved through the town and NE to Houplines. 12 Bde, on its left and still on the N bank of the Lys, got to Le Gheer in front of Ploegsteert Wood, and 11 Bde remained in reserve about Steenwerck. The prisoners taken belonged not only to German Cav Corps but also to XIII and XIX German Corps, fully confirming the presence of these formations. The advance had caught the enemy in the process of a relief; again the speed and direction of III Corps' advance had outmanoeuvred a much stronger force.

However, the enemy had begun to entrench a position on the high ground in front of III Corps, Prémesques-Pérenchies-Verlinghem. This low clay ridge, known as the Pérenchies Ridge, was a very important feature. At the same time the Germans pounded the positions about Armentières with heavy artillery and mounted strong counter-attacks.

That day HQ III Corps moved forward to Bailleul which was in a semi-ruinous state, and was established in the Hotel de Ville in the main square. Putty, as usual, was close up behind the advance; at 8 am he was at the cross roads two miles NW of Nieppe presenting crosses of the Legion of Honour to 57 all ranks including Captain Jack (James Lochhead Jack 1880-1962) 1 Cameronians, now SC 19 Bde and of whom more later. Refugees from liberated areas were causing problems but now there were also several thousand Belgian refugees, hoping to return to their homes, following up III Corps into the area of operations. They were becoming a nuisance, blocking the roads and slowing the overall forward movement.

At 11.55 pm 17 October III Corps issued OpO No.28:

> Enemy reported to be holding position from Radinghem to Pérenchies and thence in a NE direction but report received this evening from a patrol to effect that it has been through Prémesques and found Germans retiring seems to indicate that the enemy is withdrawing. He is also holding right bank of River Lys from Frelinghien to Wervicq. III Corps has been ordered to move down the valley of the River Lys attacking enemy vigorously, supported on right by French cavalry and on left by Cav Corps. As there is no enemy in front of the corps on the left bank of the river and as right flank of corps would be threatened if it were to try and pass by enemy's position at Pérenchies certain preliminary operations are necessary before orders received can be carried out. First it will be necessary to drive back the enemy reported to be between La Vallee and Pérenchies and second to gain possession of Frelinghien so as to be in position to pass troops of 4th Division across the river at Houplines so that the corps may act with its full force in direction chosen for ultimate operation. The following operations will therefore be carried out tomorrow morning commencing 6.30 am. 6th Division is to reconnoitre line La Vallee-Pérenchies by pushing forward infantry supported by artillery in sufficient strength to test the character of defence. Should enemy

be found in strength no attack will be delivered until 4th Division is in a position to cooperate. Should the enemy be weak and give way he should be pushed back at once towards Lomme and contained while division prepares to advance on Quesnoy. 4th Division will attack Frelinghien from both sides of the river and prepare to pass the bulk of the division over river at Houplines when Frelinghien has been taken.

Putty did not just give orders but explained his uncertainty of the German intentions and his own intentions in some detail. He had been ordered to turn his corps 90 degrees to advance N while in contact with the enemy and crossing a major obstacle. While doing this III Corps' right flank would be vulnerable from the Pérenchies Ridge and also from forces in Lille, so he was determined not to take undue risk and maintain a degree of balance at all times. This had to be explained to his divisional commanders so that they in turn could ensure their plans were equally measured.

Events on 18 October were somewhat complicated as both divisional commanders executed Putty's plans. At 6.30 am Keir sent 18 Bde against the enemy S of Prémesques and 17 Bde against Prémesques-Pérenchies, each with an artillery brigade. 16 Bde was subsequently ordered forward on the right, one battalion to small groups of houses in front of Radinghem at the foot of the ridge, to feel for the enemy. 1 E Kent, which was given the task, encountered no one. 18 Bde reached its objectives towards 11 am after only slight resistance but on their left 2 Leinster and 3 RB (17 Bde), sent against Prémesques and Pérenchies respectively, met continuous opposition as they moved up the slopes in front of them; but by 10 am 2 Leinster were on top of the ridge, in Prémesques and in sight of Lille. They could not get further, so dug in and waited. 3 RB made some progress but, its left flank not being covered, was eventually forced back from the houses.

HQ III Corps had come to the conclusion that the enemy in front of 6th Division was weak (it was indeed the weakest point of the defence) and at 11.30 am ordered it to press the enemy vigorously eastwards, and 4th Division to contain them in the N. The order explained that before the corps could advance down the Lys to Menin it was essential to drive the Germans off the ridge and over the River Deule beyond it, and to prevent them debouching from Lille.

Shortly before noon Keir sent 16 Bde to attack Radinghem in cooperation with 10th French Cavalry Division. On receipt of Putty's orders he instructed 18 and 17 Bdes, each supported by a brigade of artillery, to press forward on either side of the Armentières-Lille road, and 16 Bde (less two battalions in divisional reserve) to wheel NE from Radinghem, to turn the enemy's flank from the S. They did not start until about 2.30 pm: on the right 16 Bde had some difficulty approaching Radinghem but took the village, held by part of 139 Regt XIX German Corps, and were at once ordered to entrench the ground gained. The strength of the Germans evidently lay half a mile to the SE of the village, and on their flank. The next advance lay across open ground, and in attempting it 1 E Kent and 2 Y&L came under heavy fire, and were immediately afterwards counter-attacked. Eventually 2 Y&L threatened to outflank the enemy and they hastily withdrew. Instructions were now received to handover Radinghem to I French Cav Corps, still on III Corps' right, but only 150 men appeared so it was decided that two battalions should remain there.

On the left of 16 Bde, 18 Bde's objective was the line Ennetières-Capinghem, on top of the ridge, roughly a mile to its front. 2 DLI on the right secured its objective about 5 pm and entrenched just E of Ennetières. 1 E Yorks on its left, was held up by enfilade machine-gun fire from its left, because 2 Leinster 17 Bde, although in the village of Prémesques, were unable to take Mont de Prémesques just S of it. At nightfall 1 E Yorks was still half a mile short of Capinghem. 17 Bde, the left brigade, was unable to make progress and at 5 pm on the line Prémesques-Epinette (two miles E of Armentières) was ordered to entrench. Its right battalion, 2 Leinster, had got nearer to Lille than British troops were to be for many a long day. Thus at night on 18 October, the general line of 6th Division was convex towards the enemy, and some points of the Pérenchies Ridge were in its hands.

Ordered to capture Frelinghien, 4th Division moved forward at 6.30 am. 10 Bde, with a howitzer battery attached, advanced on the right (S) bank, and 12 Bde on both banks of the river. It then became evident that the main enemy line in front of Lille did not run as first supposed. Instead of continuing northwards it turned W at Verlinghem to Frelinghien; the latter, in a salient, could be attacked from both sides, S and W, but the right of any advancing force against the southern face would be caught by enfilade fire from its right. 2 Seaforth and 1 R Irish Fus led the attack here, with 2 RDF acting as right flank guard and connecting with 6th Division. They were stopped by fire from houses in front and on their right by short range artillery fire. 12 Bde, moving against the western edge of the salient, reached the railway without encountering resistance; but after crossing it came under heavy fire from front and flank, and halted to allow 10 Bde to draw level.

Thus when Wilson (GOC 4th Division) received Putty's revised orders issued at 11.30 am for 6th Division to press on, and for 4th Division to contain the Germans on the line Verlinghem-Frelinghien he was still short of this objective. 10 Bde, with enemy in front and on its right flank, and without support from 6th Division on its right could make no progress. Assistance was sent to it, first 2 Essex from 12 Bde, and then two battalions from 11 Bde in corps reserve, but to no avail. 12 Bde fared better as it was easier on the W bank of the Lys to support it with artillery, and by nightfall it had captured Le Touquet, opposite Frelinghien, although the village was strongly held and supported by continuous fire from across the river.

At 7.22 pm III Corps issued orders to both divisions to hold the ground gained and organise strong reserves. CinC visited Putty at Bailleul during the day; he summed up the situation: 'III Corps had captured Bois Grenier and Armentières, and were on the line Radinghem-Prémesques-Houplines, after an excellent advance for which Pulteney deserves great credit'. Putty had issued simple orders that made his intentions clear, given each division its objective, and provided such coordinating instructions as absolutely necessary. Subordinate commanders were then allowed, even encouraged, to use their initiative in developing their own plans. This flexible approach was only possible because of the level of training in the Regular Army divisions. 4th Division had been weakened at Le Cateau and subsequently but this was the first time 6th Division, commanded and trained by Putty before the war, had been committed as a division to battle. III Corps casualties in the nine days 9-18 October were 1,550, comparatively few when considering the strength of the German defence.

When Putty held a conference at 7 am 19 October he was faced with a difficult situation. At 8.50 pm the previous evening GHQ had issued orders: 'CinC intends to continue attack at 6 am tomorrow (19 October). III Corps will continue to attack on the line which it was engaged today'. Information was then received that strong German forces were advancing and this led to further orders that the overall offensive was to be temporarily abandoned with III Corps ordered to maintain its present position, and to collect all possible reserves. This uncertainty resulted in a day of consolidation. 10 Bde did attack Frelinghien; well supported by artillery it reached the outskirts of the village, but the attack was not pressed further, as Putty did not consider the gain of ground was worth the inevitable expenditure of life. But there was still a mood of optimism that the advance could and would be continued, and HQ III Corps was moved forward from Bailleul to Armentières. At 2 pm French, Smith-Dorrien and Putty met: as a result of this meeting 19 Bde was returned to III Corps, to fill the gap between it and II Corps, still held by Conneau's French Cav Corps. However, GHQ OpO issued at 9 pm directed that 19 Bde would remain under GHQ even when deployed, and this caused some confusion.

Early on 20 October, Putty realised that III Corps' advance had been checked, and, anticipating a violent counter-attack he ordered his men to dig in and prepare to hold on. He gave orders that as many men as possible should be collected to build up local and divisional reserves and that a number of strong points should be prepared behind the front line. His aim was to give the corps' position the depth it lacked. However, the Germans struck before much could be done and attacked along the whole front of 6th Division. At 11 am all corps commanders were summoned to meet the CinC at Bailleul: Smith-Dorrien wrote: 'I heard from Pulteney that his III Corps was being heavily attacked, German troops having been heard coming up by train in the night, and that he feared that his right flank might be turned'.

Although an attack was expected, the appearance of XIII German Corps previously identified on the N bank of the River Lys and now on the left of XIX Corps, was not. 6th Division's positions were pounded by artillery of all calibres up to 8 inch before the infantry attacked covered by heavy machine-guns. The Germans had become wary of British rifle fire and their infantry attacked using fire and movement. This was not a local counter-attack but the beginning of the great German offensive, the First Battle of Ypres. 6th Division was caught in a position that was over-extended and tactically unsound for defence. The scattered and broken nature of the line, merely the night positions of a series of advanced guards, mattered little when III Corps was moving forward, but, now that it was on the defensive, was highly dangerous during the hours of darkness. All three brigades of 6th Division were attacked but the main weight fell on 18 Bde and especially 2 Sher For holding a salient in advance of Ennetières. They withstood all attacks until 4 pm but were then overwhelmed and the enemy captured Ennetières. 6th Division was forced back about 2 miles in the centre and on its right, but only a quarter of a mile on the left. The new position covered Bois Grenier where 18 Bde was brought back in reserve, as the line shortened. 6th Division's fighting withdrawal under a strong and ferocious surprise attack, and in heavy drizzle, was a remarkable achievement. It did suffer about two thousand casualties but 1,119 of these were in 18 Bde, and most of these in 2 Sher For.

10 Bde (4th Division) continued to attack Frelinghien to improve communication across the Lys. At daybreak they secured some further trenches and houses on the southern border of the village, took fifty prisoners of 40th Division XIX German Corps, and counted over a hundred of its dead. However, the supply of lyddite (HE) shells for the attack of houses was not equal to the demand, and after this success the operation was stopped. Further to the N, 12 Bde, about Le Gheer in front of Ploegsteert Wood, was attacked from noon onwards with increasing strength, and at dusk enemy infantry established themselves within three to five hundred yards of the brigade line.

From 8 am 20 October onward the enemy shelled Armentières with heavy guns; two of HQ III Corps' staff were wounded, Captain James (APM) and Rothschild (ADC). Harington (GSO2) recalled: 'I recollect so well Hunter-Weston (Comd 11 Bde corps reserve in Armentières) coming to beg the corps commander to return to Bailleul. He was right'. Putty took his advice and HQ III Corps did return to Bailleul.

By the evening of 20 October French still did not seem to have appreciated the full seriousness of the situation. GHQ's OpO issued at 9 pm stated: 'CinC intends to contain the enemy with II, III, IV and Cav Corps and to attack vigorously with I Corps (about Ypres)' and 'These corps will hold the enemy opposed to them to its ground and at the same time take every opportunity of seizing tactical advantages'. The reality was that the initiative had passed to the enemy and there was now a serious risk of the defence being broken, if not overrun. The threat of this came soon enough when GOC Cav Corps (Allenby) requested two battalions be sent to Hill 63 in case they needed assistance. Comd 11 Bde was given this task at 3 am 21 October with two of his battalions and 2 Essex (less two companies) of 12 Bde. As he marched he was also to drop off 1 E Lancs (less a company) to support 12 Bde which was holding Le Gheer. He was only able to take one (1 Som LI) of his own battalions to Hill 63 because 1 Hamps had been sent to assist the left of 6th Division earlier in the day and 1 RB, his fourth battalion, was still under 10 Bde before Frelinghien. Such was the way III Corps was now stretched.

Putty wrote to Ettie Desborough on 20 October:

> My dear Chief, You have not written for some time. Have had hard fighting all this week, the casualties have been heavy but we have more than pulled our weight and but for a fog which came on on Wednesday morning should have rounded up a good lot of Germans. The refugees from Lille and these big manufacturing towns is going to be a very serious question in the future as it is even now, the Germans have been occupying all these towns and taking all the food out of them now places like Armentières which we have reoccupied they all come flocking back to and there is nothing for them to eat. We have just had three 'Jack Johnsons' (German 6") arrive in the middle of the town Jemmy Rothschild had the nearest shave I ever saw, he got off with a covering of dust and a few cuts and my provost marshal who was with him with a splinter in his neck Jemmy is never good looking but his face at this moment is a picture of which I should much like a coloured photograph, I expect they will have me out of the place before very long, anyway it has had the desired effect of making the refugees bolt just as they had begun to intimidate the local inhabitants for food. Yours ever Putty.

By dawn on 21 October Putty realised that III Corps was faced by both XIII and XIX German Corps on a front of 12 miles. 4th Division in the N was under attack by XIX German Corps, mainly from across the corps boundary with Cav Corps. 6th Division and 19 Bde, on the right, were opposed by XIII Corps probing S to find a weakness. Putty had few reserves and Armentières itself was weakly held. Now, in addition to a shortage of artillery ammunition, the infantry discovered that the cartridges they were being issued with were slightly too large for the breeches of their rifles. When their rifles were cool this was not a problem, but as they heated up the cartridges began to jam. Men could not flick open the bolt to eject the spent cartridge and reload; it was necessary to kick open the bolt and feed in the rounds by hand, and this was compounded by a lack of rifle oil to clean and lubricate the action. With large enemy concentrations advancing against their positions rapid rifle fire was much needed.

On the left the Germans attacked the whole front of 12 Bde, driving in the left and occupying Le Gheer. This endangered the cavalry at St Yves so a counter-attack was mounted by elements of 11 and 12 Bdes supported by 4th Divisional Artillery on Hill 63; it was entirely successful, the Germans (104 Regt) being driven back with great loss and the abandoned trenches reoccupied. About 200 prisoners were captured and one battalion of 104 Regt was practically annihilated; 40 of 4th Division's prisoners were released. But it was not without cost, 12 Bde alone had 468 casualties. Meanwhile at the other end of the line 19 Bde was under severe attack at Le Maisnil but, supported by three French horse artillery batteries, were able to maintain their position until nightfall. Jack (SC 19 Bde) recalled:

> The situation is growing acute. Le Maisnil is burning. Since the right of the brigade is now compromised and the three remaining companies of 1 Cameronians are insufficient to restore the situation Comd 19 Bde (Gordon) orders his command to fall back forthwith to La Boutillerie. Here the brigade rather mixed up and in little more than one extended rank, lies lining the road and buildings, rifles ready and bayonets fixed, expecting the Germans at any minute.

For Putty it was a time of more than usual anxiety. III Corps' long front was holding firm but at 4 pm the Cav Corps to the N needed urgent assistance and two companies of 2 Essex and a section of 9 Fd Coy RE were despatched to strengthen Messines. There seemed every prospect that XIII German Corps would next attack Conneau's French Cav Corps on the right of 19 Bde, threatening the corps right flank. The CinC's view which he expressed in telegraphing Kitchener was that the enemy was playing his last card; but this was far from the view of his subordinate commanders in contact with the enemy. Smith-Dorrien wrote in his diary:

> In the evening Colonel Davidson (GSO2 HQ III Corps) arrived from III Corps to say that in consequence of our Cav Corps N of the River Lys having to fall back a short distance, III Corps had been ordered to extend its line N of the Lys, and, therefore, it would be necessary to draw 19 Bde nearer towards them – thereby increasing the gap between us and making a bigger task for the French cavalry. Davidson also told me that 18 Bde had lost heavily yesterday and that he feared the Sher For heavier than any other regiment.

The withdrawal of 19 Bde had widened the gap between II and III Corps to 3 miles. Although this was covered by Conneau's French Cav Corps, GHQ wired III Corps at 3 am (22 October) to close the gap. However, at 2.35 am Putty had instructed 19 Bde: 'It should be clearly understood that my G.381 does not justify you in giving up a yard more ground than absolutely necessary, and while keeping in touch with the right of 6th Division your right should extend as far in the direction of Fromelles as you reasonably can'. At 8.15 am he placed 19 Bde under 6th Division and by 9 am the gap was satisfactorily closed.

At 9.30 am (22 October) HQ III Corps established an Advanced Reporting Centre at Nieppe. This greatly reduced the time for communication to and from the divisions, now of critical importance, and provided Putty with a tactical headquarters to speed up the decision making process. At 12 noon French held a conference at Bailleul, attended by Putty, at which it was decided to entrench a reserve position. No-one was now in any doubt about what was to come.

During the day 4th Division was attacked but in all cases positions held without difficulty. The severity of the fighting was indicated by a report at 11.15 am from 12 Bde that there were 800 to 1,000 dead and wounded Germans still lying out in front of them from Touquet to St Yves. 4th Division were learning that straight shooting over the parapet, supported by crossfire of artillery and flanking machine-guns could stop an attack of almost any weight. 4th Divisional Artillery (Milne) was extraordinarily effective, with arrangements now made to switch nearly the whole weight of it to any sector that was menaced. On the right, 19 Bde was again attacked; Jack (SC HQ 19 Bde) noted:

> Yesterday (22 October) 19 Bde lost 8 officers and 300 other ranks, chiefly 2 A&SH. Entrenching is carried out under some shelling, and therefore promptly. The covering companies, although close to the Germans and rather pressed by them, succeed in holding their ground until retiring on their battalions at nightfall. The Lahore Division and a brigade of II Corps are behind us in Estaires, ready to give help if necessary.

The pressure on III Corps was increasing every day. All the brigades were committed and had been in continuous action for some time; inevitably everyone was very tired, including Putty, but there was to be no let up. III Corps was fighting for its very survival. Putty's letter to Ettie Desborough that day (22 October) gives an indication of the strain felt by everyone:

> My dear Chief, It has been desperate fighting on a very extended front for some days now and a very anxious time we have had of it, our losses have been very considerable but those of the enemy simply enormous now we have had time to dig ourselves in we are more comfortable and every day makes us stronger, there is little doubt but that a most determined attack will now come from the N and all our forces may be required to meet it once that is expended and the line is still unbroken all will be well, I don't say that we shall not have to give up some ground but it will be to get more interior lines and shorten our front to economise troops and collect reserves with a view of making our advance in the required direction in due course. One thing I know viz that is the trained troops that do the deeds and win the fights, it is drafts to our present formations that are required and not new units and I don't hold for Lord K's new army, he should prepare drafts from his new army for the regular units and the Territorial Force both of which are properly staffed and organised and the men should be sent to the various depots now with that object, Hythe school should be turned into an instruction camp for maxim detachments and the sections ready to go to units when qualified, the maxim plays the most important part in this war it has no nerves and seems to give unlimited confidence in defence as well as attack. I wish I had room for Julian[12] on my staff but rest assured if there is the smallest opportunity I will have him applied for at once. Our guns will soon be worn out they must be prepared to replace them, guns and ammunition must never fail us, the power of production of both of these should be trebled. I saw Colonel Cook and young Astor[13] in the hospital here yesterday they will both be soon all right again, poor old John Cavendish[14] it was very sad about him. It

---

12   Ettie's son Julian Grenfell RD (1888-1915) died of wounds.
13   Probably John Jacob Astor (1886-1971) LG Eton later 1st Baron Astor.
14   Major Lord John Spencer Cavendish LG killed in action 20 October 1914.

seems funny to see the Indian troops out here, they take every precaution I saw them doing advance and rear guards along the roads with all our troops miles out in front of them I thought some Frenchman was the most probable billet for their bullets but they will soon learn. All blessings Yours ever Putty.

At 10 am on 23 October Putty held a conference of his divisional commanders and GOC Cav Corps, and at 11.10 am sent this message to GHQ:

I have conferred with my divisional commanders and Allenby this morning and arrived at the decision to strengthen my right by extending the line now held by 4th Division to the right so as to allow 6th Division to increase the strength of its reserves. Provided the line now held can be maintained I am of the opinion that it should be reasonably secure on the understanding that General Conneau's cavalry are relieved as soon as possible by British infantry and the infantry of the Lahore Division now with the Cav Corps remain so that Messines is securely held. I am putting my (Fortress Company) to work at once assisted by civilian labour on the line Fauquissart-Fleurbaix-Nieppe-Neuve Église but it will of course be some days before the line can be made really strong. In the meantime I have no faith in General Conneau's cavalry being able to resist another serious attack and should they fall back today behind Rue de Tilleloy this line above mentioned will already be compromised.

Even as the conference was taking place 6th Division was reporting 16 Bde being hard pressed between Bridoux and La Boutillerie. This area was intersected by deep drainage ditches, referred to in 16 Bde's report by the Indian word 'dongas', which when full of water were an obstacle to movement. Now, only partially filled, they provided a covered approach for the enemy to get close, cut the wire, and rush the trenches. 16 Bde's report ended: 'These trenches have been re-occupied at the point of the bayonet. A few German prisoners are held and a large number of German dead remain on the ground'.

During the afternoon Putty attended a conference at Estaires with the CinC, GOC II Corps and GOC Lahore Division present. III Corps GS log recorded:

Question raised (at conference) regarding relief of Gen Conneau's cavalry and following wire sent at 5.35 pm to II Corps: 'This is to confirm the arrangements arrived at the conference at Estaires this afternoon to the effect that 6th Division will not take over from General Conneau tonight'.

Late that afternoon, in preparation no doubt for the general attack of 6th German Army on 24 October, XIII German Corps drove the French cavalry out of Fromelles; thus, as Putty had feared, the right flank of III Corps was seriously endangered.

At 5 pm that day Maude (GSO1) left to take command of 14 Bde in 5th Division. He would be much missed; Putty wrote of him:

His greatest asset in South Africa and in the European War was the way he would see everything for himself where any doubt existed; in fact he gave one so much confidence in this respect that it prevented one as a commander from going oneself on occasions.

Lieutenant General Pulteney, 1914.
(*War Illustrated*)

At dawn on 24 October 6th German Army attacked on the whole front from the La Bassée Canal to the Lys. It was everywhere repelled in III Corps except on the front of 16 Bde which, as it faced S, was exposed to enfilade. After a few lucky shots had wiped out some of the trenches, German infantry from the cover of factory buildings penetrated for a time into the line of 1 Leics; they lost 225 men before the gap was closed. Fighting continued all day and into the night, and at 11 pm Comds 16 and 18 Bdes met: it was decided, with divisional and corps' approval, to withdraw 16 Bde to a prepared line five hundred yards in rear, if the Germans attacked again.

Meanwhile Putty's reorganisation was taking place with 12 Bde 4th Division taking over 17 Bde 6th Division's trenches, so that 4th Division was now holding a front of 8 miles. DDMS III Corps noted: 'From 18 to 24 Oct there had been 3,294 wounded in III Corps, an average of 470 daily. During this period there had been six ambulance trains and one truck train to evacuate them'.

Also this day French's despatch was published:

> Lieutenant General WP Pulteney took over command of III Corps just before the commencement of the Battle of the Marne. Throughout the subsequent operations he showed himself to be a most capable commander in the field, and has rendered very valuable services.

Putty wrote to Edith Castlereagh on 24 October:

> Dear Lady C, We have had the most desperate fighting every day lately, the casualties have been very heavy but those of the Germans simply terrific we have got two more

days to stick it out, then the situation should be easier, the times are anxious but it is the second big coup which the Germans have tried to bring off one more fresh army corps in these parts would settle the show. My cold is better, Charley is also quite right again but with this changeable weather it is rather difficult to gauge the temperature one is hot one minute and cold another which is all very well in connection with your sex but is useless out here where one has no opportunity of (outlet), hence the cold, it is rather involved but you must try and grasp the meaning!! There is terrible congestion of traffic on the railway here owing to fresh army corps being brought out up into these parts the result is that it is difficult to get our hospital trains away, they are all right in the towns here but we like to get them straight on to the trains and away to England to free more of the staff, why does not Miss Florence (probably a nurse serving with Scottish Women's Hospital at Royaumont, and later in Serbia) come down here to lend a hand instead of going down to the Aisne to lend a hand to French Generals after we have gone, it was not very kind of her to go flirting even with the allies when there were all of us about. The Indians have arrived, they will probably be in the firing line at any moment now they look quite splendid fellows and should have a good chance of distinguishing themselves, don't suppose the Germans will have any compunction in shooting them when they catch them but they will easily get quits with them if they do. All the German army corps in this part are so mixed up it is impossible to tell what we are fighting against it is a good sign and means they have been unable to keep up their original formation, formations are necessary even with the production of children, therefore when they alter their formations it is a sign of decadence. What made George Digby[15] do that? Had he found Lady Muriel[16] unfaithful to him! It is a great nuisance as the Copper Horse cannot arrive today. Goodbye dear thing. Yours ever Putty.

Putty's letters to Edith Castlereagh invariably did not go through the censor, especially when they contained detailed information on the fighting, although he never wrote about future plans, or his views which were often indiscreet, or sexual innuendo. The latter was to increase and must have been reciprocated.

Early on the morning of 25 October the enemy again made desperate efforts to break in especially against 1 Leics (16 Bde 6th Division). The planned withdrawal was therefore ordered: although in close touch with the enemy, 16 Bde that night withdrew in heavy rain and pitch darkness to its new line without interference, and the right of 18 Bde conformed. Jack (SC HQ 19 Bde attached 6th Division on the extreme right) wrote:

Since 23 October the Germans have also been entrenching, 500 to 700 yards from us; their earthworks are visible here and there. The two mile front held by the brigade is so extensive that the advanced battalions form practically a single line, with gaps between them and most of their companies. Scarcely any men can be spared for local supports. At night the gaps are guarded by standing posts or patrols. Where the trim, deep, willow lined ditches (the dongas) of the country are suitably placed they have been adopted as trenches in order to

15   Major George Hugh Digby (1867-1914) Eton Dorset Yeo accidentally killed 20 Oct 1914.
16   Lady Muriel Augusta Digby (1876-1920) daughter of 5th Earl of Ilchester.

provide cover from fire, and are being widened and improved. Battalions are now well dug in; their HQ are in inconspicuous houses about the La Boutillerie road, 300 to 400 yards from the trenches. A few rolls of barbed wire, made up on wooden reels in one-man loads, are arriving for battalions nightly. They are pegged out after dark so as to trip an incoming enemy. No work is possible in close view of the Germans in daylight. The Germans pound our trenches daily for about three hours in the morning and three in the evening with heavy howitzers. Our artillery reply is relatively feeble since we have few howitzers and not enough shells for them. Field gun shrapnel and high explosive shells, while effective against troops in the open, are useless for dealing with men in good trenches.

On the III Corps' right flank Indian troops relieved Conneau's French Cav Corps without incident. Also that day French visited Bailleul where he saw Putty, Allenby and Smith-Dorrien. While HQ III Corps GS wrestled with the numerous issues arising from attacks by a greatly superior force on a very wide front, the AQ Staff worked to keep it administered and supplied. That day the first significant reinforcements arrived at St Venant, 47 officers and 997 other ranks; they had to be received, administered, and then moved to their respective units, and in the middle of the battle this was difficult. Another arrival was a special cable section to allow the corps to control aeroplane work and especially reporting of the enemy's gun positions. Within 24 hours this arrangement was working well with the enemy's trenches and heavy howitzers engaged.

During the night and morning of 26 October the enemy continued to shell 6th Division, mainly 19 Bde, but there were no serious infantry attacks. It was a relatively quiet day which allowed the reorganisation planned by III Corps to be completed. At 7.15 pm GHQ ordered I and IV Corps to attack in the N, and II and III Corps to maintain and strengthen their present positions. III Corps OpO No.33 implementing this was issued at 9 pm and with it a memorandum:

> The enemy has for the time being abandoned his infantry attacks and has resorted to a heavy bombardment of our trenches. Till the corps is in a position to resume the offensive, the reply to this method of attack will be as follows: deepen trenches; make communication trenches; withdraw as many men as possible from the front line; collect as strong divisional reserve as possible; improve facilities for artillery observation.

Telegraphing Kitchener at 8 pm that evening French, who had visited HQ III Corps during the day, expressed his confidence that it (and II Corps) would be able to hold its own.

Putty was not so convinced; his corps was now very stretched. One problem was administering the town of Armentières in the front line which was now an unacceptable burden for 4th Division; HQ III Corps, therefore, asked AG GHQ for 200 French Territorial troops to control the civilian population and relieve 4th Division of this task.

After a quiet night 27 October was again relatively undisturbed apart for an attack on 18 Bde 6th Division which they repulsed with heavy loss, some 150 enemy dead being found in front of the trenches. At 12.10 pm Putty sent this telegram to GHQ: 'It is now clear that the enemy has not withdrawn to any appreciable extent from my front; shelling and infantry are active in places; the offensive of I and IV Corps has not as yet resulted in the contraction of the front of III Corps which still holds from Rouges Bancs to the River Douve, a front of 12 miles. I do not wish to make any suggestion that would weaken the offensive movement ordered to take place today so long as it is possible to persevere with this movement but I must point out that the extension of my front continues to exhaust the troops which have already been subjected to a great strain and that the result of the present extension is to render it impossible for me to collect adequate reserves so that even were the enemy to weaken on my front I should have no troops available with which to take offensive action. The point at which relief can be afforded is from Le Gheer to the River Douve. This portion of the line is of great importance owing to the large number of guns grouped about Point 63 and as it is now held by infantry I cannot weaken my line there at present. It would ease my situation if circumstances were to allow the Indian Bde attached to Cav Corps to take over this portion of the line'. The reply from GHQ was: 'Length of the line you hold fully realised. First opportunity will be taken to contract your front'. There was little that they could do to help.

That evening Putty wrote to Ettie Desborough:

> My dear Chief, The fighting has been desperately heavy daily, practically continuous either attacking or defending, my corps has had the full weight of one and a half of the best German corps against it, the strain has been very heavy, many a time the staff came in in the night one had to make momentous decisions which horrified the local situation by telling them to hold on by their eyelids to certain pivots where one knew there would be terrible losses but which had to be held not only for the safety of my army corps but for those on either side of me, they have stuck it out magnificently but I scarcely dare face the regiments for fear of seeing the gaps among the officers, it cannot possibly last at this pace one side or the other is bound to crack. Have had lots of congratulations about the Dispatch but really didn't deserve them as the poor fellows in the fighting line should have got it all, one wants to go there oneself the whole time but if one did one would be drawn away at one point without looking after the main problem. Seely goes about like a madman, drives his motor car up to the firing line etc he is certain to be killed, how such an irresponsible person could ever have been made War Minister defeats me, he pulls his weight though in the number of shells he draws daily and shall be sorry when they finish him on account of his pluck, the stories he tells of himself are simply priceless. What I told you a long time ago about supply of gun ammunition was looking well ahead and now we have to be careful, all new plants for the supply of an inexhaustible amount should have been erected on 5th August but alas they were not, pray God they are now, don't repeat. Bless you. Yours ever, Putty.

The enemy appeared to be making preparations for a greater effort. On the morning of 28 October, after a heavy bombardment, they struck again against 18 Bde. Creeping up through the ruins of cottages, parts of two German regiments reached the trenches of 2 DLI and forced out the defenders, some men actually getting in rear of the British line. The invaders were ejected by a counter-attack of the reserve companies (including one from 2 LF of 4th Division), and nearly 200 of the enemy were buried. They and the prisoners belonged not only to XIII German Corps but also 24th Division of XIX German Corps, which would seem to have been brought S for the attack. Putty's decision to readjust and reinforce III Corps' right proved to be correct and timely.

He wrote to Edith Castlereagh that day:

Dear Lady C, Many thanks for yours of 25 October which Cyril Hankey brought yesterday. Have had a very anxious time since I last wrote hanging on by the eyelids to an enormous front, swept in all directions by terrific shell fire, men unnerved by the casualties want of sleep, the continuous strain etc., the losses break one's heart but those of the German have been colossal, you cannot get near the front trenches by daylight one place was attacked yesterday morning we knew nothing about it until relieved last night, the subaltern in charge counted 56 dead Germans in front of him two of whom fell on the top of his own bit of trench, that represents 200 casualties in one place, but the shell fire is what does it to the nerves. Charlie is all right again and full of life the tales he tells us of his dreams are somewhat disquieting they scarcely show a pure mind but having slept with you so often must have had that effect indelibly stamped into his person. We have got an uphill time before us for another two months and then the tide will turn, we must have big guns and endless supply of ammunition just when one wants it they are short, it makes me mad but that is all right now, the authorities at home don't realise what colossal expenditure there is in these terrible conflicts, I blame K for not having started double the producing plant for guns and ammunition the moment the war began I know it was the first thing I thought of, I know how cheese pairing Secretary of States deplete the reserves. Of course I should like your little perfect pet of a Shetland 'woolly' I hope it won't make me feel too naughty thinking of you when I wear it. The Indians have had a bad time from shell fire and ignorance but will hold their own now that they know more, they lose their way all over the country and cannot make anyone understand what they want. Every blessing Yours ever, Putty.

Jack (SC HQ 19 Bde attached 6th Division), wrote on 29 October:

There is little change in the local situation, the brigade has not been seriously attacked, but apart from definite actions the daily German shelling and sniping continue to be severe. Battalions continue to put out more wire, and higher, so as to form a fence which will prevent the enemy from rushing them in the dark. They are also improving their defences and digging short communication trenches to enable men to pass to and from fire trenches in greater safety. Further work is on shelters, for the construction of which damaged buildings are being stripped of timber. The weather has rather broken, and all men coming from the trenches are plastered in mud from head to foot.

An usual incident was the surrender of about a dozen men from XIX Saxon Corps to 18 Bde during the morning. In the N, 4th Division had a quiet day until about 6 pm when the enemy made a sharp attack on Le Gheer and the line to the N of it, but were repulsed. III Corps' situation, opposed by between three and four divisions seeking, fortunately in vain, a weak place was perilous enough; and the desperate efforts of the Germans to break through near Ypres began to have repercussions. But on 30 October the action started in the S when at 2 am the enemy made a heavy attack on 19 Bde S of La Boutillerie. It was beaten off except at one place where the enemy actually entered some of 1 Middx trenches and held them for several hours until, with the assistance of 2 A&SH from the brigade reserve, they were recovered, all the enemy being bayoneted or captured. Over two hundred dead were counted and forty prisoners taken belonging to a new formation, 48th Reserve Division of XXIV German Reserve Corps, which had come into the line between XIII and XIX Corps.

Jack described the attack:

> Last night, just after midnight, the enemy suddenly opens intense shell and machine-gun fire on the brigade front. Our batteries reply immediately in order to stop an infantry assault. The brigadier (Gordon) turns to me 'Inform the artillery, and ask them to open fire' (Their targets having already been arranged in case of emergencies). In two minutes, or less, from the commencement of the bombardment, the couple of 18 pdr batteries supporting the brigade are hard in action; a few seconds later they are joined by the 4.5" howitzer battery and the two 6" howitzers further away. HQ 6th Division are informed by telephone and by motor cyclist that this seems to be a real attack. At 2 am the enemy's guns lift to our support line; their machine-guns redouble their fire for a minute or two before stopping abruptly. At once the German infantry advance with consummate courage, cheering and bugles blowing, the survivors getting right up to the trenches. A little later reports from battalions say that they are hard pressed and want reinforcements. The word comes that the enemy has penetrated 1 Middx line. 2 A&SH are therefore ordered to turn them out, 1 Leics about 200 strong, sent from 6th Division, taking their place. The attacks cease at dawn. 300 bodies counted lying in front of our trenches.

Jack's description of this action shows how effectively coordinated the defence had become in 6th Division, as it had in 4th Division.

In the N 11 Bde reported at 8.23 am that the enemy was advancing against its whole front, Le Touquet-River Douve. This made no progress but, across the corps boundary, Cav Corps was now under heavy attack and at 2.25 pm GHQ instructed III Corps: 'If you have not received other orders from CinC who is with Cav Corps move what reserve you have to your left and report action you take'. At 4.30 pm Putty updated GHQ on his deployment and added: 'Considering the extension of my front, the distance from my left to the area in which 2nd Cavalry Division and 7th Division are fighting, and the vital importance of maintaining the position held by the right of the army, I do not consider it advisable to move more troops to my left'. At 5.15 pm orders were received from French that all available reserves of 4th Division were to be N of the Lys by daylight next day (31 October) prepared to assist the Cav Corps, and Putty was instructed to redistribute his 6th Division reserves so as to be able to support 4th Division S of the river. He was being pulled to both flanks but the CinC clearly thought the threat was now much greater in the N and, without further delay, Putty issued the necessary orders.

The situation was worsening in the N. At 7.45 pm HQ III Corps reported to GHQ: 'Heavy attack being pressed on St Yves after very heavy and severe bombardment throughout the afternoon; 11 Bde preparing counter-attack from direction of Point 63; whole front of 4th Division N of the river heavily engaged; no attack S of the river but enemy's trenches in very close touch at several points. Reserves being distributed in accordance with my G352'. The attack had fallen on 1 Hamps; as the front was 2,000 yards long, Le Gheer to River Douve, almost every man was in the trenches, and these were not continuous but isolated lengths without communication trenches to the flank or rear. For ten minutes the Germans were in the trenches of 1 Hamps, but were expelled by a counter-attack of the 11 Bde reserve. Comd 11 Bde (Hunter-Weston)'s report was: 'Major Prowse and 1 Som LI, God bless them, have restored the situation'; but the whole platoon in the trench entered were found dead at their posts. The prisoners captured belonged to 134 Regt, 40th Division of XIX German Corps.

At 10 pm that night these orders were sent by III Corps to 4th Division, copied to GHQ and Cav Corps:

> Cav Corps reports Messines being heavily attacked. Your efforts should be directed firstly towards providing adequately for the security of your artillery at Point 63 and secondly towards collecting as large a force as possible near Ploegsteert for offensive action either towards St Ives or towards Messines as circumstances may dictate. Should Messines be captured during the night its recapture should not be attempted with an inadequate force.

Some time that day, most likely after 10 pm, Putty wrote to Theresa Londonderry:

> Dear Lady Londonderry, The fighting has been most desperately heavy for the last fort-night; the Germans are massing every available man, their attacks have been quite magnifi-cent, their losses stupendous, but they must have had marvellous reserves for them to come on again in the manner they do. They ought to send every available foot soldier there is in the country to meet what will be the last final effort of attack before the winter comes; supply of ammunition and guns are what the Government ought to have concentrated their urgent attention in the first week of August, we shall see if they have done their duty. The weather has turned very much colder now at night which is trying for the men in the trenches but it cannot be otherwise alas. Charlie is very well, quite fit, there is not much exercise for him in these days of telephones etc as the messages come so much quicker that way than the man on the horse. What a pity you are not here to shoot the rabbits in the shape of the Germans; we want every rifle in the firing line and good straight eyes like yours. Yours very sincerely WP Pulteney.

The following morning (31 October) GHQ was told by III Corps at 7.45 am:

> After successful counterstroke by 1 Som LI (11 Bde) on St Yves the enemy did not renew its attack and the front of 4th Division was quiet during the remainder of the night. Arrangements were being made to repair the trenches which had been much knocked about by yesterday's bombardment. A consultation took place between 4th Division and 1st Cavalry Division with the result that 4th Division has extended its line slightly to the N of River Douve so as to allow 1st Cavalry Division to strengthen its posts in Messines.

By 9 am Cav Corps was under severe attack at Messines and to its N; and at 10.35 am 1st Cavalry Division informed III Corps: 'Regret to inform you that owing to gap made by 57 Rifles (Ind Corps att Cav Corps) shall not be able to hold town of Messines, shall fall back slowly to a N and S line through Wulverghem, am bringing up infantry to this place and shall of course retake the town if possible'. 4th Division had sent two companies of 2 Innis Fus (the battalion was now holding the extended line N of the River Douve) to assist in the defence of Messines and at dark they held the W edge of the town, by which time the Cav Corps had regained most of the ground it had lost in the morning. S of Messines and between it and the River Lys, the southern line of the great German attack, the enemy made no progress.

However, the retirement of Cav Corps from Messines made III Corps' position critical and on 1 November Putty reported to GHQ that the line was so extended and the men so exhausted that he doubted whether a serious attack could be stopped. He took the precaution of making preliminary arrangements for the withdrawal of 4th Division, now with all but two battalions N of the Lys, to a rear position which had been partially prepared. At 9 am the CinC sent him two battalions from II Corps and they were moved to Wulverghem with the caveat 'the CinC earnestly hopes that III Corps will not find it necessary to use them'. Although now under constant attack from the N and the E Putty was able to draw back his left towards Neuve Église and form a flank facing N, covering the important artillery position on Point 63. 4th Division outnumbered and under unceasing attack held on.

The right of the corps was quiet that day with just one entry in the AQ log worth high-lighting: 'A court martial was held at Bois Grenier on a man for a self-inflicted wound. During the proceedings the court was heavily shelled, but the only man hit was the prisoner. The court then decided that as the prisoner was now legitimately wounded they did not intend to proceed with the case'. Bois Grenier was almost in the front line and it does seem a somewhat farcical situation but normal administration, including discipline, had to continue. Interestingly discipline so far had not been a problem but this was about to change with the arrival of large numbers of older reservists.

2 November was the official end of the Battle of Armentières which overlapped in time and to a limited extent in geography with the First Battle of Ypres and the defence of the Messines Ridge, and in which III Corps was still fighting. Since 13 October, in the eighteen days taking and holding Armentières and the line of the River Lys, III Corps had 5,579 casualties, more than half in 6th Division but this included 19 Bde.

At about 8.30 am, after a heavy bombardment that included trench mortars, I German Cav Corps with two battalions of 134 Regt XIX German Corps attacked 11 Bde. The enemy pressed forward, particularly in the vicinity of St Yves, but were everywhere repulsed with heavy loss. At 1 pm 4th Division reported that:

> The left of their line along Ploegsteert Wood which is being held by 1 Hamps (11 Bde), 2 Innis Fus (12 Bde) and 1 Som LI (11 Bde) is being shelled very heavily it seems doubtful how long it will be possible to hold there. Dorset and Worcesters (from II Corps) which are still in hand have been moved up but have not much faith in them. Unless pressure is taken off soon must have two or three reliable battalions to restore situation on our left this evening as it is essential not to give up an inch of our line. Our men who have held this line practically unaided for the last four days without relief are splendid but there is a limit to human endurance.

This highlights the ongoing superiority of the German artillery; the British lacked ammunition for their field artillery and had pitifully few heavy guns. It also brings out the danger of assuming that reference to a battalion is always indicative of a fighting unit of one thousand men or more. The lack of confidence in the two battalions from II Corps was that they were well under-strength and had come from severe fighting further S, from which they were about to have a break. Again, and despite all, 4th Division held on. On the right 6th

Division was in close touch with the Lahore Division on its right and reported no problems on that flank.

Putty wrote to Ettie Desborough:

> My dear Chief, Many thanks for your letter of 31 Oct which I got last night a record. I don't mind what you tell Arthur Balfour[17] because I have more faith in him at the present crisis than any man in England. The fighting still continues to be terrific, the casualties on our side are heart rending, those of the Germans colossal, the German shell fire has been beyond all description and owing to having to economise our gun ammunition we have not been able to cope with it, it has been a terribly anxious time for me as am holding nearly double the front of any other English corps and am the pivot of all the Army of the North if I was forced back five miles Douglas Haig would have to run too – the poor cavalry have stood it in the most wonderful manner, outside their role in defending positions against superior numbers of attacking infantry, hopelessly outnumbered in guns as well, the pace is too terrific, it cannot last, exhaustion must come, how the Germans can keep up their supply of big gun ammunition defeats all our organising imagination it seems to be perfectly endless. What we want now at this period of the war is infantry and artillery the cavalry should be in rear of the fighting line ready to support a break in the line or dash through when we break the German line. Poor Sir John French he has had an anxious time this week, if all is well by this day week the blow will have been spent, the fighting may be continuous but not with the same driving power. Boulogne is where the organisation of nursing is most required at the present moment. Yours ever Putty.

It was to be a quiet night and this continued throughout 3 November. The GS log recorded at 1.40 pm: 'From enquiries made by 4th Division it has been ascertained that the enemy's losses about Le Gheer and St Yves during the attacks in the last three days have been heavy' and 'In front of 1 RB 11 Bde the Germans were seen to be pushed out of the trenches to make an advance, no officers apparently leading them, and retired in disorder as soon as fired on'. Unusually it then went on: 'Behaviour of 11 Bde under very heavy shellfire has been excellent and they have been well handled by Comd 11 Bde (Hunter-Weston) and CO 2 LF (Butler)'.

The following day (4 November) was again quiet although 6th Division reported an attack on 19 Bde during the previous night which they had driven off. Putty continued to press GHQ for some relief, a reduction in the length of his line, but GHQ was concerned with the recapture of Messines. This was to be done by Conneau's French Cav Corps supported by Cav Corps and 5th Division. It must have been a surprise when an officer sent by Conneau arrived at HQ III Corps expecting III Corps to cooperate with their attack on Messines by attacking simultaneously with its infantry. Putty reported to GHQ at 8.25 am: 'Explained to him that this does not come within the spirit of my orders and that the most I can do is support his attack with artillery fire'.

Putty also wrote to Edith Castlereagh on 4 November:

> Dear Lady C, Charlie wants to be off to his regiment he is right in wanting to go because he is ambitious and wants to get on in his profession so much against my will I shall have

---

17   Prime Minister 1902-1905 and First Lord of Admiralty from May 1915.

to let him go after the present crisis is over. He has a rotten time now with me as he sees none of the fighting, with no chance either of making a name for himself as a soldier, he is really only a flunkey now he feels and comes round in the motor with me but all the same I cannot tell you how I will miss him, have seen so much of him fretting lately I cannot stand in his way, but further he is doing the right thing now that his regiment is short of officers, write and tell me what you think in your heart of hearts. Yours ever Putty.

These few days, mainly fine, gave III Corps a welcome respite to reorganise and improve its defences. They would have known it was not to last. Everyone would have been aware of the intensity of the fighting around Ypres since they would have been able to hear the continuous roar of the guns, and feel the ground shake under them. It would have been brought home to Putty when he went to meet 2 SG in the early morning of 6 November. The Scots Guards' history records:

> Who that remembers 1914 will ever forget Locre (about 4 miles from Bailleul), town of tragic, glorious muster! Here come the Scots Guards, and the Commander of III Corps, Lieutenant General Pulteney, comes up to meet his old regiment, and rides with them to Locre – one captain and 69 men.

On the morning of 7 November 4th Division was again heavily engaged, the main weight of the attack by six infantry and two jäger battalions falling in front of Ploegsteert Wood. This part of the line was held by 3 Worcs lent by II Corps. They had been driven from their trenches, by the severe bombardment, to the shelter of the wood and then at 7.30 am, in thick mist, the Germans broke into the wood and began to spread out. Comd 11 Bde organised a series of counter-attacks which cleared the wood and expelled the Germans from almost all their gains, except a group of houses in front of the wood N of Le Gheer. Efforts to retake this went on into the night without success. One officer and 70 men were taken prisoner: they confirmed that the whole of XIX German Corps was opposite 4th Division.

During the afternoon 1 RB at Le Touquet were also attacked; after a heavy bombardment the enemy charged with unusual enthusiasm and disregard of casualties, but they never managed to break in. For a time 4th Division's situation was precarious; the divisional reserve was re-deployed from S of the Lys and Putty placed three battalions of the corps reserve in Armentières at GOC 4th Division's disposal, but they were not needed. Owing to its good trenches, the losses of 4th Division for the day only amounted to four hundred, of which 208 were in 3 Worcs. 6th Division was also attacked but the enemy were beaten off and the attacks not pressed home.

At 8.50 am (8 November) III Corps informed GHQ that the situation at Ploegsteert Wood was still not clear: it seemed that 11 Bde was holding a continuous line on the edge of the wood but had lost about 500 yards of their old trenches which were outside the wood. 4th Division were waiting for Comd 11 Bde to return from visiting the line; nevertheless GHQ decided not to wait and to send 21 Bde 7th Division (1500 strong) to help restore the situation. 4th Division were informed that this help would not arrive until 4.30 pm. In view of this, and the need to reorganise his brigade after the fighting of the previous days, and the time needed to get a howitzer in a position to engage the enemy in what was now a small salient, Hunter-Weston decided to postpone a further attack. Trench mortars would have destroyed the enemy in the houses of the salient which were surrounded by tall trees, but none were yet available; the two field batteries that were available were limited to six rounds per gun per day; and the size and shape of the salient meant that they could only fire if the infantry first withdrew, risking further enemy advances. This made the deployment of that single howitzer all-important.

Putty's letter to Theresa Londonderry that evening conveyed some of his concerns:

> Dear Lady Londonderry, Many thanks for your letter of 5 Nov which Stavey[18] brought with him yesterday. Charlie wants to go off to the Blues on account of the paucity of officers left with them. I don't want him to go but feel that he is right himself in his decision so shall not stand in his way if the situation here becomes any easier and I find that I can spare him, but I can't tell you how I shall miss him. Of course you ought to make up your minds to conscription and that without delay as if you try keeping up a standing army of one million men in peacetime on the present lines the country will never be able to stand it, it will improve the nation from every point of view and must be done, whether they like it politically or not. We have had an anxious time of it lately and expect to have for some time to come, the Germans seem to have no end to the number of men they are able to reinforce with. Love to all. Yours very sincerely WP Pulteney.

The following day (9 November) was reported quiet as 4th Division prepared to attack the salient that night. The word 'quiet' was only relative because 1 RB was recorded that day as having 'repulsed all attacks made on it inflicting loss on the enemy of whom about 70 lie in front of the trenches'. To their left the enemy in the salient was shelled during the day and the ground carefully reconnoitred; at 11.30 pm the attack by 1 E Lancs (11 Bde), 2 A&SH (19 Bde) and 2 LF (12 Bde) went in. The two battalions of 21 Bde moved up in reserve but were not employed. Success was gained on the right, but as no progress was made elsewhere, the trenches regained were abandoned in daylight. The composition of the attacking force shows the extent to which III Corps was now stretched; again the question must be asked, on this and many occasions later, whether it was necessary to try and retake every piece of lost ground.

Putty wrote to Edith Castlereagh that day:

> Dear Lady C, Thanks for your letter, I cannot let Charlie go just at this moment as the times are too anxious for me to be bothered about a change besides I mean to hang on to him as long as I can. Kitchener makes me very angry, these Territorial battalions have come out here badly equipped and without having done a proper course of musketry, all the Territorials should be put through a proper course before coming out, drafted down by divisions to Aldershot and Salisbury for a month's thorough practical training instead of filling up the place with his army you must have trained men to fight these Germans, above all they must be able to shoot, he made a great mistake in not developing the Territorial system, making new rifle ranges round all the training centres and being practical, you could have got the money for the ranges at the asking and the sooner he gets it done the better all the training centres should have rifle and artillery ranges, just see to it at once!

---

18   6th Earl of Ilchester (1874-1959) Coldm Gds Eton Lord Stavordale until 1905 but still called 'Stavey' married to Lady Helen Vane-Tempest-Stewart, Charlie's sister.

The fighting is still of the most desperate character it really seems a matter as to who can bring up the most men, so far the Germans have, the question is can they continue to do so. Yours ever Putty.

Next day (10 November) it was decided to desist from further attacks and organise a new line W of the salient, thus the 'Bird Cage', as it came to be called, a small projection about three hundred yards square surrounded on three sides by British trenches, remained in German hands and continued so until 1917. Putty was still concerned with the length and the strength of III Corps' line and wrote to GHQ later in the day (G514):

As stated in my G513 the situation to the E of Ploegsteert Wood does not cause immediate anxiety but at the same time matters cannot be allowed to remain as they are indefinitely. There are now two vulnerable salients at St Yves and Le Gheer which cannot be held by the troops now occupying them against a determined attack prepared by artillery fire. Unless therefore the Messines-Wytschaete Ridge is recaptured very shortly the maintenance of the line now held by my corps will become increasingly difficult. The French make little progress in their attack on Messines and there seems little prospect of the situation improving. It is impossible therefore to disguise the fact that a withdrawal to the Neuve Église-Nieppe-Fleurbaix line may shortly be necessary. I hope I may be allowed to point out most forcibly the grave disadvantage of conducting such a retirement under the pressure of an attack and the necessity of giving this question the most serious consideration at the present moment. Considering the condition of the troops and depleted ranks of 21 Bde I do not consider it advisable to renew the attack at present and I am taking steps to make a short retrenchment behind the salient of St Yves which I hope may be of service. WP Pulteney Lt Gen Comdg III Corps.

11 November was quiet; but a German account noted that 26th German Division and 11 Landwehr Bde should have advanced but 'the enfilade fire of artillery and machine-guns from Ploegsteert Wood compelled our men to remain in their trenches'. Putty wrote to Edith Castlereagh:

Dear Lady C, Many thanks for your letter of 9 Nov have still got Charlie and shall not part with him until the next application arrives which I expect hourly now ever since his lot have been about in these parts. We have had an easier day today so far but expect that it means an attack tonight unless all of them have gone off to the First Corps at Ypres. The fogs and cloudy mists have prevented the aeroplanes doing anything the last few days which is a nuisance as we cannot use our big guns Mother and Baby, the former is the howitzer and the latter the 6 inch fortress gun, cannot imagine what kind of maternity skirt mother had before it was born for it is the most enormous gun I have ever seen. We had an easier night yesterday but expect it means walking about one's room wondering where the supports and reserves are to come from now that they are all in the firing line. The Queen's Westminsters [QWR] have arrived and they come into my corps tomorrow but don't want to use them unless am obliged it is much better to let them get their legs first. We have got Lord Roberts coming here tomorrow he is a grand old fellow to come at his age, will take good care he goes nowhere near any shells, the Indians will give him a tremendous cheer.

Billy Lambton[19] came to luncheon here with us today he is rather bored just at the moment and feels Pickles[20] death a great deal. Every blessing Yours ever Putty.

At last there was to be some relief: III Corps OpO No.38 issued on 13 November gave orders that 'IV Corps would take over a portion of the line now held by 6th Division tomorrow night (14 November)'. Lord Roberts visited HQ III Corps during the day which Putty noted in his letter to Theresa Londonderry that evening:

Dear Lady Londonderry, Thank you for your letter, am not going to let Charlie go until he breaks away; I wish the Blues had never come near here but if the situation gets easier he will have to go. We had Lord Roberts over here yesterday and today, he is a great man for 82, the men cheered him which did both good. I Corps have had very desperate fighting and I hear that the Scots Guards have suffered but know no details, the other battalion is here within two miles and has been made up to over a thousand, George Paynter[21] seems to be the hero with them but they are all right and will give a good account of themselves when their time comes again. Any amount of rain which is uncomfortable for the men in the trenches but which is a good thing to wash this town of Bailleul which smells like nothing on earth. Get the Government to make a proper rifle and artillery range in Ulster and a depot for the Army. Yours very sincerely WP Pulteney.

Winter was coming and it was to prove at times a greater enemy than the Germans. Much was done by III Corps AQ Staff to improve conditions for the front line troops. This and the care of the wounded were matters in which Putty took the closest interest. On 14 November AQ log noted: 'One field ambulance 4th Division has been organised temporarily as a rest camp for men slightly sick who are likely to be fit again in a few days. Several houses have been taken over in Steenwerck and a number of men limited to 150 come in for 3 days at a time to receive a hot bath, haircut and clean clothes, and then allowed to sleep for 48 hours before returning to the trenches'. It also noted that day the arrival of 16 officer and 2901 other rank reinforcements, a very large number to be received, administered and assimilated. French visited during the day and saw Putty.

It was very cold with sleet showers on 15 November but the relief of part of 6th Division was completed. Nevertheless Putty felt that III Corps was still stretched too thinly and sent this memo to GHQ:

Now that it has been decided to extricate the British troops in the neighbourhood of Ypres from amongst the French and redistribute them on the line La Bassée-Hollebeke, the moment is opportune to consider the situation of III Corps with a view to future action. The attached map shows the situation as it exists at present and the entrenchments that have been constructed, as well as those of the enemy as far as they are known. It is proposed as soon as circumstances permit to make the River Lys the dividing line between 4th and

19   Brigadier General Hon William Lambton (1863-1936) late Coldm Gds Eton MS GHQ.
20   William Lambton's brother Second Lieutenant Hon Francis Lambton (1871-1914) RHG killed in action.
21   George Camborne Beauclerk Paynter (1880-1950) SG 1899-1927.

6th Divisions and to move 10 Bde to the left bank. The effect of this will be to shorten the line held by 4th Division to enable that division to withdraw some of its battalions from the trenches and give them the rest they so greatly need. It will however leave 6th Division, to which 19 Bde and the Queen's Westminsters are attached, occupying approximately the same extent of front that it has been occupying for so long, and these troops will experience no relief. I must, therefore, again urge the imperative necessity of carrying out further relief on the right of III Corps up to the railway at Rue du Bois, which was foreshadowed in your O(a) 312, if the troops are not to suffer still further from the exhaustion imposed by their prolonged occupation of the trenches, which are now becoming daily more waterlogged and insanitary. I am especially anxious for my front to be contracted so that I may be able not only to give my troops their much needed rest, but also in order that I may be able to collect some reserves and prepare for offensive operations. The attached map shows the purely defensive nature of the trenches now held. They consist of a front line and a supporting line at an average distance of 1000 to 2000 yards apart. There is little or no means of communication between these lines, and it is under existing circumstances impossible to assemble troops for attack or counter-attack except under cover of darkness. The map also shows how different the enemy's position is. At the points where he has pressed his attack he has numerous parallel trenches with zigzag communications, in which he can assemble his troops under cover at any time of the day or night. We fight, therefore, at a disadvantage in this respect and if we gain a local success, cannot confirm it. The reason for this state of affairs is to be found in the shortage of men for the front occupied, and the shortage of engineers. If the front is contracted I shall at once endeavour to remedy this state of affairs, by selecting suitable objectives, distributing the artillery with a view to the bombardment of these points, opening up parallels and communicating trenches so as to be able to mass troops for an assault, sapping forward, destroying obstacles and, if necessary, mining so as to import an energetic offensive into my operations. As regards objectives, I do not think I can do much at present to improve my position between Bridoux and Frelinghien so I would propose that this front should remain a defensive front but I would propose to attack Frelinghien, Le Touquet and the enemy's position between Le Gheer and St Yves. A fact in the situation of great importance is Messines. It is essential for the ultimate success of any operations of this character that Messines should be retaken. It is, however, outside my sphere of operations. I submit the above proposals therefore with the twofold objective of asking the CinC to approve them and also of ascertaining as early as possible what his intention may be as regards the attack of Messines. WP Pulteney Lt Gen Comdg III Corps.

On 16 November Lowther (CO 1 SG) called on Putty and 'dined and breakfasted with his cheerful staff'. Lowther had been wounded at the Battle of the Aisne and resumed command of 1 SG, only one officer and 73 other ranks, that day. Three years later he was Putty's best man at his wedding. The III Corps Intsum that day produced by Major Davidson GSO2 included: 'It is important to ascertain whether the troops opposed to III Corps still consist of XIX Saxon Corps and 48th Reserve Division of XXIV Reserve Corps'. The capture, identification and interrogation of prisoners was an important source of information.

The following day (17 November), another cold and wet one, Putty wrote the first of his monthly letters to the King. These letters, in his own hand, covered an operational summary for the month which was collated from the GS log. On most occasions the letter was addressed to Wigram:[22]

> In reply to your letter of 13 Nov, I enclose a diary of the movements of my corps since I took over command of it. I would have gladly submitted it before if I had been aware of His Majesty's gracious wishes. The fighting has been of a severe and arduous nature during the last three weeks, the strain of the continuous shelling is great, the fortitude shown by the men in the trenches would bring pride to any heart, the nearer to the front you get the better the spirits of the individuals. Rain in this clay country is a great obstacle, it is nearly impossible to keep trenches dry. On the whole our men are better than the Germans all round we suffer from not having a gun that can reply to the Black Maria, a gun should be constructed for the army in the future a 6 inch howitzer with a range of 8,000 yards would meet the case. Our 4.5 howitzer is an excellent weapon and a further increase of this gun (and) in the personnel of each division is necessary in the future. All attacks have to be prepared by artillery fire and the necessary searching of the ground means a supply of ammunition that none of us calculated on. Light maxims used by the Germans are much handier and better in every way than ours. We have arrived at a stage in the war where soldiers feel like the Russians at Plecona who carried their spades on their backs from that place to Constantinople rather than ever part with them again. Yours sincerely WP Pulteney.

The Prince of Wales visited HQ III Corps on 18 November and that night the reorganisation of the corps was completed: 19 Bde, previously on the right of 6th Division, relieved 10 Bde (4th Division) so that it could rejoin the rest of its division N of the River Lys. III Corps now held from Bridoux in the S to the River Douve in the N which was the boundary with II Corps. Snow fell throughout 19 November and it was a very cold day. Putty wrote to GHQ on the subject of artillery:

> Many suggestions continue to reach me for regrouping, reorganising and rearming the artillery. In order to save time and correspondence I have decided to embody my thoughts on these questions in one communication.
> 1. Regrouping. 6th Division before leaving England rearranged its divisional artillery, breaking up the howitzer brigade and distributing the batteries among the three 18 pdr brigades. One 18 pdr battery was taken away from each of the 18 pdr brigades and a fourth brigade formed. The divisional artillery thus consists of one 18 pdr brigade, three mixed brigades and the heavy battery. This regrouping has my approval and has been found to work satisfactorily.
> 2. Reorganisation. Proposals for reorganising the divisional artillery on systems similar to the above, but involving an increase in howitzers have been submitted to me by both 4th and 6th Divisions. While I am favour of mixed brigades of guns and howitzers, and am also in favour of an increase in howitzers, I do not consider it practical to reorganise the artillery during the course of the war. As regards proposals to reorganise

---

22   Lieutenant Colonel Clive Wigram (1873-1960) Bengal Lancers APS to HM King George V.

in 4-gun batteries, in my opinion nothing has taken place during the war to justify a decision arrived at before the war to postpone this reform till the artillery is armed with a better gun.

3. Rearming. There is of course no possibility of changing our principal artillery weapons during the course of the war, but a demand has arisen for certain natures of weapons for certain definite purposes.

   a) Some form of trench mortar is required to throw a heavy projectile for a short distance into a trench. It is chiefly advocated because the enemy use such a weapon which has a bad moral effect if it can not be replied to.

   b) A mountain howitzer, or mountain gun, is required to accompany the infantry closely in situations when the field artillery cannot do so. Such occasions are not infrequent and a mountain howitzer with pack transport would on occasion be invaluable.

   c) A better anti-aircraft gun than either the pompom or the converted 13 pdr is urgently required.

   d) An answer is required to the 'Black Maria'. In my opinion this is a matter of very great importance, as it greatly affects the moral of the infantry. The 6 inch siege howitzer is an excellent weapon, but it is deficient in range and there are very few of them available. It is very necessary to obtain an adequate supply of up-to-date 6 inch or 6.5 inch howitzers throwing a projectile of 100 to 150 lbs to range of 8,000 yards or more. Such a weapon can accompany troops in the field without loss of mobility and is in every way superior to the 60 pdr gun.

   e) Before the war is over we shall probably want an adequate supply of heavy siege howitzers. The 9.2 inch howitzer now attached to the corps shoots accurately, but the means of transport are unsatisfactory and require further consideration. It is doubtful whether it will suffice as regards weight of metal and a heavier weapon may be required.

WP Pulteney Lt Gen Comdg III Corps.

It was almost certainly this that produced the GHQ internal memo the following day from French to his CGS:

I have already spoken to GOC III Corps on the subject of discussing such questions as these on paper and I trust I shall not have to remark on it again. The GOC knows perfectly well that I am ready to listen to any suggestion or representation he may desire to put forward verbally and in secret but I must again strongly deprecate the circulation of such memoranda as the above – written in type – seen by many staff officers – and no doubt in some extraordinary way brought to the knowledge of one of the numerous spies which abound everywhere. I deeply regret that I am obliged to take exception to any of the work done by a command and staff which has done such splendid services but as this is not the first time such a document as this has appeared I am obliged to do so. I feel sure I shall not have to do so again. JF.

It was sent on to Putty 'Please note the remarks of CinC. To be returned. AJ Murray Lt Gen CGS'

The document was not returned and kept by III Corps GS. Presumably Putty was not concerned about the CinC's 'rocket' or that his staff should be aware of it. He may have discussed it with the CinC personally and this would explain why the document was not returned. The CinC's paranoia about security and the use of the staff system does seem very strange. That day his despatch covering the Battle of Ypres was published:

> I am anxious to bring to special notice the excellent work done throughout this battle by III Corps under General Pulteney's command. Their position in the right central part of my line was of the utmost importance to the general success of the operations. Besides the very undue length of front which the corps was called upon to cover (some 12 or 13 miles), the position presented many weak spots, and was astride the River Lys, the right bank of which from Frelinghien downwards was strongly held by the enemy. It was impossible to provide adequate resources, and the constant work in the trenches tried the endurance of officers and men to the utmost. That the corps was invariably successful in repulsing the constant attacks, sometimes in great strength, against them by day and night is due entirely to the skilful manner in which the corps was disposed by its commander, who has told me of the able assistance he has received throughout from his staff, and the ability and resource displayed by divisional, brigade and regimental leaders in using the ground and means at their disposal to the very best advantage. The courage, tenacity, endurance and cheerfulness of the men in such unparalleled circumstances are beyond all praise.

The First Winter

The III Corps AQ Staff were continuing their efforts to look after the men in the trenches and prepare for the winter. The laundry at Bailleul lunatic asylum was got into working order, and used for washing large quantities of clothes sent in by divisions. On 21 November a German aeroplane dropped a bomb on the hospital in Bailleul doing serious damage. Also that day, as the cold weather continued, 10 cases of frostbite were reported amongst troops of III Corps in the trenches.

Putty wrote to Edith Castlereagh on 24 November:

> Dear Lady C, Thanks for yours of 22 Nov, my imagination won't run to being hugged by you just because I sent Charlie back besides the effect would mean my sitting down in the snow to cool myself after it, but fortunately I don't dream often but if I do trust it will be about you if it is to be a naughty one. Marlborough[23] is going back tonight so will send this by him. We had the American Military Attaché out here yesterday and sent him round the 6th Division trenches, he was delighted, got shrapnel and Black Marias at him and tell it not but he took a rifle and had a pot at a German too, he was lost in admiration of the decoration the men had put up in their trenches, photos of their girls, straw mats, carved names etc, never saw a man so pleased with himself on his return. Colonel Repington[24] was

---

23 Probably Lieutenant Colonel Charles Richard John Spencer-Churchill 9th Duke of Marlborough (1871-1934) Ox H.
24 Charles à Court Repington (1858-1925) Eton RB War Correspondent *The Times*.

here this morning, gave him some useful hints about K's Army, artillery and other matters, he must have been in Ireland from his fulsome speeches about the 3rd Corps. All blessings Yours ever Putty.

As the front became more static, and with winter setting in, III Corps concentrated on improving its positions. Operations were restricted to sniping and shelling whenever a target presented itself, patrols were sent out both to cover defensive works and to disrupt those of the enemy, and large raids mounted from time to time. Alcohol was becoming a problem to such an extent that III Corps had to issue an order on 27 November forbidding the sale of all alcoholic drinks to troops except beer. That same day Putty wrote to Theresa Londonderry:

Dear Lady Londonderry, I did not answer your letter of 18 Nov because I know having Charlie go home to see you was much better value. Much milder again here, no more frost bites, the life in the trenches means so little circulation to the body, the men become particularly liable to chilblains and that class of annoyance. The casualties have been fewer every day lately in my corps, so have been able to clean, refit and rest most of the troops. The Monmouthshire Territorials were digging in the reserve two days ago, when a shell burst killing two of them, the remainder lay down their tools, when expostulated with they said oh we never work in the coal pits on the day when anyone is killed. The Prince of Wales is up here going round the troops, he is bored to death with us generals and much prefers to dine with the boys of the Grenadiers and no wonder. Love to all. Yours sincerely WP Pulteney.

As the letter indicated it was now possible to allow short periods of leave to England and the weather, almost always unpleasant, varied from periods of extreme cold, to snow and torrential rain. On 29 November Putty wrote to Ettie Desborough:

My dear Chief, Thanks for yours of 24 Nov. Julian has answered me also this morning though his letter was written ten days ago unless you get the proper official channel out here it takes just ages, he is quite right to stay with his regiment, I admire his decision which is correct from every point of view as a soldier who wants to be a success in his profession. The idea of fleecy lined gloves rather appeals to me so shall look forward to their arrival but so far have not put on any thicker underclothing or made any change to my apparel with a view to hardening myself up should we have a severe winter, now it is much milder and have far more fear of flood in the trenches than from frost. You must write and let me know when you come to Boulogne, Stavey or Cyril Hankey must run you out in their car to have a day with us. Tell me the truth about Ireland we hear that there is nothing but sedition among the Nationalists, that Larkin[25] is the channel by which German money is disseminated, this I scarcely believe but there is money coming in to make the anti-British propaganda worth preaching, the best thing to do is to start building large barracks in Ulster with rifle and artillery ranges with a view to the future, the army has got good recruits from there why not encourage it, spend the money on the part of the country that

25   James Larkin (1876-1947).

brings in the men. To my mind this cry against stopping football is all Tommy Rot as the boys say, if they don't go to the football matches they will go to the public houses, you won't get any more recruits from doing it and you will send up the drink bill and take fresh air from those who want it most, the men are practical enough if you deal with them in the proper way. My corps has suffered fewer casualties every day lately, but then the fighting is only of the nature of sniping and snarling while we dig ourselves in, wire ourselves in and pray against flood and frosts. Bless you Yours ever Putty.

On 30 November the CinC held a conference of his corps commanders to discuss plans for the winter. In the period since 14 October III Corps' casualties were 344 officers and 10,864 other ranks, a total of 11,208.

Putty wrote to Ettie Desborough again on 30 November:

My dear Chief, Charlie arrived just after I had written to you yesterday, he tells me Julian is at home which is splendid for you, tell him I got his letter of 19th all right. HM arrives today all the anti-aircraft guns are glued to the skies to hunt away the Taube with the bombs Reggie Pembroke gets to London today for a week so you may see him. Yours ever Putty.

On the first day of December the QWR, one of the Territorial units attached for instruction, captured two men opposite Bois Grenier; they were both from XIX German Corps, confirming that they were still the immediate opposition. Also Putty wrote to Edith Castlereagh:

Dear Lady C, Many thanks for yours of 25 Nov, am glad you liked my remarks. Have sent a cheque to Lord Rothschild today for 25£ for a bed in the Waterloo Hospital and told them to affix a tablet with 3rd Army Corps on it, each of the divisions want to give one too and if a few more people gave one we might get a 3rd Army Corps room in it, do you know who runs it for Lord Rothschild if so could you get to see him and find out how many beds go to a room also if it would be possible to get a whole room of the 3rd Army Corps, there could be no more practical memorial, am writing to my sister today and telling her to give another one from the family in honour of the corps. Am tremendously glad at the despatch in yesterday's paper and so is the gallant 3rd Corps but wish I had not had so much praise myself for the brave deeds done by other people. We have got HM coming to luncheon tomorrow and round the troops afterwards, it is a good thing and will be much appreciated. Excuse more am busy this afternoon Yours ever Putty.

On the following day (2 December) the King had lunch with Putty at HQ III Corps in Bailleul. He then inspected troops of 4th and 6th Divisions and visited both divisional head-quarters, at Nieppe and Croix du Bac. Putty also took him to the convalescent hospital and charcoal burning site at Steenwerck, and to the bathing place at Pont du Nieppe. Putty wrote to Ettie Desborough on 4 December:

My dear Chief, I too was absolutely delighted at French's despatch, wish I had felt that all the praise was due to me, it was the troops themselves that did the deed, one only had to be the judge of where was the right place to reinforce when so many places were wanting help. The King's visit to the Third Corps was the greatest success, have never heard the men more genuinely giving cheers or so downright honest in saying they were pleased to see him, they are all talking about it still, there is no doubt that it was the right thing to do. My blessings. Yours ever Putty.

As December progressed the constant rain caused the trenches to flood so continuous repair work was needed. On 6 December HQ III Corps escort or defence platoon of one officer and 51 other ranks provided by 2 Innis Fus of 4th Division was relieved by 1 Leics of 6th Division. To those who had been fighting in the front line for the past six weeks it must have appeared a 'cushy number' but it is unlikely that the soldiers doing the job would have seen it that way.

On 7 December Putty wrote to Theresa Londonderry:

Dear Lady Londonderry, Many thanks for your letter of 30 Nov, the capons arrived all right yesterday, we thought they had been for some time on the journey but my servant[26] described them as 'sweet as honey', so they were, we devoured them last night most excellent they are, never were such fine birds eaten on active service before. We are suffering from too much rain, the water in the trenches on this low lying clay soil is very difficult to deal with and impossible to drain off. I had one of my best aeroplane officers wounded yesterday by a bullet at 5,000 feet which was very unlucky, they always seem to hit the good ones, he will have to go home but should be all right. Charlie seems to look fitter every day but personally liked him much better with his moustache but he was evidently ordered to take it off 'at home'. Yours very sincerely WP Pulteney.

There was little to report during the next few days apart from successful engagements by the heavy artillery against enemy trenches, strong points and batteries. The rain continued; HQ III Corps AQ staff obtained a pump from Dunkirk, as used in fishing boats, and it was tried as a means of pumping water from the trenches. So successful was this trial that 36 more were ordered with certain modifications.

Putty again wrote to Theresa Londonderry on 9 December:

Dear Lady Londonderry, Many thanks for your letter of 6 Dec and the gratifying remarks on French's despatch, all III Corps are very pleased with it. Rain has been abominable lately, buckets of it just when it was not wanted, result trenches full of water which on this low lying clay soil is very difficult to get rid off, so please pray for fine weather even if it is cold, at present it is too muggy to be wholesome. The Durhams had a bad time at the beginning of the war, they were very unlucky but now are in great heart and will do well when their chance comes.

What we want to know out here is the real truth about sedition in Ireland nobody seems quite clear and Pantaloon Birrell[27] does not know. Yours sincerely WP Pulteney.

On 11 December he wrote to Ettie Desborough:

26 Private George Hogbin SG son of a Ramsgate butcher.
27 Augustine Birrell (1850-1933) Chief Secretary for Ireland.

My dear Chief, Only got your letter of Sunday this morning, the post is quite hopeless except by the messengers it is the one failure of the British Army. I don't know what to say about your coming out here to Bailleul because between ourselves we begin a move on Monday and will most probably take a week before it is finished, of course if it collapses come on the 16th, find out by the messenger or will endeavour to send you a line but if there is a fight on I shall not be here in the day time and very doubtful at night at certain stages, you could always find out at General Headquarters at St Omer if I am likely to be here and you must motor that way, oh I do hope you will be able to manage it it could be fun and this week would have been quite feasible. Am sending this by Cyril Hankey and you ought to get it before you leave. The floods and water in the trenches causing much anxiety. Yours ever Putty.

On 12 December Putty attended CinC's conference at Bailleul to discuss the attack planned for 14 December, and later visited divisional and brigade HQs. The CinC's orders (OA 816) were issued at 7 pm that evening:

1. It is the intention of the CinC that an offensive will be commenced on 14 Dec by II and III Corps in conjunction with the French on the left, with the object of reaching the line Le Touquet-Warneton-Hollebeke …
4. The attack on the Messines Ridge-Warneton will be conducted by Lieutenant-General WP Pulteney. The attacking troops will be III Corps (less whatever troops are required to assist 19 Bde in holding the trenches apportioned to III Corps south of Le Touquet) and one infantry brigade of IV Corps. The attack (is) to start from the line of the trenches now held by III Corps from opposite Messines to Le Touquet. The left of the attack will be directed on Messines. The right will be held back. The advance on Warneton to be delayed until Messines is taken, when further orders will be issued to meet the situation which the course of action will have produced. AJ Murray Lt Gen CGS.

Putty had told French how important it was to retake Messines; now he was being told to do it. But the orders issued by French at his conference differed in some respects to those issued by his CGS. French had ordered divisions to attack in succession from the left; indeed he impressed on every commander that he was on no account to get ahead of his neighbours in the attack, everybody was to 'wait for the man on his left'. The attack was to be made in three stages. First Wytschaete in the N was to be captured by the French and 3rd Division; then Spanbroekmolen by II Corps from the W; and finally Messines by II Corps from the W and III Corps from the S. During the early stages of the attack, III Corps was to make demonstrations (feint attacks) against the enemy with the object of holding him to his trenches. These piecemeal attacks were not supported by well planned and coordinated artillery fire, essential if such a plan was to succeed.

On 13 December 18 Bde 6th Division was moved to Armentières to come under 4th Division for the forthcoming attack; III Corps' ten mile front was now really stretched with few reserves to deal with anything unexpected. Putty wrote to Ettie Desborough:

My dear Chief, I don't know what to say to you about coming here as there will be heavy fighting from tomorrow on and shall never know where I am to be found, the best day to come would be Thursday 17th, you ought to get to Bailleul about one and we will have luncheon for you, you would have to motor via St Omer, it would take you about three hours and we could have luncheon there. It all depends how the fighting is going on Tuesday as to whether we shall be finished by Wednesday night, so will try to send you word on Tuesday night by the messenger but if you don't hear you will know that fighting is still going on and that it would not be safe to come on the chance of finding me as you could not come to the fighting centre. Julian can show you the way as he is back in reserve to start with and if he is drawn in to it you will know we all are. I do hope I shall see you. Yours ever Putty.

The following day at 11 am III Corps opened an advanced report centre at Nieppe and in the early afternoon 21 Bde IV Corps also arrived there and came under Putty's orders. The French and II Corps attacked but made no progress; the artillery of 4th Division supported II Corps' attack and the rest of III Corps made feint attacks. These operations continued in a half-hearted way on 15 and 16 December: the German positions were now too strong to be attacked without adequate artillery preparation and even with it the deep mud prevented an advance by the most determined troops. During the night of 15 December Armentières and Houplines were shelled continuously setting fire to the billets of 1 W Yorks (18 Bde) and forcing the battalion to move to L'Armee for the night.

While Putty was waiting to attack N to Messines the enemy was active on the rest of his front; 6th Division artillery were used effectively to silence the enemy's batteries and interfere with sapping. He wrote to Theresa Londonderry on 16 December, possibly from Nieppe:

> Dear Lady Londonderry, Thank you for your letter of 12 Dec. Two more or less fine days have made the trenches more comfortable, we have now got more pumps in what is known as Plugstreet Wood than there are trees left, on all occasions we pump the water in the direction of the Germans. We have had some fighting here on Monday but little result on either side but II Corps got some prisoners which located what Germans were in front of them, my corps has the Saxons[28] in front of them, we know each other's tricks. It was good of you giving that bed to III Corps at Waterloo Hospital, we ought to get the Government to give it over permanently as a military hospital. Yours sincerely WP Pulteney.

Many of Putty's letters also included his views on the situation in Ireland perhaps because of his experience in the Country or because of the considerable time he spent with Charlie Castlereagh.

Rawlinson (then GOC IV Corps) had lunch with Putty on 16 December, one of their frequent meetings at this time when both were commanding corps. No progress was made on 17 December and at 10.40 pm GHQ issued orders that: 'It was the intention of the CinC to attack vigorously all along the front tomorrow with II, III, IV and Indian Corps'. In the details of the order, however, II Corps was told merely to resume its attack in conjunction with French XVI Corps and III, IV and Indian Corps were directed 'to demonstrate and seize any favourable opportunity which may offer the capture the enemy's trenches on their front'. No more

---

28   XIX German Corps – General Maximilian von Laffert (1855-1917).

than forty rounds per 18 pdr gun and twenty rounds per 4.5" howitzer were allowed for the operation.

These orders which were issued very late, allowing no time for proper planning or reconnaissance, must have caused further confusion since they lacked clarity of purpose and will. The next day (18 December) not much happened; 4th Division carried out a demonstration attack but, since the Germans counterattacked French XVI Corps, II Corps again made no progress. HQ III Corps GS log noted: 'Arrangements made to attack eastern edge of Ploegsteert Wood postponed as the readjustment of the guns which had previously been working with II Corps had not been completed'. III Corps were trying to use these demonstrations, which by now must have lacked any credibility, to improve their tactical position; this operation was intended to drive the enemy out of the salient E of Ploegsteert Wood between Le Gheer and St Yves, and readjust 4th Division's line. An enemy salient was not just a nuisance; it gave local tactical advantage to the enemy and required additional troops to contain it.

Putty wrote to Ettie Desborough that day:

> My dear Chief, We stayed in yesterday in the vain hope that you might come to luncheon, or during the afternoon, the plans were altered on Wednesday night but too late to let you know. We are going to have a small attack tomorrow just to straighten out a bit of my line and if the artillery observation is good we should be successful. Tell me what you did when you came over here, did you get to see Julian, Sir John French etc., how did your hospital work out and were you satisfied with all the arrangements. My casualties have been few this week have inflicted more than I received which is always an asset, but there has been little change, have got the same German corps opposite me, they are inferior in artillery as most of their big guns have gone to Russia, they have like us received their drafts and our strength is much the same, one of my regiments the Essex speak to them every day until some gun puts a stop to it or their officer comes along, but this will probably cease after tomorrow, their trenches are wetter than ours you can see the water splash out of them when one of our shells pitch into the trench which is consoling. The French interpreter was very funny yesterday 'I do not understand at all'. I go to all the French and say how terrible the bombardment of Scarborough and Hartlepool and they all cry I go also to the English I say the same and you all laugh and say splendid it will do the country a bit of good, we do not understand. I never saw such splendid gloves as Leo Rothschild[29] sent out General Du Cane on my staff to give to the officers there must have been about £100 worth, am sure half of the officers will send them back home to their best girls. God bless you and bring you good tidings at Xmas. Yours ever Putty.

At 2.30 pm on 19 December, in heavy rain, the postponed attack was carried out by 11 Bde after a very heavy bombardment which concentrated the limited amount of ammunition available: it was supported by 10 and 12 Bdes with enfilade fire, and by mountain artillery lent by the Indian Corps. These pack guns carried by mules could be got forward in the mud to positions impossible to reach with field artillery. 11 Bde captured the most advanced enemy trench and some of the houses but further progress was stopped until dark by machine-gun fire from houses

---

29   Leopold de Rothschild (1845-1917).

further back; the ground gained was consolidated and held. The cemeteries in Ploegsteert Wood bear witness to the severity of the fighting.

At dawn that day Private Brown 2 Essex, by sentence of a FGCM, was shot for desertion at Nieppe. This was the first recorded case in III Corps but there may have been others earlier. One of the problems was the recall of reservists without giving them any training; many had left the army years earlier and had no time to sort out their affairs or readjust. Some had mental illnesses. They are mentioned in this narrative because Putty would have been involved in the process but the number of these cases and other disciplinary problems in III Corps were remarkably few.

Orders were issued by III Corps to continue the attack on 20 December preceded by another heavy bombardment. It was, however, found that the ground was quite impassable and decided that 11 Bde should hold the eastern edge of Ploegsteert Wood with sniper pits in front. The same day orders were received from GHQ for III Corps to take offensive action to prevent the enemy moving reserves to the Indian Corps' front. An operation was therefore planned against Frelinghien, and again Putty was being pulled from both flanks with no change to the length of his front or the enemy opposite him. This operation was abandoned on 22 December, another wet day. The ground had now become very heavy and boggy, and the difficulty of advancing over it increased daily.

Putty wrote to Ettie Desborough on 21 December:

My dear Chief, What do you think of the 4th Division Xmas card it is really rather funny. Am depressed as at the end of my attack on Saturday when I had taken the place I wanted I found the ground was so wet I could not hold it, I did manage to straighten up my line but not as much as I would have liked to have done, we have to keep pricking them to prevent their sending troops away to Russia or down S where the French are attacking. Best wishes to you for Xmas and may 1915 bring us all back victorious to you all. Yours ever Putty.

He wrote to Edith Castlereagh next day:

Dear Lady C, Thanks for yours received by the Copper Horse (unidentified messenger) – glad the explanation about the ward was lucid, heaven knows how it will all end up if many more beds arrive. The ending to your letter, must go and dress for dinner, dinner is nearly ready and am not even dressed, sounds as if you were writing in your birthday suit, how ravishing I wish I had been there but not with a 'letter' although Jemmy Rothschild is the universal provider of Bailleul, have just read this remark out to Charley who is jealous!! I have not heard about 'M' yet but think it very likely but F went over to meet K two days ago so no doubt much has been settled. The Indians got a bit of a bulge in their line so 1st Corps had to go to straighten it out, the first named are stale and want a rest. Am sending Gen Du Cane [BGGS] off for a holiday then all my staff will have had a turn. Jemmy went to Dunkirk yesterday he saw Emily Sutherland[30] in bed she says she is coming over here next week to see me, I wonder!! Bless you dear thing all good wishes for Xmas and good Tidings for 1915. Yours ever Putty.

30   Probably Millicent Sutherland-Leveson-Gower Duchess of Sutherland (1867-1955), a Soul, whose Red Cross Hospital was at Dunkirk.

He wrote to her again on 23 December:

> Dear Lady C, Have done the business part of the letter and now a multitude of thanks for all the trouble you have taken, you are a dear. There will be plenty of odd sums coming in which can all be devoted to making the wards more comfortable, lots of brigades would send things for their own cots, photos of their brigadiers!!! best girls, girls they love but ought not to!! Photos of the trenches in Armentières. There ought to be a plate outside the door with 3rd Army Corps on it. I don't think we want any names on the tablets at all, just the corps division or brigade. Fine weather at last for two days the result is that the water has gone down nearly two feet and hope that in consequence the trenches will be more habitable. The attack on Monday was not a success owing to want of being able to observe the artillery fire but my corps was not committed so did not suffer, on the contrary with 6th Division we gave them (beans) in the trenches the shells falling in them and bursting the water up in the air out of them which showed how wet theirs were, but this wire fence is a bit of a problem, if we had endless gun ammunition we could blow them out but we haven't alas. I loved your story about Margaret[31] she will be a nice handful when she reaches years of discretion, sure to come home with the milk if she comes at all. The Monmouth Territorials were sniping with great accuracy yesterday through an iron loophole, causing much annoyance to the Germans when at last a big German shouted out 'Stop it you … and go and have your dinners', the answer is not related. Expect Scarborough bombard will stir the nation up the fact that we really are at war. The local girls are having a rare time in Bailleul and the demands on the chemist's shop where Jemmy Rothschild lives increase daily. Yours ever Putty.

There is only one entry in the III Corps GS log for Christmas Eve: 'Much singing in the German trenches'. Jack, back now with his battalion, wrote:

> The lines (at Houplines) are in a terrible state. The incessant rain has caused large portions of the trench walls to subside. We are hard at work revetting the broken edges and filling sandbags to stop the breaches after dark. Except at the posts where the parapets have been built higher than the other parts of the line and the men stand fairly dry on wooden gratings, the trenches are knee-deep in water and mud. Two hand pumps, when not clogged up, are constantly at work in the company [C Coy 1 Cameronians 19 Bde], but the men are convinced that their exertions are fruitless and that the bottom of the trench is below sea-level!

So concerned was Putty that he asked his DDMS[32] for a report on the probable effects on health of men of prolonged occupation of trenches under present conditions; this was produced the same day. The problems were greatest for those troops in the flood plain of the River Lys, and their problems were going to get much worse. On Christmas Day an informal armistice was held in certain places to allow the dead to be buried. It was a fine day, a prelude to colder weather

---

31 Lady Margaret Frances Anne Vane-Tempest-Stewart (1910-1966).
32 Colonel Menus O'Keeffe from Cork – his chief medical officer.

to come. That day the 'army' level of command came into existence with II and III Corps, and 27th Division, being formed into 2nd Army under Smith-Dorrien. Haig was given command of 1st Army.

Putty wrote to Edith Castlereagh on Christmas Day:

Dear Lady C, Thank you dear thing for your Xmas letter, every good wish for 1915 may it bring you a centenary Waterloo colt to crown the victory that the year will bring with it, all good women ought to bear sons for two years to come to fill up the gaps, as a rule it is the men that fill up the gaps!! Have fixed all about the beds up with Cyril Hankey and you must let me know if you have any other points to raise. Yes you must come out here you can easily do it for a weekend and my room is always at your disposal. We have had a devil of a luncheon and have been to church twice this morning once with 4th Division and once with 6th Division, the roof came in on neither occasion, Charlie and Cyril spent the morning going round the trenches they thought the language would be worse there and they arrived back in time to let some of it loose to the Chaplain at luncheon. God bless you and bring you luck in 1915 Yours ever Putty.

On 26 December DDMS III Corps reported:

Enteric fever has broken out amongst the civilian population. Cases strictly isolated. Steps taken to clear out refugees and prevent others coming in. All water and milk is boiled and all the troops have been inoculated. The beer was found to be of inferior quality and on analysis bacillus coli was discovered, the water used for beer was taken from a stream close by, it is badly contaminated with sewage matter and this water is used for washing out the barrels.

That evening Putty wrote to Ettie Desborough:

My dear Chief, A 1000 thanks for the shortbread which we have demolished together with many other Xmas delicacies am expecting a return of gout daily from the amount that has showered in to this mess. They are altering all the formations over here, Douglas Haig and Smith-Dorrien are to have two armies of three corps each and I believe Fergusson and Monro are to get their vacant corps, I see the hand of K I think because all my own people are being bagged to make up the staff and am miserable at losing them, no clerks or anything else arranged how well I know these changes but we shall shake down to it somehow. The ordinary post has been well organised out here and we get letters now in 3 days instead of five and sometimes in 2. Let me know if you really do come out here again I should bag the Duchess of Sutherland's pass the next time you come she seems to go where she pleases and I believe comes here this week to luncheon, it must be Jemmy Rothschild!! God bless you in 1915 Yours ever Putty.

There was a heavy storm during the night of 28 December which caused much damage to III Corps' aerodrome, one aircraft being completely destroyed and another much damaged. The position of the aerodrome was now becoming a cause for concern, despite a recently made cinder track and efforts to drain the site. The River Lys rose considerably and overflowed its banks N of Frelinghien, causing even more problems in the trenches. The year ended with the arrival of two more 6 inch guns to join the corps and trials of a caterpillar tractor to pull them. At last the corps was to have more heavy artillery which it could use to influence the battle and support its divisions.

Putty had now commanded III Corps, which he had formed in the most difficult circumstances, for four months without a break. During this time the corps had crossed three major rivers in the face of the enemy, carried out a relief in the line with the French and then moved to the northern flank without the Germans being aware of it, mounted a coordinated corps attack to take Armentières and the German defences covering it, and then held the line to its E astride the River Lys against overwhelming German attacks while under constant threat on both flanks.

Success is often more attributable to a team effort of the commander, his staff, and his subordinates. Failure has to be attributed solely to the commander for a bad plan or poor leadership. In such cases it would be surprising there were not criticisms of the commander from those above or below him: Putty's performance in this, the first year of the war, seems devoid of such criticism. Orders from GHQ were often unclear or delivered late, or both; despite this III Corps seemed to know what it had to do and achieved almost all that was required of it. The standard of administration within the corps was good and improved all the time; most of the unsolved problems were caused by matters outside its control. Putty showed decisive and strong leadership and a care for those under him; he was quite prepared to do what he considered right for III Corps even if this got him into difficulties with the CinC and other corps commanders.

From a personal point of view Putty would have lived with the mental pressure of almost constant noise of battle and its consequences. At this stage of the war he would have known many of the officer casualties and, in 6th Division especially, a large number of the other ranks. There would also have been the physical pressure caused by constant lack of sleep, exacerbated perhaps by gout or the treatment of it, at least at the beginning. There is no evidence that any of this affected his performance.

There were two occasions in 1914 when III Corps had the enemy 'trapped' retreating over a major river, the Aisne and later the Lys, and with greater boldness might have captured or destroyed a large German force. The circumstances in both cases argued strongly for prudence; even if Putty had the information in time to make the necessary decisions, and there is no evidence that he did, lacking any uncommitted resources he would have put his corps and the success it had so far achieved at considerable and unjustified risk. A number of other criticisms have been raised subsequently of III Corps' advance to Armentières: 'Putty had stayed at his HQ on 13 October rather than going forward to observe the ground, thereby missing the opportunity to outflank the German cavalry on the Méterenbecque'; 'Putty did not press the advantage gained by 10 Bde 4th Division in reaching the outskirts of Méteren by mid-morning 13 October'; and 'Putty was reluctant to exploit the crossing secured over the Lys until he was sure the far bank had been cleared, holding back 4th Division until 6th Division had accomplished this task'. Had Putty gone forward on 13 October he would have seen nothing and been out of contact with his HQ at a critical time when the advance was starting and the corps shaking out. The enemy were withdrawing because III Corps were advancing on a broad front and any position held was quickly outflanked. It was essential to maintain balance during this advance; Putty focussed on his orders and the mission that he had been given. When he got to the Lys Putty had to cross it and then swing NE across the front of the Pérenchies Ridge. If the ridge was strongly held he could be taken in the flank with the river behind him: this had to be his first objective. Again it was a matter of maintaining balance. The evidence suggests these criticisms are without substance.

Smith-Dorrien considered that Putty was a taking an unacceptable risk during the advance by allowing the gap to widen between the two corps, a gap which was covered by Conneau's French Cav Corps. This was exacerbated by Smith-Dorrien's belief that he had Putty's agreement to close the gap. The problem stemmed from lack of clarity in GHQ's orders; Putty's priority was his mission to move E, then NE, around Lille, keeping in touch with the Cav Corps on his left. To be able to do this he had to keep III Corps concentrated and those on the outer flank, Conneau's Cav Corps and II Corps, had to conform to him. When asked to arbitrate, French concurred with Putty, and there seems little doubt that this was the right course of action.

French considered Putty a friend and respected professional colleague; it seems highly likely that he asked for Putty to be appointed to command III Corps, on the basis that he was the best man for the job. There were occasional disagreements but they never affected this relationship. By the end of the retreat, however, French's relationship with Smith-Dorrien was very different and it was perhaps inevitable that it would affect the relationship between Putty and Smith-Dorrien; and this was to deteriorate still further.

Putty corresponded regularly with three women of extraordinary influence and did not hesitate to voice his concerns on the conduct of the war. They in turn must have used this information in informal discussions with government ministers and many others; and it would not have taken long for them to realise where it was coming from. Kitchener was irritated by this and he probably was not the only one. Putty also corresponded with Jessie on a personal basis; their love, for him a source of strength, is covered in a later chapter.

A reasonable conclusion is that Putty did well in 1914 but it was just the start, and the worst of that first winter was still to come.

8

1915

Holding the Line

Putty started and ended 1915 with his corps deployed in the flood plain of the River Lys. In the centre of the British line opposite Lille, he was required to hold an extended front and cover the right flank of 2nd Army in its battles around Ypres and the left flank of 1st Army in its battles of Neuve Chapelle and Loos.

January

At the beginning of the year III Corps had 4th Division (Wilson) on the left from Ploegsteert to Houplines and 6th Division (Keir), including the independent 19 Bde, on the right. HQ III Corps was still at the Hotel de Ville in Bailleul: the corps reserve, 16 Bde, was in Armentières. The greatest enemy was the weather; as the River Lys rose, and the drainage ditches and trenches filled with water, it required a major effort by both sides just to survive.

In his letter to King George V on 2 January Putty wrote:

> My dear Wigram, There is little of interest in the diary of the 3rd Corps for the period [December] I am forwarding you for the information of His Majesty today. The corps has lost no ground during the last month but on the contrary have pushed a little forward in Plugstreet Wood. The difficulty of water in the trenches has been increasing daily, the clay soil is so waterlogged at present I see no solution of being able even to pump it out except at a few points, this fortunately affects both sides, neither of us can use our communication trenches, the ground is also in such a dreadful state that you cannot advance across it. There is no doubt that we are behind the Germans in all fortress work, they have better steel loopholes, hand grenades, flares for lighting up the ground at night, electric torches for each section, portable search lights, mortars, all of which show study in peace time that has been neglected on our part. We are all very depressed at the present output of the 4.5" howitzer ammunition and if the armies are going to be increased out here other arrangements will have to be made as with all the economy that we have exercised we are in no position to attack on account of the lack of it, it is our most important weapon. The health of the corps has been quite wonderful considering the strains that are put on the men, the number of sick is little above normal, the wet trenches give the men a description of mud

fever similar to what a horse gets, the only prevention is cleanliness and rubbing the feet with oil but taking all things into consideration the health is very satisfactory and from all accounts rather better than in the other corps. Brigadier General Anley [Comd 12 Bde] and his staff had a near shave yesterday a Maria went through the roof of his house and another through the yard door if the first shell had been 20 feet lower it would have killed him and his staff I went round to see him just after it happened and cannot imagine how they escaped. There has been an increase in the amount of the enemy's shelling again lately, probably their supply of ammunition has improved. Yours Sincerely, WP Pulteney.

This letter provides a good summary of the situation and Putty's priorities; indeed this and all Putty's letters must have given the King an invaluable insight to the war. Also that day Putty sent a memo (G418) to 2nd Army (extract):

14. At present the attitude of the corps is defensive. That is to say there is no definite objective against which offensive operations are being conducted by sapping or other means, and the efforts are concentrated on maintaining the present line and nullifying any attempts that the enemy may make to advance. At present he is not making any such attempts, and his offensive is limited to desultory shell fire. The conditions prevailing in front of the corps make any offensive enterprise most difficult to carry out and of doubtful value to attempt. WP Pulteney Lt Gen Comdg III Corps.

As tactfully as he could Putty was telling Smith-Dorrien that offensive action was impossible, at least for the time being.

Putty also wrote to Edith that day (2 January):

Dear Lady C, Weather awful, rain has ruined all the trenches the water level in the soil comes to within two feet of the surface which makes pumping impossible. There was no gazette yesterday so all the soldiers remain unrewarded it is perfectly sickening, I can't tell you how many have been killed since I sent in the original lists and will be ignorant that any honour has been done to them, Sir John French has done his part and sent the lists forward now they say they must have them made up to the end of the year which will mean another months delay. Everything is delay the supply of the 4.5 howitzer ammunition and its future is a disgrace. Went with Reggie to pay General Anley [Comd 12 Bde] a visit for New Year greetings he had a shell through the roof of his house and another through his motor two hours previously if the first had been 20 feet lower it would have killed him and his staff. Charley is fearfully well and leads Jemmy Rothschild a dog's life I don't know what they did not do to him on New Year's Eve. Bertie's[1] Xmas card he sent Charlie has been an unqualified success it really was a winner. Sir Archibald Hunter[2] was here two days ago, he is to have command of the 3rd Army, he will have to be younger than he looks now if he is going to be any good. Hope Robin[3] is all right again. Yours ever Putty.

1   Probably Vere Frederick Bertie (1878-1954) Eton with Castlereagh.
2   General Sir Archibald Hunter (1856-1936) late RLR GOC Aldershot Command.
3   Edward Charles Stewart Robert 'Robin' Vane-Tempest-Stewart (1902-1955) later 8th Marquess of Londonderry.

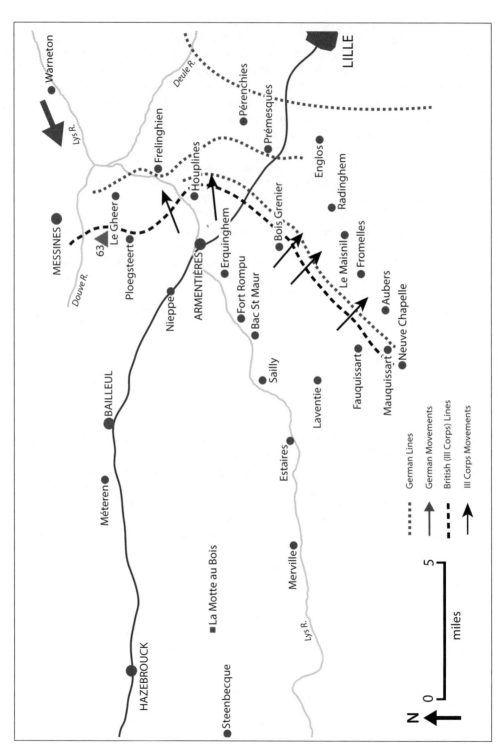

Map 7 1915/16.

The bad weather continued with the River Lys still rising. Work was concentrated on the improvement of communications, and erection of breastworks and high command trenches. Breastworks were invariably built on high ground, even if only a few feet higher, behind the line in case the trenches became completely flooded and had to be abandoned. Strong points were constructed in rear from houses and bomb proof shelters.

Smith-Dorrien (GOC 2nd Army) made his first recorded visit to Putty at HQ III Corps on 3 January; in his diary he noted his meetings with Putty while III Corps was under his command, but these notes are terse and lack detail.

On 4 January Putty wrote to Ettie Desborough:

My dear Chief, Thanks for your letter of 30 Dec which only arrived yesterday so must have got hung up somewhere, the ordinary post out now is so good that unless the messenger is going the next day it is not worth bothering to use other means. We have come to a dead-lock out here both sides have made their lines impregnable, we batter down anything that can be observed by artillery fire during the day, then up it all has to be built again at night. We have had a hard time with the water in the trenches, there is no description of pump that we have not tried where we get beat is when the level of the water all round comes within two feet of the surface because then as fast as you pump in it comes again but taking all things together the result is good if we don't get much more rain, the sickness is very little, a kind of mud fever on the feet which is largely avoided by making the men wash their feet directly they come out of the trenches and letting the foot dry in the air before they put on their socks again. Sir Archibald Hunter was here four days ago he has aged a great deal, he did not inspire one with confidence and took a most gloomy view of things I hope he will change before he comes out here in command of 3rd Army. The officers were all disappointed at there being no gazette for them on the 1st January, I don't think K wants it as we all sent in our lists up to the end of the battle of the Aisne and today we have worked hard all day to get it done up to the end of the year and they talk of getting a gazette out by the end of this month but such numbers have been killed since one made out the last lists that can never know that their services were rewarded it depresses one and their relations even more so. Was too delighted to see that Julian got a DSO congratulate him a 100 times from me, it is a real good fence to have got over as we soldiers say. Mind you let me know when you come out again as if they wont give you a pass I will motor in to Boulogne to see you. Bertie Paget[4] was in Bailleul yesterday and is off to London today, he is very distressed at his father A.P.[5] not getting one of the commands, personally would sooner have him than either Hunter, Rundle[6] or Bruce Hamilton,[7] the last named is a ridiculous appointment, it only has one redeeming point that he is too deaf to hear even a shell, I do think they ought to have given A.P. one of the commands at home at any rate he is the only general not employed. Just insist on an endless supply of 4.5" howitzer ammunition being made and you will confer national benefit to the troops. Best love Yours ever Putty.

4   Captain Albert Edward Sydney Louis Paget 11 H (1879-1917) died on active service.
5   General Sir Arthur Paget (1851-1928) late SG GOC Central Force at Home.
6   General Sir Leslie Rundle (1856-1934) late RA GOC Eastern Command and later GOC Central Force at Home.
7   General Sir Bruce Hamilton (1857-1936) late E Yorks GOC Home Defence.

Hunter never did command 3rd Army.

Still the rain continued. On 5 January Captain Jack (C Coy 1 Cameronians 19 Bde) wrote:

> Allowing for windings, the battalion holds about 1500 yards of front with all four companies in the line. One other battalion of the brigade and two companies of 5 Cameronians [TA attached] are also in the trenches. The Prussian trenches, one to two hundred yards from ours, must also be flooded as we are delighted to see buckets of water being thrown over their parapet.

And on 7 January:

> It is raining hard and the trenches are in an indescribable state, necessitating our having to be dragged out of bogs at times when on rounds. The enemy appear to be in a similar way, to judge by their baling. The parapets have fallen dangerously low, and the men are confined to their posts which are like islands in a morass. Both we and the Germans are far too busy trying to improve conditions to bother each other too much; so the front is quiet and the shell fire trivial.

The aerodrome of 5 Sqn RFC attached to III Corps had also become waterlogged, and a new site had to be found.

On 8 January Putty decided to do away with a corps reserve and the following day held a conference to readjust 6th Division's line into four (brigade) sections, to reduce the time spent by the men in the trenches. As the GS log noted, with the River Lys rising eight inches in the previous 24 hours: 'Water the dominating factor in the present situation'. Late that afternoon Smith-Dorrien recorded: 'I went thence to Bailleul to see the corps commanders, Pulteney and Fergusson, to discuss certain points'.

The AQ Staff were closely monitoring the discipline situation. In the week ending 6 January there were 44 FGCMs, 17 in 4th Division and 27 in 6th Division which included 19 Bde. 23 of these 44 were for drunkenness.

On 10 January the weather was still very bad and in the previous 24 hours the River Lys had risen another 8". Putty's views on the continual encouragement from Smith-Dorrien to take offensive action must have become widely known for on 11 January Smith-Dorrien wrote to him:

> My dear Pulteney, From what Walker[8] tells me of a conversation between your CSO and himself, I gather you find difficulty in reducing to action certain principles which in a recent memo I laid down for guidance and that you are also doubtful as to the military soundness of them, or some of them. I should naturally like to know if you at any time find it impossible to carry out those instructions, and I need hardly say that I am always glad to hear your views regarding the soundness of the principles on which I want the corps to act. I have then an opportunity to reconsider and if necessary modify them. Will you therefore please forward officially a memo dealing with these points. I prefer the matter in writing as it gives me a better chance of considering your views. Yours sincerely H Smith-Dorrien.

---

8   Major General George Townshend Forestier-Walker (1866-1939) late RA MGGS 2nd Army.

Putty's reply the following day, after another night of rain, was short and to the point (extract):

While I am extremely anxious to adopt as aggressive and offensive attitude towards the enemy as circumstances permit, I am afraid there are certain practical difficulties in giving effect to the policy laid down in your memorandum G235 as far as the corps under my command is concerned. They arise from: (1) The extended front occupied by the corps (10.5 miles astride the River Lys which is in flood) (2) The weather (3) The physical condition of the troops (4) The shortage of artillery ammunition.

Discipline issues were a continual concern; the AQ log recorded that at 7.30 am that morning Private F Sheffield and Private J Ball both of 2 Middx, having been tried and convicted by FGCM of desertion, were shot. 2 Middx (8th Division) was not in III Corps but this fell within its jurisdiction.

That evening Putty wrote to Ettie Desborough:

My dear Chief, Thanks for your letter of 8 Jan, am so grieved to hear about Monica[9] do hope she is all right again, you must have had a horrid time. My 3rd Corps is in the 2nd Army under Sir Horace Smith-Dorrien all the army commanders are a long way senior to me so cannot complain at not being given one of them, they have made a great mistake in forming them so soon, each army corps should have been given an extra division until we had got them trained out here and then formed the new armies about April as it is enormous staffs have been formed to the detriment of the army corps before the situation demanded it or before there were enough troops, personally should have preferred to have been under Douglas Haig as he is a better fighting man but one cannot pick and choose. We are having terrific contests with the floods, neither side can do anything, we are all busy making breastworks instead of trenches fortunately the Germans like ourselves have not got enough gun ammunition to knock them down if we had made them in October or November they would have been flat an hour after daylight. Best love Yours ever Putty. I think I may be over for a few days on 1 Feb.

The following day (13 January) the weather improved, the Lys began to fall, and the enemy shelling and sniping increased. Next day Rawlinson noted in his diary: 'Called III Corps and saw Putty'. The improvement in the weather was short-lived and rain returned on 15 January and then it snowed on 18 January Constant work was required to maintain the defences. The AQ log recorded sick wastage for week ending 17 January at 3.3 per 1000 men per day; this rate was constantly monitored and rarely exceeded 3. On 17 January Smith-Dorrien wrote: '6 pm. General Pulteney came to see me and I had an hour and a half talk with him about his corps'. Again there is a surprising lack of detail or comment.

Putty wrote to Ettie again on 19 January:

My dear Chief, Thanks for yours of 15 Jan which I got this morning. We had quite a cheery night as had Billy Lambton (MS GHQ), Hugh Lonsdale[10] and Ilchester ('Stavey') staying

9   Monica Margaret Grenfell (1893-1973).
10   Probably Hugh Cecil Lowther 5th Earl of Lonsdale (1857-1944).

night and I sent a motor car over to the 7th Division and brought in G. Trotter[11] for dinner, a change of conversation among a lot of pals did us all a lot of good. Hugh did not startle us as at present he is a little out of his ground, however sent him off with Billy Lambton and Reggie Herbert (ADC) to the famous Plugstreet Wood which will give his imagination plenty of scope and expect he will return to London full of startling tales. Unless there are any new developments shall be back on the 1st for a few days it will be heavenly seeing you and you are an angel to stay. How splendid Monica going on so well don't let her return too soon. The snow came down in heavy flakes all yesterday not stopping until noon today, result the river floods etc all up higher than the highest level we have had them it is enough to cause one despair just when we thought we had got to the end of our anxieties. The men are truly wonderful, some of the North Stafford [1 N Staffs 17 Bde 6th Division] were playing football near Armentières yesterday afternoon, three shells pitched among them, killing one man and wounding nine within ¼ hour they were back playing football again, of course it was unaimed fire but still it gives you an idea of the callous value of life. Charlie, Reggie and self went to see a performance of The Follies yesterday afternoon at Armentières, the troop was got up by my 4th Division with the addition of two local ladies (on whom some of the troop seemed to be on very intimate terms) it was awfully good, some of the talent above the ordinary especially a corporal from the Army Service Corps they have two performances a day 4 and 7 pm the men come in batches and pay ½ franc entrance, with the profit they run a cinematograph show and all sorts of things an excellent thing which takes the strain quite completely off their minds. Best love Yours ever Putty.

It rained again on 20 January with the River Lys still rising when Putty sent this memo to 2nd Army:

Attached is a table showing the frontage held by the corps of 1st and 2nd Armies. I do not know the strengths of the various corps, but III Corps has an extra brigade and may be considerably the strongest corps numerically. I would point out, however, that its front, if these figures are correct, slightly exceeds that of the whole of the remainder of the army, exclusive of IV Corps, which means that it is holding much more than its share of the front whatever the strength of other corps may be. This corps held a front of 11.5 miles from 20 October till relieved of 1.5 miles on its right by IV Corps on 19 November 1914, since which time it has held its present front. I am aware that the health of the men compares favourably with that of the rest of the army, but it does not seem to me that this affords an adequate reason for subjecting them to the further strain on their endurance by constant work in the trenches with only short periods of rest. In order that troops under my command may have a fair opportunity of recuperating before they are called upon to undertake offensive operations in the near future, I feel compelled to ask that the question of shortening the frontage held by the corps may be fully considered, unless it is contemplated to increase the number of troops at my disposal shortly. WP Pulteney Lt Gen Comdg III Corps.

---

11   Major Gerald Frederick Trotter (1871-1945) 1 Gren Gds 20 Bde 7th Division.

On 21 January it rained yet again but on 22 January the weather was fine albeit colder with a frost. Captain Jack (1 Cameronians 19 Bde) noted: 'It is very cold and a sharp frost has made the narrow paths trodden in the trenches hard and level. This change in the weather immensely lightens our tasks and discomforts'. The only other event that day was at 7.20 am when Corporal Latham 2 LF (12 Bde 4th Division), having been convicted by a FGCM of desertion, was shot.

Rawlinson wrote in his diary on 23 January: 'Putty and JP (Du Cane BGGS III Corps) to lunch'. Liaising with flanking corps was important especially when the focus was close to the inter-corps boundary. The River Lys started to go down and on 25 January was only 3 feet above normal. That day the AQ Staff received and distributed 26 officer and 1600 other rank reinforcements.

Putty wrote to Ettie Desborough:

> My dear Chief, There is a little bother about my getting away because Sir John has taken my staff officer General Du Cane away to his own staff [to be MGRA] but still I hope to arrive in London either Sunday or Monday morning if nothing turns up with the Kaiser's Birthday. Send me a line by return if you are going to Grimsthorpe[12] for this weekend as if I arrive on Sunday would come down there for the day. There is no news here but the water in the river Lys has gone down a lot, all the staff at Hazebrouck and St Omer have got the 'Flue' but up here and in the trenches we are pretty free from it. All blessings Yours ever Putty.

The following day was again fine, but Putty was forced to write to Ettie:

> My dear Chief, There is no chance of my being able to get away at present, they have not appointed another chief general staff officer and I must wait until he knows the ropes, things are more lively too and the Germans more active. Let me know if you can come over here. Afraid the Scots Guards caught it yesterday but have heard no details. Best love Yours ever Putty.

Brigadier General Milne was appointed BGGS III Corps on 27 January as a stand in for a month; problem solved, Putty tried again and wrote to Ettie:

> My dear Chief, Things are quieter, I hope to arrive in London on Tuesday evening 2nd Feb shall only be over for a couple of days name a time for an appointment on Wednesday a line to 3 Lower Berkeley St will catch me. Very cold here Yours ever Putty.

On 30 January Putty attended GOC 2nd Army's conference during the afternoon; even after a month it had already become apparent that the introduction of 2nd Army had greatly increased the volume of staff work with numerous additional reports and returns required. The weather continued fine; the GS log noted that a brigade of artillery opened on a column

---

12   Home of Gilbert Heathcote-Drummond-Willoughby 2nd Earl of Ancaster (1867-1951) Eton Politician.

approaching Pérenchies within 35 minutes of an aviator seeing it, reflecting the improved coordination between ground and air.

January can be best summarised as a month of rain, snow and flood. The River Lys rose 7 feet, and in places spread out over one hundred yards in width: many of the dykes became running streams. Some trenches could not be pumped out and had to be abandoned; in places troops occupied only isolated sectors of fire trenches, dammed at each end and bailed dry, a system of cross fire from posts on these islands being relied on for defence; and breastworks often took the place of trenches. In many parts of the line men stood knee-deep in mud and water and had to be relieved twice a day. The enemy's guns dominated the situation and added to the general misery; owing to the shortage of ammunition there was little that could be done to counter this fire. The field artillery was limited to four rounds per gun per day.

III Corps casualties for January were 25 officers and 724 other ranks = 749. The strength of the corps on 31 January was 1,364 officers and 43,127 other ranks = 44,491.

February

February started as January finished with shelling and sniping, sometimes desultory, sometimes concentrated and occasionally severe. Putty never did get home to England; on 1 February he wrote to Ettie Desborough:

> My dear Chief, Was prevented coming at the very last minute [probably by Smith-Dorrien with whom his relationship was now bad].The enclosed wire made me laugh I got it this morning, somebody must have interfered with me by bringing papers or something for my brain to have wandered. I don't see my way to making further arrangements to get over there are too many rows going on. Will write to you fuller in a day or two as Kings Messenger just going. Yours ever Putty.

Enclosed was a Telegram: 'Have received a letter. Written to Chief. To whom should it be addressed. Both it and mine addressed to me. Isabel Pulteney'. His sister would not have been amused.

Summarising the previous month in his letter to the King, Putty wrote on 2 February:

> My dear Wigram, Am afraid this is a dull summary of operations to send you, the whole month has been occupied in getting above ground, instead of underneath it, luckily the Germans had to do likewise and they know if we shelled their breastworks that they could retaliate, as the weather improves we shall both get underground again where we shall feel much safer and warmer. Yours Sincerely, WP Pulteney.

The dreadful weather made it unlikely that the Germans would attempt an attack on his front but Putty decided that he had to prepare now for the better weather to come. That day a memo was sent to both divisions: 'The corps commander has decided that the reconstruction of the second line of defence should at once be taken in hand. Instructions to this effect have been issued to the BGRE, on the corps staff, who will carry out the necessary work with civilian labour directly under the orders of the corps commander. No responsibility will be placed on divisional commanders but General Pulteney desires that they should instruct their CREs to give Brigadier General Glubb all the assistance they can, even to the extent of placing an officer at his disposal. GF Milne BGGS III Corps'

For the next few days the weather was fine and the shelling and the sniping increased. Smith-Dorrien called to see Putty on 4 February. On 5 February the enemy used a searchlight to direct artillery on to 16 Bde 6th Division prior to an attack on the right of the corps.

Putty wrote to Ettie Desborough again the following day:

> My dear Chief, Have just got your note of last Tuesday it was too sad not getting over after all, now that things are more lively don't suppose there will be any opportunity unless one gets ill. Eddie Wortley[13] came here today to get a few tips, he looks older but in good form you will know all about it when he gets home (he is coming here to luncheon on Sunday). They attacked my 16th and 19th Brigades last night but I knocked them back with artillery fire before they could do any damage. Mind you let me know if you come out again you must find your way to Bailleul and see the 3rd Corps. Weather much improved with any luck we shall soon be back again in our trenches which are much safer and much warmer than the breastworks. We expect the Canadians out here soon and I believe they come to my corps which will give me a lot of necessary stiffening though expect they are a wild crowd. Yours ever Putty.

The AQ log recorded that at 8 am on the morning of 5 February Private J Byers and Private A Evans both of 1 RSF, having been convicted by a FGCM of desertion, were shot.

On 7 February the GS log noted that a patrol shot three of five snipers who were lying out in front of a German trench. The drier weather allowed an increase in patrol activity by both sides; offensive (fighting) patrols and defensive (covering) patrols.

On the morning of 8 February another soldier, Private A Pitts 2 Warwicks, also convicted of desertion, was shot. Later that day the King of the Belgians visited HQ III Corps and had lunch with Putty.

The weather continued generally fine for much of February; some days there was rain causing the River Lys to flood. On those days it was again a matter of survival. Then the fine and cold weather would return allowing repairs and improvements to be made to the positions. It was tough and there were problems of desertion: at 7.45 am on 11 February Corporal G Povey 1 Cheshire, having been convicted of leaving his post, was shot. Yet it is of note that of the 7 men executed since the beginning of the year only one was actually in III Corps.

Captain Jack recorded on 13 February: 'We shall be glad when the breastworks are ready for occupation as the trenches have become almost impassable. The posts are practically isolated in daytime'. As soon as there appeared to be grounds for some optimism more rain fell. Putty wrote to Ettie Desborough next day:

> My dear Chief, Thanks for yours of 9 Feb we are much depressed this morning for we had reclaimed so many trenches from the floods, yesterday buckets as if it had never rained before and all of them are full up again now it all has to begin again. Charlie is staying

---

13   Major General Montagu-Stuart-Wortley GOC 46th Division.

over in England until about the 19th so perhaps you may see him, he feels poor C's[14] death terribly as they were such tremendous pals, should imagine it would be just as well for Charlie to come back here and let things settle down naturally. The first lot of cavalry Byngs (GOC 3rd Cavalry Division) lot came out of the trenches yesterday they have done splendidly I hear during the ten days they have been in much better than the 27th and 28th Divisions who were on their right, there is no doubt that the troops from India have been sent out too soon, their blood is not in a fit state to stand the cold they get malaria, are soft and the result is there is not enough heart in them. To my mind this fortress warfare will go on for a long time yet until the process of exhaustion makes the German narrow his front. I don't say we shall not break through here and there for a mile or two but the loss of life will not compensate for the success gained, it is merely a matter as to who can bring his manufacture of gun ammunition up to the highest pitch to support the number of men he is engaged with, ours never get any more forward to the outward show because just as we get up a reserve out comes more men which means guns have to cover more front, more front means more ammunition, still it is gradually going on in the right direction. Will go to see Evan[15] the next time I go to St Omer. Best Love Yours ever Putty.

Plans were being made for offensive action and on 15 February French approved Haig's (GOC 1st Army) plan (for Neuve Chapelle) and ordered him to be ready to carry it out as soon after 9 March as the weather and the condition of the ground permitted. To concentrate for this operation, French decided to postpone any independent action by 2nd Army: it was to assist 1st Army by containing the enemy on its front. II and V Corps were to undertake minor attacks and act as if an offensive was about to be launched from the high ground E of Ypres. III Corps, on the right of 2nd Army, was to make active demonstrations towards the front Pérenchies-Fort Englos (Ennetières), the outer line of the Lille defences, with the ulterior motive of preparing a way for an eventual attack on Lille. Smith-Dorrien wrote on 16 February: 'I held a conference with my corps commanders and discussed future operations, the conference lasting 3 hours'.

Putty wrote to Ettie again on 19 February:

My dear Chief, Cyril Hankey goes back tomorrow so send this line by him. There is no news much here. Billy Lambton and Fitz[16] came to luncheon after having been round the famous Plugstreet Wood, I did not have much time to talk to Fitz but told him all I could on main points, we have got to make up our mind that this war is not going to end for another year and get the British public to recognise this fact. We have had another dose of floods but scraped out by the skin of our teeth again without having to give up any of our line. The last divisions that have come out here have not been home from India long enough to get their blood in to proper order, the result is they are cracking up and we shall have to nurse them until the warmer weather comes. Charlie is returning on Sunday. Much love Yours ever Putty.

---

14   6th Marquess of Londonderry died 8 February.
15   Possibly Captain Evan Edward Charteris Coldm Gds (1864-1940) Eton SC GHQ close friend of Ettie Desborough also a Soul.
16   Possibly Lieutenant Colonel Sir Frederick Edward Grey Ponsonby (1867-1935) Gren Gds Keeper of the Privy Purse to George V later Baron Sysonby.

The CinC visited Bailleul on 20 February and saw Putty and his divisional commanders. Shelling and sniping continued throughout the week then, on 21 February, 2 Cdn Bde joined 4th Division for instruction. It was the start of a programme of attaching Dominion, Territorial and New Army Divisions to III Corps and its divisions in the line, so that they could gain essential experience. This involved considerable additional staff work for HQ III Corps at a time when they had to hold the extended line and prepare for the forthcoming battle. That morning Putty watched 1/2 London set off from Bailleul in the morning and march the seven and a half miles to Armentières where it joined 17 Bde 6th Division. Under a separate programme a territorial battalion was to be added to each brigade giving them now five in all.

French visited Putty at Bailleul again on 24 February. Also that day Putty wrote to Ettie:

My dear Chief, Just a line by Stavey to say all is well. Weather abominable, rain and snow with fine intervals just to buoy one up and then throw one down. Charlie has returned, he is very different and depressed but will give him plenty of work to do to distract. Don't you think the case of the incapacitated soldier who has lost a foot or a leg is a good opportunity for starting a school to teach telephonic work, all these men will commute their pensions and be on the rates in a few years' time, if they are taken in hand at once they would learn a trade and be able to start before the mighty influx of the men at the end of the war when they will have no chance. The 16th Lancers had a bad time up North and lost 16 officers killed in trying to retake a trench that their men had been blown out of by a mine. Best love Yours ever Putty.

He also wrote a long letter that day to Edith, now Marchioness of Londonderry:

Dear Lady C, Thank you dear thing for your letters which I meant to answer before, am very pleased at my KCB [LG 15 February] it is a very good fence to have got over. It has been a very uphill job lately almost as much as anyone without the hide of a rhinoceros could stand but have played the game have not complained and worked steadily along and now I think begin to see daylight. We have got Forestier-Walker [MGGS 2nd Army] out of the way though am afraid shall have to give up Milne [BGGS III Corps] to replace him which means having to get another man into my ways, shock him very gradually by my depraved conversation at the same time get him to go the devil for me, however I shall let him go as I think it is the only chance of 2nd Army ever being a success and though I could probably have got my corps put into the 1st Army it was dog in the manger and except for saving the 3rd Corps would not have dreamt of it, all of this for your private ear as you know the ropes. Charley seems a different man since he went away but will give him plenty of work and try to keep his mind interested, he is so nice about his mentioned in despatches, of course I should have liked to have got a him a DSO or a brevet but had to consider what others had been through in the trenches in comparison, however he will get his reward for his work in due course. Took Charlie round the hospitals and convalescent homes yesterday, if you have any old packs of playing cards, magazines or cheap boxes of dominoes drafts, send them along they are a godsend to these poor devils, we have a good room for inoculation against enteric where by making them comfortable for three days they all volunteered instead of resisting all this owing to weakness at home in not making it compulsory. Tell me how the 3rd Corps ward stands am sending you a tenner as a thanksgiving for my KCB you must

Lieutenant General Pulteney, 1915.
(Image courtesy of Lady Rose Lauritzen
and PRONI D4567)

spend it on fittings etc necessary for the room. I enclose you a couple of photos one of your humble servant alone the other with General Wilson who commands the 4th Division, they appear on the cinematograph at Armentières without too much hissing. A dull letter Yours ever Putty.

Much paper flowed from HQ 2nd Army including this memo to III Corps on 26 February:

In confirmation of my secret memorandum (G448 of 23 Feb) and with the object of facilitating the eventual advance of the Army when the time arrives, the army commander considers it advisable that your efforts should be primarily directed in front of 6th Division, opposite which the Pérenchies-Fort Englos ridge offers a definite objective. He desires that you will have a reconnaissance carried out of the ground within your present line and report on the number of heavy guns and howitzers that, in your opinion, can be usefully employed now and at a later stage against the same objective, and the position they should occupy. He understands that this has already been done as far as field guns are concerned. He would be glad to have a report at an early date. Milne MGGS.

Milne had been Putty's BGGS until the day before and it is not clear to what extent he was involved in the drafting of this memo which seems strangely lacking in resolve about III Corps' mission; asking Putty how many heavy guns he could use and where they should go is also peculiar since the allocation should have been based on the corps' task and the ammunition available.

The same day Putty wrote to Ettie Desborough:

My dear Chief, Am going through changes of my General Staff Officer as General Milne has been moved up to Sir Horace S.D. they have sent me Lynden-Bell who I had not met before, he seems a nice fellow with one eye out of repair. No news here, the snow that fell here yesterday disappeared in the night we cannot get the ground dry which distresses me. We all howl for carpet slippers for the men to put on in our convalescent homes they rest their feet so, the hospitals are all provided but these homes we put the men in for only two or three days rest, nobody seems to make a wool slipper now. Yours ever Putty.

February came to an end with a cold day of brilliant sunshine. Casualties for the month were 10 officers and 172 other ranks killed, 29 officers and 694 other ranks wounded = 905. This slight increase over the previous month was again a reflection of the drier weather and consequent increase in enemy activity. The drier and colder weather was also responsible for the greatly improved sickness rate in III Corps down to 1.5 per 1000 men per day for the last week of February (compared with 3.3 in mid-January). The strength of the corps was now 47,991.

March

1 March brought stormy weather, and a group of 12 Belgian officers, including 6 generals, to visit HQ III Corps and then the defences at Ploegsteert Wood. Everyday there were visitors; some could be dealt with by the staff but many required Putty's time and attention. Another memo arrived that day from 2nd Army:

The army commander desires that you will make the necessary arrangements for an active demonstration along the front of your 6th Division against the enemy's trenches. The scheme should consist of a systematic advance by sap and mine especially from the fronts held by 16 and 17 Bdes.
   All initial arrangements such as the sinking of mines and construction of saps should be at once commenced and he hopes that the operations may be carried through with the utmost energy. It is regretted that for the moment the daily allowance of ammunition cannot be exceeded. Sir Horace also desires that you will draw up a considered plan for a further advance against the Pérenchies-Fort Englos ridge, embodying your probable requirements in RE personnel and material. The contents of this communication should be in the hands of only such members of your staff as is absolutely necessary. GF Milne MGGS 2nd Army.

The difficulties of sapping and mining in the flood plain of the River Lys, with the water table so high, are self-evident; this, compounded by the shortage of artillery ammunition, made the task an extremely difficult one if the demonstration was to be convincing.

The following day Putty sent his monthly letter to the King:

Dear Wigram, I send you the diary of the 3rd Corps for the month of February. The casualties increase a little every week now which I attribute to the increased number of hours of daylight. The art of sniping has been reduced on both sides to as near perfection as possible, new units on arrival in trenches suffer accordingly from want of experience. We have trained the Canadians during the last fortnight and they took over a portion of the line last night, splendid material, full of enterprise, and only too anxious to learn, it would have repaid us many times over to have had British regular officers commanding each battalion. We have had desperate contests with the floods, in despair one week jubilant the next, just as we begin to dig the communication trenches we get drowned out at once but we have made the lines very much stronger than they were with many supporting points, the Germans have also put up a great deal more wire lately all round our front which look as if they anticipated an attack. Stuart-Wortley's Territorial Division (46th Division) we begin to train on Thursday in fact the 3rd Corps has been rapidly turning itself into a training school. The health of the troops is very good considering the weather. Yours Sincerely, WP Pulteney.

But that morning at 7.5 am Private T Hope 2 Leinster (17 Bde 6th Division) and Private A Atkinson 1 W Yorks (18 Bde 6th Division), having been convicted by a FGCM of desertion, were shot.

3 March was a day of particularly heavy shelling against 6th Division inflicting damage and casualties. However, III Corps' howitzers did considerable damage to the factory in La Houssoie, the brewery and farm at Wez Macquart, and attacked the enemy's salient at Rue du Bois in cooperation with two field batteries. Considerable damage was done to the parapets and stretcher parties were seen afterwards. The heavy battery did further damage to Wez Macquart brewery and to the house near the railway at La Houssoie. Enemy guns which replied to this fire were silenced by the 'Churchill' armoured train. Such artillery battles were now common-place with III Corps artillery well-coordinated and able to engage targets more quickly and effectively across its front. Invariably it was to get the better of such actions. During the day French rode over to Bailleul and had lunch with Putty and Stuart-Wortley.

Putty was presented with the Grand Croix of the Legion of Honour on 4 March, the day that 46th Division began to arrive for instruction. In Ploegsteert the following day he was hit in the shoulder by a spent shrapnel bullet which broke two windows of his car and grazed the driver in the neck. It did not penetrate and Putty was not hurt.

Earlier he had written to Ettie Desborough:

My dear Chief, Many thanks for your congratulations [for KCB] and those of Willie and the family, it is good fence to have got over. Was further honoured yesterday by being given the Grand Officier of the Legion of Honour the highest one, Allenby Willcocks and self while Sir John French was given the Medaille Militaire which is the most coveted decoration in the French Army. General Lynden-Bell that is with me is a brother of the medical one that you met at Boulogne, he is a nice energetic man but lacks a little of the experience of the front line but think he will get all right, he has lost an eye on the ranges some time ago. I will let you know how the slippers suit when they arrive it is very dear of you to have thought of sending them. Julian came over to see me on Tuesday, he looked the picture of health, energy youth and manliness with an eye as clear as crystal he had put his name down to go in the Scots Guards but all that movement is off, the energy and direction are in him all right, he does not want office work from what I could grasp but has got the right ambition for deeds in the field, I must look out for an opening for him if the present role of the cavalry does not alter, he made me roar with laughter over firing the rifle grenade as he fired it from the shoulder instead of from a rest on the ground, how he stood the kick of it I do not understand. The Canadians have taken over a bit of the line, they are shaping well and if they get over the next week without losing their confidence will be a great asset. Reggie Pembroke came back here yesterday full of life, he has not stopped talking since he returned and the name of Jackdaw that the Blues gave him when he joined hit the right nail on the head. Weather very hopeless in this low lying section of ground that my corps operates in, sapping, mining and communication trenches nearly break one's heart. Much love Yours ever Putty.

At the end of a week of more rain it was reported in the Opsum: 'Work has been continuous on strengthening the lines of defence of the corps. Many flooded trenches have been reclaimed, supporting points strengthened and wired, breast works erected and communication improved. In addition, sapheads are being vigorously pushed forward and mining operations are in progress at certain selected points'. Gradually the conditions were being mastered. However, at 7.5 am on 6 March Private E Kirk 1 W Yorks (18 Bde 6th Division), having been convicted by a FGCM for desertion, was shot at Armentières.

Also on 6 March III Corps received another memo from 2nd Army:

The army commander desires that from tomorrow morning [7 March] there should be a considerable increase in activity in front of II and V Corps, and on the left of III Corps. For this purpose the daily allowance of artillery ammunition is doubled. Every endeavour should be made to push forward saps and mines against the enemy's front.

Up to now the focus for Putty and his staff had been on his right (6th Division), now, at short notice he was required to concentrate on his left (4th Division). On 7 March Smith-Dorrien wrote: 'I afterwards visited HQ III Corps and discussed certain matters with General Pulteney'.

Brigadier General Lambton (MS GHQ) writing to the King that day noted: 'The Canadians have been gaining experience of trench life under General Pulteney's divisions, he reports very well of them, says they show a fine fighting spirit, and are very keen and willing, and that the officers are trying hard to learn'. Some regular officers were particularly unfavourable towards the lax discipline of colonial troops but Putty was not one of them, perhaps because of his experience with the VMR in South Africa.

The AQ log recorded on 7 March: 'French interpreter sent to Dunkirk to purchase some small mesh fishing nets, to erect in front or over the trenches, as an experiment, with a view to stopping or deflecting the enemy's rifle and hand grenades'. It also noted that sick wastage for the previous week was 1.7 per 1000 men per day, and it was now to be consistently low.

Next day Putty wrote to Edith Londonderry:

Dear Lady C, Thanks for your charming letter. As you say it is not a bad move Milne going up to S.D. [Smith-Dorrien] as one knows how the land lies, if one could only have realised to what excess vanity can be carried by a man, one would have been diplomatic long ago to some extent but it was impossible to conceive. The new man Belinda [Lynden-Bell] seems to be shaping all right but jumps much too quickly at conclusions, he has already had some shocks which will do him no harm. I think he will be all right if I can get him out of the office. Charlie is picking up well, is in far better spirits, the surroundings are becoming much more interesting for him, forward plans are on the tapis I don't tell him of them on purpose so as to make him like Jemmy Rothschild ask his friends like Tim Harington [GSO2] and Pitt-Taylor [GSO3] until he gets to the bottom of the business. The Ritz has been very full this week we have had Eddie Wortley [GOC 46th Division], Dick Cavendish,[17] Charlie Kerr[18]and Northampton[19] to dinner. Charlie Willoughby[20] and Roger Tempest[21] arrived to be trained in the division [6th] yesterday but have not seen them yet, will ferret them out today. We are beginning to make a push all along the line it will not develop much to the outward eye for some time but the arrangements for passing from the defensive to the offensive are all in progress. Will try and get you another photo some time with the evil eye. Best love and all blessings Yours ever Putty.

Every Wednesday from early 1915 a group of friends, known in due course as the members of the Ark, met for a late dinner on the top floor of Londonderry House, most of the rest of the house having been turned into a hospital. The Ark was originally formed to give Edith's friends a chance to relax away from their wartime work. It quickly became the nearest thing to a salon in wartime London. There was something of the school secret society about it: you had to be invited to join; every member had to take the name of a real or mythological beast and was given a matching 'address'; silly games were played; jokes were told; gossip exchanged; and skits acted. It was a long way below the intellectual and spiritual level of the Souls; but then, as Edith had rightly judged, for someone who had spent all day grappling with the arduous and depressing realities of the war the chance to drink the excellent Londonderry House champagne, to be frivolous, playful, even absurd in the company of beautiful women was irresistible. What the Ark offered above all was fun. Ark appellations had to begin with the first letter of Christian name or surname, or they had to rhyme, or be amusingly apropos. The QMG, Sir John Cowans, was Merry John the Mandrill; Princess Helena Victoria was Victoria the Vivandière. Edith found herself christened Circe the Sorceress.

A first list of about 30 members (c1915) contains four groups of people – the family, those involved with Edith in her wartime work especially the Women's Legion, King's Messengers of which her brother in law (Stavey married to Lady Helen Vane-Tempest-Stewart) was one, and politicians. It includes Princess Helena Victoria as the Grand Mistress, General Cowans as Vice President; other King's Messengers include Lord Hindlip and Lieutenant Colonel Cyril Hankey; the politicians include Arthur Balfour, Winston Churchill (First Lord of Admiralty up to May 1915) and Sir Edward Carson (Attorney General May-October 1915). Others include Lord and Lady Desborough, Duchess of Portland (Winifred Anna Dallas-Yorke 1863-1954 wife of 6th Duke of Portland) and Percy Chubb, the American industrialist. Both of Putty's first ADCs are on the list, Reggie and his wife and Charley. Finally this first list includes 'Putty

---

17 Probably Lieutenant Colonel Lord Richard Frederick Cavendish (1871-1946) Eton CO 5 RLR 28th Division brother of 9th Duke of Devonshire.
18 Charles Ian Kerr (1874-1968) RHG later 1st Baron Teviot.
19 William Bingham Compton 6th Marquess of Northampton (1885-1978) RHG.
20 Probably Major Hon Charles Heathcote-Drummond-Willoughby (1870-1949) SG 1890-1908.
21 Probably Major Roger Stephen Tempest (1876-1948) SG 1898-1921.

the Polecat' with the name of Lady Pulteney added later. No other soldiers appear on Edith's various lists. A significant later addition is Sir Philip Sassoon noted then as Private Secretary to Field Marshal Haig CinC and also a member of the Rothschild family.

On 9 March Smith-Dorrien (GOC 2nd Army) recorded: 'Thence to Bailleul in a heavy snowstorm. There I saw General Pulteney'. Again there was no detail, no warmth. Also that day Putty wrote to Ettie Desborough:

> My dear Chief, A line to say the slippers have arrived all right, am afraid that they are too small for what I want, it wants a very soft woollen slipper that will go over a man's foot with a bandage on, something that wont press him and that is very soft to tread on. There is no news here we are all preparing to push our line a little forward but it is long tedious work without much apparent result to the onlookers' eye. We had the press correspondents here last week and sent them to the famous Plugstreet Wood which was interesting for them to see and quite different to the ordinary line of trenches. Had a near squeak on Friday as a bullet from a shrapnel came right through the two front windows of my car and just missed Reggie Pembroke and self, of course all sorts of stories got about that I was wounded but neither of us was touched. Ilchester goes back today so send this by him. Much love Yours ever Putty.

At 5 pm III Corps issued OpO No.44 (implementing orders in 2nd Army OpO No.5):

> III Corps, in conjunction with II and V Corps, will open at 7.30 am 10 March artillery bombardments on selected objectives. These will be followed by fire attacks and offensive enterprises both by day and night, in order that, when opportunity occurs and necessary preparations have been made, any selection of the hostile trenches may be captured.

The aim was to hold the enemy in front of III Corps to his ground and prevent the despatch of reinforcements to the Neuve Chapelle battle area. Duly at 7.30 am (start of the Battle of Neuve Chapelle) on 10 March the artillery of III Corps shelled the German wire and defences to mislead the enemy as to the point of attack and, from time to time for periods of 15 minutes, the infantry opened bursts of machine-gun and rifle fire followed by cheering as if about to assault. The next day (11 March) the attacks by fire were continued by both divisions; the enemy's response was ineffective. Then at midnight 17 Bde 6th Division assaulted and by 3.15 am had captured L'Epinette and consolidated the position. The result of this operation was that an advance of 300 yards was made on a front of half a mile. More importantly as the GS log noted at 7.30 pm (12 March): 'Enemy has shown considerable activity all along III Corps front and there are no signs of any depletion of his strength whatever'.

Field Marshal French noted: '12 March was ushered in by a brilliant night attack carried out by the 6th Division under General Kier in the very early hours of the morning. This division formed part of the III Corps under Pulteney, which, although nominally forming part of the 2nd Army, was now acting independently on a front of which Armentières was the centre. The attack resulted in the capture of the village of L'Epinette'. This gave an indication of the problems to come.

Putty's diversionary action had been very successful and also gained some ground. During the night of 12 March several enemy bomb attacks were repulsed near L'Epinette; three prisoners were taken who stated they were from 2 Bn 133 Regt and that the remainder of their party, 17 men, had been killed when they came under heavy fire. 6th Division reported that the enemy was by now thoroughly stirred up in front of their line and decidedly jumpy, using flares and searchlights continually during the night.

Putty next wrote to Ettie Desborough on 13 March:

> My dear Chief, You will have got my letter about the slippers. The fighting serious has begun so far with tremendous success, the 1st Army have taken over 2,000 prisoners and have killed a great many Germans, the fire of our grandmothers mothers and aunties was too terrible it blew one village in to a shapeless mess, you could not distinguish which were the roads, everything was killed in it, scores of them by the concussion alone. The crisis is now coming we feel that the great effort is going to be made, you have got to get the hospitals ready at home and care for them as they arrive wounded for now is our time to put every man in to the field and hit Germany while economic strain is on her besides we want to cause them every single casualty that we can to prevent her raising new formations, once this ceases the end will begin to come and if our gun ammunition will last come quicker than most people imagine, provided the pressure is kept up on Constantinople etc. Very pressed with work with best love and blessings. Yours ever Putty.

Milne (MGGS 2nd Army) sent another memo to III Corps on 13 March; this was about the planning of an attack on Wez Macquart. By now Putty must have been more than irritated by Smith-Dorrien's conduct of operations and especially the direction given to him.

The next three days were fine and quiet apart from the continual shelling and sniping. On the right of the 4th Division, 2 Monmouth 12 Bde were attacked by about 200 Germans at 5.30 am on 17 March, as the morning mist lifted, and were driven off by rapid fire. At 2.30 pm that afternoon Smith-Dorrien wrote: 'Accompanied by General Pulteney I saw 1 Warwicks and 2 Seaforth (both 10 Bde) marching through Nieppe'. On 18 March it was the turn of 1 QWR 18 Bde 6th Division who were bombed by the enemy and suffered several casualties; and it was probably no coincidence that both were Territorial battalions. It was cold with frequent snow squalls on 19 March; 6th Division reported that the water in the ditches between the lines was still five feet deep. That night in compliance with 2nd Army orders, III Corps issued OpO No.45 extending the corps' line left to the Wulverghen-Messines road on the night 21/22 March, an addition of 1000 yards. The GS log noted that the corps' front was now 17,300 yards.

Putty wrote to Ettie Desborough again next day:

> My dear Chief, Thanks for yours of 17 Mar which reached me last night. George Paynter [CO 2 SG] is shot in the lung, the bullet went clean through but made a large hole where it came out of his back he was very bad on Tuesday night, rather inclined to chuck it but now is all right bar a relapse. Yes Eloise Ancaster's brother[22] was killed at St Omer experimenting with bombs, the beastly thing did not go off and he went to see what had happened, he was blown to pieces. It is a sign of the times that here we are already in possession of Douglas Haig's orders for the Neuve Chapelle fight in a German paper it is a

22   2nd Lieutenant William Lawrence Breese (1883-1915) RHG killed 14 March.

Nieppe Chateau HQ 4th Division, 1915. Pulteney (left) with Generals Wilson GOC, Fox CRA and Lynden-Bell BGGS. (© IWM Q56715)

great pity that it should have ever fallen in to the hands of the Germans as they have made the most of the superior numbers quoted, the whole thing would have been a far greater success if the artillery had calculated the error of the day caused by the difference of the atmosphere in comparison to the day they registered their ranges on, you can understand. Laurence Drummond [now Major General and Director of Infantry] is here getting tips to train the infantry at home on the proper lines, he really of course is itching to get out here again in any capacity but between ourselves you can tell from his looks after two days here when he has done nothing at all except the ordinary rounds that his constitution would never stand it. There is only one thing you must all be in one accord over in Great Britain at the moment viz that no man or woman or child that can help to make gun ammunition is away from work more than eight hours, all the strain is coming the next two months and whichever side can bring up the most will win the fight quicker, what we have got to realise is that all the ammunition that arrives now shortens the duration of the war by so many days. Winston was here on Thursday [18 March] but he had not much news, optimistic as usual which is a great asset though we Flanders soldiers think that the Constantinople side issue may be a good move from a diplomatic point of view but not likely to shorten the war, further that it is likely to lead to complications with Russia as regards the Dardanelles, it is

Germans you have to kill not Turks or Austrians, besides the summer down there will kill hundreds. Best love Yours Putty.

In this letter Putty also talks about Ettie's first meeting with Jessie Arnott, the woman he had loved since at least 1911. This was an important milestone in their relationship; but they still had a long way to go, and there was a war to be fought which would keep them apart. Ettie played an important role behind the scenes.

He wrote to Edith Londonderry on 21 March:

Dear Lady C, Charley is off to 'join' you once more, I hope he will make a good job of it this time!!! Why he can't leave all the things for you to sign I can't imagine you seem to have a splendid business head. Charley is much better, is coming in to form rapidly (I don't mean yours) but public, he begins to take an interest in all military matters together with a most (appreciable) sense of humour which is always worth its weight in gold, our interesting time has not yet come though in the next attack my right flank may be involved if this is successful then my turn will come next, have been gradually working towards it for a long time but I think it will be successful as the troops are in good heart. I think I see signs of Reggie breaking out, this sun on his back is too much for him, the thin end of the wedge has come to the fore with two girls in Armentières whose nicknames are Vaseline and Glycerine ye gods if you saw them in Piccadilly you would deny them thrice. Jack Durham[23] is coming here [France] tomorrow have told Billy to bring him to Bailleul for the night on Tuesday [23 March]. Laurence Drummond has been touting round he wants a job most evidently but it is hard to tell a man that you can see he would not stand the strain a fortnight when it comes to hard fighting. Neuve Chapelle was very nearly a great victory, it would have been if the artillery had registered their ranges in the morning of the fight and found out the error of the day caused by the atmosphere, the infantry were magnificent, the state of the troops after the losses magnificent, all the old fighting spirit is coming back to the nation and they take their ground like their forefathers used to. Write me a line to tell me how you are settling down to your new position I mean at the head of the table not any other posture on or under the bed. How long have I told you that the supply of gun ammunition is what we ought all to centre our efforts on, it is no use to double our present supply we want to quadruple it with the increasing size of our army. Best love Yours ever Putty. This is not meant for the censor.

The successes of the artillery were not often recorded but on 22 March 6th Division reported excellent shooting by 24 Hy Bty in which an anti-aircraft gun was destroyed and three direct hits obtained on a howitzer battery.

On 23 March III Corps received another memo from 2nd Army: 'Order to corps comds to meet army commander at HQ III Corps at noon 24 Mar – to report progress in sapping and mining in their district (in response to GHQ request to brief CinC dtd 22 Mar)'. The corps, and Putty in particular, did not need repeated encouragement to take offensive action. There were practical problems; a memo to III Corps from 4th Division (23 March) stated: 'Ref offensive

---

23   Probably John George Lambton 3rd Earl of Durham (1855-1928) Lord Lieutenant of Co Durham.

spirit and ammunition shortages – 549 rifle grenades since 1 March for a front of 4.5 miles, 50 rds for the trench mortars; 4th Division have only been supplied with 2 telescopic sights'. It was not just the adverse weather and ground conditions, and the shortage of artillery ammunition, which had to be overcome. There were shortages in many areas.

The AQ log recorded that at 6 am that morning (23 March) Lance Sergeant W Walton 2 KRRC, having been convicted by a FGCM of desertion, was shot. He was not in III Corps; indeed up to now only 4 of the 10 men tried and convicted for desertion in III Corps' jurisdiction were actually serving in III Corps. It is worth repeating that some of them would have been recently recalled reservists, out of the army for many years; they received little training or preparation for the appalling conditions in the trenches and even less time to assimilate amongst men they would have not known. Such men were likely to be married and in the haste left problems unresolved; inevitably a few would have been suffering from physical or mental health issues. This may help to understand these men but they had volunteered for service that included a reserve commitment, and knew the punishment for desertion in the face of the enemy.

Putty wrote to Edith Londonderry:

> Dear Lady C, I rather agree with the enclosed cutting don't you? (Letter to *Daily Mail* 17 Mar 1915 ref disclosure of information to the public – trust them). Billy Lambton and Jack Durham are coming to stay here tonight, am taking them to see the Durham Light Infantry in their billets tomorrow. I hear that the ladies in London when they find they are in the family way say they have been 'mobilised'. Germans are getting pretty active at present, cannot help thinking that they will have a (punch) at me instead of St Eloi this time, let them come. Tell Charlie to order another 10,000 postcards to be sent out to me for the Hospitals. Hope the 'Carpentering' has gone on well. Yours ever Putty.

Smith-Dorrien wrote on 24 March: '12 noon. I had a conference with my corps commanders at Bailleul'. By then relations between Putty and Smith-Dorrien must have deteriorated further, with the CinC aware or even involved.

Military attachés from Russia and Japan visited III Corps on 25 March, a day of heavy mist in the morning and later being cold and wet. Putty sent a memo (G579) to 2nd Army ref planning of attack with first objective La Houssoie-Wez Macquart-La Bleue-La Fresnelle. It concluded:

> Speaking very generally my idea is, whilst pivoting my attack on L'Epinette, to drive a wedge into the enemy's front line on a front of about 1200 yards ie 600 yards on each side of the main road Lille-Wez Macquart near the point where it enters the latter village.

He also wrote to Theresa Londonderry and Ettie Desborough:

> Dear Lady Londonderry, Many thanks for your congratulations it ought to give one a command of entry in the future in French circles, I am very proud of having got it. There has been a lull after the Neuve Chapelle fight but expect that the Germans will make the next move as they appear to be collecting troops for the offensive. We had the ground well dried up but now the usual downpour has begun again. Jack Durham is staying here am taking him to see the Durham Light Infantry (2 DLI 18 Bde 6th Division) in their billets this morning You ought to be there too. Yours sincerely WP Pulteney.

My dear Chief, Many thanks for yours of 23 Mar. Yes I think I am more than satisfied over Neuve Chapelle, it was the first time we had taken the offensive against what are practically siege works, it was very nearly a great victory, it made the Germans show their hand as nearly all the guns that they brought in to action had been quiet for two months obviously in readiness but saving ammunition and keeping their existence dark. You must not believe what they tell you about the ammunition, the supply is an absolute failure and none of the army has any confidence in the arrangements made for the future especially with the demands of the Constantinople side issue. Charley has been home to sign some papers but we expect him back again today, he seems to be cheering up in a wonderful way. Evan came with Jack Durham to tea yesterday the first time I have seen him since he came out. The Germans appear to be side slipping some troops from N to S which is probably the prelude to an attack probably in the direction of Sailly or La Bassée but wherever it is it will accompanied by a massing of artillery, as a counter stroke to ours at Neuve Chapelle. The Stellenbosch stories were very rife here for some time I call them Marseilled now that being the southernmost place we can think of, Joey Davies[24] came out all right between ourselves I think Rawlinson [GOC IV Corps] tried to cart him, Carter [Brigadier General FC Carter Comd 24 Bde 8th Division invalided Mar 1915] was ill and did not deserve the nickname of 'Cartem' that I gave him on first arrival. Lynden-Bell is doing very well he works hard gets on well with the other staff officers but has not the experience or the knowledge of the field work that Milne had nor is he anything like so accurate, he does not weigh things in the balance long enough in fact reminds me of the Irish character and nature, Milne went as Chief of Staff to Smith-Dorrien where he is competing with his temper in a diplomatic manner. Best love and blessings Yours ever Putty.

Next day (26 March) he wrote to Edith Londonderry:

Dear Lady C, Thanks so much for your letter. Re the 'Carpenter', Charlie joins you, as a rule a joiner is a carpenter, but trust the grooves fitted well enough to require no nails. Jack Durham made an excellent speech to the Durham Light Infantry at Armentières yesterday, I took him to see them in their billets, they gave him three real good cheers afterwards, Charley must go to pal with them as several asked after him, there are only two officers left who came out originally with the battalion. You are splendid with intrigue, yes old S.D got it in the neck and has been different ever since, Milne is going to be master you can see that he is too clever for him and as both sides have strong tempers that side is equal. The expenditure of ammunition at Neuve Chapelle was the dickens, two attacks never came off that the artillery prepared the way for, they could not collect the brigades in time to carry them out, the communications between the batteries in rear was much easier and they got ready in time, we all live and learn, people at home must realise that we can never have enough ammunition and that every increase to the output shortens the duration of the war. The Germans are collecting all the reserves that they can get hold of and are evidently intent on making a push somewhere, both sides are saving up ammunition, we are like boys only allowed to load one barrel in a double barrelled gun. Bestlove Yours ever Putty.

24   Major General FJ Davies GOC 8th Division.

The rest of the month was dry but colder. AQ log noted that FGCM for week ending 27 March were: 4th Division 18 (8 drunk) and 6th Division 21 (12 drunk). The overall number was gradually declining as conditions improved but drunkenness continued to be a problem with cheap alcohol so readily available.

Summing up the month the GS log recorded:

> Great advantage has been taken of the better conditions to improve communications throughout the front trenches, old communication trenches have been drained and boarded and new ones dug, thus making it possible to get to any portion of the front line in daylight with comparative safety.
>
> III Corps has completed training of the Canadian and North Midland Divisions (46th), while the South Midland Division (48th) is about to commence its training. Continuous and systematic patrolling has been carried out every night all along the front held by the corps; the object being to capture or kill and bring in one of the enemy for purposes of identification.

III Corps casualties for the month were: 19 officers and 272 other ranks killed, 32 officers and 1,031 other ranks wounded = 1,354.

April

Enemy aircraft bombed Armentières on 1 April; also that day 2nd Army issued OpO No.7. It allocated 48th Division to III Corps, the first change to its divisions other than for instruction since the corps was formed, and heavy artillery of three hy btys (24, 31 and S Mid) and two siege btys (7 and 12 less one how).

The following day Putty wrote to the King:

> Dear Wigram, Herewith the diary of the 3rd Corps for the month of March for the information of His Majesty. The longer days, the drying ground has brought fresh life in to the men you can see the blood returning to their faces. We have trained the Canadian Division, the North Midland Division (46th) and commenced yesterday on the South Midland Division (48th), both the two Territorial divisions shape well but neither have done sufficient musketry, good shooting in this trench warfare pays its way, regiments like the Queens Westminsters [1 QWR 18 Bde] more than hold their own, in fact the crack Bisley shot is coming to the fore as accurate shooting is absolutely essential, telescopic sights worth their weight in gold. Failure of supply of gun ammunition especially 4.5" howitzer breaks one's heart, it is not a case of just being recognised but it has been foreseen ever since we reached the Aisne, all the promises of improvement have apparently signally failed, after the war there will be a good many attacks on the Ordnance. One could understand a failure in the supply in big gun ammunition but a shortage in rifle grenades does seem faulty management for the corps we get about 100 a day and we could do with a 1000 easily. How is the army going to expand if the supply is going to fail like it is at present with this sized army. Naturally the army in Flanders does not view the Constantinople side issue with favour, there will be more casualties from disease than there will be from bullets besides it is the Germans we want to kill not Turks, Smyrna on the other hand was sound

strategy. I think the feeling of the troops against the Germans at the present time is more bitter than it ever was. Yours Sincerely, WP Pulteney.

The next few days were relatively uneventful. Smith-Dorrien visited HQ III Corps where he had 'discussions with General Pulteney'. He may have known that III Corps was about to be removed from his operational command, so the discussions could have been difficult to say the least. On 4 April Putty wrote to Ettie Desborough:

My dear Chief, The last week has been splendid for getting on with the communication trenches, we have all strengthened our foothold and are preparing to push forward our lines in various directions, all at present is the engineer and the artillery pitted against one another in due course the former will win, the supply of periscopes with a very small mirror (on account of the target it represents) telescopic sights and rifles grenades is absolutely inadequate the Bisley shot with all his aids is coming to the fore, the care of the rifle our first consideration, look at a man like Corporal Fulton[25] in the Queens Westminsters he picks men off at 800 yards you see the next day parados built up right across the valley of the river Lys to avoid his bullets, we want fifty telescopic sighted rifles a battalion not 'two' which we have at present (and these nearly all private), I know the gun makers in London are supplying the W.O. I know one man who gets out 4 a week, well on this scale we ought to be getting them out 20 a week to each corps but they don't arrive, they should put some expert Bisley shot on it like Waldegrave,[26] Mellish[27] or Freemantle.[28] [They were all long range rifle specialists to distances beyond the maximum 1200 yards of Bisley competitions] class and make a man's name in dealing with the subject, a good sniper will always kill two or three Germans a day. There was a Servian officer here last week who had seen a lot of the fighting, he says the Servian Army is all right, fit and well, well stocked with ammunition but that the state of health of the country is deplorable the Austrian prisoners of whom they have about 60,000 are dying from typhus etc and the whole thing is a matter with our money we ought to take in hand and rectify, an act for which Austria will be for ever grateful. An aeroplane took up a football on 1st April, marked in white paint on it April Fool, flew over a German platoon at drill dropped it in the middle of them we saw it bound in the air, the Germans fleeing from it in all directions. Yours ever Putty.

On 6 April III Corps received a memo from 2nd Army: 'In reply to III Corps letter 25 March ref attack to seize line La Houssoie-Wez Macquart-La Bleue-La Fresnelle. Army commander agreed objectives and desires that plans should be prepared'.

That same day III Corps was withdrawn from 2nd Army and placed directly under GHQ, although a formal instruction about this was not issued by GHQ until 8 April. Nevertheless on 7 April a memo was sent to Putty by Robertson (CGS GHQ):

25 Arthur G Fulton winner Kings Prize Bisley 1912.
26 William Frederick Waldegrave 9th Earl Waldegrave (1851-1930) Eton Evans House London Rifle Corps.
27 Lieutenant Colonel Henry Mellish (1856-1927) Eton Sher For.
28 Hon Walter Fremantle (1869-1936) Eton Captain Ox & Bucks.

1. I have already verbally explained to you the general intention with regard to operations in the near future, and the approximate date on which they will commence. In connection with them the CinC wishes you to attack the enemy's trenches opposite Frelinghien and Le Touquet with the object of gaining ground in that neighbourhood and of forcing the enemy to use up reserves by counterattacking you.

2. You will have at your disposal 4th, 6th and South Midland (48th) Divisions and 19 Bde but it will not be possible to reduce the front you now hold. The following heavy artillery will be placed under your command: 2 × 9.2" hows, 8 × 6" hows (4 Siege Bty from 1st Army), 1 × 15" how. Brigadier General Uniacke will be placed at your disposal for command of this artillery.

3. The following ammunition will be available: 18 pdr – 7,500 rds, 500 of which will be HE; 4.5" how – 600 rds, 300 of which will be HE; 4.7" guns – 100 rds, 50 of which will be HE; 9.2" how – 100 rds, all HE; 6" how – 400 rds, all HE; 15" how – 25 rds, all HE.

    If you desire to use your 5" Hows and 15 pdrs in the operation, please submit an estimate of ammunition you are likely to require. 5" ammunition is, however, very scarce, and there is no 15 pdr available except in ammunition echelons.

4. In forming your plans you should not take into account the 60 pdr guns now on your front, as it may be necessary to employ them elsewhere.

5. You will be notified as soon as possible of the actual date on which your attack will take place. The attack should be timed so that the enemy's trenches will be occupied about dusk.

6. I am to ask you to forward your plans for the above operation for the information of the CinC.

It was not till the following day (8 April) that the GS log recorded receipt of another memo from CGS GHQ to III Corps and 2nd Army:

III Corps will for the present be under the direct orders of the CinC for the purpose of operations. For administrative purposes it will continue under 2nd Army. The Heavy Artillery Reserve and Army Artillery now in III Corps area will remain under III Corps for the present.

The exact sequencing of the formal instructions is not important since other verbal instructions might have been given. What does seem strange is that on 6 April Smith-Dorrien was ordering Putty to attack in his S (on 6th Division front) and yet within 24 hours GHQ had taken direct command of III Corps and was ordering Putty to attack in his N (on 4th Division front). Since this was a 2nd Army diversionary attack, it was an extraordinary state of affairs and one that must have required a phenomenal amount of staff work for HQ III Corps to sort out; at least Robertson's orders, on behalf of the CinC, were very clear and in sharp contrast to anything that had come from 2nd Army. History records that French had now no confidence in Smith-Dorrien and sought to undermine him by reducing the size of his command. Haig writing on 30 April 1915 noted: 'Sir John told me Smith-Dorrien had caused him much trouble. He was quite unfit (he said) to hold command of an army and so Sir John had withdrawn all troops from his control except II Corps'. There is no evidence that Putty played any part in all of this; Milne too must have been in a difficult position having served in III Corps as BGRA 4th Division and then BGGS before becoming MGGS 2nd Army. It is very easy to forget how few major generals and above there were serving in the regular army at this stage of the war; and they knew each other very well not least because most had served in the South African War. Furthermore, appointment and removal at this level were not matters for the CinC alone. Another possible explanation for the removal of III Corps from 2nd Army was French's plan that Putty would command the new 3rd Army in due course and this might have been a preliminary move in that direction.

Meanwhile trench warfare continued: on 9 April 4th Division exploded a mine (1200 lbs) near Le Touquet and 27 enemy wounded were seen later being evacuated to the rear. The following night a patrol of 1 Som LI (11 Bde 4th Division) attacked an enemy working party inflicting up to 10 casualties.

In the evening of 9 April Putty wrote to Ettie Desborough:

> My dear Chief, Thanks for yours of 7 Apr from Panshanger it seems only yesterday I met you there with a fuzzy head having come over from Brocket but for all this it must be thirty years ago. We have had a lot more rain the river Lys is over its banks once more. Polly-Carew[29] is staying here with me by way of inspecting Territorial Forces needless to say he has not been near one of them spends his whole time looking at Plugstreet Wood etc, the nearest he has been to seeing a Territorial is I got hold of Eddie Wortley [GOC 46th Division] to come and dine last night to meet him. I exploded a mine at Le Touquet this morning, I did not mean to do it for some time but found out the night before last that they were countermining me, their gallery was within 12 feet of mine but luckily we heard them first but I had to alter my plan so drawing as many into the house and trench as possible we fired it at 8.30 am this morning it was a glorious explosion, every sort of thing being flung about 300 feet in the air, it will not be possible to ascertain the damage for another 24 hours but it blew a house clean down beyond the barricade we were aiming at which means that we did all we wanted and must have completely smashed in their mine, the question is if it has hurt one of my other galleries, you listen by collecting water on the ground in a small pool and put your ear inside the water you can then hear a watch ticking 10 feet away, there are also sticks for it but the water is the best, it is very dangerous work and fearfully exciting, it took 16 hours to tamp the powder in alone, what devilish people we are to one another.
>
> Billy Lambton [MS GHQ] has gone to England for a couple of days so you may see him. Best love Yours ever Putty.

At 11.30 pm on the night of 12 April an enemy airship bombed the aerodrome of 5 Sqn RFC and HQ III Corps at Bailleul. Some civilians and horses were killed but only one man of IH was wounded. Brigadier General Lambton writing later to the King noted: 'Bailleul was bombed by a Zeppelin on the 12 Apr, and dropped a good many large bombs all round General Pulteney's house; very little damage was done'.

Putty described the same incident in his letter to Edith Londonderry (13 April):

---

29   Probably Lieutenant General Sir Reginald Pole-Carew (1849-1924) late DCLI.

Dear Lady C, How are you, you have not written for some time. Charlie is very fit again at one time I nearly sent him back again he was such a wreck from the 'Flue' which at first he said was a cold caught from me. A Zeppelin bombed us last night about 11.45, it must have carried a tremendous quantity of high explosives about 10 bombs in all fell, one old woman 80 one girl 25 one child were killed, about four of the bombs about 200 lbs weight the remainder 100 lbs fortunately the effect very local though desperately violent, the child in the cot being blown clean over the roof of the next house, five horses of the Irish Horse killed but no soldiers, Reggie ran out bagged the sentry's rifle and fired fifteen rounds at it used awful language. Things have been pretty quiet lately but we shall warm up to pull our weight again about the end of the month. South Midland Territorial Division (48th) are just beginning to take their place in the line while we give a rest to all the troops in turn that have never had one all these months. Copper Horse has been with Charlie in to the Durham trenches to give them their telescopic sights. What do you hear about the opening of the hospital ward I conclude pretty soon now. Am going to St Omer tomorrow to see some experiments with a torpedo bomb of the rocket description from which we anticipate good results but they are dangerous things to handle and look diabolical in the air. The Germans are shelling us a great deal more than they have for some time which means that they are angry contemplate an attack or are moving troops about. Yours ever Putty.

Robertson (CGS GHQ) sent a further memo to Putty on 14 April in response to one from him (III Corps G783 of 11 Apr – proposed attack on Frelinghien and Le Touquet):

The operation shall commence on the day preceding the main operation, the date of which will be notified to you in due course.

It is understood that you prefer to time the assault for 6 pm and to this the CinC has no objection [The ammunition request was significantly reduced by GHQ].

5. The CinC would not wish to commit you to an operation in which you are doubtful of success, but on the other hand he must give priority to the needs of the main attack and also have regard to the extent to which the result of your operation may justify ammunition expenditure. He attaches no importance, at present, to the capture of either Le Touquet or Frelinghien except as a means of achieving the object (prevent the enemy from withdrawing troops from in front of you and also attract as many reserves as possible in your direction). If, therefore, you are of opinion that the operation here in question, is rendered impracticable, or unduly costly by the amount of ammunition allotted, you should submit at once other proposals for attaining the object in view. If you cannot see your way to do this, it will be necessary to consider whether the project must not be wholly abandoned so far as your command is concerned.

Putty would have been well aware of the importance of such diversionary attacks, and that they should be convincing, yet, at the same time, would have wanted to do everything possible to minimise casualties. The key was the effectiveness of the artillery, hence Putty was pressing for as much ammunition as could be spared. He replied to Robertson on 15 April:

Has every hope of being able to carry out the role assigned to me by the CinC.

I made the demands for ammunition contained in my G806 because I hoped, if possible, to capture the whole of the village of Frelinghien (which contains a large number of strongly fortified houses) and thus make quite certain of drawing a large force of the enemy into the neighbourhood.

I suspect, with the ammunition allotted, to be successful in capturing the enemy's trenches opposite Frelinghien and Le Touquet as well as the latter village and the houses in Frelinghien up to and including the brewery.

His reply also included discussion of armoured train (later confirmed to be deployed to Bailleul initially and to Armentières Annex later).

Meanwhile 48th Division had arrived and Private Raymond Smith 8 Worcs (144 Bde) recalled:

That evening [some time before 15 April] a comrade and I visited Armentières. The town was a blaze of light, despite the fact that it was so near the front line, and the sound of rifle and machine-gun fire came distinctly to our ears. The shopping centre was crowded with khaki-clad officers and men, and there were many civilians about. There were several big shell holes in the roads, and we were told that occasionally a shell burst in the street, but that ordinary life went on the same as ever. On 15 Apr we had our first experience of the front line trenches. This was at Houplines, just to the south of Armentières. It was practice in those days for a battalion just out from England to go into the trenches for twenty four hours 'instruction' with a battalion of the old professional army. Our hosts were 2 RWF (19 Bde). It was almost dark when we started from our farm billet, in next to no time we found ourselves in the front line. The first thing that struck me were the lights from the hundreds of candles stuck into the wet mud of the 'funk holes'. In this part of France the ground is so flat that trenches, as we knew them later on the Somme, were impossible and protection from rifle and machine-gun fire was afforded by breastworks of sandbags, with a parados made in a similar way. The actual trench was only about two feet below ground level. The parapet was high enough to enable an average sized man to walk upright.

Over the next few days Putty reorganised his line which he completed by the morning of 18 April. 6th Division now held the right with 19, 16 and 17 Bdes, the centre was held by 4th Division with 18 and 12 Bdes, and the left by 48th Division. 10 and 11 Bdes 4th Division which had been continuously in this line since October were at last withdrawn.

The night before Brigadier General Lowther (late SG now Comd 1 Gds Bde) recalled:

Gave a lecture to all company and platoon commanders, and after that Pulteney's car fetched me away to Bailleul to dine and spend the night with him. As always, a cheery party with Lynden-Bell (BGGS), Pembroke (ADC), Londonderry (ADC), Hindlip (3rd Baron Hindlip and Messenger), Phipps-Hornby (BGRA) etc.

On 18 April Putty wrote to Edith Londonderry:

Dear Lady C, Thanks dear thing for your letter. K is a curious creature he kicks up a devil of a row one minute because of the losses at Neuve Chapelle and then gets impatient the next because Sir J is not going on, I blame Von Donop[30] for not putting the case in a proper view to him because he will not come and see for himself what the wants of modern fighting are, they wont realise what the preliminary bombardment means, first the defended houses within 2000 yards have to be knocked down, then the wire has to be cut, this wire takes on an average one shell a yard if it is perfect shooting and can be observed if it cannot be observed or the forward observing officer is killed it takes double that, then you have the trenches and the covering of the advance the curtain of fire to prevent enfilade and finally the counter-attack. They cannot even supply us with a little thing like a rifle grenade or telescopic sights, the Germans fire at my corps between 150 and 200 rifle grenades a day for the last eight days the issue to my corps has not averaged 30 a day and I could do with 300 yet K says why don't we go on, just compare what organisation has done to Germany in the matter of supply of ammunition since the war began, she has increased her army by more than the whole British Army out here and yet knocks us sideways by the amount of stuff she can supply her troops with, tell K to put his own house in order before he wants us out here to do too much. Charlie is very fit again, did he tell you about the disgraceful copulation of the frogs that we three witnessed on our walk the other day, they are wonders no sooner disturbed by sticks and stones than they started again as Charlie very funnily remarked and they don't want any fixed platforms either!! And mind you there is a good deal in that platform question don't you think! I quite agree you ought to come out here to have a look round it would do you good besides cheering us up beyond all expectations but I should not be content with only a good laugh with you, you would have to pay for your 'footing' on entering 3rd Corps, the GOC must have every knowledge of things 'under him'!! Write to tell me how your cricket match went off I expect you are very good in the field, are you best at 'Cover Point' or being 'Stumped'. Reggie has intentions on a nurse out here you never saw such a person but hope she will do him good, I dare not commence as it would make one much worse afterwards. Meat Lowther stayed here last night he is in good form but quite gigantic, no dug out will hold him unless it is made for two. Best love Yours ever Putty.

During the night of 19 April a patrol of four privates of 8 Warwicks (48th Division) encountered an enemy patrol and took a prisoner of 5 Regt, 4th Bavarian Division, just one indication of the effectiveness of this division. The following evening a German aeroplane dropped 4 bombs in Armentières; it would not be long before the lights went out.

Three soldiers were shot that morning, have been convicted by FGCMs of desertion; at 4.40 am Lance Corporal JSV Fox Wilts att 3rd Division Cyclist Coy; at 5.35 am Lance Corporal A Irvine 1 RLR (12 Bde 4th Division); and at 7.05 am Gunner W Jones 43 Bty RFA (6th Division).

Private Raymond Smith 8 Worcs (144 Bde) again recalled his experiences:

On the afternoon of 21 April we moved up into Ploegsteert Wood, known to all the British Army as 'Plugstreet'. Here we took over a line of trenches immediately in front of the wood.

30   Major General Stanley Brenton Von Donop (1860-1941) late RA MGO.

At this time of the year we usually did four days in the line and four days out. One great institution which was appreciated by everyone was the weekly bath we were able to take while occupying this part of the line. The bathing house was a huge jute factory on the banks of the River Lys, and our baths consisted of large vats, capable of holding about half a dozen men.

Constant mining was going on with the GS log recording: 'One of ours at Le Touquet was blown up at 7.15 am 22 April in order to forestall a German mine which had approached to within two yards of our main gallery. Considerable damage was done to the enemy's front walls. At 1 am 23 April the enemy exploded a mine at the same place; it was short and did no damage'. That evening 4th Division was ordered N to join V Corps which had been heavily attacked NE of Ypres (start of the 2nd Battle of Ypres) and by 30 April the whole division had left III Corps. From now on there would be continual changes in the divisions within the corps placing a much greater burden on both the corps commander and his staff.

Putty wrote to Ettie Desborough on 25 April:

> My dear Chief, Thanks for your letter of 21 Apr. We are all amazed at a splendid fighting nation like the Germans having been reduced to use asphyxiating smoke, it must mean they are on their last legs, this of course is the thin end of the wedge because although in their wireless put that it is in hand to hand fighting it means that it will soon be coming along in their shells as it has been for over a week in their bombs. The space covered by the smoke is simply phenomenal, it is heavier than air and comes rolling along in a low cloud about three feet from the ground, it has chlorine and some kind of pepper mixed with it, at 2000 yards behind the front line of the French trenches the gunners fell on the ground vomiting with their eyes streaming, men's eyes were affected over 5 miles away. Arthur Balfour will have told you all about his visit to me, I took him right in to the front trenches was determined that he should do one better than George Curzon, showed him all real life in the trenches what one's wants really are, he saw wounded men brought out, shells falling everything entitling him to a war experience unique in every sense. I wish I was as happy about the ammunition as you all are at home you swallow more than we can, the figures produced by the Government are misleading as they merely represent the proportion since the commencement of the war as regards the original force which landed viz six divisions and does not allow for its expansion in the same proportion, nor does it allow for the difference in attacking fortified positions in comparison to hastily thrown up entrenchments, personally I blame Von Donop [MGO]. Yes dear thing you must let me know when you come to Wimereux shall break my rule of not leaving the corps since I left England to come to see you if you dont find your way up here. We have had a lot of shelling this last week but not much else except mining and counter mining the other night my men were firing down the counter gallery against the Germans and could not continue because of the smoke from the rifles it is wildly exciting but desperately dangerous work, counter galleries make it practically impossible to be blown up provided that they are deep enough. Best love Yours ever Putty.

Much had been achieved during the month: III Corps Opsum noted: 'It is now possible to walk all along the front line trenches and more than 6,000 yards of communication trenches are available. The whole front has a complete double row of wire and in some places there is a zone of entanglements 40 to 50 yards broad. There is a second line and here and there a third and fourth, at close supporting distance behind the front line. Finally the dugout accommodation is now almost sufficient for all men off duty by night and, in many places, for the much larger number off duty by day'. III Corps and its two regular divisions had not just survived the appalling conditions of the winter of 1914/1915, they had made the line more secure against enemy attack and improved conditions dramatically; at the same time the enemy had been dominated so that he remained pinned to his front, never able to reduce his strength for employment elsewhere.

III Corps casualties for April were 5 officers and 233 other ranks killed, 35 officers and 830 other ranks wounded = 1,103.

May

The new month began with the GS log recording on 1 May that the enemy were strengthening their defences of Wez Macquart-Houssoie road; the AQ log noted the issue of III Corps Q/2839/15 – Instructions as regards protection against asphyxiating gasses. Some time during the day Smith-Dorrien visited HQ III Corps and noted he 'had a talk with General Pulteney'.

Putty wrote to Ettie Desborough that day:

My dear Chief, Thanks for yours of 29 Apr. I have not been in the fighting myself but all my 4th Division have been, my best Brigadier Julian Hasler[31] was killed and my 12th Brigade lost 50 p.c. have not heard yet who was responsible but this trench warfare seems to have driven tactics out of the leaders heads, the attacks were inconsequent, unsupported by artillery, and made piece meal, I think it was Smith-Dorrien's fault but dont know for certain. Write to Billy Lambton [MS GHQ] for a pass to come up here, make the excuse that you want to see me on my birthday 18th May, I should have to write to Billy for the pass in any case, and it would be heavenly to see you, you could say that Monica wants to see the hospital at Bailleul, if they wont give you a pass I must motor over to Wimereux to see you but expect that there will be heavy fighting about then. Tell Arthur Balfour that the Territorial divisions out here must be armed with the 18 pdr gun and not the old useless 15 pdr they have got now, they have got the new 18 pdrs with Kitchener's army and it is unfair on the Territorials to send them out handicapped to this extent nor is it fair on us corps commanders to have our lines defended by such guns in comparison to what the Germans are now beginning to concentrate against us, mark my word the Germans will make a dead set against us for the next two months every modern gun will be brought up of longest range and big calibre and that this and next month will decide the final issue. The weather has been divine the last few days it has seemed to be almost sinful to fight in such sunshine but really it seems that the harder the fight the lovelier the day, the wheat you can see growing. They were bombarding Neuve Chapelle this morning at 5 am as if they the Germans had enough ammunition to waste as they used to have men, I can't imagine how they supply it we seem to be children at it in comparison. Personally I think the salient at Ypres will have to be readjusted it ought to have been last winter except for that stupid

31   Brigadier General Julian Hasler (1869-1915) late E Kent Comd 11 Bde killed in action 26 April.

sentiment of not giving up a yard of ground. I think the Canadians are coming down to me here to be put in to order again but even with their draft of 2,000 arriving directly they will be very weak. Yours ever Putty.

The following day (2 May) S Mid Hy Bty engaged La Petite Douve Farm and reported 3 machine-guns destroyed and 30 casualties inflicted. III Corps Artillery was becoming more effective.

Also that day Putty wrote to the King:

My dear Wigram, I enclose a summary of operations of the 3rd Corps for the month of April for the information of His Majesty. The losses in the corps have been about the same as usual, though the proportion of killed to wounded is high as it always is when sniping is the chief factor dealt with, with little but the head exposed. The weather has enabled many communication trenches to be dug which have greatly facilitated reliefs and reduced casualties. I am expecting the Canadian Division down here next week to replace 4th Division but must give them all the rest I can after their splendid deeds. The asphyxiating gases are a problem which we are at present trying to circumvent, the moral effect produced is very great and no respirators that we have got up to now seem able to combat with it, to my mind it is the best sign of deterioration in the German Army, that such splendid soldiers should stoop to it would have been incredible six months ago, one thing is certain viz that the French will beat them at it. Mr Arthur Balfour came here and I took him to the front trenches within 70 yards of the Germans, showed him their trenches through a periscope, all the items of trench warfare, which must have interested him, he behaved well except he would stop to look round at all the open places in the communication trench and had to be hurried on, he must have realised how much we wanted gun ammunition to reply to the German artillery fire. We badly want telescopic sights. The manufacture of rifle grenades seems to be a hopeless failure, the Germans fire 150 to 200 on my front every day and I can only reply with 30 which is a one sided affair. Obviously strong German pressure is going to be brought to bear on us between Lille and the sea and probably the Ypres salient will become impossible if many more German guns are brought to bear on it. We ought to get many tents up now so as to get our men out of the stuffy billets and away from the flies which will soon commence. Yours Sincerely, WP Pulteney.

The Canadian Division arrived on 4 May and went into corps reserve SE and SW of Bailleul; they were not to stay long, departing for 1st Army on 14 May. The line was now held by 6th and 48th Divisions, and 19 Bde. The following day 6th Division recovered the body of an enemy soldier shot in the morning; he belonged to 179 Regt of XIX Corps.

Much attention was being given to the design of a respirator to counter the increasing threat of gas attack. DDMS III Corps recorded (6 May): 'He [DMS 2nd Army] brought in an improved pattern of mask which is practically the same as one approved by GOC III Corps and designed after experiment by Lieutenant Barley Cameronians'. Putty took the greatest interest in the development of equipment and any new ideas that could improve the effectiveness of the corps. A respirator was a very high priority.

Barley was a graduate in chemistry of Oxford and Kiel Universities and had been considering the gas threat ever since it was first rumoured. Writing in the *Covenanter* many years later Barley recalled:

A laboratory was found in the Lycée [at Armentières] which was occupied by a Scottish medical unit who put me up with the utmost kindness and hospitality. I got down at once to experiments, spraying various gases such as chlorine, fromine and nitrous fumes and found that I got constantly gassed myself in the process. It was therefore necessary to prevent this and I thought that some cotton waste in a bag of muslin would be the best answer. This turned out to be satisfactory. The cotton waste was impregnated with sodium hyposulphite and with the addition of a little sodium carbonate I was then able to fill the laboratory room with chlorine and to destroy it effectively with my spray solution. By 6 May, therefore, my respirator enabled me to give a demonstration of the destruction of the yellow chlorine gas in this room. Suddenly I was surprised to see the large window obscured by the faces of many officers with red tabs etc of which I was told chief was Lieutenant General Sir William Pulteney GOC 3rd Corps. I did not have speech with them that day, but they were sufficiently impressed to think that my respirator would work that General Pulteney immediately gave instruction for the troops of his corps to be protected with it. I elaborated it to being a square bag containing about one inch thickness of impregnated cotton waste and along the top and bottom were tapes, the top of which closed the nostrils when tied in front with a bow and the bottom effected satisfactory cover for the mouth. All cars available were sent to Paris to buy the necessary materials and 80,000 were made up in the course of a few days at nunneries and workshops behind the line. I was removed immediately after the demonstration at Armentières to 3rd Corps Headquarters in order to help with the production and I was placed on the Q side of the staff where I had a delightful companion in Major Howard, the DAQMG, who set about the organisation of the manufacture.

At 9 am on 7 May Putty attended a conference at Sir John French's house at Hazebrouck. There were present GOCs 1st Army (Haig), Cav Corps (Byng), Indian Cav Corps (Rimington), besides CGS, AG and QMG. The subject was 1st Army's attack that was to become known as the Battle of Aubers Ridge, in which III Corps was to play a diversionary role. Later that evening at 5 pm III Corps issued G1106:

III Corps (less Canadian Division) will tomorrow make a vigorous demonstration against the enemy on its front with the object of attracting the enemy's attention and pinning him to his ground. It is essential that the demonstration should be continued until further orders.

Later he wrote to Ettie Desborough:

My dear Chief, Let me know when you come to Wimereux. Sir Horace Smith D has been dégommé[32] at last, high time too his temper was quite impossible and his vanity greater still

32   The British used the word 'stellenbosched' in the Boer War as a euphemism for being sacked, Stellenbosch being on the route back to Cape Town and thence to England. The word was carried to France in 1914 but soon replaced by 'marseilled' for much the same reason ie it was on the route to the Middle East and India. 'Dégommé' meaning 'unstuck' was taken from the French and replaced it.

than ever, am really very sorry for him as he is a fine fighting soldier but he had not the gift of being able to get fellows to work for him, Plumer has been given the command of the 2nd Army and will do it well. We are desperately busy in making respirators and inventing things to deal with these asphyxiating gases, fortunately they are entirely dependent on the wind which is sure to average more in our favour than theirs. We have got heavy fighting ahead of us all this week, personally am confident of success the more we can push now the greater the strain on Germany, she has got a tremendous lot of guns in position up by Ypres being always nervous of a big landing in the neighbourhood of Ostend, the ammunition question too is better but then the fighting up at Ypres has been a heavy strain on what we had accumulated for the push. Sir John was in London yesterday and had a long talk with K. I should imagine a successful one, he is the most optimistic man I have ever met at the conference this morning he was almost at the Meuse. Best love Yours ever Putty.

He wrote to her again on 8 May:

My dear Chief, Got yours of 5 May last night just after I had written to you. Have failed to get a pass for you so far what I can make out it is all Macready[33] who has the issuing of them, am going to see Billy tonight and will have another shot he is trying all he knows but the difficulty takes some solving. Yes I remember telling you about the Ypres salient it has been a hobby of mine all winter but of course we had not thought of poisonous gasses. There is hard fighting going on for the next week I expect. Yours ever Putty.

By now III Corps had experience of diversionary operations; to be successful they had to be convincing. This time would be more difficult since the enemy was now alert to deception and the length of the operation was indeterminate. Worse still GHQ had greatly reduced III Corps Artillery for this operation and it was left with 36 × 15 pdr (obsolete), 102 × 18 pdr, 20 × 4.5" how, 8 × 4.7" guns (obsolete), 4 × 5" how (obsolete) and 4 × 6" guns. Throughout 8 and 9 May III Corps carried out this diversionary operation. The Opsum noted: 'Dummy assembly shelters prepared. Trucks shunted in and out of Armentières station. Registration of guns and wire. The enemy's wire was cut and his trenches were bombarded at daylight. A mine at Le Touquet was fired. Machine-guns used to good effect. Colonel Currie's artillery group (Currie had replaced Uniacke) employed against enemy's guns with aeroplane observation. The operations as a whole appear to have kept the enemy on the qui vive and prevented him from withdrawing any troops from his first and second lines before the evening of 9 May at the earliest'. From all reports the operation achieved its objective; III Corps was required to repeat it on 16 May to further assist 1st Army. One inevitable consequence was to provoke enemy action, both mining and shelling. Armentières station received special attention.

By now Lieutenant Barley was on his new task:

I was quickly diverted from manufacturing to training. Indeed this happened so suddenly as to terrify me for a few hours because I was ordered to give an address in the Town Hall at Bailleul to 400 officers and NCOs from a division which was about to be moved up to

---

33   Lieutenant General Sir (Cecil) Nevil Macready (1862-1946) late Gordons AG GHQ.

the Ypres salient. However, I got through not too badly and went out to outlying battalions to give them the same sort of talk. The vehicle in which I went to these appointments was either a Douglas motor-cycle or the Rolls-Royce of Baron James Rothschild who was supernumerary ADC to General Pulteney.

On 17 May, 9th Division (Major General Landon) joined III Corps for training and administration. Then, on 25 May, orders were received for the transfer of 6th Division to V Corps; it was to be relieved by 27th Division (Major General Snow who had commanded 4th Division until injured in 1914) on 27 May. The division consisted of regular battalions withdrawn from overseas stations mainly in hot climates. 6th Division had been in III Corps almost from the beginning of the war and Putty had commanded it for the three years before that; it left on the day that Congreve (Comd 18 Bde) assumed command of the division. The amount of additional work for Putty and his staff to implement all these changes in the face of the enemy must have been considerable, and there was much more to come.

Putty wrote to Ettie Desborough on 17 May:

My dear Chief, I hope you met poor Julian [wounded 13 May] at Boulogne, I heard nothing about it until yesterday, have traced him as far as Hazebrouck going on well, he has such vitality he will soon recover, I heard of him in the thick of the fighting at Ypres strolling about among the shells as if he was on the river, he met Ricardo[34] in the Blues and took a message. Jim Foster[35] in the Blues had his leg off last night but is going on well. Tweedmouth[36] was hit by a bit of a shell while shaving, no damage, but Ricardo said it was beastly bad luck on the fuze. Have just been out to see the 9th Division K.1 the horses of the artillery are the most beautiful sight I have ever seen, it seems incredible that such horses should arrive after we have been fighting nine months, the troops certainly do K credit they are simply quite magnificent, am going to train this division I do hope I can get them in hand for a fortnight before they are sent in. The attack of the 1st Army is going well as I write, a great number of prisoners have surrendered which is a good sign of deterioration on the side of the Germans, they are using these beastly asphyxiating gases in their shells. One of the men this morning as I was watching a brigade go past heard me tell the CO there were several surrenders exclaimed oh I hope they won't all have before we get there!! The failure of the attack last Sunday week (9 May) was owing to want of the artillery support the fire being too much hurried, not properly observed either, further the Germans were nervous after Neuve Chapelle and they were too far over the parapet which was practically untouched. Ian Hamilton ought to hang over the hospital arrangements in the Dardanelles, I should send Smith-Dorrien to take command in Egypt where I understand Maxwell (Lieutenant General John Grenfell Maxwell 1859-1929 late BW GOC Egyptian Exped Force) is hopeless, that the Turks keep approaching the Canal with calm equanimity. Write and tell me how Julian is. Yours ever Putty.

34   Major Ricardo RHG BM 7 Cav Bde wounded three times 13 May.
35   Possibly Captain Arthur William Foster RHG leg amputated 13 May.
36   Lieutenant Colonel Dudley Churchill Marjoribanks 3rd Baron Tweedmouth (1874-1935) RHG.

He also wrote to Edith:

Dear Lady C, Thanks dear thing for your letter you owed me one for some time and was rather hurt, but I really wiped the floor so with you in mine no wonder you could not receive me lying down!! The attack of the 7th Division the night before last was decidedly good, the enemy have but few reserves in hand so expect the Canadians and Highland Division will both be put in today (and tomorrow) to endeavour to consolidate the position especially with a view of closing in in conjunction with the French at La Bassée for which there will be desperate fighting if only that ammunition and men had not gone to that blasted Dardanelles we should take Lille this month now we shall have to sit and look at it. The 9th Division came to me today to be trained, Landon who commands them tells me they are very green but if I can get them in to their stride before they are smashed up they will be all right. The main feature that requires attention at once is the organisation of drafts especially for the Territorials at present it is a hopeless failure and not on sound lines. Champagne for my birthday tomorrow All blessings Yours ever Putty.

Putty wrote again to Ettie on 19 May:

My dear Chief, Your wire only reached me at 2 pm yesterday, the delay with telegrams is hopeless the letters get here much quicker. Mind you write to tell me how Julian is getting on, whatever happens don't let him get about too soon, with his marvellous constitution he will be wanting to be about again much too soon, a good patient means quick and permanent recovery. The fighting of the 1st Army has been a success this time, we have come to a standstill at the present moment, probably the line will have to be consolidated and fresh plans initiated, the whole secret of success is accurate shooting and power of direction, as regards numbers we are now equal to and in most cases superior to the Germans in front of us, as regards numbers of machine-guns we are hopelessly deficient for they have ten where we have one I conclude that we cannot manufacture them, ammunition they still defeat us at, how they supply it is a marvel to me, things like rifle grenades they use 500 a day against the front of my corps while my resupply does not average 300 a week to reply with. What we all shouted for on the Aisne was a six inch howitzer with a range of 10,000 yards, plenty of 60 pdr guns and heaps of ammunition for the 4.5 howitzers, all of these the supply has failed, the new divisions are coming out with 4.7 guns instead of 60 pdrs, an inaccurate gun which is more dangerous to our own troops than the enemy, the 6" howitzer with a long range they have never made the result is we have no weapon to answer Black Maria with, the 9.2 howitzer is an excellent weapon but it is not a fighting gun for it is too heavy, all of this I blame Von Donop for he is the wrong man I am certain and probably the reason is that his opinion carries no weight if he ever was a good man, if he is a good man I am much mistaken. Had a great birthday dinner last night and feel none the worse this morning. What is the truth about Winston why doesn't Arthur Balfour go there to the Admiralty instead of him? Yours ever Putty.

Two days later (21 May) he wrote to Ettie again:

My dear Chief, So glad to get your news about Julian he seems to be getting on well. Steele[37] I am afraid must die, his brother in the Coldstream is here he tells me it would be better for him to die as he could never move again, they are going to try to move him tomorrow to Boulogne and if so they will wire his wife to come over there but there is little chance of his recognising her. The Canadians attacked last night and carried two out of the three strong points they went for, the Germans have massed an enormous quantity of guns round La Bassée which they are using against the French and ourselves, this has eased the whole northern situation up at Ypres. What joy it was just seeing you the other day it gave one new life we did not get back until 11.30 but feel young and refreshed after the trip. The 9th Division of the K.1 Army went in to the trenches last night to learn the ropes and by the end of next week shall have put all the division through the tuition part after which they will have to take their place in the line. Did Billy turn up all right? The fighting will continue for some weeks yet awhile as we cannot afford to allow any troops to be taken off to Russia and if Italy comes in we want her to pull her weight as well. Love to all Yours ever Putty.

Ettie must have come over to see her son, Julian, who was in a hospital in Boulogne; she probably stayed in Wimereux where Putty visited her. Julian died of his wounds on 26 May.

Rawlinson (GOC IV Corps) wrote in his diary on 21 May: 'Went Bailleul – arranged for guns with Putty'. Meanwhile anti-gas precautions continued with III Corps AQ staff on 25 May ordering 50 bells from Paris for use in the trenches to give warning of the approach of gas; on 28 May detailed orders were issued on the provision and use of respirators.

Putty wrote to Ettie on 28 May:

Oh poor dear, may God bless and comfort you in your hour of trial, brave you will be for you could not have been his mother without that greatest of characteristics, he would have wished it thus and thank God you were spared to see the last of him, a joy that is prevented from so many. Love to all. Yours Putty.

The CinC inspected 27 and 28 Bdes 9th Division in billeting areas and 18 Bde 6th Division in Bailleul on 29 May. By 31 May the reliefs had taken place and III Corps now had 48th Division on the left and 27th Division on the right; 9th Division was in reserve, albeit under instruction. That day the Prime Minister (Asquith) visited III Corps; he saw 16 Bde on parade at Bailleul, visited 48th Division at Nieppe and, at Putty's request, 2 CCS. He also had lunch with Putty and his staff.

Lieutenant Barley 1 Cameronians 19 Bde, whose unofficial work had greatly improved III Corps' effectiveness against gas attack, had been appointed III Corps Gas Officer. Putty must have been frustrated when Barley was posted to 2nd Army in the same role on 16 June.

DDMS III Corps recorded the number of infection cases during May: 'Enteric Fever (including Typhoid) – 7, Cerebro-Spinal Meningitis – 2, Diptheria – 2, Measles – 66, German Measles – 24, Scarlet Fever – 7'. III Corps casualties for May were: 15 officers and 209 other ranks killed, 48 officers and 944 other ranks wounded = 1,216.

---

37   Lieutenant Colonel George Frederick Steele CO RD, Julian Grenfell's CO, died of wounds 22 May.

June

The month of June began with the withdrawal of III Corps' navy, the armoured boat 'Mary Rose' which had operated on the River Lys. Putty wrote to Edith Londonderry on 1 June:

Dear Lady C, Thanks for your letter 30 May. If my letter to Jack Cowans[38] has done any good tant mieux, it put things on some practical lines instead of London theoretical which has rather been developing lately, what we are all suffering from now is an excess of units arriving before the old formations are properly filled up, the training of drafts is what is more required at home than anything else, large depots to feed each army corps should be formed and a proper system of making good waste prepared the men should be enlisted for general service in the infantry and drafts got ready to fill up casualties, a large section of Aldershot, Salisbury etc should be devoted to training drafts and nothing else, K has made all these armies without a proper provision of depots for drafts of these same armies which is unsound, staff and personnel are therefore wasted out here. Am pretty well in despair at what I have seen of the 27th Division it breaks my heart to see my old brigades going away and replaced by such stuff, they look to me like the old order and counter order division which never knew where the devil it was still I hope that the Germans are too busy elsewhere to put much pressure on me here before I have time to pull them together. I cannot see Charlie's point in wanting to go to the cavalry now, to say that he is sheltering behind me is absolute nonsense, the crisis at Ypres is over and the cavalry will do nothing for a long time to come they keep on thinking the war is over and that there will be no opportunity of pulling their weight whereas their hour of trial has not come what Charlie does not realise is the help he is to me in arranging things and saying the right thing to the various people that come in to touch with me, I know I could give Charlie more work and should have but for the continuous changes in my own staff, some people like to share their experience some don't like to be interfered with and one has to watch all these things, I am a fair judge of man or at least think I am, the one thing to avoid is friction of one's own staff the next is to avoid one's own staff making friction with other staffs, don't let Charlie think for one instant he is not pulling his weight because he is, he has and will continue to do so, when all these moves are going on I think by myself and can play patience while I think besides I have the experience gained by years of watching men with a critical eye as to whether they are deteriorating or not and imagine I can tell, when I see a weak spot I bring pressure gradually until it is rectified without making too much trumpet blowing about it. If they give me an army I will come over for 48 hours just to pass the time of day, get some new clothes etc. Yes it is a pity you don't come out as liaison officer but it would only result in a duel between Charley and myself if I was too much in your company so perhaps you had better stay away. Charlie will have told you all about 'Squiths' visit, he is a big man if you can only keep that brain in the right channel. Reggie has gone off and Charlie follows next week, so you in luck so just keep me in luck by making Charley stay with me if he won't just refuse to let him 'tuck up' with you. Yours ever Putty.

---

38   General Sir John 'Jack' Cowans (1862-1921) late RB QMG.

Two days later at 3 am on 3 June, in another innovation, a mountain gun which had been placed in position during darkness in the trenches opposite the barricade on the Le Gheer road, fired ten rounds at a German emplacement, and a breach 5 feet across was made in the enemy's parapet.

The same day Putty sent his monthly letter to the King:

My dear Wigram, Herewith the diary of the 3rd Corps for the month of May. The Germans and ourselves have both strengthened our lines now to such an extent that an attack on either side means great preparation by artillery. I have trained the 9th Division the first of K's army to arrive in the country and it shapes very well, the artillery show excellent promise, horses were the best I have seen in the country and a wonderful feat of production after nine months of war, the engineer & pioneer companies are very good, excellent class of men who combine a great variety of trades, except two battalions the infantry are very good, platoon commanders and NCOs their weak points. The South Midland Division (48th Division) have become very good, the drafts for filling up this division is a constant source of worry, it does not seem to have been taken properly in hand when the division left England, it is a great pity to let these trained cadres dwindle down at the expense of new formations at home, am sorry to say that General Heath who commands the South Midland Div has had to be invalided home for heart trouble, I understand that it is only temporary and that he will soon be able to work again he has been succeeded out here by General Fanshawe, but I hope General Heath will be given further employment at home. Alas the 3rd Corps have lost both the 4th and 6th Divisions, they have gone to strengthen the line round Ypres and replace troops that were pretty well exhausted. The 27th Division under General Snow has replaced the 6th Division, it will take some time to pull them into shape, they look worn out and never seem to have had a real chance since they came into the country ... about by fever on arrival and fighting as they got over the Indian climate, if I get time and drafts I hope to get them in to a very different state of fighting efficiency. Mr Asquith [Prime Minister] made the 16th Brigade an excellent speech the day before they left for Ypres, a speech is no effort when one has such command of expression in language, he was much amused by seeing all the men in their baths at Nieppe. Just this last week German artillery & aeroplanes have been distinctly more active, we are deficient in number of anti-aircraft guns but like Mr Micawber we keep waiting for some to turn up. I long for the appearance in the field of a 6 inch howitzer with a range of 10,000 yards, for 60 pdrs to replace the 4.7 guns and for a good supply of ammunition for the 4.5 howitzer the best weapon we have got in the army either for offence or defense. Yours Sincerely, WP Pulteney.

He also wrote to Lord Desborough that day:

My dear Willie, Many thanks for your letter, that was a very fine remark by Billy's[39] Colonel, all the army seem to feel the same about Julian, nobody seems to have been so universally liked and consequently deplored for his age since we came to France. The Ypres situation is

39   Gerald William Grenfell 8 RB (1890-1915) killed in action 30 July.

being gradually restored but only because pressure is being brought to bear on other parts of the line and the Germans have no men to continue that area at present but their artillery positions up there are so dominant and the superiority of their observing stations so marked it can only be a matter of time before they begin to prick the bubble there again, they will meet some good troops though this time and more artillery. Submarines are going to make the Dardenelles operation very difficult. Yours ever Putty.

Next day (4 June) Putty wrote to Ettie:

My dear Chief, There is little news from these parts except a small local attack up at Ypres and another down by the 7th Division in the First Army, the shelling has been much less the last few days except just in front of me where obviously a new lot are registering. Have finished training the 9th Division, they move off tomorrow into reserve behind the 1st Army and the 12th Division takes their place on Monday [7 June] to go through a similar training, have no idea what sort of lot they are but only trust they are as good as the first two divisions of K's army. Asquith went home yesterday he was very interested out here, came to luncheon and made an excellent speech to the 16th Bde who were just on their way to Ypres, they gave him three cheers after it which pleased him immensely, I wish I could make as good speech as that on the spur of the moment what a pity it is not always in the right channel. The wind has gone round to the S it looks and feels like rain, we want it badly as the water supply is causing us some anxiety it does seem an irony after what we suffered last winter. A Danish General and his ADC came to dinner here last night, we drank the King's health, he said that Denmark was quite ready to fight but I think they had better wait a bit. Kitty (Drummond) keeps writing me despairing letters about Laurence not getting command of one of the divisions at home I must say judging by some of those one hears of I think he might have one with some advantage. Reggie Pembroke is at home for a bit and Charlie goes when he returns next week, the latter is inclined to think that he ought to go back to the Blues but it is all nonsense as they very likely won't be in the line except in reserve for ages. Best love Yours ever Putty.

On 5 June III Corps' divisions changed with 9th Division departing to GHQ Reserve and 12th Division (Major General Wing) arriving in their place. The history of 5 Sussex (36 Bde 12th Division) recorded (6 June):

Parading at 6.10 am we marched by brigade 15½ miles to Steenwerck, being inspected at Merris by the III Corps Commander, Lieutenant General Sir William Pulteney. The day was intensely hot, and in spite of extra halts many men fell out exhausted.

The GS log commenting on the arrival of 12th Division noted:

A hot sunny day (7 June): 35 Bde (12th Division) and 36 Fd Amb continued march to billets in Nieppe and Armentières. Although the troops had only been 3 hours on the road this brigade was so visibly distressed by the time Bailleul was reached that the Corps Commander ordered it to be halted for the day and continue the march in the evening. The poor marching powers of both 9th and 12th Divisions have been noticeable. The causes seem to be that the pace is set too fast, the troops have not been trained to carry a full load, the pavé roads are uneven and make walking more tiring than on ordinary roads, and finally faulty administrative work in not seeing that the troops are properly fed before the march is started.

Mine warfare continued with 48th Division exploding a mine at 10.30 am on 6 June under the German trenches opposite Ploegsteert Wood; about 30 yards of both front and rear parapets were destroyed. The enemy replied with rifle grenades and shrapnel and by shelling the support lines and Ploegsteert with HE. Another mine was exploded in the same place on the following day provoking a similar response. The enemy's working parties were frequently driven to shelter by machine-gun and artillery fire; it was reported that one large enemy working party was wiped out by a howitzer shell. Such was the almost daily menu of trench warfare: each new division had to learn the skills and then gain experience in the line. Only then could they dominate the enemy and minimise casualties.

For the army in France the problem of choosing the right men to command at the higher levels was a difficult one. There was a case for appointing those at home, inevitably older but rested and with experience in previous wars, and their case was pressed by the War Office and themselves; there was also a case, arguably a much stronger one, for appointing those recommended by the CinC in France. On 8 June Brigadier General Lambton (MS GHQ) wrote to the King on this subject:

Wigram asked me to give Your Majesty some information as to officers suitable to command armies which I have the honour to forward. I went carefully through the list of possible commanders with Sir John quite recently, the conclusion came to was that Sir A Paget and Sir W Pulteney were the most suitable; the best of our other Generals and Lieutenant Generals were Rundle, Bruce Hamilton and Codrington,[40] none of whom were considered suitable. There is no Major General senior to Pulteney fit and the next best is Allenby a corps commander now.

Also that day Putty wrote to Ettie Desborough:

My dear Chief, At last this afternoon we have had a thunderstorm which may clear the air at any rate it has laid the dust, it may save the hay crop and if it will only continue it may quiet our anxieties about the water supply. Of course you heard the lady who made the recruiting speech to the Territorials 'Your arms our defence, our arms your recompense, to Arms'. Of course the funniest episode of the war so far is the fact that Asquith had tea with Hubert Gough what price such a thing a year only from Ulster. Have finished training the 9th Division and have just begun on the 12th, they were knocked out by the heat on marching up here, the NCOs are the weak part of K's Army and the men have not sufficient confidence in them. I inspected what was left of Princess Patricia's Regt of Canadians (80 Bde 27th Division) yesterday they have fought quite splendidly and deserve more praise even than the other Canadians, of course there is colonial intrigue to get them to join the

---

40 Lieutenant General Alfred Edward Codrington (1854-1945) late Coldm Gds GOC 3rd Army in Home Forces.

other Canadians but the men don't want to go, I think it would be a 1000 pities to do away with the original formation but one never knows what ropes they may be pulling in Canada. We blew up a mine on Sunday [6 June] very successfully, yesterday we photographed it from an aeroplane it is a wonderful piece of work you can see the two craters made by the mines exactly in the right place, they were nearly on top of us with theirs so we were lucky to get it off when we did, their galleries all blown to pieces. The situation at Ypres is straightening out with my old troops having gone in to the salient but it is a bad position and never will be a good one. I trust this will find you able to rest better with much love Yours ever Putty.

The next three days were relatively quiet although the mine warfare in the Ploegsteert Wood area continued with the enemy exploding a small mine on 10 June and 48th Division occupying the crater the following day. On 12 June Putty sent a memo to GHQ, part of the continuing correspondence on demolition of bridges (including the road bridges at Houplines, Pont de Nieppe, Erquinghem and Bac St Maur, and two railway bridges). Contingency planning was essential but agreement with the French authorities on when and how such bridges were to be demolished very difficult to achieve.

The same day Brigadier General Lambton MS GHQ again wrote to the King:

The question of the new army commanders will have been submitted to Your Majesty before you receive this, of the three considered viz Pulteney, Keir [GOC VI Corps] and Monro (GOC I Corps) I think there is no doubt that of these Pulteney is the best, he has more experience and has done well in command of III Corps, on the whole I think better than Monro, though of course he has not been called upon to make any big attacks but he has held a long line with success and his forward position in front of Armentières was due to good work when he first came to the area. His staff all say he is very good to work with, knows his own mind and does not fuss.

The enemy exploded another mine at 7.15 am on 13 June which demolished a house between the lines in Le Touquet and buried two miners. Then at 2.15 am on 14 June the enemy exploded a counter-mine NW of Ploegsteert Wood. The force of the explosion caused the collapse of III Corps' mine shaft in this vicinity and buried eleven miners, who were subsequently extricated.

Putty wrote to Ettie Desborough on 13 June:

My dear Chief, Thanks dear for your letter of 10 June, the quiet and surroundings of Taplow are good for you, I can read between the lines the relief the mutual memories of the courageous aspirations you had instilled little by little, step by step in to the willing receptacle, the glory of his character will always be with you. Arthur Paget came to luncheon here on Friday [11 June], when sufficient troops come out here he is to command the 3rd Army, it is a blow to me as had been given to understand I was to have it, they said I was not senior enough, some of those out here being senior, this is true in rank but next to Douglas Haig I am senior as corps commander which fact they conveniently forget, however there is no one I would rather serve under than A.P. we have been comrades together for 35 years and I owe him much, for he has always fought my battles as I have always and always shall fight his, it came as a sad blow on top of the III Corps being ruined by taking the 4th and 6th Divisions away from me to pull them round at Ypres, however I have always shone best at an uphill fight and am sure will come out top once more. Charley Beresford[41] came to luncheon yesterday [12 June], very fat and puffy he is, as easily drawn as ever over Fisher and Churchill but his spirits just as good as ever. He was in khaki dressed as a Colonel of Marines, his coat was so big and his neck so full in it that when I laughed he said he looked like a boiled bull dog and he absolutely described the picture. The 27th Division are shaking down but they have got too much accustomed to looking over the shoulder to suit me when they get more in them I hope to be able to stir up the right spirit once more. The gun we want is a six inch howitzer with a range of 10,000 yards, this is the gun which is a reply to their Black Maria the only gun they have ever got the best of us with since the war began they know it and never cease to hammer us with it when in a hole, theirs is a 5.9, a fighting and not a siege weapon. After all of this you will be able to lecture Von Donop and put him straight. The Belgian and local farmers all round here are the admiration of every one of us, they clear their land in the most remarkable manner, there is not a weed left in the ground, not an inch left uncultivated, scarcely a hedge to harbour weeds, ploughed right up to the road, a proper succession of crops each equally cared for. Bless you Yours ever Putty.

Next day he wrote to Theresa Londonderry:

Dear Lady Londonderry, I hope you have given me a good mark for letting Charley home to see you again. Organisation at home on practical principles is what now is required we have formed as many armies as we are ever likely to be able to supply in the field now the army centres should be formed in to huge training establishments for the drafts of the four armies, then depots should be arranged so as to admit a system of universal training at the end of the war in the future we shall have to keep a standing army of twelve divisions at home which we must supply with men at a less rate of pay than at present or we as a nation would be broke in no time. I do wish they had pressed for a division to be kept in Ulster and barrack accommodation provided for it would have done more good to bring the S of Ireland to their senses than anything else if they had seen money being spent in Ulster and not in the S or W. Knaresborough[42] is here at Bailleul at the moment, his son Meysey-Thompson[43] in the Rifle Brigade has been very badly wounded, if anything kills him it will be listening to that dullest of dogs his father, the boy has got three shrapnel bullets in his back and one in the stomach the last named they have not been able to locate. Expect we shall make a bit of a push in connection with the French before long, Waterloo Day will have to have a clasp added to it to celebrate the centenary, though honours will probably be with the French this time. Plugstreet Wood is well shelled every day now on account of pictures allowed to appear in the Illustrated paper. All good wishes Yours sincerely WP Pulteney.

The next five days were fine and unusually quiet. The only interruption for Putty was the order from GHQ to place 12th Division (less 35 Bde) at 4 hours readiness to march, such were the problems to III Corps' north. This order was cancelled on 18 June. The same day, between

---

41   Lord Charles Beresford (1846-1919).
42   Henry Meysey Meysey-Thompson 1st Baron Knaresborough (1845-1929) Eton.
43   Hon Claude Henry Meysey-Thompson RB died of these wounds 17 June.

7 and 7.30 am, opposite Frelinghien, 5 mines were exploded with as the GS log recorded 'good results'. Then, during the night of 21 June, an encounter took place between a patrol of 19 Bde and an enemy patrol; several Germans were killed. Articles picked up pointed to 179 Regt being opposite as was expected; III Corps was continuing to dominate the enemy.

On 18 June Putty wrote to Ettie Desborough:

> My dear Chief, Little good news to tell you, the attack at Ypres was very nearly a big success there was a mistake on the part of the artillery or it would have been, we had about 2,000 casualties but the Germans suffered very heavily, in one part of the field no quarter was given by either side, in another they took 150 prisoners, three German officers were killed by one shell as they were being marched to the back line while the corporal with them was only wounded, it has restored a lot of confidence to the troops up in that part, after a bit perhaps they will be able to straighten it still further out. Am blowing up three mines this evening just to celebrate the centenary of Waterloo, one of them must be successful for it is right under the German trenches to which by device we draw them in to occupy quite easily, it is rather fiendish isn't it the more especially as they are Saxons. The Saxons really loathe the Prussians I believe it would pay to put them in a separate prison camp by themselves and give them better treatment, it would not make any difference while the war lasts but it would afterwards and might in the future prove an asset. Poor Meysey-Thompson in the Rifle Brigade died yesterday, he had been going on well but yesterday peritonitis set in and it was soon over, Knaresborough was with him all the time, he takes the body back with him tomorrow, he is an only son. Reggie Pembroke got a letter from Egypt telling us all about the Dardanelles fighting, the Australians and New Zealanders fought quite magnificently, the Marines ran like rabbits, the 29th Division was very good and the Territorials just doubtful, they have been now sandwiched in to the 29th man by man and are all right. I wonder if you were able to see Charlie Castlereagh while he was at home I expect him back on Monday [21 June], he comes over with Ilchester. Two of my brigadiers Freddy Gordon [Comd 19 Bde] and Ingouville-Williams (Comd 16 Bde) have gone home to command two of the new divisions they should both do well but are a loss here. K's Army are shaping very well and will be a success. Bestlove Yours ever Putty.

III Corps was about to be reorganised again, and orders for this were issued on 22 June. The moves took place over the next week at the end of which the Canadian Division (Major General Alderson) was on the left (having joined III Corps on 28 June); on their right was 12th Division which had relieved 48th Division (the latter left III Corps also on 28 June), then came 27th Division unchanged. On the extreme right III Corps took over 8th Division (Major General FJ Davies) and its sector of the line down to Picantin (from 1st Army on 30 June). The staff work to achieve all these changes smoothly would have been enormous; the divisional artilleries did not change at the same time as their parent division so each new division would have to coordinate with the appropriate field and heavy batteries of the division it replaced, as well as those of the Corps Heavy Artillery. III Corps AQ staff would also have had to realign all the logistic arrangements; then all the changes required time and close supervision before they were working smoothly. Putty was also very busy visiting divisions and brigades to ensure their commanders knew what was required of them, and also thanking those leaving the corps for what they had done.

Before 48th Division left III Corps, a lieutenant of reserve was killed (24 June) on its parapet S of the Douve whilst leading a bombing party: his identity disc showed he belonged to 5 Bavarian Reserve Regt. 48th Division had done well to the last.

Next day (25 June) Putty wrote to Edith Londonderry:

Dear Lady C, Thanks for your letter dear person. Cyril is going back tomorrow so will send this by him as it is for you and not the censor. Charley won't stay on any longer as ADC. He doesn't realise that he is learning more about the various arms of the service every day out here than he would learn in ten years in command of a cavalry regiment, it upsets me that he is going away at this time just as Reggie is doing the same thing but there it is he wants to command men and he does not get an opportunity, am afraid I cannot give him one, I tried to introduce him to learning staff duties but he does not want to do that, of course this infernal trench warfare is stagnation itself for both of them and they are bored to eternity. I wish they only knew how I shall miss them then neither of them would leave me just as there is extra stress on, just as the whole corps is changing its divisions, it will mean a very different ménage because I can't have pals again as ADC but just 'beck and callers', Charley I shall miss many times more than Reggie but then I have known him ever since he was a lad, he keeps his tongue quiet which the other doesn't have always been able to tell and talk to him about things which I could not to Reggie when they go I feel I shall turn in to a Smith-Dorrien and make them all frightened to come near me. Well here I am mixed up in the settling down of the Canadians, 8th Division, 12th and 27th, a tough job on the face of it, all except the 12th have been knocked about, the 27th will take another three months to pull together and old Snow who commands them is always looking over his shoulder to see where he is going to retire to but with ginger and getting the confidence of his brigadiers I think I shall pull it through in time, Indian fever is at the bottom of most of the trouble with the men, they have not got it out of their system yet. I don't want to come home until I feel seedy, my staff is very different to what it was six months ago and there is much more responsibility besides I see all sorts of trouble and friction ahead between Alderson [GOC Canadian Division] and the Canadian authorities. Sam Hughes[44] is trying to down him with the result that there are two parties among them which prevents them becoming united. Joey Davies [GOC 8th Division] has got away from Rawley [Rawlinson GOC IV Corps] and he feels his staff say as if he could throw himself in to my arms which I hope to goodness he won't as have no taste for such figures. All blessings Yours ever Putty.

He wrote to Ettie again on 26 June:

My dear Chief, Thank Willie for his letter of 20 June and for your note at end of it. We had a thunderstorm yesterday that washed this dirty Bailleul to some tune, it did more good in one hour than our disinfectants for the last month, I wish I could think that it had filled up all the wells again. My corps has been a good deal changed or will be by the end of the month, shall have four divisions, the Canadians, 8th, 12th and 27th. There is great political trouble going on over the Canadians, Sam Hughes has got a down on Alderson chiefly

44   Sir Sam Hughes Canadian Minister of Militia.

because the men have thrown away their Ross rifles and taken ours instead, the Ross rifle jammed up at Ypres from the dirt and the result of the gas so the men threw them away and picked up the other ones from the wounded and dead, of course all the Canadians have got shares in the Ross rifle and there is the 'divil' to pay, Alderson is scarcely man enough to engineer these troubles with success from what I can see of him. The 27th are pulling round bit by bit they have never got over the Indian fever they came with. The 12th are a good lot but very green, the 8th will be all right they were sent to me because Joey Davies and Rawlinson did not hit it off the latter carted him badly without compunction. Reggie Pembroke is going home to the Blues and I expect Charley Castlereagh won't be long after him as the War Office have kicked up a row about my having two such senior officers on my staff. I shall miss them but changes are the order of the day but it will be a great blow changing from real friends, of course in this trench warfare there is very little for them to do, Charley is ambitious but Reggie not unless stirred up by his better half, I should not wonder if he returned on A.P'.s staff. We had some champagne on Thursday (24 Jun) night, Lynden-Bell (BGGS) had got the CB, Capper (CE) made a Major General, Stokes (BGRA) CB, Reggie full of wine called the two CBs, the two ladies in the Bath and hoped they would not be found with their legs up in the morning. Have you seen these flower cards they are rather wonderful, hang it up in the light in your bedroom. Yours ever Putty.

On the last day of June he wrote to her again:

My dear Chief, Thanks for your letter 27 June. Those are brave lines of Clough,[45] full of sustenance. Yes I will go and find Billy [Billy Grenfell 8 RB] the next time I go up Ypres way, I suppose he could not endure office work if I found him a job could he? They all hate leaving their brother officers so much. There is little news since I wrote except that the shift of divisions has gone off all right and my lot are all in their places they are new to the ground which makes a difference in the casualties always the first few days, the Canadians are on my left, that idiot Seely[46] has arrived with them of course he goes and plants his brigade headquarters in Neuve Église which is out of my area, which we purposely have not put anyone in for ages so as not to draw fire, am glad to see I soon had him kicked out aided a little by German shells, was it not like him. Sam Hughes is trying to get rid of Alderson he wants to command the Canadian Corps when it comes out so he has written the most abusive letters to K about Alderson up at Ypres, these political rows are trying this one is accentuated by some of the Canadians refusing to use the Ross rifle which Sam Hughes & Co are all interested in from an investment point of view. Snow's Division the 27th is the biggest problem I have got, they never seem to have had any life in them since they arrived in the country, I think he is too old for the work and would do better with a corps. Some of the 10th Hussars are here now digging some supporting lines was up with them last night,

45   Arthur Hugh Clough (1819-1861).
46   Major General Seely late Hamps Yeo S of S for War 1912-1914 Comd Can Cav Bde.

Dudley's[47] & Wentworth Beaumont's[48] boys were there, all of them as careless as cavalry soldiers should be, what they were doing or going to do!!! But doing splendidly when put to it. Very thundery but the rain has done no end of good. Best love and blessings Yours ever Putty.

III Corps casualties for the month of June were: 11 officers and 155 other ranks killed, 36 officers and 666 other ranks wounded = 868.

July

The month started quietly. Putty wrote to Edith Londonderry on 1 July:

Dear Lady C, Many thanks dear thing for your letters of 28 and 30 June. Am sending this back by Cyril and am going to have a talk to him this afternoon about his own affairs, I think the best thing is for him to come out here on my staff for a bit as ADC to enable him to look round after which we can fit him in to a billet of some sort, it is quite impossible to give an opinion at this moment until the policy of the Government shows itself, the whole question is does the 2nd Army go to the Dardanelles or to France, if to the former then the 3rd Army will not be formed out here, it looks on the face of it as if it was to go to the Dardanelles to support the former policy of the Government, however you will probably hear the result of today's Cabinet meeting before I shall, Robertson and French have gone strong and if it does not come off should not be surprised if the former resigns. The drafts for the divisions out here is the present difficulty it is criminal not to fill up the Territorial divisions just as they are trained and seasoned they don't realise what training these NCOs means, they are the failure of the new armies because they have never had the opportunity of learning. I think A.P. will get the 3rd Army all right if it is formed I hear there is a row about it in England at the moment but if it did come to me to have it eventually I should not have much to fear in being able to do as well as the other commanders Smith D. and Plumer. The Canadians are shaping well and killing some of these damned Germans already, have already straightened out the line in parts, in fact have generally shown resource. Billy Lambton stayed here last night and enjoyed himself, played bridge after dinner and (breked) quite in his old form. Jemmy Rothschild has returned quite thin but as full of questions as ever, the French crosses are pretty colossal according to him. Best love Yours ever Putty.

On 3 July Putty wrote to the King:

Dear Wigram, I forward herewith the diary of the 3rd Corps for the month of June for the information of HM The King. The divisions have completely changed, the

---

47   William Humble Eric Ward Viscount Ednam (1894-1969) 10 H son of Lieutenant Colonel William Humble Ward 2nd Earl of Dudley (1867-1932) Eton at this time serving as CO Q Worcs H in 1 Mid Mtd Bde Egypt.
48   Probably Wentworth Henry Canning Beaumont (1890-1956) 2 LG son of 1st Viscount Allendale (1860-1923) Eton and Lady Alexandrina Vane-Tempest daughter of 5th Marquess of Londonderry and Charlie's aunt.

Canadians are now holding my left flank next to them the 12th Division, then the 27th with the 8th on the extreme right. The front of the corps now is about 17 miles which is a very considerable slice out of the front held by the BEF. The Canadians are weak and badly want some reinforcements, there is no doubt but that they are the most excellent material with any amount of resource, their staff work too has greatly improved since they were under me on their arrival in the country, they shoot well and have already made their presence felt. The 12th Division are shaping very well, the NCOs are the weak point in the new divisions but the class of men in the K army is decidedly better than the ordinary line and the necessity of the good NCO is therefore to an extent neutralised. The 27th are recovering, the defensive attitude of the enemy opposite them is giving me the chance of pulling them round that I was anxious to obtain, they are getting confidence in themselves which is a great asset, the warm weather has suited them after their service in India. The 8th Division I like the look of, the discipline is good and they will give a good account of themselves. With all the changes it has been necessary to be on the defensive, we are now strengthening our line in every possible manner in case the Germans should come to pay attention here after their victories in the East. Each side has dug itself in wired itself to such a degree that the result is a fortress pure and simple on an enormous front without reference to the tactical position which one would have naturally chosen to fight upon, the Germans have conformed to ourselves in that respect. The question of breaking through the lines presents a more difficult problem every day, without fresh army corps, stupendous supplies of ammunition it is not feasible and to be successful must be in the nature of a surprise at an unsuspected vulnerable spot. The artillery of the new divisions is improving daily but you cannot expect of them in the attack to do what our troops did at the beginning of the war. We tried some incendiary shells last week on a house that we built up, but they were a hopeless failure and not nearly as efficient as an ordinary HE shell. The German infantry in front of me both Bavarians and Saxons appear to have lost a lot of their initiative, they snipe the same are splendid shots, they fire about 200 more shells a day than we do but their patrols are not so daring nor have they the same dash in fact I should say they are thinking of their homes and live and let live policy, they do not seem to change their troops to any extent and they fill up casualties almost at once, in fact the organisation of their system of drafts is a masterpiece. My ADC Pembroke has gone back to the Blues and I much doubt if shall be able to keep Londonderry much longer as it is against the policy to keep such senior officers doing that work, the authorities are correct in their attitude in this matter but I do hate changing such excellent officers whom I know and who know me so well. Yours Sincerely, WP Pulteney.

The following week was generally fine and the front line quiet. 3rd Cavalry Division (Major General Briggs) was lent to III Corps from 8 to 14 July to work on the rear defences.

Then, on 9 July, Brigadier General Lambton (MS GHQ) wrote to Kitchener (S of S for War) recommending Putty for command of 3rd Army:

My dear Kitchener, You may want an explanation about the selection of the army commander. The three names considered were: Pulteney, Keir, Monro. Of these the reports on Keir both as a divisional and corps commander were not very good. He has only had a corps for about one month and is reported to be slow, rather obstructive and wanting in decision. The respective claims of Monro and Pulteney were carefully considered and the latter's record comes out best. In spite of the adverse opinion of Haig and others his record is not bad. His corps was the first to cross the Aisne and to establish itself on the northern bank, and maintained its position there. In the advance to the present position he again did well as his forward position in front of Armentières proves, and though he has not been called on to make any attacks his corps has held a very long line with success and such small enterprises as he has been allowed to undertake have been as a rule successful. I write so fully because (I/we) discussed this question on your visit and because I think Pulteney's merits have been (undervalued) at home while Keir has been given undeserved credit. Yours truly, W Lambton.

Haig's preference for Monro is understandable because Monro had commanded 2nd Division in I Corps under him, and then took over I Corps when Haig was promoted to command 1st Army. So he would have seen a great deal of his performance.

Next day (10 July) Putty wrote to Ettie Desborough:

My dear Chief, Thanks so much for yours of the 7 Jul, Cyril Hankey is going back from here this morning so you ought to get this tomorrow. Arthur Paget's appointment to the 3rd Army has been knocked on the head and I am in the running for it, Sir John has recommended me for it and it now rests with London for the final decision there is a good deal of opposition first because I am so junior as a General 2nd because I have not been to the Staff College the first point did not stand in the way of the War Office when the corps was formed at the beginning of the war the Staff College is not the only place that produces soldiers for neither Roberts, Kitchener or French were ever there besides when I ought to have gone to the Staff College I was so broke I had to go to East Africa for 2½ years to avoid the sheriff, Sir John told me he had recommended me for it and after all that was all I cared about as far as my services out here were concerned. The 2nd [New] Army has begun to arrive the 15th are here, Pilcher,[49] Gleichen[50] and Davies[51] follow in that order I gather that the ammunition cannot be really satisfactory much before the end of the year, no doubt Von Donop [MGO] has not been a success but I would not make him a 'Bride in the Bath' half as much as Sir Charles Hadden[52] and Sir Charles Harris[53] both of whose legs I would gladly hold up. There seems to be a large concentration of Germans round Lille, they seem to think an attack on Armentières marching down to the Bassée is contemplated, let them come against me as much as they like for I am jolly well prepared for them personally I have always said they would attack St Eloi, La Bassée to Arras, St Elois or Arras are the two valuable directions as far as the British line is concerned. All blessings Yours ever Putty.

49   Major General Pilcher GOC 17th Division.
50   Major General Lord Gleichen GOC 37th Division.
51   Major General RH Davies GOC 20th Division.
52   Major General Sir Charles Hadden (1854-1924) late RA President of the Ordnance Board.
53   Sir Charles Harris (1864-1943) Financial Secretary War Office.

On 11 July the GS log recorded:

> Opposite and immediately S of Ploegsteert Wood sniping was heavier than usual. Then, about 2.30 am, the enemy was noticed to have their 2nd Line trenches N of Le Gheer fully manned. Artillery and rifle fire was directed on them, it is believed with good results.

That same day orders were received for the formation of 3rd Army and reorganisation of III Corps. Kitchener wrote to French:

> My dear French, On Sat at the Cabinet I told the Prime Minister [Asquith] about your wish to have Pulteney and of Lambton's letter regarding him. He quite recognised Pulteney's good [services] as we all do. But, for an army command, the Government consider that Monro would be the right selection. I have just returned from the King to whom I submitted the matter; he entirely concurred in the view expressed by the Prime Minister although he mentioned that Pulteney was a personal friend of his. Kitchener.

Meanwhile Putty was dealing with the problems of drunkenness in 27th Division which, as explained before, was made up of regular units brought back from overseas stations throughout the Empire. The AQ log recorded 52 cases of drunkenness in the division for the month of June, due to the 'large number of estaminets in Armentières which is in 27th Division's area'.
French replied to Kitchener on 13 July:

> I have duly received your letter with the Government's decision about command of 3rd Army. Of course I am sorry for Pulteney but Monro is an excellent man and I have full confidence in him. French.

Putty wrote to Ettie:

> My dear Chief, I am sore at heart. They have given the 3rd Army to Monro over my head. French backed me for all he was worth but K went against me for some reason, obviously if the man in the field is not supported they have not confidence in him. My corps has not lost a yard of ground and I have saved more lives than all the others put together. Bless you Yours ever Putty.

Monro was a year older than Putty and only six months junior to him as a Major General, so neither would have been relevant to the decision. The most likely explanation is the one that Putty suggests: they 'have not confidence in him (French)' and had probably sounded out others. Of these the most likely and credible would have been Haig, and he would have recommended Monro. The strangest aspect of this is that Putty never would command an army in France but was to continue in command of III Corps, almost continually in the line, for another three years.
Putty would have had little time to consider all this since he had more than enough to do implementing the numerous changes he was required to make. At midnight on 14/15 July the Canadian Division together with the frontage it was holding was transferred to II Corps; 12th Division and its frontage followed at midnight 15/16 July. On 16 and 17 July 50th Division which had just joined III Corps for instruction provided brigades to 27th Division in the line;

on 18 July GHQ placed III Corps under 1st Army (Haig); and, on 19 July, 19 Bde took over an additional part of the line extending III Corps' right to the Fauquissart-La Flinque road. Putty and his staff would have been thankful that the enemy were quiet and inactive while this was all going on. When it was all over III Corps had slipped to the right and come under command of 1st Army.

On 20 July Putty wrote to Ettie:

> My dear Chief, Thanks dear thing for your letter, it was a disappointment not getting the 3rd Army but as long as I was recommended by the man in the field I don't care a blow about a government at home that cannot even deal with a coal strike, it made me feel like a ship between the Atlantic waves in a storm but have recovered and full of energy once again, all my staff are new as they had moved all mine to the 3rd Army in anticipation of my getting it, have got new ground, new troops in the old 3rd Corps so have plenty to do, thank goodness am in the First Army under Douglas Haig it is a real good going concern and we will make it better. Several of the Tommies have married French women out here the old 6th Division who have gone up to Ypres write letters in French to the girls they have married at Armentières, the censor is convulsed with laughter but what complications there will be after the war, are they going to get separation allowances now? It looks as if K was dead set against Sir John with Asquith backing him up, What do you think? Hebester will take this letter back with him tomorrow. Yours ever Putty.

It was still quiet on III Corps front as the new organisation settled down; 19 Bde on the right of 8th Division was put under its command on 23 July with its and the corps right boundary now the Fauquissart-Aubers road (inclusive).

The following day Captain Lord Gavin George Hamilton of Dalzell[54] was appointed as Putty's ADC. Hamilton had been the Government Chief Whip in the House of Lords from 1905 to 1911 during the Campbell-Bannerman and Asquith Governments. His stepson, Lieutenant William Bernard Webster Lawson, had been killed at Ypres on 22 October 1914 while serving in 1 SG. Hamilton was to serve Putty until March 1917.

That evening Putty wrote again to Ettie:

> My dear Chief, Ever so many thanks for your letter of the 22 Jul. I have pulled Gavin Hamilton out of the trenches and put him in Reggie Pembroke's place, he looks too ghastly ill he will take this letter back with him this evening for am sending him back to get some clothes (& colour in his face). My staff now consists of General Romer (G) General Chichester (B) General Stokes (B) Major Wingfield (G) Major Bartholomew (V.G.), G stands for good and B for bad all except Bartholomew and Wingfield are new to their posts, another Chief Engineer in Capper's place has not yet been appointed he was the greatest loss I have had as he is much more level headed than his brother Tommy Capper. George Milne commands the 27th Division and Joey Davies the 8th which are the only two divisions I have got under me now, Milne is A.1. and Davies is a good steady going methodical Grenadier. Rawlinson had been writing to Kitchener about me and talking more but he

---

54   Gavin George Hamilton of Dalzell (1872-1952) SG Eton.

hasn't done himself any good over it but things cannot be going well when they don't take the advice of the man in the field, however I should never be surprised if Sir John French were to resign if he does Douglas Haig is the proper man to take his place. The settlement of the strike is a display of weakness that makes one tremble for the future of the country I wish you would tell me what A.J.B. says about it. Monro takes the 3rd Army down S of Arras to release some French divisions there which are required for an attack it separates the British force but I do not think that should matter though it gives an opportunity for distrust if you are not a large enough minded man but I think Monro will do all right. There is great excitement over the Guards Division that is being formed personally I think it is a mistake to form a corps d'élite like that but if they do want to compete with the Prussian Guard they should have started with a division of nine battalions instead of twelve for I don't believe they will be able to get sufficient officers and drafts to feed so many bns, 4 bns of Grenadiers & Coldstream will be a terrible strain and take no end of men away from other branches of the army, but the NCOs of the Guards are so far superior to the rest of the army I daresay they will pull them through we all realise that it is the young gunner and the platoon commander who will win this war, I hear Corry [Colonel Corry CO 3 Gren Gds arrived 27 July] comes out again with a Grenadier battalion so conclude the old controversy about him has died a natural death tant mieux. We have had fewer casualties this week than any since the war began but then we have done practically nothing, we have been saving up ammunition and taking matters easily while all the divisions were changing their positions to make up the new army and new corps it has been a very fine piece of staff work altogether. I think I shall change my headquarters about 7th August but will let you know later. All blessings Yours ever Putty.

On the next day (25 July) Putty sent a memo to 1st Army giving details of his preparation for the defence of the present line during the coming winter (summary of subjects only):

Use of concrete for strengthening machine-gun emplacements and look-out posts in the front line and for dug-outs for that part of the garrison which must be maintained in it during a bombardment
Raise the level of communication trenches to above water level
Employment of motor-driven and hand pumps
Clearing drains and ditches using civilian labour
Strengthening of the wire throughout the line
Construction of splinter and weather proof shelters
Additional requirement for lamps, torches and braziers
Scheme for the provision of tramways

Putty was determined to improve security of the line and conditions for the troops in it, before the onset of another winter. Next day, and another sign of improved planning and coordination, BGRA III Corps and Comd 8 Bde RGA held a conference to consider the most suitable targets for retaliation and methods by which retaliation was to be made.

Meanwhile German working parties were busy both by day and night: they were engaged with artillery, machine-gun and rifle fire. Overall, it was still relatively quiet although activity was increasing.

On 28 July Putty wrote to Ettie Desborough:

My dear Chief, You owe me a letter. The Russians are making a grand stand before Warsaw it is just a question of arms and ammunition to meet their needs. Joey Davies who commands the 8th Division in my corps was ordered away to the Dardanelles at ½ hours' notice yesterday via Paris to Marseilles I almost doubt whether he was able to catch the train at Paris, he is to succeed Hunter-Weston but what is the matter with him we don't know though he gets so excited he may have broken down from the strain. It has been very quiet on our front, have had fewer casualties during the last ten days than at any time since last October we could do little while all the changes consequent on the formation of the 3rd Army were going on. I hear my enemies were Asquith and Rawlinson why the P.M. I don't know have never come up against him that I can remember you might tout Mrs A. the next time that you see her. I don't know how they are going to keep up the supply of officers for the new Guards Division, I wish they had made it only nine battalions instead of twelve, it will be a fine division but their mixture in the line was doing more good to the army as a whole, one thing is they ought to keep it going after the war is over. This is only just a line as Hebester is just off. Yours ever Putty.[55]

Over the next two hot days (29 and 30 July) 20th Division arrived to join III Corps; each division in the line was now able to hold one brigade in reserve. III Corps casualties for July were: 7 officers and 186 other ranks killed, 60 officers and 836 other ranks wounded, 2 other ranks missing = 1,091.

August

August started much as July ended with the enemy relatively inactive. The situation around Ypres was, however, sufficiently serious that Haig recorded on 1 August: 'I have been ordered to send a brigade of 8 inch howitzers which recently arrived from England and is now with III Corps to be attached to 2nd Army'. The following morning at 8.45 am a shell from a German naval gun fell among the tents of 3 CCS at Bailleul killing 4 men of RAMC. Also that day HQ III Corps sent 1st Army a proposal for a light railway system.

Then on 3 August Putty sent his monthly report to the King with this covering letter, still as always in his own hand:

My dear Wigram, Attached is the diary of operations of the 3rd Corps for July for the information of HM The King. Am afraid it is a dull record, none of the original 3rd Corps are left in it, it now consists of the 27th, 8th and 20th Divisions. Practically all my head-quarter staff were taken to form the staff of the 3rd Army so have had new troops, new staff and new ground to work with lately which has somewhat accentuated the strain caused by other disappointments. General Milne has succeeded General Snow in command of the 27th Div, this division is beginning to pull round bit by bit after its Ypres experiences, there

---

55   Hebester, Copper Horse and the Howler were three of the messengers whose names have not been identified.

are not so many sick, the majority of those suffering from Indian fever seem to be getting over it, the discipline is I hope on the mend and I am much more hopeful than I was originally at it turning in to a really good division if fortune will favour it. General Davies has gone to the Dardanelles and been succeeded by General Hudson in the 8th Division. The 20th Division under General Davies (Major General RH Davies) arrived last week, I have inspected them they appear most excellent material but are at present unfit to go in to the line but they are a good class and will train easily if willingness helps them for I never saw men more keen, the men suffered a great deal from sore feet on the march up here as have practically all the new divisions that I have seen, the reason being:

1st. They are not marching at home with the weight of ammunition in their pouches, the addition of respirators, clasp knife etc issued on arrival increases the shock on the foot in marching.
2nd. The training at home is done on the heather or downs in the majority of cases.
3rd. The boots are not issued soon enough to have become shaped to their feet by the time they arrive here.
4th. They march on the other side of the road in England, my theory is that this fact has a great deal to do with it as the roads out here are more arched than those at home, it would be a good excuse for altering the rule of the road at home so as to come in to line with other countries.

The 3rd Corps has now come in under the command of the 1st Army under Sir Douglas Haig, personally am very glad as lately we had been nobody's child and I find it a real good going concern properly directed. There has been an increase of shelling all round by the Germans and their naval gun was ranged on Bailleul yesterday for the first time, it was aimed at the Flying Corps ground at a range of nearly 20 miles, it really was an extraordinary fine piece of gunnery for it pitched on a tent of the RAMC just the other side of the road unfortunately killing three men of the RAMC, the German aeroplane was up with its wireless marking for them, they only put in one shot, it went very close to the asylum where there are 1600 female lunatics. I tried to get them cleared out when I arrived here last October but the French authorities did not see their way to it, it will be a calamity if they pitch shells among them which is what happened to the male lunatics in the asylum at Armentières last October. I had to march them to the station with soldiers as warders but managed to get them away by train. Princess Patricia's Canadian Bn got a draft of 250 men last week and soon will be a splendid bn again. Yours Sincerely, WP Pulteney.

Putty wrote to Ettie Desborough at Taplow Court on 5 August (postmarked London 6 August):

Oh you dear thing I only heard it yesterday afternoon (Her son, Gerald William 'Billy' Grenfell, was killed in action 30 July), had the most extraordinary presentment that he would follow the call of his brother so as to be happy together once more; may God help you to live long to remind us of them both is the one wish I can think of. Your friend Putty.

Chateau La Motte au Bois prior to the First World War, HQ III Corps, 1915-1916. (de la Grange)

Trench warfare was increasing in tempo as the nights got longer. On 7 August III Corps issued its 'Defence Scheme' to its divisions, now that the deployment was settled at least for the time being. 8 August was a busy day with HQ III Corps moving to the Chateau La Motte au Bois, a better location for the new deployment of the corps; it opened at 12 noon. Shortly afterwards opposite 2 A&SH 19 Bde (under command 8th Division) a German patrol was encountered and one prisoner taken of 16 Bavarian Regt.

Putty wrote to Ettie Desborough again early that morning:

> My dear Chief, I had not the heart to write you any news on Friday but Hindlip is here today and will take this over with him tomorrow. Am shifting my headquarters this morning to Chateau la Motte in the Forest of Nieppe after a ten months sojourn in Bailleul, just fancy on the 14th October should have been here a year, my new headquarters are rather far back from the front line but not so much on the flank of the front my corps is holding, ten minutes more in a motor makes no difference, one end of the chateau is occupied by a Baroness la Grange who is a sprightly widow of 60 summers I believe, she has the reputation of flirting a good deal and of having gone further with Allenby, Charlie L & Gavin Hamilton don't report very favourably on her but Dozie Brinton has been taking French lessons from her & says she is a good sort, I imagine she is a person who requires being kept in her place. Had a long letter from Granard[56] in the Dardanelles, he says that Hunter-Weston got a touch of the sun and was practically off his head which he was always liable to with his mass of nerves, no name is bad enough for Johnny Hamilton[57] and his staff

56   Lieutenant Colonel Bernard Arthur William Patrick Hastings 8th Earl of Granard (1874-1948) SG 1899-1911 CO 5 R Irish 10th Division.
57   General Sir Ian 'Johnny' Standish Monteith Hamilton (1852-1947) late Gordons CinC Allied Med Exped Force.

Pulteney at Chateau Motte au Bois.
(de la Grange)

apparently the guiding hand is all criticism instead of help, the one bright spot appears to be Freddy Stopford,[58] I understood there was to be another landing this week but where don't know but wish it has been Smyrna in the first instance from a strategical point of view as it would have made Egypt secure and drawn the Turks from the Caucasus having drawn the Turks down there to have had a dash for the Dardanelles anyway they must clear up the situation in the peninsula by end of next month or clear out as they cannot land the boats there after that date. We are trying to make our lines shell proof but without much success as the lines are of such a great extent the amount of material required is impossible to obtain, further our line is just where we could get to last year and not one chosen from tactical reasons there is but one consolation viz that the German line conforms to it as far as my corps is concerned. The situation up at Ypres is still none too good and I calculate they would have saved 100,000 lives if they had gone back to the back line last winter when the weakness of the line held was just as obvious. I believe the Welsh Guards begin to arrive this week I hear the sight of the presentation of colours was the rain in Lloyd George's hair where it hung like a mop head, they ought to keep them three weeks before they put them in the line, it will be a splendid division but its formation a mistake from the good of the army point of view. My 20th Division under New Zealand Davies seem to be a very good lot but these new K divisions want hardening up for at least three months before they are really fit to go into the line, they have not got the stamina of the 7 years soldier to stand the shelling though they have plenty of dash, I wish I had had my way and formed the corps on three divisions each division having one brigade Regulars one Territorials and one Ks army it would have made the best blend. Best love Yours ever Putty.

Patrol activity by both sides increased over the next four days especially on 8th Division's front; meanwhile enemy artillery increased opposite 27th Division.

DDMS spoke to Putty on 12 August about 'the probability of scorbutic taint among men, caused as noted yesterday, and recommended to Q the daily issue of lime juice to men in trenches, and green vegetables when possible – also fresh meat in lieu of tinned meat'. The following day, the AQ log noted: 'Entomological Committee visited the corps area to investigate the prevalence of flies'. Keeping the corps fit and healthy in the trenches, particularly in the summer months, presented numerous challenges; most mornings Putty discussed these matters with his DDMS.

19 Bde was taken out of the line on 16 August prior to leaving III Corps on 19 August, the last of the units that had been with Putty since the formation of the corps the previous year. It was replaced in the line by 59 Bde 20th Division.

The same day (16 August) DDMS recorded:

Called on ADMS 27th Division at 11.10 am who was out but left word asking him to let me know if he could ascribe any medical reason for sentries sleeping on their posts. I understand new arrivals in these parts are those who have been found to do so. Corps Commander tells me he has tried insisting on night sentries having a rest before going on duty but this has made no difference.

Putty wrote to Edith Londonderry on 16 August:

Dear Thing, Naughty girl, you are safe away from the Snipy crowd once more, would to God you had slept in my bed to make the whole tour complete, look out for Jack Cowans[59] and humour him a bit is my advice as an old soldier. I feel years younger for having seen you, the devil there is in you, the risks you will take; if I only had a dozen brigadiers like you we should be in Berlin by Xmas. Yours always Putty.

The evidence suggests that Edith visited HQ III Corps.

In the line the enemy continued to be particularly active opposite 8th Division with several enemy working parties being dispersed during the night of 18 August.

On 18 August Putty wrote again to Ettie:

My dear Chief, Charlie Londonderry is going home tomorrow for good, he wants to go to the Ulster Division on the staff, now he is Lord Lieutenant of Co Down all his thoughts are

---

59   General Sir John 'Jack' Cowans (1862-1921) late RB QMG.

in that direction I shall miss him very much he has been so thoughtful about my comforts and household arrangements, however Gavin Hamilton is shaping well and I think I shall ask Hebester to come when he returns from the Dardanelles as Birdie[60] says he would like to and it is not taking away a serving soldier. Lord K is out here, he is going to meet all the corps commanders of the 1st Army tomorrow morning also inspect the 19th Bde on the march, the 19th Bde is leaving me to take the place of the 4th Guards Brigade which goes to the Guards Division, I shall miss them for they have been with me ever since the beginning they were very demoralised in the retreat but are now a very fine brigade. I took Jack Cowans (QMG) all round my front trenches when he was here he got shelled as we were coming away, this is the first time he had ever heard a bullet or a shell fired in anger during his service, he told me he had no conception of the amount of work there had to be done to make the trenches and parapets and quite realised now why we wanted so much material, it would do K good to go down to see it all. Billy Lambton is going home to command a division he is taking one Joe Maude had, he having been sent off to the Dardanelles, expect he will be succeeded as Military Secretary by Cecil Lowther. Freddy Stopford is coming back from the Dardanelles being no good, Byng has left here to take his place and Fanshawe gets the Cav Corps. The Welsh Guards are due to arrive this week I call them the ('Prizeaux') but the rest of the Brigade call them the 'Foreign Legion'. I hear there is a subaltern come out with the Scots Guards aged 51 with snow white hair the boys have named him the 'White Ensign'. The Germans have been very quiet opposite us all this last week the casualties have been lower than they have ever been since I came round here in October, am pulling round the 27th Division with any luck it will turn all right now, was in despair about it when it first arrived from Ypres the discipline was so bad. My baroness who lives in this chateau has gone to Paris, she put her age on her passport as 51 but we know she is 60, she tells me she knows she is old but has a very young heart from the way she pressed my hand should say that she had. Well good bye dear thing may some comfort come to you and Willy with all love and blessings. Yours ever Putty.

He also wrote to Edith Londonderry that day:

My dear Motte, Thanks for your letter, was glad to hear that you had got back safely from the clutches of the YMCA or otherwise the Young Maidens C. Association which you had talked yourself on to. Of course I will be godfather it ought to be named Flare or Nightshade. The old baroness came to me and said I have a secret with you, she is charming, but come to see me I am old but have a young heart!! Well here is your Charlie back safe and sound after a year I am miserable at his going have got so fond of him. Write me often Yours ever Putty.

That Edith visited Putty in his headquarters seems beyond doubt, probably around 15 August; how long she stayed and what occurred during the visit are less clear. Her visit coincided with the end of Charley's time as ADC; he departed for England next day.

---

60   Lady Helen Vane-Tempest-Stewart (1876-1956) married to 6th Earl of Ilchester – Lord Stavordale until 1905 but still called Stavey.

On 19 August, as Putty mentioned in his letter and Haig described:

> Lord Kitchener went into the garden [of Haig's HQ] and called the four corps commanders (of 1st Army) round him. There were present General Willcocks (Indian Corps), Pulteney (III Corps), Rawlinson (IV Corps), Gough (I Corps). After asking us all what we wanted in the way of bombs etc, he then explained his views on compulsory service. All the four corps commanders agreed with what I [Haig] said, and added that compulsory service would improve the discipline of the army. Lord K argued strongly against compulsory service.

III Corps received orders from 1st Army on 21 August to take over part of the line held by Indian Corps as far S as the Piètre-Winchester road, just N of Mauquissart, to be completed on night 27/28 August. III Corps order (G386) to implement this brought 20th Division into the line on its right, with 8th Division in the centre and 27th Division on the left; each division was able to keep one brigade in reserve. Trench warfare continued with mines, artillery and snipers. Patrols from both sides each night attempted to disrupt the other's working parties.

Putty wrote to Edith again on 23 August:

> My dear Motte, Thanks for yours of 19 Aug, will send this by the Howler this morning. Have received a charming letter from Charley which I will answer tell him in due course. Old Phipps-Hornby (BGRA HQ III Corps until 5 June 1915 invalided) sent me this story. Boys in school were made to write short sentences which brought in any particular word given them, the word given to them was 'notwithstanding' the boy that got first prize put down 'I had a button off my trousers this morning, notwithstanding.' The grouse you sent me were quite excellent we feel all the better for them. Saw K last week have no further doubt now why I did not get the 3rd Army he showed his hand much too much, I don't know though how I have offended him, he looks well and is full of ideas which is something. Send out some better news at the end of this week by the Howler. The 3rd (K) army is coming here at the beginning of next month also the other Canadian division, the Welsh Guards the Foreign Legion have arrived and look a good lot. Howler is off so excuse more take care of your dear self. Yours ever Putty.

Putty sent a memo to 1st Army on 24 August reporting on preparations for the winter. Much progress had been made but the constant changes to the line must have caused some frustration.

Treatment and evacuation of the wounded had been of great concern to Putty since the war started but he was now to focus on two separate aspects; as a result significant improvements were made. At 9.30 am 25 August DDMS noted:

> Corps Commander asked me whether it was essential to move abdominal cases to CCS. I said no, but it was essential to operate early and he conceived that in such cases it would be better to have the operation done as near the spot where the wound was received as possible. The best way of doing this would be to have a surgical team attached to the corps and an operation room and ward placed as near the front as possible. In this area the best solution would be a barge fitted up for the team and the hospital near the pontoon at Bac St Maur. Failing this a launch for transporting such cases to Merville would be better than

River Lys at Bac St Maur, 2012.

the journey by road. Bad chest and head cases should be dealt with similarly. GOC's query arose on the death of Captain Makins KRRC shortly after arrival at CCCS Merville (and other horrific cases).

The following day (26 August) III Corps AQ sent a letter to 1st Army recommending that two hospital barges be allotted to the corps and stationed on the River Lys near Bac St Maur for the conveyance of the seriously wounded by water to Merville instead of by road. This seemed to have missed half the point but DDMS recorded at 2.30 pm:

> Corps Commander put in a recommendation today that the corps should have a special surgeon and staff and a barge for the treatment of abdominal and other severe cases. I believe this would help to save life; at the very least it would add to comfort by avoiding jolting along the roads, some of which are pavé.

Putty was determined to pursue both concepts 'surgical teams to conduct certain life saving surgery as far forward as possible' and 'the subsequent rapid evacuation by river and later railway'. He was to meet much opposition before they were both accepted and adopted. III Corps was already using the river for the movement of supplies; on 28 August the AQ log recorded: 'Steps taken to lay in a stock of 9000 tons of coal for use in the winter, to be brought in by barge and stored near Bac St Maur'.

He wrote to Ettie again on 28 August:

> My dear Chief, I enclose you a little postcard which was sent me from Paris by the Baroness la Grange in whose chateau I am billeted, she has 60 summers to her credit but says she

has a warm heart! The Russians do not seem to be doing much better, am much afraid they are fairly on the run, however, there is a possible chance of our offensive doing some good before the end of next month in which case it will mean that they are unable to send drafts to the E and may have to recall an army, have every hope this time for we really have got some ammunition and all the preparations are on a good scale the troops too are in much better heart, Ypres too is quite safe, the front line may be pierced but behind that the whole place is quite impregnable. Had luncheon with Douglas Haig yesterday where I met Sir Frank Swettenham[61] but he was dull diffident and apparently ill at ease with his replies on press censorship, he is a man I never should trust either from his face or his manner. We had a great Scots Guards dinner last night in the Maxim gun school at St Omer about 45 of us sat down, a cheery gathering no speeches allowed, just the King's health drunk, then the pipers came round the table they really played capitally after this they cleared the table away and danced reels, they seemed to have a capital lot of young fellows with wonderful spirits headed by Charlie Mills[62] who seems a capital boy. Weather quite glorious, all the harvest is being collected much of it is thrashed so as to clear the barns which are bringing in a goodly income from being hired for billeting. Cecil Lowther is succeeding Billy Lambton as Military Secretary and John Ponsonby[63] gets Lowther's Brigade, the 11th Corps has been formed and given to Haking[64] it consists of the Guards Division and two new ones of the 3rd (K) army one of which is in the country and the other has begun to come along. I saw K when he was over here, he left no doubt in my mind as to who had stood in my way from getting the 3rd (BEF) Army why he should have taken a dislike to me I cannot tell you. Charlie Hindlip comes today so will send this by him on Monday and add anything that may come to mind.

Sunday
The wind has gone to the N it is much colder and inclined to rain. A deserter came in to the Indian Corps last night and said that the Germans were waiting to attack, they had sunk many mines and had a great quantity of gas cylinders stored in their parapets ready for the first wind that favoured them, there may be some truth in it for he was the first German we have seen with a proper gas helmet, anyway we are bombarding the parapet where he says they are on the chance of bursting a cylinder for the wind is just right to take it over the German lines at that point. We have made some experiments with bombs to make a thick black smoke and find the composition of napthaline, linseed and tar makes a good cloud we want it to cover our advance across the open and screen the actual point of attack from the enemy. Do you do any dealings with the Red Cross people because we find that their stretchers are very valuable for getting the wounded along roads where you cannot take the ambulances they are quite light too and have the further advantage of being fire proof. I wonder if you are going to get a little Scotch air it would do you good in a quiet place. Love to Willy Yours ever Putty.

---

61   Sir Frank Athelstane Swettenham (1850-1946) Director Official Press Bureau.
62   Probably 2nd Lieutenant Hon Charles Thomas Mills 2 SG killed in action 6 Oct 1915 aged 28.
63   Brigadier General John Ponsonby (1866-1952) late Coldm Gds.
64   Major General Richard Cyril Byrne Haking (1862-1945) late Hamps GOC 1st Division.

He also wrote to Edith Londonderry:

Dearest La Motte, La Baronne is still away when she returns next week I will give her your letter, she wrote to me this morning enclosing some postcards one of which I forward to you it should bring back many pleasant recollections!! [Postcard of young woman on bed with breasts exposed. Man standing by bed, perhaps a doctor. Caption 'Vous me cachez encore quelque chose' – 'You are still hiding something from me']. Further I send you the submarine account which is most interesting it really sounds like a tale of dreams. Am expecting the Howler this afternoon and will send this by him on Monday.

Much of the rest of the letter repeats the information in his letter to Ettie but referring to the Scots Guards dinner:

'Alby' Cator[65] whose nickname is 'Forni' was in great form recounting his experiences in Paris last week with G. Trotter,[66] they had a pretty good time and consummated the friendship to some tune.

On Sunday Putty added:

Howler brought the grouse and the cakes, the former were quite excellent the latter may last a little as Jemmy went off to Paris this morning to buy some periscopes. All blessings Yours ever Putty.

Next day (29 August) Putty wrote to Marquess of Londonderry now back with his regiment:

My dear Charlie, Very many thanks for your nice letter of the 20 Aug which I honestly very much appreciated, of course if you get on the staff come here to be attached you will find Karslake [GSO2] is just as good as Bartholomew only not quite such a charming manner but he has had a good deal more practical experience in the field. The 20th Division are shaping well, your (fat) friend still makes hurdles and they now have created a record of making 135 in one day. Everybody goes to Fleurbaix to see Shreiber's [BGRE III Corps] folly in the way of the defences. We have got a herd of Scots Guards coming to dinner tonight also G Trotter [CO 1 Gren Gds], he and Forni Cator had a devil of a time in Paris, they returned like the proverbial rag. Best of luck Yours ever Putty.

Baronne de la Grange recorded (30 August) the arrival of HQ III Corps earlier in the month at the Chateau La Motte au Bois:

I hardly had time to get the house cleaned, when General Pulteney, head of III Corps, arrived. As everyone had always spoken of him as 'Puttey', I so addressed him when we

---

65   Lieutenant Colonel Albermarle Bertie Cator (1877-1932) CO 2 SG.
66   Lieutenant Colonel Gerald Frederick Trotter (1871-1945) CO 1 Gren Gds.

first met and, and there was never any frigidity. He is what we call a 'bon vivant' with a lively and twinkling eye. His staff is a very cheerful one, and I see extremely frivolous Parisian papers lying on tables mixed up with ordnance maps and plans of attack. The III Corps, formed by Lord Kitchener, is composed of varied elements. One sees as many kilts as khaki trousers, and the glengarry of little Colonel Rose (Camp Commandant) is to be seen bustling about everywhere, in every part of the billet, superintending the general installation. From the moment of rising he has his revolver in his belt, as though he were camped in a wood, reconnoitring the enemy. He is never separated from a certain weird instrument, which, he says, indicates the presence of springs of water! When the little wand twitches and turns in his hand, that means water is near. And, as in Flanders water is often only a few inches below the surface, the wand waggles merrily. I see very little of General Pulteney's cheerful presence, being much more favoured with the company of Lord Hamilton of Dalzell, a charming man, whom I liked at sight. Very tall, with grey hair and fine blue eyes, I should think he must have been something of a 'lady-killer'! As he is fond of inventions, I often see him in the park experimenting with trench tools and poison gas, which spoil my lawn. There is a very original artist on the staff who has a talent for the mischievous arrangement of cuttings from *La Vie Parisienne*. The most unexpected and surprising juxtapositions are to be found in these composite pictures. He has arranged a screen like a staircase; on each step are curious neighbours, as, for instance, Mr Lloyd George with a modern Eve on his knee, or Lord Balfour carrying on his shoulder a Venus well known to the world of the grands boulevards! When I cross the office I lower my gaze primly, but I manage not to miss a single detail of the screen all the same!

On the last day of the month (31 August) DDMS noted: 'Fort Rompu. Arranged with MOs to vacate the residential part of the brewery in event of battle, all but 2 rooms, to make room for Report Centre of HQ III Corps (DDMS also refers to it as Advanced HQ III Corps)'. Fort Rompu is on the S bank of the River Lys, slightly E of Bac St Maur. All three divisional head-quarters were close with HQ 27th Division at Croix du Bac and Advanced HQ at La Rolanderie Farm, 8th Division at Sailly, and 20th Division at Nouveau Mande.

III Corps casualties in August were: 7 officers and 97 other ranks killed, 24 officers and 536 other ranks wounded = 664.

September

Putty sent his monthly report to the King on 2 September:

My dear Wigram, I enclose you the diary of the 3rd Corps for the month of August for the information of His Majesty the King. As far as the Germans are concerned there is very little to tell you for they have been very much on the defensive and very quiet. The 27th Division have improved in the most satisfactory manner quite a different spirit, any amount of energy in fact it is almost impossible to believe it is the same division that came down from Ypres, their health at last is quite excellent, all the Indian fever is now I hope out of them. The 8th Division are doing very well under General Hudson. The 20th Division have taken their place in the line and are shaping splendidly, any amount of dash and enterprise

Pulteney with Baronne de la
Grange, 1915. (de la Grange)

right through, they seem to be learning quicker than any I have trained yet. We have done a great deal of work in making bomb proof covers for the men, also increased the number of communication trenches, it has been very hard fatigue work but I attribute the reduction in the number of casualties to the completion of this work. The artillery are improving as well in their shooting and have far more confidence in themselves than formerly especially in the 27th Division, the supply of ammunition has been better and this keeps the Germans in their proper place. I hope this finds you quite recovered from your accident. Yours Sincerely, WP Pulteney.

The following morning (3 September) Putty with his BGGS, BGRA and CE attended a conference at Advanced HQ 1st Army, the first for the forthcoming battle – the Battle of Loos.

At 9 am on 5 September DDMS recorded that at his morning meeting with Putty: 'The Corps Commander selected a factory near Bac St Maur bridge (for the barge etc) should it be sanctioned'. Meanwhile another division, 23rd (Major General Babington), joined III Corps on attachment; by 7 September it had moved to Borre-Vieux area with its HQ at Merris.

Captain Jack, now with 2 Cameronians (23 Bde 8th Division), recorded his experience in the line this day:

The 1914 trenches in this [Cordonnerie Farm] area had to be abandoned last winter as they became water-logged. In their stead we hold a line of breastworks, on top of the ground, which we were building in February. There were no communication trenches; the front line could only be reached across the open; this has been remedied. The breastworks are some 7 feet high, 7 feet wide at the top and 18 inches at the bottom. About 6 feet behind the front wall there is a similar wall, with a trench 2 feet deep between the two. The inner face of both walls is revetted with sandbags, and solid traverses every ten yards protect the men in the bays from enfilade fire as well as localising shell bursts. Small recesses, shored up with timber, in the parapet give shelter to officers and men. On the enemy's side of the parapet a wide ditch, boggy in wet weather, and a thick belt of barbed wire to prevent a surprise attack. There is practically no support line, redoubts taking its place. One feels less confined behind breastworks than one did in the trenches, and the range of view, although little enough, is better.

Coincidentally Jack had served with 1 Cameronians 19 Bde and as SC HQ 19 Bde in the same place during the previous winter so was better placed than most to report on the improvements that had been made to the defences.

On 6 September, a day of increased artillery by both sides, Putty with his BGGS, BGRA and CE attended a second conference at Advanced HQ 1st Army.

It was also that day that Lord Stamfordham, Private Secretary to the King wrote to Lord Kitchener, SofS for War: 'Pulteney stands almost first among the LGs (Lieutenant Generals) who might fairly look for advancement'.

Writing on 7 September Haig noted: 'My orders are to break the enemy's front and reach Pont à Vendin. With this objective IV and I Corps attack south of the La Bassée Canal. The Indian Corps and III Corps must also attack to the full extent of their power'.

Putty wrote to Edith Londonderry on 7 September:

Dearest La Motte, I enclose you a circular that General Macready[67] issued I think it may amuse you, we call him Gen Make Me Ready. Am down in my luck again as they are going to take the 27th Division away to form the 12th Corps just as I have pulled them together, am going to get the 23rd Division in its place it arrived in my area this morning, the roads looked as if there had been a battle it is commanded by Babington who is a nice fellow but was quite useless in S Africa, David Kinloch[68] was one of the brigadiers but has already been sent back as too old. Billy Lambton was here all the afternoon he is going to command the 7th Division but as there are some operations in view he is going to wait until they are over and leave Tommy Capper there until then, T.C. has been given a corps and my friend Wilson who commands 4th Division is to command the next, when I finish training the 23rd Division shall have trained ten divisions more than three army corps so have pulled some weight for them whatever the government may know of my shortcomings. George Paynter[69] is now with Sir John French as ADC he does not look fit to be out here, unfortunately both Forni Cator [CO 2 SG] and Norman Orr-Ewing [SG] are both in St Omer now and they gave him big dinners, he eclipsed himself on Sunday by asking Gavin

---

67   Lieutenant General Sir (Cecil) Nevil Macready AG BEF.
68   Brigadier General David Kinloch (1856-1944) late Gren Gds.
69   Major George Camborne Beauclerk Paynter (1880-1950) SG 1899-1927.

Hamilton how Minor Lawson[70] was. The Baroness has just returned, her son is engaged to Miss Sloan who is coming here next week, an American with a Scotch mother (which may be the saving of her), the whole place has been tidied up in the most wonderful manner in anticipation of her arrival but she says they are not to be married until after the war which may keep her some time, I hope there won't be any precious arrivals. The Speaker's son[71] is going on pretty well at Merville but has had a narrow squeak, if you go and dig maxim gun emplacements within 200 yards of the front trenches in broad daylight you must expect something. The 20th Division are doing well they snipe the Boches well and are up to all sorts of mischievous games at night with their wire. Do you realise that we have nearly 2,000 more guns out here now than we had this day last year no wonder the ammunition takes more supplying. Much love Yours ever Putty.

It was a busy day for Putty on 8 September. At 5.45 am the GS log recorded: 'Two prisoners of 17 Bavarian Reserve Regt were taken on 20th Division front. One prisoner was badly wounded. Valuable information particularly with regard to enemy's telephone and mines was obtained'. The day had started well and the morning staff meeting would have been upbeat. Putty then went to HQ 8th Division at Sailly where he held his first corps conference on the forthcoming attack; 4 Group and 16 Sqn RFC also attended. Later in the day he inspected 23rd Division.

That evening he wrote to Ettie Desborough:

My dear Chief, Delighted to get your letter of the 3 Sep and find you in the northern air at this time of year instead of by the river it will do you good. The rains are over and we have got back in to decent crisp weather again though somewhat on the chilly side which is not a bad thing as it hardens the men up before the winter. Am rather depressed as they are taking the 27th Division away from me at a critical period especially after having pulled it together however they are making new corps and they must have a blend of the old stagers among the new ones, where I feel it most is that the new corps has no Territorial battalions in it which means 3,000 less men to hold back the line with and the artillery absolutely untrained this is a trial amid operations. The best story of the war is Granard having written to Ian Hamilton as a Privy Councillor on the conduct of the war in the Dardanelles, it beats anything we have had happen out here. I fancy Sir James Willcocks is disappearing from command of the Indian Corps as he is no use out here and does not get on with Douglas Haig either. Just fancy we have 2,000 more guns in the British force out here now than we had this time last year, 33 divisions instead of 8 which shows the magnitude of the army and the pace that it grows, enough credit has not been given to Kitchener for this although I say it who he does not like, the fault is in the training which is chiefly due to Archie Murray[72] who will not keep in with the times or rather up to them. Conscription will be no good unless they pass it without exemptions. All blessings Yours ever Putty.

70 Probably Hamilton's stepson killed in action on 22 October 1914.
71 Probably Christopher William Lowther (1887-1935) Suffolk Hussars Eton son of 1st Viscount Ullswater Speaker 1905-1921.
72 Lieutenant General Sir Archibald James Murray (1860-1945) late Innis Fus DCIGS.

He mentions Jessie Arnott in this letter to Ettie, which he had not for some time, but there was nothing to reveal his feelings or his intentions. He had been corresponding with others, including Jessie herself, but considering the frequency of his letters to Ettie and his openness on every other subject, there is surprising lack of detail: the impression is that Putty was very unsure of himself and how to pursue his love. By now Jessie must have been well aware of his feelings for her but she too seemed uncertain and reticent.

III Corps OpO No.50 was issued on 11 September giving orders for the relief of 27th Division by 23rd Division (left sector III Corps) on 14 September. On 12 September, Captain Jack 2 Cameronians (23 Bde 8th Division) noted: 'Company commanders have just been told "Secretly and Personally" to prepare for an early attack on the enemy'.

Putty wrote to Edith Londonderry:

Dearest La Motte, Mille thanks for your letters of 6 and 10 Sep will send this back by the Howler tomorrow. Enclose you a letter from Granard[73] which is rather interesting, should imagine that Ian Hamilton and Braithwaite[74] are both good fighting men but should let somebody else bring their troops up for them to the required points, everybody says the same thing that there was absolutely no coordination and no division knew what the one on his right or left were doing or what their orders were, to have allowed them to have landed without guns was nothing more or less than an inhuman jest, I suppose you heard the story of Granard writing to Sir Ian Hamilton as a Privy Councillor regarding the conduct of the campaign, it is really the funniest incident of the war everybody ought to put P.C. after his name instead of K.P. for the future, burn Granard's letter after you have read it. We have been trying the new HE which has been bursting some of the guns after making alterations we had to test 3,000 rounds but alas after we had fired 1,500 and thought all was well we burst a gun a foot from the muzzle, no casualties because we had taken proper precautions, we gave the salient at Rue de Bois which Charlie knows well the devil of a dusting, it drew very little reply from the Germans which looks as if the chief gunner had gone to Lille for the weekend and was unable to give the necessary authority to spend more, they have all their girls in Lille, the lucky dogs. Have been bothered all the afternoon by visitors, first of all Haking came, with all his plans about the 10th Corps which includes the Guards Division, he stayed two hours, it is an ill wind which blows no good, Haking published a book just before the war, when he went back on leave a short time ago he asked his publishers if it was being bought they said rather we had an order from America last week for a thousand copies. I chucked up all idea about the Stoat as an ADC for I could not make out what he wanted to do he could not make up his mind so had to make up mine, no regular officers in future are to be allowed so shall have to look for someone 'irregular', will you come! Allenby came here this afternoon to see the Baroness but she went away to Paris last night so he had all the motor drive for nothing, he showed his disappointment, obviously he could not stand the simple life of Ypres any longer. How splendid about the Zeppelins you must have had a grand time of it, George Milne saw them on two nights at Woolwich and has applied for two clasps in consequence, his division 27th leaves me on the 17th and

---

73   CO 5 R Irish 10th Division.
74   Lieutenant General Sir Walter Pippon Braithwaite (1865-1945) late Som LI COS Allied Med Exped Force.

Babington's 23rd a raw lot takes its place, he has already ousted one of his brigadiers David Kinloch as useless, he always was a damned bad soldier but he gave up 2,000£ a year to try and retrieve his reputation as a soldier but has failed, poor old chap he is dreadfully cut up about it and has not taken it in the right spirit. What you say about the promotions really does lick cock-fighting it would be the absolute limit, there really would have been a boil over if it had happened I for one could not have stood that, I really think even Sir John could not have expected me to swallow that pill. The 4th Army is a long way off if they are going to stick to four army Corps in each army there never ought to have been more than three. The other Canadian division arrive this week and Alderson gets the corps. We are all dying to know the result of the conference about the Dardanelles, K has come over here to ask for two trained divisions. Best of love, tell Charlie will answer his letter later. Yours Ever Putty.

Meanwhile the enemy were not idle, exploding three mines early on 13 September; one, at 5.30 am, was under a small salient of trench held by 7 Som LI (20th Division). About twenty men were buried by the explosion. In spite of heavy artillery, machine-gun and trench mortar fire which the enemy poured in to the area of the explosion the crater was occupied at once, and the rest of the company began to rescue those buried, five of whom were killed and twelve injured. Two of the rescuers were also killed and five wounded.

Putty wrote again to Ettie on 13 September:

My dear Chief, Charlie Hindlip is just off so will send a line by him. All sorts of rumours and intrigues on K's part as regards promotion of generals keep reaching us out here but I don't know with what amount of truth yet, Birdwood[75] and Robertson[76] were the two I heard quoted to go over my head but don't think that will happen if Sir John gets wind of it in time. The Germans are very jumpy in front of me at the present time they are exploding defective mines nearly every night, we have been successful as well in bringing down their artillery observation aeroplanes, we got three last week and another was chased out to sea and had to land near Calais for want of petrol and they are all their best men. Best love & blessings Yours ever Putty.

When 23rd Division took over the line from 27th Division on 14 September, the front was 4,500 yards in length with the left boundary being the Armentières-Wez Macquart Road. It is described in 23rd Division's history:

The defensive system consisted of a front line, which, except for a short length of trench on the right, was formed by a continuous line of breast-work; a close support line of trench, wired throughout and furnishing dug-outs for 75 per cent of the front line garrison; and the Bois Grenier (reserve) line, a continuous line of breast-work, 1000 yards in rear of the front line, partially wired, with fire bays at intervals, and containing dug-outs. Six main

---

75   Major General William Birdwood (1865-1951) late RSF and Bengal Lancers promoted Lieutenant General 28 October 1915 to command Dardanelles Army.
76   Major or Lieutenant General Sir William Robertson (1860-1933) late 3 DG COS GHQ and CIGS Dec 1915.

communication trenches connected the Bois Grenier line to the front line. There were, in addition, numerous short lengths of communication trench between the front and support line.

This was the part of III Corps' front that they had held for nearly a year and reflected Putty's efforts to make the line secure and as habitable as possible.

At 5 am on 15 Sep Rifleman P Sands 1 RIR (25 Bde 8th Division) having been convicted of desertion by a FGCM, was shot at Fleurbaix. Perhaps the records are incomplete but this was the first execution recorded in III Corps' jurisdiction for nearly six months.

Sir John French's orders for the participation of the BEF in the allied offensive, in accordance with General Joffre's plan, were issued on 18 September. The main assault between Lens and the Bassée Canal was to be carried out by 1st Army. The six divisions of its IV and I Corps were to deliver the assault while its two other corps, Indian and III Corps, N of the canal, made subsidiary attacks. III Corps' subsidiary attack was to be made near Le Bridoux, 3½ miles S of Armentières; this was a 'subsidiary' attack not a 'diversionary' attack, and both corps were to be prepared for a general advance immediately the situation permitted.

DDMS noted that day that DMS 1st Army called on him at 11 am: 'I pressed the question of an operating barge for abdominal cases, which he said was not available, but he would ask for it. Meanwhile he would send a surgeon and sisters to deal with these cases to 26 Fd Amb retaining them here for treatment till fit to remove in evacuation barge'. Progress was being made.

At 11 pm on 19 September 1st Army issued its orders: 'III Corps will assault (on 25 Sep) the enemy's trenches in the vicinity of Le Bridoux. It will take full advantage of any weakening of the enemy on its front to operate with a view to effecting a junction with Indian Corps on the Aubers ridge ... The attack by III Corps will take place at daylight. It will not be preceded by smoke unless the hour of Zero is suitable'. The orders also allocated 4 HAG to support both Indian and III Corps. As written, Haig's orders lack clarity and resolve: however, it may well be that his verbal orders at the conferences provided both.

Putty issued his orders (III Corps OpO No.51) on 20 September, five days before the offensive was due to begin but only one day before the start of the preliminary bombardment. The plan was simple: 8th Division was to attack the Bridoux salient; 20th Division on its right was to cover its right flank and join up with the left of the Indian Corps, on the Aubers Ridge.

He also wrote to Edith Londonderry:

Dearest La Motte, Thanks for yours of 14 Sep, I agree with you about Granard expect he would take any billet where he could get in an office after the beach under shell fire his American dollars don't do him any good out there. If you will come out I will certainly turn La Motte Chateau into my Lille it would be a case of Corps to Corps or 1 × 1 = 1, you would always have to be in waiting and never off duty except when you were spoilt which would be impossible. Frankie de Tuyll[77] came and dined here on Friday, he looks blacker in the chin than ever, he has gone as 2nd ADC to General Milne, he was trying all round for that sort of job. K arrives in these parts this morning to inspect some of the Indians,

---

77   Probably Baron Francis 'Frank' Owen de Tuyll (1885-1952).

he seems extraordinary keen on keeping them in the country. Sir John French has been far from well, Atkins kept him in bed for two days last week, he got a bad chill and nearly had a go of pneumonia, his heart is none too strong. Bend D'Or[78] came here yesterday but was out, Gavin Hamilton said he was very fat, he hopes to canter in behind the cavalry with his motor guns but personally have no faith in them they are too big. I made a speech to each of the brigades of the 27th Division before they went away, they gave me three hearty cheers which I don't think were to order. The 23rd are shaking down but they are very green still. Maurice Wingfield [DAA&QMG HQ III Corps] is going off as AQMG to the 7th Division under Tommy Capper until after these operations when he will be under Billy Lambton he is being succeeded by Ailwyn Fellowes boy in the Rifle Brigade[79] who they say is a capital boy but have never met him. The Speaker's son is still very bad at Merville, his wife and mother are out here at present there is a fragment of shells in his lungs. The Russian news reads pretty bad notwithstanding K's optimistic speech but we will change all the tone of things by this day week the ammunition has come along really very well and if we don't get through this time we never shall, the smoke things are really good and should like to put one in your bedroom so that nobody like that beastly Charley could see in, it ought to make it impossible for the German aeroplanes to tell where the decisive point of attack is meant to be. My servant [Private Hogbin SG] came back on Saturday from a bust, he went to his home in Sussex where he got bombed by an aeroplane, he said London talked about nothing but Zeppelins altogether he thought it more peaceful here. There is the most splendid oak in the forest here which must be about 400 years old, a grand stem about 30 feet round and very straight, it is rather lost in the middle of the forest. Jemmie Rothschild had to fast all last Friday, he was not allowed to eat or drink for 24 hours, his stomach must have thanked that day of atonement. Philip Chetwode[80] came over here yesterday he has been training the cavalry hard W of St Omer, was delighted to get back to the work after all the digging, they have been swimming the canals on improvised bridges and only managed to drown one man which was pretty good for the cavalry. One of the girls in the village has got some killing letters making appointments with her by a cavalry brigadier am going to make Jemmy buy them off her as a memento. Tim Harington[81] has gone as Brig General Staff Officer to the Canadian Corps so all the 3rd Corps leaving get on well. Best of love Yours ever Putty.

The GS log recorded the start of the bombardment on 21 September:

Offensive operations commenced today with the bombardment of the enemy's defences, all along the front of the corps. For these operations the artillery of 8th Division has been reinforced by 3 Cdn Arty Bde, 92 (How) and 93 FA Bdes from 20th Division, and 103 and 105 (How) FA Bdes from 23rd Division. The following guns of No 4 Group HAR also

78   Hugh Richard Arthur Grosvenor 2nd Duke of Westminster (1879-1953) RHG/CY.
79   Major Ronald Townshend Fellowes RB Eton.
80   Major General Philip Walhouse Chetwode (1869-1950) late 19 H Eton GOC 2nd Cavalry Division later Field Marshal 1st Baron Chetwode.
81   Major Charles 'Tim' Harington GSO 2 HQ III Corps until April 1915 then Lieutenant Colonel GSO 1 HQ 49th Division.

cooperated on the front of III Corps: 30 Siege Bty (8" How), 26 Siege Bty (6" Guns) and Warwick 118, 110, 1 Sec Canadian and 1 Sec 14 Hy Btys (60 pdr). The enemy's wire and parapet at certain points were the principal target for our field guns, whilst the howitzers were engaged upon the enemy's support lines, houses and strong places in rear. During the day the enemy made only a feeble reply. Intermittent firing was continued throughout the night, especially at those points where wire had been cut or parapets breached.

Putty reported on the progress in a memo to 1st Army: 'Wire cutting batteries report satisfactory work done today. Aerial observers report fire of 4.5" howitzers on support line satisfactory. Hostile artillery fire has been very small'.
He also wrote to Ettie that day:

My dear Chief, Thank-you for your dear letter which I got yesterday, how right you are about the living principle being destroyed in you but then it has paved the way for the golden future which we are unable to measure, how different to things on this earth where we see the American worship the dollar, the Balkan State the winner without any distinction between right and wrong. The bombardment has begun, the preparations are practically complete, the big effort of the French and ourselves will be launched in its way by Saturday by Monday you will know whether success has crowned it or not, it augurs well for it is the anniversary of Lucknow the light hearted men have turned it to Luck Now, if we have a little luck with the wind there is a great chance of success, it is the first time we have attacked with proper reserves in hand, the first time ammunition has even admitted of a chance of success and with an enormous preponderance of guns unless our calculations and information are incorrect as far as we know they have put one army corps in general reserve at Valenciennes and a division at Lille and this is all the available reserves in the West and they certainly are not sufficient to meet us if we break through if we don't get through it means just settling down for the future to attrition pure and simple if it had not been for the Dardanelles it would be a certainty but as it is I am more confident than I have ever been before, it is just 33 years since I had my first big fight in 1882 in September and I feel fortune will favour us. I don't know when you will get this letter as believe they have taken off the mails for some days to prevent information getting across the Channel a jolly wise precaution which they ought to carry on for a week. All love and blessings For ever Putty.

The bombardment continued on 22 September, which was fine and clear with a NE wind. The GS log recorded:

8" hows continued shelling the enemy's front line about Le Bridoux – field guns wire cutting – 4.5" hows on strong points in enemy's support and reserve lines. More wire was cut during the day and fresh breaches made in the parapet. The enemy's reply was rather greater than yesterday but still very small. The bombardment was continued throughout the night.

Again on 23 September, another fine day with wind still changeable, being E in the morning changing to S in the afternoon, with heavy rain in the evening:

> Places where wire had been cut were kept under fire during the night. The bombardment was continued throughout the day in accordance with the previously arranged programme. At 4.30 pm a burst of fire as if the prelude to an attack was opened from all 18 pdr batteries. The enemy, however, did not reply to any extent. Although a slightly greater increase in hostile shelling during the day, the enemy's reply is still feeble. At 8 pm another false alarm bombardment took place but again there was little reply from the enemy.

From 10 pm (23 September) a facsimile of the programme for the night 24/25 September was carried out. Then, at 4.25 am (24 September) a bombardment prior to assault took place but little reply was made by the enemy. The GS log recorded: 'During our bombardment today the field guns were principally engaged in cutting wire and destroying the enemy's parapet. Our wire cutting is reported to have been particularly successful in places'.

HQ III Corps opened its Advanced Report Centre at Fort Rompu at 4 pm; since most of the staff had moved there it was in effect an Advanced HQ. HQ 23rd Division moved forward to Rolanderie Farm and the division threw three pontoon bridges across the River Lys so that it could move forward rapidly when required.

During the night (24 September) 8th Division moved forward to its positions for the attack. At 11 pm 1st Army confirmed that III Corps' attack was to take place at 4.30 am on 25 September; everyone was now in position for their part in the Battle of Loos, in itself a subsidiary attack to the main allied effort to be made by the French armies in Champagne. There was a general spirit of optimism from Putty downwards that their part in the offensive next day would succeed, indeed that the whole 1st Army attack would be successful.

At 3.40 am on 25 September HQ III Corps received a message from 1st Army that Zero hour for the main attack was to be 5.50 am. At daybreak there was a slight wind from the SW; the morning was dull and turned to heavy rain. The weather became so bad, with so much mist and heavy rain later, that it became impossible to see what was going on.

The assault by 25 Bde 8th Division took place at Zero hour, 4.30 am, supported by two trench mortar batteries and six 18 pdr guns which had been manhandled up to embrasures in the front parapet; smoke appliances were deployed to screen the flank. Instantly the three assaulting battalions (L-R 2 Lincoln 2 Berks 2 RB) advanced in the mist and rain from their 'jumping off line', a dry ditch joining the horns of a deep re-entrant in the line, through the cut wire, to carry the German trenches. The frontage of the attack was about 1,200 yards between Corner Fort and Bridoux Fort two works in the German front line, and the distance of advance about 250. The German front trench, including both Corner and Bridoux Forts, was carried in the first rush; 3 officers and 120 men of 1 Bavarian Regt were taken prisoner.

At 5.56 am a wall of smoke was put along III Corps' front as part of 1st Army's plan to conceal the point of main effort; the smoke drifted slowly and was about 100 feet high.

On the right of 25 Bde 8th Division, two battalions of 60 Bde 20th Division (12 RB and 6 KSLI) assaulted at 8.25 am; by 9.30 am they had gained the enemy's trenches and begun to consolidate a line running NE and E of Mauquissart. They got into contact with the left of the Bareilly Bde and bombers were pushed along the enemy trenches. Although fighting was still going on in the German lines between Corner Fort and Bridoux Fort, the overall situation looked promising.

Two hours later the situation changed. On 8th Division front 25 Bde were still holding their own but being hard pressed by bombing counter-attacks and liquid fire. Captain Jack 2 Cameronians, who observed the attack, related: 'Among other difficulties which they (25 Bde) had to contend with, the fuses of their bombs became damp from rain and would not light' and 'there were 12 patterns of hand bomb in British use and few mastered completely the mechanism of all of them'. But the problems started on the right when the Germans launched a strong bombing attack on the Bareilly Bde, forcing it to retire. This exposed the right flank of the two battalions of 60 Bde 20th Division; they were heavily attacked by bombers on the front and both flanks and at 12.30 pm forced to retire.

On the left of 25 Bde 8th Division a determined counter-attack at 1 pm drove 2 Lincolns back on to Bridoux Fort and shortly afterwards German bombers forced them back from the captured front trench. By 2 pm the position of 2 Berks also became untenable and they were withdrawn to their original trenches. At Corner Fort 2 RB, on the right of 25 Bde, continued to hold and beat off several counter-attacks, two trench mortars assisting greatly in keeping off the German bombers. It was felt, however, that the retention of this isolated position was not worth the losses it would entail, and at 3.30 pm the defenders were ordered to withdraw, the movement being skilfully carried out with little loss. Shortly thereafter all the III Corps' battalions were back in or behind their original front line.

III Corps had done what was asked of it: the left flank had been protected until the Bareilly Bde of the Indian Corps was forced back and III Corps had to conform. Haig himself recorded: 'Considerable numbers of the enemy's troops have consequently been drawn off from our main attack – by III Corps'. III Corps had broken in to the enemy's defences, which were very strong, and inflicted many casualties. Advantage had been taken during the attack to dig a new trench, which was completed during the night, across the re-entrant in the British line.

Much should have been learnt by Putty and HQ III Corps from their part in this phase of the Battle of Loos: a long preliminary bombardment compromised any attempt at achieving surprise, yet without surprise a very strongly defended position could only be taken if the artillery had completely destroyed all resistance, and this was impossible; field artillery could cut wire given sufficient ammunition but was totally ineffective against deep dugouts and strong points; counter battery fire could suppress the enemy's artillery that had been identified but there would always be 'silent' batteries to contend with; the beaten zone of the British guns when firing overhead rendered close support of the infantry almost impossible and made them very vulnerable; the inflexibility of the fire planning meant that artillery fire very quickly had little relevance to the tactical situation; the infantry placed too much reliance on the artillery and neglected its own tactical principles and the weapons at its disposal; its bombs were inadequate in dealing with German bombers; these were just some of the lessons. Some of them should have been learnt already: the probability of a gun hitting the target it is aimed at is the sum of a number of errors associated with the gun, target and weather. The result is that the rounds fall not on the target but in a beaten zone whose length is significantly greater than its width. If, therefore, the gun is fired over the heads of the attacking infantry it is supporting there are two consequences; firstly it is unlikely to hit a linear target at right angle and secondly the gun will have to stop firing on the enemy's line at a very early stage, probably before our infantry have left their trenches. The solution was to fire from defilade but this required more effective command and control.

III Corps casualties on 25 September were 52 officers and 1,283 other ranks in 8th Division, 19 officers and 542 other ranks in 20th Division, a total of 1,896. Since only six battalions actually took part in the assault, and would have sustained most of the casualties, the number is proportionally high. Captain W Paynter's 14 Bty RFA was supporting the Indian Corps. At 7 am his FOO with 2 Leics was wounded and he went forward and took his place. He noted: 'When they were withdrawn that night 2 Leics had only one officer and 130 men left out of 800'. This proportion is very much higher.

The ammunition expended by the corps artillery was 21 Sep – 4,965, 22 Sep – 5,590, 23 Sep – 7,850, 24 Sep – 9,393 and 25 Sep – 30,517 rounds.

Haig sent orders to Putty at 2 am on 26 September that he was to continue to pin the enemy to his trenches and orders were given to divisions to this effect at 4 am. Putty then went to HQ Indian Corps at 8.30 am to confer with its GOC (Willcocks). Later in the day at 6.30 pm HQ III Corps issued OpO No.52 setting out the coordinated details for a demonstration by artillery and machine-gun fire in support of I and IV Corps. Captain Jack 2 Cameronians noted: 'We kept expecting a German counter-attack but nothing of the kind happened. Many dead of 2 RB were seen lying close up to the enemy's parapet'.

Early in the morning of 27 September Haig called a halt to offensive operations. At 2 pm HQ III Corps issued OpO No.53 readjusting the line held by divisions. Throughout the night work on the new line continued to join up Well Farm Salient to the Bridoux Salient.

DDMS had called on Putty that morning to tell him that the arrangements for forward surgery at 26 Fd Amb had been excellent, there had been 4 deaths out of 15 abdominal cases.

On 28 September 1st Army ordered III Corps to extend its right and 20th Division was ordered to take this over (OpO No.54). This brought the right flank of the corps to a sunken road about half a mile NE of Neuve Chapelle.

It rained throughout the night of 28 September and then all day on 29 September. At 9.35 am DDMS noted: 'Visited barge. Patients are quite comfortable, the transfer having been affected without disturbance. Corps Commander visited the barge just as I was leaving. He sanctions a landing place being arranged nearer the bridge at a spot which will not be flooded in winter'. Putty was still at Advanced HQ III Corps so this would have been only a short walk along the river.

He wrote to Edith Londonderry on 29 September:

> Dearest La Motte, Multitude thanks for your letter of 23 Sep which only reached me last night for some reason or another. The great effort is now about expended and we shall now settle down to the winter campaign the results on the whole have been satisfactory, they were not as great as we had hoped for but we gave the Germans a real good shaking but the amount of ammunition that has now been expended prevents much further being done by either side for the present. Nothing but big guns such as 6 and 8 inch howitzers are any good against the breastworks the HE of the 18 pdr made no impression and many rounds were wasted at it (parapet), the feature of the German trenches was the extraordinary depth they had dug down to under their parapet, they were absolutely immune from shell fire, they beat us at bombing because they were practical and only used one kind of bomb, we have ten, the men get mixed up tried to light the percussion ones and threw the timed fuzed ones all the German bombs have instructions how to use the bomb printed on it we have none not even different coloured labels. The men fought magnificently and went in like lions, the officers leading were the weak points, they did not understand the principle of blocking up the communication trenches quick enough and lost the tactical features of the ground in advancing, the discipline of the young troops was not proof against searching for curios instead of attending to business but on the whole they did

well, considering what a little time the K divisions had been in the country they did wonders but they will take the whole winter to make them into proper fighting troops. The gas cylinders are a mistake what we want is gas shells like the Germans have got and which the French are coming along with, these burst over the deep dug outs and make it impossible to resist an attack, the wind is so shifty that the gas in the cylinders can only be used if the wind is actually in the right direction, the Indian Corps gassed themselves and some of my lot. Some of the deeds done were diabolical on both sides all the animal seems to come out in the heat and preparation for the fight, one man went in with his shirt sleeves tucked up, four bombs a dagger and the cooks knife, he was a mass of gore when he came out and said he had done in two of the … with the cooks knife. One prisoner was brought up to the engineer officer in the 8th Division, he shook all over turned out his pockets and said 'No shoot, No shoot, we very sorry about the Lusitania'. The 8th Division took 3 officers and 123 prisoners which arrived at the railhead they say they took more but I only believe what I get receipts for a subsidiary attack it was only fairly successful but it still held the Bavarian Corps to their ground as did the Indian Corps with the 7th, I straightened out the extraordinary re-entrant there was in the line which I renamed Hudson Bay (as he commands the 8th Division) but had to be firm about it as they wanted to go back to the old line, all sorts of excuses about wet in the winter etc. but it is a fait accompli, at present moment the old 3rd Corps is holding eleven miles of front not bad. Will write about what went on down S later, Poor Tommy Capper[82] am so sorry. Yours ever Putty.

DDMS came to see Putty again on 30 September to report on the bad distribution of rations to the men of 20th Division in the trenches. For III Corps AQ staff it was an enormous task to compete with the numerous supply problems in the line, and they were compounded by battle and by the changes in the deployment; also many AQ staff officers and others in the supply chain were totally inexperienced.

III Corps casualties for September were: 37 officers and 422 other ranks killed, 76 officers and 1,792 other ranks wounded, 9 officers and 453 other ranks missing = 2,789 (1,898 on 25 Sep).

October

DDMS and Putty had frequent discussion on improvements for the health and welfare of the troops in the corps. On 1 October it was about improving the laundry at Sailly baths and the following day about wet feet and getting boots off once a day in the trenches. In an army that had expanded so rapidly there was much for the newcomers to learn, matters that would have been taken for granted or accepted in the pre-war professional army.

On 2 October Advanced HQ III Corps closed at Fort Rompu and moved back to the Chateau la Motte au Bois after more than a week forward. Putty sent his monthly report to the King that day:

My dear Fritz,[83] Thank you for your letter of the 16th inst, I forward herewith the diary of the 3rd Corps for the month of September for information of His Majesty. The 8th

82 Major General Sir Thompson Capper (1863-1915) late E Lancs GOC 7th Division died of wounds 27 September.
83 Lieutenant Colonel Sir Frederick Edward Grey Ponsonby (1867-1935) Gren Gds Keeper of the Privy Purse later Baron Sysonby.

Division had hard fighting on the morning of the 25th, they attacked the Bridoux Salient, 2 RB on the right, 2 Berks centre and 2 Lincolns on left, Lincolns and RB both got in with not too many casualties but the right of the Berks was caught by a searchlight and one company wiped out, the result being a gap between the RB and them, the Lincolns went right through and captured 120 prisoners but did not consolidate their left sufficiently with the result that they were eventually counter-attacked and driven out, the Berks later on being dealt with similarly, the RB were all right but Stephens (Lieutenant Colonel RB Stephens) who had been at Neuve Chapelle where all the RB were cut up after hanging on a long time ordered them back at 4 pm, this they accomplished without heavy losses, the whole thing would have been a great success except for the bombs they beat us completely at it, the Germans have only one kind of bomb which is quite simple to use and very effective we have ten different kinds, some percussion, some time, some you light others you pull the pin out, unfortunately it was a very wet morning the bombs that they light had got wet and there was not time to cut the end of the fuse off to light it, then when bombs were sent up from reserve some of the men did not know the different kinds tried to light the percussion ones and threw the others, there is no doubt the percussion is the best and you must have no bomb in the attack that requires lighting and the sooner we fix on one or two bombs only faut mieux. We had about 1500 casualties altogether in the 8th Division which includes the 4 day bombardment, there is no doubt we killed a great number of Germans. The German trenches were so deep the men could not get at them from the top to bayonet the men, the dug outs were eight feet below ground level, what the bombers wanted was a short spear weighted in the handle similar to a pig sticking spear in India. Now as regards the bombardment it was on the whole disappointing for the amount of ammunition expended, we only had an 8 inch battery for the first two days and then they went S to the main attack but the 8 inch and the 9.2 knock down the breastworks all right but the 18 pdr with HE is useless it never reached the dug outs at all, the Germans never left the front trenches at all during the bombardment but stayed in their dugouts, so that when the men attacked they were caught as they had not time to get out of them, we had knocked out all the machine-guns except one, that was concreted in so that nothing but a 15 inch could have smashed it. We had no gas which was just as well as the wind was wrong for my part but from what I saw of the men in hospital at Merville our gas is nothing like so powerful as the Germans as all the men recovered in a few hours. You want the gas in shells not cylinders, the Germans use simply devilish shells which not only make you sick but make your eyes run till you can't see, if we had gas shells to burst over these deep trenches we should have them at our mercy. The wire was well cut by the shrapnel but it requires very careful observation and a great deal of ammunition but it must be done before you attack otherwise I believe a short bombardment of four hours would be better than four days. 12 RB in 20th Division joined up with the left of the Indian Corps and for a new Kitchener bn did most extraordinary well in fact all the 20th Division showed good promise. The 23rd Division under Babington is coming on gradually, in time will be all right, but they had no business to have sent it out with the long rifle with all the others with the short one, the men are all bagging the short one when they get a chance and changing because they get chaffed by divisions on their right and left of being Territorial. The weather has been too vile for words, the old mud has brought back last winter memories very vividly. Yours Sincerely WP Pulteney.

On 3 October HQ III Corps issued OpO No.55, orders for a demonstration by 20th Division in support of a further attack by I and IV Corps. At 9 am that morning DDMS spoke to Putty about the quality of the food for the men in the trenches and the problems of carrying forward cooked rations.

Later Putty wrote to Ettie Desborough:

> My dear Chief, Have got an afternoon to myself before we begin again tomorrow. My corps has done its job and is only going to demonstrate in the attack on Tuesday. Oh the weather has been so very disastrous it has made all the difference to the offensive operations but the deed is done there is not the smallest doubt that between the French and ourselves we have wiped out a total of two German army corps and we have made them bring back three corps from Russia, this ought to save the situation as far as she is concerned enable her to pull herself together and gradually take the offensive. I went to poor Tommy Capper's funeral on Thursday [30 September], he was shot through the lung, but had no business to have been there where he was as he rode across the open to lead on a battalion instead of doing his proper work but he is a loss. Poor Thesiger[84] was killed on Fosse No. 8 and they have not got his body yet. Today I hear that poor Freddy Wing[85] and his ADC have been killed by a shell, it is a great pity for he had a very good New Army division and they are going to be in the attack on Tuesday [5 October]. The divisions of the New Army 21st and 24th did not do well the former simply could not stand the shelling and bolted, I was very much afraid when I heard the experiment was going to be made and Haking [GOC XI Corps] would have done much better to have put the Guards Division straight in with a brigade to each of the others, the officers of the New Army cannot possibly have the experience until we break them in gradually by which means they get accustomed to it. The German parapets were a masterpiece, the dug outs were eight feet below the ground level and underneath their parapets, nothing except the 8 inch and 9.2 howitzers had any effect on them but it had its objections because my lot attacked at dawn and we kept the bombardment up until the last seemed the result being they could not get out of their dug outs in time to man the parapets. I think after this week it will come to a full stop as neither side will have the men or ammunition to go on with it at this rate, we shall then sit down for the winter and by February be able to take the offensive with practically all our resources mobilised and large accumulations of ammunition. The piece of ground captured by the 1st and 4th Corps is a mass of desolation and it is desperate work making all the communication trenches and parapets when all the material has to be carried up in the open so far. Best love Yours ever Putty.

It was probably not just the bombardment being kept going to the last which was responsible for the infantry reaching the enemy parapets before they got out of their dugouts. There were three other factors: it was a very misty morning; the distance to be covered was 250 yards or less

---

84   Major General George Handcock Thesiger (1868-1915) Eton late RB GOC 9th Division killed in action 26 September.
85   Major General Frederick Drummond Vincent Wing (1860-1915) late RA GOC 12th Division killed in action 2 October.

and the rate of advance does not seem to have been restricted; and the Germans seem to have been caught out which did not happen often.

Putty also wrote to Edith Londonderry on 3 October:

Dearest La Motte, Thanks for your letter of the 29 Sep, have got an easy morning at last so will tell you what news I can and send it back by the Howler tomorrow. I don't know Nugent [GOC 36th Division] but am writing a letter to Jack Cowans which he can pass on, recommending Charlie if it is not too late. We got back to the chateau from our advanced post last night but we begin to fight again on Tuesday [5 October] with a bit of a bombardment tomorrow but we can't do much attacking as we hold such an enormous front we have taken over half of the Indian line as well as what we held before Charley went away so you can gauge what it is. I enclose you a letter from Maurice Wingfield (now AA&QMG HQ 7th Division – letter described 7th Division's attack and death of General Capper) which should interest you and Charley when you have done with it send it me back, I went to Tommy Capper's funeral and had to walk with Sir John French and General D'Urbal[86] so was a bit of a swell. Now to tell you about things in general since 25 Sep, the fighting has been on a desperate scale, the casualties are very high but the results justified it on the whole, the weather did us badly, it turned hopelessly wet and cold, the wind was wrong in direction for the gas except for the 1st and 4th Corps, the Indians tried to use it but only gassed themselves and stopped the rest about the 8th Division I told you Haking's corps was too late coming up when it did Forestier-Walker's division 21st was leading, it arrived at 6.35 pm instead of 2 pm it had not been fed so could not attack until next morning when it did it got badly shelled and turned around and did a 'bunk' now they are called the 'Hookey' division and will be ever afterwards, the 24th were not much better and Thesiger [GOC 9th Division] left the 9th to try and rally one of its brigades and was killed on the Fosse, of course he ought never to have left his own division which had been terribly cut up but he tried to pull round the whole situation, this beastly Fosse which is in reality a heap of stuff out of the mine commands the whole country and we must take it to do any real good and that is what they are going for next week. The Guards Division did very well there were 100 casualties among the officers, Harold Cuthbert in the Scots Guards is missing which I am very sorry for he was on my staff in S Africa, Norman Orr-Ewing has been hit again etc. Poor Freddy Wing who commanded 12th Division was killed with his ADC yesterday, he is a great loss the more especially as his division is to attack on Tuesday, they must take this Fosse No 8 before they can do any more good. All blessings Yours ever Putty ... Binning[87] is coming to dine tonight.

Next day Putty inspected 1 RIR (25 Bde) at Pont Mortier and other troops of 8th Division that had been relieved and withdrawn for a brief rest.

The operations planned for 5 October were postponed by 1st Army, mainly because of the adverse weather. That day General Sir John Cowans (QMG WO) wrote to Theresa Londonderry with whom he corresponded regularly:

86   General Victor D'Urbal (1858-1953) GOC 10th French Army.
87   Brigadier General Lord George Baillie-Hamilton Binning (1856-1917) late RHG Eton Comd 41 Bde 14th Division.

I quite concur in a great deal of what you say particularly about C. I have been doing all I can and stirred up Carson (Sir Edward Carson Attorney General) to do likewise; but of course it lay entirely with the General commanding the Ulster Division, and I wrote again to him yesterday, enclosing a letter from Putty on the subject. Of course there is a certain amount in what the General urged when approached, that C had no infantry experience, and that it meant the lives of about 4000 men being put under a man without sufficient experience. Against this I urged that he had a year's experience out there, and that they might give him good staff officers, as no doubt the Ulstermen would follow him far better than any other man; and after all, local influence and experience of war combined, seem to make a pretty good case for him. We will have to see what the General replies from France, as they have now gone over there.

Theresa Londonderry's attempts to get her son, C (Charlie), and previously Putty's ADC, command of a brigade in the Ulster (36th) Division did not find favour with the GOC[88] Putty also wrote to Ettie on 5 October:

My dear Chief, Your letter of 1 Oct reached me after I had posted one to you yesterday by Charlie Hindlip, will send this by Hebester tomorrow. My part of the attack is over and what was to have taken place today has been put off on account of the absolutely vile cold weather so it probably won't take place for a week. Douglas Haig was bitterly disappointed by the two New Army divisions the 21st and 24th, not so much that they failed in the attack but they lost ground that had already been won in front of which two battalions were still fighting which of course have never been heard of since. Winston has no business to go about saying the attack has already failed we have given them a tremendous knock, have practically wiped out three corps and pulled the weight off Russia at a critical moment, further if it had not been for the Dardanelles our resources would have been nearly doubled and many more trained troops in the field, you cannot make armies in a year, the staff does not exist nor can the officer learn enough in the time, these new divisions knew nothing about a bomb it had to be explained to them but they had never seen a live one except as a rarity. We shall go on in about a week's time as there is a prominent position we must take after that it depends whether the French will be able to continue or not, they have simply wasted their shells in a manner in which even their supplies could not stand. How charming of Kitchener to have telephoned you while the fighting was on I like him a million times better for his having done it. Bestlove Yours ever Putty.

He also wrote to Edith Londonderry along the same lines; additionally:

Dearest La Motte, The enclosed cutting from a German paper (cartoon of delivery of black baby to white woman with caption 'C'est La Guerre') should amuse you. The young baroness is expected back this week we are wondering whether the young man pulled off a push in the air! Bestlove Yours ever Putty.

88   Major General Oliver Stewart Wood Nugent (1860-1929) late KRRC.

The 1st Army attack was again postponed on 9 October; these were days of fine weather and light winds. On 11 October HQ III Corps issued OpO No.56 giving 20th Division revised orders for its demonstration in support of I and IV Corps' attack, and coordinated with a similar demonstration by the Indian Corps. Once again the aim was to hold the enemy to his ground, and prevent him moving reserves to the main point of attack.

On 12 October Putty wrote to Edith Londonderry:

> Dearest La Motte, Thanks for yours of 9 Oct which Stavey brought along with him. Am sorry about Charley and the Ulster Division but understand that Nugent was opposed to it. I do wish Miss Florence (nurse) was not out there (Serbia) one thing if anyone is able to look after herself she is, suppose Reggie's sister is out there too[89] I heard she was engaged to young Chichester who died of typhus but don't know if it was true. Winston throwing 15 Army Corps of the Western Front in to Greece is the maddest thing I have heard of the 'Curio Crew' attempting yet why the devil we have not let these Balkan tribes kill one another without entering in to it defeats me I suppose the failure of the Bulgarian diplomacy will be put down to the army instead of the Dardanelles enterprise which caused it and will cause much more, what possible good can it do our sending an expedition to Salonika you cannot save Serbia which has pulled its weight jolly well, as for the others let them fight it out, if we had only gone to Smyrna in the first instance we should have made the Turks come to us instead of using absolutely no strategy but going bald headed at the main earth it serves us jolly well right for being so weak as to be led by politicians instead of a War Board. K did wonders in raising the armies organising their equipment but he is absolutely ignorant of tactics, strategy or the training of troops, the lawyers laugh at him and turn him round their fingers, how can anyone expect new divisions to fight like the old ones you might just as well try to ride a yearling in the Grand National. We are going to have a go tomorrow at Fosse No 8 and the Hohenzollern redoubt if it is a day like today I think they will just about do it it should make us a good front line for the winter instead of a very bad one. The German counter-attack on 8 Oct was real good business, about 11 battalions attacked on the front held by the Guards Division of which only two battalions were holding the trenches, they came on in dense lines and were mown down by machine-gun and rifle fire, after the first repulse they came on again and after being driven back they attempted to form behind the Bois Hugo where they caught it from the artillery. The organisation of the Guards bombers was entirely responsible for the great success, on the other hand the 28th Division lost the Hohenzollern redoubt from being completely bombed out by six Germans, simply because Bulfin [GOC 28th Division] did not believe in bombing and the men were ignorant, the new divisions arriving in the country had never thrown a bomb which shows the sort of situation we have to deal with when one has to attack with them directly they arrive in the country but we live and learn though it is an expensive way. The Ulster Division went down to 3rd Army where they ought to be able to train them all right, am afraid that the discipline is none too good from all accounts but they will pull themselves together out here just like the Canadians did. Gavin Hamilton has had the flue also two of the others but have escaped all right myself. The young baron

---

89   Lady Muriel Herbert (1883-1951). She was.

arrived in his aeroplane yesterday to see his girl and left again in the afternoon, I don't know how his engine worked going back!! The baroness says she sent you a book from Paris but does not think you can have got it as you never acknowledged it. Bestlove Yours ever Putty.

Putty wrote to Ettie Desborough early on 13 October:

My dear Chief, Many thanks for your letter of 11 Oct which I got Monday night, Hebester goes back today so will send this by him. The attack is going to be continued about 2 pm this afternoon we hope to get Fosse 8 and the Hohenzollern redoubt, the wind seems pretty right for the gas if it does not turn later, personally I don't think much will be done after this show there is sure to be a big counter-attack and all our efforts will be concentrated on making the line impregnable and then dividing out the line for the winter, train the new divisions, and get ready for the Spring. My corps is only demonstrating today am holding too extended front to do anything else viz practically half that held by the First Army but the smoke will bring down a lot of artillery fire until they ascertain where the main attack is to be. We got down two German aeroplanes yesterday, their pilots are all mechanics with an officer as observer, one of the observers yesterday was scowling at his pilot for he said he had no business to have come down, the other officer in the other machine had his leg broken for the machine turned over on getting to the ground the English one that shot its petrol tank was down on the ground all right almost as soon as he was like a hawk on a bird, they are fine fellows these aviators and give no information away. We are busy making shelters and beds for the winter, the amount of material we are getting is very good in comparison to the meagre allowance last winter. Must finish. Bestlove Yours ever Putty.

That morning (13 October) at 11.50 am DDMS noted: 'Special Ward (26 Fd Amb) doing well. There will be 10 cases for transfer in barge by 15 Oct. Corps Commander visited while I was there'. They were both determined to make the system work; both were there again the following morning at 11 am. DDMS recorded:

Landing stage for barge set up. Not far enough out from the bank, while Lieutenant Colonel Thomson and I were pointing this out to the workmen the Corps Commander came up and gave them an order to make the water end of the stage almost flush with the bank, which involves using 12' instead of 10' poles (several barges with heating now in use).

III Corps' part of 1st Army's attack started with wire cutting by 18 pdrs; at 12.30 pm smoke was released along the whole front and the guns turned on the enemy's front and second line parapets. Two battalions of 60 Bde 20th Division made a feint attack using dummies which were made of sacks stuffed with straw, clothed in old salvaged greatcoats and with caps also salvaged or else lent by the men. The enemy opened heavy rifle, machine-gun and artillery fire, with the dummies attracting particular attention. The demonstration was successful and the enemy suffered heavily from the shell fire; 20th Division had 50 casualties.

20th Division continued to attract the attention of the enemy's artillery on 15 October; perhaps, because of the success of the demonstration two days earlier, the enemy still expected to be attacked. The Battle of Loos officially ended on 16 October. III Corps had been mainly involved on 25 September, and since then its efforts had been diversionary to prevent the enemy moving troops to the S. Putty had done all that he had been asked to do within the constraints he was given, and should have learnt some important lessons for future offensive operations.

Meanwhile Haig (17 October) was concentrating on other matters: 'I had come to the conclusion that it was not fair to the Empire to retain French in command. Moreover, none of my officers commanding corps had any opinion of Sir John French's military ability or military views: in fact, they had no confidence in him'. That an army commander should canvas his corps commanders on the abilities of the CinC is extraordinary; Putty was one of them and it must be presumed had also given his views, but this is strange given his loyalty to French. Perhaps he too had realised the time had come for a change.

To improve the training of the new troops 70 Bde 23rd Division exchanged with 24 Bde 8th Division on 18 October. In 8th Division battalions of 70 Bde were then exchanged with battalions of 23 and 25 Bdes to form three amalgamated brigades. A similar rearrangement took place in 23rd Division so that at least one battalion of the older formation was in each brigade. The advantage was not all one way, the men of 23rd Division brought a 'keenness and enthusiasm that acted like a tonic'. This arrangement was completed on 24 October and continued in part into the Battle of the Somme; it ceased on 16 July 1916.

Putty wrote to Ettie Desborough on 19 October:

> My dear Chief, Thanks for your letter of 16 Oct, no the attack last Wednesday [13 October] was a failure but at the same time the Germans do deserve credit for having stuck to Fosse 8, I honestly do not think any other troops in the world would have stood the artillery fire of 380 guns of every calibre which was directed on it, the gas did not come off the drift of the wind was the wrong way, my demonstration was a great success for I drew an enormous quantity of shelling and rifle fire, I lost one officer killed 5 wounded and about (fifty) other casualties I really think we killed a good lot of them as we arranged dummies climbing over the parapets which they fired at like mad while we raked their trenches with maxims from a flank, one of the dummies had 12 bullet holes through it. Troops are evidently going off to Salonika from here I regret to say the 28th Division leave for Marseilles at once but I don't know what other divisions, they asked for eight but they could not be spared at the present time. I heard Charlie Londonderry was to leave London today to rejoin the Blues, all the cavalry are being sent out another 100 men to each regiment to ensure that the horses are properly looked after when they go in to the trenches, this is a sound policy. What a fright your poor people at Panshanger must have had with the Zeppelins, the shooting of our anti aircraft guns leaves much to be desired, they should invent an aerial torpedo to be directed by electricity, everybody I hear is buying fire extinguishers. The stories about the behaviour of the Welsh Guards last month are none too pleasant hearing several of them surrendered without cause, that is the worst of having no traditions to keep up. I don't think we shall do much before the beginning of next month, if only this lovely weather would last we should soon be well over part of the winter. All love and blessings For ever Putty.

On 21 October HQ III Corps issued OpO No.57, orders for an attack by all three divisions in support of another 1st Army attack. The hope of a further offensive that year was still well alive and it was essential to maintain an offensive spirit behind the line, a line that became ever stronger.

There was mist every day with a light E wind for much of the time. Trench warfare continued with the enemy exploding a mine on 22 October opposite the right of 20th Division and close to their own parapet. They attempted to occupy the crater but were prevented by fire from doing so.

Next day DDMS noted: '12 noon. 71 Fd Amb. I took some slippers presented by the Corps Commander and handed to OC for use in Rest Station'. Putty was determined that men in the Corps Rest Station should be able to keep their boots off but the army provided no alternative footwear, so he, with the help of Ettie Desborough, provided slippers at his own expense; this was the first of many such consignments from England.

The staff work generated by 1st Army was nowhere near as onerous as that by 2nd Army under Smith-Dorrien, but there was still a lot of it; on 25 October HQ III Corps sent a return (G1157) to 1st Army describing the state of defences in rear of front line and another (G1159) describing the preparations for the winter.

On 26 October Putty wrote to Ettie:

> My dear Chief, Hebester goes back tomorrow so will send you a line. Am more depressed at not getting 3rd Army again than I can say, I know that squint eyed Agrippa Kitchener has got a down on me but don't mind that half so much as to think Sir John French won't stand up about it. Yesterday was terribly wet, all the assembly places are full of water and the question is how we are going to get them dry again in time to attack. Except for shelling the Germans have been very quiet all this week opposite my corps though down S the fighting has been pretty incessant. Some of the munition workers were round my trenches on Saturday [23 October], I sent Gavin Hamilton with them, he was much interested especially as one came from his place, they said they were paying off all the young unmarried men and filling up their places with old ones, giving the young ones a card saying 'Your King and Country need you'. Have not seen the King yet but hope to on Thursday [28 October] when he is going to inspect the Guards Division, I wish he could have come round my corps but he can't do them all, they appreciated it so much last year. Poor Jack Trefusis[90] was killed on Sunday morning looking over a parapet, it is a great pity for he was one of the most promising young soldiers, you can only do it for a few seconds or else you are playing the Germans' game, owing to the telescopic sights their shooting is wonderfully good, it does seem ages to get those things out here, have only got twenty three rifles fitted with them in my corps even now. The bombs at last are coming along well, they are absolutely essential in this cads' warfare. Have got Linlithgow[91] coming on Sunday in Charley's place, they say he is a very capable keen young fellow and full of fun. The roads are just beginning to get too awful slippery for the motors one sees the drivers glaring at one another as which is going to give way from the middle of the road. Bestlove Yours ever Putty.

---

90   Brigadier General Hon John Frederick Hepburn-Stuart-Forbes-Trefusis late SG (1878-1915) Comd 20 Bde 7th Division died of wounds 24 October.
91   Lieutenant Victor Alexander John Hope 2nd Marquess of Linlithgow Lothians and Border Horse (1887-1952) Eton.

He also wrote to Edith Londonderry:

> Dearest La Motte, I apologise about Charley, though why you should not tell me it was on the cards I am d...d if I know instead of letting all the gossips like Jemmy Rothschild give it me as information. Am so sick about not getting the 3rd Army I really can only just hold up my head, it is that squint eyed Agrippa nigger who is at the bottom of it he gets some of my home truths thrust at him, he knows as much about European fighting as the King of Siam, but I don't mind that part but what cuts me to the core is Sir John French not sticking up for me and insisting on it. Beef (probably CO RHG) and Reggie came over for luncheon here one day last week to tell me about the 'Charley' muddle as you say there must be something very radically wrong for such a thing to happen. Have got Linlithgow coming as my ADC on 1 Nov in Charley's place, Binning[92] gives me a very good account of him, from the things he and Doreen[93] write to one another about, he ought to be all right in our company. Doreen tells me she is very glad to have had a girl as a War Baby instead of a boy, I tell her she is stupid as what you want is a man with a 'gun' though if she is any child of hers she will probably be able to place 'the guns' well in the coverts. I heard from Salonika on Sunday the 10th Division under Mahon[94] got there on 8 Oct. We are preparing for more offensive down in these parts, there is no doubt we have got the Germans well bustled and cannot allow them to settle down comfortably for the winter. Every blessing Yours ever Putty.

3rd Army had become vacant again when Monro was sent to Gallipoli, and Allenby was appointed. Linlithgow was to be one of Putty's ADCs for eighteen months: after the war he was to be a Minister in the Conservative Governments of the 1920s and 1930s before being appointed Governor General and Viceroy of India from 1936 to 1943. His son, 3rd Marquess, served in the Scots Guards.

On 27 October III Corps received orders from 1st Army that preparations for offensive operations were to be completed by 7 November. Four days later offensive operations were postponed by 1st Army because the Indian Corps was to be withdrawn and the other corps' frontages would have to be adjusted.

III Corps casualties in October were: 7 officers and 164 other ranks killed, 34 officers and 731 other ranks wounded, 1 officer and 7 other ranks missing = 944.

November

On 1 November Putty held a conference of his divisional commanders to plan the next offensive operation. Also that day the enemy shelled the rear areas of 20th Division heavily, an indication that they still expected an attack on that part of the line; also a reminder that the enemy's artillery was able to reach deep behind the front.

---

92   Son of the 11th Earl of Haddington and late RHG Comd 41 Bde.
93   Doreen Maud née Milner Marchioness of Linlithgow (1886-1965).
94   Lieutenant General Bryan Mahon (1862-1939) late 8 H GOC 10th Division and British Expeditionary Force Serbia.

Putty sent his monthly report to the King that day with his usual covering letter:

My dear Fritz, I trust when this reaches you His Majesty will have got back none the worse for his journey and that the recovery may be rapid, he must have been very fit to have stood the shock so well, it was too unfortunate and I only thank my stars I did not provide the horse or the cheers, otherwise should have expected orders to proceed forthwith to Mesopotamia. There is very little in the monthly diary of the 3rd Corps for this month, the whole corps has been spread out covering a front nearly equal to the whole of the rest of the First Army, this has put a considerable strain on the troops but am glad to say that my line is going to be shortened and I shall be able to give the troops rest. Both the New Army divisions 20th and 23rd are shaping very well, if they continue at their present rate they will surpass the regular divisions. I was doubtful at first of the 23rd but now have every confidence in them and the training does Babington credit. We are preparing for offensive movements this month, there is no doubt the preparation for offense does the troops good and wakes up the proper fighting spirit. Bombs have come along well this month and we are well supplied with one kind 'Mills' which is very good indeed. Trench mortars and bombs for same is what we are behindhand in, ours have been a failure because of the supply of ammunition for them and those bombs which were supplied having such a large proportion of 'blinds' the fault of the fuse. I took Charles Cust[95] round my trenches so he can tell you what Flanders mud is like at present, we don't anticipate getting much worse before the middle of December taking last year as our guide, from that date until middle of February it is a case of water existence in the part of the line which I hold but thanks to all the breastworks, tram lines, floor boards etc that we have put down it will be a picnic to what they went through last winter. Yours ever, WP Pulteney.

Some senior officers were unsympathetic to the New Armies: Putty seems to have been very supportive from the outset. Next day (2 November) orders were received from 1st Army for XI Corps to relieve Indian Corps on III Corps' right and for XI Corps to take over line from III Corps as far N as Fauquissart cross-roads (exclusive to XI Corps) on night 14/15 November. III Corps' line was to be significantly shortened.

Putty wrote to Ettie:

My dear Chief, Many thanks for your letter of 27 Oct, Gavin Hamilton is going on leave tomorrow so will send this by him. I did not know Ivo Charteris[96] but from all accounts he is a very great loss in every way. Am at last depressed, very sore at heart, I consider that I have been treated in an unjust manner and I want to know if you will ask Mr Balfour his advice, my idea is to appeal to the King but should like to know if he thinks that is the correct course to take. As you know the original three army corps were commanded by Haig, Smith-Dorrien and self so you will see I am a long way the senior corps commander in the country. I maintain that the 3rd Corps has done better than any other corps all the way through from the beginning of the war, I have had no less than eleven divisions

---

95   Commander Sir Charles Leopold Cust (1864-1939) RN Equerry to The Prince of Wales.
96   2nd Lieutenant Hon Yvo Alan Charteris (1896-1915) Gren Gds son of 11th Earl of Wemyss killed in action 17 October.

through my hands, eight of which have served in my corps and three others I have trained fit to take their place in the line the 4th and 6th Divisions were each taken away in their turn to save the situation at Ypres which they did, the 27th came down from Ypres a mob and I sent it away one of the best, I was recommended by Sir John French for the command of the 3rd Army when it was given to Monro and now as a recompense they put five Lieutenant Generals over my head, whereas if there had been no war I was to be promoted a Lieutenant General in October 1914, it makes me feel as if I had been a failure in serving my King which wounds me deeply, I enclose you a list of the divisions so as to give you an idea of the work, am afraid I am boring you with my grievances and asking you to do so much but must unburden myself to someone I can trust. The weather is very bad, the trenches are full of water once more, the leaves are nearly all off the trees and memories of last Flanders winter returning very vividly, we are much better prepared than we were last year but then the men expect more and there are many much younger men and inexperienced to deal with. The Indian Corps is going away to Mesopotamia which is a very wise decision, the troops would not have stood the winter, they represented a positive danger in the line and when offensive operations were in progress four or five used to desert to the enemy which gave the show away, am glad to say 11 [XI] Corps is coming to take their place with the Guards Division in it, they will be next to me in the line which will be jolly. Poor Monro I do not envy him his job, nor have I the smallest confidence in his staff officer Lynden-Bell,[97] [Pulteney's initial reports were good so something must have happened in July 1915 to change his opinion] who is as crooked as his eye, but I wish the Gallipoli lot well without disaster whatever Monro may decide for they have made a splendid fight all the time with their backs to the wall, the whole business is the fault of not having a proper General Staff in London to manage things, so to mend that they make Archie Murray[98] a failure out here Chief of the General Staff we really are a marvellous nation. I took Charlie Cust all-round a section of my trenches, he was like a school boy looking through the periscope and seeing all the trench arrangements he really did enjoy it but seemed tired after the walk. Best of love For ever Putty.

He also wrote to the Marquess of Londonderry:

My dear Charley, Many thanks for your letters of the 21 and 30 Oct have been in such a bad temper lately have not been in the mood to write letters. I entirely agree with you that my being passed over for promotion will have to be challenged, am just going to make sure of my ground with Douglas Haig and Sir John French and then move in the matter in the meantime am asking the advice of a man in whose judgement I have implicit trust. From all I can get hold of at present Swivel Eyed Agrippa, Rawlie, Smith-Dorrien and a snake in the grass Lynden-Bell are the only people who have ever had a single word against me, Agrippa's reasons I know not except that my criticisms of his policy may have reached his ears, Rawlie was jealousy combined with the red herring to cover his own faults, Smith-D was merely trying to hit Sir John through me in addition to vanity and

---

97   Brigadier General Lynden-Bell BGGS III Corps 25 Feb-13 Jul 1915.
98   General Sir Archibald James Murray (1860-1945) late R Innis Fus CIGS Sep-Dec 1915.

egotism, Lynden-Bell was a spy with a cock instead of a swivel eye. Few people realise the divisions that I have trained, pulled round and made efficient but they are: 4th, 6th and 19 Bde, 8th, 9th, 12th, 20th, 23rd, 27th, 46th, 48th, 1st Canadian Division. Every single one has done well, the pulling together of the 27th Division from an undisciplined mob was worth promotion to Lieutenant General alone, the above are hard facts for the Army Council or Coalition Government of HM to get over even if Agrippa can, what makes it still harder is that without this war I should have been a Lieutenant General in September 1914 and had been picked for same by the Army Council. Best of luck Yours ever Putty.

He wrote to Edith Londonderry on 3 November:

Dearest La Motte, Many thanks for yours of the 28 Oct have been too angry to answer it before, I have applied to see Sir John French about being passed over for promotion but he has gone to England so must wait until he returns if I get no satisfaction out of him shall apply to see the King, when one is the senior corps commander out here and have had eleven divisions through your hands, all of who have done well one is entitled to be heard, further the 3rd Corps got further E than any other corps, has held the longest front of any corps in the army for a whole year, has never lost an inch of ground, has got the best trenches and the best system of defences, although in the wettest ground, it was bad enough being passed over as an army commander but to have five Lieutenant Generals put over one's head is beyond the limit, just because of a crooked eye Agrippa K and a swivel eyed spy Lynden-Bell. The rain has been perfectly awful the last few days and all the old floods are out again the Lys is back high, the communication trenches are like ladies legs accommodating themselves to water channels as well as communication purposes, of course we are much better prepared than we were last year but then the men expect more, they are younger and not so experienced, however we shall hold our own against the Boche in everything except trench mortars which we are hopelessly deficient of and for which the ammunition is hopelessly inadequate besides being almost worthless from bad fuzes, in eleven shots last week only four detonated the other seven being blind. The King's accident was a great misfortune, the men cheered too soon, the horse had a different bit in its mouth and came right over on top of him in fact he got well out of it, thank goodness I did not supply the horse or should have been sent off with the Indian Corps to Mesopotamia. Gavin Hamilton is going home this morning so will send this by him, Linlithgow has turned up to take Charley's place he is tall enough under all conscience. Hear from Granard at Salonika on Saturday [30 October] dated 20th they had not moved up country, I gather the British troops are only to guard the railway and protect the port, of course they ought to send all the mountain guns out there without delay. I don't envy Charles Monro his job, if he retires he should be sent out an enormous quantity of gas and smoke and retire under cover of it but I don't suppose they will allow anything so practical. What news have you had of Miss Florence in Serbia I do hope she is all right. The 11th Corps is coming with the Guards Division next to us I am glad to say so shall see some pals when I go through Merville of a morning. The baroness is away, my servant is taking on the governess which shows the dearth in the land, it does him great credit being able to manage it for she is positively hideous. Best love Yours ever Putty.

For the next week the weather was fine but it was getting colder and there was a frost on the night of 6 November. The pattern of trench warfare continued with shelling and sniping, mining, patrols and working parties: there was never any let up. At 12 noon on 7 November III Corps issued OpO No.58 – Relief of Indian Corps by XI Corps on right of III Corps and adjustment of corps boundary at 10 am 10 November.

Also that day Haig recorded a conversation he had when Robertson told him: 'Lord K recently promoted Birdwood to be a Lieutenant General over the heads of Rawlinson, Pulteney and many others'. This seems to confirm that Kitchener made the decisions on appointment and promotion of senior officers, and, for some unexplained reason, was against Putty.

Putty wrote to Ettie again on 9 November:

> My dear Chief, Many thanks for your two letters, I quite agree with all you did. I went to see Sir John French yesterday [8 November], he said he had done all he could, he blamed Kitchener entirely for all that had happened but I gathered that Haig had been running Rawlinson, however as long as I had French's confidence I did not mind though personally much doubt his lasting much longer either from health or from other causes, I did not mind being passed over for the command of the army half as much as I did having five Lieutenant Generals put over my head, but whatever happens one must go on doing one's best for the main cause. Kitchener should go back to Egypt if things go wrong in the Balkans he would pull more weight, carry more authority and do more good in that country than anywhere else. The ground is getting in a dreadful state not so much from the rain as from the water which is coming down from Béthune and Festubert direction it is filling up all the ditches sending down all the rats in to our trenches, reminding us too vividly of last winter, we are better prepared but we expect more. The Guards Division has come next to me in the line am glad to say so shall see many pals now. All blessings For ever Putty.

Orders were received on 10 November for the redistribution of artillery in 1st Army and from 13 November III Corps was allotted:

> Corps Artillery
> 25 Bde RGA – 23 and 24 Siege Btys each with 4 × 6" hows (range 6800 HE)
> 4 Bde RGA – 109, 110, 118 and Warwick Hy Btys each with 4 × 4.7" guns (range 12000 HE and 8500 S)
> Attached to III Corps from 1st Army HAG:
> HQ 26 Bde RGA
> One section 34 Siege Bty with 2 × 9.2" hows (range 9500 HE)
> 30 Siege Bty (less one section) with 2 × 8" hows (range 11000 HE)
> One sub-section 29 Siege Bty with 1 × 6" gun (range 18000 HE and 13500 S)

That day HQ RA III Corps was formed from existing staff with Brigadier General Stokes as CRA. III Corps was now much better able to support its divisions but there were also greater demands for planning and coordination both of fire and the logistic support required to sustain it.

On 14 November, with the Guards Division now on its right and the line shortened, III Corps was able to withdraw 8th Division and hold the line with two divisions, each division having two brigades in the front line and one in reserve. 8th Division was to be in Corps and Army Reserve. Orders (III Corps OpO No.59) to implement this were issued on 15 November.

Captain Jack 2 Cameronians (23 Bde 8th Division) wrote of conditions at that time:

> The nights are cold. I manage, however, to sustain a little heat in my body by means of an open coke stove in the shelter. The fumes partially asphyxiate callers with less sound lungs than mine. Muddy as the line is, it is dry compared with its knee-deep state all last winter when the infantry were not nearly so often out of it.

Putty wrote again to Ettie on 16 November:

> My dear Chief, Thanks for your letter of the 11 Nov I think we shall leave the matter to take its natural course without taking any further steps by saying anything to A.J.B., there is a very strong undercurrent in my favour in the army over here and my own divisions will do anything for me, also all those who have served under me and after all that gives me a far better feeling of life in one's blood than any personal promotion can. There is no doubt but that we are gradually getting the best of the Germans on the Western Front, we have got to train our army as a fighting machine before the spring, you cannot expect us or our staffs to be able to turn out new formations in a minimum time, however gallant the material you must have the old experienced hands at the right moment to give the necessary confidence, musketry is the chief failing, the new divisions cannot shoot, rifle ranges and rifle clubs want organising at home and each division should have its own depot at home. The rain has brought us to a standstill, the ground is full of water, the height of the river Lys is the dominating factor with us here, all is a repetition of last year, we are much better prepared but then the men expect much more, last year we hung on by the eyelids this year we grieve because it prevents one attacking. Have got the Guards Division next to me which is delightful. Cavan,[99] John Ponsonby, Esmé Lennox,[100] Geoffrey Feilding[101] have all found their way here to luncheon or dinner it does me real good to see fellows so pleased to see me. If the King ever visits King George's Hospital have a look at the 3rd Corps Ward and see if there are any additions to its comfort that you can suggest to me. All blessings For ever Putty.

Putty never received any explanation as to why he was passed over for promotion to Lieutenant General.

He wrote to Adv 1st Army on 18 November (Ref 1st Army 137d/d 15 Nov) on the 'destruction of three church towers and one culvert, in addition to the bridges over the River Lys – contingency planning in the event of retirement'. Putty tried to make several contingency plans

---

99   Major General Frederick Rudolph Lambert 10th Earl of Cavan (1865-1946) Eton late Gren Gds GOC Guards Division.

100   Lieutenant Colonel Lord Esmé Charles Gordon-Lennox (1875-1949) Eton CO 1 SG son of 7th Duke of Richmond – Putty was his son's godfather.

101   Brigadier General Geoffrey Feilding (1866-1932) late Coldm Gds Comd 1 Gds Bde.

but it was difficult to make any for a possible withdrawal because the French authorities had to be consulted, and were reluctant to agree to any demolitions.

The same day at 7 pm HQ III Corps issued OpO No.60 for bombardment by artillery and machine-gun fire on 20 November and vacation of trenches from 10.30 am to 2.15 pm. This was the first recorded III Corps Artillery attack linked to a vacation of the front line trenches, which were very close at this point, thus allowing the heavy artillery to fire on the enemy mine shafts and to do as much damage as possible to personnel and material in the front line. Machine-gun fire was to be brought to bear on the area in rear of this point at certain periods during the day and night with the object of preventing and hindering repairs. This attack seemed to be very successful and provoked little enemy reaction.

It continued to get colder with overnight frosts. HQ III Corps issued a memo to divisions (G29) on 20 November stating the policy to be pursued during the winter. There were four main principles: 'Fitness, short as time as possible in trenches, planning for counter-attacks, and small enterprises'.

Putty wrote to Theresa Londonderry on 20 November:

> Dear Lady Londonderry, Thank you for your letter of the 19 Nov. The 3rd Army Corps paid for the sixteen beds of the ward at King George's Hospital and further they paid for the equipment of the ward itself and I hope you will convey this fact to Lady Ripon.[102] As I told you in my last letter, if there are any more things which each bed could require in the 3rd Corps room I am sure I could get the money for the necessary equipment. Yours very sincerely WP Pulteney.

He also wrote to the Marquess of Londonderry on 21 November:

> My dear Charlie, I owe you a letter though I have no news, many thanks for the cake and ginger breads, the latter were excellent. I don't think that I got much good over my case as Sir John simply referred to the scores of others who had been passed over and swore at Agrippa for doing it, further I found that Haig had been pressing Rawlinson's case without having taken up mine, further that Haig had not backed me in the first instance about 3rd Army but had somewhat naturally gone for Monro who had been under him all the time, so altogether I wish I had held my tongue as it has made me look as considering self too much. The trenches and parapets stood the first lot of floods very fairly well though most of last year's sandbags have gone burst, was in the old Rue du Bois salient this morning the blighters had the cheek to shell the communication trench all the way up just as we walked up the famous Shaftesbury Avenue which was pretty fair impertinence. It is very jolly having the Guards Division at Merville near one [,] one sees a lot of pals, Alby Cator, G Trotter, Stanley[103] etc have all been to dinner. Count Schreiber [BGRE III Corps] is splendid with his pumps from what I can make out he puts the water back in the same trench he takes it out of. Best of luck Yours ever WP Pulteney.

---

102 Possibly Constance Gwladys née Herbert Marchioness of Ripon (1859-1917).
103 Hon Ferdinand Charles Stanley (1871-1935) late Gren Gds later Comd 89 Bde.

8th Division was withdrawn from the line between 22 and 24 November. DMS 1st Army wanted 26 Fd Amb to accompany its parent division but Putty wished it to remain because it provided the Special Ward. This provoked considerable correspondence and debate but Putty prevailed and 26 Fd Amb remained. On 24 November 20th Division assumed command of the right sector from 10 am, with its HQ at Sailly now vacated by 8th Division: 23rd Division held the left sector and 8th Division was in reserve between Hazebrouck and Aire.

On 25 November Putty wrote again to the Marquess of Londonderry:

> My dear Charley, Thanks for your letter of 23 Nov, am delighted to hear there is a chance of your coming out again it will do you and the regiment both good. Sir John French is coming over here tomorrow to do the usual talk with the divisional generals so he may have some news but we have none at all. We have pulled the 8th Division out of the line and it has gone right away back to train and rest for a month, it is the first time it has been out of the line since it came into the country, it wants some more fighting spirit put in to it as well it has sat down in those trenches too long. Am glad there are other people you can catch the flue from besides me, I had my usual three day cold last week but quinine knocked it out all right. Let me know when you come out. Yours ever Putty.

Putty had been despondent and this is reflected in his letters. Considering his performance over the previous eighteen months it was surprising that he should have been passed over for promotion but perhaps more extraordinary that no-one should have told him the reason for it. Putty's own thoughts on this matter may well be correct, considering the outspokenness in his letters to Ettie Desborough and Edith Londonderry. Inevitably they would have discussed the contents with others including members of the government, and Kitchener would have had little difficulty in discovering where such views had come from. In any event Putty seems to have put his disappointment to one side very quickly and got on with his job.

Snow fell during the afternoon of 26 November. The CinC visited HQ III Corps and saw the corps staff and divisional commanders: an inspection of 8th Division was cancelled because of the weather. Putty wrote to GOC II Corps that day (Ref II Corps G30 dtd 24 Nov 1915) – emphasising the importance of Wez Macquart road on his left flank as a probable enemy approach should they take offensive action.

He also wrote to Ettie on 26 November:

> My dear Chief, Many thanks for yours of 20 Nov. Charlie C. wrote to me yesterday telling me he was probably coming out, everything having been arranged satisfactorily they were quite right not to leave Harold in command he is a very charming personality but lazy and indifferent as a soldier. Linlithgow seems an intelligent person with a certain amount of ability which should have been developed on different lines, you can see he has been spoilt, he had to be put in to his place which he took well and shows he is made of the right stuff, his mind is as much of a sink as Doreen's or Putty's which is saying a good deal. Tom Guerney[104] apparently wrote to his wife giving her full particulars of an offensive movement which was in preparation at the moment, the absolute indiscretion of a cavalry

---

104 Probably Major Tom Claud Gurney (1880-1963) LG Eton.

soldier to his wife but which were little short of criminal to put on paper if viewed from the fact that the German General Staff should have given evidence to the information coming from such a reliable source, of course the boys are hopeless in what they write but they are mere joke to the things they say when they go on leave or return wounded neither of which shortcomings ever reach the eye of the censor even if they do his ears indirectly. Practically no news from this part of the world, I have pulled the 8th Division out of the line and am holding my front with two of the new divisions both of whom shape very well, the 8th are I hope going to have a rest until 1 Jan it is the first time they have been out of the trenches since they came out in November last year, discipline is what they want taught, the company and platoon commanders get no chance in the trenches now they will train their men not less themselves and go back in 1916 quite a different sort of soldier. The Germans feed their soldiers well twelve prisoners taken last week had their blood examined by Bowlby[105] he says the quality of their blood is higher than our men as regards power of circulation and resistance, this is the result of discipline and careful feeding, trench feet is unknown to them, here they have the best of us because we cannot train new formations to learn these things quick enough though am glad to say that the 3rd Corps wins easily in all the statistics of immunity so far, soldiers friends and parents at home should be instructed what are good things to send out to the men, my idea is what he wants as a gift is condensed milk, cocoa, tea, porridge, postcards, writing paper pretty well in the order named, you would never believe the amount they write, I have started writing rooms for them in some of the barns, it seems to make them more human than anything else. Yes do go and see the 3rd Corps ward at the St George's Hospital tell me if there are any little things you can think of as practical adjuncts to the comfort of the patients such as book rests, holdalls etc. Bestlove Yours ever Putty.

There was a sharp frost overnight 27/28 November. The GS log recorded (28 November):

Bombardment of gun positions at Satte Rue arranged for today was abandoned. During registration hostile aeroplanes interrupted. After they had been driven off insufficient time remained to carry out the programme.

Also that day DDMS noted:

9 am. Corps Commander thinks puttees are a mistake as they constrict the circulation. I agree. He thinks a canvas gaiter put on loose over the lower ends of the legs would meet all requirements. I think 'loose trousers' is the best – a bicycle clip might be provided for use when necessary to march over rough ground or obstacles.

Ideas such as these were invariably discussed at DDMS' conferences with ADMS of divisions and DA&QMG HQ III Corps, and then frequently acted on.

The postponed bombardment of the enemy guns at Satte Rue was carried out by heavy artillery on 30 November; the shooting was reported effective. III Corps casualties for November

---

105 Major General Sir Anthony Bowlby (1855-1929) Consulting Surgeon to the Forces.

were: 5 officers and 91 other ranks killed, 10 officers and 403 other ranks wounded, and one other rank missing = 510.

December

On 1 December Putty sent his monthly report to the King:

My dear Fritz, I enclose you the monthly diary of the 3rd Corps for the information of HM The King. Very little of importance has happened during the month except that our front has been shortened which has enabled us to hold the line with two divisions and rest one for a month. I have taken out the 8th Division which has not been out of the line before since it went in November last year. I hope to keep the 8th out until 1 Jan which will give us a chance of really training it as a division, it is lamentable to see how bad the NCOs are from want of training and this I attribute to bad depots where their instruction is neglected, units like the Guards, Rifle Brigade with good depots seem to be able to keep up the standard. The parapets have stood the first heavy rains very fairly well but it is a case of constant repair especially after a frost, the water we are coping with much better than last year but alas so are the Germans opposite me where unfortunately the fall is towards us. Trench feet we have got well in hand, these are a matter of discipline viz keeping the feet rubbed with oil and cleanliness, in my opinion the puttees are the chief cause of the stoppage of the circulation, I should like to see them abandoned and a canvas gaiter worn not higher than the calf of the legs in fact an anklet made of sacking to keep the mud off the trousers and out of the boot. I hope that HM has quite recovered. Yours ever, WP Pulteney.

That same day III Corps Signal School opened at Racquinghem. Also Putty wrote to Ettie:

My dear Chief, Have no news for you but as Hindlip is here and returns tomorrow I send you a line. Snow and frost have gone and it looks like our first flood to be dealt with, we are much better prepared than last year and hope to deal with it all right. The 8th Division are out of the line training until 1 Jan, one does not realise how bad they are until one sees them out of the trenches the NCOs are the weak point, the proper standard is not kept up at the depots at home except with the Guards and the Rifles. I wish the government at home would be firm and insist on a strong General Staff for the army, to my mind either Douglas Haig or Robertson ought to be Chief of the Staff at home, strong men who could advise the government, the latter for choice I should say for he would be better there than in the field. Johnnie Willoughby[106] tells me he is going with Smith-Dorrien[107] to Uganda with his machine-guns, personally should have given the command to Botha and told the Boers we would give them farms there at the end of the war, I understand that the Germans have armed about 30,000 natives and are well off for ammunition which has been run in in dhows etc from Mozambique, I cannot help thinking if they destroyed about ten miles of railway with bridges and culverts the Germans would find some difficulty in repairing

---

106 Probably Lieutenant Colonel Sir John Christopher Willoughby (1859-1918) RHG who provided armoured cars for the campaign.
107 Smith-Dorrien got pneumonia on way out and Smuts was appointed in his place.

it, what a lot of porters they will require and whatever will those herds of game think of it all. We have got no mails today because the Germans have put navies outside Boulogne, we ought to able to catch the submarines doing it I should have thought. Yours ever Putty.

On 3 December BGGS III Corps (Romer) issued a memo (G159) to the divisions copied to BGRA (Stokes):

After reading the weekly programme of artillery action sent in by the divisions, the Corps Commander is of the opinion that his wishes have not been entirely understood. (In the light of less restriction in the use of artillery ammunition) Our aim should be to annoy the enemy and do him as much damage as possible. This can be affected by: (1) Breaking down his parapet, especially his MG emplacements (2) Cutting his wire (3) Bombarding communication trenches, especially junctions, observation posts, battalion headquarters etc. As regards (1), divisions should select points which are of tactical importance from the point of view of an offensive or where the hostile parapet is weak and shows signs of subsidence, or to which the enemy is devoting special attention, or which can be enfiladed. Fire should be concentrated on these points and the damaged parapet should be kept frequently under fire of machine-guns and artillery, especially at night. Where possible guns should be pulled out of their ordinary day positions when required for night firing, in order that flashes may not betray the day position. We shall thus gradually weaken the enemy's line, diminish his efficiency, and facilitate our own offensive when the time comes. In the same way wire must be cut at several points and the gaps kept open. This will force the enemy to come out in the open in order to make repairs, during which we can inflict loss upon him, or if he cannot mend it, his morale and confidence will suffer. Of course these wire cutting operations will also be carried out in accordance with such raids etc, as are planned by divisions. But divisions should remember it is important to cut wire frequently at several points. As a general rule, no day should pass without some portions of the hostile wire and parapet being damaged.

The GS log recorded on 5 December:

Artillery operation against Turks Head and a parapet in vicinity carried out today by Heavy and 20th Divisional Artillery. The enemy parapet was much damaged and 10 direct hits by Heavy Artillery were observed on the culvert (one of the points to be destroyed) wire was effectively cut in places. In retaliation enemy shelled Boutillerie and Convent Wall.

Putty was determined to dominate the enemy during the winter, thus making it difficult for the enemy to mount offensive operations against him and reducing III Corps' casualties. This was the beginning.

Putty wrote to Ettie again that day:

My dear Chief, Thank you for your delightful letter of 3 December, Hindlip is going back tomorrow so will send a line, they seem to be working these messengers pretty hard now as it is the 3rd time he has been over in seven days. Floods are out everywhere, a week earlier than last year and so far not up to the highest level, they have driven all the rats and mice up to the trenches, the former are an intolerable nuisance the men bag all the dogs and cats out of the billets to take up to the trenches to guard their dug outs all the farms they used to live in are destroyed and there is plenty of food distraction round the trenches. Tell Willie [Lord Desborough] to let me know when he comes out and to propose himself here when he wants to come, no I don't know what he is coming out for. If I come over will certainly ask you to (meet) me at Panshanger but I am funny about coming home unless I feel ill. I do hope Smith-Dorrien is taking the advice of the people on the spot in Uganda who know the climate the conditions and the possibilities, I don't know to what part he is actually going but for any part he must be late as far as weather is concerned he (ought) to have started his expedition on 1 December at latest as the rains will begin in February, the difficulty of transport will be great and the Uganda railway quite unequal to the task of carrying the stores, as far as I know only the light engines can go on it just beyond Nairobi, on account of the bridges, large sidings will have to be made at once if they are going to cope with it. I dined with Haking last night and met Cavan we laughed over the rumour from London that Forestier-Walker [GOC 21st Division] was schooling a horse at Loos instead of paying attention to the fight, really people should be shot for saying such a thing, the truth was that Haking [GOC XI Corps] got a report that the 21st Division was in difficulties so he ordered Walker and his staff to go to the critical point, Walker jumped straight on to his horse, jumped all the trenches and told his terror stricken staff to follow him which they endeavoured to do through shot and shell. I wish I had confidence in the General Staff at the War Office it appears to me that they are not realising what the transport of supplies to all these divisions abroad means, I don't believe it possible on the present lavish scale of rations, look at coal for example we buy coal from the French out here on conditions that we repay with Welsh coal imagine the strain of one item like this even. All blessings Yours ever Putty.

III Corps Heavy Artillery bombarded the enemy parapet opposite Cordonnerie on 6 December, where mine shafts were known to exist. The GS log noted:

Eight rounds 9.2" hows were observed to detonate well on the site of suspected shafts. Heaps of timber and sandbags were thrown into the air. 23rd Divisional Artillery carried out operations against the enemy parapet S of Wez Macquart. Considerable damage was done. 6 German stretcher parties were seen moving away subsequently.

On 7 December:

The Heavy Artillery carried out an operation against enemy works called Lozenge. 13 effective hits observed in front line and support trenches. Timber and sandbags thrown up. 20th Divisional Artillery breached enemy parapet in several places. 23rd Divisional Artillery cut wire and damaged parapet. Enemy retaliated today by shelling groups of houses and villages in rear of line with 4.2" and 5.9" shells. A billet was burnt down at Petillon, otherwise little damage.

There were fine days interspersed with storms and some very heavy rain. This began to cause problems for both sides as III Corps Opsum noted:

> In spite of the difficult state of the ground between the lines, some very good patrol work has been carried out during the week. Their reports show that the enemy is experiencing considerable difficulty in keeping the water out of his trenches.

III Corps Artillery was relentless; the GS log recorded on 8 December:

> Hostile parapets in front of De La Porte Farm and elsewhere were bombarded with good results, two breaches being made. A direct hit was observed on a loaded wagon near the Brewery. Enemy shelled infantry billets and some battery positions. Enemy aeroplanes were active.

Again on 9 December:

> 20th Divisional Artillery did considerable damage to enemy trenches. 23rd Divisional Artillery breached enemy parapet, thus allowing accumulated water to flood enemy lines. Repairs were attempted at once but were stopped by our fire. Enemy active in the afternoon against several defended posts and also shelled Erquinghem and Armentières with 4.2" and 5.9" howitzers. Corps Artillery retaliated successfully against certain active batteries.

At 9 am on 8 December DDMS wrote: 'Spoke Corps Commander about returns called for from DGMS re severity of wounds and applicability of armour. He agreed with my notes pointing out that chain trunk armour loose, over leather jerkin, would prevent many otherwise fatal wounds, that a shield would probably do the same in addition to protecting the arms but that armour on legs and arms, which show the bulk of wounds during an attack, would hamper the mobility of the soldier'. Body armour was not developed; had it been the casualties might have been much reduced.

The artillery of both sides continued their attacks but the weather was now causing a greater problem. The GS log noted on 11 December: 'River Lys reached 15 ft today. Local records show this is the highest mark for 21 years. On the Well Farm and Bridoux Salients the water is up to the firing step'. Again on 12 December: 'River Lys still rising. Roadway N approach to Erquinghem Bridge under water'. There was now serious flooding. DDMS noted: 'I suggested to the Corps Commander that during this wet weather the stay in the trenches should be limited to 2 days. He said he had been asking them for some time to do this, but they seemed to prefer the longer period as it was such a business getting their things down to the trenches. He will try again'.

Also that day Haig recorded: 'As regards my successor as GOC 1st Army, I recommended Sir Henry Rawlinson. Though not a sincere man, he has brains and experience. Robertson (CGS GHQ) agreed that he was the best choice'.

Putty wrote to Ettie Desborough on 12 December:

> My dear Chief, Willie [Lord Desborough] came to luncheon here yesterday, I took him over to see one of the army workshops and got hold of a certain amount of information

for him which should be useful. I read a letter from Mahon, also one from Howell[108] at Salonika written 20 November, evidently both were looking over their shoulders at Greece which was not the way to fight the Bulgars or impress the Greeks for if the latter turned against they were done in anyhow, they said Maxwell[109] wants twenty divisions for the safety of Egypt I should kick Maxwell out tomorrow if I was the government, can't you see Clive turning in his grave at the idea of the modern British General I should be inclined to send Smith-Dorrien to Egypt he would run that sort of show very well. We are enduring a heavy flood, the river Lys is nearly a foot higher than it was at any time last year and there really seems little chance of it going down if these squalls continue, part of my line is very bad and the parapets seem to slide away every night. I sincerely hope the rumours here that pressure from home was put on Nixon[110] to hurry on the Baghdad operation is not true for it is simply criminal to aim for diplomatic effect under such circumstances, find out for me if it was the case. Hubert Gough[111] came to luncheon today he really was too funny over Winston Churchill and Allenby it really does one good to hear straightforward honest abuse from a man who does not care who hears him. Gavin Hamilton is going off on leave for a week tomorrow and Linlithgow goes when he returns they are very busy making a screen the morals of which are perfectly appalling, I should think the screen will be finished by the time we get to Berlin at the present rate. The attitude of the Germans opposite is very different to last year and I cannot help thinking they cannot be too well off for gun ammunition as they only reply feebly, further there have been one or two deserters lately which was never the case last winter. Best love Yours ever Putty.

He also wrote to Edith Londonderry on 12 December:

Dearest La Motte, You and your pen are a couple of rotters. The enclosed remark about Jack Cowans [QMG] is rather funny he evidently always says nice things to ladies (this was about them sending out Bovril to the troops). We have got a desperate flood on, the river Lys is a foot higher than it was any time last year one cannot get near the barges as no tow path is to be seen, every description of wood is floating down also much filth. Willie Desborough came to luncheon here yesterday by way of looking for overseers for munition workers who may be serving in the ranks, they say each man looks after 40 at home but must be absolutely experienced men, he wants 2,000 should imagine they would pull more weight making ammunition at home than being shot at in the trenches. Jemmy Rothschild excelled in conversation of filth last night, he lied about his prowess with women until I had to damn him. They nearly caught me on Thursday [9 December] had been in the trenches and my car was waiting behind a house they must have seen it go there for as we started off luckily at a fast rate as a Jack Johnson (German 15 cm artillery shell that threw up cloud of black smoke, named after black US boxer) ploughed the road up just behind us a damned good shot but not quite quick enough for WPP. Yours ever Putty.

108 Brigadier General Philip Howell (1887-1916) late 4 H COS Salonika Army.
109 Lieutenant General John Grenfell Maxwell (1859-1929) late BW GOC Egyptian Expeditionary Force.
110 Lieutenant General John Eccles Nixon (1857-1921) late Indian Army GOC Mesopotamia.
111 Lieutenant General Hubert de la Poer Gough (1870-1963) Eton late 16 L GOC I Corps.

Trench warfare continued; the GS log recorded:

> Early this morning [16 December] two parties of 59 Bde [20th Division], 11 KRRC and
> 10 RB, raided the German trenches. 11 KRRC, in hand to hand fighting against superior
> numbers, claimed to have killed at least 39 Germans, including two officers, and then
> regained their own trenches with a loss of 5 killed and 8 wounded. 10 RB abandoned the
> attempt when discovered getting through the wire.

III Corps Artillery Report for week ending 16 December recorded: 'The enemy fired about
6,500 rounds of which about 650 were 5.9". Nineteen hostile batteries were recorded as active
this week'.

Haig succeeded French as CinC on 17 December. Also that day Putty wrote to Ettie:

> My dear Chief, Thanks for your letter of the 11 Dec. We had just got over our flood which
> reached a foot higher in the Lys than any time last winter when down comes the rain again
> in torrents before we had got the water off the country. Alas! We have got Sir John French
> coming here to say good bye tomorrow to all the corps commanders before he leaves us on
> Monday, I for one shall miss him because I have served him for so long and know his sterling
> optimistic value, besides one knows that it is political influence that is now removing him
> and the Cricket Pitch Government as I call it has none too good a wicket to boast of itself
> when it dismisses its bowlers, the sooner it gives the boot to Margot and Johnny Walker
> Asquith[112] the better for this country. One of my battalions carried out quite a successful
> raid on Wednesday night [15 December], going in and out of the Boche trenches, they were
> led by Edward Warre's[113] son who got wounded in the arm going out after the show was
> over to bring in a wounded man altogether he behaved well and I shall recommend him
> for a Military Cross, was glad to hear they had a foot of water in their trenches, in some of
> the dug outs they had electric light which filled our men with envy, one rather clever dodge
> they had put a light coloured cloth on their side of the parapet so that if their trench was
> rushed they could see our men moving from the trenches in rear, they killed about twenty
> of them, and would have done more but their fingers were so cold they could not pull the
> ring out of the grenades, they had crawled all across no man's land on their stomachs and
> the ditches were icy cold as well, young Warre shot two Boches with his revolver. Have seen
> nothing more of Willie so don't know how he got on with his munitions workers but trust
> he got some, I did not think him looking too well and he did not appear able to explain his
> points besides having to look continually at his note book for reference which was unlike
> his old self, I tell you this as you asked me to. Robertson goes to London but I don't know
> yet who succeeds him here, that is a good appointment and he should never have left the
> War Office, I do hope he will take up the organisation and training of drafts. I dined with
> Pa Heyworth[114] and a lot of Scots Guards last night, pipers round the table and many jovial
> faces of the old regiments. All love and blessings Yours ever Putty.

---

112 Herbert Henry Asquith (1852-1928) Prime Minister.
113 Probably Edmond Warre (1837-1920) Provost of Eton, son Lieutenant Felix Walter Warre
     (1879-1953) Eton 11 KRRC 59 Bde 20th Division.
114 Brigadier General Frederick James Heyworth (1863-1916) late SG Comd 3 Gds Bde.

Field Marshal Sir John French visited HQ III Corps on 18 December: GOC I, III, IV and XI Corps were present to bid him farewell. Putty wrote again to Ettie afterwards:

My dear Chief, Thanks for yours of 15 Dec, Hebester goes back tomorrow so send a line by him. Have had a sad day saying good bye to Sir John French, I feel my friend has gone and that the reason is chiefly political, he is taking Cecil Lowther[115] with him as his General Staff Officer and he will do him well, he goes tomorrow morning to say good bye to the 3rd Army then to Paris in the afternoon to bid adieu to Joffre he goes back to his old rooms at Horse Guards on Wednesday [22 December], nobody could have said nicer things to me thanking me a 1000 times for all I had done for him. Am glad to hear what you say about Bagdad [sic] but there are so many bad bowlers in this Cricket Pitch Gov't one can really believe almost anything. Hubert Gough says Allenby is a bull in the office but in the field useless, he never was to be found when the fighting was on except miles away in rear tearing his hair at the losses of his men, he certainly is the most unpopular man in the army out here but except knowing never to trust his reports I really don't know much about his capabilities, he used to allow my hostess in to his offices and accept her eulogies if nothing more which annoyed Hubert Gough more than anything, I put her in her place and never let her inside my side of the house as don't believe in moves of troops being discussed with those sort of people, am much afraid in consequence I am sadly unpopular with the baroness, Allenby comes all the way over from Béthune to see her so am afraid it is a bad case! Yours ever Putty.

The next two days were comparatively quiet, except for artillery engagements. Putty wrote to Theresa Londonderry on 20 December:

Dear Lady Londonderry, Many thanks for your letter. Am depressed at the departure of our CinC Sir John French, he went off yesterday and gets to London on Wednesday to go to his old rooms in the Horse Guards, of course his recall is the result of machinations of Asquith and the weak attitude of this Cricket Pitch Government who don't seem to have a good bowler among them, one thing I am glad of which is that Robertson is going with him for a great many of our failures have been entirely due to want of good advice in strategy with a strong man like Robertson the government may listen with conviction instead of turning round a man like Archie Murray with their larger brain. Am glad to think that Charley is coming out again he is badly wanted to train the men in the Blues, all our army has expanded so much we have not had time to train it efficiently but now that we have begun to get the best of the Boche in the W we have time to look round and put our house in order. We have had a foot worse flood than we had last year but have got through it all right with much less damage to our parapets and trenches than anticipated, the men too understand how to prevent getting trench feet, we don't get one case when we got ten last year. Every good wish for Xmas and luck for 1916. Yours very sincerely WP Pulteney.

---

115 Brigadier General Henry Cecil Lowther late SG MS GHQ.

It was again quiet on 21 and 22 December. At 6 pm that day HQ III Corps issued OpO No.62, orders for the relief of 20th Division by 8th Division; reliefs to commence 1 January 1916.

III Corps Artillery Report for week ending 24 December recorded: 'The enemy fired about 7,680 rounds of which 760 were 5.9" how. Twenty seven hostile batteries are recorded as active this week'. With the formation of HQ RA III Corps this information was used for planning artillery operations. Artillery engagements continued right through Christmas to the end of the year. III Corps Artillery engaged the front line, including the enemy wire to give patrols access, as well as strong points further back. The enemy's retaliation was weak and III Corps' counter battery fire invariably silenced it. The weather was very changeable with fine days interspersed with much rain; the GS log recorded on 25 December: 'Today the River Laies rose to 7 ft 4 ins which is the highest it has been this year, and the River Lys rose to 14 ft 10 ins'.

On 25 December Putty wrote to Edith Londonderry:

> Dearest La Motte, Many thanks for your letters of 23 Dec and 19 Dec both of which reached me on the same day, you have all my love and good wishes for this day and 1916 with many years to follow. You are a dear to send me such a splendid useful present, I feel a brute at not having been home to get one for you but there is nothing here. The cake is perfectly splendid and my felicitations are please to go to Flora for her work it really is excellent, the recipe of it does your father's taste the very highest credit, I have been quite unable to face tea after the pudding and mince pies at luncheon but Jemmy R is still going strong but should be guinea colour tomorrow if there is any justice in this world. I cannot quite make out whether Monro is coming back here or not if he does it will kick Rawley out though he tells me he expects the 4th Army to be formed at once and that he will get it, from what I can make out Haig, Rawley and K made a dead set against French and Robertson over the Battle of Loos and they got Haking in on their side while Lady Haig did the trick with the King, anything that is told the King is repeated that way back to Haig, I mean to let the whole damned lot go their own way they are sure to quarrel again before long among themselves. I like the photo of the ward and should like some more copies to give one or two of the subscribers if you can get me some. Ben D'or[116] was to have come to luncheon yesterday but he never turned up he is off to Egypt on Monday with Ernest Bald to run his motor cars. Ben Tillett[117] is coming here this evening en route to the trenches of the 20th Division, he was quite interesting last year when I sent him down to Plugstreet, I will pump him about the Labour Party if I can, he is a tremendous egotist what we want organised now is the labour question after the war it would be better for Germany if America was dragged in on our side for then she would make a dead set for Brazil as she would have no chance in North America. I wish I could find out what Smith-Dorrien was actually going for in East Africa is he going in from the coast or in from the Lake Victoria end, I expect all this conquest of country is required for diplomacy at the end of the war or otherwise I am sure we don't want any more of Africa, teaching all these tribes to fight means endless trouble in the years to come in a part of Africa that is not a white man's country. The Boche tried to make a truce with the Guards Division this

---

116 2nd Duke of Westminster.
117 Benjamin Tillett (1860-1943) Union Leader later Labour MP for Salford.

morning but of course they would have none of it, the shelling all day has been practically continuous all along the line, the feeling is 100 times more bitter than it was last year, the treatment of our prisoners has a good deal to do with it, also the men in the K divisions mean business. Tell Charley to come and look us up here the first opportunity he gets when he comes out here and bring Reggie with him we will have a good laugh over old times, you must come out again but mind that Lady Haig does not get wind of it. The floods are all up again but not quite so high as a week ago, needless to say the big pumps that the engineers were going to do such wonders with have not started working yet because some of the parts are still in England. Best love Yours ever Putty.

HQ III Corps gave the baroness a Christmas present as she recorded:

I [Baronne de la Grange] must mention another Christmas present I have had. III Corps have given me a charming silver inkstand, with a flattering inscription, Really, although I am no longer exactly young, I feel I am the spoiled child of the British Army!

On 28 December Putty wrote again to Edith:

Dearest La Motte, A line today to say that the turkey more especially cold was the best bird that was ever eaten, Jemmy R produced one but it was a tough old rooster, the walnuts, gingers etc. all good, am still alive. Floods reached their zenith last night and now are beginning to fall the local liar says that they are the highest they have had for twenty years. The Guards Division is going away down to the 3rd Army in to Cavan's Corps I shall miss them from round me here I expect that Geoffrey Feilding [Comd 1 Gds Bde] will get the division. The Howler and Gavin Hamilton are spending all their time making a screen, the former has procured some fearful postcards from Hazebrouck which Jemmy brought for him, they really are the limit. We are having the most desperate artillery duels every day now it does sound funny after last year when we could not answer with more than two rounds a gun a day. Repington puts it pretty straight about conscription in yesterday's Times, he is quite right for once too. Best of luck for 1916 Yours ever Putty. PS: We gave A.J.B. a great day yesterday. Birdie[118] tells me Johnnie Willoughby keeps on proposing to Maggie Greville[119] I say Johnnie ought to bring her out here with his armour motor car she would make an excellent 'sandbag' with a ready-made loophole, if she survived she would turn in to the necessary 'money bag'. The 2nd Corps had a good show yesterday and did very well, about 1000 casualties but they killed an awful lot of Germans. W.P.P. so many Ps it looks rather 'watery'.

He wrote to Ettie on 31 December:

My dear Chief, Thanks for yours of 27 Dec, which I got last night, have no news for you. We had a great concert here on Wednesday of which I enclose the programme. I think

---

118 Lady Vane-Tempest-Stewart married to 6th Earl of Ilchester.
119 Margaret Helen Greville (1863-1942) later Dame Margaret Greville.

the Warre boys name was Felix, I have got him the Military Cross all right which will please the Provost. Absolutely no news here, the floods have gone down but the canal is still too flooded for the barge traffic and the country is one vast flood. The papers describe daily artillery duels, one of my officers told me they were misnamed as they consisted of our artillery shelling the German infantry in their trenches and the Germans retaliating on our infantry, it is rather true. Mrs baroness returned yesterday she had spent one night at Allenby's chateau with the 3rd Army!!! I told her I was shocked but she had a long string of excuses, she told me she had met Regane[120] and that she had promised to come here soon to give us an entertainment. I think conscription will cause a large immigration in to Ireland! But we must have it. Linlithgow is laid up at home with boils, the doctors say he won't be fit to come back for a month. Best of luck and all blessings for 1916. Yours ever Putty.

III Corps casualties for December were: 8 officers and 92 other ranks killed, 17 officers and 480 other ranks wounded, 1 officer and 2 other ranks missing = 600. III Corps total casualties in 1915 were 12,793.

During the year Putty had been passed over for command of an army on two occasions and for promotion to Lieutenant General, yet he had done all that was asked of him. His corps had held its line, often a very long one, in the flood plain of the River Lys; and this line had been adjusted on several occasions during the year. It had mounted diversionary and subsidiary attacks in support of the offensives at Neuve Chapelle and Loos; it had trained a number of new divisions; above all it had dominated the enemy opposite it. Putty had done much to improve conditions for his corps, reduce sickness, care for the wounded, and seek better and more effective equipment. It is hard to criticise his performance as a corps commander in 1915; on occasions he had a difference of opinion with his superiors, but he was usually right. He could have tried to use the patronage of others but did not do so. The evidence suggests that he was not treated fairly: he was promoted to Lieutenant General by the end of the year and his seniority as a Lieutenant General was backdated to May 1915, above Monro and the other four, but this only makes the earlier decisions harder to understand. The 'grave displeasure' of the Army Council in 1911 might have been a factor but this seems unlikely.

Several decisions attributable to Putty deserve to be highlighted: the introduction of forward surgery for the more serious head and abdominal casualties and their subsequent evacuation by barge on the River Lys undoubtedly saved lives. Recognition of Barley's ability and the manufacture of sufficient gas masks to equip the corps are worthy of note for the same reason. His use of a forward headquarters in the brewery at Fort Rompu during the Battle of Loos indicates a commander determined to be in touch with the battle and one who did not shirk from its dangers. During 1915 there were at least three reported occasions when he came close to being killed when visiting forward positions.

The letter from Kitchener to French on 11 July 1915 appears to convey two important messages: that the cabinet had decided that Monro not Putty should command 3rd Army and that the King had agreed with this decision. One interpretation of this is that Kitchener,

---

120 Gabrielle Rejane stage name of Gabrielle-Charlotte Reju (1856-1920) French actress.

being well aware of the King's and French's preference, was making sure neither could try and influence the matter further. If this is so it suggests that Putty did have a level of patronage from the King; such a suggestion is reinforced by the phrase 'He (the King) mentioned that Pulteney was a personal friend of his'. If this is true, and there is an absence of evidence of such a friendship, there is no suggestion that Putty used such patronage to his advantage. Putty was very loyal to French and was perhaps closer to him than the other corps commanders. Kitchener, Haig and others were scheming to replace French with Haig, and Putty may well have become caught up in this. If that was so, it was surprising that Haig kept Putty as a corps commander in France until 1918; he could have sent him back to England to another appointment, perhaps even on promotion. Maybe Haig could not do so because of patronage but there is no evidence to support this. This leaves the other possibility, that Haig had confidence in Putty as a corps commander.

Putty considered seeking advice from Arthur Balfour on the way he had been treated but decided not to do so. Balfour had been Prime Minister 1903-1905 and was at this time First Lord of the Admiralty in Asquith's coalition government; he was also a friend of both Ettie Desborough and Edith Londonderry. As to the decisions themselves it is more than likely that Putty's own assessment is correct. Kitchener would not have taken kindly to being questioned about his policies by other members of the government who seemed to have direct access to military information: it would have taken him little time to trace this back to Putty. It is difficult to be certain who was responsible and why for Putty not getting command of 3rd Army or being passed over for promotion but there is more than a suspicion that the decision was Kitchener's and not made on ability and performance alone.

It is possible that Asquith, the Prime Minister, might have had a hand in this. According to Field Marshal French, he had wanted Wilson to succeed Murray as his CGS and the Prime Minister was 'obdurate in the extreme' and had vetoed the appointment because of Wilson's involvement in the Curragh incident. Asquith was against Paget for the same reason and maybe Putty's name became linked.

Letters written by Lambton (MS GHQ) to his brother 3rd Earl of Durham provide invaluable background. Writing on 14 January 1915 about the deployment of Kitchener's new armies he said:

> Sir J has not approached the matter with any sort of tact and instead of going straight to K, sent him a memorandum on the subject and at the same time one to some of the cabinet, Asquith, Winston and some others. Naturally K has been annoyed, and a settlement is made more difficult. I am in despair over Sir J's attitude to K and there are too many politicians of the Winston type and other busy bodies who encourage him to go at K in this roundabout way. He will get the worst of it, as K is far more tricky, and can work that sort of business much better.

Clive Wigram wrote to Lambton on 21 March in the same vein:

> It is a great pity that Sir J does not handle Lord K more tactfully, and does not give Lord K more credit for what he is doing – Sir J seems to think (he) is always trying to let him down, and is vindictive, which is wrong.

Later in the year (30 October) Lambton (then GOC 4th Division) wrote to his brother 3rd Earl of Durham:

> We have got Allenby as army commander in place of Monro, not a very good exchange as far as individuals go, but I think he is a good soldier, but rather hard and drives too much, hence he is not popular. I had hoped Putty would have got it, but he seems to be under a cloud.

On 16 December he wrote:

> I wait with some trepidation to see what Haig's appointments will be as he always sticks to his own men, and will look at no-one outside the 1st Army.

These letters again show the extent that politics and personalities influenced decisions on command at army level.

It is not possible to assess Putty's relationship with Ettie Desborough or Edith Londonderry with any certainty. Both visited France in 1915, and Edith got to HQ III Corps. Good friends they were without a doubt: he may well have wanted more, indeed he may have been in love with both of them, but there is a danger in reading too much into the flirtations and, in Edith's case, the sexually explicit and rather puerile suggestive humour. Yet they, Edith in particular, could easily have called a halt to this but on the contrary seemed to have encouraged him, and they kept his letters for the rest of their lives. In the background all the time was Jessie, the woman he was eventually to marry. What really matters is that his letters were not only being read by Ettie and Edith but there seems every likelihood that the information and ideas were passed on to Souls and members of the Ark in numerous informal meetings. Both women were highly intelligent and would have taken care not to promote anything that they had not first considered and discussed with others, and there are constant hints that they challenged Putty in their letters to him. However, they were very influential and it does seems likely that through them Putty was able, perhaps unknowingly, to press his views to the highest levels. There is no evidence that he used them, as he could have, to further his personal interest although his disappointment on not getting command of 3rd Army and being passed over for promotion must have become widely known in their circles. It could be argued that Putty's contacts in some way strengthened his position: Secretaries of State for War and others might have been cautious; Haig and Rawlinson too had achieved what they wanted, to deny Putty further advancement, and were prepared, because of his ability or his potential influence or both, for him to continue in command of III Corps. But this is all speculation.

9

1916

January-March

The New Year started with a windy day. III Corps was still in 1st Army with 8th, 20th and 23rd Divisions under command and its HQ at Chateau La Motte au Bois. Early that morning 23rd Division raided the enemy's trenches. The enemy had been alert and used searchlights but on the left 9 Yorks 69 Bde managed to get into the German trenches; a few of the enemy were killed but most ran away. The enemy then counter-attacked and a further 20 were killed. The right attack by 10 NF 68 Bde was abandoned because of the searchlights and heavy fire.

That day Putty sent his monthly report to the King:

> My dear Wigram, I forward herewith the diary of III Corps for the month of December for the information of His Majesty. The raid of the 20th Division on 16 December was quite a successful affair and was well carried out, the 23rd Division did one last night which was also successful but the details are scarcely to hand and of course it is not included in this diary. The 8th Division has benefited a good deal by their months training out of the trenches, the weather has been against them but it has been a great asset getting the officers of a battalion together and in some cases starting sergeants messes, the men have improved in smartness and one can notice the difference in esprit de corps. The health of the corps has been wonderful, January was the worst month last year so I do not anticipate keeping such a good record this month. The floods have been a great nuisance the River Lys is a foot higher than it was at any time last year, according to the local people it has not been so high for twenty years, the parapet or rather breastworks sink in many places and entailed a vast amount of repair work, sandbags burst, dug outs fell in with many of the usual inconveniences which reminded us of last winter but on the whole we are getting through it famously and are altogether 100 pc better all round than last year, our superiority over the Boche is now becoming more marked every month. Good luck to you for 1916. Yours Sincerely, WP Pulteney.

Next day was wet and quiet apart from shelling by both sides: an enemy OP was destroyed on 20th Division's front. III Corps AQ log recorded that the corps had been ordered to provide 100 NCOs and men for the formation of a new mining company.

III Corps Artillery were very active over the next two days (3 and 4 January) with the heavy artillery breaching the enemy's parapet opposite La Boutillerie during the morning of 3 January and much damage done by both divisional artilleries on 4 January. A 4.2" hostile battery was silenced. Also on 4 January HQ III Corps issued G367/4 altering date of relief of 20th Division by 8th Division to 8 January.

Putty wrote to Ettie on 4 January:

> My dear Chief, Thank you dear person for your letter of 27 Dec which I ought to have answered sooner. There is no military news from these parts, the Germans shelled us heavily at the beginning of the week but it is all normal again now. We have had a desperate gale for the last 24 hours which sent the glass down with a hop but it is on the rise again and there was but little rain. The Eastern news does not sound good, some of us can not understand the appointment of Lake[1] to succeed Nixon [as GOC Mesopotamia] he has never done any fighting, it was a most peculiar choice of Beauchamp Duff![2] The Zeppelins must have caused a great deal of damage we shall never do any good until we get a very small fast air ship which can show up the Zepp and fight it as well, we are on the wrong tack trying to take them on from the ground or with aeroplanes, have scarcely read anything more ridiculous than the article in the Times on the subject. The Primate of Ireland was with me for Sunday, he preached two capital sermons in the morning and I handed him over to the Irish Guards for the afternoon where he met several friends, McCalmont,[3] Desmond Fitzgerald[4] etc. but he [Primate] was pretty tired when he came back in the evening. Charley L (Londonderry) also came over for the day and went back to his cavalry in reserve, he had had an interesting time in the trenches and on the whole enjoyed it, his position as regard Fitzgerald coming out still seems rather doubtful but I tell him he had much better stay where he is instead of going to an infantry battalion, he is ambitious which is a good sign. Harold Brassey[5] came over the other day he is commanding an infantry battalion, he likes the work but feels lonely without a pal among his brother officers. I like the 34th (Division) from what I hear of them, the men are A1 but the staff and the brigadiers leave much to be desired, I don't believe the men who have been out here a long time will ever be able to go back to town life, they all say they can never face an office again after the healthy air of the country, it will drive many to Canada and Australia I am quite certain, perhaps the bon dieu sent it to put us back on the land, give votes to women and efface the self of trade unionism. Yours ever Putty.

The artillery of both sides engaged overnight and during the day (5 January) with III Corps Artillery generally having the upper hand. A 6" gun fired five rounds at Lille Station with a smoke barrage used successfully to conceal its flash.

---

1   General Percy Henry Noel Lake (1855-1940) late E Lancs CIGS India.
2   General Beauchamp Duff (1855-1918) late RA CinC India incl Mesopotamia.
3   Lieutenant Colonel McCalmont CO 1 IG.
4   Captain Lord Desmond Fitzgerald (1888-1916) Adjt 1 IG killed in an accident at Calais 3 Mar 1916.
5   Lieutenant Colonel Brassey (1877-1916) RHG CO 8 S Lancs killed in action 15 Jul 1916.

DDMS III Corps wrote at 11.15 am: 'I wrote to DMS about evacuation from 26 Fd Amb by barge, as Corps Commander told me this morning that the Estaires bridge is to be open again tomorrow (closed because of the high level of the River Lys)'. Evacuation of the wounded was of continual concern to Putty, and the use of the river was far better for their survival than the paved roads. Later that day he visited 23rd Division to congratulate the men who took part in the raid on 1 January.

It was quiet on 6 and 7 January except for III Corps Artillery which again dominated the enemy. The field artillery and trench mortars engaged the front line and working parties while the heavy artillery took on the enemy batteries and strong points.

III Corps GS log recorded on 8 January:

> During the day the wind worked round to the NW and it was decided to carry out the gas attack by 20th Division [whose relief by 8th Division had been further delayed] tonight if conditions were favourable. Of the 800 cylinders which had been placed in the line S of Cordonnerie Farm for an attack on 20/21 December, 400 were withdrawn on the nights of 6/7 and 7/8 January there having been no favourable wind during the time they were in position and the cylinders were required elsewhere. Only 400 cylinders still in the line were therefore available for this attack, and as the original scheme required considerable modification, the conduct of the operation was left entirely in the hands of 20th Division. This attack started at 2 am 9 January. Some 90 cylinders failed to work and the gas out of the others vaporised very slowly. The enemy was alert and it was decided that an assault in these conditions could not have much chance of success. The assaulting columns were waiting, but were therefore not employed.

The relief of 20th Division by 8th Division then began and continued over the next three days.

III Corps Artillery continued to dominate the enemy, the heavy howitzers frequently engaging with the assistance of aeroplane observation. The GS log recorded on 11 January: 'Generally a quiet day except for hostile shelling of battery positions by 100 5.9" shells of which 60% were blind. Our heavy artillery engaged hostile batteries and direct hits obtained on gun-pit and front apron: much material thrown up'. The accuracy of III Corps Artillery and the problems the enemy was having with the reliability of its ammunition meant that on some days it was ineffective, and others inactive.

At 9 am 10 January Putty asked the CE [Brigadier General Schreiber] to try and arrange more frequent openings of Estaires bridge 'which at present opens only at 1 pm daily'. Again the rapid evacuation of the wounded and their survival was uppermost in his mind.

The weather had been gradually improving with W/SW winds, fine days and occasional rain. 13 January was a quiet day on the whole corps front. DDMS wrote: 'Lieutenant Colonel Rose Camp Commandant cut his right instep 2.5" with an axe while wood cutting. I saw him with Major Ritchie [MO] and sent him to 2 London CCS Merville (he returned to duty on 31 January)'. Putty was very fortunate with his staff, none more so than Rose who was to be with him throughout his time in command of III Corps. Rawlinson wrote in his diary that day: 'Putty and Hamilton [ADC] to dinner'.

On 14 January the GS log recorded that the water levels in the Lys and other streams had fallen steadily over the past week. Then at 4.15 pm: 'Left bn 23rd Division opened demonstration with smoke bombs, artillery co-operating with good effect on enemy parapet. Enemy at once sounded bugles and gongs and his artillery then concentrated about 200 rounds upon our fire and support trenches. At 4.20 pm he opened heavy rifle and machine-gun fire, his fire trench then fully manned. Individuals were observed wearing gas helmets'. Such deception unsettled the enemy, provided valuable information, and often allowed the artillery to inflict heavy casualties. That evening HQ III Corps issued G1260/3 – precautions against gas attack (orders, training and equipment): this was another subject in which Putty continued to take a close interest. The weekly sick wastage recorded by the AQ staff that day was 0.62 per 1,000 per day, extraordinarily low considering the conditions and time of year.

Artillery exchanges were again the only action on 15 January: as usual III Corps was able to fire more rounds, more accurately than the enemy, silencing btys, destroying OPs and sniper posts. A Sergeant of 21 Bavarian Reserve Regt was captured in the early morning, he said he had become separated from a small patrol, lost his way in the dark, and mistook 'our parapet for his'. Such intelligence windfalls were though rare.

Putty wrote to Ettie again that day:

> My dear Chief, I owe you a letter and never thanked you for your last delightful note. Very little news here except that the floods have disappeared the River Lys is lower than it was at any time last year so with the lengthening days we need only anticipate one more flood that won't get absorbed quickly enough not to matter. There has been great activity in the artillery line on both sides which indicates that the state of the ground is too bad for any general attack, that the killing is reduced to making the enemy man his trenches and then bringing guns on to them. Our aeroplanes have suffered a good deal lately because we are behindhand in anti aircraft guns and the Germans possess faster fighting machines besides I think those air raids unless on a colossal scale are very doubtful value judging by the result of the German ones on us. I dined on Thursday with Rawlinson [GOC 4th Army] to meet George Warrender[6] who had been well shelled, going round the trenches near Loos, he is so deaf poor man it is almost impossible to carry on conversation the whole ship must have heard any information being imparted to him by voice, he seemed quite contented at the prospect of Plymouth. Granard tells me he is off back to Salonika today to take up the post of Military Secretary to Mahon.[7] Charley L [Londonderry] I believe came over on Thursday to rejoin the Blues I hope he will get the regiment all right in due course. I think the retirement from Gallipoli the finest feat on military record and they ought to make Monro a full General at once. All my blessings Yours ever Putty.

During the night a number of enemy working parties were dispersed by rifle and MG fire and during the next day (16 January) the artillery engagements continued with III Corps in the ascendency. Putty wrote to Edith Londonderry that day:

> Dearest La Motte, Thanks for your letter of 12 Jan. So glad Charley has come out once more he will be glad to turn his hand to the wheel once more in the field, although some

6   Vice Admiral Sir George Warrender Bt RN (1860-1917).
7   GOC 10th Division and BEF Salonika.

of them are taking their turn in the trenches it does them a lot of good from a disciplinary point of view, they look so funny marching as infantry and how they get their kit up to the trenches without packs I don't know. Have got to receive some Belgian decoration tomorrow but what it is I don't know I never thought they would give me one after being a spy against them on the Congo but it is immaterial in these days on which side one fights judging by the Balkans. Am glad you 'packed Charlie up' I hope he fitted the lining all right!!! The Copper Horse went off this morning he says Birdie[8] has taken to cutting down trees I always thought your sex liked to see things upright but I suppose stumps have their advantage. I did not see Jack Cowans [QMG] when he was here, what a man to send to study economy one thing I bet he gave a sound opinion. We went down to Calais yesterday to see some shooting experiments with 18 and 60 pdrs in cutting wire, Frank Bingham[9] came over for it but between ourselves it was not very satisfactory in fact with good wire the defence takes a tremendous lot of beating down, am off this morning to see some of the new 6 inch howitzers fire the other side of Armentières they are a top hole gun I wish they were coming along quicker, the trench mortar is a thing we ought to be much better at for it is an undoubtedly useful weapon. We took a sergeant prisoner yesterday but he would not tell us much, a Bavarian who whenever we got on to military matters said I can't disclose because it may effect [sic] the victorious national cause, they are well trained aren't they? So glad to hear Miss Florence is all right, what an experience for her. Best of luck Yours ever Putty.

The artillery engagements continued throughout the next week. On 17 January 23rd Division reported:

A hostile battery was silenced by howitzers, and others were successfully engaged by two siege batteries. Enemy rifle-fire on our observing aeroplanes was again kept down by gun-fire. An enemy machine-gun cupola was damaged by shells. Of 18 shells fired by enemy after dark at pumping station, E of Erquinghem, only three exploded.

This was the ongoing pattern of events with the enemy's armoured steel cupolas built in to the parapets receiving particular attention. III Corps counter-battery fire was especially effective with some batteries destroyed and others silenced.

CinC (Haig) visited 8th and 23rd Divisions in the line during the afternoon of 17 January and HQ III Corps later in the day. At 9 am on 20 January DDMS wrote:

DMS 1st Army wrote last night that CinC considered Lieutenant Sampson [surgeon Special Ward] should have higher rank and a better post and asked my views. Replied that he ought to have rank of major being a highly skilled surgeon, but that he ought not to leave. Spoke to Corps Commander this morning and he is of this opinion.

It seems more than likely that Haig was taken to the Special Ward during his visit for this very purpose. Later on 20 January Putty visited 6 KSLI and other units of 20th Division (now

8   Lady Vane-Tempest-Stewart married to 6th Earl of Ilchester.
9   Major General Francis Richard Bingham (1863-1935) late RA DDRA War Office/Member of Ministry of Munitions Council.

relieved by 8th Division) and 'thanked all ranks for the good work they had done while under his command'. 20th Division then left III Corps.

On 21 January HQ III Corps issued OpO No.63: Orders for the attachment of 34th Division to 8th and 23rd Divisions for instruction and subsequent relief of 23rd Division in the line by 34th Division. 34th Division joined the corps next day. Also on 22 January Major Jack wrote:

> After dusk, following a march of 2½ miles, we [2 Cameronians 23 Bde 8th Division] took over from 2 W Yorks (also 23 Bde) the identical line held (at La Boutillerie) by 1 Cameronians [then 19 Bde III Corps] when trench warfare first began in October 1914. Conditions are, however, not nearly as bad as they were then.

Also Putty wrote to Ettie:

> My dear Chief, Many thanks for your letter of 17 Jan. Little news to tell you from these parts. On Monday [17 January] the Belgians presented me with the Grand Officer Cross of the Crown, at which I made pretty speeches about having fought with them on their beautiful river the Congo, (where I expected a bullet for being a spy instead of friendship). On Thursday [20 January] I went to pay my respects to Joffre, he looked pale and worn but he has a charming voice which appeals to me far more than his bourgeois figure, Rawlinson had made very good arrangements I really believe he would lick Douglas Haig's feet from the way he goes on. Am very depressed at the 20th Division having been taken away from me, it was the best division I had and the best of the K divisions, after they have been in the country six months I think the K divisions are better than the regular ones, there is no doubt they are out to kill Boches while the old ones are just like the Germans you have to keep driving them or they would sit still. I have got a new K division arriving in my area tomorrow the 34th under Ingouville-Williams[10] whom I know well, he says they are a good lot but I have not seen them yet, this will make the fourteenth division I shall have had through my hands more than twice as big as the original expeditionary force. Have been reading some very interesting accounts of the last German gas attack up at Ypres, I think there is little doubt but that they used two kinds of gas as several men were affected long afterwards who seemed all right until they took violent exercise when they were seized quite suddenly by a heart attack and a good few died, those who rested 24 hours without exertion were all right, the 2nd gas was more volatile I think and not heavy as it only affected men in the front trenches. Stavey takes this tomorrow. All blessings Yours ever Putty.

23 January was dull and chilly, with a morning mist; enemy patrols tried to take advantage of this but were discovered and engaged. 34th Division joined III Corps in corps reserve while they carried out their familiarisation with 8th and 23rd Divisions. The story of 10 Lincolns 101 Bde is illustrative of most other bns in the division: it was formed by 19 October 1914 and the first six months were devoted to individual training and gathering equipment. On 17 June 1915 the battalion, about 950 strong, moved into a tented camp at Studley Royal near Ripon and joined the rest of 101 Bde. Early in August they moved to Perham Down, Salisbury Plain

---

10   Comd 16 Bde when Putty was GOC 6th Division and later III Corps.

for collective training. Then on 10 January 1916, two weeks earlier, they had crossed to France. Their weakness was in the officers, NCOs and specialists who also had only sixteen months training; now they had to make a further leap to master the evolving doctrine of the forces in the field: time was not on their side.

At 9 am on the morning of 23 January DDMS noted:

> Corps Commander spoke about gas attack reported by Captain Adie and wanted to know what medical recommendations had been made about late symptoms in gas poisoning. The special measure recommended was that men who had been gassed should not be employed for some time on heavy work, as it was when they exerted themselves that the symptoms appeared.

This discussion continued next day with Putty trying to prepare his corps for such attacks.

January continued with artillery and patrol engagements; the enemy retaliated but III Corps was usually dominant. On 25 January Putty sent HQ III Corps G620 to HQ 1st Army: Update report on preparations for the winter (considerable progress now that flooding has ceased). Also issued was HQ III Corps G631 giving dispositions of the corps: HQ 8th Division was at Sailly, HQ 23rd Division at Croix du Bac, and HQ 34th Division at Blaringhem. On 27 January Rawlinson wrote: 'Rode to Sailly and saw Putty'.

This pattern of activity continued for the next few days which were generally dull although warmer. Putty wrote to Edith Londonderry on 28 January:

> Dearest La Motte, You must have got writer's cramp from the rarity that your pen puts pen to paper to me. The usual sort of changes have been taking place in my corps they have just taken away my best K div the 20th and given me another one to train viz the 34th, most of the division come from Newcastle Tyneside, some Scotch some Irish, two of the brigades are very good the other one is rather moderate, this one makes the four-teenth division I have had through my hands. Poor Bobby Filmer[11] died in the hospital at Merville yesterday, I saw him the day before, they were just going to take his foot off as a last recourse but Bowlby [Consulting Surgeon to the Forces] told me he did not think there was any chance of his recovering, he had a terrible wound as well in the buttock and never could have been anything beyond a wreck if he had lived so on the whole it was merciful, he was a fine brave fellow though a trifle mad, he dropped his spectacles coming out of the trenches and rode back next morning to try and find them, a shell pitched on the road behind him, killing the horse of course he had no business to have been where he was on a horse. The Germans have got up a pretty good hate against us at present, the artillery fire on both sides is very heavy indeed but we hold our own as long as Lloyd George does not cart us. I have got the Primate of Ireland coming to stay with me tomorrow for Sunday so shall have to be on my best behaviour. Wombat Howard-Vyse[12] came to stay the night of Wednesday (26 January) he was in good form and told us about your Charley and Reggie who seem to be in very good form, he started us off with their cavalry joke which is after

11   Captain Sir Robert Marcus Filmer 10th Bt Gren Gds (1879-1916).
12   Lieutenant Colonel Richard Granville Hylton 'Wombat' Howard-Vyse RHG (1883-1962).

every sentence to say 'What the bride said' for example say it after 'Come again quickly' 'Turn over another leaf' 'You will come again wont you'!!! Yours ever Putty.

It was dull and warm on 29 January, a day that the enemy artillery dominated for the first time for some days. Next day was cold with a dense mist and 31 January was much the same; consequently both days were quiet. III Corps casualties for January 1916 were: 5 officers and 99 other ranks killed, 29 officers and 562 other ranks wounded, 2 officers and 3 other ranks missing = 700.

1 February was bright and cold but still hazy, and another relatively quiet day. Putty sent his monthly report to the King:

> My dear Wigram, I enclose a copy of the diary of III Corps for January for information of His Majesty The King. The health of the troops has been wonderful. The floods have all disappeared the River Lys is at its normal level, the country is very forward indeed for the grass has begun to grow, lilac and other shrubs in leaf. I have had a great loss in the 20th Division being taken away from the corps it was a good way the best division I had in the corps and the best of the K divisions I have had through my hands. The 20th have been replaced by the 34th whom we are teaching and hope to get in the line in about three weeks time, they mostly come from Newcastle-on-Tyne and two of the brigades promise very well, this makes the fourteenth division that I have had in my corps since I came out originally. There has been considerably more artillery fire on both sides this last month we had much the best of it for a long time but lately they have knocked a great many of our houses down which is a nuisance because of billets but you can't expect to hit a man without getting something back. These constant raids have made the Germans very alert at night and they hold the parapet quite as strongly again as they used to in consequence. I had the Primate of Ireland staying with me last Sunday he is a wonderful man for his age 61, he preached twice in the morning to two of my divisions and twice to the two battalions of the Irish Guards, with the latter it was somewhat difficult to find a Protestant congregation for him, he certainly preached excellent sermons which the men much appreciated, a change from their own padre does them a lot of good. The dry weather this last week has enabled us to repair nearly all the subsidence of the front breastworks and cut a lot of new drains, we may expect one more flood but I do not think it will matter much. Yours very sincerely, WP Pulteney.

2 February was cold and hazy, with early and late frost. HQ III Corps recorded:

> Night patrolling was active. Nine of ours were out, while three hostile parties and two covering parties were seen. One patrol, 20 or more strong, was driven in by rifle fire from our parapet. The enemy appears to be taking advantage of recent fogs to effect considerable alteration in his trenches about Bridoux Fort and the Lozenge, and they appear to be heavily manned.

The artillery, trench mortar and MG engagements continued on 3 and 4 February. At 9 am 4 February DDMS recorded: 'Corps Commander gave GS an order to close ADS at Bois Grenier (69 Fd Amb) and to find another. This appears to be due to the MO there having stopped the

RE working the pump which he held to be distressing to the patients. The pump was moved by the RE to the next door building. On my speaking to the CE about it, and pointing out that it was not possible to get another adequate ADS, he spoke to the Corps Commander who consented to the ADS not being removed for the present, provided the pump was not interfered with'. Putty was clearly prepared to get involved in resolving such matters and did so, at least on this occasion, with commendable flexibility.

There was little change over the next three days with artillery, MG and patrol engagements continuing with equal intensity by both sides. On 7 February several of the enemy were hit by III Corps' snipers and both divisions were convinced that reliefs had been carried out on the enemy's line.

HQ III Corps G728/1 was issued on 9 February setting up a Corps Sniping School and the courses to be run at it. Also that day HQ III Corps (Brigadier General Romer BGGS) issued G760: WngO for the extension of the corps' right.

III Corps GS log 10 February recorded the patrol activity the previous night:

> A NCOs patrol attempted to examine some sapheads when work was in progress, but was stopped when MG fire was opened on them under flare lights for the second time; a wounded corporal had to be carried back. A MG in an LP opposite La Boutillerie was silenced with grenades by another patrol. Another patrol bombed an enemy patrol which challenged them while cutting a sample of wire. The enemy's patrol was reinforced and the officer in command of our patrol was clubbed with a rifle; but the German officer was shot in the stomach and all our patrol regained our lines. Frozen grass, where at all thick, prevented close patrol work.

Such was the nightly battle for information and domination of no man's land on the corps' front. At 6 pm that evening HQ III Corps issued OpO No.64: Orders for the extension of 8th Division's right (and that of III Corps) at 8 am 16 February; 8th Division would then have all three bdes in the line.

Putty wrote to Edith Londonderry:

> Dearest La Motte, Thanks so much for your letter of the 2 Feb which I meant to have answered ages ago but hoped there would be some news to tell you but there isn't so here goes. To start with my hostess has a large luncheon party today to introduce the man who took (Houget's) place at GHQ I believe he is a nice fellow, Allenby is coming so have to take 2nd place and sit next to the young baronne whom we have named the 'plum' it will be a dreadfully long business as there are 16 to table. She declares she has got Rejane coming next week but shall believe it when I see it not before. Saw Cis Bingham[13] yesterday he looks pretty fit but wanted the barber on his fast becoming white hair, had gone down for the day to Vermelles to see an experiment with a sounding machine which was intensely interesting, am going to have one put up in my rooms in London to hear the conversations of the various bedrooms in the neighbourhood. Linlithgow's boils are so bad I much doubt his being able

---

13   Probably Major General Hon Cecil Edward Bingham (1861-1934) late LG GOC 1st Cavalry
Division until October 1915.

to come back as ADC so must look for another one, do you know of anyone that would suit he must be someone unfit for trench life or I would send for you. I like the looks of my new division but there are so many changes going on I spend the whole of my time taking up more ground while the others get their new formations in to shape, it is wonderful to see the vast army growing at the pace it is but the question is will they be able to give us enough ammunition when it is completed I have grave doubts myself. I think the Germans will plan an attack against us here next month and that in May they will have another go to try to crush Russia, we had a real cheery Russian over here the other day he is to report at the end of each 'year' the state of things this side. Charley [Londonderry] gave me excellent news of Reggie Herbert [Pembroke] when he was here says he is doing top hole with his squadron, he has any amount of brains if he would use them. A dull letter but best of love Yours ever Putty.

On 11 February the GS log recorded:

The 'Courou' flowing from the enemy's trenches opposite Boutillerie was dammed last night, when its bed was found to have been recently cleared out towards the enemy's parapet.

Next day (12 February):

The level of the 'Courou' dammed the previous night was found to have risen considerably on the enemy's side of the dam.

The rain had made no man's land sodden once more, and stealthy work was impossible in many parts: manipulation of the water levels could catch out the enemy.

The enemy's artillery was active all day, devoting particular attention to the salient at Cordonnerie, Well Farm, Bridoux and Rue du Bois, and their vicinities. Fire was also directed upon posts, billets and villages, and an OP was considerably damaged. There were fifty casualties in our trenches. Our howitzers retaliated upon billets and villages, while field guns bombarded the enemy's lines, destroyed MGs and breeched the parapet in several places. The heavy guns carried out a retaliation scheme in co-operation. Three of the hostile batteries ceased fire as soon as fired upon.

At 10.15 am DDMS recorded:

Went on to the jute factory S of river (with DMS 1st Army) and looked at site for a hospital barge. At request of Corps Commander, I raised the desirability of the wounded being treated on a barge under shelter of this tall factory. DMS objected that this would entail splitting up the work of 26 Fd Amb which he thought would be carried out best at its present site.

Putty was still pressing for a less rigid approach to the treatment and evacuation of the wounded, and for greater use of the river. During the afternoon GOC 1st Army (Monro) visited HQ III Corps and met the divisional commanders.

On 13 February III Corps patrols found no man's land sodden with the ditches full of water: they met none of the enemy. During the afternoon two enemy aeroplanes came over and dropped bombs on Fleurbaix and Bac St Maur but no damage was reported. Putty wrote to Theresa Londonderry that day:

Dear Lady Londonderry, Very many thanks for your letter of 9 Feb which I so much appreciated getting. Yes the casualty lists look heavy but then people do not realise the number of people who are exposed to danger daily in comparison with what it was a year ago, you have to remember that whereas we had ten divisions out here last year we have more than four times that amount now the only person who seems to realise our army is expanding at this rate is Mr German and it is making him very uneasy, if we go steadily until our army is properly formed we shall win the war at the end of this year but if we go rushing at it before it is trained we shall be at it another year. I may come back over later on but with these incessant changes it is difficult to make plans, have kept my leave up my sleeve until I felt ill and the strain too much for me. Charley gave me a wonderful account of your health and energy which is splendid. Yours very sincerely WP Pulteney.

It was quiet on 14 February with very little artillery fire on either side. During the course of the day the preliminary moves were made for the extension of III Corps' line to the right and for 34th Division to replace 23rd Division in the line. Putty's discussion with DDMS is again recorded:

9 am. Spoke Corps Commander about moving Special Ward as I consider cross roads, bridge and ordnance workshop are all objects likely to draw fire. He does not consider ordnance workshop would draw fire, and does not know where the Special Ward could be moved, as it must be near the river.

It was windy and raining on 15 February: during the evening 23 Bde 8th Division relieved a bde of Guards Division, extending the corps' right flank.

Baronne de la Grange (owner of Chateau la Motte au Bois) wrote:

I am a woman who is exceedingly fond of her personal belongings – furniture and the like. Perhaps I love them too much! Yesterday while in the park I noticed a mirror, evidently mine, fixed up in the branches of a tree. 'Now who,' thought I, 'can be the lunatic, even among Englishmen – notoriously original – who goes up a tree to shave on a bitter February morning?' Feeling my temper rising and determined to have my property respected I turned back, and, meeting the General, expressed my indignation at once. He listened attentively and promised to inquire into the matter. I have now had the explanation. Lord Hamilton [Putty's ADC], always busy with inventions and experiments, has had an idea that he can perfect a system of reflectors to look into enemy trenches when they are very near. Acting upon this notion, he bought a glass in Hazebrouck – one exactly like mine – so the mirror really was 'honestly come by', and is Lord Hamilton's own property. The staff now consider me a marvellously good housekeeper to have spotted such a thing, but since I realized these British Army ambitions, I have dreamed of little mirrors passing their secrets from one to another.

That afternoon at 3 pm DDMS noted:

> Corps Commander has approved the other factory (at Bac St Maur) being taken (for 26 Fd Amb Special Ward) up if possible. I am to consult 23rd Division tomorrow about it.

Early that night (15/16 February) the enemy's trenches in front of the Cordonnerie Salient were shelled, light mortars, MG and rifle fire cooperating. The enemy retaliated with a dozen trench mortar bombs all of which fell behind III Corps' line, and later by shelling the trenches near La Boutillerie. The day (16 February) was very quiet but with a strong westerly gale. A few enemy working parties were dispersed: an observer with a telescope reported fifteen of one party hit by our combined artillery and MG fire. GOC 8th Division assumed command of the new right extension of the III Corps front, extending it to Chapigny.

Putty wrote to Ettie Desborough on 16 February:

> My dear Chief, You owe me a letter. The gales have been terrific, trees and telegraph lines are down in all directions the latter interfering more than anything else. Lord K was round here on Thursday [10 February], he saw my new divisions but it was a hopeless day he is looking much older I thought and walking lame, he Monro [GOC 1st Army] and Prince Arthur [Prince Arthur of Connaught] were a limping trio, he thinks the Germans have only got 900,000 more men to draw on which should only last them at the ordinary rate until August, it will be somewhat doubtful if Europe will stand the strain more than this year. Hunter-Weston was here last week quite recovered and looking better than I have ever seen him for a long time, he is going to get a corps out here when a vacancy occurs. The Germans shelled my line very heavily indeed on Saturday and Sunday [12 and 13 February], I had more casualties than I have had for a long time but it has done the men good for they were getting much too accustomed to think themselves immune and had got lazy about digging themselves in. The Germans seem to be massing a good many men expect they will have a minor attack against the Ypres-St Elois salient and make a big attack down S in the neighbourhood of Verdun after which they will have a go against Russia is my prophecy and they will use a good proportion of Turkish troops to do it by which means they will save their men and prevent trouble with Bulgaria. Desperate row going on in the park here testing various kinds of fog horns for gas alarms, it seems impossible to wake the British soldier in his dug out in time. Pa Heyworth[14] dined here last night, he goes off today to Calais with his brigade for a week's rest before they go up N, am very distressed at their departure for it was very jolly having them all so near. Where will you be about the beginning of March if I come over for a week, am not certain of my plans yet so don't say anything about it. Am afraid the news from Mesopotamia is none too good but trust they will be able to pull the show through by the end of next month. I like the looks of my new division the 34th if they are not rushed at it they should form a valuable asset. Best love Yours ever Putty.

---

14   Brigadier General Frederick James Heyworth (1863-1916) late SG Comd 3 Gds Bde killed in action 9 May.

Little changed at the front 17-21 February except the days were cold and usually dull. Sometimes at night it cleared and then owing to the extreme brightness the GS log noted: 'our patrols did not go far afield'.

La Baronne de la Grange wrote:

Yesterday (21 February) Madame Rejane,[15] whose son Jacques Porel, is an interpreter with the British Army, came here to see him. She passed forty-eight hours under my roof, and was gracious enough to recite us passages from Madame Sans-Gêne and the Blue Bird. I invited all the General Staffs and officers in the district, and it was a great success. The main staircase, which goes from the entrance hall up to the first floor, formed the auditorium, and the officers sat there, pretty well packed, producing a general effect of beautifully cleaned boots and a background of khaki, among which showed up here and there a rare French 'cornflower'. The High Command surrounded Madame Rejane, to do her honour, but I did notice that she cast a friendly glance now and then in the direction of the younger officers of the staff.

Next day (22 February) it snowed for most of the day; the ground in front of the lines was found to be very marshy and consequently there was little activity. DDMS recorded: '11.50 am. 103 Fd Amb took over finally yesterday and is fairly well established. Gave them 15 pairs of slippers from the Corps Commander'. 23 February was frosty and more snow fell; patrolling was again hampered by the moon. Major Jack 2 Cameronians wrote:

In line Fauquissart. The weather is vile following a few sunny days. Snowfalls have replaced incessant rain. The lines are in a terrible state of mud, and pumps are kept going all the time to persuade the water to flow along – not down – to the Layes stream.

Baronne de la Grange wrote:

The intense cold continues, and the staff officers, deprived of their usual sports, are replacing them by another sort of exercise. General Pulteney gives the example, and armed with a shovel, he throws himself passionately into the absorbing occupation of shovelling snow in the avenues and clearing the courtyard! The officers made a snow woman – a statue of me – just opposite my window, and while they were at mess I looked out some old clothes – feathered hat, a parasol, and shawl, skirt and boots – and dressed it up. Unluckily, they were delayed, and a ray of warm sunshine – like that of Austerlitz – shining upon my image melted it piteously, and when the officers arrived they only found a pathetic heap of snow and old garments! A shell could not have wrought greater destruction on its objective, but great was the amusement of my guests in fishing out the sorry 'glad rags' from the snow.

---

15   Gabrielle Rejane (1856-1920), the stage name of Gabrielle-Charlotte Reju, famous comedienne. In 1895 she performed her most famous role in New York as Catherine in Sardou's Madame Sans-Gêne – the story of Marshal Lefebvre's unreserved and good-hearted wife Catherine Hubscher (1774-1861), a French female soldier.

Pulteney and ADC (Hamilton) clearing snow at Chateau La Motte au Bois February 1916.
(de la Grange)

34th Division took over from 23rd Division in the line on 24 February, another frosty day. 10 Lincoln 101 Bde recorded in its history: 'Now no longer under instruction, moved into the front line trenches near Bois Grenier. During this spell suffered first serious casualties, losing 4 killed and 5 wounded'. There was more snow and little enemy activity on 25 February, the day that the last readjustment was completed. At 11.15 am DDMS wrote: 'Special Ward. Machinery still going. I gave them 10 pairs of felt slippers from Corps Commander'.

Yet more snow fell on 26 February although a thaw set in. No enemy patrols were encountered although there were a number out on the corps' front. III Corps Artillery also had the upper hand destroying two armoured emplacements opposite Cordonnerie, a MG emplacement at Picantin, and obtaining several hits on the Distillerie and neighbouring station buildings. Having been relieved by 34th Division, 23rd Division went into corps reserve and on 27 February orders were issued for it to join IV Corps.

At 9 am 27 February DDMS wrote: 'At request of Corps Commander arranged with 'Q' for an extra ½ ton of coal daily for 10 days for 24 Fd Amb to provide extra baths for itch cases [Scabies caused by the itch mite which burrows beneath skin – leads to intense itch]'. The health and welfare of his corps received Putty's constant attention, and he missed little.

He wrote to Ettie that day:

> My dear Chief, You have been remiss with your pen. The Verdun reverses have not been as bad as I anticipated, there was a big salient there, the Germans have dealt with one side of it and in due course will deal with the other side, they are sensible and go for smashing in salients instead of trying to break through which would be bad policy on their part, of course they could do it at Ypres or Armentières whenever they wanted to,

we on the other hand break through and make more salients like Loos, these salients cost us more men to hold than we ever lost even in taking them, what we want to do is to gain tactical points while our army is being formed and trained. Training of staff officers at home is what our army wants more than anything, next to that schools of instruction for NCOs, plenty of disabled officers have gone home who would do the work splendidly, this sort of work comes on our shoulders out here when we are not in a position to carry it out from want of officers and necessary accommodation. The aeroplane at night is going to be a great factor it is almost impossible to see them to shoot at them and if it was not for the difficulty of landing after a raid in the dark they would be desperately vulnerable to railways [sic], you would laugh to see the shutters being closed in the chateau here by my thoughtful staff directly the lamps are lit, I have taken little interest in it myself for there is no object in going for single houses in the middle of a forest when you can take on towns like Béthune which are alive with troops, what is required in these days are very fast machines that are handy to land which is a very difficult combination. The frost and snow are the finishing touches to the road at the end of the winter, the regulations for the thaw are long enough to be quite impracticable but if we break them the French say we have ruined their roads in which statement they have mush justice on their side. You would have smiled to have seen the cessation of the artillery on both sides when the snow came down, everyone afraid of giving away their position by the mark left on the snow by the blast of the gun and the dread of the footmark to the eyes of the aeroplane. Bestlove Yours ever Putty.

It was dull and cold on 28 February: owing to the thaw, no man's land was found to be very swampy everywhere in front of 34th Division, less so in front of 8th Division. It was a leap year; 29 February was fine and breezy, and 23rd Division left III Corps. There was as yet no inkling that Putty knew what was about to happen or that he and these three divisions were to play a part in it. Now, as winter ended, he was required to hold his part of the line with just two divisions. III Corps casualties for February 1916 were: 4 officers and 92 other ranks killed, 26 officers and 509 other ranks wounded, 1 officer missing = 632.

It was fine and warm on 1 March but otherwise little changed at the front. An increase was authorised in the number of staff officers in each corps HQ from 18 on mobilisation to 24 by July 1916. Five of the extra six officers were for the artillery – the CHA (to command two or more HAGs), his BM, SC and ADC, and a SO for the BGRA. The greater responsibility of the corps was evident by the increase in the number of corps troops: from only a cable section in 1914, they now included a corps cavalry regiment, corps cyclist battalion, corps signal company and associated troops, corps ammunition parks, three supply columns, ASC companies, mobile ordnance workshops, several HAGs, engineer and RFC units. This expansion was to continue, but the established number of GS and AQ staff officers remained the same.

Patrol and artillery engagements continued into 2 March with only desultory retaliation from the enemy. Putty sent his monthly report to the King:

My dear Wigram, Attached is the diary of the 3rd Corps for the month of February. Am afraid that there is but little to tell you except that now the 23rd Division have left me and the 39th Division is expected to begin arriving in my area tomorrow, the 23rd under General Babington had done very well, they are a good division but not as good as the 20th and they wanted a little more time before taking over a bad bit of the line but am sure they will do well. The 39th is commanded by General Barnardiston[16] who I used to know well at one time as my central African work was under his section at the Intelligence Department, I have no idea what they are like. The Verdun fight was typical of German methodical coordination, they surrounded the salient with an overpowering number of guns then advanced by stages but never before they had already consolidated the line that was already captured, they went for tactical points and did not go breaking through on lines of least resistance and then find themselves hung up with a salient to defend like we have at Loos. The war is fast developing in to an artillery duel it looks like whoever can make the most gun ammunition being ahead for the day, the great thing is to keep them fighting this side while Russia gets ready. I meant to come over this week but had to postpone until later date will let you know if I do come. Yours sincerely, WP Pulteney.

The III Corps GS log noted on 3 March that 'two more sentries' lives were saved by the new steel helmet' otherwise nothing of significance was reported. Next day it snowed again; the GS log recorded:

A small combined scheme was carried out by the corps heavy and 34th Division's light artillery, a large breach being made in the enemy's parapet. The 6" guns got 8 direct hits out of 10 rounds fired on the Distillerie. Out of 61 4.2" shells fired by the enemy at our front trench in front of Picantin, 45 were blind, and out of 11 5.9"s fired behind the same front four only exploded, due no doubt to the softness of the ground.

III Corps' patrols were very active overnight (4/5 March) in spite of the sodden condition of the ground, several reaching the enemy's wire. An enemy LP was bombed: no hostile patrols were encountered. III Corps Artillery retained the upper hand bombarding the Distillery and Sugar Loaf salient in conjunction with a 6" gun; the latter had ten direct hits and much damage was done.

Putty wrote to Edith Londonderry on 5 March:

Dearest La Motte, Thanks for your letter of 26 Feb. There is no news to tell you more especially as I hear you have got your Charley with you. The Verdun coup has made a lot of alterations, it was well planned by the Boche, the salient was so large he was able to concentrate about 800 guns on it, the French knew it was coming and for that reason I blame them for keeping the Moroccan Division there for they knew they would never stick the heavy shelling, they bolted as did another French division with the result that the remaining division that stuck it was surrounded and they constituted the bulk of the prisoners, the amount of ammunition expenditure was colossal and it only convinces me that we shall never have enough at our present rate of increase, if they only made a less complicated fuze we could go ahead double the pace. I lost the 23rd Division last week just as it was getting trained it was not nearly so good as the 20th but was just beginning to come on it has gone down to take over ground from the French and in due course we shall have taken over all the ground

16   Major General Barnardiston (1858-1919) late Middx.

between 1st and 3rd Armies and shall all be in a line instead of having a sandwich of French, this will be a better arrangement though it means holding more line about 85 miles but still it was quite time we were pulling more weight for the French. The 39th Division begins to arrive tomorrow under Barnardiston who is a good man, I know nothing about his division, this will make the fifteenth division I have had under me I am a bally old school master with new boys coming each term. How is Miss Florence? Did any of the Bulgars try to take advantage of her lovely person!! I expect she had some pretty interesting experiences. Cis Bingham[17] came to luncheon here yesterday very down in his luck, he has been recommended for a billet at home but has no idea if there is anything vacant, the drop in his pay affects him a good deal, poor devil they just telephoned to him to say that his command was broken up voila tout, manners are curt in these days. Harold Brassey[18] came to tea yesterday he seems very fit and well as an infantry CO his division goes off S this week to join the 3rd Army. The recapture of the International Trench up Ypres way was very well done, they bombarded it for two days stopping in the evening, then rushed them at 4.15 am it was a complete surprise and they killed an awful lot of Boches, they collared 47 in a steel dug out who stuck it out inside for 24 hours before they surrendered. One of the Canadians swam down the River Douve the other night under the German wire put a mass of explosives in the trenches with a time fuze and swam back under the wire again all right. Bestlove Yours ever Putty.

It snowed again on 6 March, although it thawed later in the day. The GS log recorded: 'Numerous patrols were out, but encountered only two enemy patrols, both of which retired. Enemy MGs were inactive. Hostile artillery was very quiet. Our field artillery shelled the enemy's parapet at various points, destroyed a MG, cut wire, and dispersed working parties. Our heavy guns again bombarded the Distillerie successfully, inflicting casualties. They also dispersed some working parties. Our snipers hit several of the enemy, and of his periscopes'. III Corps' aggressive defence was still dominating the enemy in front of it.

Also on 6 March, five days after taking command of the 4th Army front and the preparations for the offensive on the Somme having been transferred to him, General Rawlinson held a conference of his corps commanders at Querrieu. At this meeting he told them the general nature of future operations, and that 4th Army would probably be reinforced by another corps and by heavy artillery. Subject to modification, the order of the corps, each brought up to the strength of four divisions, would be, from S to N: XIII (Congreve), new corps, X (Morland) and VIII (Hunter-Weston). The first phase would be the capture of the enemy's 1st position; the date would probably be June or July, although an offensive of some kind might be necessary in April in order to relieve pressure on the French at Verdun. He ordered the corps commanders, X Corps acting for the new corps, to prepare their plans and to get on with all the preliminary preparations, such as the selection of sites for batteries, construction of observation posts, and laying of telephone cables, so that no time would be lost.

There is no firm evidence that Rawlinson or Putty knew that III Corps would be a 'new corps' at this stage. In fact there were to be two 'new corps' with III and XV Corps coming in to the line between XIII and X Corps. Putty did not attend this meeting.

---

17   Probably GOC 1st Cavalry Division until October 1915.
18   RHG CO 8 S Lancs killed in action 15 July.

There was snow and sleet all day on 7 March and no man's land was in a very marshy state; nevertheless the patrol and artillery engagements continued. DDMS noted that day: '9 am. At request of Corps Commander wrote to DMS 1st Army that 23rd Division may have a lot of itch still, having left 140 cases here when they left'.

Putty also wrote to Ettie on 7 March:

> My dear Chief, Many thanks for your letter of 28 Feb. The weather here has been atrocious, heavy snow, floods, thaw and frost alternately, it really has made the roads difficult to deal with and work in the lines next to impossible. Tell me what you think of the American attitude, I never can take a fair view of them because I have always disliked them as a nation, this war I compare them to a woman who looks on the mantelpiece for payment before doing business with her man. It is a good thing getting the whole British Army in one line instead of having French corps sandwiched as heretofore, it makes a long line and the process of taking over makes the offensive on our part very difficult especially with two new untrained divisions as in my case but still there we are expanding at a great rate, all of it means more shells and more bullets to go at the enemy on the Western Front this is where we want to keep him until August by which time Russia will have got a few arms and shells up her sleeve. I have got a young engineer officer who was fighting with the Russians for the first eight months of the war, his description of the way they were armed and the number of rounds they had to fight with baffles all description I can't imagine how they still exist as an army, he says the men are absolutely splendid and will go on killing Germans so long as ever they are allowed to. All blessings Yours ever Putty.

Artillery and patrol engagements continued on 8 March, a fine day but with snow still lying. To the right of Cordonnerie a hostile mine gallery was broken into and entered; enemy were encountered and one fell to pistol fire. Two 15 lb charges of gun-cotton were fired and the remains of one or two Germans were found. Also that day, in the afternoon, Monro (GOC 1st Army) visited HQ III Corps and the HQs of 8th and 34th Divisions. The underground battle continued into the next day as the GS log recorded:

> The charges yesterday having failed to close the enemy's mine gallery, this was further explored in the night. The enemy, who used rifles, were kept at bay by pistol, while a 30 lb charge was laid and fired. Finally a charge of 200 lbs was blown at 4.5 am and a shaft head was located a little later by the escaping gas. It was bombarded with considerable effect during the morning by 4.5" hows.

On 10 March there was more snow: the GS log continued:

> Our 9.2" hows fired 20 rounds at the enemy's shaft head located yesterday, breaching the parapet and scattering timber. At the fourth shot, a fire was started which burnt all day and night, emitting continuous thick smoke. This may possibly have been a ruse to prevent further shelling. More probably the gallery broken into yesterday communicates with more than one shaft; the enemy fired a camouflet there at 1 pm, followed five minutes later by a small mine, which made a small crater outside our wire.

Above and below ground III Corps continued to dominate the enemy. That day the movement of 39th Division in to the corps reserve area was completed.

The nature and scale of the fighting was little different on 11 and 12 March. An LVG aeroplane descended E of Laventie on 11 March owing to engine trouble and its occupants, a captain and an 'unter-offizier' were captured. On both days according to the GS log 'our snipers claimed a dozen hits, a little more than the daily average'.

There was bright sunshine on 13 March, the day that 39th Division started its instruction with 8th Division. No man's land was still very swampy and no hostile patrols were met. The good weather continued for the next three days and no man's land began to dry out, although the ditches remained full which impeded movement. Patrol and artillery engagements continued with particular attention paid by III Corps to the enemy's working parties on the front line. Baronne de la Grange wrote on 15 March: 'III Corps is leaving me. General Pulteney and his officers have just been to bid me farewell'.

The good weather continued on 17 and 18 March although there was much mist which restricted artillery operations. On 18 March the GS log noted: '11.30 pm. We exploded a counter-mine 40 yards in front of our wire – on the right of the Cordonnerie Salient. The enemy was heard working about 20 feet away at the time. The crater formed was 50 ft across and 15 ft deep'. There was bright moonlight on the night 18/19 March which made it impossible for patrols to work very close to the enemy's lines, and there was little activity on 19 March.

Putty wrote to Ettie:

My dear Chief, Charlie Hindlip tells me Willy [her husband] has been unwell but trust that he is all right again. The weather is glorious again, the floods have disappeared, one forgets there ever has been such a thing as winter, flies have begun, all the farm yards are being cleaned to kill all their breeding places together with the mosquitos. I enclose you a letter from McCalmont [CO 1 IG] about poor Desmond Fitzgerald burn it when you have read it, there have been a terrible lot of these accidents all through the army but it is very difficult work training all these boys to handle such things without accidents. The Germans have been very quiet opposite my corps and pretty well all along the British line, the Vaux (Fort Vaux) repulses at Verdun really did cost them very dearly and the defence of the French has been very brilliant but it is a good thing we are collecting some of the Egyptian divisions to shorten their line for them, two have arrived safely and I don't think all the fuss about the Egyptians rising will be heard any more of. Are the government really shaky everybody out here says so, the married even have a grievance, the Derby[19] figures too seem to be all wrong and all the exemptions on the lines that you must be a trade unionist to become exempt. Winston has returned I hear if there is any justice he should be wounded in the mouth to stop him making those sort of speeches in the future. Have you seen Arthur Paget[20] or Reggie Pembroke since they came back from Russia? Wonder what sort of impression they returned with from all accounts that reach us the munition question is nearly as bad as ever and their railway arrangements contemptible. The leave begins again tomorrow and the boats tomorrow will be crammed with the lucky ones who are able to get

19   Edward George Villiers Stanley 17th Earl of Derby (1865-1948) late Gren Gds SofS for War 1916-1918.
20   General Sir Arthur Paget (1851-1928) late SG Head British Military Mission to Russia 1915-1916.

away, my new division the 39th gives me fits when I think of their ignorance one just has to hope for the best while they are learning. Bestlove Yours ever Putty.

The enemy were ineffective 20-22 March with III Corps' patrols, MGs and artillery continuing to dominate. At 7 pm 21 March HQ III Corps issued OpO No.66 – Adjustment of III Corps' front; then, at 4 pm 22 March OpO No.67 – Transfer of 8th and 39th Divisions to XI Corps and 34th Division to II Corps at 10 am 24 March: HQ III Corps was to be transferred to 4th Army at 12 noon 24 March.

23 and 24 March were again relatively quiet. HQ 4th Army issued 32/3(G) on 23 March – Transfer of HQ III Corps and 8th Division to 4th Army. HQ III Corps to be located at Montigny and 8th Division to take over the new corps' front opposite the villages of Ovillers and La Boisselle. On 24 March at 10 am the line and most of III Corps was divided between II and XI Corps: two hours later HQ III Corps with III Corps Signal Company, defence platoon, and III Corps Troops Supply Column came under command of 4th Army. The HQ closed at Chateau la Motte au Bois, where it had been since August 1915, at 9 am 26 March and re-opened in Montigny at the same time. Writing of that last day Major Jack 2 Cameronians 23 Bde 8th Division noted: 'In line at Fauquissart. The weather is infamously wet, cold and snowy; the pumps are on the go all the time trying to reduce the floods at the breastworks. We get back from inspections of companies plastered with mud from head to heel'. 8th Division, which had been in III Corps for nine months, started its move S on 27 March. At 8 am 28 March HQ III Corps issued OpO No.68 – 8th Division to take over portion of the line now held by 32nd Division X Corps at 10 am 5 April with HQ at Hénencourt; GOC III Corps assumes command of III Corps area at same time and date.

Battle of the Somme April-December 1916

Preparation

Putty wrote to Ettie from Montigny on 28 March: 'My dear Chief, Thanks for your letter of 24 Mar. I hope to arrive in London on Friday next 31 March, shall stay at the Ritz, hope to be over for a week, send me a line to the Turf as to where you will be that Sunday 1 April All news then Yours ever Putty'.

It was bright sunshine on the morning of 29 March with a snowstorm in the afternoon. 8th Division continued to arrive in III Corps rear area and was complete there on 30 March; its HQ opened at Flesselles. That day HQ III Corps issued G216:

Memorandum to divisions on important points for consideration on taking over portion of 4th Army area (summary): 'The Corps Commander wished GOCs divisions (8th Division, and 19th and 34th Divisions on arrival) to impress the following points on all their subordinates:

1. Importance of preventing the enemy learning of the arrival of new troops in 4th Army area.
2. The very different country with the enemy having very good observation of many of our positions and the area behind – and the impact of this on our movement in daylight.
3. The need to reduce road movement to a minimum in daylight – to conceal the arrival of new troops.

4. For 8th and 34th Divisions to adopt the same methods as the troops they are relieving
   – and any changes to be adopted gradually.
5. Conceal from the enemy the concentration of artillery on this front'.

It was a fine day on 31 March. HQ III Corps issued G225 – List of positions of HQs and
G228 – Boundaries of III Corps. III Corps casualties for March 1916 were: 7 officers and 70
other ranks killed, 16 officers and 408 other ranks wounded = 501. Putty set off for England on
leave; it was his first recorded leave and the first time that he had seen Jessie since the war started
twenty months earlier. Putty mentions one week but he did not return until 10 April

The weather at the front was generally fine for the next ten days: during this time 8th Division
took over command of the new III Corps front from 32nd Division X Corps at 10 am 5 April,
with HQ 8th Division now at Hénencourt, and HQ III Corps began to assemble its corps
troops. 21 Motor Ambulance Convoy (MAC) joined on 1 April; one section 4th Army Horse
Transport Coy and C Coy 2 Labour Bn on 2 April; HQ 27 Group RGA, 57 Siege Bty (4 × 8"
hows), 1/1 London Hy Bty (4 × 4.7" guns), one sect 26 Siege Bty (2 × 6" guns), 214 and 221
AT Coys RE, D Coy 2 Labour Bn, two coys 6 Entrenching Bn, 179 Tunnelling Coy, HQ and
1 Sect 5 Bridging Train RE on 5 April; 22 Hy Bty (4 × 60 pdr guns) and C Bty RMA (4 × 2
pdr pompoms) on 8 April; and 23 Hy Bty (4 × 60 pdr guns) on 9 April. III Corps had a very
narrow front and consequently the allocation of space and control of movement in the rear areas
were extremely difficult. There were very few routes forward and movement on them restricted
in daylight because of the need for secrecy and because they were in many places overlooked by
the enemy. III Corps' area began to resemble a vast military encampment, and there were still
three divisions and numerous other units to come. The organisation and administration of the
corps was a monumental staff exercise, and that was before any battle. There was no room to
manoeuvre, barely room to move: but what was being planned in Putty's absence was a battle
of attrition.

Haig wrote to Robertson (CIGS) on 4 April a letter that had a chilling effect on the government. It made it clear what lay ahead; he told them the attack was to be all out and the casualties
might run into the hundreds of thousands.

Writing in April before his meeting with Haig (on 5 April) Rawlinson said: 'If the artillery
did its work well, the rest would be easy'. It was impressed on all, at conferences and at other
times, both by Haig and Rawlinson – to use the latter's words: 'Nothing could exist at the
conclusion of the bombardment in the area covered by it' and 'The infantry would only have to
walk over and take possession'. Much later in the context of La Boisselle Rawlinson said: 'The
village would have been rendered untenable and the Germans in it wiped out by the preliminary
bombardment'. This belief in the total supremacy of the artillery was to prove the greatest of
several flawed planning assumptions.

Before going to see Haig (on 5 April) Rawlinson held a conference of his corps commanders
at 10 am at HQ 4th Army (Querrieu). He noted:

I asked each corps commander in turn to give me briefly his plan of attack. Hunter-Weston,
Morland and Hudson (GOC 8th Division representing Putty) all showed by their descriptions that they realised the problem before them and they were working on the right lines.
Congreve (GOC XIII Corps) I was less satisfied with and I therefore called him up into my
room afterwards and gave him a talking to pointing out that he saw too many difficulties.

Considering how little time they had to prepare and what else was going on Hudson and Romer (BGGS III Corps) did well to present any plan at this conference.

Meanwhile Putty was on leave. King George V in his private diary noted on 3 April: 'General Pulteney came to see me and I gave him the KCB and knighted him'. On 6 April Putty sent his monthly report to the King: 'My dear Wigram, I enclose the diary of III Corps for the month of March as His Majesty told me that he would like to see it. The enclosed statistics* also might interest the King from a general point of view, they are only those of course of III Corps but might give a general idea. I return on Monday 10 April Yours sincerely, WP Pulteney'

* III Corps September 1915 – March 1916. Casualties: Officers – 73 killed, 208 wounded and 14 missing = 295; Other ranks – 1,030 killed, 4,885 wounded and 465 missing = 6,380; Total – 1,103 killed, 5,093 wounded and 479 missing = 6,675. Evacuated sick: 0.95 per 1,000 per day = 9,147. Reinforcements received: 9,410. Ammo (arty) expended: 313,089 (18 pdr: 254,698).

For much of his leave Putty was pursuing his love for Jessie Arnott (Chapter 11). On 7 April he wrote to Ettie Desborough from the Ritz Hotel:

> My dear Chief, I went to see her again and you have won your bet but on no account will you tell a soul for the present, you will understand why I don't come down am just walking on air. Yours Putty.

Again from the Ritz he wrote to Ettie twice on 8 April:

> My dear Chief, Thanks for your letter which however only reached me this morning you must forgive my not coming down but you do understand the circumstances don't you? All goes well so far but she is particularly anxious that no one should know at present for reasons which I won't write. I shall see her at luncheon but from what I know of her I don't think that she will come down tomorrow [9 April] I wish she would. Yours ever Putty.

Later that day he wrote:

> My dear Chief, I could not persuade her to come down tomorrow she is so nervous about anyone knowing for the present. I do wish I had seen you again for there was much I wanted to talk to you about. I return on Monday [10 April]. Yours ever Putty.

He wrote again to Ettie from the Ritz Hotel on 9 April:

> My dear Chief, I just couldn't get her to face Panshanger, she is so frightened of anyone knowing it, it just makes me laugh the reason but I cannot write it but if I hadn't known that you were at all times a tomb I never would have told you, I am just the happiest man in the world and mean to smash the Germans to finish the war and make me free. I shall want you to do some commissions for me, still my Chief. Yours ever Putty.

Portrait photograph of Pulteney by
Russell of London 1916.

The ADOS log recorded on 6 April (during Putty's leave): 'Sample number 24 periscope to DA&QMG for Corps Commander'. Putty was very interested in any new equipment that could improve the effectiveness of the corps or the welfare of the men in it.

While Putty was on leave Rawlinson wrote (8 April) of his imminent arrival to Wigram (APS to the King): 'Putty who is now home, and has no doubt seen you, will have told you that he has brought his old III Corps down here to join my army in place of the Australians. I am delighted to have him especially as he has brought with him the 8th Division'. He also wrote to Robertson (CIGS): 'The four corps commanders I have are Hunter-Weston, Morland, Putty (Pulteney), and Congreve. They are now well-staffed and I ask for no changes though the last is I think the weakest'.

Putty returned from leave on 10 April, a cloudy and wet day. Next day DDMS wrote: '9 am. Corps Commander returned from leave. He approves of a Corps Itch Hospital'. He then visited HQ 4th Army at Querrieu with Rawlinson noting: 'Putty came to lunch all the better for his weeks leave'. Afterwards Rawlinson went to 8th Division opposite La Boisselle and noted: 'It did not come out well'. It was a bad day for 8th Division with the GS log recording at 6.55 pm: 'The German artillery commenced a heavy bombardment of our front, reserve and communication trenches, in the right section, trench mortars and MGs cooperating. A good many lachrymatory shells were used. The bombardment lasted one hour and 15 minutes. Considerable damage was done to the trenches and about 60 casualties were caused by it principally to 1 RIR. A German raiding party got into our trenches and captured 28 men and one Lewis gun. Our artillery and the heavy artillery of X and XIII Corps retaliated'.

HQ III Corps AQ log recorded that day the issue of QC113 – 'Instructions on the control of use of water'. This was but one of the many logistic and administrative problems requiring the staff's attention.

Putty wrote to Ettie Desborough again on 11 April:

My dear Chief, A 1000 thanks for your letter which I got on Sunday. She's very funny and won't let us mention it to anyone at present, she tells me all her family have been the same in this respect, when the embargo is off I will make her see you, I quite agree with you about getting married and suggested coming back in July to do so but she wanted time to make up her mind so have just left her to think it over. Had a wonderful passage over with my 2 ADCs, I think Linlithgow is bigger than ever at least he seemed so at the end of the motor drive. Today it has been horrid nothing but rain besides turning much colder, the Germans have been pretty active down opposite me, a great amount of shelling and raiding has been going on, they seem to have an endless supply of gun ammunition which is astounding with Verdun going on all this time. I went to see the Sussex [Cross-channel passenger ferry torpedoed 24 March] in Boulogne Harbour, the torpedo just cut the fore part of the ship clean off, you could not have done it better with an axe, luckily the explosion was outwards and the bulkhead under the captain's bridge held all right or she must have gone down. Am afraid they are not going to be able to relieve poor Townsend[21] and he will have a sorrowful journey to Constantinople. Best love Yours ever Putty.

The III Corps GS log recorded on 12 April, a day that was cloudy and wet:

Throughout the day and well into the night, the enemy fired various trench mortar bombs, canisters, and rifle grenades against our trenches opposite La Boisselle. At least 250 were fired. Our 4.5" howitzers replied but failed to silence the enemy.

For the next four days the 4.5" hows tried to neutralise the enemy's trench mortars, only succeeding on 16 April, as the GS log again noted:

German trench mortars again active about La Boisselle. They opened fire at 10 pm with them but were speedily silenced by combined fire of 4.5" hows, Mills bombs and rifle grenades.

On 13 April Putty wrote to Edith Londonderry:

My dear Circe, Here we are at it again but all the better for the London air which beyond going to Kew I never went outside of, after all it is the healthiest place in the world. Had a great night with Bertie and Rock on Sunday, felt most extraordinary well considering the next day too. The blighters raided us on my return after a terrific bombardment of course they chose the worst battalion in the corps to take on and they chucked it (between

---

21   Major General Charles Vere Ferrers Townshend (1861-1924) late Indian Army GOC 6th Indian Division surrendered Kut 29 April 1916.

ourselves) so 29 of them are marching to Berlin, they are all Irishmen I much doubt if they knew which brigade they belong to and am sure they don't know what division so much doubt if they get much information out of them. We had a lot of rain the last two days with bright intervals of April sun, the roads dry up very quickly here which is a good thing. The French are very pleased with themselves at Verdun and claim to have killed a vast number of Germans altogether besides they have only used their divisions once and not twice like the Boche. Mind you write me with the news. Yours ever Putty.

On 15 April Putty sent HQ III Corps G378 to 4th Army: 'Report on raid on 1 RIR 25 Bde on 11 April. GOC 8th Division placed OC C Coy 1 RIR under arrest and ordered a court of inquiry. Apparently no officer was in the front line'. More corps troops continued to arrive with 60 Siege Bty less one sect (2 × 6" guns) and 83 Siege Bty (2 × 12" hows on railway mountings) joining the corps that day.

Rawlinson held his next conference on 16 April noting: 'At 3 pm I had a corps commanders conference which lasted till 4.30 pm. I gave them the conditions of the new problem and discussed many important questions – all went well and I was pleased with the tone and keenness of the meeting'. Rawlinson explained to them the CinC's plan: the objective of III, X and VIII Corps would be the Pozières-Grandcourt-Serre line, which was to be gained, not necessarily in one bound, but on the first day, and not in two operations as he had previously indicated. Putty would have been briefed by Hudson (Acting GOC III Corps in his absence) and by his BGGS on return from leave. According to the III Corps GS log, Putty briefly explained his plan for attack at the conference (III Corps objective for the first day was Pozières/Contalmaison).

The engagements between the enemy trench mortars and III Corps' 4.5" hows continued on 17 and 18 April. 18 NF (Pioneer bn 34th Division) joined III Corps on 18 April and went into billets at Bresle; the rest of 34th Division would follow. In a letter by Rawlinson on 18 April to Clive Wigram he wrote: 'Putty who was lunching with me today is in his best form, all the better for his weeks leave which was long overdue'. It was a very short distance between Montigny and Querrieu, and Putty must have seen Rawlinson frequently: however, clearly Putty did not reveal that he was now unofficially engaged to Jessie.

Also that day (18 April) DDMS recorded: 'I spoke to Corps Commander about probability Fd Amb would become blocked owing to slowness of evacuation, as Heilly is not allotted to us alone, and Amiens is a long journey and trains are not likely to be plentiful'. They discussed the problem again next day – DDMS again: '9 am. I saw Corps Commander with Q re evacuation problem. He suggested Pont Noyelles as light cases station, and getting a CCS there'.

28 Siege Bty joined III Corps on 20 April: the arrival of so much heavy artillery allowed the softening up of La Boisselle to be started as the GS log recorded that day:

Our heavy artillery carried out a bombardment of La Boisselle with 6" and 8" hows; 4.5" hows, 18 pdrs and trench mortars co-operated. It is believed a considerable amount of damage was done, but owing to the depth of the trenches it is very hard definitely to say. The enemy retaliation was weak, being confined to a few 77 mm shells and a few trench mortar bombs.

The artillery on both sides was fairly active on 21 April. A few shrapnel were fired at the German wire S of La Boisselle; 4.5 hows obtained two direct hits on an OP, one on a MG emplacement, and two on a dugout into which some Germans had just gone. Five siege btys and elements 90 Hy Bty joined the corps that day.

It was a wet day with fair intervals on 22 April. Between 9.45 am and 11 am the German wire was cut in two places by Ovillers, it was also fired at S of La Boisselle. At 9.20 pm that evening the GS log recorded:

> Our artillery, field and heavy, opened fire. Under cover of the bombardment a party of 1 RIR attempted a raid S of La Boisselle, with the object of obtaining an identification. Two Germans at least were killed, but no identification could be obtained. Our casualties were three wounded and one missing. The enemy retaliated vigorously to our bombardment.

On 24 April Rawlinson rode over to Montigny; he wrote:

> I am displeased with the part taken by the RIR [1 RIR 25 Bde 8th Division] in the raid on Sat night (22 April). They would not follow their officer who behaved very well and shot two Germans himself. The report of their behaviour when the Boches raided them (11 April) is poor reading and I shall hope to try an officer and at least one corporal for cowardice. They are a very bad battalion. I rode over to Putty today and gave him my views on the RIR.

Next day Putty visited Querrieu (HQ 4th Army). Rawlinson noted: 'Putty came this morning to enviegle against losing Dernancourt'. The loss of Dernancourt would have further narrowed and constricted III Corps' area around Albert. Putty also wrote to Ettie:

> My dear Chief, There is not much news for you from these parts, we have had dreadful weather followed by two glorious days, the glass is high and it looks like lasting. The Russian arrival was a great excitement we had expected them so long we had given them up, General Horne[22] who had just arrived from Egypt told me he had seen them in the canal, nice young yokel class of men, clean shaven with old officers covered with medals, they were packed like herrings on the ships, the French have armed them with their old rifle with the long bayonet, about a division have arrived, I thought Joffre's welcome speech very fine we have no one who could have expressed himself thus. The Germans have raided us, the chief features being the great accuracy of the shooting of the artillery at night due to their superior gun platform and their guns never being changed from the sector they are covering. Have been doing some gardening lately here, Gavin Hamilton and Linlithgow both work well under the guiding hand, the amount of seed which has arrived from London is enough to stock ten gardens of double the size, am not sure that Gavin Hamilton is not going off to command one of Ferdie Stanley's[23] battalions he might be able to do it in the summer but

---

22   Lieutenant General Henry Sinclair Horne (1861-1929) late RA GOC XV Corps Suez Canal until March 1916: XV Corps now transferred to 4th Army.

23   Probably Brigadier General Hon Ferdinand Charles Stanley (1871-1935) late Gren Gds Comd 89 Bde – Hamilton did not go.

never could stand the winter. Went down to Tréport last Thursday for the day to see Lady Murray's hospital[24] there and Mrs Roberts who was staying with her, the military hospital has been built on the most wind swept place they could possibly have found it must have been looking for a penal settlement. All blessings Yours ever Putty.

It was fine and warm on 26 April. Putty wrote to Edith Londonderry:

Dearest Circe, A 1000 thanks for the glorious Easter parcel you sent me, cakes and ginger breads with a darling little Easter egg, I should have liked to have seen you lay it, have put the little charm on my chain, I must try and find you a little egg with good fortune to send in return. If you come over to Paris mind you let me know a week end there would be glorious in this weather, the country is drying up at a great rate, they say they have heard a cuckoo but have not personally, swallows have arrived in great numbers they seem to think our telegraph wires have been put up on purpose for them to sit on. There has been little news on our front the Boche seems to have an allowance of ammunition which he keeps to blaze off in one day, jolly good shooting he makes too at night, he has the advantage because he does not shift his gunners about from area to area like we do and his gun has a better platform besides he has not had to make an army like we have had to do. I do hope they will shoot Roger Casement[25] at once, the Boche have sent him over on purpose to make trouble in Ireland, what a pity that he was not drowned, the man is a crank but that should not save his neck. Have done a lot of gardening at my new house, pansies, daisies, antirrhinums, while the kitchen is loaded with things for a permanent occupation, if we sow ½ of the seed that has been sent out to us we should go on until 1918 without any trouble whatever. Bestlove Yours ever Putty.

The rest of April was fine and warm: the pattern of activity, with artillery, trench mortar and rifle grenade exchanges continued, and the artillery exchanges were particularly heavy early in the morning of 30 April. On 27 April HQ III Corps issued G496 – Orders in connection with Anti-Aircraft defence on III Corps front. Next day (28 April) DDMS wrote: '9 am. Corps Commander this morning asked me about scabies, whether prevalent, and steps taken to combat it'. He also recorded on 30 April: 'DA&QMG (Brigadier General Hambro late 15 H) called this morning on me; spoke about providing tarpaulins to make bathing places for troops. Corps Commander has already discussed it'.

Putty wrote to Edith Londonderry again on 29 April:

Dearest Circe, Thanks for your letter of 25 Apr which I hasten to answer. Nugent [GOC 36th Division] said that he had gone carefully in to Charley's qualifications as a soldier; beyond the fact that he had been my ADC and an adjutant of the Blues he knew nothing that could justify his appointment as a brigadier, he would not entertain his local influence which to my mind was the greatest stumbling block, he then told me about Merry

24   No. 10 British Red Cross Hospital Tréport 1916-1918.
25   (Sir) Roger David Casement (1864-1916) Consul Boma 1903 Irish activist Easter Rising 1916 captured tried for treason and hanged.

John[26] who to my mind made a great mistake in his estimate of Charley's qualifications by answering oh give him a good brigade major and he will be all right, this of course showed weakness and to my mind put the whole thing out of court, he has got a good friend in Douglas Haig [CinC] and to all intent and purposes he has a far better chance with the cavalry than he ever will have with a battalion if he gets command of the Blues he will get what he deserves and well on his way to become a brigadier, this is for your private ear from one who has his whole career at heart. I feel so sore at heart at all this Irish business I cannot help thinking Charley ought to be with his people in Ireland, they ought to put Birrell[27] with Roger Casement in the Tower Ditch tomorrow morning, now they have sent the worst General[28] in the British Army to command in Dublin as a climax. Am so glad your father[29] is going to stick to his own name except Squire which was impossible it was for the best. We have had the most glorious weather the last few days; the glass is like a rock and we shall soon be howling because we are short of water which always does happen in these chalk countries. Am afraid Kut will fall this next week, it is a pity but cannot be helped I blame Fleetwood Wilson[30] for the whole thing except Hardinge[31] should have been a stronger man over the whole business and not allowed the cheese pairing policy in the campaign, they should keep a threatening force out there to pull the weight off the Russians and if they had sent a division to Alexandretta a month ago they would have relieved Kut and Egypt now they have done neither. Things out here are going along well and our increasing pressure on the Boche is making itself felt. Best of love Yours ever Putty.

III Corps casualties for April were: 4 officers and 54 other ranks killed, 9 officers and 245 other ranks wounded, 29 other ranks missing (all 1 RIR) = 341.

The good weather continued at the start of May and the enemy was increasingly active on the front line. The GS log recorded on 1 May: '7.15 pm. Last night enemy opened fire with MGs on right bde, followed immediately by two minenwerfer shells. This appeared to be the signal for a general bombardment of the right bde sub-sector. Our artillery replied very promptly and vigorously. Hostile fire slackened about 8 pm. An active hostile MG was knocked out by our gun-fire. Two parties of the enemy were seen to leave their trenches apparently with the object of raiding us, but both fell back under our shrapnel curtain and MG fire. Bombing parties were sent out on cessation of bombardment, but found no enemy'. The build up of heavy artillery continued with the arrival of 75 Siege Bty (4 × 6" hows) and 137 Hy Bty (4 × 60 pdrs).

III Corps MGs and artillery dominated the enemy on 2 May dispersing working parties and patrols, and causing damage to their front line. Putty sent his monthly report to the King that day:

26   General Sir John 'Jack' Cowans (1862-1921) late RB QMG.
27   Augustine Birrell (1850-1933) Chief Secretary for Ireland 1907-1916.
28   Lieutenant General John Grenfell Maxwell (1859-1929) late BW Military Governor of Ireland.
29   Henry Chaplin (1840-1923) created 1st Viscount Chaplin of Blankney 1916 known as the 'Squire of Blankney'.
30   Sir Guy Douglas Arthur Fleetwood Wilson (1851-1940) Financial Member and Vice President Legislative Council of India 1911-1913.
31   Charles Hardinge 1st Baron Hardinge (1858-1944) Cheam Viceroy of India 1910-1916 PUS Foreign Office 1916-1920.

My dear Wigram, Herewith the monthly diary of III Corps for the information of His Majesty. There is little to read in it for April because it is only the work of one division the 8th, the 34th begin to arrive tomorrow and the 19th on Saturday. The Irish Rifles [1 RIR] did not do very well when they were raided on 11 Apr but the blame is due to the officers and not the men I have made changes which I trust will have good effect, they have always been the worst battalion in the division. The Boche on this front confines himself entirely to making spasmodic raids, presumably with the object of obtaining prisoners for identification purposes, they are accompanied by a very intense artillery bombardment which is very accurate, all the trenches are smashed in and the difficulty is to prevent the men going in to the deep dugouts for safety where the exits are bad and from which there is no field of fire, they saturate the ground in rear of the point they are going to raid with lachrymatory shells also with gas shells both of which are very effective. Beyond these raids the mining is very active on both sides and in this chalk carried out at great depths with heavy charges, there is more defensive in the system on both sides at present but later on we hope to take more offensive action, the chief difficulty is the distance that working can be heard in this chalk in comparison with the blue clay we were accustomed to in Flanders. They have a very objectionable type of trench mortar which throws what the men call oil tins, a tin canister with a very thin covering, the weight is about 200 lbs chiefly high explosive, no noise is made when the bomb leaves the mortar, the difficulty is to locate the mortar accurately among all the mine craters among which they hide them. We have had the most wonderful weather for the last ten days which has dried everything up and made us realise that one must husband one's supplies of water to enable us to get through the summer. Yours sincerely, WP Pulteney.

The weather continued fine and warm. On 3 May the siege batteries of the heavy artillery in the corps were grouped under 3, 7 and 30 HAGs. Next day 34th Division began to arrive on joining the corps and its HQ opened at Baizieux. HQ III Corps issued OpO No.69 at 10 am 5 May – 34th Division to take over that portion of the line now held by right bde 8th Division at 8 am 10 May. Also that day Rawlinson (GOC 4th Army) noted: 'Today I went through the III Corps scheme of attack and saw both the div and corps commanders about it'.

In the front line the artillery, trench mortar and rifle grenade exchanges continued. 123 Hy Bty joined III Corps on 5 May; the GS log recorded on 6 May: 'At midnight we bombarded the enemy's trenches in accordance with a pre-arranged scheme. Two large dug-outs were blown to pieces'. Later that day, at 9.45 pm, HQ RA III Corps issued its OpO No.1 – Bombardment and CB with RFC. The number of guns in the corps had been significantly increased; now they were being used more effectively.

DDMS wrote that day: '9 am. I saw Corps Commander and mentioned the proposed move of 21 MAC (GOC 4th Army considered they blocked a road at La Houssoye). Corps Commander said they could remain at La Houssoye provided they got off the road'. This report is a minor illustration of the difficulties in maintaining the corps in such a small area and with so few roads forward. The motor ambulances had a very poor performance across country, and needed to be available at short notice to go forward and clear casualties from the front: La Houssoye was very close to Querrieu (HQ 4th Army) so inevitable that 21 MAC came to Rawlinson's attention.

34th Division was complete in III Corps on 7 May and 19th Division began to arrive that same day with its HQ opening at Flesselles. 90 Hy Bty joined III Corps as the artillery build up continued. Putty was in Paris staying at the Ritz Hotel from where he wrote to Edith Londonderry:

Dearest Circe, Many thanks for your letter of the 3 May I hope you have got Charley with you and got everything settled up to your satisfaction. Am spending another week end in Paris, it was the last chance of getting away this summer so bolted here with my two ADCs, we behaved fairly well last night but the preparations for tonight look like being pretty heavy work, but I trust we shall catch the train back all right in the morning. Neil Primrose[32] was here last night he was rather interesting about Egypt he said the submarines outside Malta at present were the very devil. Jemmy Rothschild also arrived from Boulogne, they have given him three months sick leave but won't decide yet whether they will let him go to England to recoup or not, the whole crew were in my sitting room last night ringing up the bordels that they used to know but as it was midnight they got no response to any of their calls that I could make out, the war has shut all those places up here which is one good thing anyway. Shall look forward to the stick bomb if you and Robin[33] are able to find one, I want revenge on Linlithgow for some of his school boy habits when he is gardening. Mrs Ronnie Greville[34] is staying here she held my hand so tightly yesterday I thought she was going to go further but luckily she stopped and only told me the number of my room, she is the stupidest woman in Europe I always think, though she did walk in to my room at the Hospital in Dublin one night by mistake I never could have taken it on!! Yes those Zepp raids must be most unwelcome guests in a country house coming at that time of night however it makes a good excuse for being found in the passage even if you are on the wrong floor you can claim you went to wake someone in case of fire!! There are so many kinds of fire which require extinguishing at times! Our garden is becoming the show thing of the place, the vegetables too are all coming up aussitôt que possible though the geese got in and devoured the young lettuce, the goat has had two kids, a record performance she began to squeal at 3 pm at 3.15 pm the two kids were born and 3.30 all three were standing up as if nothing had happened as the French refugee woman said to me, it is very easy like that Monsieur le General! The Boche has been very quiet opposite me all this last week in about a fortnight's time he is due to make another raid on me but am ready for him, he has some beastly gas shells that he puts in to the batteries that he knows the positions of which are very unpleasant. All love and blessings Yours ever Putty.

It continued quiet on 8 May with very little artillery activity due to the high wind. Rawlinson wrote in his diary: 'Did III Corps scheme and pm visited 34th and 8th Divisions to talk things over. All going well VII, X and III Corps. XIII Corps and Montauban not so satisfactory'. Putty wrote to Ettie that day:

---

32   Probably Captain Neil James Archibald Primrose (1883-1917) R Bucks H son of 5th Earl of Rosebery former Prime Minister killed in action 15 November 1917.
33   Edward Charles Stewart Robert 'Robin' Vane-Tempest-Stewart (1902-1955) later 8th Marquess of Londonderry.
34   Margaret Helen Greville (1863-1942) widow philanthropist and friend of Queen Mary.

My dear Chief, You owe me a letter, though I quite agree that mine to you have been dull and devoid of news. Have been the last two weekends in Paris where I enjoyed myself but now shall not be able to get away again, Paris was very full of people, much less like war than it used to be, it appeared that their spirits were better. The weather turned cold yesterday after the rain but then we have had it glorious for nearly a month. There is little news from these parts, we each raid one another but never stay in the trenches that we have raided, the chief point being the extreme accuracy of the German guns in night shooting together with the inconvenience of their lachrymatory and gas shells. We have done a lot of gardening at the chateau [Montigny] here lately after tea, really the place is looking quite pretty from the tidying up, Gavin Hamilton and Linlithgow are both good workers, the kitchen garden too is improving, though the lettuces were raided by the geese just as they were coming up, they are down for bombing if it occurs again. What is the real situation of things in Ireland now, we get bad rumours about the growth of the Sin Fiends as the men call them especially in Clare or Galway, but Maxwell seems to have handled the situation well it has done one good thing in removing Birrell but cannot imagine who they will put in his place. I think Charley L. went home last week, don't quite know what he intends to do but personally think in these times all Lord Lieutenants should be with their counties. All blessings Yours ever Putty.

The artillery exchanges continued on 9 May with III Corps Artillery shelling various points between Ovillers and La Boisselle. 37 Siege Bty joined III Corps that day. DDMS recorded:

9 am. I spoke to Corps Commander re men not using raisins, dates and lime juice; owing to shortage of potatoes it is important they should take these antiscorbutics (to deal with scurvy caused by vitamin C deficiency leading to weakness, anaemia and bleeding gums). Suggested an order to platoon officers to instruct their men as to the values of these articles. He concurred.

It was a fine day on 10 May with III Corps GS log noting: 'La Boisselle was shelled during the morning by the artillery of 8th and 34th Divisions and by the Corps Heavy Artillery, the latter firing some 130 8" shells. It is believed the bombardment was successful. The German reply was weak'. Few villages in history can have received such a sustained artillery bombardment and for La Boisselle it was just beginning.

At 2 am 11 May as the GS log recorded:

A party of 2 Middx [23 Bde 8th Division] attempted a raid on the German trenches in front of Ovillers. A heavy bombardment was carried out by 8th Divisional Artillery, assisted by the artillery of 34th Division and that of the corps on our right and left. The raid was not very successful, owing to the German wire not being cut properly (by a bangalore torpedo which broke in two). Bombs were thrown into the trench, but the Germans opened a heavy fire on the party struggling in the wire and forced them to return. A wounded German was captured and brought in. Our casualties were somewhat heavy (2 killed and 2 officers and 17 other ranks wounded). The artillery retaliation in reply to our bombardment was not great, but trench mortars were used freely.

At 10 am GOC 34th Division assumed command of the right section of the corps' front: this was now held with two divisions in line, but with each division having one bde in line and two bdes in reserve. The bdes holding the front line each had two bns in the trenches and two in brigade reserve. 19th Division was in army (and corps) reserve. So narrow was the corps' front that it was held by just four bns, less than 10% of the number in the corps. That day HQ and one sqn Wilts Yeo and one sqn DLOY joined the corps.

Haig and Rawlinson visited HQ III Corps during the afternoon. Rawlinson noted: 'I have again spent the day with CinC going round X and III Corps. We visited Pulteney who has much to do in getting his scheme in order'. Haig wrote that day: 'Pulteney (III Corps) while a plucky leader of a brigade or even a division' had 'quite reached the limits of his capacity as a commander' and had 'not, however, studied his profession sufficiently to be a really good corps commander'. Haig's view of Putty was much the same as it had been in 1915 when he did not support Putty's appointment as an army commander. Since then he could have sent Putty home without any difficulty, but he did not; furthermore it was he who brought Putty S to play a key part in the battle ahead. The comment of Haig's that Putty had not studied his profession sufficiently to be a really good corps commander, taken with Rawlinson's comment, indicates a difference of opinion on III Corps' plan. The overall plan was academic and theoretical, and based on numbers of guns per yard of front, weights of artillery fire in lbs, and fixed rates of advance: it was rigid and inflexible, and ignored the ground or the enemy deployment. Neither GOC 8th Division nor GOC 34th Division were convinced especially as it meant by-passing La Boisselle before it had been secured. Both knew Putty very well, and he them, which would not have helped when Putty argued the case for a different approach. Rawlinson would not have questioned the CinC's plan which also put Putty in a difficult position.

On 12 May III Corps Cyclist Bn assembled at Beaucourt: with the Corps Cav Regt, they were to play an important role in the command, control and communications of the corps. Little of significance occurred at the front on that day or the next. HQ III Corps issued G649 on 13 May – GOC III Corps wishes divisional commanders to ensure artillery barrages on every part of the line can be satisfactorily established at any time. Much effort was being put into the fire planning for the offensive battle ahead: Putty wanted sufficient attention to be given to defensive fire planning so that the great weight of the corps artillery could be used effectively whenever and wherever it was needed. III Corps AQ log recorded that day that sick wastage for the week was 0.46 per 1000 per day. The corps' strength was 65,000 so about 300 were sick on each day, a very low number considering the conditions.

Putty went to see Rawlinson at Querrieu (HQ 4th Army) on 14 May in the morning. Rawlinson noted: 'Putty came to see me to ask for an explanation regarding our memorandum on attack. He has evidently not got it into his head and we shall have to look after him as his plan is far from good'. It seems unlikely that Putty did not understand Rawlinson's intentions, more probable that he did not agree with them.

Next day, 15 May, Putty held his first conference with those attending being GOCs 8th and 34th Divisions with their GSO1, CRA and CRE, GOC III Corps HA, OC 179 Tunnelling Coy RE, OC 3 Sqn RFC, BGGS, BGRA, CE and GSO2. It was a fine day on 16 May with the GS log noting: 'The German trenches opposite the Nab (small salient on 8th Division's front) were bombarded by Corps HA and the guns of the left division in retaliation for hostile TM fire. The results were very satisfactory'. At 9 am DDMS recorded: 'I spoke to Corps Commander about Special Ward, suggesting some spot might be found near Millencourt and tents used. He said I might find a convenient place on the Albert Road'.

Rawlinson visited 34th Division engaged in training that day; he also received a letter from Haig which said: 'After the most serious examination, the attacks outlined in GHQ Instructions of 12 Apr, involving the over-running of part of the German 2nd Position in the first phase should be prepared, and that the bombardment would be a prolonged one, depending on the amount of ammunition available'. Haig was now expecting even more, especially of the artillery.

17 May was a quiet day: it was also fine. DDMS wrote: '9 am. Corps Commander thinks good site for Special Ward would be on Albert Road, near ordnance workshop at junction of road to Baizieux. Looked at this later. Site available, but some distance from water (1½ miles)'. Putty then went to Rawlinson's conference of his corps commanders at Querrieu at 10 am; Rawlinson noted: 'It lasted nearly two hours but we got through a lot of good work and I think I made it clear to corps comds what I required of them in the way of drawing up their schemes of attack and training their troops for that purpose. There was little or no argument and I certainly carried the sense of the meeting with me'. Rawlinson's artillery adviser, General Budworth,[35] calculated that one heavy howitzer (which he defined as 8" or above) was required for every 100 yards of front attacked. It was quite clear that Rawlinson regarded this as satisfactory. On 17 May he told his corps commanders: 'As regards the bombardment, looking at the operations as a whole, we shall have twice as many guns for the bombardment as we had at Loos, and we shall have an unlimited supply of ammunition'. Putty had 31 heavy howitzers for III Corps' front: this may have satisfied Budworth's formula and Rawlinson but took no account of the increasing depth of the objective, the strength of the various targets or the number of targets to be engaged simultaneously.

Rawlinson wrote in his diary on 18 May: 'We (Furze – probably Furse GOC 9th Division) dined with Putty'.

Artillery exchanges continued on 18 and 19 May. DDMS wrote on 18 May: '9 am. I spoke Corps Commander about Special Ward. He is anxious that we should start one and asked me to tell DMS 4th Army about this. Did so later'. On 19 May the subject was again discussed: '9 am. Corps Commander is very keen on the Special Ward and said to me that he would speak to Surgeon General O'Keeffe[36] about it'. Putty remained determined to have forward surgery available for those severely wounded, rather than risk them dying during evacuation. On 19 May III Corps Cav Regt was finally completed (DLOY with one sqn Surrey Yeo) and billeted at Beaucourt.

The III Corps GS log recorded on 20 May, another fine day: 'The Germans were very active along the whole front of the corps with trench mortars. There was also considerable artillery fire; the Nab and the trenches opposite Ovillers being the chief targets. Considerable damage was done to our works but the casualties were light. Our batteries replied vigorously'. Despite the number of guns III Corps Artillery had yet to gain the upper hand.

Putty wrote to Ettie Desborough on 20 May:

> My dear Chief, Got your letter of 17 May this morning just in time as had determined to go to Boulogne to ferret you out, thought you had forgotten to send me the address, not having

---

35   Major General Charles Edward Dutton Budworth (1869-1921) RA.
36   Probably Menus William O'Keeffe (1859-1944) from Cork DDMS III Corps 1914-1915.

heard that all leave to enter the war zone was stopped. Thanks dear for the good wishes for my birthday (55) we had a very cheery dinner here on Thursday [18 May] to celebrate it, managed to collect six guardsmen (Rawlinson was one) of sorts, some of the stories very delicate as you can imagine. The weather here is absolutely glorious though it enables the Boche aeroplanes to make night raids with impunity, it is impossible to see them except by chance. We were making experiments with mines this morning, you have no idea how beautiful the effect of the chalk is going up in great waves in the air in comparison to the mud one used to see go up in Flanders, we blew these craters near our instruction schools then practice the men at putting them in a state of defence also getting in and out of them which is no easy task as some of the big ones up at St Elois and N would almost hold the Albert Hall. The Boche has been very quiet opposite me for some time, he has registered one or two points which generally is the forerunner of a raid but we are ready for him if he comes on those expected places, he has increased his trench mortars in the most remarkable manner lately and is evidently going to make them a feature in his attacks in the future, he uses them with great effect in battering down the wire and front trenches also full of gas which makes the ground nearly untenable. The only sign of slacking off one notices is the amount of ammunition he fires from his anti aircraft guns he doesn't fire one round for every ten he used to up N so evidently that class of gun has been put on an allowance. Saw Farnham[37] today who gives me a very gloomy account of Ireland, Nathan[38] and Birrell come very badly out of this evidence so far before the commission, should imagine that it was highly necessary to keep on martial law until the end of the war, I hear John Dunnville's boy[39] was put up against a wall and shot in cold blood but luckily it only went through his lung and he is recovering, why are the real number of casualties held back all the world knows about them. My garden here is quite the show place, all the departments compete with one another and do ½ hours digging before dinner which is very good for them. Bless you Yours ever Putty.

The fine weather continued on 21 May and both divisions fired a test barrage. Putty wrote to Edith Londonderry:

Dearest Circe, You have not written for a long time, heard from Charley this morning proposing a visit here for the weekend with Reggie so have told both of them to come next Saturday 27 May. We have had the most glorious weather lately, I cannot get my summer under linen out quick enough result being that I lose many pounds daily and if I had anyone in bed with me should do the same at night but alas there is no one, a hug with you would do me a lot of good so come out for next Saturday or if you can't do that what do you say to the week end in Paris of 10 June. Suppose that you have heard the story of the girl who used 'Nugget Polish' for her shoes, she showed them to her young man saying they are so well done you can see your face in them so lifting her skirt she told him to look and all he

37   Major Arthur Kenlis Maxwell 11th Baron Farnham (1879-1957) NIH.
38   Lieutenant Colonel Sir Matthew Nathan (1862-1939) late RE Under Secretary for Ireland 1914-1916.
39   Lieutenant Robert Lambart Dunnville (1893-1931) Eton Gren Gds captured and shot by Irish republicans.

said was, the next time you ask anyone to look you should wear drawers. The Boche has been fairly quiet lately in our front, in front of me very quiet, he just registers a few places preparatory to a raid as a rule, I hope to have got him settled this time if he will come where he has been registering. Had the very dickens of a dinner on my birthday last Thursday, the table covered with flowers, lovely wax models of ladies 'Cockado Mimi Pinson' [1915 operette La Cocarde de Mimi Pinson] which Gavin Hamilton had bought on the quiet in Paris and kept for the occasion, just fancy my being 55, must own I don't feel it even though I look it. The Boche is now pinning his faith in endless supply of ammunition for his heavy howitzers which he knows the French are deficient of and he has also made a great feature of heavy trench mortars which he now uses to batter down the front trenches with, they are noiseless when it leaves the gun also smokeless but very violent when it bursts but effect local, the war is fast developing into an artillery duel, the best gun we can make ammunition for is the new 6 inch howitzer, a gun I told you of on the Aisne and which I have never left urging the supply of. How is your garden in Springfield [Londonderry shooting box near Oakham]? The roses up to the tennis court screen etc? Here I have made a show place, people are already flocking to see the results of the evening work from 6 to 7 pm. I make all the officers and clerks dig like blazes, they are getting such muscles on their backs they want to go home to be photographed. The way that Lansdowne[40] upholds Asquith [Prime Minister] completely defeats me, I wish Charley had gone back to look after his country but apparently from his letter he don't mean to. All love Yours ever Putty.

There was heavy rain overnight 23/24 May and it was overcast next day: artillery exchanges continued. III Corps GS log noted: 'Our heavy howitzers bombarded the southern face of La Boisselle salient in search of TM emplacements'. DDMS wrote:

9 am. Corps Commander said slightly wounded were not to go to Frechencourt, but to La Houssoye. I pointed out that as Frechencourt had been selected by 4th Army it would be necessary to obtain their sanction to the change, and that the change to La Houssoye would cost me as many ambulance cars as if I removed them direct from Lavieville. He said he would refer the questions. Later, I mentioned this to DMS [4th Army], who said he was not prepared to give up Frechencourt.

The discussion continued next day:

9 am. I saw Corps Commander. He had no objection (refers to conversation the previous day). But later Q [DA&QMG] told me Corps Commander objected to the train emptying at Vecquemont. He considers that once men are in a train they should go through. I was not present when this was said. It is clear that the men must go to a CCS and if they are not to go to Vecquemont, the CCS must come here.

Putty's concern, as always, was care of the wounded.

40   Henry Charles Keith Petty-Fitzmaurice 5th Marquess of Lansdowne (1845-1927) Minister without portfolio 1915-1916.

Little changed on 26 or 27 May other than the weather which was fine. With only one bde in the line both divisions rotated their bdes frequently to allow time for rest, training and other preparation. On 27 May HQ III Corps issued G835 – Orders in connection with exercise to take place on 1 June. Attack by 8th and 34th Divisions (-) on flagged trenches between La Houssoye and Franvillers; exercise to end with debrief by GOC III Corps. The day had not started well for DDMS as he noted:

> Corps Commander was not informed of Sir J Kingston Fowler's[41] visit to III Corps [on 25 May]. We informed Q who passed it to G for permission to visit the trenches but no one informed the Corps Commander. He directs that in future he is to be informed of all such visits, as he wanted to see Sir J Kingston Fowler.

The rest of the month of May was fine and warm. On 28 May the III Corps' GS log recorded: 'All available guns of 8th Division fired 3 rounds at 1.50 pm and again at 1.55 pm on points opposite the Nab, in retaliation for shelling of that salient. Enemy breached our parapet in four places'. Next day a dummy man was discovered in no man's land with wire connections to the rear. HQ RE noted on 30 May: 'CE [Brigadier General Schreiber] visited a demonstration at 3rd Army School at Auxi le Chateau with Corps Commander – a mine was exploded and the crater consolidated'. In the afternoon, at 3 pm, Rawlinson held a conference of his corps commanders at Querrieu mainly to arrange about raids. The artillery engagements continued with the enemy paying particular attention to the Nab on 31 May. III Corps casualties for May 1916 were: 2 officers and 84 other ranks killed, 34 officers and 370 other ranks wounded = 490.

The first three days of June were fine with little change at the front. III Corps exercise took place on 1 June with Rawlinson visiting 8th Division to watch them training. 57 and 58 Bdes 19th Division meanwhile started training in the St Ricquier area.

The exchanges between Rawlinson and Haig in deciding on the specific tactics of the Somme offensive continued to show the tension between the realistic principles of artillery warfare and over optimism of the offensive. Rawlinson, supported by his corps commanders, had in mind an infantry assault only as far as the artillery could support the infantry, without the guns having to be moved forward. Rawlinson had summarised his concept: 'Our object rather seems to be to kill as many Germans as possible with the least loss to ourselves, and the best way of doing this appears to me to be to seize points of tactical importance which will provide us with good observation and which we may feel quite certain that the Germans will counter-attack'. This sounds laudable but the eventual plan was very different.

Putty sent his monthly report to the King on 2 June:

> My dear Wigram, Herewith the diary of III Corps for the month of May for the information of His Majesty, am afraid that there is little of interest. The 34th and 19th [Divisions] have joined the former are in the line the latter are training. The weather has been very fine indeed, generally a good breeze on the hot days. The Boche aeroplanes have been remarkably quiet on my front during the whole month, last week only five came over the front watched by my anti

---

41   Lieutenant Colonel Sir James Kingston Fowler (1852-1934) RAMC physician and expert on TB and the lungs.

aircraft section while 214 of our own were recorded during the same period, this fact is of very considerable importance to our artillery and very different to what we used to experience in Flanders. I wish we could encourage the soldier in the field to be more thrifty, there never was such an opportunity for men to invest in the war loan but the regulations are so cumbersome, entail so much red tape the men won't do it, men should be able to buy bonds out here like the ordinary person at home, many men would welcome a stoppage of their pay if it was invested in the War Loan or would pay bonds direct at the Field Post Offices, I don't know what opportunities the Navy have but I cannot see why a special Navy or Military Voucher should not be printed and the men enabled to purchase them in his AB 64 Pay Book, am certain that we are throwing away great sums of money that would be invested if it were made simple to the soldier to purchase bonds instead of requiring vouchers signed by commanding officers together with other formalities which don't exist outside the Service, premium bonds would attract men out here who are not accustomed to putting money in savings banks but would put their savings in the hands of the government to carry on the war. Have managed to make quite a bright garden, turn them all out of their offices between 6 and 7 pm to do digging and watering which does the plants and themselves both good. We have got rumours of a big naval fight [Jutland 31 May-1 June] and are very anxious to get the statistics. Yours sincerely, WP Pulteney.

There was considerable activity on 3 June, and 102 Bde relieved 101 Bde on 34th Division's front. The enemy was alert to this relief as HQ III Corps GS log noted:

1.30 am [4 June]. Enemy raided 21 NF 102 Bde in the Right. Raiders were the right party of 200-300 who attacked division on our right. They attempted to bomb along our trenches, but were repulsed. In first surprise they took a few prisoners, most of whom regained their liberty in our trenches, while the remainder all made good their escape before reaching hostile trenches. Enemy left one dead and one prisoner in our hands, and many dead in front of our lines. 9.45 pm. Enemy 200-300 strong attacked 21 NF. He was repulsed by artillery barrage and rifle fire before reaching our lines, except for a small party which gained an entry into our trenches. A party of 15 bombers who advanced at once to eject this party and to counter-attack the retreating main party have not been heard of since. Both these raids were accompanied by intense bombardments, which caused us many casualties and severely damaged sections of our front trenches.

That evening there was an Eton dinner at Amiens – 167 sat down. It was in Rawlinson's diary so it seems highly likely that he and Putty were there.

34th Division got their own back the following night, again recorded in the GS log:

11.40 pm. A double raid was carried out by 24 NF and 26 NF 103 Bde. The right party (24 NF) was prevented from entering by heavy shells falling just in front of the enemy's trenches, and had one killed and 5 wounded, all of whom were brought in. 26 NF on the left threw 100 grenades into a dozen dugouts – all apparently occupied – cut all the wires of a telephone exchange, and brought back some useful information, without suffering any casualties. The fact that they were only allowed five minutes in the trenches, and that the enemy's dugouts in the chalk just here communicate with one another, accounts for the failure to capture any prisoners.

The planning and preparation continued: on 5 June MGGS 4th Army sent GX3/1P to III Corps and others: '6. The Army Commander wishes every corps to draw up their scheme of operations in detail, to include all their tactical and administrative arrangements'. Rawlinson visited III Corps again on 6 June as he noted:

> This afternoon I visited 34th Division and found they were not as far forward in their preparations as I could wish. Williams (Major General Ingouville-Williams GOC 34th Division) and Mayles[42] had not thought out their details sufficiently. Hudson and 8th Division were better prepared.

The scale of the training is indicated by the experience of 16 RS 101 Bde 34th Division:

> At 6.30 am 6 June they marched four miles W of La Houssoye to find several thousand yards of red ribbon pegged across the adjacent field. Drawing closer, they saw several dozen sign-posts: 'Bloater', 'Kipper', 'Sausage Redoubt' and all the rest. It was a full-scale model of the front at La Boisselle. Since the entire brigade was present, only one conclusion was possible.

There was intermittent artillery activity on 7 June. DDMS recorded:

> 9 am Corps Commander asked me for short statement on evacuation arrangements – wrote it out and took it up to Corps Commander later with 4th Army arrangements.

Intelligence on the enemy in front of III Corps and their defences was vital but difficult to collect. Rawlinson was aware that in the Somme chalk dugouts of any strength could be constructed (info gained from the raiding party on the night of 5 June. 4th Army Intelligence Summary 8 Jun). Details of a dugout near Ovillers, 17 feet deep and capable of holding a garrison of 12 men, had been obtained from a prisoner as far back as January 1916.

Many units recorded the 'fatigue-duty in all kinds of labour behind the line' resulting – in the case of one unit – in only one week being available for training. Major Jack 2 Cameronians 23 Bde 8th Division summed up the result:

> We have done our level best to instruct all ranks and tune them up for the battle ahead. But the very heavy all-nightly and daily fatigues have swallowed up almost all the officers and men who should have been putting the finishing touches to practice for operations, and who in my opinion are still not properly trained, although full of courage.

A long line of deep dug-outs, called the Usna-Tara-Bécourt line, was constructed on the reverse slope of those hills by the RE and pioneers. They were at a depth of about twenty feet and in two groups, one each side of the Bapaume road. Each group was linked by underground passages, and in rear 19th Division dug a long assembly trench: two tramways were also laid.

The first ammunition trains for filling the dumps began to arrive on 8 June. In addition to the holdings in the batteries and ammunition columns there were to be dumps near the

---

42   Probably Lieutenant Colonel Mangles W Surrey GSO1 34th Division and previously BM 16 Bde.;

guns (1,000 rounds per 18 pdr, 650 per 6" how, 500 per 8" how) and behind them divisional and corps dumps (the former with 250 rounds per 18 pdr, the latter with 200 per 6" but none for 8" and higher calibres). There was so much to be done in a short time, and it was perhaps inevitable that training and briefing would be curtailed; but this only encouraged a rigid plan of attack.

The weather continued fine on 9 June and that day Putty held his second conference at 11 am. He also sent G992 to 4th Army – Report of raids by 34th Division on night 5/6 June: '24 and 26 NF deserve commendation; the training of the parties was carefully supervised and (the raids) carried out with proper offensive spirit. I call attention to the part played by the medium trench mortars which deserves credit'. Rawlinson wrote on 9 June: 'I went to St Riquier to see 19th Division under Bridges (Major General Bridges GOC 19th Division). They had two bdes out and were working capitally over a long advance – there has been a great improvement in this div – they were working with their Lewis guns well forward'.

Next day, with little change in the front line, 57 and 58 Bdes 19th Division returned to the reserve division area on completion of their 10 days training in St Riquier area. 16 RS 101 Bde commented on the conclusion of its training: 'Divisional training (34th Division) was effectively bde training – a series of "sham" attacks on German trenches. We came home each day in motor transport' and 'It rained constantly and lasted only six days': by 10 June they had apparently been trained. '4th Army's "Red Book" was the principal tactical authority for the operation, but it was a far from satisfactory document'. 4th Army was not just telling its corps what they were required to do but also how to do it – the consequence was even more inflexibility and even less scope for common sense and initiative.

Heavy showers fell on 11 June: that day came General Joffre's request that the assault (fixed on 3 June for 1 July) might be brought forward to 25 June, the wire-cutting beginning on 20 June. Rawlinson, after consulting his corps commanders, thought it might be done, although all the additional heavy batteries and five of the divisions had not yet arrived. A provisional programme based on the new date was issued, and the dumping of ammunition hurried up, which greatly upset the railway, road transport and labour arrangements.

A combined artillery and trench mortar bombardment was carried out against the trenches S of La Boisselle on 12 June, a wet and chilly day. The enemy concentrated its efforts on the front and support trenches W and SW of La Boisselle; they also shelled the Nab. That morning DDMS wrote: 'At 9.15 am I spoke to Corps Commander about CCS Albert – he will speak about it'. Putty would have had to hurry because Rawlinson held his next conference that morning; he wrote: 'I had a conference of corps comds this morning at 10 am and it lasted till nearly 12. I told them the date had been accelerated and that U Day would be the 20th the assault taking place on the 25th. They took it very well. Not many questions and I think I managed to remind them of many useful points in connection with the attack. I further allotted to them the tasks they would have to undertake in the 2nd and 3rd phases of the operations'. In fact the date of the assault was to change several times.

It continued cold and wet with daily artillery and trench mortar exchanges. On 14 June at 7.30 pm 4th Army OpO No.2 was issued:

5. The first day's operations will include the capture of Montauban, Contalmaison, Pozières and Serre (Green Line). As soon as this line has been gained and consolidated, preparations will immediately be undertaken to commence the second phase of operations. The Army

Commander wishes to impress on all commanders that the success of the operations as a whole depends on the consolidation of the definite objectives which have been allotted to each corps. Beyond these objectives no serious advance is to be made until preparations have been completed for entering on the next phase of the operations.

7. The five corps of 4th Army will attack simultaneously on the fronts shown on the map at Zero on Z Day.

So Rawlinson expected III Corps to take and secure both Pozières and Contalmaison on the first day. Before them stood Ovillers and La Boisselle which Rawlinson expected to be by-passed, because they and everything in them would be destroyed by the artillery bombardment. Pozières was in a dominating position on the ridge: Contalmaison was at the junction of several roads, surrounded with redoubts, and defended by the Prussian Guards. It had a perfect field of fire in all directions and was trenched with a wire line, which was strongly held. The chateau was just to the N of the church and slightly above the rest of the village which at the beginning of the war had 72 houses, making it one of the largest villages on the Somme.

There was little change on 15 June: next day the weather improved and it was a bright, cool day. 19th Division moved E of the Amiens-Doullens road with its HQ now at St Gratien, the next village to Montigny (HQ III Corps). At the same time 12th Division began to enter the area vacated, establishing its HQ at Flesselles. Here final training took place for its expected role, the capture of Martinpuich. That morning DDMS noted: '9 am GOC 34th Division having asked for rum on 21 June and following days, I spoke Corps Commander about it. He does not approve of rum except for inclement weather which seems now to be past'.

Rawlinson wrote on 17 June: 'I went round III Corps and discussed their schemes with corps and div comds. All seems in order and going well. 34th Division have improved'. There were patrol engagements on 18 and 19 June as both divisions sought to gain information on the enemy opposite them. The weather further improved on 19 June being a day of bright sunshine. DDMS wrote:

> 9 am Corps Commander remarked to me on the paucity of house flies this summer and attributes it to the killing off of larvae by inclement weather, the early fly induced out by early warm weather having failed to propagate his offspring, these having been scotched by the subsequent cold. This seems a scientifically adequate solution.

Putty sent a memo to 4th Army on 19 June:

> It is essential that information regarding the length of time the poison shells used by the French 75mms continue to be effective (is obtained). The official French pamphlet gives no data regarding the poison, as opposed to lachrymatory, shells. The effects of the poison are probably transitory, but the question ought to be cleared up. WP Pulteney, Lieutenant General.

III Corps had been allocated three btys of French 75mms for the gas attack; evidently Putty's staff was not getting the required information.

At 6.30 pm 20 June HQ III Corps (BGGS) issued OpO No.70:

1. 4th Army will take part in a general offensive with a view to breaking up the enemy's defensive system and of exploiting to the full all opportunities opened up for defeating his forces within reach. 21st Division of XV Corps will attack on the Right of III Corps and 32nd Division of X Corps on the Left; the dividing lines are shown on Map A issued with the III Corps scheme.

2. III Corps will attack the enemy's position on Z Day the 30th instant (amended to 1 July), at an hour to be notified later between the points X.20.d.7.2. and R.31.d.9.0. and will seize and consolidate the line Acid Drop Copse (inclusive)-The Cutting-Pozières-R.28.c.2.0., marked Green on Map A issued with III Corps scheme. 34th Division will be on the Right and 8th Division on the Left. 19th Division will be in Corps Reserve and 12th Division in Army Reserve. The latter will be ready to move S to the assistance of XIII and XV Corps if required or will be available for use by III Corps during the 2nd Phase.

3. Details of the previous artillery and other operations commencing on U Day have been issued to all concerned.

4. Mines will be fired at X.20.a.3.6. at one minute to Zero and under Y Sap at Zero.

5. III Corps Cav Regt, III Corps Cyclist Bn and 6 Motor MG Bty will remain at Beaucourt.

6. Reports to Montigny.

A strong patrol again searched the ground in front of the Nab during the night (20/21 June) in the hope of taking a prisoner for intelligence purposes, but without success. Both sides registered during the day provoking retaliation. III Corps' kite balloon (14 Kite Balloon Sect 1 Sqn) also received attention from the enemy's artillery.

Putty wrote to Ettie Desborough on 21 June, his first letter to her since 20 May:

My dear Chief, Shall have to wipe you out as a correspondent, do you realise that you have only written twice since first week in April. At last the weather has turned warmer, it has been a great effort not to go back to winter underneath during the last fortnight, now the dust is our difficulty, the various convoys can be traced by the clouds on the roads but fortunately in this chalky soil the dust is not dense and does not rise to any height if we had been in your Thames Valley it would have been very different. That was a fine speech of Arthur Balfour's [First Lord of the Admiralty] at Admiral Craddocks memorial but I do wish they would be more practical in their war memorials something that would do good to the nation in the future, there is a grand chance now in the memorial to Lord K they ought to buy that hospital in the Waterloo Road and call it the Kitchener Hospital, it is all fitted up, it is close to the Union Jack Club and would be a memorial that many sailors and soldiers would see besides being a public benefit. In front of me the Boche have been absolutely quiet either it is the lull before the storm or else he is husbanding all his munitions for the unfortunate Verdun. Have made a nice garden here, we have had to wage war on the moles who upheaved our best beds and this morning I killed one in the open which I have never done before. Much love Yours ever Putty.

On 22 June it was warm and bright; the GS log noted:

> 40 emplacements for gas cylinders are now ready on 34th Division front and 43 on 8th Division's. Each emplacement has been made to hold 20 cylinders – 8 more each than was finally ordered (1,660 cylinders). Most of these gas cylinders were put in last night. One emplacement was damaged by hostile trench mortars, a cylinder being apparently broken, for 23 men were gassed, of which several have died. There is no broken cylinder unburied, but some cylinders were buried and are being dug out.

Putty attended Rawlinson's final conference on 22 June. Rawlinson wrote:

> I had a conference of corps comds at 10 which lasted 1½ hours and at which I explained the new ideas and the framework of the battle indicating that our efforts would be directed northwards via Achiet le Grand instead of S eastwards to help the French cross the Somme. The corps comds took it very well and few questions were asked.

The official 4th Army record of the conference was more detailed: having informed the corps commanders that the British attack had become the main operation and although the first objective remained the same, subsequent ones had been added by the CinC. Distant towns such as Bapaume, Monchy, and Douai were to be captured in due course by the cavalry. Rawlinson then went on to say:

> An opportunity may occur to push the cavalry through, in order to confirm success, and in this connection I will read you the orders which I have received on the subject from the CinC this morning. But before I read them I had better make it quite clear that it may not be possible to break the enemy's line and put the cavalry through at the first rush. In the event of our not being able to capture the first line until the afternoon, it would not be possible to send the cavalry through on the first day at all. A situation may occur later when the attack on the second line takes place for pushing the cavalry through; but until we can see what is the state of the battle, it is impossible to predict at what moment we shall be able to undertake this, and the decision will rest in my hand to say when it can be carried out.

Rawlinson then proceeded to discuss what action the Germans might take, suggesting that should their reserves not have been used up during the first advance of 4th Army, they might be employed to counter-attack, when it would be best to hold on and defeat the counter-attacks, and then proceed without delay to the second objective; each corps would have a division to relieve tired troops, but he hoped that it would not be necessary to use them. He then touched on many things to be done in case of success; such as getting up ammunition and supplies; moving forward guns; joining up the British roads and railways to the German communications. Finally, he reminded the commanders they would be working with New Army troops lacking the discipline, training and traditions of the men they had led at the beginning of the war.

It was hardly surprising that there were no questions; if Putty and the other corps commanders thought that what was expected of the artillery bordered on fantasy, they would have been dumb-struck by Haig's expectations of the cavalry. Caught between fantasy and reality Rawlinson had wandered between introducing reality into the orders he had received from Haig and telling his corps commanders what they already knew.

On his return to Montigny Putty would have reflected on the difficulties ahead. Behind III Corps front line there was no cover of any kind on the bare, gentle slopes of the Tara-Usna hills. This entire area was overlooked by the Germans so that even moving forward small numbers of troops to the front could bring down on them a hail of artillery shells and MG bullets. In marked contrast, the German positions were of great strength: to the N of the Albert-Bapaume road on a small ridge which dominated the surrounding countryside stood Ovillers; to the S of the road on lower but still dominating ground stood La Boisselle. These villages were small, but the houses had substantial cellars, ideal for the protection of small groups of men and MG posts. Between Ovillers and La Boisselle was a long, narrow re-entrant (called Mash Valley by the British) which could be dominated by enfilade from the villages. Finally, the whole northern section of III Corps front was also overlooked by two strong positions in front of X Corps. It was essential, if 8th Division was to get forward, that these positions be eliminated by X Corps artillery.

Such was the reality facing Putty: he had given 19th Division, his corps reserve, a number of possible tasks depending on the progress or lack of it of the two forward divisions. The fantasy, however, was continued in secret orders given to GOC 19th Division that if the general attack was successful, a cavalry division, two battalions of cyclists and several mobile batteries would be placed under his command, and 19th Division was to march on Bapaume as the spearhead of the army.

Faced with the realities of the ground, the enemy, and the constraints of Rawlinson's orders, Putty had very little choice. Even if he and his divisional commanders did not share Rawlinson's confidence in the ability of the artillery to overwhelm all resistance, and they did not, they had to accept it and in doing so dismiss the possibility of resistance from La Boisselle or from the left flank.

Putty wrote to Edith Londonderry on 22 June:

Dearest Circe, How goes the world with you? Your pen is intermittent, have come to the conclusion that Ireland has a bad effect on you when you go there with Charley I attribute it continually calling out 'Mount' Stewart to him!! The Boche has been absolutely quiet opposite me for ages, he must be hatching some devilry but if he does not look out he will get Johnnie up the Orchard for going to sleep for it is high time he is woken up from his slumbers. [Large part of the letter devoted to the wider conduct of the war omitted.] Up to yesterday the cold had been intense, one had to be very spartan not to go back to winter underwear but I argued it was better to keep those parts cold so that they could fully appreciate the warmth of other parts when they got into them!!! My garden here is quite good, mowing the lawn has taken many pounds off myself and staff, the moles are an infernal nuisance they burrow right through the flower beds besides throwing up mighty mounds which deface the 'gazon', however we have killed three in traps and I beat all records by killing one in the open yesterday before he got back from his nocturnal visits bad luck being caught by an early bird like me who knows the habits of those returning from other peoples' beds in the dawn. It was a great pity you two did not come to Paris, we had a good time but were hauled back on the Sunday night, so had not much time to commit many atrocities but considering the short period we were there we came to the conclusion that we cemented our friendship pretty well, Charley Kerr[43] and his wife were there, she seems rather a good sort but as far as I know had not seen her before. That man Esher[44] was there though I did not speak to him, what is his vocation in Paris for from his conversation with one of my generals should say that he was a most indiscreet fellow to have there, he pretends to be very much in the know but never have trusted him with men!! Write me the news. Best love Yours ever Putty.

It was quiet on 23 June with fine weather in the morning and heavy thunderstorms in the afternoon. The III Corps GS log noted: 'At the beginning of the thunderstorm this afternoon 14 Sect Kite Balloon (F19) broke from its moorings as it was being towed in, and after being hauled down as the storm approached. The occupants had just got out. It came down near Senlis in X Corps area. Examination revealed that the valve had opened through some part being fused by lightning and this caused it to descend'. It was the lull before another storm planned for next day: during it the reserve bdes of 8th and 34th Divisions were moved forward. The AQ log noted that day that 2,466 red flares were issued for communication between infantry and aeroplanes.

On 24 June (U Day) the preliminary bombardment started. It had three aims – to cut the wire in front of the German trenches, to neutralise the occupants of the German trench system and to overwhelm the German artillery. It was planned to last 5 days. Brigadier General Uniacke was Putty's BGRA; he was described by Liddell Hart as 'one of the most eminent artillery experts of his generation' and 'later, in the perfecting of the creeping barrage as GOC first of III Corps Artillery and then of 5th Army Artillery, had an influential part'.

MGRA GHQ (Birch) claimed that at the time of the Somme, Haig did not understand the artillery, 'poor Haig – as he was always inclined to do – spread his guns'. Instead of guns and infantry concentrating, therefore, the guns were spread out evenly along the whole line. Also, where the Green Line objective included the German second line trenches, the wire there was distant enough to be difficult to cut. The lack of artillery tactical direction from above, particularly in regard to counter-battery work (whose staff was still being organised during the battle), meant that corps had to devise their own tactics from experience. In fact the direction of the artillery, the most important element of the offensive and on which all else depended, existed in a vacuum. Time and again mistakes were made at corps level, for example Major Broad (then HQ RA 5th Army) later remarked that 'III Corps Artillery did not understand the barrage, and jumped from one trench system to another without searching the shell holes or destroying the concrete MG'. Since Broad was GSO 3 RA HQ III Corps at this time (he left August 1916 to go with Uniacke to GHQ) this is not a criticism of Uniacke but of the difficulty of getting their ideas implemented in the corps artillery.

For the fireplan in the days preceding the attack and on the day itself, III Corps had available the artillery of 8th, 19th and 34th Divisions, in total 144 × 18 pdrs and 36 × 4.5" hows. The artillery of the New Army received considerably less training before going to France than the infantry. The artillery programmes gave the impression of haste and it seems unlikely that the technical detail for even rudimentary gunnery could have been absorbed in the short time

43   Probably Charles Ian Kerr (1874-1968) RHG later 1st Baron Teviot.
44   2nd Viscount Esher (1852-1930).

available. Lack of sufficient guns and ammunition for training was also a major problem. For some btys of 34th Division there was time for only three days' practice before embarkation in January 1916.

In addition to the divisional artillery, there was III Corps Heavy Artillery consisting of:

7 HAG (HQ Dernancourt – Hy Res Gp):
10 Bty RMA – 1 × 15" how, 83 Siege Bty – 2 × 12" hows railway mounting (rlwy mtg), 18 Siege Bty – 2 × 12" guns rlwy mtg, 53 Siege Bty – 1 × 12" gun rlwy mtg and 1 × 9.2" gun rlwy mtg, 48 Siege Bty – 4 × 9.2" hows, 26 and 60 Siege Btys – 2 × 6" Mk VII guns, 45 Siege Bty – 2 × 9.2" guns rlwy mtg
22 HAG (CB Gp):
21, 22, 23, 90 and 126 Hy Btys – each 4 × 60 pdrs
34 HAG (HQ Albert – CB Gp):
17, 35 and 137 Hy Btys – each 4 × 60 pdrs, and 123 and 1/1 London Hy Btys – each 4 × 4.7" guns
27 HAG (HQ Moulin Vivier – Hy How Gp with 34th Division):
10 Siege Bty – 4 × 9.2" hows, 19 and 39 Siege Btys – each 4 × 8" hows, and 1, 37 and 75 Siege Btys – each 4 × 6" hows
30 HAG (HQ Hénencourt – Hy How Gp with 8th Division):
69 Siege Bty – 4 × 9.2" hows, 57 and 61 Siege Btys – each 4 × 8" hows, and 40 and 109 Siege Btys – each 4 × 6" hows

Finally, there were V/III Hy TM Bty, C Bty RMA (4 × 2 pdr pompoms) and 52 AA Bty (4 × 3" AA Guns), 3 btys 18 French FA Regt (12 × 75mm guns), 110 and 111 Siege Btys (each 4 × 220mm mors).

In total III Corps had 180 field guns/hows and 98 heavy guns/hows for the corps' front of 3,500 yards (8th Division – 1,500 and 34th Division – 2,000).

GOC RA III Corps (Uniacke) issued 'Artillery Instructions for U Day (24 June)' on or before 14 June:

1. As much wire cutting as possible to be done by the 18 pdrs.
2. Care must be taken not to have too many 2" TMs firing at the same time so as to avoid disclosing the concentration that has taken place. The heavy TMs will not be used on this day.
3. As soon as our 18 pdrs provoke retaliation by wire cutting, the heavy batteries will commence active counter battery work on all known emplacements, concentrating fire on each in turn. The heavy howitzers will be prepared to take up calls and co-operate in this counter-battery work but again, like the 2" TMs, care must be taken not to have too many of these firing at the same time.
4. The 12" and 9.2" guns will register Flers and Le Sars during the afternoon.
5. All batteries of whatever nature will complete any outstanding registration.
6. Firing on approaches will take place throughout the night in accordance with instructions already issued.

39 Siege Bty at Battle of the Somme. (© IWM Q5817)

He also issued 'Artillery Instructions as regards special concentrated bombardments ordered for V, W, X and Y Days in the programme already issued' on 14 June:

1. Advantage will be taken of these bombardments to 'drill' all batteries in the tasks which they will have to perform during the advance of the infantry on Z Day and so, as far as possible, render everything 'foolproof' as far as the artillery is concerned.

2. These bombardments consequently will coincide in every particular, except intensity of fire, timing of lifts, and actual duration, with certain phases of the final bombardment on Z Day. The particular phases to be dealt with at each particular bombardment will be detailed on a programme which will be shortly issued. For instance, referring to the map of artillery lifts which has already been issued – on one day fire may be opened on the Blue line, remain for a certain time and then lift successively to the various intermediate lines until it reaches the Brown line. Another day fire may be opened on the Orange line and lift successively to Black, Light Blue and Crimson lines.

3. During these bombardments special officers should be posted where they can see the ground, to watch closely the various lifts, note if they appear to be working smoothly, see that no marked gaps occur in the various barrages, and report if they notice any shell falling short of the objective and if so where, when and of what nature. The reports of these officers should be collected by divisional and heavy artilleries and forwarded to Corps HQ RA as early as possible, GOCs noting that they have taken steps to correct any errors that they can trace down to their own units.

4. Careful synchronisation of watches in the whole of the artillery of the corps is naturally essential. Signal time will be taken as correct as arrangements have been made by which this time will be sent from Corps HQ as often as required.

These instructions had been issued on 14 June or before; on 22 June GOC RA III Corps issued:

Artillery Instruction No 26
1. In order to comply with instructions just received from 4th Army, the following amendments will be made in the programmes already issued:
    V Day. Ref: Artillery Instructions No 21 for this day para 3 (B) Fire will now be opened at 4.15 pm in lieu of 4 pm and will cease at 5.15 pm in lieu of 5.20 pm. All intermediate timing of lifts will remain exactly as before. Rate of fire not to exceed one round per gun every two minutes
    Y Day. Ref: Artillery Instructions No 24 for this day para 2 (B) Fire will now be opened at 4.5 pm in lieu of 4 pm and will cease at 5.15 pm in lieu of 5.20 pm. Rate of fire not to exceed one round per gun every two minutes
2. The whole of the rest of the daily programmes already issued will as far as the artillery is concerned hold good in every respect.

Artillery Instruction No 27
1. The French gas shell will only be used on Z Day and subsequent days. The gas is very volatile and can be used with perfect safety on ground over which our infantry is subsequently to advance provided that all our men do not reach the gas area until 30 minutes after the last shell has been fired into that area. This interval gives a large margin of safety.
2. The 12" and 15" Howitzers will not be fired until U Day.

These orders, a small selection from the many issued, show the top-down and inflexible nature of the fire plan, caused in part by the method of rotating the artillery and by the inadequate training of many btys. On U Day (up to noon) ammo expenditure in III Corps was: divisional artillery (DA) – 5,314, heavy artillery (HA) – 498, trench mortars (TM) – 237 = 6,049.

V Day (25 June) was a day of low cloud which restricted registration, and the wind was unfavourable for gas. The III Corps GS log recorded:

General bombardment repeated as yesterday. Between 10 am and noon the three villages of Pozières, Contalmaison and Bazentin le Petit were bombarded for 12 minutes each by all guns and howitzers which could be directed upon them. Divisional artillery co-operated with shrapnel in the case of the first two named villages, and 60 pdrs with shrapnel in the case of the last. The medium trench mortars cut front wire most successfully.

4.15 pm. A practice of timed lifts, to cover attacking infantry, was practised by all guns and howitzers. Two hostile kite balloons were brought down. There was hostile retaliation on Albert and Aveluy. A few hostile aeroplanes were seen but very distant.

At night a successful raid was made by 2 RB 25 Bde 8th Division who report having killed and wounded some 50 of the enemy. They brought back a wounded prisoner of 108

Regt. Our casualties were 1 killed and 10 wounded. The enemy's trenches were found full of Germans all wearing gas masks. A simultaneous attempt to raid by 34th Division was frustrated by a collision with a strong hostile patrol lying out.

Artillery Instruction No 21 for V Day issued 15 June gave the detailed fireplan:

1. Wire cutting and bombardments by all natures will take place throughout the day, and searching operations of all approaches etc during the night.
2. Counter-battery work must be very active throughout the day.
3. In addition the following special bombardments will take place:
   A) At 10 am precisely every gun and howitzer in the Corps Heavy Artillery that can be brought to bear will open fire simultaneously on Pozières village and fire at their highest rate for 12 minutes when fire will stop. At 10.30 am an exactly similar procedure will be followed as regards Contalmaison. All available divisional artillery guns will co-operate in these two bombardments by covering the whole area of the two villages and their outskirts with shrapnel fire during the time of the respective bombardments, the 8th Divisional Artillery dealing with Pozières, the 34th with Contalmaison. In addition the 18 pdrs will open a sudden burst of fire on Pozières at 10.35 am and over Contalmaison at 11.15 am – in each case the fire will be maintained for 5 minutes.
   B) At 4 pm (amended to 4.15 pm – see Artillery Instruction No 26 issued 22 June) the artillery will open fire exactly as arranged in every particular, except rate of fire, for the intense bombardment prior to zero on Z Day.
   At 4.30 pm fire will be lifted to the Blue line.
   At 4.45 pm fire will be lifted to the Pink and Yellow line
   At 4.55 pm fire will be lifted from the Pink line to the Green line
   At 5.5 pm fire will be lifted from the Yellow line to the Green line
   At 5.20 pm (amended to 5.15 pm) this special bombardment will cease and the ordinary deliberate bombardment will be resumed.
4. For the above and for all bombardments of this nature prior to Z Day the average rate of fire will not exceed one round per gun per two minutes with the necessary modifications as regards the heavier natures.

The Green line was the objective on Z Day and for III Corps this included both Pozières and Contalmaison: it was an advance of over two miles.

Artillery Instruction No 25 issued on 20 June is also relevant to this day:

1. If no gas attack takes place on the night V/W, Martinpuich will be bombarded as directed in Artillery Instruction No 22 at 10 pm on the night of V/W. If a zero hour for the gas attack is ordered, Martinpuich will be bombarded at 1.27 hours on the night of V/W whether gas is actually liberated or not.
2. If the gas attack takes place on any other night than the night of V/W Martinpuich will be bombarded a second time in accordance with the programme.

3. The following will be added to Artillery Instruction No 21 para 1 (A) 'At 11 am an exactly similar procedure will be followed as regards Bazentin le Petit. In addition all 60 pdrs that can be brought to bear will open a sudden burst of shrapnel at 12 noon on Bazentin le Petit. Fire to be continued for 5 minutes'.

4. Official night time for the purpose of artillery fire is amended to '9 pm to 5 am'.

5. The first brigades of 19th Divisional Artillery to advance will not be used to cut the wire of the main hostile second line but, if no suitable target presents itself, will keep their ammunition to deal with counter-attacks.

III Corps ammo expenditure for the 24 hours was: DA – 10,518, HA – 5,236, TM – 981 = 16,735. Lieutenant Colonel Cordeaux (then aged 50) CO 10 Lincoln 101 Bde 34th Division wrote to his wife:

> I have little time to write, the din and constant concussion is tremendous. I have much to do and it is a very wearing life and one only gets sleep in small doses and sometimes a whole 24 hours without any. You will someday read in the newspapers all that is going on, it is simply titanic, the big thing of the war perhaps.

W Day (26 June) was showery, and the GS log recorded:

> General bombardment as on 24 June. All villages opposite our front were bombarded during the day and fired on at intervals during the night. Special attention was paid to the railway loop SW of Martinpuich. 'Lifts' practise from 9 am to 10.20 am. There was a large explosion in La Boisselle (The detailed fireplan for W Day was in Artillery Instruction No 22 issued on 15 June).

> 10.10 am. Smoke was liberated, drawing a barrage, mostly from trench mortars on the Nab and to the S thereof.
> 11 am. Smoke was liberated in conjunction with a discharge of gas by XV Corps on our right. It drew some retaliation including a barrage in front of Bécourt Wood. Medium trench mortars cut wire steadily in front, 60 pdrs in enemy's rear lines. The heavy trench mortars fired with excellent results. There was retaliation with trench mortars and howitzers, nothing heavier than 15 cm has been reported as yet. There was hostile shell fire all night.

The bdes of 19th Division moved forward and 12th Division closed up behind them.

III Corps ammo expenditure in the previous 24 hours was: DA – 31,141, HA – 8,314, TM – 1,857 = 41,312 (more than twice V Day and six times U Day). Cordeaux (CO 10 Lincoln) wrote to his wife:

> Am in the chateau (Bécourt) for about 24 hours, the noise and the concussion is more than ever and continuous; the house is shaken to its foundations. The last 48 hours have been about the worst I have ever spent but I expect there are worse to come, however they will probably be over by the time you get this. Have only had 10 hours sleep in 96 hours; this and my responsibilities are trying me near to breaking point.

Putty managed to write to Lady Lyttelton that day:

> I only got your letter about the two Chevrillons[45] today so conclude they have been in the country some time as your letter is dated 26 Apr, I will do what I can for them, but at the moment we are all very busy. Things are going well and we are gradually getting the better of the Boche. Trust this finds you all in best of health. Yours very sincerely, WP Pulteney.

X Day (27 June) brought a steady SW wind by 4 am with low cloud and rain later in the day. The GS log recorded:

> General bombardment as on 24 June and subsequent days. Practise 'lifts' 4.30 am to 7.30 am [Artillery Instruction No 23 for X Day issued on 15 June gave the detailed programme]. Gas from 1600 cylinders was liberated with smoke by a detachment of the Special Brigade on a 5 mph SW breeze from 5.30 am till 7 am. The artillery carried on from their 'lift' practice with a special scheme of co-operation culminating in a general bombardment of Martinpuich by the heavies. The enemy put a barrage along our front N of La Boisselle. 2" trench mortars and 18 pdrs cut wire. 10 pm. divisional artillery bombarded the enemy's front trenches, 2" trench mortars, MGs and rapid rifle fire co-operating. Our heavy howitzers then fired a general salvo on the front trenches.

19th and 12th Divisions continued to close up with 19th Division now just forward of HQ III Corps at Montigny and 12th Division just behind. With so few routes forward, movement was now becoming very difficult indeed.

Rawlinson noted on X Day (27 June): 'I visited the divs of III Corps in the morning'. III Corps ammo expenditure for the 24 hours was: DA – 31,934, HA – 9,374 and TM – 1,231 = 42,539. The experiences of the infantry are best illustrated by 16 RS 101 Bde 34th Division:

> The day was damp and overcast; in the evening the battalion trudged back to the wood in order to complete their final preparations for the assault. The noise and concussion had now been continuous for more than 100 hours and the men were getting rattled. 'We couldn't sleep' recalled Private James McEvoy 'and the ground would not keep still'.

It was very wet on 28 June (Y Day later renamed Y1 Day); the III Corps GS log was very brief:

> General bombardment as on preceding days. Lifts practise from 6 am to 7.20 am. Concentrated bombardments during day of each enemy salient in succession, by heavy artillery. At midday intimation was received that Z Day is postponed from 29 June to 1 July [Rawlinson ordered postponement at 11 am]. A heavy trench mortar (9.45") fired a few rounds at Ovillers, with great effect, a very great amount of debris being thrown into the air near the church.

---

45   Possibly André Chevrillon (1864-1957) French writer with the British Army at the front and his wife.

The weather after all proved the determining factor in fixing the date of the assault. There was so much rain on 28 June that even next day the trenches and gun emplacements were in places full of water. Zero Day having been postponed 48 hours, two extra days called Y1 and Y2 were put between X and Y; and the programme of Y, one of the days devoted to the destruction of defences, was fired on each with such economies of heavy gun and heavy howitzer ammunition as were necessary.

That morning DDMS wrote: '9 am. Corps Commander told me German prisoners reported that their mask was a perfect protection against our gas, none of their men having suffered, whereas our men had been poisoned heavily'. Rawlinson noted later: 'I held a conference of Goffy (Gough) and the corps comds of III, XV and X Corps to explain the situation and to put in force arrangements for use of reserve divisions once Green line is taken. Attack postponed because of torrential rain'.

Major Jack 2 Cameronians 23 Bde 8th Division wrote that day:

> I have been writing my orders for the two companies acting under my command when the battle opens. Before us no man's land is some 750 yards wide – exceptionally wide – the long rank grass plentifully sprinkled with bright scarlet wild poppies. The country ahead is perfectly open, treeless and devoid of buildings save for those lying in broken heaps in the shell-blasted villages. One thousand yards in front of the battalion left flank, and on rather higher ground, lie the pulverised ruins of Ovillers amid a maze of trenches and posts half a mile in depth, heavily wired and reported to be full of machine-guns. This fortress is the first objective of 23 Bde. Slightly below us and 1200 yards to our right front are the ashes of La Boisselle, similarly fortified, the first objective of 34th Division. These two villages form the horns of a re-entrant in the hostile line with the shallow Mash Valley, to be crossed by our battalions, leading into it.

III Corps ammo expenditure for the previous 24 hours was DA – 38,007, HA – 11,559, TM – 3,486 = 53,052.

Y2 Day (29 June and the original Z Day) was showery: the GS log noted:

> General bombardment as on preceding days. Practice 'lifts' 4 pm to 5.20 pm [Artillery Instruction No 31 for Y2 was issued on 28 June and gave the amended fireplan]. Hostile retaliation more severe than on previous days; gas and tear shells used. A party of infantry and sappers of 34th Division blew up some 'knife rests', which had escaped previous destruction. From 8th Division a patrol of 1 officer and 15 men set out to enter the hostile trenches, but were stopped by a strong patrol lying out. 34th Division attempted a triple raid, but were frustrated by machine-gun fire, only one party reaching the enemy's fire trench, which was found strongly held. 102 Bde moved to the new reserve line between Tara and Usna redoubts; 103 Bde moved to the railway cutting SW of Albert.

Haig wrote that day: 'I went on to HQ III Corps at Montigny and saw General Pulteney. He is also quite satisfied with the artillery bombardment and wire cutting'. Ammo expenditure in III Corps for the previous 24 hours was: DA – 26,500, HA – 5,865, TM – 1,442 = 33,807 (much less than the previous day).

Y Day (30 June) was fine; III Corps GS log recorded:

> General bombardment as on previous days. Practise 'lifts' from 8 am to 9.10 am. Concentrated bombardments by heavies of each salient of enemy's line in turn. Practise 'lifts' from 4.5 pm to 5.15 pm. General concentration of fire on valley opposite the Nab, which will lie along the left of 8th Division's advance in the attack. 12" gun registered Achiet le Grand, and bombarded Bapaume day and night. In the evening an observing aeroplane signalled that four shells fell in Bapaume Square. On its way home it brought down a hostile aeroplane. Pozières church spire (undoubtedly used as an OP) was broken off by a shell.

103 Bde moved forward into the Usna and Tara redoubts; 19th Division closed up into the areas vacated by 34th Division, and 12th Division closed up into areas vacated by 19th Division.

Artillery Instruction No 24 for Y Day had been issued by GOC RA III Corps on 15 June (and amended by Instrs No 26, 30 and 31):

1. In general work will be carried out as on preceding days.
2. The following special bombardments will take place:
    A) At 6 am Fire will open as for the intense bombardment on Z Day.
       At 6.35 am Fire will lift on to the Blue Line.
       At 6.55 am Fire will lift on to the Pink and Yellow line.
       At 7.10 am Fire will lift on to the Green line.
       At 7.20 am This special bombardment will cease and the ordinary deliberate bombardment will be resumed.
    B) At 4.0 pm (amended to 4.5 pm) Fire will open on the Brown line.
       At 4.15 pm Fire will lift on to the Mauve and Orange line.
       At 4.25 pm Fire will lift from the Mauve to the Orange line.
       At 4.55 pm Fire will lift from the Orange to the Black line.
       At 5.10 pm Fire will lift from the Black line to the Light Blue line.
       At 5.20 pm (amended to 5.15 pm) Fire ceases and the ordinary bombardment is resumed.
    C) At 6.0 pm a concentrated fire of heavy howitzers lasting until 6.40 pm will be brought on to the valley in R.32.c (valley on the left of 8th Division attack).
3. The GOC Heavy Artillery will ensure during this day that the following places are completely destroyed: Salient X.20.d.7.2 – Heligoland – Y Sap – salient X.8.c and salient X.7.b.
4. The 12" Gun will bombard Bapaume during this day and throughout the night Y/Z.

A summary of the corps artillery tasks for the battle is in this unreferenced and undated document produced by HQ III Corps:

5. This provides for a deliberate bombardment for destruction for 5 days and nights terminating with a set timetable of 'Lifts' on the 6th Day [the day of the attack].
   During the 5 days bombardment each division will cut the wire on its front up to and including the easternmost trench of the hostile front line system. The wire in the intermediate system will be dealt with by the 60 pdrs and by the general bombardment

of the heavy howitzers. During the 5 days every trench and every strong point will be bombarded under a general programme arranged by the GOC RA. Such places as Ovillers-Boisselle-Pozières-Contalmaison-etc will be dealt with by the 12" and 15" howitzers and the 9.45" TM in addition as regards the two former places. Fire, once commenced, will be continuous night and day. The 60 pdrs and 18 pdrs will fire throughout the night so that no rest will be allowed to the enemy and no repair of his works will be possible. The daily programme will be elastic so that any point not thoroughly dealt with on a preceding day may be completely destroyed on a later one.

6.   On the day of attack the general principle of the plan is to form a devastating barrage of HE and shrapnel behind which the infantry will advance. The barrage will not lift, but will gradually roll back upon itself so that as the physical strain on the infantry increases so the weight of the barrage in front of them will increase until practically the whole of the available artillery is collected onto the final objective, from which it will rake back and form a wall of fire which will be maintained until the position is consolidated.

A bty comd in 34th Divisional Artillery wrote:

24-30 June. Wire cutting every day for an average of five hours per day. Also at least one special bombardment each day, and several abortive attempts to loose gas. The latter eventually went over one morning, about 28 June. Shooting all night on approaches and wire cutting. Am living in the OP on sardines and bread. The seven guns average nearly 2000 rounds per day, and are beginning to give buffer trouble; seldom more than five in action at the same time. Boche prisoners say that they are finding great difficulty in getting food and other supplies.

Communications next day would be vital. Major Frost RE OC 8 Sig Coy 8th Division wrote many years later:

Before the battle a very complete system of deeply buried telephone cables, with numerous by-passes and small exchanges for circumventing breaks during repairs, was laid by 8th Division, extending even along the tunnel (I went there myself) below no man's land, towards Ovillers. This line was to connect HQ 8th Division, when they advanced, with HQ III Corps. These lines gave an uninterrupted service, during the battle, throughout 8th Division area. A central visual signal station was established at Hénencourt, with heliograph, to communicate, during the expected advance, with units advancing through and beyond Pozières, whilst cables were being laid. I visited both this central station and the 'moving station' in our front system, ready to advance through Ovillers. The visual stations were in touch, and messages passed to relieve the wires till the afternoon. Carrier pigeons were carried (two in a basket) by men during the advance. I think I am right in saying that only two birds (in 8th Division) failed to return. One bird, after being captured by the enemy, returned with a message to say that such dainty fare did not suit German stomachs. The attackers also carried several power buzzers by which messages could be morsed by sending the message to earth. Receiving sets were placed in deep dug-outs along the front to receive these messages (or intercepted enemy messages) and pass them back to division along a buried cable.

At 2.30 pm that day (30 June) DDMS recorded:

> I saw Corps Commander about need for special ward at Albert as our front advances and the distance to Warloy which is excessive already, being too great to be of any real use to abdominal cases. He concurred entirely. Wrote to DMS 4th Army asking permission to start one, he providing a surgeon and special surgical equipment, and sisters later. Orderlies of 26 Fd Amb could carry on in the interim, being well-trained. Asked for Captain Sampson [Surgeon in III Corps Special Ward on Lys] as surgeon.

Rawlinson wrote on 30 June: 'The corps and div comds are the best we have got and there are few weak spots in them. All know their job and the great majority are proved fighters. VIII Corps is the weakest'. Haig wrote that day: 'I have personally seen all the corps commanders and one and all are full of confidence. The only doubt I have is regarding VIII Corps (Hunter-Weston) which has no experience of fighting in France and has only carried out one successful raid'.

Putty had his doubts as did his divisional commanders but the time to express them had passed. He now had to fight the battle with an inflexible plan that depended for success on the artillery overwhelming the German defences. Every strongpoint had to be destroyed: if even a few of the enemy survived in the front line they could jeopardise the attack; and they had to be kept in their bunkers or from engaging the advancing infantry. Many did indeed consider that taking of the Green line would be the culmination of an 'advance' rather than an 'attack', and many of them were in GHQ and HQ 4th Army.

Ammo expenditure in III Corps for the previous 24 hours was again low: DA – 28,770, HA – 8,296, TM – 999 = 38,065. III Corps casualties for June 1916 were: 13 officers and 174 other ranks killed, 52 officers and 1,114 other ranks wounded, 29 other ranks missing = 1,382.

Putty wrote to Ettie Desborough that evening:

> My dear Chief, Was delighted to get your dear letter of 26 June, you must not expect much from me today as we are all at concert pitch, for the last seven days the air has screeched with shells by day and night, am glad to say that so far my casualties have been a good way under my estimate, the men get so deep down in this chalk they are practically safe against the enormous shells but of course this applies to the enemy as well, had we had this fire on our breastworks in Flanders there would be nothing left of them. I think Willie's address about Lord K to the wounded Canadian soldiers as good as anything I have read for some time, the natural pride of the gifts of your dear sons who had gained his friendship to their King and country enabled him to speak with the emphasis that can only come straight from the soul of a parent, I always trust that poor Lord K lays buried in the ship, a fitting covering in the depths. Weather has been bad, a cheerless June only brightened by Russia's great victories. Am so sorry to hear what you write about George Essex,[46] he has little chance I fear. Best love Yours ever Putty.

---

46   Probably George Devereux de Vere Capell 7th Earl of Essex (1857-1916) late Gren Gds died 25 September.

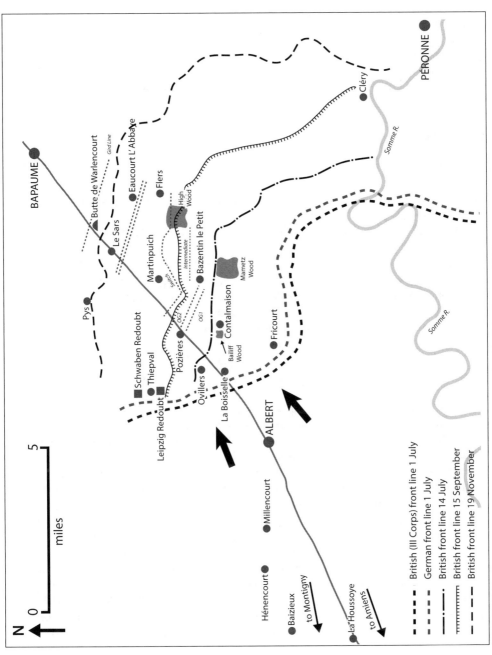

Map 8 Battle of the Somme 1916.

On the night of 30 June/1 July, the eve of the assault, the usual patrols were sent out and raids were made in order that there should be no difference from the routine of the previous nights. Meanwhile in the clear moonless summer night the approach march to the battle positions began. Major Jack 2 Cameronians 23 Bde 8th Division wrote of his experience:

> Leaving Millencourt after sunset, the headquarters and four companies of 2 Cameronians, some 20 officers and 650 other ranks, filed at intervals by road to Albert. The River Ancre was next crossed by a temporary wooden bridge and we followed along the marshy valley to Aveluy. The track then mounted the slopes eastwards until we entered Preston communication trench for the last part of the 5-mile march to our assembly positions in Ribble Street. The assembly was completed shortly after midnight without incident.

Battle of Albert 1-13 July

La Boisselle

The morning of 1 July was 'breathless and shimmery blue: a cool mist lingered in the valley, but the sun was already burning through'.

The official history summarises the ground, enemy and III Corps' outline plan:

> The position of III Corps, between Bécourt and Authille, lay on the forward slopes of a long low ridge between Albert and La Boisselle, marked by Tara (S) and Usna (N) hills, a continuation of the main Ginchy-Pozières ridge on which the village of Ovillers stands. Behind this ridge the divisional artillery was deployed in rows, one brigade behind the other, dug in on bare and open ground. The observers were on the crest, with a perfect view of the whole German position spread out before them like a map, each trench shown up by its chalk parapet. The enemy 1st position, with its front line higher than the British, lay across the upper slopes of the three spurs which reach out south-westwards from the main ridge towards Albert.
>
> The distance between the opposing lines varied from 800 to 50 yards, the trench nearest the enemy, opposite La Boisselle, being known as the 'Glory Hole'. The right of the corps faced the western slope of the long Fricourt spur; its centre, the La Boisselle spur, with the village of that name almost in the German front line; whilst in front of its left was the upper part of the Ovillers spur, with the village within the German front defences. The depressions running into the enemy position between the three spurs were known as Sausage Valley and Mash Valley. Neither was more than a thousand yards wide so that, being bare and open, any advance up them could be effectively met by crossfire from both sides; whilst the spurs themselves were covered with a network of trenches and machine-gun nests. The great Thiepval spur – actually opposite X Corps, next on the left – overlooked practically all the first belt of ground over which the divisions of III Corps had necessarily to advance.
>
> The German defences consisted of a front system with four main strongholds in its southern half: Sausage Redoubt (or Heligoland), with Scots Redoubt behind it; Schwaben Hohe; and La Boisselle village. A fifth, Ovillers, was situated centrally in its northern half. Behind the front defences were two intermediate lines; the first from Fricourt Farm

to Ovillers, and the second, incomplete, in front of Contalmaison and Pozières. Behind these again was the 2nd Position from Bazentin le Petit to Mouquet Farm, consisting of two lines. The 3rd Position was three miles in rear of the second. The German front line opposite III Corps was held by 110 Regt of 28th Reserve Division and 180 Regt of 26th Reserve Division. Each regt had two bns in the line and one in reserve.

The high road Amiens-Albert-Pozières-Bapaume cut through the centre of III Corps front. In its straight course from Albert up to the Pozières ridge it ascends aslant the northern slope of the La Boisselle spur, and thence rises steadily to Pozières. This highway was roughly the demarcation between the two divisions to make the assault, the actual dividing line being at first about five hundred yards to the left of it, but near Ovillers passing to the right. 34th Division, on the right, was to attack and capture the German defences on the Fricourt Spur and astride Sausage Valley as far as La Boisselle (inclusive). It was then to advance to the line Contalmaison-Pozières (exclusive), halting some eight hundred yards in front of the German 2nd Position. 8th Division, on the left, was to capture the German front defences N of the Bapaume road, including the whole western slope of Ovillers spur and the village. It was then to push forward to a line facing the German 2nd Position between Pozières (inclusive) and Mouquet Farm.

The two assaulting divisions had thus to capture two fortified villages and six lines of trenches, and to advance into the German positions to a depth of roughly two miles on a frontage of four thousand yards – a formidable task.

19th Division, in corps reserve, but with its guns in action under the other divisions, was to be in a position of readiness in an intermediate position N of Albert, and as 34th and 8th Divisions moved forward to the assault, the two leading brigades of 19th Division were to take their places in the Tara-Usna Line, ready to move forward to relieve them when they had secured their objectives.

Extracts from III Corps Opsum also help to set the scene:

Some weeks before the assault the whole system of German trenches on the corps front was reproduced on the ground in the neighbourhood of La Houssoye and Franvillers which roughly resembled the ground over which the actual attack would take place. The assaulting troops were repeatedly practised over this ground; the artillery lifts being represented by lines of men with flags who retired in accordance with the artillery programme. Communication with aeroplane contact patrols was practised. As a means of providing covered communication across no man's land after the assault, three tunnels were constructed from our trenches to within a short distance of the enemy front line. The tunnels were 5' 6" high, 3' 6" wide at the bottom and 2' 6" at the top – one in 34th Division area (410 ft long) and two in 8th Division (both 600 ft long). HQ III Corps established an OP just in front of Labour Redoubt on the high ground SW of Albert which was connected to Corps HQ by telephone, and a communication centre was established at Laventie. The pigeon-cote was also in this farm. Very few messages came through by pigeon on the first day but the system proved of great value during subsequent operations. During the bombardment, the progress of wire cutting was recorded daily at Corps HQ on a large scale map. On the evening preceding the assault, the wire was reported to be well cut both on the front and rear lines. This proved to be the case.

The official history continues:

> As the infantry commanders were by no means satisfied with the results of the bombardment of La Boisselle and Ovillers, a battery of eight Stokes mortars was told off to shell the former at Zero. It was speedily knocked out by shell fire, but before this happened considerable effect appeared to have been produced on La Boisselle.

Of more significance:

> The programme for 1 July provided for eight lifts of the heavy artillery, and laid down that after the assault the subsequent movement of the infantry will be assisted and regulated by a system of barrages which will move back 'slowly' in accordance with a time table. In this programme the sixth lift, to fall behind Contalmaision and Pozières, took place 1 hour and 25 minutes after Zero, and the final lift, roughly one thousand yards further back, 22 minutes later. The 'slowly' referred to the general pace of the advance of the barrage, which was about two miles in 1 hour and 47 minutes. It was made in 'jumps' by the heavy artillery as in XIII and XV Corps: the divisional barrage, on the other hand, was to go back 'very slowly', and the instructions issued in 34th Division Artillery made clear what was intended. They state: 'Lifts are timed to commence at the same time as the heavy artillery. But instead of lifting straight back on to the next line, divisional artillery will rake back gradually to the next line'. The rake, however, the speed of which was given in an appendix, was not continuous, but a series of short lifts of 50, 100, or 150 yards. It was further said that: 'The speed at which the rake goes back to the next line will be calculated so that the shrapnel barrage moves back faster than the infantry can advance'. This was not therefore a creeping barrage, but only an attempt to deal with every small intermediate trench.
>
> There were frequent complaints of bad gun ammunition during the preliminary bombardment and on 1 July, for the field-gun ammunition proved to be very faulty, causing numerous premature bursts with consequent casualties as the guns were ranged in several lines. Many of the heavy howitzer shells fell short, and many failed to burst: an officer with the successful right wing of the corps reported 'a dud shell every two or three yards over several acres of ground'. On the other hand, it should be mentioned that the 12" railway gun firing at Zero from behind Albert at 13 miles' range, drove the HQ XIV [German] Corps out of Bapaume.

BGRA III Corps issued one final instruction (No 33) – Cooperation with No 3 Sqn RFC on Z Day and thereafter:

1. Z Day Period -65 to 2.15. There will be two machines for counter-battery work. One machine will work in the area allotted to the right counter-battery group and one in the area allotted to the left. The task of these machines will be to report active hostile batteries to the HQs of their own groups as quickly as possible. In order to make certain of transmitting the signals, the machines will fly back until they are over their group HQs before sending the signals. If corrections on the fire can be given, it will be done, but the first task of these machines is to report all active hostile batteries.

2. Z Day Period 2.15 and afterwards. One of the above machines will be detailed to do actual counter-battery shooting at any batteries which still remain active. One 12" howitzer will be detailed for this duty and targets will be sent down by the aeroplane and ranging carried out in the ordinary manner. It may perhaps be necessary for this machine to fly back over the 12' mast before sending corrections. The other machine will be for reconnaissance duties only. Its primary duty will be to report any movement or collection of hostile troops or any preparation for a counter-attack. It will in addition report all batteries which are seen to be active.

The rest of this instruction was largely overtaken by events.
Again the official history:

Two very large mines, to be fired two minutes before Zero, were laid by 179 Tunnelling Coy RE under the shoulders of the salient formed by the trenches round La Boisselle in order to destroy any flanking arrangements, and by the height of their lips to prevent enfilade fire along no man's land on either side. The southern one, known as 'Lochnagar', under Schwaben Redoubt, contained 60,000 lbs of ammonal; the other 'Y Sap', 40,600 lbs of ammonal. As mine warfare had been going on in the La Boisselle area, infinite precautions were necessary to prevent discovery of this new enterprise.

Major Hance OC 179 Tunnelling Coy RE wrote many years later:

The gallery of the crater, known as the Lochnagar tunnel, had been driven by 185 Coy from the redoubt of that name. The enemy had certainly become aware of these operations for he put down a defensive mining system considerably deeper than our tunnel. Early in 1916, the tunnel came into the charge of 179 Coy for maintenance, work being temporarily stopped. It was later decided to continue this tunnel to get nearer the two objective points in the German front line. The work was done in silence. A large number of bayonets were fitted with handles. The operator inserted the point in a crack in the 'face', or alongside a flint, of which there were any number in the chalk, gave it a twist which wrenched loose a piece of stone of varying size which he caught with his other hand and laid on the floor. The men worked bare-footed, the floor of the gallery was carpeted with sandbags, and an officer was always present to preserve silence. As sandbags were filled with chalk they were passed out along a line of men seated on the floor, and stacked against the wall ready for use later as tamping. Air was forced in from bellows through armoured hose and 'exhausted' out thro' the gallery. The dimensions of this latter length of tunnel were about 4'6" × 2'6". The work was extremely laborious, and if we advanced 18" in 24 hours we thought we did well. We could hear the Germans quite plainly in their mining system below and in the dug-outs in the upper part of the system.

He continued about Y Sap:

The large mine fired two minutes before Zero hour under the northern side of the La Boisselle salient was not under La Boisselle or any portion of it. It was under a redoubt connected to the German front line at La Boisselle immediately to the N of the Albert-Bapaume road. The

German line then made a big re-entrant round Mash Valley, running first alongside the main road, and then swinging away to the N and W. The Germans attached enormous importance to the Y Sap redoubt. As fast as we bombarded it they repaired it with concrete and steel. It was protected by a deep mining system. So long as it existed, and its machine-guns were in action, no human infantry could cross no man's land (800 yds wide at most) in front of Ovillers. I knew it was no good going straight at the place, so we began the drive from a point on one of our inclines 200 feet in front of our front line trench, thence drove 500 feet about N-NW, and thence 500 feet E by N, which brought us under the Y Sap. Ventilation was assisted by a new shaft sunk from a chamber in front of our front line. The actual drive was 1030 feet long, the longest offensive drive in the chalk of the War. It will be observed that the gallery had a bend of nearly a right angle, about the middle of its length. The chamber was 75 feet below the surface; we could hear the Germans working in their mine system above us.

However, it is his comments on the decision when to blow these mines that is of the greatest interest:

For hours, if not days, before Zero I could have blown up the Y Sap any time I liked, and I, accordingly, saw the Corps Commander, asking for permission to do so. Sir Wm Pulteney, whilst agreeing that the destruction of the Y Sap would save life locally, was of opinion that the explosion of such a great mine would have warned the Germans for 5 miles N and S that the attack was imminent, and caused every German machine-gunner for 10 miles to be on the qui vive. In my humble opinion they would be in any case, and what if the mine had been blown two days before? However, having put forward my view, and having been overruled by the Corps Commander, with all his infinitely wider knowledge of the issues at stake, and the possibilities of success on the front involved, I could only abide by his decision.

Putty's decision would have been a difficult one but blowing the mines close to Zero was one of the few surprises left to him. Hance also wrote: 'All my life, I shall be proud of my connection with the corps (III) of the red, white and blue (should be black) triangle'.

Putty's planning was meticulous within the constraints he was given by Rawlinson but neither divisional commander was happy with the plan; GOC 8th Division (Major General Hudson) protested that his front was excessive particularly in view of the enfilade fire which his division would suffer from the Thiepval spur to the N and La Boisselle to the S. He suggested that his attack should be delayed until the flanks had been secured: the proposal was put to Rawlinson, presumably by Putty, but he rejected it. GOC 8th Division moved his assaulting bns into no man's land before Zero hour to reduce the distance to cover but this did little to reduce their casualties.

By 2.15 am everyone was in position and gaps made in the wire to allow passage. The GS log recorded the main events and decisions taken that day:

6.25 am. Intense bombardment of the enemy's front line by all available artillery.
7 am. Heavy artillery lifted to support lines. Divisional artillery continued to fire on front line till 7.30 am when they lifted in accordance with the programme.
7.28 am. A large mine was exploded under German trenches (Schwaben Redoubt) and another under Y Sap at 7.30 am.

7.30 am. The attack was delivered along the whole front occupied by the corps, with the exception that no direct attack was made on La Boisselle, the two front line bns of 102 Bde passing to the N and S of it respectively [XV Corps planned the same indirect approach to Fricourt which suggests this tactic was on direction from 4th Army]. Smoke curtains were put on La Boisselle and Ovillers by a detachment of Special Bde. The front lines of both divisions reached the German lines with comparatively few casualties.

The wire was found to be well cut. Subsequent lines came under heavy machine-gun fire from Ovillers and La Boisselle and from the high ground S of Thiepval. Right bn of 101 Bde was reported to be holding Scots Redoubt.

9 am. The position of 8th Division was that 2 Middx had reached the enemy support line. 2 Devon had carried the front line, but had lost heavily and were unable to advance further. 2 W Yorks, who were ordered to support them, came under heavy machine-gun fire from La Boisselle and failed to cross no man's land. Both leading battalions of 25 Bde reached the enemy's front line, but further advance was prevented by machine-gun fire from Ovillers. 70 Bde had reached the enemy's second line and, in places, his third, but had been unable to hold on.

11 am. Report received that elements of 34th Division have passed Peake Wood.

12.15 pm. GOC 8th Division reported that two of his bde comds had not sufficient troops to make any further attack. Corps Commander placed 56 Bde of 19th Division at disposal of GOC 8th Division.

12.35 pm. Orders were issued by GOC 8th Division for 56 Bde to attack Ovillers, joining up with the right of 70 Bde, 23 Bde supporting 2 Middx with all available reserves. Attack to be delivered at 5 pm, after re-bombardment of Ovillers

3.05 pm. 34th Division was ordered to use a battalion of 19th Division to clear up situation at La Boisselle.

4 pm. Report on situation of 34th Division and line held

4.15 pm. Attack by 56 Bde countermanded and orders issued to 19th Division to attack La Boisselle to form a defensive flank to 34th Division (III Corps OpO No.71 at 4.30 pm – Zero hour to be fixed by GOC 19th Division).

4.40 pm. 12th Division placed at the disposal of GOC III Corps.

6.10 pm. 12th Division ordered to relieve 8th Division and to prepare to attack Ovillers tomorrow. 8th Divisional Artillery to remain in position (III Corps OpO No.72). HQ 12th Division moved to Hénencourt Chateau and shared it with HQ 8th Division.

7.30 pm. Zero hour for attack on La Boisselle by 19th Division fixed at 10.30 pm today.

7.45 pm. Corps Cavalry and Cyclists placed at disposal of 34th Division.

11.05 pm. 4th Army OpO No. 3 received. III Corps to secure La Boisselle, Ovillers and Contalmaison and a line joining the two latter. VIII and X Corps to pass under control of General Gough (GOC Reserve Army) from 7 am tomorrow

Prisoners taken to corps cage: 6.

8th Division attacked with all three bdes in the line: 70 Bde was on the left (Left: 8 Y&L, Right: 8 YLI, Sp: 9 Y&L, Res: 11 Sher For); 25 Bde was in the centre (Left: 2 Berks, Right: 2 Lincolns, Sp: 1 RIR, Res: 2 RB); and 23 Bde was on the right (Left: 2 Devons, Right: 2 Middx, Sp: 2 Cameronians and 2 W Yorks). 70 Bde had to attack up Nab Valley with the high ground on its left the responsibility of 32nd Division across the corps boundary; its objective was Mouquet Farm and a line S towards Pozières. 25 Bde's objective was Ovillers and the defences covering the village; 23 Bde was to attack up Mash Valley with La Boisselle and high ground on its right the responsibility of 34th Division, and its objective was Pozières.

Opposing 8th Division was 180 Regt holding four lines of defence. Two bns were forward, each with two coys in the front line, one in the second, and one in the third. The third bn was in the fourth line covering Pozières. The six assaulting bns of 8th Division, therefore, faced two bns of the enemy. Neither of the division's flanks was secured; the preliminary bombardment had not destroyed all the enemy positions; and the consequences were inevitable, and as GOC 8th Division had feared.

70 Bde found the open ground of Nab Valley an utter death-trap. The first wave made some progress breaching the German lines, but as the German defences reorganised and their machine-guns began to intervene from the flanks, the supporting bns found it almost impossible to cross no man's land. Corporal Tansley 9 Y&L recalled many years later:

Zero hour, the whistles were blown, ladders were put to mount out of the trench and lanes had been cut through the 30 foot British wire. We had been told: 'There's no need for this short rushes and getting down on your stomach, go straight over as if you were on parade. That's the orders, there's no fear of enemy attack, that's been silenced by the British guns'. Up we went through the lanes cut in the wire, spread out and tried to follow this instruction. Myself, I was a bit sceptical about it. Anyway we tried to adhere to it as far as possible. We spread out, I and my section made for this slight ridge marked by an old farm instrument. Looked around for where the line was, they seemed to disappear – lying about on the ground.

25 Bde fared no better as Captain Hanbury-Sparrow Berks GSO3 HQ 8th Division recalled:

I was given a place with my signallers about 400 yards behind our front line on a bank where you could see very clearly on a fine day. The troops advanced out of the trenches, but by this time although the sky was clear the shells had thrown up so much smoke and rubble, and a reddish dust was over everything. There was a mist too and hardly anything was visible. One saw these figures disappear in to the mist and as they did so, so did the first shots ring out from the other side. I thought our men had got into the German trench – and so did the men with me. I reported as much to division. Presently as the barrage went forward so did the air clear and I could see what was happening. In the distance I saw the barrage bounding on towards Pozières, the Third German Line. In no man's land were heaps of dead, with Germans almost standing up in their trenches, well over the top firing and sniping at those who had taken refuge in the shell holes.

Brigadier General Tuson Comd 23 Bde noted in his report that throughout the attack his bde had been 'deprived of artillery support' and that it was futile bombarding distant objectives 'if we are ourselves unable to maintain our hold on the enemy's front line'.

Major Jack 2 Cameronians 23 Bde noted that day:

7 am. The intensity of our barrage increased to drum fire and I led my two companies up Hodder Street to the rear of [2] W Yorks in Houghton Street, as well as in the new assembly

trenches off it, which had been for some time, and still were, under terrible blast from the enemy's howitzers. For over an hour my men, crouching at the less exposed side of the trench, were subjected – as were the W Yorks – to an infernal pounding from the enemy's howitzers. Our mortars joined in the tumult. Simultaneously 2 Middx and 2 Devons, climbing out of their trenches by short ladders placed on the fire-steps, crept through the lanes in our wire. Each battalion then extended in four waves to cover about 300 yards of frontage and crawled forward to begin crossing the six to eight hundred yards of no man's land. Eight minutes afterwards (7.30 am), on the tick of Zero hour, and following the explosion of mines under the La Boisselle salient, our field gun barrage, till then falling on the first German trench line, lifted to a further line. Both battalions (2 Middx and 2 Devons), rising to their feet, now advanced in quick time through the rank, knee-deep grass, the four waves at one hundred paces interval, to close on the foe with the bayonet. A hail of bullets from shell holes clear of the blasted German trenches in front, as well as from either flank at La Boisselle and Ovillers, mowed down the three leading waves now breaking into a charge. Those of both battalions who succeeded in gaining an entry fought hand to hand with bayonet and bomb till they had either become casualties or were forced to retire some two hours later to the scanty cover afforded by the grass and weeds in no man's land there to await the friendly mantle of night.

Some of 8th Division got to the German 2nd Line, a few – very few and mainly from 70 Bde – got to the 3rd Line, but none were able to hold on. By 2.30 pm the Germans had regained all their lines opposite 8th Division; many of the wounded and unwounded were forced to remain in no man's land until darkness fell. At 12.15 pm Putty placed 56 Bde 19th Division at the disposal of GOC 8th Division for another attack on Ovillers. However, when he became aware of the full extent of 8th Division's losses he cancelled this plan, and at 6.10 pm ordered 12th Division to relieve 8th Division and be prepared to attack Ovillers next day (2 July).

8th Division had 5,121 casualties on 1 July, almost all in the infantry bns: of these 1,927 were killed. This loss of 50% was reflected almost equally in the attacking bns – 23 Bde: 2 Middx – 623, 2 Devons – 450, 2 W Yorks – 429; 25 Bde: 2 Berks – 374 incl CO, 2 Lincolns – 471, 1 RIR – 446 incl CO, 2 RB – 119; 70 Bde: 8 YLI – 539, 8 Y&L – 597, 9 Y&L – 423, 11 Sher For – 437.

A last word from Major Jack 2 Cameronians:

We relied far too much on our artillery not only in pulverising the hostile works, which it did, but also on its maiming and cowing into inertia practically all the defenders of each trench line in succession, which it did not. Indeed the enemy, with great acumen, generally vacated their blasted works effectively to man shell holes clear of our barrage, from which they were able to maintain very heavy small arms fire during our assault.

Nothing illustrates this more clearly than 180 Regt's casualties that day: 4 officers and 79 other ranks killed, 3 officers and 181 other ranks wounded, 13 other ranks missing = 280.

On the right of the corps, 34th Division's task was equally formidable, and again the official history provides a helpful summary:

The full weight of the twelve battalions of 34th Division was to be thrown into the first assault, by successive waves, against the German position. It was to attack in four columns, each column three battalions deep on a frontage of four hundred yards. Between the third and fourth columns opposite La Boisselle there was to be a gap. La Boisselle, the key of the front system owing to its salient position, was not to be attacked directly; the two left columns, passing on either side of it, were as they advanced to send into it special bombing parties (amounting in all to one platoon) to clear it from both flanks. Brigade and battalion commanders who expressed doubt as to the feasibility of this course were reminded that the commander of 4th Army (Rawlinson) had said the village would have been rendered untenable and the Germans in it wiped out by the preliminary bombardment, while the flanking shoulders on either side of it would be destroyed by the great mines. On 30 June, however, the front line troops had found the garrison very much on the alert, for parties put over the parapet to clear passages through the wire in front of it were fired upon. It was arranged, therefore, that at Zero when the barrage lifted, the bombardment of the village should be continued by trench mortars until the flanking parties could enter. To deal with Sausage Redoubt, a dangerous flanking work, during the night an emplacement for a trench-mortar battery was dug in no man's land – there about 500 yards wide – and its fire proved very effective until all its personnel were killed or wounded. It was subsequently discovered that the damage done was superficial; in one of the deep dugouts an overhearing station had remained in action to the last. At 2.45 am it had picked up part of a telephoned British order which pointed to an assault in the morning.

The two right columns were formed of 101 Bde, each having one battalion in front and one in support with a battalion of 103 Bde [Comd 103 Bde was wounded soon after Zero and replaced until 4 July by CO 27 NF] in rear. The two left columns were similarly composed of 102 Bde, with the two remaining battalions of 103 Bde in rear. As 103 Bde contained, as did the division as a whole, a large number of miners, extensive galleries had been dug in Tara Hill for the first assembly of its battalions. At the hour of the assault all four columns were to advance in extended order in lines of companies, each in column of platoons at 150 paces' distance. Comd 101 Bde ordered the headquarters of his battalions to stand fast when the troops advanced, and not to go forward until ordered by the brigade. They therefore remained intact and available to reorganise their commands at night, whilst practically all the other battalion staffs became casualties.

The first objective of the two leading lines of battalions was the German front system, consisting of four trenches. The fourth trench, requiring an advance of about two thousand yards, was to be reached forty-eight minutes after Zero hour, 8.18 am. The second objective was the German second intermediate line, the Kaisergraben, in front of Contalmaison and Pozières villages. This was to be reached by 8.58 am, when 101 and 102 Bdes were to halt and consolidate. 103 Bde, forming the third line of battalions and following close in rear, would then pass through 101 and 102 Bdes, capture Contalmaison village, and advance to the third, and final, objective of the division, a line close to the outer or eastern edge of the village and Pozières; this line was to be reached by 103 Bde at 10.10 am. 34th Division was opposed by German 110 Regt on a similar frontage, two battalions holding the front, the third battalion being in reserve in the intermediate lines and 2nd Position.

The divisional plan was flawed in several respects. The decision to bypass La Boisselle may have been an inevitable consequence of Rawlinson's orders but GOC 34th Division's orders provided no effective command and control above bn level after Zero hour, and in 101 Bde there was none at bn level either. He committed all his bns at the same time leaving no reserve in case of any problems, and, even worse, the bns of 103 Bde closed up on those in front as soon as they were stopped presenting ever better targets for the enemy.

Each column had a different story to tell and the official history provides a good overview:

The right (First) column (15 RS, 16 RS 101 Bde and 27 NF 103 Bde) was faced by the steep convex slope of the long western side of the Fricourt spur. The front companies of 15 RS moved forward to within two hundred yards of the German front trench before Zero hour, covered by the final bombardment and trench mortar fire. On the barrage lifting, they overran with great steadiness and with little loss of life the German front trench which lay along the upper part of the slope. At this very early stage flanking machine-gun fire from Sausage Valley and La Boisselle forced the leading companies of 15 RS, which were ahead of those of the second column, from their proper direction, and practically destroyed the left wings of the rear companies and of the lines of 16 RS, which were following. The intended line of advance lay north of east, but owing to the hail of fire from the left the lines instinctively veered due eastward, moving straight up instead of aslant the rising slope, leaving parties of 15 RS to clear up the German trenches in the sector, which included Sausage Redoubt. This divergence was maintained and accentuated as the advance progressed, carrying the right column into the zone of XV Corps. Thus by 7.48 am 15 and 16 RS were well on top of the Fricourt spur, but had left uncaptured both Sausage Redoubt and Scots Redoubt. The error of direction was not discovered until half-an-hour later (8.18 am), when, after advancing nearly a mile and crossing the German first intermediate line, RS reached Birch Tree Wood beyond Sunken Road, in the depression leading down to Fricourt village and ran into units of 21st Division (XV Corps). The remains of the two battalions, now considerably intermingled, edged away therefore to their left, northwards, to rectify the mistake. Those of 15 RS moved along Birch Tree Trench in the German second intermediate line, towards Peake Wood, and those of 16 RS took up a position to support two hundred yards in rear.

Before this northward movement along Birch Tree Trench was completed, the enemy attacked from the direction of Peake Wood, chiefly with bombing-parties along the trench; simultaneously heavy machine-gun fire was opened from the left flank and rear. This counter-attack caused heavy loss, and forced the RS to withdraw southwards. They then initiated a movement towards Wood Alley and Scots Redoubt: both objectives were secured, Scots Redoubt in an almost undamaged condition.

The RS were now astride the Fricourt spur, even a little beyond their first objective along the eastern side of it, and faced Contalmaison spur, a thousand yards away across the valley. One party of 16 RS, according to German accounts, actually penetrated the village and was there annihilated. 27 NF, which was to follow close behind 16 RS, was stopped by the intense and accurate machine-gun fire which dominated no man's land. Parties got through to the Fricourt-Pozières road and some men, with others of 24 NF of the next column on the left, reached Acid Drop Copse and the outskirts of Contalmaison. But such isolated advances could not change the fortune of the day. On learning what the situation was, Brigadier General Gore (Comd 101 Bde) selected CO 16 RS (Lieutenant Colonel Sir George McCrae) to go forward and take command. The position reached by the RS was consolidated, and as it flanked the eastern side of the Fricourt spur towards Contalmaison, it formed a strong defensive flank on the left of XV Corps. The casualties that day were: 15 RS – 513 and 16 RS – 466.

On the left of the second column (10 Lincoln 11 Suffolk 101 Bde and 24 NF 103 Bde), opposite the gap of two hundred yards which divided it from the third, the Lochnagar mine was successfully exploded at 7.28 am, blowing up the German garrison and causing a crater ninety yards across and seventy feet deep, with lips fifteen feet high. Immediately S of the mine, however, the German front trench, following the contour of Sausage Valley, formed a pronounced re-entrant; and the infantry of the second column, delayed five minutes by order (there was no necessity for this wait) in view of the mine explosion, was not only behind the columns on either side in crossing no man's land, but had further to go than that on its left. The barrage had lifted and the Germans had plenty of time to man their position, including Sausage Redoubt, the northern face of which flanked the advance. Their fire, combined with that of the flanking machine-guns in Sausage Valley and La Boisselle, turned first on the right column and then on to the second, was fatal to the success of 34th Division. Within two minutes of Zero hour, before the lines of 10 Lincoln had cleared the front trench, machine-gun fire raked them and those of 11 Suffolk following. The latter, in addition, suffered from a weak artillery barrage placed on the British trenches by the German batteries soon after the assault had been launched. Men fell fast, and the lines were gradually reduced to isolated small parties.

On the extreme right, a party which tried to storm Sausage Redoubt was burnt to death by flame throwers as it reached the parapet; but some of the Suffolks got through and joined the RS of the first column on top of the Fricourt spur. Still the courageous efforts of the mass of the Lincolns and Suffolks to cross the 500 yards of no man's land were unavailing, and 24 NF following them was ordered to halt in the front trenches. The survivors took any cover available in the open fire-swept zone; some men, from all three battalions, reached and consolidated a position in the Lochnagar crater. The party of 15 RS left by the right column to deal with Sausage Redoubt attempted to bomb northwards, but was not strong enough to do so. Two attempts by 27 Fd Coy RE and a company of 18 NF (Pioneers) to reinforce this party across no man's land also failed owing to machine-gun fire; it was obvious that until the Germans could be cleared out of the redoubt, the troops of the second column lying out in no man's land could neither be reinforced nor relieved during daylight. Casualties in this column were: 10 Lincoln – 477 and 11 Suffolk – 527.

Major Vignoles OC D Coy 10 Lincoln was wounded early in the day; he wrote when he was in hospital in England:

Zero was at 7.30 am but we had to move to another position about 5.30 am and were to breakfast at 4.30 am. Rum was to be issued early on and, as I had some letters to write, I did not turn in till well after midnight, in the end I only had a couple of hours sleep on my bed frame. We were all ready in good time and moved off to our final positions about 5.30 am. We found the trenches full of men but there was no confusion as each unit had been allocated a separate trench and the routes were laid down. At 6.25 am the artillery, which had been firing in a desultory manner, began to speed up and within fifteen minutes there was a perfect hurricane of sound. Every gun, large or small, started firing rapid, the trench mortars in the front line joining in while above all could be heard the tearing rattle of the

Vickers machine-guns firing from somewhere near us. The morning was fine and the sun shining, but the enemy's trenches were veiled in light mist, made worse, no doubt, by the smoke from the thousands of shells we were pumping into his lines. Nearby I could see our machine-gunners out in the open already, trying to get the best position to enfilade certain parts of the Boche line. My company got out of the trench to carry forward our stuff and a Boche machine-gun kept sweeping over us. I got the men down and while getting them all together I tried to stop a bullet with my left hand!

Private Baumber 10 Lincoln wrote of his experience many years later:

The mine went up and the trenches simply rocked like a boat, we seemed to be very close to it and looked in awe as great pieces of earth as big as coal wagons were blasted skywards to hurtle and roll and then start to scream back all round us. A great geyser of mud, chalk and flame had risen and subsided before our gaze and man had created it. I vividly recall as the barrage lifted temporarily and there was the slightest pause in this torment, several skylarks were singing – incredible! With enfilading machine-gun fire from the flanks it was simply a massacre and although a few struggled into the German defences, we who were left were simply pinned down where we lay. There was no going forward and at this point no way of going back to our lines.

Not everyone in the column was an infantryman; Corporal Maw RA wrote, again years later:

It went up, the ground suddenly jolting and then rocking below our feet. Muck was thrown some two or three hundred feet into the air to land later like a load of coal dropping for what seemed an age. The instant it stopped we went over the top with the lads to claim the new crater. Amid heavy supporting fire, I and a handful of men brought up the field telephones and cables essential for the communications between the front-line troops and our artillery.

Lieutenant Colonel Cordeaux CO 10 Lincoln wrote:

The battalion was immediately exposed to heavy shell-fire, shrapnel and HE, and the most intense enfilade machine-gun fire from La Boisselle and Heligoland Redoubt. Advancing with the utmost steadiness and courage, not to be surpassed by any troops in the world, yet the distance they were from the German trenches (800 yards) and the intensity of the machine-gun fire did not allow of the possibility of rushing and penetrating the enemy line. It is doubtful if any troops have ever been subjected to a more intense machine-gun fire than was experienced in the assault, a fire which made it absolutely impossible to relieve or reinforce units during daylight.

The official history again:

The third column (21 and 22 NF 102 Bde, 26 NF 103 Bde) tried to pass immediately S of La Boisselle, but N of the Lochnagar crater. Starting immediately the mine was fired, and having less than 200 yards of no man's land to cross, it succeeded in overrunning the trenches of Schwaben Hohe. The leading lines then moved along the western side of Sausage Valley, and immediately below La Boisselle village, and crossed the next two lines of trenches. Their right flank was, however, exposed owing to the failure of the second column to advance at Zero. Detachments of bombers were sent out towards La Boisselle, but were unable to make progress. Up to this time, twelve minutes after Zero hour, the bombardment of the village had been continued by trench mortars, so as to cover the advance of the assaulting columns to the N and S of it; but this did not prevent the Germans from emerging from the deep dug-outs under the ruins. They opened machine-gun fire on the columns and enfiladed the lines of infantry moving past the southern front of the village, and they drove back the bombing parties. Very heavy losses were incurred by all three battalions at this stage. Nevertheless, the German first intermediate line, astride the Contalmaison road, was reached in places, some men being reported as far E as Bailiff Wood only 500 yards from Contalmaison itself. The Germans now counter-attacked and the NF, unable to retaliate effectively owing to a shortage of bombs, withdrew to the remains of the third German front trench. Reduced to 7 officers and about 200 other ranks, they held and consolidated this trench on a front of 400 yards, their right on the road up Sausage Valley.

The fourth (left) column (20 and 23 NF 102 Bde, 25 NF 103 Bde) was to pass by the northern side of La Boisselle, while the Glory Hole between this column and the third was held by a company of 18 NF (Pioneers). Here, too, the German front line followed the contour of Mash Valley, forming a pronounced re-entrant, so that on the left nearly 800 yards of no man's land had to be crossed. All depended on the bombardment having obliterated the defences of the two villages. In spite of the successful firing of the Y Sap mine (1 officer and 35 men were taken out of a dug-out just beyond the radius of the mine; the officer said that nine dug-outs equally full must have been closed in) immediately the NF left the trenches they encountered cross machine-gun fire, not only from Ovillers on their left front, but at short range from La Boisselle and its trenches on the right, besides some shelling. The two leading battalions were almost annihilated before they reached the German front trench. 25 NF, advancing behind them, also lost heavily.

GOC 34th Division watched the attack from a forward OP on Tara Hill. At 11.25 am, four hours after Zero, he telegraphed HQ III Corps asking for reinforcement to press the attack on La Boisselle from the S. It is difficult to understand how he could have expected this to succeed but perhaps he was still not aware of the extent of his division's losses. 9 Welch from 19th Division in corps reserve was placed at his disposal but then Putty countermanded this order during the afternoon when he too fully appreciated the situation, and decided that 19th Division should be ordered to take La Boisselle. 34th Division had lost 113 officers and 2,367 other ranks killed, 148 officers and 3,439 other ranks wounded, 3 officers and 291 other ranks missing, and 1 officer and 18 other ranks taken prisoner = 6,380. The officer casualties included Comd 103 Bde (wounded), 7 of its 12 COs (5 killed and 2 wounded): 103 Bde lost 3 of its 4 COs and 15 of its 16 Coy Comds. Only 101 Bde could be considered a fighting force, and then only just.

During the day Putty was about to reinforce failure but once he knew the full situation he made three important decisions. Firstly, he countermanded his orders that committed the corps reserve piecemeal: secondly, he ordered 12th Division to relieve 8th Division that night: and thirdly, he ordered 19th Division to attack La Boisselle again that night (Zero 10.30 pm). As he made these decisions, the full extent of the losses in the corps would have been coming in. The total casualties were 11,501 or more than 50% of the infantry in the two attacking divisions. In the 24 hours from 6 am 1 July 5,000 wounded were evacuated. This and the relief of 8th Division made it impossible for 19th Division to get forward and its attack was therefore postponed until next day.

III Corps failed to make any significant progress on 1 July and suffered appalling casualties because of its total reliance on the artillery's ability to overwhelm the enemy's resistance. Both GOC 8th and 34th Division were concerned about this and made representations to Putty, and he in turn made them to Rawlinson: almost certainly the divisional commanders also made them direct to Rawlinson when he visited. Yet Rawlinson did not alter the plan in any way and, even more extraordinary, any contingency planning seems to have been discouraged. The tactics of the two divisions bordered on suicidal if their commanders had any doubts about the artillery.

They all would have known the basic facts – the low probability of a shell hitting its target given the beaten zone of the various guns, and that they were firing overhead; the low probability of a shell exploding given the unreliability of the ammunition; and the low probability of a shell that did hit and explode destroying enemy positions given their strength and depth. The overall probability of success, a multiplication of these three, was very low indeed: to achieve it would have required a phenomenal amount of ammunition, and this was not available. A creeping barrage might have been more flexible than a timed one but with so many guns firing across the front it would have been difficult to implement, and the beaten zone problem would have remained: to reduce the risk of hitting their own troops the barrage had to be lifted early and kept well ahead of them, allowing the enemy time to recover before the attacking infantry could arrive.

Brigadier General Benson CHA V Corps wrote in his report:

> Most wire-cutting guns fired 18 pdr shrapnel or HE shells. On bursting, a shrapnel shell propels steel balls forward and downwards. So to penetrate the wire at the high velocity needed to cut it, the shell had to explode a few yards short of and above the target. It is a reasonable supposition that at least a proportion of the gunners had not the experience to achieve consistent accuracy of this sort. HE 18 pdr shells required less accuracy but the problem here was that many of the shells travelled through the wire and only exploded on impact with the ground. This tended to throw the wire into the air and down again without cutting it. The distant wire presented a particular difficulty. Here the results could not be checked by patrols and aerial photographs, which in the case of wire-cutting were notoriously difficult to interpret, had to be relied on.
>
> In III Corps the artillery men warned that, while they were willing to try and cut a few lanes 'favourable results are not anticipated'.
>
> Finally, the overall task was, despite the number of guns employed, too great for some corps. III Corps calculated that to cut all the wire within 3,500 yards of the front line would require quantities of ammunition which were simply not available (III Corps Artillery only fired 70,963 rounds on 1 July). Their only solution was to suggest that the infantry provide a priority list of wire whose removal was essential.

Benson must have been talking to Brigadier General Perkins CHA III Corps or more likely Brigadier General Uniacke BGRA III Corps, considered to be one of the foremost experts in the use of artillery. Uniacke (or Perkins) would also have made their concerns known to Putty and to MGRA 4th Army (Major General Budworth). Again these concerns would have got to Rawlinson.

General Broad (at that time Captain Broad SO to BGRA III Corps – Uniacke) wrote many years later:

> There is no doubt that we began the Battle of the Somme without really understanding the barrage. As far as my recollection goes, the barrage of the III Corps front was made to jump from one trench system to the next. We did not realise that the Germans would be driven out of their trenches and would occupy their shell holes with machine-guns and riflemen. It was this defence combined with the concrete machine-gun emplacements, especially around Ovillers that caused the trouble on the first day. The second point was that we did not in the least realise how slowly attacking troops must move in fighting of this description. Our experiences this day led to the creeping barrage. The next point of interest was how slowly this barrage must go in order to search out thoroughly the shells holes at normal rates of fire. The matter was not settled in our own minds until the attack on 15 September.

For Putty it would have been a bad night. After the defeat on 1 July he would have been determined to prevent the enemy reinforcing or reorganising his front: speed was essential. Yet GOC 12th Division (Major General AB Scott) wanted time for reconnaissance before attacking Ovillers and GOC 19th Division (Major General Bridges) needed time to get his division into position through trenches blocked by stretcher bearers and others before he could attack La Boisselle.

Commenting on Edmonds' draft history, Putty wrote many years later:

> 1 July. I do not think enough credit is given to the Tunnelling Company who made the mines, their sap head was in the front trench, if anything in front of it. The main thing overlooked was the fact of the trenches being obliterated giving us no cover for the attackers when reached, no one realised the depth of the German dug outs, our own dug outs were miserable attempts, the ground was absolutely strewn with our own dud 8" shells.

As dawn broke on 2 July Putty had 34th Division on his right; now reduced to one weak brigade it was holding forward beside the corps boundary. In the centre 19th Division had moved forward and was preparing to attack La Boisselle, and on the left 12th Division having relieved 8th Division was preparing to attack Ovillers. HQ III Corps also had to move 8th Division back out of the corps and bring forward 23rd Division as the new corps reserve.

At 5.30 am HQ III Corps issued OpO No.73, carrying out the orders in 4th Army OpO No.3 received at 11.5 pm the previous night: 'III Corps to secure La Boisselle, Ovillers and Contalmaison and a line joining the two latter'. According to the III Corps Opsum at 8 am: 'Southwards (from La Boisselle) the German front and support lines were in our hands with the exception of an isolated party of Germans who were holding out in Heligoland (Sausage Redoubt), a redoubt in the front trench system – 1,000 yards S of La Boisselle'.

At 8.5 am the GS log recorded: 'XV Corps asked to assist III Corps by bombing towards Heligoland still held by the enemy'.

9 Cheshire 58 Bde were the first bn of 19th Division to arrive and relieved men of 34th Division holding Schwaben Hohe (Lochnagar) crater. Captain James Trench Mortar Officer HQ 34th Division was LO between 34th and 19th Divisions. He wrote:

> I went with the CO 9 Cheshire to explore La Boisselle. On the way we discovered that the tunnel (Kerriemuir) was choked with dead and wounded. We straightened that out and went across no man's land. When we got to the village, at about 12.30 pm, we found an officer and a few men in possession of the left flank – skirting Mash Valley. I took over, and the Colonel went back to bring up reinforcements. The Hun started a bombing attack so I counter-attacked shortly after 1 pm, drove him back until my party was blotted out by shrapnel and I was sent to earth myself. Later I crawled back out of their bombing range, found I could still walk – I had bullets in my back and right lung, but did not know that – so I decided to hobble back to divisional headquarters (34th) and report to General Williams (Ingouville-Williams). I staggered into my tent, near the mill (Moulin Viviers), and my orderly helped me change my shirt and tunic, then I saw the General.

During the afternoon two coys 7 E Lancs (56 Bde 19th Division) were lent to 34th Division to capture Sausage Redoubt. The Germans offered little resistance to a resolute bombing attack which began after an advance across the 500 yards of no man's land. 7 E Lancs then entered the enemy trenches beyond the redoubt, occupying and consolidating a frontage of 1,000 yards. They sent back 58 prisoners, mostly hauled from dug-outs.

GOC 19th Division (Major General Bridges) wrote of his division's attack on La Boisselle:

> 4 pm. We arranged to simulate an attack on Ovillers on our left. We got all available guns to concentrate on that sector for a short and intense bombardment, and infantry to show their fixed bayonets in the front line. My orders were 'La Boisselle will be taken this afternoon without fail and regardless of loss'. Under cover of the demonstration three companies of the Wilts [6 Wilts 58 Bde] in the lightest fighting order raced across no-man's land and got into the village with scarcely a shot fired at them, while at the same time the Welch Fusiliers [9 RWF 58 Bde] effected a lodgement to their right. They were speedily reinforced, and a lot of hard hand-to-hand fighting ensued. The place was a rabbit warren, the result of two years' tunnelling by the people actually holding it who did not mean to be dislodged. But in an hour and a half (5.30 pm) the western portion was in our hands and a line across it consolidated and parties were bombing their way through the village, nearly every house of which was a strong point with dug-outs thirty to forty feet deep. Desperate fighting went on all night, the German bombers counter-attacking with great gallantry and two battalions of reinforcements had to be put in.

To deceive the enemy as to the point of 19th Division's attack, Ovillers was bombarded from 3.30 pm to 4 pm and the approaches to it covered by a smoke screen. The show of bayonets mentioned by GOC 19th Division must have been made by 12th Division, suggesting the deception plan was made by Putty. In any event it had the desired effect for the Germans put a barrage around Ovillers and left La Boisselle alone. GOC 19th Division does not mention

9 Cheshire: this bn joined in on the right of the attack. By 9 pm 19th Division had cleared the western part of the village as well as its southern defences, and had also consolidated their defensive positions along the lane just W of the church. However, it had not yet been able to join up with 34th Division.

Meanwhile at HQ III Corps OpO No.74 was issued at 2.30 pm ordering the movement of 8th Division to Picquigny and out of the corps area. At midnight 23rd Division came under Putty's command and began to move into the corps area with its HQ at Baizieux. OpO No.75 was issued at 3.30 pm ordering an attack next day by 19th Division against La Boisselle and by 12th Division against Ovillers, in cooperation with X Corps on its left. Zero hour was to be 3.15 am 3 July, following an hour's intense bombardment. 12th Division therefore had at least some of the day for reconnaissance and preparation. Having secured La Boisselle, 19th Division was to connect up with 12th and 34th Divisions.

Haig (CinC) wanted to exploit the success on the right and turn the German positions from the S but Rawlinson (GOC 4th Army) wanted first to improve the position of his centre and to secure Thiepval. Putty with his III Corps, in the hinge, was in the midst of it all. The success of III Corps on 2 July was in marked contrast to its failure the day before, and further demonstrated the futility of Rawlinson's original plan.

Putty managed to send his monthly report to the King on 2 July:

> My dear Wigram, Herewith the diary of the 3rd Corps for the month of June for the information of HM The King. We are all at concert pitch at the present moment so must ask you to excuse my writing any details of the fighting yesterday, it was a disappointment in some ways but I have never seen men go better than the 34th Division who covered themselves with glory though their losses are severe. Yours Sincerely, WP Pulteney.

With La Boisselle partially secured and X Corps attacking the Leipzig Salient on its left, 12th Division had a much better chance of taking Ovillers on 3 July. However, at 2.30 am, just 45 minutes before Zero and 15 minutes after the start of the preliminary bombardment, HQ III Corps GS log recorded:

> Telephone message from BGGS X Corps that they are unable to make an infantry attack before 6 am but will carry out smoke and artillery programme. Only half the ammunition allotted can be used for latter on account of requirements of their own attack at 6 am. Message taken by Captain Lord Hamilton. BGGS informed at once.

There is also some suggestion that GOC Reserve Army (Gough) himself telephoned at 2.55 am and said that it had not been possible to get his attacking troops ready in time, but as an example of disgraceful staff work it is difficult to surpass.

It might seem strange that Putty did not postpone the III Corps attack: he could have considered this was a matter for Haig or Rawlinson, or that with the right flank of 12th Division more secure there was a better chance of success. However, neither was the case: the tragedy was that it was impossible to cancel the attack at such short notice as there was not the time for the order to reach everyone taking part. Putty wrote to Edmonds many years later: 'Am glad my language is not repeated on the cancelling of the X Corps attack, it was enough to break anyone's heart'.

The morning of 3 July was dark for the time of year, with high cloud, but the weather continued fine until the afternoon when there was a thunderstorm. The GS log recorded the key events that day:

> 2.40 am. 12th Division informed (X Corps would not attack): Attack to take place as arranged.
> 8.56 am. 19th Division report that, with the exception of two points in rear, La Boisselle is now in our hands.
> 9.9 am. 12th Division report that they now have no troops in German trenches.
> 12.30 pm. III Corps OpO No.76 issued ordering 12th Division to stand fast and reorganise, 19th Division to hold and consolidate line captured in La Boisselle, and ordering relief of 34th Division by 23rd Division.
> Prisoners taken: 236.

12th Divisional History is very concise:

> Division attacked with 35 Bde on right (5 Berks and 7 Suffolk in front, 9 Essex in support and 7 Norfolk in reserve) and 37 Bde on left (6 Queens and 6 RWK in front, 6 Buffs/E Kent in support and 7 E Surrey in reserve). Attack failed to capture village because 1. The flanking machine-gun was unmolested. 2. Attack was carried out at night by troops who did not know the ground. 3. The artillery fire cut the wire but failed to reach the deep dugouts. 4. Recent storms made shell-holes and trenches almost impassable. Casualties in the two brigades amounted to 97 officers and 2,277 other ranks (out of 3,350).

The machine-gun fire was mainly from the front and the left flank, although a bn of 36 Bde had been put on this flank to cover the attack with a discharge of smoke. All four assaulting bns entered the enemy front trench, which appeared to hold only a few sentries. By the time the support line was reached, however, Germans were pouring out of deep dug-outs to counter-attack with bomb and bayonet. Dawn broke, but observers could see little: smoke obscured the action whilst German machine-guns rattled on without a pause. Of the men of the bns who had entered the German position very few returned; they fought until their supply of bombs ran out and were then gradually overwhelmed. One coy 9 Essex (35 Bde) lost its way and drifted to the right towards La Boisselle where it cut off 220 Germans and handed the prisoners to 19th Division.

GOC 19th Division (Major General Bridges) was equally brief; he wrote:

> 3 am [should be 3.15 am]. Ovillers on our left was attacked by 12th Division and 57 Bde of ours seized the craters and trenches to the N of La Boisselle, taking two hundred prisoners [probably those taken by 9 Essex], and during the day we mopped up to the eastern outskirts of the village where the enemy still hung on.

In fact there was to be some very hard fighting in the mopping up. 8 N Staffs (57 Bde) with bombers of 5 SWB (Pioneers) led the advance between La Boisselle and the Albert-Bapaume Road with 10 Worcs covering the outer flank. Much of the fighting was hand to hand as parts of the village were taken, re-taken, and eventually secured. The Germans counter-attacked against

57 Bde (according to the official history this was by 190 Regt 185th Division relieving 110 Regt 28th Reserve Division: 110 Regt was withdrawn at the end of the day, having lost 1,251 officers and men). The supply of bombs ran short, and the enemy gained the eastern end of the village, but reinforcements of 10 Warwicks and 8 Glos were sent forward, and the fight continued.

The situation remained confused all day and the report received at HQ III Corps at 8.56 am clearly premature. The village itself, when finally taken, was unrecognisable as ever having been the habitation of human beings. GOC 19th Division again:

> Its strength lies underground, in a complicated series of dugouts twenty to forty feet deep, all connected with each other, that no artillery can touch and no charge clear, however recklessly pressed home. If attackers go too fast and leave garrisons in any of these holes unaccounted for, machine-guns rise from the bowels of the earth behind them and shoot them in the back. If they go too slow there is a danger of exhaustion before the objective can be reached. Their (the enemy) shelling of the part of the village in our hands was very heavy. Reports were very confused and I was anxious there should be no misleading orders given. Remembering the tragedy of Spion Kop, I went across into the village at 6 pm with my GSO2, Haskard. We made our way up to the consolidated line which we found full of men, and had a talk with Carton de Wiart commanding 8 Glos. Two commanding officers [CO 8 N Staffs and CO 10 Worcs] had been killed and two wounded, so I placed the whole of the troops in the village under his command.

The battle for La Boisselle was far from over and would continue throughout the night 3/4 July. During the day 34th Division made three bombing attacks from its forward positions to link up with 19th Division, but failed to do so. When darkness fell, 23rd Division (Major General Babington) began the relief of 34th Division, 69 Bde taking over the captured trenches. 23rd Division's history describes this operation:

> The relief in the front trenches, which were taken over after dark, was a trying experience for troops unaccustomed as yet to the aftermath of a great battle. The trenches, now battered to bits, had been the scene of terrific carnage. They were literally choked with dead bodies, which it was impossible to avoid treading underfoot.

On arrival in reserve, the shattered 102 and 103 Bdes 34th Division were replaced by 111 and 112 Bdes of 37th Division. 34th Division was not reformed as originally constituted until 21 August, but it was to be back in action long before then.

Rawlinson held a conference of his corps commanders during the afternoon, as a result of which HQ 4th Army 32/3/16(G) was issued at 9.45 pm. A change of boundary between 4th and Reserve Armies would mean that Ovillers was no longer Putty's problem: Rawlinson wanted Putty to secure La Boisselle on the left and then get forward on his right to take Contalmaison. The AQ log estimated III Corps' casualties in the battle so far as 16,140 (8th Division: 5,123, 12th Division: 2,823, 19th Division: 1,288 and 34th Division: 6,906).

To compound Putty's problems the weather, which so far had favoured the attacks, began to change during the night 3/4 July when some rain fell. Heavy showers on 4 July culminated in a thunderstorm which lasted all afternoon; the troops were soaked, the trenches filled with water, and the ground became inches deep in mud. The GS log recorded the key events that day:

2 am. III Corps OpO No.77 issued giving orders for 19th and 34th Divisions to occupy
and consolidate the line running from Round Wood by Horseshoe Trench to the SE
corner of La Boisselle, preparatory to an attack on Contalmaison and Bailiff Wood.
23rd Division was to take over part of front from 17th Division.

2 pm. La Boisselle cleared by 56 and 57 Bdes (19th Division).

3.55 pm. GOC 23rd Division assumes command of right sector of corps front. HQ III
Corps G.525 issued – orders to 19th Division to secure NE part of La Boisselle
tomorrow. 24 Bde (23rd Division) placed at disposal of GOC 19th Division for this
purpose.

11.15 pm. 4th Army inform III Corps that 12th Division is transferred to Reserve Army
from 12 midnight tonight.

GOC 19th Division wrote about 4 July, the day La Boisselle was finally taken:

By eight the next morning the place was reported clear of the enemy, but it is probable
that snipers and bombers still lurked in ambush, for soon began a series of counter-
attacks, that drove the Wilts [6 Wilts], Cheshires [9 Cheshire] and Welch Fusiliers [9
RWF] of 58 Bde back to their starting positions. But bombers of 9 Welch gradually
regained the lost ground. Meanwhile the northern half of the village was again wrested
from 57 Bde, and they were also driven back to the consolidated half-way line of the
hedge. The situation was desperate. Had the line given at this point it is probable that the
enemy would have recaptured the whole village. That they did not do so was, according
to eye-witnesses, due to the gallantry of Carton de Wiart, who led men from one danger
point to another, himself bombing the enemy out of their positions. By late afternoon
the whole of the village was again in our hands. As de Wiart had already lost an arm
and an eye in action I recommended him for the VC. This was one of three VCs given to
the division for this action and a fourth was awarded later. Carton de Wiart was shortly
afterwards shot in the neck making the fourth battalion commander in his brigade to go
down. This officer was wounded eleven times and each time returned to the war. That the
casualty list was 3,500 in an area not much larger than Trafalgar Square speaks for the
desperate nature of the three days' struggle. It was a real dog fight, a soldier's battle, and
the Germans never fought like that again.

Haig wrote on 4 July:

I reached Montigny, HQ III Corps, about 5 pm and saw Generals Pulteney and Romer.
I urged them to press their advance because, by delaying, the enemy was given more time
to strengthen his second line. The 34th Division had fought splendidly. The losses were
severe, but it was anxious to remain in the corps. 8th Division had been withdrawn and will
be sent to 1st Army to replace the 1st Division.

Rawlinson wrote that day: 'I visited all the corps comds and had some difficulty in urging
Putty in to more vigorous action. He is not good at keeping his end up – I have little trouble
with the other two who are first rate and full of energy'. This has to be taken in the context of the
battle so far and 12th Division's failure to take Ovillers; it suggests Putty was no longer prepared

10 Worcs (19th Division) escorting German prisoners La Boisselle, July 1916. (© IWM Q763)

to accept Rawlinson's orders without question: Rawlinson was equally uncomplimentary about Cavan, Congreve and Morland when events did not go his way, or they too challenged him.

The AQ log recorded: '50 Siege Bty (4 × 6" guns – Naval mountings), 29 and 31 French Siege Btys (4 × 120 mm long guns each) and 110 and 111 French Siege Btys (4 × 220 mm mortars each) rejoined III Corps Heavy Artillery'. Their arrival must have further complicated an already complex and overworked logistic system.

Contalmaison

5 July was a relatively quiet day: at 9 am DDMS wrote: 'Corps Commander thinks Albert liable to be shelled heavily from Thiepval and therefore not suited for a special operation ward yet'. HQ III Corps issued OpO No.78 at 2.30 pm: 'stopping relief of 34th Divisional Artillery, who will remain in support of 23rd Division. Divisional artillery of 23rd Division to come into action between Bécourt and Fricourt under orders CRA 23rd Division'. It also confirmed the transfer of 12th Division to Reserve Army and alteration of the boundary between III and X Corps.

12th Division had left III Corps at midnight on transfer to X Corps (and a change in the army boundary). Putty issued this order of the day: 'As the 12th Division is leaving III Corps, the Corps Commander wishes to thank all ranks and to express his appreciation of the gallantry and dash shown in the attack on Ovillers. He is also grateful for the very efficient support which the division rendered to their comrades of 19th Division, who were fighting in La Boiselle'. 12th Division were still in the line but 34th Division were out of it. At about noon Putty addressed all three bdes at Hénencourt Wood. He complimented them on their bravery and tenacity, drawing particular attention to their stout defence of 21st Division's vulnerable left flank. He singled out 16 RS for its efforts and said 'they fought like regulars, maintaining their discipline and structure when almost every officer was gone'.

Rawlinson noted: 'After lunch I had a meeting of the corps comds and gave them orders for the next attack on 7 July'. The orders were confirmed in 4th Army 32/3/23(G) issued at 9.45 pm:

> 3. The final advance to within attacking distance of the enemy's 2nd line between Longueval and Bazentin le Petit Wood (both inclusive), will be made at 8 am on 7 Jul, in conjunction with an attack by the Reserve Army on Ovillers.
> 4. Objectives are allocated as follows:
>   III Corps. The Cutting, Contalmaison, Contalmaison Cemetery, Bailiff Wood, a line running through X.15.central to X.14.central. The attack on Contalmaison itself to be made on 7 July by strong detachments with Lewis and Maxim guns, after it has been demolished by artillery fire. The advance to the remainder of the line allotted to III Corps to be made by stages which should be commenced at once and continued unremittingly, so that as much of this line as possible may be in our possession when the final advance on Contalmaison is made.

During the day 19th Division endeavoured to straighten out the re-entrant on the eastern side of La Boiselle, but the bombers of 56 and 57 Bdes met with little success. The arrival of 1 Sher For (24 Bde 23rd Division) to reinforce coincided with that of 9th Grenadiers (3rd Guard Division), and practically no progress was made. At the end of this day 19th Division was still on the left of the corps (having handed over La Boiselle to 12th Division now in X Corps and about to attack Ovillers again). 23rd Division was on the right of the corps having taken over Horseshoe Trench, and 34th Division was reorganising well to the rear. The front of the III Corps had been reduced to less than 2,000 yards and its objective was Contalmaison.

With so much reorganisation to be done there was little progress on 6 July. 1st Division joined III Corps that day, as did 111 and 112 Bdes to replace 102 and 103 Bdes in 34th Division. At 9 am HQ III Corps issued OpO No.79 'ordering attack on objective given in para 1 of OpO No.77 and 19th Division to take over left of present 23rd Division's front (12th Division having taken over left of 19th Division). 34th Division to take over present front when 19th and 23rd Divisions advance to attack' The AQ log recorded latest estimated casualties since 1 July: 725 officers and 17,202 other ranks.

The weather on 7 July was miserable: the official history recorded that the trenches became knee-deep, in some cases waist-deep, in clinging slime, and under shell-fire collapsed beyond recognition. Movement was often agony; men fainted from sheer exhaustion while struggling through deep mud. The III Corps GS log recorded the key events:

> 6.15 am. XV Corps have failed to take Quadrangle Support Trench. It will be attacked again by 17th Division at 8 am and Mametz Wood by 38th Division at 8.30 am. 23rd Division informed.

7.30 am. 19th Division report they have second line from eastern edge of La Boisselle to western end of Horseshoe Trench and have joined up with 12th Division (L) and 23rd Division (R).

7.58 am. 23rd Division report enemy have regained junction of Shelter Alley and Quadrangle Trench. Situation well in hand

11.40 am. Both divisions have gained their objectives. 250 prisoners taken. 19th Division reached objective at 9.30 am.

5.15 pm. 23rd Division report that 24 Bde has been driven out of Contalmaison and Intermediate Line.

5.25 pm. HQ III Corps G649 issued: Orders issued to 23rd Division to attack Contalmaison and Bailiff Wood at 8 pm tonight in conjunction with attack by 17th Division on Quadrangle Support Trench.

8 pm. 23rd Division inform Corps Commander by telephone that they have been unable to carry out the orders given in G649. The bombardment ordered has taken place.

8.55 pm. Telephone message from 34th Division Artillery that FOOs report 17th Division have taken Acid Drop Copse and are advancing on Contalmaison. XV Corps deny latter part of the message.

Prisoners taken: 5 officers and 311 other ranks.

The official history describes 19th Division's attack:

Its objective was a trench running from Bailiff Wood SW and then W, and another which led towards the NE end of La Boisselle (taken over by 12th Division the previous night), involving an advance of some 600 yards on the right and half that distance on the left. With patrols and bombers leading, 9 Welch (58 Bde) and 7 RLR (56 Bde) moved forward at 8 am behind a barrage, carrying out to the letter their instructions to 'approach the objective as near as possible before the bombardment lifts' (In III Corps the field artillery lifted back slowly 100 yards at a time, different batteries being detailed to lengthen their range in succession). The bombardment was accurate and effective, but owing to some mistake in the timing the infantry ran into the barrage almost at once, and considerable loss and disorganisation ensued. Fortunately communications held, so that lines of fire could be adjusted without much delay, and the advance was restarted at 9.15 am after reinforcement by 6 Wilts (58 Bde). The three battalions then rushed the whole of their objective, capturing over 400 Germans belonging to six different regiments and five different divisions (185 and 190 Regts 185th Division, 110 Regt 28th Reserve Division, 23 Regt 12th Division, 95 Regt 38th Division believed to be at Verdun, and 210 Regt 45th Reserve Division believed to be at Messines). The dead lay thick at the dug-out entrances which seemed to show that those who had been first to leave cover had been caught by the barrage. Consolidation began forthwith, the infantry being heartened by the quick appearance, in spite of the mud, of 56 MG Coy. 9 RWF (58 Bde) was brought up to secure the right flank where there was no sign of 23rd Division. This success had cost less than 600 casualties, most of them wounded.

The attack by 23rd Division was to be carried out by 24 Bde with the objective Contalmaison and 68 Bde with the objective Bailiff Wood. In preparation for the attack a French 75 mm battery at 5.30 am would bombard Contalmaison Wood. At 6.30 am

Contalmaison itself would receive 100 incendiary shells. At 7.20 am the heavy artillery was to open an intense bombardment on Contalmaison and on a line running westerly from the NE corner of Bailiff Wood, lifting gradually as the infantry attack developed. At the same time 23rd Divisional Artillery (with 34th Divisional Artillery under command) would bring an intense bombardment on Contalmaison, Quadrangle Trench to the W of the village, the near edge of Bailiff Wood, and the trench just W of the wood. At 8 am they would lift to form a barrage to prevent enemy supports being brought forward, and at this hour the infantry would advance.

Such was the plan as outlined in 23rd Division's history. It continued:

A preliminary attack by 17th Division (on III Corps' right) failed to secure its objective and a heavy counter-attack forced back their left. 1 Worcs on the right of 24 Bde became involved and this delayed the advance on Contalmaison; this in turn delayed the advance of 68 Bde on Bailiff Wood. In the meantime the artillery programme had been carried out according to plan. But, owing to the delay, it was not until 9.15 am that 11 NF advanced to attack Bailiff Wood. The troops, dragged down by the weight of sodden equipment and blinded by torrents of rain, were operating over flooded ground, water-filled craters, and trenches waist-deep in mud. Although 11 NF managed to secure the southern edge of the wood (It had been planted with saplings before the war and these were only a few feet high), they came under heavy enfilade machine-gun fire from the N and NE and were forced to retire. Seeing that this withdrawal had uncovered the right flank of 19th Division, 12 DLI now pushed forward and dug in on a line immediately S of Bailiff Wood, and further succeeded in capturing the German trenches in the SW corner of the wood.

24 Bde, on the right of 23rd Division, was to take Contalmaison (held by 2/9 Grenadiers and 3/163 Regt); their attack was delayed by the lack of progress on its right. However, there was further delay when Comd 24 Bde (Brigadier General Oxley)'s orders were held up, and the movement of troops up trenches deep in mud and blocked by dead and wounded proved very slow. It was not until after 10 am that 24 Bde's attack was launched. 1 Worcs (on the right) advanced over the open from the southern end of Pearl Alley; 2 E Lancs came forward on the left, from Shelter Wood, at the same time. In spite of the German machine-guns 1 Worcs breasted the slope and forced their way into Contalmaison, clearing the ruins as far as the church after a struggle which lasted half an hour. Many prisoners were taken and two counter-attacks were repulsed, but hand-to-hand fighting continued whilst the German gunners shelled the whole village indiscriminately. Meanwhile the advance of 2 E Lancs on lower ground was much impeded by the mud and a heavy rain-storm (at 1 pm), and came under accurate machine-gun fire from Contalmaison, Bailiff and Peake Woods. To add to their difficulties a shell which fell on HQ 2 E Lancs buried the CO and his Adjt, and killed or wounded the rest of the staff. The efforts of 2 Northants to support 2 E Lancs were of no avail. Amid the ruins of the village three companies of 1 Worcs carried on the struggle throughout the afternoon but, with both flanks exposed, they were obliged to fall back when their supply of bombs and ammunition failed. 24 Bde then established a line S of the village having lost nearly 800 officers and men, almost half belonging to 1 Worcs.

Rawlinson wrote of 7 July: 'Day of heavy fighting without much success. We took Contalmaison in the morning: in the pm we lost Contalmaison without sufficient excuse I think as it is reported we were shelled out'. On 8 July Rawlinson told Haig that 24 Bde had abandoned Contalmaison without just cause and Haig approved of Brigadier General Oxley Comd 24 Bde being sent home. This might appear hard but the staff work at HQ 24 Bde failed to get the bde forward to attack at the required time, and failed again to reinforce or re-supply 1 Worcs in Contalmaison. The conditions were dreadful but an opportunity had been missed.

Putty wanted to attack Bailiff Wood and Contalmaison again at 8 pm, when 17th Division would also attack again, and before the enemy had time to recover: but the deep mud, the heavy German barrage, and the absence of fresh troops made this impossible. GOC 23rd Division (Major General Babington) telephoned Putty to make him aware of the situation: the trenches were blocked with wounded and passage over the open was impossible owing to the enemy barrage. It was decided to wait until next day before attempting a further operation against Contalmaison. Meanwhile on III Corps' left Reserve Army had still not managed to secure Ovillers. Putty wrote of 7 July to Edmonds many years later: 'One of the worst days I ever remember for orders and counter orders'.

By the morning of 8 July the mud in the trenches S and W of Contalmaison was so thick and deep that often men could not move in their depths; many became stuck fast unable to move without assistance. The battle continued as the GS log again recorded:

> 6.40 am. 23rd Division instructed to order 24 Bde to bomb up towards Intermediate Line.
> 8.45 am. HQ III Corps G664 (Wng O) issued ordering 34th Division to relieve 19th Division (8/9 July). 19th Division to leave one bde in billets round Albert as divisional reserve for 34th Division. 1st Division will be billeted tonight as follows: HQ at St Gratien, bdes to Baizieux, Frechencourt and Franvillers.
> 1.30 pm. Bailiff Wood reported evacuated. Strong patrols sent by 68 Bde found enemy in strength with many machine-guns.
> 3 pm. 1 Worcs (24 Bde) attacked the trenches S of Contalmaison, some men penetrating to southern end of village, but were driven back by machine-gun fire.
> Prisoners taken: 3 officers and 117 men.

24 Bde's efforts that day were half-hearted, possibly because of the mud but the lack of leadership was also likely to have been a factor. 1 Worcs attack on Contalmaison was made by only two coys, those that had suffered least the previous day: it was stopped by machine-gun fire and a heavy barrage. 1 Northants tried to advance from Peake Wood to link up with the forward line of 68 Bde on its left, but was similarly checked.

19th Division, by contrast, made significant progress, as recorded in the official history:

> Only the bombers had been engaged during the day but at 6 pm, after warning had been received from the air, a movement of German troops from Contalmaison to Bailiff Wood was stopped by rifle and machine-gun fire. Later, an advance of the left was ordered, to co-operate with an attack of X Corps. The objective, nearly a thousand yards ahead, was a German trench which ran into the northern end of Ovillers, and this fell, after little opposition, to 13 RF, one of two battalions of 111 Bde (34th Division) attached to 56 Bde as a step towards its relief. Consolidation proceeded, and during the night 58 Bde on the right was relieved by 112 Bde.

At 5.30 pm that day Rawlinson held a conference of corps commanders and their BGRAs to discuss the next operation, and also the attack on the enemy's 2nd Position, Longueval-Bazentin le Petit. The record included:

> Rawlinson: 'We want to carry out this operation as early as possible, and, for that reason it is necessary for all of you to go on pushing to your utmost, working forward both by night and by day in order to improve your positions and get closer to the enemy's second line'.
> Pulteney: 'Is the Reserve Army going to do anything?'
> Rawlinson: 'The Reserve Army are going to work on Ovillers, to establish themselves north of that place, and, in conjunction with our attack towards Longueval, to get forward from Hindenburg Trench on towards Pozières'.

Unusually, 4th Army OpO No.4 was issued at 3.30 pm, before the 'conference':

> 1. 4th Army will attack the enemy's second line between Longueval and Bazentin le Petit Wood at Zero on Z Day (3.25 am 14 July: 4th Army 32/3/41(G) issued 5 pm 12 July).
> 2. The following objectives are allotted to III Corps: In order to protect the left flank of the attack of XIII and XV Corps, III Corps will establish a strong defensive flank (N of Contalmaison on a line E-W). As soon as this line is secured strong patrols will be pushed out towards Pozières. III Corps will also assist XIII and XV Corps with enfilade fire from its heavy artillery.

Essentially 4th Army was to swing N, pivoting on III Corps.

During the day Haig visited Rawlinson. According to the official history: 'He was chiefly concerned with the situation at Mametz Wood (XV Corps). General Rawlinson reported to him that the leading of some of the higher commands was unsatisfactory, with the result that the officers in question were soon afterwards replaced'. Putty stayed, so presumably Haig and Rawlinson did not consider his performance 'unsatisfactory'. Neither does it appear that his subordinates were concerned. Putty must have been very tired but the only evidence of this is the absence of any letters to Edith Londonderry or Ettie Desborough, but this too was about to change.

At 12.30 am 9 July HQ III Corps issued a Wng O for the relief of 23rd Division by 1st Division. OpO No.80 followed at 9 am confirming Wng O G664 issued 8.45 am 8 July for relief of 19th Division by 34th Division and other moves; OpO No.81 was issued at 2 pm confirming the relief of 23rd Division by 1st Division.

The situation at 6.45 am was that 23rd Division was holding a line short of Bailiff Wood and Contalmaison, with 68 Bde on the left and 24 Bde on the right. 19th Division held a line running NW from the left flank of 23rd Division towards Ovillers. Both flanks were in touch with neighbouring corps. At 11.50 am HQ III Corps issued G702: '23rd Division ordered to seize trenches immediately W and S of Contalmaison in conjunction with attack on Quadrangle Support Trench by 17th Division (XV Corps)'. Contalmaison was to be taken step by step and Putty was determined that his right flank would not again get ahead of XV Corps. By 7.40 pm the III Corps GS log recorded: '68 Bde have cleared Bailiff Wood and are establishing a post in it' and 'Prisoners taken: 2 officers and 64 men'. By the end of the day 19th Division's relief by 34th Division was completed.

The official history provides the clearest account of 23rd Division's operations on 9 July:

> 24 and 68 Bdes had been ordered to improve their positions S and W of Contalmaison. 69 Bde had been ordered to assault the village on the morrow (10 July), passing through the other brigades. Reports were current that the enemy seemed to be preparing a counter-attack from Contalmaison, and many casualties were caused by a bombardment of the trenches of 68 Bde which were shallow and full of men. A number of Germans who then advanced were speedily disposed of by the artillery and machine-guns. As a preliminary measure 10 DOW (69 Bde attached to 24 Bde) sent forward bombing parties which established, S of Contalmaison, a post from which machine-gun fire could sweep nearly the whole area. Patrols of 12 DLI (68 Bde) (on the left) entered Bailiff Wood but could not stay there as it was still under the fire of British artillery. Comd 68 Bde decided to seize the wood by an advance of two companies from the west at 6.15 pm, but a German attempt at counter-attack delayed them (German record speaks of a counter-attack delivered at 4.30 pm by 2 and 3/183 Regt west of Contalmaison to strengthen the weak line between that village and Pozières. The advance melted away under fire, one battalion losing all its officers). The barrage was fired (at 6.15 pm) and, as the telephone wires were cut, it was impossible to provide another when 12 DLI went forward at 8.15 pm. Nevertheless the two companies captured nearly the whole of the original objective of the brigade: Bailiff Wood and the trenches on either side of it (behind the wood were found four undamaged field guns). Only on the right was success not quite complete, and here the trench was barricaded, a counter-attack which soon followed being repulsed with loss. The capture of the wood proved of great advantage in the following day's operation, for the Germans were no longer able to bring short-range enfilade fire to bear from the north.

Putty found the time to write to Ettie Desborough on 9 July:

> My dear Chief, Thanks for yours of 4 Jul. Just a line to say that the fighting is still very severe on both sides but this time we have dictated and made the Boche move all his reserves down to us instead of the usual method which he used to inflict on us before. The French guns are simply quite wonderful once you can get the Boche out of these deep dug outs or away from villages, with an absolutely steady platform once they are on the targets it is merely a matter of how many times they can load the gun. Some of the sound catching instruments we captured in Boisselle are very clever, I actually had a copy of one of my own messages asking where certain wire was cut put down on the Boche's paper and we had no telephone instrument within 200 yards of his listening post and even that was forbidden to be used except for SOS signals. The one feature of all the fighting so far has been the entire absence of counter battery work by the Germans they have never fired at anything except the infantry since we began with the result that we have had no casualties among the gunners at all, thanks to the present superiority of our aeroplanes we have done in a good lot of their batteries, the guns do not affect them but the trained gunners do. The weather on Friday broke our hearts you could not believe so much rain could come down in 12 hours outside the tropics, digging trenches was impossible, men had to be hauled out by ropes out of the trenches, today is lovely again though. Best love Yours ever Putty.

The weather had now much improved and was generally fine, although cooler. Conditions now favoured offensive operations, but cases of trench feet had already occurred among men who had stood in mud and water for several days with little chance of taking off their boots. At 8 am 10 July the III Corps GS log recorded: 'Situation: 68 Bde are holding eastern edge of Bailiff Wood and line N of it. 24 Bde hold a post where Intermediate Line crosses Contalmaison-Fricourt Road. 19th Division situation unchanged; their task could not be executed owing to hostile fire'. By 8.30 am the relief of 19th Division by 34th Division was completed.

HQ III Corps OpO No.82 was issued at 11.17 am ordering 23rd Division to attack Contalmaison from the W at 4.40 pm and giving details of the artillery programme. The GS log continued:

> 4.50 pm. 23rd Division assault on Contalmaison delivered.
> 5.50 pm. 23rd Division report that our men have been seen entering Contalmaison and enemy retiring E. A later report states that the church was reached at 5.45 pm.

Then at 6 pm HQ III Corps OpO No.83 was issued giving orders 'for cooperation by III Corps in attack by XIII and XV Corps on Bazentin le Grand and Petit by forming a defensive flank'. This implemented Rawlinson's 4th Army OpO No.4 swinging the right of 4th Army N against the enemy's 2nd Line, pivoting on III Corps. But first Contalmaison had to be taken.

Putty was by no means certain that 23rd Division would succeed this time in taking the village: that morning BGGS III Corps (Romer) sent this instruction to 1st Division (Major General Strickland), about to relieve 23rd Division:

> 23rd Division are attacking Contalmaison this afternoon. If this attack fails the Corps Commander will require you to attack Contalmaison again as soon as you can make the necessary preparations which for the sake of the combined operations should be pushed on with all speed. He suggests that a simultaneous attack from the W and from the S would be the surest means of gaining the village. 34th Division would be directed to attack at the same time. Each attack should be given definite sectors to gain and consolidate and strong points should be selected beforehand. It is important to bring up Stokes mortars into the line from which the assault is to be launched.

Putty would have hesitated before giving such detailed guidance himself to GOC 1st Division, so the instructions came from his BGGS, but it shows where he thought mistakes had been made in previous attacks on the village.

The official history again provides a clear account of 23rd Division's attack:

> Careful reconnaissance of the ground preceded the attack of 69 Bde (8 GH, 9 GH, and 11 W Yorks) at 4.30 pm on 10 July, and close cooperation with the artillery of 23rd and 34th Divisions was arranged. Comd 69 Bde assembled 8 and 9 GH in and near the northern part of Horseshoe Trench on a front of 1,000 yards, some 2,000 yards W of Contalmaison. He sent two companies of 11 W Yorks 500 yards forward to Bailiff Wood to make a flank attack and join up with 8 and 9 GH at the NW corner of the village.
> The village and the trench in front of it were bombarded from 4 to 4.30 pm, the batteries firing in enfilade from the S and quickening their rate to cover the

infantry during its approach. Fire then swept in five short lifts from the trench W of Contalmaison to its eastern edge. A smoke barrage was to have been put down by 4" Stokes mortars in position 400 yards W of Bailiff Wood, but although the wind was favourable it proved impossible, in the time available, to carry up sufficient ammunition to produce an effective screen. The advance was, however, well covered by fire from all the machine-guns of the division which enfiladed the flanks of the village and all the approaches to it.

Moving out steadily in four waves, with searching and consolidating parties in rear, 8 and 9 GH were met by fire of all kinds, and, on the right, uncut wire caused some delay. Yet the trench in front of the village was carried, and the Germans broke back into the ruins. Going on, over ground broken by innumerable shell holes and intersected by wire, 8 and 9 GH, now in small groups, ran into the creeping barrage, so that the times of all lifts had to be advanced (owing to the initiative of CRA 23rd Division, this alteration was accomplished with very little delay). Soon Contalmaison was entered and, although some Germans still fought stoutly, all resistance was overcome. 8 GH, reduced to 5 officers and 150 men, had the satisfaction of taking prisoner a force greater than its own: 8 officers and 180 unwounded men of 122 Regt. The flank attack of 11 W Yorks was also successful; they caught with their fire the enemy retreating northward from Contalmaison and joined up with 8 and 9 GH about 5.30 pm. In all 280 unwounded prisoners, among them a battalion commander, and nine machine-guns were taken. Unfortunately the buffer springs of many of the 18 pdrs gave out so that the artillery could not take proper toll of the Germans in retreat (the German record states: 'One dug-out after another collapsed, one machine-gun after another was destroyed, the cellars of the chateau were full of wounded. Scarcely more than a hundred men escaped to the 2nd Position'). Consolidation proceeded with the assistance of 10 DOW, the remainder of 11 W Yorks, and 101 Fd Coy RE. Throughout the night a box barrage was maintained round Contalmaison. Towards 9 pm a strong body of the enemy advanced from the N, but was driven back by bombers, and no further attempts to counter-attack were made. According to German reports 1/Lehr Regt lost 618 officers and men in the defence of Contalmaison.

Every record has to be considered with caution but this account shows just how much had been learnt since the start of the battle.

23rd Division was now relieved by 1st Division: its total casualties during the seven days fighting amounted to 3,485 officers and men. HQ 23rd Division now moved to St Gratien; 24 Bde returned to 8th Division; and 68 Bde remained detached to 34th Division until 20 July.

Rawlinson wrote: 'III Corps took Contalmaison: pm I visited my corps comds (after CinC visited at 3 pm)'.

Some have commented on the number of attacks 23rd Division launched on Contalmaison between 5 and 10 July, and that many of these were uncoordinated with 19th Division or with XV Corps. Some of these attacks were GHQ operations (involving more than one army), some 4th Army operations (involving more than one corps), some III Corps operations, and some at a lower level. The objective of each was often different with lower level operations on many occasions being preliminary to a later larger scale operation, and with a limited objective. Nevertheless poor coordination with flanking formations was often the cause of failure.

69 Bde's capture of Contalmaison was in marked contrast to 24 Bde's attempt at the beginning of the battle. Lieutenant Colonel Grogan then CO 1 Worcs 24 Bde wrote a report many years later making the following points:

> Insufficient preliminary reconnaissance by those responsible for executing the attack; lack of co-ordination between neighbouring units as regards time of attacks, these were disjointed and should have been simultaneous; no proper liaison between units and those on their flanks; too many attempts to gain vital ground by bombing attacks up trenches, instead of well mounted, well gunned, simultaneous attacks in strength across the open; lack of properly regulated and well timed artillery support, and no proper liaison between front line troops and artillery by means of artillery liaison officers attached to attacking units; Contalmaison was attacked from the wrong direction; Bde HQ was too far back to appreciate the situation at the front; CO of the battalion which attacked Contalmaison did not know his job.

Since he was unlikely to have been criticising himself, these points suggest various problems in 24 Bde. The first point was a common complaint at all levels: orders arriving too late to carry out a proper reconnaissance, make a plan, give orders and do some rehearsals. Sometimes it was inevitable and then training and confidence in the higher commander had to be relied on: such confidence seems to have been lacking in this case.

BM 24 Bde wrote many years later:

> As regards operations of 24 Bde against Contalmaison, my mind is a confused mass of order, counter-order and disorder; insufficient maps and no reconnaissance. All communication was cut with Bde HQ and the brigadier was away all day trying to straighten things out.

Brigadier General Oxley Comd 24 Bde wrote about the same time:

> It is the first time I have heard that the brigade was blamed for not being able to hold on and I absolutely disagree that such a report was justified. 1. 1 Sher For had been committed at La Boisselle and suffered heavy casualties; the brigade only had three effective battalions. 2. The whole brigade had been warned for La Boisselle and we were carrying out reconnaissance there. 3. 52 Bde [17th Division] failed to secure our right flank. 4. The trenches were in a very bad state and evacuation of 52 Bde's casualties made it impossible for our machine-guns and RE to get forward to consolidate. I have since visited the ground and in my opinion the attack, as ordered by III Corps, was not the way to attack Contalmaison and without Pearl Alley and the Quadrangle it was doomed to failure.

Oxley may have been sent home but seemed to be unaware of the reasons for his removal. The GS log recorded the situation at 6.30 am 11 July:

> 23rd Division (1st Division took over at noon) holding N edge of Contalmaison; line runs S along eastern edge of village. Strong patrols of 34th Division met an attack by enemy and retired on their trenches. Enemy were counter-attacked by 10 Warwicks and 13 RB with the bayonet, when 50 yards from our trenches, and were driven back with considerable loss. 34th Division are holding all their trenches intact.

HQ III Corps issued Addendum No.1 to OpO No.83 at 2.30 pm, orders for consolidating and holding the line established the previous night. The GS log also confirmed: 'Prisoners taken 6 officers (including one CO of bn) and 312 other ranks, and 9 MGs'.

There was still disagreement between Haig and Rawlinson, and Haig told Rawlinson to confer again with his corps commanders. This he did at 2 pm (11 July); as result of this conference Rawlinson reported that all were strongly in favour of the original plan (a dawn attack on 14 July by XIII and XV Corps between Longueval and Bazentin le Petit, with III Corps providing left flank protection by an advance on Contalmaison Villa, a fortified place some 1,000 yards ahead, and beyond). Rawlinson then wrote: 'Late pm. I then rode over to see Putty and give him his orders for attacking Contalmaison Wood and Villa simultaneously with Horne'.

III Corps AQ log recorded: 'Reinforcements: 15 RS – 300 other ranks, 16 RS – 299 other ranks, 10 Lincolns – 179 other ranks and 296 more on 12 Jul'. Absorbing these numbers, as 101 Bde 34th Division had to, must have been extremely difficult. III Corps ADOS log noted that day: 'Major Orpen Salvage Officer called and brought two 12" mortars for Corps Comd'. Presumably they had been captured, and hence Putty's interest.

Rawlinson wrote on 12 July: 'Heavy fighting still continues. We are firmly in possession of Contalmaison'. In fact, there was little fighting on the front of III Corps. The morning of 13 July was dull, cold and fairly windy. The previous night Contalmaison had been shelled more heavily than usual with tear shells from 8 pm to midnight. The GS log recorded at 4 pm 13 July: 'Situation unchanged – 1st Division report capture of two 4.2 hows; 34th Division report capture of 3 field guns. Contalmaison heavily shelled during morning. Prisoners taken: 2 officers and 74 other ranks'. At 10.45 pm that evening, 1 BW (1 Bde 1st Division) captured Lower Wood, just N of the NW corner of Mametz Wood. This gave 1st Division a springboard for its attack on Contalmaison Villa the following day.

Putty inspected 69 Bde (23rd Division), the bde that took Contalmaison, in Molliens au Bois during the day: 23rd Division moved two of its bdes to the rear of the corps area on 13 July to make room for another division moving through. Later Haig visited Putty at Montigny and recorded: 'He (Putty) had not thought how to employ his divisions to capture Pozières village. I said he should not attack direct, but take it from the rear to avoid loss. For this he should plan with General Horne (XV Corps on III Corps' right)'. Putty had not been ordered to take Pozières at this time, perhaps because it was also in front of Reserve Army.

At 5.45 pm 4th Army issued 32/3/45(G):

> General idea of future plans in the event of the attack of the enemy's 2nd Line between Longueval and Bazentin le Petit being successful.
> 3.   III Corps (1st, 34th, 19th, and later probably 23rd Division). The task of this corps will be to secure the enemy's second line between Bazentin le Petit Wood and the Albert-Bapaume Road, Pozières and Mouquet Farm. Later on to secure Courcelette and Le Sars
> 5.   To Sum up; should events progress satisfactorily it is intended that the following will ultimately be the position of 4th Army:
> III Corps. Eaucourt L'Abbaye (exclusive) – Le Sars (inclusive) with flank thrown back to Courcelette till the Reserve Army advances into line with the left of III Corps.

The disagreement between Haig and Rawlinson inevitably affected III Corps' direction of advance and objectives: GOC 4th Army had given III Corps very limited objectives for 14 July but now not only Pozières but also Mouquet Farm had been included. It seems that III Corps' direction of advance changed dependent on the progress or lack of it of 5th (Reserve) Army, on its left, and XV Corps on its right. This meant that Putty had to take one small step at a time.

On 13 July he wrote to Edith Londonderry:

> Dearest Circe, Charley and Beef[47] dined here on Monday [10 July] in good form, they reeled away at a late hour. We have had four fine days which made the dust bad but there was so much of it I don't think the Boche could tell which were the roads through the cloud now we have got some more sharp showers which we trust won't last long. It was a great feat taking Contalmaison, the troops went in with great dash, we completely annihilated the Boche battalion who fortunately had only come in the night before and did not know the ground, we have now established ourselves there and are pretty snug it is a good tactical point to have gained, there were a great many dead Boche in there, we got over 300 unwounded prisoners out of it besides ninety which were too bad to move but which we hope to get away by degrees they have got a Boche doctor looking after them in a cellar, of course they are now bringing up a lot of reinforcements but still we keep wearing them down and gradually reducing the pressure from other places which all tells in the long run. We have collected some very curious trench mortars which throw what the men call oil cans, a canister of about 200 lbs, devilish things, the track they ran the shell on came from Alexandria and must have been captured at Gallipoli which is rather curious isn't it? I suppose that you are all pretty busy with the wounded in London now, fortunately the great proportion are light. Very busy. Best love Yours ever Putty.

Battle of Bazentin Ridge 14-17 July

Pozières

By first light on 14 July 1st Division had occupied Contalmaison Villa and Lower Wood. At 7.45 am Rawlinson noted: 'I spoke to the corps comds on the telephone. All is going exceedingly well at present. We are in possession of all our first objectives'.

At that stage 21st Division (XV Corps) on the right of III Corps had overrun their objective and had managed to link up with 1st Division. The official history continues:

> At 8.50 am. General Horne (GOC XV Corps) settled on his further plan; 21st Division to move northwards and clear the enemy communication trenches between Bazentin le Petit and the light railway to Martinpuich, in order to facilitate the capture by III Corps of the German 2nd Position between the corps boundary and Black Watch Alley. This Lieutenant General Pulteney had agreed to undertake. Arrangements were then made between 21st Division (XV Corps) and 1st Division (III Corps) for a combined operation at 2.30 pm, when 34th Division was to push strong patrols towards Pozières.

47   Possibly CO RHG.

HQ III Corps OpO No.84 was issued at 11.25 am giving orders for 'an attack by 1st Division on German 2nd Line; 34th Division to cooperate by gaining ground towards Pozières'. At 12 noon, Zero hour was fixed for 2.30 pm (14 July). According to the III Corps GS log this attack was made at the request of XV Corps in cooperation with a further advance by them. Just one hour later, at 1 pm, the GS log recorded: 'XV Corps notified III Corps that they were unable to carry out this operation. Attack by 1st Division was consequently countermanded'. Rawlinson was not aware of this at 2.30 pm when he noted: 'Horne is making an attack against the second line trenches which lead up behind Pozières in conjunction with III Corps at Contalmaison Villa'. Apparently the infantry of 21st Division was now so reduced in numbers that further offensive action by it was not possible.

While all this was going on HQ III Corps was getting conflicting reports about whether Pozières was still held by the enemy. At 3.20 pm HQ III Corps issued OpO No.85 ordering 'any artillery firing on the neighbourhood of Pozières at 6 pm tonight shall lift to N of a line, when patrols will reconnoitre the village'. Further reports were received that the enemy was retreating in large numbers and great disorder from Pozières at 7 pm; but at 10.5 pm 34th Division reported that their patrols (S of Pozières) were being driven back.

At 6.15 pm HQ III Corps issued G885. 1st Division was ordered to take over from 21st Division up to the western edge of Bazentin le Petit Wood and prepare to attack the German 2nd Line, as already ordered, in conjunction with advance of XV Corps towards Martinpuich. At 8.10 pm G885/1 was issued ordering 34th Division to attack Pozières at the same time (on 15 July) as 1st Division attack 2nd Line. These two Wng Os were then embodied in HQ III Corps OpO No.86 issued, after further orders from 4th Army, at 10 pm. It had been a difficult and frustrating day but Putty was now swinging N; 34th Division was to take Pozières from the S with 1st Division on its right attacking up the German 2nd Line. Much would depend on the progress made by XV Corps on his right.

Rawlinson wrote to Robertson (CIGS) that day:

> I only write to say how splendidly the troops have done. Only one division, the 38th (Welshmen), turned out badly and if it had not been for their failure at Mametz Wood we would have brought off the action of today [Bazentin Ridge] at least 48 hours sooner. Our corps commanders Horne and Congreve have done and are doing splendid work – so is old Putty (Pulteney) though he is of course not up to the standard of the other two.

Rawlinson's views of his corps commanders seemed to change frequently, depending on his frustration and the level of their disagreement.

15 July was misty and overcast until the evening: at 9 am 1st and 34th Divisions attacked. The official history provides an overview:

> 34th Division attacked Pozières at 9.20 am, 8 E Lancs 112 Bde starting from the line Contalmaison-Bailiff Wood after an hour's preliminary bombardment. The battalion had to cross some 1,300 yards before reaching the first German trench, the forward posts previously established by the brigade having been vacated. When the advance began the barrage raked slowly through Pozières to reach the German 2nd Position N of the windmill at 11 am and there remain; 112 Trench Mortar Battery and a section of machine-guns fired in close support. Fire from hidden machine-guns took a heavy toll of the attackers, and

the advance eventually came to a halt 300-400 yards S of Pozières. GOC 34th Division secured the assistance of the corps artillery for another attempt, and the Reserve Army promised aid of X Corps heavy guns for the second half of the hour's bombardment which was to open at 5 pm. Nevertheless, when the fresh assault was launched at 6 pm it seemed to 8 E Lancs that the artillery preparation and support were quite inadequate; they were not able to get forward quickly enough to anticipate the German machine-gunners, who promptly emerged from their undestroyed dug-outs and cellars as soon as the guns lifted. The advance, however, made some ground, and the position eventually consolidated by 112 Bde, with one battalion of 111 Bde, was half a mile in length, and ran WSW from a point on the Bapaume road 300 yards short of Pozières.

This should probably be ESE; but the main point is that III Corps Artillery fired 30,200 rounds that day, much less than might have been expected, and mainly because of the mist. On the right of 34th Division, 1 N Lancs (2 Bde 1st Division) attacked NW up the trenches of the German 2nd Position and gained about 400 yards of the front line and 200 of the support line. Accurate machine-gun fire and the battered state of the trenches prevented further progress. A fresh attempt was made at 5 pm by 2 Welch (3 Bde); this was checked at the start by the German machine-guns (German reports state that the attacks failed in the face of rifle and machine-gun fire of 1/184 and 2/27 Regts); but after darkness fell 3 Bde linked up with 34th Division, 600 yards to the NW, by establishing a line of posts.

The III Corps GS log provided further detail:

11.30 am. 1st Division instructed to push forward and capture communication trenches on N of German 2nd Line, in order to help 34th Division on the left and 33rd on the right.

11.50 am. 1st Division report that fighting is still going on in NW corner of Bazentin le Petit Wood which makes it impossible for them to deploy eastward and carry out instructions given. XV Corps informed.

3 pm. XV Corps report Bazentin le Petit Wood now clear of enemy. 1st Division informed.

4.30 pm. 1st Division report both trenches forming old German 2nd Line are levelled by shell fire and afford no protection from machine-gun fire. This makes it difficult to support 36th Division (should be 33rd Division). An assault to be made at 5 pm on communication trenches running NE from support line.

This attack was stopped by MG fire from the open right flank as was another at 11 pm.

All considered III Corps had done well to make so much progress. If the right wing of 4th Army had got further forward this would have helped 1st Division and, because this in turn would have threatened to cut off Pozières, made 34th Division's task easier: but this was not to be.

HQ III Corps issued OpO No.87 at 8 pm 'ordering an attack by 1st Division on German 2nd Line and communication trenches running NE from it in conjunction with an attack by 33rd Division tomorrow at an hour to be communicated later; and the establishment of strong posts by 1st Division from Contalmaison Villa and by 34th Division from line established today to left of 1st Division'. However, at 11.58 pm HQ 4th Army issued orders postponing its attack until 17 July.

Somehow Putty managed to write to Edith Londonderry that morning (15 July – first page is missing):

> Kiggell (CGS GHQ) is a real good man, I have the utmost confidence in his ability, in many ways he is more brilliant than Robertson who if anything erred on the side of caution. The Irish problem is quite impossible simply and solely because the infernal people cannot get away from politics, what is required is a non political man to form a judgement, fair and square that is not affected by politics for the welfare of the country without reference to party. Am changing my quarters tomorrow (must have been postponed), shall be sorry to go as had made the garden so nice, everything in apple pie order, the result of much exercise in the evenings by Gavin Hamilton, Hopie[48] and self at our new place the surroundings are better, lovely hornbeam hedges with Countess[49] in to the bargain have already told Hopie off to do her down she is very small and has little chance under his weight, unfortunately they burnt down one of the wings last winter which has done away with much of the accommodation and spoilt the look of the house. Well I must finish for I see them beginning to arrive with their papers after their breakfast. Best of love Yours ever Putty.

This letter tells much of Putty's character and his resilience.

At 2 am 16 July 2 Welch (3 Bde 1st Division) made another attempt to bomb up the trenches of the German 2nd Position, but without much success. The mud proved a great handicap to movement and the fire of the Stokes mortars, although effective, could not be maintained; it was impossible to carry forward sufficient ammunition. HQ III Corps GS log recorded at 8 am:

> OpO No.88 issued, stating that 33rd Division are not attacking today and ordering 1st Division to extend today and tonight their hold on German second line and communication trenches running NE, and, in particular, German 2nd Line overlooking approaches to Pozières, preparatory to an attack on Pozières by 34th Division and on Switch Line by 1st Division, in conjunction with a general attack by 4th Army on 17 July.

DDMS noted that morning (before 9 am): 'Corps Commander asked about medical units of 1st Division. I said they were not bad but not as good as 34th, 23rd and 19th'. At 9.30 am Putty and Horne (GOC XV Corps) with their BGRAs attended a conference at HQ 4th Army. Rawlinson wrote: 'I had a conference of corps comds and gave them orders for the attack on Pozières and the Switch Line at dawn on 18 Jul' and 'As the enemy had now had time to bring up new troops, the time for isolated attacks had now finished and an organised attack on a broad front was now necessary'. 4th Army orders were issued at 4.45 pm.

---

48   ADC: Marquess of Linlithgow.

49   Suzanne Virginie Marie Ghislaine Crombez Comtesse de Lameth (1883-1963) married to Thibaud Marie Baudouin Henri Clement de Lameth (1875-1956). In 1916 they had 3 children aged 7, 8 and 10. She became the Marquise when her father in law died on 25 October 1916. A Belgian who did not like the country or the weather, she is described as having a very strong and independent personality. Her husband was in Amiens during the war.

HQ III Corps GS log continued:

> 7.45 pm. Addendum No.1 to III Corps OpO No.88 issued, stating that the main attack is postponed until 18 July and giving instructions for artillery preparation. Both divisions report a quiet day. 34th Division hold a line S of Pozières, 200 to 300 yards from the German trench.

4th Army orders for artillery preparation which was to begin at once were to bombard (the German positions) sufficiently both by day and night to prevent movement and work taking place, and to destroy strongpoints.

1st Division was still trying to get forward, mainly because it was vulnerable to counter-attack in its present position but also to be prepared for 18 July. The official history notes:

> The divisional artillery (1st Division) had spent the whole day (16 July) wire-cutting, the batteries which fired in direct enfilade from Caterpillar Valley N of Montauban doing very effective work. At 11.50 pm the bombardment became intense and ten minutes later fire lifted back from the objective. In darkness and rain 1 Glos and 2 RMF then attacked north-eastward, keeping close behind the barrage, whilst 2 Welch bombed in from the right. Success was gained at little cost, for the Germans fled in confusion before the bayonet, leaving in their shattered trenches large numbers of dead and wounded. The stormers advanced some three hundred yards beyond their objective, to which they withdrew at dawn; strong posts were established some distance up the communication trenches – now named Welch Alley and Gloster Alley – running north-eastward. On the left (probably should be right), 1 SWB formed a defensive flank in Black Watch Alley, another communication trench running back to the Switch Line.

The III Corps GS log further added that this attack was made frontally by 3 Bde: 1st Division was now facing N (in line with 34th Division) and NE up the German communication trenches behind their 2nd Line.

During the night 16/17 July 68 Bde (23rd Division but under command 34th Division) relieved 112 Bde: 34th Division now had 68 Bde and 111 Bde in the line. 111 Bde during the night occupied SE corner of orchard SW of Pozières linking up with X Corps (Reserve Army).

The GS log recorded on 17 July:

> Heavy rain from midnight to 3 am; misty all day. The weather for the past two or three days has not permitted bombardment with aeroplane observation, which now appears to be an essential preliminary to a successful attack.

At 2.50 am HQ III Corps issued Addendum No.2 to OpO No.88 stating:

> That the attacks by XIII and XV Corps are postponed to 19 Jul, to coordinate with French attacks N and S of the Somme, and ordering 34th Division to attack German trench on S side of Pozières at 8 pm tonight preparatory to attack on village tomorrow (18 July) at 3 am.

At 8 pm 12 DLI 68 Bde duly attacked the line (a wired trench) defending S and SW of Pozières. Ten minutes before the assault the enemy put down a heavy barrage. The moment the infantry left the trench and shell holes where they were dug in, with 200 yards to cross, the enemy opened fire with a number of machine-guns mostly from the left front (SW of Pozières). GOC 23rd Division sent in a report, presumably having spoken to Comd 68 Bde, that he thought it probable that the enemy had found out about the intended attack by overhearing telephone conversation with his listening apparatus. In consequence of this, and of the number of machine-guns revealed still in action after the bombardment, the attack on the village, timed for 3.30 am 18 July, was cancelled.

1st Division spent the day consolidating the positions it had taken the previous night. Three deserters of 27 Regt surrendered N of Black Watch Alley, an unusual occurrence. 1st Division was also to have attacked at 3.30 am 18 July to further improve its hold on the German 2nd Line but this too was cancelled.

The weather caused much of the uncertainty. Rawlinson issued 4th Army 32/3/50(G) at 7 pm (17 July):

2. III Corps have captured the enemy's second line as far N as X.5 central.
3. Owing to present weather conditions the attacks of XIII, XV, and III Corps on the Switch Line will be postponed to 19 Jul.
4. III Corps will attack Pozières at 3.30 am 18 Jul, assisted by the artillery of XV Corps and Reserve Army.

As previously mentioned this order, issued after III Corps order, was later cancelled. To complicate matters further Haig called on Rawlinson during the afternoon and suggested that the Reserve Army should deal with Pozières, allowing him to slip his three corps to the right.

Putty wrote to Ettie Desborough on 17 July:

My dear Chief, Thanks for your note of 12 Jul. The fight continues with little less ferocity, we are making the Boche bring down all description of units by milking other parts of the line besides the 7th and 8th Division which he brought complete and which have already suffered heavily, he fights grandly and sticks it out to the end every time. We got Ovillers last night after 14 days endless struggle of bombs and machine-guns and if we get Pozières we shall soon be on the top of the plateau and have much the best of the observation. Charley L and Tweedmouth[50] came to tea here yesterday they were very restless at not being able to have a ride through yet, personally think the battle has to go on a long time yet before that will be possible. The soldiers are just realising what it is to have plenty of gun ammunition but all of you at home can never make as much as we can fire if it comes along, thousands of tons of iron have gone in to this chalky ground and the wells will be quite toxic before long, the 'duds' are strewn all over the place, one curses the fuse on each occasion. Weather is thundery which is bad for observation and the air is very close. Best love Yours ever Putty.

---

50   Lieutenant Colonel Dudley Churchill Marjoribanks 3rd Baron Tweedmouth (1874-1935) RHG.

Tancred (BGRA III Corps from 26 July) wrote many years later about a conversation he had with Putty on the effectiveness of the bombardment before 1 July:

> I cannot say what happened over the whole front but Sir W Pulteney Comdg III Corps told me that on the front captured by his corps our heavy shells were lying about unexploded in enormous number.

18 July was a dull day with drizzle: the clouds were again very low, and aeroplane and KB observation impossible. HQ III Corps GS log noted:

> 11 am. A conference took place at corps HQ, attended by Lieutenant General Kiggell (CGS) and other officers GHQ, Major General Montgomery (MGGS) and other officers from 4th Army, General Gough and other officers from Reserve Army, the Corps Commander, and members of his staff. It was decided that the attack on Pozières should be undertaken by the Reserve Army, and, in consequence, a portion of the front now occupied by III Corps will be taken over by ANZAC Corps.

It was a momentous decision: gone was any attempt by Haig to manoeuvre his armies and with it a return to frontal attacks aimed at fixing and wearing down the enemy. For III Corps the direction of advance was again towards Bapaume.

At 2.30 pm Putty, accompanied by his BGRA (still Uniacke), attended Rawlinson's conference at HQ 4th Army, when it was decided that III Corps should take over the frontage occupied by the left division of XV Corps. HQ III Corps OpO No.89 was issued at 4 pm, probably on Putty's return, ordering both divisions to improve the positions gained, and to form a continuous trench S of Pozières to guard what would be an open left flank. It was a quiet day on III Corps front although the official history recorded that 1st Division:

> began to establish a line of battle outposts, supported by strong-points, running NW from Bazentin le Petit Wood parallel to and half way between OG 2 (Old German 2nd Line support trench) and the Switch Line; these posts, practically on the crest of the Pozières ridge, were established without much interference from the enemy.

Rawlinson wrote that day: 'I decided to postpone attack until 22 Jul'. At 7.30 pm 4th Army 32/3/52(G) was issued:

> 1. Owing to the weather conditions, attack by 4th Army on 19 Jul has been postponed.
> 3. After the readjustment of the front has been completed, the attack of the enemy's Switch Line and of Ginchy and Guillemont will be undertaken by 4th Army. This attack will take place on 22 Jul at an hour to be notified later.
> Objectives will be as follows:
> III Corps. Switch Line (Munster Alley was added by 4th Army 32/3/56(G) issued at 2.40 pm 21 July) (Time of attack was given as 12.30 am 23 Jul by 4th Army 32/3/58(G) issued 10.10 pm 21 July).

It was quiet overnight 18/19 July and 34th Division made substantial progress with the trench S of Pozières. At 8 am 19 July HQ III Corps issued OpO No.90:

> giving effect to the alteration of the front decided on yesterday (34th Division relieved by 1st Australian Division, 1st and 19th Divisions shift to the right), same to be carried out tonight. As soon as completed, preparation for attack on German Switch Line to be started.

III Corps carried out some complex operations in the war and this was one of them – to side slip the corps at night, in contact with the enemy, and over appalling ground required meticulous staff work. III Corps AQ log recorded that III Corps Admin Instr No.1 was issued to support OpO No.90 reflecting the logistical complexities of the change.

1st Australian Division ANZAC Corps relieved 34th Division; this relief was completed by 7.30 am 20 July in spite of heavy bombardment by gas and lachrymatory shells. For the period 6-20 July 111 and 112 Bdes reported total losses as 169 officers and 2,818 other ranks. 68 Bde, attached to the division 16-20 July, had casualties of 13 officers and 240 other ranks (101 Bde was absorbing replacements, 102 and 103 Bdes were ineffective after 1 July). On the other flank 56 Bde 19th Division took over the left sector of XV Corps' front from 19 Bde 33rd Division; during the relief the enemy shelled Sausage Valley and Bécourt Wood with a new type of small gas shells.

At 6.45 pm 19 July HQ III Corps issued OpO No.91 giving 'orders for 1st and 34th Divisions to attack the German Switch Line on 22 July'.

It was misty on the morning of 20 July, and not clear enough for aerial observation until the afternoon. In the early hours of 20 July 1st Division made two attempts to secure Munster Alley junction with OG2 but these failed in the face of heavy machine-gun fire: otherwise the day was relatively quiet. The III Corps GS log recorded at 7.45 am: 'XV Corps report capture of southern part of High Wood'. It was to be two months before High Wood was fully secured, and then by III Corps. DDMS wrote at 9 am: 'Corps Commander said the present smoke helmet handicapped men in their military duties and asked me if the German mask was efficient. I told him Chemical Adviser had informed me that it was'. Sometime during the afternoon, probably late, Rawlinson rode to HQ III Corps to see Putty.

21 July was fine and much clearer than it had been for sometime. Overnight the extension of the front to Bazentin le Petit was completed, and XV Corps reported that the Germans had retaken most of High Wood; otherwise the day was quiet. At 9.30 am Putty and his BGGS (Romer) attended a conference at HQ 4th Army to discuss the attack on 22/23 July, the orders for which had already been issued. In view of the success of the 14 July assault, and at the strong urging of Haig, Rawlinson opted for another night attack by 4th Army in the early hours of 23 July. Zero hour was eventually fixed for 12.30 am 23 July. III Corps was to take the Switch Line in front of Martinpuich in conjunction with an attack by the Reserve Army on Pozières. Details of the attack were issued in Addendum No.1 to III Corps OpO No.91 at 10.15 am. The preliminary bombardment was to begin at 7 pm 22 July, the previous evening, with five minutes intense fire before the infantry advanced.

The deployment of III Corps was now: 1st Division on the left with HQ at Moulin Vivier, 19th Division on right with HQ in Albert, 34th Division in support with HQ also in Albert, and 23rd Division in reserve with HQ at Hénencourt. The shortage of locations for the HQ of divisions resulted in three of them now being in Albert: HQ 23rd Division was in Hénencourt which explains the delay in moving forward HQ III Corps. III Corps Cav Regt (DLOY) log noted that it had a troop providing a corps OP at Bellevue Farm: the name of the farm and the fact that the OP was still there on 10 September suggests that it provided good information on the battle, and probably forward observation for Putty.

Advance to Martinpuich

III Corps' responsibility for Pozières was now at an end: the next village in front of it was Martinpuich, and in front of it was the Switch Line much of which was on the reverse slope. 22 July was fine but not very clear; at 5.55 am 19th Division reported that the Germans were in force half way between Bazentin le Petit and High Wood, and that patrols attempting to get in touch with 33rd Division in High Wood were driven back. III Corps was now to advance NE but its left flank was still insecure until the Reserve Army took Pozières, and its right flank was in the air because of an oblique gap between it and XV Corps. This was described as:

> a 1,200 yard diagonal gap across the field from High Wood's southern corner to the right of
> the cross-roads NE of Bazentin le Petit. The field was in name only, cratered as it was beyond
> belief, and literally spread with human flotsam that dated back to the 14 Jul engagements.

However, this was the least of Putty's problems on what was to be a particularly difficult day. At 12 noon the III Corps GS log noted: 'Various reports have been received that the enemy were digging trenches N of Bazentin Le Petit in advance of the Switch Line. Owing to misty weather the Flying Corps had not verified this. Lieutenant Pearson 34 Sqn RFC arrived at corps HQ and reported that this morning he had dived down out of the mist to 900 feet over the area in question and had observed a trench running beside the road from S.2.a.5.3. to S.2.c.8.4. when it turned E and ran through S.2.d. to S.3.c.4.4. It was full of men'. The trench was to be called 'Intermediate Line'.

This altered the situation on the right of III Corps' front (19th Division) and left of XV Corps (now 51st Division). It was decided, after much discussion, that this would have to be taken in a preliminary operation one hour before the Zero hour of the main attack which had been changed at the request of the Reserve Army. The effect was that III Corps would attack the Intermediate Line at 12.30 am and Switch Line at 1.30 am. In the confusion 51st Division did not receive the changes and did not attack at 12.30 am with III Corps. Rawlinson wrote:

> After visiting corps comds in the morning and thinking that all was settled and ready for
> the attack I found photos taken yesterday reveal a new trench in front of the Switch Line
> NW of High Wood. The right of III Corps and left of XV Corps must therefore undertake
> the attack of this as a preliminary operation and will not be able to attack the real Switch
> Line till 1.30 am instead of 12.30 am.

During the afternoon Major General Ingouville-Williams ('Inky Bill') GOC 34th Division was killed by a shell at the Queens Nullah near Mametz after reconnoitring the area and while walking back to his car at Montebaun. He had taken over 16 Bde in 6th Division from Putty in 1912, when Putty was appointed to command the division, and served under him in Ireland until the outbreak of war; he continued to do so when 6th Division was in III Corps 1914-1915. For Putty it was a personal loss; coincidentally the new GOC 34th Division was to be Major General Nicholson at that time Comd 16 Bde in 6th Division and who had been Putty's BM in 16 Bde.

At 7 pm 22 July the preliminary bombardment started for the attack which was badly planned and even worse coordinated by both GHQ and 4th Army. III Corps attacked at 12.30 am and the result was a disaster, as the official history recorded:

On 19th Division front heavy shell-fire greatly hampered the despatch of orders to battalions and the movement of the troops to their assembly positions. In 57 Bde, next to but not in touch with 51st Division (XV Corps), 10 Warwicks carried out a last minute relief of 10 Worcs which had been engaged in several attempts to rush forward machine-gun posts of 3/93 Regt. Before the barrage lifted at Zero hour, the infantry was to creep forward to within seventy-five yards of its first objective, Intermediate Trench; but 10 Warwicks on the extreme right of the attack was not ready in time to take part. Next on the left, 8 Glos was checked by machine-gun fire from the front and from High Wood; it lost heavily, Lieutenant Colonel Carton de Wiart being again wounded. 7 S Lancs and 7 N Lancs of 56 Bde could do no better, although the former hung on for some hours in shell-holes outside the German trench. Between 3 and 4 am therefore a general withdrawal was carried out, and the line reorganised under persistent shell-fire.

1st Division fared much the same:

The attacking battalions formed up before Zero hour outside the British wire, the Germans sending up lights as they did so and opening fire with machine-guns. Nevertheless, the assault was pressed with great determination. On the right 1 Camerons (1 Bde) and 10 Glos, next on the left, were heavily punished by the fire of machine-guns concealed in the long grass. Neither battalion could reach the Switch Line, and no better fortune attended the assault of 2 Bde, made by 2 KRRC and 2 Sussex, which had for objective the re-entrant formed by the Switch Line and Munster Alley. The two battalions were under machine-gun fire from the outset, and the attempt to rush the trenches under cover of the barrage (and darkness) stood no chance of success. Although some of 2 KRRC, which lost its CO mortally wounded, entered the trenches of 3/27 Regt, they were obliged to withdraw again. At 2.30 am 2 Bde sent in 1 N Lancs to attack Munster Alley, but no progress was possible in the face of concentrated machine-gun fire.

At the end of the day everyone was back in their original trenches with the exception of 7 N Lancs 56 Bde on the left of 19th Division which were reported dug in 70 to 100 yards in front and in touch with 1st Division on the left.

Putty wanted to be certain what had occurred and ensure it was not repeated. The GS log recorded: '4 pm. Both divisions report heavy casualties from machine-gun fire from their outer flanks. This was confirmed by a staff officer who visited all brigades who took part in the attack. Brigadiers all of opinion that failure of attack was due to machine-gun fire from W corner of High Wood and dug-outs on the right and from the high ground in direction of Pozières Windmill on the left'. It was the failure of Reserve Army and XV Corps on III Corps' flanks that had caused the casualties and prevented its progress.

Rawlinson had mentioned air photographs of Intermediate Trench in his note on 22 July but they could not have reached HQ III Corps. The III Corps GS log recorded on 23 July:

> No photographs or reports of new trench system between High Wood and Bazentin Le Petit. The intelligence officer of corps (probably the GSO2) went up late in afternoon and brought back report and eye sketch of trenches.

At 12.20 pm Haig came to HQ III Corps: he may not have seen Putty because he was forward but the GS log noted:

> CinC emphasised the necessity of close liaison between us and 1st Australian Division and the importance of having fresh British troops in the neighbourhood of Munster Alley and of seizing point X.5.b.4.1.

The CinC's concern was the army boundary and presumably he made similar points to the Reserve Army.

HQ III Corps issued Addendum No.2 to OpO No.91 at 12.30 pm

> ordering 19th Division to capture German trenches and dug-outs in S.3.c.8.5 to S.2.c.8.3 and the construction of a line of trenches between our present right and High Wood, and 1st Division to capture Munster Alley and German Trench running X.6.a.4.6 to S.1.d.3.8 and to join it up to S.2.c.8.3 as a preliminary to an attack on German Switch Line.

Putty was now concentrating his efforts on taking Intermediate Trench, securing his flanks, and working into position from which a successful attack on the Switch Line could be launched.

At 3.30 pm a conference took place at HQ III Corps attended by CGS GHQ and GOCs Reserve Army, ANZAC and III Corps. III Corps GS log noted: 'A decision was arrived at which is embodied in Memorandum G100'. As a result of this HQ 4th Army issued 32/3/63(G) at 6.15 pm:

> The enemy has pushed forward small posts with machine-guns and has dug advanced trenches in front of his Switch Line in order to interfere with a direct attack on this line. These posts must be driven back and the advanced trenches captured before a general attack can be undertaken.
>
> 2. The tasks allotted to the corps will be as follows:
>   III Corps: (a) To capture Munster Alley (X.5.b.4.1 – X.6.a.4.5) and the trench running from S.1.d.3.8 to X.6.a.4.6. (b) To join up S.1.d.3.8 to S.2.c.8.3. (c) To capture the trench and dug-outs between S.3.c.8.4 and S.2.c.8.3. (d) To connect with XV Corps at S.3.c.8.4.
>
> The above to be carried out as soon as the objectives have been adequately prepared by artillery and the necessary preparations have been made. The closest touch must be kept on the left with 1st Australian Division whose right flank must be protected by III Corps by every possible means.

This order merely confirmed what Putty had already instructed at 12.50 pm. The reaction of HQ III Corps to the last sentence can only be guessed at.

Rawlinson himself noted at 6.30 pm:

> The result of this morning's attack has been unsatisfactory. III Corps (1st Division) succeeded in gaining possession of some 300 yards of the Switch Trench (presumably refers to 2 Bde) but were unable to remain there as the bde on their right (1 Bde) had failed in their attack. 19th Division did not reach the Switch Trench on account of the new trench (Intermediate Trench) that the Boche had constructed in front of our present line and owing to machine-gun fire from the direction of High Wood.

He makes no mention of the machine-gun fire from III Corps left flank, from the direction of Pozières Windmill across 4th Army's boundary.

GOC Reserve Army (Gough) issued orders to I ANZAC Corps at 7 pm that they were to capture the OG trenches SE of the Bapaume road. Zero hour was to be 'before daybreak' on 24 July. However, 1st Australian Division was not able to be ready in time and I ANZAC Corps OpO issued at 11 pm ordered the operation to take place on night 24/25 July at a time to be decided by GOC 1st Australian Division.

Major General Ingouville-Williams was buried at Warloy at 4 pm. It is not certain whether Putty attended as the conference which started at 3.30 pm was a most important one. However, Warloy being so close to Montigny he and others from the HQ may well have done.

3rd Cavalry Division was placed at the disposal of III Corps at 5.30 pm for work, and there was much to be done carrying forward ammunition, defence stores and supplies of all types. The AQ log recorded the artillery ammunition expenditure for 23 July as 54,345, higher than any day since 1 July.

24 July was fine, but cloudy, although it cleared late in the afternoon. Both divisions reported a quiet night and the day was much the same. III Corps was now deployed with 19th Division on the right: 58 Bde was in the line (HQ at Bazentin le Petit); 56 Bde in support in area of Mametz Wood; 57 Bde in reserve at Bécourt Wood. 1st Division had 1 and 3 Bdes in the line (HQs were at Contalmaison and Shelter Wood); 2 Bde was in support in Horse Shoe Trench. 23rd Division was in support with its HQ still in Hénencourt and 34th Division in reserve with its HQ now at Baizieux. At 9 am HQ III Corps issued OpO No.92 ordering relief of 1st Division (less divisional artillery) by 23rd Division; the relief was to begin on 25 July and finish on 27 July. This was a strange order with the attack about to take place and must presume that it would not be prolonged.

Equally strange is the report in the III Corps GS log: 'Again no photographs or reports on new trenches. Intelligence officer again went up and reported'. The low cloud was restricting air photography and the state of the ground made patrolling by day impossible but it was still unusual for the GSO2 at corps HQ to have to collect information himself, and for the second day running when that information was available at HQ 4th Army. After dark the flank units of XV and III Corps began digging to join up securely between the southern point of High Wood and Bazentin le Petit windmill: at 9 pm a new trench was occupied by 9 Welch 58 Bde. The AQ log recorded on 24 July that 34 Sqn RFC joined III Corps for administration and 300 Canadian lumbermen arrived to work under CE.

Putty wrote to Ettie Desborough that day:

My dear Chief, Thanks for your letter of 20 Jul. The fighting is still very violent but we are gradually making ground. First one way then another but it all means more room to manoeuvre the forces in, we have nearly got Pozières what the men call 'Poser' and it is an extremely important tactical point, the Boche defence of which has been magnificent from the start. I lost a great friend on Saturday [22 July] in General Ingouville-Williams he was a splendid fighter who had been under me in Ireland, his energy was simply astounding, he was all on wires very much the Tommy Capper[51] type of man, he was quite reckless and I knew too well it was only a matter of time but now it is over I miss him very much. Bobby White[52] dined here last night the picture of health, I rotted him well told him that two years training in the open air with soldiers had made him look like an honest man again instead of the pinch anything look he had grown in to in his nefarious dealings in the City. Simon Lovat[53] stayed a night with me, he doesn't look well by any means but he is very keen he was very interesting about the cutting of his forest trees with the Boche prisoners, it seems quite a sound idea. Charley and Tweedmouth dined here last Friday night (21 July), both of them very restless not knowing whether to mount their horses for the break through or not, there is no ride for them at present I am quite sure. All blessings For ever Putty.

It was misty on 25 July: at 2 am 1st Division attacked Munster Alley in conjunction with an attack by 1st Australian Division on OG1 and OG2 as far as the Bapaume Road. The attack was made by 1 SWB (3 Bde) and was initially successful but machine-gun fire from Pozières Windmill forced them to withdraw. 1st Division reported at 8.30 am that the attack had failed. HQ III Corps issued OpO No.93 at 12.15 pm ordering 'the seizure of the junction of Munster Alley and of the old German support line this afternoon; also for the seizure of the German Switch Line this evening'. The problem appeared simple: the right of 1st Australian Division was exposed to fire from Munster Alley and the left of 1st Division, when it tried to take Munster Alley, to that from Pozières Windmill. However, the shape of the ground and coordination across the army boundary made it more complicated.

To make matters even more difficult, at 12.30 pm the III Corps GS log noted:

A reconnaissance was made by 34 Sqn RFC which discovered the existence of a new German trench starting from Munster Alley at a point 250 yards from its junction with the old German support Line (OG2) and running almost due N to the Bapaume Road.

It was not surprising that 1st Division was having such difficulty working their way forward, and many of the trenches had been shattered beyond recognition. In consequence of this report HQ III Corps modified OpO No.93 and ordered 1st Division to capture the junction of Munster Alley (with OG2), to capture 100 yards of Munster Alley and to dig a trench thence to connect

51   Major General Sir Thompson Capper (1863-1915) killed in action Battle of Loos.
52   Brigadier General Hon Robert White (1861-1936) late RWF Comd 184 Bde 61st Division and brother of Luke White 3rd Baron Annaly SG 1877-1896.
53   Major General Simon Fraser 14th Lord Lovat (1871-1933) late Camerons GOC 4th Mounted Division.

with Lancashire Trench. Meanwhile on the right of the III Corps 19th Division had a quiet day with 51st Division now holding the new trench on their right.

Rawlinson recorded that day:

> I held a meeting of corps comds (at Querrieu) at 9.30 this morning and arranged a concerted attack on Longueval and Delville Wood for the morning of 27 July. I visited 1st and 19th Divisions this afternoon and found the div comds all right but they say that the troops are having a hard time in the forward trenches from continual shelling.

At 2.30 pm 4th Army 32/3/65(G) was issued: '2 (2). The operations by III Corps to capture Munster Alley (X.5.b.4.1 – X.6.a.4.6) and the trench S.1.d.3.8 to X.6.a.4.6, in conjunction with the Australian advance against the Windmill, will be pressed unremittingly'.

It was again dull and misty on 26 July. The official history tells of 1st Division's last effort:

> At 3 am 2 Welch of 3 Bde made an attack. A preliminary bombardment was dispensed with to give no warning to the German machine-gunners, and 2 Welch reached what appeared to be the junction of Munster Alley and OG 2, where they found Australians established. By noon of 26 July, 23rd Division had carried out the relief of 1st Division (11-27 July 1st Division's casualties were 123 officers and 2,955 other ranks), which left behind two companies of 2 Welch to deliver another attack at 3 pm [they were relieved in the early hours of 27 July]. This made considerable progress up the trench towards the Switch Line, but the Germans counter-attacked with bombs and also over the open; in spite of the heavy losses inflicted by the fire of their Lewis guns, 2 Welch were driven back (parts of five battalions 18th Reserve Division were engaged in this fighting. According to German reports, the situation in the OG lines SE of the Bapaume road was a constant anxiety to the divisional commander).

The GS log noted of 2 Welch's attack in the afternoon that 'they took 200 yards of Munster Alley but, when the enemy counter-attacked, were forced back and now hold 70 yards of it. They claimed to have killed 100 Germans with Lewis gun fire'.

23rd Division deployed with 68 Bde (left) and 70 Bde (now back from 8th Division on right) on a frontage of 1,600 yards on either side of the Contalmaison-Martinpuich Road; HQ 23rd Division moved forward to Albert. They reported at midnight that 'men of 1st Australian Division and their men (68 Bde) are having bombing fights with enemy in Munster Alley. 100 yards of latter still held. They are sapping communication between X.5.b.4.1 and X.5.d.7.8 as the old German trench there is destroyed by shell fire'. On the other flank 19th Division reported that they had dug a continuous trench in front of their existing line from S.2.d.1.2 to the right of the area overnight 25/26 July, and would deepen it the next night.

HQ III Corps issued OpO No.94 at 4 pm ordering: 'cooperation of artillery of III Corps in operation of XIII and XV Corps tomorrow [27 July]'. At 11.40 pm HQ III Corps issued OpO No.95 ordering 'attack on German intermediate line by 19th Division tomorrow at an hour to be settled by GOC 19th Division. Corps HA and Motor MG Bty to cooperate'.

The morning of 27 July was again dull, although it did clear later. At 5.30 am 23rd Division reported that after stiff bombing fights through the night they held 200 yards of Munster Alley;

during the day this was consolidated. Zero hour for XV and XIII Corps attack was 7.10 am: 12"
and 9.2" guns of III Corps HA cooperated by engaging targets in the enemy's rear. At 12.35 pm
Putty issued Correction No.1 to III Corps OpO No.95 cancelling 19th Division's attack. This
was probably because XV Corps' attack, although successful, had not got far enough forward to
secure his right flank. Some have suggested that III Corps made too many small scale attacks
but in the hinge of the two armies this was sensible tactics, making limited attacks on the left
and right, coordinated with those on the flanks. This allowed the corps to fight its way forward
to a position from which it could attack the Switch Line.

It was quiet overnight on the front of both divisions: 28 July was a clear day and at last air
photography was again possible. The GS log recorded at 11.15 am: '23rd Division report that a
new trench has been dug for 250 yards NW from X.6.c.8.6 to Switch. They are holding it. Net
result of night operations: position of left stationery and right half of line advanced to within
200 yards of trench, and improvement made in communication trenches'. However, the enemy
did not allow this sapping to continue unopposed and all day 68 Bde had a heavy bombing
fight in Munster Alley with its forward post changing hands on more than one occasion. On
the other flank 19th Division's junction with XV Corps was again secure, and consolidation
proceeded under heavy shell fire.

Rawlinson wrote that day:

> I held a conference of corps comds (at Querrieu) at 9.30 this morning and arranged to
> attack Guillemont and Falkemont Farm in conjunction with the French at 4.45 am on 30
> Jul. After lunch I visited 1st and 23rd Divisions.

At 3.15 pm 4th Army 32/3/66(G) was issued:

2.   III Corps have established themselves in the southern end of Munster Alley for about
     200 yards from its junction with the German second line. III and XV Corps have
     connected up in S.9.a.

3c). III Corps will capture the trench running approximately from S.3.c.8.5 to S.2.c.8.4
     (Intermediate Trench), and join this up with our present line. III Corps will push
     up Munster Alley towards X.6.a.4.6 and in the event of the Reserve Army having
     captured the windmill prior to 30 Jul III Corps will capture the Switch Line between
     S.1.d.3.8 and X.6.a.4.6. The hour of attack will be communicated later. (6.10 pm 30
     Jul – 4th Army 32/3/67(G)).

At last HQ III Corps was able to move forward and opened at Chateau Hénencourt at 3 pm.
OpO No.96 was issued at 7 pm 'ordering attack on German Intermediate Line on 30 July and
the capture of the remainder of Munster Alley to its junction with Switch in conjunction with
an attack by XV Corps on the German position on the W of High Wood. A bombardment
to precede attack orders for which will be issued by GOC III Corps Artillery. OpO No.95 is
cancelled. Zero hour was to be 6.10 pm 30 Jul'. Putty was taking Rawlinson's orders one step
at a time. At 8.15 pm HQ III Corps issued OpO No.97 ordering the relief of 19th Division by
34th Division (less divisional artillery) to be completed by 1 August.

29 July was fine and clear. HQ III Corps GS log recorded: '12.15 am. Attack by 2nd Australian
Division on 2nd Line N and E of Pozières. Corps artillery cooperated. Attack failed'. In their

Chateau Hénencourt, HQ III Corps 1916

morning report at 5.30 am 23rd Division reported they had gained ground by bombing in Munster Alley but were driven back later to their original position. It was a familiar story but on their right in Gloucester Alley (600 yards SE of Munster Alley) a point was reached beyond the crest of the ridge and only twenty-five yards from the Switch Line.

At 7.30 am Addendum No.1 to III Corps OpO No.96 was issued giving orders for a rehearsal of the bombardment at 3.30 pm (29 July) and a feint attack accompanied by smoke and a bombardment on the morning of 30 July. Addendum No.2, 3 and 5 followed giving further details of the bombardment, and Addendum No.4 issued at 2 pm fixed Zero time for the feint attack at 4.45 am 30 July. HQ III Corps, at 11.30 am, ordered 3rd Cavalry Division to find 6 detachments to construct and garrison strong posts in rear of the line now held. It is not clear why this small number of men could not have been found by the forward divisions: using 3rd Cavalry Division seems outside the spirit of their deployment, as well as complicating command and control.

Putty wrote to Ettie Desborough again on 29 July:

> My dear Chief, Thanks for your letter of 25 Jul. We have at last got glorious weather with some warmth in it which will ripen the barley quicker than they can deal with it, the worst of it is that we always have a mist and the aerial observation has been next to useless and photography very difficult. The fighting still continues to be of a very fierce description the gun fire is terrific but we keep gradually gaining ground for position of observation which will prove the dominating factor in the long run, there is no doubt but that the German troops are rattled, as a Brandenburg officer said yesterday if this strain continues of the Boche troops being sent first East, then South, then West and back again no troops in

the world can stand it. Have just changed my quarters as found that I was too far away am in a large chateau of the Louis Quatorze period, typical for its want of money and labour to keep such a lovely place going, the gardens are dead not like those at Versailles, the hornbeam hedges are beautiful but they want trimming very badly and it is work that the ordinary gardener cannot do, the head gardener is stone deaf, a shell pitched in the grounds here about four months ago close to him, he looked up and said 'I heard something'. You will find that part of Scotland lovely I went up there with Charley Londonderry to Loch Assynt [Sutherland], the old railway porter at Lairg used to be there in the old giant Fizhardinge's[54] days. We got a rather curious spring man trap among other things at Boisselle, they evidently meant to catch patrols with them, cannot imagine anything more horrible if one was crawling along on one's hands and knees. Best love Yours ever Putty.

30 July was again fine and clear. At 2.40 am 23rd Division reported:

They have occupied 250 yards of Munster Alley, also Switch Line from S.1.d.1.9 to S.1.d.3.8. Considerable machine-gun fire and shelling, our men holding on well. Request that this part of Switch shall be excluded from all barrages.

Once again the gains made in Munster Alley were later lost due to fire from the left flank across the army boundary.

At 6.10 pm 19th Division attacked Intermediate Line. Ahead of this the Switch Line at the NW corner of High Wood had received special attention from the corps heavy artillery, and a smoke screen fired by mortars of Special Bde RE screened the right of the advance from the German machine-gunners on the western side of the wood. The attack was made by 57 Bde (R-L 7 RLR attached from 56 Bde, 10 Warwicks, 10 Worcs and 8 Glos). The first two battalions pressed forward close behind the new creeping barrage. When it lifted they rushed the German defenders, and captured half of the Intermediate Trench, about 250 yards of it, and the strongpoint at its eastern end; over 30 prisoners of 75 Regt were captured (a company commander who was captured said that the British infantry got in so quickly after the barrage lifted that his machine-gunners had no chance to come into action). On the left, however, 10 Worcs and 8 Glos were later in advancing, and the German machine-guns were able to open fire with deadly effect: and their attack failed. The captured part of Intermediate Trench was consolidated with the assistance of 5 SWB (Pioneers) and 81 Fd Coy RE, a barricade being erected on the left of 10 Warwicks. A counter-attack was repulsed, but the enemy shell-fire made work and movement difficult and communication with the front was very precarious. This was the only permanent success that day on the 4th Army front but GOC 19th Division (Major General Bridges) writing later 'attributed the failure of his division at Bazentin le Petit to the lack of more to time to prepare'. Nevertheless the division had done well and shown what could be done.

During the afternoon Rawlinson had visited HQ III Corps and 34th Division; he later wrote: 'The attacks of III and XV Corps this evening at 6.10 pm were generally successful and we have improved our positions'.

---

54   Possibly Charles Paget Fitzhardinge Berkeley 3rd Baron Fitzhardinge (1830-1916).

31 July was a relatively quiet day and one of consolidation. HQ 4th Army ordered the withdrawal of 3rd Cavalry Division but they were replaced by 2nd Indian Cavalry Division; they provided both working parties and the garrisons for the new posts dug behind the front line. During the morning the III Corps GS log noted: 'Air photographs received this morning show that a new German trench starts from Munster Alley'. This trench running almost E-W was protecting the left flank of the enemy facing Reserve Army and making it very difficult for 68 Bde 23rd Division to make any permanent progress.

At 9.30 am Rawlinson held another 4th Army conference attended by his three corps commanders and their BGRAs. It was recorded that 'the policy to be adopted by III and XV Corps was to be offensive, troops to press forward with a view to the capture of the Switch Line'. During the day 34th Division relieved 19th Division; this was completed by 10.30 pm that evening. At 9 pm HQ III Corps issued OpO No.98 ordering 15th Divisional Artillery to relieve 19th Divisional Artillery on nights 3/4 August and 4/5 August.

III Corps casualties in July 1916 were: 311 officers and 2,978 other ranks killed, 894 officers and 20,668 other ranks wounded, 149 officers and 7,989 other ranks missing = 32,989 (1st Division 3,091, 8th Division 5,445, 12th Division 2,374, 19th Division 7,875, 23rd Division 4,944, 34th Division 9,893, 3rd Cavalry Division 9, Corps Troops 179). The difficulties of evacuating and treating this number of casualties, replacing them, and absorbing such large numbers of reinforcements during the battle are obvious. During July III Corps took 22 officers and 1,664 other ranks prisoners.

The AQ log recorded that during the month III Corps Artillery fired 609,593 18 pdr rounds (472,035 shrapnel and 137,558 HE), consequently many of the 18 pdrs required repair in ordnance workshops (17-30 July: 90). This meant fewer guns available and lower levels of accuracy because of the excessive wear, and but one example of the logistic problems that Putty's staff had to tackle.

The pressure on Putty during the month must have been relentless: keeping up to date and knowing what was happening all the time, making the necessary decisions sometimes on very limited information, and providing leadership in the face of setbacks and appalling losses would have severely tested his strong constitution and iron will: and the battle was far from over.

The GS log recorded that 1 August was a fine day, although Rawlinson wrote that the weather was getting very hot. DDMS noted: '9 am Corps Commander asked me how the heat was affecting the men. The only noticeable disease is an increase of febrile (fever) attacks diagnosed as influenza'. At 12.45 pm HQ III Corps issued OpO No.99 giving orders for the move of 19th Division to the area W of Flixecourt on 2 August and to be transferred to V Corps (2nd Army) 3/4 August. OpO No.100 was issued at 6 pm ordering 34th Division to extend to its right and to take over 51st Division's front up to High Wood by 3 August. It was quiet that day at the front but, as always, there was intermittent shelling of the rear areas with one bn 112 Bde 34th Division in Mametz Wood having 40 casualties.

Haig wrote that day: 'On the fronts of XV and III Corps preparations for a renewed attack must, for the time, follow the accepted practice of semi-siege warfare by pushing out saps and digging parallels close to the German advanced positions'. Some time on 1 August Putty addressed a bde of 1st Division: 'He thanked the bde for their share in recent operations and hoped that the men clearly understood that they were now in open warfare and must use their own initiative without waiting for the commands of their superiors'. Too often an opportunity was being missed as III Corps fought its way forward while orders were awaited from commanders who could not see what was happening.

Next day (2 August) was again fine. At his meeting with DDMS that morning Putty 'spoke about shell gas and demoralising effect on men, and exhausting effect of wearing smoke helmets for a long time, wanted to know if a remedy was not possible'. HQ III Corps issued OpO No.101 at 1.15 pm ordering the march of 15th Division into the corps rear area (Bresle-Franvillers-La Houssoye-Behencourt) on 5 August. Then, at 2 pm, HQ III Corps issued OpO No.102 giving orders for attack on night 3/4 August by 34th Division on the Intermediate Line and by 23rd Division on Munster Alley as far as Torr Trench, in conjunction with an attack NE of Pozières by ANZAC Corps. The line was to be advanced and strengthened by construction of several trenches joining advanced points and by the construction of communication trenches. This might seem at variance with Haig's orders to Rawlinson: 'No serious attack is to be made on the front now held by XV and III Corps. Preparations for a subsequent attack on this front must, however, be carried out with energy and method. The decision as to when a serious offensive is to be carried out on this front is reserved by the CinC'. The key is Haig's use of 'serious'.

Putty sent his monthly report to the King on 2 August with this covering letter:

My dear Wigram, I attach for the information of His Majesty the diary of my corps for the month of July, there is little to add to what it contains. The attached table would perhaps be of interest as it shows the amount of ammunition that my corps has fired in a month [946,270 rounds of artillery ammunition] which gives a fair idea of a modern battle; it practically means that neither side could ever have enough ammunition. The heroism of the men astounds me they all seemed to think that this fight was going to rid them of the horrid trench work and they fought simply magnificently, the great secret now is to follow the artillery barrage right in to the enemy lines in the attack the few casualties you get from your own artillery are compensated for many times over by the fact that the enemy is unable to man his parapets. There is no doubt that the Germans have had very heavy losses, my men alone have buried 2,000 besides which there are all they have buried themselves and those lying between the lines which neither side can bury. We are gradually advancing, gradually getting hold of ground from which we can get observation there is no doubt that we are gradually wearing him down, the casualties are heavy but considering the amount of gun ammunition one only wonders that they are not heavier. The Germans have a very effective gas shell and the German mask is superior to ours, this and their lachrymatory shells are the only things they are ahead of us at the present moment. The death of General Ingouville-Williams who commanded 34th Division was a great blow, he was a very fine trainer of men, never rested, never took any precautions and was quite fearless, he was all nerves and reminded me in many ways of poor Tommy Capper, he was killed by a chance shell quite dead he has been succeeded by Nicholson who used to be my brigade major in Fermoy. The German aeroplanes have greatly increased in numbers the last ten days, for three weeks they scarcely crossed the line but they have evidently got some of their best men up lately to cope with the situation but they will want many more to keep pace with us. Yours very sincerely, WP Pulteney.

It continued fine on 3 August. Correction No.1 to OpO No.102 was issued by HQ III Corps at 10.30 am postponing ANZAC Corps' attack and that of 23rd Division by 24 hours, but continuing with that of 34th Division: Zero for this latter attack was fixed for 1.10 am 4 August. Later that day III Corps G318/1 was issued giving details of coordination with ANZAC Corps and Zero hour for this attack as 9.15 pm 4 August. During the day Rawlinson came to see Putty and told him of CinC's intentions as regards the future conduct of the battle.

34th Division's attack was made by 101 Bde (16 RS and 11 Suffolk): only one coy of 11 Suffolk gained its objective in Intermediate Trench and it had to be withdrawn about 5 am (4 August) for want of bombs. Putty was clearly displeased with this result and asked for an explanation. GOC 34th Division's (Nicholson) report on operations of 16 RS and 101 Bde on 3/4 August was submitted to HQ III Corps (A) for GOC III Corps on 18 August:

> I [Nicholson] enquired into the whole question of the conduct of operations on 3/4 August in the presence of Sir George McCrae [CO 16 RS] on 16 August and subsequently directed Comd 101 Bde (Brigadier General Gore) to submit a report. I have no doubt in my own mind that the failure of the operations, as far as 16 RS was concerned, was due almost to an entire absence of detailed arrangements by the commanding officer; to a complete misconception of his duties in the matter of such arrangements; and failure to understand the orders issued to him, especially with regard to the necessity of adhering exactly to time-table. Two companies were engaged [of 16 RS], each under a separate commander, one of whom was very young. No senior officer or member of the battalion staff was sent to supervise either the assembly of the companies in the forming up trench, nor the conduct of the attack. No forward report centre was established, and the only alternative means of communication to the telegraph was an order to send runners to bn HQ. Sir George McCrae's personal gallantry is well known and unquestioned, as also is his unfailing cheerfulness under all circumstances, and the devotion to him of his men, but he does not appear able to grasp the fact that it is necessary in this war to think out every detail and make every possible arrangement to secure success; that is necessary not only to issue orders, but to ensure their being carried out; and that an order issued to him must be carried out, no matter what loss may be incurred. For these reasons I do not consider that he is qualified to command a battalion in the field, and I concur in the opinion of Comd 101 Bde that he should be given command of a reserve battalion. I am forwarding a separate application for the removal of the adjutant of the battalion [Capt WB Robertson] from his appointment.

McCrae was admitted to hospital on 19 August (discharged 14 September) and left 16 RS on 25 November.

On 4 August III Corps was deployed with 23rd Division (left) and 34th Division (right): 1st Division was in support with its HQ at Montigny; 15th Division was in reserve with its HQ at St Gratien. At 2.15 pm that afternoon HQ III Corps issued OpO No.103 ordering 34th Division to attack Intermediate Line again that night with Zero hour to be 11 pm. OpO No.104 was issued at 6 pm ordering 15th Division to relieve 23rd Division on the nights 7/8 and 8/9 August.

Later that evening, at 9.15 pm, 23rd Division (mainly 13 DLI 68 Bde) attacked Munster Alley in conjunction with the Australians on their left. These smale scale attacks were considered essential preliminary operations: in this instance Munster Alley and Torr Trench were previously enemy communication trenches and from them the enemy could enfilade to either side. The attacker had to bomb up these trenches and try to outflank any blocking position across the open. Such was 13 DLI's attack which gained 60 yards of Munster Alley that night.

On the right 34th Division attacked at 1.10 am 5 August and quickly reported that their right bn (15 RS 101 Bde) had entered Intermediate Trench. 10 Lincoln were unable even to start because of a crushing enemy barrage: indeed 15 RS were soon also forced out. Fighting continued throughout the day: the problem for Putty was simple – across his front lay Intermediate Trench (covering the Switch Line), the right of which was held by 34th Division and the left by the enemy. 34th Division were trying to take the left part by bombing along it and by flanking attacks, and meanwhile 23rd Division was working up Munster Alley. Coordination between these two preliminary attacks was very difficult: coys worked forward with support of machine-guns and trench mortars, often out of contact with other coys and their bn HQ.

At 2.30 pm 5 August HQ III Corps issued OpO No.105 ordering 23rd Division to take over 100 yards of front from 34th Division to include W corner of Intermediate Trench. Both divisions were then to extend their trench systems towards Intermediate Trench and improve communication trenches connecting with it. At 9 pm another OpO No.105 was issued (in error) ordering preliminary operations and work on positions with a view to ultimate attack on Switch Line – pushing forward saps and strong points and bombing up trench lines.

Both divisions were slowly fighting their way forward. At 5.50 pm 23rd Division reported: '4 prisoners including one badly wounded officer. Enemy busy evacuating wounded from Munster Alley. Their snipers got 40 enemy'. On 34th Division's front, after a day of attack and counter-attack, 15 RS 101 Bde managed to capture 50 yards more of Intermediate Trench. The corps artillery fired 46,232 rounds on 5 August; a very large amount considering most of it was in support of these two small but important attacks.

Putty wrote to Edith Londonderry that day:

> Dearest Circe. Thanks for your letter of last Sunday [30 July] which I have been meaning to answer the last two days. Charley and his crew have been taken away from me so expect they are on other roads now they have got out of my good influence. The weather has been glorious, the last two days cooler but the dust is a horrid nuisance and seems to penetrate everything. Things on the whole are going well, the gains are small but we are gradually working our way up to the high ground in several directions what strikes one most is that the Boche counter-attacks rarely amount to anything more than terrific artillery prepara-tion which means that the men wont face it or that our artillery fire is too well organised to admit of success, there is little doubt but that the fighting here will go on for a long time yet and that the strain that it will bring on the Boche in this particular Western Front will tell on him at a time when he would like breathing space, he is getting in a desperate mood but his organisation for the supply of ammunition is unimpaired, what we have got to do is to make ours unlimited and see that Russia's is ditto, our fuses are bad, damned bad one might say and the proportion of 'duds' is still much too high. We ought to keep the Boche so employed on this Western Front that he cannot afford to send another man away, we ought to make the Mesopotamian Force so that it is a perfect piece of organisation, a going concern to move ahead as soon as ever the weather is cool enough to admit of it, am glad that Merry John[55] is taking an interest in it expect it is the 'Pot' that attracts him, anyway

---

55   General Sir John 'Jack' Cowans (1862-1921) late RB QMG.

it is a long time since we heard anything of the Russian Baratoff[56] but expect he will be striking south from Mosul about the same time we move on Kut. Send me a few of those fly wisks you sent Charley last year, I wish you would try a thing called Heppell's Fly Spray in a room and see if it is any good I think it costs about 7/– if they are any good we ought to get them for the hospitals out here, one never ought to leave a fly open ought one? Not even Hugh Cecil's?[57] The *Quarterly Review* that you promised me has not turned up yet but like a good girl daresay it will in time! Have done a lot of work in my new garden here, the Countess is beginning to take a great interest in my weeding! It is a lovely Louis Quatorze old chateau in the most hopeless repair you ever saw, you ought to come out to see it, say you are on a special mission to enquire in to the 'Flies'. The troops are still fighting quite splendidly, the Australians too are covering themselves with glory as well they might as their forefathers were sent out there by the best judges in England. Best love Yours ever Putty.

6 August was another fine day as III Corps continued to attack. The enemy replied with heavy shelling of the front line, and of Bécourt and Albert in the rear. By the afternoon 8 GH (69 Bde) had bombed the Germans out of another 150 yards of Munster Alley and also secured the eastern part of Torr Trench; at 10.55 pm 23rd Division was able to report that the junction had been captured and a block established 200 yards beyond on Munster Alley. One under officer and 30 other ranks had been taken prisoner; there were men from three different regiments, each belonging to a different division, which had reinforced 18th Reserve Division. Meanwhile, on the right, 34th Division made little progress bombing in Intermediate Trench but had made contact with 51st Division on its right near NW corner of High Wood.

At 2 pm HQ III Corps issued an addendum to OpO No.104 ordering 23rd Division to march to Allonville area on 10 August, prior to leaving III Corps next day. During the afternoon Rawlinson visited III Corps. Later, at 9 pm, HQ III Corps issued OpO No.106 ordering the bombardment of Martinpuich, Switch Trench, W of High Wood and other points on 7 August between 5.30 pm and 6.30 pm and on 8 August between 4 am and 6 am in support of XIII Corps.

34th Division reported at 5.30 pm 7 August that another attempt to bomb westwards down Intermediate Trench by 8 E Lancs 112 Bde had failed. 23rd Division beat off several counter-attacks but were unable to make further progress. At 2.15 pm HQ III Corps issued OpO No.107 ordering the arrival of 47th Division and relief of 23rd Divisional Artillery by 47th Divisional Artillery on nights 13/14 August and 14/15 August: 'Guns of 23rd Divisional Artillery to be taken over by 47th Divisional Artillery; unserviceable guns to go to Mobile Ordnance Workshops to be replaced by guns from 47th Divisional Artillery'. That day CE III Corps (Schreiber) noted: 'Visited Reserve Line-Mametz Wood-Contalmaison with Corps Commander'.

Lieutenant Colonel Cordeaux CO 10 Lincoln 101 Bde 34th Division wrote on 7 August:

We have been relieved in the front trenches although we are still very near them: we had six days of it and my total casualties must amount to 20% including three officers killed.

---

56   General Nikolai Nikolaevitch Baratoff (1865-1932) Russian CinC Persia.
57   Probably Lord Hugh Richard Heathcote Gascoyne-Cecil later 1st Baron Quickswood (1869-1956) Eton politician RFC WW1 later Provost of Eton.

All the trenches were subject to enfilade shell-fire and there are practically no communication trenches so there had to be a great deal of movement across the open. In this sweltering weather it is trying never to be able to take off one's clothes, bath or shave and our surroundings are so filthy and horrible, so many unburied dead about.

The fine weather continued on 8 August: it was quiet overnight and during the day, apart from some heavy shelling. 15th Division (Major General McCracken) relieved 23rd Division and noted:

Owing to the recent fighting and the newly established line, the division found their trenches in a deplorable condition. Many had practically ceased to exist, while others were merely a series of shell-holes linked together by shallow ditches, giving little or no cover from either fire or view.

During its time in the line (25 July-7 August) 23rd Division's casualties were 96 officers and 1,547 other ranks. The Intermediate Line had still not been taken but preparations for the attack on the Switch Line began: at 7 pm HQ III Corps issued G431 ordering bombardment of Switch Elbow by heavy and divisional artillery from 12 noon to 4 pm tomorrow (9 August).

9 August was again fine and hot. The GS log recorded at 1.20 am:

GOC 34th Division (Nicholson) reports that he has ordered discontinuance of operations against Intermediate Trench as the troops engaged have lost heavily and it is too late to put in fresh ones.

Throughout the night and for much of the next day 34th Division were heavily shelled, including gas. However, at 9.50 pm an interesting report was received from 1st Divisional Artillery, still in the line:

Excellent results of shelling Intermediate Trench. 30 Bty fired 200 rounds and 40 Bty 350. Series still proceeding. Germans seen running out of trench fired on with Lewis guns. Five hit.

There was a slight drizzle all day 10 August which must have been a welcome relief. Other than artillery engagements there was little enemy activity. At 11.20 am 4th Army issued 32/3/80(G):

1. The general situation has never been better …
2. Continuous pressure must be kept on the enemy all along the front …
3. Preparations will be made for the following operations to be carried out:
    III Corps
    1) Capture of Intermediate Trench in S.2.d and S.2.c. The date and time of this attack will be notified later.
    2) The capture of the N end of Munster Alley and the Switch Line from about S.1.d.9.8 to its junction with Munster Alley at X.6.a.4.6. This attack to take place on 12 Aug at an hour to be fixed by III Corps.

There was nothing new in these orders: the enemy had dug the Intermediate Trench to cover the Switch Line and it had to be taken in a preliminary operation. Putty went to lunch with Rawlinson at Querrieu to meet the King and Prince of Wales. Later that day (at 6.15 pm) HQ III Corps issued OpO No.108 'ordering 15th Division to attack Switch Line from S.1.d.9.9 to junction Munster Alley on night 12/13 August in conjunction with an attack by 4th Australian Division on left. Zero time later'.

III Corps Opsum noted (10 August): 'IX Prussian Corps which had been in action opposite III Corps appears to have been relieved by XIX Saxon Corps. This is the corps which held the front opposite III Corps during the time it was in the neighbourhood of Armentières'.

At last 34th Division was making progress against Intermediate Trench. At 2 am 10 N Lancs (112 Bde) advancing both up the trench and across the open, and in spite of desperate resistance, won 300 yards more of this trench. At 7.15 am 34th Division reported:

> Intermediate Trench captured to a point 50 yards from road in S.2.d where a block has been made. Trench flattened for 50 yards either side of road. At 5.45 am enemy made strong counter-attack on newly captured trench, down trench and across open. This was repulsed with heavy loss to enemy.

At 11.45 am (11 August) HQ III Corps issued Addendum No.1 to OpO No.108 fixing the time for 15th Division's attack as 10.30 pm 12 August. At 12 noon the GS log noted the dispositions of the corps:

> HQ at Hénencourt. Right sector of front held by 34th Division: HQ in camp SW of Albert. Left sector held by 15th Division: HQ in camp W of Albert. 1st Division in support: HQ at Montigny. 23rd Division is moving out of corps area to be replaced on 12 August by 47th Division. Right sector of line defended by artillery of 1st and 15th Divisions, and 27 HAG; left sector by artillery of 23rd and 34th Divisions, and 30 HAG. The remainder of Corps Heavy Artillery, with one brigade of 34th Divisional Artillery, is in action under GOC Corps HA.

During the afternoon (4 pm) HQ III Corps issued OpO No.109 ordering 1st Division (less artillery) to relieve 34th Division (less artillery) in right sector of corps front, to be completed by 6 am 16 August. Also that afternoon 15th Division reported their forward post in Munster Alley was now within 20 yards of the junction with Switch and that four prisoners of 174 Regt 24th Saxon Division had been captured (by 6/7 RSF).

At 9 am that morning (11 August) DDMS noted: 'Corps Commander on being told gas used (10 August) was mine gas wished me to ascertain if it could be used in ordinary shells (this gas goes through smoke helmets, which miners are forbidden to wear)'. Later that day Rawlinson wrote: 'I visited all the corps comds and after discussing plans agreed to make an attack all along the line on 18 August in conjunction with the French'. Putty was under pressure to make progress so that he could meet this date.

Overnight 11/12 August 15th Division continued to make progress: patrols entered Switch and found it lightly held and full of dead. Another four prisoners of the Saxon Corps were taken. The day (12 August) was quiet, and again fine. At 11.45 am HQ III Corps issued Addendum No.2 to OpO No.108 : '34th Division to attack Intermediate Trench at the same time as 15th

Division attack Switch Line tonight (10.30 pm 12 Aug)'. At 12 noon 4th Army 32/3/87(G) was received, ordering attack by III Corps on Switch Line and Intermediate Trench on 12 August: not only was this repetition of Rawlinson's previous orders but it was also issued very late; its likely purpose was coordination and support across boundaries. More relevant to Putty would have been another order issued under the same reference that 50th Division was posted to III Corps from midnight 16/17 August.

III Corps attacked at 10.30 pm 12 August. On the right 34th Division (11 Warwicks 112 Bde) again failed to take the part of Intermediate Trench still held by the Germans. Despite the intensity of the supporting bombardment, they were driven back by the enemy's artillery and machine-gun fire having suffered 162 casualties. 34th Division never did succeed in taking the rest of Intermediate Trench: GOC 34th Division (Nicholson) wrote:

> The Intermediate Trench which gave us so much trouble was eventually taken by 1st Division, which relieved 34th. The method adopted was to dig a line of trench from a point in our trench E of the barricade, in such a way that it eventually ran in rear of the portion of Intermediate Trench which was held by the enemy. The result was that all reinforcements and supplies for the enemy were cut off, and the garrison eventually surrounded.

This was for the future but Nicholson went on:

> The failure of the attacks made by 34th Division was due to various causes: (a) not only the Intermediate Trench, but our own front line, were under enfilade observation from High Wood; (b) the enemy's artillery could bring enfilade fire on both trenches; (c) last, but not least, the attacks after that of 3/4 Aug (owing to circumstances beyond divisional control), were carried out as isolated operations, and never as part of an attack on wide front.

On the left 15th Division patrols had already reported Switch Line to be lightly held and for four days the division had bombarded the enemy's trenches with every available gun of 15th and 23rd Divisional Artillery, and two bdes of 34th Divisional Artillery in conjunction with the Corps Heavy Artillery. So heavy was the fire that it was found, when the position was captured, to have obliterated many of the German trenches. On the right 12 HLI 46 Bde was checked by machine-gun fire, but on the left 6/7 RSF and 6 Camerons of 45 Bde took and consolidated the objective from Munster Alley to a point 400 yards south-eastward. 6 Camerons on the left were in touch with the Australians at the head of Munster Alley. 6 Camerons war diary noted: 'The artillery support was excellent, a "wall of fire", and the men advanced under it'. Pipe-pushers were then blown to form communication trenches to the new line. Although the division had not gained all its objectives, those won were of great importance. From the captured Switch Line an extensive view was obtained and observers in it were able to direct effective artillery and machine-gun fire on enemy advancing from Martinpuich to attack or conduct reliefs.

13 August was a fine, hot day, and one of consolidation after fighting for most of the night. On the left 15th Division was in Switch Trench up to Switch Elbow but to the E 34th Division was unable to get forward because the enemy was still holding the western end of Intermediate Trench, and had managed to dig a 'New Trench' across the front to High Wood. At 3 pm HQ III Corps issued OpO No.110 giving preparatory orders for 1st Division (relieving 34th Division) to attack New Trench on 18 August. At 3.30 pm HQ III Corps issued Addendum

No.1 to OpO No.109 ordering the move of 34th Division to Allonville-Cardonette-Poulainville on 17 August, and to leave III Corps at midnight 18/19 August: also that day the relief of 23rd Divisional Artillery by 47th Divisional Artillery started. Artillery ammunition expenditure continued high with 53,936 rounds fired that day, much of it in the early hours.

During the morning of 13 August General Foch[58] and General Rawlinson settled that when XIII Corps [on the right of 4th Army] attacked Guillemont on the evening of 18 August, in conjunction with subsidiary attacks by XV and III Corps, the French would capture Maurepas.

It was a close muggy day on 14 August; for the next three days the weather was wet and little could be done. The ground at the front was impassable on account of numberless shell-holes, now full of water; scarcely a square foot of earth had not been broken up by shell-fire. 15th Division continued to consolidate and push forward, and the GS log noted at 6 pm: '15th Division report successful bombing raid on Switch; two prisoners taken and block established. Two bombing raids carried out in morning by 46 Bde on Switch old saps, entered trench and caused several casualties. Enemy retreating over open were caught by MG fire from occupied portion of trench'. At noon HQ III Corps issued OpO No.111: 50th Division was to join III Corps on 17 August. During the evening 4th Army 32/3/94G was received ordering attack on 18 August by III Corps on new German trench W of High Wood and on uncaptured portion of Intermediate Trench: these operations to be in conjunction with attacks by XV and XIII Corps and by 6 French Army. Effectively Rawlinson was binding Putty's planned attacks into 4th Army's overall plan; also, earlier in the day, Rawlinson wrote: 'I visited Putty to arrange with him details of the attacks on 16, 18 and 22 Aug'.

At 9 am next day (15 August) DDMS recorded:

> Corps Commander asked if there is not some method of burning or getting rid of bodies lying out in places inaccessible for burial, or where buried corpses are thrown up again by shells, or where as in Delville Wood there is no soil for burial purposes owing to roots of trees. The most satisfactory chemical is C Solution, the supply of which is limited. Next to that is quick lime which is heavy and no use in damp weather.

During the afternoon of 15 August (2 pm) HQ III Corps issued Addendum No.1 to III Corps OpO No.110 ordering bombardments, 'Chinese' attacks and other deception measures including the use of dummies in connection with operations 16 August to Zero 18 August. At 7.55 pm GOC 1st Division assumed command of the right sector of the corps front: 34th Division then moved back and left III Corps having had nearly 3,000 casualties since the beginning of the month.

Putty wrote to Edith Londonderry on 15 August:

> Dearest Circe, Many thanks for your letter of 12 August, the fly wisks have arrived they have duly removed vast numbers, you recounted most of the fly stories except the one of old Seymour Portman[59] who was told his fly was open, he asked how many buttons to which the reply was one, oh said Seymour it takes two to let him out. The Howler has just given

---

58   General Ferdinand Foch (1851-1929) GOC French Army Group North.
59   Probably Seymour Berkeley Portman 6th Viscount Portman (1868-1946).

us your Y.M.C.A. postcard last week personally I consider that the C must have stood for something else than Xtian either CK or CT what do you think. As you say there are no flies on you, the life would not suit you as although they copulate and breed quicker than anything else in the world the performance is over in under a second, true they don't have to take their clothes off but otherwise there are no redeeming features I never can make out how they can tell which sex they are on top of. G Trotter[60] dined with me last night, his lot are going out of the line, he hoped to get home for a bit to settle up his brother's estates etc so get hold of him if he does tell him to tell you of the photo the boys sent me of Beatrice Sinclair she must be a flier if she strips as well as she comes out in the camera she looks as if she would not fail her name as far as the 'Sin' is concerned. The Australians have taken some more ground since I wrote but did no good last night, they are born fighters, the Boche tries to make them angry by calling them coloured troops in his dirty communiqué if they were as good collectively they would be hard to beat. That was very interesting what you said about shortage of meat in Germany but should doubt the veracity of the statement their worst crisis is at this moment until the next harvest is thrashed out but that will not stop him fighting, we must go on making good mortars and 6 inch guns while if could only get decent fuses we should have been in Bapaume long ago, the number of 'duds' is a terrible blow, that expression will be used by your sex for many years to come. We have had a good deal of rain the last two days, a depression has been coming from the north for some days but should imagine it is on the turn. The War Office scandal they call the Cow and West affair,[61] how they can spend their time over such a ridiculous affair I cannot imagine, the Mesopotamia thing was really serious and has lead to dismissals already this may well be called the 'Pot' Scandal as it begins with a mess and is likely to end in one, it is a great pity for the Turks want beating in the direction. Bestlove Yours ever Putty.

Apart from intense shelling on 1st Division there was little change overnight or next day (16 August). HQ 50th Division opened at Montigny in the morning and at 4.45 pm HQ III Corps issued OpO No.112 giving 18 August as the date for the attack by 1st Division specified in OpO No.110; details of the bombardment and discharge of smoke were also given. However, before this, 1st Division had to make a preliminary attack. That evening three officers from 1 SG, then at Sailly-au-Bois, came to dinner with Putty – Sherard Haughton Godman,[62] Miles Barne[63] and Charles Cecil Boyd-Rochfort.[64] Miles Barne wrote:

The corps HQ was in a very beautiful very big chateau. This was a very interesting outing as we heard a lot of what was going on, the 3rd Corps even then being very hotly engaged between Pozières and High Wood, though to look at corps HQ one would have thought everything very peaceful. From a point just outside the garden we watched the huge battle in the dim distance, thousands of gun flashes, being able to see the whole line from Thiepval

60   Brigadier General Gerald Frederick Trotter (1871-1945) late Gren Gds Comd 51 Bde 17th Division.
61   General Sir John 'Jack' Cowans (1862-1921) late RB QMG and Mrs May Cornwallis-West (1858-1920).
62   Sherard Haughton Godman (1865-1938) SG 1887-1919 CO 1 SG.
63   Miles Barne (1874-1917) SG 1893-1917 2IC 1 SG died of wounds.
64   Charles Cecil Boyd-Rochfort (1887-1983) Eton SG 1914-1920.

right round to the French's right near Péronne. General Pulteney himself was looking very well though much aged.

At 10 pm 1st Division attacked and by 12.15 am were able to report that it had captured the greater part of the 'new' German trench. The assault was made after a 5 minute intense bombardment by 2 Sussex and 1 Northants 2 Bde: about 25 prisoners from 181 Regt were taken and the captured part of the trench consolidated with blocks at either end. However, on the left, 1 Bde (1 BW) failed to clear the Germans from Intermediate Trench by bombing and a flanking attack over the open. Meanwhile 15th Division tried to clear more of the Switch Line by bombing to the right. 7 Camerons 44 Bde made a successful frontal attack but afterwards lost heavily and had to be reinforced. 10/11 HLI 46 Bde on its right succeeded in extending the hold on the Switch Line to a point 120 yards E of Switch Elbow. Opposite 15th Division was 179 Regt holding the left sector of 24th German Division (which had relieved 18th Reserve Division) and 181 Regt in the right sector of 40th German Division: 181 Regt extended into 1st Division's front. Overall III Corps had made significant progress on each flank but in the centre was still held up, especially by Intermediate Trench. Rawlinson noted that day: 'III Corps got on well'.

At 2.45 pm 18 August the main 4th Army attack started: it failed almost everywhere. 15th Division discharged smoke to support 1st Division but did not itself attack. 1st Division did take more of 'New' Trench but failed to take the rest of Intermediate Trench, the W edge of High Wood and the trench running to its W, partly because XV Corps (33rd Division) failed to take the rest of High Wood. However, its artillery support was inadequate, both missing Intermediate Trench and destroying one coy 1 N Lancs W of High Wood. Finally on a bad day for 1st Division, Lieutenant Colonel Longridge Indian Army its GSO1 was killed.

It was wet again in the morning of 19 August; during the night the enemy made a weak counter-attack against 15th Division but this broke down under rifle and machine-gun fire, and on retiring the enemy were caught by a barrage. 1st Division, meanwhile, continued to consolidate the positions it had captured and to push forward patrols. W of High Wood patrols of 1 Northants (2 Bde) entered the Switch Line at noon and found that part of it empty, and no enemy was seen in the N portion of High Wood. A line of posts was established and that night working parties were sent up to dig an outpost position almost on the crest of the ridge midway between High Wood and Martinpuich. All this seemed to indicate that the German resistance in front of III Corps was weakening. Rawlinson wrote that day: 'The Saxons are tired and demoralised in front of III Corps. Eleven more surrendered this morning. Rode out to Hénencourt after tea to see Putty and III Corps – all very cheery'. The problem of the Intermediate Trench, however, continued. Putty must have been very frustrated about it because the GS log recorded that day: 'Major Battye (GSO2 HQ III Corps) carried out a reconnaissance of the Intermediate Line and reported on the problems in capturing it. He concluded that the tactics of siege warfare had to be used'. Interestingly Brigadier General Tancred (BGRA III Corps) wrote many years later on the numerous failures to take the Intermediate Trench:

> The division (1st) holding the portion of the Intermediate Trench placed their left flank 200 yards further to the left than they really were. The various bombardments consequently left the vital part of the enemy's trench entirely untouched. Finally an officer of the division with an air photo, by counting each traverse from our end of the trench, found the right spot on the map and the next attack succeeded.

Also on 19 August Putty wrote again to Edith Londonderry:

Dearest Circe. The enclosed cutting from a Cork paper might amuse you, expect it is a long time since Dillon sang 'God Save the King'. Your Heppell's Fly Sprayer has arrived all right and Gavin Hamilton has been spraying all in sight I think they take a long time to die but anyway I trust it makes them impotent. Yesterday [18 Aug] was a desperate days fight and altogether quite 1000 prisoners must have been taken, I gave the old XIX Saxon Corps a real good doing in, it was rather funny their coming opposite me after all the time we had faced one another at Armentières, the shelling eclipsed anything we have seen up to date but taking all things in to consideration it was very satisfactory and the Boche will have to relieve these corps at once. We have had a lot of thunder rain the last two days which I trust has come to an end as we want our roads in good condition for this work, but it does good in one way for it fills up the shell holes with water that the Boche wants to hide in. Bestlove and all power to you Yours ever Putty.

Overnight 19/20 August both divisions pushed forward patrols without encountering enemy: by morning 20 August the new outpost line had been established. However, on the right 2 Bde (1 Northants) was forced back and two counter-attacks failed to retrieve the position. The enemy opposite (181 Regt) had been reinforced with 3/104 Regt 40th Division and 3/3 Regt of 1st Bavarian Reserve Division. Severe fighting continued all day on 1st Division's front.

Rawlinson held a conference of his corps comds at 9.45 am (20 August), at HQ XV Corps. He explained that there were just three weeks for them to reach the high ground from which the CinC intended to launch the assault on the last German line between Morval and Le Sars. Relentless pressure was to be maintained, including surprise night attacks. In his record that day he wrote:

I gave out the programme of our next attacks on 21, 24 and 27 August. I impressed on the corps comds the need for pressing forward with patrols in order to gain ground. III Corps are doing this well and have got a line of outposts W of High Wood which they are making into a trench.

At 12.30 pm HQ III Corps issued OpO No.113 ordering 15th Division to liberate smoke at 4.25 pm 21 August to assist the attack by XIV Corps. Later in the day, at 10.30 pm HQ III Corps issued OpO No.114 'ordering continuing offensive operations to take advantage of the successes on 18 August and low morale of Saxon Corps (a considerable number of deserters have come in on front of III Corps). Divisions to push out patrols and gain ground'. Putty held his meeting with DDMS when he got back from Rawlinson's conference, and DDMS wrote: 'I saw Corps Commander who will not place any obstacle in way of Major Ritchie (MO/DADMS HQ III Corps) going to Étaples (as DADMS)'. Personnel matters took up much of his time and there were continual changes in the HQ, divisions and corps troops; Major Ritchie had been with HQ III Corps for nearly two years.

It was another fine day on 21 August: both divisions reported heavy shelling, including gas, overnight and next day on their front and rear areas. At 3 pm 1st Division reported that an extensive view could now be obtained to N and NE from its forward post. At 10.45 pm they reported that contact had been obtained with the enemy in Intermediate Trench and later the

GS log recorded: 'Air photographs received this evening show that enemy are digging a new communication trench towards Switch. This trench is converging towards old communication trench now held by us. Division (1st) informed and it was arranged for a trench to be dug eastward in order to intercept this'.

Soon after 20 August (possibly on 21 August), Major Henderson Garhwal Rifles GSO2 HQ 15th Division wrote many years later:

> General McCracken (GOC 15th Division) and I attended a conference at HQ III Corps at which Sir W Pulteney explained the arrangements preparatory to the battle of 15 September, one of these was to pull out of the line and rest as many divisions as possible, the divisions remaining in the line stringing out to cover twice their frontage hitherto. General McCracken protested that by 15 September his division would have been continuously in the line for over a month without relief, and that if in addition they were to run a double portage for a fortnight before the battle and do all the preparatory work on that double portage, they would begin the battle worn out. Sir William replied in effect that this was realised but was in some cases unavoidable.

The exact date of this conference is unknown but Putty provided 15th Division with a brigade of 34th Division as a consequence of McCracken raising the issue.

It was quiet overnight and 22 August was another fine day. That morning 15th Division captured another 100 yards of the Switch Line. Later in the afternoon 1st Division reported that the enemy had shelled his own trench in the Intermediate Line, and that the occupants had fired green lights. 47th Division joined III Corps that day and its HQ opened at Baizieux.

Some time on 22 August Putty wrote to Theresa Londonderry:

> Dear Lady Londonderry, Many thanks for your letter, you seem to be as full of energy as ever. Well we have had had hard fighting ever since 1 July and it looks like going on until winter stops us, we have made good progress besides killing a great number of Boches, taking all things in to consideration our losses have not been very heavy nothing like what I anticipated they would be, the men have been magnificent the whole tone altered directly we began to take the enemy's works and although they cannot stand the shelling more than a certain time they are all right after a rest, there is no doubt but that we have pulled great weight at a critical period, the pressure on Verdun has been relieved and our offensive has certainly stopped five corps being sent to Russia from the West. Have not heard anything of Mrs Roberts for some time between ourselves am bored with her, she does not know her own mind two days together. Charley Hindlip[65] was here today and I think goes back tonight he had no news. The War Office scandal is ridiculous, if it had not been for Markham it would never have been allowed to see daylight, they call it the Cow and the West case if they would pay attention to business and find out in one month instead of one year who was responsible for Mesopotamia or making bad fuses one could understand them, they were quite right to move Beauchamp Duff[66] but they haven't got the right man

---

65 Charles Allsopp 3rd Baron Hindlip (1877-1931) 8 H/Worcs GSO Messenger.
66 General Sir Beauchamp Duff (1855-1918) late RA CinC India incl Mesopotamia.

yet. I believe the best speculation at the present time would be to buy brood mares, after the war there will be a tremendous shortage of horses for racing and every other purpose. You will enjoy your visit to the sea I know, can picture you going in to all the details and longing to pull the lanyard of the big gun yourself. Have not seen anything of Charley lately but all the mounted troops have had a somewhat dull time but their time will come in due course. We have had wonderful weather lately, just enough thunderstorms to make the wells all right and the dust not too impossible. Yours very sincerely WP Pulteney.

Little changed overnight or during the next day (23 August). At 3.15 pm HQ III Corps issued OpO No.115 giving orders for the attack on 24 August in conjunction with attack by XV Corps. 1st Division was to attack remainder of Intermediate Trench and on the right to push forward to NW; 15th Division to seize N end of new German communication trench and gain more ground in the Switch Line by bombing. Details were given of the two hour bombardment prior to the attack and Zero hour was to be 5.45 pm 24 August. Some time during the day Rawlinson visited HQ III Corps because he noted: 'I then went round the corps to give instructions for the attack of 29 August and to impress on the corps comds the urgency and importance of the attack'.

III Corps' attack on 24 August failed to make any progress. 15th Division's bombs, which were stored for the attack, were blown up by a shell soon after the attack started. 1st Division made no progress on the right; its attack on Intermediate Trench by 2 RMF 3 Bde, after some progress, was driven out by heavy rifle and machine-gun fire from men of 113 Regt 24th German Division. The enemy had been reinforced but the artillery bombardment was again ineffective. At 10.40 pm HQ III Corps issued OpO No.116 ordering the bombardment of the eastern end of Intermediate Line from 3 to 5 pm 25 August. The infantry were to withdraw along the part of the trench already held; the GS log noted that the enemy's part of the trench had never been bombarded because its location was not accurate, and had only been confirmed by air reconnaissance that morning.

Both divisions reported very heavy shelling throughout the night 24/25 August and next day. To compound Putty's difficulties the weather which had been fine for most of August deteriorated on 25 August. There followed a week of heavy rain which rendered operations impossible.

On 25 August Putty attended another of Rawlinson's conferences. Rawlinson wrote: 'I held a conference of corps comds at Heilly at 9.30; I gave orders (for 29 August); I reached St Riquier at 3 to see the tanks, on the whole I was rather favourably impressed but the personnel is green, went into the wood well'. At the conference, with the first indication that tanks were soon to arrive, III Corps was ordered to take the northern part of Wood Lane and the German front trench in High Wood, in addition to joining up the captured portion of Switch Line with the forward trenches W of High Wood. There were two problems with these orders – High Wood and Wood Lane were in XV Corps' area and Intermediate Line had yet to be taken.

At 8.30 pm that evening HQ III Corps issued OpO No.117: 1st Division was to take over part of 33rd Division's front on its right by 8 pm 27 August. 15th Division was to take over part of 1st Division's front: it would be reinforced with one bde of 34th Division but that would not arrive at Lavieville until 27 August. There was much consequent alteration of boundaries and re-grouping of artillery; and it was perhaps fortunate that bad weather forced postponement of the attack to 30 August, then 1 September, and then 3 September.

1st Division was to have made another attempt to take the rest of Intermediate Trench during the night 25/26 August but postponed the attack to the following night due to delay in getting troops in position. It was relatively quiet during the day except for artillery engagements: III Corps Artillery was firing 20,000-50,000 rounds a day. At 6.30 pm 1st Division attacked Intermediate Trench and by 8 pm was able to report that 1 SWB 3 Bde had been successful in taking most of it. At 8.15 pm HQ III Corps issued OpO No.118 ordering 1st Division to attack Wood Lane and the German front line in High Wood on 30 August (later postponed) in conjunction with attacks by XV and XIV Corps (4th Army) and by the French; 15th Division and Corps Heavy Artillery were to provide fire support. 103 Bde 34th Division rejoined III Corps that day for attachment to 15th Division.

It was wet again on 27 August. The adjustment of the corps' front took place and by 11.40 pm the GS log recorded that GOC 1st Division had assumed command of his new front. Prior to that 1 SWB 3 Bde made further progress and with the assistance of 2 RMF had taken some prisoners of 23 Regt but the enemy still held out: late that night this part of the line passed to 15th Division, as did the problem of taking the rest of Intermediate Trench. Rawlinson wrote in his diary that day: 'Visited III Corps tea time to discuss tanks'.

Very little happened on 28 August as III Corps settled down to its new deployment. At 12 noon HQ III Corps issued Addendum No.1 to OpO No.118: 179 Tunnelling Coy to establish a Pipe Jack at head of Sap A (S.10.b.9.5). The heavy rain continued and restricted activity except for the artillery. At his morning meeting with DDMS Putty suggested: 'Having one MDS for this and XV Corps, as the wounded of both corps go through what is practically the same defile'. DMS 4th Army was against this idea as too cumbersome. Later in the day Rawlinson again visited III Corps.

30 August was very wet. At 12 noon 15th Division reported that during the night a line of posts had been put out, W and E from Switch Line, cutting off the retreat of the enemy garrison in Intermediate Trench except for a gap of 120 yards. However, it was not until 11 pm that the HQ III Corps GS log recorded: '15th Division report that garrison of Intermediate Trench consisting of 4 officers, 3 NCOs and 122 other ranks have surrendered'. They were from 17 and 23 Regts 3rd Bavarian Reserve Division. Now, at last, the whole III Corps' line was advanced just beyond the crest of the rising ground S of Martinpuich. From the new line the ground sloped gently downwards to the village, the next objective on the left flank.

Putty wrote to Ettie Desborough on 30 August:

My dear Chief, You have been selfish in not writing when you yourself are enjoying peace and good air. The fighting has been continuing at a high rate of fierceness ever since I last wrote to you, at the moment we are hung up by the weather, the glass is lower than it has been this year, tropical thunderstorms which are accompanied with gusts of wind which has three eddies all going different ways in fact if one was in the land of earthquakes one would bet on their presence to have caused the disturbance, luckily we are in a hilly country where the water runs off the tops but the valleys beneath are all flooded, we must just hope that the gale which is blowing will dry it up because the horse standings are in a terrible state and our chalk surface roads which we are pleased to call emergency ones are like drifts in S Africa which used often to nearly break our hearts. We have been bringing constant pressure on the Boche all the time down here, every day we have gained ground, his losses have been very heavy indeed in fact he has had to relieve his corps in the lines as often as we have had to, this is good but it must be kept up for we cannot allow him to send another man across to Russia who already looks like having to be on the defensive though I daresay it is also caused by the slide slip of troops to Romania. Cavan[67] is better and will be back for duty in a few days have had several of my old regiment to dinner the last few days, it does me good to see their discipline and bearing. Flies have been very bad, we kill thousands with things they call 'What the Fly' and Keatings Insect Powder. Best love Yours ever Putty.

He also wrote to Edith Londonderry:

Dearest Circe, You have not written for some time. How is the Mandril,[68] all sorts of rumours reach me about my conduct as described by the Snipe, that I have deserved the censure of the Army Council, that there were to be questions in the House, they can mark up as much against me as they like, would do the same again any day to allow husband and wife to come together though I own should have much preferred to have been the husband myself instead of that spoilt Charley. The weather has been too abominable for words, endless rains accompanied by tropical thunderstorms with gusts of gales of much violence, it makes the ground to attack over very difficult, the shell holes filled with water, the chalk roads of the emergency description become impassable which is a serious item in the supply of ammunition. Have gradually been gaining ground since I last wrote all along the line, the advance has been steady gradual but of the wearing down description which has certainly told its tale because the Germans have now employed as many fresh divisions as we have but we must stick to it hammer and tongs so as to prevent a single man being taken off to Russia. The Flies have been unbearable if it was not for 'Swat the Fly' we should have been eaten up, all the staff have been ill with diarrhoea which the doctors attribute to flies but I tell them it is corrupt youth and rotten insides as I am not attacked. A lady wrote to me to ask what motto I liked best. I answered 'Upright' since which she has not written. Yours ever Putty.

The last day of what had been a very hard month was fine with a good drying wind. At 9 am HQ III Corps issued Addendum No.4 to OpO No.118 announcing the postponement of attacks by 4th Army and the French to 2 September. Most of the day was devoted to the support of 24th Division XV Corps on III Corps' right. It reported attacks all afternoon and the loss of several trenches. By 8.15 pm 1st Division, which had repelled the enemy attacks on its front, had formed a defensive flank on its right and was providing artillery fire support. 1 Bde had been ordered to cooperate with 73 Bde 24th Division in a counter-attack.

Putty attended a 4th Army conference that day, and Rawlinson wrote:

I held a conference of corps comds (Cavan, Horne and Pulteney) at 9.30 [at Querrieu] and laid out before them the scheme which I had worked out with CGS yesterday ie to go all out with 9 fresh divs in the front line on or about 12-15 Sep. I gave them the reasons and

---

67   Lieutenant General Frederick Rudolph Lambert 10th Earl of Cavan (1865-1946) Eton late Gren Gds GOC XIV Corps.
68   General Sir John 'Jack' Cowans (1862-1921) late RB QMG.

discussed the use of the tanks. I think they understand what is required and am sure they will all do their best but time is short.

As far as III Corps was concerned, on the inside of the attack, its left would only have to advance about 300 yards and its right about 2,000. Most of the tanks were allotted to the other two corps.

Since this was the first time that tanks would be employed their use provoked much discussion. Rawlinson's view was that the tanks should work in groups and precede the infantry to beyond their objective. In the minutes of the conference he is quoted: 'The tanks should go forward with the shrapnel barrage and should be concentrated in groups in trench junctions and strong points, and the shrapnel barrage should be put between the groups of tanks'. Although there was discussion it was his view that inevitably prevailed. When asked for his views on the plan Putty said: 'His chief difficulty will be artillery support and the supply of the right portion of his lines'. He was going to receive very few of these tanks and, to him, it was essential that their activities did not reduce the effectiveness of the artillery support; and the routes forward on the right of the corps were particularly bad.

During the month of August III Corps divisional artillery had fired 793,076 rounds. If the corps heavy artillery is added the total approaches one million rounds: it was hardly surprising that the forward area was so devastated. III Corps casualties in August were: 94 officers and 1,462 other ranks killed, 346 officers and 7,451 other ranks wounded, 18 officers and 845 other ranks missing = 10,216.

Major Lewer (SO2 HQRA III Corps) wrote:

> At that time camouflage was in its infancy and stocks very short; however, I had been to a demonstration of the use of camouflage so as the reinforcing bdes [field arty] could not get covered positions and nets could not be obtained from camouflage depots, I obtained permission from GOCRA III Corps [Tancred] to arrange with my opposite number SO RE, if Corps Commander agreed, to try and buy some netting and raffia grass. This permission was given so in a corps car and with cheque book and a borrowed lorry we proceeded to Dunkirk for a couple of days, where we bought up all the fish netting, gardeners bars and raffia grass and took the lot back to corps HQ in triumph.

The GS log recorded:

> The line held by III Corps now runs from McDougall Trench on the E through High Wood to Munster Alley on the W, a distance of nearly 4,500 yards. The right sector is held by 1st Division, the left by 15th Division plus 103 Bde. HQ 47th Division is at Baizieux and HQ 50th Division at Montigny.

So much space is devoted to the fighting and the intensity of it that it is easy to forget the level of effort required to support it. The complexity of the administrative and logistic choreography is indicated in Appendix C which covers the corps troops; they had to be pulled together by Putty to play their vital parts within the corps, yet none were permanent and space for their deployment and movement was very limited.

Battle of Flers/Courcelette 15-22 September

September started quietly with little activity on 1 September except by enemy artillery on 15th Division's front. The Prince of Wales wrote to King George V that day:

> On 1 September I motored to a place called Yvrencheux with General Morland [GOC X Corps] to watch the trials of ½ dozen of these 'land submarines' of which you have heard about I expect. We watched them assault some trenches with infantry. The scheme is that they should be launched against the Huns behind the 1st wave and go right on to the second objective in front of the 2nd wave of infantry. Personally I think they are nice toys and worth trying; but not to be in any way relied on for success for I don't think they will be a success. General Putty and a whole crowd of staff officers were also at these trials and we lunched together afterwards.

At 11.35 am 1 September HQ III Corps issued OpO No.119 ordering the bombardment of Wood Lane and High Wood in support of an attack by 24th Division XV Corps.

Again it was relatively quiet on 2 September. DDMS recorded at 9 am: 'Corps Commander does not like new mask (gas) – too cumbersome and heavy. He wishes me to ask Chem Adviser if a small respirator could not be devised which could be put on at once, while the man is adjusting the smoke helmet'. Putty held a conference at 10 am to discuss the attack next day, the preliminary bombardment for which had already started. Addendum No.6 to III Corps OpO No.118 was issued at 1.30 pm giving Zero hour as 12 noon 3 September. At 6.2 pm the GS log noted: 'Our bombardment of Wood Lane by heavies on the whole was good'. Rawlinson had spent the afternoon at St Riquier looking at the tanks and wrote: 'I was not pleased with them. They are green and do not understand fighting the Boche and it does not seem to me that anyone is taking them in hand and teaching them'. A note in the AQ log is also worth mention: 'Repairs carried out in ordnance workshops 23 June-2 September: 627 guns, howitzers and mortars. The main problem was buffers, springs and piston rods'. Very large numbers of rounds were now being fired every day; fewer guns were available, those in the batteries were firing even more rounds, and the inaccuracies becoming an ever growing problem.

No rain had fallen since 30 August, and conditions promised to be favourable for 3 September's attack by XIV, XV and III Corps. In the III Corps' case the attack was to be made by 1st Division with the objectives of Wood Lane and the German front line in High Wood. Rawlinson wrote on 3 September: 'After breakfast I went to see 1st Division to wish them good luck in their attack on High Wood returning by way of III Corps'. 30 seconds before Zero hour (at 12 noon) a mine was exploded at the eastern end of High Wood. 178 Tunnelling Coy RE had dug down 25 feet to burrow a gallery 310 feet in length which brought them under the German redoubt. They had worked in hazardous conditions and all material had to be brought over the devastated battlefield, culminating in placing 3,000 lbs of ammonal at the end of the gallery.

1st Division attacked with 1 Bde: 1 Camerons were on the right with their objective being Wood Lane. They attacked with all four companies in the line and a detachment of 8 Berks on their right. Here on the corps boundary no progress was made, but in the centre and on the left 1 Camerons took the trench and gained another hundred yards before beginning to consolidate. 1 BW on the left had the objective of the German front line in High Wood, and here no preliminary bombardment had been deemed possible because the lines were so close together.

Much has been written about the tactic of evacuating the front line to permit a preliminary bombardment but little attention has been given to the difficulties or the risks. 1 BW did have the assistance of the mine at the eastern corner, blazing oil drums, 'pipe pushers' and flamethrowers. Unfortunately the 'pipe pushers' in the wood blew back and a Stokes mortar, firing short, ignited the oil drums prematurely. The result was considerable confusion and the bn, with the exception of one coy which secured the mine crater, was held up by machine-gun and rifle fire. It was to become a familiar story in the days and weeks ahead.

The Germans counter-attacked from the NE at 3 pm and re-took the mine crater: from there they were able to enfilade 1 Camerons which was forced to retire. Again the proximity of the enemy prevented the use of artillery support. The Germans did suffer heavy loss as evidenced by the 80 prisoners taken, mostly from 5 Bavarian Regt. III Corps GS log recorded at 5.54 pm: '1st Division report that 1 Bde has returned to the old front line and had been ordered to consolidate owing to heavy counter-attacks. During these attacks the enemy are reported to have lost heavily'. At 11 pm that night 4th Army ordered (299/12(G)) III Corps to 'undertake operations' against High Wood and Wood Lane – again. If High Wood was to be taken it would not be done by courage alone, or by sheer numbers because the front was narrow, but by effective coordination of all arms.

Putty sent his monthly report to the King on 3 September:

> My dear Wigram, Attached is the diary of the 3rd Corps since 1 August. There is little to add which is of interest except the capture of the Intermediate Line on the 30th was good, although I say it as shouldn't but I made a dash of connecting up a chain of posts the previous night a distance of nearly 500 yards, perhaps it was risky but it came off without the loss of a man and they surrendered the next afternoon, these were Bavarians and not gentle Saxons, real tough fellows who had been opposite Hohenzollern all the summer. We have made progress every day, have caught prisoners every day if the Boche has not got fresh troops to relieve this front with we have a good chance of giving him a severe blow, the strain is heavy but the men have borne it with wonderful fortitude flies and want of rest from the continual shelling tell most, the Boche uses a far greater number of gas shells at night than he used to but ours are coming along well and we pay him back in his own coin, the men sleep so soundly that the shell does not even wake them some times, one of my brigadiers had to wake up two men the other night to make them put their masks on although the shell had only pitched 30 yards from them, nothing like being tired with an easy conscience. The thunderstorm of last Tuesday was the most severe I have seen out of Central Africa, I thought our emergency chalk roads were done for but we have had three fine days since and everything has dried up well again. Have had to send Gavin Hamilton away for a week, he has got the universal complaint of diarrhoea, they put it down to the flies, it apparently is very catching though the men in the front trenches don't seem to get it nearly so much as those in the billets behind, perhaps they don't eat so many green apples. Yours sincerely, WP Pulteney.

At 1 am 4 September HQ III Corps issued OpO No.120 ordering the bombardment of High Wood from 8 am to 9 am by III Corps Heavy Artillery followed by a Chinese attack; for this the infantry were to be temporarily withdrawn from the front line. Later, at 6.35 am, Addendum No.1 to III Corps OpO No.120 was issued giving Zero hour as 3.10 pm. Apart from shelling by enemy artillery, it was an uneventful day: even the Chinese attack with gas and smoke bombs produced little retaliation. The corps artillery fired 51,336 rounds that day, considerably more than usual.

It was quiet again on 5 September. Rawlinson recorded: 'I held a conference of corps comds at 5.30 pm and arranged for attacks on 8 September. We also discussed the attack of 15 September and the use of tanks'. Much has been written about events leading up to and including 15 September and records are often confusing and conflicting. The record of the conference on 5 September includes:

> Rawlinson: Taking III Corps on the left first. If your operation for the capture of High Wood, which you propose carrying out, is successful, will it enable you to carry out the task which has been allotted to you for 8 Sep? [Presumably this should be 15 September]
>
> Pulteney: On 9 Sep I was going to get into Wood Lane. If the attack from the west (on 8 September) is successful, the 1st Division will just be able to do it.
>
> Rawlinson: By undertaking that on 8 and 9 September, you will be in a good position to jump off from for the further operation. There is a trench just inside the Switch Line. You will probably want to get that first. With your two extra divisions (47th and 50th) on the day of operation, you think you will be able to undertake to get as far as the trench junction west of Flers, which is the point that has been allotted to you?
>
> Pulteney: Yes
>
> Pulteney: The strong point just north-west of Munster Alley is the only piece of high ground we have got before us, I should like to get that.
>
> Rawlinson: I do not know whether they (tanks) will be able to go over crumps at top speed downhill. At the present time I think you could drive down Flers and avoid crumps. Make a scheme showing exactly how you are going to use them.
>
> Pulteney: I have done so.

It was a fine day on 6 September with the situation unchanged. At 9 am DDMS wrote: 'Spoke Corps Commander re gas. Told him of my interview of yesterday with Chemical Adviser. He said he would himself write a letter about it (light weight respirator)'. At 9 pm HQ III Corps issued OpO No.121 giving details of reliefs in the front line: 50th Division to relieve right sector of 15th Division front by 12 noon 10 September; 47th Division to relieve 1st Division by 6 am 12 September. At 11.50 pm 4th Army 299/14(G) was received giving orders for attacks on 8 and 9 September – the objective on 8 September being the W end of High Wood and on 9 September the E corner of High Wood and Wood Lane. It may seem that 4th Army is telling Putty to do what he was already planning to do, but this is much more: 4th Army is coordinating it with those on right and left, and ensuring army level support for it. That day HQ 44 HAG joined III Corps.

Putty wrote to Edith Londonderry on 6 September:

> Dearest Circe, Many thanks for yours of 2 Sep. Had never dreamt of Eddie Derby[69] probably the information came from there instead of Snipe, anyway for all I can make out there

---

69   Edward George Villiers Stanley 17th Earl of Derby (1865-1948) late Gren Gds SofS for War.

is nothing in the rumour as regards affecting myself, so shant bother my head any more about it but write to tell me what the Mandrill says, also tell him in future to traverse his trenches against enfilade as well as indirect fire and to give up dug outs that have been used by other people so often in the 'West'. The French have done simply quite splendidly both N and S of the Somme I think the latter attack was quite unexpected by the Boche, old Foch caught them napping and made a splendid coup, they must have knocked out at least five divisions I should imagine, this will put a stop to any more troops being sent to the East. We have done well lately, the weather has been against us or we should have done better, now it has cleared and become warmer again which is a good asset for the emergency roads become quite impossible in the wet chalk. Your cricket match must have been grand fun should have loved to have been there, should have asked you to be cover point when I was in!! It must have been nice having Charley, suppose you aired your views on military matters as well as other matters shall hope to see him in a few days time. How splendid to have got a Zepp one or two more and they won't be so fond of the journey across the North Sea. My love to all Yours ever Putty.

It was another fine and sunny day on 7 September. At 12 noon HQ III Corps issued OpO No.122 'Ordering 1st Division to attack W portion of High Wood on 8 Sep. 15th Division was to cooperate by joining up Bethell's Sap with left of 1st Division along N edge of wood. 6 hours bombardment to precede attack. Zero hour 6 pm 8 Sep'. There was increased aerial activity for much of the day which was otherwise quiet. At 8.30 pm HQ III Corps issued OpO No.123 'Ordering 1st Division to attack E portion of High Wood (and W part if not taken on 8 Sep) and Wood Lane on 9 September in conjunction with attacks by XV Corps on W end of Tea Trench and its junction with Wood Lane and by Canadians on N of Pozières; a mine to be exploded and flammenwerfer to be used. 15th Division to liberate gas and to bombard German trenches S and SW of Martinpuich. Zero hour to be given later'. Rawlinson noted that day: 'CinC wanted us to attack Martinpuich on 15 September with 23rd Division. I consulted Putty and find we shall be very short of troops having no reserves behind corps except tired troops. I visited Putty after tea to consult him on future prospects and plans'. 23rd Division had not yet joined III Corps and all Putty's divisions were either in the line or due to be in it by 15 September.

The good weather continued on 8 September. At 2 pm HQ III Corps issued Addendum No.1 to OpO No.123 fixing Zero at 4.45 pm 9 September. The day was quiet apart from enemy artillery and air activity until 6 pm when III Corps attacked. The GS log is brief:

> 7.25 pm. 15th Division report that 44 Bde captured their objective. 11 prisoners.
> 8 pm. 15th Division report enemy counter-attack repulsed.
> 10 pm. 1st Division report that attack on enemy's trenches in High Wood did not succeed. Right attack succeeded but owing to failure of left had to retire to original position. 15th Division report that owing to failure of left of 1st Division's attack they had to retire.

III Corps and 1st Division had learnt lessons from the failed attack on 3 September – Wood Lane could not be taken until the western portion of High Wood had been secured and there needed to be more than fire support on the open flank. Nevertheless it was another failure.

1st Division had attacked with 1 Bde: on the left was 1 Glos and on the right 2 Welch. 1 Glos attacked the SW face of the wood: very weak in numbers, it had to deal with Germans in wired shell craters. Losses were heavy; and German artillery and machine-gun barrages then prevented reinforcements reaching them. They repulsed a counter-attack but eventually were ordered to withdraw, which they did at midnight. 2 Welch took the right of its objective without too much trouble but made no progress on the left. It hung on to what it had taken until 4 am 9 September and then it too withdrew. 9 BW (44 Bde 15th Division) which had successfully secured the open flank was also forced to withdraw. Many of the enemy were killed and nearly 50 prisoners taken, mostly from 18 Bavarian Regt. The reason for the failure was simple – the enemy was able to isolate the attackers with artillery fire, preventing support reaching them: unsupported and under counter-attack they were forced to withdraw.

Failure on 8 September made 1st Division's task on the following day even more difficult. It was misty in the morning, then the day became fine: at 5.55 am 9 September the GS log recorded: '1st Division report that a bombing attack has been made on Gloucesters (probably 10 Glos 1 Bde) in new trench W of High Wood. 2 officers and 19 men of 23 Bavarian Regt taken prisoners'. It seems likely that this was close to the divisional boundary and to where 15th Division had been successful the previous day. At 9 am HQ III Corps issued OpO No.124 extending the scope of the attack as required by 4th Army; this late intervention was unhelpful but had little effect on events.

At 4.45 pm 1st Division attacked with 2 Bde tasked to take Wood Lane and E of High Wood, and 3 Bde to take High Wood with the assistance of 10 Glos attacking from the W. 2 Bde captured all its objectives: 2 KRRC on the right obtained contact with 55th Division (XV Corps) on its right; 2 Sussex dug a defensive flank to connect with the line in High Wood where again the attack failed. A mine was exploded at E corner of the wood 30 seconds before Zero (the charge was again 3,000 lbs ammonal) cutting into the crater made on 3 September and inflicting considerable loss on the Germans occupying it. 1 Northants (2 Bde) took the crater but lost it after bitter fighting about 90 minutes later. In the wood 1 Northants and 2 RMF (3 Bde) could make no progress, and on the western side 10 Glos entered the wood only to be forced out again by bombing attacks and enfilade machine-guns. 55 unwounded prisoners were taken, mostly 5 Bavarian Regt (4th Bavarian Division). According to the AQ log III Corps Artillery fired 58,179 rounds, much of it in support of this attack. At 10 pm 1st Division reported that Sap D was being joined up to Wood Lane to form a communication trench. This time the failure to take High Wood was not caused by the enemy artillery but by the well-coordinated and determined defence of the Bavarian infantry. Three times 1st Division had attacked the wood and on each occasion it had failed.

Some time that day CE III Corps (Schreiber) noted: 'Visited Bécourt Hill with Corps Commander re camp and town water supply'. The supply of water to so many men and animals was a constant problem.

The weather on 10 September was much the same as on the previous day with mist in the morning clearing to a fine day. At 8.30 am 1st Division reported that the position in Wood Lane had been consolidated and communication trenches dug to it. Meanwhile 50th Division (Major General Wilkinson) was taking over the right of 15th Division's front, in the centre of the corps, and at 12 noon this was completed. At 2 pm HQ III Corps issued OpO No.125 giving details of the move of 23rd Division into the corps area and its deployment; two bns 70 Bde were to join 15th Division on 12 September. The day itself was quiet with little reported activity.

Rawlinson held a conference at Heilly during the morning of 10 September, apparently in optimistic mood despite III Corps' failure to take High Wood. He laid down four lines of objectives for 4th Army on 15 September – Green, Brown, Blue and Red. It would mean an advance of 2-3 miles (on the right of 4th Army) on a front three and a half miles wide. The record noted:

Rawlinson: I called this conference to discuss how to get into a position to obtain a line from which to jump off for a larger operation … We have not allotted so many tanks to III Corps, because its objectives are not so distant, but has III Corps worked out any details as regards the method of using them?

Pulteney: I propose using six of them against the southern end of Martinpuich. I have three different roads for getting them up. Two of these are sunken roads and the third is on the other side of the trench that runs close up to the very southern extremity of Martinpuich. We thought of sending one down the Martinpuich road because there is probably a barricade there.

Rawlinson: Can you tell from the photographs whether the road is negotiable?

Pulteney: I cannot tell.

Rawlinson: You will have to put the tanks right into the village in front of your infantry. They will have to start very early because the infantry will move faster than they will. What about the barrage?

Pulteney: That will be a difficult matter. The tanks will go quickly through High Wood because they will have cover all the way … Is there any reason for going so far forward towards the north of Martinpuich?

Rawlinson: We want to get the trench in M.33.a, in order to secure ourselves in M.33.

Pulteney: It depends where the right of the Reserve Army rests.

Rawlinson: The right of the Reserve Army will come down to the trench which joins the main western exit of Martinpuich in M.31.b.8.2.

The records of these 4th Army conferences have to be treated with caution. Much has been made of Putty's reply that the tanks would go quickly through the wood because they would have cover all the way. Assuming that he did say this, it is difficult to be certain what he meant. It is possible that, as some have suggested, he envisaged the tanks smashing down the trees. Haig wrote in his diary after seeing a tank demonstration on 26 August: 'One entered a wood … and easily walked over fair sized trees', and Putty had attended at least one such demonstration. However, this does seem unlikely: Putty knew what High Wood was like and contemporary photographs show what was left of it. He may well have been thinking of the next phase after High Wood had been taken.

At this stage Putty is devoting much of his attention to the 6 tanks that would support 15th Division, an allocation that would be reduced to 2 before 15 September. The main issue of concern to Rawlinson and to him was how best to coordinate the untested tanks with the creeping barrage. There were two options – the tanks could move ahead of the barrage or the tanks could move in designated safe lanes within the barrage. Putty favoured the latter and it was this tactic which was adopted.

It was again quiet on 11 September, another fine day. At 6 pm GOC 47th Division (Major General Barter) assumed command of the right sector of the corps front from 1st Division, and the problem of High Wood. This extract from the divisional history sets the scene:

We walked into a new world of war. Fricourt, where the line had stood for so long, was now out of range of any but long-range guns and we could see freshly-devastated country without being in the battle. Farther forward in Caterpillar Valley heavy howitzers stood in the open, lobbying their shells at a target miles away. Up near the line by Flat Iron Copse and the Bazentins the ground was alive with field-guns, many of them hidden by the roadside and startling the unwary. All these things, later the commonplace of a successful 'push', were new. But we never saw anything quite like High Wood. It had been attacked by 7th Division on 14 July, just two months before our arrival, and had indeed on that day been entered by a party of cavalry. But it had been an insuperable obstacle to subsequent attacks, and the trench which we took over ran through the centre of it, leaving more than half still in Boche hands. As for the wood, it was a wood only in name – ragged stumps sticking out of churned-up earth, poisoned with fumes of high explosives, the whole a mass of corruption. Outside the wood the country was a featureless wilderness. The absence of natural landmarks must always be borne in mind, for it explains what might seem to be instances of confusion and bad map-reading in the progress of operations.

Martinpuich and High Wood

4th Army orders for the attack on 15 September were issued on 11 September. The first phase of the offensive involved a series of trench-to-trench assaults, with limited objectives, carried out methodically according to a pre-arranged timetable. For III Corps these objectives were: 1st (Green Line) – The Switch Line, together with its connecting defences which covered Martinpuich; 2nd (Brown Line) – Series of subsidiary defences between Flers and Martinpuich; 3rd (Blue Line) – Envelopment of Martinpuich and threaten the German gun positions S of Le Sars; 4th (Red Line) – III Corps was the inner hinge of the offensive and when XIV and XV Corps arrived on the Red Line they would have broken through the German 3rd Position.

Zero hour was fixed for 6.20 am 15 September. III Corps' role was an important one in that it would secure the flank of 4th Army, and support the Reserve Army: its success would give observation over the low-lying country running NE to Bapaume. For this attack by three divisions on a frontage of less than 2 miles Putty had 15th, 23rd, 47th, 50th and 55th Divisional Artilleries – 228 × 18 pdrs, 64 × 4.5" hows; and 5 HAGs containing 1 × 15" how, 12 × 9.2" hows, 16 × 8" hows, 28 × 6" hows, 1 × 12" gun, 1 × 9.2" gun, 40 × 60 pdr guns and 8 × 4.7" guns. This was a total of 399 guns and hows.

Brigadier General Clifford Comd 149 Bde 50th Division was killed by a sniper on 11 September: he had gone forward with his SC to reconnoitre the assembly trenches.

Also that day Putty wrote to Ettie Desborough:

Dearest Chief, I got your letter of 5 Sep two days ago, yesterday Julian and Billy's book arrived but otherwise no letters of any kind have reached me from you ever since you went up to Loch Merkland [Sutherland], it is very curious as all letters as far as I know have turned up all right except about a year ago when a week's letters written I never received, somebody is gloating over the news you sent me. I read the Family Journal last night until a late hour, it is absolutely charming how wise of you to have kept all those records of life and affection, all the frankness of youth without a sign of the cunning of old age or the diplomatist, some of the illustrations are speaking it is hard to say which one would treasure most but I think the one of Julian, Billy and Monica at Swanage in 98 and the one of the hills of Assynt [Sutherland] in 02 you must put me by a copy of those two, unmounted if you have them to put in my book of photos. I liked the message of the nurse catching a 10 lb salmon it reminded me of a trick we played Jeanine Combe's girl of tying on a salmon when we were baiting her hook with a worm we managed to pull the string away as we brought up the gaff and she would not let anyone touch it but carried it off straight away to be cooked as we told her it ought to be cooked within one hour of being caught, as a matter of fact it had been killed five hours before. The weather has been good after terrific thunderstorms last Tuesday (5 September) which filled us with despair on these chalk roads of emergency, all goes well the fighting is very desperate and the shelling a great trial on the mens nerves, however we are hitting the Germans very hard indeed when I tell you that on my front alone I have had identifications of no less than seventeen different divisions you will see how the wearing down process is telling on him, if our gun had such a good platform as the French or our fuses half as good we should be in Bapaume by now. Charley is back again I hear and tomorrow ought not to be very far off, if he can he is sure to come over to give me all his news, he is disappointed at not being higher up but he would not begin at the bottom of General Staff work and he changed his mind too often about an infantry battn which between ourselves I did not encourage as he is essentially a cavalry soldier and has no idea of the drudgery of the infantry life in its realities, poor Harold Brassey[70] used to tell me how he never had a pal he could really talk openly to and Hugh Warrender[71] who dined here the other night told me the same. They don't realise the luxury that serving with one's brother officers means, how well I know the difference. Cavan is back but looks none too well, this diarrhoea has laid out an extraordinary number of fellows, they put the cause down to the flies which certainly are numerous enough to bring any thing, he has lost a stone in weight but could well afford it if it has not left him too weak. Bestlove Yours ever Putty.

Putty had spoken too soon because the weather changed on 12 September and it was wet, with heavy showers late in the day. Putty now had five divisions with three in the line, 23rd Division in reserve with its HQ at Baizieuz, and 1st Division further back with its HQ at Allonville. At 9 am HQ III Corps issued Addendum No.1 to OpO No.125 – two FA bdes of 23rd Divisional Artillery to go into the line, one each to 15th and 47th Divisions. At the same time DDMS noted:

Corps Commander wishes every SB to be in possession of 2 handle carriers and the regimental MO to see that ground sheets are placed so as to be available readily; also wheeled carriers to be concentrated as far forward as possible.

Appendix No.1 to HQ III Corps OpO No.126 was issued at 9.15 am (before the OpO itself): it set out the allocation of tanks to divisions, assembly positions, routes to be followed, rates of advance and timings. Correction No.1 to OpO No.126 altered the routes for the tanks. At 11 am the GS log recorded:

70   RHG CO 8 S Lancs killed in action 15 July 1916.
71   Gren Gds CO 15 London.

III Corps OpO No.126 issued ordering 15th, 47th and 50th Divisions to take part in an attack on a large scale by 4th Army and Reserve Army on a date to be given later. Map issued giving objectives – breaking through enemy line and taking Martinpuich.

After the battle the controversy was about III Corps' right (47th Division) but at this stage the GS' focus was on Martinpuich and 15th Division. At 1 pm, in Addendum No.1 to OpO No.126, III Corps MMG Bty was placed at the disposal of 47th Division for indirect fire.

The preliminary bombardment started on 12 September and continued right through to 15 September. Its effectiveness on the first two days was restricted by the weather (13 September was again wet) since the artillery was dependent on spotting aircraft to achieve the necessary accuracy. The night 12/13 September and the next day were otherwise very quiet with little enemy activity. HQ III Corps modified the plan for the tanks three times during the day, as the GS log recorded:

9.30 am Correction No.2 to OpO No.126 issued, giving further details regarding tanks.
11 am Correction No.3 to OpO No.126 issued, giving revised table of routes and timings for tanks.
6 pm Correction No.4 to OpO No.126 issued, further amendment of tank routes especially those allocated to 47th Division.

This was III Corps and its divisions' first use of tanks and the issues were mainly of coordination. It is evident there was much discussion.

At 12.30 pm Addendum No.2 to OpO No.126 was issued ordering III Corps Cav Regt and III Corps Cyclist Bn to be prepared to move at one hours notice on Z Day; should there be a breakthrough on the corps front they would form the advance guard. Also, at 3.30 pm, Addendum No.3 to OpO No.126 was issued, making alterations in the timing of the artillery barrage, and coordinating between 15th Division and Can Corps across the corps boundary.

Rawlinson held another conference at Heilly, at 3 pm that afternoon. The record includes:

Rawlinson: I called this conference to ensure everyone knew what was required of 4th Army in the offensive to be undertaken on 15 Sep and also the action that should be taken in the event of a decisive success being obtained.

Corps commanders then stated the situations on their fronts: III Corps Commander (Pulteney) said: He was going to attack with his divisions in the following order from the right: 47th, 50th and 15th. 2 battalions from 23rd Division had been placed under 15th Division, but would not go into the assault: they will chiefly be used for carrying parties. All arrangements had been satisfactorily made with Canadian Corps on his left. Junction will be at the western end of Martinpuich in the trench running from that village to the Courcelette Sucrerie. The subsequent objective of III Corps would be Eaucourt L'Abbaye.

Rawlinson: III Corps must push on towards Le Sars as soon as possible; 47th Division should get on the ground in square 29.c and, if possible, Eaucourt L'Abbaye.

Putty's III Corps Routine Orders published 13 September announced the award of the VC to Captain (Temporary Lieutenant Colonel) de Wiart CO 8 Glos (19th Division La Boisselle), Lieutenant Bell 9 S Yorks (23rd Division Horse Shoe Trench killed in action 10 July), Private Miller 7 KOL (19th Division Bazentin le Petit killed in action 31 July), Private Short 8 S Yorks

(23rd Division Munster Alley killed in action 6 August) and Private Turrall 10 Worcs (19th Division La Boisselle) – five men whose courage had helped get III Corps thus far.

That night the tanks moved forward to their assembly places; for 47th and 50th Divisions (now with 4 and 2 tanks respectively) this was behind Bazentin le Petit and for 15th Division (now with 2 tanks) S edge of Contalmaison.

It was a return to fine weather on 14 September with little enemy activity. Coordination of the tanks continued to occupy HQ III Corps:

> At 1.30 pm Addendum No.4 to OpO No.126 was issued, fixing Zero hour at 6.20 am 15 September. It also allocated letter/number to each tank. At the same time Correction No.5 to OpO No.126 was issued; it dealt with problems associated with tank (E1) allocated to 47th Division and allocation of drivers diagrams. Then at 2.45 pm Addendum No.2 to Arty Instr No.71 was issued, giving tank routes A to E.

During the morning Rawlinson wrote:

> I went round this morning saw all the corps comds and saw Comd 47th Division. Shortly after my return CinC turned up to say he wanted III Corps to attack Martinpuich in earnest. I pointed out we were short of troops but he insisted so I had to give way.

Rawlinson then sent Putty further instructions at 7 pm and HQ III Corps issued yet another addendum – Addendum No.5 to OpO No.126 was issued at 11.30 pm, ordering scope of attack to be extended in case of success. Considering how much discussion there had been in the days leading up to the attack this was an extraordinary late intervention by the CinC, and just as extraordinary that GOC 4th Army should then issue further orders. Putty's objectives were not so very different to those required by the CinC: certainly this intervention was unnecessary and unhelpful, and would also prove to have been irrelevant.

Sergeant Horne 6 NF 149 Bde 50th Division wrote:

> On our way up to the trenches we passed groups of large objects concealed under camouflage netting, but in the dark could not see what they were. Also we noticed that at intervals white tapes had been laid on the ground leading in the direction of the trenches. When we got into position we had the job of filling in the trench at each place where the tapes met it to provide a crossing place for the 'tanks'. After we got into position, we were told that 'tanks', a kind of armoured vehicle, were coming up to lead the attack.

At 6.20 am on 15 September, a typical sunny early autumn day, III Corps attacked. There might have been a sustained preliminary barrage on the rest of 4th Army's front but the ammunition expenditure in III Corps up to 15 September was normal, confirming that the barrage had been very heavily restricted by the weather. However, on 15 September the corps artillery fired 88,669 rounds.

III Corps Opsum gives an overview of the situation at 9.30 am:

> 15th Division had gained the S edge of Martinpuich and were consolidating. 50th Division were holding Starfish Line on their left in the neighbourhood of Martinpuich, their right

being swung back as far as Hook Trench. The right battalion and part of the left battalion of 47th Division had progressed in line with 50th Division and NZ Division while the centre of the division was held up in front of the German front trench in High Wood. The Corps Commander ordered 50th Division to hold Starfish Trench as the main line of resistance and to push out as far to the right as possible in order to help fill the gap.

Referring to the whole of the first day of the battle, the Opsum continued:

Three 77 mm guns were taken intact which were subsequently used to fire on Le Sars. Two 5.9" guns (one damaged) and a 15 cm mortar were also taken with a large amount of ammunition and several machine-guns. Prisoners taken during the day amounted to three battalion commanders, 34 other officers and 1,300 other ranks (from 3rd Bavarian Division, 24th and 45th Reserve Divisions).

Also in the Opsum is this note:

The three tanks in High Wood were examined by a staff officer of the corps on 17 Sep. One which had a broken track was in a deep shell hole; one which had been burnt was on level ground; one which had been ditched appeared to have tried to cross one of our trenches at too acute an angle with the result it had fallen over on its side. In no case was a tank stopped by a tree.

This was to be a controversial issue.

15th Division's story is one of unqualified success. Its OpO stated: 'Under the barrage the infantry were to advance at the rate of 50 yards per minute, and in order to allow the tanks to accompany them, a lane 100 yards wide was left in the barrage'. The division was supported by two tanks: one was knocked out very early by a shell, but the other did excellent work. On 15th Division's right, 45 Bde (11 A&SH and 13 RS in front; 6 Camerons, 8 Y&L attached from 23rd Division and 6 RSF behind) met no great opposition because the bombardment had been effective and most of the Germans were disposed to surrender. 46 Bde on the left (10 Scottish Rifles, 7/8 KOSB and 10/11 HLI in front; 12 HLI and 9 Y&L attached from 23rd Division behind) with the one tank was equally successful. By the end of the day the division had captured all its objectives including the ruins of Martinpuich, and had taken nearly 700 prisoners. It had linked up with 2nd Canadian Division on its left and 50th Division on its right, albeit not quite as far forward.

Initially 50th Division's line was slightly in front of the divisions on either side and the GOC had to decide whether to delay his attack to allow for this, or to start at the same time thus helping them to get forward. He decided on the latter and in the event was only partially successful. The left bde, 150 Bde, attacked with 4 E Yorks, 4 GH and 5 GH in front and 5 DLI behind. It was supported by two tanks: one was hit early but the other proved invaluable in knocking out three machine-guns on the eastern outskirts of Martinpuich. On the left 150 Bde secured its third objective and linked up with 15th Division in the Starfish Line. On the right 4 E Yorks, its flank in the air, was forced to withdraw to Martin Trench. 149 Bde, the right bde of 50th Division, attacked with 4 and 7 NF: at 7 am Hook Trench (the first objective) was entered by both bns, few Germans except dead and wounded being encountered, and they were in contact with 4 E Yorks on their left. However, the advance to the next objective (Starfish Line) proved much more difficult. Brigadier General Ovens, who had only been in command for a few hours, pushed forward 5 and 6 NF to support the attack, and GOC 50th Division sent forward 9 DLI 151 Bde to further assist. It was all to no avail: the failure of 47th Division on its right to take High Wood prevented 149 Bde taking Starfish Line and at 3.30 pm all were back in Hook Trench. Meanwhile HQ 50th Division was getting reports that 150 Bde had been shelled out of the Starfish Line. The situation was confused but Major General Wilkinson was determined to secure not only the Starfish Line but his final objective (Prue Trench) beyond it. At 5.45 pm he ordered 151 Bde (right) and 150 Bde (left) to take Prue Trench and after a special bombardment the attack was eventually launched at 9.40 pm. 5 Border, 6 and 9 DLI were the attacking bns of 151 Bde but 5 Border was not in position. Even with the advantage of darkness the other two bns could not take and hold Prue Trench and were driven back by machine-gun and rifle fire, much of it at close range.

47th Division also attacked with two bdes. On the right 140 Bde had 7 London (right) and 15 London (left) in front with 6 and 8 London behind. The first objective was Switch Line and the northern point of High Wood; the latter was the objective of 15 London. On the left was 141 Bde: 17 London was to clear the enemy from the rest of High Wood before its other three bns passed through and on to Starfish and Prue Trenches. The division was supported by four tanks, all of which were to be employed against High Wood. 7 London on the right of 140 Bde reached the Switch Line without meeting much resistance and linked up with the NZ Division across the corps boundary. Part of 8 London passed through and took the second objective: 6 London then passed through it and despite heavy casualties took Cough Drop (between Starfish and Prue Trenches) and again linked up with the NZ Division.

Once again the problem was High Wood. Because the lines were so close together the front line in the wood had been evacuated to allow a preliminary bombardment and only reoccupied just before Zero hour. 17 London 141 Bde and 15 London 140 Bde attacked and were stopped almost at the outset by machine-gun fire. Behind them the remainder of 8 London 140 Bde and 19 and 20 London advancing to attack the second objective came into the wood. With four and half battalions now in High Wood, all under artillery and machine-gun fire, confusion ensued. The day was saved by Comd 140 Bde (Brigadier General McDouall late Buffs) who organised a special bombardment by 140 TM Bty. They fired 750 rounds in a few minutes and when the infantry again advanced the Germans began to surrender: several hundred stained and filthy men, mainly from 23 Regt 3rd Bavarian Division were collected as well as two 10.5 cm hows and six machine-guns. At last, at 1 pm, 47th Division was able to report that High Wood was cleared of enemy.

Now the division had to take its next objective, the Starfish Line about 700 yards ahead. The German artillery was shelling all the captured ground very heavily, and placing barrages on all approaches to the new forward positions. At about 3.30 pm 21 and 24 London 142 Bde were ordered to carry on the attack. With no time for reconnaissance they (24 London with only one coy) went forward round the E of High Wood but were brought to a halt in front of the Starfish Line by machine-gun fire. When night fell 47th Division had taken its first objective with heavy loss, and had 6 London 140 Bde well forward in Cough Drop on its right.

Five individual accounts are of particular interest. Sergeant Horne 6 NF 149 Bde 50th Division wrote:

The hour before zero, while crouching in the trench and looking at one's watch, was an almost unbearable strain. Eventually we heard the hum of machinery coming up behind us, and saw through the mist great toad-like things with caterpillar tracks, a gun projecting forward and at the back a tail with two small wheels, come lumbering over the shell-holed ground at walking pace. One tank followed the tape to the filled in place in the trench where I was and went on towards the German line. A few moments later it was our Zero time and we got out of the trench and followed.

Lieutenant Colonel Karslake RA GSO 1 50th Division wrote many years later:

I was personally interested in the employment of the tanks against High Wood on 15 September. I attended a conference at HQ III Corps when this was decided. High Wood had been attacked several times without success and on 15 September the attack of the division I was with depended for its success on the subjugation of fire from High Wood. My divisional commander therefore begged that the tanks should move in single file on our right just outside the wood. He pointed out that the tanks were bound to be stopped by the tree trunks if they attempted to go through the wood. He was over-ruled with the result that both 47th and 50th Divisions lost terribly from fire from High Wood, the tanks failing to get into the wood and being quite useless.

Karslake had been GSO2 HQ III Corps until June 1916 but makes no mention of Putty. Also relevant to this is an extract from 50th Division's history:

On the high ground at the NW corner of High Wood the enemy had a very strongly defended position, part of his defence system which commanded the whole of the ground held by 50th Division.

Lieutenant Colonel Warrender Gren Gds CO 15 London wrote to Major General Cuthbert (late SG and previously Comd 140 Bde) on 1 November 1916:

On 15 Sep my battalion had to take the right half of High Wood and a trench beyond it, and 7 Bn were on my right outside the wood. 17 Bn was on my left, and had to take the left half of the High Wood, and we had 3 tanks to help us. As a matter of fact they let us down badly, for they failed utterly to get through the wood. The Corps (III) were warned that the tanks would be no good in the wood, but they would not listen. The result was my unfortunate battalion had to do a frontal attack in broad daylight without any artillery preparation. We were hung up at the start by enemy machine-guns and I had a lot of casualties in the first 10 minutes. I got Goodes [OC 140 TM Bty 140 Bde] to give the Boche 15 minutes rapid with his Stokes mortars and that settled the matter and we pushed right through.

Captain Carlisle Civil Service Rifles, then GSO3 HQ 47th Division, wrote many years later:

I was in close touch with the tanks as I was detailed to lead them up to their jumping off positions. You cannot bring out too clearly the fact that owing to the proposed advance of the tanks through High Wood, the close artillery support of the infantry was dispensed with in the wood and to this we, at the time, attributed our very heavy casualties.

Finally, Major Fair CO 19 London:

> It has always seemed to me that the confusion and heavy casualties were largely due to the formation laid down for us by which each company of each battalion in each of the two assaulting brigades of 47th Division were to advance in a series of waves. No local reserves were kept in hand, with the result that after the first check in the wood every minute brought fresh troops into the front line with little or no possibility of exploiting success on the flanks, so as to 'pinch out' the wood itself. I know that both Hamilton [CO 19 London until killed that day] and Macdonald [should be McDouall Comd 141 Bde] protested against the formation as ordered, and I have often wondered since if it was the reason why Barter ceased to command 47th Division a few days later.

Three issues are said to have contributed to 47th Division's problems in High Wood: the use of the 4 tanks allocated to the division, the artillery support which was inaccurate due a map reading error and failed to neutralise the enemy, and the deployment of the infantry. It was the last two which caused the high casualties; they were Barter's responsibility and led to his removal. Both Barter and Wilkinson had apparently argued that the tanks should go round not through the wood but Putty was not convinced. It was Haig who ordered the tanks to be used in very small numbers and with limited training, as Lloyd George wrote: 'Haig insisted on throwing a few specimen machines into the fight without waiting until a sufficient number had been manufactured to enable him to hurl a resistless mass of them against the enemy lines'. It was GHQ and 4th Army that insisted they be used in direct support of the infantry to overcome objectives in depth, where so often the artillery had failed. It seems highly unlikely that Putty was expecting the tanks supporting 47th Division to smash their way through the wood but to use it as a covered approach to Starfish and beyond. Strangely, Barter does not seem to have told Rawlinson of his concerns when he visited on 14 September.

Brigadier General Tancred (BGRA III Corps) wrote many years later:

> The real reason for many costly failures at High Wood was not discovered until the 5th Army took Pys where they found a battery of 15 cm high velocity guns which pointed at High Wood and enfiladed our trenches there. I am firmly convinced that all troops, however good, when they were enfiladed by guns whose shells arrived before the sound, believed they were being shelled by their own guns. Every time we shelled High Wood our troops said we were firing short. We consequently lengthened and I am sure the bombardments were quite ineffective.

If this is accurate, it merely provides another perspective.

Orders for the resumption of operations next morning (16 September) were telephoned by 4th Army to corps at 5.50 pm, with written confirmation following at 8 pm. The first task of III Corps was to capture the third objective along the whole front, then to push forward its right, and, in two stages reach Eaucourt L'Abbaye and the spur SW of it. At 7 pm the HQ III Corps GS log recorded: 'WngO G13 (OpO No.127) issued. Consolidation at end of 15 Sep and renewal of attack on 16 Sep'. This was followed at 11.45 pm by OpO No.129: 'Renewal of attack on 16 Sep to secure outstanding objectives'. OpO No.128 was issued at 7.30 pm ordering moves of 1st Division.

16 September was fine although little progress was made. On the left the enemy made a weak counter-attack on Martinpuich which was easily repulsed; otherwise 15th Division consolidated during the day and pushed out posts NW of the village, took over the front from the Canadians up to the Albert-Bapaume road, and were in contact with 50th Division on their right. More prisoners were taken from 12 and 13 Regts 3rd Bavarian Division and 229 Regt 50th Reserve Division. 47th Division attacked Cough Drop on its right with 23 and 24 London (142 Bde) and found it still held by 6 London. The intention was then to swing left and take Prue Trench and the spur behind it in the flank but the left (141 Bde) had been heavily shelled and machine-gunned during the advance and could not get beyond Starfish. By the end of the day 140 Bde was well forward holding the junction of Drop Alley and the Flers Line, in touch with NZ Division on its right. 18 Bavarian Regt opposite 47th Division recorded that a counter-attack had been planned but could not be launched because of this further advance by 47th Division. Meanwhile 50th Division, in the centre of the corps, was able to make little progress on its right, as the left of 47th Division, but 150 Bde on its left was well forward with 15th Division: it tried to bomb down Prue Trench from its junction with Martin Alley, but little was gained.

Towards the end of the day Putty was faced with two problems. He had by then received information of the enemy's intention to counter-attack on his right (47th Division). The III Corps GS log recorded: '9.50 pm. Instructions issued to 47th Division regarding precautions to be taken against the counter-attack stated by prisoners to be launched tomorrow morning'. However, there was to be no pause because five minutes later the log recorded: '9.55 pm. Orders issued to 47th Division to endeavour to take Flers Support Line as well as front line, by tomorrow morning if possible'. The problem in the centre was dealt with in III Corps Wng O (OpO No.130) issued at 10.55 pm: '47th Division to organise Drop Alley and Cough Drop, and join up with 50th Division in a continuous line. 50th Division to establish strong posts (afterwards to be made a continuous line) in Prue Trench. 15th Division to establish a line of posts'. The corps was fighting its way forward right across the front with the intention of outflanking Prue Trench, in the lower ground, and at the same time breaking into it. Putty must have been confident of success because at 11.4 pm HQ III Corps issued a Wng O (OpO No.131) for a further attack on 18 September.

Artillery ammunition expenditure was very high on 16 September with 95,985 rounds fired in support of the three divisions. The AQ log recorded the corps strength for the week ending 16 September as 114,112 (1st Division 18,823, 15th Division incl att 27,102, 23rd Division 13,542, 47th Division incl att 21,584, 50th Division incl att 19,709, Corps Troops 13,370).

For III Corps, 17 September was a day of consolidation and reorganisation for the next attack. 15th Division continued to make progress and at 1.7 pm reported they had taken the mill NE of Martinpuich. However, in the centre and on the right the situation was not so good or even clear: for much of the day neither division was certain where its forward positions were but it eventually transpired that 50th Division had not secured Starfish on its right and 47th Division's front was on a line running through Cough Drop to its junction with NZ Division. According to the GS log, Putty intervened at 2.20 pm issuing instructions that trenches were to be joined up so that the boundary between 47th and 50th Divisions was secure. The enemy heavily shelled much of the forward area during the day, especially Martinpuich and Cough Drop, which added to the difficulties.

Rawlinson held a 4th Army Conference at Heilly at 12 noon which Putty attended. In the record are these extracts:

> Rawlinson: The results of the operations on 15 and 16 September were very satisfactory, since very considerable advantage had been gained by reaching nearly all the important positions on the high ground, as well as the villages of Martinpuich and Flers. Great loss had been sustained by the enemy. 3,000 prisoners had been captured. A WngO had been issued for a further attack by 4th Army on 18 September – every corps to complete the capture of the objectives given for 15 September with an additional advance for III Corps.

> Corps commanders then gave their views on the proposed objectives for 18 September. III Corps Commander said he wanted to work on to the Spur in M.29, also up the Flers Trench to M.29 Central and then back along the main road. He was not particularly anxious to take Prue Trench as it was in a hollow. Later Rawlinson again drew attention to the necessity of getting good roads within the shelled area.

> Pulteney: They (roads) were getting on fair, but he had some difficulty in getting rations up to the right of 47th Division. The railways in III Corps area were, however, getting on well.

HQ III Corps issued OpO No.133 (replacing OpO No.132) at 8 pm: '23rd Division was to relieve 15th Division on night 18/19 Sep on corps left: 1st Division to relieve 47th Division on night 19/20 Sep on corps right'. Other orders issued during the day returned attachments to their parent divisions. HQ III Corps OpO No.134 and Addendum No.1 to it were also issued at 8 pm: 'postponing 4th Army attack to 21 Sep; divisional objectives and boundaries given – III Corps (50th Division) to attack remainder of objective allocated for 15 Sep; confirming WngO No.131 of 16 Sep. Zero hour 5.50 am 18 Sep'.

Following a wet night, rain fell nearly all day on 18 September. There was now not enough labour and material for work on tracks and roads which in places were dissolving into deep slime. Inevitably the weather also affected operations. On the right 140 Bde 47th Division attacked and took Drop Alley and Flers Line to within 50 yards of their junction, but on the left 23 and 24 London 142 Bde made little progress and failed to secure Starfish Trench to the divisional boundary. 50th Division was unable to assault until the afternoon (4.30 pm) owing to the state of the ground and the enemy bombardment. Then 150 Bde (elements of 5 DLI, 4 and 5 GH) bombed eastward along Starfish and Prue Trench and almost reached Crescent Alley. However, 8 DLI (151 Bde) failed in its attempt to bomb up this trench. For 15th Division it was another day of consolidation until relieved by 23rd Division: it had been in the line for six weeks during which it had 6,732 casualties. Putty again intervened that day, at 1.30 pm, ordering 50th Division to keep the Sunken Road running from M.29.a.0.0 under periodical bursts of machine-gun fire day and night. With both flanks now reasonably secure the corps was vulnerable to counter-attack in the centre where 50th Division was still held up.

If there was any frustration in the objective not yet being completely secured it did not show in Rawlinson's letter to the King that day: 'Putty with his old III Corps captured Martinpuich and High Wood, the latter after considerable difficulty and heavy fighting in which 47th Division lost heavily'.

Putty wrote to Edith Londonderry:

> Dearest Circe, You don't deserve a letter but here goes all the same for it is raining in such buckets I should only lose my temper if I did anything else except write to you! Well we had a great fight on 15 and 16 September, my lot did top hole and I amassed 1500 prisoners to my own check 6 guns and 40 machine-guns, the 'tanks' were a success on the whole, they fairly did frighten the Boche the predicament was when they wanted to surrender the men did not know what to do because they are all shut up inside, one lot of Boches climbed on to the top of the tank for safety, they really are the most weird things I have ever seen going across country, they look exactly like armadillos of a huge size. They brought Charley and his lot up but they have sent them back for a day or two I believe again they drank too much water!! There is no doubt we gave the Boche a good deal more than he expected nor have we done with him yet we cannot afford to let him send a single other man to Russia which of course is Hindenburg's idea viz to hold the line as lightly as possible here and do in Russia and Roumania. Gavin Hamilton brought me back the most beautiful bit of china from Paris, the subject is highly edifying it rests on my table here but would be a case of the smoking room back home. How is your hospital going on? You never say anything about it in your letters. Believe the Howler comes late this evening but unless they bring grouse we don't welcome them, have not eaten a partridge yet although there are plenty of them about, we are not allowed to shoot but when we have time we might net some. Bestlove Yours ever Putty.

It continued very wet on 19 September; after a quiet night it was to be another day in which positions were taken and lost. At 10 am 23rd Division assumed command of the left sector; then, at 5.15 pm, they reported that the enemy had been seen crawling from shell hole to shell hole between Prue and Starfish trenches. Later, at 9.55 pm, the III Corps GS log recorded: '23rd Division report that nearly 120 yards of Prue Trench has been captured by the enemy and that none of Star Fish is in their hands. Situation well in hand. Lost portion of trench bombarded and counter-attack will be launched shortly'. 47th Division, on the other flank, was able to report at 9.35 am that it had taken most of Starfish Line; and by 7.15 pm that evening confirmed that 142 Bde had taken it all. However, on the extreme right, most of Drop Alley was reported captured by the enemy at 9.30 pm, and then retaken by 11 pm. While this was all going on 47th Division was being relieved by 1st Division. In the centre, 50th Division postponed its attack (at 8 pm) owing to the wet state of the ground for a few hours. The same problems caused HQ III Corps to issue OpO No.135 at 8.30 am, postponing 4th Army attack until 21 September.

At 12 noon there was another 4th Army Conference at Heilly. The record included:

Rawlinson: General Fayolle[72] told him that it would be impossible for him to undertake an
attack while this weather lasts. He had concurred, it being decided that postponement
of 24/48 hours would be necessary according to the weather.

Pulteney: As regards jumping off places, the III Corps Commander said at present they
were not satisfactory but they hoped to be able to improve them.

Rawlinson: The Starfish Line must be occupied by them before the attack is launched.

Pulteney: He proposed to attack this line and obtain possession of it on the early morning
of the day of the attack and to use tanks for this purpose (III Corps said they had three
for certain and hoped to be able to obtain a fourth).

Later Rawlinson asked the corps commanders what divisions they considered should be
sent away. III Corps said 47th Division should go. This division was only at the present
moment doing its first tour in the battle, and Rawlinson thought they ought to be withdrawn for a week or so, to pick up and reorganise, with a view to doing a second tour. At
any rate the question of their leaving the army could not be considered at present.

At 5.15 am 20 September HQ III Corps GS log recorded: '50th Division reported the attack
on the Crescent failed. Trenches were four or five feet deep in water and mud and the country
generally very wet and muddy, making movement extremely difficult'. Prue Trench, the objective of 50th Division, was in relatively low ground and their difficulties consequently greater.
47th Division managed to re-take the part of the Flers Line and Drop Alley that they had lost
but at 6.15 am reported that they had been unable to hold on to it. At 11 am GOC 1st Division
assumed command of the right sector of the corps front: 47th Division was withdrawn having
had 4,554 casualties since 10 September. By 11.10 pm 1st Division was able to report: 'The
whole of Drop Alley has been taken (by 1 BW). We are in touch with New Zealanders half way
up'. 23rd Division, now on the left of the corps, had lost much of their part of Prue and Starfish
in an enemy counter-attack at about 7 pm the previous night, but then itself counter-attacked at
11 pm and re-took most of the lost trenches. So, on both flanks, the divisions had been relieved
and despite the heavy fighting were still well forward. 50th Division in the centre was stuck in
the mud further back; 8 DLI are recorded as standing in mud two and a half feet deep along the
whole trench it was holding.

At 10 am (20 September) HQ III Corps issued orders to all divisions 'that their energies
are to be directed towards consolidating positions gained, with a view to providing jumping
off places before a fresh attack'. This attack (OpO No.135) was postponed until 22 September
(Addendum No.1 issued 10 am) and then indefinitely (Addendum No.2 issued 10.15 am). Putty
intervened at 10.30 am: 'Corps Commander wishes Prue and Star Fish Trenches to be joined up
by communication trench near the present blocks'. This would allow reinforcements to reach the
blocks without having to cross the open ground, and make them more effective for jumping-off.

With 47th Division withdrawn from the line, Putty removed Major General Barter from
command of it. This was done with the agreement of both Rawlinson and Haig. Some historians argue that it was Putty's decisions on the deployment of the four tanks at High Wood
which caused 47th Division's heavy losses in the battle, and that he sacked Barter to avoid being

72   Marie Emile Fayolle (1858-1928) GOC 6th French Army.

censured himself. Interestingly, in 1915, Rawlinson wrote in his diary: '15 August. Went to see DH about Barter' and '3 Sep. I censured Barter'. So, Barter's performance in command of 47th Division had already been poor and come to the attention of Haig and Rawlinson when they were army and corps commanders respectively. Writing on 5 October Haig said: 'I had to send home General Barter on Pulteney's recommendation. He mishandled his division on 15 and 16 Sep at High Wood. Two brigades were actually sent in to the wood, when 2 battalions would have sufficed to engage the enemy in it, while the others might have been pushed on to the next objective'.

As far as Putty was concerned Barter's removal had little to do with the tanks: it was his bad divisional plan and the consequent heavy losses that were unacceptable to Putty. The evidence suggests that Wilkinson and Barter both argued for the tanks going round the western side of High Wood. They were over-ruled by Putty or someone on his behalf because 4th Army doctrine was that the tanks with their poorly trained and inexperienced crews should be used in close support of the infantry; or because the greatest problem at High Wood was always breaking through the German front line and the use of the tanks in the wood was an acceptable risk; or because this was the only way of effectively coordinating infantry, artillery and tanks, as done by 15th and 50th Divisions; or a combination of these reasons. What matters is that they were over-ruled. Before Barter left he replied to a 4th Army/III Corps questionnaire on the use of tanks in the battle: 'The tanks were able to make so little progress in High Wood it is quite impossible to give any valuable information' and 'the routes followed by the tanks were given by you'. However, GOC 47th Division could have taken High Wood much more easily had he planned the attack with fewer infantry in the wood, more effective close artillery and trench mortar support, and greater coordination between all arms. More than 40 divisions were to pass through III Corps during Putty's time in command, many several times. He tended to give orders to his divisional commanders and then leave them to get on with planning their own part in the operation. He was rarely criticised for interfering in the detail, to being unreceptive to advice, or for being inflexible, rather the opposite; and Barter was the only divisional commander that he removed.

21 September was fine albeit dull, and no rain fell. The day was quiet: orders were received from 4th Army at 1.15 pm for four tanks from XV Corps to be attached to III Corps. Later, at 10.15 pm, the GS log recorded:

> 1st, 23rd and 50th Divisions, Heavy Artillery and RA informed that in consequence of Star Fish Line and Crescent Alley having been enfiladed all day, there is reason to suppose that the enemy has suffered severely. Energetic efforts will be made to seize these trenches tonight. RA will arrange for barrage to be maintained on these trenches.

Patrols were pushed forward and it was discovered that the enemy had abandoned Starfish and Prue Trenches and they were gradually occupied.

Also of note is DDMS log at 10 am:

> Corps Commander asked this morning if the party of wounded out near Flers had been brought in. Colonel Macdonald (probably ADMS 1st Division) says not, and that he was informed there were 70 of 6 London left there by 47th Division in a German dug-out (dressing station) at the Cough Drop.

Putty wrote to Edith Londonderry that day:

> Dearest Circe. Many thanks for your letter and enclosed which I return. Am afraid that the Snipe must blame me because I very wrongly attributed the information to have come from her, her letter quite removes any suspicions I had for it is as straight as a die and I hope the next time you write you will apologise for me, find out if E.D.[73] told Rawlinson, he either did him or Douglas Haig I should imagine anyway I have never heard any more about it, it might have come through Johnnie Du Cane[74] who always knows all the gossip and who would have fought on my side if he had been consulted, anyway D.H would have been only too glad to put a spoke in my wheel but know no earthly reason why E.D. should. I laughed over your visit to Wynyard, can see them all having a quarrel I should have joined in out of mischief. Have you heard why a man after breakfast is like a committee? 'Because he sits in the chair and arranges his papers and then the matter drops' if you have not heard it it is excellent. The tanks were a great success in places, their fault is that they go too slow and therefore have to start before the infantry, the Boche directly he saw them called for a barrage of artillery which catches the attacking troops but some of them did wonders, one of mine sat on a dug out and bolted a battalion commander out of it, of course every single machine-gun was put on to them which was what was wanted because they did no harm and the troops rushed in, as long as the artillery cannot see them or be directed on them they are splendid, they break down the wire like a piece of paper, they are an infernal nuisance when they stick in a road for nothing on earth can move them, for they weigh 28 ton, they are capable of improvement and no doubt will be. The New Zealanders have done most awfully well in the fighting of 15 September and onwards as have the Canadians also Black Watch and Camerons, latter especially so. I think we shall capture all the high ground, have all the good observation and be able to give the Boche the most unpleasant winter he has ever had. The Howler was here on Tuesday (19 September) he gave me the book 'How Europe Armed for War' quite a good 1/- worth if you have not read it. The rain has been enough to break our hearts, it has been a great asset to the Boche. The French caught them well in an attack yesterday a deserter gave them away. My love Yours Putty.

It was a fine autumn day, at last, on 22 September. During the night 21/22 September Starfish and Prue Trench were consolidated: 50th Division reported that Prue Trench was now nothing more than a wet ditch. Patrols pushed forward and did not locate any enemy S of the line Le Sars-Eaucourt L'Abbaye-Flers. The weather continued fine and warm on 23 September and there was very little activity at the front; also, very little artillery ammunition was used reflecting that contact was almost broken. Rawlinson wrote that day:

> I rode to III Corps this morning. 23rd Division made some ground E of Martinpuich. Putty tells me that the Boche bolted from Prue Trench as they thought we were getting round their flanks. They evidently left in a hurry for the trench was full of helmets, equipment, ammunition and debris of all sorts.

---

73   Edward George Villiers Stanley 17th Earl of Derby (1865-1948) late Gren Gds SofS for War.
74   Major General John Philip Du Cane (1865-1950) late RA BGGS III Corps 1914 DG Munitions Design 1916.

At 2 pm DDMS recorded:

Asst to 4th Army Chemical Adviser called and showed a new design of respirator which is placed in the mouth at once, and the nose clipped. Breathing then takes place through 2 lateral tubes lined with smoke helmet material. These remain on the neck. Goggles are worn separately. Took the officer with his respirator to Corps Commander, who was impressed with its handiness and wishes to put it forward to the authorities.

Also on 23 September Putty wrote to Ettie Desborough:

My dearest Chief, Mille thanks for your letter of 17 Sep it was a delightful one every line of it brings out your bravery. Well we have had bad weather up till yesterday but the last two days have been fine and once more it looks as if the men can get over the ground, repair the roads that have been obliterated by our combined shell fire [they] present an obstacle which one has not allowed for, it is really a matter of light railways [III Corps were the first to build light railways having proposed them in August 1915] fed by heavy ones which (one) has to look forward to in the future, my lot have got on well the Boche was afraid of being surrounded like he was before when I had gained the two horns he bolted in the night leaving all his equipment behind him but this gradual pushing back is telling on his nerves and he is no longer the man he was, the surroundings make it impossible for the same troops to remain long in the trenches at a period it is really too appalling. The censor pays no attention to rank Hubert Gough[75] was furious because they opened his, personally I don't mind for I never write anything about future movements and a few home truths about the past do no harm. Have not seen Charley L or Reggie this time it was too far for them to ride and I could not spare a motor to send for them. Billy[76] was here today with one of Lambton's as ADC typical Lambton he was too, I thought Billy looking very fit and well. Some of the stories about the 'tanks' are really too funny for words, some of the Boches wanted to surrender but the fellows in the tank could not get out so the Boche climbed on top and rode back with them, one that was burnt inside by petrol catching fire now makes the most perfect observation post for artillery nothing but a direct hit from a big gun could knock it out. I don't believe much in Sarrail's[77] telegrams. Bend D'Or[78] does not seem any too well from the accounts that reach us from Paris, he ought to take a lot of care of himself for some time to come. Have you read a book called 'How Europe Armed for War' some of the statistics are very interesting and show we took things too easily as usual. The morals of the Bavarians are the worst I have come across judging by the picture postcards they all carry with them and send to their relations. My love and blessings to you Yours ever Putty.

75   General Sir Hubert de la Poer Gough (1870-1963) Eton late 16 L GOC Reserve Army.
76   Possibly Major General Hon Sir William Lambton (1863-1936) Eton late Coldm Gds GOC 4th Division.
77   General Maurice-Paul-Emmanuel Sarrail (1856-1929) French Army Commander Allied Forces in Macedonia.
78   Hugh Grosvenor 2nd Duke of Westminster (1879-1953) IY/CY.

Both the weather and the situation at the front were little changed on 24 September. 23rd Division made some progress overnight but an attack, in the thick morning mist, by 12 DLI (68 Bde) against 26th Avenue E of the Bapaume road was repulsed by machine-gun fire. At 11 am HQ III Corps issued Addendum No.3 to OpO No.135: 4th Army attack now to take place on 25 September – divisional objectives given. Addendum No.4 was issued at 2.10 pm: Zero hour for the attack to be 12.35 pm. At 4.15 pm Addendum No.5 was issued 'giving general scheme for employment of cavalry on 25 September, if the infantry attacks are successful'. Correction No.1 was issued at 7 pm, giving alterations to 23rd Division's objectives and allocation of two tanks to them; an hour later, at 8 pm, HQ III Corps sent maps of routes for use of tanks on 25 September to their commander.

Battle of Morval 25-28 September

Le Sars and Eaucourt L'Abbaye

III Corps' part in operations that started on 25 September was minor since the main effort of 4th Army's attack (to be known as the Battle of Morval) was on its right. At Zero hour it began an advance to close with the enemy, now 50th Reserve Division. The only fighting was on the flanks: 1st Division (1 BW 1 Bde) bombed up the Flers Trenches at Zero and gained about 300 yards; at 5.35 pm it reported 'Blocks established in the Flers front line 100 yards beyond objective and in the support line just beyond objective'. On the left 10 NF (68 Bde 23rd Division) supported by the two tanks attacked 26th Avenue. The enemy position was on the reverse slope and held in greater strength than expected, probably to cover the withdrawal to Le Sars. This and one tank breaking down before Zero resulted in the attack failing with heavy loss; 10 NF had 205 casualties.

At 3.25 pm a Wng O (OpO No.136) was issued by HQ III Corps for attacks on 26 and 27 September. HQ III Corps then issued OpO No.137 at 10.20 pm ordering the further attacks on 26 September and 'giving instructions for new trenches to be dug tonight'.

At 7.55 am on 26 September, a very fine and warm day, 1st Division reported that it had progressed another 100 yards down Flers front line and taken 6 prisoners. HQ III Corps issued OpO No.139 at 8 am – contingency for further attack if objectives not secured by morning 27 September. At the same time HQ III Corps issued Addendum No.1 to OpO No.137 giving Zero hour as 12.35 pm 26 September ie that day. However, 23rd Division was continuing to make progress without fighting, reporting that patrols had found much of 26th Avenue now unoccupied. Progress on this flank was only held up by the Can Corps of Reserve Army which had not advanced. At 2.30 pm HQ III Corps issued OpO No.138 ordering the relief of 1st Division by 47th Division on night 28/29 Sep.

That day Putty wrote to Edith Londonderry:

> Dearest Circe, Many thanks for your letter of 21 Sep. Things have gone well the last two days, the French and the XIV Corps did A-1 while the capture of Thiepval is a crowning success, it has bothered us ever since we started fighting on 1 Jul besides costing us thousands of shells and lives, you can't imagine what a relief it is to us besides it quite puts a stop to the Boche trying to send any more troops to Russia. I believe the caves at Combles are wonderful and full of ammunition for trench mortars how they could have amassed

such stores defeats me, their power of production must be truly wonderful no wonder their women regret their absence. I think the captured order was genuine but the shortage is only owing to having to provide more stuff for Bulgaria and Turkey than before. Poor Robin[79] he will feel lonely going to Eton at first but will enjoy it when he is in Pop and the eleven, I only hope he will do more work than I did, don't let him have too good looking a maid as a valet. The 'tanks' did very well indeed today again, with good men in them that do not lose their heads they are A.1. the bullets make the weirdest noise on them. Trust from what you say the Mandrill is all right but he seems to have been paying more attention to the under clothing than the Clothing Dep? Weather has been good if it still holds up all will be well. I think the Boche will announce his new War Loan at a moderate moment. My love to you Yours ever Putty.

The fighting continued on 27 September with more progress made across the front: on the left 23rd Division worked its way up 26th Avenue towards Le Sars; in the centre 50th Division up Crescent Alley towards Eaucourt L'Abbaye; and on the right 1st Division, already in the Flers trenches fought its way up both, NW towards Eaucourt L'Abbaye. Overnight it was 5 Yorks and 5 DLI 150 Bde that achieved most: attacking at 11 pm they had by morning taken much of Crescent Alley.

At 12.5 am Brigadier General Greenly arrived to take temporary command of 47th Division. Later, at 8 am, HQ III Corps issued Addendum No.1 to OpO No.139: Zero hour was to be 2.15 pm that day. This may have been relevant to the rest of 4th Army but on III Corps' front the fighting was continuous. 23rd Division reported at 5.25 pm:

> Enemy evacuated 26th Avenue this morning leaving a considerable amount of equipment, rifles and bombs. A 77 mm gun was discovered. Patrols are pushing down 26th Avenue and endeavouring to gain touch with 50th Division. Party has been sent to reconnoitre Destremont Farm (in front of Le Sars). Much material for dugouts discovered in trenches.

On their left Can Corps had also made further advances and 2nd Canadian Division reported enemy to be withdrawing. In III Corps' centre 50th Division reported at 8.10 pm that a patrol of 5 DLI had worked up a communication trench and entered the Flers line with no enemy seen.

HQ III Corps issued orders at 7.30 pm that the ground gained was to be consolidated and a continuous line dug from the Flers Line to the Bapaume Road, and communication trenches with the present front to be dug as soon as possible. Then at 10.20 pm the GS log recorded: 'Orders issued to 1st Division to the following effect: Corps Commander wishes you to make a point of strengthening your position in the captured line'. It was becoming even more difficult than usual to maintain control over the advance and ensure that the ground won was not then lost in an enemy counter-attack. Rawlinson wrote that day: 'III Corps getting on well'.

---

79   Edward Charles Stewart Robert 'Robin' Vane-Tempest-Stewart (1902-1955) later 8th Marquess of Londonderry.

HQ 4th Army (MGGS) held a conference at Heilly at 11.30 am attended by BGGS III Corps. The key extracts from the record include:

> III Corps. The next objective will be Eaucourt L'Abbaye ... The next operation, which will take place on 4 or 5 October, will be to get the Butte de Warlencourt and Le Sars village, and join up with the Reserve Army ... III Corps will then round off from Butte de Warlencourt through Little Wood and out towards Pys.

Later:

> III Corps. BGGS said: he would prefer to attack on 1 October instead of 30 September for reasons of command (MGGS said he hoped that this might be arranged, and agreed with views set forth). The first attack would be undertaken by 47th, 50th and 23rd Divisions. After that it is hoped that the 50th Division might be squeezed out of the line, which will be held by 47th and 23rd Divisions only. The attack on 4 or 5 October would thus be undertaken by 23rd and 47th Divisions. If, however, later on it was found that 23rd Division was not in a fit state to undertake the whole of the objectives proposed to allocate to them it would be necessary to put 15th Division in, but III Corps Commander did not want to do so.

The enemy on III Corps front was not only falling back to the Eaucourt L'Abbaye line but 50th Reserve Division was also being relieved by 6th Bavarian Division from Flanders as it did so. III Corps was carrying out its own relief with 47th Division replacing 1st Division on the right. Major Fair (CO 19 London 141 Bde) wrote:

> We received a draft of 250 other ranks on 24 September and on 27 September we were back at Bazentin le Grand having had only two days to absorb the new men, after losing the commanding officer and all four company commanders at High Wood on 15 September. Consequently it was largely an untried battalion under officers they hardly knew which was ordered to make a bombing attack up the two parallel Flers lines on 29 September.

28 September was a fine day and one of consolidation. At 10 am 4th Army 299/41G was received: 'Alterations to all corps boundaries consequent on French taking over line to a point between Morval and Lesboeufs. III Corps front runs from 100 yards E of the point where Flers Line crosses Bazentin le Petit-Le Barque road to W side of Destremont Farm, frontage due N. Objectives for further attacks: (a) 1 Oct: Destremont Farm and a line E to 200 yards E of Eaucourt L'Abbaye (b) 5 Oct: Butte de Warlencourt and a line E and W of it (c) 10 Oct: A line due E of Pys parallel to present corps front and one mile E of village'. At 10.45 pm HQ III Corps issued a Wng O (GO417/1) giving preliminary details of OpO No.140: 'Zero hour will be 3.15 pm 1 Oct. Two tanks allocated to 23rd Division to assist in taking Le Sars'. 4th Army orders suggested there was to be a pause but this was not the case: 23rd Division was to try and take Destremont Farm that night.

23rd Division reported at 12.5 am 29 September that the first attempt by 70 Bde to take Destremont Farm had failed but the next attack succeeded, and at 7.41 am the GS log recorded: '70 Bde (8 Y&L) have captured Destremont Farm. One machine-gun taken. Casualties slight'.

50th Division dug assembly and communication trenches overnight but two attempts to enter the Flers Line during the night failed owing to heavy rifle and machine-gun fire. On the right 47th Division's relief of 1st Division was complete by 10 am but their attempts to bomb down Flers front and support trenches during the day failed.

At 9 am DDMS recorded: 'Corps Commander has decided that 1 MDS go to Bécourt Chateau and a Corps Rest Station be formed at Bécourt'. Two other instructions of note were issued during the day. At 11.10 am the GS log noted: 'All divisions and 34 Sqn RFC informed that from 1 Oct inclusive yellow flares will be used by infantry; 1000 yellow flares issued to each division'. There was obvious confusion with the red flares but this change in the middle of the battle would have been difficult. Also 23rd Division had been told that it would have the support of two tanks but this was changed. At 1.30 pm OC Tanks reported that tanks would only be used against Eaucourt L'Abbaye and not against Le Sars and later, at 8.5 pm: 'Two tanks are proceeding to Cough Drop tonight and will remain there until morning'.

Also on 29 September Putty responded to 4th Army's questionnaire on the use of tanks two weeks earlier:

> The routes followed by the tanks on 15 Sep are shown on the attached map. Route diagrams as per copies attached were issued to each driver together with a set of aerial photographs with the route marked on them, and where possible a panorama aerial photograph showing the ground from above. The skippers state that these diagrams proved absolutely invaluable and that they worked on them entirely. There is no doubt that all the tanks which were not ditched early in the fight proved very effective against hostile troops, enfilading trenches causing many casualties and shooting down enemy when retiring.

This is further evidence that HQ III Corps planned the use of these first tanks with great care to ensure close support to the infantry and to coordinate their movement within the artillery barrage.

The weather became unsettled on the last day of the month with the wind NNE; however, the fighting continued without let-up. On the left 23rd Division patrols were in touch with Can Corps at Destremont Farm but had found the Le Sars line strongly held. 50th Division, by contrast, reported at 8.30 am: 'Flers Line can easily be captured if barrage is closely followed up. Enemy has local reserves in Le Sars'.

At 9.45 am HQ III Corps ordered a bombardment of the Flers Line by heavy artillery fire from 1 pm to 4 pm with the infantry being withdrawn during it; then at 4 pm 47th Division was to bomb up the Flers front line with the NZ Division operating in Flers support on their right. By 6 pm 19 London 141 Bde had reached its objective and was in contact with 20 London on its left and the NZ Division. In summary, most of III Corps was closing up to the Flers Line and on the right 47th Division was working up it. All were poised for the next step.

III Corps casualties in September 1916 were: 179 officers and 2,362 other ranks killed, 577 officers and 11,314 other ranks wounded, 37 officers and 3,118 other ranks missing = 17,587 (about 15%).

Battle of Le Transloy 1-18 October

October started very fine and clear: during the night of 30 September/1 October jumping-off trenches had been constructed. Then, at 3.15 pm, III Corps attacked with 47th Division on the right, 50th Division in the centre and 23rd Division on the left.

Major Chammier (OC 3 Sqn RFC)'s report, requested by Putty, provides a very clear view of events from the air:

> At 3.15 pm the steady bombardment changed into a most magnificent barrage. The timing of this was extremely good. Guns opened simultaneously and the effect was that of many machine-guns opening fire on the same order. As seen from the air the barrage appeared to be a most perfect wall of fire in which it was inconceivable that anything could live. The first troops to extend from the forming up places appeared to be the 50th Division who were seen to spread out from the sap heads and forming up trenches and advance close up under the barrage, apparently some 50 yards away from it. They appeared to capture their objective very rapidly and with practically no losses while crossing the open. The 23rd Division I did not see much of owing to their being at the moment of Zero at the tail end of the machine. The 47th Division took more looking for than the 50th, and it was my impression at the time that they were having some difficulty in getting into formation for attack from their forming up places, with the result that they appeared to be very late and to be some distance behind the barrage when it lifted off the German front line at Eaucourt L'Abbaye and immediately to the W of it. It was plain that here there was a good chance of failure and this actually came about, for the men had hardly advanced a couple of hundred yards apparently, when they were seen to fall and take cover among shell holes, being presumably held up by machine-gun and rifle fire. It was not possible to verify this owing to the extraordinary noise of the bursting shells of our barrage. The tanks were obviously too far behind, owing to lack of covered approaches, to take part in the original attack, but they were soon seen advancing on either side of the Eaucourt L'Abbaye-Flers Line, continuously in action and doing splendid work. They did not seem to be a target of much enemy shell fire. The enemy barrage appeared to open late, quite 5 minutes after the commencement of our own barrage, and when it came it bore no resemblance to the wall of fire which we were putting up. I should have described it as a heavy shelling of an area some 3 to 400 yards in depth from our original jumping off places. Some large shells were falling in Destremont Farm but these were again too late to catch the first line of the attack, although they must have caused some losses to the supports. 30 minutes after Zero the first English patrols were seen entering Le Sars. They appeared to be meeting with little or no opposition.

47th Division attacked with 141 Bde: on its right, 19 London was initially checked by machine-gun fire 50 yards from the German trenches, but once the two tanks arrived took its objective in Flers Support and linked up with the NZ Division on the Le Barque Road. 20 London, in the centre, had Eaucourt L'Abbaye as its objective; again with the help of the two tanks it crossed the Flers trenches, pushed through Eaucourt L'Abbaye, and linked up with 19 London. 17 London, the left bn, was less fortunate; it was checked by uncut wire and machine-guns, and both the tanks had become stuck in the Flers lines, so were unable to assist. These two tanks now isolated had to be set on fire and abandoned when 2/17 Bavarian Regt counter-attacked SE down the trench line.

In the centre of the corps front 151 Bde 50th Division attacked with 6 DLI on its right and 5 NF (attached from 149 Bde) on its left. 6 DLI, its flank exposed by the failure of 47th Division's left, lost heavily from the fire of German machine-guns, and could do no more than gain a precarious footing in Flers Trench. Lieutenant Colonel Bradford, whose 9 DLI was in support, came forward and a renewed assault by both bns secured Flers Trench by about 9.30 pm (for his gallantry that day Bradford was awarded the VC). In the centre and on the left 151 Bde captured the Flers lines without too much trouble, the Germans being allowed no time to organise an effective resistance.

23rd Division, on the left of III Corps, attacked with 70 Bde. On the right 11 Sher For took Flers Trench and most of Flers Support, where they linked up with 151 Bde 50th Division. However, there was stubborn resistance to be overcome beyond the Bapaume road before the Germans could be bombed back up Flers Trench by 8 KOYLI, which joined hands with the Canadians. 9 Y&L provided much needed reinforcement, but patrols which tried to enter Le Sars were checked by fire from the houses.

Overall it was a very successful operation with most of the Flers trenches taken. However, there was still much fighting to be done before Le Sars was captured, and the Flers lines and Eaucourt L'Abbaye fully secured. This was made more difficult by the change in weather that evening bringing rain and mist, and it continued to rain with little break for the next two days.

2 October was a day of consolidation. Although German accounts show that Eaucourt L'Abbaye was regarded as lost on the afternoon of 1 October, there was no such certainty at HQ III Corps where the situation was considered at best obscure. 47th Division had sent forward 23 London (attached from 142 Bde) during the night to renew the attack over the same ground where 17 London had failed the previous day. At 6.45 am 2 October this bn attacked: tired and very weak in numbers it had little chance of success and was withdrawn after sustaining 170 casualties. Perhaps the best development for this division during the day was the arrival of Major General Gorringe to take over command from Greenly (temporarily in command since the removal of Barter); he came direct from Mesopotamia and was to transform the division.

50th Division completed its task before dawn on 2 October: Lieutenant Colonel Bradford, with 6 and 9 DLI, had driven the Germans from Flers Support. He then barricaded his right flank, where 47th Division had failed to get forward, against the persistent attacks of the enemy, and kept them back by bombing and Stokes mortar fire. 3/17 Bavarian Reserve Regt had rallied along the Eaucourt L'Abbaye-Le Sars road, where it was reinforced by 3/16 Bavarian Reserve Regt; meanwhile, detachments of 362 Regt 4th Ersatz Division had taken over the defence of the village.

During the day Putty attended Rawlinson's conference at Heilly with his BGGS (Romer). The conference had been called in order to discuss the objectives that corps commanders considered they would be able to reach in the attack arranged to take place on 5 October. Rawlinson noted: 'The most important objectives being those of III Corps, who would take for their right division the Butte de Warlencourt and the Chalk Pit (M.15) for their left' and 'As regards divisions in the line, III Corps at the present moment had 47th, 50th and 23rd Divisions in the line, but the GOC (Putty) was most anxious to get both 50th and 47th out and he had 1st and 15th behind'. This was partly because these two divisions were tired, but III Corps' front had narrowed and only two divisions were needed.

At 5.30 pm HQ III Corps issued a WngO (G417/2) giving preliminary instructions for the attack to take place on 5 October:

> 47th Division to clear up situation around Eaucourt L'Abbaye and Flers Line so that they can prepare jumping off trenches for the attack against Butte de Warlencourt. 23rd Division will take over front held by 50th Division.

At 7 pm HQ III Corps issued OpO No.142 giving detailed orders for 23rd Division taking over 50th Division's front, to be completed by 2 pm 3 October.

It continued to rain very heavily all night 2/3 October and the ground became a quagmire. At 7 am 4th Army 299/42(G) was received: Orders for attack on Brown Line – 'Attack is to take place on 5 Oct, in conjunction with 1 Can Corps (on left) and XV Corps (on right), and 6th French Army on right of 4th Army'.

During the night 50th Division (151 Bde) repulsed enemy counter-attacks with artillery and trench mortar fire. However, the relief proceeded and GOC 23rd Division took over his extended line at 2.5 pm 3 October. Meanwhile 47th Division (8 London) had by the evening of 3 October secured Eaucourt L'Abbaye and were in contact with 20 London on their right and 68 Bde (23rd Division) on their left. 50th Division were withdrawn having had 4,072 casualties since 10 September. At 8.30 pm HQ III Corps issued OpO No.143 giving details of objectives and artillery fire for the attack (by 47th and 23rd Divisions) to take place on 5 October. One (female) tank was allocated to 23rd Division: the pressure from above to press forward was continuous and relentless.

Putty sent his monthly report to the King on 3 October:

> My dear Wigram, Attached is the III Corps diary for the month of September, the month has been full of interest and the corps has made good progress, the way the British soldier sticks it out is truly wonderful, it is a matter of endurance as he knows, luckily he fancies himself in that direction and from all appearance is correct. It is interesting to note the number of divisions of the Boche opposite the 4th Army since 1st July, there have been elements of 38 divisions from which I have taken prisoners from no less than 28. There is no doubt but that the present pressure has told heavily on the Boche, his resistance gets weaker on each occasion, the counter-attack has less sting in it, the best sign is the continual call of SOS signals that he keeps sending up, one cannot help thinking that they have not too much ammunition for their guns at the present moment or we should get more in retaliation than we do, they may be saving it up until things quiet down a little for the winter on the Eastern side but otherwise I can't help thinking the task is beyond them to keep up a supply on so many fronts. We have had a good deal of rain lately which takes the few remaining hairs off my head when I consider the making of roads and railways in front of me, there is no doubt but all advances in future will have to be made with the assistance of light railways as roads disappear under shell fire. Yours sincerely, WP Pulteney.

1st Division (less its artillery) left III Corps for X Corps on 3 October: this was a short notice and temporary deployment but reduced Putty's options for the rotation of his divisions.

The day cannot be concluded without mention of 2nd Lieutenant Kelly 10 DOW 69 Bde 23rd Division. Comd 69 Bde was determined to improve his position and ordered 10 DOW to capture a portion of the Flers line still held by the enemy. Kelly's citation for the VC stated:

> For most conspicuous bravery in attack. He twice rallied his company under the heaviest fire, and finally led the only three available men into the enemy trench, and there remained bombing until two of them had become casualties and enemy reinforcements had arrived. He then carried his company sergeant major, who had been wounded, back to our trenches, a distance of seventy yards, and subsequently three other soldiers.

Putty presented him with the ribbon of the VC on 29 November.

There were heavy showers on the morning of 4 October, probably the main reason for the postponement of the attack on the Brown Line from 5 to 7 October. At 9 am DDMS recorded: 'Spoke Corps Commander about increase in dysentery. He recommends men washing their seats with antiseptic after using latrine'. HQ III Corps issued orders to 23rd and 47th Divisions at 9.25 am to establish a line of posts in the Flers Support Line and at 10 am 47th Division was ordered to take over, maintain and extend the tramway constructed by 50th Division from Bethell Sap towards Eaucourt L'Abbaye. Despite the weather, consolidation had to continue.

Putty also wrote to Ettie Desborough that day:

> Dearest Chief, Thank you dear person for your letter of 29 Sep. Yes the pictures of the tanks are perfect. Was so afraid of it getting lost I sent your book home for safety. It is not often I get time to read now that the evenings are longer I daresay I shall read more I used to at Bailleul but while this Somme battle lasts it is a chance. The rain has been bad, nothing can describe the roads either made or unmade, it is a nuisance as we ought to be getting on for winter will soon be on us. Yes if I can I will come to shoot the pheasant in January there shall be no interference so hold you to your bargain. The fighting since 1 October round Eaucourt L'Abbaye has been pretty stiff but it is all ours now or at least what was left of it which is mighty little, at the junction of two valleys it has been a Boche artillery position for a long time besides a store in its caves etc. We found a very interesting German document yesterday giving a description of the fight in High Wood early in September when I got a footing and then lost it again after heavy fighting and no wonder as had two whole divisions counter-attacking me and had only attacked with a brigade, they always claimed to have killed an enormous number especially the artillery, there is no doubt they did too. Have you heard about the young lady who wished for employment in the munitions works, when asked by the foreman what she could so she replied I can shell a 1000 peas in an hour, all he said was 'Do you Reverse?'! I wonder if you read the enclosed cutting in the Times, it is a remarkable discovery, the last sentence is essentially narrow minded as it is typical of the medical profession. Another Zepp is splendid work it is obvious that the nerves of these men are already affected by the indiscriminate way they are dropping their bombs, no wonder either, Had a long letter from Joe Maude[80] in Mesopotamia but as it is dated 8 August and only reached me on 2 October the news is stale, what with him

---

80   GSO1 HQ III Corps 1914 now GOC III Indian Corps.

writing and Gorringe[81] being under me now I have been able to piece the whole tale pretty well together, it is a sorry page in the history of the war but what annoys me is that the system of transport is not perfected in any way or have they devolved a system of seasoning the troops they send there by keeping them in India or Aden, Hardinge and the Indian authorities want a really good kicking over the whole affair. The Canadians are now called the Bing Boys because Julian Byng commands them but expect you have already heard the joke. Bulgaria looks as if she was weakening what do they tell you? All my love Yours Putty.

It was cloudy but there was no rain on 5 October, a relatively quiet day except that 6 London 140 Bde 47th Division captured the old mill 500 yards NW of Eaucourt L'Abbaye; the enemy counter-attacked at 6.30 pm but was completely repulsed. More rain fell on 6 October: during the day Addendum No.1 to OpO No.143 was issued (1.40 pm) giving Zero hour for the attack next day as 1.45 pm; at 6 pm a WngO was issued for the probable relief of 23rd Division by 15th Division on 8/9 October; and at 7 pm 4th Army told III Corps that 9th Division less artillery would be posted to it from 12 Midnight that night (6/7 October).

The main German defence now opposite III Corps was the Gird Line running from Guedecourt to Warlencourt, and including the Butte de Warlencourt an ancient mound of excavated chalk about 70 feet high, cunningly tunnelled by the enemy, and used as an observation post from which machine-gun and artillery fire from positions in depth was directed with devastating effect on the western slopes.

47th Division attacked with 140 Bde: first it had to capture a German trench 'Snag Trench' dug across the eastern slope of the depression leading N to Warlencourt; the centre of this objective lay 500 yards ahead, half-way between the British front line and the Butte. 8 London was checked by terrific machine-gun fire, and 7 and 15 London which were to pass through and continue the advance suffered a similar fate. All that could be done was to establish a few posts near the Le Barque road in touch with 41st Division (XV Corps). In a letter dated 1 November 1916 Lieutenant Colonel Warrender Gren Gds CO 15 London wrote to Major General Gerald Cuthbert late SG Comd 39th Division and previously Comd 140 Bde:

> After that we came out for a week and got reinforcements, and then came back to take part in the operations of 7 Oct. 140 Bde relieved 141 who had taken Eaucourt L'Abbaye, and we were to take the Warlencourt Line some 1,200 yards in front of Eaucourt L'Abbaye. However things didn't go well from the start. The aircraft kept on discovering new trenches between us and the Warlencourt Line, and the plan of attack had to be altered several times. Eventually the 7th, 8th and 15th attacked and the 6th were in reserve. None of us got anywhere near our objectives for a small German trench with half a dozen machine-guns in it, and which had never been touched by our bombardment, stopped our advance and simply mowed the men down. The casualties were again very heavy. My right company were partially protected by the slope of the ground and managed to get on about 300 yards and dig themselves in. That the division failed (as did the one on our right) was in no way its own fault; no troops could have advanced more gallantly than they did. I think the failure was due to the preparation being too hurried and to bad artillery observation.

81   GOC III Indian Corps before Maude now GOC 47th Division.

In the same letter he wrote:

> I dined with Putty several times whilst I was down there (on the Somme). No doubt he has had a very arduous time since the offensive began, but I was rather shocked to notice how aged he is. In fact he seemed rather to have gone to seed altogether.

He also wrote about the removal of Barter:

> At the division there are great changes; after 16 Sep operations CB [Barter] got the sack. The authorities said that he had remained too far behind and was out of touch with his brigadiers; also that his orders were bad, and that the div had had too many casualties. There is no doubt that they were wanting to get rid of him, but at the same time it was rather rough on him to sack him just when the div had done so well. Everyone loathed him and was glad when he went, but there was a feeling that he was hardly treated. It was a bad day for old CB and for the whole div when Burnett Hitchcock[82] left us. Weatherby[83] who was very nice and had a sweet smile, was quite incompetent and could not stand up to the old man, and so became a real nuisance to the brigadiers and to the COs as well; Weatherby has now been evacuated, sick, with dysentery.

It was 23rd Division which achieved the striking success of the day. The official history recorded:

> At Zero hour 68 Bde, on the right, sent forward 12 DLI, supported by a tank. It did excellent service in assisting to clear the Germans from the Tangle but, after turning left at the sunken Eaucourt L'Abbaye-Le Sars road beyond, it was hit by a shell and destroyed. 12 DLI found the road enfiladed by machine-gun fire from Le Sars, and was held up for a time. Meanwhile 9 GH (69 Bde) had advanced into the SW part of Le Sars towards its objective, the cross-roads in the village. Between these two battalions, 13 DLI (68 Bde), whose mission it was, in the second stage of the advance, to push through and complete the capture of Le Sars, was thrust into the fight about 2.30 pm and joined up with 9 GH at the cross-roads. After stubborn fighting the German resistance collapsed and the village was cleared. 12 DLI had consolidated the sunken road in front of the Tangle and established forward posts to protect the right flank of the division. 13 DLI and 9 GH now put out posts round Le Sars, and Lieutenant Colonel Lindsey CO 13 DLI asked for two fresh companies and a tank in order to attack the Butte from the W; these reinforcements were not available. Twenty minutes after Zero hour 11 W Yorks (69 Bde) had made a frontal assault against Flers Support beyond Le Sars, only to be checked by the enemy's barrage and by machine-gun and rifle fire from the exposed left flank. A renewed attack, assisted by bombers who advanced up the trench from Le Sars, was, however, successful, the fleeing Germans coming under effective fire from the village and from the divisional artillery. That

82   Lieutenant Colonel Burnett Hitchcock Notts and Derby GSO1 47th Division until 15 June 1916.
83   Lieutenant Colonel Weatherby Ox & Bucks.

night 69 Bde was in occupation of the two Flers trenches to a point some three hundred yards inside the army boundary.

At 7 pm HQ III Corps issued OpO No.144 ordering 15th Division to relieve 23rd Division in the left sector of the corps front on 8/9 October. 9th Division less its artillery joined III Corps on 7 October, as did 52 Bty and C Bty RHA both equipped with AA guns, further evidence of the increasing air threat.

It was cloudy with yet more rain on 8 October. At 4.50 am 23rd Division renewed its attack, the same time as Can Corps Reserve Army on its left attacked. By 9.45 am its left bde (70 Bde and mainly 8 Y&L) had captured the Flers lines up to the corps boundary, and during the afternoon a post was established 750 yards NW of Le Sars commanding the quarry/chalk pit on the Pys road. 47th Division held on to its line of posts but was unable to make further progress. At 3.30 pm HQ III Corps issued OpO No.145: 9th Division was to relieve 47th Division in the right sector of the corps front 8-10 Oct. Both forward divisions were exhausted and to change over both at the same time involved considerable operational and administrative risk, although the enemy was in no position to take advantage of this.

In the two days 7/8 October 23rd Division captured 11 officers, 517 other ranks and 8 machine-guns at a cost of 627 casualties. Nearly all the prisoners were from 360, 361 and 662 Regts 4th Ersatz Division. Except for this success, no significant gains were made by 4th Army. The main problem had been the weather with the mud making it impossible for the infantry to maintain a steady advance and the mist having a disastrous effect on the artillery support. Also the Germans had been greatly reinforced with new divisions and increased artillery; this may go some way to explain the failure of 47th Division but it also makes 23rd Division's achievement all the greater.

The relief of 23rd Division by 15th Division was completed by 9 am 9 October, at last a fine day. This extract from 15th Division's history provides an overview for the rest of their month:

> With the exception of the usual patrol activities, no actual fighting took place during the tour [until 3 November]. Conditions could not have been worse, and towards the end of October frost added to the difficulties; in spite of all this an enormous amount of work was accomplished by the sappers and pioneers. At first work was concentrated in assisting the infantry to construct a series of strong posts in front, and later in connecting these up to form a new front line north of Le Sars. Directly the front line was continuous, strong posts were pushed out in front, and a new front line, about 200 yards ahead, formed by joining them – a jumping off trench. The pioneers also dug a cable trench, 6 feet deep, from Martinpuich to the front line, 400 yards in length. Owing to the shell-riven state of the ground, few communication trenches, and weather, it was difficult for reliefs and carrying parties to find their way to and from the front line. Two overland routes were therefore laid out. These were bounded by pickets painted white at the top, fenced with wire, and trench-boards laid down over the worst places. The tramway was put in good working order from Peake Wood to Martinpuich: sidings were put in, and a regular service run. The Contalmaison-Martinpuich road was cleared, drained and repaired. Four sites for battalion camps were prepared at Contalmaison, and about eight nissen huts erected up to the time the division left the line – as well as drying sheds, divisional baths, wells, and covered horse standings.

Meanwhile 47th Division was relieved by 9th Division: since 20 August its casualties had been 296 officers and 7,475 other ranks, a total of 7,771. Its attack on 7 October had been unsuccessful but it had managed to establish posts in front of its line and 9th Division would join them up and form them into a new front line and a starting point for fresh operations, with 26 Bde on its right and 1 SA Bde on the left. The division's history gives a good account of what it found:

> The whole drainage system of the country had been smashed by months of shelling and the roads, poor at their best, seemed to have no bottom. The ruins of whole villages were thrown into them but even that never appeared to make them any firmer: on the front taken over by us the principal feature was the Butte de Warlencourt, a mound of chalk about 50 feet high, which stood at the far end of the spur that ran from the main ridge through Flers. NE of this the ground sloped into a depression, which led into the valley of the Ancre, and beyond it lay a spur running from the road towards Morval, on which the enemy had his fourth position. Behind the British front line lay the vast waste of wilderness created by three months of savage warfare. Its general colour was a dull uniform grey, which changed to a dingy yellow when the sun shone. The whole area was covered with the debris of battle and camps, but worst of all, from Mametz Wood to the front line were scattered fragments of corpses and a heavy fetid odour pervaded the atmosphere.

The III Corps AQ log recorded that the corps artillery fired 76,160 rounds that day, mainly to cover the reliefs. 23rd Division concentrated at Albert and was then transferred to X Corps in 2nd Army on 11 October. In his message to GOC 23rd Division (Babington) Putty said: 'Please convey to the troops of your division my congratulations on their gallant and successful attack on Le Sars'. There was no let up: at 4.30 pm 9 October HQ III Corps issued OpO No.146 – Preliminary Instructions for the attack on the Butte de Warlencourt on 12 October.

On 10 October, another fine day, Putty made a farewell inspection of 47th Division and on 14 October they entrained at Albert for a journey northwards. At 10.30 pm HQ III Corps ordered both front line divisions, 34 Sqn RFC and the HA to: 'Make special arrangements to note where the enemy places his barrages during the Chinese attacks on 11 Oct, and to report to corps HQ immediately'.

The weather continued fine on 11 October. At 3.15 pm the GS log recorded:

> The (one) Chinese attack did, however, take place and reports on the enemy barrage and retaliation produced by it were furnished by officers of corps HA and of both divisions. A report was also furnished by an officer of HQ III Corps GS who flew over the lines during the bombardment. The information obtained from these reports was furnished to both front line divisions.

Later, at 5 pm, Addendum No.3 to OpO No.146 was issued giving Zero time for the attack on 12 October as 2.5 pm. The five batteries of French Artillery attached to III Corps left and 9th Divisional Artillery joined it on 11 October. Finally that day, DDMS noted: 'Visited CRS. Took some slippers presented by the Corps Commander'.

When III Corps attacked at 2.5 pm 12 October, it was its third corps attack in twelve days, although on this occasion it was with only two divisions and 15th Division's role was in the main a supporting one. Both Scottish divisions had taken over in the previous three days and had had little time to prepare. GOC 9th Division (Furse) apparently protested strongly to Putty and to Rawlinson that the operation was being conducted in too much of a rush: he suggested that the attack be postponed for 24 or 48 hours, in order that the artillery would have no doubt whatever as to the position of his infantry and that of the enemy. There is no III Corps record of such a protest; moreover Putty was determined to maintain the momentum that had now been built up and not allow the enemy any time to reorganise and prepare further positions. The Butte had to be taken as a preliminary to the Reserve Army's attack on the Ancre, and no-one wanted to spend the winter in their present positions. Furse was proved right and the attack failed because the barrage though heavy was inaccurate; it did not demolish the trenches and neutralise the machine-guns of 6th Bavarian Reserve Division.

9th Division had first to capture Snag Trench, then the Butte de Warlincourt and the Warlincourt line. They attacked with 26 Bde (7 Seaforth and 10 A&SH) and 1 SA Bde (2 and 4 Regts) but were checked half-way to Snag Trench where the survivors entrenched themselves. 15th Division provided fire support and 4 Special Coy RE released smoke to blanket Little Wood and the Butte, and they made considerable progress on their right without having to fight for it.

The rain had held off on 12 October although it was a dull day, and it was much the same on 13 October. By 5.28 am 9th Division was able to confirm that none of its troops was in the first objective: the best that had been achieved was a line about 50 yards in front of the original line and this at considerable cost. During the day both divisions were shelled intermittently both on the front line and in the rear. At 3 pm Rawlinson held another of his conferences at Heilly chateau; Putty attended with Romer (BGGS) and Tancred (BGRA). The failure of the previous day was discussed and again the weather and its effect on artillery observation considered the primary cause. It was just not possible in the appalling terrain to locate the enemy positions and adjust the artillery with any certainty without aerial observation, and the dull days had greatly restricted its effectiveness. The enemy's machine-guns in depth were a special cause for concern.

In the record of the 4th Army conference is: 'Operations of 12 Oct. 1. III Corps. The line is practically the same as it was before the attack. Reasons for failure: GOC 9th Division states the preliminary bombardment was not sufficient; it did not knock out the intermediate line (1st objective of the division). In addition the troops were met by heavy machine-gun fire from the front and flanks. Three quarters of the casualties were caused by bullets'. Since GOC 9th Division was not at the conference, this must have been reported by Putty. Rawlinson proposed to attack again on 18 October (Zero hour 3.40 am two hours before sunrise), with certain positions to be taken before the general attack – one of these being Snag Trench to be taken by III Corps.

It was quiet overnight and for much of 14 October; the morning was again dull but it became fine and sunny later. At 4 pm 4th Army placed two tanks at the disposal of III Corps; they were still being used in very small numbers which greatly limited their effectiveness. HQ III Corps OpO No.147 was issued at 5.15 pm ordering 9th Division to attack trenches in M.17.c. and d. on 18 October (in conjunction with 30th Division XV Corps on its right). During the night both bdes 9th Division worked their way slowly forward. 15 October was again quiet although there was an increase in enemy aerial activity with 14 kite balloons up behind the enemy's lines and four German planes flew over Le Sars and Martinpuich, with one firing into 15th Division's trenches. 66 HAG joined III Corps that day.

16 and 17 October were both remarkably quiet. The days were fine and cold with a further increase in enemy aerial activity: 5 enemy aeroplanes machine-gunned the trenches of 15th Division at 5.45 pm 16 October. The railhead at Bazentin was opened on 17 October but CE (Schreiber) noted: 'Went with Corps Commander to Bécourt and Bazentin by train – which could not reach the latter place'.

At 3.40 am 18 October III Corps again attacked Snag Trench: smoke and lachrymatory bombs were discharged from the front of 15th Division to keep down the aimed fire from the Butte and Warlencourt Line. In pouring rain across a sea of mud 9th Division attacked with 5 Camerons (26 Bde) on the right and 1 Regt (1 SA Bde) on the left. Progress was desperately slow but by the end of the day, after very heavy fighting, they had secured most of Snag Trench and were in contact with 2 Wilts 30th Division on the right. Twice Putty intervened personally (6.15 am and 7.30 am) to ask XV Corps to assist 9th Division by providing fire support on the Gird and Gird Support Trenches.

Later, at 9.50 am, the GS log recorded that 4th Army was told: 'III Corps had only received 280 tons of road metal on 17 October with a further 300 tons expected today (18 October). This was against a daily requirement of 1,000 tons'. That it was recorded in the GS log indicated that this was a now a major concern and that Putty had become involved. Unless the roads were maintained no further progress could be made. Integrating the delivery of more than 300 lorry loads of road metal daily with all the other logistic requirements was difficult enough but if the roads were allowed to deteriorate the problems would become very much worse.

At 2 pm DDMS wrote:

> Spoke G (BGGS) and Corps Commander about keeping 2 MDS at Bottom Wood, where they are at end of Contalmaison tram line. They agreed this was best site in view of possible further advance.

An hour later Putty was at Rawlinson's 4th Army conference at Heilly with his BGGS and BGRA: the discussion this time was not about past problems but about the next attack by 4th Army coordinated with Reserve Army's (on its left) attack on the Quadrilateral on 23 October.

It was quiet overnight 18/19 October and then on 19 October it again rained heavily. 1 SA Bde had established a block in the Tail, in effect an enemy communication trench running from the Butte to Snag Trench. At dawn on that day German bombers, supported by flammenwerfer, moved forward up the Tail, driving the South Africans back on 8 BW (26 Bde) which had relieved 5 Camerons during the night. At the same time another counter-attack against the right of 8 BW was repulsed. These counter-attacks were made by a storm detachment of 104 Regt 40th German Division. By the evening 9th Division had managed to stabilise the situation and 27 Bde was sent forward to relieve the exhausted 26 and 1 SA Bdes. An extract from the divisional history says it all:

> One Lewis gunner of 6 KOSB in 27 Bde going forward was so firmly embedded beyond the waist in mud that when he was finally extricated with ropes both his ankles were broken. Many highlanders coming back discarded their kilts as being too heavy, but indeed so glutinous was the abundant mud that it was difficult to tell whether a man wore a kilt or not.

At 11 am HQ III Corps issued OpO No.148:

> In accordance with 4th Army 299/51(G) of 18 Oct, III Corps is to take part in an attack by 4th and Reserve Armies on 23 Oct (later amended to 24 October and then postponed to 25 October). 9th and 15th Divisions are to attack both trenches of Warlencourt Line, including the Butte. Divisional boundaries and objectives shown on map. 9th Division to capture remainder of Snag and Tail as soon as possible. 15th Division to join up to left of 9th Division by a continuous trench. Two tanks allocated to 9th Division.

Later Putty managed to write to Ettie Desborough:

> My dearest Chief, Many thanks for your letter of 16 Oct which I got this morning also for returning the cutting. The weather once more is heartrending, we wanted another week of fine to allow us to get well on with the roads and railways, the latter have been progressing well, I went to open a new station on Tuesday [17 October] but we could not get there as the cutting had been made on the top of an undiscovered Boche 'dug out' and although the light engines had gone over all right the heavy one that morning had done it in, it just shows how the shelling had quite obliterated the entrance because a month ago a dug out of that description was worth anything in that neighbourhood and we never knew of its existence. I had a hard fight yesterday [18 October] only managed to get ¾ of my objective but lost ¼ of it again in the mist this morning but have got it all back again this afternoon and the missing ¼ of yesterday as well so am well contented but the men are fighting up to their knees in mud. Willie did extraordinary well at Langwell, have never been there but believe most of the stalking is on the flat isn't it? I never saw anything of Sir John French when he was out here, it was an extraordinary thing of Lloyd George to send him out to study 'barrages' unless the best artillery experts had accompanied him, the whole thing is volume of fire and it all depends whether you can afford to wear out your guns or not, the French can get 600 rounds out of theirs we can get 200 but then they burst two to everyone that we do but theirs is the best gun of the war and the Boche 5.9 the best howitzer. You seem to have seen a lot of people on leave there is no chance of my being over until January at the earliest, personally I hope we fight all the winter so as to keep the pressure up here and take it off the East, I don't see how we can slack down if we want to end the war am quite absolutely certain we shall finish it off much sooner by keeping the fight up, it does seem so funny one never hears the name Verdun mentioned he has taken them off to Roumania and given up the offensive there. The Boche prisoners are doing good work on the roads there is no doubt but that they surrender more easily to the French than to us, there are several reasons advanced 1. That they put the best men against us 2. That the Boche has spread about the rumour that we kill all our prisoners 3. The French have made the most admirable comfortable camps for their prisoners which probably depicts a happier life in letters home. One of the Australians going over the other day on the boat was bucking about what they had done on the Somme but he ended up but we all take our hats off to the British Tommy and I

think he was right. Gathorne-Hardy[84] looks too dreadful without his moustache I tell him he looks like a clergyman who has gone wrong in his parish and has been obliged to enlist. Much love Yours ever Putty.

On 20 October, another fine and cold day, 15th Division prepared to support Reserve Army's attack the following day. Zero hour for this was 12.6 pm. The GS log recorded at 7.30 pm 20 October: 'Corps Commander orders 15th Division to bring indirect machine-gun fire to bear on Below and Gallwitz trenches from the Quadrilateral to assist in operations of II Corps tomorrow morning'. 6 KOSB (27 Bde) attacked again at 4 pm 20 October and during the night became firmly established in Snag Trench, and a coy of 11 RS was pushed up the Tail. 104 Regt 40th German Division recorded that by the evening of 20 October, when the trenches were nearly obliterated by shell-fire, a withdrawal was ordered in accordance with the new OHL policy to give up forward positions of no tactical value rather than incur useless loss. However, it was not until 5.27 am 21 October that III Corps GS log recorded: '9th Division report all Snag Trench occupied. Patrols are going down the Tail' and at 8.40 am: '9th Division post established 200 yards N of junction of Tail and Snag Trenches. Enemy dead in large numbers in the Tail'.

It was quiet overnight 21/22 October and next day. At 4 pm the enemy left his trenches with the object of attacking 9th Division's right. SOS signal was sent up and the SOS barrage fired which drove the enemy back to his trenches.

At 9.30 am HQ III Corps issued OpO No.149: 48th Division to join III Corps from midnight 24/25 October with its HQ at Baizieux. At 5.15 pm Addendum No.1 to OpO No.148 was issued ordering 50th Division to move tomorrow (23 October) to Millencourt-Albert-Bécourt with two bns going forward to Bazentin le Petit to work in the front line under orders of 9th Division. Addendum No.2 to OpO No.148 was issued at 8.30 pm giving boundaries between divisions for the operations to take place on 25 October, and details of artillery barrages.

It was a day of thick mist on 23 October with the enemy shelling the front trenches of both divisions during the afternoon. At 12 midnight 4th Army 299/54(G) was received, postponing the attack from 25 to 26 October. At the same time HQ III Corps issued OpO No.150: 50th Division less artillery was to relieve 9th Division; relief to be completed by 9 am 25 October.

Haldane (GOC 3rd Division and not in III Corps) wrote during October: 'I am told that in III Corps, Pulteney and his BGGS Romer, never go to the trenches, so get little first-hand information. What corps commanders do all day I cannot imagine'. It is not clear what sparked this second-hand remark but it reveals a complete lack of understanding of the situation in III Corps. It was fighting on a very narrow front; getting there was extremely difficult and took a very long time; once there nothing could be seen other than the very limited confines of one trench. The situation was very different to that in 1914 and 1915 when Haldane last served in III Corps, and Putty was a frequent visitor to the front line.

There was yet more heavy rain and mist overnight 23/24 October. At 12.30 pm 24 October the attack now planned for 26 October was again postponed, to 28 October. 48th Division less its artillery joined the corps that day. More rain again fell on the morning of 25 October although

---

84   Brigadier General John Francis Gathorne-Hardy (1874-1949) Eton late Gren Gds BGGS XIV Corps.

it did clear up later in the day. At 9 am the GS log recorded that GOC 50th Division had taken over command of the right sector of the corps front. HQ III Corps issued OpO No.151 at 2 pm ordering redeployment of divisions. 9th Division, now relieved by 50th Division, was to move to the rear area on 26 and 27 October, and to leave III Corps on 29 October; in the period 12-24 October the division had 3,137 casualties. 48th Division was to move from the rear area to Albert, Bécourt and Millencourt on 26-28 October vice 9th Division. 1st Division was to re-join the corps on 28 October and move into the areas vacated by 9th Division. III Corps' GS log recorded at 2.35 pm: '15th Division call attention to a number of batteries of 4th Canadian Division in their area, and asks to be given exact location of each'. The strange aspect of this is not the deployment but that HQ 15th Division were unaware of it.

At 9 am that morning DDMS noted: 'Corps Commander again spoke about trench feet and said MOs should instruct battalion officers as to proper care of feet'. With so many new men who had not experienced such terrible conditions as existed in the front line, lessons had to be re-learnt. Also, in a further reminder that the enemy artillery reached well into the corps area, OC III Corps Sig Coy recorded: 'III Corps Sig Det Dernancourt (CHA) shelled and demolished. 2 RE wounded'. This was more than 12 miles from any enemy gun.

Putty wrote to Edith Londonderry on 25 October; unusually the letter went through both field and base censors:

> Dearest Circe, The news from Verdun is splendid, what glorious deeds for the French, what a twinge it must give old Falkenhayn and his amputated leg, what stage management to pull off such a coup just as their War Loan was in the balance of issue, I don't suppose that they took many guns but now they have all the observation on to the Boche guns that they could ever want, they ought to give them a real good doing in. I wonder if you still intend to go to Paris, alas there is no possible chance of my being able to get away nor do I see any prospect until snow and thaw do the roads in, the rain again has been hopeless the ground is a sea of mud, the glass has fallen lower than any woman could do in the time. Uffy Craven[85] dined here the other night he was really very funny about his son's marriage he told Gavin he was quite pleased with the marriage for he was certain that the boy would have married a 'Screamer' in a year or two, am told the young lady had a rare time among the sailors but in looks she can give old Bradley Martin[86] the ma in law about two stone and a beating. Have neither seen nor heard a word of your Charley for ages the brute never writes just stoke him up in Paris although that is his business towards you I know!! The days are beginning to shorten up very quickly now have not begun to wear my under linen yet have you? But soon shall if it continues to be so parky. Have made a bit of ground the last few days by means of peaceful penetration, this I am good at as you can imagine the Boche as a rule does not find it out until an aeroplane does a photo of it, with this weather that is generally too late. Best love Yours ever Putty.

It was wet for the rest of October which greatly hampered operations, apart from artillery engagements and patrolling. At 11.30 am 26 October Addendum No.5 to OpO No.148 was

---

85 William George Robert Craven 4th Earl of Craven (1868-1921) Eton.
86 Craven married Cornelia Martin (1877-1961) daughter of Bradley Martin, wealthy American banker in 1893.

issued postponing the attack from 28 to 30 October, and then at 9 pm 27 October in Addendum No.6 from 30 October to 1 November. Meanwhile the redeployment of divisions was taking place.

The GS log recorded on 28 October: 'Q report closing of all roads NE of a line between Contalmaison and Bottom Wood to mechanical transport till further orders'. The AQ log noted that day: 'Repairs carried out in ordnance workshops to guns, howitzers and mortars 1-28 October: 253 of which 230 were 18 pdrs, mainly buffer springs and pistons'. The weather and constant fighting were taking their toll. 180 Tunnelling Coy RE joined III Corps that day.

29 October was very quiet: the only event of significance was a report from 50th Division at 4.50 pm: '6 men 4 NF killed in Snag Trench about 3.30 pm by our howitzer firing from direction of High Wood. Same gun was firing short yesterday. BGRA informed – states none of our hows firing there, must belong to XV Corps'. Little is said about the numerous accidents: in this case the weather, inadequate maps, poor training and worn equipment would all have played a part.

Putty wrote again to Ettie on 29 October:

> Dearest Chief, Mille thanks for your letter of 25 Oct. There is little news from these parts except the weather which absolutely breaks one's heart every twelve hours, how the roads stand it I don't know. I never saw A.J.B. when he was over this time at which I was much distressed one does love to meet an honest politician in these days. You make me laugh over the Asquith ménage had heard rumours to that effect before however it is only consistent with the man. Yes I meant Frank Gathorne-Hardy who shaved off his moustache he does not realise that he has not the best of mouths. The Channel raids show a certain amount of daring on the part of the Germans it is probably the forerunner of the sink at sight submarine policy again which would be pretty serious if he really did begin on the Atlantic side. Was so pleased that young Congreve was given the VC he really won it on Hill 60 three or four times over, Excuse a very dull scrawl. All love Yours ever Putty.

30 October was an even quieter day as both sides struggled with the greater enemy, the wet. At 7 pm HQ III Corps issued OpO No.152: 'Operations to take place on 3 or 5 Nov according to weather conditions'.

The month ended with a fine day. At 1.45 pm, perhaps encouraged by the change in the weather, HQ III Corps issued Addendum No.1 to OpO No.152 ordering 50th Division to attack on 2 November, weather permitting. Later, at 9 pm, HQ III Corps issued WngO (GO971) for the relief of 15th Division by 48th Division in left sector of the corps front, to be completed by 9 am 3 November. The AQ log recorded that Det W India Regt left the corps, as the constant rotation of the diverse units of corps troops continued. III Corps now consisted of 1st, 15th, 48th (less artillery) and 50th Divisions, and 9th and 23rd Divisional Artilleries. During October III Corps casualties were: 161 officers and 2,038 other ranks killed, 297 officers and 7,654 other ranks wounded, 22 officers and 1,535 other ranks missing = 11,707.

Battle of the Ancre 13-18 November

Butte de Warlencourt

There had already been a lot of rain and conditions in the line were dreadful; November was to bring no let up. The GS log recorded on 1 November: '15th Division state many communication trenches are impassable in right brigade area owing to mud and water up to a man's hips'. HQ III Corps issued a preliminary defence scheme that morning:

> An intermediate defence line is to be formed by means of 'nests' of machine-guns placed in shell holes, old gun pits, present gun positions etc right across the corps front, so placed as to cover the whole front with long range fire. When these are completed 'cruciform posts' (strong points) are to be established right across the front.

Putty realised that in the worsening conditions it would be difficult to reinforce the front line, hence the importance of a strong intermediate line.

HQ III Corps also issued OpO No.153 that morning (1 November) detailing the relief of 15th Division (left) by 48th Division. Meanwhile preparations for the attack continued: despite the conditions the corps artillery was bombarding the enemy positions every day with ammunition expenditure daily about 25,000 rounds (22,000 DA, 3,000 HA), all of which had to be resupplied over roads requiring constant repair. Apart from this bombardment it was relatively quiet at the front overnight and next day but the rain continued. At 12 noon in Correction No.2 to OpO No.152, 50th Division's attack was postponed to 5 November.

Putty sent his monthly report to the King on 2 November with this covering letter:

> My dear Wigram, Attached is diary for the 3rd Corps for the month of October, the chief features are the capture of Le Sars and Eaucourt l'Abbaye, the latter place was very difficult as regards its position and configuration of the ground, it broke up the attack on the 1st. The capture of Le Sars was a great feather in the cap of the 23rd Division and all the arrangements did General Babington great credit, further we actually captured more prisoners (11 officers and 517 other ranks) with that division that day than it had casualties. The description of wounds on Page 8 are interesting [DDMS III Corps' figures regarding the causes of wounds in September: rifle and machine-gun fire 1,956 (15%) of which 217 were severe, shell fire 10,554 (81%) of which 4,066 were severe, and bombs and grenades 443 (3%) of which 111 were severe]. It took us until the 18th to get the Snag Trench completely which covered Eaucourt l'Abbaye. I forgot to answer your question about the pipe pusher which blew back in High Wood, it is a hydraulic machine for pushing a pipe full of explosive under the ground, it is an excellent device in ordinary soil, but stone and chalk stop it, in this case we had gone under the roots of trees and resistance above was too much for it and the force came backwards instead of upwards but it is a good thing from which we have had very good results. The weather has broken our hearts, it has trebled all our difficulties with roads and communication trenches, it is now just a matter of corduroy and revetting, the health of the men has been quite wonderful considering the climatic conditions but it has given the Boche the breathing space he was badly in need of. Yours sincerely, WP Pulteney.

After a wet night the morning of 3 November was misty, although there was less rain during the day. The GS log recorded at 10.20 am: 'Addendum No.2 to OpO No.152 issued – Attack of left division on Green Line to take place on 7 Nov, weather permitting; Attack of right division in conjunction with left division of ANZAC Corps to take place on 5 Nov'. At 10.35 am 48th Division reported that it had completed its relief of 15th Division: it now had four days before its attack.

HQ III Corps also issued OpO No.154 on 3 November, at 2.15 pm. 1st Division which had been in the corps rear area resting and training was to move forward to Bécourt, Albert and Millencourt, and 15th Division just relieved in the front line would replace it. HQ 15th Division would then be at Baizieux two kilometres behind HQ III Corps at Hénencourt. These moves were to be completed by 6 November. The workload on the AQ staff in these conditions would have been very high indeed: they had to administer and supply the corps, prepare for the forthcoming attacks and manage the redeployment of divisions. Additionally, there was the constant rotation of corps troops' units, all of which required direction and supervision if they were to do their jobs effectively. The AQ log recorded that 3 Cavalry Reserve Park joined III Corps on 3 November, 11 POW Coy joined III Corps for administration on 4 November, and 2 Cavalry Reserve Park and Det Bermuda Artillery left the corps the same day.

4 November was again relatively quiet although the bombardment continued; it was also a day of heavy rain. 50th Division history recorded the night of 4/5 November:

> The night was a horror. Heavy rain again fell and a gale howled about the trenches making the going even more difficult as, staggering under their equipment and usual heavy loads, the troops detailed for the attack floundered through mud and water to their assembly positions. In some parts of the line the mud was now thigh-deep; it is impossible to describe the physical and mental agony of waiting for hours on end, drenched through, caked with dirt, shivering cold and with clothes rain-sodden, for Zero hour. 6 DLI are reported to have had several men drowned in the trenches before the attack began.

III Corps had a minor part in the Battle of the Ancre, the sixth and last phase of the Battle of the Somme. The objective of 50th Division in this preliminary operation on 5 November was the Butte de Warlencourt and Warlencourt Line: the Butte being this small isolated hill of little consequence other than it gave good observation in all directions, and might affect the main attack by 5th (previously Reserve) Army to the N. In the view of some it was imperative that it was captured before the main attack took place. 50th Division's attack was to be made by 151 Bde and two bns 149 Bde in cooperation with I ANZAC Corps (2nd Australian Division) on its right; Zero hour was 9.10 am. Reports during the day were very confusing but the attack was unsuccessful on the right: on the left, however, the Butte was taken and a post established to the N of it. After heavy fighting these too were to be lost.

The official history provides one perspective:

> In touch with the Australians, the attack of III Corps was delivered by 8, 6 and 9 DLI (151 Bde 50th Division). The corps HA concentrated on the Gird lines, the Butte de Warlencourt and the area between Warlencourt and Le Barque-Thilloy. 8 DLI on the right, where men had to pull each other out of the mud before they could advance, struggled on, far behind the barrage, almost to the German front line, but was then stopped by

enfilade machine-gun fire from both flanks. A gradual withdrawal was carried out during the day. 6 DLI suffered a similar experience, except on the left where some of the battalion entered the German trench with 9 DLI. The latter broke through two lines of German trenches, reached the Butte, and established a post on the Bapaume road. Observers could see Durham men on the Butte itself so that a notable success was expected. Fighting continued all day, and at 10 pm the quarry, W of the Butte, was still held and also 500 yards of the German front line. Then, about midnight, German counter-attacks at last prevailed: the weary survivors of the DLI were forced out of the captured trenches and compelled to withdraw altogether.

1st Guard Reserve Division was relieving 24th Division and elements of most regiments were involved in the fighting. Lieutenant Colonel Bradford was CO 9 DLI that day and wrote in his report:

> There were many reasons why 9 DLI was unable to hold on to its ground. The failure of the troops on the right to reach their objectives and the fact that the division on the left was not attacking caused both the flanks of the battalion to be in the air. The positions to be held were very much exposed and the Germans could see all the trenches and control their fire accordingly. It was a local attack and the enemy was able to concentrate his guns on to a small portion of our line. The ground was a sea of mud and it was almost impossible to consolidate our posts. The terrible intensity of the German barrages and the difficult nature of the ground prevented reinforcements from being sent up to help 9 DLI. Four hundred yards N of the Butte the enemy had a steep bank behind which they were able to assemble without being molested. The terrain was favourable to a German counter-attack. On looking back at the attack it seems that the results which would have been gained in the event of success were of doubtful value, and would hardly have been worth the loss which we would suffer. It would have been awkward for us to hold the objectives which would have been badly sited for defence. The possession of the Butte by the Germans was not an asset to them. From our existing trenches we were able to prevent them from using it as an observation point. The Butte would have been of little use to us for the purposes of observation. But the Butte had become an obsession. Everybody wanted it. It loomed large in the minds of soldiers in the forward area and they attributed many of their misfortunes to it. The newspaper correspondents talked about that 'Miniature Gibraltar'. So it had to be taken. It seems that the attack was one of those tempting, and unfortunately at one period frequent, local operations which are so costly and rarely worthwhile. But perhaps this is only the narrow view of the regimental officer.

Lieutenant Colonel Bradford won the VC for his conspicuous bravery and leadership on 1 October (although he might not have yet known because it was not published in the London Gazette until 24 November). He was to be killed in action on 30 November 1917 when Comd 186 Bde 62nd Division: he was then 25.

There are two sides to the debate in respect of such attacks. Local attacks allowed the enemy to concentrate his forces against them and were invariably costly: on the other hand they often deceived the enemy as to the point of main effort and drew his reserves away from it. As for the Butte itself, Bradford must be right about its limited value. III Corps Artillery fired 45,518 rounds that day most of it in support of this attack. The resources might have been better applied on the day of the main 5th Army attack astride the Ancre and yet this preliminary operation may well have diverted the enemy's attention and contributed to its success.

It rained overnight 5/6 November and the next day was one of reorganisation with 50th Division back in its original line. In the previous 24 hours the division had almost 1,000 casualties. Early that morning the attack by 48th Division planned for 7 November was postponed by Putty, probably because of other postponements. It never took place.

At 3 pm 6 November Putty attended a 4th Army conference at Heilly with his BGGS, BGRA, DA&QMG and CE. Rawlinson explained the CinC's future intentions and told his corps commanders that the big operation of 5th Army had been reduced in scope and was now expected to start on 9 November when I ANZAC Corps and III Corps would repeat their attacks, weather permitting. He continued:

> Our operations had been very much hampered by the weather recently. The organisation of 4th Army was now fixed; III Corps would retain 1st, 15th, 48th and 50th Divisions. The organisation and selection of positions for defensive purposes, particularly villages like Lesboeufs, Flers, Martinpuich and Le Sars must be taken in hand at once. Behind these villages the big ridge running by High Wood, Longueval and Ginchy would be our main line of defence [for the winter].

The weather and ground conditions were so bad that it was hardly surprising there was so much indecision, order and counter-order. The objective was to secure the best possible position for the winter but now had come the realisation that it would have to be on the devastated battlefield. The artillery battle continued with III Corps firing 49,561 rounds that day before this too was scaled down.

There was again heavy rain overnight 6/7 November and for much of the next day, again relatively quiet. More rain fell overnight, and at 10.15 am 8 November III Corps issued Addendum No.1 to OpO No.155: Attack of 50th Division and I ANZAC Corps on the Butte de Warlencourt and adjacent trenches postponed indefinitely on account of the bad weather. Later that evening, at 10.20 pm, the GS log recorded: '48th and 50th Division, and I ANZAC Corps informed that there will be a concentrated bombardment of hostile trenches on this corps front tomorrow'.

Putty wrote to Ettie Desborough on 8 November:

> Dearest Chief, Mille thanks for your letter of 4 Nov which only reached me this morning, the post is all disorganised as Charley Hindlip wrote to me on the 3rd and it has not reached me yet, he was here yesterday and returned today. I agree with you about the submarine but am afraid we are to blame in not having built ships to meet the loss, on the same principle as we do guns, I understand that it is the engines that we are behind hand in, we ought to have been teaching black labour more than a year ago to help in our ship building yards. Percy Chubb was here yesterday I met him right away in the front area walking through a sea of mud, he had brought out Edie L with him and she and Charley are in Paris where Chubb goes to meet her tomorrow as C has to return to his regiment, do you know him at all, he is an intelligent American with a nice manner, he told me that the Hamburg and Dresden merchants that he has dealings with in New York told him they

were heartily sick of the war, they all entered in to it thinking it would only last six months, that it was a pretty sure gamble and now they would like to realise with a loss instead of becoming bankrupt. The fuss the people made about the Channel Raid was ridiculous to start with I understand it was so dark nothing could be seen but we have to be thankful no more damage was done, when we heard the 'Queens'[87] was lost we thought we had heavy losses as she is one of the leave boats but luckily they were not on board. The Boche is still shaky opposite me although the weather keeps us from attacking, nearly every night there are two or three of them desert, they always say they were on patrol and lost their way, six months ago a deserter would have been a feature now one thinks nothing of it, this with their best troops is a good sign. All love Yours ever Putty.

At 3.5 pm 9 November the Chinese attack and bombardment of the enemy's positions was carried out by the divisions and the corps artillery: there was heavy enemy shelling in response, particularly on 50th Division. Otherwise it was another quiet day, and the first fine and clear day for some time. DDMS wrote: '12 noon. Corps Commander inspected 1 MDS and CRS. Site of latter unsatisfactory'. The AQ log recorded: 'Trench boots to be worn in front and support trenches'.

There was a further Chinese attack and bombardment by the divisions and the corps artillery at 9.10 am 10 November, all to maintain the pressure on the enemy. Overnight 9/10 November it was fine and cold with the day again bright but III Corps Opsum noted that day: 'Since the beginning of the month there have been two fine days. A great deal of rain has fallen during the period which has made the roads in the forward areas worse than they were last month; the front trenches are also very wet and muddy. The sick rate of 50th Division, holding the right of the line, has been high: on the last three days of the period to 10 November it averaged 160 per day'. The problem with the location of the CRS had been resolved; DDMS noted: 'The CRS at Bécourt is to be given up. Instead the Corps Commander has allotted billets in Millencourt, which will be cleared of troops except bde HQ. 2 Fd Amb will take this on'.

At 12.5 pm 11 November there was yet another Chinese attack and bombardment by the divisions and the corps artillery. Then, on 12 November, HQ III Corps issued OpO No.156 at 3.15 pm: 'To assist operations of 5th Army a Chinese attack will take place at 5.45 am 13 Nov'. At 5.15 pm the same day Addendum No.3 to OpO No.155 was issued: 'Attack on German trenches by 50th Division, in conjunction with Australians on III Corps' right will take place on 14 Nov'. This attack by 50th Division was to be made by 5 NF (right) and 7 NF (left) with the other two bns of 149 Bde in support; 150 Bde was then also in support. Zero hour was to be 6.45 am 14 November.

It was misty on 13 November but there was no rain: at 5.45 am the bombardment and Chinese attack in conjunction with 5th Army's attack took place, provoking heavier retaliation than usual especially on 50th Division and suggesting that the deception had been effective. That evening, at 6.15 pm, HQ III Corps issued OpO No.157 ordering the relief of 50th Division by 1st Division in the right sector of the corps front, to be completed by 12 noon 19 November. For 50th Division the end was in sight but first there was a job to be done.

---

87   SS *Queen* torpedoed 26 October 1916.

The attacking bns of 149 Bde took over the front line that night. Captain Buckley 7 NF wrote:

> Mud was everywhere, in parts up to the waist, and what was worse, the thicker, more tenacious kind that just covered the boots and clung in heavy masses. The exertion of forcing our way step by step in an already heavily-burdened state during our various moves about this line remains in my mind as some of the most strenuous and exhausting times of the whole war.

At 6.45 am half an hour before sunrise on 14 November III Corps in conjunction with I ANZAC Corps attacked. Taking the enemy's trenches ahead of them was the objective of the two attacking divisions astride the inter corps boundary, but the strategic objective of GHQ was still to divert the enemy's attention and resources away from 5th Army's attack on the Ancre. Captain Buckley 7 NF again:

> Eventually a grey line appeared in the eastern sky, and slowly the low outline of the Butte de Warlencourt took shape half-left of our position. Suddenly the sky seemed to split as our barrage came over. Pencils of golden rain, the German SOS, rose all along the opposite line. Machine-guns opened up from all directions and crash came the German barrage.

There was no rain that day but the mist often made observation difficult.

50th Division got into the German trenches and linked up with 2nd Australian Division on its right. The situation then became very confused as they tried to consolidate their positions: the layout of the enemy's trenches was very complex; many of them and the surrounding ground were in a terrible condition; the enemy's artillery and machine-gun fire was very heavy; and there were frequent counter-attacks with much of the fighting hand-to-hand. 3/5 Guard Grenadier Regt was holding the front attacked and German records state that immediate attempts to counter-attack were stopped by British artillery fire. III Corps Opsum recorded that one officer and 15 other ranks 5 Guard Grenadier Regt were captured that day by 50th Division; many more were in fact taken but could not be got back to the rear.

During the night 14/15 November the battle continued as the other bns 149 Bde tried to get forward in support. 15 November was a fine day, albeit cold with an E wind. The fighting continued all day and into the night with 4 E Yorks and 4 GH 150 Bde being sucked in. The enemy's barrage was very heavy and at times developed into an intense bombardment: this and the counter-attacks were unceasing but 50th Division managed to hold on.

At 12 noon 15 November 4th Army 299/63(G) was received:

> 4th Army will take over from the French up to N edge of Bouchavesnes. III Corps will take over from I ANZAC Corps up to Factory Corner-Ligny-Thilloy road. Western boundary as at present. Relief to be completed by 8 am 22 Nov.

That afternoon must have been a particularly difficult time for Putty with 50th Division now fully committed and under heavy attack, and now he had to take over more front to his right where 2nd Australian Division was also under attack. Nevertheless at 7 pm that evening III Corps OpO No.158 was issued extending the corps front and giving the new corps and divisional boundaries. The AQ log recorded one consolation that day – the arrival of two additional heavy and siege btys to join the corps; they would have been quickly into action.

The weather now changed with frost overnight and days that were invariably bright and sunny. At 3 pm 16 November a heavy German bombardment began, preceding a counter-attack which came in gathering darkness shortly before 5 pm. One of the first shells landed on a blocking party and knocked out all the men and two Lewis guns. The captured portion of Gird Trench, where casualties from German shell-fire had been very heavy, was then enveloped by strong parties bombing in from both flanks and assaulted from the front (5 Guard Grenadier Regt recorded that the Divisional Storm Coy delivered the flank assaults, detachments of 1 and 2 Bns attacked from the front). In little over half an hour the remnants of 50th Division and 2nd Australian Division were forced out of the position, and those who could do so withdrew to the original front line. Further attacks were then cancelled. During these three days 50th Division's casualties were 37 officers and 852 other ranks.

It was much quieter on 17 November. At 5.30 pm HQ III Corps issued OpO No.159: 'To assist operations of 5th Army on 18 Nov, 48th and 50th Divisions will open intense fire on the Butte, Galwitz trench, and Below trench as far as its junction with Coulee trench from 6.10 am to 6.40 am'. Snow fell overnight and it was very cold on 18 November. After making this last Chinese attack 50th Division was relieved by 1st Division in the right sector. The Battle of the Ancre was over and work could begin on consolidation of the line for the winter. Rawlinson noted: 'Glad to be going away on leave tomorrow. Putty takes my place'.

Putty wrote to Ettie that day:

> Dearest Chief, Thanks for your letter of the 15 Nov, the mails have been hopeless lately both coming and going, sometimes 3 and sometimes 6 but now the army has grown to this size it is wonderful how they come at all, as far as I know have lost none. The victory on the Ancre was a great feather in D.H'.s cap, it came most opportunely before the Paris Conference, we must have done in quite two divisions the making good of which will prevent his sending any more troops to the East, with the ground in this condition one can only keep up communicating trenches with the very greatest difficulty in fact as a rule it pays to go above ground in the dark than through the mud in the day, one has much more chance of not losing one's boots. I did not mention Lucas[88] because his fate was so indefinite but personally am not too hopeful because there is a sort of freemasonry among the Flying Corps of both sides they generally drop messages to one another if there is a casualty but if he dropped some way from an aerodrome he would perhaps not get in touch with the Flying Corps and go along as an ordinary prisoner, anyway they are always practically speaking traced which is not the case in the trench fighting. I don't wonder at poor Arthur Balfour[89] being worn out with the work I can scarcely imagine a man of 70 being able to stand the strain, but who could they find as his successor, there is nobody straight who would not be a figure head, anyway I trust that Winston will not come back, the versatile L.G. would no doubt like to try his luck at the post, am sure the army will not stand in his way. Linlithgow is at home, he is a martyr to boils and I much doubt if he will be well enough to come out again this winter but still have the faithful Gavin Hamilton with me.

88   Auberon Thomas Herbert 9th Baron Lucas (1876-1916) Captain 22 Sqn RFC killed in action 3 November – cousin and friend of Ettie: considered as older brother to her sons. Lost leg in SA.
89   First Lord of the Admiralty until December 1916 then Foreign Secretary.

Geoffrey Feilding[90] came to see me one day last week am delighted to see that the King has ordered him to grow his moustache again, Frank Gathorne-Hardy has followed suit which is as well as it did not suit him. All love Yours Putty.

At midnight 18/19 November Major General McCracken GOC 15th Division assumed temporary command of III Corps (III Corps RO No.68). Putty took temporary command of 4th Army during Rawlinson's absence, returning to III Corps on 3 December. The next three days in III Corps were quiet: the rotation of corps troops continued with 1 Indian Cavalry Pioneer Bn joining and ½ 26 and 60 Siege Btys leaving III Corps on 21 November. Next day the redeployment took place with 1st Division, having relieved 50th Division on 19 November (48th Division extended its front to the right on the same day), relieving part of 2nd Australian Division.

It continued quiet on 22 November; at 12.30 pm HQ 4th Army asked what duties were being performed by III Corps MMG Bty. HQ III Corps' reply to this strange question (at 2.30 pm) was: 'All MMG Bty's guns are being employed on AA work. Bty gives continuous courses of instruction in AA work to Vickers and Lewis gunners of divisions'. It was strange because 4th Army GS should have known what the corps MMG btys did. Then, at 5.20 pm, HQ III Corps issued GO986/3 III Corps Defence Scheme with explanatory map:

1. The corps consists of four divisions. Of these two hold the front line, one is in corps reserve with its bdes at Fricourt Farm, Bécourt and Albert, and one in training W of Albert. 3. The corps defences consist of: (a) Front line system (b) Intermediate line (c) Corps second line (d) Defended localities such as Martinpuich and strongpoints such as Bazentin Windmill, Bazentin le Petit, Mametz Wood and Contalmaison Cutting.

A Bty RHA joined III Corps on 22 November: on 23 November, another fine bright day, there was little activity at the front other than artillery engagements which included a concentration of III Corps Heavy Artillery on the Butte for twenty minutes at 3 pm. At 11 am that morning 4th Army 311/160(G) was received, a WngO that 48th Division Artillery was to be transferred to III Corps on 1 December. The division itself had joined III Corps on 24 October: again, it was clearly sensible not to take a division out of the line at the same time as its artillery but this was nearly a month later during which coordination and cooperation would inevitably have been weaker.

Also that day (23 November) HQ III Corps issued OpOs No.161 and 162. These transferred billeting areas in accordance with 4th Army No.19/4 received on 22 November:

Accommodation in Contay, Vadencourt and Warloy from 5th Army to 4th Army (III Corps) from 26 Nov inclusive. 5th Army to give up right to billet one bde in Albert. Accommodation in St Gratien, La Houssoye and Franvillers from III Corps to I ANZAC Corps from midnight 26/27 Nov. Two maps issued showing new boundaries.

This order gives a small insight into the difficulties of providing accommodation in the rear areas for divisions resting but available to support the front line if required. The amount of suitable accommodation in each corps area varied and so it was controlled at army level.

90   GOC Guards Division.

The Battle of the Somme was now at an end. One view of it was:

> that it raised the morale of the British Army. Although we did not win a decisive victory, there was what matters most a definite and growing sense of superiority over the enemy, man to man. The attacks of mid-July were more successful and better managed than those of 1 July. In August and September things went better still.

III Corps was one of only two corps (of 8 that took part in the battle) that fought right through the Battle of the Somme. Eleven divisions had served under Putty during the battle (1st, 8th, 9th, 12th, 15th, 19th, 23rd, 34th, 47th, 48th and 50th Divisions). Up to 16 November (from 1 July) III Corps had a total of 48,935 casualties: of these 23rd Division had the highest number with 9,801.

On 24 November Putty wrote to Edith Londonderry:

> Dearest Circe, You have gone to the devil since your visit to Paris as far as your pen is concerned I conclude that you dare not write the atrocities that you and Charley committed, it was rather funny my meeting Percy Chubb while walking one morning wasn't it? You seem to have ruined his heart among many others I can't imagine what they see in you!! Well things have quieted down in these parts in comparison this last week, both sides are really trying to put their house in order after all the rains that have taken place, I never want to hear anything about either roads or railway in the future, the making of them and the repair of the former are rapidly driving me in to an early grave, the greatest bother is to prevent the mud coming on to the roads from the fields, it simply does the road in in no time besides making it impossible for the lorries, we are now making wooden door mats to try and obviate, dig ditches by the sides of the roads that are too big to drive over besides wiring in the fronts of the camps. Have heard from Charley twice this last week, had hoped that his lot were coming to me, however I expect to see him the week after next when I return to my proper abode again, am going to try to persuade him to come to Paris again for Xmas, you had better come along again too your children won't want you, they are sure to be playing snap dragons with ma in law, they will want your good advice for the New Year, I hope to get away to England about the 2nd week in January and to play as much hell as I can in those ten days. I don't suppose that the old Emperor's death [21 November] will make any difference except that his successor is more Boche than he was, am afraid that the Monastir pressure is not sufficient to make much difference for the Boche does not care a damn how much of that part Bulgaria loses all she wants is the main road to Constantinople and Bagdad. Much love Yours ever Putty.

It rained again on 25 November and that day the GS log recorded: '11 am. III Corps Ammunition Park ordered to supply divisions in the line with a new SOS signal consisting of a rifle grenade bursting into two red and two green stars at the top of its flight. To be taken into use at noon 28 Nov'. The AQ log noted: 'Repairs carried out in ordnance workshops of guns, howitzers and mortars 29 Oct – 25 Nov: 157 of which 135 were 18 pdrs, mainly buffers and broken springs'.

There was yet more rain on 26 November as the adjustment of the billeting areas took place. HQ III Corps issued OpO No.162 bringing 15th Division forward to Bécourt, Albert and

Millencourt changing over with 50th Division; the latter moved into the corps rear area for much needed rest and training.

The last four days of November were cold, often misty, but there was less rain. At the front it was quiet apart from intermittent shelling. On 27 November 9th Division Artillery left III Corps for 3rd Army, yet another example of the way a division's artillery was detached from its division. Next day, 28 November at 10 am, OpO No.163 was issued confirming the arrival in III Corps of 48th Division Artillery. Finally on 30 November the GS log recorded: '4th Army GG105/92 with 4th Army 432(G) dated 17 Nov and 25 Nov and GHQ OB909 of 16 Nov received. Reorganisation of AA btys: 4th Army AA Group HQ formed. Necessary extracts repeated to divisions and heavy artillery'. As the air threat in the rear area had now increased significantly, coordination of AA defence was becoming much more important.

III Corps' casualties in November were: 46 officers and 531 other ranks killed, 108 officers and 2,286 other ranks wounded, 18 officers and 633 other ranks missing = 3,622. At least 2,000 of these casualties were in 50th Division.

The start of December was cold with hard frosts and frequent thick mists. 1st Division was on the right and 48th Division on the left in the line; 15th Division was in support around Albert, and 50th Division having just been relieved behind them. At 8 am 1 December 4th Army No.299/68(G) was received: Orders for future operations. HQ III Corps OpO No.164 was issued at 11.30 am: 1st and 48th Divisions were to capture Hook Sap, Butte (Warlencourt) and Quarry on W or X Day. Then on Z Day III Corps was to carry out a Chinese attack to assist attack of neighbouring corps.

The front line and the area behind it, right back to Albert, were in a dreadful state. The Opsum for December recorded:

> The wet weather has had a bad affect on the front trenches which were hastily dug in heavily shelled soft ground and are very difficult to keep up. Duck board tracks have been made by both divisions for the last 3,000 yards of the journey up to the front line which makes the passage of reliefs and carrying parties over the shelled area much easier than was formerly the case.

48th Divisional Artillery joined the corps that day, almost a month after the rest of the division: again, changing over artillery and infantry at different times was sensible but it did make coordination and fire planning especially difficult. P (AA) Bty also joined III Corps as the air threat and consequent difficulties of moving in daylight continued to increase. Overnight, in a rare event, an enemy patrol surprised a 7 man post of 48th Division killing two men and capturing two more, the other three escaped; the next day (2 December) was relatively quiet.

Also that day Putty sent his monthly report to the King:

> My dear Wigram, Attached is the diary of the 3rd Corps for the information of His Majesty. I am afraid there is little of interest. The weather was simply abominable at the beginning of November, it greatly affected the 50th Division in the operations round the Butte de Warlencourt although they lost it after once gaining it the enemy had very serious losses indeed and much of the fighting was hand to hand. We have had an uphill time with the trenches for the shelling has broken up the ground so much that trenches dug in it do not stand up after heavy raining or heavy shelling, the result being heartbreaking for

the earth once it has fallen in gets in to a muddy state and is very difficult to handle, these conditions have caused a good deal of sickness while the trench feet have also bothered us a good deal but if we can get one more fine week I trust we shall get our communication trenches through and get the best of everything. The roads which looked so hopeless are now well in hand, the railways and trams have also made good progress, I must say the troops deserve every possible praise for the way they have either faced or overcome extraordinary difficulties in the offensive so late in the winter. The nissen huts are a great success and whoever invented them deserves the greatest credit with all our thanks added. The attitude of the Boche is very encouraging for he is evidently much in need of a quiet time, he scarcely ever replies to our shelling except the infantry send up SOS signals, we have had 14 deserters come in to our line during the last two days, such a thing never happened all last year, personally I think we ought to keep these desertions out of the paper otherwise it gets back to Germany who take measures to prevent it, such a thing as a deserter this time last year was never heard of, all this shows that the moral of the Boche is deteriorating, there are many signs which one cannot mistake, from what I learn from those who come home from leave there is much greater confidence out here than in England. There is a very intelligent Boche prisoner in one of the camps here who speaks English, he says Germany will take Rumania and then propose terms of peace, he says the war will be over by March at the latest I fancy this is the tale that is told to all merchants. The fogs on the Somme would prevent anyone wishing to live in its villages in the future. All good wishes for Xmas Yours sincerely, WP Pulteney.

Putty resumed command of III Corps at 6 pm 3 December: he had been in command of 4th Army for two weeks. The GS log recorded for the second day running that the Town Major of Albert had reported shelling in the town. Also HQ III Corps issued Addendum No.1 to OpO No.164 giving further details of the planned attack. The AQ log recorded that pack animals lent by 2nd Cavalry Division left the corps to rejoin their division, and DDMS noted: 'Corps Commander directs that the attention of all medical officers be drawn to the seriousness of trench feet, as there are a large number of cases daily in this corps. Confidential memo sent to ADMS'.

Also on 3 December Putty wrote to Ettie Desborough:

My dearest Chief, Many thanks for your letter of 27 Nov which only reached me this morning as you had put 3rd Army instead of Corps on it. I expect to be over the second week in January and will come down to Panshanger to stay with you whether you like it or not. With us down here the Boche is very docile, have had 14 deserters in within the last three days, last winter we never got sign of one, this shows the signs of deterioration which we have so anxiously been looking for. Am glad D.H. said nice things about me, though have got quite callous on the subject, I used to allow personal matters to worry me but have quite broke myself of it now, we have got to beat the Boche and differences of opinion can wait until peace time when they will keep us fit. Arnold Albermarle[91] turned up today to

91 Arnold Allan Cecil Keppel 8th Earl of Albermarle (1858-1942) Eton SG 1878-1883 ADC to the King.

see his son but he is in the line and I don't think he will be able to see him, he is a nice old thing but quite absolutely without a brain of any description, I don't think Bury[92] has many either though he wants to get command of a battalion, he won't get one of mine I know that, Find out for me why Eddie Derby has got a down on Edie Castlereagh if you can. Have just rung up the Flying Corps about Lucas but alas there is no news and am now much afraid of the worst. My love and blessings Yours ever Putty.

He also wrote to Edith Londonderry:

Dearest Circe, Thanks for your letter of 27 Nov. It is a pity you cannot come to Paris for Xmas but your reasons are sound and if you really go over for the New Year I will come back for that weekend. No I will not take you on at golf your maxim of never up never in is sound but always understand the first rule of golf was 'to keep your eye on the ball' even though it does only tip the lip of the hole sometimes anyway I hope the greens will be in order and the grass not too long. Have you heard the story of the soldier who stayed at a house and put all three daughters in the family way, the father was absolutely furious and said though he could not marry all three he must one, which would he take, without hesitation he said the eldest because she T.U. most like her mother!!! Am glad you think D.H. has got a better opinion of me. Some do some don't but it matters not as long as the only cause goes on all right, my lot had 14 deserters give themselves up in the last three days, last winter we never got one, this is a splendid sign and shows that the moral is beginning to give under the strain, further they have practically never bothered us although we were floundering in the mud wilderness it shows they respect us and want to be quiet. Charley am afraid is going back to his old Blues but have sent him over a note to try and get him to dinner tonight if he comes will send you some messages. Have got Simon Lovat staying with me have got some of his men [Lovat Scouts], a real good lot they are too, I am going to try some experiments with them and use their trained eyes to discover the wiles of the Boche, he is fully in accord with my views and takes great personal interest, he tells me he has to pay the Boche prisoners 25/- a week up at Beauly because the trade unionists refused to allow them to work for less, the government are a lot of cowards. I hear the report they brought over that Jemmy Rothschild's wife was going to have a baby is untrue it was only flatulence. My love to you Yours ever Putty.

An interesting note in the ADOS log on 4 December shows the efforts being made to ameliorate the effects of frost in the front line: 'DA&QMG spoke about small bottles for whale oil and small tins so that each man could carry his own. Went to Amiens and arranged for 1,000'. By 14 January the two forward divisions had 10,000 each.

It was quiet overnight and throughout 4 December: after a frost during the night the day was bright and clear. Again that evening the Town Major Albert reported about 60 shells had fallen in the town the previous night mostly in the neighbourhood of the civil hospital, which had been seriously damaged. Two British soldiers had been killed and 2 wounded; 1

---

92   Walter Egerton Lucian Keppel Viscount Bury (1882-1979) Eton SG 1901-1919 OC MG Coy Guards Division.

French gendarme and 2 Germans had also been wounded. On the evening of 5 December 15th Division reported that this long range enemy shelling had hit 47 Fd Amb in Bécourt Chateau just outside Albert killing 7 and wounding 40.

That day (5 December) Putty inspected 50th Division: 151 Bde at Warloy, two battalions of 150 Bde at Contay, and 149 Bde at Bresle next day. According to the divisional history: 'To all these he expressed his great appreciation of the fine fighting qualities of the division and its good work generally on the Somme since 10 Sep'. Lieutenant Colonel Allan CO 6 DLI 151 Bde writing to his wife that day was less than appreciative: 'We got a telegram in the middle of the night saying the Corps Commander, Pulteney, was going to inspect the brigade at 10 am this morning. The parade went off alright but the Corps Commander, another Guardsman, was as different as possible from the last two Generals Fergusson and Congreve. He walked round the battalion without saying a word to me, in fact if I had been a lamp post he couldn't have taken less notice'. It was an almost impossible conundrum for any corps commander faced with constant changes in units and formations under him. If he wanted to thank them on leaving his command any parade had to be short, otherwise it would be completely counter-productive; but if it was short he could only speak to a tiny proportion of the officers and men. Without public address equipment it was almost impossible to speak to more than one battalion at a time, and this was very difficult. Issuing congratulatory orders lacked any personal touch and anyway they rarely reached all concerned.

Albert was shelled again in the evening of 6 December, this time it was the station. The indiscriminate shelling must have caused problems for Putty. He had a division in the town, and the flow of men and supplies through the town was constant in both directions: routes were few and any disruption could easily affect operations in the front line. It was quiet again on 7 December, a misty and cold day. At 11 am 4th Army issued 299/70(G) postponing the Chinese attack in support of 10th French Army S of the Somme to 11 December: it was later further postponed and then cancelled.

The next two days (8 and 9 December) were wet and very quiet except for artillery exchanges. At 4 pm HQ III Corps OpO No.164 was issued giving further details of the artillery bombardment for the projected attack on the Butte. It also cancelled the attack by 48th and 1st Divisions; major offensive operations were no longer possible. At 6.15 pm 9 December III Corps issued OpO No.165 ordering 15th Division to relieve 48th Division in the front line.

Rain continued to fall on 10 and 11 December At 5.8 am 10 December the GS log recorded: '48th Division reported that 6 prisoners of 1st Bn 1st MIR [possibly Marine Inf Regt] have been taken'. The AQ log recorded on 11 December: '61, 111, 141 and 187 Siege Btys and 17, 127 and 137 Hy Btys left III Corps. 500 men Kaffir Labour Bn joined the corps'.

It snowed during the night 11/12 December and the next four days were generally wet. There was some shelling by both sides but the winter weather was now the greater enemy. Putty wrote to Ettie again on 15 December:

Dearest Chief, Thanks for your letter of the 6 Dec it was too sad about poor Bron Lucas but one can only be thankful that he died in the air instead of on the impure ground. I told you Germany would offer peace terms at Xmas, the dirty dogs they know they have arrived at any zenith there was for them and this is their course sooner than face the smash which awaits them next year 'the dirty dogs'!! Have had the Flue [sic] this last week, am still rather a wreck but gradually getting back my strength again, ought to have gone to bed but didn't, there is a good deal about but not a very virulent type. The weather is past writing about as also is the mud, I will back clay on top of chalk to beat any mud in this war Galicia included which the Boche prisoners say was the worst they had seen before this. Gavin Hamilton has made me a splendid fire place in conjunction with the engineers there is nothing like fire bricks properly arranged I thought they had ruined the whole thing the first day as the bricks were so damp there was no heat and the fire would not burn. I like the composition of the new government there is some chance of a decision, Seeing before Waiting should be their motto and then 1917 will bring them their reward, I only hope A.J.B'.s health will be equal to it he has the heart of a lion to have faced it at all. There is practically no military news from these parts just artillery duels that's all. With love Yours ever Putty.

On 16 December 15th Division relieved 48th Division, and 15th Division history recorded:

> HQ 15th Division just behind Shelter Wood. The line ran almost due E and W opposite the famous Butte de Warlencourt. Conditions were bad, if not worse than formerly. The front line consisted of a series of shell-holes linked up in places by shallow trenches. There were no defences in the shape of wire or other obstacles, and no communication trenches between the front and support lines.

There was thick mist again on 17 and 18 December but still quiet at the front. On 19 December the mist cleared but there was a hard frost and snow fell in the evening. The AQ log recorded: 'Daily train service for sick and wounded commenced. Leaves Bazentin for Bécourt, stopping 5 minutes at Bottom Wood'. This was a considerable achievement by the engineers being a distance of more than five miles over the most appalling ground.

Activity on the front line was now restricted to artillery engagements and patrolling: for the infantry it was a matter of survival and rotations were frequent. On 21 December the GS log recorded:

> 15th Division report a creeping barrage, having for its object the clearance of enemy posts, shell holes etc, was carried out by our artillery today. This drew retaliation on Le Sars and OG Line which was effectively stopped by our counter battery work.

A patrol of 15th Division captured four prisoners in no man's land early on 22 December and another during the night 22/23 December. It was important to dominate the enemy especially as the defences were so inadequate but this was very difficult. To add to the problems there was now much rain and high winds which restricted the use of the heavy artillery.

At 4 pm 23 December HQ III Corps issued OpO No.166: 'In accordance with instructions received from 4th Army, the enemy trenches opposite III Corps are to be heavily bombarded from 11 to 11.30 am on Christmas Day'. The following day (24 December) III Corps OpO No.167 was issued: in another rotation, 48th Division was to vacate the reserve area (Albert) and move back into the training area; 50th Division was to relieve 1st Division in the front line on 1 January.

Little changed and nothing of significance occurred during Christmas, apart from the planned half hour bombardment on Christmas Day. The GS log recorded on 28 December: 'Air photographs were taken yesterday, the first for some time, which show a large hole has been dug in the Bapaume Road W of the Butte, presumably to stop tanks'.

1916 petered out with periodic enemy shelling, sometimes very heavy: it was warmer but that brought more rain and made conditions even more miserable, especially in the front line. III Corps' casualties for December 1916 were 11 officers and 251 other ranks killed, 37 officers and 806 other ranks wounded, 2 officers and 24 other ranks missing = 1,131. They were surprisingly high given the intensity of the fighting, reflecting the state of the front and of communication trenches and the lack of protection they now provided.

So much has been written about the Battle of the Somme that Putty's contribution should stand out clearly, but it does not. The reason is simple; the picture is clouded by those around him and the circumstances in which he lived and fought. To complicate matters further those that have analysed other people and events have drawn inaccurate or incomplete conclusions about Putty, perhaps because they have not had all the evidence.

Some time at the beginning of 1916 Haig decided that Putty and HQ III Corps should move S to 4th Army. It seems highly likely that he consulted Rawlinson before making this decision, and Rawlinson was pleased to have Putty under his command for the battle ahead. There was no compelling reason for them to have selected Putty and put him in such a key position; they did, and it can only have been because they thought he was the best man for the job. Neither man knew that Putty had got unofficially engaged during his leave but if they had it would probably have made no difference. During the battle both recorded occasional reservations about Putty's ability or his performance, and these have to be considered in context. If either Haig or Rawlinson had any real concerns about Putty they could have removed him, but they did not. Putty does not criticise either in his letters, as he did Smith-Dorrien in 1915, but neither does he give them any praise, as he did French: the implication is clear.

Haig talked of breakthrough and of exploiting it with cavalry but his overall strategy for the battle, especially on 1 July, lacked the concentration of force and surprise to make this possible. The strategic objective was attrition – to suck in and destroy as many German divisions as possible so that they could not be sent to other fronts. Because Germany was fighting on interior lines and because of their ability to improvise, this objective required constant offensive operations.

On 1 July the artillery was applied with mathematical uniformity along the whole front and expected to achieve overwhelming domination at the end of the preliminary bombardment: the six corps, with an equal uniformity that took no account of the ground or the enemy's deployment, would then advance against what was expected to be minimal resistance, at least initially. The flaws in this are self-evident and should have been challenged but Rawlinson the only man who might have done this did not do so; he embraced the consequent plan. Rawlinson's style of leadership was one of frequent conferences at which genuine discussion and new ideas discouraged, and this merely compounded the problems.

The evidence shows that Putty understood the strategic objective, and that the taking of a few ruined villages or enemy trench lines was only important in that it supported this objective: yet he had to lead his men against them. Putty was also constrained by the ground; his front was never more than 3 miles wide and the corps area at most 20 miles in depth with only one or two routes through it. Throughout the four and a half months of the battle, and in this very confined area, Putty organised, supplied and fought his corps of about 100,000 men. Eleven divisions passed through his command, some he knew and some he did not: the corps troops, including the artillery, were also continually rotated. During the battle III Corps attacked 25 times with one, two or three divisions, usually as part of a 4th Army or GHQ operation. The narrowness of the front made manoeuvre very difficult; when he was able to concentrate his artillery in support of one division and that division could get round the enemy's flanks this invariably led to success with fewer casualties, but that was not often.

Two criticisms have been made of senior commanders in the battle: the first was that they were too far back and out of touch. HQ III Corps started at Montigny about 12 miles behind the front line: it moved forward to Hénencourt at the earliest opportunity, again 12 miles from the front. Any examination of the deployment of III Corps shows that the HQ could not have been further forward. Communications from both places were good, HQ III Corps deployed forward OPs for direct observation if this was deemed necessary, and Putty visited his divisions frequently. The second criticism is that they did not visit the front line often enough, and Putty certainly did not visit the front as much as he had done in 1914 and 1915. There were several reasons for this – the fighting on the front line was almost continuous and visiting units during the day, when most were sleeping, counter-productive; the time to get to and back from the front line, sometimes days, was rarely available; and he would been out of touch with the battle for far too long. It was usually better to visit units before and after they had been in the line.

At the beginning of the battle Putty was fighting in a straight jacket of Haig and Rawlinson's making. Often he was told not just his objective but when and how it was to be taken. The inflexibility of 4th Army's plan might not have mattered if the total reliance on the artillery had been justified, but it was not. The artillery could never have destroyed the enemy's deep dugouts: it might have been able to neutralise them by keeping the enemy in them until the infantry arrived but the doctrine of a timed barrage fired overhead was both inflexible and ineffective. The infantry started too far behind, for safety, and inevitably the barrage got further and further ahead. During July all this improved with more limited attacks allowing greater concentration of fire, some of it in enfilade, and the introduction of the creeping barrage. The unreliability of some artillery ammunition was another factor.

Rawlinson was so confident in the artillery's ability that he insisted that La Boisselle could be by-passed on 1 July: the consequences were both predictable and inevitable. Putty and both his divisional commanders represented their concerns, to no avail. Yet he cannot be absolved from all responsibility for what happened. Ingouville-Williams' plan for 34th Division was equally bad. The whole division was committed at the outset; he did not have a reserve should La Boisselle resist, as it did, and the corps reserve could not be committed until the next day. Arguably Putty did not represent his views strongly enough, nor did he ensure that he was able to deal with the unexpected, or in this case the expected.

The first attack on Contalmaison by 23rd Division failed and Comd 24 Bde was removed because of it, attracting little controversy. Matters then became even more complicated for Putty: Haig and Rawlinson could not agree whether or not the right wing of 4th Army should swing N. The consequence for III Corps in the hinge was considerable confusion; on occasions III Corps was facing both N and NE and coordination became even more complex when Reserve Army took over those corps to the left of III Corps. Reserve Army would deal with Ovillers and then Pozières but the latter was on the high ground so any progress of III Corps' left would be dependent on that of Reserve Army. On Putty's right the swing of XV Corps, if it was successful, would bring it almost across his front. It was not successful and Putty eventually reverted to a NE axis but it meant that his right division was limited by XV Corps' progress.

So III Corps worked its way forward throughout the month of July punching with its left and right as the situation permitted, taking the German trenches in front of its Switch Line. On occasions Putty was able to influence the battle by concentrating the fire power of the corps in support of one attacking division and by limited turning movements, but the corps' front was very narrow. Coordination across the corps' boundaries which were matters for GHQ (on the left) and 4th Army (on the right) was invariably very poor and often the cause of unnecessary casualties. There is very little evidence of criticism of Putty in July from those in his corps, either at the time or later. 34th Division, which had the greatest number of casualties on 1 July, chose to remain under his command.

Logistics were difficult throughout the battle. Everything required by the corps had to be moved forward over the two roads which could be maintained as far as Albert. Further forward the situation was more precarious with roads often impassable, some help from the new tramways, but much had to be carried. The further the corps advanced the worse this became. Consider just the artillery: the number of rounds that were fired, the food for the horses, the water for men and horses, and the constant rotation of the batteries. All had to pass along the two roads through one if not both of the two reserve divisions, and they were competing for space on these roads with the evacuation of casualties from the front and the resupply of the forward divisions especially the huge amount of defence stores. The day to day running of the corps would have taken much of Putty's time but this had to be done during a battle that lasted more than four months.

During August III Corps closed up to the enemy's Switch Line and this was made more difficult and much slower because the enemy dug several new trenches to delay its progress. III Corps reverted to the tactics of siege warfare to get forward, sapping and then joining up the saps. Putty was criticised for his lack of 'education' but he took a very close interest in every aspect of his corps: the health of the men, evacuation of the wounded, response to gas attack and even the purchase of camouflage nets. His resilience was remarkable, both his physical health and his determination, although by the end of August the pressure was taking its toll as evidenced by the SG officers that visited him. Death was all round him but that of Ingouville-Williams had a greater impact than most. However, again, there was very little controversy about anything to do with Putty personally during the month. One exception might have been the time 15th Division was to be in the line but when GOC 15th Division raised the matter Putty gave him a bde of 34th Division to ease the pressure. It was probably Putty who sent forward one of GSO2s at HQ III Corps to see why the Intermediate Line was causing so much of a problem.

During September III Corps eventually closed up to the Switch Line and then, on 15 September, attacked with three divisions taking both Martinpuich and High Wood. It then advanced to the Flers Line beyond. The attack on 15 September was in many ways one of the most successful that Putty conducted in the war. It was the first time that tanks were deployed and their numbers were small. Shortage of time and the need for security meant that few had seen them and even fewer had considered their use. Many, including Lloyd George, thought that the deployment was premature and others that the tanks should be concentrated for maximum effect, but Haig over-ruled all of them with the result that they were deployed in ones and two across the whole front of the 4th Army attack. Because the crews were so inexperienced their tactics had to be rigid and unimaginative. GHQ and 4th Army decided that they should be used in close support of the infantry but this caused problems of coordination with the artillery.

The doctrine that emerged was to give the tanks clearly defined and marked safe lanes in the artillery barrages.

On the left of III Corps, 15th Division did well taking Martinpuich but on the right 47th Division had great difficulty and many casualties taking High Wood. Two controversies arose from the latter. 47th Division had been allocated four tanks and both GOC 47th Division (Barter) and GOC 50th Division (Wilkinson) wanted them to go round the NW side of the wood where there was an enemy strong point. There is no evidence that either represented these concerns to Putty. HQ III Corps decided that they should be used to support the infantry in High Wood, maybe because this was 4th Army doctrine or possibly because High Wood had caused so many problems. Putty may have become involved but this is irrelevant because he was responsible for the decision. To complicate the controversy is the issue of whether or not the tanks could get through High Wood: in the event this was also unimportant because none of the three that went into the wood was stopped by a tree. However, because the tanks went in to the wood it did make coordination with the artillery even more difficult.

The second controversy was Putty's decision to sack GOC 47th Division (Barter) after the battle. This has become confused with the first: Putty is said by some to have sacked Barter to cover himself over the tank decision. There is no firm evidence to support this and it would have been out of character for Putty to have acted in this way over a matter that was comparatively trivial. He had seen the demonstration of tanks and knew their limitations, knew 4th Army's guidance on their use, and knew High Wood; his decision, if he made one, would have been based on this knowledge. Any alternative would have had just as many problems. Putty sacked Barter because his plan of attack was flawed in many respects and resulted in unnecessarily high casualties, and the evidence supports this. Again there is little criticism of any of Putty's decisions during the month; even Lieutenant Colonel Warrender CO 15 London does not criticise him directly: his remark about him looking seedy (unwell) shows that Putty was not impervious to the constant pressure.

During October III Corps closed up on and took the Flers Line, the village of Flers and the hamlet of Eaucourt L'Abbaye. When the battle ended because of the deteriorating weather and the beginning of winter III Corps was facing the Butte de Warlencourt which it had found easier to take than to hold. Now the logistic problems which had been growing more and more acute as the corps advanced over what was now a wasteland would get even worse.

III Corps advanced about 12 miles in the battle at a cost of about 50,000 casualties: the enemy's losses can only be guessed at. In his letters Putty remarked that these casualties were less than he might have expected. This apparently casual and callous remark reflects the dominance of III Corps Artillery. Almost all the enemy artillery fire during the battle was on the attacking infantry, and there was comparatively little counter-battery fire or shelling of the corps rear area. This suggests that the German front line was constantly under pressure and they could do no more than keep the attacking divisions out.

Overall and within the constraints that have been mentioned Putty did well in 1916 and during the Battle of the Somme. It was a test of command more exacting, more testing than most battles in history. He made mistakes but the absence of any significant criticism from those above or below him is truly remarkable: if nothing else it showed that his leadership commanded considerable loyalty.

10

January-September 1917

Stuck

The New Year began as the old year had ended – in mud. III Corps was now in sight of Bapaume, or what was left of the town, but the German line astride the Butte de Warlencourt was still holding it up and any major offensive was out of the question. Survival was difficult enough at the front, traversing the ten miles from Albert required all the efforts of an unencumbered fit man; for the wounded, carrying parties and even fully equipped reliefs it was a journey of nightmares.

III Corps started 1917 with 15th Division on the left and 50th Division, taking over from 1st Division, on the right. 1st Division was now in support with its HQ in Albert and 48th in reserve with its HQ in Baizieux: HQ III Corps was nearby, still at Hénencourt. On 1 January Putty inspected the Corps Rest Station at Millencourt and opened a new recreation hall; he continued to do his best to improve conditions and facilities especially for those in support and reserve.

He also wrote to Edith Londonderry on 1 January:

> Dearest Circe, Am so sorry to hear that you have had the flue so badly, it must have been from sympathy that I caught the beastly thing, however, am all right again now and trust that this finds you the same. Shall not be over in time for your theatricals on the 8th as do not cross until the next day I mean the sea not you, cannot tell whether the boat is early or late but hope to roll up at the Ritz Hotel some time on the 9th send me a line there as to your whereabouts on that date. What does Mandril[1] tell you about his case, it reads too bad in the papers, that ass Lord Nicholson[2] is I imagine at the bottom of it all, but it is a scandal that a woman like Mrs Birch [wife of owner of nursing home in which Barrett resided] should come out on top of the Mandril however often he may have been on top of

1 General Cowans QMG.
2 Field Marshal Lord William Gustavus 1st Baron Nicholson (1845-1918) late RE headed inquiry into Barrett and Thomas cases. He was CGS when Putty incurred the 'grave displeasure of the Army Council' in 1911. Cowans was criticised for involving himself in matters of no concern to him but remained as QMG.

her. The weather has been worse and worse, the rain perfectly hopeless have got the roads pretty nearly all right but the trenches are simply drains, however the men are keeping wonderfully well under the circumstances. I see they have made me a KCMG alias a Night Commander of Much Good, it is another fence to have got over, my breast is becoming full of these decorations, I expected to see you made a Grand Cross of the WC not what you think but Women Cooks. All love and blessings to you for 1917 Yours ever Putty

Next day he sent a rather more carefully drafted report to the King:

My dear Wigram, Attached is the diary of the 3rd Corps for the month of December for the information of His Majesty. Am afraid there is little of interest as the weather has been so hopelessly wet it has been a case of existence for both sides however behind the lines we have made great strides with the railway, tram lines and roads, the huts are nearly all up and the comfort of the troops has improved all through the area, the men have kept wonderfully well considering the weather, not many trench feet chiefly flue and colds which they probably would have got at home from all accounts. The wet has had a very bad effect on the front trenches and the communication trenches, there is no doubt but when the ground has had so much shelling the earth is much more shaken than would appear from the surface the result is that after rain it gives and falls in. The men seem to be in very good spirits judging by the letters that they write home and Lloyd George as Premier seems to be very popular among them, I don't think they bother much about the political side but they are good judges of men of action. I hope to arrive in London on 9 Jan for ten days leave, shall make my headquarters at the Ritz Hotel, shall be glad of the change. We are all delighted at our Chief being made a Field Marshal he well deserved it for the Somme. Yours very sincerely, WP Pulteney.

Action at the front was very limited; patrols had to be sent out to protect working parties, gather information, and prevent enemy patrols operating. The artillery engagements continued with both sides attempting to dominate the other; III Corps Artillery was now only firing about 10,000 rounds each day. Putty's brief letter to Theresa Londonderry summarised the situation:

Dear Lady Londonderry, Many thanks for your nice letter of good wishes, I reciprocate all good fortune to you for 1917. Am so sorry to hear that you have broken your collar bone, you ought not to have ridden too soon or you will get a lump on the bone it doesn't matter to a man but it shows on a low dress! Our battle at the moment is versus mud. I hope to be in London next Wednesday. Yours very sincerely WP Pulteney.

Next day (6 January) a deserter from 2nd Marine Infantry came in, a very unusual circumstance given the difficulty of crossing no man's land.

Putty handed over to Major General Wilkinson (GOC 50th Division) on 8 January and proceeded on leave. Before he left he would have known change was coming and that III Corps was to be relieved by I ANZAC Corps at the end of the month; he probably also knew that he was then to move his corps S of the River Somme and take over the line held by XVIII French Corps, although 4th Army's orders to this effect were not issued until 15 January. His staff would have been left with much detailed planning to do, and as he drove along the well-worn road to Boulogne he would have had much to think about – but there was now Jessie.

During the middle of the month (18 and 19 January) snow fell again, and it was followed by a sharp frost. The whole countryside was now under a white pall, with here and there the stumps of trees or a lonely wooden cross. The hardened ground now made the going up to, or coming down from, the front line much easier, but it had the disadvantage of showing up more clearly tracks to and from trenches and the outline of the trenches themselves: and as a consequence the enemy's artillery had good targets. Patrols usually wore white coats in order to be less conspicuous.

Putty wrote to Ettie Desborough from the Ritz Hotel on 18 January:

> Dearest Chief, I hoped to have heard from you this morning that you might be coming up today, but now am afraid I shall not see you again as am off back tomorrow morning. Have had a glorious time on the quiet with my girl and if the war looks like lasting a long time shall come over at the end of the summer and marry her, she still persists in not announcing it (from shyness I think) she came as far as Laszlo's house to see me being painted but bolted back at the door so I just hauled her there myself the next afternoon. All my love and blessings Yours ever Putty.

He would have had little time to think about Jessie when he got back on 19 January. The corps staff had done much of the detailed work while he was away but the forthcoming operation was a complex one and many decisions would have waited his return. III Corps OpO No.169 issued

Sir William Pulteney Pulteney by Philip Alexius de Laszlo oil on canvas, 1917. (© National Portrait Gallery, London)

on 15 January had covered the hand over to I ANZAC Corps 23-28 January: III Corps OpO No.170 issued 21 January covered the relief of XVIII French Corps with three divisions in the line (48th, 1st and 50th) 8-13 February. HQ III Corps was to open at Villers Bretonneux at noon 28 January, settled in a place to oversee the operation. To extract his corps from one front and move it to another posed challenges enough for Putty and his staff but between these two fronts was the flooded valley of the River Somme crossed by only two very minor routes with narrow bridges. Along and across them had to pass nearly 100,000 men with their artillery and logistics, and this had to be done when it was bitterly cold with NE winds and hard frosts, and the snow still lying.

On 23 January DDMS III Corps visited Villers Bretonneux to see the new HQ; he recorded: 'Main office and Corps Commander's house still in occupation as ambulance. French propose to disinfect, but San Sect will also attend to this'.

Rawlinson wrote in his diary (28 January): 'Putty came on his way to Villers Bretonneux'. 15th Division signed off III Corps' part in the Battle of the Somme on the night 29/30 January. Strangely they were still in III Corps but in the line that was now the responsibility of I ANZAC Corps albeit very briefly. At 1.45 am 30 January 15th Division reported:

> Mounted a very successful raid on the Butte de Warlencourt. Two companies (8/10 Gordons 44 Bde) wearing white for camouflage in the snow took part. 5 machine-guns and teams destroyed, 1 trench mortar and team destroyed, 2 dug outs smashed and set on fire – one of which contained a company, 17 prisoners taken, a large number of Germans killed. Own casualties 16.

Putty wrote to Ettie Desborough again the day HQ III Corps moved (31 January):

> My dearest Chief, Many thanks for your letter of the 24 Jan. Had heard nothing about the reconciliation dinner, how like French not to turn up, I wonder if Derby had arranged it properly or whether he did not let them both know, I should have bet against it coming off, Haig came back the same day as I did. I saw Maurice Baring[3] at luncheon today looking the picture of health I think he was bear-leading some Russians about. The cold is intense the wind cuts right through one. I feel it more tonight than usual as have just changed my quarters having left my beautiful chateau and come in to an empty house but have no doubt after a week we shall have settled down, cleaned the place up and forgotten the lovely garden of last summer. The attack yesterday morning was a great success, the Germans had some big dug outs and the cold no doubt had driven them all in to them, the result was they were fairly caught and our casualties were very small. Things seem to be going on all right out here, probably the Boche will attack as soon as he can in order to forestall us, he seldom varies his programme and I expect he will have a similar one to Verdun of last year with more massed artillery if it is possible! Let me know if they send you a photo of my picture, I told them to. All Love Yours ever Putty.

3   Maurice Baring (1874-1945) HQ RFC Eton.

III Corps' casualties for January were: 10 officers and 134 other ranks killed, 31 officers and 634 other ranks wounded, 1 officer and 16 other ranks missing = 826.

On 1 February Putty was back N of the Somme with his CE (Brigadier General Schreiber) to say good bye to 179 Tunnelling Coy RE: he then went on to 35 POW Camp and to 15th Division. On his return he discussed with his DDMS the prevalence of dysentery which was now a matter requiring serious attention. Providing clean drinking water for so many men on the move and in such cold weather was extremely difficult. All the support arrangements which III Corps had developed over the past eight months had now to be re-established on the new front. Rawlinson came to see Putty in his new HQ on 2 February: they would have had much to discuss.

Putty wrote to the King on 3 February:

> My dear Wigram, Herewith the diary of the Third Corps for January for the information of His Majesty The King. The first part of the month was spent fighting the elements in the shape of either rain or mud, lately it has been the cold but so far fortunately with but little snow. In comparison with the other corps we have been very fortunate in the matter of trench feet but we took it in hand earlier and it paid us well. The French theory is that it is a microbe which exists only in dark places and grows like a fungus on a cheese, there is little doubt in my mind that this is correct and we have found certain section of trenches much worse than others and in these trenches the soil has been more moist than the others, they also treat the ... entirely with camphor with quite extraordinary success, we have tried this new treatment for a month and it seems alright but we shall know more definitely after another month's trial. The raid by 15th Division on the Butte de Warlencourt was a great success, they brought back 17 prisoners with only 17 casualties to themselves, they bombed the dug outs with Stokes and Phosphorous bombs setting fire to all three of them, they also had an element of luck as a machine-gun was holding them up when a shell (one of our own which came short) fell right on top of it destroying the gun and team. We are now in the course of moving S of the Somme with the corps and have already taken over the left part of the line we are going to hold and shall have completed by the middle of the month, the French have done a lot of work down in these parts, up to now my front seems fairly calm which I trust will continue until the relief is completed. We found our new quarters very cold at first but our stoves are gradually making it more habitable, being unfurnished made it look colder too, we are gradually collecting articles besides papering up any unnecessary passages of air. I dined this week with the French Corps Commander in the neighbour-hood, the German aviators very rudely bombed the village while we were at dinner causing some casualties outside, the effect was very local and did not even break the windows of our house. Gavin Hamilton has had a cold but wisely went straight to bed and has got rid of it. I enjoyed my leave but the weather was impossible. Yours very sincerely, WP Pulteney.

Just as the divisions were beginning to move to their new fronts and HQ III Corps was beginning to sort out the deployment of the artillery and corps troops behind them, 4th Army issued orders for further change. 15th Division, at last in corps reserve, was to be transferred to 3rd Army, and two new divisions (42nd and 59th) now arriving in France, were to join the corps. A more welcome change was the increase in the number of Lewis guns per battalion to 14, although this would further add to a now very heavy training requirement.

On 6 February Putty wrote to Edith Londonderry (much of the letter was about the wider progress of the war):

> Circe dearest, Put your pen to paper to tell me all the news from London town, did that man ever send you the photo of the picture, I think he has made me look too old but perhaps it was the only way to bring respectability in to it. Am in a new house that has no furniture, the cold in consequence has been pretty severe, have hired several articles, brought a large carpet and am gradually getting more comfortable. Raids are all the order of the day as a whole the Boche has had very much the worst of it, some of my fellows the other day counter-attacked after a raid and made them drop three Frenchmen they were taking away as prisoners that was promoting the Entente with a vengeance wasn't it? When are you coming over to Paris again or are you frightened of more remarks from Derbyshire! It would be fun to make up an Easter party though 8th April is rather late, the first week in March would probably be better and sooner. Those rhymes that Charley Hindlip sent Gavin about the West case and Miss Eaton of Exeter were quite excellent, did he get them from you? Mind you grow potatoes in all your pots those in your greenhouse not under the bed, they will pay you ten times over and under if you get the roots! My love to you From Putty.

A new challenge

At 10.4 am 8 February Putty took over the fronts now occupied by 1st and 48th Divisions from General Hirschauer[4] Commanding XVIII French Corps. It must have been a considerable relief that this front was relatively quiet since there were still so many units on the move: 50th Division was still moving to its position on the right of the corps and that day the advance party 59th Division arrived to take over from them. German aircraft paid particular attention to HQ III Corps at Villers Bretonneux, bombing it by day and night 9-11 February, adding to the difficulties of Putty and his staff. Nevertheless on 13 February 50th Division took over its sector and Putty was now responsible for a front of 12,000 yards that extended from the River Somme on the left to Genermont on the right. There was still much to be done but a major complex operation requiring meticulous planning and involving considerable risk had been successfully completed.

OC 388 Coy ASC recorded at this time:

> On 12 Feb sent workshop officer to Base for parts for Corps Commander's car. Temporary car arrived for Corps Commander; I tested the same, and driver, and found both unsatisfactory, and reported to SMTO. I was sent to Paris on 13 February for parts for Corps Commander's car, had gearbox fitted and car on the road that day [15 February].

For some journeys Putty could ride but for longer ones a car was essential and yet the roads were appalling.

---

4   Auguste Edouard Hirschauer (1857-1943).

48th Division now held the left sector with its HQ at Cappy; 1st Division was in the centre with its HQ at Méricourt-sur-Somme; and 50th Division was on the right with its headquarters at PC Gabrielle. However, Putty was given no chance to oversee the essential coordination of defence; this had to be left to Major General Wilkinson (GOC 50th Division) who assumed temporary command of III Corps on 14 February, while he again temporarily commanded 4th Army.

An issue that General Wilkinson had to deal with in Putty's absence concerned the water transport on the Somme, although no doubt they would have discussed it. Putty had ordered two barges for evacuation of the wounded by the Somme Canal and these arrived at Cappy on 14 February but were immediately ordered to return to Froissy by DDIWT. As in so many areas increased GHQ bureaucracy was tending to stifle initiative and common sense but Putty was more than prepared to fight his corner especially when the welfare of his soldiers was concerned.

59th Division joined III Corps on 16 February and then on 17 February the advance party of 42nd Division arrived from Egypt and was attached to 1st Division. That day 4th Army issued orders to its four corps to carry out attacks on 27 February: these were later postponed until 2 or 3 March because of the weather and in the case of III Corps, postponed indefinitely. It was presumably from 4th Army that Putty wrote next day to Ettie Desborough:

> Many thanks for your letter of the 13 Feb which I got on Friday, would have answered you yesterday only Gavin Hamilton was going over today so put it off as thought you would get it sooner. I had General Nivelle[5] to luncheon yesterday, he has aged since I saw him in London a month ago but is the best optimist I have come across, he caused a great deal of inconvenience by coming ¾ hour before he was due entirely owing to Gough[6] who brought him not knowing what to do with him, had just returned at the moment from seeing an attack being practised, was in a filthy state but made some excuse, did a lightening change then made my servant clean his boots by which time the excess had nearly vanished and we went through the programme of decorations he was giving away, Archie Montgomery[7] rubbed his cheek unconsciously after being kissed which made us all laugh. Robertson [CIGS] stayed the night here last night, he seems in good form, he says that Haig is better off than all the other Commander in Chiefs because he is not bothered by the political side but he inferred he was himself, he is really a simple man with tremendous power of working and concentration on points he thinks correct. George Milne[8] wrote me yesterday from Salonika obviously very bored and dying to bring the whole of his Army round to this country but we are too much committed to allow that now, the Bulgar and the Turk must be kept busy for the next four months, from all accounts Joe Maude[9] has done well in Mesopotamia he has had about 6,000 casualties but the Turks have had more than double but soon now the Grand Duke will be moving against them which will make a lot of differ-ence. Am doing Rawlinson's [GOC 4th Army] work for ten days while he goes to recruit

5   Robert Georges Nivelle (1856-1924) CinC French Armies on Western Front.
6   GOC 5th Army.
7   Major General Archibald Armar Montgomery (1871-1947) late RA MGGS 4th Army.
8   GOC Salonika Army.
9   GOC III Indian Army Corps.

his health down in the south of France with Bend D'Or[10] for ten days but my new 'quartier' is getting more habitable although they nearly got me there with a bomb last week just after dinner fortunately the effect of those bombs is very local, it demolished a house but did not break the windows of the house opposite. Go to my sister's house in 3 Lower Berkeley Street and ask to see my picture any time you are up that way she would be delighted. All love Yours ever Putty.

When he got back to his corps Putty would have found the weather yet again the greater enemy, and especially the mud. 48th Division was routinely reporting that their communication trenches were impassable. An officer of 7 NF (149 Bde 50th Division) wrote:

We left the trench at 3.30 am this morning [21 February] and it is now 2 pm and I do not think we have got all the men out yet. You cannot imagine the mud. And no mother's son would recognise him. They are really plastered from head to foot, and soaked through and through. There is such a maze of trenches here (mile upon mile of them) that we are constantly losing people. They wander about for hours in old disused trenches, and that is no joke with mud up to your knees and German shells chasing you all the time.

The ground to their front differed little to that which they had just left. The towns of Berny and Belloy by this time were practically only places on a map; an officer described one of them: 'All you could see of the town were a few odd bricks lying here and there'.

On 24 February III Corps received a report from 5th Army that a number of trenches on their front were believed to be evacuated by the enemy. As a consequence strong patrols were pushed out that night to re-establish contact with the enemy, they found them still holding the same line but this was the first hint of what was to come. The same day III Corps Signals recorded the erection of a Corps Wireless Directing Station, a major enhancement to the corps' ability to command and control its divisions.

The month ended with III Corps issuing OpO No.175 on 28 February ordering the relief of 50th Division by 59th Division on nights 6-9 March. For III Corps and its divisions it had been a month of considerable operational success – changing front across a major obstacle and in contact with the enemy. Casualties for the month had been low with 7 officers and 178 other ranks killed, 22 officers and 598 other ranks wounded, 1 officer and 28 other ranks missing = 834.

At 9.15 pm on 1 March 48th Division reported that fires had broken out in the village of Mons-en-Chaussée E of the Somme; then, at 11 pm, 4th Army issued 540/6(G): 'All reports from prisoners and other sources still tend to show that the enemy means to retire to the Hindenburg Line'. In III Corps' case this would mean that the Germans would have to break contact and withdraw across the Somme, then a further 15 miles E to their new line W of the St Quentin Canal; as yet there was no sign of this happening.

Despite this intelligence, little changed on 2 March except that 42nd Division started arriving from Egypt and concentrating at Hallencourt. Putty wrote to Ettie Desborough that day telling her of his troubles with Jessie:

10   Hugh Grosvenor 2nd Duke of Westminster (1879-1953) IY/CY.

Dearest Chief, I am in trouble as my girl has just written to me to say she goes in for Christian Science and gets all her diseases healed that way, her sister made her tell me, personally have strong convictions on that subject and have told her I would not stand any nonsense about not calling in a doctor if I thought it necessary and that she would have to give in on that point, most of her family go in for it too, have not had her answer but am afraid there is going to be trouble over it, tell me soundest of advisers your views on this subject, you know the way I always scoff at these sort of ideas but have never studied the subject but unless someone can produce some convincing arguments in favour of it am going to be obdurate as it is no use marrying and having an everlasting quarrel straight away. The ground is in a very bad state after the thaw, trench feet have come back again and everything has fallen in which should not have but still we shall soon get the grass growing to say nothing of the drying March winds. Was immensely struck with Lyautey[11] who I took round the Somme battlefields, he asked more intelligent questions than any French officer I have met, it is a great pity he did not come earlier on the scene in this country but his shout of vengeance on German towns on seeing the church of Albert was worth going a long way to hear! Bestlove Yours ever Putty.

Next day (3 March) Putty sent his monthly report to the King:

My dear Wigram, Attached is the diary of III Corps for the month of February, for the information of His Majesty The King. There is not very much of interesting detail in it this time it has been a case of taking over from the French; getting them out of the area and seeing what havoc a thaw after the severe frost can do, we are over the worst of our troubles now but defend me in the future from any road with a chalk foundation after frost there seemed to be a sort of spontaneous combustion which raised the road up into heaps. Am sorry to say that we have lost 15th Division which under McCracken did me so splendidly in the Somme fighting, the 59th under Sandbach [Major General Sandbach] has arrived, they are very green and have much to learn but the class of men is above average, when one gets a new lot like that it makes me feel as if one was encountering a new school class that had to learn from the beginning. So far there is no sign of retirement in front of my sector but it appears a clever move if you are able to spare the men to make the new lines behind, the Boche is shortening the line by this retirement further he is destroying all the villages as he goes in which to my mind there is a good deal of method he seems to be doing it purposely to show France what state her country will be in if this class of retirement continues. Am sorry to say that Gavin Hamilton is laid up in London with his old trouble in his lung. Am glad he got there as was afraid he was going to crack up here from the cough he had, it was sure pluck his sticking as long as he did. Yours very sincerely, WP Pulteney.

Patrol operations continued on the front line both to protect their own positions and to gather information on the enemy. On 4 March 9 DLI 50th Division carried out a successful raid and brought back six prisoners from 10 Grenadier Regt and with no casualties. Next day (5 March)

---

11   General Hubert Lyautey Morocco 1912-1915 Minister of War 1916-1917.

59th Division relieved 50th Division, the latter was withdrawn into corps reserve and given much needed time for training. The indications of a German withdrawal continued to mount but patrols still found the front to be firmly held; another successful raid, this time by 48th Division on 8 March, took 2 unwounded prisoners and 2 MGs. That day III Corps Cyclist Bn was reorganised into a HQ and two fighting companies each of 130 men; this battalion and the Corps Cavalry Regt would have a vital role to play if and when the corps was required to advance against a retreating enemy.

Putty wrote to Ettie on 9 March:

Dearest Chief, Mille thanks for your letter of 5 Mar which was full of cheerful news. I went to Paris on Tuesday [6 March] for the night and had great fun with Charlie and Edie, Reggie Pembroke was also there so it was quite an original III Corps gathering, I had to come away the next morning but Edie did not know when she could get a boat to bring her back. We have had more snow which fortunately disappears soon after it falls but the wind has been icy. Raids continue on both sides every single night, there is no doubt but that they keep up the fighting spirit of the troops besides being invaluable for identifications. You are quite right about the excitement about the Curzon dance it reached us here with many exaggerations. Gavin Hamilton writes a better account of himself this morning, he has been staying with Millicent Duberly,[12] he says she has made the house very nice down there near St Neots, I do hope he will be able to come back to me at the end of the month, I miss him so much when he is away, to have a man of the world about with one is worth anything. The Boche still seems to be retiring, what he fears is a concentration of guns on our part and by moving back he shortens his line and makes such a concentration very difficult, I wish we could re-populate the desert as we go along it all looks such a sinful waste of land. Much love Yours ever Putty.

On 10 March Putty went with his CE to see the site of a new camp for HQ III Corps W of Foucaucourt, nearly eight miles in advance of its present position, but still the Germans held firm. Two days later Rawlinson held one of his conferences at HQ 4th Army: Putty attended with his GSO2 and AQMG. The main subject of discussion was the possibility of a German withdrawal and the record included: 'It can be assumed that the first bound will be approximately for III and IV Corps to the line of the Somme and the German Intermediate Line'. Putty raised the question of lateral roads in addition to the main forward road; Rawlinson replied that the forward road was of main importance, but, as the weather improved, the difficulties of establishing lateral communications would decrease. Putty was concerned about the prospect of the Germans imposing endless delays on an advance restricted to a few forward routes especially with a major water obstacle ahead. Rawlinson tended to be defensive and negative when questioned at his conferences on matters to which insufficient thought had been given. Rawlinson then drew attention to the necessity to continue training, and pointed out that III Corps were just receiving two very inexperienced divisions (59th and 42nd): he considered that, as far as possible, 'GOC III Corps should concentrate on the platoon organisation'; he went on to point

12   Hon Millicent Florence Eleanor Wilson (1872-1952) married 1 Sir Charles Edward Cradock-Hartopp Bt SG 1879-1888, 2 3rd Earl Cowley, 3 Major Grey William Duberly Gren Gds killed in action 1915.

out that 'with the difficulties of transport in the Mediterranean it is unlikely that 42nd Division will be able to go into the line before 1 Apr'. All the corps commanders pointed out the difficulty of carrying out any training with the limited troops at their disposal; and told Rawlinson it was probable that reliance would have to be placed almost entirely on schools.

There is no record of what Putty thought of Rawlinson's instructions on training. He was contemplating an advance by his corps across the Somme valley against an enemy that would fight rearguard actions at every opportunity; being told to train two of his four divisions, one of which was in the line, in the basic skills might have led him to question the army commander's judgement. When he got back to his headquarters he wrote to Ettie:

> Dearest Chief, Mille thanks for your dear letter, your advice is exactly what my feelings are but she is not taking it very well at present, rather on the line that the other men who married her sisters do not mind. However, I shall see her on Sunday [18 March] and will let you know or come down to see you to talk it over. Well done Joe Maude and Baghdad, it won't matter his being Ld Baghdad for his father is dead, I think it will have a very good effect in India and the East generally, the appointment of a faithful Arab governor of Baghdad will take much discrimination of choice, he will be a rara aris. Really a spring day and again ever so many thanks for your letter. Yours ever Putty.

On 13 March 59th Division reported more fires behind the German lines and 1st Division that the Germans were registering their own front line, but for three more days the Germans held that front line and strongly resisted any penetration. Then, on the morning of 17 March, the Germans withdrew leaving isolated posts to cover and delay. By 10.15 am 48th Division on the left was E of La Maisonette and in the German 3rd Line; shortly afterwards 1st Division in the centre was through Barleux and into Éterpigny; and on the right 59th Division reported that Mazancourt and Misery had been taken by the end of the day. Few Germans had been encountered and by nightfall all three divisions of III Corps had reached the Somme. Though they had expected the German withdrawal for some days, the enemy had managed to break contact and withdraw across the Somme valley without significant casualties.

From Offoy to Péronne the Somme ran roughly parallel to the front. It was a very formidable obstacle with a canal following the left bank, the main stream under the right, and in between them marshy ground cut in places by narrow channels with osier beds. Every bridge had been destroyed by the enemy. The roads crossed the marsh on causeways, which banked up the water into pools nearly half a mile wide. Where there were mills there had been bridges over the mill-pond and spillway, as well as over the flood water channels already mentioned, the canal and the main stream; crossings were practicable only where the causeways existed. So this was not one water obstacle but several, with marshy ground between them: it should have been a slow and difficult operation to cross the valley.

Putty handed over command that night to Major General Fanshawe (GOC 48th Division) and proceeded on leave. He would have had few qualms about leaving at this time since there was no indication that the Germans would attempt to do more than delay the corps crossing the Somme. There were three separate crossing operations to be supported and coordinated; the planning had been done and Fanshawe was more than capable of overseeing the execution. A hint of what might be to come was in DDMS' report before Putty left that 1st Division had found arsenic in the water at Barleux.

Advance to the Hindenburg Line

His relationship with Jessie was in crisis with her revelation that she was a Christian Scientist and this would have been uppermost in his mind as he drove through the night. Two months ago, when he was last on leave, everything had been going so well with the prospect of marriage: now that was in jeopardy and there was little likelihood of leave again until later in the year.

Meanwhile on the left of III Corps very rapid progress was being made. 48th Division had launched six pontoons near the junction of the Somme Canal and the Canal du Nord. The canal was full of snags, tree trunks had to be sawn through, and ice an inch and a half thick had to be broken, with the enemy a quarter a mile away. By noon 17 March a floating bridge 60 feet across the canal was complete and that evening a company 8 Warwicks crossed the canal by the bridge and was ferried across the river on pontoon rafts. It was the first unit to enter the once beautiful town of Péronne, now a pitiable sight. By the end of 18 March patrols of all three divisions were on or across the Somme: on the left 48th Division patrols were on a line Mont St Quentin-Péronne; in the centre 1st Division was in Brie; and in the S 59th Division was approaching St Christ. There was almost no resistance.

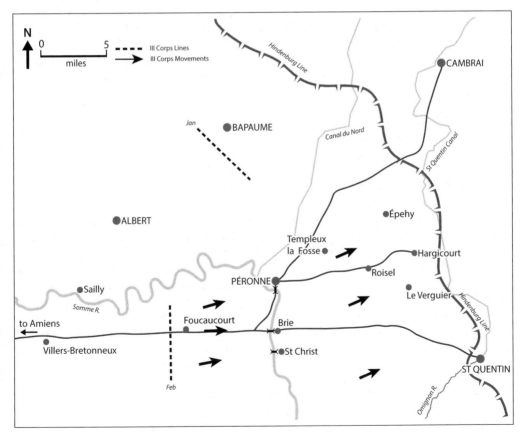

Map 9   Advance to the Hindenburg Line 1917.

Behind the advanced patrols bridging was being rapidly constructed. The heavy timber piles of the river bridge at Péronne had been destroyed to the water line by fire and explosives, but the shore bays on either bank were fairly sound. 475 Fd Coy RE simultaneously prepared a raft for ferrying field artillery and built a new bridge on the piles of the old one, with four pontoons in the centre bays. This was completed at 3.30 pm 18 March. 1st Division (3 Bde) also built a rough footbridge at Brie that day and formed a bridgehead to cover the work of the engineers, and this was secured by first light 19 March.

III Corps OpO No.182 which was issued at 2.30 pm 18 March ordered an outpost line to be taken up on the banks of the Somme, preparations made at once for bridging the river and suitable positions secured for covering their construction: it confirmed verbal orders given earlier but the speed of advance meant that it was in danger of being overtaken by events.

4th Army issued 540/14(G) at 4.15 pm:

> 1. The enemy are retiring along the whole front of 4th Army and in front of 5th Army on our left and French 3rd Army on our right.
> 3. Corps will continue to follow up the enemy with advance guards of all arms.

III Corps did not need any encouragement to press forward as rapidly as possible. An advance guard had already been formed of Corps Cav Regt, an infantry battalion, two field batteries and some sappers, all under the command of Brigadier General Ward CRA 48th Division and this was moving ahead on the left of the corps.

Consolidation of the bridgeheads continued on 19 March. Rawlinson held a conference at HQ 4th Army that morning: at it the acting III Corps Commander (Fanshawe) said:

> The bridge at Brie would be through tomorrow. In addition, the bridge at Halle[s] should be passable for light traffic at 12 noon today. He would then be able to get traffic through La Quinconce and Péronne to Doingt. He pointed out that the high ground N of Doingt was very important and had been occupied by III Corps this morning.

Meanwhile that day the Corps Cav Regt crossed the Somme on rafts with orders to keep in touch with the retreating enemy.

20 March was a day of rapid advance by III Corps, as much as 5 miles in some places: by the end of it 48th Division was just E of Péronne; 1st Division had completed the bridge at Brie and was now advancing; and 59th Division had just completed its bridge at St Christ for use by cavalry. Remarkably, III Corps mounted troops had reached the line Tertry-Bouvincourt-Tincourt with patrols in front of that. The crossing at Brie was the most important because it carried the main Amiens-St Quentin road over the river; its reconstruction also entailed the greatest amount of work. There were in all six gaps to be bridged: the canal, the canal flood-water channel, the millstream, the mill spillway, a breach blown in the 600 yard causeway, and the river itself. Working through the night by the light of bonfires and using local material, the engineers of 1st Division completed the crossing for horse transport by 5 am 20 March; twenty four hours after the work had started.

Late that night III Corps issued OpO No.184 withdrawing 1st Division into reserve and reducing its front to two divisions. The advance continued next day (21 March); out front were the Corps Cav Regt and Corps Cyclist Bn pushed against the German rearguards (6th

III Corps Cyclist Battalion, Vraignes, March 1917. (© IWM Q1886)

Dragoons and infantry) with occasional minor engagements and by nightfall they had reached the line Poeuilly-Fléchin-Bernes-Marquaix. The threat at this stage was an attack by a German cav bde against the corps mounted troops, now widely dispersed. Behind the advanced guard the three divisions continued to cross the Somme. Heavy bridging material arrived by barge at Cappy and by rail at La Flaque, nine and ten miles respectively from Brie, and was delivered to 1st Division.

III Corps mounted troops began to meet stronger resistance on 22 March. Enemy infantry attacked their post at Bernes and were driven off with 6 casualties. They reported Vendelles strongly defended by machine-guns, and also that Roisel was also strongly held. At 5 pm HQ III Corps issued OpO No.186 which gave new boundaries between corps and divisions, the arrival of 42nd Division and departure of 1st Division. Of more significance was the arrival of 5th Cavalry Division to be inserted in front of III Corps on 23 March, reporting direct to 4th Army. This was a strange decision of Rawlinson's at such a late stage in the advance: it suggests that he thought the army vulnerable to counter-attack until such time as III Corps had consolidated E of the Somme, rather than any attempt to bounce the Hindenburg Line. However, it involved two risks – holding up the advance and allowing the Germans time to prepare covering positions, and getting the new command and control arrangements to work effectively and quickly. III Corps had the Ambala Cav Bde now on its front and coordination must have been difficult, but seemed to work well. On 24 March, for example, III Corps took Roisel but the Ambala Cav Bde had one squadron in Hamelet just to the S. The divisions continued to advance but their progress was slow for the Germans had destroyed every bridge, cratered every road, destroyed everything of military value and much else, and placed numerous booby-traps, all designed to impose delay.

Putty had been appointed KCMG on 21 March: he returned from leave on the evening of 24 March to a very different situation from that which he had left a week earlier. Although he would have done much of the planning before he left, Major General Fanshawe had overseen its execution: he had done an excellent job in instilling a sense of urgency and coordinating the various elements of the corps, for which Putty gave him the credit.

At 10.30 am 25 March Putty attended Rawlinson's conference with his BGGS and DAA&QMG, and reported:

> The cavalry were on the line Bois de Tincourt-Marquaix-Hamelet-Bernes-Fléchin. Bernes and Fléchin were commanding positions on this line. Work in filling the craters E of the Somme was progressing, but the difficulties of supply would be considerable in the event of the main line of resistance being advanced, unless a reserve park or some additional horse transport became available. The chief difficulty lay in the fact that all available lorries were required for bringing up stone and if a portion of the lorries worked E of the Somme there would not be sufficient to cope with the required work on the roads.

Despite the warning from Putty, 4th Army issued 540/20(G) at 3 pm:

> Corps will advance their main lines of resistance to the line Germaine-Beauvois-Poeuilly-Bernes-Marquaix-Longavesnes-Liéramont-Équancourt-Ytres-Bertincourt. The above line will be occupied, under cover of darkness, on night 28/29 March and its occupation will be completed by 6 am 29 March.

By the end of 25 March 5th Cavalry Division was on the line Villévèque, across the Omignon River-Poeuilly-Fléchin-Bernes-Hamelet-Marquaix-Aizecourt-Nurlu and were in touch with the enemy on this line. III Corps mounted troops and advanced guard were also on this line but mainly concentrated in the centre. There was very little opposition that day except that the enemy drove out the post of 4 Ox & Bucks which had occupied Roisel the previous night. Putty had just three days to advance his main line of resistance to what was now only a very weak outpost line but, as he had pointed out to Rawlinson, this was not in itself difficult; the problem would be supporting his divisions on this line.

Next day 48th Division made particularly good progress with 4 Ox & Bucks assisted by two squadrons of 18 Bengal Lancers and two armoured cars re-taking Roisel, and 143 Bde occupying Longavesnes to the N. The division was effectively on the line it was required to consolidate on two days later. The detailed orders for occupying the new line were not issued by III Corps until 10 am 27 March but divisions were now required to be in position on the night 27/28 March, twenty-four hours earlier than required by 4th Army; this merely reflected the speed of events. 5th Cavalry Division was still covering III Corps: in several places it was forward of the new position, in others actually on it. They did particularly well in front of 48th Division carrying out a mounted attack on a copse E of Longavesnes in which 6 Germans were killed and 9 taken prisoner. 8 H took Villers Faucon and other units Saulcourt and Guyencourt. All of this was done with few casualties.

59th Division was progressing more slowly but by the end of the day 178 Bde was in Bouvincourt. One of the problems was still the bridging. To make way for the new (heavy) bridge at Brie, the medium bridge had to be dismantled and a deviation bridge thrown to take traffic in the meantime; but as there was no room for the deviation bridge at the mill spillway, traffic had to be stopped for over twelve hours for one period. The breach in the causeway had widened under the scour, so a pile dam filled with rubble from the houses of Brie was built upstream, and charges were exploded in the bed of the river to guide the water back into the old channels; the roadway was also made good with bricks from the village. Despite all the difficulties CRE 1st Division, whose task it still was, had the heavy bridge open by 4 pm 28 March.

The AQ log recorded that day that HQ 29 HAG, 208 Siege Bty and 12 Hy Bty joined the corps and that seven siege and hy btys left it. This constant rotation of the artillery was necessary if only to give everyone some rest but to coordinate this with the operational requirement to support the forward divisions must have been extremely difficult for the staff. Later that evening III Corps issued OpO No.190 transferring 50th Division to 3rd Army on 31 March.

The following day (29 March) HQ III Corps moved forward to Bichat Camp, comprised of nissen huts, W of Foucaucourt. 5th Cavalry Division was withdrawn with 48th and 59th Divisions now occupying the new main line of resistance; a new CRS was opened at Cerisy on the Somme. Little changed on 30 March apart from 178 Bde 59th Division being ordered to advance and take Vendelles and Jeancourt; the new defensive line was to be held if they were

Pulteney talking to 2 SG in Péronne March 1917. (© IWM Q1961)

counter-attacked but the advance was to be continued and the Germans given no opportunity to prepare delaying positions. Both villages were taken by 59th Division next day in a very successful attack that earned Putty's congratulations in corps orders. 48th Division also secured the village of St Émilie well forward of its defensive line. Overall opposition had not been significant and the enemy pulled out of its delaying positions as soon as seriously challenged.

The ADOS log noted on 30 March: 'Saw DA&QMG who also wanted special tents for Corps Comd and staff'. Suitable buildings were now difficult to find and perhaps they already had intelligence on the enemy's use of delayed action mines.

At the end of March III Corps had 59th Division on its right and 48th Division on its left. 42nd Division was in corps reserve with its HQ at Hallencourt well to the rear. 1st Division had left the corps on 20 March and 50th Division on 31 March. Considering all that had happened in the month, III Corps' casualties for March were remarkably light with 8 officers and 163 other ranks killed, 34 officers and 576 other ranks wounded, 1 officer and 21 other ranks missing = 803. Despite the weather, the difficulties of twice crossing the Somme valley, and the German delaying tactics, III Corps had achieved much in the month.

April started with high winds from the NW and heavy rain. III Corps continued to push forward to the Hindenburg Line while covering and consolidating the new line of resistance, and repairing the roads. On 1 April 48th Division took Épehy and Pezières in a surprise attack without preparatory artillery fire capturing 26 prisoners and a field gun. HQ III Corps issued OpO No.192 that afternoon ordering 48th Division to consolidate a new advanced line from Villers Faucon to Saulcourt, to conform with the corps on the left. Separately III Corps ordered 59th Division to take Le Verguier and the high ground nearby on 2 April.

The bad weather continued next day (2 April) with very high winds, rain and even snow during the afternoon. Both divisions reported progress against increasing opposition. It was at last possible to move 42nd Division up and HQ 42nd Division opened at Méricourt that evening. The roads had been improved to such an extent that on 3 April BGRA III Corps was able to order the heavy and siege batteries in corps reserve up to Roisel, and assist operations of the forward divisions. 59th Division (7 Sher For 178 Bde) was involved in heavy fighting that day near Le Verguier.

Heavy snow fell most of 4 April. 59th Division was stopped by strong German defensive positions; on the right the attacking battalion fell back to its original position under heavy machine-gun fire from S of Le Verguier, and with heavy casualties, and on the left the division found the defences NW of Hargicourt covered by very strong and thick wire. III Corps therefore cancelled the orders for the division to take Le Verguier and ordered it to establish a line of posts short of it: 59th Division was now far too extended to do more. 42nd Division started to cross to the E of the Somme with battalions sent forward to 48th Division for experience and others employed in Péronne to clear roads and the railway station.

Putty sent his monthly report to the King on 4 April:

My dear Wigram, Herewith the 3rd Corps diary for the month of March for information of HM The King. The last ten days of the month is very interesting and great credit is due to General Fanshawe of the 48th Division for pressing his reconnaissance on the 17th and getting across the Somme through Péronne so quickly to Mt Saint Quentin which dominated all the crossings over the river to the south, when one goes over the ground east of the river and looks at their dispositions for preventing our crossing one can only marvel at their not even staying with a rearguard, I calculate that it would have cost me 20,000 men at least to have forced the crossing. The joy of the men at getting out of the trenches in to the open to fight you can well imagine, notwithstanding the appalling weather the health of the troops has been excellent, the acts of vandalism have left practically no shelter but after all it is like the winter of 1914 when I had 4th and 6th Division round Armentières you could not flog the men in to the houses because of fear of shelling, the same applies here on the open downs where the few isolated villages are all shell traps. The delay action mines which we discovered here worked on the principle of acid eating its way through a small rod thus releasing a strong spring, cleverly made and quite evidently thought out a long time beforehand. The evacuation of the poor refugees that had been left behind was a great strain on our ambulances, it took us about five days averaging 400 a day, some of them of great age but beyond five who died before we could move them we got them all away alright. The sight of Péronne will make every Frenchman vow revenge for the rest of his life, no fruit tree is left nor those delightful sycamores which are trained to make lattice work of shade in the summer have been spared, the bricks of the houses enable us to repair roads which otherwise would have been a very difficult question from the amount of metal required we make diversions round the craters and in the summer when one can go across the fields they will be no obstacle. My engineers covered themselves with glory in bridging the Somme, the main difficulty was damming the river so that it went back through its proper channel instead of the course the Boche had blown for it, it meant working day and night fortunately without any molestation from either shelling or aeroplane. Was very sorry not to have seen you when I was over in London. Yours very sincerely, WP Pulteney.

Some time that day Putty met his CE (Brigadier General Schreiber) at Le Catelet, the next location of HQ III Corps.

48th Division had a day of hard fighting on 5 April and made more progress. It reported:

All objectives gained and held on frontage of at least 3,000 yards including Ronssoy and Lempire. Enemy garrisons totalling about 400-500 men were driven out. Many enemy killed. Our casualties about 188.

It also reported capturing 45 prisoners and 12 machine-guns. HQ III Corps again ordered 59th Division to take Le Verguier and the associated high ground by 6 am 7 April (OpO No.194).

III Corps issued two OpOs on 7 April: OpO No.195 postponed 59th Division's attack 24 hours to allow it to be coordinated with 61st Division of the corps to its S, and the capture of Le Verguier and the rest of the objective was now to be completed on 9 Apr; OpO No.196 altered the inter divisional boundary, with 48th Division taking over a portion of the line from 59th Division. 125 Bde 42nd Division was placed under command 48th Division to help with this change. 59th Division's attack on Le Verguier and the high ground was further postponed on 8 April (OpO No.197); this may well be because Major General Romer, up to then BGGS III Corps, took over command of the division that day. OpO No.198 was also issued on 8 April ordering demonstrations to be made against the Hindenburg Line to identify its positions and the strength of its defences.

Putty wanted 59th Division to get on and take Le Verguier but the division was very extended; the first delay was to coordinate the attack with the corps on the right, the second to reduce the length of the division's front, and the third to give the new commander time to look at the plan.

Also that day Putty wrote to Ettie Desborough:

> Dearest Chief, Delighted to get your letter of 4 Apr yesterday. Yes have been hard at it all this last week, have captured several more villages in most cases inflicting more casualties on the enemy than we suffered ourselves, we have been fighting for observation etc, the bridging of the rivers has been vastly interesting work especially damming the river so as to divert it back to its proper channel instead of the one a Boche explosion had made it go down. America coming in is real good business, there are many things such as the construction of aeroplanes, guns, ships etc that she can be of the utmost assistance in, she especially can help Russia and I hope she will do that more than anything else because if we get sympathy between those two it will be the making of Russia and personally I think she is the most important asset to keep on the right path of the moment. The weather is impossible, we have had everything in the last 48 hours except an earthquake and really it seems curious that we did not have that as evidently there is some very disturbing influence among the elements, no leaf on the tree, no growth of grass, the only living thing in this wilderness are the magpies and one has got its nest close to my camp on the main road, I can't think how she can keep the eggs warm. My love and blessings to you From Putty.

Little changed next day (9 April) except that 59th Division continued to fight its way forward to Le Verguier on the right and Hargicourt on the left, and 4 Balloon Wing RFC joined the corps. The weather was appalling on 10 April with a strong W wind, snow and hail; progress was minimal. III Corps OpO No.199 was issued at 11 am 11 April setting out an offensive policy – divisions were to push forward posts with a view to obtaining direct observation of the Hindenburg Line. Brigadier General Bonham-Carter was appointed BGGS III Corps that day; his brother had been Private Secretary to the Prime Minister Herbert Asquith 1910-1916.

Also on 11 April Putty wrote to Edith Londonderry:

> Dearest Circe, How are you? What have you been up to? The weather is useless to discuss because we daily get everything except an earthquake, but fortunately the wind has been in the right direction viz bang up in the Boche's eyes which must have been most unpleasant in these terrific hailstorms. I think the whole attack [Battle of Arras] has gone off well, the Vimy ridge was the nut to crack like all positions are when they form a flank to an attack and the Canadians have covered themselves with glory, I should imagine that we must have knocked out about eight Boche divisions which is good for he had just brought 8 over from Russia, a few more knocks like this and he will have no more troops left to make an offensive with even if he wants to. The aeroplane fighting has been desperately severe I should say that we are 3 to 2 up on the Boche and this branch will probably be highly developed by the Yank. Gavin Hamilton has gone away to 4th Army as Mil Sec[13] which he should do well but I shall miss him very much indeed it was such a comfort having a man of the

---

13   Putty's new ADC was Captain Giles Harold Loder SG.

III Corps Cavalry Regiment, Vermand, April 1917. (© IWM Q2928)

world as ADC have also just lost my chief staff officer and have got another one arriving this evening, have never met him before but they tell me he is a good man. We are tidying up the destroyed villages and already they begin to look like habitations once more. Much love Yours ever Putty.

Very little changed on 12 April including the weather; the strong winds, rain and snow continued. III Corps closed up to the Hindenburg Line with its artillery and other corps troops coming in behind the forward divisions. A site for a new CRS was selected at Doingt between road and railway.

On 14 April Putty again wrote to Ettie Desborough:

Dearest Chief, Things are going well, the Boche is evidently fighting to a time table and the Arras attack defeated him because he did not think that the Vimy Ridge could be taken, now he is apparently retiring from Lens which will be a considerable asset, the long and the short of it is that his troops will not face another Somme bombardment, the prisoners' letters this time disclose very serious disturbances at Kiel and Hamburg and if Russia can pull herself together we may see the beginning of the end much more quickly than we anticipated, for the next five months we have got to put every effort we can in. Was very glad to hear last night that Charlie L and Reggie P were both all right, was nervous when I heard that their brigadier had been killed. The Boche will make another (definite this time) peace offer before June is my prophecy at the moment. My love Yours ever Putty.

The corps rear area was becoming increasingly congested as more and more specialist units arrived: that day 12 Mobile (Hygiene) Laboratory joined.

59th Division (6 N Staffs 176 Bde) took Villaret on 16 April. 4th Army, however, was getting concerned about the possibility of a German counter-attack and issued 540/33(G) extract:

2. The heavy counterattack made against I ANZAC Corps on our left on 15 April emphasises the necessity of undertaking every possible preparation to meet and defeat such counterattacks on the 4th Army front. As our line advances to close quarters with the Hindenburg Line, the chance of counterattacks by considerable forces will undoubtedly increase.

4. The Brown Line will remain the main line of resistance until orders for a further advance are issued, and it is to this line that the outposts will withdraw if driven-in by a serious counterattack.

5. Corps commanders are to take this matter in hand and personally ensure the Brown Line is made into a strong defensive position along the whole front of 4th Army. Special attention must be paid to points of junction between corps and neighbouring armies.

This order of Rawlinson's lacks any clear strategic aim: the Hindenburg Line was very strong and would require a deliberate attack to breach it, so reference to 'further advance' suggests a further German withdrawal which must have been unlikely. Therefore to close up to the Hindenburg Line was unnecessary and forced 4th Army into holding a line that had limited tactical importance or strength. However, the advance to close with the Hindenburg Line went on and now involved battles for farms rather than villages. That night, which was wet and stormy, 48th Division captured Le Tombois and Petit Priel Farms, NE of Lempire; Gillemont Farm on the Ronssoy-Bony road held out on this occasion. Rawlinson sent his congratulations next day:

Please convey to 48th Division my admiration of their success last night. To have carried out a successful night attack on a wide front in the midst of such a storm reflects highest credit on all ranks especially on the leadership of subordinate infantry commanders. My congratulations to all troops engaged including artillery.

HQ III Corps moved forward from Foucaucourt to Le Catelet on 18 April. Brigadier General Home BGGS Cav Corps wrote later of this location: 'HQ (in an apple orchard) consists of huts. The chateau and farm are in ruins, fruit trees are cut down'. Bonham-Carter (now BGGS HQ III Corps) wrote many years later:

Our hutted camp was comfortable. I had a nissen hut to myself, a most luxurious provision of accommodation for one man. It was divided into two rooms, a bedroom and a sitting room: both of course contained only camp furniture. The Corps Commander had similar accommodation. I always thought that rather an attractive trait in his character was his love of birds. In his hut a swallow raised two or three broods. He used to explain to us the careful sanitary arrangements of the parent birds. On the GS with me were BC Battye (GSO 2), a Sapper, who had been in 50th Division with me. He was one of the well-known family who served India for generations. Like them he was very religious and I think he must have found some of the talk in Putty's mess a bit trying.

Pulteney with Rawlinson in Péronne 1917. (NAM)

On the night of 19/20 April 48th Division mounted another unsuccessful attack on Gillemont Farm, otherwise little changed. HQ III Corps issued GO2334/7 on 21 April – Outline of General Policy of Work on Defences: 'Now that troops are approaching the Hindenburg Line, the Corps Commander considers it necessary to outline the general policy of work on defences in the III Corps'.

P(AA) Bty joined the corps and HQ 48th Division moved forward from Tincourt to Roisel; but there was still no clear overall direction reaching III Corps. 4th Army's orders hovered between attack and defence, fortunately the Germans stayed within the Hindenburg Line.

Putty wrote to Ettie again on 23 April:

> Dearest Chief, Ever so many thanks for yours of the 19 April which I got last night. Was delighted to read your news about Russia for I have had grave misgivings during the last six weeks, am nervous about their navy and am afraid the Boche will get in behind their right flank if they do not pull themselves together at sea, am afraid they shot a lot of their best officers, evidently the Boche does not anticipate bother from the East as he keeps on withdrawing divisions from there to come here. Our offensive has been a great success up to now, the putting in of the cavalry under the circumstances was the only fault I can find, can only imagine they were fretting so much at having had nothing to do they let them

have a go with the result that we have lost a great many horses at a time when we have none too many, besides dead horses on ground you have to advance over has the most nauseating effect, am delighted to read what you say about Charley had hoped to have heard from him, have always told him that if got a chance it should be with his regiment he never would have done with an infantry battalion and between ourselves he is not brainy enough to go on the staff. Had a long talk to Repington[14] last week, he is more optimistic than I remember seeing him before, manpower is the only difficulty as it was and always will be but personally think we are wise not to have taken everyone at once otherwise there would have been no reserve for the final pinch and remember telling Kitchener that two years ago. No I had not heard that they had found poor Bron's grave am so glad for it is a great consolation, it is very remarkable the trouble the Germans have gone to in bringing in all flying people everywhere it is the same, yet I was in a cemetery on Friday [20 April] which had been shamefully desecrated, vaults used as dug outs besides far more shameful things but what does gratify one is to find so many German graves in all these villages their losses must have been colossal even behind the line. These delay action mines are still a great nuisance nobody except the De Crespigny[15] family will sleep in a house or near a cross roads, some of them were set to 48 days so we shall not be safe from them for another month as a matter of fact the men are much better in tents for all these villages are pure masses of filth besides being shell traps. Joe Maude seems to have done wonders in Mesopotamia but conclude the heat there will hinder him a good deal now, I wish I felt the same confidence in Archie Murray in Palestine but can only hope I have misjudged his capabilities. Best love Yours ever Putty.

Putty mentioned the problem of long delay mines, one of which went off in Tincourt close to HQ 48th Division; other large mines exploded in Épehy on 24 and 26 April. There is no record of casualties, probably because everyone kept out of buildings.

Both divisions had attacked during the night 23/24 April. 48th Division attacked Gillemont Farm and the high ground known as 'The Knoll'. Gillemont Farm was captured but retaken by the enemy; 144 Bde suffered over 400 casualties before the spur on which it stood was secured as a result of a further attack late on 24 April. Three counter-attacks were repulsed on 25 April, in one of them 20 Germans were killed trying to enter the farm. Such attacks and counter-attacks for ground of tactical importance took place all along the front, and continued to the end of the month; sometimes casualties were heavy.

Brigadier General Bonham-Carter wrote to his father two weeks after taking over as BGGS:

My General is Sir William Pulteney an old Scots Guardsman and a charming man to work with. We are now living in a camp in the grounds of what must have been a very nice house and farm. With two exceptions the houses are now nothing but heaps of rubble. The two exceptions are two farm houses probably occupied I should think by the sons of the owner. They were without roofs or floors, but we have put a covering over them and use the lower floor rooms as a dining room and kitchen.

14   Lieutenant Colonel Charles à Court Repington (1858-1925) Eton RB War Correspondent.
15   Probably Brigadier General De Crespigny late Gren Gds Comd 1 Gds Bde.

On 28 April III Corps issued OpO No.203 ordering 42nd Division to relieve 48th Division with command of the left sector to pass at 10 am 3 May. Summarising their captures during the month of April, 48th Division reported 68 other ranks, one light field gun, 16 machine-guns and 2 trench mortars; 59th Division reported 16 other ranks and 4 machine-guns. III Corps casualties for the month were: 49 officers and 469 other ranks killed, 125 officers and 2,518 other ranks wounded, 17 officers and 601 other ranks missing = 3,779. A high proportion of the casualties were towards the end of the month in the small but now fierce battles close to the Hindenburg Line.

At the beginning of the month of May the corps was holding an outpost line consisting entirely of detached posts. The policy of the corps, as stated in the Opsum, was to continue to push on towards the Hindenburg Line by seizing successive points of tactical importance and so enabling the whole line to advance. One justification of this was the aim of pinning down as many German divisions as possible to allow attacks to succeed elsewhere but, arguably, pinprick attacks across the whole front were less likely to achieve this aim than the threat of much larger attacks at selected points: such threats could have been made more credible by the use of deception and cavalry to cover the main forces. 4th Army's policy seems unimaginative but there is no record of it ever being challenged.

Putty attended one of Rawlinson's conference at HQ 4th Army on 1 May. The record included:

3.   4th Army was to prepare an attack on the extreme left of the army, with a view of distracting the enemy's attention and helping 3rd Army.

4.   For this purpose a readjustment of the dispositions of the troops on the army front would be necessary, but definite orders for the movement of troops had not yet been received. Corps would be reconstituted in accordance with 4th Army 540/36(G) (issued at the conference).

The conference did not give any clear direction and this vague warning order can only have added to the uncertainty.

Next day Putty sent his monthly report to the King:

My dear Wigram, Herewith the III Corps diary for the month of April for the information of HM The King. There has been hard fighting all the month every inch of ground has been disputed as we get nearly to the Hindenburg Line, a good deal of the fighting has been at close quarters and very desperate, our casualties are high but there are a large number of German dead which on the same proportion as our own killed to wounded would make his losses to be heavier. The Germans have adopted a new system of defence in the shape of very numerous rifle pits in rear of their lines, the object being to keep the men in the rifle pits during the shelling of the trenches, the trench line can often be seen by artillery observing officers but the rifle pits cannot be seen as the earth used in excavation is removed, however they are plainly discerned in the photographs where they look like very numerous shell holes, this will mean an increase in shrapnel in the future. Altogether things have gone well all along the line, the Boche has used up most of his reserve divisions besides those that he has withdrawn from the Eastern Front, the air fighting still continues at a high rate and if the American flying men come along in the autumn they will probably arrive at a time when both sides are pretty well-nigh exhausted, the main feature is that as long as we and the French can keep up this offensive we are keeping the Boche off Russia and Italy, the best sign being the wireless telegrams from Ludendorff which are savouring very much of the bucket shop, all the prisoners say the same thing that they are now entirely trusting to their submarine policy, none of us will be surprised if food parcels are disallowed pretty soon nor to hear of you being on rations at home. The weather for the last ten days has been all that could be desired, clouds of dust have replaced acres of mud but better still the grass has begun to grow and the horses will begin to pick up at once, the cold in April gave them a bad time, it has been good weather for burning all the filth in and around these villages which the Germans left behind them, their sanitation must have been very defective and I can quite believe the rumours last year that we received that they were suffering greatly from diarrhoea. The swallows have arrived and are the tamest I have ever met they fly in and out of one's nissen hut quite irrespective of one's presence. Yours very sincerely, WP Pulteney.

The number of corps troops' units was still increasing; and the AQ function was getting more and more difficult with the corps operating on a narrow front with few forward routes. The corps rear area contained the reserve division, the Corps Heavy Artillery and the numerous other corps troops' units each with its own functions and logistic requirements. The allocation of real estate was one of the most difficult tasks. On 2 May one company 1 Canadian Railway Battalion and 3 Mobile X Ray Unit joined the corps. Training of these units could be done given continuity, time and resources but III Corps was allowed none of these.

Putty also wrote to Ettie Desborough on 2 May:

Dearest Chief, We have no great news of any kind to give you except that I think things are going quite well, the Germans are fighting hard and mean to contest every yard of ground but as long as the French and ourselves can keep up the present pressure, keep on gaining tactical points we pin him to this theatre where he has to submit to terrific artillery fire instead of his delivering the same on the Russians to my mind it is absolutely necessary to go on hammering him now for all that we can so as to make his losses felt in Germany at a time when they are badly pinched for food, I think all Ludendorff's wireless telegrams now show signs of the bucket shop. No, I did not believe in the corpse manufactories though I understand that the 3rd Army captured a German doctor who said they existed, personally do not believe that the Roman Catholic Bavarians would stand it and the proportion of R.C.s in the German Army is very high much higher than I would have believed until one sees the number among the prisoners. I only just know Suffolk,[16] he was a very nice fellow but his father[17] I knew very well, he used to encourage me in my wicked deeds of my youth and laugh at the atrocities I had committed. I wonder which battn of Grenadiers Ivo[18] will go to, they ought to send them all to Caterham to start with to really learn the ground work from the beginning, I was adjutant at the depot there once for a year and never regretted

16   Major Henry Molyneux Paget Howard 19th Earl of Suffolk (1877-1917) RA killed in action 21 April – sister Agnes Isabel married Poynter, Putty's ADC, 23 January 1917.
17   Henry Charles Howard 18th Earl of Suffolk (1833-1898) Politician.
18   Ivo George Grenfell (1898-1926) – Ettie's youngest son, the older two having already been killed in this war.

it as got all the foundation work in to my head. I saw Harry Dalmeny,[19] G. Trotter[20] and Ferdie Stanley[21] on Monday [30 April], they all seemed to be well pleased with their efforts (probably Battle of Arras), Ferdie is quite enormous and must die of apoplexy unless he takes a pull, the Boche has a new system of defence now, besides machine-guns in front of his wire he has innumerable little rifle pits behind his line, he puts the men into these as they are more difficult to locate than the line of works I foresee we are going to have much necessity for heavy shrapnel in the future and use more of that than high explosive, his supply of barbed wire is simply beyond belief. Of course it would be a great thing if the Russians could push now but feel it would come better in about six weeks time when we have got him thoroughly pinned to the Hindenburg Line. My blessings and love Yours ever Putty.

The relief of 48th Division by 42nd Division, on the left of III Corps, was completed on 3 May: as Brigadier General Ormsby Comd 127 Bde was engaged in marking out the new front line of his brigade he was struck in the head by a piece of shell and killed. Meanwhile, on the right, 59th Division attacked Malakoff and Cologne Farms that evening capturing the former after a hard fight.

Putty wrote to Edith Londonderry on 3 May:

Dearest Circe, I was glad to get your letter of 28 April though it took a long time to come exactly the opposite of what I should be if I was tucked up with you. Am very well though a fortnight ago the weather was bothering my insides a bit but that marvellous constitution of mine has thrown it off and now I feel like staying the course as usual. Yes the food question is serious it was always bound to be but the arrangements made to deal with it are puerile, politics creeping in to all the arrangements as usual and the people in consequence not being united or taken in to confidence, look at the amount of food sent out to the army by parcels post every day, why not say that a soldier can only have the Field Force Canteen and that the parcels post must cease say after 1st June as long as they know they would not mind they never do, the amount sent out to the Field Force Canteen can be legislated the other cannot. Percy Chubb is a cool headed man who works for the common cause in his ideas and is the sort of man who can run a practical supply of a certain quantity of food to this country; several ships have landed passengers and then been done in going round to some other disembarkation port which sounds ridiculous to the amateur. Have heard nothing about Murray returning though am quite sure that he ought to, he was a mass of inefficiency and indetermination out here and why he was sent in command to Egypt goodness knows, I understand that he was completely surprised at Gaza that further his despatch was full of untruths to go on with, I believe Wingate[22] has given him away but

19 Albert Edward Harry Meyer Archibald Primrose Lord Dalmeny (1882-1974) Eton Gren Gds ADC to General Allenby GOC 3rd Army.
20 Brigadier General Gerald Frederick Trotter (1871-1945) late Gren Gds Comd 51 Bde 17th Division.
21 Probably Brigadier General Hon Ferdinand Charles Stanley (1871-1935) late Gren Gds Comd 89 Bde 30th Division.
22 General Sir Francis Reginald Wingate (1861-1953) late RA and Egyptian Army High Commissioner for Egypt 1917.

am not sure. Am delighted to read what you say about A.J.B. and America he was the right man to send, you had to send an honest politician and not a man who had had unfulfilled bargains with Irishmen. I agree with you about the cavalry business it was the act of a lunatic but then when a. [probably Allenby] makes plans of going across no man's land as if you could smooth out roads in 48 hours what else can you expect, they will not realise that you cannot go more than 4000 yards in front of your 18 pdrs in your bounds and if they had stuck to that and taken things in a methodical manner we should now be much further on than we are at present with a good deal more up our sleeves but still we knew all this before they started and a. took no heed from all that I hear. I wish that H [probably Horne] had the command he is far away in front of the other man and is a gentleman into the bargain which the other is not. I never see Reggie or hear from him but how anyone can take any notice of what he writes I can't imagine, I hear your Charley did A.1. if only Beef had been able to pull through the business and get a brigade all would be well but those things never do come right for some people. Charley has had his luck in marrying you so can't have it all ways. Well we have got the spring at last and to look at this country even in this present devastation shows what a jolly part of the world it must have been far far better than the west side of the river, the swallows are the tamest that I have ever come across, they are trying to build inside my nissen hut but they make too much mess on my maps so have told them to build outside. My love and blessings Yours ever Putty.

59th Division's fighting in the area of Malakoff Farm continued on 4 May with posts taken and then lost. Many were very isolated and vulnerable to surprise attack but equally, if taken, were difficult for the Germans to hold.

That day DDMS III Corps wrote to DA&QMG recommending: 'That sweetened lime juice be issued instead of unsweetened as the latter is unpopular and advantage is not taken of it. Corps Commander agrees'. Such was the complexity and variety of the numerous issues with which Putty now had to deal.

In the early hours of the morning of 5 May 59th Division was driven out of Malakoff Farm. Next day III Corps issued GO3747:

Intention of the Corps Commander to continue the policy of pushing forward towards the Hindenburg Line by seizing Malakoff Farm and the ridge running SSE from this point. Operation to be undertaken by 42nd and 59th Divisions in combination on a date to be notified later. Conference to be held at HQ III Corps on 8 May and to be attended by GOC, GSO1 and BGRA of 42nd and 59th Divisions.

At some stage this must have been postponed 24 hours.

On 7 May Putty drew the attention of his DDMS to the need for more supervision of sanitation. It was a particular problem in the rear area and DDMS recorded next day (8 May): 'saw Q (DA&QMG) who said Town Major Péronne had been impressed by him that sanitation of the town was the first necessity'.

At 8 am 9 May III Corps issued OpO No.204: 'III Corps will continue its advance towards the Hindenburg Line on Z Day. Combined attack by 42nd and 59th Divisions on hostile positions including Malakoff Farm'. The order was cancelled 11.20 am. At 9 am Putty held a conference at HQ III Corps: the subjects discussed included consolidation of the line, training (men must be taught to hold their ground even under heavy artillery fire), telephone security and sanitation. Putty must have known what was about to happen and changed the agenda of his conference accordingly.

All change

III Corps was very different to the corps of seven weeks ago when the German withdrawal started. Of the divisions then Putty now only had the excellent 48th Division: 59th Division was improving all the time but 42nd Division was completely green. Behind the forward divisions Putty was at last able to sort out the numerous support and logistic units so that they began to operate effectively as a team. But just when he thought he was beginning to get on top of the numerous organisational and administrative challenges facing him, Rawlinson issued 4th Army 540/38(G) at 4.40 pm (9 May) cancelling his previous orders (making all the work Putty had done that morning nugatory). He ordered (extract):

> 2b) Cav Corps will take over the front now held by III Corps. (c) On relief III Corps will go into reserve, and ultimately take over the northern half of XV Corps area as soon as IV Corps has been relieved by the French.
> 3. The ultimate composition of the corps, after the reliefs have taken place, will be as follows: III Corps – 42nd and 48th Divisions (This was later cancelled by 4th Army 540/42(G) dated 11 May 1917).
> 11. HQ III Corps into corps HQ prepared by XIV Corps at Etricourt.

Next day Putty issued his own orders in OpO No.205. Further detail followed in OpO No.206 issued on 11 May ordering the move of 48th Division, the corps reserve, to 5th Army on the night of 13/14 May; and in III Corps letter GO3799 issued the same day which transferred the Corps Heavy Artillery and RE units to the Cav Corps on 19 May. 4th Army 540/41(G) ordered the transfer of command of the line from III Corps to Cav Corps to take place at 9 am 19 May.

Somehow Putty found time to write to Edith Londonderry that day:

> Dearest Circe, Mille thanks for yours of 6 May. No your Charlie never did send the Rasputin literature, please direct him to at once, expect that continual erection would be a nuisance as one's clothes would have to be made differently but intermittent would be a good investment as a stock to your sex, I had hoped to see Charley next week but think now that his lot are not coming down until later but they ought not to be far off, I can't understand why he was not given leave. (Most of this letter is devoted to the requisitioning of the Londonderry horses and the wider conduct of the war). This day week is my birthday alas am 56 and have lived pretty hard all the time but no matter can still stay the course. The swallows are building away in my hut as I write but are more shy curiously enough than they were a fortnight ago, the female must feel like Eve and put a fig leaf on when she comes in to my room expect it is the first time a war map has been built on, curiously they never make a mess in the room and are obviously broke to the house. My love and blessings From Putty.

Putty seems to have had no warning of the change: he must have been irritated and frustrated, but none of this comes through in his letter to Edith.

It was very hot on 12 May with HQ III Corps struggling to avoid organisational chaos. In response to endless questioning, III Corps issued Addendum No.1 to OpO No.205 at 11.15 pm that night making it clear they did not know the ultimate composition of the corps. Every unit had to be dealt with separately: that day 311 Road Construction Coy was transferred to XV Corps and 51 Siege Bty to IV Corps. While all this upheaval was going on both 42nd and 59th Divisions continued to gain and lose posts of tactical advantage forward of their main positions. On 13 May Putty attended 2 SG Sports Meeting at Cartigny and had dinner with the battalion that evening. The Guards Division's presence behind the corps rear boundary in army or GHQ reserve is a reminder that the deployment of the British Army stretched back to the coast.

By 14 May III Corps had got over the worst and was able to issue OpO No.207. This ordered the relief of 59th Division by 5th Cavalry Division and of 42nd Division by 2nd Cavalry Division. HQ III Corps was to close at Catelet and open at Etricourt when command changed. The following day (15 May) Putty was presented by Rawlinson to the King of the Belgians at Villers Carbonnel.

Everything then proceeded relatively smoothly: 42nd Division having been relieved was transferred to XV Corps, and 59th Division on relief was transferred to Cav Corps, as corps reserve. By 21 May HQ III Corps had only a few corps troops' units under its command in and around its new HQ at Etricourt.

Any thoughts Putty may have had on all of this he kept to himself when he wrote to Ettie Desborough on 21 May:

> Dearest Chief, So many thanks for your letter of 14 May, which I meant to answer two days ago but being on the move was not able to, handed over my old camp to the cavalry including my swallow's nest which was complete and in good order, it was curious how tame they became, they did not mind my electric light in the evening but the hen was much more confident than the cock and always took the initiative, they would almost touch me when I walked into the kitchen garden catching flies at my feet as they rose out of the grass. Tell me did anyone ever send you a photo of Bron's grave? I had the ground round it tidyed [sic] up last week but did not do anymore because I did not know whether you had made any arrangements about it. Had the great satisfaction of seeing an aeroplane shot down by machine-gun fire as I was making a reconnaissance in the morning yesterday the observer fell out but the pilot landed all right though he was pretty badly wounded, he had only just come over from the Russian side where he said there was nothing doing, they have withdrawn nearly everything from the East so if the Russians pull themselves together they ought to have a good chance of dealing them a heavy blow. Yes I used to know Philip Hardwicke[23] when he was in the Royals in S. Africa but have not seen him since. If Charley L. has come back shall hope to see him this week, my other late ADC Reggie I hear is in Paris with B [Beatrice]. The country is lovely now even the dandelion is coming through the old shell area and changing the colour. My love to you ever Putty.

23 Lieutenant Colonel Philip Edward Hardwick (1875-1919) RD.

Bonham-Carter (BGGS) wrote to his sister on 22 May: 'We have moved our headquarters and are now a staff in reserve. I am employed at present making some reconnaissances and shall not be free for another week or more'.

Putty and his staff were to have just three days of comparative rest before Rawlinson issued new orders on 24 May in 4th Army 540/47(G):

1. HQ III Corps will take over command of the present XV Corps front at 9 am 2 June. HQ III Corps will remain at Etricourt.
2. The following will be transferred from XV Corps to III Corps at the above hour:
    a) Divisions. 35th, 40th, 42nd (less one how bty and one med TM bty) and 59th (less divisional artillery, one heavy, one medium and one light TM bty)
    b) Heavy and Siege Artillery. HAG: Nos 21, 62, 92 and 89. 60 pdr btys: 1/1 Kent, 127, 150, 155, 1/1 London, 110, 115, 125. 6" how btys: 9, 15, 240, 119, 216
    c) RE Units. AT coys: 238, 239, 142, 232, 574, 8 Rft Coy. Tunnelling coys: 178, 256. Pontoon Park: ½ No 4 Pontoon Park
    d) RFC. 52 Sqn (for administration only). 15 Balloon Coy (6 and 41 Sections). 16 Balloon Coy (12 and 43 Sections)

III Corps GO3932 issued 25 May implemented these 4th Army orders and provided further detail: included was the return of some staff and personnel that had been attached to the Cav Corps to provide continuity but did not deal with the other corps units, especially the logistic ones. It did specify that the new front would be held as follows: Right – 35th Division, Right Centre – 40th Division, Left Centre – 59th Division, Left – 42nd Division.

The rest of May must have been a time of frenetic activity as the staff worked out the detailed arrangements and issued orders in time for subordinate commanders to make their plans and issue their orders. There was just one week in which to ensure this new III Corps would operate effectively against the enemy on 2 June. III Corps casualties for May 1917 were: 4 officers and 89 other ranks killed, 13 officers and 367 other ranks wounded, 4 officers and 67 other ranks missing = 544. These casualties were surprisingly low; most were incurred in a small number of minor but bloody engagements in the outpost line.

The new front of III Corps extended from Villers Guislain (inclusive) in the S to the Canal du Nord (exclusive) in the N and was about 15,000 yards long. The front line defences consisted of a single line of trench which was not continuous, a few communication trenches, and some portions of support and reserve trenches. An intermediate line and second line were also in course of construction. The front included the villages of Gonnelieu, Villers Plouich, Beaucamp and Trescault. The main position held by the enemy was the Hindenburg Line from Banteux and the St Quentin Canal in the S to Havrincourt in the N, a double line of trench strongly wired and sited on the reverse slope of a series of spurs in such a way as to make observation of it very difficult. The distance between front lines varied from 1,000 to 2,000 yards but the enemy had succeeded in pushing forward posts along the line and also held the villages of Honnecourt and La Vacquerie; opposite Gonnelieu and Villers Plouich he had established a continuous advanced line.

The policy of the corps, as stated in III Corps Opsum and taken over from XV Corps, was to prepare the front for an attack on the Hindenburg Line between Banteux and Havrincourt. The most important part of the work to be done was to advance the front line to within assaulting distance of the Hindenburg Line; before this could be done, however, the existing front system and intermediate line had to be improved.

There is nothing in any of the orders to indicate why III Corps and Putty were put through such a period of redeployment and reorganisation, or who instigated it. What seems beyond doubt is that HQ III Corps implemented the changes with commendable slickness.

Cambrai in sight

On 2 June Putty sent his monthly report to the King with a covering letter:

> My dear Wigram, Herewith the diary of III Corps for the information of Their Majesties, am afraid it is a very dull month the whole time lately has been spent in side slipping, handing over my old ground to the cavalry and taking over the front of XV Corps however it is all finished now and am once more settled down. If it was not for the desolation of the villages the bit of country we are in is delightful, after all that shell area you cannot believe the relief it is being able to ride about on green grass once more, it is eminently suited for the cavalry whose horses will be able to supplement their ration with grass besides really pulling their weight in holding the line, I handed over my nissen hut to Kavanagh[24] obtaining a receipt for a swallow's nest which had been built on the edge of my map of the area which had in consequence to be left behind, the hen bird was much the most daring and after the first storm had driven them in they did not mind me or the electric light at night in the smallest. The Boche is evidently trying to save men all he can whenever we slack down owing to reliefs etc he does the same, the more blows we can deal him in the next three months the better for he is gradually using up all his strategic reserve that he had collected and at the present rate it will cease to exist by the winter. The greatest developments seem to be in the wireless, there is no doubt before the end of the year all the artillery aeroplane observation machines will have wireless on them in which they can receive as well as send, our men get to know the operators from the way they send their messages although they continually alter their code calls to try and deceive us. Yours very sincerely, WP Pulteney.

AQ HQ III Corps summarised the size and complexity of the new corps on 2 June: 'III Corps took over from XV Corps at midnight. Now composed of 35th, 40th, 42nd and 59th Divisions. Corps troops incl III Corps Cav Regt, det Lovat Scouts, III Corps Cyclist Bn, III Corps School. RA, RE and logistic units also transferred – corps troops now 121 units incl III Corps Rest Camp, 7th Guards Entrenching Bn, 54 Pigeon Loft and III Corps Cinema'.

The battle to dominate no man's land with artillery, patrols and forward posts started immediately. Putty now had three tasks: to maintain the pressure on the Hindenburg Line to prevent the enemy withdrawing troops for use elsewhere – the argument whether this was best done by constant pinpricks rather than the use of deception and the threat of larger attacks remains; to prepare a strong defensive position in depth in case of German attack; and to prepare for a major

---

24   Lieutenant General Sir Charles Toler MacMorrough Kavanagh (1864-1950) late 10 H GOC Cav Corps 1917.

attack on the Hindenburg Line. 4th Army does not appear to have presented them in this way; they have to be extracted from various sources, so there was no indication of overall intent or priority for Putty to work on.

It was very hot on 4 June when he wrote to Ettie Desborough:

> Dearest Chief, Many thanks for yours of 29 May, I will see about the photo but it may be some time before I can get hold of the official photographer to do it, he is very good and I enclose some samples of his work I don't want them back. I went to Paris on Thursday for 48 hours and had a glorious time, had luncheon at Compiègne then on to the races at Chantilly, they only allow owners, trainers and jockeys on the course, no betting, just absolute trials of horses for small stakes in fact everything practical that will keep up the breed of race horses in war time with nothing that anyone could object to, on Friday we went down to Versailles where it was glorious, there are no food restrictions in Paris and plenty of lovely women, we also went down to the flower market on the Quai D'Orsay and had great fun buying some plants for our garden about ¼ the price one pays in England and all the best but of course nobody except we sort of people buy such things in war times. We have got a great Etonian dinner tonight the Boche would get a good bag with a bomb if he knew it was going on. I don't see any chance of leave at present am very busy at a new area with a lot of work in front of me. How did you think Charley L. was as from what I could make out from Reggie he was very down in his luck over his military chances, they made a most ridiculous fuss about B. Pembroke being out here could not see that she did the smallest atom of harm. So is it true Asquith has made it up with Lloyd-George? That is the latest out here. All love forever Putty.

Next day it was still very hot when Putty held a conference at HQ III Corps (Etricourt); it brought together his staff and the GOC, GSO1 and BGRAs of his four divisions. The focus was on taking over from XV Corps, defensive measures and closing up to the Hindenburg Line. Also discussed were establishment of bathing places, musketry training for officers, and accommodation for reserve bdes. DDMS noted that day that Putty approved the site of a new CRS at Moislains on the Canal du Nord, established for 20 officers and 715 other ranks. Once again this was but one of several indications of the close interest he took in the welfare of those under him.

The corps carried out a coordinated action to identify the enemy's artillery positions on 6 June. III Corps GO4038 dtd 5 June had directed 40th and 59th Divisions to carry out an intense bombardment of the enemy's lines from 5 pm to 5.15 pm to simulate an attack. Hostile responses were feeble but good results were obtained by aeroplane observation.

42nd Division reported on 9 June that:

> a new front line had been dug during the night by joining up saps, being an advance of 400-500 yards on a front of about 1,500 yards. Hostile patrols were active but did not break through our covering parties. Our casualties were very slight. The new line was wired throughout.

It was classic siege warfare but nonetheless successful. On 11 June HQ III Corps issued III Corps GO4126 – III Corps Buried Cable Scheme. Each division was required to detail a permanent excavating party of two companies to carry out this work; this must have been an unpopular duty but it was essential since the corps still relied on telephone.

Artillery and patrol engagements continued throughout the month as did work on the defensive lines. Putty wrote to Ettie Desborough again on 14 June:

My dear Chief, So delighted to get your letter of the 8 June. Am very grieved at not being in the Messines show for it is what I have longed to do for over two years, at last there was some strategy in the conception for it threatens his communication with Lille besides saving 100s of lives in the Ypres salient, it has been far the most popular victory among the rank & file than all the others put together, Plumer deserves every bit of credit for it and as he is a great personal friend of mine am doubly pleased at his victory, I only hope they will change their policy and go for Belgium which is where we shall hit the Boche and prevent his using those naval bases at Ostend and Zeebrugge. Am very glad that they have at last moved Murray from Egypt, a mass of indecision who never ought to have been sent there after his most signal failure here. I went to see my swallows that I left behind in my last camp, they have hatched off 4 very hungry little chippies on my situation war map. Is it true Charley L. [Londonderry] has gone as private sec. to Eddie Derby that is the news I have? The country now is simply glorious nature has defeated the hands of man even in the awful shell area of the Somme battle, the thistle, dandelion & poppy have come through while every stump of tree has thrown out shoots, you see half a tree shot away the other half in brilliant foliage. My garden was quite beautiful but has had great assaults by moles which uplifted everything, have purchased traps and have been the death of two but there are so many they have rather bested me. I want to see the joy of France when the first American division arrives it will be the equivalent of six in the effect it will have, it will be interesting to see what type of gun she will adopt whether she sticks to her own field gun or not for if she does she will complicate the production powers I should imagine. All love and blessings from Putty.

Siege warfare continued as the corps fought its way forward. On 15 June 15 Cheshire (105 Bde 35th Division) successfully jumped an advanced trench N of Honnencourt Wood in order to gain better observation. 15 Sher For supplied patrols to protect the digging parties and one of them had an encounter with a hostile patrol which was driven off. Eventually a trench 800 yards long and 4½ feet deep was dug and wired during the night.

Putty wrote to Edith Londonderry on 16 June:

Dearest Circe, Your pen like yourself is naughty and I have much missed your news, having Charley at home has done you no good so put yourself in front of your writing and tell us your news. Personally have had a dog's life without the luxury of getting stuck, what with a change of quarters, change of ground and getting lumbered with four of the worst divisions of the British Army I have had grey becoming white on my head to say anything of trials of temper almost beyond human control. Is it true your Charley is now a private secretary? I trust he has learnt to file the French Letters properly. The Messines fight was the best done thing of the war, the first relief to the pressure on the British Army at Ypres that has taken place and the first move with a little British strategy in it that has aimed at fighting for position instead of that everlasting chestnut of breaking through, old Plumer ought to be stuffed and put up in the United Service Institution with the motto 'Patience Rewarded' put in gold letters underneath. Is there any truth in the rumours that reach us about Wimborne?[25] He seems a pretty hot bit of stuff if they are true? I went to see my swallows in my last camp on Tuesday (12 June) they have got four jolly little young ones Kavanagh is just as much a martyr to them as I was but then they got the necessary encouragement to breed and build from me before he took over. We have got two jolly good cows which roam about by themselves and sleep outside the hut of the man who milks them without any constraint, the only bother is we have got no bull for them, the War Office ought to send one out with you in charge the only one we had has gone to Egypt! We have cut an enormous amount of hay already this year, Nipper Poynter my ADC[26] is in charge of it, should say that it is coming out at 2½ tons an acre which means something when we have cut 500, we stack it and thatch it with rushes from the Somme. It has been desperately hot and the ass that built my camp built it where no air could ever reach it but notwithstanding all my health is good and I trust this also finds you. Much love and blessings Yours ever Putty.

That night, 16/17 June, 59th Division carried out a raid on the enemy trenches. The GS log recorded:

Raiding party left our line at 11.10 pm and reached a point 25 yards S of the enemy wire. A large body of enemy came out through their wire and were fired on and scattered. We secured two prisoners, one of whom died. Enemy casualties believed to have been heavy; ours slight.

For some time Putty had been working on a plan to break the German defences of Cambrai SW of that city. The origin of this was an instruction issued by Haig on 25 April to 4th and 5th Armies. Sometime later the responsibility for preparing a plan was given to Putty and it is possible that this was the reason behind Rawlinson's decision to move III Corps N. The idea of such an attack was an attractive one. Between Banteux and Havrincourt the enemy line curved to the W and then again to the N. A deep thrust beyond Cambrai would pose a serious threat to the whole German defensive system. Putty submitted a plan on 19 June for taking the Havrincourt-Flesquières ridge with a force of six divisions as a prelude to further attacks to the N. GHQ approved the plan and ordered 3rd Army to begin making preliminary arrangements for it as a diversion, subsidiary to the operations which were about to begin in Flanders. If this planning was of such vital importance it seems strange that Haig did not do it himself, or that it was not done by Rawlinson or Byng. It could be that they had confidence in Putty's ability to plan such an attack or that the attack was not considered of particular importance, even as a diversion, and restricted in objective and resources. Given this Putty's focus on the enemy's vital ground, the Flesquières Ridge, was sensible; once this had been taken other options became available.

---

25 Probably Ivor Churchill Guest 2nd Baron Wimborne (1873-1939) Eton Lord Lieutenant Ireland 1915-1918.
26 Captain Arthur Vernon Poynter SG.

For several days the corps rear area was being shelled by two 24 cm guns firing from the railway S of Cambrai. Fins was the target on 21 June: fortunately the effect was not serious because 60% of the shells were blinds.

During the afternoon of 22 June a particularly daring raid was carried out by Sergeant Sugden of 10 Manchesters (126 Bde 42nd Division). Annoyed by a small trench mortar, which he had then reconnoitred, he chose two men whom he posted on a flank while he crawled unobserved to a few yards of the dug-out. He then quietly informed the sentry, in fluent German, that he was covered, and that he would be shot if he showed the slightest hesitation in obeying orders. Sugden had the satisfaction of bringing in four very sullen Germans, carrying a trench mortar, across no man's land in broad daylight. Putty sent a complimentary letter to the CO 10 Manchesters praising the initiative and aggressive tactics of his men, and congratulated Sugden personally, and also gave him special leave for fourteen days. This and other earlier examples show that III Corps was very much the master of no man's land.

On 24 June Putty wrote to Ettie Desborough:

Dearest Chief, Many thanks for your letter of 19 June. Was delighted to get the news about Arthur Balfour's impressions, had been hoping that you would send them, it appears to have been the one successful mission during the war, he was the absolute right man to send, Asquith's past record never would have done to deal with a straight, trustworthy man like Wilson, I gather that they are not very far advanced in the matter of war material but they don't do things by bits and will soon become a going concern, in the mean time they should train squadrons of air men, artillery and engineers, by the spring they will be marching to victory, conclude they will rename Alsace & Lorraine, Stars and Stripes. I went to Boulogne on Weds night to get a tooth put right by Villadier on Thursday morning, he is a marvel fixed up my tooth in ¼ hour, gave a very good account of my mouth which I was not prepared for as it is thirty years since I went to a dentist and thought I had probably allowed all sorts of evils to develop from my carelessness. Had a letter from Congreve[27] last night, he is going on well, he has lost his left hand but is able to walk about and hopes to get home next week he is in the Duchess of Westminster's Hospital at Le Touquet he was very fortunate not to get killed, he talks about being back again in six weeks which I should imagine is optimistic. The Boche seems to be making very determined efforts against the French on the Chemin des Dames probably with the object of preventing another offensive on their part. The Paris intrigue is quite interesting am much inclined to back Esher [2nd Viscount Esher] who has a certain following in that city, I don't think Henry Wilson would be up to it, he is not a big man. Had not heard about Henderson's[28] departure but it would be a good thing for he has not got big or audacious enough ideas what we want are schools for training the young aviators, the future of flying will consist of air flights to prevent aeroplane battery observation for the whole war is now fast developing in the artillery duel of counter battery work in which wireless is becoming a greater asset every day. All love from Putty.

27   Lieutenant General Walter Norris Congreve (1862-1927) late RB GOC XIII Corps before war Comd 18 Bde under Putty.
28   Lieutenant General David Henderson (1862-1921) late A&SH DG Military Aeronautics.

There is no indication in this letter that Putty knew what was about to happen; maybe he was just taking more care with the censor, or perhaps he did not know – if so that would be very strange.

More change

On 25 June HQ III Corps issued GO4312 which ordered all work in connection with the offensive scheme to be stopped, and work to be concentrated on the defences ('The Corps Commander directs that from receipt of this order work will be concentrated on the defences, and that work in preparation for the offensive, with the exception mentioned in para 2 (burying cables to the next test point or dug-out) shall cease'.). No explanation was given: perhaps the idea of an attack on this front had been abandoned or possibly it was a first step towards security and deception for another planned attack; more likely it was because of what was about to happen.

Bonham-Carter (BGGS) wrote to his sister on 26 June: 'I am not overworked now though have pretty long hours 8.30 am till about 11 pm, but am not working at full pressure and can usually take my time over most of my jobs'. Perhaps he did not know what was about to happen.

Next day (27 June) 4th Army issued 540/53(G):

1. Command of the present 4th Army front will pass to 3rd Army at 10 am 5 Jul, together with all the troops in the area.
2b) III Corps will take over the front and area now belonging to Cav Corps.
3. The ultimate composition of the corps after reliefs have taken place will be: III Corps – 40th, 35th and 34th Divisions.
4c) Command of Cav Corps front will pass to III Corps at 10 am 10 Jul.

If Putty knew the aim of this reorganisation which took III Corps back to where it had been at the beginning of the month, he did not get it from Rawlinson in this order, and there is nothing to indicate it in III Corps OpO No.208 issued 29 June: 'III Corps will come under command of 3rd Army at 10 am 5 Jul. Command of 59th and 42nd divisional areas will be handed over to IV Corps and III Corps will take over the command of Cav Corps area and front at 10 am on 10 Jul. Ultimate composition of the corps will be: 34th Division on the right with HQ at Nobescourt Farm; 35th Division in the centre with HQ at Villers Faucon; 40th Division on the left with HQ at Sorel'. This reorganisation involved even greater movement of units in and out of the corps and to new locations than the previous one.

III Corps had been in its present position for almost all of June during which its casualties were: 20 officers and 175 other ranks killed, 43 officers and 889 other ranks wounded, 18 other ranks missing = 1,145.

Fighting continued on the front most nights but the night of 30 June/1 July was a busy one for 35th Division, as recorded in the divisional history: '104 Bde, after careful reconnaissance, had planned an attack on Honnecourt Wood, and this was delivered at 1.30 am 1 July under a barrage of 159 Bde RFA as well as Stokes mortars (the medium mortars had been lent to 2nd Cavalry Division) and machine-guns. Despite the darkness and rain several Germans were killed and wounded and one captured who provided valuable information. Meanwhile a hostile barrage was placed on three posts of 105 Bde. When this was lifted 14 Glos was able to see a party of Germans in the act of negotiating the wire. After a fight, the enemy withdrew leaving behind three dead and one slightly wounded officer of 123 Regt. Another party made an attempt to break through further N, again they were beaten off and a prisoner was taken. For this action the battalion (14 Glos) received the congratulations of GOC III Corps'. Putty took a very close interest in the activities of the front line battalions and was quick to praise those that did well.

In the early hours of 3 July it was 7 Manchesters (127 Bde 42nd Division) on the left of the corps who carried out a successful raid on Wigan Copse, SW of Havrincourt:

> At 11 pm [2 July] the guns opened on the enemy's lines behind the copse, and Lieutenant Hodge's platoon, after a crawl of more than half an hour, rushed the copse. After five minutes rough-and-tumble, in which none of the 7th was hurt, though a number of the enemy had been bayoneted, or shot by the officer's revolver, Hodge returned with the three prisoners indented for. It had been a model raid.

Putty's letter of 3 July covering his monthly report to the King provides some context for this fighting:

> My dear Wigram, Herewith the diary of III Corps for June for the information of His Majesty, am afraid there is little of interest in comparison with the fighting in the north. We have done a lot of preparation work during the month we have been here and are leaving it a going concern for the time it is required, as you will see we are shifting back to our ground that we held in May until the Cavalry Corps took over from us. We have stacked about 700 tons of hay besides having nearly as much again cut, this should be a considerable saving in £ s d to say nothing of the importance of (saving) of freight, thunderstorms have interfered a good deal with the drying, they have further found out many weak points in the trenches. The Boche has been raided a good many times but this last week he has been very persistent in raiding us entirely to get hold of the identification of divisions, we have been very fortunate as we have only lost one man a sergeant who had only joined his unit five hours and as the German officer we caught on Monday said was quite useless as he did not even know what division he belonged to. I took HRH The Duke of Connaught a circular tour on the Decauville system (trench railway system – light, narrow gauge track fastened to steel sleepers, easily assembled and transported) in my area which gave him a first rate general view of the ground after which we went to Péronne where I showed him how we got across the river in March, he was looking most remarkably fit, he took my ADC's name Poynter for not having a moustache but he has a very good one himself which Poynter never had. The Boche is going in for heavy counter battery work, he is frightened of our sound ranging machines and fires from many batteries at the same time on the one object to prevent their use, if the wind is in the east there is no doubt we get wonderful value out of the sound ranging machines, he is increasing his number of high velocity long range guns which you can only stop by knocking out his aerial observation. Shall hope to see you soon. Yours very sincerely, WP Pulteney.

At 10 am 5 July III Corps transferred to Byng's 3rd Army (General Sir Julian Byng 1862-1935 late 10 H Eton). That day Putty inspected the horses of the Corps Cav Regt at Moislains, returning again on 7 July to inspect the Surrey Yeomanry part of the regiment. Putty's interest in the regiment and in the welfare of its horses was noted and much appreciated.

Also on 7 July he wrote to Ettie Desborough:

Dearest Chief, Thanks for your letter of the 2 Jul, there is no news from my part of the world this week. I saw Henry Wilson over the Paris intrigue he told me that the Bull Bertie[29] stays on until the end of the year, he would not do there, he declares Austen Chamberlain[30] is the right man I told him anyone except Esher[31] and himself, Hardinge[32] is dead after that report. You interest me about Bend D'or, the sooner they are divorced the better for it is impossible as it is, do you think she will follow mother's footsteps as regards a young man wanting a commission? We have had intense thunder off & on during all this week the result has been an arctic temperature generally with very bad visibility. Have had two letters from Horace Farquhar[33] the last two days, both imploring me to come to Paris, he came over with K & Q [King and Queen] and evidently is on the bust, cannot get away because have got a change of quarters in the (tapis) to say nothing of two meetings of K. The Russian news has been exhilarating an unexpected asset which is always doubly welcome, it could not have come at a better time and was before I had expected it though it was up to the original programme if they continue the pressure it will have the greatest significance for they (the Boche) have concentrated great pressure against the French on the Chemin des Dames as well as Verdun, gambling on not having to send any but tired out divisions to Russia, The Boche is unable to keep his divisions up to strength even with the 1919 class so am absolutely certain he is [hardly] pushed but the best sign is to read Hindenburg's speeches as regards placing absolute confidence in the result of the U. boats instead of his armies. Have you heard about the officer going on leave who wrote to his best girl a little time before he put it thus: 'I drink to England, Home and Blighty; I in Pyjamas you in your Nighty. She replies: Now that you seem so very flighty; Why the Pyjamas, why the Nighty?' Would you do a commission for me viz get a wedding present for Irene Denision[34] for me, anything that you like to choose up to ten pounds, put the enclosed chit with it, have known her for many years and am devoted to her. My love to you for ever Putty.

Patrol encounters continued but at 10 am 10 July III Corps handed over the northern half of its front to IV Corps and assumed command of the Cav Corps front with 34th, 35th and 40th Divisions in the line. The corps thus held a front approximately 24,000 yards long, extending from the Omignon River in the S to Villers Plouich (inclusive) in the N: XI French Corps was on its right. That morning Putty visited GOC 34th Division (Major General Nicholson) at Nobescourt Farm; he went again on 13 July.

29   Lord Francis Leveson Bertie 1st Baron (1844-1919) Eton Ambassador Paris 1905-1918 later 1st Viscount Bertie.
30   Resigned as SofS for India in 1917.
31   2nd Viscount Esher.
32   Lord Hardinge (1858-1944) Cheam Viceroy of India 1910-1916, PUS at Foreign Office 1916.
33   Lord Farquhar (1844-1923) Lord Steward to the Household later Earl Farquhar.
34   Probably Lady Irene Francis Adza Denison (1890-1956) daughter of 2nd Earl of Londesborough married Alexander Mountbatten 1st Marquis of Carisbrooke Gren Gds 19 July 1917.

Closing up to the Hindenburg Line

Putty wrote to Ettie again on 11 July:

> Dearest Chief, Here are two photos of poor Lucas' grave [now at Écoust-St Mein], he must rest happy in his surroundings as you will see they have a football ground quite close you will see the goal posts in one photo and a camp in the other. There is no news from these parts, have got old Horace Farquhar staying the night with me so shall get all the Paris news from where he has just come I must take him up to see some shellings it will do him good. The Russian news is again excellent if they can do that once a month it will be splendid, the Boche is evidently putting every man he possibly can against the French to try and knock them under before the Americans are in force, every gun the Americans land is a nail in the Boche coffin, ditto every aeroplane. Yours ever Putty.

At 12 noon 15 July HQ III Corps moved from Etricourt to Le Catelet. The new front, namely that held by 34th and 35th Divisions, consisted of a series of disconnected posts protected by a continuous belt of wire, the main line of resistance being the Intermediate Line. The enemy front line was a continuous, well wired trench running approximately 2,000 yards in front of the Hindenburg Line. No man's land varied from 500 to 1,000 yards in width, but at certain points, the Unnamed Farm E of Hargicourt, Gillemont Farm, and the Birdcage W of Vendhuille, the enemy trenches approached very close to the British; these points were the scenes of most of the fighting. The old front, held by 40th Division, now consisted of a continuous front and support line with a considerable number of communication trenches.

It was about this time that Byng (GOC 3rd Army) began to develop plans for a tank attack S of Cambrai. The idea was that the tanks, covered by smoke, would break a way through the wire for the infantry, who would be supported by artillery barrages. But because of silent registration, now possible with improved technology and gunnery, no gun would be fired before Zero hour. Surprise would be complete, and if it could be achieved and the advance swift it might be possible to unleash a large force of cavalry into the enemy rear and gain a spectacular success. Haig was favourably impressed by the possibilities offered by this concept.

On 18 July Putty wrote again to Ettie:

> My dearest Chief, Many thanks for your letter of the 13 Jul. How good of you to have found such an excellent present for Irene, I wish you always did my shopping as you always find things so useful and much cheaper than I ever do, have not received the bill yet. Yes the Nieuport news was bad but it is the first reverse we have had since Vimy more than a year ago, I gather it was a position that the Boche could have taken from the French at any time that they had wished to, looking at the map I should say the position we are forced back to will cost us much less in casualties than the old one but will be a barricade for an advance owing to the difficulty of crossing the river under fire. You ask me about our little friend, yes he looks tired, he ought to go to Scotland to get the air, he wants hardening up he gets hot much too easily, a fortnights grouse driving would make another man of him. The fault of the Mesopotamian enquiry is the time it has taken to come out, they have not hit the

right man on the hand who was Fleetwood Wilson[35] who Meyer[36] succeeded and natural followed the false economy the former had got credit for, for Hathaway[37] there is no excuse and very little for Beauchamp Duff,[38] none had the courage of opinion to represent case to Hardinge who apparently showed much egotism on it all. Yours Putty.

Artillery engagements and raids by both sides continued throughout the month. The emphasis was on defence: on 19 July HQ III Corps issued GO2334/17 to 34th and 35th Divisions (Policy in Construction of MG Emplacements in Second Line of Defence): 'III Corps GO4569 dtd 20 July "Employment of MGs on III Corps front" contains paragraph stating principles on which Corps Commander wishes machine-guns sited'. The same day HQ III Corps issued 2334/18 – III Corps Provisional Defence Scheme. Putty's plan for an attack on Flesquières Ridge had been abandoned by 3rd Army and there was no indication of any future offensive action by his corps.

In the early hours of 20 July the enemy attempted two raids simultaneously on the front of 35th Division under cover of a heavy artillery bombardment and smoke barrage. One was driven off with the loss of two killed; the other on Gillemont Farm, was driven off by Lewis gun and rifle fire, and by bombs. 35th Division casualties were about 30 all ranks. Another raid by three parties of enemy took place on 26 July and again under cover of a heavy barrage and smoke screen, this time on 40th Division; about 25 men were reported missing, many of them buried. 35th Division also suffered considerable casualties from the shell fire. Such raids were a regular occurrence on the corps front but overall it was relatively quiet.

On 25 July a memo was issued to the staff of HQ III Corps 'Implementation of GHQ Reduction of Establishment of Horses'. HQ III Corps was reduced from 45 to 38, a reduction of 7. Putty was reduced from 3 to 2 and each ADC (Loder and Poynter) from 2 to 1. The horse was still the quickest and easiest way to get round most of the corps area.

Bonham-Carter (BGGS) wrote to his father that day:

Since my last letter written to Joan [sister] we have moved our headquarters back to the small hamlet two or three miles out of a well-known old French town [Péronne] which lies in the valley below us. We have a very comfortable camp here very beautifully situated on the top of rising ground with wide views in every direction across the uncultivated fields but showing a riot of colour, just now the fields are especially lovely with the brilliant reds of the poppies and blues of cornflowers showing through the greys of the flowering grasses. Here and there are big patches of thistles and showing in masses of purple.

Putty wrote to Ettie Desborough on 27 July:

Dearest Chief, So many thanks for your letter of 20 Jul, I am sending you two more photos also a water colour drawing that Colonel Rose [Camp Commandant] of my staff did for me I thought you might like it. Have got the bill for Irene's present all right. There is no news from my part of the world except that we raid one another daily as a rule the defence gets

---

35   Sir Guy Fleetwood Wilson (1851-1940) Financial Member Supreme Council of India till 1914.
36   Sir William Stevenson Meyer (1860-1922).
37   Major General Hathaway late RAMC Surgeon General.
38   General Sir Beauchamp Duff (1855-1918) late RA CinC India including Mesopotamia 1914-1916.

the best of it, one of my lot they have had six goes at and never been able to get an identification which is very creditable. My swallows have hatched off four young ones, it is most
interesting to see them feeding, the male brings in the most food but feeds from the side of
the nest while the female gets down and feeds them down in the nest, the male is just like
he should be quite unable to get in to the nest and evidently wont trust himself to try but
when the female is out he sits as sentry on the side of the nest without moving, at night she
is on the nest and he is on the telephone wires over my head, they are both absolutely broke
to the house and never make a mess inside. I saw Douglas Haig on Thursday, he is looking
very well and very confident of success, each time he tries to go one better than the last
which is the proper spirit, he seems to be greatly improving at conferences which is a great
asset to him. I heard from Edie this morning at Mt Stewart where she had enjoyed the rest
but she is coming back very soon to the strife of London, Charley was off to Dublin, write
to tell what A.J.B. says about the Convention, it does not read hopeful and what on earth
made them put Granard on it? Best of love for ever Putty.

35th Division carried out two successful raids on 29 July. At 2.45 am a raiding party of 20
LF entered an enemy trench under cover of an artillery barrage. No enemy were encountered,
but many dead were found, and a deep dug-out was bombed; two machine-guns, one of the new
light pattern, were captured. At midnight 17 LF carried out another raid: two Germans were
captured (8 Jäger Regt) and a dug-out containing six bombed.

On the last day of the month HQ III Corps issued OpO No.209: 'III Corps front to be
extended in the N up to the Beaucamp Valley, and all the divisional boundaries to be adjusted
accordingly. Reliefs to be completed by 10 am 3 Aug'. This adjustment added about 2,000 yards
to the corps front making it even more stretched and even less able to contemplate offensive
operations. HQ III Corps also issued GO4783 that day: Instructions for signal communication
in the forward area.

Most of July had been spent on this line; during it III Corps casualties were 15 officers and 182
other ranks killed, 63 officers and 1,094 other ranks wounded, 50 other ranks missing = 1,404.

It rained for much of the first week in August; on 2 August Putty sent his monthly report to
the King:

My dear Wigram, I send herewith the diary of III Corps for the month of July, there has
been a good deal of changing of ground as you will see and the front held is a wide one.
There have been a great many raids on both sides though I think we raid on an average of
3 to 1 in our favour, the 35th Division have done most successful raids and up to now the
Boche has failed to get an identification of them, there is no doubt but that a successful raid
puts better fighting spirit in to the men than anything else. I trust His Majesty was none
the worse for the walk I took him round Péronne it was a very hot day and it took longer
than I allowed for [King and Queen visited France 3-14 July]. We have got a great quantity
of hay now in stacks over 3,000 tons which should be an asset in the winter and save [the]
freight. It is most unfortunate this wet weather coming while the operations in the north
were taking place, it must have been desperate hard fighting especially as regards the air,
there is no doubt the production of guns and aeroplanes to replace losses is what we have
got to keep up to the mark in especially now that Russia is going to pull so little weight.
I think the great feature recently has been the success of our sound ranging apparatus we

Pulteney with the King on bridge in Péronne 13 July 1917. (© IWM Q5665)

Pulteney with the King walking through Péronne 13 July 1917. (© IWM Q5671)

not only get the position of the enemy guns most accurately but we can carry out shoots with them, lightening causes bother as it destroys the microphones, of course we should do better if the east was the prevailing wind. Yours sincerely, WP Pulteney.

On 4 August III Corps issued OpO No.210. 4th Cavalry Division was to provide a dismounted brigade and this was to take over the left sector of 35th Division on the night 6/7 August; III Corps Cyclist Bn was also placed at the disposal of 35th Division from 8 am 6 August for duty in the trenches. Then, on 5 August, III Corps issued GO4849 WngO: Operations will take place in the near future:

1.   35th Division will capture Gillemont Farm and The Knoll, and high ground near these points. 35th Division will also raid the enemy's trenches between Ossus Wood and Canal Wood.
2.   34th Division will capture Cologne Farm and the ground E of it.

In the misty early hours of 6 August the enemy, 100-150 strong, raided 35th Division's trenches at Gillemont Farm. There was no preliminary bombardment and the forward posts fell back but, after hand to hand fighting, all were eventually reoccupied. The inevitable conclusion was that the enemy suspected an attack.

Next day (7 August) Putty held a conference at HQ III Corps attended by divisional commanders and their GSO1s. Putty's points at the conference were:

> Coordination between patrols and artillery in no man's land; protection of dug-outs; use of artillery against hostile raids (to engage them when they withdrew); and wiring of outpost line and use of knife rests.

III Corps GO4884 issued that day provided a dismounted brigade of 4th Cavalry Division to free one brigade of 34th Division after the operations of 35th Division had been completed. On 11 August III Corps issued OpO No.211 for the attack and capture of Gillemont Farm, The Knoll, Cologne Hill Farm and Farm Trench, and for a raid on Ossus and Canal Woods. Additional heavy artillery was placed at the disposal of III Corps for these operations: 77 and 156 Siege Btys (8" how), 42 and 117 Siege Btys (9.2" how), and 355 Siege Bty (6" how). The following day in Addendum No.1 to OpO No.211 further heavy artillery was allocated – 15, 24, 109, 115 and 171 Siege Btys (all 6" how).

The 'Grimsby Chums' noted that on 13 August:

> 10 Lincoln [with the rest of 101 Bde 34th Division] moved to camp at Hancourt for ten days rehearsal for the coming action. On this occasion Major General Nicholson [GOC 34th Division] had been given enough time by III Corps to make adequate preparations and he was determined to take full advantage of the opportunity.

Raiding continued with 40th Division being successful on 14 August. Two parties entered the enemy trench after cutting their way through the inner belt of wire. Two prisoners were taken and 10 Germans known to be killed. Two dug-outs whose garrisons refused to come out were bombed; 40th Division's casualties were 1 officer and 8 other ranks wounded.

Putty's continued interest in every aspect of the corps' activities is shown in two entries in DDMS' log that month. On 17 August: 'Corps Commander suggests that sawdust be kept at given positions to throw over ground affected by new gas if used. Saw Chemical Adviser about this'; and again on 18 August:

> Corps Commander wants Roads Officer to improve the crater at Villers Faucon and the ground into 35th Division MDS there. Saw Roads Officer with Q [DA&QMG] last night. Has been finished today. This is a great improvement.

He also wrote to Ettie that day:

> Dearest Chief, Delighted to get your news of the 13 Aug. It is a great pity that the King cannot get away to Scotland for a fortnight's rest he ought to or he will break down. It is

very sad about the Minto boy,[39] he was such a capital fellow and worth ten of the others, Charlie Harbord says his boy[40] is getting on all right and hopes to be out again in a month's time. Have not seen Evan his headquarters are a very long way off me or would have looked him up there is a chance of seeing him tomorrow as am going to see some experiments which he may be at will be like Ascot Race Meeting if all go who are summoned. No I had not heard about Burgline and the De Trafford girl[41] what a pity there is no money for he wants it so badly. The weather has been quite hopeless up till yesterday when we had a glorious day which dried up everything and made us forget all our troubles. They have blown up St Quentin Cathedral it was burning hard on Wednesday night the Boche accuses the French and vice versa if I was asked to bet should back the French to have done it any way there was a heavy explosion so he must have stored ammunition there. Am quite pleased with the Ypres show, the eastern attack has not progressed but it is very difficult country and the Boche has got all his reserves there but the western attack is splendid and the Boche will have to look to his flank, the Lens show too is splendid am more pleased at that beastly Hill 70 being ours than anything since Messines, I think the Boche is feeling the strain a great deal for there have been a great number of deserters to the French down south, the first time in any numbers since the beginning of the war. I think from reading between the lines that Henderson[42] was carted by Lloyd George am I correct? I met H. last year when he came out to see his son's grave[43] at High Wood and liked him. Do you get Muirhead Bone's[44] drawings if not I will send you them the July volume is very good with sketches of all the parts I was in the Spring. I don't understand the Pope's proposals they might have been issued by the Boche what has always astonished me is the large p.c. of Roman Catholics there are among the Boche prisoners had always thought the Protestants dominated in that country. My love For ever Putty.

At 4 am on 19 August 35th Division attacked and successfully carried The Knoll and Gillemont Farm. The assault was preceded by an intense artillery, machine-gun, and trench mortar bombardment, which lifted on to the enemy's trenches in rear and on the flanks of the objective, and on the enemy's line of approach. At the same time Stokes guns fired thermit and gas shells into Quennet Copse. In the case of Gillemont Farm the attack was carried out by two companies (18 HLI) and The Knoll by two battalions (15 Cheshire and 15 Sher For) all of which reached their objectives, and a new line was consolidated 200 yards E of the old German line. One officer and 30 other ranks, 2 MGs and 5 TMs were captured; many Germans killed and dug-outs bombed. Counter-attacks were made immediately and again later that evening but were broken up by artillery and machine-gun fire. In the early hours of 20 August the enemy attacked again but were repulsed before they reached the new trenches. All day the Germans

39   Hon Gavin William Esmond Elliot 2 SG, second son of 4th Earl of Minto, killed in action 6 August 1917.
40   Lieutenant Hon Victor Alexander Charles Harbord later 7th Baron Suffield 2 SG gassed 24 July 1917.
41   Probably Violet Mary De Trafford (1893-1968) who married Captain Rupert Oswald Derek Keppel Coldm Gds son of 8th Earl of Albermarle SG 1878-1883 in 1919.
42   Arthur Henderson (1863-1935) Minister without portfolio.
43   Captain David Henderson (1889-1916) Middx/19 London killed in action.
44   Sir Muirhead Bone (1876-1953) war artist.

heavily shelled The Knoll and then at 3.51 am 21 August they attacked at four points, using flammenwerfer on the right; again they were driven back. Meanwhile 35th Division raided the enemy's trenches between Canal Wood and Ossus Wood with two parties each 250 strong (17 LF and 23 Manchesters). The advance was made under cover of heavy artillery and MG fire, and smoke barrage, but was delayed by uncut German wire. When the obstacle was passed the remaining Germans in the trench were dealt with; four dug-outs were bombed and destroyed, 15 prisoners from the newly arrived 10th Bavarian Division were captured.

Major General Ponsonby arrived on 23 August to take over as GOC 40th Division, and had lunch with Putty at HQ III Corps. Putty visited HQ 40th Division at Sorel le Grand next day with his BGGS and Giles Loder (ADC). Ponsonby in his journal noted that Putty visited him most days.

For the rest of the month the enemy bombarded the positions captured by 35th Division and mounted counter-attacks against them. Only on 31 August did they succeed: at 4.50 am under a heavy barrage they attacked The Knoll and captured the trenches on the very top, after severe fighting. A block was then established in the communication trench leading up to The Knoll.

A week after 35th Division's attack it was 34th Division's turn; at 4.15 am 26 August 101 Bde (11 Suffolk, 10 Lincoln, 15 and 16 RS) attacked the system of trenches on the Cologne Ridge about 2,000 yards W of the Hindenburg Line, and overlooking III Corps' positions in the Villeret-Hargicourt Valley. Under cover of a short preliminary bombardment, the attacking infantry crept out into no-man's land and lay down. At 4.30 am the main barrage opened (one of the batteries was Q Bty RHA – Major Paynter) and it smothered the front line for three minutes while the infantry dashed in behind. 16 RS went over in two waves with 10 Lincoln on their left and 15 RS on their right. Red 'Bengal lights' were set off in the captured trenches as a signal to the RFC; a squadron of SE5s was covering the assault and any trench without a flare was strafed. Consolidation then began; trenches were deepened, and a continuous belt of barbed wire was thrown out along the slope. 34th Division suffered little in the actual assault but paid dearly for its success when the enemy bombarded its late trenches very heavily; several unsuccessful counter-attacks were made during the day all of which were defeated with severe loss. The corps artillery fired nearly 40,000 rounds that day much of it in support of 34th Division. Almost every objective was taken and overall the front was advanced to a maximum depth of 800 yards on a frontage of nearly 2,000 yards; one officer and 135 other ranks of 35th and 195th German Divisions were captured.

This was a very successful operation by 34th Division but as the divisional history records:

> Although the operations at the end of August had driven back the Boche, and given us a good view over parts of the Hindenburg Line, while denying him observation over much of our own, his continued possession of some high ground made the situation in the Hargicourt Valley and the rear of Cologne Farm Ridge unhealthy for reliefs, ration parties etc. It was therefore decided that the Hun must be driven off this ground. On 31 August a reconnaissance was made by GOC 34th Division with a view to settling exactly how much of these Boche trenches we must take.

40th Division continued to raid the enemy to their front during the second half of August. At 5 am 29 August they raided an enemy trench NE of Gonnelieu and brought back one prisoner. They also killed 14 of the enemy, bombed 2 dug-outs and destroyed another with a mobile charge. 40th Division's casualties were 2 officers and 8 other ranks wounded, 1 other rank missing believed killed.

The last four days of the month saw strong SW winds, sometimes very strong, and much rain, compounding the difficulties for those in the front line. III Corps casualties for the month of August 1917 were: 22 officers and 431 other ranks killed, 121 officers and 2,277 other ranks wounded, 9 officers and 186 other ranks missing = 3,046.

The comings and goings of corps troops continued throughout the month. The AQ log recorded in the last ten days of the month: 12 American Railway Troop joined (20 August), 5 AA Searchlight Sect left (22 August), 13 CCS and 2 Canadian Labour Bn left (23 August), 55 Indian Labour Coy joined (25 August), 3 Sqn RFC left (26 August), 11 American Railway Coy joined (27 August), 119 Railway Construction Coy left (28 August), and 293 Army FA Bde joined (29 August).

On 1 September HQ III Corps issued GO2334/14:

> Reorganisation of front (Outpost Line from Omignon River to Targelle Ravine and Front Line thence to Beaucamp) into a series of defended tactical localities. Each locality would comprise a self-contained defended area of sufficient size to enable the garrison to maintain a prolonged defence. The wire on the whole front would be maintained, but the post or trenches between the tactical localities would be abandoned.

The outposts were increasingly vulnerable to isolation and surprise attack, especially in bad weather; this development that only held ground of tactical importance, covered gaps by obstacles and patrols, and allowed penetration where it could be contained was of considerable significance.

Also that day GOC 34th Division discussed the findings of his reconnaissance the day before with Putty and it was decided that 102 Bde should attack and take the ground required on 8 September.

Putty wrote to Ettie Desborough on 1 September:

> Dearest Chief, Thanks muchly for yours of 29th August. The weather has been quite too abominable for words, trees falling in all directions buckets of rain with arctic evenings everything detrimental to consolidation work which I am engaged on, this is very unfortunate for us as with the moon being nearly full we generally got a lot done. The Boche gave me a bit of a knock yesterday morning & took back a little post I wrestled from him about three weeks ago but my other show went off very well indeed and am well dug in considering all things besides which it has improved my observation very much and put a hitherto dickey division right facing on its toes again. Old John Ponsonby [GOC 40th Division] is now under me at which I am very glad, of course he has got all the fellows under him already devoted to him, he is very amusing about part of the line which both sides hold very thinly he said he could only flush a few partridges just here and there! Have sent you the Muirhead Bone's drawings up to date which please accept with all my blessings. The gale drove all the swallows back to the shelter of my hut which they have not been near since they flew a fortnight ago, now they sleep every night on the telephone wires but they are not broke at the house the 4 young ones like the two old ones who never by any chance made a mess in the hut. Am glad A.J.B. has gone for a result he is absolutely right and it is a

great pity that the Windsorites don't do likewise. Have written to chaff Edie Londonderry about being a Dame (made DBE) and have made some of my usual class of rhymes on the event. Am going to try and get over on a bit of leave the early part of next month if things are fairly quiet. Best love For ever Putty.

There is no indication in this letter that he was aware of what was being planned by 3rd Army or that he had yet made any firm plans of his own. Maybe he did not know, or perhaps he was just being wary of the censor.

On 2 September Putty sent his monthly report to the King with this letter:

My dear Wigram, I enclose you the diary of III Corps for the month of August. Both 34th and 35th Divisions have had some hard fighting during the month, although the latter have been turned out of Gillemont and The Knoll they gave the Boche a most tremendous dressing-down, the two divisions opposite instead of having a rest have been so knocked about they are quite useless for the Boche at present in fact one of them is already in process of relief so we have pulled a lot of weight down here in comparison with the forces at our disposal besides having greatly improved the fighting spirit of the 34th and 35th especially the former who had a bad time at Arras earlier in the year. The only thing that the Boche is superior to us at is his long range trench mortar, which he masses some distance off and completely outranges our 2" one and this is a very considerable asset unless the trenches are very close to one another, as soon as the 6" Stokes comes along we shall be as good as him. The weather has been quite impossible, it has interfered with the consolidation all through the operations to a marked degree which hit us hard, for the whole matter is speed, further it made quite double the work for the carrying parties. The gales we have had for August must be almost without precedent, every apple in the orchard where my hut is is down, the noise on the roof of tin being continuous, a good number of the trees that the Boche had half sawed have succumbed. Ruggles-Brise[45] has gone home for six months and John Ponsonby has taken his place, he seems in capital fettle and has already endeared himself to his division. I do hope His Majesty will be able to get up to Scotland to get some good air and a rest for he must badly need it. Yours very sincerely, WP Pulteney.

Bonham-Carter (BGGS) wrote to his sister on 3 September:

I have strained the muscles of my back and have had to spend the last 48 hours in bed. I hope to get up tomorrow and to be perfectly fit by the end of the week. I have had a busy time lately as we have been doing a little attacking down in this part. Cecil Lothian's division (34th) took the Cologne Farm Ridge and at present holding their ground without difficulty. Another division (35th) took Gillemont Farm and The Knoll but have lost them both again. Our total losses have been under 2,000; we know that we have knocked out a whole division of Jägers and part of another division completely.

Apart from frequent enemy shelling, the GS log recorded little activity in the first week of September: on 5 September Putty visited 40th Division and went round all the gun positions in

---

45   GOC 40th Division severely wounded 1914.

the right sector with the GOC and BGRA. They went to an OP in Villers-Guislain from where Ponsonby recorded 'you can see all the Boche lines for miles'. On 6 September Putty visited the 2nd Line defences with his CE (Schreiber), and next day 102 Bde (34th Division) returned to the line having trained and rehearsed for the forthcoming attack. Orders for this attack were issued at 8.15 am 8 September in III Corps OpO No.214: '34th Division will undertake the capture of Railway Trench and Farm Trench (part) on the night 8/9 September'. Addendum No.1 was issued later that day giving Zero hour as 12.15 am 9 September.

III Corps GS log recorded:

> After artillery preparation 34th Division attacked Railway and Farm Trenches, E of Villeret, in order to extend the right flank of the positions already captured by them on 26 Aug, and thus deprive the enemy of observation down the Hargicourt Valley. The hostile trench was entered with slight opposition, but it was subsequently found that the attack had lost direction and the right flank was about 200 yards too far N. Thus the whole of the objective was not gained. Simultaneously, by another attack, 34th Division captured and consolidated a portion of Triangle Trench immediately E of Malakoff Farm. 52 prisoners were taken.

Later that evening, 34th Division attempted to take the remainder of their objective by bombing attack but made no progress.

The attack had been made by 21 and 23 NF (102 Bde) leading under cover of a creeping barrage. In many places the enemy were seen to bolt as they neared the trench, and in it were found many rifles and sets of equipment. The next morning (10 September) at 2.30 am the enemy counter-attacked under cover of a heavy barrage and thick mist, and succeeded in regaining most of that E of Malakoff Farm which had been taken the previous night. However 24 hours later, at 3 am 11 September, 34th Division attacked and took the rest of Farm Trench, thus gaining the last of their objectives E of Villeret. There were few casualties and little opposition: at 6.20 am the enemy counter-attacked but was driven off. During the three days fighting 34th Division captured 70 prisoners and 8 machine-guns.

Putty met his CE (Schreiber) at Templeux-la-Fosse on 12 September to look at potential sites for HQ III Corps, the first indication of another change. Next day III Corps issued WngO GO5312: 24th Division was shortly to arrive in III Corps area and would relieve 34th Division in the line, the latter being withdrawn into army reserve. The dismounted bde 4th Cavalry Division was also to be withdrawn. Artillery engagements and raids continued. Putty visited 40th Division on 13 September to tell them: 'To make preparations for the capture of La Vacquerie. Tunnels are to be made; also we are shortly to have a 6" trench mortar battery in the division'.

At 8 pm 16 September 35th Division carried out a successful raid on the enemy trenches just S of Canal Wood. After a 3 minute bombardment by artillery and Stokes mortars the raiding party (17 RS) attacked through the enemy wire, which was found to be thin, and entered the trench. Two prisoners of 16 Bavarian Regt were captured and 11 Germans killed. The relief of 34th Division by 24th Division was confirmed in III Corps OpO No.215 issued on 18 September: command of the front was to be handed over at 10 am 29 September. III Corps Cyclist Bn was to be attached to 24th Division once it had taken over.

Also on 18 September Putty wrote to Ettie Desborough:

Dearest Chief, Mille thanks for your letter of the 10 Sep from Melbury,[46] cannot imagine why my last took such ages to get to you but they have been very erratic lately, two of my sister's letters from Scotland have never reached me yet. I have Dick Molyneux[47] staying with me here for a couple of days so if you see him he will be able to give you all the news I think he gets back about the 20th together with the party that have been visiting the Ice Creamers. It must have been lovely at Melbury how I wish that I had been there with you, Stavey can never get down my way now it is such miles away. The weather has been fine but much colder, the French are well on with their harvest but they waste a great deal by not having it thrashed earlier especially near the fighting zone where the rats have increased so much, there are several stacks of last year still unthrashed. Have had a good deal of successful fighting on my front lately and the Boche wireless has lied a good deal about it which is always a good sign. One of the men in hospital yesterday told me he had been in that ere 'Bombery' which is a new expression for a bombing attack. I hope to be over about 3rd Oct. All love. Yours ever Putty.

Have just rung up to ask how Billy Lambton is, they are very anxious indeed about him, his horse put its foot in to a shell hole and threw him over on to his head, they are much afraid that he has dislocated his neck. 14 9/17 WP.

Putty visited Nurlu, School of Rifle Grenade Bombs, on 19 September with GOC 40th Division to see a demonstration. Next day GOC 40th Division and his staff visited Putty at HQ III Corps to discuss future raids. Also on 20 September HQ III Corps issued another WngO (GO5380): '55th Division (less artillery) will leave 5th Army area and will relieve 35th Division (less artillery) at an early date'.

34th Division captured 4 prisoners of 141 Regt on 21 September. The following evening 14 HLI (120 Bde 40th Division) carried out a highly successful raid: in order to confuse the enemy, a smoke barrage of P bombs, smoke cases and 4" Stokes mortars of 3 Special Coy RE was employed and dummies ostentatiously deployed on the left of the real attack. Under cover of an artillery barrage the raiders rushed the hostile line and found the trench held in considerable strength. Many Germans were killed, five dug-outs were completely destroyed, and an ammunition dump was blown up. Ten prisoners were brought in: our casualties were slight. Interestingly, Q Bty RHA (Major Paynter), last reported supporting 34th Division, was used to support 40th Division in this raid, demonstrating much more flexible use of the corps artillery.

The enemy attacked 34th Division under a heavy barrage E of Villaret early in the morning of 23 September; the attack was a complete failure and was driven off with loss before reaching 34th Division's lines by artillery, MG and Lewis guns, rifle fire and Stokes mortars. Late that evening HQ III Corps issued OpO No.216 confirming that 55th Division was to relieve 35th Division in the line with command being handed over by 10 am 3 October.

35th Division carried out another successful raid late in the evening of 24 September. The wire had been cut during the afternoon and the assault was made later in two parties (17 and

46   Melbury House in Dorset home of 'Stavey' 6th Earl of Ilchester.
47   Possibly Major Hon Richard Frederick Molyneux (1873-1954) RHG son of 4th Earl of Sefton.

18 LF) under cover of a heavy artillery, TM and MG barrage. The wire had been temporarily repaired but four Bangalores were fired and gaps successfully blown. The left party encountered a second belt of wire which they crossed with traversing mats and entered the trench. Four Germans (440 Reserve Regt) were captured and two bayoneted.

Next day 40th Division again raided, this time E of Gonnelieu. 12 Suffolk (121 Bde), 200 strong, carried out the raid:

> The engineers did splendid work with a smoke screen and with thermite, a very valuable incendiary agent. Dummies were again used, but the Germans were not caught napping this time. The Suffolks entered the enemy trenches and brought back 5 prisoners and a machine-gun but lost 6 killed, 74 wounded and 22 missing.

HQ III Corps issued WngO GO5455 on 26 September: 20th Division (less artillery) was to relieve 40th Division (less artillery) in the line at an early date. All three divisions in the corps were now about to be replaced.

Putty wrote to Ettie again on 26 September:

> My dear Chief, Thanks for yours of 19 Sep, I went to see Billy Lambton yesterday found him very much improved in appearance from a week ago, not nearly such a drawn look on him, there was not so much improvement in the movement of his hands and legs but it was still obviously improvements. The weather has been glorious but more like October than September, mists every morning with slight touches of ground frost. I went to Paris for the day last Saturday (22 Sep) the forest of Compiègne was absolutely lovely with the change of tint had luncheon with Prince Arthur[48] and Johnny Ward who were very full of their French peregrinations, they both said the enthusiasm for the English was now very marked indeed besides being unanimous. Paris is very full of Americans and the price of food in the restaurants almost prohibitive, they seem to be very forward with their harvest, in some cases were already sowing again, they lose a great deal by very late threshing, keeping the corn for a higher price but don't gain in the end from the ravages of mice and rats. The Ypres show on the 20th was a great success, admitted by everyone, am so delighted Plumer pulled it off he may be slow but he is absolutely methodical and sure. Best of love for ever Putty.

On 28 September Putty inspected the nearly completed Malassise Farm defences with his CE. At 10 am the following morning 34th Division handed over their front to 24th Division; later that day HQ III Corps issued OpO No.217 confirming the relief of 40th Division by 20th Division: 40th Division were to move to Péronne and thence by road and rail to VII Corps. III Corps casualties for the month of September 1917 were: 18 officers and 244 other ranks killed, 78 officers and 1,136 other ranks wounded, 3 officers and 64 other ranks missing = 1,543.

The front was relatively quiet at the beginning of October but HQ III Corps had much to do implementing the changes of divisions and then all their supporting units. 55th Division took over the centre divisional front at 10 am 3 October. III Corps OpO No.219 issued that

---

48   Prince Arthur of Connaught (1883-1938) grandson of Queen Victoria 7 H Eton ADC to CinC.

afternoon transferred three siege batteries of III Corps and seven siege batteries now attached to III Corps temporarily to XVII Corps, the move to be completed by dawn 9 October.

Also that day (3 October) Putty sent his monthly report to the King:

> My dear Wigram, Herewith the diary of III Corps for the information of Their Majesties. It has been an interesting month, there has been a lot of hard fighting for the retention of Cologne Farm also for the extension which was necessary to prevent the enemy's observation, the 34th [Division] did very well indeed and I much regret that they have been relieved to go away, the raids of 35th and 40th [Divisions] have been very successful and they inflicted heavy casualties on the Germans. The weather has been splendid this last fortnight and we have been able to consolidate, prepare for winter at a much greater rate than we anticipated, the enemy have been very nervous opposite us and has adopted an attitude of trying to be let alone if possible as if he was getting ready to go up north for hard fighting but anyway he is saving men all he possibly can. I went to see Billy Lambton last Tuesday and a great improvement from the week before, doubt his being fit for service out here again until well in to next year, it is bad luck on him. The French are clearing the ground in the back areas at a wonderful pace, they are well off for mechanical implements but very short of man labour but those that are there work as soon as it is light until dark. We are delighted to hear Joe Maude's news from Mesopotamia. Yours very sincerely, WP Pulteney.

The enemy raided 40th Division on 4 October after a heavy bombardment of Highland Ridge (N of Villers Plouich) with HTMs, 77 mm and 150 mm. At 7.25 pm an enemy party about 40 strong attempted to penetrate the wire. Heavy rifle, Lewis and Vickers gun fire was opened and the enemy were driven off. 40th Division's artillery put down a heavy barrage and probably inflicted casualties on the enemy party while they were withdrawing. 40th Division raided the enemy lines next day W of La Vacquerie. All the enemy in the area were killed and two dugouts destroyed. 40th Division's casualties were slight. A Chinese attack carried out on the right diverted a considerable amount of hostile artillery fire.

CE III Corps (Schreiber) recorded that he visited the Gouzeaucourt Road with Putty on 7 October, perhaps a preliminary reconnaissance of what was to come. III Corps OpO No.220 issued on 8 October transferred 35th Division, now in III Corps rear area, to 5th Army (XIV Corps). By the end of that day 24th Division was on the right (HQ at Nobescourt Farm), 55th Division was in the centre (HQ at Villers Faucon), and 40th Division on the left (HQ at Sorel le Grand). 20th Division was in corps reserve (HQ at Péronne).

Next day 20th Division took over from 40th Division. If the decision had been coordinated with future plans for this sector it was a very strange one of Byng's. 40th Division knew the ground and had mastered both it and the enemy opposite. 20th Division was new to the area, and had suffered 3,204 casualties between 6 and 19 August and a further 1,409 between 20 and 25 September. This total of 5,000 was a significant proportion of the infantry in the division; it needed rest, time to absorb the numerous drafts, and the opportunity to re-train: it got none of them. Major General Ponsonby wrote: 'We seem rather to shift from one corps to another. Personally I wish we had stayed in our original corps under Putty'.

Bonham-Carter (BGGS) wrote to his sister on 8 October: 'My news is that I am leaving this corps almost at once I expect on Thursday and am going to GHQ as BGGS Training (no reason given)'.

Putty wrote to 3rd Army on 10 October (GO5681) following the departure of 4th Cavalry Division:

> Now that the RHA Batteries of the 4th Cavalry Division have left the III Corps, I wish to take the opportunity of expressing my appreciation of the work that has been done by the various units of the division which have been attached to the III Corps.
>
> When in July the III Corps took over the front previously held by the Cav Corps, A, Q and U Batteries RHA remained attached to my corps. They have done invaluable work during the whole time they have been under my command. These batteries took up very exposed positions, on occasions being brought right forward for the night and withdrawn before daylight. The work of their forward observing officers has been excellent.
>
> During the offensive operations undertaken by 34th and 35th Divisions, 4th Cavalry Division held a portion of the front with a dismounted detachment to enable these divisions to be concentrated for the attack, and the detachment remained in the line while consolidation of the newly won positions was carried out. The detachment did admirable work when holding the line, their patrol work being especially praiseworthy. Without the assistance of this detachment it would have been quite impossible to carry out the operations which took place in August and September. During July and August a working party of 400 men was also provided which carried out much important work.
>
> I should be grateful if my thanks may be conveyed to the Cav Corps and to Major General Kennedy and to the officers, NCOs and men of the 4th Cavalry Division for the assistance they have given to the III Corps during the past three months.

III Corps Cyclist Bn left 24th Division on 12 October and returned to Le Catelet beside the corps HQ. Putty wrote to Ettie Desborough that day:

> My dear Chief, Many thanks indeed for yours of 9 October from Scotland am delighted to think that you got up there in the beautiful air. I saw Billy Lambton a few days ago, he has improved a great deal but it will be a very long case am much afraid, he will never come out again in this war is my opinion. How I laughed over Lady Moyra[49] she really is very naughty to give way to her feelings like that but as you say I do hope it is a boy. Who is Alan Graham[50] that is going to marry Norah Brassey?[51] Well all my plans are changed they have told me to go away soon as I probably shall not be able to go away later in the year so I hope to arrive in London next Monday and shall be staying at the Ritz. The weather has not even been neutral this last week, am much afraid that unless there is a great change it will be impossible to make the Ypres show the success it was otherwise certain to be, the trans-

49 Probably Lady Moyra de Vere Beauclerk (1876-1942) married Lord Richard Frederick Cavendish 1895. They had a son b 23 November 1917.
50 Major Alan Charles Douglas Graham.
51 Lady Norah Brassey née Hely Hutchinson (1880-1964) daughter of 5th Earl of Donoughmore married (2) Graham on 27 August 1917.

port difficulties will be impossible to overcome, the shell holes are full of water and D.H. must have a very anxious problem. I can't help thinking that the German moral is really on the decline, they are obliged to have officers going round the various regiments answering questions and giving lectures on the situation, the men know jolly well that there must be something up for this necessity, what view do you take about Count Czernin's[52] speeches he does practically accept the whole programme of the League of Peace, anyway he has got a good rise out of Tirpitz.[53] I had Harry Milner to dinner last night wonderfully well but very grey which is not to be wondered at considering he married the Duchess of [M] in 88! I hear Windsor is having a bit of a shoot and Horace is with him it is a capital thing, he would have broken down if he had not some recreation of that description. Let me know if you shall be in London shall probably arrive late Monday evening, 15th. All love and blessings for ever Putty.

On his way back to England (14 October) Putty visited the Corps Convalescent Depot at Cerisy on the River Somme. He would have much to think about on the journey. Next day (15 Oct) HQ III Corps would issue OpO No.221:

> HQ VII Corps will relieve HQ III Corps. VII Corps will take over command of the present III Corps front at 12 noon 18 Oct. On relief HQ III Corps will move to Querrieu (on 17 Oct this was changed and HQ III Corps was ordered to remain at Le Catelet). Details of troops and personnel to accompany corps HQ are included. III Corps Cyclist Bn and 6 MMG Bty temporarily detached to VII Corps.

For the fourth time in six months III Corps was to be stripped of almost all its units, only to be re-built. On this occasion it seems inconceivable that Byng had not by now given Putty at least an outline of the role he was to play in the forthcoming 3rd Army attack even though no date had been decided.

To complicate matters his BGGS at HQ III Corps was to handover on 15 October. Brigadier General Bonham-Carter had only been in the appointment for six months. He wrote many years later:

> Old Putty (not so old) was the most completely ignorant general I served during the war and that is saying a lot. I relieved Cecil Romer who was transferred to command a division. He left a message for me 'Never let Putty out of your sight. If you do it he will either give you an order you cannot carry out or give a promise which you cannot fulfil'.

Much depends on the context; this could just mean that Putty had had very little formal education or training, having left Eton at 16, and never been to Sandhurst or the Staff College. It is also at variance with his other comments about Putty: it could be the reaction of a man who has been sacked but this seems improbable given the timing and other indicators. The most likely reason for his premature departure is in the letter of Bonham-Carter's dated 3 September:

---

52   Ottokar von Czernin (1872-1932) Austrian Foreign Minister 1916-1918.
53   Admiral Alfred von Tirpitz (1849-1930).

'I have strained the muscles of my back and have had to spend the last 48 hours in bed'. He was replaced by Brigadier General Fuller (late RE) who came direct from being GSO1 HQ 29th Division, previously in Gallipoli and now involved in the 3rd Battle of Ypres. The divisional history records: 'He was a tower of strength. A finished product of the Staff College, he was a rapid and accurate thinker, clarity itself on paper, and an indefatigable visitor of the forward positions'. Putty would not have been unduly concerned about this change: his new BGGS, who he probably briefed before he left, was clearly outstanding, and would quickly get to know the staff and start work on future plans so that Putty could take the necessary decisions on his return.

... and then there was Jessie ...

Putty must have started 1917 physically and mentally exhausted after six months continuous fighting in the Battle of the Somme; his painting by de Laszlo shows the toll it had taken. He went on leave at the beginning of the year and may well have got engaged to Jessie but there continued to be difficulties with their relationship.

At the beginning of February Putty had to extract his corps from the line, move it across the Somme valley, and take over a new front from the French. There were only a few, very poor roads and it was bitterly cold with snow still lying, hard frosts and NE winds. The operation would have been a major organisational and administrative challenge for his staff: Putty would have had to make the key decisions; if it had been a shambles he would have been rightly to blame, so he must be given credit for its success. When the Germans withdrew to the Hindenburg Line they sought to impose delay on III Corps in its advance; fortunately they did not take advantage of the Somme itself for it was a formidable obstacle. Putty was away on leave for a week during this time, sorting out his relationship with Jessie, but he would still have planned and remained responsible for much that took place. The rapid bridging of the Somme and the passage of III Corps across it was an exemplary operation and again he must be given some of the credit for that.

The events of May to October are difficult to fully understand. Four times Putty built up III Corps into an effective fighting formation only for it to be taken apart, with all the consequent upheaval, and rarely was any explanation given. Each time Putty appears to have accepted it and got on with the job; if he tried to argue against these decisions with Rawlinson or Byng he must have done so in private and then kept his thoughts to himself. Some of the decisions, such as the relief of 40th Division by 20th Division, presumably taken by Byng, make little sense.

As III Corps closed up to the Hindenburg Line Putty was rarely given clear direction on the army's intention. Without this it must have been difficult for him to determine operational priorities for the corps especially between offense and defence. Three priorities seems to have emerged: securing ground of tactical importance to gain observation of the Hindenburg Line and denying it to the enemy, dominating the enemy by aggressive patrols and raids along the front so that troops could not be withdrawn for use elsewhere, and preparing strong defences in case of enemy attack. The order of these priorities was never stated. However, in each of them III Corps seems to have excelled. The fighting by 34th and 35th Divisions at the end of August showed the increased operational proficiency of the corps in the preparation of an attack, concentrating and switching resources, the use of deception and the coordination of close air support. III Corps had come a long way since July 1916.

In this period of nine months it is difficult to find anything of substance with which to criticise Putty; the operational successes speak for themselves. His continued interest in all aspects of the working of his corps and the welfare of the men in it come through in his letters, most now subject to the censor, and in his actions: the development of sound ranging, inspection of the horses of the Corps Cav Regt, cutting of hay, provision of clean drinking water, evacuation of the wounded, and dealing with delayed action mines are just some examples. Furthermore the corps was now a much bigger and more complex formation, and very different to that of 1914.

Putty was now a very experienced corps commander but he had to operate within the constraints given by his army commander. Byng and his HQ 3rd Army operated with more flexibility than Rawlinson and HQ 4th Army but still interfered in the detail and some of their decisions defied logic. A corps like any other unit required training and continuity to achieve a high level of cohesion and operational effectiveness; and as its complexity increased this requirement became ever more important.

11

Time out – marriage to Jessie Arnott

On 17 October 1917 Putty married Jessie Arnott at the Church of the Annunciation in Bryanston Street, London. In London for 15 October, he had two days to prepare for his wedding: Hogbin would have been on hand to assist with his morning coat and one of the ADCs, most likely Giles Loder,[1] to help with the arrangements. Putty could have stayed with his sister, Isabel, at 3 Lower Berkeley Street which eventually was to become their home after the war, but the comfort of the Ritz after the hut at Le Catelet was too great a temptation. Jessie may well have spent the time before the wedding with another member of her family or a friend in London, but this cannot be confirmed.

Jessie was born at Woodlands in Shandon, a suburb of Cork, on 9 October 1875. Her father, John Arnott (1814-1898), the son of Robert Arnott and Jessie Page from Auchtermuchty in Fife and a Presbyterian by birth, came to Cork in 1837 where he became a successful and wealthy businessman, politician and philanthropist. Amongst his many commercial interests were Arnotts Department Stores in Dublin and Glasgow which he founded, the *Irish Times* which he bought in 1873, and shipbuilding, ship repair, steamship, brewery, railway, linen manufacture and gas supply companies. One of the largest employers in the UK, in Cork alone he employed 5,000 women just in the manufacture of crochet needlework. He was MP for Kinsale 1859-1863, three times Lord Mayor of Cork 1859-1861, and High Sheriff of Cork City in 1875. Knighted in 1859, he was granted the baronetcy of Woodlands St Anne in Shandon, County of Cork and Baily in County of Dublin on 12 February 1896. His political career focussed on the poor and children, and he was instrumental in the passage of the Irish Poor Law Relief Bill. He was a very popular politician and at end of his term as mayor he was carried through the streets of Cork. His immense popularity was also due to his philanthropic generosity. In 1861, the year that Putty was born, he forced down the price of bread in Cork by 25% by setting up bakeries in competition with the established ones to help the poor and prove that a profit could be made at his reduced price. When his goal was achieved he made a gift of the bakeries to those who had helped in their establishment. This is but one example of his help for the poor; others in Cork and elsewhere in Ireland included provision of coal, blankets and housing.

John Arnott had married Mary Mckinlay from Stirling in 1852 and they had 3 sons and 2 daughters. Twenty years later, in 1872, he married Emily Jane Fizgerald (1853-1938), the

---

1   Giles Harold Loder (1884-1966) Eton SG 1903-1929.

daughter of Reverend Edward Loftus Fitzgerald Rector of Ardagh and Lily Anne née Maxwell. They had 2 sons – Loftus Percival (1873-1956) and Cecil John Maxwell (1882-1954), neither of whom married, and 5 daughters – Emmeline Louisa (1874-1966), Jessie Alexandria (1875-1971), Lily Eleanor (1878-1967), Florence Geraldine (1879-1958), and Mary Louisa Mabel (1886-1982). All four of Jessie's sisters were married before her, with Mabel being the last and marrying Francis Hugh Brooke[2] in 1915.

Sir John Arnott's life was not entirely without its difficulties. Extracts from an article about the Cork and Macroom Railway Company tell of one:

> Sir John Arnott was Chairman of The Cork and Macroom Direct Railway Company, the owner of a branch line of about 24 miles opened on 12 May 1866. The new railway was an instant success. In February 1878 a dividend of seven and a half percent was declared, this being possible because the directors were drawing money from the company's reserve funds. When questioned about the wisdom of this policy, the directors opined that there was no need for the company to maintain a large reserve fund because their railway was a very short and simple line upon which there was 'no chance of a collision or anything of that kind occurring'. This somewhat rash statement was surely tempting fate, and a few months later on 8 September 1878 an accident occurred in which five people were killed and twelve seriously injured. The subsequent investigation revealed no less than three thousand defective sleepers and over one hundred defective lengths of rail. The Cork and Macroom directors were held responsible and warrants issued for their immediate arrest. An appeal was made to the authorities in Dublin and the charges against the company were eventually withdrawn; the company paid compensation to victims but suffered financially for the next eleven years.

He was not held to account for the accident but it must have dented his reputation in Cork; he did not hold public office again but he must have recovered from this to receive a baronetcy in 1896. However, the setbacks were few in a life that was devoted to making money for his family and for those less fortunate than himself.

Jessie was presumably named after her grandmother; her early life would have been spent between the family's two homes, Woodlands in Cork and Darnardagh in Blackrock Co Dublin. Her education was probably in the hands of a governess, and a music teacher. By the time she was a teenager her parents were moving in the highest levels of Irish society.

Sir John Arnott's Presbyterian upbringing and standing within Cork society almost certainly meant that Jessie's early life was very sheltered. Since she was 23 years old when he died in 1898 this may well explain why she married so late in life.

On 28 April 1890 the *Irish Times* recorded:

> A grand concert in aid of Castlelyons Organ Fund was given in the Assembly Rooms, Fermoy under the distinguished patronage of the Lord Lieutenant and Countess of Zetland.[3] The entertainment was in every respect, financially and otherwise, a decided

---

2   Francis Hugh Brooke (1882-1954) KRRC later 2nd Bt.
3   The Earl of Zetland was Lord Lieutenant 1889-1892.

success to which Miss Arnott, Miss Jessie Arnott and Mr (Loftus) Percival Arnott (children of Sir John and Lady Arnott) contributed in no small degree. The violin duets of Miss Jessie and Mr Percival Arnott were much admired; the youthful violinists biding fair to become performers of no mean merit.

Jessie was then 15 years old but it was another three years before she came to note again. On 18 February 1893 the *Irish Times* reported:

> Lady Aberdeen[4] accompanied by Lady Marjorie Gordon, Lady Arnott, Miss Jessie Arnott, Mr Loftus Arnott, Mr Peter White Hon Sec of the Irish Industries Association and Mr Edmund T Murray travelled in a saloon carriage today to Youghal, where they were joined by Colonel Fitzgerald, Lady Arnott's brother.[5] They visited the Presentation Convent where they were received by the Reverend Mother and sisters.

In 1896 her father purchased the Bandon Estate of 18,500 acres from the Duke of Devonshire. Jessie visited the estate on 7 May 1896 with her mother for two days, and stayed at French's Hotel.

The *Irish Times* reported the activities of the Arnott family in some detail and Jessie in particular. On 16 September 1896 she was a bridesmaid when her oldest sister, Emmeline Louisa, married Godfrey Herbert Bloomfield late Bengal Artillery (1864-1946), and on 12 August 1902 she was again a bridesmaid when her sister, Lily, married Arthur Edward Rogers (1871-1950).

The *Cork Examiner* also reported the activities of the family and on 7 November 1896 described Woodlands in its Social Review:

> The drawing rooms at Woodlands are in faultless taste of white and gold effectively combining with the beautiful mirrors that adorn the walls. The curtains of black and gold brocade, with just a suspicion of crimson, are superb. Passing from the drawing room, you enter a finely constructed dining room, which has a second entrance from an inner hall. The ballroom is a really splendid apartment, decorated with gold and panelled alternately with mirrors and pretty floral paintings. It is in her boudoir that Lady [Emily] Arnott accomplishes such a noble philanthropic work, and evolves from her busy brain so many kindful and thoughtful plans. The apartment is simply but elegantly furnished.

It was also reported that on 21 November 1901 Jessie, then aged 26: 'Attended a dance given by five bachelors at Richmond Barracks. Miss Jessie Arnott looked sweet in a white and silver dress'. Again the following year, that on 20 February: 'Attended (with Emily, Lady Arnott and her other daughters) a ball given by the Duke of Connaught, Commander of the Forces, at the Royal Hospital. Miss Jessie Arnott was in white satin relieved with pale turquoise'. And again on 5 September the same year: 'Attended the Racing (at the New Race-Course). Sir John (2nd

---

4   Probably Ishbel Maria Countess of Aberdeen (1857-1939): 7th Earl of Aberdeen was Lord Lieutenant of Ireland 1885 and 1905-1915.
5   Possibly Colonel Sir Charles John Oswald Fitzgerald (1840-1912) who married Lady Alice Fitzgerald daughter of 4th Duke of Leinster.

Jessie Arnott 1908
aged 32.

Bt) and Lady Arnott dispensed hospitality in the Vice-Regal Stand and brought a large party of guests. Miss Jessie Arnott had a very stylish grey voile costume, with sacque bolero over a white bodice' and a week later on 13 September: 'Attended the first day of the Autumn Meeting at the Cork Park Race-Course. Miss Jessie Arnott wore pale blue voile, smartly made'. Jessie and her clothes were matters of increasing interest.

The evidence suggests that Jessie was tall, perhaps 5' 11", and certainly taller than Putty; that she was strikingly beautiful judged by the times in which she lived; and was very talented. Some who knew her in later life have said that she was the greatest fun and sparkled, and in her youth was perhaps rather wild. In 1898, when her father died, she inherited at least £5 million (2014).

Putty arrived in Ireland in February 1908 by which time Jessie was 32 years old and he fifteen years older at 47. They might have met beforehand but it seems unlikely. That they did meet could have been mere chance because their paths probably crossed at numerous social occasions but there are also two other possibilities that could have brought them together.

The first concerns part or all of a triangular network of people and places. The northern point of this network was Beaufront Castle near Hexham, the home of the Cuthberts. Harold Cuthbert[6] who lived in the castle had been the Signals Officer of Putty's Column in South Africa; his uncle, Gerald Cuthbert,[7] was also a close friend of Putty's.

6   Harold Cuthbert (1876-1915) Eton SG killed in action.
7   Gerald Cuthbert SG and in 1908 Colonel AAG Egypt.

Gladys Cuthbert[8] was Harold's sister; she married Henry Heneage[9] in 1904. By 1907 they were living at Springmount, Mallow Co Cork. Heneage was the son of the 1st Baron Heneage[10] and Lady Eleanor Cecilia Hare.[11] He fought with 12 L in South Africa and since two squadrons served in Putty's column, albeit briefly, he may have met Putty and Harold Cuthbert there. The Heneages must have got to know Jessie very well too because it was their address that she put in the register when she married Putty; he may have known both Henry Heneage and Gladys Cuthbert before their marriage at Hexham Abbey and reception at Beaufront Castle, but he certainly knew them in Ireland later.

If Springmount in Co Cork was the western point of the triangle, the eastern point was Riverhill in Kent. This was the home of John Rogers and his wife Muriel,[12] who he married in 1899. Rogers served in South Africa and, since the RD were also in Putty's column, it is very likely that they met there. Muriel Morrison-Bell grew up in Northumberland and would have known all the Cuthberts from childhood. The collections of rhododendrons at Beaufront Castle and in the Himalayan Garden at Riverhill are one aspect of this link; another is that Muriel's brother was Arthur Clive Morrison-Bell,[13] so he too would have known the Cuthberts.

John Rogers' brother, Arthur, had married Lily Arnott in 1902; they lived close to Riverhill and were frequent visitors there. Muriel Rogers was a strong and fervent Christian Scientist and it was probably inevitable that Lily would be influenced by her. Christian Scientists believe illness is due to sin, and that it is not God's will that they should receive blood or treatment for any disease. Lily was to die of cancer, rejecting the removal of the tumour.

During Putty's first year (1908) in Fermoy, commanding 16 Bde and living in the Royal Hotel, Gladys and Henry Heneage stayed at Riverhill 6-9 June; later in the year, 18-21 November, Jessie and her brother Loftus stayed there in a house party that included her sister Lily and her husband. Jessie was also to fall under the influence of Muriel Rogers and this may well have been the start of it.

On 22 December 1908 Gladys Heneage wrote a letter from Hainton Hall, Lincoln (home of Lord and Lady Heneage) to Gerald Cuthbert (AAG British Forces Egypt):

> I have seen General Pulteney once or twice over in Ireland, he was at Convamore (home of Earl and Countess of Listowel, Gladys Heneage's mother-in-law's parents) when we were there, he is a most charming person.

Jessie did not go to Riverhill in 1909 but Harold Cuthbert and his wife, Kathleen, did (1-4 November); this may be connected with the shared interest in Himalayan plants and trees, and especially rhododendrons.

There may have been another force at work. General Sir Neville Lyttelton[14] and his wife frequently invited Lady Arnott to lunch or dinner; Lady Arnott also invited the Lytteltons,

8   Gladys Mary Cuthbert (1879-1957).
9   Hon Henry Granville Heneage (1868-1947) Eton 12 L.
10 1st Baron Heneage (1840-1922) Eton LG.
11 Daughter of the 2nd Earl of Listowel.
12 John Middleton Rogers (1864-1945) RD: Muriel née Morrison-Bell (NK-1919).
13 Arthur Clive Morrison Bell (1871-1956) Eton SG 1890-1908 & 1914-1919 later 1st Bt.
14 General Sir Neville Lyttelton (1845-1931) Eton Evans House RB CinC Ireland 1908-1912.

the first occasion being 21 April 1910. From time to time the Arnott girls were invited; both Mabel and Jessie attended a dinner party at the Lytteltons on 24 September at which, according to Lyttelton's diary, Harry Lauder sang very well. But that year Jessie and Mabel stayed at Riverhill on three occasions, twice in May and again in October, and yet again in January 1911; it seems that the influence of Ireland was competing with that from Kent.

In February Putty attended a Fancy Dress Ball in aid of Queenstown Hospital, as did a Miss Arnott; it might have been Jessie. However, by now Putty must have met Jessie because on 17 March 1911 General Lyttelton wrote to his wife from The Royal Hospital, Dublin:

> This morning began with family prayers, Lady A [Aberdeen] playing the harmonium indifferently and singing a hymn with very slight support from the minute congregation. Pulteney, who is said to be deeply in love with a youthful Miss Arnott from Cork, told me that Lady Paget had made £60 by the sale of work.

This information could have reached Lyttelton from several sources but the most likely is the ADCs network. Putty had as his ADC at this time Henry Sturgis,[15] the same regiment as Lyttelton and his ADC. It does, however, seem strange that Lyttelton has not made the connection with the 'Jessie Arnott' that they had entertained on several occasions the previous year. Perhaps he needed to be reminded by his wife.

Just over two weeks later the National Census shows that on 2 April 1911 staying with Sir Richard John Musgrave (5th Bt 1850-1930) and his family at Tourin, Cappoquin, Co Waterford, were General Pulteney, Sturgis (his ADC), Private Hogbin SG (his orderly) and several others including Jessie Alexandria Arnott. General Lyttelton must have known the Musgraves because he stayed there on 10 September 1909 and wrote 'Putty came over from the camp (probably Camp Aglish) for dinner'; so this may be when Putty first met the Musgraves. However, Putty was to stay there a further 29 times, on many occasions for several days. It is possible that Putty became a close friend of the Musgraves and was invited to shoot and fish, and it is also possible that he stayed with them when visiting training at Camp Aglish. But the Musgraves were also good friends with the Arnotts, or at least their children, because Loftus, Mabel and Jessie stayed there frequently: Jessie stayed at least 13 times 1910-1912, on many occasions coinciding with Putty, and sometimes they were the only visitors. Other visitors included Gladys Heneage and the Earl and Countess of Listowel. It is possible to imagine Putty staying at Tourin, riding off to visit troops, and returning to Jessie at the end of the day, especially in the knowledge of Lyttelton's letter and frequency of their visits to Tourin, but any more can only be speculation. Putty may well have been in love with Jessie but it was to be more than six years before they married. Jessie was now 36 years old and either she was not in love with him, or loved someone else, or there was some other impediment. She did not go to Tourin in either 1913 or 1914.

Putty attended the Lord Mayor of Cork's Reception on 14 June, according to the guest list published in the *Cork Examiner* with 'Mrs Pulteney and Party'. Two days later he was at the High Sheriff's Garden Party along with Sir John Arnott, Loftus Arnott and Misses Arnott. Jessie may well have been there on both occasions.

15   Captain Henry Russell Sturgis (1879-1967) Eton RB.

Tourin before the First World War.
(Jameson)

Ethel Anne Priscilla ('Ettie') Grenfell (née
Fane), Lady Desborough by Bassano, whole-
plate glass negative, 1914. (© National Portrait
Gallery, London)

The visits to Riverhill continued in 1911 with Harold and Kathleen Cuthbert there in May, Gladys and Henry Heneage in June and Jessie, with her sister Lily and husband Arthur Rogers, there in November. On 13 July that year Lady Arnott presented her youngest daughter, Mabel, at the King's Levée in Dublin Castle; Putty was also presented on that occasion by the CinC but it seems improbable that Jessie was there too. Lady Arnott dined with Lyttelton on 25 October; so, if they were match-making, there was at least one opportunity to continue to do so.

Harold and Kathleen Cuthbert were again at Riverhill in June 1912 suggesting that the annual visit at this time of year had more to do with rhododendrons than anything else. Jessie stayed there twice that year in May and November; on the latter occasion Mabel was also in the party, as was Lawrence Beesley (1877-1967). Beesley had been a science master at Dulwich College since 1904 but resigned to go to the United States. He sailed on the Titanic which was sunk on 15 April, survived, and had then returned to England. He was a widower, interested in spiritualism and a member of the Psychical Research Society. It seems probable that he was just a guest of Muriel Rogers and had no connection with Jessie, but even so it gives some indication of events at Riverhill. Jessie returned there three times in 1913, in January, May/June and July, each time on her own, or at least without her sister Mabel.

Jessie was at Riverhill again in April 1914. Three years had passed, at least, since Putty had fallen for Jessie and there is no firm evidence of progress in their relationship; Putty left Ireland in July and after that, up to the time of their wedding in October 1917, could only have seen Jessie on his brief spells of leave, and they were very brief. He did write to her and she to him, sometimes very frequently, but these letters have not been found. The only evidence is contained in the small extracts from his letters to Ettie Desborough who became a close confidante.

On 24 September 1914 Putty wrote to Ettie:

> Be a darling and do a commission for me. Buy a birthday present for this lady for me and send it off to her on the 2nd October to Ireland with the enclosed note. I suggest a real good pair of hair brushes or something useful for herself that she is likely to use, spend the enclosed cheque and if they or whatever it is costs more let me know.

Again on 29 September:

> What an angel you are to have written to Miss A have heard twice from her but she didn't mention it so you must have done it cleverly, you are a darling, I hope you got my letter asking you to get a birthday present.

The following month after her birthday Jessie was again staying at Riverhill and her sister, Lily, was also there on this occasion. It is perhaps worth considering whether Lily was also there on some of the previous occasions, but not recorded because she lived so close.

In his letter to Ettie on 27 October Putty wrote: 'How darling of you to write to Miss A you are a diplomat I wonder if she answered she would be like a coursed hare at the idea of answering I know and hide in her fawn to avoid'. By November he was thinking about a Christmas present for Jessie, writing on 2 November to Ettie: 'Thanks for sending me the bill from Barrett it was dear of you, yes do look out for a Christmas present for her about the same price' and again on 4 November: 'Don't know what to advise for Xmas present for Miss A you must find it, get her something for her dressing table that will go with the brushes you got her before, spend the enclosed cheque on it, it should be sent off about the 20th addressed Miss Jessie Arnott Castlemartyn (home of the Fitzgeralds), Co Cork. She is sure to be going back there for Xmas, though believe she is at present in London and stays at the Athaneum Club at 31 Dover St'. On 30 November, just in case, he again wrote: 'Don't forget to look out for Xmas present for the Irish lady She (Jessie) is still in London and lives from what I can make out at the Ladies Athaneum Club at 31 Dover St'.

Finally, on 13 December he wrote: 'So many thanks for doing the commission also for the one pound note duly received plus receipt am sure it will do her splendidly'. The matter of Jessie's Christmas present was again mentioned in his letter to Ettie on 18 December: 'I think Miss A is going to stay in London for a bit so wrote and told her to go to MacMichael to send the mirror to wherever she was, I had to give her a good dressing down for not writing, she got out of it by saying I had promised never to scold her again, she has rooms from what I can make out in the Ladies Athaneum Club in Dover St but cannot realise that they are very comfortable'. The saga of the mirror continued into 1915 with Putty writing on 19 January: 'She never went home so never got the looking glass but she knows all about it she still writes from the Ladies Athaneum Club in Dover St No 31'. This constant mention of where Jessie was living could be merely that he had so much correspondence and wrote so many letters to Ettie that he could not remember what he had said in a previous one, or that he wanted Ettie to go and see her but could not find the words.

Ettie seems to have taken the hint, if one was intended, as indicated in Putty's letter to her on 26 February: 'Yes Miss A is still in London you will find her in a tiny little house 108 Beaufort St Chelsea do write to her to come and see you, I can't quite make out what is the matter with her but she does not write as if she was any too well'. This is further evidence that they were corresponding although, as indicated, even this was not going very smoothly. His instructions to Ettie in his letter of 5 March were hardly tactful: 'If you see Miss A give her a good talking to, she deserves it and tell her so from me'.

The meeting did go ahead. First, Putty wrote to Ettie on 13 March in reply to her report:

> Thank you dear thing for your letter of 10 Mar which I got last night. What an angel to see Miss A but how dull of you to have talked of things quite impersonal I don't believe any women could, of course she is beautiful but surely I had told you so, do make her come to see you again when she returns from Ireland.

On 20 March he wrote to Ettie and reported on what Jessie had said about their meeting:

> Miss A she wrote to say that she shook all over walking up to your hotel, but you were a great success she says that 'you were awfully nice and quite extraordinary attractive' which is no news to me, she is by way of going to Ireland on Monday [22 March] but it is no certainty she does not change her mind from previous knowledge.

They may have spoken about Putty but neither woman would have been likely to have mentioned this part of their discussion.

On 5 May 1915 Jessie attended her sister Mabel's wedding in London to Francis Hugh Brooke and some time that month she also went to Riverhill, her only visit there that year. Interestingly it was to be her last recorded visit before her wedding in 1917.

With another Jessie birthday approaching Putty wrote to Ettie on 8 September:

> Will you look out for another birthday present for me anything near ten pounds that you can find that would suit perhaps you could find something to match the other things that you got, I will tell you where to send it later it should leave London about 1st October.

Something must have gone awry because his next letter on 5 October said:

> It was such a pity about the commission as made Kitty Drummond [wife of Laurence Drummond SG] do it by letter only the day before and would have much sooner have trusted you but keep your eyes open for something for Xmas.

If Ettie was irritated by these instructions she did not seem to show it. On 1 December Putty wrote to her: 'Have you seen anything that would do for a Xmas present?' and again on 5 December: 'The idea of the motor bag rather appeals to me but I will write again on the matter later'.

Putty had not been home on leave since the war started and he can only have kept his relationship with Jessie going through letters, and the occasional help of Ettie and others. His first leave came at the beginning of April 1916 (31 March-10 April), after nearly eighteen months; even then it was only just over a week including travelling time.

Putty based himself at the Ritz Hotel London from where he wrote four letters to Ettie: On 7 April he wrote:

> I went to see her again and you have won your bet but on no account will you tell a soul for the present, you will understand why I don't come down am just walking on air.

Next day:

> Thanks for your letter which however only reached me this morning you must forgive my not coming down but you do understand the circumstances don't you? All goes well so far but she is particularly anxious that no one should know at present for reasons which I won't write. I shall see her at luncheon but from what I know of her I don't think that she will come down tomorrow [9 April] I wish she would.

Later on 8 April:

> I could not persuade her to come down tomorrow she is so nervous about anyone knowing for the present. I do wish I had seen you again for there was much I wanted to talk to you about. I return on Monday [10 April].

Finally from the Ritz on 9 April:

> I just couldn't get her to face Panshanger, she is so frightened of anyone knowing it, it just makes me laugh the reason but I cannot write it but if I hadn't known that you were at all

times a tomb I never would have told you, I am just the happiest man in the world and mean to smash the Germans to finish the war and make me free. I shall want you to do some commissions for me, still my Chief.

When he got back to France he wrote to Ettie again on 11 April:

She's very funny and won't let us mention it to anyone at present, she tells me all her family have been the same in this respect, when the embargo is off I will make her see you, I quite agree with you about getting married and suggested coming back in July to do so but she wanted time to make up her mind so have just left her to think it over.

He had been to lunch with Rawlinson (GOC 4th Army) that day. Rawlinson commented: 'Putty came to lunch all the better for his week's leave'.

By now they must have been unofficially engaged but there was no further discussion about Jessie or his plans in his letters to Ettie for the rest of the year. His thoughts of a July wedding were somewhat overtaken by his prior commitment to the Battle of the Somme but Jessie's prevarication is difficult to understand: the reason, at least that put in Putty's letter, does seem improbable if she loved him given her age and that the country was at war.

However, their engagement may have become official by the end of 1916 because Putty's sister, Isabel, commissioned de Laszlo to paint a portrait of him as her wedding present: the artist finished the portrait in February 1917 so it seems likely that it was commissioned at least a month earlier. Putty was on leave 9-19 January 1917, during which time some progress must have been made but there were still troubles ahead. Nevertheless, Isabel must have been sufficiently confident that a wedding would take place to spend the equivalent of £20,000 on her present to them.

He wrote to Ettie when he got back to France after his leave (22 January):

Have had a glorious time on the quiet with my girl and if the war looks like lasting a long time shall come over at the end of the summer and marry her, she still persists in not announcing it (from shyness I think) she came as far as Laszlo's house to see me being painted but bolted back at the door so I just hauled her there myself the next afternoon.

It is difficult to know what the 'glorious time on the quiet' could be. Mr and Mrs Smith would not have worked because he was too well known, and if they had stayed with someone that would not have been very quiet. But it does seem that they were now officially engaged; but still no announcement was to be made.

Then, at last, Jessie told Putty at least part of the reason for her reticence. He wrote to Ettie on 2 March:

I am in trouble as my girl has just written to me to say she goes in for Christian Science and gets all her diseases healed that way, her sister made her tell me, personally have strong convictions on that subject and have told her I would not stand any nonsense about not calling in a doctor if I thought it necessary and that she would have to give in on that point, most of her family go in for it too, have not had her answer but am afraid there is going to be trouble over it, tell me soundest of advisers your views on this subject, you know the way

I always scoff at these sort of ideas but have never studied the subject but unless someone can produce some convincing arguments in favour of it am going to be obdurate as it is no use marrying and having an everlasting quarrel straight away.

Ettie must have written back agreeing with the line he was taking or about to take because Putty wrote again on 12 March:

Mille thanks for your dear letter, your advice is exactly what my feelings are but she is not taking it very well at present, rather on the line that the other men who married her sisters do not mind. However, I shall see her on Sunday [18 March] and will let you know or come down to see you to talk it over.

Her sister, Lily, had become a Christian Scientist but this letter suggests there was at least one other and this could only have been Mabel since she was the only one that was a frequent visitor to Riverhill.

Putty went to England on 17 March as the Germans were falling back on the Hindenburg Line: he was invested with KCMG by the King on 21 March but was then recalled, and back in command on 24 March. At most he had six days' leave to sort out his relationship with Jessie, but he must have succeeded because there is no evidence of the issue arising again, at least before the wedding.

Three possible reasons for Jessie's reticence have now surfaced: a family tradition of long unofficial engagements, her shyness, and her reluctance to tell Putty that she was a Christian Scientist. The first seems improbable: Jessie was now 42 years old and had known Putty for six years. Shyness as a reason is at odds with her character as rather an extrovert, fun-loving person. It is possible that Jessie, who may have been a Christian Scientist when she first met Putty, kept putting off telling him until she had to, and that was the primary cause of her reticence, but there may also have been another reason.

Two impressions of Jessie have been passed down the family: one is of a girl at ease with her male admirers being chased round the gardens of Riverhill; the other is of a girl averse to sex. The latter, if true, and whatever the reason for it, could provide an explanation for her reticence to marriage. It is also possible that this is too simplistic and that fear of the consequences of sex combined with her Christian Science beliefs may have been the reason.

Yet another possible explanation is in the content of Putty's letters to Edith Londonderry. These were personal and never intended for publication but the sexual exchanges, presumably encouraged, go beyond mere flirtation. They even suggest sexual frustration. If Jessie got wind of this in his letters to her this might have made her hesitate.

All of this is speculation: it had taken six years but at last a wedding was about to take place and the Germans were now the only obstacle. In the meantime Ettie was to be enlisted again to help Putty with a present for Jessie. On 8 April he wrote:

When you next go to London I wish you would find me two combs, really good ones to put in the hair at the sides, fair hair and the ones she has now are about two inches long, have no idea where you get such things but I meant to get her some before I came back but being recalled was unable to, tell me what sort of price those things are for I have no idea but I want them good.

The discussion continued in his letters for on 14 April he wrote: 'I too like the dark tortoise-shell much the best, yes just plain tortoise-shell'. Again on 23 April:

> Ever so many thanks for yours of the 19 Apr which I got last night, I like the 'Comb' not the 'Prongs', the one I have numbered No.4 only I think you have given it a lot of teeth for its size, you draw as well as I do have never been able to, when I opened the letter I thought No.1 was a picture of lady's legs they look just like some of the ladies up the Congo who wear grass round their waist, yes I want you to decide 'out and out' please send them with the enclosed note, sending the bill to me at the same time.

Finally on 2 May:

> You are an angel to have chosen those combs for me, am sure they are delightful and hope to soon hear of their arrival, have not had the account from Floris yet but suppose I shall in due course, I thought they would be much more expensive.

On 3 May Putty wrote to Edith Londonderry: 'No I have not been divorced again, really believe that Jessie is genuinely devoted to me though I cannot imagine why she must be going dotty because she writes nearly every day now'. So Edith knew of their relationship but this is the only time throughout the war that Jessie gets a mention in his letters to her, and he did not write again to Edith after 16 June. This suggests a rather different relationship to that with Ettie.

Putty continued to correspond with Ettie but without any mention of Jessie until 12 October when he wrote:

> Well all my plans are changed they have told me to go away soon as I probably shall not be able to go away later in the year so I hope to arrive in London next Monday and shall be staying at the Ritz, my girl is down at Dunraven's place in Wales[16] staying with Lady Ardee[17] have ordered her up to London but do not know if she will obey because she has only just gone down there.

There was uncertainty right up to the wedding day on 17 October. It is not known who attended at the Church of the Annunciation except those listed as having signed the register. Loftus Arnott, Jessie's brother, was there to give her away and Mabel, her sister, as bridesmaid. Putty's best man was Major General Sir Cecil Lowther.[18] Reverend Arthur Wykeham Pulteney, Putty's brother and Rector of Ashley, performed the ceremony. Undoubtedly there was a reception, possibly at the Ritz, and then a very brief honeymoon that was cut short; Putty was back in France preparing for the Battle of Cambrai by 26 October.

16   Dunraven Castle near Bridgend – Windham Thomas Wyndham-Quin 4th Earl of Dunraven and Mount-Earl (1841-1926) LG politician.
17   Lady Aileen May Ardee née Wyndham-Quin (1873-1962) daughter of 4th Earl of Dunraven and wife of Reginald Le Normand Brabazon, Lord Ardee Gren Gds later Brigadier General and 13th Earl of Meath.
18   Henry Cecil Lowther (1869-1940) late SG Secretary of the AFA after Putty and IO of Putty's Column in South Africa.

Edith Londonderry, c. 1900. (Image courtesy of Lady Rose Lauritzen)

On 19 October the marriage was announced in the *Morning Post*.

Information about Jessie and Putty's relationship up to the time of their marriage is sketchy and the lack of anything first-hand from Jessie makes it a bit one-sided. It would, therefore, be tempting to speculate on the gaps that exist, a temptation that should be resisted as much as possible. Also this is about Putty and his life, so Jessie is only directly relevant when and if she influenced him.

Most of Putty's contemporaries were married with children long before the start of the war, in many cases with grand-children. They would not have escaped completely from family pressures but their wives in particular would have tried to shield them from problems rather than pass them on to their husbands in France. Few were actively courting a much younger woman, and one who was proving inexplicably reluctant. When this relationship was progressing smoothly it would have provided positive support for him, at other times it might have been a distraction especially when Putty needed to be fully focussed.

The first three years, 1911-1914, of the relationship are of less importance. They were both in Ireland and by 1911 Putty had fallen in love with Jessie; she must have got to know him reasonably well in these years and developed some feelings for him, otherwise the next three years when she saw very little of him might have been somewhat different. Putty must have left for France in August 1914 with at least some hope that their relationship would progress. It may well be that his love was reciprocated by then but this cannot be confirmed; it is just possible that for her this was a relationship of convenience. Whatever it was, it and her letters must have sustained him for the next eighteen months. It also seems inconceivable that Jessie would have accepted Putty's presents or met Ettie Desborough if she had no feelings for him: or that she would not have told Ettie if that was the situation.

Everything points to Putty returning on leave in April 1916 confident that Jessie would accept his proposal of marriage. Even though he could not announce his engagement officially this would have sufficed to sustain him through the Battle of the Somme. His leave in January 1917 must have moved their relationship further forward with at least their families now knowing that a wedding would take place. Putty's letter of 22 January 1917 suggests much, but it seems beyond doubt that he returned to France a happy man; all that had to be done was to arrange the wedding. So, Putty must have been very low when he got Jessie's letter a month later telling him about her being a Christian Scientist. However, he returned to England for six days in March 1917 during which time he managed to sort out the problem, so the period of low morale would have been short-lived. Jessie's feelings for him seem to have prevailed over her leanings towards Christian Science. Putty's determination to stand firm on this issue shows considerable moral courage because it could have resulted in the end of their relationship.

Overall Jessie's support, perhaps more than that, seems to have sustained Putty through the first three years of the war; there is little doubt that she was the most important person in his life, with Ettie Desborough, Edith Londonderry and perhaps others in a lesser role. If he had any doubts they would have been in the past on 17 October; it would have been a married man with renewed strength and vigour that attended Byng's briefing for the Battle of Cambrai on 26 October.

12

Battle of Cambrai

October-December 1917

When Putty returned to Le Catelet on 25 October from his very brief honeymoon it was to find III Corps in army reserve with no divisions and very few corps troops under command. He must have had some idea what was to come, and it was likely that his new BGGS (Brigadier General Fuller) was involved in the planning while he was away, but it was not till 26 October that Byng (GOC 3rd Army) briefed his corps commanders on the plan for the battle just over three weeks away. It is also important to remember that, at this stage, the attack was seen as a diversion and subsidiary to the operations in Flanders. Byng pointed out that to achieve any success at all the battle should be going on in the N. As he saw it there were three possibilities of creating a diversion: the first was to break through the enemy line and cut their communications N and NE of Cambrai; the second to take and hold the Hindenburg Support Line; and the third to carry out a major raid and destroy enemy troops and equipment. While he hoped for the first, the third option in his view would still meet the requirement of creating a diversion.

The operation would be divided into three phases. In the first, seven divisions of III and IV Corps, with three brigades of tanks, would break through the German defences (the Hindenburg Line), capture crossings over the St Quentin Canal at Masnières and Marcoing, and gap the Masnières-Beaurevoir line to the E. Then, in the second phase, Cav Corps would pass through the infantry, advance around the E of Cambrai, and seize the crossings of the Sensée. Finally, in the third phase, Cambrai and the area bounded by the St Quentin Canal, the Sensée River and the Canal du Nord would be cleared and the German divisions to the W of that area would be destroyed. From the outset Byng made it clear that III Corps was to establish defences to protect the southern flank of the penetration along the Gonnelieu-Bonavis-Crèvecoeur Ridge and to widen the breach by raiding towards Walincourt, five miles to the SE.

Much had been asked of Putty and HQ III Corps in the previous three years. Now, in just three weeks, he had to assemble, organise, brief, and prepare a new corps for battle: this new corps was then to smash through the Hindenburg Line that the Germans had spent so much time and effort preparing, cross a major obstacle, conduct the very difficult operation of passing another corps through, and expand the breach to the S. The secret for success was to be surprise but it was still a tall order.

III Corps OpO No.223 and Addendum dtd 27 October set events in motion. On 29 October that part of VII Corps front held by 20th Division, less the extreme right up to Villers-Guislain

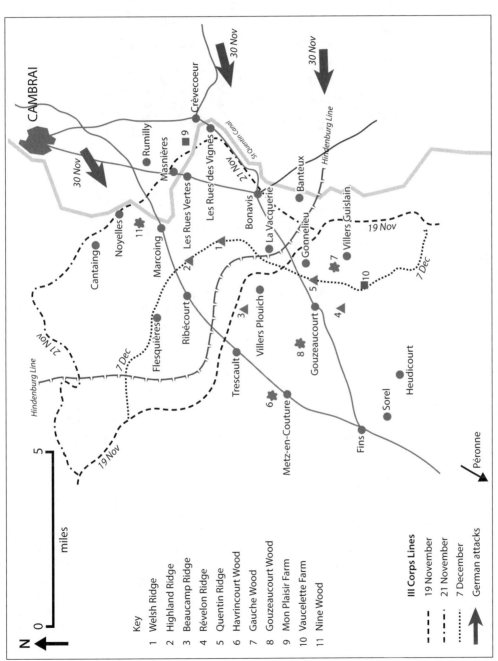

Map 10 Battle of Cambrai 1917.

CAMBRAI

Crèvecoeur

Rumilly

Masnières

Les Rues des Vignes

9

30 Nov

30 Nov

30 Nov

30 Nov

St Quentin Canal

Hindenburg Line

21 Nov

Banteux

Bonavis

La Vacquerie

Gonnelieu

Villers Guislain

Les Rues Vertes

Noyelles

11

Marcoing

Cantaing

2

1

7

5

10

19 Nov

7 Dec

Flesquières

Ribécourt

Villers Plouich

3

Gouzeaucourt

4

8

Hindenburg Line

21 Nov

7 Dec

19 Nov

Trescault

Metz-en-Couture

6

Sorel

Heudicourt

Fins

Hindenburg Line

Péronne

N

miles

0   5

Key

1   Welsh Ridge
2   Highland Ridge
3   Beaucamp Ridge
4   Révelon Ridge
5   Quentin Ridge
6   Havrincourt Wood
7   Gauche Wood
8   Gouzeaucourt Wood
9   Mon Plaisir Farm
10 Vaucelette Farm
11 Nine Wood

III Corps Lines

--- 19 November
-·- 21 November
··· 7 December
     German attacks

Nissen huts in ruined village of Templeux-la-Fosse, HQ III Corps, 1917. (Mairie)

inclusive, was transferred back to III Corps. 20th Division, HQ 21 HAG, 270 and 449 Siege Btys, 144 and 2/1 Midland Hy Btys, and 239 AT Coy RE joined the corps that day. 12th Division joined the corps for administration, and HQ III Corps moved to Templeux-la-Fosse. III Corps now held the front on which it was to attack.

The last two days of October were quiet. On both days the mornings were misty, clearing later. A small but nevertheless interesting development was that the BGGS was now signing the GS log: the standard of staff work in the headquarters had always been good but improved further under Fuller's leadership. III Corps casualties in October were: 33 other ranks killed, 9 officers and 193 other ranks wounded, 1 officer and 6 other ranks missing = 242.

Captain Dugdale KSLI SC HQ 60 Bde 20th Division wrote:

> The first signs of activity started on 1 November with a visit from the corps commander General Sir W.P. Pulteney and his staff to our headquarters. Such important visitors gave me much anxiety about the luncheon menu. However, it passed off to the satisfaction of the General, who was very thoughtful after the subsequent secret meeting. He told us later that he was informed confidentially about the projected attack on the 20 November at this meeting.

The same day HQ RE log recorded:

> Provision of extra accommodation for additional troops in 20th Division area proceeding: (a) Right Forward. Steel structures in banks and sides of sunken roads (b) Farther Back. 'A' Frame tarpaulin shelters tarred or painted in neutral colours. Erected amongst village ruins and beside hedges and walls (c) In Dessart Wood and Back Areas. Stained tents. Existing tented camps increased in size as far as possible without making noticeable alterations.

Orders for the movement of troops into the corps area continued to be issued daily, on 2 November for 6th Division Pioneer Bn (11 Leics) (G79) and HA units (G60). There was both a shortage of routes forward and limited space on arrival: the moves had to be carefully planned to ensure units arrived in the correct order of priority, and to avoid compromising security.

Putty sent his monthly report to the King that day:

> My dear Wigram, I forward herewith the diary of III Corps for the information of Their Majesties. Many thanks for your letter of the 28th and the congratulations that it contained. Am afraid that there is little of interest in the diary this month because the corps was taken out of the line on 15 October but went in again on 29 October, it was rather an interesting fact that this is the first time the corps has been taken out to rest since it first commenced in August 1914 which I imagine establishes an easy record. We are getting pretty well accustomed to change of camps as the one I am now in is the seventh this year. The weather is characteristic of November and we can look forward to fog and drizzle until the March winds blow them away. Am glad that Allenby[1] has made such a good start with the Turks, I wonder who will dare fire the first 9.2 into Jerusalem? I see that they made a determined aeroplane raid on London again, there must have been a lot of ammunition fired during the various flight formations. I too saw Billy Lambton when I was in London and thought that he had stood the journey well. Yours very sincerely, WP Pulteney.

HQ RE Log recorded (2 November): 'Whole output of saw mill at Bois Bais (37 Canadian Forestry Corps) made available for III Corps for 3 weeks, for tarpaulin shelter construction in forward areas'.

The enemy raided 20th Division at Newton Post early in the morning 3 November capturing an NCO. Such actions were routine and he would have known nothing of the forthcoming attack at this stage but nearer the time it would be a matter of concern. At 11.30 am that morning HQ III Corps held its first 'G' conference attended by representatives of 6th, 12th, 20th and 29th Divisions: the detailed planning had now begun.

It continued quiet throughout the next week except for patrol activity, with mist in the mornings and much rain. 20th Division captured a prisoner from an enemy patrol on 4 November; while it was important to prevent enemy patrols operating and to gain identifications in case of any change in the enemy opposite, patrol activity had to be kept at normal levels. On 4 November Putty attended a 3rd Army demonstration by the Tank Corps near the Bapaume-Arras Road.

HQ III Corps continued to plan and issue orders for the forward movement of troops: on 7 November 1/2 Monmouth (pioneer bn 29th Division) GO5880; on 8 November 6th Division Artillery GO5931 and 50 HAG GO5929; on 9 November 87 HAG GO5957 and 78 HAG GO5958. III Corps MMG Bty was moved to Aizecourt-le-Bas on 8 November where it could both cover corps HQ and be in reserve. While HQ III Corps was organising the operational and logistic movement of the corps it also had to ensure that orders were disseminated to allow planning, preparation and rehearsals, and all of this had to be done within the constraints of security.

---

1   General Sir Edmund Henry Hynman Allenby (1861-1936) late 6 D CinC Egyptian Expeditionary Force.

At 11 am 8 November Putty attended Byng's conference at HQ 3rd Army (Albert). Two days later, on 10 November, HQ III Corps held a conference attended by representatives of the four divisions and that evening HQ III Corps issued III Corps Instructions Nos.1 and 2:

Instruction No.1 GS1/1 Orders for attack by III Corps:

2. The object of the operation is, with the aid of tanks, to break the enemy's defensive system by a coup de main between Canal de l'Escaut at Banteux and the Canal du Nord, west of Havrincourt, and to pass the cavalry through the gap thus made, with a view to operating in a NE direction.
6. The present dispositions of the enemy opposite the above frontage are as follows: From Banteux to Welsh Ridge 2 inf regts 9 Res Divn (6 or 395 and 19). From Welsh Ridge to Havrincourt 3 inf regts (90, 27 and 84). The 204th Division is north of Havrincourt. The total enemy forces available immediately for defence and counter-attack amount therefore to 15 battalions.

Instruction No.2 GS1/2 Further Instructions for Attack. Movement and Administration. It included establishment of III Corps Advanced Report Centre at Sorel le Grand.

That day HQ III Corps also issued GO5967: Instructions for move into III Corps area of 32 and 203 Siege Btys; the build-up continued.

Putty wrote to Ettie Desborough on 10 November:

Dearest Chief, Have settled down to my recall after being desperately homesick without owning it, it was fortunate to find any amount of interesting work to do on my return otherwise the climatic conditions would have damped any ardour under the tottering walls of a figure which endeavoured to show no outward sign of minding about being hauled back as we generally express it. The Germans to my mind have taken a great many more divisions down to Italy than the papers give credit for, they have practically skinned the Russian front, I still think that with these rains, snow etc the rivers brought to our aid by the Bon Dieu we shall be able to stem the advances as long as the revolution does not get hold of the organ grinders and thus complete the debacle. Am planning to get my better half to come to Paris as shall not be able to get to England at any rate before February. All love and blessings for ever Putty.

His letter mentioned that he was 'recalled' which suggests that no decisions on the attack had been made by Haig and Byng before he left, and that he had been told very little about it at that stage. If this is so it makes III Corps' achievement, in the context of the war so far, all the more remarkable.

On 11 November, a day of bright sunshine, it was again quiet. The build-up continued with HQ III Corps issuing GO6012 – move of 67 HAG into III Corps area, and GO6011 – move of 12th Division Artillery, 179 and 232 AFA Bdes into the corps area. III Corps Instruction No 2 GS1/3 was also issued – Further Instructions for Attack: Security Arrangements.

HQ RE log recorded:

Advance Party of 2 Army Tramway Coy RE arrived. This coy will be used to lay 60 cm line from British light railway to German light railway terminus (to link up British and German systems) making all possible preparations beforehand so that this connection may be made as rapidly as possible after Zero.

Next day (12 November) must have been another busy day at HQ III Corps. That evening GO6033 was issued giving the timetable of moves by train to Péronne of 6th Division (15 November), 12th Division (16 November) and 29th Division (17 November) – 6 trains each. III Corps Instruction No.2 GS1/3 Further Instructions for Attack – Dissemination of Orders within Corps, was also issued. Finally that day NH again joined the corps as Corps Cav Regt.

It was again misty on 13 November as the concentration of the new corps continued. HQ III Corps issued GO6062 – Instructions for the move into the corps area of 431 Siege Bty, No 1 15" how RMA, 60 pdr Group 29th Division Artillery, 3 and 16 Bdes RHA, 169 and 277 AFA Bdes.

General Byng issued his final plan that day with the three stages of the offensive now described as:

1. The breakthrough of the Hindenburg position; the seizure of the canal crossings at Masnières and Marcoing; and the capture of the Masnières-Beaurevoir line (Red Line) beyond.
2. The advance of the cavalry, through the gap thus made, to isolate Cambrai and seize the crossings of the Sensée River; and the capture of Bourlon wood.
3. The clearing of Cambrai and of the quadrilateral St Quentin Canal-Sensée River-Canal du Nord and the overthrow of the German forces thus cut off.

Haig wrote on 13 November:

I left soon after 9 am by motor and met General Scott GOC 12th Division at Vacquerie (W of Frévent) at 10 am. 37 Bde (Webber) then carried out an attack across country with tanks represented. I walked with the troops for an advance of fully 3 miles. I explained to the divisional and subordinate commanders whom I saw today that the object of the operations of the infantry aided by tanks was to break through the enemy's defences by surprise and so permit the Cavalry Corps to pass through and operate in open country. This requires bold and determined action on the part of subordinate infantry commanders. This was not, I thought, fully realised in all units I saw today, especially in 6th Division.

It was again misty on 14 November hindering German air reconnaissance. At 11.30 am a 'Q' Conference was held at HQ III Corps with many issues still to be resolved. That evening HQ III Corps issued GO6115 – Orders for the move into the corps area of 95 Siege Bty, 25 and 135 Hy Btys, 1/2 Lancs Bty (less 2 Sects), 1/1 Wessex Bty (less 2 Sects); GO6089 – Orders for the move into the corps area of 261 Siege Bty, 71 Hy Bty, 1 Section 449 Siege Bty, 4 Bde RHA and 6th Division; and GO6129 – Orders for the move of 12th Division and its transport into the corps area. Also issued that evening were III Corps Instruction No.2 GS1/4 Further Instructions for Attack – Regulation of Movement over last 4 nights prior to attack, III Corps Instruction No.2 GS1/6 Further Instructions for Attack – Codes and Ciphers, and III Corps Instruction No.2 GS1/7 Further Instructions for Attack – Communications.

Haig wrote that day:

> At 1.45 pm I witnessed an exercise carried out by 6 SLI with tanks. This battalion is in
> 60 Bde 20th Division (III Corps). A very good battalion. The tanks were part of Colonel
> Hardress Lloyd's command. I thought the tanks went very well, and were better manoeu-
> vred and at a faster pace than I have seen hitherto.

15 November was again quiet, and Haig, his CGS (Kiggell) and Putty were at Basseux in the
morning to see 29th Division's final day of training. Haig wrote:

> At 10.30 am I motored to HQ 29th Division at Basseux where General de Lisle commanding
> the division met me. We then rode towards Ransart. The scheme was based on the idea that
> the 29th Division will have to pass through the divisions which have gained the first of our
> objectives, and capture two villages and a system of trenches beyond a canal as a second
> objective, the flanks of the division being covered by other troops. Monchy on the right and
> Ransart on the left represent the two villages; while the ditch in the low ground between
> these two places was taken as the canal and crossing places were marked with flags. The
> ground represented the reality very well, and the old British and German trench lines are
> very much like the actual defences over which our troops will have to pass. The division
> advanced with its three brigades in line. Right brigade on Monchy, and left brigade had to
> capture Ransart. I was very pleased on the whole with the way battalions worked. I noticed
> two points however of importance: 1. In some cases platoon and company commanders did
> not arrange for covering fire with machine and Lewis guns to help forward the advance from
> stage to stage. This should have been arranged for automatically whether it was necessary or
> not to support the advance, and 2. The advance should be from ridge to ridge. That is to say
> before leaving the line gained, all arrangements should be made for occupying the next ridge
> and then everyone, knowing his objective, should move forward on to it without any hesita-
> tion or delay. Partial advances here and there should be avoided. I also spoke of the need
> for brigadiers having artillery at their call. The brigades seem to me well commanded: 86
> Bde (Cheape) was on the left, 87 Bde (Lucas) in centre and 88 (Nelson) on right. I was very
> pleased with the general appearance of the division and the spirit and keenness of the men.

The divisions were now beginning to arrive at Péronne railway station by tactical trains and
moved in to the III Corps area the following night; 6th Division arrived on 15 November.
Also on 15 November HQ III Corps issued AQ 40/1/17 giving details of CCS, ADS and III
Corps MDS on Fins-Nurlu Road. The movement of all the logistic units and stores, dumping
of ammunition, casualties and prisoners of war, food for animals, water, communications, traffic
control and many more required detailed planning taking into account the constraints of time
and space, and the operational plan.

With four days to go and the front still quiet, Haig wrote on 16 November:

> At 11.30 am I had a conference at Villers au Flos (HQ IV Corps) with Generals Byng (3rd
> Army), Pulteney (III Corps), Woollcombe (IV Corps), Kavanagh (Cavalry Corps). We
> discussed plans of divisions and corps in detail. All very confident and everything so far has
> gone very smoothly indeed. We finished about 1 pm.

At 3 pm (16 November) III Corps issued OpO No.224: III Corps, in conjunction with the corps on the left, will on a date and at an hour to be communicated later attack the enemy on their front. It is in full in Appendix E. HQ III Corps Instruction No.2 GS1/8 was also issued. Further Instructions for Attack – Additional measures to speed up the passage of information.

Meanwhile 6th Division had arrived and joined III Corps: and, as Second Lieutenant Taylor 6 Buffs 37 Bde 12th Division recorded: '12th Division was ready to move and on that day marched 9 km to Bouquemaison near Doullens when it proceeded by train to Péronne, arriving there in the dark at 6 pm. A march of 5 km to Haut Allaines ensued, where we billeted for the night'.

17 November was again foggy and the front quiet. HQ III Corps issued GO6251 ordering the move of NH, Corps Cav Regt, to Moislains on the night 18/19 November. III Corps Instruction No.2 GS1/9 was also issued – Further Instructions for Attack: The subsequent (Third Stage) operations to clear Cambrai and deal with German divisions cut off. Lastly, III Corps Instruction No.2 GS1/10 was issued – Further Instructions for Attack: Orders for Lucknow Cav Bde to cross the Canal de l'Escaut (often called Canal St Quentin at this point) at Masnières or E of it and moving N of Crèvecoeur advance as rapidly as possible in the direction of Walincourt in order to (a) Destroy any guns they may meet, burn villages and destroy bridges, and (b) By the direction of its advance turn the Masnières-Beaurevoir Line, thus assisting in the capture of Crèvecoeur and enlarging in a southerly direction the gap made, and threatening the enemy's exposed flank S of Crèvecoeur.

Meanwhile 61 and 60 Bdes 20th Division, which were to deliver the assault on the 20th Division front, were relieved by troops of 12th and 6th Divisions; outposts belonging to 20th Division were left, however, covering the original front. 20th Division had a critical and difficult role in the attack both preparing itself and doing much to aid the rest of the corps: CRE 20th Division with 83, 84 and 96 Fd Coys RE and 11 DLI (pioneer bn 20th Division) had made and completely camouflaged the concentration camps in the forward areas; 20th Division Signals Coy had prepared communications for all the divisions and laid 137 miles of armoured cable to the various battle headquarters of all arms. Wireless was to play an important part in the forthcoming battle.

There was much concurrent activity. Second Lieutenant Taylor 6 Buffs 37 Bde 12th Division recorded: 'After dusk we continued our march to Heudicourt (12 km) where we found ourselves in our last billets before the attack. Throughout these preparations the utmost secrecy was observed. All movement took place at night, and during the hours of darkness the roads and communications were thronged with moving troops and transports of all descriptions'. 12th Division joined III Corps that day.

Putty also wrote to Ettie:

Dearest Chief, I refuse to add the (Ess) because you are always the Principal and I cannot make you a Viscount like the deposed Field Marshal. All the letters from London are depressed but I think personally if the Italians can hold on until about the 22 November, that all will be well the allied forces will have got in to line and the necessary stiffening given them even if they are not strong enough to take a counter offensive, after all Italy is wonderfully well off for man power, the loss of material is the only serious part of the whole thing, there seems to have been very bad staff work everything being held in breadth instead of in depth, if we can kill Germans there in the winter it is an unexpected asset. We have had no rain for nearly a week only a succession of fogs which not only make everything wet but produce the weirdest sounds as regards artillery fire completely defeating the ordinary person but also the sound ranging machines which I do not understand, the barometer is higher than it has been this year, my staff call it St Martin's summer which I had not heard of, the only St Martin's I know is the Irish celebration of the 3rd November when he is the patron saint of the drunkard and they kill all the wrens they can. I see Charley L. has gone over to Ireland again, news from there is not good though have only heard of one row at Listowel, I don't believe they will rise again unless we are beaten which we shall not be. I saw D.H. [Haig] this week he looks much better than he did in the summer. What did you hear about Billy Lambton? Best love for ever Putty.

At 5.11 am 18 November, with the situation at the front still quiet, 6th Division reported reliefs completed and that it had taken over the left sector of the corps front. At the back 29th Division was in the Allaines area and had joined III Corps.

Orders were now being passed down. Second Lieutenant Paish 53 Bty 2 Bde RFA 6th Division recorded:

> On I think 18 November the colonel called a meeting of battery commanders in our mess, and afterwards the major gave junior officers instructions for the attack, including maps of a creeping barrage, to be fired without preliminary bombardment, or even registering, lasting over three hours. Our battery had an opening range of 1,300 (the shortest I have ever fired at), and a closing range of over 4,700 yards. The rate of fire was to be two rounds a gun a minute, with each round of shrapnel followed by one of high explosive and one of smoke.

During the night 18/19 November 12th Division relieved 20th Division and took over the right sector of the corps front. By the morning of 19 November III Corps front was held with 12th Division on the right with HQ at Heudicourt; it was commanded by Major General Scott late RA, a very experienced artillery commander who had commanded the division for nearly two years. 20th Division was in the centre with HQ at Sorel where Putty's Advance Report Centre was also located; it was commanded by Major General Douglas Smith late RSF. Haig wrote (23 June 1916) that Lord Cavan (GOC XIV Corps) 'spoke in high terms of Major General Douglas Smith commanding 20th Division which had become quite a different force since his appointment'. Another source recorded 'Major General Douglas Smith was quite happy to crawl round trenches to see things for himself'. 6th Division on the left had its HQ at Etricourt and was commanded by Major General Marden late Cheshire who had only taken over in August 1917. Colonel Grove (GSO1 6th Division 1917-1919) wrote of him: 'A man of restless energy, and a first class regimental officer, with an exceptional knowledge of detail who left no one in any doubt who commanded the division'. In reserve was 29th Division with its HQ established in a quarry near Quentin Mill E of Gouzeaucourt at 5.10 pm, and commanded by Major General de Lisle late DLI and RD. He had commanded 1st Cavalry Division in the early years of the war then 29th Division in Gallipoli before bringing it back to the Western Front. A man of iron will with no concern about his personal safety, one source recorded: 'At Arras de Lisle went up to the front most days regardless of shelling'.

6th and 29th Divisions were Regular Army; 12th and 20th were of the New Army. However, such distinctions were of less relevance by 1917 with all divisions having been involved in heavy fighting, suffered casualties, and absorbed large numbers of reinforcements. The effectiveness of each division was more a measure of the ability of its commander and the time that he had been given to reconstitute and re-train it. Each of the four divisions was a cause for concern. After the Battle of Arras (April/May 1917) in which 12th Division had more than 3,500 casualties it went straight into the line at Monchy for four months where it had another 3,000 casualties. It was not until 30 October that GOC 12th Division was able to start preparing what was in effect a new division for its next battle, less than three weeks. 20th Division had been the first to arrive, taking over all of what was to be the III Corps' front on 10 October; but it had come direct from the 3rd Battle of Ypres (where 11 RB 59 Bde alone lost 66% casualties including 11 of their 16 officers) and the artillery did not arrive until after 20 October having suffered exceptionally heavy casualties. 29th Division arrived on 16 October, also from the 3rd Battle of Ypres: in the six months between 10 April and 10 October the division's casualties had been 644 officers and 13,792 other ranks. Arguably 6th Division was in the best state having come from the Loos Salient, arriving about the beginning of October.

Some men of 20th Division were taken prisoner that day (19 November): this was now a cause for concern but, if they knew anything, the attack was not compromised. The Lucknow Cav Bde arrived at Longavesnes and came under orders III Corps: all was now in place. At 6 pm HQ III Corps issued Addendum No.1 to III Corps OpO No.224: 'Zero Day will be 20 Nov, Zero Hour will be 6.20 am'.

The original plan for the attack at Cambrai had been drawn up in August. What started as a large scale tank raid gradually developed into a major attack, but by this time most of the available reserves had been committed in the N. The strategic objectives made timing an issue; if the attack was solely a diversion to draw the enemy down from Flanders it could be limited in its scope but if it was also to draw the German effort away from the French and from other fronts it had to aim to do much more. The consequence was an attack launched without the reserves needed to sustain it.

III Corps had to break through the Hindenburg Line, a title that bore no relation to reality: more appropriately called the 'Hindenburg System' it relied on defence in considerable depth for its security. An attacker was to be caught in a crossfire from a complex of trenches and strongpoints. The sentries and listening posts were five or six hundred yards in advance of the first major defences and the area in between was dotted with machine-gun nests, often of reinforced concrete. The main line of resistance was dug into the reverse slope with observers concealed in concrete bunkers overlooking the Hindenburg system ready to direct shells on troops trying to cross the ridges. From the air the barbed-wire entanglements appeared impregnable, four belts some 50 feet deep and 3 feet high with 20 feet between them. Aerial photographs showed them laid out geometrically, broad arrows to funnel advancing infantry into killing grounds covered by machine-guns. The trenches themselves were up to 12 feet wide at the top, a serious obstacle for the tanks. The whole complex was honeycombed with underground headquarters, signals installations, aid posts, ammunition stores and barracks. Ventilation shafts enabled whole companies to shelter 25 or 30 feet below ground. Shored up tunnels, six feet high and four feet wide led to the firing line and connected nests of pill boxes. All were lit by electric light.

German troops had been trained in new defensive tactics. No longer did they occupy their front-line trenches during bombardments. When shells began to fall, the bulk of the troops took

Marcoing railway bridge over St Quentin Canal, 2012.

cover deep underground, leaving a few sentries in well-protected posts to look out over no man's land and warn them when the barrage lifted. The pillboxes of reinforced concrete, impervious to anything but a direct hit from a heavy gun, and equipped with machine-guns covering the belts of wire, would allow the main line of resistance to be occupied if and when the enemy breached the wire. The Germans had calculated that to break though this section of the front would take weeks.

The St Quentin Canal was itself a major obstacle. At that time there were six main bridges across it: Crèvecoeur (iron bridge – road), Masnières (iron girder bridge – road), Marcoing (iron girder bridge – double track railway), Marcoing (iron bridge – road) and Noyelles (two iron bridges – road). There were also at least 8 wooden bridges and lock crossings in this sector.

The essence of the plan was to surprise the enemy, and overwhelm him with a sudden rush of tanks followed by infantry. In order to ensure secrecy of the concentration of troops, III Corps area was divided into three zones. The front, that under direct observation of the enemy; the centre, where movement and roads could be seen from observation balloons on fine days; and back, which could be observed by hostile aircraft. Movement in the open by day was restricted: in the front zone, no party was to exceed two men, and they were to move at 100 yards distance; working parties of ten were permitted to proceed to the front line along selected routes, and no horse or vehicle was allowed to enter this zone without a pass. In the central zone no party was to exceed thirty-two men on foot or sixteen men mounted, and all parties were to proceed in single file along the edges of the metalling or under the trees, at intervals of 100 yards, convoys being limited to ten vehicles. In the back area men and transport were not to be in larger bodies than the equivalent of one company, and at intervals of less than 200 yards. From the fourth day before the battle, fires were restricted to one per platoon and none were allowed at night.

To ensure success the troops which were to undertake operations practised with tanks in back areas, and officers and men went through the operation on carefully made ground models without being aware what ground they represented. Units were brought up just before 20 November, the day of the attack, marching by night and hiding in woods and villages by day. In some cases battalions were quartered in flat canvas erections looking like ammunition or supply dumps. No unusual activity on the ground or in the air was allowed, no guns registered, even the home mails were stopped for a short period. The extent and thoroughness of the planning and briefing is illustrated by Second Lieutenant McMurtrie 7 Som LI 61 Bde 20th Division:

> Our part in the attack was to take La Vacquerie; Sorel was made to represent this village. Over and over again we practised attacking it. All the German trenches were marked with tape and the REs constructed a model of the whole ground we were to advance over. It was about 50 yards wide and 30 yards long and was very well made. All the roads, canals, villages, railways and light railways, tracks, trenches and hills were shown, the hills being modelled correctly. There was a large wooden platform about 2 ft wide going the whole length of the model about 2 ft off the ground, so that one could see the model properly. We spent a whole morning on the model, the officers were shown where we were to attack and then every NCO was shown what to do. The officers went to see the model nearly every day to make sure they knew the exact lie of the ground.

Supply railheads for III Corps were at Roisel, Fins and Rocquigny with railheads for ammunition at Tincourt and Quinconce.

Two hundred and sixteen tanks were to operate with III Corps (2 and 3 Tank Bdes with six battalions each of 36 tanks). The 'male' tank with its 2 × 6 pdr guns was the heavier at 28/29 tons and wider at 12'9"/13'6". The 'female' with 5 MGs weighed 27 tons and was 10'5"/10'9" wide. 72 tanks were allotted to 12th Division on the right. The special role of the division was to form a defensive flank to the SE, keeping in touch with 55th Division of VII Corps on its right. The attack was to be carried out on a 1,700 yard front with 35 Bde on the right and 36 Bde on the left. First the German outpost line and a strong position at Sonnet Farm had to be taken. Fresh companies were then to pass through and gaining some 1,500 yards of the Hindenburg Line, establish themselves on the far side. This was an advance of 2,000 yards. After a pause of 48 minutes to allow 37 Bde to assemble the advance was to be continued a further 2,000 yards to capture the Hindenburg Support trench and the strong positions of Bleak House, Bonavis, Pam Pam Farm, Le Quennet and Lateau Wood. As the advance continued the new line of defence on the flank was to be formed, but with the exception of some trenches in Lateau Wood, none of the German trenches faced the required direction. Forming this defensive flank was the most difficult part of the 12th Division operation.

6th Division, on the left of III Corps, attacked on the front Villers Plouich-Beaucamp, with 71 Bde on the left, next to 51st Division of IV Corps, and 16 Bde on the right, next to 20th Division. These two bdes were to advance about 3,000 yards to the first objective, Ribécourt and spur SE of it, and then a further 1,000 yards to the support system. 18 Bde was then to advance through 71 Bde and secure the third objective about a mile further (Premy Chapel Ridge), throwing back a defensive flank towards Flesquières for the further operation of 51st Division on its left and securing the flank of 29th Division on its right. Two battalions each of 36 tanks were allotted to the 6th Division.

20th Division in the centre had as its main objective Les Rues Vertes with the bridge across to Masnières on the other side. It was supported by 60 tanks. On its left was 6th Division, with the railway the boundary, and on its right 12th Division: it would have to extend the defensive right flank secured by 12th Division and eventually join up with 29th Division's right flank once it had passed through and crossed the canal. 20th Division's task sounds complex and it was. 60 and 61 Bdes had to break through the German defences which included taking the village of La Vacquerie and Welsh Ridge. 59 Bde was then to pass through the 60 and 61 Bdes, take the canal crossings between Masnières and Marcoing, and form a defensive flank by holding a line from Les Rues Vertes to the S for a distance of about 2,000 yards. 29th Division had to pass through 6th and 20th Divisions and capture the high ground S of Rumilly, Nine Wood and Premy Chapel, most of it on the far side of the canal.

The importance of the bridges was recognised in III Corps OpO No.224. Once the objectives of 6th, 12th and 20th Divisions were taken companies of tanks were specifically tasked to secure the bridges. The words used at the two Marcoing bridges were to 'occupy as soon as possible'. In between Marcoing and Masnières the tanks were to 'seize' specified locks and bridges' and 'clear' the canal bank. At Masnières the tanks were ordered to 'seize' specified bridges and 'form a bridgehead there'. Since the tanks themselves could neither seize nor hold ground, and would have to wait for the infantry to catch up, this left much to the interpretation and initiative of individual tank coy comds. Only at Masnières was there a specific requirement for the tanks to cross the canal to 'form a bridgehead'. Speed was essential and it was important for the tanks and infantry to get to the bridges as soon as possible.

The repair and maintenance of the bridges was made the responsibility of 29th Division which was also to provide additional crossings (pontoon bridges) on the western side of Masnières. An AT coy RE was to be held in readiness to construct any heavy bridges that might be required. However, if Brigadier General Schreiber (GOC RE III Corps) understood the limitations of the existing bridges from his intelligence or reconnaissance, or the implications of their loss, and was prepared for the rapid deployment of pontoon and heavy bridging, this is not immediately apparent from any of the orders.

III Corps Artillery was under command Brigadier General Tancred (BGRA) and Brigadier General Perkins (BGHA). In addition to the artillery of the 6th, 12th, 20th and 29th Divisions it had: 40th Division Artillery, 3 Bde RHA (2nd Cavalry Division), 16 Bde RHA (4th Cavalry Division), 169, 179, 276 and 282 Army FA Bdes and 21, 26, 32, 34, 50, 78, 82 and 87 HAGs. The heavies were organised into seven groups, one to each attacking division (three), two counter-battery groups, one 60 pounder group and one super heavy group. After capture of the Blue (Hindenburg) Line, the guns of 12th and 20th Divisional artilleries were to move forward, if possible at Zero plus one hour. There were 36 × 13 pdr, 264 × 18 pdr, 66 × 4.5" how, 54 × 60 pdr, 72 × 6" how, 8 × 6" gun, 14 × 8" how, 16 × 9.2" how, 1 × 9" gun, 4 × 12" how and 2 × 15" how. This was a total of 537 guns and about 10,000 gunners.

At Zero hour the barrage was to come down on the front edge of the German outpost zone opposite III Corps; it was to be a lifting one of equal proportions of shrapnel and HE, the amount of smoke to be added up to a similar proportion dependent upon meteorological conditions. The times of successive lifts varied on different parts of the front, being calculated according to the infantry method of attack, the nature of the ground, and the character of the defences, tank speeds under varying conditions being taken into account. Special smoke barrages, if the wind proved favourable, were to be laid in particular areas (The forecast was wind WSW 8 mph which proved correct, the conditions being ideal for full smoke). On the southern flank of III Corps, 55th Division VII Corps was to assist 12th Division by firing a protective machine-gun barrage across the Banteux ravine. On the front of 6th Division twelve 6" Newton mortars were to open a 22 min bombardment at Zero hour on certain machine-gun and mortar emplacements.

The enemy deployment opposite III Corps had changed little since the assessment on 10 November. Opposite 12th Division was 19 Regt of 9th Reserve Division. On the right of 9th Reserve Division was 54th Division with its 90 Regt facing 20th Division and 387 Landwehr Regt (attached from 20th Landwehr Division) facing 6th Division. 54th Division had nine field artillery batteries (34 guns and howitzers), four batteries of medium artillery and a battery of heavy mortars. Of major significance, 107th Division had arrived in Cambrai from the Russian Front on 19 November.

Little has been said up to now about the cavalry who were to be passed over the canal in due course. There were three divisions of the Cav Corps (1st, 2nd and 5th). 1st Cavalry Division was to pass through Ribécourt and Marcoing and move N; 2nd and 5th Cavalry Divisions were to cross at Masnières and Marcoing moving NE. There was also the Lucknow Cav Bde, with most of III Corps Cav Regt attached, directly under III Corps, with its task to cross at Masnières going SE. More than 30,000 cavalry were in or about to come into III Corps area, greatly adding to the movement and logistic problems.

On a front of about 7 miles and stretching back 10 miles III Corps had assembled its force of 100,000 with their guns, tanks and logistics for the attack. In addition the cavalry were ready to exploit a breakthrough. All of this had been achieved in less than three weeks and without apparent detection by the enemy. At HQ III Corps in its nissen huts hidden in the ruined village of Templeux-la-Fosse the night of 19/20 November would be a very long one: Putty and everyone under him could only wait.

Brigadier General Seely (previously SofS for War now Comd Can Cav Bde) wrote:

> The distance to be travelled by the tanks in order to arrive in open country was about four miles. Will it be believed that at the point selected for attack there was one obstacle on the whole of the Western Front which formed an insurmountable barrier to the cavalry – the Canal de l'Escaut [St Quentin Canal]. Horses can cross almost anything; they can even swim broad rivers, as they have often done in war. But the one thing they cannot get over, unless they can bridge it, is a canal with perpendicular banks. They can get in, but they cannot get out. We were told that the tanks would cross by the existing bridges – in the case of the attack which I was to lead, by the bridge at Masnières. On the night before the battle as I always did on the eve of any attack or indeed on every occasion when I was in the front line, I went to the nearest aerodrome and got a pilot to take me over the country. I saw the canal at Masnières, and wondered what chance there was of our crossing it by the bridge. Clearly it was impossible to get over at any other place in that neighbourhood.

Apart from the irresponsibility of his action, it seems strange that Seely was not aware of the wooden bridges and locks, nor apparently did he see them when he had the opportunity of doing so; further he makes no mention of military bridging.

Captain Dugdale HQ 60 Bde 20th Division was waiting in the darkness:

> At midnight a continuous roar in the distance informed us that the tanks were moving up to their positions. Everybody was in a dither of excitement. The noise of their approach got louder and louder; minute by minute our anxiety increased, as we could not think it possible that the enemy could help hearing the outrageous noise they were making. As they approached their positions in the dark the guides in front were shouting directions at the top of their voices. We were expecting every minute the German batteries to open up along the whole front line with all the guns they could bear. The tank close to me made the most shattering noise. It seemed to have an open exhaust and the captain, or whoever was in charge, seemed to have no realisation of his close proximity to the enemy. However, he got the great hulk into its allotted position, and at last stopped his engine, and still nothing happened.

The last word must go to Private Adams 6 Queens 37 Bde 12th Division:

> On the evening of 19 November we marched up towards the line with fighting order, shovel, flares, 3 bandoliers of ammunition and a tin of bully beef. After marching all night we arrived at the assembly point at 4 am (20 November) where we found everything quiet. The cooks came up with us and made porridge and tea before we went over.

Zero

III Corps GS log recorded on 20 November:

> 6.20 am. III Corps in conjunction with IV Corps on the left and assisted by 2 and 3 Bdes Tank Corps attacked the German defences on a frontage of about 8,000 yards from Newton Post [E of Gonnelieu] to Beaucamp Valley. There was no preliminary bombardment. The line of tanks followed by infantry advanced from their assembly positions at Z-10 and the artillery and machine-gun barrages opened at Zero. The attack was carried out by 12th, 20th and 6th Divisions in the front line; on reaching the second objective or Brown Line, 29th Division passed through and proceeded to capture the final objective or Red Line.

The key reports that Putty would have received from his GS during the day were:

> 8 am. 20th Division report tanks and troops have passed Hindenburg Line; 8.30 am. 12th Division report Blue [Hindenburg] Line taken; 9.20 am. 6th Division report Hindenburg Line taken and well into Ribécourt; and 10.15 am. Corps OP reports tanks have passed round NE end of Ribécourt – no infantry seen with them – all going well – casualties light – enemy barrage weak.

Based on these reports Putty ordered '29th Division to move forward without waiting for confirmation of the capture of Bonavis Ridge, but to do so with caution, watching their left (probably right) flank'.

Progress was then much as planned:

10.35 am. 6th Division report objective gained on left flank and probably on right. Officer prisoner says attack was a complete surprise.

10.40 am. 59 Sqn RFC reports enemy still in Lateau Wood where there is heavy open fighting going on. Many tanks engaged there – some disabled – aeroplanes heavily engaged by enemy from Brown Line. Cavalry seen moving up Gonnelieu-Lateau Wood road.

11 am. RFC report reconnaissance of bridges over canal failed through bad visibility. Our troops in front and support trenches of Hindenburg Line.

12.10 pm. Both 60 and 61 Bdes (20th Division) reported in Brown Line and in touch on both flanks.

12.15 pm. 12th Division report 37 Bde have passed Lateau Wood and are forming a defensive flank.

All three divisions had made good progress; there was still a problem on the left but that on the right had been overcome:

12.45 pm. 29th Division report their leading battalions in Masnières and have secured bridgehead.

1.25 pm. 29th Division report 86 Bde in Nine Wood and Marcoing. One bridge blown up.

2.30 pm. Prisoner taken by 6th Division states that Masnières bridge is mined.

2.45 pm. OC 5 Coy Tanks reports 13 tanks of B Bn tanks are in Marcoing. Hostile infantry retired and left only 20 prisoners – bridgehead intact – infantry arriving – a few snipers still in the town.

2.50 pm. 29th Division report (from 88 Bde) bridge at Masnières is in good condition – 4 tanks now crossing.

3.15 pm. 6th Division report that Flesquières (IV Corps) is still apparently uncaptured.

3.25 pm. BGGS orders BM Lucknow Cav Bde to try and cross at Crèvecoeur if patrols report that this is feasible; if not, they are to follow 2nd Cavalry Division over the canal at Masnières and then push out to the E and S as originally ordered.

3.35 pm. 29th Division report that at 2.20 pm 88 Bde were fighting in Les Rues Vertes, assisted by 4 tanks and by 59 Bde. 87 Bde are believed to be across the canal at Marcoing and are moving their HQ up to Marcoing.

3.45 pm. Cav Corps report one squadron Secunderabad Bde 5th Cavalry Division are E of the canal at Marcoing and are helping infantry who are held up in railway cutting. Can Bde are opposite Masnières and Umbala Bde are in rear. 2nd Cavalry Division are behind Umbala Bde and Lucknow Bde are behind 2nd Cavalry Division.

4 pm. 15 Sqn RFC report at 1.40 pm that Cantaing is empty and enemy retiring in scattered order.

The GS log recorded the time an event was reported at HQ III Corps and is merely a brief summary of a much more detailed report. The event itself occurred much earlier; if Putty was at his Advanced Report Centre or visiting the division concerned he would also have seen the report much earlier. The wording can sometimes cause confusion, even more so if not used correctly: for example an objective may be 'taken' sometime before it is fully 'secured', especially if it is a wood or village and has underground bunkers. The log included two decisions taken by Putty: to order 29th Division to pass through the forward divisions at the earliest opportunity and before the first objectives had been secured; and to order the Lucknow Cav Bde to try and cross at the Crèvecoeur Bridge in variance of his original orders, this probably under pressure from 3rd Army.

It was still dark at 6.10 am when the engines of the tanks roared into life and they began to move forward. Few Germans would have heard them amid the noise of the aircraft, flying low over their lines. For ten minutes the tanks clattered forward; as they crossed the front-line trenches, followed by the infantry, the first light of dawn began to glow and at the same moment, with a deafening roar, the thousand guns of 3rd Army's artillery opened fire: it was Zero Hour.

The artillery was extremely accurate partly due to the now 90% accuracy in fixing gun positions and partly to the effectiveness of flash-spotting and sound-ranging. It was described by Arthur Pries 90 Regt 54th German Division: 'Suddenly all of the enemy's artillery began to fire madly right along our division's sector. The incendiary shells illuminated the whole front, left and right, as far as the eye could see, as if the entire area was on fire. We barely had time to instruct this battalion to follow our orders, when our own position and likewise the other commands in our rear were covered in a veritable hailstorm of shells of every imaginable calibre. Our telephone lines were shot to pieces straight away and could not be restored despite the utter fearlessness of our radio operators and engineers'.

Second Lieutenant Paish 53 Bty 2 Bde RFA 6th Division recorded:

> As the nearest tank passed me I was alarmed to see that it was heading slightly across my line of fire. At our very short opening range the guns had very little trajectory, and although care had been taken to see that our shells would clear the low crest three or four hundred yards in front of us, I was by no means sure they would clear the crest with a tank on it, especially if it was carrying a fascine. When, therefore, the tank approached my line of fire, I ordered my section to stop firing until it was over the crest.

and:

> As soon, therefore, as the paint began to burn, the guns were taken out of action, one at a time, while buckets of water were poured down their elevated muzzles, and poured out again, black and boiling, from their depressed ones. With one gun out of action most of the time, the battery was effectively reduced to five guns firing at any one time; even so, we must have fired about two thousand rounds.

The leading tanks carried a bundle of fascines, tightly-bound stout brushwood, to drop into German trenches to make them easier to cross. The first tank dropped its fascine into the front-line trench, crossed and turned left, shooting up the trench garrison as it did so. The remaining two tanks made for the next trench, where the second tank repeated the process, leaving the third tank free to proceed to the third trench. The infantry followed up, moving through gaps ripped in the wire and capitalising on the 'tank fright'.

Second Lieutenant McMurtrie 7 Som LI 61 Bde 20th Division recorded:

> We had formed up in artillery formation. When we came to the gap in the wire, each section and each platoon ran through the gap and took up the same formation on the other

side. This manoeuvre we had practised over and over again at Sorel, men going in front with flags to represent the tanks. Everything seemed to be going very well. We were all smoking hard and all of us officers had our whistles ready and were giving directions just like a field day.

Lieutenant Lee 46 Sqn RFC saw it all from above:

It was 6.30 am before we could see to take off in formation [from Izel les Hameaux about 50 kms from Gouzeaucourt], when we were immediately in the clouds to Bapaume, then SE over the wide empty Canal du Nord to Gouzeaucourt, then along the straight road to our objective, a wood [Lateau Wood] at the junction of three roads. We passed over a succession of unoccupied camps and horse lines, then as we approached the lines, saw large assemblies of cavalry waiting, and reserves of infantry moving up in scattered columns (12th Division). A few seconds later we passed over the deep wide trenches of the dreaded Hindenburg Line, with its vast belts of barbed wire, through which the first waves of tanks had crushed hundreds of lanes. From then on the mist was made denser by the smoke-screens laid in front of the advancing tanks, which still hung around. We pass over the rear wave of the advance, reserve and supply tanks, field artillery, support troops and so on, then quickly catch up with the first wave. Everything flashes by like a dream, and as we rush forward at over ninety miles an hour, twenty feet up, I get split-second glimpses that remain vividly in my memory. I see the ragged line of grey diamond-shaped monsters, thirty to fifty yards apart, stretching into the mist on either flank, rolling unevenly forwards, their tracks churning round, their exhausts throwing out blue-grey smoke. I see, behind each tank, a trudging group of infantry, casually smoking, looking up at us. To a flank, I see a disabled tank, flames leaping up the troops standing helplessly around. A chance enemy shell bursts between two tanks, knocks down a small bunch of soldiery like ninepins. The ground slopes upwards, trapping us under the clouds, so that our wheels almost touch the grass. I have to rise to clear a tank ahead, skim over it, dip down in front. It seems to be standing still. Then we've passed them, we're ahead of the advance and approaching the Boche. Now we reach the Hindenburg defence system, two lots of trenches, with troops in field grey waiting in them, their forward view blocked by the pall of smoke. We issue out of the screen so low and so fast that they have no time to fire and as we skim over their heads, I see them staring up at us in incredulous amazement. Then they're behind. More smoke-shells burst ahead, and suddenly, unexpectedly we're at the wood, at the Y-junction of our road and the two others. All this time we've managed to keep in loose formation, but now we break up and climb, in order to dive and bomb. At once, we're in the clouds, and have to drop. The 5.9s below are firing, producing more smoke. In a sharp turn I saw a bunch of guns right in line for attack, so dived at 45 degrees and released all four bombs. As I swung aside I saw them burst, a group of white-grey puffs centred with red flames. One fell between two guns, the rest a few yards away. I dive at another group of guns, giving them 100 rounds, see a machine-gun blazing at me, swing on to that, one short burst and he stops firing.

Captain McCudden 56 Sqn RFC (one of the most decorated pilots in the war with VC DSO and bar MC and bar MM) was over the left flank of III Corps (6th Division) sometime later:

> About 8.30 am we left the ground, and flew along the Bapaume-Cambrai road at 300 feet, as the heavy clouds were down at this height. We arrived at Havrincourt Wood and saw smoke and gun flashes everywhere. From 200 feet we could see our tanks well passed the famous Hindenburg Line, and they looked very peculiar nosing their way around different clumps of trees, houses etc. We flew up and down the line for an hour, but no sign of any Hun machines about, although the air was crowded with our own.

The French had been pressing Haig for the use of the Crèvecoeur bridge so that they could use it to break out to the S. On 19 November Haig impressed on Byng that he must establish a strong bridgehead at Crèvecoeur in readiness for the passage of the French. This was passed to III Corps which at 8.40 am on 20 November (2 hours 20 mins after Zero hour) telegraphed 29th and 20th Divisions and Lucknow Cav Bde that a vigorous effort must be made to capture the Crèvecoeur crossings and establish 'a bridgehead of all arms' beyond the canal as soon as the second objective was captured. It seems that they had no prior knowledge of the importance of this task. The Lucknow Cav Bde was behind 2nd Cavalry Division and only at 3.25 pm was HQ III Corps suggesting that they try and cross at Crèvecoeur.

Before looking at each division it is important to remember that there were very many other supporting units with detachments well forward. Lieutenant Ross RE Signal Service III Corps was with one. Supplied with 16 miles of cable, 4 miles to be carried by each of 4 mules, his task was to establish a forward report station:

> I never passed through so much scrap iron in all my life. Yards and yards, thick, ugly, terribly rusted, long, barbed. Tanks had rolled it flat into the soft soil, completely hidden in places by the matted growth of weeds. Easily negotiable by men but I had men and mules, four-legged raving lunatics. As soon as we reached this wire, these mules seemed to sprout dozens of pairs of legs to which were attached the most ticklish feet that ever animal had. Tread ever so lightly and before a yard had been traversed they would be in the most terrible tangle. The flattened wire seemed to writhe in devilish glee round their limbs; the more they kicked, the more hopelessly they became entwined, like a swimmer stuck in the reeds.

12th Division on the right had a more difficult task than might at first be assumed. To seize the Bonavis Ridge it had to break through the Hindenburg defences which included a number of fortified buildings and farms that had been turned into strongpoints. The first of these was Bleak House on the Péronne-Cambrai road; it had not been shelled by the heavy artillery but eventually fell to tanks and infantry working in close cooperation. Pam-Pam Farm proved tough; it required the attention of ten tanks and only surrendered when the buildings caught fire. By contrast, Bonavis Farm, specifically targeted by a 15" how during the first hour of the attack, was easily captured – a good indication of how important the artillery's contribution was to the day's success.

Bonavis and Lateau Wood were taken by 12th Division about 11 am. Lateau Wood's capture was important as until it was taken 29th Division could not advance on Masnières. Its objective captured the division now had to swing to face SE and secure the right flank of the corps. In securing its objective 12th Division had made an advance of nearly 5,000 yards. Twelve of the 72 tanks (C and F Bns) had been hit; but 55 eventually rallied on the second objective. 5 officers and 378 other ranks, 12 guns and howitzers, 4 TMs and 22 MGs were captured. Second Lieutenant Taylor 6 Buffs 37 Bde 12th Division, who was left out of battle for the attack, noted: 'Spoke to some prisoners in the cage: They said the attack was a complete surprise'. 12th Division's casualties were 144 killed, 841 wounded and 160 missing. By 10.50 am 12th Division had pushed patrols through Banteux, across the canal and into Bantouzelle, without encountering Germans.

20th Division in the centre attacked with 61 Bde on right (7 Som LI right with 12 Kings in support, 7 DCLI left with 7 KOYLI in support) and 60 Bde on left (6 Ox & Bucks right with 6 KSLI in support, and 12 KRRC left with 12 RB in support). 59 Bde were in reserve initially but were then passed through to seize crossings over canal. The division's objectives included the villages of La Vacquerie and Les Rues Vertes. The attack went exactly as planned and all the objectives in the Hindenburg defences were secured by 10 am: 17 officers and 700 men were captured.

The meticulous planning and briefing paid off at La Vacquerie when it was taken by 61 Bde (7 Som LI) at 7.30 am with mopping up completed by 9 am. 60 Bde had taken its objectives on Welsh Ridge by 9.30 am. Lieutenant Austin 12 KRRC 60 Bde 20th Division recorded:

> I commanded a company and was given four tanks. We had some machine-gun fire that was very troublesome and killed and wounded a lot of men. In the battle, when I tried to communicate, I couldn't do so because of the noise all around us. I wanted to alert the tank to the machine-gun that was shooting us up but the tank saw the machine-gun itself, tackled it, and cleared the way.

Captain Dugdale SC HQ 60 Bde 20th Division again at 10.40 am:

> We could see our tanks and troops entering the village of Marcoing. This was most important news, so a message was sent to division and corps headquarters to acquaint the Generals of this fact. It meant that we were right through the Hindenburg Line, and advancing into the open country beyond. General Duncan [Duncan took over 60 Bde on 27 October three weeks before the battle] told me afterwards that this message was so incredible, that so far as he was concerned he sent it forward adding a note to say that he could hardly believe it.

59 Bde passed through the two leading bdes of 20th Division to seize crossings over the canal at Masnières and Marcoing, both of which had tanks in position at them. This they achieved about 11 am. Fourteen more tanks (B Bn) reached Marcoing at about 11.30 am and it seems that the enemy then made a further attempt to blow the railway bridge. The tank gunners opened fire, dispersing the Germans running out a wire to the explosive charges; a section of RE then arrived and the charges were removed. Meanwhile several other bridges and locks were also seized.

Captain Smith 11 RB 59 Bde 20th Division (previously Pte 8 Worcs 144 Bde 48th Division) noted: 'Our attack was completely successful; the tanks crushed the enemy barbed wire into the sodden ground and our infantry were able to follow them through the lanes they made, without so much as catching a foot in the wire'. By 12 noon 59 Bde occupied a bridgehead across the canal at Marcoing and troops of 29th Division were crossing unopposed. The situation at Masnières was not so good. At about 12.40 pm 11 RB was held up at the main bridge: when a tank crossed the centre of the bridge, the bridge collapsed and the tank became wedged. COs

10 and 11 RB both pointed out other bridges to the waiting cavalry. At about 4.30 pm 11 RB had handed over its canal crossings to 29th Division and 59 Bde began to establish itself in the northern part of the defensive right flank, on the left of 12th Division. However, it was not until 9 pm, with 10 RB on the right and 11 RB on the left, that 59 Bde pushed forward along the spur and were established between Les Rues des Vignes (opposite Crèvecoeur) and the canal S of Mon Plaisir Farm.

Consolidation was proceeding from about 11 am. Second Lieutenant McMurtrie 7 Som LI 61 Bde 20th Division again:

> We saw several gun and ammunition columns come galloping around the hill across the other side of the valley and get under the shelter of the hill where they unlimbered and immediately opened fire again. Meanwhile the ammunition columns dumped their loads and went back for more. It was a fine sight seeing the horses racing along with the guns.

This is confirmed by Captain Dugdale SC HQ 60 Bde 20th Division's report at the same time:

> Here we found one of the German artillery observation posts wonderfully fitted up with an elaborate range-finding apparatus. We seized all the maps we could find in this dugout. There appeared to be no Germans left at all. Everybody was walking about on the top and in front doing just as they liked.

20th Division had achieved all its objectives: 60 and 61 Bdes had broken through the Hindenburg defences; 59 Bde had then been passed through and secured bridgeheads through which 29th Division was now passing, although the main bridge at Masnières had collapsed. 59 Bde had also secured all the other bridges and locks included in its objectives: once relieved by 29th Division it began to concentrate on the right defensive flank (on the left of 12th Division) from where it began to approach Les Rues des Vignes and the Crèvecoeur bridge.

6th Division on the left was focussed initially on Ribécourt and Premy Chapel. By noon all its objectives had been secured and the division was in good shape. By its accounts it had a most successful day: 'The division had very light casualties (about 650), captured 28 officers and 1,227 ORs, 23 guns, 40-50 MGs and many TMs, and received the congratulations of the Corps Commander (Putty). Everything had gone like clockwork: the artillery had pushed forward to advanced positions to cover the new front before darkness came on; the machine-guns were likewise established in their new forward positions thanks to careful arrangements and the use of pack animals'.

The first objective of 71 Bde included Ribécourt village. Its capture was the task of 9 Norfolk. Lieutenant Colonel Prior CO 9 Norfolk had decided to go over with his battalion, to observe its progress after it had crossed the ridge. He noted:

> B Coy had gone through and were in the village. I saw A Coy make a beautiful attack on a line of houses on the left of the village, supported by a male tank whose gun was in action. A Coy was attacking by sectional rushes, covering the advance by rifle fire, and I could not help feeling that my efforts at open warfare training whilst at Tinques had not been wasted.

On 6th Division's front the tanks' (H Bn) advance on the third objective (Flesquières Ridge) at 11 am initially suggested that the Germans would offer little opposition. However, the tank battalion had several tanks destroyed by a battery of German artillery firing at short range on the ridge N of the Ribécourt-Marcoing road. Despite these losses H Bn reached their final objective at about 1 pm. Some German infantry around Premy Chapel and a few machine-guns on the outskirts of Marcoing were dealt with, but otherwise the advance was hardly contested at all.

Flesquières village had not been taken by IV Corps. The continuing hold up on the ridge was obvious to 6th Division as Major Boxer CO 2 DLI 18 Bde noted at 1.15 pm:

> My objective was the farthest one, on the Premy Ridge, so we did not follow immediately behind the tanks, but went over the heads of those people who took the 1st and 2nd objectives, and then forward to our own objectives. The show went like clockwork except that Flesquières village was not taken, and as I had been informed that this village had to be taken by the brigade on my left (IV Corps) before I could advance to the Premy Ridge, I naturally thought it was so when it hove in sight. I was speedily undeceived by a hail of machine-gun bullets from it, but the shooting was high and did not hit anybody, and we got our objective in spite of it, capturing 11 Hun guns and killing or capturing all the gunmen.

At 3.15 pm the cavalry, who would have been of great assistance in capturing the enemy guns holding up 51st Division, reported that they could not advance owing to snipers in Ribécourt. The village had been in 6th Division's possession since 10 am and 18 Bde were now two miles beyond it. By 4.30 pm the division had thrown out a defensive flank along the high ground N and NW of Marcoing, where it was in touch with the left of 29th Division. The tanks of H Bn and later 18 Bde had managed to get past Flesquières village because of the convex shape of the slope: the German guns firing from the village could not see into the valley below them.

Behind the three leading divisions came 29th Division. Its advance went without a hitch and it reached its allotted positions in the old British front line sometime after 7.30 am. At 10.15 am the division received permission to advance, being warned to watch its right flank. HQ III Corps was still uncertain if the important defensive flank along the Bonavis ridge had been established; it was not until 12.30 pm that III Corps was able to confirm that Lateau Wood was in British hands. Lieutenant Colonel Allen Hamps GSO1 HQ 12th Division wrote many years later: 'Comd 37 Bde assumed responsibility of presuming the capture of Lateau Wood before any report was raised by 6 W Kents thus obviating any delay to the advance of 29th Division'.

The three brigades of 29th Division advanced towards their objectives preceded by twelve tanks, four being assigned to each brigade; machine-guns went forward on mules. There was no opposition at first. Captain Dugdale described events at 10.15 am:

> Bugles sounding in the British assembly trenches between Gonnelieu and Beaucamp had signalled the advance of all three brigades of 29th Division. They marched, three brigades in line, each battalion in fours. I cannot describe what a wonderful sight it was. The only thing missing was a band in front of each battalion. We cheered.

GOC 29th Division (de Lisle) noted at 10.30 am:

> I sent orders to start my three brigades. 88 Bde (Nelson) had to move NE to Les Vertes and Masnières, two adjacent villages separated by the canal; 87 Bde (Lucas) to Marcoing a village south of the canal; and 86 Bde (Cheape) to Nine Wood at the top of the spur 1200 yards NW of Marcoing.

Bridges and bridging of the canal were to be issues throughout the battle. In CRE 29th Division's Instruction No.1 dated 18 November one fd coy was detailed for the crossings from Masnières to the bridges and lock E of Marcoing Copse and one fd coy from N of Marcoing Copse to Marcoing (inclusive) with the task of: 'making practicable crossings for infantry, under cover of our artillery bombardment and rifle fire; after the passage of the infantry to make them practicable for cavalry'. Pontoon bridging equipment was allocated to both coys. There was no mention of bridge classification or provision for tanks to cross the canal or river. The division was concerned first with its infantry and then the cavalry.

Reports were now reaching HQ III Corps of two fresh German divisions around Cambrai, one being 107th Division. At 11.30 am Brigadier General Fuller (BGGS III Corps) questioned HQ 3rd Army on the advisability of pressing on over the canal. His caution was swept aside in the euphoria at HQ 3rd Army: it was only 11.30 am. Major General Vaughan, Byng's MGGS, pointed out that the reports were not confirmed, and in any case, if they were, then vigorous action might involve these divisions 'in the debacle'.

During the afternoon 29th Division pushed forward to the next line of defences. At Marcoing with the bridgehead over the canal established 87 Bde had two bns confronting its final objective (Masnières-Beaurevoir Line known by the Germans as Siegfried II) and two in reserve in Marcoing. Two tanks from A Bn were taken across the canal and then sent forward towards 87 Bde's final objective. Captain Raikes of 3 Coy A Bn Tank Corps recorded:

> On receipt of a message from the infantry, stating that there were machine-guns still firing from Talma Chateau, I ordered these two officers to fire into the rear of it as they went by, and also arranged for two platoons of infantry to move up on the left side of the canal to clear out the chateau. I sent both these tanks to the right and left of Flot Farm and returned myself to bring up the other two. When I arrived with the other two tanks at Marcoing Station, I found that the infantry had not gone forward, but were prepared to go forward again if supported by tanks.

In the meantime, the three infantry companies that had crossed the canal had been reinforced by 1 Innis Fus (87 Bde) who now led the advance on the wire of the next line of defences. Despite their courage by cutting the wire by hand, it soon became clear that tank or artillery assistance was needed and they were forced to dig in for the night. The close cooperation that existed between tanks and infantry earlier in the day was gone: the infantry tried to lead out of the bridgehead and take the final defence line on their own; they failed. That there were only two bns and four tanks at this critical stage of the attack shows how stretched 29th Division had become. There was also insufficient artillery forward to support the infantry onto this part of the Masnières-Beaurevoir line: part of the problem was the mud and rain, but all the trenches needed bridging to get the guns across and this took time. By 4 pm it was beginning to get dark and there was much reorganisation to be done.

On the left of 87 Bde, 29th Division's history recorded:

> 86 Bde took its objectives (Nine Wood and Noyelles) by 1 pm. So far forward were the troops by 11 am that the Bde Comd (Cheape) asked the LO to summon the cavalry. These did not, however, appear for three hours, too late to develop the attack northwards.

1st Cavalry Division had been delayed by snipers in Ribécourt but this does not fully explain the lack of urgency: the days were short and it was inevitable that they and the rest of the Cav Corps would be fighting in the dark at some stage. Cav Corps reported at 3.45 pm that one sqn Secunderabad Bde 5th Cavalry Division were E of the canal at Marcoing; this suggests that the rest of the bde was nearby.

At Masnières the bridge had been destroyed by 12.40 pm. As a tank, with a number of bombers from 11 RB clinging to its sides, approached the main span of the bridge, Private Bollard Flying Fox II 17 Coy F Bn Tank Corps recorded: 'The Boche blew the far end of the span in, and we dropped smack into the canal'. Other reports had said that the tank itself caused the bridge to collapse either because of its weight or because of its width.

The loss of the bridge did not delay 88 Bde. Shortly after 12 noon two bns had crossed the canal: the village was strongly held and progress was slow but by 2 pm 88 Bde had captured most of Masnières and had three bns across the canal and one in Les Rues Vertes.

As early as 11.40 am Can Cav Bde (5th Cavalry Division), which had been waiting since 9 am, was ordered to begin its advance from behind Gouzeaucourt towards Masnières, keeping in touch with the infantry in front. Captain Williams LSH Can Cav Bde 5th Cavalry Division noted: 'Finally, just after 12 noon, orders came to move. Off we went as fast as we could over the fifteen miles between Fins and Masnières, where we halted in a sunken road, about a mile from Masnières, while a patrol went forward to ascertain the conditions of the canal crossings'.

Brigadier General Seely Comd Can Cav Bde said:

> It was wonderful to be cantering along behind one of the tanks, with hardly a British casualty to be seen. I left my brigade about a mile short of Masnières, and galloped with my BM, my ADC and six orderlies close behind the tank which was making for the bridge. My instructions were, as soon as the tank had crossed the bridge, to take my brigade over towards and beyond Cambrai. As the event proved, had the bridge remained intact, this we could have easily done. With the thousands of horsemen and machine-guns supporting us, the results might well have spelt a disaster of the first magnitude to the German Army. The tank rumbled along the street leading straight to the bridge, I, on my faithful Warrior, cantering along behind it. It got on to the middle of the bridge, but then there was a loud bang and crash, and down went the tank and the bridge into the canal. At the same moment there was a burst of rifle fire from the opposite side of the canal, and one or two of my orderlies were hit. I sent back a message at once reporting this disaster, saying that I would endeavour to bridge the canal elsewhere.

It was about this time that Lieutenant Marchant 1 Essex 88 Bde 29th Division was killed. Sergeant Collins, wrote from 24 Gen Hosp Étaples on 23 November:

> Should there be any inquiries regarding the personal effects of my platoon commander, the late Mr Marchant, any articles of value that were on him I was unable to save, he was shot through the head by a sniper as we were crossing the bridge and fell into the canal at the part where the bridge was broken. He was killed about 2 pm 20 Nov.

FGH Can Cav Bde entered Les Rues Vertes around 2 pm; unable to cross, they moved E to the lock discovered by 4 Worcs (88 Bde). Brigadier General Seely again:

> I sent for my brigade to come to the outskirts of Masnières. One squadron was sent to find a means of bridging the canal further to the S. That redoubtable soldier, Tiny Walker, my machine-gun officer, took on the job. He managed to find two baulks of timber near a demolished lock, and, under cover of continuous rifle fire directed on every nook and cranny in the buildings opposite, got this narrow structure into position. The squadron, commanded by Strachan, of FGH, led their horses across and galloped into the open country.

This must have been between 3 and 4 pm.

At 3 pm Major General Greenly GOC 2nd Cavalry Division rode into Les Rues Vertes and conferred with Seely and Nelson (Comd 88 Bde 29th Division). Given the state of crossings at Masnières and that it was then too late in the day for enough light for cavalry to operate, Greenly came to the decision (around 4 pm) to stop FGH, bring them back and to defer the crossing until the next morning. B Sqn FGH already across had meanwhile moved N from the canal, charging a battery of field guns and killing or capturing their crews. They reached a sunken road about one kilometre E of Rumilly and, isolated, held out there until dark. They then abandoned their horses and fought their way back to Masnières on foot.

Captain Williams LSH Can Cav Bde 5th Cavalry Division was there when Greenly was conferring with Seely:

> The reason I happened to be at HQ Can Cav Bde was that Macdonald [OC C Sqn LSH] had learned of another bridge to the left of Masnières, and wanted permission from Seely to send a patrol to report on the possibility of crossing there. Seely told him to send a patrol round and to take his squadron round if he thought it wise to do so. I thought it funny to tell him that, after just giving word to stop the FGH from crossing. However, it was not my place to question. I dashed back to my troop and called for number one patrol. This was all organised beforehand and in no time at all, we were on our horses and away. We got to the bridge without being fired on at all, and found on reaching it that it was held by a detachment of the Newfoundland Regt [88 Bde 29th Division]. I found the bridge to be quite passable for cavalry, its only fault being that one end was about a foot out of plumb. I sent back word. Macdonald brought the squadron round and was able to size up the situation for himself. He very wisely decided that nothing worthwhile could be accomplished by trying to operate with one squadron unsupported, and especially with the light fading

so rapidly. We watered our horses while the opportunity was at hand, and went back to where we had been.

Kavanagh's (GOC Cav Corps) plan was to pass his leading divisions through 'as soon as the infantry had secured crossings at Masnières and Marcoing, and have ensured the possibility of passing over the Masnières-Beaurevoir Line, which could happen at any time after zero hour plus four and a half hours (ie 10.50 am)'. This is somewhat vague and optimistic but there is no suggestion of waiting for 29th Division to have secured the Masnières-Beaurevoir line. The Cav Corps, at Masnières at least, were inadequately briefed on the bridges, had poor coordination with III Corps, and lacked any real sense of urgency. Nightfall seems to have come as a surprise: it would have found them somewhere across the canal even well on to the Cambrai plain. There is also no mention of any III Corps military bridging in Cav Corps planning.

Adv HQ Cav Corps was at Fins where BGGS Cav Corps recorded: 'It went very successfully but there were two points which affected us: the first was that the Boche had two divisions in reserve behind the line where we hoped he had none; secondly the want of confidence in some of the infantry in the powers of the tank (a reference to GOC 51st Division IV Corps). The result of both was loss of time and therefore less time to get to our objectives. At one time it looked as if we were going to get through, but the failure of 29th Division to get over the Canal de St Quentin at Masnières and on to Rumilly en Cambrésis before dark, did not give us the opportunity we wished for'. Again the arrival of darkness seems to have been unforeseen in 3rd Army's planning.

By nightfall III Corps' line ran from the right of IV Corps forward (6th Division) to Premy Chapel where 29th Division carried it on to Nine Wood and Noyelles and across the St Quentin Canal to Masnières. E of the village it crossed again to the southern side. Before Crèvecoeur the line turned once more to the S, 20th and 12th Divisions holding it along the Bonavis Ridge to join the front line occupied before the attack at Gonnelieu. Three of III Corps' four divisions were therefore securing the flanks of the breakthrough with just one, the over-stretched 29th Division, continuing the direction of attack.

At 7.30 pm 5th Cavalry Division ordered Can Cav Bde to make Rumilly their objective that night. Comd Can Cav Bde ordered LSH to carry out this operation: the order did not reach the regiment until 10.15 pm at which time a conference was held, all officers and men of the regiment attended. However, just as they were filing out of the big barn word came that the project was abandoned. The regimental war diary states that the night was a continuation of orders and counter orders.

Byng issued his orders for 21 November at 8 pm: III Corps was to 'make every effort' to gain the Masnières-Beaurevoir line E of Marcoing and Masnières and to capture Crèvecoeur so as to allow early passage of the cavalry. Unfortunately he also redeployed 3 Bde Tank Corps from III to IV Corps, because he believed III Corps had the easier task next day. This move had an unwelcome side effect, however, for in their move across the rear area the tanks managed to sever many of the telephone lines linking forward units with their headquarters, with the result that a severe communications problem arose at a critical time. This clear direction to continue the offensive was undermined by Byng's orders late in the evening telling III Corps 'to select and prepare a strong defensive line overlooking the canal crossings, as the ground beyond it might prove untenable in the face of strong counter-attack. Bridges should be prepared for demolition'.

At 10 pm Putty issued his orders for the next day. 29th Division assisted by 12 additional tanks (it had 12 in the initial attack) was to capture the Masnières-Beaurevoir line as far E as Crèvecoeur, whilst 20th Division also with 12 tanks pushed along the near bank of the canal to seize the bridges at Crèvecoeur where the two divisions would join up; they were to agree a suitable Zero hour (11 am 21 November). As soon as the objectives had been secured the Lucknow Bde would cross the canal and sweep southward. By this time 11 RB 59 Bde 20th Division had pushed forward down the slope to the canal and were just half a mile from Crèvecoeur. Captain Smith 11 RB noted:

> At the ghastly hour of 2.30 am [21 November] I received orders to take my party up to our new front line, near the canal bank. It was a grim struggle through the mud in the pitch dark, and long before reaching our forward position my men were tired out.

Overall it had been a very successful day: it had shown that it was now possible to break through the strongest defences, and in doing so had dealt a serious blow to German morale. DDMS III Corps log recorded that the total number of casualties dealt with by III Corps medical units up to 6 pm was 1,733. 54th German Division had almost been destroyed with 5,785 officers and men reported missing at the end of the day. The AQ log recorded that III Corps Artillery had fired an estimated 150,000 rounds, a figure that seems extraordinarily high.

There was little rest for the tired troops who in the rain and the darkness had to consolidate their positions and reorganise in preparation for fresh efforts: orders would come. III Corps had no fresh infantry in reserve. All four divisions reported the night 20/21 November was quiet; the enemy too, briefly, had nothing left. When dawn came it was still raining, as it would all day. The first effect of this was greatly to hamper flying operations and the movement of tanks.

Many civilians had remained close to the front line, basing their decision on three years' stagnation of trench warfare; now they were in the middle of battle. Unwittingly they added to the chaotic mix already created by the poor weather and the disruption caused by blocked roads and blown bridges. The Germans had also blown mines, creating large craters in the roads. The combination had severe implications for the supply and reinforcement of the attacking divisions.

At 8.30 am HQ III Corps received its first report of progress. 6th Division informed them that the attack (by IV Corps) on Flesquières was progressing well and there was no enemy opposition. At the same time Cav Corps reported that they (probably 1st Cavalry Division) were held up at Cantaing. At Noyelles on the left of 29th Division there were both cavalry and infantry in the village; 29th Division reported that the bridge had been blown up at 10 am but that they intended to try and get a bridge across during the morning.

A report (timed at 6.15 am) from 2nd Cavalry Division was received at HQ III Corps at 9.32 am:

> Infantry hold Masnières with exception of extreme N of village. Situation between Masnières and Crèvecoeur uncertain – cavalry patrols left before dawn to clear it up but not yet returned. Rumilly reported held by the enemy.

Then at 10.42 am Cav Corps reported 'Can Cav Bde in trench with 88 Bde who have extended their right flank to Mon Plaisir Farm'.

A more important report was received at 11.07 am from Captain Rolls GSO3 HQ III Corps who had been sent forward so that Putty could get immediate and accurate information on the situation. He was at Rues des Vignes and reported that:

> Crèvecoeur was still occupied by the enemy at 8 am. 59 Bde attacked and hold Rues des Vignes and bridge at M.5.c.4.7. Enemy attacked last night from Révelon Chateau but was repulsed. 29th Division have one platoon at farm [Mon Plaisir] at G.27.d.9.9. and hold front line of Beaurevoir-Masnières Line but enemy still in support trench. 59 Bde are not in touch with 12th Division on their right and the gap between M.3.d. and Lateau Wood should be filled and consolidated early.

This is confirmed by Captain Dugdale SC HQ 60 Bde 20th Division:

> Our line was now in the form of a very acute salient. We had penetrated about four miles deep into the German lines. Therefore we had two flanks to defend, which were very much open to counter-attack. 12th Division on our right were facing one of these flanks; our front extended from Crèvecoeur along the canal bank to within a quarter of a mile of Masnières; from there 29th Division held the line. Our left flank ended by a [wooden] bridge over the canal on our side; on the other side of this bridge 29th Division held the front.

At 11.11 am HQ III Corps received a copy of 6th Division instructions to 16 Bde to proceed with the relief of 86 Bde: this would bring 86 Bde into reserve. Then at 12.25 pm it received a report from Major Battye GSO2 HQ III Corps on the left flank (sent via 29th Division) that at 11 am the infantry advance on Cantaing had started with cavalry and tanks cooperating. Cantaing was taken by 14 DLI 18 Bde 6th Division in conjunction with the cavalry at 2.50 pm.
Brigadier General Schreiber wrote years later:

> It was in the morning of the second day that I went down to the front Marcoing-Masnières to see what the situation was chiefly in connection with crossing the canal, as a tank had broken down the bridge at Masnières. Although I had an AT bridging coy on the way down our front line was such a short distance over the canal that bridging there would not have been feasible but possible near Marcoing – at a lock. I think by that time the situation was such that any bridge was no longer required.

All was not going so well on the right. At 12.20 pm 20th Division reported 59 Bde had been driven out of Rues des Vignes at 9 am. They also reported that 59 Bde could not make contact with 37 Bde 12th Division on their right (as Captain Rolls had reported earlier) so one battalion 61 Bde had been ordered up to protect 59 Bde's right flank. 20th Division's next report at 4 pm stated that 59 Bde had 'crossed canal but not the river at Crèvecoeur and are held up by wire and MG fire. They could see troops of 88 Bde 29th Division on the left and the operation against the bridge at Rues des Vignes was progressing'. A later report from 20th Division at 8.08 pm said that at 4.30 pm 59 Bde was attacking Crèvecoeur.

Second Lieutenant McMurtrie 7 Som LI 61 Bde 20th Division described his battalion's part that day:

> 7 Som LI was moved up to Masnières. To do this we had to cross a piece of very marshy ground and the enemy started shelling heavily. We got across however without any casualties, crossed the canal by pontoon bridge and got under cover of some buildings on the right edge of Masnières. Here we had to dig in as a battalion in reserve to the brigade holding the front line. We were expecting the enemy to counter-attack at any moment and if he did we would have to go up to support our front line troops. The place we were in was as nasty as it could be.

29th Division reported at 4.43 pm that 88 Bde had captured Mon Plaisir Farm confirming the earlier report from Cav Corps. Major General de Lisle reported personally at 7.25 pm:

> 29th Division are 200 yards from enemy front line – an attack by tanks today was a failure owing to heavy MG fire with armour piercing bullets only 3 tanks out of 16 came back and their commander reports 50% of his personnel were casualties. Comd 87 Bde reports the operation will require 20 tanks and an artillery bombardment.

He reported again at 8.50 pm:

> 86 Bde is to rest tonight, very exhausted after fierce fighting all day and many casualties. 87 Bde are also very exhausted and not fit to attack Red Line tomorrow unless three hours artillery bombardment and cooperation by 20 tanks. 88 Bde are most exhausted and cannot be relieved; they have beaten off 2 heavy counter-attacks in the course of the day. This being position the only course to follow is to hold on for the present.

There was now no doubt that the Germans had been reinforced including by 107th Division, and the momentum of the attack had gone.

The attack by 87 Bde 29th Division with 16 (other reports say 18) tanks was due to take place at 11 am but did not start until an hour later. 2 SWB and 1 KOSB with the tanks attacked from Marcoing Station towards Flot Farm. It was hastily prepared with little or no opportunity for liaison between the tank commanders and the infantry. Without supporting artillery, the infantry waited for the tanks; without fascines for their tanks, commanders were wary of attempting to cross German trench lines, often moving laterally along them instead. When 87 Bde did attack, the tanks were met by a storm of machine-gun fire: the Germans used large quantities of armour-piercing bullets which frequently pierced the tanks' armour. However, it was the use of field artillery over open sights that knocked out several tanks. Another source said that the 'infantry had little success in its frontal assault against wire which was mostly intact. At 3.30 pm when the fighting died down most of the battalions were back at their starting line'. 87 Bde was opposed by 3/1 Guard Reserve Regt and 3/13 Bavarian Regt, part of the substantial reinforcements now deployed against III Corps.

20th Division was still persevering opposite Crèvecoeur and reported at 10.15 pm:

> Tanks unable to cross bridge at G.35.d. which is not strong enough. Tanks however are in position guarding bridges from the N bank – 11 KRRC met by rifle and MG fire from

villages and trenches N, have established themselves about Révelon Chateau – 11 RB have formed a defensive flank facing E covering crossing over canal at G.34.a.2.9. and G.34.b.2.9. One coy 10 RB has held bridgehead in M.5.c. all day. Attempt will be made to destroy bridge tonight.

MGGS 3rd Army discussed the situation by telephone with Putty at 3.10 pm: the enemy's resistance E of the canal appeared to be stiffening and it seemed that a further advance might not be possible as the troops were very tired and no reinforcements were in sight; it was advisable to select and prepare a strong defensive line overlooking the canal crossings, as the ground held E of the canal might prove untenable in the face of a strong counter-attack. Following this conversation CE III Corps ordered 29th Division to prepare for demolition all the bridges on its front. No decision, however, had yet been made at GHQ. Haig had to decide whether the prospect of securing the Bourlon ridge, always of paramount importance in his eyes, justified continuing the offensive. He displayed no hesitation in closing down III Corps' operation on the St Quentin Canal, for he had always regarded the advance eastward as primarily of value in safeguarding the flank of the northward thrust. The conclusion of Haig's deliberations at 9 pm was that III Corps would go over to the defensive and hold the line of the canal while IV Corps would devote its strength to the capture of the Bourlon position.

Byng, now acting on the decision of the CinC, spoke to Putty at 10.30 pm agreeing that there was 'very little chance of breaking through', and confirming the defensive proposals which had been discussed in the afternoon. III Corps, which had already issued a warning with regard to defensive preparations, at once issued its orders: HQ III Corps G706 to 6th, 12th, 20th and 29th Divisions, III Corps HA, 59 Sqn RFC, 3 (probably 2) Bde Tank Corps, 3rd Army, IV Corps, VII Corps, Cav Corps, Lucknow Cav Bde, GOC RE. 'Reference Wire No.G661 of 20 November: Divisions will consolidate all ground gained with a view to meeting counter-attack. 6th Division will establish a well wired line of resistance from and including Nine Wood to the river in L.11.d. with an outpost line established north of Noyelles village. Touch must be gained with 51st Division near L.4.central. 29th Division will make every effort to strengthen their present position north and east of Masnières and across Triangle through G.13.d. Bridges will be prepared for demolition at once in following order of precedence. 1. Both bridges in Masnières. 2. Station Bridge in 23.b. 3. Railway Bridge in 23.c. 6th and 20th Divisions will supply the two fd coys of 29th Division with any explosive required for bridge demolitions. Acknowledge'.

29th Division reported relief of 86 Bde by 16 Bde complete at 11.30 pm: '86 Bde remaining in billets in Marcoing. Relieving coy on house to house search took 29 prisoners'. The last part emphasises again that taking a village or strongpoint might be quick but securing it, having cleared all the bunkers, cellars and tunnels, took a long time and much infantry effort.

Further advance for III Corps was no longer possible: now, with the enemy reinforced, all their experience would have told them to expect a counter-attack. 20th Division history noted:

> The position held by the division at this time was most important. The line formed a deep salient, overlooked by the high ground which the enemy occupied. Not only did the enemy hold the bridges across the canal but on the SE face of this salient the steep convex slope of the ridge left a strip of dead ground along the front, so that even from the outpost line the bottom of the valley and the village of Les Rues des Vignes were out of sight.

That GOC 20th Division (Douglas Smith) seemed to accept this situation was to have serious consequences.

AQ HQ III Corps estimated the casualties in the infantry for the two days fighting (20 and 21 November) to be: 6th Division 29 officers and 425 other ranks, 12th Division 45 officers and 1,311 other ranks, 20th Division 45 officers and 1,085 other ranks, 29th Division 71 officers and 2,700 other ranks = 5,711. This is an average of about 100 casualties per battalion which considering the experience of the previous three years and what had been achieved is remarkably low.

Two other AQ HQ III Corps reports that day are also of interest. One stated that 450 civilians were evacuated from Masnières to Péronne, most very elderly, an added complication in the middle of the battle; the other report stated that ammunition expenditure was 17,000 rounds, slightly more than 10% of the previous 24 hours (20 November), if that figure is correct. The problems had been hinted at during the day. Some batteries had managed to get forward but they had been very few: congestion on the available routes, difficulty of crossing the trench lines, and the weather all contributed to the difficulties. Ammunition resupply could have also been a problem.

Any examination of Putty's planning and conduct of the battle on 20 and 21 November must focus on the failure of III Corps to take its final objective, the Masnières-Beaurevoir (Red) line. This was a strong well-wired position with adequate defenders. Experience should have told him that 29th Division would not be able to do this with infantry alone; they would need artillery, air and, perhaps most important of all, tank support. In the first phase each attacking division was supported by two bns of tanks (72 tanks). 29th Division initially had only 12; those that were redeployed later had used their fascines and there had been no resupply. The tanks, and the cavalry, had to cross the canal by one of the existing bridges or by a military bridge when it had been built but there seems to have been an absence of engineer intelligence and inadequate planning in this regard. Lastly Haig was pressing Byng, and he was pressing Putty, about the importance of securing the crossing at Crèvecoeur. Initially, on 20 November, this would have been relatively easy, as 12th Division had shown at Bantouzelle but 20th Division, whose task it became, had first to break through the Hindenburg defences and secure the crossings over the canal for 29th Division; only then could it consider Crèvecoeur. Tied in with all of these issues was the absence of any III Corps reserves both at the outset or reconstituted later. Yet without reserves Putty's ability to influence the battle was limited.

Major General Fuller then SO HQ Tank Corps wrote many years later:

> The whole trouble about the tanks was that Byng would not hold any in reserve. I urged him to do so, but all he replied was 'I cannot go against the wishes of my corps and div comds'. He was far too soft to be a good general, and Louis Vaughan [MGGS 3rd Army] was quite useless. Had the cavalry gone in dismounted on the afternoon of 20 November, they might have done some good, but Kavanagh – surely the worst cavalry general in history – was miles away and no move could be made without his orders.

By the morning of 22 November everyone, including Putty, was beginning to get tired: some were exhausted. During the night 5th Cavalry Division was withdrawn into the Cav Corps concentration area easing the congestion and, with the exception of 20th Division, III Corps had a relatively quiet night. In the salient opposite Crèvecoeur 59 Bde 20th Division was counter-attacked and driven back from Révelon Chateau at 4.50 am. During the morning RFC was able to operate over the front line and reported it still quiet.

At 11 am 29th Division reported: '88 Bde in touch with 87 Bde on Cambrai Road and in touch with 59 Bde at Mon Plaisir Farm – situation in Masnières improving – several underground passages being occupied'. There were numerous caves under Masnières which had been used by the Germans and it seems that 29th Division had received little intelligence on them beforehand.

12th Division reported two loud explosions heard in Bantouzelle at 4.50 pm. At 5.19 pm 20th Division reported:

> 11 RB holding bridge G.28.c. 11 KRRC covering lock at G.28.d. but are not across it. None of our troops in Crèvecoeur tanks have retired from lock at G.35.d. Enemy known to be occupying Révelon Chateau. Troops not in Rues des Vignes but on the spur at M.4.4. Enemy thought to be in Rues des Vignes.

From last light the previous evening neither division had observation on the dead ground to their E.

That evening (22 November) HQ III Corps issued instructions for consolidation which went into more detail than those sent out the night before. The main defensive line was to run from VII Corps boundary, at the Banteux ravine, along the Bonavis ridge to Lateau Wood (inclusive to 12th Division); thence E of the main Cambrai road to the St Quentin canal (20th Division); beyond the canal, taking in that part of the Masnières-Beaurevoir line in III Corps possession and the spur W of Rumilly, to the lock opposite Marcoing station (29th Division); and thence to the near side of the canal north-westward behind Noyelles to the junction with IV Corps near Cantaing (6th Division). In front a series of posts was to be established; the captured Hindenburg support system was to be converted into a second line, its right on Lateau Wood.

Special tasks were laid upon each division. 12th Division was responsible that Lateau Wood was strongly organised against attack from the NE and N, and was ordered to push forward its line above Banteux in order to free the main Cambrai road from close-range machine-gun fire and obtain observation over the canal valley (this matter of observation had been mentioned in III Corps OpO for 20 November. On that day, it will be remembered, a 12th Division patrol had crossed the canal at Banteux and found the entire location abandoned by the enemy; but unfortunately no advantage had been taken of this). 20th Division was to establish forward posts in the canal bend opposite Crèvecoeur. 29th Division was to convert the caves in Masnières into a defended locality, take an early opportunity to capture the spur E of Rumilly, establish a strong bridgehead at Marcoing station, and make that portion of the village lying between the canal and river into an 'impassable obstacle'. 6th Division was to form an outpost line in front of Noyelles, dig a reserve line from Marcoing to Nine Wood, and entrench the Premy Chapel ridge as a defensive flank. These four divisions which had carried out the attack on 20 November were not relieved, and received no reinforcement; the fighting strength of many battalions was low and there is no doubt that their efficiency was further impaired by the hard work, in bad weather, of consolidating the ground they had won.

This extract from the official history summarises the situation and the main issues:

> III Corps was now required to hold all the ground it had won. Some of it was of no tactical importance and would be very difficult to hold. It made III Corps very stretched and unable to reconstitute reserves to counter-attack should that be necessary. Because the divisions

were holding forward in the right angle of the line, this part lacked depth and made communication, artillery support and logistics difficult. Some of the likely approaches were not covered by observation or fire. Above all III Corps was going to need time to carry out all these tasks and to get some rest; and the enemy was not likely to provide this time.

Captain Dugdale SC 60 Bde 20th Division reflected a different mood than two days earlier:

We were not relieved after the attack as we expected to be; the men had no overcoats and the weather was very cold. It was also very difficult to provide the troops with hot food, therefore their spirits became rather low as time went on, especially as prospects of relief were dim.

Putty visited GOC 29th Division that day (22 November). Major General de Lisle noted: 'Corps Commander came to the Chalk Quarry where my HQ were established to congratulate us. I told him I was more proud of my troops than ever before'.

It was again quiet overnight and throughout 23 November apart from shelling and machine-gun fire. 12th Division reported Bonavis Ridge and Cambrai Road between Bonavis Farm and Sonnet Farm shelled intermittently during the day with all calibres up to 15 cm, as was 29th Division at Masnières. With hindsight the enemy were evidently registering targets early to ensure surprise for their counter-attack. During the afternoon 3rd Army ordered 2nd Cavalry Division to move at once from Villers Faucon to a concentration area about Fins. This brought them behind III Corps; even more welcome news came when 59th Division arrived in Etricourt and came under command of III Corps – Putty had a reserve at last.

Snow fell during the night followed by rain: conditions were miserable, and so were many of the men. Although there had been local counter-attacks, the Germans appeared to have had their first thoughts of a counter-offensive on 23 November when reinforcements began to accumulate. The main effort opposite III Corps was to be made on the southern sector of the battlefield in the direction Banteux-Gouzeaucourt. The bombardment was to be intense but brief, the attack timetable staggered along the front and aircraft used on a scale not seen previously. The Banteux-Gouzeaucourt thrust was to be delivered towards Metz-en-Couture, situated on the only good road to the Bourlon position. Bantouzelle, found deserted on 20 November, was used as an assembly point for enemy troops. The bridges had remained intact and, despite costly attempts, 12th Division had been unable to secure Pelican Trench which overlooked the crossing. From Banteux-Bantouzelle the Germans had access to Banteux Ravine which featured prominently on British maps as it lay at the junction of III (12th Division) and VII Corps (55th Division).

Most of the fighting on 24 November was on 12th Division's front. At 11.34 am it reported: 'Attack was carried out by 35 and 36 Bdes at 8 am against Quarry Post-Pelican Avenue and Bleak Quarry. All objectives taken. Casualties light. 43 prisoners taken – 395, 76 and 19 Regts identified'. At 4.20 pm 12th Division reported the situation at 3 pm: 'Quarry Trench (part) including Quarry Post taken and Hindenburg Line (part). Pelican Trench blocked (in two places) between these points in enemy hands also Bleak Quarry'. 12th Division's evening report at 5.15 pm said: 'New line near Quarry Post heavily shelled with 77 mm, 10.5 cm, and 15 cm from 11 to 12 noon. Hostile snipers active firing from Banteux on Hindenburg main line inflicting casualties. Bleak House, Sonnet Farm heavily shelled during day, vicinity of Pam Pam Farm heavily shelled from 8.30 am – 1.30 pm from direction of Cheneau Wood'. 12th Division was seeking to achieve the two tasks given to it by III Corps – to push forward its line above Banteux to free the main Cambrai road from close-range machine-gun fire and establish observation over the canal. It had some success but there was still much dead ground in the valley over which it had no observation. At 9.30 pm 12th Division reported considerable enemy movement in Les Rue des Vignes suggesting it had a patrol or listening post forward, but there was no report of any action taken on the report.

HQ III Corps issued Instruction No.2 GS1/11 at 9.30 pm 24 November. Further Instructions for Attack – Orders to 29th Division to capture the high ground S of Rumilly. That evening IV Corps made it clear to Byng that nothing but a major effort would secure the objectives set by the CinC. Byng therefore ordered III Corps to take over the right of IV Corps' front including Cantaing. Byng was still determined to hold on to all the ground that had been taken.

25 November was again quiet on the whole front, although VII Corps reported shelling of Villers-Guislain at 6.27 am and 12th Division reported shelling of the village from 9 am to 2 pm. At 9 am III Corps reported captures since 19/20 November: 70 officers and 3,590 other ranks, 35 × 77 mm guns, 5 × 15 cm guns, 11 × 10.5 cm guns, 1 × 11.5 cm gun, 6 anti-aircraft guns, 71 machine-guns and 34 trench mortars. Later, at 11 pm, HQ III Corps issued G795 warning 6th Division to be prepared to take over on the evening 26 November part of Guards Division IV Corps' line (as ordered by 3rd Army). It also issued HQ III Corps GO6740 amending the boundary between VII and III Corps. 29th Division's attack planned to take place next day was cancelled after Putty consulted de Lisle and the brigadiers concerned.

It continued quiet throughout the night 25/26 November and through 26 November. At 11.15 am III Corps issued OpO No.226 confirming the WngO (G795) issued to 6th Division. Also that day, after 'spending two or three days reconnoitring III Corps' front', 59th Division was suddenly transferred by 3rd Army to IV Corps. Both moves were designed by Byng to strengthen IV Corps and its offensive at Bourlon but in doing so he had made III Corps significantly weaker and even more stretched.

Since it was on 26 November that the corps heavy bridging opened at Marcoing this is a suitable place to tell the full story of this part of the battle, mainly from the HQ RE log:

On 16 November CE III Corps [Brigadier General Schreiber] issued Instr No.1: 574 AT Coy RE will be ready to carry out heavy bridging, or other duty as required. Spans, material and launching gear for crossings at Marcoing and Masnières was in stock at Fins RE dump. In addition there were 30 complete bays of heavy type Inglis bridge. At Roisel there was also a heavy bridging dump. 42 GS wagons (19 Reserve Park Etricourt) and 8 pontoon wagons (LH 3 Pontoon Park Nurlu) were placed at the disposal of 574 Coy for moving material forward when required. 15 bays of heavy type Inglis bridge and other materials were loaded on the morning of 20 November. Loaded wagons were then parked E of Fins, the horses returning to their lines at Etricourt and Nurlu to await orders from 574 Coy. Nothing is then recorded until 12.15 am 21 November when Schreiber telephoned CRE 29th Division: 'Please can you say by what bridges other than the main road bridge the tanks got across at Masnières and whether you are taking any steps to repair Masnières main road bridge'. CRE 29th Division replied: 'It is difficult owing to conflicting reports to answer this, but personally I think it is very doubtful whether the tanks crossed by any other bridge at Masnières. I intend to arrange for the repair of this bridge to carry ordinary wheeled traffic'. After this call Schreiber decided that no action need be taken till the morning [21 November] when an order (A93) was sent to 574 Coy (CRE 29th

Division informed): 'Be ready to move on receipt of telephone message at 7.45 am with horses hooked in. Coy go with bridging wagons. Inglis bridge only. Acknowledge'. At 7.30 am he postponed movement; then at 12 noon he visited 574 Coy and ordered bridging to go forward which it did about 3.30 pm. Sometime that afternoon CE III Corps sent S306 to CRE 29th Division: 'A portion of heavy bridging ie heavy Inglis bridge is being sent via Villers Plouich and Marcoing to Masnières. About 14 wagons. Remainder will follow tomorrow. This is in accordance with orders from army'.

This is an extraordinary message but more was to follow: At 10.30 am 22 November Schreiber sent A99 to CRE 29th Division: 'Get in touch with 574 Coy and instruct cancel Masnières bridge and make subsidiary bridges over canal and river about L.23.b. Report map reference of camp and have messenger at nearest signal office'. The reply from CRE 29th Division (M3) was: 'I saw CSM of this coy in Marcoing today and your orders were left at HQ 87 Bde there to be called for. I could not find any officer of the coy, but told the CSM what the orders were'. Then, at 5.10 pm, Schreiber received a message from OC 574 Coy: 'Have examined crossings at Marcoing. Have found two heavy bridges intact one being double track railway bridge which was used by tanks. The enemy mines from both bridges have been removed by 29th Division. Site unsuitable for Inglis bridge. Propose returning tonight [22 November] with Inglis and loading two twenty one foot six bridges. No trestles required. Please wire instructions'. Inevitably nothing happened until 24 November when Schreiber visited Marcoing and saw the site. Meanwhile 574 Coy again set off for Marcoing with one 30' and one 21'6" bridge (one lock at Marcoing is wider than the other). At 7.30 pm OC 574 Coy reported (M3): 'Am offloading transport and starting assembly'. The following morning at 8 am he reported again: 'Twenty one foot six bridge completed. Thirty foot sixty per cent. Road approach still to be made'. It was not until 12.20 pm 26 November that he was able to report (P99): 'Canal bridge [Marcoing] ready to take all A Class loads'.

59th Division left III Corps on 27 November otherwise the situation was unchanged. Putty wrote to Ettie Desborough:

> Dearest Chief, Thanks for yours of 24 Nov which I got this evening. The show on 20 November was what I was called back for, it had all been arranged before then cancelled and I was given a month's leave to get married with the sequel of a recall after 12 days, my crew did A.1 and but for an unfortunate incident of a tank going through the canal bridge should have done still bigger things, have not had much beyond the ordinary fighting and consolidation since the 21 November as my role was to form a defensive flank, have been all over the captured ground which is intensely interesting the rows of wire, dug outs, etc show what the Boche can do in the way of work, now we shall winter in his line while he digs himself another, the dirty dog. Was so glad to hear what you say about Billy Lambton as reports before were not too cheerful, suffering from boils and other painful things. Lionel Tennyson[2] was wounded again but they told me at the casualty that he was alright, it was a great pity as he was just going to be given command of a battalion. Jessie is very well, she is working daily at a canteen at London Bridge which she enjoys, she was passing St Paul's as they were pealing the bells so went into to thank for Putty's victory, I wish you would

2   Lionel Hallam Tennyson 3rd Baron Tennyson (1889-1951) Eton RB wounded three times.

suggest something to give her for Xmas so if you see anything out of the way nice let me know. The weather has been bad lately, including snow last night which however melted before 10 am now it is as mild as it was cold. Some of the captured maps giving details of what they knew of our front are full of the most astonishing accurate detail from aeroplane reconnaissance, their staff work is admirable and little wonder that they were too much for the Russians and Italians. All blessings for ever Putty.

Putty seemed to believe, as did most others, that the Masnières bridge was collapsed by a tank rather than destroyed by the enemy. More importantly, there is nothing in this letter to indicate that he was expecting a major German counter-attack, although perhaps the censor would have prevented him mentioning the possibility.

28 November was again quiet except for shelling and enemy aircraft flying low over III Corps' lines. By now Snow (GOC VII Corps), on the right of III Corps, was convinced that the Germans were planning a counter-attack in strength. He could not get this point across to Byng or Haig, even after he sent a warning on 25 November that such an attack seemed likely on 29 or 30 November, and would probably come in against the Banteux Ravine. Reports of the German build-up were also coming in from RFC patrols and from observers on points overlooking the battlefield. Enemy activity, ranging artillery fire, the presence of observation balloons, the sound of transport moving up at night, increased patrolling, all hinted strongly at an attack. Byng and his staff took no notice: according to reports coming from GHQ, the Germans were as exhausted as the British and, after their losses at Passchendaele and Cambrai, were in no condition to launch a major offensive.

III Corps was in a more difficult position than IV Corps. Next to 6th Division, 29th Division had the St Quentin Canal immediately behind it and was overlooked from the high ground N of Rumilly, and from the spur behind Crèvecoeur to the E. Covering the right and rear of 29th Division beyond the canal, 20th Division faced E and SE, its front extending up the slope of the Bonavis ridge from the canal towards Lateau Wood; but even from the outpost line only the roofs of some of the houses in Les Rues des Vignes could be seen and there was no view over the canal crossings. 12th Division, holding the remainder of this side of the salient, was at a similar disadvantage as regards observation over the canal valley, the minor operations of 24 and 25 November having failed. This lack of observation would be a severe handicap if the Germans attacked, particularly at the junction of III and VII Corps on the northern edge of the Banteux ravine where the permanent trench system had been dislocated by the forcing back of the German front in the attack of 20 November (as early as 3 November, III Corps had pointed out in a memorandum to VII Corps the need for special precautions against counter-attack at this point when the defensive flank had been formed along the Bonavis ridge).

The exact line of the boundary on 30 November is still unclear. 12th Division's history includes a map showing the S boundary of 12th Division running E-W from E of Gonnelieu. This is of interest because this boundary does not stretch back as far as Gonnelieu and because 12th Division had posts to the S and across this boundary. It is of even more interest because Major General Scott was one of the authors of the history and drew the maps.

There is also some doubt whether the canal crossings between Crèvecoeur and Banteux had been destroyed but neither 3rd Army or III Corps seemed concerned about their possession or denying them to the enemy. Perhaps this is unimportant; since III Corps could not observe this stretch of the canal the Germans could do as they liked.

On 28 November GOC VII Corps made another attempt to arouse HQ 3rd Army to a sense of emergency. At 7 pm BGGS VII Corps (Burnett-Stuart) telephoned MGGS 3rd Army whose record of the conversation was:

> BGGS VII Corps rang regarding unusual enemy activity opposite their front. GOC 55th Division thinks the enemy is going to attack. Discussed question and agreed that an attack from the N and S was a good and likely operation from the enemy point of view. VII Corps are in touch with III Corps about it and are on alert. Told VII Corps we would arrange to keep Guards handy to help if required. Cavalry also could move up if required. 61st Division coming down on 30 November.

This reassurance was not followed by action. 3rd Army issued no warning order, ordered no movement of reserves (other than the Guards Division which was concentrating behind III Corps), and took no steps to ensure that troops in rear areas were readily available. On two occasions III Corps had appealed to 3rd Army for the relief of its tired divisions, with no success: two artillery bdes were withdrawn from III Corps on 29 November.

At the end of 28 November intelligence assessments varied from those coming down from GHQ that the Germans 'were in no condition to launch an attack' to those from 55th Division that 'the enemy is going to attack on 29 or 30 Nov'. 12th and 20th Divisions must have had patrols forward of their observation line yet neither division reported any unusual activity on 27 or 28 November. Putty and the staff of HQ III Corps, lacking any intelligence of their own, would have reached the inevitable conclusion that, if the enemy was about to counter-attack, it would be one limited to its right flank and to VII Corps, and be small in scale. That night (28/29 November) and the day of 29 November were quiet apart from intermittent shelling of Marcoing and Masnières. There was some heavy counter-battery fire that evening but this does not seem to have caused alarm at HQ III Corps. The only order issued that day was III Corps GO6806 allotting new boundaries to 6th and 20th Divisions on the likely withdrawal of 29th Division before their departure for another corps.

At 10 am 29 November GOC Guards Division handed over command of his sector in IV Corps area to 59th Division, and by about 6 pm HQ Guards Division was at Neuville; 1 Gds Bde was concentrated at Metz, 2 Gds Bde at Ruyaulcourt and Bertincourt, and 3 Gds Bde at Trescault. The division was in 3rd Army reserve but much of it positioned behind III Corps.

That afternoon the commanders of the two divisions in position by the Banteux Ravine, Major General Jeudwine (55th VII Corps) and Major General Scott (12th III Corps) met at the village of Villers-Guislain to consider the situation. As a result, GOC 12th Division moved his reserve machine-guns to cover Villers-Guislain; COs 6 Queens and 11 Middx (12th Division reserve at Heudecourt) were informed of the probability of an attack and ordered to reconnoitre the ground from Vaucellette Farm to Gonnelieu as soon as possible. Warning orders were issued by the division, and four 18 pdr batteries were directed to carry out harassing fire on Honnecourt from 5-7 am 30 Nov.

Writing many years later Snow (GOC VII Corps) said:

> The junction [VII and III Corps] was not satisfactory as immediately N of it the permanent trench system had been dislocated owing to the bending back of the German line on 20 November. GOC 55th Division ordered the digging of a N and S trench just N of

the Banteux Ravine and established a post in front of that line. We discussed putting a battalion from the resting brigade into Vaucelette Farm. This farm was in the III Corps area and occupied by details. I got III Corps to give over the farm and put 1/4 N Lancs into it on 29 November and it was fortunate that we did as the battalion barred the German advance W from Villers-Guislain on 30 November.

The left battalion 166 Bde 55th Division, 1/5 S Lancs, was across and astride the Banteux Ravine. The reserve battalion 35 Bde 12th Division, 7 Suffolk, was behind them between Newton Post and Cheshire Quarry; HQ 35 Bde and some other units of III Corps were in Villers-Guislain; some or all could have been across the corps boundary, a consequence of the salient. Comd 35 Bde (Vincent) telephoned GOC 12th Division on 29 November reiterating his fear of an enemy attack. Lieutenant Colonel Collen RA AA&QMG HQ 12th Division noted that day: 'On our right was a weak division holding a long front and their left was the weak spot. We thought it was so weak that we would not put any more batteries at Villers-Guislain and General Vincent felt so certain of an attack that he packed up and sent away most of his papers'.

In III Corps, which had allowed some of its troops and commanders to assume that a period of normal trench-warfare had set in, Brigadier General Fuller (BGGS) visited the brigade commanders to impress upon them the need for vigilance; but no warning was issued. GOC 29th Division shared the opinion that the Germans were too weak to undertake a major operation but was impressed by the opposite view of GOC VII Corps whom he met by chance on the afternoon of 29 November when on his way to HQ III Corps. Putty must have been convinced by now that a German counter-attack was imminent and sending his BGGS to visit the bde comds was going to be more effective than issuing yet another general warning.

12th Division Artillery had six FA bdes to support the division: in addition it was covered and supported by 50 HAG consisting of one bty 9.2" hows, two btys 8" hows, two btys 6" hows and one bty 60 pdrs. Each of its three bdes also had 3×6" mors. The issue was not, therefore, the amount of artillery available to support 12th Division but its effective use, particularly in the early stages of an enemy attack. Scott (GOC 12th Division) had commanded artillery at division, corps and army level in this war so had all the experience required to do this. He wrote many years later: 'The formation of the terrain led me to wish to push forward the front line and we were unfortunately not able to bring this off. Artillery fire from 12th Division area was not good as the front line was on a ridge and it was not possible to cover the ground in the immediate front from that area'. However, as the Cambrai Enquiry was later to record, the front of the division was 4,800 yards much less than the other divisions.

Brigadier General Thomas BGRA 12th Division wrote:

On the morning of the 29 November 55th Division requested assistance from the 12th Divisional Artillery to put down counter-preparation on the village of Honnecourt, the wood and the entrance to the Banteux Ravine. The usual harassing fire programme in conjunction with the heavy artillery was arranged [the heavy artillery programme was not carried out as VII Corps did not wish any fire to take place on their front until the SOS signal was sent up], special attention being paid to the approaches in this area, and from 5 am onwards counter preparation from every gun of the field artillery that could reach this point was turned on Honnecourt and the approaches from the wood.

The official history gives a different impression:

> As regards artillery assistance, CRAs of 55th and 12th Divisions had arranged that at 6.30 am 30 November III Corps heavy batteries (50 HAG) in and about Gouzeaucourt should open intense fire on the obvious German assembly positions S of Banteux; but when III Corps was consulted and HQ VII Corps did their best to get this arrangement confirmed some misunderstanding arose. VII Corps believed that III Corps had refused to allow the guns to open as requested; III Corps was left with the impression that fire was not required unless called for at the time by VII Corps, or the SOS was sent up from the British front. Six field batteries, also of 12th Division, which could enfilade the front of 166 Bde (55th Division) would then assist, in addition to the heavy howitzers.

This apparent misunderstanding surfaced again after the battle. MGRA 3rd Army was responsible for coordination of artillery across corps boundaries and for ensuring that there were no such misunderstandings. If Snow had asked Putty for artillery support and he had declined to give it for any reason, Snow would have put the request to 3rd Army (and his GOC RA would have put the request to MGRA 3rd Army): it would then have been for Byng (advised by his MGRA) to decide the priorities and resolve the matter. This did not happen which suggests that Brigadier General Thomas' recollection may be the more accurate.

That they possessed no tanks was of little consequence to the Germans who saw artillery as the chief means to make a breakthrough. Consequently the plan was for a short, intense, artillery bombardment of between thirty minutes and an hour's duration, with gas and smoke shell mixed in with it. Suspected HQs, battery positions and OPs were to be subjected to special attention. Some of the 77mm field guns of the type used so successfully as anti-tank weapons on Flesquières Ridge were to accompany the infantry in the attack, whilst light trench mortars, supposedly relatively static weapons of position warfare, but which could be moved on wheeled carriages, were to offer close support.

The German plan (2nd German Army OpO issued 29 November) as far as it concerned III Corps involved an attack by 9 divisions. In the S 183rd and 208th Divisions would protect the left flank. In the centre the point of main effort was the 34th Division on left and 28th Division on right followed by 185th Division attacking in general direction Gouzeaucourt-Metz in order to take the British in flank and rear. On the right 220th Division (left), 30th Division (centre) and 107th Division (right), followed by 9th Bavarian Reserve Division provided right flank protection. The German infantry were to employ a new form of infiltration tactics; the first waves would pass round strong points and villages, leaving them to be isolated and overcome by the following formations.

It should not have come as any surprise when the blow fell and the Germans launched their counter-attack at 7 am 30 November. Their thrust centred on the line Gouzeaucourt-Metz struck the left of VII Corps and 12th Division; the northern thrust struck 20th and 29th Divisions. Both 12th and 20th Divisions were forced back with many units in disarray, and it was some time before Putty was able to restore the situation. HQ III Corps GS log recorded the times that reports were received, decisions taken, and orders issued:

6 am. Situation fairly quiet. Marcoing and approaches heavily shelled.

9.20 am. 59 Sqn RFC report at 8.20 am heavy German barrage from Rues des Vignes to Honnecourt and on Bourlon Wood.

9.30 am. VII Corps report attack of enemy and occupation by latter of Eagle Quarry and front line Honnecourt to north. 20th Division report brigade holding Cemetery Spur forced to fall back. Enemy in force from Lateau Wood.

9.45 am. Instructions to 2 Bde Tank Corps to send all available tanks to Quentin Ridge and Révelon Farm. Report that enemy have broken through to Quentin Mill and advancing from E in force. 29th Division report enemy hold railway E of Gouzeaucourt and advancing into village.

9.50 am. Instructions to 6th Division to move their reserve brigade to Dead Man's Corner (blocking position N of Gouzeaucourt).

10.10 am. 86 Bde report fighting in Les Rues Vertes and enemy attacking down Cambrai Road.

10.15 am. 3rd Army asked to direct Gds bde from Metz on to Quentin Ridge.

10.30 am. Corps Commander orders two bdes 2nd Cavalry Division (Greenly) to hold Révelon Ridge. 59 Sqn RFC report enemy in E portion of Gouzeaucourt and in all ground between La Vacquerie and Gouzeaucourt.

From this alone it is evident that HQ III Corps knew the direction and extent of the enemy's attack by 9.30 am. That the southern thrust which started first was not identified earlier may well have been because all communications forward of HQ 12th Division had been destroyed. HQ 35 Bde (outside Villers-Guislain) was overrun about 7.45 am and was in no position to pass a report even if it had communications to 12th Division. From 9.50 am HQ III Corps had identified that the priority was countering the S thrust which threatened the whole corps. For this counter-penetration task it was beginning to assemble 2nd Cavalry Division and Guards Division, in addition to some 12th Division and 2 Bde Tank Corps' units. Its reserve (bde 6th Division) was also moved to a blocking position. The GS log continued:

10.55 am. 86 Bde (29th Division) report enemy in Les Rues Vertes and right forward on ridge.

10.57 am. Wire from V Corps re transfer of 61st Division from V to III Corps.

10.59 am. 3rd Army wire ordering Guards Division under III Corps.

11 am. 2nd Cavalry Division are moving troops on to Révelon Ridge to cover left flank of advance of Cav Corps from Épehy to cut off enemy in Gouzeaucourt. Cav Corps wire places 2nd Cavalry Division at disposal of III Corps.

11.11 am. Guards Division orders 1 Gds Bde to hold Gonnelieu-Révelon Ridge, 3 Gds Bde to prolong right of 1 Gds Bde, and 2 Gds Bde to prolong right of 3 Gds Bde'.

The intention now was not just to contain the enemy attack but a counter-attack by the Cav Corps against the southern thrust, once it had been checked, was being contemplated. The GS log continued:

11.15 am. 86 Bde report enemy still in Les Rues Vertes and attacking us from S (HQ 29th Division had been forced out of its position in the quarry near Quentin Mill and lost communications with its bdes and with HQ III Corps, but its bdes held on reporting direct to corps HQ).

11.35 am. III Corps instructions to 29th Division to hold on to Welsh Ridge if forced to withdraw from Marcoing, and to withdraw by Marcoing. Also hold on to Highland Ridge (These orders may have been given to GOC 29th Division when he called in to HQ III Corps).

11.40 am. 86 Bde report enemy in great strength attacking them. Three attacks already beaten off.

12.55 pm. 2nd Cavalry Division report our infantry holding line (Révelon Ridge). Cavalry are on line behind.

12.57 pm. 86 Bde report enemy massing and advancing.

1.16 pm. 12th Division report they are in good position astride Révelon-Gouzeaucourt Road, and SE towards Vaucelette. Cavalry reported in touch with left flank of this force. Enemy is in considerable strength, but has failed to push on SW from Gouzeaucourt.

59 Sqn RFC reports our troops fighting NE of Gouzeaucourt – we hold Chapel Crossing.

1.35 pm. III Corps asks IV Corps to send any spare troops to help to Highland Ridge; also grateful if some of their guns could be turned on to Crèvecoeur. 20th Division report line held with left bde in Brown Line – thence to La Vacquerie – NW of Gonnelieu – along NW edges of Quentin Ridge. Counter-attack ordered on Quentin Ridge, but result not yet known.

This summary recorded a time of great difficulty (and was probably edited at a later date); it indicates that the enemy's southern thrust was being countered. The problem was to the N: 29th Division was holding firm although it's right (86 Bde) was under constant attack. However, 20th Division and 12th Division had been forced back, with some units destroyed or in disorder, and were still threatened. The GS log again:

2.10 pm. III Corps instructions that 70 Bde RFA should report to Guards Division.

2.15 pm. 6th Division instructed to fill up gap between 20th and 29th Divisions.

3.35 pm. III Corps GF21 issued. Instructions to Guards Division and Cav Corps: After capturing Gouzeaucourt you will seize the Quentin Ridge from Gauche Wood to Gonnelieu both inclusive. Your left will be in touch with the 20th Division. Cav Corps will advance in a northerly direction with a view to attacking the enemy flank between Villers-Guislain and Gouzeaucourt and seizing the Gonnelieu Ridge. 5th Cavalry Division will move at once with objective the enemy's flank between Villers Guislain and Gouzeaucourt. It will be supported by 4th Cavalry Division in accordance with the situation as it develops.

4.15 pm. 86 Bde report large bodies of enemy moving from Crèvecoeur side of the ridge towards Marcoing.

4.25 pm. Cav Corps message saying Gouzeaucourt is in our hands.

5.21 pm. 86 Bde report having beaten off another counter-attack on Les Rues Vertes.

5.25 pm. Cav Corps report two bdes 5th Cavalry Division attacking Gauche Wood, one on foot and one mounted, third cav bde moving between Gauche Wood and Villers-Guislain.

5.33 pm. 6th Division report 88 Bde line is intact – they have driven the enemy southwards, clearing the area behind Masnières.

6.30 pm. III Corps wire G888 ordering 6th Division to send two battalions to 20th Division to fill gap. III Corps wire: Two bns 59th Division holding Highland Ridge will come under orders of 6th Division.

7 pm. III Corps wire GF21 to 2 Bde Tank Corps and 12th Division: You will collect all available tanks in the hollow W of Vaucelette Farm tonight in order to be ready to make an attack with cavalry on Villers-Guislain and Villers Ridge at dawn tomorrow. Orders regarding the attack will be issued later. Your tanks should keep N of the Fins-Heudicourt Road.

9.40 pm. 6th Division report enemy party cutting wire in front. One of the party shot (232 Regt). Enemy have captured one of our posts in Noyelles.

With elements of seven divisions now under Putty's command, the enemy pressing hard and a confused situation, he and HQ III Corps could easily have lost control, but they seem not to have done. In the S the enemy was now being contained and about to be counter-attacked; in the N the situation was less stable but improving, although there was still much chaos to be sorted out.

At 10 pm HQ III Corps issued OpO No.227 – Attack for 1 December to be made by Guards Division and Cav Corps. This is reproduced in full in Appendix F. Later, at 12 midnight, III Corps wire G899 was issued giving Zero hour for this operation as 6.30 am 1 December. Also at midnight III Corps issued GO7835 – re attack of 6th and 20th Divisions at 1 am 1 Dec: 'if latter successful Guards and Cavalry will not attack, if unsuccessful attack to be made'. HQ III Corps might not have had much confidence in these night attacks by 6th and 20th Divisions; but they might temporarily halt the enemy's thrust and buy some time.

So much for HQ III Corps' record of this day: other sources provided more detailed accounts.

The German attack began with a pre-dawn bombardment which lasted about an hour before the infantry assault. In the early hours and while this was going on they emerged from cellars and dug-outs in Bantouzelle and other villages, crossed the canal undetected and formed up at the entrances to the ravines (there was another on the 55th Division front accessible at Honnecourt within the enemy lines). The morning was dark, with a mist which lay thick in the valleys so that no sign of the German assembly could be discovered by the patrols of the RFC.

At 6.50 am it was just getting light when the enemy's bombardment came down on Villers-Guislain. No SOS went up and the comds of the two btys of 169 FA Bde (12th Division), who were on the outskirts of the village by the cemetery, temporarily withdrew their men from the guns, which were being heavily shelled. Subsequently SOS was ordered, and the guns were at once manned and fire opened. Very shortly afterwards the Germans were seen topping the crest just in front of the guns. The btys kept up their fire until the very last moment, and then withdrew with their breech-blocks, the gunners joining up with the infantry. The guns were lost, and both btys suffered heavy casualties. The enemy swarmed over the hill and were now on the crest overlooking HQ 35 Bde. In the meantime masses of German infantry were seen advancing up the Banteux Ravine towards Gonnelieu. Also in Villers-Guislain was 34 HAG: III Corps lost twenty 6" hows and four 60 pdrs, in addition to the twelve 18 pdrs of 169 FA Bde. In total III Corps HA was to lose 41 × 6" hows and 16 × 60 pdrs that day with the losses in Villers-Guislain (24) being nearly half of them.

The first Brigadier General Vincent (Comd 35 Bde) knew of the Germans' swift progress was when they appeared beyond Villers-Guislain. His BM (Broadwood) dashed down into the HQ 35 Bde dugout to burn any useful papers and was captured along with the clerks. Lieutenant Colonel Collen RA AA&QMG HQ 12th Division recorded:

> The Boches were through Villers-Guislain before anybody had any warning and no one here knows how they got through the division on our left [right] without any SOS signal. One of our fd ambs had an ADS there and the CO and some men were taken prisoners. The divisional burial party got away by the skin of their teeth and lost everything they possessed.

The German 34th Division was supported by seven heavy trench mortar companies, six field gun, six howitzer and nine additional 5.9" howitzer batteries. Advancing from Honnecourt, its main strike was against the left of 55th Division (VII Corps). Its assault waves moved in small columns and, in some cases, led by men armed with flame-throwers. Although in places stands were made around various strong points behind the front defensive line, the German infantry swiftly overwhelmed the weakened infantry battalions. 34th German Division was thus able to press on towards Villers-Guislain and into the flank and rear of III Corps, almost without tackling the front-line defenders of 12th Division.

For some time it was thought that the attack was focussed solely on 55th Division's front (VII Corps), chiefly because the attack N of the Banteux Ravine started an hour later than that to the S. Thus, the left bde of 12th Division, together with 20th Division, were still surprised in much the same way as units further S when two further German divisions attacked. Second Lieutenant Taylor 6 E Kent 37 Bde 12th Division noted:

> Shortly after daybreak we were awaked suddenly by the unmistakable sound of bursting shells, and the din of a hostile bombardment. I dashed upstairs and a glance showed me that our front line was being heavily shelled, and that a box barrage was being placed on our communications. An enormous flight of enemy planes appeared, coming up fast from the direction of Cambrai, and flying very low. The sky was black with them, and throughout the day they dominated the situation, firing on our infantry, harassing communications, and putting many btys out of action. I never saw a friendly plane all day.

Taylor was wounded in the thigh and taken prisoner that day.

The Germans, who had concentrated in the wood near Grenouillère Bridge, advanced from there about 7.45 am, forcing the advanced posts (37 Bde), well down both sides of the road from Bonavis to the canal, back on their trenches; they then mounted a strong attack and drove the defenders across the Cambrai road beyond Pam Pam Farm. The bombardment spread to 20th Division about 7.30 am when three barrages, which included smoke and mustard-gas shells, fell simultaneously between the outpost line and sunken road from La Vacquerie and Masnières. The infantry attack in the same manner developed from the S. 55th and 12th Divisions had been heavily engaged for some time, when, at 8 am, the Germans advanced on the whole of 20th Division front. Covered by a thick mist the enemy moved forward very rapidly and the outpost companies were soon overwhelmed; the majority were entirely cut off and were never heard of again. Calls for artillery fire brought little response, for already many of the heavy batteries and some of the field guns were being over-run.

Captain Dugdale SC HQ 60 Bde 20th Division noted:

> Very soon after this the Germans lengthened their range; their barrage was now concentrated just in front of the sunken road where we were. I was ordered to proceed at once to my observation post in the rear as best I could. When I got there an astonishing sight met my eyes. On our bde front I could see our troops retreating with the Germans following them. The enemy were then amongst our btys.

Captain Smith 11 RB 59 Bde 20th Division wrote: 'The situation is a nasty one. I can see our men occasionally and the enemy not at all, but there is a barrage before and behind us and the smoke is very thick'.

An officer of 6th Division, Standish Crawford (probably Brigadier General Crauford late Gordons Comd 18 Bde) recorded: 'The whole of the high ground in our rear was covered with men like Epsom Downs on Derby Day, and we realised some great disaster had taken place. The men we saw were 20th and 12th Divisions coming back from the front line in full retreat'. Later on, Crauford met GOC 29th Division (de Lisle) who asked him 'if he knew where his division were'. 20th Division's defence had been greatly weakened by the decision of its commander, Major General Douglas Smith, to send several units of his reserve brigade, 60 Bde, to assist 12th Division when the first German attack was launched.

Captain Dugdale visited HQ 20th Division about this time:

> The scene at divisional headquarters at Villers Plouich was sensational. There were crowds of officers from the division on our right [12th Division], many of them in a state of undress, but although it was reported at the time that these officers were caught in their pyjamas I did not see it for myself; the General received me in his dugout perfectly calmly. He said he was pleased to see me; would I have a cup of tea? He also said that as far as 61 Bde was concerned he had no idea where they were, and he would be very glad if I would tell him something about them. I did my best to explain what had happened, and showed him our position on the map.

The officers of 12th Division included HQ 36 and 37 Bdes: now forced back to their reserve lines W of the Cambrai road, Villers Plouich was now the best location for them to command their bdes and re-establish contact with HQ 12th Division.

6th Division's history records:

> The Germans reached Gouzeaucourt at 9 am but were stoutly opposed by transport details of 18 Bde who checked the enemy in a portion of the village until it was re-taken by the Guards about midday. Staff officer HQ 29th Division arrived at 6th Division HQ reported that HQ 29th Division just NE of Gouzeaucourt had been captured. 16 Bde [6th Division reserve] ordered to take up position on ridge between Beaucamp and Gouzeaucourt (Dead Man's Corner E of Gouzeaucourt Wood). Situation by now very confused.

The order to move 16 Bde was given by HQ III Corps at 9.50 am (see GS log).

Soon after 10 am 14 DLI (reserve battalion 18 Bde 6th Division) was sent to Highland Ridge to take up a position facing SE astride the Hindenburg support system. Later (at 1.35 pm) III

Corps asked IV Corps for assistance in manning the ridge and in the course of the afternoon 59th Division provided two battalions for this purpose.

By this time the three (10 and 11 KRRC and 10 RB) forward battalions of 59 Bde (right of 20th Division) north of Lateau Wood had been destroyed; 11 RB in reserve occupied a position in front of the Hindenburg support system through which stragglers made their way. During the morning the Germans made four attacks on this line, but all were repulsed. Similarly on the left of 20th Division, 61 Bde's two forward battalions were overwhelmed and destroyed. 7 DCLI in support in the La Vacquerie valley was ill-prepared for the onset of the Germans. For a time, however, the enemy's advance was held and considerable loss inflicted upon him, but eventually the battalion gave ground and rallied on 7 KOYLI in the reserve position immediately E of the Hindendurg support system, where touch was maintained with the remnants of 59 Bde on the right and, on the left, with 29th Division. As a consequence 20th Division was thrown back to the lower slopes of Welsh Ridge; but here the fire of the infantry, with that of the batteries and such machine-guns as remained in action, turned the Germans northward, away from their intended line of advance. 30th German Division, after its initial success, swung right-handed towards Marcoing and thereby lost touch with 220th German Division, the 9th Bavarian Reserve Division pushing forward to fill the gap.

Unopposed (having forced back 61 Bde 20th Division), the enemy entered Les Rues Vertes from the S. The village was held due the leadership and bravery of Captain Gee RF SC HQ 86 Bde 29th Division who organised its defence (and was awarded the Victoria Cross) until Comd 86 Bde brought back additional troops from Masnières. Shortly before 9 am a frontal attack (by 107th German Division), preceded by low flying aeroplanes, developed against 86 Bde holding the right of the bridgehead at Masnières. This was checked by the fire of rifles and Lewis guns and the guns of the machine-gun company. No German got within four hundred yards of the main position but 86 Bde was forced to withdraw its posts at Mon Plaisir Farm and bridge.

About 9 am the first alarm was received in Marcoing, a message from 86 Bde to Comd 87 Bde: he ordered his reserve battalion (1 KOSB) to move out at once and establish a defensive position on the southern edge of Marcoing Copse. A little later, GOC 29th Division, having escaped from Gouzeaucourt when his HQ was attacked, ordered 88 Bde (in reserve at Marcoing) to move across to the right flank of the division. Comd 88 Bde assembled his brigade S of the village, then 88 Bde and 1 KOSB 87 Bde, advancing from Marcoing, drove the Germans back steadily SW across the lower slopes of Welsh Ridge. The Germans retreated along the whole line, losing many killed and wounded, and the left of 88 Bde was eventually joined with 86 Bde at Les Rues Vertes.

Major General de Lisle (GOC 29th Division) wrote:

> On 30 November we were surprised. It is useless to disguise this fact. The Germans made a secret concentration, and at dawn advanced in three columns from the E. On arrival [87 Bde Marcoing] at 12 noon, I found all was well, although desperate fighting was in progress. My messenger had only just got through to 88 Bde [in reserve Marcoing] and they were assembling in the streets prior to marching off to Les Rue Vertes which is about 2,000 yards due E. Before they could start, however, the German advanced troops were approaching the town from the SE. HQ 87 Bde in a deep dug-out just S of the town, was surprised by a machine-gun firing down the sunken road, not from the N

where our troops were facing, but from the S. 88 Bde were fired at in the streets before they left the town. In spite of this and its consequent confusion all the four battalions of this bde, and the reserve bn of 87 Bde [1 KOSB] attacked at once. No orders were issued for none could be issued. Companies were mixed, and even platoons were made up of men from all bns. The troops, without any artillery support, advanced, firing by alternate platoons, drove back superior numbers of Germans flushed with success some 2,000 yards, killed large numbers, and linked up with the right of my line at the village south of Masnières and there dug themselves in on a line 5,000 yards long, connecting with the old Hindenburg support line to which the division [20th Division] on our right had withdrawn.

Captain Miller Sher For ADC to GOC 29th Division wrote to de Lisle many years later recalling that day: 'and then you calling for me with my notebook and dictating a message as if we might have been in the Long Valley – a message not only that told the corps (III) what was happening but, and this is the important thing, advising them the best way of countering the German advance. Then our moving off – a call at a neighbouring division HQ (probably 20th Division) where we found the commander, I can't remember his name, wringing his hands! You spoke to him rather sharply I remember which pulled him together'. If this was GOC 20th Division the picture of him is very different to that painted by Captain Dugdale.

On the right of III Corps Gonnelieu, like Villers-Guislain, lay open to attack from the Banteux ravine. It provided accommodation for 70 Fd Coy RE and 5 Northants (pioneer bn 12th Division). HQ 36 Bde were on the northern outskirts, and five artillery batteries were located to its NW. The approach of the German infantry (34th German Division) about 9 am came as a surprise. SE of the village in the old British front line 7 Suffolk (reserve 35 Bde 12th Division) was destroyed. Faced with so little opposition, it is remarkable that the German advance should have stopped; that it did so is largely to the credit of the artillery batteries that played havoc at short range with the parties of Germans seen among the houses.

Meanwhile Comd 35 Bde (Brigadier General Vincent), despite being badly surprised, had collected a force consisting of his headquarters personnel, a company of REs, and a machine-gun crew. Initially they held a rise W of Villers-Guislain before falling back to the shelter of Gauche Wood. Here he organised his force, further increased by survivors from other units, into four platoons; he then conducted a fighting withdrawal to Révelon Ridge half a mile to the rear. Help came from a variety of sources. When the first reports from allied airmen of Germans massing opposite Villers-Guislain had arrived at HQ 12th Division, Lieutenant Colonel Collen (AA&QMG) had collected about 800 reinforcements encamped nearby and formed them into a provisional battalion. By 9 am, this battalion was moving to engage the Germans. Meanwhile the divisional reserve consisting of two bns, 6 Queens and 11 Middx, advanced from Heudicourt. In due course Vincent's force, as it became known, reached 2,000 men and was supported by 11 × 18 pdrs and 1 × 4.2" how.

Lieutenant Colonel Wollocombe CO 11 Middx recorded:

At 7.30 am, the BM [36 Bde] rushed into our billets and told me to get on parade as soon as possible as the line had been broken. The bn was actually at breakfast. I had to collect the company and platoon commanders and had no time for a proper preliminary reconnaissance, though I made a personal one as soon as possible, and rode forward with the vanguard most of the way into action. We were moving off in ¾ hour. It was one of the most interesting and, in many ways, enjoyable days of my life. I was one who hated the trench warfare routine, into which we all fell of necessity, and insisted for the year I had command of that bn on at least one open warfare scheme every time we came out of the line. So you can imagine my joy when the chance came to carry out an advance guard show in open country. My instructions were that the Germans had broken through the front and we were to march on a certain objective, find them and stop them.

Captain Cook's company of 11 Middx was on the move within a quarter of an hour, receiving an extra iron ration and ammunition as they filed along the road. He noted:

We went to Quentin Mill Ridge where we met details coming in the opposite direction in all states of attire – gunners, sappers, pioneers, signallers. I well remember meeting General Vincent [Comd 35 Bde] just before I reached the brow of the ridge. He was in gum boots and British Warm over his pyjamas. He asked me where I was going. I said my orders were to hold Quentin Mill Ridge. He walked up the ridge a short way with me and there was a target such as we had longed for, for the Boche were about to ascend the further side of the ridge like rabbits.

Lieutenant Colonel Collen and his provisional battalion also arrived at this point. He wrote:

When we arrived, I met General Vincent with about forty men and some gunners, pioneers and sappers. He had fought a rearguard action from Villers-Guislain. Just as they had prac-tically fired their last round, up came these three battalions and the Boches were stopped there. This mixed force really saved the situation on this side. I saw the Boches come over the rise and they were received with five rounds rapid.

Help was also coming from unexpected quarters. Brigadier General Hyslop (Comd 59 Bde) was at Rear HQ 20th Division at Sorel on his way home on sick leave; he took command of the head-quarter details of 20th and 29th Divisions and also of the details of the 20th Division at Nurlu. Part of this force was rushed forward towards Gouzeaucourt and part took up a position near Révelon and helped to repel the attack. Now that III Corps held the higher ground in the S (including Révelon Ridge), they could effectively block any further German advance in that direction.

2 Bde Tank Corps was in the process of withdrawing to winter quarters: to move tanks by train and pass under the narrow bridges, the tank sponsons had to be unbolted and swung into the tank body to reduce their width. BM 2 Tank Bde (Foot) was about to leave their HQ at Templeux-la-Fosse (co-located with HQ III Corps) on an inspection tour when Putty telephoned with news of the German breakthrough and ordered all available tanks to Quentin Ridge and Révelon Farm. Foot ordered H Bn to prepare for action; they had to swing out the sponsons again, load ammunition, petrol and rations and set off in improvised companies. Foot then rode forward to reconnoitre the situation on Révelon Ridge. H Bn went forward in two companies each of about 20 tanks; one supported Guards Division's counter-attack on Quentin Ridge and the other Cav Corps on Gauche Wood and Villers-Guislain.

Captain Lee 46 Sqn RFC wrote about: 'Twenty minutes of shooting up groups of Boche infantry, mostly while they were attacking pockets of resistance, farms and other isolated buildings, N of Gouzeaucourt'.

Later, having refuelled and rearmed at Bapaume:

Almost at once I found a body of infantry moving in mass along the very road along which, ten mornings ago, C had led C Flt in the bombing of Lateau Wood. I flew along the column at 100 feet and released a bomb. I could not miss. I circled back and shot them up as I switchbacked along, then returned on a repeat, until only corpses and wounded were on the road.

Again, after refuelling and rearming once more:

There was a big fight going on in and around Gouzeaucourt, but it was the sort of thing that you can't join in, so I went further E looking for opportunity targets, the best being a battery, with limbers and wagons, passing through a village, which got three bombs. The fourth went to a large group of infantry waiting by a wood.

By 10.15 am HQ 35 Bde (Vincent) had established its defence on Révelon Ridge. It had under its command 11 Middx (36 Bde) and 6 Queens (37 Bde) – 12th Division reserve, one coy 5 Northants (pioneer bn 12th Division) and three guns 235 MG Coy; and it seems likely that Lieutenant Colonel Collen's provisional bn was also under Vincent's command at this stage. About this time Vaucelette Farm was handed over to III Corps by VII Corps: NH (III Corps Cav Regt) was in a position on the railway S of Vaucelette Farm to secure the corps right boundary.

In the meantime Gouzeaucourt had fallen to the enemy. Situated mainly in a hollow on the Péronne-Cambrai road the village had no prepared defences; but in it were five batteries of heavy howitzers (4 × 6", 8 × 8", 4 × 9.2" and 2 × 12" hows), HQ and one coy 11 DLI (pioneers of 20th Division), 470 Fd Coy RE, 18 Bde transport details, detachment of III Corps Cyclist Bn and detachment of 11 (American) Engineers (Railway). There was also HQ 29th Division abruptly forced out of its position in the quarry near Quentin Mill. The defenders resisted for some time: eventually CO 11 DLI with his battalion and others took up a position astride the main road about a thousand yards W of Gouzeaucourt and extended their left flank beyond the Gouzeaucourt-Metz road. However, the Germans never managed to secure the village completely. While the Germans paused, III Corps' defences got ever stronger. Some disorganisation had been caused by the very rapidity of the German advance whilst their losses, especially in officers, had been heavy, and 34th German Division reported that it had become 'leaderless'. But by 10.30 am they were pressing forward again.

The German infantry were now closing in on the artillery batteries holding out near Gonnelieu, but 60 Bde 20th Division now appeared from the N where it had been in reserve at Villers Plouich. At about 10.45 am 3rd Army placed 2nd Cavalry Division (at Fins) less its artillery under III Corps. 20 H 5 Cav Bde was the first to reach the line held by 11 DLI and others, and extended it to the right. Here touch was obtained with 11 Middx on the left of the troops under Comd 35 Bde on Révelon Ridge.

The right of the corps was getting ever stronger but many artillery batteries were still in difficulty from the northern attack, especially those in rear of 20th and 29th Divisions. Lieutenant Colonel Murray CO 17 Bde RFA 29th Division noted:

> We were encircled. About 10.45 am 15 Bde RHA, who were completely isolated, were obliged to abandon their guns, all of which were captured. Very shortly after this German infantry appeared on the crest above us. I turned two batteries on to them This was not easy as they were on our right rear, but we got our guns round in time and were able to hold them up until some of our infantry were found to counter-attack, when the Germans were driven back to the crest beyond. All day my batteries were hanging on by their eyelids, expecting to be cut off at any moment. But the men were as steady as rocks. 29th Division infantry didn't yield a yard of ground. If they had broken it would have meant the whole line going. I constituted myself CRA, collected another brigade and organised a defensive barrage. Very weak it was, but it sufficed, and we were able to give the infantry a good deal of support.

It was not until 88 Bde's counter-attack late in the afternoon that this area behind Welsh Ridge was secured.

From HQ III Corps' and Putty's perspective the overall situation at 11 am was that the enemy had pushed back 12th and 20th Divisions and had broken through in two places. On the right the enemy had come through VII Corps and turned this flank, taking Gonnelieu and Gouzeaucourt. The enemy had also come through on the left of 20th Division leaving 29th Division across the canal isolated. Even though an attack was expected, they had been surprised by its momentum, its strength and its speed, and by its direction.

Putty's extreme right was now a little more secure with the Corps Cav Regt around Vaucelette Farm and the Corps Cyclist Bn near Révelon Farm: they could observe and delay any wider outflanking movement. Révelon Ridge was held by Vincent's Force (HQ 35 Bde and three bns, although none of its own) and 2nd Cavalry Division. There was still a gap at Gouzeaucourt but the Germans had still not completely secured the village, and there was a screen of sorts made up of 11 DLI (20th Division) and other troops pushed out of Gouzeaucourt to its W and N. NE and E of Gouzeaucourt 12th Division, with the help of 60 Bde 20th Division, was holding its reserve line on the high ground astride La Vacquerie.

The northern breakthrough on the left of 20th Division had forced back 59 Bde (right) and 61 Bde (left) S of the canal to Welsh Ridge over-running many batteries of artillery deployed to its E. Its reserve (60 Bde) was around Villers Plouich behind 12th Division: because of its location and because 12th Division was the first to be attacked, it had been committed to support this part of the line. 29th Division was still holding with 86 Bde and most of 87 Bde across the canal, and was counter-attacking with 88 Bde and 87 Bde's reserve bn to secure its right flank.

6th Division on the left, although attacked, was secure with 71 Bde and 18 Bde deployed forward. One bn 18 Bde (14 DLI) and two bns 59th Division (IV Corps) were in depth on Highland Ridge covering its right rear and Marcoing. 16 Bde (6th Division reserve bde) was on route to a blocking position NW of Gouzeaucourt.

It is doubtful if Putty had such a clear picture of the situation although he was in communication with all his divisional commanders most of the time (GOCs 6th and 29th Divisions were out of telephone communication for much of the morning). Some of them, however, were having difficulty getting an accurate picture from their bde comds since several of their HQs had been over-run or had moved. Thanks to an alternative emergency ground line which 20th Divisional Signal Coy had laid to corps through the outskirts of Gouzeaucourt, to supplement the poled cable route, signal communication between HQ 20th Division and corps was successfully maintained throughout the day, in spite of the fact that at one time a portion of the line passed into German hands and out again. The line also proved of great value to the other divisions. That night HQ 20th Division moved from Villers Plouich to a point half-way between Gouzeaucourt and Gouzeaucourt Wood.

At 11 am the Guards Division was transferred to III Corps and GOC Guards Division (Major General Feilding) went to HQ III Corps to be briefed by Putty. By 2 pm Adv HQ Guards Division was established at Metz-en-Couture.

At 12 noon 16 Bde 6th Division, which had been at work all night, began approaching their destination (E of Gouzeaucourt Wood). Comd 16 Bde (Walker) had been ordered to report to GOC 29th Division at Gouzeaucourt; he narrowly escaped capture, and meanwhile GOC 29th Division had passed through HQ 6th Division on his way to his division. Without telephone, communications between Putty and these two GOCs would have been slow: and there would have been further delay in communications between GOC 6th Division and Comd 16 Bde. This bde having been ordered (by Putty at 9.50 am) to take up a line covering Beaucamp and to await the arrival of tanks before attacking Gouzeaucourt, found the Guards Division in the village at 3.30 pm. It then advanced eastwards at the same time as 3 Gds Bde came up to cover the left of 1 Gds Bde. Naturally there was some confusion. In the gathering dusk 16 Bde took up a position on the road between Gouzeaucourt and Villers Plouich, to the left of the Guards (and well in rear of 60 Bde 20th Division), and prepared to attack Cemetery Ridge between Gonnelieu and La Vacquerie, so as to re-establish the line.

Coordination between Guards Division and 16 Bde was inevitably poor but it was not the only problem of command and control in this area. Both GOCs 12th and 20th Divisions had realised the importance of re-taking Gouzeaucourt and were acting accordingly.

1 Gds Bde were drawn up in artillery formation behind the crest of the high ground W of Gouzeaucourt by 12.30 pm. Assisted by the fire of the bde machine-guns, they advanced rapidly through 11 DLI and 470 Fd Coy RE, and carried 20 H forward with it. The fight for Gouzeaucourt was brief; a number of Germans were shot or bayoneted and about a hundred taken. The remainder retreated quickly, so that by 1.30 pm 1 Gds Bde had reached a line on the eastern edge of the village, the abandoned siege batteries with their dumps of ammunition being recovered almost intact: other sources noted 'British artillery men who followed up the attack recovered four abandoned 6" hows and reopened fire'. 3 Gds Bde came up on their left after 1 Gds Bde had taken Gouzeaucourt village and 2 Gds Bde moved to Gouzeaucourt Wood.

Lieutenant Colonel Wollocombe CO 11 Middx 36 Bde 12th Division recorded:

> At about noon HQ 12th Division signallers, cooks, orderlies etc attached themselves to our line and a few tanks came up. We were ordered to do an attack on Gouzeaucourt at 2 pm, but very shortly before this hour we were suddenly informed that the Guards had retaken the place. We did not know they were there even, but they came in on the left flank much to our surprise. Of course I had no telephone communication with the rear.

Presumably Major General Scott had decided to move his HQ personnel to join Comd 35 Bde on Révelon Ridge and either he or Comd 35 Bde had ordered this attack on their own initiative.

Somewhere between Gouzeaucourt and Gonnelieu, Captain Dugdale SC HQ 60 Bde 20th Division watched as 20th Division's reserve brigade arrived to bolster the survivors (from the two villages) before launching their counter blow, supported by dismounted Indian cavalry:

> I had a wonderful view of the counter-attack made by 60 Bde and the Guards. They put up a wonderful show, driving the Germans out of Gouzeaucourt and part of Gonnelieu. An SOS at this time was sent for the cavalry to come to the rescue. Their arrival gave us great encouragement and was a magnificent sight. They dismounted and came into battle as infantry.

60 Bde's attack was on the left of the Guards Division (to re-take Gonnelieu and secure 12th Division's right) and most likely made on Putty's orders.

By about 2.30 pm the Guards in Gouzeaucourt were joined there by about twenty tanks (H Bn), which took up position round the village and helped to consolidate the defence.

In the meantime 5th Cavalry Division (see GS log GF21 issued 3.35 pm) had come up on the extreme right and advanced to attack Gauche Wood, but mounted effort failed under artillery and heavy machine-gun fire. Eventually a line was secured along a sunken road west of the railway and as the light began to fail it was extended astride the railway to a point E of Vaucelette Farm (still held by III Corps Cav Regt).

By last light Putty had the equivalent of three divisions containing the breakthrough on his right flank. From Vaucelette Farm his line ran N along the railway to Gouzeaucourt which had been re-taken, then E through Gonnelieu which was still in enemy hands. The enemy (34th German Division) still held Villers-Guislain, Gauche Wood and Quentin Ridge.

All afternoon 12th Division was fighting to hold on to its reserve line. 37 Bde (on the left) had been reduced to a force of one bn (mainly 6 E Kent) and was holding a position in the Hindenburg support system NW of Pam Pam Farm where it was able to inflict heavy loss on the Germans (220th Division). The defence owed much to the support of 179 Bde RFA located E of La Vacquerie; guns were run into the open and fired over open sights. Before noon the force's left flank was threatened and it withdrew to a communication trench between the Hindenburg support and front systems, only about 100 yards in front of some battery positions and in touch on the right with what remained of 36 Bde. The three regiments of 28th German Division facing it made little attempt to advance beyond the main Cambrai road, and all accounts emphasise the obstinate resistance they faced. Because the German 220th Division could not overcome 12th Division's resistance, 185th Division in army reserve was ordered forward about this time to take La Vacquerie.

As evening approached, it became known (to the Germans) that the Arras Group had only made slight progress on either side of Bourlon Wood. But Rupprecht's particular frustration was that in the southern attack, despite repeated reminders, 2nd Army had failed to shift its point of main effort to the left flank of the attack. Night fell on a very hard day for III Corps and with it matters quietened down. 12th Division was still holding its reserve line covering La Vacquerie with a forward position across the Hindenburg Line SW of Bleak House.

Guards Division and Cav Corps knew Putty's intentions for 1 December as early as 3.35 pm (30 November) when GF21 was issued (see GS log). Confirmatory orders were issued by Cav

Corps to 5th Cavalry Division (and Lucknow Bde 4th Cavalry Division) at 6.40 pm to attack Gauche Wood and Villers-Guislain with tank assistance. Orders were issued by HQ III Corps to 2 Tank Bde at 7 pm to collect all available tanks in the hollow W of Vaucelette Farm ready to attack Villers-Guislain and Villers Ridge at dawn, but to leave 20 tanks to cooperate with the Guards Division.

At 9.50 pm Putty spoke to GOC VII Corps (Snow) on the telephone; the latter promised to support III Corps' attack with the fire of his available artillery. Then, at 10 pm, HQ III Corps issued OpO No.227 giving confirmatory orders for the attack by the Guards Division and Cav Corps (Appendix F). Later at midnight Zero hour for this operation was set as 6.30 am 1 December.

Also at midnight HQ III Corps issued clarification (GO7835) of the respective attacks by 60 Bde (20th Division) and 16 Bde (6th Division), and that by the Guards Division and Cav Corps. Putty's objective was to take advantage of darkness and the apparent lull to push these two bdes forward: if they succeeded in driving back the enemy in Gonnelieu and to its NE, even in retaking Villers-Guislain, the main attack planned for the next day would not take place and the Guards Division would relieve them; if they failed it would go ahead. Putty also needed to give 12th Division time to reorganise without the risk of further attack from this direction. Its casualties on 30 November were 164 officers and 3,362 other ranks (75% of their casualties in the whole battle: 2,341 of these were taken prisoner and most of them were captured on 30 November).

For the renewal of the offensive on 1 December the 2nd German Army named 'Beaucamp–Trescault' heights as the objective. The point of main effort was entrusted to 185th Division (right) and 9th Bavarian Reserve Division (left). 34th Division* (on left of 9th Bavarian) was to envelop Gouzeaucourt from the N and the 208th and 183rd farther to the left again, were to straighten out the defensive flank running roughly SE from Gauche Wood. 28th Division* on the right of 185th Division was to take La Vacquerie, whilst 220th* and 9th Reserve pushed forward to the Couillet Wood valley but no farther. 30th Division was to capture Les Rues Vertes. Eight divisions to participate, although those marked * had significant casualties on 30 November, with four more in reserve). Zero hour was fixed for 8.30 am (British time) and all divisions were warned that the British might counter-attack before this time.

29th Division has not been mentioned for some time. They were still holding across the canal with 86 Bde in Masnières and 87 Bde in Marcoing. Following its counter-attack 88 Bde was in Les Rues Vertes and on the lower slopes of Welsh Ridge. The division was under constant attack from almost every direction but was still holding on.

DDMS recorded that day at 10 am that part of the personnel 36 Fd Amb (ADS) at Villers-Guislain was captured, also some motor ambulances. This fd amb belonged to 12th Division again demonstrating that Villers-Guislain was considered to be well behind the front line. He also recorded: 'Wounded admitted from 6 am to 6 pm 1,090 which included 1 German'.

HQ RE III Corps noted that Brigadier General Schreiber handed over his duties as CE III Corps to Brigadier General Rolland on 30 November. It may appear strange that he should have handed over in the middle of the battle but his son (OC 106 Bty 22 Bde RFA) had died of wounds on 22 October: his departure and Rolland's arrival may well have been arranged to take place after the offensive on 20 November and Putty would have been reluctant to keep him any longer, and he had been his CE for more than two years.

III Corps total casualties for November (mainly the Battle of Cambrai but not including 30 November) were: 74 officers and 737 other ranks killed, 237 officers and 3,995 other ranks wounded, 9 officers and 948 other ranks missing = 6,000. This compares well with AQ HQ III Corps' estimate following the offensive on 20/21 November of 5,711.

Overnight 29th Division held on across the canal and at 6 am 1 December reported 'situation at Masnières unchanged, but more satisfactory, heavy shelling ceased'. However, at 8.15 am, under an intense barrage, waves of infantry (30th German Division) advanced on Les Rues Vertes; they were checked with heavy loss. According to the HQ III Corps log nothing more was heard until 11 am when 29th Division reported 'the line is still intact in Masnières and W of it, though enemy are barraging heavily'. Sometime during the morning Comd 87 Bde (holding the bend in the canal), who had been placed in command of all forward troops, reported to GOC 29th Division (HQ 29th Division at Villers Plouich was shelled out at 9.55 am and moved to Trescault. Communications were frequently cut by German bombardment during the day) that 86 Bde must be reinforced otherwise it might be necessary to evacuate Masnières. At 2.30 pm a heavy bombardment opened on Masnières and Les Rues Vertes and it was evident that 29th Division's position was becoming untenable. Major General de Lisle noted: 'That afternoon I motored to HQ III Corps to ask for sanction to straighten out the point of my salient giving up Masnières and Les Rues Vertes. Owing to casualties, my strength was reduced by 50% and I was holding a double portion of the line in this acute angle. This proposal met with approval (presumably Putty's); we proceeded to carry out the plan that night, and by dawn (2 December) had withdrawn to a line facing E half way between Masnières and Marcoing'. At 3.20 pm HQ III Corps issued GF21: Instructions to 86 Bde to withdraw to a line W of Masnières, and 88 Bde to conform. Convey: 'Corps Commander's heartiest congratulations to 86 Bde on their fine performance'.

The situation continued to deteriorate during the evening as III Corps GS log recorded:

> 4.56 pm. 86 Bde report situation critical.
> 5 pm. 29th Division report 86 Bde on right have beaten off 8 attacks during the day.
> 5.5 pm. 29th Division report numerous enemy gun locations. Crèvecoeur full of hostile troops. RA informed.
> 5.50 pm. 29th Division report enemy have pierced line of 88 Bde.
> 6 pm. 86 Bde report enemy driven out of Les Rues Vertes and 50 prisoners captured.

The fighting then died down and preparation for the withdrawal of 86 Bde began. The first move out of Masnières was at 11 pm and the whole operation was so well conducted that it entirely escaped detection by the enemy.

In the S, the Guards Division reported at 12.30 am (1 December) enemy holding Gauche Wood and Chapel Crossing strongly. Half an hour later 16 Bde 6th Division attacked the ridge between Gonnelieu and La Vacquerie in moonlight. This attack was ordered by GOC 6th Division because patrols had reported no enemy activity, and as there were no guns available he thought a surprise attack by moonlight might succeed in capturing this important ridge before the enemy could reinforce it. Comd 16 Bde knew nothing of 60 Bde 20th Division's attack on his right until 12.45 am but he nevertheless put his troops in; the attack failed because of machine-gun fire and the difficulty of operating at night over strange ground.

60 Bde 20th Division carried out a hasty reconnaissance before the light failed. At 1 am 6 SLI advanced on the right, working forward along the railway and then turning left-handed to assault Quentin Ridge from the W. Although an advanced trench was captured and a number

of Germans killed, strong opposition barred further progress; and a combined attempt of 6 Ox & Bucks and 12 RB to enter Gonnelieu under cover of trench-mortar fire was also stopped.

These attacks failed because there was insufficient time to carry out the necessary reconnaissance and because the enemy was in greater strength than expected. That they were ordered by Putty sometime late on 30 November is evident from HQ III Corps GO7835 issued at midnight 30 November. Arguably, there appeared to be an opportunity and by taking the initiative during the night the enemy was discouraged from continuing their offensive, and this gave vital time for reorganisation. By 2.45 am the failure of these attacks was known to the Guards Division.

Their attack at 6.30 am 1 December with 1 Gds Bde on the right and 3 Gds Bde on the left, had for objectives Gauche Wood-Quentin Ridge-Gonnelieu and was supported by two field btys. As for heavy artillery, there was little left at the disposal of III Corps (of twenty-nine siege and heavy artillery batteries that had been in action on 29 November, the equivalent of ten remained), and most of the surviving btys were engaged further N. The attack was, however, supported by 20 tanks.

3 Gds Bde with four tanks had the task of capturing the part of Quentin Ridge N of the mill, and the village of Gonnelieu. On the right 1 WG took its objective and was able to dig in beyond the crest of the ridge; about 300 prisoners were captured mainly from 9th Bavarian Reserve Division. On the left 4 Gren Gds attacked through 60 Bde (20th Division) still in position astride the Gouzeaucourt-Gonnelieu road. They fought their way into the village, but more and more Germans entered it because they were about to resume their offensive, and 3 Gds Bde were forced out.

On the right sixteen tanks led that attack by 1 Gds Bde against Gauche Wood, spraying the trees and stumps with fire as they advanced, 2 Gren Gds running close behind them to take the wood at the point of the bayonet. The fight went on all morning with cavalry troopers coming up to help the Guards snuff out the last of the German machine-guns. Gauche Wood was taken by 11.30 am. 3 Coldm Gds on the left of 1 Gds Bde carried the crest of Quentin Ridge as far as the mill; several hundred Germans were captured (from 34th German Division).

If the Guards Division had failed to capture Gonnelieu they had secured their other objectives and stopped the attack of two enemy divisions and part of another. Zero hour for these attacks was 8.30 am British time, two hours after III Corps' attack. The German attack which forced 3 Gds Bde out of Gonnelieu struck 60 Bde 20th Division which continued the defensive front to La Vacquerie; with the assistance of 3 Gds Bde the line was held. In front of La Vacquerie the enemy (28th Division) had even less success. All ground lost was recovered by counter-attack after some hand-to-hand fighting. Air reconnaissance reports reaching HQ III Corps during the morning identified a large body of enemy E of Villers-Guislain and the attack from Gonnelieu; there could have been little doubt as to the threat on this flank.

On the right of the Guards Division Cav Corps also attacked at dawn (6.30 am). 4th and 5th Cavalry Divisions attacked Villers-Guislain and Gauche Wood from the S. These attacks were said to 'have been ill-coordinated in small packets and without the promised tank support or adequate artillery support accomplished little'. They did contribute to the taking of Gauche Wood and they were supported by 19 tanks (mainly H Bn), at least one of which reached Villers-Guislain.

III Corps GS Log recorded Cav Corps reports on 1 December:

8.5 am. Attack on Gauche Wood and Villers-Guislain progressing.

8.50 am. Tanks moving well: one seen north of Gauche Wood and two south.

9.45 am. Ambala Bde has taken Gauche Wood.

10.30 am. Gauche Wood captured. 4th Cavalry Division's advance on Villers-Guislain failed through MG fire.

1.45 pm. Taking over responsibility from Gauche Wood to Chapel Crossing (HQ III Corps G918).

4.9 pm. Filling gap between III and VII Corps with 4th and 5th Cavalry Divisions.

7.30 pm. Enemy counter-attack succeeded in getting behind advancing squadrons of dismounted cavalry, who were therefore withdrawn.

The various records are contradictory: at times it seems Cav Corps was under Putty's command, at other times not. The two corps were also mixed up with both apparently commanding troops and tanks in the same area. There were also no clear boundaries between Cav Corps and VII Corps, or with III Corps. It is strange that 3rd Army who had failed to coordinate adequately before 30 November seems to have again neglected the matter.

On the left of 60 Bde 20th Division the troops of 12th Division and of 59 and 61 Bdes 20th Division were less heavily engaged on 1 December. It was just as well since both divisions were in a bad state and exhausted. Neither is recorded in HQ III Corps GS log as having made any reports on 1 December. 12th Division was still occupying its reserve line centred on La Vacquerie but only four of its original ten bns in their part of the front could be considered effective. These were the four not holding the front line on 30 November; although they too had taken casualties, they had been reinforced by men from other bns. 20th Division had effectively taken them (and HQs 36 and 37 Bdes) under command at some stage when its HQ was at Villers Plouich and this arrangement seemed to continue into 1 December, although it was never confirmed by HQ III Corps.

According to the records, Putty first influenced the battle at 9.58 am when HQ III Corps G903 was issued reorganising the corps' front: 'Guards Division was to take over from Gauche Wood exclusive to Gonnelieu inclusive: 20th Division to take over from Gonnelieu exclusive to R.5 a.central: 29th Division from R.5.a.central and original sector: 6th Division to hold their original line: 61st Division to take over right portion of 20th Division front tonight (1/2 December), and remaining portion tomorrow night'. This is of interest for several reasons: there is no mention of III Corps from Gauche Wood to the right which is now Cav Corps area (HQ III Corps G918) or the III Corps troops still there; there is no mention of 12th Division now effectively under 20th Division; and there is no mention of 16 Bde 6th Division, now returning to its parent division.

6th Division was still holding its original line and although attacked had never been under the same pressure as the other divisions. Its reserve (16 Bde) had attacked Cemetery Ridge between Gonnelieu and La Vacquerie during the night without success. At 5.10 pm 6th Division reported enemy attack on Cantaing at 2.30 pm beaten off. HQ III Corps had ordered 6th Division to assist 20th Division and one bn was provided that evening. Later still, at 9.14 pm, HQ III Corps issued GF24 warning all divisions of likely attack (from prisoner's statement) on La Vacquerie-Gonnelieu line, and two bns 6th Division were placed at disposal of Guards

Division to strengthen left flank (probably from 16 Bde). 6th Division had under its command the two bns 59th Division on Highland Ridge but was now very stretched.

Assistance was coming at last; at 1.10 pm HQ III Corps issued G918 ordering one bde 61st Division to take over right portion of 20th Division front. At 1.18 pm HQ III Corps GS log recorded: 'Whole of 61st Division, less artillery, placed at the disposal of III Corps by 3rd Army'. More help was on its way with 9th Division moving into army reserve and at 7.50 pm HQ III Corps issued G931 'Instructions for the march of 65 and 150 AFA Bdes after detraining at Bapaume on 2 Dec'.

Captain Wyatt 2/4 Glos 183 Bde 61st Division had been sent up in the afternoon of 1 December to arrange the relief. At Villers Plouich, he found HQs of three infantry bdes:

> There were two brigadier generals of the 12th Division, Vincent [Comd 35 Bde] and Owen (Comd 36 Bde) by name, and a colonel acting as bde comd of a bde of 20th Division [Lieutenant Colonel Priaulx CO 11 KRRC in temporary command of 59 Bde vice Brigadier General Hyslop]. These three brigades were pretty well mixed up in the Welsh Ridge-La Vacquerie area and had been having a pretty tough time for the past two days keeping their end up against the Boche. Vincent seemed to be the directing spirit.

If this report is accurate the appearance of Comd 35 Bde, up to then commanding the force on Révelon Ridge, suggests the beginning of 12th Division's reconstitution and that he was now able to resume command of what was left of his bde (perhaps two bns based on 9 Essex and 5 Berks).

Rupprecht received no news until 8 pm, and so concluded that no success worth mentioning had been gained. Marwitz,[3] commanding 2nd Army, admitted that the attack had 'run itself out'. Orders for 2 December called for a halt; the day was to be devoted to consolidation. However, 30th German Division was to capture Masnières (evacuated night 1/2 December by 29th Division) early 3 December when 28th German Division was to storm La Vacquerie. The German attacks that day had succeeded in pushing back III Corps from Masnières but little more. Like the British attack ten days earlier, the German counter-offensive had been halted, though the battle was not yet over. It continued for another six days until 7 December when snow and rain made further attacks by either side unprofitable.

The position of the troops of 29th Division beyond the canal continued to give Putty cause for anxiety, and as a precaution 16 Bde 6th Division was brought back from the Gonnelieu front on the night 1/2 December and positioned on Highland Ridge (with one bn 18 Bde 6th Division and two bns 59th Division).

DDMS III Corps log recorded: 'Wounded admitted 6 pm (30 November) to 6 am (1 December) 1,374 which includes 10 Germans; wounded admitted from 6 am to 6 pm (1 December) 1,226 which includes 26 Germans'. Added to 1,089 wounded in first 12 hours 30 November, 3,653 III Corps wounded had been evacuated in the first 36 hours of the battle. The HQ III Corps AQ log recorded 104,857 artillery rounds fired (79,000 by divisional artillery and 25,857 by heavy artillery). Since there was no record of 30 November expenditure, this is likely to include the first 36 hours: considering the number of guns lost it is a remarkably high figure.

---

3   General Johannes Georg von der Marwitz (1856-1929).

Putty was quick to recognise the contribution the Guards Division had made in countering the German offensive. In a Special Order of the Day he said:

> The Corps Commander wishes to express to all ranks of the Guards Division his high appreciation of the prompt manner in which they turned out on 30th November, counter-attacked through chaotic mobs of retreating men and retook Gouzeaucourt. The very fine attack which they subsequently carried out against Quentin Ridge and Gauche Wood, resulting in the capture of these important positions, was worthy of the highest traditions of the Guards.

This shows Putty's relief at holding and defeating the German offensive and exasperation at the performance of 12th and 20th Divisions, some of whose units were a 'disorganised rabble'. Haig wrote that day:

> pm. I motored to Albert and had a talk with Byng. He was much happier with the situation than when I saw him yesterday. Indeed he has every right to be pleased. The determination of 29th and 6th Divisions on the Masnières front quite justifies a feeling of satisfaction. Guards have re-taken Gonnelieu with 3-400 prisoners and 40 machine-guns, and the cavalry with tanks pressed the enemy eastwards from Gauche Wood and further to the S of the latter place.

The CinC's record is inaccurate in some detail but his exclusion of 12th and 20th Divisions from his praise leaves little doubt where he and Byng placed at least some of the blame for 30 November.

At 12.45 am 2 December HQ III Corps issued OpO No.228 confirming the divisional moves and reliefs for night 2/3 December (as outlined in WngO G903); 61st Division was to put in one bde for the first time and boundaries between divisions allotted.

20th Division reported a quiet night apart from heavy shelling of La Vacquerie. Normality was slowly being restored with 20th Division sending an evening report at 5.10 pm:

> Enemy at 3 pm made three strong attacks on La Vacquerie, covered by a heavy artillery barrage. Enemy were met with heavy MG and rifle fire, and were completely repulsed. Our artillery SOS barrage, in addition, inflicted casualties on the enemy.

This does not report the reorganisation and resupply that must have continued during the previous night and during the day: every hour 20th Division and the units of 12th Division 'under it' would have grown stronger.

By 4 am 2 December the withdrawal of 86 Bde 29th Division from Masnières was complete and 87 Bde had swung back its right to cover the lock. On the opposite bank 88 Bde had thrown back its left to conform. At 8 am 29th Division reported that 86 Bde was back in reserve and gave details of the new line they were holding. However, they were to have little time to prepare: the enemy shelled Masnières throughout the early morning, and at 9.20 am 29th Division reported the enemy was massing in Masnières and that artillery was being directed on to them; then at 10.5 am they reported 'enemy attacked from Masnières on line N of Canal about 8.30 am. He was driven back in disorder'.

Throughout the day (2 December) Putty was working to consolidate III Corps' position. The GS log included:

> 12.35 pm. Guards and 20th Divisions informed that 16 tanks are concentrated in the Villers Plouich Valley, covering Gonnelieu and La Vacquerie. Only to be used in case of enemy attack.
>
> 1.30 pm. III Corps GF26 issued ordering consolidation of Reserve Line as follows: Vaucelette Farm-Beaucamp Ridge-Highland Ridge. All divisions to get to work on this line and to keep in it a garrison with machine-guns.
>
> 1.35 pm. III Corps GF25 issued. The two bns 6th Division placed at disposal of Guards Division to revert to 6th Division tonight.
>
> 4.15 pm. III Corps GF22 issued places bde 29th Division (88 Bde) holding the line from the canal to the left of 61st Division under orders of 6th Division.
>
> 7.20 pm. III Corps GF23 issued. Instruction to 61st Division re organisation and strengthening of front system. Ground to be gained, where possible, in the direction of Foster Lane, and the Cambrai Road near La Vacquerie.
>
> 7.30 pm. III Corps G961 issued. Divisional artillery of all divisions and MGs to carry out brisk night firing at irregular intervals throughout the night, especially at 5.15 am, 6.10 am and 6.40 am.
>
> 11.30 pm. III Corps GF34 issued places 59 Bde 20th Division under orders 61st Division.
>
> 11.55 pm. III Corps G972 issued, instructing 6th Division to relieve 29th Division by a bde, on night 4/5 Dec, and to reconnoitre front now held by 88 Bde.

Apart from attacking from Masnières and at La Vacquerie, the enemy were also active on the III Corps' right flank. Cav Corps reported at 12.50 pm that the road Honnecourt-Villers-Guislain had at least one bde of enemy moving along it, that the wood in S.8.c. and d. was packed with troops and transport, and that their heavy guns were directing their fire on to them. Nothing more was heard from them until 11.40 pm that night when they reported a Hotchkiss Post established in copse 300 yards N of Vaucelette Farm. The intermingling of the two corps in this area without any defined command and control arrangements continued.

At 5.50 pm that evening the GS log recorded: 'Enemy artillery active on Gouzeaucourt Wood. Otherwise situation quiet, with exception of attack on La Vacquerie. Three 77 mm guns reported captured by us in Gauche Wood'. One other report deserves mention. At 6.24 pm 12th Division reported enemy seen in large numbers consolidating on Gonnelieu Ridge. It is possible that this was seen from Révelon Ridge rather than by troops still in and around La Vacquerie but this is the first recorded report from 12th Division since 7.20 am 1 December: 36 hours had elapsed and it is difficult to believe that Major General Scott had not re-established command and control of his whole division in that time.

61st Division had begun to relieve the remnants of 12th Division in the early hours of the morning (2 December) but it would have taken some time to find and extract all the units, as well as those of 20th Division in this area. After 183 Bde 61st Division had carried out this relief the line facing the Péronne-Cambrai road was far too close to La Vacquerie to permit an effective defence of the village (this was realised by III Corps which instructed 61st Division to push forward towards the road, if possible – HQ III Corps GF23 issued 7.20 pm), whilst an awkward salient existed farther E where the trenches of the old Hindenburg front line ran into the defence line. It was at this salient that the Germans renewed their attacks with a bombing assault at 5.30 am, an advance over the open at 6 am and another effort in greater force at 6.30 am; none met with any success for 220th German Division. The Germans were obviously well aware of what was happening and pressed their attack at this vulnerable time.

The enemy attacked again in considerable numbers S and SE of La Vacquerie at 3 pm and, although the advance over the open was everywhere checked and driven back, the bombing attacks drove in 183 Bde 61st Division leaving 500 yards of the Hindenburg front system in German hands (the enemy's objective was not La Vacquerie; it was to improve its position for the attack next day). During the night (2/3 December) 182 Bde 61st Division relieved the remnants of 61 Bde (and some of 59 Bde) 20th Division, and were in contact with 88 Bde 29th Division on their left.

Also that night 87 Bde across the canal was relieved by 16 Bde 6th Division. 6th Division eventually became responsible for the whole front including that portion S of the canal held by 88 Bde. HQ RE III Corps recorded that day: 'III Corps to 6th and 29th Divisions and CE: All bridges over St Quentin Canal will be prepared for demolition'.

By now Putty and his staff must have been very tired, yet this was a critical time in the battle with much to be done. Tired and depleted divisions had to be relieved by new divisions that did not know the ground; the line had to be shortened which meant a limited withdrawal; and new defences prepared. All of this had to be done in contact with a superior enemy. The new main line of defence included the vital ground of Quentin Ridge, the high ground NW of Gonnelieu and Welsh Ridge: this had to be held. The Reserve Line behind (essentially Révelon Ridge-Beaucamp Ridge-Highland Ridge) was still in most places little more than a line on the map. It was on that day that Haig instructed Byng to select a good winter line and make arrangements for withdrawal to it.

Overnight 2/3 December there was a great deal of activity in III Corps but the overall situation was quiet. 3 December (the fourth day) was to be a really difficult one for Putty and his staff. One of the first reports came at 9.10 am from 1st Cavalry Division (Cav Corps) on their left flank: 'Hostile batteries in action on the forward crest'. The left was not to be threatened during the day but could not be ignored. The danger was in the centre and on the right.

According to III Corps GS log, at 9 am 61st Division reported: 'Enemy attacked their front at 8.15 am under heavy barrage. Believed that enemy did not enter our trenches'. However, their next report at 10.10 am said: 'Enemy, as a result of their attack, have gained a footing in La Vacquerie. Steps being taken to recover the place'. Then at 11.55 am 61st Division reported: 'We hold Corner Work and N part of La Vacquerie. Enemy still in S part' and at 1.30 pm: '3 coys now on their way to clear enemy out of southern portion of La Vacquerie'. These regular reports are in marked contrast to the absence of reports from 12th Division.

Other sources provided a more detailed account. At 7.30 am 183 Bde 61st Division endeavoured to recover the trenches lost the previous afternoon, without success. Soon afterwards an intense bombardment opened upon La Vacquerie and the neighbouring positions. Infantry of 28th German Division advanced in waves over the open whilst bombing parties attacked up the trenches. Artillery (field artillery still under CRA 20th Division), machine-gun and small-arms fire did great execution above ground, but bombers made headway. 183 Bde was forced out of La Vacquerie (or most of it); and 182 Bde on left of 61st Division was also forced back.

HQ III Corps issued GF37 at 2.35 pm instructing G Bn Tank Corps to place 16 tanks now at Trescault at disposal of 61st Division for counter-attack purposes: 'To OC G Bn Tks copy to 61st Division. G Bn Tanks have 16 tanks disposed along the reverse slope of the Trescault Ridge. These tanks are placed at the disposal of the 61st Division for use in case of enemy attack when they will be used to restore the situation. Colonel Hankey CO G Bn will keep in close touch with 61st Division. Colonel Hankey's HQ is in Havrincourt Wood. A tank liaison officer will live with one of the forward bde HQs of 61st Division. CG Fuller BGGS'.

So serious was the situation on 61st Division front that at 9.50 am Putty directed the Guards Division to turn their guns on Gonnelieu, and at the same time to warn the reserve artillery bde to keep a look out to the S. However, by the afternoon the situation to the N was to be an even greater cause for concern.

HQ III Corps issued GF36 at 10.55 am – Instructions that 12th Division will relieve Guards Division on right bde front on the night 5/6 December. Exhausted and greatly reduced in strength the division was to have little time to recover. At 12.30 pm (3 December) III Corps issued OpO No.229: '(i) Transfer of 36th Division from V to III Corps 12 noon 4 Dec (ii) Relief by 36th Division of portion of 6th and 61st Divisions' front on 4/5 Dec and 5/6 Dec (iii) Relief by 61st Division of portion of Guards Division front on night 4/5 Dec (iv) Relief by 12th Division of portion of Guards Division front on night 5/6 Dec (v) Guards Division, on relief, to be in corps reserve (vi) 20th Division to embus on 4 Dec (vii) 29th Division to entrain on 5 Dec'.

By the time this was completed late 5 December (36 hours away) a shortened line would be held by (L-R) 6th, 36th, 61st and 12th Divisions. For the first time there would be a reserve (Guards Division); 20th and 29th Divisions would have left III Corps. The two omissions are the artillery which was slowly being built up again (143 Siege Bty was detraining on 4 December – HQ III Corps G893) and the tanks. 16 tanks G Bn had been allocated to 61st Division but there is no mention of any others. However, Putty now had to deal with the more immediate problems in the N.

At 1.32 pm 29th Division reported: 'At noon enemy attacked Marcoing from the S under heavy barrage. First wave of attacking infantry caught in our barrage and dispersed. Attack has extended S, but he is still strong on our front'. Then at 2.10 pm (3 December) 29th Division reported enemy was reinforcing his line in front of Marcoing and Rumilly. It seemed that the enemy was pressing to cut off and destroy the salient across the canal just as 6th Division was in the process of relieving 29th Division.

6th Division reported at 2.15 pm that: 'Enemy has broken through S of the canal. 2 Y&L (16 Bde) were on their way up at 1 pm to restore the situation'. Five minutes later came the report from 6th Division that their line N of the river had been heavily attacked and pierced, but subsequently restored. Then at 2.35 pm 6th Division reported: 'Enemy have broken through and are marching on Marcoing. 88 Bde have suffered heavy casualties – line very weak – no reserves in hand. 59th Division has placed one bn at our disposal'.

The Germans put down a heavy barrage on 88 Bde 29th Division, S of St Quentin Canal, and on 16 Bde 6th Division in the bend of the canal beyond Marcoing at 10.30 am; infantry then advanced to the attack. The left of 88 Bde had suffered heavily, some of the troops having been blown out of their posts by trench mortar bombardment; but the Germans coming forward along the S bank of the canal were checked by fire when they reached the first positions, and heavy fighting raged in the bend of the canal. The first attack was repulsed by 16 Bde, and then a second; but the enemy was now left in possession of the lock house, and when they put in a third attack at 12.15 pm a close, confused struggle ensued. The Germans, in much superior force, pressed on regardless of loss, penetrating the position. The fight continued with rifle, Lewis gun, bomb and bayonet as the remnants of the two battalions (14 DLI and 1 KSLI) fought their way back across the canal. 14 DLI were reorganised and eventually re-crossed the canal by the railway bridge and a barge bridge near it (part of 8 Bedford coming up on their left). In gaining these trenches a number of Germans were killed and taken prisoner (from 107th Division).

Early in the afternoon alarming reports began to reach HQ 6th Division in Havrincourt Wood: the Germans were said to have broken through and to be entering Marcoing. GOC 6th Division sent a bn of 16 Bde to reinforce 88 Bde S of the canal, manned the Hindenburg support system on the forward slope of Highland Ridge with the reserves available, ordered 71 Bde, holding the Noyelles sector, to establish a line along the southern edge of Noyelles and Nine Wood facing Marcoing, and sent two bns to dig in on the Premy Chapel-Flesquières ridge. All field batteries E of the Hindenburg support system were ordered to withdraw W of it. GOC 6th Division knew that Comd 16 Bde considered his position in the bend of the canal was untenable in the face of serious attack, and he represented this view to III Corps. He was told that a general withdrawal to the Hindenburg support system would shortly take place; but a withdrawal and readjustment was carried out by 6th Division order without delay (it is most unlikely that this was done unless ordered by Putty).

According to the HQ III Corps GS log nothing more was heard until 4.45 pm when 2 Bde RFA 6th Division reported that the enemy were in Marcoing; this was confirmed five minutes later (4.50 pm) when GOC 29th Division said (probably on the telephone) the enemy were moving into Marcoing in parties of 70 and 80. Later (5.40 pm) he clarified this: 'He does not think the enemy are in Marcoing, but in Marcoing Copse. 29th Division are digging a line in L.29.central, and hourly patrols are being sent out to report on situation'.

At 6.50 pm (3 December) 29th Division reported this message received from Comd 88 Bde at 6.30 pm re situation in Marcoing:

> A few of 16 Bde in Marcoing defences – remainder driven back. GOC 16 Bde on his way up to restore situation with one bn. My bde is very cut up as a result of the morning's bombardment under which the enemy attacked and occupied trenches of SWB [2 SWB 87 Bde who had not yet been relieved by 16 Bde were almost annihilated]. On the left I have a post on lock, but the enemy are very strong opposite this point. Other reinforcements are arriving. CO 14 DLI is trying to re-establish the Reserve Line, and cover bridges across the canal, but he is very weak in numbers.

A later message from GOC 88 Bde reported: 'Failure of DLI to take up Reserve Line. State of all troops in that sector is very bad, and reinforcements are urgently required. Should the enemy capture Marcoing, the position of whole of 88 Bde will be critical'.

For Putty the situation was now very serious indeed: there was little that he could to help 6th and 29th Divisions; they would have to hang on. More help was beginning to arrive. The GS log recorded:

> 3.30 pm. 3rd Army Instructions received that VII Corps will extend their left so as to include Vaucelette Farm.

3.50 pm. 3rd Army wire placing 9th Division at disposal of III Corps from 3 pm today (3 December).

4.30 pm. III Corps G991 issued. 9th Division (less artillery) transferred to III Corps.

Also III Corps WngO G992 issued: Move of one bde 9th Division to relieve right bde of Guards Division (instead of 12th Division).

4.35 pm. III Corps G994 issued. Instructions to 20th Division that 59 Bde will be withdrawn tonight to Sorel. Also III Corps G993 issued: 108 Bde (36th Division) to occupy Reserve Line under orders of 61st Division.

5 pm. III Corps OpO No.230 issued, transferring 20th Division to IV Corps on 4 December.

5.45 pm. III Corps G998 issued. Instructions to 12th Division to withdraw those troops hitherto kept in reserve to Cav Corps to Heudicourt but to keep 500 men in reserve at Révelon Farm to be ready for any emergency (This clarifies that elements 12th Division on Révelon Ridge had remained there: also by concentrating 12th Division at Heudicourt Putty was effectively extending his right behind VII Corps).

6.30 pm. III Corps GF40 issued giving instructions to 36th Division for 108 Bde to take over on the night of 4/5 December from 88 Bde 29th Division.

11.30 pm. 3rd Army wire transferring 36th Division from V to III Corps.

The burden of staff work at HQ III Corps that day was exceptional, yet they had managed to monitor the situation with commendable accuracy so that Putty made the necessary decisions in a timely manner, and then put these decisions into effect. His four divisions had resisted the attacks of seven German divisions: now he had eight divisions under his command, all to be directed and supported in a very confined area. This support included both the reorganisation of the artillery, the redeployment of the numerous corps troops, and the many logistic requirements. Much of the performance of the AQ staff and the corps logistic units (under the DA&QMG HQ III Corps Brigadier General Hambro) is unrecorded; yet their achievements in maintaining and reconstituting the corps throughout the battle deserves as much recognition as that given to the men in the front line.

That day (3 December) Byng told Haig that he had selected a rear line which corresponded generally with the Hindenburg support system and included the defences of Flesquières (on III Corps' left flank). Haig ordered the withdrawal to commence without delay. GOC 3rd Army saw the commanders of III and V Corps that afternoon so that preliminary preparations could be put in hand. Haig wrote:

> Evening reports state that the enemy delivered repeated strong attacks from Gonnelieu NW to Marcoing. His attacks were repulsed with great loss to the enemy. All our troops seem to be on the W bank of the canal now, and we hold Marcoing to canal bank. Written orders issued to Byng in confirmation of my verbal ones this morning [withdrawal from Marcoing salient]. We impress on him the importance of some position about La Vacquerie to cover his right flank.

Putty must have represented GOC 6th Division's concerns to Byng, and he to Haig, and forcibly, for the decision was taken and the necessary orders given very quickly.

Putty must have had a long day. In the morning the priority was 6th Division and Marcoing; having been to see GOC 6th Division (Marden) in Havrincourt Wood he must have immediately telephoned Byng. His meeting with Byng later in the day could have been at his HQ in Albert (it is not recorded as having been at HQ III Corps). Guards and 61st Divisions were in the line so he would have tried to visit them, and there were also GOCs 12th, 20th and 29th Divisions to see before they left III Corps. At 7.30 pm that evening Putty awarded Military Medals to six other ranks of Corps Cav Regt at Heudicourt for gallantry in the field between 19 and 21 November. This was probably worked in with a visit to GOC 12th Division but nevertheless shows efficient staff work by all concerned including Putty's ADCs (Captain Poynter SG and Captain Loder SG) at a difficult time.

During the night 3/4 December Vincent's force 12th Division was at last broken up, its positions being taken over by 64 Bde 21st Division. Since 21st Division was not in III Corps this suggests the inter corps boundary was still awkward; with Quentin Ridge and Heudicourt in III Corps, the boundary must have given 64 Bde little depth if as seems likely it was facing E to NE.

It was not to be a quiet night for HQ III Corps with the pace of staff work and decision-making relentless. The GS log recorded (4 December – the fifth day):

> 1.45 am. 3rd Army GB326 received. Wng O for 20th Division, less artillery and pioneer bn, to be ready to entrain from Albert and Aveluy on 5 and 6 Dec. HQ III Corps issued its WngO (G17) to 20th Division for this move at 2.10 am.

The morning reports then came in:

> 4.25 am. 29th Division report Brigadier General Lucas [Comd 87 Bde] returned from reconnaissance in Marcoing, where everything is now satisfactory. Rumour that enemy had crossed bridges quite unfounded. No enemy had ever crossed, and at 8 pm [3 December] were still shelling bridges, while RE were preparing them for demolition. Junction between 6th Division and 88 Bde quite satisfactory.
> 5.45 am 12th Division morning report stated hostile artillery more active than usual. On remainder of corps front a quiet night.

Comd 87 Bde's report would have been good news.
At 6 am 4 December HQ III Corps issued OpO No.231:

i)   36th Division, less artillery, to be transferred from V to III Corps at noon 4 Dec (ie no change to OpO No.229).

ii)   36th Division to take over sectors of the front from 6th and 61st Divisions (it was also to take over 88 Bde 29th Division – HQ III Corps GF40 issued 6.30 pm 3 Dec).

iii)   9th Division to take over portion of Guards Division front and Cav Corps front (this is the portion of the Guards Division front that was to be taken over by 12th Division – HQ III Corps OpO No.229 and G992).

iv)   29th Division (less artillery) to entrain on 5 Dec (88 Bde and part of 87 Bde still in line but due to be relieved by 36th Division).

v)   Guards Division, less artillery, to entrain on 5 Dec (still in line but due to be relieved by 61st and 9th Divisions).

vi) 12th Division, less artillery, to be assembled in Etricourt area by 6 Dec and entrain on 7 Dec (subsequently amended with 12th Division marching to Tincourt).

vii) Boundaries between divisions after above moves are completed are laid down.

While this was going on the Germans were again about to attack. At 7 am HQ III Corps GS log recorded: '61st Division reported that at 6.35 am enemy put down a heavy barrage on left bde front from La Vacquerie northwards. Our own barrage came down in reply, and by 7 am all was quiet. Uncertain at present whether any infantry attack developed under enemy's barrage'.

Before describing the action on 61st Division's front it is necessary to complete the orders issued by Putty and HQ III Corps during the day (4 December). OpO No.231 had been got out quickly and there was a need for further detail or amendment:

11.20 am. III Corps G25 issued (Amendment to III Corps OpO No.231). Instructions to 9th Division to take over from Cav Corps the front from Gauche Wood to Chapel Crossing on the night 5/6 Dec, relief to be carried out under orders of the Guards Division. One bde 12th Division to remain in support until completion of relief, and then to rejoin 12th Division at Tincourt. 4 MMG Bty to corps reserve

12.28 pm. VII Corps wire. Vaucelette Farm taken over from Cav Corps (Once 9th Division was in position VII and III Corps would again be in direct contact).

1.30 pm. Cav Corps informs III Corps party of 12th Division is not required at Révelon Farm any longer. This force to be withdrawn to Heudicourt after 5 pm.

At 1.45 pm came a report from 29th Division (from Comd 88 Bde) that all was quiet near Marcoing.

The staff work continued at HQ III Corps:

4 pm. III Corps OpO No.232 issued. Transfer of 29th Division from III to IV Corps on 5 Dec.

4.30 pm. III Corps OpO No.234 issued. Guards Division transferred from III to XVII Corps on 6 Dec.

6 pm. III Corps OpO No.233 issued. Evacuation of Marcoing, Nine Wood and Bourlon Wood.

6.10 pm. III Corps G36 issued. Instructions re Reserve Line. Front and Support Lines to be dug and well wired.

8.10 pm. III Corps G44 WngO issued. 12th Division, less artillery, to be ready to move by rail on 7 and 8 Dec from Albert and Aveluy.

11 pm. III Corps G52 issued. Places 107 Bde 36th Division and 26 Bde 9th Division in corps reserve.

At 11.20 pm HQ III Corps received a copy of 6th Division's instructions to 88 Bde (under 6th Division) 'to throw back its line from the point of junction with the 61st Division to join 16 Bde covering Marcoing (its line to continue along the canal to Chateau Talma). All bridges over canal to be demolished, and approaches commanded by MG positions. 16 Bde to be responsible for guarding bridges over river, and destroying them if driven back. 9 R Irish Fus placed at disposal of 88 Bde, but only to be used to restore the situation if necessary'.

All of this represents a very considerable amount of work by HQ III Corps and by Putty. Each order and instruction had to be planned in detail and coordinated within the overall plan. There were very limited routes; the AQ staff had to ensure that logistic support was provided at all times; orders had to be disseminated in a timely way so that everyone knew what was required of them; command and control of the numerous artillery batteries left behind had to be sorted out; and all of this had to be done in contact with the enemy. Again, it reflects on the abilities of all concerned that it all worked so well.

All troops were brought back across the canal and early on the morning of 4 December the bridges were blown (five bridges were blown by 455 Fd Coy RE 29th Division). On the right now 88 Bde's line ran almost due N down the slope of Welsh Ridge to join the main position of 16 Bde which extended along the near bank of the river in and through Marcoing, all river bridges having been prepared for demolition. Forward posts covered the old crossings of the St Quentin Canal, the detachment on the left at Chateau Talma being in touch with 71 Bde which still defended the Noyelles sector.

Having captured La Vacquerie the enemy was concerned to improve its position on the slopes of Welsh Ridge and consequently 182 Bde 61st Division bore the brunt. The Germans attacked about 8.30 am after a vigorous bombardment, and fighting continued all day. Although the enemy gained ground at times he was always thrust back by counter-attacks. At 11 pm an attempt was made to clear the trenches leading to La Vacquerie, but all that was won was lost again by enemy counter-attack.

3rd Army had issued orders for the withdrawal at 9.30 am, an operation which gave up Marcoing, Nine Wood and Noyelles. III Corps issued its orders at 6 pm but 6th Division had received sufficient warning to issue its own orders nearly four hours earlier. The main bodies of infantry moved at 11 pm when platoon after platoon began to dribble back from the front. In 6th Division the retirement of 88 Bde 29th Division on the right to the new line was followed by its relief by 108 Bde 36th Division. From Premy Chapel (inclusive) for a thousand yards southward the covering position was manned by 71 Bde; 18 Bde withdrew from Cantaing and took over the left portion of the covering position. On being relieved Brigadier General Nelson Comd 88 Bde collapsed and for three days was unconscious; he did not fully recover for six months.

On 4 December, the day that 20th Division left III Corps, HQ RE log recorded III Corps with 6th Division (HQ Havrincourt Wood), 12th Division (HQ Liéramont), 29th Division (HQ Trescault), 61st Division (HQ Metz), Guards Division (HQ Neuville), 9th Division (HQ Haut Allaines) and 36th Division (HQ Léchelle).

Haig wrote on 4 December:

> At Templeux I saw General Pulteney, III Corps. He looked tired and had obviously passed through an anxious time. He told me about the enemy's attack on 30 November. Apparently patrols had gone out as usual in the early morning, found nothing unusual, and all then proceeded to breakfast. There seems to have been no warning of the attack, and the enemy swept through the front held by the left of 55th Division (VII Corps) and parts of 12th and 20th Divisions. The position rushed is immensely strong, but the defenders seem to have put up little or no fight at all. The enemy attacked in great numbers preceded by 'stoss-truppen'. Some of the latter were taken prisoner a mile W of Gouzeaucourt. Luckily the Guards Division happened to be near the latter village and were marching back to rest (ie westwards) with bands playing. On hearing of the trouble troops were at once faced

about, and they advanced eastwards. Crowds of fugitives of all branches of the service were streaming back, some without arms or equipment. By this time the enemy were on the ridge W of Gouzeaucourt so the Guards at once deployed and after some heavy fighting cleared the ridge and retook Gouzeaucourt which is in the valley beyond. I also went round the artillery office of III Corps, and complimented the CRA Tancred [Brigadier General Tancred] on what he had done. He looked very tired. Most of his heavy artillery had been taken, but we have managed to reinforce him with more than he has lost.

The CinC's record is inaccurate in several respects, particularly about the Guards Division. The artillery may have been reinforced but the ammunition expenditure seems very low (DA 10,604 and HA 3,104) considering the severity of the battle.

It was quiet overnight but the sixth day (5 December) brought no let up. On the left of III Corps, 6th Division reported at 7.10 am: 'Withdrawal of left brigade completed without difficulty. No news from other brigades as wires cut'. Then at 8 am: '16 Bde withdrew from Marcoing successfully. Centre bde (71 Bde) all complete except one bn'. Finally at 8.40 am they were able to confirm that all movements of infantry and guns had been completed. The division had withdrawn to its new position with an outpost line forward, but there was to be no rest. 6th Division reported at 12.58 pm that the enemy were still shelling Cantaing heavily with 5.9s; at 2.15 pm they passed on a message from 59th Division that the enemy was coming down side of Bourlon Wood in large numbers; and at 3.40 pm they reported 'Left bde (18 Bde) reports enemy advancing on NW corner of Nine Wood; also advancing from Bourlon Wood on Graincourt'.

HQ III Corps issued G77 at 3.50 pm to 36th, 61st and 6th Divisions: 'Aeroplane reports our line (gave details). If this is correct, 6th and 61st Divisions to arrange to occupy original outpost line tonight to ensure observation down valleys'. The dead ground was again giving cause for concern. But the enemy was closing fast on 6th Division and they reported at 4.35 pm: 'Left bde reports outposts in touch with enemy, who are 600 yards away, all along the line'.

Meanwhile 61st Division was also attacked; again, the III Corps GS log recorded its key reports:

At 6.45 am our artillery fired on SOS line in answer to heavy enemy barrage near La Vacquerie. From 6 to 7 am our HA and FA vigorously bombarded enemy front system and approaches.

12.41 pm. Enemy artillery active along front of left sector all morning. Posts of ours driven back by bombing attacks at 10.30 am, but since regained.

5.20 pm. At 3.15 pm enemy opened a heavy barrage along front from La Vacquerie northwards. 182 Bde report attack made on their left bn, but no news yet as wires are cut. At 3.50 pm fire slackened all along front. Two coys Innis Fus [probably 9 Innis Fus] had already arrived in relief of 182 Bde, and remainder of 109 Bde (36th Division) is now ready to move.

5.30 pm. Enemy holds part of trench. Two coys Innis Fus have arrived and have been ordered to attack this trench. Enemy attack on remainder of front believed repulsed.

10.35 pm. Enemy made three attempts in succession to advance from the western side of Corner Work against the coy in Corner Support. Attacks were made under an intense barrage lasting 30 minutes, but repulsed each time.

11.15 pm. 183 Bde report the capture of Foster Lane (part) and that patrols are being pushed out towards Cambrai Road.

The official history noted:

> After an intense bombardment, German attacks were delivered at 10.30 am along Ostrich Avenue, now almost completely shattered by shell-fire, and up the Hindenburg front system. When the German efforts slackened about 1.30 pm 182 Bde 61st Division had yielded no ground whatever. At 3 pm there was a fresh onslaught on 182 Bde, the Germans advancing eastward along Ostrich Avenue and northward over the open against the same objective. Despite a successful counter-attack the Germans were left in possession of the Hindenburg front system to a point not far below the crest of the ridge.

The relief of 182 Bde 61st Division by 109 Bde 36th Division was completed that night.

During the evening (5 December) HQ III Corps issued G81 at 7 pm: 'Reference III Corps OpO No.233. The outpost line will continue to be held N of Premy Chapel, but withdrawn S of it'. Later, at 11.15 pm, GF41 was issued cancelling this: 'Outpost Line to be withdrawn tomorrow at the hour notified to those concerned'.

29th Division left III Corps on 5 December. GOC 29th Division issued a Special Order of the Day conveying Putty's message to his division:

> The corps commander would like to place on record his deep appreciation of the fighting spirit of the 29th Division. The magnificent defence of the Masnières-Marcoing line at a most critical juncture and the subsequent orderly withdrawal reflects the highest credit on all concerned. In the fifteen days in which your division has been in action on this front all ranks have displayed an endurance which is beyond praise. He would be grateful if this could be conveyed to your troops.

The battle continued into its seventh day on 6 December; again it had been comparatively quiet overnight. III Corps now had four divisions in the line: from L to R 6th, 36th, 61st and 9th Divisions. By 9.50 am 6th Division was able to report that its outposts had been withdrawn and for the rest of the day they observed the enemy closing up and threatening their left flank. V Corps, on their left, reported at 4.15 pm that their outposts had all be driven back to the main line of resistance, and soon afterwards that the enemy was attacking Flesquières.

Having taken over part of the line from 6th and 61st Divisions, 36th Division's main problem was on its right where the enemy still held the trench it had captured during the relief. 36th Division reported that it was to be attacked early 6 December but it was not until 5.11 pm that it reported: 'Right bde succeeded in driving enemy out of trench, taking 7 prisoners (from 2/495 Regt), but were themselves bombed out by noon. Efforts by enemy to penetrate further were frustrated'. Perhaps it was the absence of information or maybe Putty had visited HQ 36th Division and realised this vital ground was again under threat but at 4 pm 6 December HQ III Corps issued G127:

> Any further advance by enemy from trench they have occupied must be stopped by MG enfilade and Stokes mortar fire. 'The corps commander directs that every possible means be taken to prevent any further advance of the enemy from the trench they have reoccupied. Machine-gun enfilade fire will be brought to bear on it in order to make it untenable by

the enemy. The trench leading from it into our trench will be blocked with wire'. SPA Rolls Capt (GSO3 HQ III Corps).

Neither 61st Division nor 9th Division had much to report during the day (6 December), both were heavily involved in reliefs. At 3.20 pm HQ III Corps issued G126 ordering 36th Division to relieve more of 61st Division. Late that evening 61st Division sent in its artillery programme for 7 December to HQ III Corps; this was unusual as was its content: '6.10-6.30 am, and 7.40-8 am FA to start barrage on SOS line, creep forward 500 yards and return at 100 yards in 2 minutes. Rate 1 round per gun per minute. HA are to cooperate'.

Later that night 3rd Army altered the boundary between III and V Corps, and the bn of 59th Division, still with 6th Division, was ordered to return to its parent division by 9 am 7 December. This order was cancelled the following day when V Corps sent a message that the bn could remain with 6th Division while in the present line. Guards and 12th Divisions left III Corps that night; now only 6th Division remained of the divisions that started the battle.

Rain fell during the night (6/7 December), a prelude to the milder weather which followed the frosty spell. Work on the defences continued, patrols were active on both sides, and artillery and machine-gun fire was opened at intervals on those localities where the Germans appeared to be digging-in. HQ III Corps GS log recorded at 6 am 7 December (eighth day):

> Morning reports from divisions show hostile artillery inactive on our front line, except on the left bde front of 6th Division, which was heavily shelled. Both artilleries, however, were engaged in heavy counter-battery work throughout the night.

6th Division had patrols out during the night but apart from the occasional patrol contact and some new wiring there was little of significance detected. At 12.48 pm 36th Division reported their attack on enemy in trench had been successful, but there was still much to be done to strengthen the line.

Throughout the day HQ III Corps was tidying up after all the changes in deployment, and there was an enormous amount to be done: boundaries had to be clearly established; artillery, engineer and pioneer units had to be returned to their parent divisions; corps troops' units had to be rested and reorganised; and logistic units had to be redeployed and new arrangements made. All of this had to be done as quickly as possible in poor weather and over roads that had deteriorated over the past three weeks. Yet by the end of 7 December III Corps had withdrawn to its main line of resistance for the winter, an operation that was carried out with complete success; the new line ran from Flesquières (inclusive) to La Vacquerie (exclusive) and Gonnelieu (exclusive).

At 1.30 am on 8 December (ninth and last day) 3rd Army GB468 was received transferring 19th Division from VI Corps to III Corps that day. The morning reports at 6 am recorded: 'Situation quiet. Hostile artillery active during the night on back areas. Left sector of 6th Division front shelled between 10 and 11 pm'. 6th Division was about to be relieved at last. At 3.50 pm HQ III Corps issued G291: Orders for 57 Bde 19th Division, arriving at Etricourt tonight (8 December), to relieve reserve bde 6th Division on night 9/10 December. Reserve bde 6th Division to proceed to Sorel on relief. At 4 pm orders were issued for 57 Bde to be in corps reserve until required for relief, and the remainder of 19th Division was to come into corps reserve on arrival at Etricourt.

The evening report at 6 pm recorded a relatively quiet day with intermittent shelling of parts of the line, Quentin Ridge and Gouzeaucourt. Two other ranks 227 Regt were captured. Later at 11 pm HQ III Corps issued OpO No.235 – Transfer of 19th Division from VI to III Corps on 8 December; GO2334/28 – arranging for defences to fit in with the defences of corps on the right; GO6944 – Trace showing boundaries between divisions in the corps; GO6948 – allotting areas to divisions for sites for artillery positions to cover Reserve Line; and GO6549 – Instructions for valleys to be well covered by MG fire. This last included: 'During recent attacks, the enemy have managed to gain considerable ground by assembling in and working up the beds of the valleys, which in some cases were not sufficiently well covered by machine-gun fire. The corps commander attaches great importance to the adequate protection of valleys, as he considers any attack launched in future will be largely directed up the valleys. He wishes divisions therefore to ensure that all valleys leading into their sectors are well wired across, and strong points established in the valleys with machine-guns sited to fire along them'.

The Battle of Cambrai had ended; the recriminations and inquiries were about to begin. III Corps casualties in the battle (20 November-8 December) were: 6th Division 115 officers and 1,754 other ranks = 1,869; 12th Division 230 officers and 4,606 other ranks = 4,836; 20th Division 148 officers and 2,816 other ranks = 2,964; 29th Division 184 officers and 4,232 other ranks = 4,416. This totals 677 officers and 13,408 other ranks = 14,085. Of this total 1,148 were killed and 2,846 missing/taken prisoner. 6,000 of the total casualties were in November and mainly 20 and 21 November: the other 8,000 were in the German counter-attack that started on 30 November. 12th Division's casualties on 30 November were 164 officers and 3,362 other ranks = 3,526 (about 75% of all its casualties in the battle). Most of the 2,341 taken prisoner in the battle were captured on 30 November (25% of all III Corps' casualties that day). These figures do not include the casualties of 2nd Cavalry Division, Guards, 9th, 36th and 61st Divisions.

That evening (8 December) Putty wrote to Ettie Desborough:

Dearest Chief, Was too delighted to get your letter of 5 December this afternoon. Practically the only consolation this week was the ejection of the Huns from S Africa otherwise it looks like a black December similar to 99 in S Africa, the Boche troops are pouring in from Russia one of the men I captured last night states he was relieved by a Polish volunteer division! The news from Italy too is none too good obviously the Boche is endeavouring to force a decision and I expect it will take us all our time to keep Italy a going concern. The counter-attack on the 30 November hit me hard owing to the left of the next corps collapsing altogether and uncovering my right, the Guards saved the day and Crawley de Crespigny[4] deserves immortal fame for the way he led the counter-attack if the cavalry had been as quick with their horses as the Guards were with their feet we should have retrieved much more it was the most anxious day I have spent this war but DH was very complimentary on what I had done. I think that Lansdowne's[5] letter was hopeless unless the Govt tried to feel the pulse of the country that way and have since played Judas to him, otherwise it was a document bordering on senile decay as far as I as a soldier am

4   Brigadier General Champion de Crespigny late Gren Gds Comd 1 Gds Bde.
5   Henry Charles Keith Petty-Fitzmaurice 5th Marquess of Lansdowne (1845-1927) Eton previously SofS for War and Foreign Affairs 1895-1905 published Lansdowne Letter in 1917 calling for negotiated peace based on situation in 1914.

concerned. Don't do anything about the Xmas present yet for as matters now stand there is a chance of my coming over some time about the 17th according to present arrangements but if I don't the diamond arrow pin appeals to me but will write again on the subject, I rather think of coming over and taking Jessie to Paris for Xmas. Best of love for ever Putty.

Overnight (8/9 December) there was considerable enemy shelling of roads and approaches in the back areas but otherwise quiet. It was not one-sided: III Corps RA reported at 11 am 9 December: 'At 4 pm 8 December 4.5" hows fired 180 rounds into Gonnelieu. Harassing fire carried out during the night on all roads and approaches. HA fired occasional bursts into Villers-Guislain and Gonnelieu'. The evening report at 5.45 pm was much the same: 'Hostile artillery fairly active on forward and back areas, Havrincourt Wood being persistently shelled. Captures 2 ORs, one belonging to 232 Regt 107th Division'. Havrincourt Wood was getting attention probably because the enemy had detected the relief of 6th Division by 19th Division.

The coordinating staff work continued as HQ III Corps issued G226 at 11 am, amending OpO No.235: Orders that 6th Division will remain in corps reserve and are being relieved by 19th Division. Then, at 5.45 pm, GO6972: NH (Corps Cav Regt) and III Corps Cyclist Bn allotted to 9th Division for defence of reserve line; GO6973: Instructions in the event of the enemy attempting to regain the lost Hindenburg Line; and GO2334/29: III Corps Provisional Defence Scheme.

During the day Putty sent his monthly report to the King with the usual covering letter:

My dear Wigram, Am afraid III Corps diary is late this month for Their Majesties but it is entirely owing to the Boche. The tank attack on the 20th Nov was a most unqualified success and I got all my objectives with 3,500 prisoners and 50 guns, if it had not been for the bridge at Masnières giving way under the tank the cavalry would have taken Cambrai from the E and personally think could have nearly done it from the W but only on the first day but I think it as well that we did not because it made our perimeter so enormous we offered weak points everywhere. Was at breakfast on 30 Nov, at 7.30 they told me the Boche was attacking the corps on my right, then we heard the barrage had died down, at 8 am!! the enemy had completely rolled up the left of the next corps and were pouring through on my right flank through the Villers-Guislain and Gouzeaucourt valleys, fortunately the Guards were in reserve not far behind, Feilding [Major General Feilding GOC Guards Division] came to see me, fortunately I knew every inch of the ground gave him his orders to hold the Beachamp (Beaucamp) Ridge and clear the Gouzeaucourt valley, de Crespigny (Comd 1 Gds Bde) was commanding the leading brigade, he galloped forward to reconnoitre through an undisciplined rabble of men, road repairers etc all mixed together, he grasped the situation deployed his brigade and cleared the valley and after hard fighting Gouzeaucourt, it was a magnificent counter-attack which was launched on the moment without any artillery support, it completely restored the situation in that valley, the next morning they pushed out and captured the ridge which overlooks Gouzeaucourt, they took Gonnelieu but could not hold on to it, La Vacquerie going two days later was a great blow as it overlooks all the valley (between ourselves it ought not to have gone) since then the attacks have been very local on both sides and much consolidation going on; 12th and 20th Divisions were disappointing but 6th and 29th fought magnificently, with only one exception the gunners were magnificent though our losses in guns were heavy the enemy paid very heavily for their capture, all the attacks were made up the valleys while the heights were barraged very extensively, they came on in great masses like they used to at the beginning of the war and drove their wedges in by sheer weight of numbers, the attack was cleverly timed because the morning patrols had come in, most of the men were having their breakfast when the attack began without any preliminary bombardment, it was a fine effort which deserved success, from all sides the bravery of the Boche on that day was duly acknowledged, I must own that I felt a good deal older after it and have not quite got over it, but all the prisoners say that their casualties have been very heavy indeed, the divisions arriving lately in front of me have all come from Russia one man declared that his division was relieved by a division of Polish volunteers! There is a certain amount of adjustment going on at present and if matters go on as at present I expect to be taken out of the line about 16th and take the fortnight's leave I didn't get the last time. It is as mild now as it was cold three days ago but alas the rain has come with it, we had 10 degrees of frost last Wednesday and the thaw has broken up any roads that had chalk as foundation, the effect of the combustion is really very curious. Am afraid the Italians are having another anxious time of it. Yours sincerely WP Pulteney.

The night of 9/10 December was again quiet apart from intermittent artillery activity by both sides. 36th Division made more progress, reporting that they had pushed along Emden Trench and established a new block. There was more activity during the day with a considerable number of enemy aircraft overhead and many enemy balloons up. Gouzeaucourt was heavily shelled, and the artillery of both sides was active on forward and back areas: one OR from 30 Regt was captured. HQ III Corps issued OpO No.236 at 12.15 pm. 61st Divisional Artillery was to be transferred to III Corps on 12 December; in a separate instruction 16 Bde 6th Division was placed at the disposal of VI Corps from 11 December and ordered to move to Courcelles Le Comte on the same day.

Again it was quiet overnight (10/11 December) and III Corps' patrols continued to dominate no man's land; one prisoner was captured belonging to 262 Regt. HQ III Corps issued G285 at 2.40 pm cancelling III Corps OpO No.236 issued the day before; G292 at 7 pm – 6th Division, less artillery, to be transferred from III Corps to VI Corps on 14 December; and G297 at 10.05 pm – one bde 63rd Division in Barastre area to move to Etricourt on 12 December. The night 12/13 December was very quiet: at 12.40 am 19th Division reported their relief of 6th Division completed. Between 6 am and 7 am all corps artillery fired on the SOS line, and concentrations were also fired during the day on Gonnelieu, Villers-Guislain and La Vacquerie (DA fired 20,660 rounds and HA 5,398 rounds).

Byng visited Putty at 12.30 pm 13 December and may well have stayed for lunch. This is his first recorded visit since before 20 November. During the day HQ III Corps issued G330 at 9.45 am ordering all detachments NH (Corps Cav Regt) to rejoin their regiment at Manancourt by 14 December and, at 1 pm, instructions to divisions to return all men III Corps Cyclist Bn to Aizecourt le Bas by same date. After GOC 3rd Army's visit, at 4.15 pm, HQ III Corps issued OpO No.238 – withdrawal of III Corps into army reserve at noon 15 December with a list showing troops to be transferred to V (on left) and VII (on right) Corps.

Putty was intending to move with Corps Cav Regiment and Corps Cyclist Bn and orders to this effect were issued at 8.30 pm (Addendum No.1 to III Corps OpO No.238) but this was cancelled at 11.50 pm when HQ 3rd Army instructions were received that they were to stay in present area and work under V Corps. Little has been said about these units but both played an invaluable part in HQ III Corps' command, control, communications and intelligence gathering during the battle.

At 9.30 pm (13 December) 3rd Army ordered HQ 98 HAG to be transferred from 1st to 3rd Army (VII Corps) in relief of HQ 26 HAG located near Fins. The next 48 hours were going to be very busy for the staff of HQ III Corps as the corps they had built up and fought during the past four weeks was dismembered, each unit requiring the same careful consideration on leaving the corps as when it joined. However, it would be easier this time because HQ III Corps was leaving the line with only a few corps troops: most of the corps would be staying put and join V or VII Corps who would extend their line to the right and left respectively. That evening Putty presented Military Medals to five other ranks of NH (Corps Cav Regt) at Manancourt.

Once again it was quiet overnight although there was much patrol activity; three ORs from 161 Regt were captured. The staff work at HQ III Corps continued with instructions issued for 20th and 29th Divisional Artillery to move out of III Corps area and rejoin their parent divisions. III Corps GO7039 was also issued transferring RE units from III Corps on 15 December. 6th Division finally left the corps on 14 December. Finally, that evening HQ III Corps issued GO7067: Relief of enemy divisions on corps front – possible renewal of enemy's offensive. This may well have been the result of new identifications achieved by the aggressive patrolling on the corps front in recent days, but it also ensured divisions were fully alert during the change in corps command.

The last night (14/15 December) was quiet on the whole corps front and at 12 noon III Corps handed over command of the line to V and VII Corps. At the same time HQ III Corps closed at Templeux-la-Fosse, the ruined village where it had been since 30 October, and moved to Beauquesne where it occupied the chateau in which Haig had his forward HQ in 1916. HQ 3rd Army issued orders that day that 36th Division, less artillery, was to be transferred from V to III Corps and to move to the area round Mondicourt 16-18 December. Next day 47th Division, less artillery, with its HQ at Baizieux was placed under HQ III Corps for administration.

The exact date of Putty's departure on leave for his delayed honeymoon is not recorded, nor is the appointment of anyone acting in his absence. It was almost certainly on 16 December because the HQ III Corps Opsum recorded:

> During the latter half of the month the weather became very cold and heavy snowfalls occurred making communications and movement of troops very difficult. For some days corps headquarters was completely isolated, and could only be reached on foot.

Also Byng wrote to GHQ on 18 December in response to the increasing political pressure for investigation and inquiry into events on 30 November:

> III Corps has been withdrawn from the line and the corps commander is at present on leave. I have therefore not been able to obtain his remarks on the reports of the 12th, 20th and 29th Divisions

For the rest of the month HQ III Corps was at Beauquesne in reserve; the divisions under its command were there primarily for administration. On Christmas Day 59th Division less artillery joined III Corps but left again on the night 31 December/1 January. 36th Division left III Corps for 5th Army on 28 December (III Corps OpO No.240 issued 11.45 am 24 December) and on 30 December at 3.20 pm 47th Division was ordered to send one bde (142 Bde) to V Corps on account of an enemy attack. At the end of the year III Corps consisted of 47th Division less 142 Bde and a small number of corps troops.

III Corps casualties for December 1917 were: 86 officers and 955 other ranks killed, 273 officers and 5,291 other ranks wounded, 106 officers and 3,472 other ranks missing = 10,183. If the November figure (6,000) is added to it this makes 16,000 casualties for the two months. 14,000 were in the four divisions (6th, 12th, 20th and 29th) of III Corps that started the battle: the other divisions (2nd Cavalry, Guards, 9th, 36th and 61st) therefore had 2,000 casualties between them. III Corps total casualties in 1917 were 30,349.

On 27 December Colonel Repington (*The Times*) wrote:

> I met at lunch Field Marshal Lord French, Sir William Pulteney and his bride, and Sir Arthur Paget. Putty's account of Cambrai is not cheering. The Boches, to the number of 6 divisions, came on in massed formations like a steam plough, and burst in. The 55th Division gave way, and then the 20th and 12th, and the Boches reached our guns and took most of them; but the Guards counter-attacked successfully, many guns were re-taken, and things more or less re-established. Putty says that the chief defence was made by small groups of old soldiers, including gunners and oddments, and that the Boche did not know what to do when he had burst in. Putty says that the divisions had enough machine-guns to mow down the enemy (as) he was mown down at Moeuvres, but he thinks our officers have become so bad that the army is not worth 50 per cent of what it was in 1914.

General Sir Arthur Paget (GOC 1st Army in Central Force at Home) in a letter to his wife on 31 December wrote:

> Pulteney is back he did gloriously and with the help of the Guards Division shoved in at the right spot and time by him there would have been disaster at Cambrai. Byng is no use a cavalry division is the outside of his capacity.

It was New Year's Eve but the sense is clear.
Also on New Year's Eve Repington wrote:

> Lunched with Sir W and Lady Pulteney at the Ritz. Putty and I told stories of our youthful days from Eton onward. Had a talk with him alone afterwards. He does not think the Boches can beat us in France but admits that the battalions are very weak. He thinks that the Boches may retake Welsh Ridge and Highland Ridge at Cambrai, as they are salients. Bits of them were bitten off yesterday. He has had 50 divisions through his hands in 3rd Army Corps since the war began. He does not think that the GHQ come often enough round the fronts, but at Cambrai a number turned up, including X, and Putty told him he must be unwell.

The spectacular success of 20 November was not that it achieved its objective; it did not. Its success was that it demonstrated British superiority especially in its ability to overcome the strongest defence. In 1914 it was the standard of marksmanship of the British infantry that gave that superiority through the period of survival. As both sides built up their numbers of heavy guns and machine-guns, neither side had superiority in the years of stalemate. Now the situation had changed again for the British because of their improvements in artillery and aircraft, and the development of tanks. When these were coordinated effectively with the infantry there was now a chance of breakthrough and ultimate victory.

Putty had just three weeks to collect together a completely new corps; then to brief, prepare and train it for an operation that was more complex than anything that had happened before. All the preparations had to be done in complete secrecy because the operation depended for its success on achieving surprise at Zero hour. More than 100,000 men with their tanks, guns and supplies had to be assembled beforehand in a very confined space, without being detected. Commanders are rightly criticised when operations go wrong, so deserve credit when they succeed. It would have been a team effort and every man in III Corps would have played a part in the preparations but Putty had to make the key decisions and ensure everyone knew what was required of them. By the autumn of 1917 HQ III Corps was well-practiced and efficient; under Putty's leadership it did exceptionally well in the preparation for battle.

Some things did go wrong on 20 November; above all the final objective of breaking through the Masnières-Beaurevoir Line, and passing through the Cav Corps, was not achieved. For this Putty must answer, along with those above and below him. To achieve that final objective, sufficient momentum had to be maintained throughout. With hindsight it is clear that momentum was lost some time around noon on 20 November, and it is also evident that this happened because too much effort had been given to breaking through the Hindenburg defence system, and too little left for the crossing of the canal and taking the final objective. The Hindenburg defence system was considered by many to be impregnable and Putty would have erred on too much rather than too little force to break through it. Some have criticised Haig and Byng for not providing more forces but this analysis is focussed on Putty and his corps.

216 tanks were allocated to III Corps (6 bns each of 36 tanks), yet only 12 of these were allocated to 29th Division. There was no plan to reconstitute a tank reserve once the Hindenburg defence system had been taken, and when an attempt was made there were no spare fascines to equip them so that they could cross the enemy trenches beyond the canal. Just one bn of 36 tanks, refuelled, re-armed and re-equipped with fascines might have made a difference. There was similar inflexibility with the infantry. It would have been possible to bring one bde from 6th or 12th Division into corps reserve at an early stage of the battle and then provide this to 29th Division when, if not before, momentum was lost. Such re-grouping occurred frequently later in the battle but does not seem to have been considered at the outset. The artillery effort also lost momentum. Some attempt was made to bridge the enemy trenches in the Hindenburg defence system so that guns could be moved forward to support 29th Division. However, the fire planning did not provide for the full force of the corps artillery to be brought to bear on 29th Division's objective; much more could have been done.

The Cav Corps have been criticised because Kavanagh (GOC) was too far back and because of a perceived lack of resolve in his corps. The first criticism overlooks the fact that Adv HQ Cav Corps was well forward at Fins. As to the latter, it is surprising that some cavalry were not dismounted to assist 29th Division when momentum was lost, but it was for III Corps to make the breech.

Some of the momentum was lost crossing the canal. There were bridges at Marcoing and Masnières and most of the focus was on them; when the Masnières bridge collapsed alternatives were not immediately apparent, and yet they should have been. There were other bridges that could have been used; military bridging could have been deployed more quickly; and some if not all the two and a half divisions of cavalry waiting at Masnières could have been switched to Marcoing. The Masnières road bridge was given much prominence in the planning, in sharp contrast to any recorded engineer intelligence on all the crossing options. Apart from the road bridges at Marcoing and Masnières, both of which may have been suspect for tanks on width and weight, there was also the railway bridge at Marcoing apparently used by some tanks. There were also two wooden bridges either side of Masnières, at least one of which was discovered by Can Cav Bde, and there were also the locks which could be crossed by the cavalry albeit with difficulty and very slowly, as demonstrated by FGH. It is strange that the cavalry were not aware of all the options; also, despite Seely's comments, it is of note that 2nd Cavalry Division had specifically trained for crossing canals in the early years of the war. It is difficult to avoid the conclusion that sufficient bridges for tanks and cavalry existed, even without Masnières, and that the issue was lack of engineer intelligence provided to and by HQ RE III Corps. This is compounded by the lack of Cav Corps LOs, their own reconnaissance, and by any preparation of their own. There is evidence of an LO with 6th Division and here liaison with 1st Cavalry Division worked well.

There was also the military bridging available, although there is no III Corps' record of when the two pontoon bridges of 29th Division were deployed on 20 November or the contribution they made other than to assist the crossing of the infantry. Brigadier General Schreiber CE III Corps concentrated his attention on the corps heavy bridging, which was deployed too late and at a site where it had no influence on the battle. However, the deployment of heavy bridging was not the main engineer contribution to the loss of momentum it was the lack of engineer intelligence. HQ RE III Corps did not appear to know where the bridges were or their classification, consequently the forward troops had to find out for themselves with inevitable delays. Some innovative thought such as prefabrication of bridges for cavalry to cross at the locks might have made a difference.

Haig had reminded Byng and he in turn Putty, albeit late in the day, of the importance he attached to securing crossings on the right flank (at Crèvecoeur) in order for the French to break out to the S. The Lucknow Cav Bde with III Corps Cav Regt was given the task of securing a bridgehead to the SE and was to cross at Masnières after 2nd and 5th Cavalry Divisions. This was changed later in the day to Crèvecoeur by which time it was too late. However, very early on 20 November, possibly by 10 am, 12th Division had crossed the Banteux Bridge and into Bantouzelle without encountering any Germans. Considering the Lucknow Cav Bde could have been there in ten minutes this was an opportunity missed but the command, control and communication arrangements made such flexibility almost impossible.

20 November was a spectacular success for III Corps but more could have been achieved. Momentum was lost before the final objective was taken and the principle reason for this was the lack of reserves to assist 29th Division: after breaking through the Hindenburg Line, Putty could have reconstituted a reserve to maintain the momentum, and if supported by the full weight of the corps artillery, the Masnières-Beaurevoir Line could have been taken on 20

November. Even with wireless it would have been difficult to arrange this during the battle but it could have been planned in advance, and it was not. The failings of the Cav Corps are not relevant to Putty's story; perhaps they could and should have done more to get forward, but they could and did argue that it was for III Corps to make the breech, and they did not.

Putty's failure to take the final objective was overlooked in the euphoria of the breakthrough of the Hindenburg Line, the last minute German reinforcement from Russia, and the consequent relief that the Cav Corps was not passed through. However, it resulted in III Corps consolidating a position of no particular importance, and one that was very difficult to defend. The decision that III Corps should go on the defensive was made quickly by Haig but, as was so often the case, Putty was not given the flexibility to withdraw to ground of his choosing: all the ground gained had to be consolidated and held. Perhaps Haig and Byng still thought further progress was possible but that seems unlikely, and all would have known that a German counter-attack was probable, if not inevitable.

The ground to be held by III Corps was in many respects immensely strong, being on dominant high ground and behind a major obstacle, the canal. 29th Division should have been the weakest link having managed to get across the canal but not secured the high ground beyond it. There were three main weaknesses in III Corps' position – the salient, the convex slopes and the right boundary, and the Germans exploited each one to their advantage and with good effect. There was little that Putty could have done about the salient with its extended line and lack of depth, other than remonstrate with Byng: he had been told to hold it. It did produce some very strange deployments which were to affect the battle: HQ 20th Division and its reserve were behind 12th Division; HQ 35 Bde and its reserve behind 55th Division (VII Corps). There was such limited space in the salient that HQ 12th and 29th Divisions could not get forward. Communications ran laterally behind the front line in many places, and there were only two routes forward into the salient. Most artillery positions were awkward with problems of crest clearance for the guns; batteries were very close together and had to be prepared to engage on a very wide front. The war had shown the vulnerability of a salient many times and this position was no exception.

12th and 20th Divisions were on high ground but the slopes in front of them were mainly convex. Commanders were faced with difficult choices: to hold forward in full observation of the enemy and under constant artillery fire; to hold back giving up ground; or to hold somewhere in between where there would be little warning and the ranges would be short. Both GOC 12th and 20th Divisions went for the third option, presumably with Putty's agreement if not under his orders; and there was in reality no choice other than to give ground: and there was very little to give. GOC 20th Division did deploy a very weak observation line forward to give warning and provide delay but in the event it did neither. Some of the most difficult convex slopes were in the valleys that run from the canal valley up and into the position. No weapon sited on the slopes could engage the bottom of the valley: a well wired strong point in the bottom was a solution but again the shape of the slope often allowed this to be isolated and destroyed. It did not help that the mist hung in these valleys until late in the mornings.

Much has been written about the boundary between III and VII Corps. At the time of the German counter-attack it ran E-W, N of the Banteux Ravine; the ravine itself was VII Corps' responsibility. After Gonnelieu the boundary was considered somewhat flexible and not delineated. Putty considered Vaucellette Farm, Chapel Crossing and Farm, and Révelon Ridge to be in III Corps' area, although VII Corps also deployed troops there. There was also a dispute about Gouzeaucourt and whose responsibility it was; there was a suggestion that it was behind

III Corps' rear boundary and therefore the responsibility of HQ 3rd Army. What seems beyond dispute is that insufficient attention was given by 3rd Army to this boundary, its location and delineation into the rear areas, and coordination across it.

The evidence suggests that III Corps was surprised by the German counter-attack but not in the way that has been suggested by some historians. The intelligence coming down from GHQ was unequivocal that the enemy was in no position to make a major offensive in retaliation for the British success on 20 November. Yet everyone knew that a counter-attack, however limited, was inevitable. Faced with the intelligence, Putty would have reasonably expected the main enemy objective to be to destroy 29th Division, forcing III Corps back across the canal, and that any other attacks would be peripheral to prevent redeployment. The surprise was in the size of the attack, its speed and its direction. Snow (GOC VII Corps) having received information from GOC 55th Division was convinced but Putty was not persuaded, perhaps because 3rd Army was not persuaded, or maybe because GOC 12th Division did not pass on the concerns he was receiving forcibly enough. The German achievement of surprise can not have been a matter of chance. They would have known that III Corps could neither see into nor bring observed fire into the Bantouzelle-Crèvecoeur stretch of the canal. Air reconnaissance would have shown them that the boundary between III and VII Corps was a weak spot and that the approaches up the valleys or re-entrants were not strongly held: all this would have been confirmed by patrols. Furthermore they would have known the limitations of III Corps' patrols and timed their attack accordingly. The mist and the short, devastating artillery bombardment did the rest.

An overall summary is that III Corps' position was potentially very strong but it did have serious weaknesses. The Germans identified and exploited them, and this was greatly assisted by intelligence assessments that under-estimated the German strength and resolve. Despite this, III Corps could and arguably should have destroyed the German attacks with little difficulty. That they did not can be attributed to a number of weaknesses in the defence planning.

III Corps had a major obstacle in front of its position but then had no observation of it: in the event it was no obstacle at all. Nearly three German divisions crossed it undetected. III Corps relied on air reconnaissance but this was of limited value at night and in the mist. The German crossing was made even easier because III Corps had not destroyed some (perhaps all) of the bridges in this sector, when they had the opportunity to do so. There should have been ground observation at all times; GOC 12th Division was well aware of this but never achieved it. Even if the right flank was considered low risk, this was still a likely enemy approach, and one that could not be observed, so it is very surprising, considering the strength of III Corps Artillery, that pre-registered harassing fire was not put down on the crossings and forming up points by the howitzers, especially those of the heavy artillery, throughout the night. This should also have been done on the entrances to the re-entrants leading up and into the positions. The Somme demonstrated the value of strong points, and the enemy provided a reminder on 20 November. They gave the defence greater strength, particularly when they were mutually supporting and in depth. Well-wired strong points in the re-entrants might have been bypassed because of the convex slopes, but they would have certainly delayed the enemy. There were very few strong points and none of the villages had been organised for defence. Villers-Guislain, Gonnelieu and Gouzeaucourt should not have been taken as easily; there were more than enough troops in them, had they been organised and prepared for defence.

Finally there was no corps reserve: each division had a bde or equivalent as its reserve, and III Corps could, and did, make use of them but it needed a dedicated reserve of its own to intervene quickly and effectively where the threat was greatest and could not be dealt with by the division. This reserve had to be mobile so that it could move quickly to counter any enemy penetration. Available for this were III Corps Cavalry Regt, at least three btys RHA, III Corps Cyclist Bn, III Corps MMG Bty and the tanks. The best reserve of all and one that could have been deployed rapidly to any part of the battlefield was the RFC, and they would have been invaluable in support of the Guards Division. The enemy achieved air superiority on 30 November but it should have been still possible to operate, and yet there is very little evidence of RFC operations over III Corps on that day.

Taken together these measures alone in the planning of the defence would have made it much more effective. They might have stopped the German offensive at the outset but at the very least they would have prevented the Germans getting into and behind the front line; they might have inflicted devastating casualties on the enemy.

The conclusion must be that III Corps defence could have been better planned and for this Putty must take responsibility for at least a degree of complacency. It has been suggested that he should have done more to support VII Corps, especially when he was asked to provide harassing fire at the entrance to the Banteux Ravine early in the morning of 30 November. Some sources speak of a misunderstanding, others that Putty refused to give this assistance; in the latter case there is no record of any request, and presumably a good reason if it was refused. If Snow (GOC VII Corps) thought this fire was vital he could have put his request to Byng and MGRA 3rd Army, and they would have decided; in any event it was for them to coordinate across the corps boundary, something they neglected throughout the battle. If Snow put the request to Byng, there is no record of him consulting Putty, let alone him ordering Putty to provide such fire support. The relationship between Putty and Snow may also have been a factor but this is only speculation.

So much for what was done or not done before the German attack; initially each division had to fight its own battle and it was inevitably some time before Putty had the information, was able to assess the situation, and make the necessary key decisions. There is no evidence of paralysis of command: overhead line communications were cut and some HQs were over-run but HQ 20th Division communicated throughout, and was of assistance to 12th and 29th Divisions; and there were other means of communication. That some HQs were well back was inevitable given the geography and the narrowness of the salient but they had advanced HQs and the GOCs were often forward with their bde comds. Putty and his divisional commanders had a difficult choice – get well forward to see what was happening in one area but then not be in a position to read the battle and influence it, or be back in his HQ where all the information came albeit sometimes slowly but where he could make the key decisions and communicate them. A balance had to be struck: to be in the right place all the time was extremely difficult.

20th Division and the actions of its GOC (Major General Douglas Smith) have been criticised; the evidence suggests much of this criticism is unfair and misdirected. The position it held was a difficult one to defend and its deployment extremely awkward. The enemy first attacked and broke through on the right of 12th Division; 20th Division's reserve (60 Bde) was in a position to assist and did so. However, when the enemy then attacked 20th Division its reserve was committed. 20th Division's outpost line which should have given warning and delayed the enemy did neither, and was overrun and destroyed. The rest of the division was forced back to Welsh Ridge which it held for the rest of the battle. However, when it went back it exposed the right of 29th Division across the canal at Masnières and the enemy poured though the gap until it was closed. The exact number of casualties suffered by 20th Division on 30 November and subsequently is unclear but did not exceed 2,000, and most of these were in the outpost line. Attacked in front and on both flanks, and lacking its reserve bde, the division did well to fall back to Welsh Ridge in some semblance of order, and then hold on it.

12th Division started the battle very weak and its deployment was in many ways more awkward than that of 20th Division. Brigadier General Vincent and his composite force did well to hold on to the right, and the left of the division clung on to the vital ground around La Vacquerie. However, 12th Division was the first in III Corps to be attacked and they were surprised; at least six bns were destroyed and a large number of men captured. It is therefore difficult not to conclude that the division and its GOC should have done better.

Putty knew of the German attack and breakthrough at 7.30 am and the detailed reports confirming this were at HQ III Corps by 9.30 am. During the morning he made four key decisions: at 9.45 am 2 Bde Tank Corps was ordered to send all available tanks to Quentin Ridge and Révelon Farm. This was the right order to get the tanks moving; it was going to take some time but they were heading to counter the main threat. Five minutes later 6th Division was ordered to send 16 Bde to take up a position at Dead Man's Corner on the Beaucamp-Gouzeaucourt Ridge, thus blocking any enemy advance in to the salient. At 10.15 am 3rd Army was asked to direct 1 Gds Bde in Metz on to Quentin Mill Ridge; although this had been lost, it was again the right decision. Fifteen minutes later (at 10.30 am) Putty ordered 2nd Cavalry Division to hold Révelon Ridge. These decisions may seem straightforward but the picture would not have been at all clear: at a very early stage Putty had identified that this was not a limited attack to force III Corps back across the canal, it was a major offensive designed to turn its right flank and destroy it. All available forces were being directed to this flank. Putty was taking risks that the rest of the front would hold but was taking decisive action to counter and defeat his greatest threat.

He must have been on the telephone very frequently that morning (30 November): by 11 am he had confirmation that 2nd Cavalry, Guards and 61st Divisions were under his command. GOC Guards Division came and received orders from Putty: he was to re-take Gouzeaucourt, then Quentin Ridge and Gonnelieu, and secure the corps' right flank. To the Guards Division's right was Vincent's Force and 2nd Cavalry Division holding Révelon Ridge and to its left securing the angle at Gonnelieu would be 16 Bde 6th Division and 60 Bde 20th Division. Shortly thereafter GOC 29th Division called in and Putty ordered him to hold on across the canal but, if forced to withdraw, it was to be to Highland Ridge and Welsh Ridge, and that these must be held.

By the middle of the day the balance was beginning to swing and the reports becoming more favourable. During the afternoon Putty (or Byng) saw the opportunity not just to block the southern breakthrough but to destroy it: presumably with 3rd Army's agreement, he instructed Cav Corps with tank support to attack the enemy from the SW. While this was going on the enemy had got between 20th and 29th Divisions in the N; 88 Bde was counter-attacking but there were no more reserves. Putty ordered 6th Division to assist and asked V Corps for help, and this breakthrough was then contained and forced back.

Putty spent the evening sorting out the many detailed coordination issues with his staff, the most important of which was between 60 Bde 20th Division and 16 Bde 6th Division who were attacking Gonnelieu from the N, the Guards Division who were attacking it from the NW, and Cav Corps from the SW. He decided not to halt the two bdes which anyway would have been extremely difficult in the dark but wait until he knew the outcome of their attacks before committing Guards Division and Cav Corps. The tanks of 2 Bde Tank Corps were by now on the right flank with the Guards Division and Cav Corps; they could have achieved much more had they been grouped with other forces in a corps reserve from the outset. On their own in small groups, and on ground they did not know, their value was limited.

Having stabilised the right flank Putty was now under great pressure in the N. Masnières could not be held any longer and 86 Bde was withdrawn through 87 Bde and across the canal at Marcoing. 87 Bde was then replaced by 16 Bde until it too was withdrawn over the canal. 6th Division then took command of this front and 88 Bde. It sounds simple but in contact with the enemy it was an extremely difficult operation. Putty was getting more help with the arrival of 61st, 36th and 9th Divisions but the new divisions required careful briefing and every relief was a risky time. The Germans realised this and pressed forward particularly towards La Vacquerie. Putty's message to 36th Division reflects another crisis point for the corps: again the right intervention was made at the right time.

Bringing in the new divisions, getting the tired and depleted ones out, and all the time in contact with the enemy, would have been very difficult; at the same time there was much reorganisation, reconstitution and resupply to be carried out. Putty would have spent much of his time now out and about visiting the new divisions, and thanking those that were departing: all the time with one eye on what the enemy were doing.

By the fifth day (4 December) when Haig visited Putty would have been very tired. The battle was to continue for another four days but the worst was over. III Corps had held the German counter-attack albeit with great difficulty and was now to withdraw to a shorter and more defensible line. Putty's planning of the defensive battle, one that he knew was coming but misjudged its size, speed and direction, had its shortcomings but he did make the right decisions at the right time, and the German offensive was defeated. Haig rightly congratulated him on what he had achieved. It was, though, close run: it did not need to have been and Putty must take some responsibility for this.

13

1918

The Oise January-February

Putty returned from leave on 1 January. It must have been a depressing journey: the Battle of Cambrai had promised much but ended with little tangible achieved, and inquiries were in full swing; it was winter and very cold with snow on the ground; and he had left Jessie uncertain when he would be back. HQ III Corps was still at Val Vion near Beauquesne with just one division, 47th Division, under command and this departed on 5 January.

On 5 January Putty sent his monthly report to the King:

> My dear Wigram, Am sending herewith the diary of III Corps for the month of December for the information of Their Majesties. Have written so many reports on the Cambrai attack on the 30 November am pretty tired of it but the conclusions that I have arrived at are as follows, that the left of VII Corps when heavily attacked by superior numbers retired south instead of west which was the front they were covering, this was entirely natural as the troops always marched up that way but it laid Villers-Guislain, Gouzeaucourt and Gonnelieu completely open, the attack on the Bonavis Road was successful from sheer weight of numbers coming on in the shape of a snow plough irrespective of losses like they used to in 1914, small knots of men of seasoned troops like artillery or engineers stood their ground and inflicted very heavy casualties, the counter-attack by troops like the Guards restored the situation at once. I don't think that there is any doubt but that the German losses were very heavy indeed for instead of his being able to follow up his success on 1 December I retook Quentin Ridge and Gauche Wood with the Guards that morning. Another lesson we have learnt is that intermediate observation posts are necessary for the artillery as the officers in the front line get cut off by the wires being broken; the batteries are always in the valleys, behind crests and get no information as regards what is happening being therefore compelled to keep on their SOS lines. All the attacks came up the valleys and not over the high ground at all, the valleys should be defended in the bottom part and not from the high ground on each side otherwise there is too much dead ground. I found it desperately cold on my return on the 1 January, the chateau I am in with its huge windows facing north and very little warmth from the stove was very different to the luxury of the Ritz, the consequence is a heavy cold in the head. Am off tomorrow for three days to do a reconnaissance down south of my new area but do not anticipate that the corps will

Sir William Pulteney Pulteney by
Walter Stoneman, 1918.
(© National Portrait Gallery, London)

function again before the end of the month. All good wishes for 1918 Yours very sincerely, WP Pulteney.

He also wrote to Ettie Desborough:

My dearest Chief, I got your letter this morning, you have indeed been very unwell but do hope 1918 will make you all right again. I landed here on 1 January, found snow everywhere had to be dug out twice on the way down, oh such a cruel chateau I found myself in with large windows facing north and no means of heating the room result a heavy cold from which I am fast recovering, the change from the luxury of the Ritz was too sudden. There is no doubt that you have got to face the man power question at home if you want to win this war, the sooner the government do it the better or else the soldiers will be demanding courts of enquiry on the politicians instead of the usual one sided cry of the other way about, the great pity of the moment is the unbridled questions and screams for enquiry are shaking the confidence of the rank and file in their officers, you could not do it in the red army and it is the old army that Lloyd George wants to see the spirit of disappear, he would like to get a shuttlecock like Ian Hamilton [then Governor Tower of London] who would say anything to keep in office, he does not like a man who speaks his mind like Robertson [then CIGS]. The general opinion seems to be the idea that a big German offensive against the West will come in the Spring, it is far the best thing that can happen for he will have such colossal losses for temporary success he won't keep the peace in his own country after it, they are only buoying them up by saying that it is the last effort they have got to make, it certainly will be the last that a good many of them will make, A German officer who deserted to the French about a week ago told them that the German losses in the Cambrai attack on 30th November were perfectly appalling and that the truth is only just now beginning to leak out in Germany. I do hope you are quite well again. Yours ever Putty.

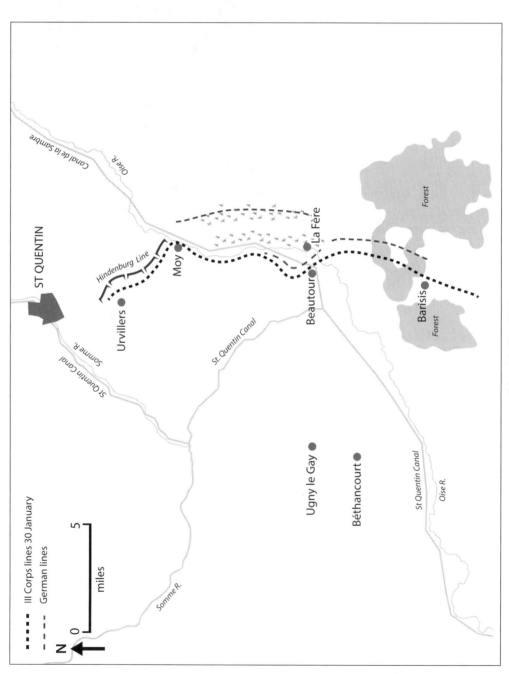

Map 11 Oise 1918.

Next day (6 January) Putty set off on his reconnaissance of the corps' new area to the S on the River Oise: he returned on 9 January. On 13 January HQ III Corps issued OpO No.242 – transfer of III Corps from 3rd Army to 5th Army at 10 am on 14 January. That day he again wrote to Ettie:

> Dearest Chief, Delighted to get your letter of 9 Jan but sorry that you don't yet give a better account of yourself for you generally pull yourself together in the most wonderful manner. Had tea with Goughie[1] yesterday, Ivor Maxse[2] came in which prevented anyone else saying anything, he declares Lloyd George sent Smuts over to Switzerland disguised to treat with an Austrian representative as regards peace terms, if he did it was the act of a low class solicitor and cannot believe it is true, he swears it is and that he has sent him again (I suggested dressed as a Turk this time) my own idea is that L.G. only made his war aims speech just in time, the pacifists and pessimists had been howling for some time to know what we were fighting for, he should be jealous and probably is of Wilson's speeches which will be handed down to history as those of a statesman. The Russian situation is quite impossible to decipher but it looks as if Lenin and Trotsky are aiming at social revolution throughout the world, what we have to guard against is a touch of bolshevism in England grasped at by the Trades Union as a counter blast to the man power scheme. I think the authorities over here are being made unduly nervous over the Cambrai affair and the proper offensive defensive spirit not being pushed nearly far enough, the whole thing is a great mistake because these infernal questions throwing blame on the superiors is now beginning to tell on the rank and file who do not have the same confidence in their officers owing to the red herring continuous criticisms, I should like five political courts of enquiry to every naval and military one, then perhaps they would think further ahead than they do and act a little sooner. The snow has all gone at last but the frost continues at night, the men have had a cruel time getting up to the trenches worse than when they reach them what those poor brutes must be going through in that shell crater area in the north I dare not imagine. Have been busy reconnoitring a new bit of the line all last week but I don't think I go in again until nearly the end of the month. Am sorry to hear Charley L. has been unwell again he keeps on breaking down which is a bad sign, of course he is not really strong. Best of love for ever Putty.

On 14 January the complex task of again building up III Corps began; 14th Division joined the corps that day and 58th Division (HQ III Corps OpO No.243) on 19 January. There were also numerous moves of support and logistic units, and at the same time the corps staff was implementing the transfer to 5th Army and planning the move S.

HQ III Corps issued OpO No.244 on 20 January which ordered the relief by III Corps of 62nd and 154th French Divisions and 5th French Cavalry Division. The relief was to start on 26 January – 14th Division to relieve the northern sector first, and 30th Division (transferred to III Corps at Midnight 26/27 January) the southern sector later. At 4 pm 20 January HQ III Corps issued OpO No.245 transferring 39th Division to the corps (on 24 January). From having

---

1   General Sir Hubert Gough GOC 5th Army 1916-1918.
2   Lieutenant General Sir Ivor Maxse (1862-1958) late Coldm Gds GOC XVIII Corps 1917-1918.

no divisions under command, there were now four divisions in or coming to III Corps (14, 30, 39 and 58th Divisions).

III Corps OpO No.246 issued 25 January dealt with the march of III Corps Heavy Artillery into the new area, a difficult operation in itself. Next day the GS log recorded: 'Relief by 14th Division of 154th French Division and northern portion of French 62nd Division commences'. DDMS noted in his log: 'Béthancourt is an excellent site for Corps Rest Station consisting of chateau and huts, total accommodation at present 250', a reminder of how much else had to be planned and organised to support those in the front line. HQ III Corps issued its Corps Defence Instructions (GO7475) for the new area on 27 January. They began: 'The frontage held by the corps extends from Barisis to N of Urvillers – a distance of approximately 30,200 yards'.

14th Division took command of the northern sector at 10 am 28 January, and next day HQ III Corps closed at Beauquesne and opened at Ugny le Gay. Finally, on 30 January at 10 am, 30th Division's relief of 5th French Cavalry Division and the rest of 62nd French Division was completed and Putty assumed command of his whole front. 39th Division left III Corps that day leaving just 58th Division in corps reserve. III Corps GS log noted that evening: 'Situation quiet. Enemy aircraft active, crossing our lines about La Fère'.

III Corps Opsum set out the situation at the end of January in more detail:

> III Corps assumed responsibility for the line from Barisis in S to Urvillers in the N (inclusive) from the French. N of R Oise it was from Groupement D'Ugny le Gay (formerly XXXVII French Corps) and S of the R Oise it was from 1st French Cavalry Corps. 14th Division were from Urvillers to Moy (both inclusive) and 30th Division from Moy to Barisis (latter inclusive). III Corps front was about 17 miles long. Southern portion of the front, about 6,000 yards long, from Barisis to the R Oise, was situated in the Basse Forest of Coucy. N of the river from Beautor to Moy, a stretch of 12,000 yards, our lines were divided from those of the enemy by the Oise River and Canal, the crossings of which had been destroyed, with the exception of a narrow bridgehead at La Fère occupied by the enemy. This river, with the marshes on either side, formed an impassable barrier, 1,500 yards wide. From Moy to the corps boundary N of Urvillers, a distance of some 8,000 yards, our line was situated generally at the foot of the slopes on which the Germans had built their Hindenburg Line. No natural obstacle separated our line from that of the enemy in this sector, while the systematic destruction by the Germans during their retreat of all cover on the long and gentle slopes behind our front rendered observation for the enemy particularly easy.

31 January was a quiet day although both 14th and 30th Divisions reported much activity in the air. That evening HQ III Corps issued OpO No.247 ordering the move of 18th Division into the corps. III Corps' casualties in January had been: 1 OR killed, 1 officer and 8 ORs wounded = 10.

The first two days of February were again quiet apart from intermittent shelling. Putty attended 5th Army conference at Le Catelet on 3 February with his BGGS and GOC RA. That evening he sent his monthly report to the King:

> My dear Wigram, I attach all there is for a diary of III Corps for January but am afraid there is nothing of interest for Their Majesties to read as we have only just taken over our

new front, I can only say that no-one could have been more civil or generous in what they have left behind for us than the French were. The region of rivers and forests is a pleasant change but we have got to put our backs well in to the defences now that the Russians have let so many divisions loose, if our fellows will only keep cool we shall do them in all right. Yours very sincerely, WP Pulteney.

Putty met the General Commanding French Northern Group of Armies in Sinceny on 4 February; that evening 14th Division reported 100 gas shells fired into Urvillers. 5 February was again relatively quiet and on 6 February at 10.30 am Putty held a conference at HQ III Corps (Ugny le Gay) attended by GOCs 14th, 30th and 58th Divisions with their GSO1s, CRAs and CREs, and GOC RA, GOC RE, BGGS, DA&QMG, DDMS, AD Signals, GSO2(O) and GSO2(I) from HQ III Corps.

Putty also wrote to Ettie Desborough on 5 February:

Dearest Chief, Have heard nothing from you for some time, but hope that you have quite recovered and are about again in your usual health. We have had wonderful weather since I came back a fortnight ago which has indeed been a blessing during the relief if it will only continue for another week we shall be very thankful. I met the French General who commands the group of armies round Soissons two days ago one Fracachet d'Esperey,[3] a little man whom the corps commanders all loathe but he struck me as very capable and grasped a situation very quickly, he spoke so distinctly I could understand him much better than usual. The bombing at night from aeroplanes is very disquieting now, one hears the humming noise and then waits to hear the bomb, this time last year the camps used to be lit up so that they looked like the hill at Epsom on Derby day but now you cannot use a light, they nearly got us in my motor car last Saturday [2 February] I fortunately pulled up my motor on hearing the first one drop or should have run in to the 2nd and 3rd which fell 100 yds ahead, hear they got a good bag of Austrian machines one day I believe the 11 pilots had got drunk before they started. The Germans are bringing over their divisions from Russia pretty quickly now and we may expect an offensive any day after the end of this month, much conjecture as to where it will be launched but have an incline to a dash at Amiens instead of Paris, they won't get either and they will lose a lot of men. The French are in better spirits than I have seen them for a long time, they are making so much money out of ourselves and the Americans all other cares seem to vanish, the Bolo[4] trial is intensely interesting our interpreters say the result is a foregone conclusion against him, that he will have to die but they know nothing. Much love yours ever Putty.

7 February was a quiet day: 5th Army issued orders that III Corps Cyclist Bn was to move by train from V Corps to III Corps and NH to move by road. Their return was long overdue, indicating their great value in the old area that they had got to know so well, but they were now much needed in III Corps. Also that day 18th Division was instructed by HQ III Corps to send

---

3   General Louis Félix Marie Francois Franchet d'Espèrey (1856-1942) CinC French Northern Army Group later Marshal of France.
4   Paul Marie Bolo (1867-1918) Frenchman tried for treason – conveying intelligence to the enemy – convicted 14 Feb executed 17 April.

forward the first two OCs Fd Coys RE as soon as possible to receive instructions re work. There was now an increasing sense of urgency (the German offensive was launched on 21 March).

58th Division relieved 30th Division on 9 February and the latter division left the corps next day. Meanwhile 18th Division was ordered to send one brigade and one field company to the northern sector of the corps front, and one brigade, one field company and the pioneer battalion to the southern sector; the reserve brigade group was ordered to move to Béthancourt on 11 and 12 February.

It was again quiet on 11 February when HQ III Corps issued an updated Defence Scheme (GO7475/30). That night a fighting patrol of 14th Division of 1 officer and 14 ORs met a party of the enemy about to raid a post, dispersed it and captured two prisoners (17 Pioneer and 128 Regts 36th German Division). Next day HQ III Corps issued GO7475/33, ordering the readjustment of forward and battle zones S of the R Oise and the boundary with the French.

Haig visited III Corps on 13 February: in the morning he went to HQ 14th Division and HQ 58th Division, and inspected a battalion on parade at each headquarters. He arrived at HQ III Corps at 2 pm and the GS log recorded that he saw members of the various staffs. At some stage he must have had a private discussion with Putty to tell him that his time in command of III Corps was at an end and that he was to return to England on 15 February to assume command of XXIII Corps. Haig in his diary wrote: 'Soon after 2 pm I reached HQ III Corps and saw General Pulteney. I told P that he had been selected to go home to command a new corps, and organise against possible raids'. There is no indication that Putty had any warning of this.

On 15 February Putty handed over to Major General Lee GOC 18th Division who commanded III Corps until 27 February when the permanent replacement arrived. Putty had commanded III Corps for more than 1,200 days, longer than any of the other 49 corps commanders who served on the Western Front; only three others served more than 1,000 days. He would have had mixed feelings as he set off on the journey back to England, accompanied by his two SG ADCs, Captains Poynter and Loder, both of whom had been with him since early 1917. Private Hogbin SG would also have been with him: and he too had served 1,200 days.

Cambrai Enquiry

The various investigations and enquiries into the success of the German counter-attack on 30 November started almost immediately and continued well into 1918. Only those parts that are directly relevant to III Corps and to Putty himself are included so that conclusions can be drawn on his actions before and during the battle: it is important to consider the motives of those involved to make certain they are not influenced for or against him.

There is the evidence of Putty's divisional commanders, and that of GOCs 20th and 29th Divisions was mainly factual. GOC 12th Division (Scott) said in his evidence on 17 December (extracts):

> The possibility of a break through by the Germans in the vicinity of Villers-Guislain had been considered and on the afternoon of 29 November the 4 reserve guns of 23 MG Coy were given a defensive position. The battalion of 35 Bde in reserve had orders to be prepared to counter-attack from the north should the Germans gain possession of Villers-Guislain. The same afternoon GOC 55th Division came to see me and informed me of having placed four of his machine-guns also in position for defence of Villers-Guislain. We then talked

over the action to be taken in the event of an attack there. I sent for the OCs of these bns (divisional reserve) at 5.30 pm 29 November, and explained to them myself the situation as it might arise and what I desired to be done viz the occupation of Vaucellette Farm, Gauche Wood and Quentin Ridge. Lieutenant Colonel Rolls CO 6 Queens was to reconnoitre the ground and make dispositions for Vaucellette Farm to Gauche Wood inclusive; Lieutenant Colonel Wollocombe CO 11 Middx the same for Quentin Ridge to Gonnelieu. This reconnaissance was to be carried out early on 30 November. Certain batteries of 12th Divisional Artillery were detailed to be prepared to fire on Villers-Guislain and the spur to the NE should occasion arise. I do not consider that the troops in the front system were in any way surprised. In my opinion the troops in the centre of 12th Division were pushed back by force of numbers.

He made two further important statements: 'I suppose that I was responsible for the defence of Gonnelieu as it was in my own area, but I had not considered it' and 'My general opinion is that my centre brigade, the 36th, were pushed back early by weight of superior numbers. I think that the officers commanding the Essex (9 Essex 35 Bde) and Berkshires (5 Berks 35 Bde) should have held on instead of going back to the line La Vacquerie-Villers Plouich. I think that was an error of judgement'.

Scott also gave his views to Edmonds many years later:

Snow seems to blame III Corps and he and 55th Division did a lot of howling for reinforcements instead of strengthening the junction with III Corps. After my talk with GOC 55th Division I arranged for the heavy artillery under my command to keep fire on the German concentration. I reported this to III Corps who said it was nothing to do with me. So I arranged to fire from my field batteries and GOC 55th Division agreed to fire along my front at Banteux as that part of the front could not be got at from my own batteries owing to the ridge. 12th Division did not get the credit it should have. Not only did the right flank get turned but the left was somewhat in the air as the 20th Division fell back. 12th Division finished in a position holding their reserve line which is what it eventually handed over on 1 December.

Scott and Jeudwine (GOC 55th Division) were the same age and both had been RA officers. GOC 12th Division was critical of CO 9 Essex (Lieutenant Colonel de Sales La Terriere) so a statement in this officer's evidence is of interest: 'I had no information either from a brigade conference or from orders as to the role allotted to my battalion'. Comd 35 Bde was Brigadier General Vincent.

Major General Douglas Smith (GOC 20th Division) offered little comment in his evidence other than the statement: 'My opinion is that 12th Division was attacked 20 to 30 minutes before my division was attacked'. Another statement in Brigadier General Banbury's (Comd 61 Bde 20th Division) evidence is also important: 'Until the intended second line was complete, the outpost line was to be held as the line of resistance'. It is difficult to reconcile these statements with events: the outpost line was surprised and overrun.

GOC 29th Division (Major General de Lisle) gave a factual report to the enquiry but quoted from his war diary when writing to Edmonds many years later:

The more I think of the performance of the 29th Division the more I marvel at their endurance. They were in the train all the night of 17 November, were marching all the night of 18 November, preparing for the battle all the 19 November and starting at 2 am 20 November they marched 10 miles to the place of concentration with fighting equipment weighing 60 lbs. On the 20th and 21st they were in action; and from the 22nd to 29th they dug a defensive position on a front of 5,000 yards with front support and reserve line of trenches. On 30 November they held the line against 12 attacks and made a brilliant counter-attack gaining 2,000 yards on a 5,000 yard front. Again they held the line on 2, 3 and 4 December and were not finally relieved until 5 am 5 December.

Brigadier General Walker (Comd 16 Bde 6th Division) did not give evidence to the enquiry but his letter to Edmonds later provides an insight to the counter-attack by the Guards Division:

Sometime about 9 or 10 am on 30 November GOC 6th Division spoke to me on the telephone – the bde was to move towards Gouzeaucourt; I was to report to GOC 29th Division there and act under his orders. We (BM and I) walked until we jumped on a lorry going south; reached some huts on the outskirts of Gouzeaucourt, no signs of life; decided to go to the station where we could see a train under steam; turning a bend we saw a number of Germans; 16 Bde was about ready for the proposed advance when the leading battalion reported the Guards advancing from the west. It was a fine sight and it appeared that they gained the village with little trouble.

GOC VII Corps (Snow) was cautious in his evidence to the enquiry but in his later letter to Edmonds he wrote:

I visited the corps commander (Pulteney) on my left and imparted my views [on the likelihood of a German counter-attack] to him. He was not impressed. Late that evening [29 November] General Jeudwine [GOC 55th Division] called up on the telephone and asked me to arrange with III Corps to put down 'counter preparation' with heavy guns on the Banteux Ravine just before daybreak. We had insufficient guns for the purpose. I did my best but the corps commander of III Corps was unable to comply with my request. It is interesting to note that the attack took place over the precise ground and at the exact moment when, had General Jeudwine's request been granted by III Corps, the proposed annihilating fire would have opened.

VII Corps log only recorded: 'On 29 November the corps commander and BGGS went over in the morning to see BGGS III Corps and again discussed the situation'.

Putty did not write his own report until he got back from leave (it was dated 4 January): Report of the Operations of III Corps on 30 November 1917 (III Corps GO7248/3rd Army GS56/250 forwarded by Byng on 11 January and received by GHQ 12 January). First, he set out the facts including details of the line he had been ordered to hold and the artillery positions. This narrative is in line with official and other records but it also included:

The chief pressure from the enemy up to the 29 November had been on the 20th Division from the Crèvecoeur direction, the 29th Division from Rumilly and the 6th Division, whereas the 12th Division had had several bombing encounters, the main pressure being on the 20th and 29th Divisions. The indications on 29 November as reported by the VII Corps showed movements of troops in front of their centre and left flanks.

It is clear where Putty thought his greatest threat lay. He then set out his conclusions:

1. Deleted [perhaps it was an error or he had second thoughts]
2. The FOs of artillery were in the front line in which the wires were cut and they became useless. The intermediate FOs for watching for SOS signals at night had been withdrawn. It is therefore obvious that intermediate OPs for watching ground are necessary, so as to give information to batteries.
3. The result of the effect of the machine-guns was unsatisfactory as there were enough to swamp any attack if the gunners had been firm.
4. The effect of the break through to Gouzeaucourt unnerved the men holding Bonavis Road (12th Division), which should never have given.
5. Weight of numbers advancing without consideration of loss was successful.
6. The effect of a counter-attack by troops like the Guards was instantaneous; also where few men like artillery and engineers got together they held their own, besides inflicting heavy casualties on the enemy.
7. The outstanding features were the behaviour of all ranks of the artillery, and the counter-attack delivered by the Guards.
8. There is little doubt in my mind that the German losses must have been very severe indeed, for he was unable on the morning of the 1 Dec to prevent my retaking Quentin Ridge and Gauche Wood with little or no artillery support, and in the face of the enemy success the day previous.
9. Tanks are a great asset in counter-attacks and were invaluable though slow to get into position.
10. Enemy low flying aircraft on the morning of 30 Nov produced a considerable moral effect on our troops by firing at them with machine-guns. WP Pulteney Lieutenant General Commanding III Corps'

3rd Army issued a questionnaire dated the same day (4 January: 3rd Army GS56/249):

Question 1(a) Did the GOC 12th Division ask, prior to the German attack on 30 Nov, for reinforcements either in men, or guns, or both?

Answer [in Putty's own hand]: I have no recollection of any demand from the 12th for either men or guns, there is no official demand existing in our records, on the contrary the 12th had troops in reserve at Heudecourt. Signed WP Pulteney Lieutenant General Comd III Corps 5 Jan 1918.

Brigadier General Schreiber CE III Corps writing to Edmonds later said:

They [the infantry] had suffered so little that it was much to their discredit that they were driven back in the way they were. General Pulteney said either to me later, or it was repeated, that if the infantry had fought like some RE tunnellers and some RA batteries the Boche counter-attack would have failed.

Schreiber left the corps on 29 November.
GOC 3rd Army (Byng)'s report to Haig was dated 18 December (extracts):

The attack of the enemy on the morning of 30 November was in no sense a surprise. The commanders of VII, III and IV Corps had realised the probability of such an attack as was actually made. Troops had been warned, and extra machine-gun defence had been established in the villages of Villers-Guislain and Gonnelieu. Their great superiority in numbers permitted the Germans to exploit their success in the direction of Gauche Wood, Gouzeaucourt and La Vacquerie. I attribute the reason for the local success on the part of the enemy to one cause and one cause alone, namely lack of training on the part of junior NCOs and men. I estimate the number of prisoners captured by the enemy to be about six or seven thousand. This number alone should have been sufficient to have at least delayed any thrust on the part of the enemy.

Lieutenant Colonel Thorpe GSO1 3rd Army said in his evidence to the enquiry:

The corps boundary was fixed for the offensive operation of 20 November. III Corps was always intended to form a defensive flank and consolidate. The boundary was fixed in order to provide depth behind III Corps for the attack, and was not modified with the result that its effect on the depth behind the left of VII Corps had not been adequately considered. The idea was that VII Corps defensive front should face east, and III Corps south-east, and that naturally gave the Banteux Ravine as the boundary. I say that III Corps was responsible for Gouzeaucourt and the area around it, and that it was not an army 'staging area' [as suggested in III Corps letter of 22 November and tracing].

Haig, in his report on 23 December, said:

Further south, however, a weaker attack on a broader front with two divisions in front line and elements of one in support (GHQ gives the number of divisions as five – see report dtd 18 Dec) succeeded in penetrating the strong positions held by us over the Banteux Ravine and south of Twenty-Two Ravine, where we held our original trench system as before the advance of 20 November. Our counter-attacks recovered part of the lost ground during the day and the following morning, but the complete recovery of Villers-Guislain, Gonnelieu and our old front line would have involved losses which were not considered worth the results to be attained.

Next day in his report to CIGS he wrote:

After consideration of all the factors I find no reason to criticise adversely the dispositions made, which in my opinion were adequate to meet an attack of the strength anticipated and actually experienced. I further consider that, if there was a miscalculation, it was not of such a nature as to reflect adversely on the competence of the commander concerned. As a matter of fact, no specific request for more troops to meet the expected attack was made by the army, corps, divisions and brigades concerned.

The German view from prisoners of war examined on 30 November (GHQ I) was:

Except on the extreme flanks and in one place in the centre there was no serious resistance on any part of this front. 34th Division, which was the most successful, advanced through the British line without difficulty, taking the villages of Villers-Guislain, Gonnelieu and occupying Gouzeaucourt. German NCOs were of opinion that the failure of the British troops to resist attack in the initial stages was the result of (1) the intense artillery bombardment (2) the complete surprise and (3) the overwhelming numbers of the attacking force.

30th and 9th Reserve Divisions on the right were held up by 29th Division. 220th Division in the centre attacked Lateau Wood 'British in the front line were demoralised by artillery fire and surrendered quite easily'; 28th Division 'Wire was easily passed and the British troops in the front line were completely surprised'; 34th Division 'Advanced with practically no resistance and captured Gonnelieu and Gouzeaucourt' and 'The British troops appeared to have been completely surprised and the fighting until about 1 pm on this part of the front was practically nil'.

The court of enquiry on the action fought S of Cambrai on 30 November 1917 was convened by the AG GHQ on 17 January 1918: 'The court will record their opinion as to the sequence of events and the cause of the German success'. The court assembled at Hesdin 10 am 21 January 1918. Lieutenant General Hamilton-Gordon GOC IX Corps[5] was the President; the members were Lieutenant General Maxse GOC XVIII Corps and Major General Pinney GOC 33rd Division.[6] The court considered the evidence and concluded that there were 9 causes (extracts):

1. Surprise in the outpost lines. Secrecy of enemy's assembly; massed troops unseen in hollows; very short but intense preliminary bombardment; lack of vigilance in the outpost lines of all three divisions (55th, 12th and 20th).
2. Warnings from above unheeded. Had been communicated; troops undoubtedly surprised; perhaps warned too frequently.
3. Aeroplane reconnaissance on 30 November. Massing of enemy infantry not detected; bad visibility given as explanation; but 13 batteries observed on III Corps front; also confirmed presence of large number of enemy low-flying machines.
4. Lack of artillery on the 11,000 yards frontage held by 55th Division. Decision by 3rd Army based on German attack expected on Bourlon front.
5. Boundaries between corps and divisions. Schemes for defence were not facilitated by the rearward boundaries allocated to corps and divisions; commanders felt that their tactical responsibilities limited to the area assigned to them; the boundary lines were not at right angles to the front – not even for 2,000 yards which perhaps might have been estimated as the forward zone; this is emphasised especially in the Banteux

5   Lieutenant General Alexander Hamilton-Gordon (1859-1939) late RA.
6   Major General Reginald John Pinney (1863-1943) late RF Comd 23 Bde in 8th Division 1915.

Ravine, where two army corps met and in which one brigade from each were detailed to fight, and here the back area of 12th Division included Gonnelieu and the ground west of Villers-Guislain, but the front trenches opposite the latter village were in occupation of the 55th Division; also the infantry holding the north side of the Banteux Ravine could not see the bottom of it from its front on account of the convex slope of the ground; no one commander was responsible for the defence of both sides of the Banteux Ravine at its eastern entrance; the troops of two army corps were involved in the defence of its western slopes; evidence was also forthcoming that neither Gonnelieu or Villers-Guislain were defended localities or provided with infantry garrisons.

6. Hostile low-flying aeroplanes. Came over in considerable numbers about the time of the assault; at altitudes described as below 100 feet; moral effect very great; our men do not seem to know what to do to minimise the moral effect of these low-flying machines.

7. Lack of defence in depth. Lack of training and of understanding on the part of subordinate and lower commanders of the method of defence in depth; universal tendency was to allocate troops to the front line system as being the main line of resistance at the expense of garrisons for defensive localities in rear and troops destined for counter-attacks.

8. Lack of doctrine for the defensive battle. This tendency indicates a want of supervision on the part of higher commanders; troops detailed for the garrisons of rearward positions and for counter-attack were in many cases exhausted by earlier fighting; they were necessarily employed as working parties and not in an efficient condition to fulfil the role originally assigned to them by commanders who had prepared the schemes of defence.

9. Propagation of rumours. Common knowledge, and it has been officially brought to the notice by the AG, that irresponsible, garbled and in many cases false information concerning the events of 30 November reached the public before any correct reports could be made use of.

One member (Maxse) submitted his own report and this was forwarded by the President (extracts):

My opinion is that the root cause is ignorance of the rudiments of successful defence and inexperience in handling sections, platoons and machine-guns as fire units in the field; but I do not see how this supervision can be effective so long as the divisions concerned do not belong permanently to one corps; it would be difficult to discover any particular corps commander who could fairly be held responsible for the defective training of any particular division; the Battle of Cambrai was a great British success which was only partially marred by a local failure on one particular date.

When forwarding the report of the enquiry to CGS GHQ, AG[7] questioned GOC 3rd Army's decisions on the allocation of artillery to 55th Division and the corps (III/VII) boundary.

---

7   Lieutenant General George Henry Fowke (1864-1936) late RE.

General Smuts was tasked by the War Cabinet to tour 3rd Army and report on the battle. His report (War Cabinet GT3198 3 January) said:

> I have gone through the papers with some care in order to find out if anybody, and if so who, was to blame for the disaster on our right on 30 November which resulted in the sudden capture of Gonnelieu, Villers-Guislain and Gouzeaucourt. I proceed to note down my impressions for the information of the War Cabinet.
>
> The general disposition of our troops on that day was quite sound, as appears from the fact that the two principal attacks of the enemy at Bourlon Wood and near Masnières were both beaten back with great slaughter, and in the third and smaller attack to the right, in which the enemy had such remarkable success, the attacking and defending forces were fairly equally matched, two of our divisions (the 12th and 55th) being opposed to two enemy divisions with elements of a third. That under such conditions of virtual equality in numbers the attack should have succeeded is most surprising, not only on general grounds, but because all our experience in this war points to the great advantage of the defensive.
>
> The evidence is fairly clear as to what really happened and the only difficulty arises as to the explanation of these facts, which does not appear clearly from the evidence collected in the enquiry. The extreme rapidity with which the attack progressed and the short time taken to reach Gouzeaucourt proves that there was some very serious breakdown and that the opposition met could not have been serious. This is corroborated by the statements of German prisoners who declare that they met with very little resistance; that the barbed wire entanglements gave them no trouble and that, with the exception of desultory machine-gun fire in some places, practically no fighting was put up by the defence.
>
> With any resistance our advance troops could easily have held the enemy back until the supports, which were rightly placed, could have arrived. As it was, the front parts were overpowered without any resistance after a very short artillery preparation by the enemy, and the supports unexpectedly found the enemy on them before they knew what had happened in front of them. This was not due to any surprise. As an attack had been expected as early as the 28th November the villages had been especially strengthened with machine-guns, and special orders had been issued to the troops to be on the alert, and these orders were repeated for the night of the 29th-30th November.
>
> In spite of all, however, what happened was that a short and intense bombardment destroyed the wire entanglements, that the enemy then poured without resistance into two ravines which led behind our lines, that as soon as our troops found the enemy behind as well as in front of them they either surrendered or retired without resistance, and that the machine-gunners, who should have held their positions (as the German machine-gunners do on these occasions) to the bitter end retired with the retreating infantry. The guns which for topographical reasons were placed very far forward were easily captured, and could not be used to stem the tide, and the situation got completely out of control until the enemy had penetrated in a very short time as far as Gouzeaucourt.
>
> What is the explanation of all this? It is clear from the foregoing that the dispositions of the higher command, army or corps command were not to blame, and that everything had been done to meet such an attack as actually occurred. The breakdown may be due to either of two causes: first, that the subordinate local commanders actually in command on the scene of action lost their heads, allowed the situation to generate into confusion,

which then spread to the rear and the neighbouring units; or second, that the trouble was still lower down with the junior officers, NCOs and men. On the first possible cause no evidence has been collected, and it is therefore impossible to come to a decision. But after reading through the papers with some care I am not at all convinced that the brigade and regimental command are free of blame in the matter, as it is difficult to conceive that with due alertness and activity on their part the situation could have got so completely out of descend. However, I hesitate to express an opinion in the absence of evidence, and hope the Commander-in-Chief will himself take up the matter as a subject of more detailed inquiry.

The second explanation is that which is suggested in the records of the inquiry. It is pointed out that the 55th Division, for instance, which had hitherto borne a very high reputation had some two months before lost about 7,000 officers and men in the fighting further north (12th Division 3,000 and a further 1,000 in the previous week), and that the division had been filled up with fresh drafts. The suggestion is that in regard to the younger officers NCOs and men and especially in regard to the machine-gunners the standard of training had not been such as to qualify them for the situation which arose with the German onslaught on 30 November.

If this explanation is correct, and it is the only one suggested on the papers and evidence collected, the position is a very serious and disquieting one. The King of Italy explained to us at Pescheira that the Italian debacle on the Julian front was due to the inexperience and inadequate training of the junior officers, NCOs and men which fitted them to hold trenches and make a simple advance but did not fit them to manoeuvre or conduct a proper retreat after a reverse, with the result that after breakthrough of the enemy at one point the Italian retreat soon degenerated into a rout. If the Cambrai reverse is, as appears from these papers, a similar case on a much smaller scale, it cannot but raise anxiety now that we shall probably be on the defensive for a good while on the Western Front, and the enemy may have been encouraged to expect a repetition on a larger scale of what has happened at Cambrai. The lesson to draw is that we must devote more time and attention to the training of our troops and especially of our junior officers and NCOs.

Seven years later (1924) Seely[8] had a long interview with Prince Rupprecht[9] at Munich. He recorded:

We discussed both battles of Cambrai. He said that the attack of 20 November fell like a thunderbolt, and that its success filled Ludendorff with alarm. The effect on the German troops was most demoralising. He realised the only way to restore confidence in the German Army was to launch a counter-attack in the same place. Rupprecht said: Yes, it was an entirely novel kind of attack. You had overwhelmed us by complete surprise with your tanks. We wanted to try and do the same thing without tanks. It all depended on finding fighting men brave enough to creep right up to and under our hastily constructed wire entanglements under cover of the mist.

8   Brigadier General General Jack Seely SofS for War 1912-1914 Comd Can Cav Bde at Cambrai.
9   Crown Prince Rupprecht of Bavaria Comd German Army Group during Cambrai.

Neither the official enquiry nor Smuts' review for the war cabinet concluded that Putty was in any way to blame for what happened. There was an undoubted difference in the performance of the divisions in III Corps. 12th Division should have stood firm but it did not. It had recently received large numbers of reinforcements and had not had sufficient time to absorb and train them but, as Maxse pointed out, this could not be attributed to the corps commander. The corps level of command was the only level where there was no continuity: divisions and corps troops came and went all the time, and it was extremely difficult for the corps commander to maintain high standards in any area. Three of Putty's four divisions had been in the corps for less than two weeks when the German counter-attack took place: this was the responsibility of Byng and Haig.

Yet Putty knew the ground well: it was awkward but nevertheless was suited to defence. All his experience would have told him that the Germans were certain to counter-attack and there were numerous specific warnings that one was imminent. Despite this III Corps was pushed back: arguably III Corps should not have just held the German counter-attack but won the defensive battle convincingly and inflicted very severe casualties on the enemy. Lloyd George wrote: 'An inquiry was set up, but it turned out to be an utter sham. General Byng, who was responsible for the battle arrangements, was never called' and 'the High Command who prepared the plans, knowing that they had not sufficient troops, guns or aeroplanes to carry them out, were exonerated from blame'.

Seven tactical issues were raised in the various investigations: each one if it had been properly addressed at the time might have changed the situation. The inter corps boundary was unsound in that it was along a likely enemy approach, and one that was not covered; the valleys, in which early morning mist was frequent, provided good approaches for the enemy and were not covered by observation or fire, nor were the valley bottoms held; the main Crèvecoeur–Honnecourt valley which also often had early morning mist, and was the obvious forming up point for the enemy, could not be observed and reliance was placed solely on aircraft and patrols; the defensive positions on the reverse slopes which should have been capable of destroying the enemy were badly sited; the villages which should have provided excellent strong points were not held; the artillery which should have inflicted very heavy casualties on the enemy in the Crèvecoeur–Honnecourt valley and during their approach were largely ineffective; and III Corps' overall deployment was much as it had finished the offensive battle a week earlier with all four divisions holding a line rather than the best ground for defence, and with inadequate reserves to deal with any breakthrough. It can be argued as to where responsibility for each lay between the commanders of 3rd Army, III Corps and its divisions but all had a share in it.

XXIII Corps and Japan

February 1918-April 1919

Putty was to command XXIII Corps in England for a just over a year, more than four months of which was spent on an official visit to Japan during which Lieutenant General Snow was temporarily in command. XXIII Corps was formed in February 1918 and Putty was its first and only commander apart from Snow: the corps seems to have had two roles – repelling enemy raids and training large numbers of men who were too young to fight at the front but in due course were to be sent in formed units out to the Army of Occupation in Germany so that men who had fought in the war could be released and sent home; its headquarters was at Bury St Edmunds.

Very little is known about XXIII Corps: Putty's BGGS was Brigadier General Tufnell.[10] Captain Loder who had been Putty's ADC since January 1917 continued with him throughout his time in XXIII Corps as did his orderly, Guardsman Hogbin SG.

Putty took up his appointment on 20 February and on 25 February was received by the King at Buckingham Palace. The following month (19 March) the King visited the Home Forces at Colchester to see education training where he was received by Putty.

He was to have little time to adjust to married life with Jessie because from 13 May to 8 September he was 'Specially employed on British Military Mission to Japan'. The mission was led by Prince Arthur of Connaught.[11] The only other people recorded as being in the party from the outset were Major Reginald Herbert 15th Earl of Pembroke and Montgomery RHG (Putty's ADC 1914-1915) and Guardsman Hogbin SG.

They sailed to Japan via the United States. Putty wrote to Ettie Desborough on 23 May:

> Dearest Chief, A line to say that we are due to arrive at New York tomorrow and go on directly to Washington. We have had an uneventful voyage except two boats fishing on the Newfoundland Bank we saw no ships of any kind until just now when we passed the famous *Vaterland*.[12] We only had two rough days which finished off Prince Arthur but the temperature has altered from 40 to 80 degrees which is somewhat trying, I can't remember when I felt any real heat last, portholes are all closed up on account of submarine restrictions, many boats I believe were lost from not taking this simple precaution. Have done a lot of reading since I came on board but chiefly military handbooks but by the time we reach our destination shall be well rested as regards the Geisha etc. Reggie Pembroke is the life and soul of the party, I don't know what we should have done without him. We are absolutely devoid of news, we got a hint in the wireless one day that there had been trouble in Ireland but nothing else, the American wireless generally consists of 'American airmen show superiority on their front and therefore help all allies' Write me news to c/o Sir C Guthrie[13] 165 Broadway New York We are sure to pick up letters written leaving England up to 8th July. Yours ever Putty.

They arrived in New York on 24 May and went immediately to Washington DC by train. Some time that day they met Colonel House.[14] President Wilson's diary recorded later: 'Received Prince Arthur of Connaught at 7 pm. British Ambassador[15] accompanied; Colonel Ridley escorted party (Putty was almost certainly one of them)'. Prince Arthur handed the President a letter from King George V.

---

10   Arthur Wyndham Tufnell (1872-1920) Eton late W Surrey murdered on the Punjabi Mail.
11   Prince Arthur of Connaught (1883-1938) grandson of Queen Victoria Eton 7 H and later RSG ADC to both CinCs in France.
12   SS *Vaterland* was unable to return to Germany in 1914 and laid up in the USA. She was seized when USA entered the war and renamed SS *Leviathan*.
13   Probably Sir Connop Thirwall Robert Guthrie 1st Bt (1882-1945) Captain Gren Gds wounded 1915 Special Representative in USA Ministry of Shipping 1916-1919.
14   Edward Mandell House (1858-1938) advisor to President and mediator and negotiator during WW1.
15   Rufus Isaacs 1st Marquess of Reading (1860-1935) Ambassador to US 1918-1919.

Next day President Wilson entertained Prince Arthur, and probably Putty and others in the party, to luncheon although not at the White House; later in the day Prince Arthur wrote:

My dear Mr President, Before leaving Washington I beg to express to you the real pleasure which I have felt at being privileged to visit the capital of the United States, at a time when our two countries are so closely bound together in the common cause. May I thank you most sincerely for the cordial hospitality extended to me in this country. My only regret is that my visit on this occasion is through force of circumstances but a short one. I venture however to hope that at some time in the future my duties may permit me to make a more intimate acquaintance with this great country. Meanwhile I carry away with me the most pleasant impressions of my short stay in Washington. In conclusion I remain Yours Very Sincerely, Arthur.

They departed from Washington DC that evening probably by special train to Chicago, connected there with the 7 pm train for San Francisco, and arrived there about 29 May. From there they sailed to Japan on board the SS *Shinyo Maru*. Her usual route took them via Honolulu and Manila and took 16 days.

They wasted little time because on 17 June they arrived at Yokohama, accompanied then by Sir Conyngham Greene British Ambassador to Japan[16] and Captain the Master of Sinclair,[17] both of whom may well have travelled in the party from England. They went on by train to Tokyo and then to Kasumgaseki Palace, Prince Arthur's residence.

Next day (18 June) the party went to the Imperial Palace where Prince Arthur presented a Field Marshal's baton to the Emperor of Japan. The Emperor also presented medals to the members of the mission with Putty receiving the Order of the Rising Sun (First Class). This part of the mission must have been concluded by 24 June because on that date Greene reported to the FO: 'Great success of Prince's mission – great satisfaction to everyone concerned'.

The mission spent about a month in Japan: after hosting receptions at the British Embassy Prince Arthur and his party travelled throughout Japan visiting historic and religious sites; they also visited HQ 4th Japanese Division. The British Ambassador had corresponded with Uchida Kosai, Japanese Foreign Minister, about an alleged plot against Prince Arthur during the visit but nothing transpired. The objective of the mission was to cement Anglo-Japanese relations at this critical stage of the war: this was achieved by the presentation of the Field Marshal's baton and Prince Arthur's tour. There may have been other secret meetings but there is no record of them.

On 10 July Prince Arthur left from Miyajima for Canada aboard the Japanese battle cruiser *Kirishima*, provided by the Emperor, and it is likely that all the party travelled with him. A warship was provided because no berths on a liner were available, probably because the mission had been arranged at such short notice. There was some speculation at the time that the Russian Grand Duchess Tatiana had escaped to Japan, was handed over to Prince Arthur and also travelled with him; this has never been substantiated and seems highly improbable.

16   William Conyngham Greene (1854-1934) Ambassador to Japan 1912-1919.
17   Archibald James Murray the Master of Sinclair (1875-1957) Eton RSG later 16th Lord Sinclair Equerry to Prince Arthur.

Pulteney with Prince Arthur of Connaught arriving in Japan 1918. (© IWM FLM4171)

The *Kirishima* was delayed two days by fog and arrived at the naval base of Esquimalt in Victoria on 24 July. The landing of the Royal party was scheduled to take place at 11.30 am but the formality of saying goodbye to the Japanese officers occupied more time than expected. It was recorded that the marine band on the warship played appropriate airs during the ceremony of departure and the wind carried the music and cheers of the sailors for miles. They were met by the Lieutenant Governor (Sir Frank Barnard), Brigadier General Gwynne representative of Militia Department and Captain Kenyon-Slaney[18] and then went by motor to Government House, Victoria; those that could not be accommodated there stayed at the Empress Hotel.

Four days were spent on Victoria starting with the provincial address and then visiting troops and military hospitals. They left Victoria by boat at 11.40 pm 28 July and travelled to Vancouver arriving there at 7 am the next morning; here the programme was much the same and included lunch with the GOC Military District No 11, and visits to troops and military hospitals. They left Vancouver at 10 pm 29 July and travelled by train to Banff Springs in Alberta, and it was from there that Putty wrote to Ettie Desborough on 1 August:

Dear Chief, Was delighted to find your letter of the 22 June waiting for me at Vancouver, We shall not be back I don't anticipate before 9 September they have lengthened the programme over here, and of course we are in the dark about our boat and point of embarkation, you will have got my letter written from the Pacific (if it was received it was not

18   Robert Orlando Rodolph Kenyon-Slaney Gren Gds ADC to Gov Gen of Canada 1916-1918.

Pulteney with Prince Arthur of Connaught at British Embassy Japan, 1918. (© IWM FLM4170)

kept) and there is not much to add from this country, except that on average we visit two military hospitals a day, convalescent homes and parades of returned wounded soldiers, the vocation industrial schools are A.1 and I am writing out a long report on them to hand in to our War Office when we get home for the idea is excellent and carried out in the most practical lines all over the country. The Russian news is terrible and I am thankful we haven't touched pitch in making advances to the bolshevists which so many of our home people wanted to do, they are all as wrong as they can be and all the German gold spent among them is stained with blood. This is the most heavenly place among the Rockies [Banff Springs Hotel], the bathing in the hot sulphur swimming bath is divine, no smell (and I should imagine very weak), we bath for 40 minutes morning and evening and although we only arrived yesterday and go away tomorrow night we have all reduced our Japanese dinner figures in the most marked manner, some of the people staying here are great celebrities, heroines of the moving picture world, the weather has been glorious and we play two rounds of golf each day all except Prince A. who likes to take matters easily. Kenyon-Slaney has joined us from Ottawa, such a nice fellow, much better looking than his father[19] used to be, he has been having swimming lessons here and is progressing well I can't imagine why he never learnt before. I loved the trees in Vancouver Island, they are very fine and the smell passing through them was delicious. Hoping to see you soon after this gets to you and with all love. Yours ever Putty.

---

19   Colonel William Slaney Kenyon-Slaney Gren Gds (1847-1908).

The Royal party travelled by train across Canada visiting the provinces of Alberta, Saskatchewan and Manitoba. In each province the official programme was the same: they were met by the Lieutenant Governor and stayed at Government House; after the provincial address they visited the GOC of the military district, troops and military hospitals. In Regina, Saskatchewan they also visited HQ RNWMP and in Winnipeg, Manitoba met Major General John Hughes Inspector General of Western Canada.[20]

They arrived in Nipigon, Ontario at 3 pm 8 August and then spent three days under canvas with a dozen Indians as guides and paddlers for a fishing trip on Lake Nipigon and River Nipigon (Lake Nipigon is the largest lake which lies wholly within the boundaries of Ontario). At 8 pm 11 August they left Nipigon by train for Niagara-on-the-lake arriving there in time for breakfast on 13 August. They were met by Colonel Caldwell representative of Militia Department and inspected troops, and then to the RAF Camp at Beamsville where they had lunch; from there they travelled to Toronto by motor boat where they stayed at Government House.[21] According to the *Acadian Recorder* they were treated to a taste of a Lake Ontario squall on the way. The next two days were spent in Ontario, Toronto and London, with the provincial address, lunch with GOC Military District No 1, visits to troops and hospitals, presentation of medals and decorations to returned soldiers and next of kin, and a visit to RAF Leaside.

They left London by train at 6.30 pm 15 August and travelled to Ottawa arriving at 8 am next morning and went to Government House[22] for breakfast. In the afternoon they played golf and there was an official dinner at Government House that evening. Five days were spent in Ottawa: on 17 August there was a visit to Rockcliffe Camp where Prince Arthur was greeted with a guard of honour, then on to Sanford Fleming Convalescent Home before lunching with the government at the country club; the Prime Minister, Sir Robert Borden, was in UK and did not return until 25 August. Next day they drove to Meach Lake for tea: Meach Lake is the official summer home of Canadian Prime Ministers located outside Ottawa on the Quebec side of the Ottawa River. On 19 August they travelled by train to visit the military base and training area at Petawawa, returning to Ottawa at 10 pm that night. 20 August was a free day in their programme, and more golf was played.

The party left Ottawa at 9 am 21 August for Montreal stopping at Lachine on route to visit the remount depot. They arrived in Montreal at 2 pm where Prince Arthur was again met by a guard of honour, and went immediately to McGill Campus for an inspection of returned soldiers and presentation of medals. During the afternoon they visited Presbyterian College Hospital, Khaki League Convalescent Hospital and Drummond Military Convalescent Hospital. The day ended with tea and a brief stay in a private suite at Ritz Carlton Hotel; but they were back on the train at 1 am 22 August and travelled on to Quebec City for a very similar programme: according to the *Acadian Recorder* they were given an official welcome by the Quebec Government on 22 August. It is possible that Prince Arthur, and Putty, may have met Taft[23] while they were in Quebec.

---

20   Brother of Sam Hughes Minister of Militia and Defence 1911-1916.
21   Sir John Hendrie Lieutenant Governor.
22   Governor General was Victor Christian William Cavendish 9th Duke of Devonshire (1868-1938) Eton.
23   William Howard Taft (1857-1930) President United States 1909-1913.

On 24 August they were in Halifax, Nova Scotia and again visited military hospitals and establishments; the visit to Halifax also included a reception at Province House, lunch at the Halifax Club, and a dinner at Government House hosted by the Lieutenant Governor MacCallum Grant. The party returned briefly to the train and then at 11.25 pm that night embarked on HMS *Shannon*, an armoured cruiser, and sailed for Scapa Flow. The voyage was uneventful apart for the threat of submarines, which required constant zigzags, and frequent iceberg alarms. On 1 September they arrived in Scapa Flow and transferred to HMS *Marvel*, a destroyer; this probably took them to Scrabster to connect with the overnight train from Thurso to London referred to as the Jellicoe Express. They arrived in London on 2 September having been away almost four months. On 9 September Putty and Jessie stayed with the King and Queen at Windsor, no doubt reporting on his travels.

On 18 September Putty wrote to Ettie Desborough from Severals Lodge, Newmarket:

> Dearest Chief, Many thanks for yours of the 14 Sep. I came down here today as our Headquarters moved to Bury St Edmunds, am staying at Giles Loder's [ADC] house until I move in to my own at Bury on 1 October. The war news continues very good but the winter accommodation for the troops is going to be a great problem especially as regards hospitals which will have to be in tents and will be a great mark for bombing. I saw Godley[24] back from the front yesterday for a couple of days, he says that the Boche is very rattled and was surrendering pretty easily, much frightened by the tanks. The American coup was good but was a good deal given away by the reconnaissance they did a fortnight previous. I gather our two battalions got away from Baku with their guns all right and our losses there were much lighter than we had been led to believe in the first instance. I had luncheon today with Birdie and Stavey [Earl and Countess of Ilchester] with their boy who was en route to Eton for the first time, Stavey had just come back from Italy where I gather our front is very quiet, in the last 6 months we have only lost 25 aeroplanes while they have accounted for 300 of the enemy. I do wish that I could do something for Laurence Drummond but there are still a great number of Generals coming back from France and we are having to kick out our present commanders to make room for them while they rest so am much afraid there is no chance but I will bear him in mind. Will see you when you come south. All love Yours ever Putty.

On 18 October Putty was in attendance, with the Duke of Connaught, to receive Admiral Prince Yorihito of Higashi Fushimi (1867-1922) at Dover. He was again in attendance, appointed by the King, to receive Prince Yorihito (representing the Emperor of Japan) on 28 October and at Buckingham Palace the following day when the Prince presented the sword and badge of a Field Marshal in the Imperial Japanese Army to the King. Finally, he attended a reception for the Prince at the Guildhall on 1 November.

At the beginning of 1919 Putty resumed his active involvement with the Army Football Association (AFA). On 4 February the records show that he, Comd 23rd Army Corps: 'Chaired meeting of the AFA Council at the Junior United Service Club. At this meeting it was proposed

---

24   Probably Lieutenant General Sir Alexander John Godley (1867-1957) late IG GOC II ANZAC
     Corps and possibly III Corps in 1918.

Arrival of Prince Yorihito of Higashi Fushimi at Dover, 18 October 1918. (© IWM FLM4172)

by Pulteney and seconded by Lowther[25] that an expression of deep sympathy of the council of the AFA with the relatives of the deceased (4 members of the council were killed in action during the war) be recorded'.

Little is known about XXIII Corps or Putty's time in command of it but his valedictory order issued at Bury St Edmunds on 24 February explains much. It is addressed to the very large number of young men who were about to be sent overseas, mainly to Germany, to replace those who were to be sent home now that the fighting had ended:

> On this occasion of your leaving 23rd Army Corps for service overseas, I desire to place on record my appreciation of the standard which you have attained during these months of your early training.
>
> Further, in wishing you good luck and happiness in the future, I earnestly trust that you will continue to keep up the same spirit of soldiering while adding to it your desire to learn in your new surroundings.
>
> I want you to recollect that you are taking the place of men who have had the good fortune of fighting against the common enemy, Germany, and that although it is not your opportunity to follow in their footsteps at the moment from a fighting point of view, yet at

25   Late SG Major General.

the same time you have much work in front of you to keep up the good name of the British Army in all your actions and military bearing, also that you are under the gaze of a foreign nation who for many years have been drilled as a mechanical machine, and whose teaching enables them to criticise accurately the behaviour and bearing of the correct soldier.

It is very much in your favour to see a foreign country at such an early age. I ask you not to waste your opportunities, but to make yourself acquainted with the history of Germany, to realise for yourselves what education has done to the masses of that country and the degree of perfection its learned men have arrived at in chemistry, medicine and industry; how by working for a common cause, namely their country, they had, before the war, practically gained control of the markets of the world, which control was only ruined by a military party who risked everything for the lust of conquest.

I wish you to pay special attention to your educational and vocational training, in both of which I am assured that you will have every possible assistance. You are at a time of life when the brain is retentive and at the most critical period of the formation of a man's character, and I want you to remember that you have a better opportunity of educating yourself than others brought up without relief from the surroundings of industrial life.

Keep yourself in good health, and above all avoid venereal disease. But should you be a victim of it you must never hide it for an instant from your doctor, and you must make it a point of honour to get it absolutely cured.

You should write to your parents and take an interest in their home life. The more cheerful the letter the more it will be appreciated; interest them in the description of your surroundings and do not bore them with your grievances.

Remember that you are doing your duty to the country in which you were born, and endeavour to uphold the memory of those who perished in the defence of their King and Country in the area of ground behind you.

It is not known whether Jessie moved up to live with Putty in Bury St Edmunds but it was from St Margarets (now part of Shire Hall) in Bury St Edmunds that he wrote to Ettie Desborough on 11 March:

> Dearest Chief, Am posting today the book on vocational training which will give you an idea how the USA have tackled the subject. I enclose a copy of my valedictory order to these graduated battalions going out, just plain language that the boy should be able to understand. I shall try and come up to see the show on 22nd. Yours ever Putty. Had a long talk at W.O. yesterday and came to the conclusion that unless we have a little more give and take with Germany we shall have the whole of that country turn bolshevists and we shall have a combination of Russia with her against us which will make the biggest war again possible.

This letter suggests that Jessie remained in London, at least for some of the time.

On 4 April Putty again chaired a meeting of the AFA this time at Headquarters Irish Guards. Then, on 15 April, his time in command of XXIII Corps came to an end, and he was on leave for the rest of the year. On 20 May he was at Eton for a photograph of eighteen generals who had been at the school and served in the Great War. He continued with his involvement with the AFA, chairing a meeting in the Horse Guards library on 15 December. Two weeks later (30

Eton Generals, 1919.
(Reproduced by permission of the Provost and Fellows of Eton College)

December) he received a letter from Lord Stamfordham[26] with the King's offer of the post of Gentleman Usher of the Black Rod, pointing out that it would require his retirement from the army. Putty duly accepted and retired from the army next day (31 December) after more than forty years' service.

It is evident that when Haig came to visit on 13 February 1918 Putty had no inkling that he was about to be sent home. This is hardly surprising since he had once again been fully involved in reconstituting the corps and taking over another new sector of the front from the French. There had also been no indication that Haig or Byng blamed him at all for the success of the German counter-attack at Cambrai on 30 November, or that Putty blamed himself. Perhaps Haig just thought it was time to change the commander of III Corps after nearly three and a half years.

Neither the official enquiry nor the Smuts review concluded that Putty was responsible for the German breakthrough; in fact they exonerated the army, corps and divisional commanders,

26   Lieutenant Colonel Arthur John Bigge (1849-1931) late RA 1st Lord Stamfordham Private
      Secretary to Queen Victoria 1895-1901 and King George V 1901-1931.

Pulteney, Pencil drawing by Percival
Anderson. (Clive Pulteney)

pointing instead to the lack of training of junior officers, NCOs and men. Yet the evidence to the enquiry suggested 7 tactical errors on the III Corps front and without further examination of them it is not possible to avoid the suspicion that there was a closing of ranks or even the whitewash suggested by Lloyd George.

The boundary between III and VII Corps was tactically unsound since it ran up a likely enemy approach. One of the corps should have been given responsibility for it when 3rd Army went on the defensive, and Byng did not do this. It seems extraordinary that an enemy force of three divisions could have formed up undetected in the Crèvecoeur-Honnecourt valley on the night 29/30 November but that is what happened. Despite all the warnings 3rd Army was surprised, and the problem was the shape of the ground. There were a number of options but both corps had to be coordinated; if only Byng or his GOCRA had coordinated the artillery fire effectively the outcome might have been different.

Putty had ordered GOCs 12th and 20th Divisions to hold the right flank of the corps' position when it was first taken on 20 November, so they had at least ten days to consider the problems and make adjustments. Neither deployed their divisions as effectively as perhaps they could have done, and both were surprised and overrun. The shape of the ground and lack of depth required observation well forward to give adequate warning, day and night; a strong outpost line to delay the enemy; a well-wired main defensive position with carefully planned artillery support; strong points making use of the villages and other tactical features; and a reserve line that integrated all those in rear. It is difficult to avoid the conclusion that both could have done more, and that there was complacency. Asking tired and poorly trained men to fight in such circumstances was inviting disaster.

The greatest mistake was to expect III Corps to fight and win a defensive battle on the same ground that the attack had ended on ten days earlier. Byng ordered his corps 'to consolidate all ground gained with a view to meeting counter-attacks'. It is the word 'all' used here as so often in the war that gave no room for any leeway – ground, however much a tactical liability, could not be given up and as a consequence reserves could not be reconstituted. It should have been possible for Haig to decide much earlier that a further advance on this part of the front was no longer possible, and to have ordered Byng to pull back to a defendable line. The delay in making this decision handed the initiative to the enemy. If III Corps had held further back with 29th Division withdrawn into reserve, there might have been an even bigger opportunity to inflict a heavy defeat on the Germans.

Some of these seven critical mistakes were Byng or Haig's responsibility, others that of GOCs 12th and 20th Division. Putty stands in the middle yet without primary responsibility for any of them; he could and should have done more to persuade Byng, especially where there was a need to give up ground or for greater coordination, and to supervise the commanders of his two weakest divisions. All of them were responsible to a certain extent but then it has to be remembered what they had achieved in the great victory of 20 November. Putty was commanding a rapidly reconstituted III Corps that he had hardly time to get to know let alone train, and must have been knackered along with many others. It should also not be forgotten that it was Putty's counter-attacks that restored the situation on 1 December.

His appointment to command XXIII Corps was a most important one for the country and the army: the mission to Japan, with its visits to the United States and Canada, had considerable political significance including as it did meetings with the President of the United States, Emperor of Japan, and the Government of Canada. Prince Arthur was the head of the mission but it seems inconceivable that Putty would have been sent with him by the King, Lloyd George or CIGS if they thought he was to blame for Cambrai or had been in any way found to be incompetent.

14

Black Rod and later life 1920-1941

In January 1920 Putty began his appointment as Black Rod, an officer of the Order of the Garter, in the House of Lords. His recorded duties were:

1. The Care and Custody, and Pre-eminence of keeping the doors of the High Court of Parliament (Garter Statute 1522). Appoints doorkeepers and controls access.
2. Disciplinary Function. Power of Detention 'taking into custody any person whom the house may order to be detained'.
3. Attends sittings of the House: subject to direction of the House, responsible for maintenance of order in the Chamber. Sits in a box immediately below the bar on the right hand side of the Chamber (as one faces the throne). Either he or Yeoman Usher has to be present during sittings of the House. When a division is called he switches on (in his box) the division bells.
4. Agent of the Administration Sub Committee. Responsible for the allocation and maintenance of accommodation and services and the control of security in that part of the Palace of Westminster used by the House.
5. Secretary to the Lord Great Chamberlain. Responsible for the Royal Apartments of the Palace of Westminster: Robing Room (used on State Openings of Parliament), Royal Gallery, and in conjunction with Lord Chancellor and Speaker of Westminster Hall. Responsible for the administration of the Crypt Chapel and keeps the Chapel registers. Responsible for administrative arrangements when the Sovereign is in Parliament.
6. Ceremonial Duties: Participates in the annual Garter Ceremonies at Windsor; First ceremonial activity is his own induction; As Sergeant at Arms duty to carry the Mace before the Lord Chancellor when he enters the House in procession at the beginning of each sitting (In practice Yeoman Usher who is deputy Sergeant at Arms normally fulfils this function. Black Rod himself follows the Lord Chancellor's procession into the Chamber and takes up his position in his box); When a new Peer is introduced into the House of Lords Black Rod leads the procession into and out of the House; and Summoning House of Commons on behalf of the Sovereign – State Opening of Parliament, Order to choose a Speaker, Royal Approval of Speaker, Lord Chancellors Royal Speech to close session, Royal Assent.

The dress was also recorded:

> Black Rod wears Court Dress – black shoes with black buckles, silk stockings, black breeches, black coat with black wig bag at back. Sword in black scabbard. Chain is worn and Rod carried only on ceremonial occasions. At State Opening of Parliament ruffles are worn at the wrists and a jabot at the neck. At Garter ceremonies Black Rod wears a scarlet mantle of an officer of the Order of the Garter with Garter badge and black velvet cap. Over his robes he wears the chain of office. He carries Black Rod.

In many ways Putty was the ideal choice for Black Rod. He knew the King and many members of the House of Lords, and they knew him from their service in the army or socially, and he was interested in the every aspect of government of the nation. The appointment also suited him since he lived in London and it allowed him more time to enjoy married life with Jessie.

The Pulteneys started their civilian life together at 4 Deanery Street, Park Lane which they rented at the beginning of 1920. This was only to be a temporary home, perhaps while Isabel, Putty's sister, moved out of 3 Lower Berkeley Street (in 1936 renamed Fitzhardinge Street) and the house was redecorated. The Pulteneys moved there in 1921 when Putty was given the lease and they lived in the house until he died: the lease was then transferred to Jessie and she lived there until 1950.

The house was owned by the Portman Estate: on five floors, it consisted of a basement (kitchen), ground floor (dining room), 1st floor (drawing room), 2nd floor (bedrooms), 3rd floor (servants), mews (carriages and cars) with accommodation (probably for Guardsman Hogbin SG), and a garden between the mews and the house.

Guardsman George Charles Hogbin was discharged from the Army in February 1920; his address on discharge was given as 4 Deanery Street and then changed to 3 Lower Berkeley Street the following year. He had married Anne Everitt in Bicklehampton, Worcestershire on 30 September 1911 and they had two daughters: it seems likely that the whole family lived in the mews accommodation in 3 Lower Berkeley Street. Hogbin was also employed as a doorkeeper at the House of Lords, a post he held until 1945.

On 2 February 1920 Putty chaired a meeting of the council of the AFA in Horse Guards. It was to be his last and he resigned from the council. Putty had been a member of the committee and involved in the management and development of football in the army for thirty years; he remained as one of the vice presidents of the AFA.

The House of Lords' records for Putty's first year show the State Opening of Parliament on 10 February, adjournment from 16 August to 19 October, and a number of 'Grantings of Royal Assent' and 'Presentations of Letters Patent' during the year. Parliament was prorogued on 23 December. It was to be the pattern of Putty's year for the rest of his life.

Putty thought that Lord Desborough had died when he wrote to Ettie on 2 December 1920:

> Jessie joins me in trying to express our sympathy with you in another great trial, may God help you in your great sorrow and bring comfort to you in the knowledge that Willy is happy and free from care with his sons. I saw him thank God in the House of Lords this week when he told me how sorry he was that I had not taken the Mill House an expression of friendship in the last words he spoke to me that I shall always cherish. May God give you health to brave this sorrow is the earnest wish of your ever affect friend. WP Pulteney.

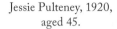
Jessie Pulteney, 1920,
aged 45.

His obituary had been published in error in *The Times* that day; in fact Lord Desborough was to outlive Putty and died on 9 January 1945.

After Christmas the Pulteneys went on holiday to Biarritz returning on 10 February. The highlight of 1921 for them was getting settled in 3 Lower Berkeley Street. On 4 March Putty (and probably Jessie too) attended the Memorial Service for Major General Lord Ranksborough[1] at the Chapel Royal, St James Palace. The following month, on 25 April, Putty was a pall bearer for the funeral of General Sir John Cowans[2] in Westminster Cathedral and the later internment at Kensal Green Cemetery.

In July the Pulteneys attended a State Ball at Buckingham Palace for the King and Queen of the Belgians: the year ended with another holiday in Biarritz, returning on 16 December. It was this that prevented Putty attending the unveiling of a memorial to 16 RS by General Sir Francis Davies[3] in St Giles Cathedral. He read a letter from Putty:

> I hope whoever unveils this memorial will allude to the magnificent work the battalion did at the first great Battle of the Somme, when they held on to the position on the

---

1   Major General John Fielden Brocklehurst 1st Baron Ranksborough late RHG (1852-1921) Comd 2 Cav Bde SA Govt Chief Whip House of Lords 1915-1921.
2   General Sir John 'Jack' Cowans (1862-1921) late RB.
3   General Sir Francis John Davies (1864-1948) late Gren Gds GOC 8th Division 1914-1915. GOCinC Scottish Command 1919-1923.

Boisselle-Contalmaison road. It enabled many subsequent advances to be made on the left flank which would otherwise have been made very difficult and more costly. Please remember me to all those who served under me and tell them how I look back with pride on their loyalty and courage.

Some time in 1921 the Ypres League was founded by Field Marshal French (Viscount French of Ypres) and Field Marshal Plumer (Viscount Plumer of Messines). Ypres of all the great battles had a very special place in the memories of those who served there, especially those of the original BEF in 1914. The League sought to remember all those who had died including the citizens of Ypres. Putty became involved from the outset because he was considered a friend by French and by Plumer, and because of the part he played in the Ypres battles during 1914 and 1915.

Three events in the life of the Pulteneys stand out in 1922. On 10 March Putty attended with Jessie a Reception given by Mrs Whiteley[4] at Speaker's House for members of both Houses of Parliament, visitors from the dominions, and officials of the House of Commons. They moved in several social circles and Parliament was one of the most active of them.

The Pulteneys stayed at Riverhill, Sevenoaks as guests of the Rogers 3-6 June. Muriel, the Christian Scientist and Lieutenant Colonel John Middleton Rogers' first wife, had died in 1919 and he had re-married Hilda Stevenson in 1921. Lieutenant Colonel Rogers' brother, Arthur Edward Rogers, was married to Jessie's sister, Lily, and they lived nearby; Lily too was a Christian Scientist. Putty did not approve and Jessie is not recorded as having been to Riverhill since they were married. This must have been a special occasion to persuade Putty and it was probably to meet the new Mrs Rogers.

The third event was the Ypres League Ball which was held in December at the Royal Albert Hall under the patronage of the King, the Prince of Wales and Princess Beatrice.[5] The Pulteneys attended because Putty was by now the Hon Treasurer of the League.

The pattern of the Pulteneys' life continued much the same in 1923. Again three events were of note. On 6 March the Pulteneys attended a dinner party given by HM The King and Queen at Buckingham Palace. Jessie sat between Sir Samuel Hoare MP[6] and former Prime Minister Asquith. Putty sat between Mrs Kipling[7] and Lady Keyes:[8] 40 people attended.

Putty unveiled a memorial to 34th Division at La Boisselle on 23 May. Interestingly the memorial is higher in the village than that of 19th Division, yet it was the latter division that eventually captured the village. It may be symbolic to reflect 34th Division's success in getting past the village on the right flank and securing part of the high ground beyond, which allowed 19th Division later to take the village.

In November Princess Beatrice laid a wreath at the Cenotaph on behalf of the Ypres League on the anniversary of the 1st Battle of Ypres. Putty attended and by now was the Chairman of the League.

---

4   Wife of John Henry Whiteley Speaker of House of Commons 1921-1928.
5   Princess Beatrice (1857-1944) Queen Victoria's youngest daughter and wife of Prince Henry of Battenburg.
6   Samuel Hoare (1880-1959) later 1st Viscount Templewood.
7   Probably Carrie Balestier (1862-1939) wife of Rudyard Kipling.
8   Probably wife of Admiral Sir Roger Keyes.

34th Division Memorial, La Boisselle, 2012.

The events of note in 1924 included Putty taking the salute at the annual Founders Day at the Royal Hospital Chelsea on 31 May. The Governor was General Sir Neville Lyttelton.[9] In August *The Times* published a letter signed by Putty and others appealing for a memorial church in Ypres. That year was the 10th Anniversary of the 1st Battle and Field Marshal Plumer laid a wreath at the celebration, at which Putty was also present.

In 1925 the Ypres League published a 'guide and record' entitled 'The Immortal Salient'. Putty was instrumental in its production: by now he was a trustee and Chairman of the Executive Committee of the League, and may still have been its Hon Treasurer. At this time HM The King was Patron in Chief, HRH The Prince of Wales the Patron, Field Marshal Earl of Ypres the President, and the Vice Presidents were Field Marshals Earl Haig, Lord Plumer and Viscount Allenby. Much of Putty's time in these years was devoted to the care of the British School in Ypres and fostering its connection with his old school, Eton, under whose auspices it was founded.

9   General Sir Neville Lyttelton (1845-1931) Eton Evans House late RB CinC SA CGS 1904-1908 CinC Ireland 1908-1912.

Pulteney with General Lyttelton at Founders Day, Royal Hospital Chelsea 1924.
(Reproduced by kind permission of The Royal Hospital Chelsea)

Field Marshal Earl of Ypres had not been at all well. On 24 April *The Times* published:

> Wednesday being the 10th Anniversary of the first use of poison gas by the Germans in the
> Second Battle of Ypres, the Ypres League sent a message to their President, Lord Ypres who
> was at that time Commander in Chief of the British Expeditionary Force. Lord Ypres is in
> a nursing home recovering from a serious operation, and the message was conveyed to him
> by Lieutenant General Sir William Pulteney, the Chairman of the Executive Committee
> of the League. It was as follows: 'On this the 10th Anniversary of the opening of the
> Second Battle of Ypres, the members of the Ypres League recall with gratitude the eminent
> services of their President and wish him a speedy recovery from his present illness'.

Lord Ypres did not recover and died the following week: Putty attended his funeral at Deal
on 27 May.

On 3 June Putty attended a dinner given by the Master of the Horse, Earl of Granard[10] at
Forbes House in Halkin Street to celebrate the King's Birthday. Granard was one of several SG
officers with whom Putty remained lifelong friends.

Later that year on 18 November the Pulteneys attended the marriage of Mr Edward Seymour
and Miss Barbara Lascelles at St Peter's Church in Eaton Square. It was a Pulteney family
occasion; Barbara Lascelles was Putty's niece, his sister Beatrice's daughter. Reverend Arthur

10   Bernard Arthur William Patrick Hastings 8th Earl of Granard (1874-1948) SG 1899-1911.

Wykham Pulteney, Putty's brother, now 70 and still living in the rectory at Ashley where he had been the rector since 1882, assisted. Arthur was to die two years later.

On 1 February of the following year (1926) Putty and Jessie attended a reception given by the Marchioness of Londonderry at Londonderry House to the meet the Prime Minister.[11] Putty would have seen the Marquess, his ADC in 1914/1915, frequently in the House of Lords but this was the first recorded meeting between Jessie and Edith.

The Ypres League again organised its annual memorial parade on 31 October on Horse Guards. Princess Beatrice was received by Putty representing the League, and placed the Ypres League wreath on the Cenotaph. The following week the appeal to build a British School in Ypres was formally announced in the form of three letters – from the Provost of Eton, Lord Plumer and Putty.

Putty's brother, Arthur Wykeham, died on 2 February 1927 and Putty with many of the family attended his funeral at Ashley in driving rain. On 31 May, as a Vice President of the AFA, he chaired the AGM at the Royal United Services Institution. *The Times* noted: 'The Chairman on behalf of the Association expressed their deep gratitude to their Majesties the King and Queen for their continued interest in and presence at the final of the Army Challenge Cup at Aldershot'.

The following month (June) Putty again attended a dinner given by the Master of the Horse (Earl of Granard) at Forbes House to celebrate the King's Birthday; it was now a regular occasion. He was at Olympia later that month with Jessie as guests of Major General Sir Cecil Lowther (Putty's Best Man in 1917) when the King and Queen visited the International Horse Show. He may well have seen both Granard and Lowther again that month when he attended the 3rd Guards Club Dinner at the Mayfair Hotel in Berkeley Square, another regular occasion in his diary.

In July Putty, probably with Jessie, went to France and Belgium. He unveiled a memorial tablet in the Cathedral in Laon commemorating the British soldiers who had sacrificed their lives in that region during the war. A few days later he was in Ypres for the unveiling of the Menin Gate Memorial: Putty was a member of the committee.

The pattern of Putty's life continued much the same each year, as did Jessie's. In November 1928 Putty unveiled the BEF Memorial at La Ferté sous Jouarre recording the names of 3,888 missing from the 1914 battles of Mons, Le Cateau, Aisne and Marne. Maréchal Foch, Field Marshal Milne (who had been Putty's BGGS in 1914 and was now CIGS) and General Weygand also attended.

In April 1928 the Ypres Memorial School, built by Etonians on a site about half a mile from the Menin Gate, was opened. The school would be attended by 62 children at the beginning, most of them the children of men employed by the Imperial War Graves Commission in tending the cemeteries at Ypres. In a statement published in *The Times* Putty said that 'every effort had been made to establish the school on modern lines'.

Putty and Jessie attended a reception hosted by Lady Melchett[12] at 35 Lowndes Square in June for the Exhibition and Sale of the Disabled Soldiers Embroidery Industry of the Friends of the Poor. The Prince of Wales also attended.

---

11   Stanley Baldwin Prime Minister 1924-1929.
12   Probably Violet Florence Mabel Mond Baroness Melchett (1867-1945) involved in numerous charitable activities including hospitals and convalescent homes during the war.

Also that year Lord Esmé Gordon-Lennox [13] was appointed Yeoman Usher of the Black Rod and continued in that appointment for the rest of Putty's time as Black Rod.

The Pulteneys went to the S of France at the beginning of 1930, and were reported staying at the Eden Hotel Cap D'Ail. On 6 September that year *The Times* published a photograph taken at North Berwick of Putty playing golf on holiday with Captain EA Fitzroy Speaker of the House of Commons.[14] At the end of the month (30 September-2 October) Putty was in Quidenham, Norfolk for three days partridge shooting as a guest of the Earl of Albermarle;[15] the other guns included Lord Somerleyton.[16] Lord Suffield,[17] Sir Langrishe,[18] L Bulteel, R Buxton, and the Earl of Clarendon.[19] Finally, in December, he attended the funeral of Lieutenant General Sir Hastings Anderson[20] in the chapel of the Royal Hospital Chelsea.

1931 was a busy year for Putty and Jessie, if judged by the number of reported events. In February Putty attended the dinner of the Royal Warrant Holders' Association at the Connaught Rooms: next month (March) they both attended a garden party at Buckingham Palace.

In May the London Committee of the Ypres League held its annual dinner and dance at the Royal Hotel Woburn Place, Russell Square. Putty was in the chair. The following month (June) Putty attended, as usual, the Master of the Horse (Earl of Granard)'s dinner at Forbes House to celebrate the King's Birthday and the 3rd Guards Club Dinner at the Savoy Hotel. Between these two dinners he was in Belgium to present a number of regimental memorial tablets for dedication by the Bishop of Fulham in St George's Memorial Chapel, Ypres. Later that same day he attended the unveiling of a War Memorial at Ploegsteert by the Duke of Brabant.[21]

Putty was at the funeral of Colonel JB Stracey-Clitheroe[22] in July. In November he was reported, with Jessie, to have attended the Prime Minister and Her Majesty's Government reception at Lancaster House in honour of the delegates to the India and Burma Round-Table Conference.

Lord Hindlip's[23] memorial service was held at St George's Hanover Square in December. Both Putty and Jessie were there. Hindlip may well have been in Putty's Column in South Africa which would explain their friendship: he was a frequent visitor to HQ III Corps during the war in his role as a War Office messenger carrying official correspondence, and on occasions Putty's private letters.

After Christmas the Pulteneys went to the South of France for a holiday staying on this occasion at the Hotel de Paris in Monte Carlo. Despite the wealth of their respective families

13   Colonel Lord Esmé Charles Gordon-Lennox (1875-1949) Eton SG 1896-1920 Putty was his son's godfather.
14   Captain Edward Algernon Fitzroy (1869-1943) LG Speaker of the House of Commons 1928-1935.
15   Arnold Allan Cecil Keppel 8th Earl of Albermarle (1858-1942) Eton SG 1878-1883.
16   Francis Crossley 2nd Baron Somerleyton (1889-1959) Eton 9 L.
17   Victor Alexander Charles Harbord 7th Baron Suffield (1897-1943) SG 1915-1924.
18   Sir Hercules Robert Langrishe (1859-1943) 5th Bart.
19   George Herbert Hyde Villiers 6th Earl of Clarendon (1877-1955) Governor General South Africa 1931-1937.
20   Lieutenant General Sir Hastings Anderson (1872-1930) late Cheshire GSO1 8th Division 1914-1915.
21   Duke of Brabant (1901-1983) Eton later King Leopold III of Belgium.
22   Colonel John Bourchier Stracey-Clitheroe (1853-1931) SG 1872-1899.
23   3rd Baron Hindlip (1877-1931) Lieutenant 8 H SA GSO WW1.

Pulteney when Black Rod. (Clive Pulteney)

neither Putty nor Jessie was ever more than comfortably off: able to mix in the highest circles of society and stay at the best hotels but not to indulge in any form of extravagance; they never owned a property of their own. Again their holiday prevented them attending another family wedding, that of Captain Lascelles[24] and Miss Manners which took place at the Guards Chapel in January 1932.

In February 1932 Putty wrote to a Mr Kitts, the first of two letters: Mr Kitts was evidently researching the history of Black Rod: 'Dear Mr Kitts, Perhaps you could find time to come to see me in the House of Lords to talk over your book on the Black Rod. You would find me in my box tomorrow (Monday) afternoon any time between 4 and 6 pm. Yours sincerely WP Pulteney'

Putty played in the Parliamentary Handicap Golf Tournament at Walton Heath in April and was reported to have beaten JSC Reid in the 1st Round and Mason in the 2nd.

In June he was in Belgium again visiting Haig House, Ypres on a Sunday with General Sir Charles Harington,[25] the Bishop of Fulham and the Chaplain General to the Forces. The following month (July) he was a pall bearer for the funeral of Field Marshal Viscount Plumer at Westminster Abbey.

He wrote to Mr Kitts again in October: 'Dear Mr Kitts, Thank you very much for returning me the Black Rod notes. Those are two very interesting points you bring out about Black Rod in

---

24   John Norman Pulteney Lascelles (1898-1939) Putty's nephew – his sister Beatrice's son.
25   General Sir Charles Harington Harington (1872-1940) late Kings Liverpool GSO 2 HQ III Corps 1914-1915 GOC Aldershot Command 1931-1933.

1510 and 1614. I like the idea of the Commons sending their Sergeant to find out if the Lords were ready and the members refusing to go as they regarded it as irregular, the refusal shows knowledge of precedent. Will try to nerve myself once more to tackle the subject, there is no doubt it is of much interest. Thank you very much for taking so much trouble in the matter. Yours sincerely WP Pulteney'

A few days later Putty attended the annual service of the Ypres League held on Horse Guards Parade; several hundred ex-Servicemen were on parade and Princes Beatrice was also present.

In November (1932) the Pulteneys again attended a reception given by the Prime Minister[26] and His Majesty's Government for the delegates to the Indian Round-Table Conference.

1933 started with the funeral of Lieutenant Colonel Henry Wickham[27] at Cotterstock, Oundle in early February; later that month Putty also attended the Memorial Service for Field Marshal Sir William Robertson at Westminster Abbey. Also in February he was reported in *The Times* as a signatory to a letter proposing a memorial to Field Marshal Lord Methuen.

In May (1933) the Queen paid a visit to the Annual Exhibition and Sale of Work by the Disabled Soldiers Embroidery Industry held at 33 Lowndes Square, the residence of Violet, Lady Melchett. The Pulteneys were also reported to have visited.

It was to be a year of memorials with Putty and Jessie attending the dedication of memorials to Field Marshal Lord Plumer and Field Marshal Lord Ypres by the Bishop of London in St George's, the British Church in Ypres, in June. The following month, July, Putty attended the unveiling of a memorial to Field Marshal Viscount Plumer in the west cloister of Eton College by the Duke of Gloucester.

In October the Pulteneys were at Chelsea Barracks when the Scots Guards were inspected by the Duke of York and later that month Putty attended the 13th Memorial Parade in celebration of the anniversary of Ypres Day held by the Ypres League on Horse Guards Parade.

Both Putty and Jessie attended the marriage of Mr John Lambton and Miss Ethel Ruth Nicholson at Christ Church Mayfair in March 1934. John Lambton[28] was the nephew of Putty's friend Major General Hon Sir William Lambton 1863-1936 late Coldm Gds.

The following month *The Times* reported:

> Under the auspices of the Ypres League 150 members of the junior OTC left London on a four day tour of Ypres and other places made famous in the Great War. Lady Plumer and Lieutenant General Sir William Pulteney were on the platform at Victoria to see them off.

At the end of the month Putty and Jessie attended a Requiem Mass at Westminster Cathedral in a tribute to the King of the Belgians.

Putty was at the Annual Dinner of the Japan Society at Claridges in May attended by Prince and Princess Kaya,[29] and he proposed their health. This was his first recorded involvement with Japanese events since 1918 but some link must have been maintained. Later that month Putty played for the Generals' team in their annual golf match with the Admirals at Camberley Heath

---

26   Ramsay MacDonald (1866-1937) Prime Minister 1931-1935.
27   Henry Wickham Wickham (1855-1933) SG 1874-1887.
28   John Lambton (1909-1941) Coldm Gds then RAF killed in action.
29   Prince Kaya Tsunenori (1900-1978) Colonel Imperial Japanese GS 1st cousin to wife of Emperor Hirohito.

beating Admiral Sir Hugh Watson (1872-1954) in the singles and, with Field Marshal Lord Cavan, losing in the doubles to Admiral Watson and Admiral of the Fleet Sir O de B Brock (1869-1947).

During June Putty attended the 23rd Division (Officers) Association Dinner at the Café Royal and proposed the toast to the division and its commanders. Later that month he was at a dinner given by the Duke of Norfolk, Earl Marshal, at Norfolk House to celebrate the four hundred and fiftieth anniversary of the College of Arms. Finally that year, 1934, Putty is reported to have attended the funeral service of Major Braithwaite[30] at Brompton Parish Church.

If Putty was beginning to slow down there was no sign of it in 1935. In April, now President of the Ypres League, Putty welcomed 300 members of the Surrey British Legion who marched to the Town Hall in Ypres, cheered by crowds of Ypres citizens. He was reported twice on the golf course during the year, in May playing in the Parliamentary Golf Handicap Tournament at Walton Heath and later in the month playing for the General's team in their annual match against the Admirals at Camberley Heath winning his singles against Admiral Sir Lionel Halsey (1872-1949).

In the period May-July Putty attended a dinner given by Sir Abe Bailey[31] to meet the Prime Minister of South Africa,[32] the 3rd Guards Club Dinner at the Savoy Hotel, with Jessie a Reception given by the Japanese Ambassador, and the Old Evansite (Evans House Eton) Dinner at the Trocadero.

When Major General Earl of Athlone[33] inspected 500 men of the London divisions of the United Service Corps at the Honourable Artillery Company in July, *The Times* reported that he was received by Lieutenant General Sir William Pulteney, Chairman of the Council: Putty had taken on yet another commitment.

In October Princess Beatrice attended the annual Ypres Day service at Horse Guards Parade and afterwards placed the wreath of the Ypres League on the Cenotaph: she was received by Putty, the Chairman of the Ypres League.

In his 75th year (1936) Putty was as busy as ever. In January was the State Funeral of King George V who had died on 20 January: as Black Rod he would have been much involved. Field Marshal Lord Allenby died in the spring and Putty attended the burial of his ashes in the Warriors' Chapel in Westminster Abbey during May. In July he and Jessie were at the memorial service for Lady Graham-Montgomery[34] at Christ Church, Victoria Street.

Also in July Putty was appointed Gentleman Usher of the Black Road to the new Sovereign, King George VI; and at the end of the month he was present as the Chairman of the Council

---

30   Major Ernest Lucas Braithwaite HLI, 13 H Egypt 1882 and Imperial Yeomanry in SA.
31   Sir Abe Bailey (1864-1940) wealthy and influential South African with house in Bryanston Square.
32   James Barry Munnik Hertzog (1866-1942) Prime Minister 1924-1939.
33   Major General Alexander Cambridge 1st Earl of Athlone (1874-1957) late 7 H Eton husband of Princess Alice, Queen Victoria's grand-daughter.
34   Probably Theresa Blanche Graham-Montgomery died 24 June 1936 widow of Sir Basil Templer Graham-Montgomery 5th Bt (1852-1928) and daughter of Lieutenant Colonel Verschoyle Gren Gds who lived in Co Kildare: she may have been an Irish Connection of Jessie's.

when Field Marshal Sir Philip Chetwode[35] carried out the annual inspection of the United Services Corps at the Honourable Artillery Company: 500 men paraded.

On 8 October 1936 a letter from Putty was published in *The Times*: 'Sir, We are continually being asked why the Belgian buglers who sound last post at the Menin Gate every night do not wear uniform, and it has often been suggested that they should do so. May we ask you to give our answer publicity through your columns. The impressive ceremony is really in the nature of two or more ordinary working men, civilian citizens of Ypres, saying "Good-night" to those tens of thousands lying asleep all round them; and we feel it is in no way a military ceremony, but it is an expression of homage from the Belgian people to those gallant British who made the great sacrifice in Flanders fields. WP Pulteney (Lieutenant General), Paul Slessor (Major), British Members of the Last Post Committee. 3 Lower Berkeley Street'.

Later that month Putty was at the memorial service for Major General Hon Sir William Lambton[36] in the Royal Military Chapel, Wellington Barracks: then, at the end of the year (17 December) he and Jessie attended the wedding of Lieutenant Commander Richard Courtenay Boyle Royal Navy (1902-1984 nephew – Putty's sister Alice's son) and Miss Guendolen Griffith at Holy Trinity, Sloane Street.

There was no holiday for the Pulteneys in the South of France that winter 1936/1937. At the beginning of January they attended the marriage of Sir John Heathcoat-Amory Bt[37] and Miss Joyce Wethered at St George's, Hanover Square. Then, in March they were both at a dinner at the Belgian Embassy. At the end of that month Putty, as Hon Sec Ypres British School, had an article written by him about the school published in *The Times*.

During April Putty and Jessie were at a Reception given by Brigadier General Sir Archibald Home and Lady Home at the Dorchester for their daughter, Miss Theresa Home. Home had been BGGS Cav Corps at the Battle of Cambrai in 1917. Later that month Putty, as Chairman of the Ypres League, saw off 100 public school boys from Victoria on a 3 day tour organised by the League of the battlefields in France and Flanders. At the very end of the month he and Jessie were guests of the Marquess and Marchioness of Londonderry at a Cocktail Party at Londonderry House for members of the Old Etonian Flying Club.

In May many overseas visitors arrived in London. Putty and Jessie were guests of the Marquess and Marchioness of Londonderry at Londonderry House at a reception for overseas visitors: a few days later they were guests of the Speaker at a reception in Speaker's House for the overseas guests of the King and Queen. Putty then attended the Coronation of King George VI, an event in which he was again much involved. At the very end of May both Putty and Jessie were at a garden party given by the Marquess[38] and Marchioness of Salisbury at Hatfield House.

A number of Putty's activities were reported in June starting with a musical at home given by Lady Hadfield[39] at 22 Carlton House Terrace. The usual pattern of events continued at the House of Lords with Putty present as Black Rod for the introduction of Earl Baldwin and Viscount Samuel. Later in the month the first Garter Service and procession for 23 years

---

35   Field Marshal Sir Philip Walhouse Chetwode Bt (1869-1950) late 19 H Eton CinC India until 1936 later 1st Baron Chetwode.
36   Major General Hon Sir William Lambton (1863-1936) late Coldm Gds Eton MS GHQ BEF 1914.
37   Major Sir John Heathcote-Amory Bt (1894-1972) Eton.
38   James Edward Hubert Gascoyne-Cecil 4th Marquess of Salisbury (1861-1947) Eton.
39   Lady Frances Belt Hadfield (1862-NK) American wife of Sir Robert Hadfield industrialist.

was held at Windsor with Putty in attendance. Still in June he attended the 3rd Guards Club Dinner at the Savoy, an event which he rarely missed, and with Jessie, a Reception given by His Majesty's Body Guard of the Honourable Gentlemen-at-Arms at St James Palace.

Later in the year (1937) he was at the Old Evansite Dinner at the Trocadero; he attended the annual meeting of the United Services Corps as Chairman of the Managing Committee; he was in Ypres for the Prize Day at the British School, when the prizes were presented by Field Marshal Lord Cavan; and he attended with Jessie His Majesty's Government's reception at Westminster Hall in honour of members of the American Legion.

In March 1938 Lady Jean Hamilton (1861-1941) wrote:

> Ian[40] and I had luncheon amongst our contempories today, a very ageing experience. It was at the Poulteneys [sic] (3 Lower Berkeley Street). Poultie, as Kitty Drummond[41] always calls him, was standing in the small downstairs room with Lady Tilworth also standing, both so bad with rheumatism they did not wish to sit down.

With this in mind it is difficult to understand how Putty managed to continue as Black Rod or his other activities. Yet in May he and Jessie were at a reception given by the Japanese Ambassador and in June they were both at the Turkish Embassy for a dance given by that country's ambassador.

The London Divisions of the United Services Corps (600 men in all) paraded at the Honourable Artillery Company in July for inspection by Princess Alice, Countess of Athlone. *The Times* reported that: 'She was greeted by the President, Major General the Earl of Athlone and members of the Council, including Lieutenant General Sir William Pulteney'. As usual at the end of October the Ypres memorial parade was held on Horse Guards Parade; 1500 men were on the parade and Lady Plumer laid the wreath on the Cenotaph. *The Times* reported: 'The Belgian Ambassador inspected the parade, accompanied by Lieutenant General Sir William Pulteney, Chairman of the Ypres League'.

At the beginning of 1939 Putty was in Ashley for the funeral of Lieutenant Colonel George Reginald Lascelles.[42] Later that month he attended the Memorial Service at the Royal Military Chapel, Wellington Barracks for Captain William Drummond Moray.[43] In early April Putty was at the 26th annual dinner of the London Branch of the Scots Guards Association at Princes' Galleries, Picadilly. This would have been a very special occasion for him, especially as there is no record of him being invited previously. Also in April he and Jessie were at the Royal Military Chapel, Wellington Barracks for the wedding of Lieutenant Colonel Sir John Aird Gren Gds (1898-1973 3rd Bt) and Lady Priscilla Willoughby. A few days later Putty and Jessie were at a reception given by the Japanese Ambassador at 10 Grosvenor Square to celebrate the birthday of the Emperor of Japan.

---

40   General Sir Ian Standish Monteith Hamilton (1853-1947) late Gordons CinC Allied Med Exped Force.
41   Katherine Mary Drummond (NK-1947) wife of Major General Laurence Drummond late SG.
42   Reginald Lascelles (1864-1939) RF husband of Putty's sister Beatrice. The Lascelles had lived at Ashley Court since Reverend Arthur Wykham Pulteney's death in 1928.
43   William Augustus Stirling Home Drummond Moray (1852-1939) SG 1871-1887.

In June Putty attended the memorial service for Brigadier General Lord Henry Seymour (1878-1937 late Gren Gds) at the Royal Military Chapel, Wellington Barracks. Later that month the annual inspection of the United Services Corps was held on the parade ground of the Honourable Artillery Company: again the parade was inspected by Field Marshal Lord Cavan. *The Times* reported: 'Lord Cavan was welcomed by Lieutenant General Sir William Pulteney and others'. Putty was probably still the Chairman of the Council because he is also recorded to have attended the annual general meeting of the Council of the United Services Corps the following month. This was to be his last recorded official event.

In May 1940 Putty and Jessie attended a memorial service for the Hon Mrs Alwyn Greville[44] at St Martin-in-the-Fields. Putty's sister, Frances, died at her home Sion House, Birchanger on 4 May 1941. Ten days later (14 May 1941) Putty also died, just short of his 80th birthday. According to his death certificate he died at Pines Hill, Stansted. There is no record of a house by this name but it is the name of the road that leads south from Stansted Mountfichet to the parish boundary with Birchanger, and Sion House is just across that boundary. A possible explanation is that Putty went to Frances' funeral and perhaps to sort out her affairs, became seriously ill, and died in Sion House. Another is that he died at Broome End which is where Mildred Mary Pulteney (c1868-1957 grand-daughter of John Apsley Pulteney – Putty's uncle), married to Harry Chester, lived. This is off Pines Hill.

The funeral was held at Ashley Church on 17 May. *The Market Harborough Advertiser and Midland Mail* recorded:

> In a grave lined with primroses and evergreen Lieutenant General Sir William Pulteney, Gentleman Usher of the Black Rod was on Saturday last laid to rest in the churchyard of Ashley close beside the church which his father Rev RT Pulteney restored 70 years ago.

Putty's gravestone is marked with a Scots Guards star. In that same churchyard lie his parents and eight of his brothers and sisters. He had come home.

Lady Oxford[45] wrote a tribute in *The Times*:

> Lieutenant General Sir William Pulteney late 'Black Rod' in the House of Lords was the best type of English gentleman. I may not be a good judge of a 'gentleman', as I have known so many, but I do not think anyone who ever met 'Putty' (as those who loved him called him) could have failed to love him. He was gay, balanced and bold. He was the first person who said to me: 'If Neville Chamberlain had not gone to face the Germans in Munich we would have had a war without an army'. I was entirely of his opinion, and I doubt if any one today disagrees with this opinion. He had great qualities of leadership; he would have had every capacity to enthuse the British public. I knew him for more years than I care to remember and I mourn his death because I am only one among many of his most devoted friends.

44   Hon Mrs Alwyn Greville née Mabel Elizabeth Georgina Smith d 19 May 1940.
45   Margot Asquith Countess of Oxford (1864-1945) widow of Henry Herbert Asquith Prime Minister 1908-1916.

Pulteney's Grave, Ashley. (Ashley Village Archive)

Hansard recorded the speeches in the House of Lords on 20 May. Lord Moyne[46] said:

He was appointed Black Rod in 1920, and since then his genial personality made him, I am sure, a great friend of every one of us. He was a man of very active habits, and he would have found an invalid life intolerable, so that we can at least be thankful that he was spared a long illness. He had lived a very full and varied life. In his early career, he alternated between the Scots Guards and employment under the Foreign Office in the African Protectorate of Uganda and in the Congo. When he first found an opening in command in

46   Secretary of State for the Colonies (1880-1944) assassinated by Jewish gunman in Cairo Eton SA WW1 Suffolk Yeomanry MP Bury St Edmunds 1907-1931.

South Africa he did very well with his column, and when the Great War came, from the start he commanded the Third Corps, retaining that command until the beginning of 1918. Some corps commanders were rather aloof from their troops, but I am sure the many noble Lords who passed through his corps will remember that was never the way with 'Putty'. He was always trusted and indeed beloved, by those who came into contact with him. He had an extraordinary power, in the army, of inspiring confidence, and I am quite sure that many will feel a deep personal loss and long miss 'Putty's' friendly presence and cheery smile.

Earl of Listowel spoke of: 'His unfailing courtesy and friendliness' 'dignity and efficiency with which he performed the complicated ceremonial duties connected with his office'. Marquess of Londonderry spoke of: 'His stern adherence to duty and determination to do his best whatever vocation he was called upon to fill'.

A Memorial Service was held for Putty at the Royal Military Chapel Wellington Barracks on 26 May: his obituary in the *Guards Magazine* was written by Major General Drummond who had been in Evans House at Eton and then in the Scots Guards with him.

Jessie lived for another thirty years and died in 1971 aged 95 years. Up to 1950 she lived at 3 Lower Berkeley Street, then moved to Upper Brook Street and finally to a nursing home close to a niece in Sussex. Guardsman Hogbin stayed on with Jessie until he too died in 1946.

After Putty's memorial service Guardsman Hogbin carried out his last duty for him taking his medals to Headquarters Scots Guards for safe keeping where they remain to tell this story to all who visit. Forty years' service Hogbin had given Putty, much of this is his story too.

Neither Putty nor Jessie left any letters or papers (or none have been found) so this chapter is mainly based on the reported events in the last twenty years of Putty's life. In many ways it is an inadequate sample since it does not include Putty and Jessie's life together or their other interests and activities: they can only be guessed at. It is likely that Putty and Jessie went to the theatre and, with Jessie's interest in music, to concerts. At weekends, whenever they could, they would probably have got out of London to stay with family or friends: Putty would have continued to fish and shoot whenever invited; eventually he gave his set of three guns made by Stephen Lang in the 1880s to Jessie's nephew, Major Sir George Brooke Bt. In considering what is known it is important to remember what is not.

Few men continue in full time employment until almost 80 years old: Putty did as Black Rod. The evidence makes clear that he was also active in many other ways: the Ypres League and Ypres School, United Services Corps, and Army Football Association to name just four. The variety and number of events reported, just the tip of an iceberg of many more, strongly supports Lord Moyne's tribute – 'trusted, beloved, inspiring confidence'. This was not a man considered a failure by anyone, including himself – he had done his duty to the best of his ability. There is no evidence to the contrary.

One of the most telling events was the organisation of the Ypres League in 1925 when Putty was Chairman of its Executive Committee. Neither the King (at that time Patron in Chief), Prince of Wales (Patron), Field Marshal Earl Ypres (President), Field Marshals Earl Haig, Viscount Plumer and Viscount Allenby (Vice Presidents) would have been involved or accepted Putty's involvement in the Ypres League if they had an adverse opinion of him. The evidence suggests quite the contrary; he was 'trusted' and 'much liked'. Differences of opinion on the limits of Putty's ability to command in war seem to have been just that, and had not otherwise influenced their high opinion of him.

At least some of the strength Putty drew on in later life came from Jessie. She was fifteen years younger than him, very attractive if not beautiful, and from the present generations' reports 'adored' Putty. The evidence suggests that she gave him a home, a sense of purpose, and the love that his life had hitherto lacked.

15

A soldier fully tested

Pulteney's detractors say that he only got as far as he did through abuses of patronage; that he was uneducated and therefore incompetent; and that he was responsible for failures in war that cost many lives. It is now for consideration whether the evidence of his life supports such views.

Everyone has a degree of patronage to give and to be taken advantage of; it is a consequence of power. The blacksmith needs an apprentice and selects his sister's son is but one example of patronage: in itself there is no harm; the blacksmith is unlikely to take on someone who would be a liability, and he would have thought long and hard if someone with more ability had been available. Taking on someone you know is not necessarily an abuse of patronage: for this to be proved the patron has to advance someone over others of greater ability as a favour to that person or a third party, or to keep him there in similar circumstances.

The Pulteney name and family links would have had limited value but Eton and the Brigade of Guards provided Putty with numerous patrons over the years. Service in Ireland brought Putty into contact with the highest levels of society in that country: friendship with Ettie Desborough and Edith Londonderry provided similar access in England. Service in South Africa at battalion and column level provided access in the army to those at the highest levels both then and for the next 15 years. Putty knew them all – the King, the Prince of Wales, Prime Ministers, members of government, peers with estates throughout the country, wealthy business men, society queens, and senior officers in the army. Few can have had greater patronage open to them. He was an extraordinarily popular man, getting on well with men and women of all ages and from all backgrounds, inspiring loyalty, confidence and trust.

The issue is whether someone abused their patronage to advance Putty, or to keep him in an appointment. Five occasions deserve investigation: Putty's advancement in South Africa and any involvement of Major General Lord Methuen; his appointment to command 6th Division and the role of General Lyttelton; his appointment to command III Corps in 1914 and the roles of General French and General Paget; the appointment of General Monro over Putty to command 3rd Army in 1915 and the roles of Field Marshal French, General Haig, Kitchener and the King; and finally the involvement of anyone in keeping Putty in command of III Corps for nearly 3½ years.

Putty made a name for himself in Uganda and the Congo and his appointment to command 1 SG when Paget departed was an obvious and uncontroversial one. The next step, to command a column, may well have been at least in part on Methuen's recommendation. However, others outside the Scots Guards, indeed outside the Guards Brigade would have been involved in the decision, and his brevet and previous experience of independent command would also have been factors. There is no evidence that he failed in command of a column; moreover, when he became ill and his first column was disbanded, he was appointed to command another as soon as he had recovered.

General Lyttelton's role in Putty's career is less clear-cut. Although 17 years older he was also in Evans House at Eton, as were his brothers. Lyttelton was very talented at all forms of sport, as was Putty. The evidence indicates that Putty corresponded with Lyttelton in South Africa when the latter was CinC. Lyttelton was then CGS 1904-1908 when Putty was commanding 2 SG; after this Putty was selected to command 16 Bde and then 6th Division in Ireland and by the time he got there Lyttelton was the CinC. It is difficult to imagine that Lyttelton was not involved, especially as the relationship was close both in Ireland and later. However, even if there was a degree of patronage there is no evidence that Lyttelton abused his position to advance Putty. In command of his column (effectively a bde) Putty had done well and fully justified his chance to command a division. Lyttelton might have preferred Putty because he knew him but that was probably the limit of his patronage. The most compelling reason for dismissing this is that Lyttelton could have sent Putty on promotion to anywhere in the army, including one of the four divisions not in Ireland. He chose Putty for 6th Division presumably because he thought that he was good.

Next is Putty's appointment as GOC III Corps in 1914. There was also the 'grave displeasure' of the Army Council to be overlooked. He had finished his time in command of 6th Division and was immediately available; he was not the most senior major general who could have been appointed, and there were others better qualified if attendance at the Staff College was a requirement. It is difficult to fathom the exact synchronisation of events on 5 and 6 August 1914. Putty was promoted to Temporary Lieutenant General on 5 August; he did not attend the War Cabinet meeting at 4 pm on 5 August although French (CinC) and the other two corps commanders did; but he knew he was going to France to command III Corps by 6.30 pm although Kitchener did not formally approve the appointment until next day. Two of Putty's 'patrons' would have been involved in his selection – General Sir Arthur Paget and General Sir John French. Paget had seen Putty in command of 6th Division, and he knew him well especially from 1 SG in South Africa fifteen years earlier: he would undoubtedly have recommended him. French also knew Putty very well from South Africa and had seen him as Inspector General but it is inconceivable that he would have selected Putty ahead of someone better; he could have asked for and would have been given anyone in the army at this critical time. He must have chosen Putty because he thought he was the best man for the job, and in 1914 and 1915 Putty fully justified his selection.

When the BEF expanded and armies were formed French asked for Putty to command 3rd Army in preference to anyone else; Monro was, however, selected by Kitchener. French, with whom Putty was linked, was on his way out, to be replaced by Haig. Kitchener favoured Haig and so Monro, who had served as a divisional and corps commander under Haig, was inevitably selected. Putty considered going to see the King about it, but did not do so; if he had the King would not have intervened on his behalf.

Perhaps the strangest of all the patronage issues is why Haig kept Putty in France as a corps commander for so long. He had no apparent need to do so; Putty could have been sent back to England or to any other command in 1916, even promoted. After two years in France, he could be considered due for a break and he had done well. Yet Haig kept him in France. Some might have considered Putty to be unsackable, especially if they knew of the influence of Ettie

Desborough and Edith Londonderry, but this could not possibly have been so. If Haig had any doubts about Putty's ability to command III Corps he would not have selected him to go S to play a key role in the Battle of the Somme in 1916, or again selected him for another key role in the Battle of Cambrai in 1917. If he had wanted to get rid of Putty and was prevented from doing so he could have kept III Corps in a relatively quiet part of the line or in reserve. He did not do so, presumably because he and his army commanders thought Putty was the best man for these jobs.

This is also relevant to the second criticism of Putty – his ability or lack of it. Haig wrote on 11 May 1916, just over six weeks before the start of the Somme offensive: 'Pulteney (III Corps) while a plucky leader of a brigade or even or a division had quite reached the limits of his capacity as a commander and had not however studied his profession sufficiently to be a really good corps commander'. Rawlinson wrote three days later: 'Putty came to see me and asked for an explanation regarding our memorandum on attack. He has evidently not got it into his head and we shall have to look after him as his plan is far from good'. Context is all important: Haig brought Putty down to Rawlinson's 4th Army for the Somme offensive and Rawlinson, who knew him well, was pleased to have him. It may be that Putty had been questioning Haig's plan, one that Rawlinson had accepted and was promoting.

Brigadier General Bonham-Carter, Putty's BGGS in 1917, wrote many years later in his unpublished autobiography: 'Old Putty (not so old) was the most completely ignorant general I served during the war and that is saying a lot'. He was only BGGS III Corps for 6 months and left on 15 October 1917, and this must have been highly inconvenient for Putty being two days before his wedding in London and about five weeks before the Cambrai offensive. Bonham-Carter did have a bad back and this might have been the reason for him being sent to GHQ but it is also possible that Putty sacked him. No-one else who served under Putty in his 3½ years in France wrote so disparagingly about him, so Bonham-Carter's motives are questionable and context is important. One interpretation is that 'ignorant' in this context means 'unlearned' or 'uneducated' which in respect of Putty is true.

Putty left Eton at 16 years old and did not go to Sandhurst or to the Staff College, indeed never held a staff appointment after adjutant. Many historians point to this and Bonham-Carter's remarks as evidence of incompetence. A commander has a staff to prepare plans and execute his orders: he does not need to be a trained staff officer himself; indeed many of the greatest commanders in history had no formal training. A good commander should not involve himself in the detail of staff work; his role is to give clear direction, make the right decisions and provide the necessary leadership on which success depends.

Putty's letters make it clear that he studied the strategic aspects of the war all the time. They and the records of HQ III Corps also show several specific areas that Putty studied in detail; and they were not matters raised by his staff but matters that he himself focussed on.

It also seems improbable that Putty would have gone to Rawlinson 'to clarify a matter in 4th Army's Memorandum of Attack'. It would have been produced by MGGS 4th Army, with Rawlinson's approval, and any clarification resolved between the two staffs. It is conceivable that Putty went to see Rawlinson without the knowledge of his staff but not on this subject. Much more likely is that Putty was briefed by his BGGS on concerns raised by his divisional commanders and he went to Rawlinson to represent them.

The orders given by Rawlinson to Putty for 1 July 1916 presented him with a very difficult task; the inflexible plan allowed no scope for tactical manoeuvre or initiative to suit the circumstances on each part of the front. Putty must have known this, and if he did not both his divisional commanders did and would have told him at every opportunity. In placing total reliance on the artillery to overwhelm the enemy III Corps had 11,501 casualties on that first day just in its two attacking divisions, yet it was not suggested by anyone that Putty was in any way responsible: the only way that this can make any sense is if the full weight of responsibility fell on Rawlinson and Haig because they told Putty both what had to be done and how he was to do it. If this were to be accepted, a Balaklava comparison, it seems peculiar that Putty neither prepared in advance for what he suspected might happen or reacted more quickly when it did. If the enemy in La Boisselle had not been completely destroyed or at least neutralised, Ovillers would not be taken, let alone Pozières. There was no reserve of artillery to neutralise pockets of resistance or mask them with smoke, no ability to stop and bring back the fire plan, no reserve bde that could be quickly put into La Boisselle, all had been committed in that first move. Putty could have done all of these within the constraints of his orders but he did not, presumably because it would make it immediately obvious that he had no confidence in the plan, and raise doubts in the minds of others. Once the offensive had started communications were the problem; not between corps and the two forward divisions but within these divisions. Putty may well have gone forward but it would have been quite impossible to get an accurate picture of the battle, certainly one accurate enough on which to base decisions: the bde comds did not know with any certainty the situation with their battalions until late in the day.

Putty may not have been held responsible but it is at least questionable whether he should have challenged Rawlinson more, to obtain greater flexibility on his front. La Boisselle had to be taken first: it could not be by-passed. If 34th Division had been given this objective in a first phase the outcome might have been different: once the offensive had started GOC 34th Division (Ingouville-Williams) with all three bdes committed was incapable of influencing the battle even if he did know what was happening. Putty should have ensured that a reserve was kept just in case La Boisselle proved difficult.

It was hardly surprising that Putty's next flirt with controversy came in the Battle of Martinpuich on 15 September 1916 since it was when the whole corps was committed to battle that he faced the ultimate test. However well-run the corps was; however well it was administered; however well it performed in the line; all counted for nothing if he was found wanting when called upon to make the key decisions in battle. This was the first time that tanks were used in action and Putty is alleged to have told GOC 47th Division (Barter) that he was to use the tanks to lead the infantry into and through High Wood. Barter wanted to use the tanks outside the wood, firing into it as the infantry advanced: in this he was supported by the commander of the tanks because experience showed that the state of the ground, difficult everywhere, would be even worse in the wood because of the stumps and fallen trees. The first attack failed; Putty allegedly sacked Barter to cover his part in directing how the tanks were to be used.

The evidence is complex and inconclusive. Putty had been to the tank demonstration which included tanks penetrating a wood, so he had some idea of what was possible. He knew the state of the ground in and around High Wood, and with the experience of La Boisselle he knew that the wood could not be by-passed and had to be taken. The attack was also to be the first use in III Corps of a creeping barrage. Because the front lines were so close together the infantry were withdrawn from the front trenches for the preliminary bombardment but re-occupied them before Zero hour and the start of the creeping barrage: it is not clear why the attack was not launched from further back or even a new trench dug for it. Lanes had been left in the creeping barrage for the 4 tanks allotted to the division. A map error meant that the creeping barrage started behind the German line and so provided little close support for the infantry or the tanks. Five infantry battalions were sucked into High Wood with inevitable confusion and casualties. The four tanks might have provided some help in getting the infantry into High Wood but three of them broke down or were knocked out before they got there.

The record of Rawlinson's conference on 10 September does show discussion on the use of tanks in the battle but it is muddled. What matters is that 47th Division ended up with four tanks, and they were to lead the infantry into and through High Wood contrary to the wishes of GOC 47th Division and the advice of Colonel Elles OC Tanks, who had not actually seen the going in High Wood. Putty must have been advised differently by his BGGS (Romer) and BGRA (Tancred) and the most likely reason was the experience of La Boisselle, and the priority was to get the infantry through High Wood and this had proved impossible up to now. It was Putty's responsibility irrespective of whether he actually made the decision.

If Barter had considered the deployment of these four tanks was a major issue for his division there were a number of ways to persuade Putty to change his mind but there is no record of any such activity. It is remotely possible that BGGS and BGRA HQ III Corps agreed with Barter in which case one or both would have would have sought to persuade Putty; in extremis they could have gone to HQ 4th Army. It would be contrary to Putty's character to act without consulting his staff and even more so to involve himself in matters more directly the responsibility of one of his divisional commanders: had he done so it would be recorded somewhere which it is not. It is for consideration that the Putty and HQ III Corps' view was the right one in the circumstances, and contemporary photographs do not show the difficulties for a tank traversing High Wood to be any greater than going round it. 4th Army 299/17(G) of 11 September 1916 makes it very clear that the tanks 'are to be used to break into the enemy's line and lead the infantry through'. However, Lieutenant Colonel Warrender CO 15 London wrote on 1 November: 'The Corps (III) were warned that the tanks would be no good in the wood, but they would not listen. The result was my unfortunate battalion had to do a frontal attack in broad daylight without any artillery preparation'. The creeping barrage was poorly coordinated with the attack of 47th Division's infantry but this had little to do with the tanks. Too many battalions became committed to High Wood and they became bunched up and disorganised, and suffered unnecessary casualties. For what was a few hours bordering on a shambles, Barter was responsible; this is why Putty decided he should go – and confirmed in Haig's record on 6 October: 'I had to send home General Barter on Pulteney's recommendation. He mishandled the division so on 15 and 16 September at High Wood. Two brigades were sent into the wood, when 2 battalions would have sufficed to engage the enemy in it, while others pushed on to the next objective'.

Commenting on the sacking of Barter, Warrender wrote: 'Everybody loathed him and was glad when he went, but there was a feeling that he was badly treated. It was a bad day for old CB and for the whole division when Burnett-Hitchcock [GSO 1 47th Division until 15 June 1916] left us. Weatherby who was very nice and had a sweet smile, was quite incompetent and could not stand up to the old man, and so became a real nuisance to the brigadiers, and to the COs as well'. Perhaps this was at the root of the problem.

Major Fair's (2IC and then CO 19 London) evidence is also important (although written many years later): 'It always seemed to me that the confusion and heavy casualties were largely due to the formation laid down for us by which each company of each battalion of the two assaulting brigades were to advance in a series of waves. No local reserves were kept in hand, with the result that after the first check in the wood every minute brought fresh troops into the front line with little or no possibility of exploiting success on the flanks, so as to "pinch out" the wood itself. I know that both CO 19 London (Hamilton killed in the battle and replaced by Fair) and Comd 141 Bde protested against the formation as ordered, and I have often wondered if it was the reason why Barter ceased to command 47th Division a few days later'. It seems likely that it was.

The context of this controversy is also important. III Corps was very successful and took most of its objectives that day, notably Martinpuich. Tanks and the creeping barrage proved, when properly coordinated together and with other arms, to give an advantage. This success had been achieved at relatively low cost with most of the casualties in the three attacking divisions being in 47th Division.

Historians have sought to establish a causal link between Putty's decision to insist that the tanks led the infantry attack on High Wood, the excessive number of casualties suffered by 47th Division, and the sacking of Barter. The evidence suggests that any such link is very tenuous. 47th Division's plan was bad in at least two respects; the re-occupation of the front line trenches before zero hour meant that the creeping barrage started behind the enemy's front line and this was made worse by a serious map reading error, and the tactics of the infantry caused congestion and confusion. These were the causes of the excessive casualties and it was they that led to Putty sacking Barter.

Tanks in much greater numbers did play a significant part in III Corps' offensive in the Battle of Cambrai on 20 November 1917. Putty succeeded in breaking through the Hindenburg Line, hitherto considered impregnable, and then getting across the St Quentin Canal beyond. However, he did not achieve his last and key objective – breaching the Masnières-Beaurevoir Line in order that the Cav Corps could be passed through into the Cambrai plain and the French to the S. For this Putty has never been criticised: partly because there was surprise in many quarters that III Corps had achieved so much and partly because there was relief with hindsight that the Cav Corps had not been destroyed.

Nevertheless Putty did fail to secure this objective and his actions should be scrutinised. The main error was that III Corps lost momentum: too often in the past III Corps had focussed on the deep objectives and then failed to take the first one: reserves had then to be committed, this took time, and the attack became bogged down. On this occasion so much effort in planning and resources had been committed to the first phases that it was the ultimate one which was neglected. Putty would not have been forgiven if there had been a repetition of 1 July 1916, nor would he have forgiven himself. As soon as the Hindenburg Line was breached and 29th Division was moving forward III Corps should have re-constituted a reserve of all arms, and this could have been incorporated into the planning.

There was one other error for which Putty was at least partly responsible, the bridging of the canal. There is no evidence of any engineer intelligence or planning for the crossing and the military bridging arrangements were chaotic. Insufficient attention was also given to bridging the lines so that guns and tanks could be brought forward, and there was no apparent re-supply of fascines. But worst was the crossing of the canal: tanks did not know which of the existing bridges would support their weight and there was no pre-planning for the deployment of the heavy bridging to make tank crossings.

In summary, Putty lost his ability to influence the battle once he had committed 29th Division: this should have been thought about in the planning stage and a corps reserve re-constituted at the earliest possible time. Because it was not, momentum was lost and the offensive halted; the bridging fiasco merely compounded the problem. Putty would probably point to all that III Corps had achieved but it could and perhaps should have been more.

The German counter-attack that was launched ten days later and the defensive battle that was fought to contain it were subject to various inquiries. None of them blamed Putty for his actions, and yet a re-examination of the evidence suggests that he was at fault. Undoubtedly serious errors were made by GHQ and 3rd Army, the assessment that the Germans did not have the capability to mount a serious counter-attack and the decision to hold on to all the ground gained on 20 November being two obvious ones. Only one person directly criticised Putty and that was Snow (GOC VII Corps) but this criticism seems to have gained in strength with the benefit of hindsight; certainly Snow did not take as strong action at the time as he could have done.

Once the Germans had broken through Putty did well to contain their offensive but it is at least questionable whether by his actions he missed the opportunity to defeat it much earlier and inflict very heavy casualties. The German counter-attack did surprise Putty and III Corps, perhaps not surprise that one was launched but certainly in its scale, direction and rate of advance. There is at least a suspicion that any counter-attack on III Corps' front was expected against 29th Division and that in the worst case it would be necessary to fall back across the canal.

In many ways III Corps' position was a strong one but there were three weaknesses. Because the salient was narrow there was very little depth on its flanks and in this case on its right flank. The slopes off the high ground were convex. III Corps would have been reluctant to hold well forward, where the canal could be covered but the positions would have been very exposed; their preference would have been to hold well back but there was not sufficient depth to do this. The result was a weak compromise made worse by several deep re-entrants that ran from the canal valley up into the position, and the slopes down into them were also convex: one, the Banteux Ravine, was just across the S boundary with VII Corps. Unless these re-entrants were blocked they provided covered approaches deep into III Corps' position: they were not and they did. Putty could have at the very least ensured the re-entrants were blocked: and he could have turned all the villages into strong points to provide greater depth to the position and a place of relative safety for support and logistic units.

The command and control arrangements could have been much better. There were four bdes in the line on the right flank. HQ 20th Division and its reserve bde were in the rear of the right bde, one of 12th Division's. HQ 12th Division and its reserve bde were completely detached from this part of the battle. One commander (GOC 20th Division) could have had responsibility for the right flank and this would have ensured much greater coordination and more effective command and control.

Putty did well to counter the penetration but he was fortunate that the Guards Division was so quickly available. His own reserves were too fragmented and uncoordinated to be really effective. A corps reserve could have been created under GOC 12th Division consisting of two bdes, at least one bn of tanks, one bde RHA, Corps Cav Regt and Corps Cyclist Bn, and air support. This would have had the ability to locate any enemy penetration and not just block it, but to destroy it.

Overall the evidence suggests that the defensive battle was close run: Putty did fight it well but he owed much to luck. He had had the time to plan it with greater care minimising the obvious weaknesses in the position and using his resources much more effectively. Yet this criticism is based on hindsight: Cambrai could be considered the first battle of twentieth century warfare; Putty came to it straight from the Somme, more akin to battles of the nineteenth century.

These two battles of Somme and Cambrai dominated Putty's life in 1916 and 1917 but there were many smaller operations; some were very complex such as the crossings of the Somme and the advance to the Hindenburg Line and Putty has to be given credit for their success. The constant reorganisations of his corps must have severely tested his leadership but there is no evidence that III Corps' cohesion and effectiveness was ever found wanting.

Historians use two derogatory words for generals in the war: a 'donkey' for someone who failed through incompetence and a 'butcher' for someone who only succeeded because of wilful disregard for the lives of those under him. If it is considered that one or both might apply to Putty it is again necessary to consider his whole life, taking due regard of his successes. Particular note should be taken of the last twenty years of his life: associating at the highest levels and yet no hint of controversy, no suggestion of failure or even that he could have done better. As for Putty he would probably be more than satisfied if history remembered him as Charley Londonderry, his ADC, did for always doing his best and for always doing his duty.

Appendix A

III Corps Higher Headquarters and Commanders 1914-1918

GHQ BEF   30 Aug – 25 Dec 1914 General Sir John French late 8 H
Later Field Marshal Viscount French of Ypres 1852-1925
GOC Cavalry Division SA, CinC BEF 1914-1915

2nd Army   25 Dec 1914 – 8 Apr 1915 General Sir Horace Smith-Dorrien late Sher For
Later General Sir Horace Smith-Dorrien 1858-1930 Comd 19 Bde SA, GOC II
Corps 1914-1915, GOC 2nd Army 1915

GHQ BEF   8 Apr – 18 Jul 1915 General Sir John French

1st Army   18 Jul 1915 – 24 Mar 1916
18 Jul– 17 Dec 1915 General Sir Douglas Haig late 7 H
Later Field Marshal Earl Haig 1861-1928 Sandhurst, psc, SA Column Comd,
GOC I Corps 1914, GOC 1st Army 1914 until 19 Dec 1915 on appointment as
CinC
Jan – 24 Mar 1916 General Sir Charles Monro late Queens
Later General Sir Charles Monro 1st Bt 1860-1929 Sandhurst, psc, SA, GOC
2nd Division 1914, GOC I Corps Dec 1914, GOC 1st Army Jan-Oct 1916,
CinC India 1916-1920

4th Army   24 Mar 1916 – 5 Jul 1917 General Sir Henry Rawlinson late Coldm Gds
Later General Lord (Henry Seymour) Rawlinson of Trent 1864-1925
Eton, Sandhurst, psc, Sudan 1898 (on Kitchener's Staff), SA Column Comd,
Comdt Staff College, Comd 2 Inf Bde 1907 and 3rd Division 1910, GOC 4th
Division 1914, GOC IV Corps 1914-15, GOC 4th Army 1916-17, CinC India
1920-1925

3rd Army   5 Jul 1917 – 14 Jan 1918 General Sir Julian Byng late 10 H
Later Field Marshal Viscount Byng of Vimy 1862-1935 Eton 1874-78, Militia,
SA – raised and commanded SA Light Horse, psc, GOC 3rd Cavalry Division
1914, GOC Cav Corps 1915, GOC IX Corps Gallipoli 1915, GOC Canadian
Corps 1916-17, GOC 3rd Army 1917-19

5th Army   14 Jan – 15 Feb 1918 General Sir Hubert Gough late 16 L
Later General Sir Hubert de la Poer Gough 1870-1963
Eton, Sandhurst, SA, psc, Comd 3 Cav Bde Curragh 1911, GOC 7th Division
1914, GOC I Corps 1915, GOC Reserve later 5th Army 1916-1918

Appendix B

Headquarters III Corps 1914-1918

ADCs

1

Aug 1914 – 15 Aug 1915 Major Viscount Castlereagh RHG
Later Major Charles Stewart Henry Vane-Tempest-Stewart 7th Marquess of Londonderry 1878-1949 Eton Sandhurst; married Edith Chaplin 1899; adjutant 1901; 1902 King Edward VII sponsored christening of first son; 1903 King visited Mount Stewart and Wynyard; MP for Maidstone 1906 re-elected in Jan and Nov 1910; in Parliament he became involved in Haldane's Territorial and Reserve Forces Bill, coal mining (owner of several mines in Co Durham), tariff reforms, women's suffrage (in which his wife was interested), 1911 Parliament Bill, and 3rd Irish Home Rule Bill 1912-1914; signed Ulster Covenant 1912; SofS for Air 1931-1935

2 Nov 1915 – 8 May 1917 Lieutenant Marquess of Linlithgow Lothians and Border Horse
Later Colonel Victor Alexander John Hope 2nd Marquess of Linlithgow 1887-1952 Eton; CO 1/10 (Cyclist) Bn RS (1917-1919); Governor General and Viceroy of India 1936-1943; son, 3rd Marquess, served in SG; Linlithgow's sister, Lady Mary Dorothea Hope 1903-1995, married Pembroke's son 16th Earl in 1936; Linlithgow's father, 1st Marquess 1860-1908, was at Eton with Putty; Queen Victoria was his godmother

8 May 1917 – 15 Feb 1918 Captain Poynter SG
Later Major Arthur Vernon Poynter 1871-1955 SG 1892-1896 and 1914-1918; SA War 10th Battalion Imperial Yeomanry – wounded; ADC Viceroy of India 1902-1905; ADC Gov Gen of Canada 1906-1907; 1 SG 1914 wounded Loos 1915

2

5 Aug 1914 – 24 Jul 1915 Captain Earl of Pembroke and Montgomery RHG
Later Captain Reginald Herbert (15th) Earl of Pembroke (1913) and Montgomery 1880-1960 Eton. Castlereagh's mother and Pembroke's aunt, wife of 13th Earl of Pembroke, were sisters of 20th Earl of Shrewsbury. Pembroke was ADC to General Sir Arthur Paget (AP) when he was CinC Ireland 1912-1914. Pembroke married (1904) Lady Beatrice Eleanor Paget 1883-1973 a relation of AP, both descended from 1st Marquess of Anglesey

24 Jul 1915 – 7 Jan 1917 Captain Lord Gavin Hamilton
Later Major Lord Gavin George Hamilton (2nd Baron) of Dalzell 1872-1952 Eton Major SG 1892-1898 and 1914-1919 AMS 4th Army Apr 1917-18. Government Chief Whip in the House of Lords under Campbell-Bannerman and Asquith 1905-1911. Married Sybil Mary, daughter of Lieutenant General Sir Frederick Marshall (1829-1900) 1912; she had been previously married to 3rd Baron Burnham who also served SG. They had 2 sons and 2 daughters – son Lieutenant William Bernard Webster Levy Lawson SG killed in action 22 Oct 1914 (1st Battle of Ypres)

7 Jan 1917 – 15 Feb 1918 Captain Loder SG
Later Lieutenant Colonel Giles Harold Loder 1884-1966 Eton Sandhurst SG 1903-1929, 2 SG 7th Division 1914, wounded 12 Mar 15, Adjt 2 SG 25 Oct-1 Dec 15, GSO3 4th Army 11 Feb 16-7 Jan 17, ADC to GOC III Corps and XXIII Corps 7 Jan 17-16 Mar 1919, CO 1 SG 1925

3

1914 – 1915 (Private) Baron Rothschild French Army
Later Baron James (Jimmy) Armond Edmond de Rothschild 1878-1957, Lycée Paris, Trinity College, Cambridge, Private in French Army at start of WW1 and later Major in British Army – 39 RF, wounded, naturalised 1919, MP Isle of Ely 1929-1945, Parliamentary Secretary to Ministry of Supply 1940-45

GOC's Orderly
Aug 1914 – 15 Feb 1918 Private (Guardsman 1918) Hogbin SG
2590 George Charles Hogbin 1878/1883-1946; born Ramsgate, Kent where father was a butcher; enlisted London 1899 (possibly age 16); 1 SG SA 1899-1902; 2 SG 1904; extended service to complete 12 years on 7 Oct 1912; re-enlisted Government House Cork to complete 21 years' service; HQ III Corps France 1914-1918 then transferred to strength of 3 SG and attached to HQ XXIII Corps Bury St Edmunds 1918-1919; discharged 15 Feb 1920; address after 1920 was 3 Lower Berkeley Street (Putty's address); married Annie Everitt 1911; door-keeper House of Lords 1922-1943

Brigadier General General Staff (BGGS)
5 Aug 1914 – 27 Jan 1915 Brigadier General Du Cane late RA
Later General Sir John (Philip) ('Johnny') Du Cane 1865-1950, Cheam, MGRA GHQ 1915, DG Munitions Design 1916, GOC XV Corps 1916-1918, MGO 1920-23, CinC Western Comd 1923-4, CinC BAOR 1924-7

27 Jan – 25 Feb 1915 Brigadier General Milne late RA
Later Field Marshal Lord (George Francis) Milne 1866-1948, Woolwich, SA, GSO1 4th Division 1909-1913, GOC RA 4th Division 1913-1915, GOC 27th Division 1915, GOC XVI Corps and GOCinC British Forces Salonika 1916-1918, CIGS 1926-1933

25 Feb – 13 Jul 1915 Brigadier General Lynden-Bell late Buffs
Later Major General Sir Arthur Lynden Lynden-Bell 1867-1943 psc, SA War-severely wounded, MGGS 3rd Army 1915-1917, DSD WO 1918-1921

13 Jul 1915 – 11 Apr 1917 Brigadier General Romer late RDF
Later General Sir Cecil Francis Romer ('Romeo') 1869-1962, GSO1 5th Division 1914-15 and 1st Canadian Division 1915, GOC 59th Division Apr 1917-Jun 1918, AG 1933-1935

11 Apr – 15 Oct 1917 Brigadier General Bonham-Carter late W Kents
Later General Sir Charles Bonham-Carter 1876-1955, psc, SA War, GSO1 17th Division, BGGS SD & Trg GHQ 1917-1918, CinC Malta 1936-1940

15 Oct 1917 – 15 Feb 1918 Brigadier General Fuller late RE
Later Major General Cuthbert Graham Fuller 1874-1960, psc, SA War, GHQ Egypt, AA&QMG 29th Division Jun-20 Aug 1915, GSO1 29th Division Gallipoli 20 Aug 1915-15 Oct 1917

Colonel General Staff/General Staff Officer Grade 1 (GSO1)

5 Aug – 6 Nov 1914 Colonel Maude late Coldm Gds
Later Lieutenant General Sir Frederick Stanley Maude 1864-1917, Eton 1878 (in Mr Cornish's House – associated with Rawlinson with whom he served in the Coldm Gds), BM Gds Bde SA 1899, GSO1 5th Division 1913-1914, Comd 14 Bde 1914, wounded in 1915, GOC 33rd Division then GOC 13th Division Gallipoli, GOC in Mesopotamia took Baghdad in 1917 died of cholera same year

6 Nov 1914 – 7 Jan 1915 Colonel Sloman late E Surreys
Later Brigadier General Henry Stanhope Sloman 1861-1945, Omdurman 1898, SA 2 E Surreys 1900-1902

General Staff Officer Grade 2 (GSO2) Operations

5 Aug 1914 – 21 Apr 1915 Major Harington Kings
Later General Sir Charles Harington Harington 1872-1940 Sandhurst psc, GSO 3 SD WO, BM 6 Bde 1911, GSO 1 49th Division 1915, BGGS Canadian Corps 1915, MGGS 2nd Army 1917, DCIGS, CinC Army of the Black Sea 1920-21, CinC Allied Forces of Occupation in Turkey 1921-23, GOC Northern and Aldershot Commands, Gov Gibraltar during Spanish Civil War

21 Apr – 16 Aug 1915 Major Bartholomew RA
Later General Sir William Henry Bartholomew 1877-1962, psc, GSO 1 4th Division 1915, BGGS XX Corps Palestine 1917, Comd 6 Bde 1923-6, DMO/I WO 1931-4, CGS India 1934-1937, GOCinC Northern Command 1937-1940

16 Aug 1915 – 23 Jun 1916 Major Karslake RA
Later Lieutenant General Sir Henry Karslake 1879-1942, psc, SA, GSO 1 50th Division 1916-1917, GSO1 4th Division 1917-1918, BGGS Tank Corps, various appointments in India including key role in Quetta earthquake of 1935, Recalled and GOC LOC BEF 1940

23 Jun 1916 – 28 Oct 1917 Major Battye RE
Later Colonel Basil Condon Battye 1882-1932, BM 141 Bde won DSO for carrying out personal reconnaissance

28 Oct 1917 – 15 Feb 1918 Major Hamilton Gordons
Later Brigadier James Melvill Hamilton Gordons 1886-NK 2 Gordons 7th Division 1914-1915, SC 1915-1916, BM 1916-1917, Comd 144 Bde 1940

General Staff Officer Grade 2 (GSO2) Intelligence
5 Aug – 26 Dec 1914 Major Davidson KRRC
Later Lieutenant General Sir John Humphrey 'Tavish' Davidson 1876-1954, Sandhurst, psc, SA, SO 1st Army 1915, BGGS Ops GHQ 1916, MP for Fareham 1918-31

General Staff Officer Grade 3 (GSO 3)
5 Aug 1914 – 1 Apr 1915 Captain Pitt-Taylor RB
Later Lieutenant General Sir Walter William Pitt-Taylor 1878-1950, Eton, BM 12 Bde 1915, GSO 1 4th Army 1916, Comd 145 Bde 1918, BGGS XIV Corps 1918-19, Comd 5 Bde 1925-28, GOC 3rd Division 1932-34, GOCinC Western Command India 1936-1939

1 Apr 1915 Captain Hewlett Devons
Later Brigadier General Ernest Hewlett 1879-NK psc

20 Nov 1917 Captain Rolls Dorset
Later Colonel SPA Rolls

Deputy Adjutant and Quartermaster General (DA&QMG)
5 Aug – 30 Sep 1914 Brigadier General McGrigor late KRRC
Later Major General Charles Roderic Robert McGrigor 1860-1927, Eton TJP Carter's House 1874-1877, DA&QMG III Corps 1914 until sick and taken to hospital in Paris

6 Oct 1914 – 13 Jul 1915 Brigadier General Campbell late Gordons
Later Lieutenant General Sir Walter Campbell 1864-1936, psc, DA&QMG 3rd Army 1915, QMG 1923-27

13 Jul – 10 Nov 1915 Brigadier General Chichester late Dorset
Later Major General Sir Arlington Augustus Chichester 1863-1948, psc, AA&QMG III Corps 1914-1915, DA&QMG 2nd Army 1915

10 Nov – 15 Dec 1915 Brigadier General Du Boulay late RA
Later Brigadier General Noel Wilmot Houssemayne Du Boulay 1861-1949, psc, AQMG III Corps 1914-1915

15 Dec 1915 – 11 Jan 1918 Brigadier General Hambro late 15 H
Later Major General Sir Percy Otway Hambro 1870-1931, DA&QMG 5th Army, GOC 46th Division 1927-1931

11 Jan – 15 Feb 1918 Brigadier General Doyle late RA
Later Brigadier General John Francis Innes Hay Doyle 1873-1919

Assistant Adjutant and Quartermaster General (AA&QMG)
5 Aug – 21 Oct 1914 Colonel Chichester late Dorset
Later Major General Sir Arlington Augustus Chichester 1863-1948, psc, DA&QMG III
Corps 1915, DA&QMG 2nd Army 1915

29 Oct – 28 Dec 1914 Major FC Dundas A&SH
Later Lieutenant Colonel Frederick Charles Dundas, DAA&QMG 6th Division

Assistant Quartermaster General (AQMG)
5 Aug 1914 – 10 Nov 1915 Colonel Du Boulay Late RA
Later Brigadier General Noel Wilmot Houssemayne Du Boulay 1861-1949, psc

18 Nov 1915 – NK Major EC Packe RF
Later Lieutenant Colonel by Jul 16

Nov 1917 – 15 Feb 1918 Lieutenant Colonel FG Harvey SA Def Force

Deputy Assistant Adjutant and Quartermaster General (DAA&QMG)
5 Aug 1914 – 22 Sep 1915 Major Wingfield RB
Later Major General Hon Maurice Anthony Wingfield 1883-1956, psc, AA&QMG 7th
Division 1915, Comd 143 Bde 1925-26 (son of 7th Viscount Powerscourt)

22 Sep 1915 – 1916 Major Fellowes RB
Later Lieutenant Colonel Ronald Townshend Fellowes 2nd Baron Ailwyn 1886-1936 Eton, SC
22 Bde 1914-1915, CO 1 RB 1916-1918

Brigadier General Royal Artillery (BGRA)
5 Aug 1914 – 5 Jun 1915 Brigadier General Phipps-Hornby VC
Later Brigadier General Edmund John Phipps-Hornby 1857-1947

5 Jun 1915 – 1 Apr 1916 Brigadier General Stokes
Later Brigadier General Alfred Stokes 1860-1931

1 Apr – 4 Apr 1916 Brigadier General Nicholson
Later Brigadier General Charles Henry Whalley Nicholson 1869-NK, wounded at Battle of
Aisne, CRA 8th Division

4 Apr – 26 Jul 1916 Brigadier General Uniacke
Later Lieutenant General Sir Herbert Crofton Campbell Uniacke 1866-1934, BGRA HA Res
BEF 1915, BGRA V Corps 1915-1916, MGRA 5th Army 1916-1918

26 Jul 1916 – 15 Feb 1918 Brigadier General Tancred
Later Major General Thomas Angus Tancred 1867-1944, BGRA VIII Corps Mar-Jul 1916

Chief Engineer/Commander Royal Engineers (CE/CRE)

5 Aug 1914 – 9 May 1915 Brigadier General Glubb
Later Major General Sir Frederic Manley Glubb 1857-1938, CE 2nd Army 1915-1919

9 May – 14 Jul 1915 Brigadier General Capper
Later Major General Sir John Edward Capper 1861-1955, CE 3rd Army 1915, GOC 24th Division 1915-17, DG Tank Corps 1917

14 Jul 1915 – 29 Nov 1917 Brigadier General Schreiber
Later Colonel (Hon Brigadier General) Acton Lemuel Schreiber 1865-NK, SA War wounded, CRE 1st Division 1910-1915 wounded

29 Nov 1917 – 15 Feb 1918 Brigadier General Rolland
Later Brigadier General Alexander Rolland 1871-NK.

Assistant Director Signals (OC III Corps Signal Company)

5 Aug 1914 – 29 Mar 1915 Major Newbigging Manchester
Later Brigadier General Newbigging Signal Officer in Chief 1919

29 Mar 1915 – 18 Aug 1917 Major Cunningham RE
Later Lieutenant Colonel AB Cunningham RE

18 Aug 1917 – 15 Feb 1918 Lieutenant Colonel Allan Camerons
Later Lieutenant Colonel AC Allan Camerons

Corps Chemical Advisor

6 May – Jun 1915 Lieutenant Barley Cameronians
Later Lieutenant Colonel Leslie John Barley 1890-1979 Oxford and Kiel Universities (Chemistry), 1 Cameronians 19 Bde 1914-1915, Chem Adviser HQ 2nd Army, Dev Dir ICI 1926

23 Mar 1917 – 15 Feb 1918 Captain RE Slade RE

Camp Commandant

5 Aug 1914 – 15 Feb 1918 Lieutenant Colonel Rose BW
Later Lieutenant Colonel Hugh Rose of Kilravock 1863-1946, CO 1 BW

Appendix C

III Corps Troops 1914-1918

When Putty took command of III Corps in 1914 he had two divisions and no corps troops. Later in the war he often had four or more divisions in the corps and the numbers of units of corps troops rose to well over one hundred; in November 1917 the strength of corps troops reached 20,627. Not only were the divisions rotated but most of the units of corps troops were too, which meant it was very difficult to build and maintain an effective and efficient team. The problems were compounded by the lack of real estate for deployment and of routes for movement. During the Battle of the Somme there would have been almost no usable space between the rear boundaries of the forward divisions and the corps rear boundary. The two routes forward through this area would have been in use 24 hours each day, every day in both directions. The administrative and logistic demands of corps command were exceptionally high; even one function badly organised could affect the best operational plans.

For reconnaissance III Corps had III Corps Cav Regt and III Corps Cyclist Bn. They were invaluable in the advance; in defence they were employed on traffic control, escort and courier duties.

III Corps Artillery was under BGRA: at corps level it mainly consisted of III Corps Heavy Artillery under BGHA. Under him there were a number of Heavy Artillery Groups (HAG), each with several hy btys, siege btys and hy TM btys. Each HAG would also have at least one ammo column for second line. However, the corps artillery also included one or more FA btys allocated by army, and sometimes one or more AFA bdes again with its HQ and bde ammo column; there were also air defence btys and specialist units for sound ranging or flash spotting.

By 1915 III Corps had a RFC sqn to provide air reconnaissance and artillery observation, and specialist balloon units. In 1916 tanks appeared in III Corps, initially in small numbers, then coys and then in the Battle of Cambrai tank bdes. All had their own command and control and logistic support.

The Royal Engineers (RE) provided many corps troops' units. There were specialist coys – tunnelling coys, railway coys, tramway coys and those that provided and released gas. General purpose coys (AT coys) built and repaired roads, airfields, field defences and accommodation, and provided water. Communications were also provided by RE, either by III Corps Signal Coy (radio, telephone, helio, buzzer or courier) or by specialist units such as pigeon lofts. The RE also provided the postal services both for military correspondence and the large amount of incoming and outgoing civilian mail. III Corps also had forestry units, at one time from 37 Canadian Forestry Corps, to meet the high demand for wood.

For the wounded the medical services provided Casualty Clearing Stations (CCS) to prioritise and allocate treatment, then Advanced and Main Dressing Stations (ADS and MDS). For the sick and those recovering from minor wounds there was a Corps Rest Station (CRS) and Corps Convalescent Station. There were horse drawn and wheeled ambulances units, and a number of specialist hygiene units to improve sanitation and reduce the spread of diseases. For the animals – horses, mules, dogs, pigeons etc – there were veterinary hospitals: there was even III Corps Horse Dip.

For the supply of the myriad of items that the corps needed, the ordnance services had ordnance parks and ammunition parks. They also provided specialist units for ammunition disposal, bathing, laundry, salvage and bakeries. There were also cavalry parks to provide saddlery and other requirements for units with horses. The two largest supplies were ammunition and forage – the first in weight and the second in bulk. Workshops, both general and specialist, serviced and repaired vehicles, guns, weapons and other equipment.

There were reinforcement units that processed and administered the drafts coming forward and movement units that dealt with those proceeding or returning from leave, and other individuals coming forward. III Corps POW cages held prisoners during interrogation prior to evacuation behind the corps rear boundary. Some POWs were employed as labourers: at one time III Corps labour units included 21 Cheshire, 35 POW Coy and A Coy 2 South African Native Labour Contingent (SANLC).

Numerous 3rd and 4th Line transport units moved supplies and men forward, returning with men proceeding on leave, salvage, equipment requiring repair, prisoners etc. In 1917 a SMTO was appointed to command the Corps Ammunition Park, Corps Siege Park and Corps Supply Columns. The Corps Siege Park and Corps Troops Supply Column both had strengths of about 1,000 men at this time; SMTO had about 800 trucks.

The provost marshal with the assistance of traffic control units had the difficult task of keeping the routes open and dealing with refugees moving up, down or across them. Welfare units of all description operated in III Corps area; many of them, such as canteens and libraries, provided by voluntary organisations. There was even III Corps Cinema. Finally, there were graves registration units with the massive task of collecting, burying and keeping records of the dead.

The problems of allocating real estate, moving these units, and assisting them to carry out their individual functions within III Corps need no further explanation: these were the tasks of the staff at HQ III Corps. However, it must not be forgotten that these units too had to be supported. Just one example – III Corps Cinema required a supply line for films, a system for the maintenance and repair of its projectors, and it too had to change over its personnel.

Appendix D

III Corps Divisions and their Commanders 1914-1918

Guards   30 Nov – 6 Dec 1917 Major General Feilding
Later Major General Sir Geoffrey Percy Thynne Feilding 1866-1932 late Coldm Gds Major General Brigade of Guards and GOC London District 1923-1927

1   8 Jul – 3 Oct 1916, 31 Oct 1916 – 16 May 1917 Major General Strickland
Later Lieutenant General Sir (Edward) Peter Strickland 1869-1951 late Norfolk, GOC British Troops Egypt 1927-1931

4   31 Aug 1914 – 4 May 1915
(1) 31 Aug – Sep 1914 Major General Snow
Later Lieutenant General Sir Thomas D'Oyly Snow 1858-1940 Eton late Somerset/Innis Fus/ Northants – injured when his horse fell on him, GOCinC Western Command 1918-1920
(2) 21 Sep – 5 Oct 1914 Major General Rawlinson
Later General Lord Rawlinson of Trent 1864-1925 Eton late Coldm Gds
(3) 21 Oct 1914 – 4 May 1915 Major General Wilson
Later Lieutenant General Sir Henry Fuller Maitland Wilson 1859-1941 Eton late RB Commander Allied Forces Turkey in Europe, British Salonika Army and British Army of the Black Sea 1919-1920

6   16 Sep 1914 – 31 May 1915, 16 Nov – 14 Dec 1917
(1) 16 Sep 1914 – 31 May 1915 Major General Keir
Later Lieutenant General Sir John Lindesay (The Matador) Keir 1856-1937 late RA, GOC VI Corps 1915-1916
(2) 16 Nov – 14 Dec 1917 Major General Marden
Later Major General Sir Thomas Owen Marden 1866-1951 late Cheshire, GOC 6th Division 1917-1919, GOC 53rd (Welsh) Division 1923-1927
'A man of restless energy and a first class regimental officer, with an exceptional knowledge of detail who left no one in any doubt who commanded the division'. (Lieutenant Colonel TT Grove RE GSO1 6th Division)

8   30 Jun 1915 – 2 Jul 1916
(1) 30 Jun – 1 Aug 1915 Major General Davies

Later General Sir Francis John Davies 1864-1948 late Gren Gds, GOCinC Scottish Command 1919-1923

(2) 1 Aug 1915 – 2 Jul 1916 Major General Hudson

Later General Sir Havelock (Huddie) Hudson 1862-1944 late Northants/19 Bengal L, GOC Eastern Army India 1920-24

Notes:

Asked for delay of 8th Division's attack on 1 Jul until La Boisselle and Thiepval attacks had started (over-ruled by Rawlinson)

Worn out and performing poorly on 1 Jul 16, 8th Division, which had been commanded 'damned badly' by his predecessor (Heneker on Hudson), 'improved beyond all recognition' under Major General Heneker (Lieutenant Colonel Hanbury-Sparrow GSO3 HQ 8th Division May-Oct 1916, CO 2 Berks 1917)

General Sir Havelock Hudson, whose 8th Division lost 'more than half its force' on 1 Jul 1916, was 'such a nice little man and very quick and sensible' but while he was 'quick enough to see what was going to go wrong' he had 'not quite enough personality to be insubordinate and refuse' pressure from above (Brigadier General Howell late C of G CO 4 H 1914-15 killed in action Oct 1916)

9   17 May – 6 Jun 1915, 7 Oct – 29 Oct 1916, 3 Dec – 15 Dec 1917

(1) 17 May – 6 Jun 1915 Major General Landon

Later Major General Herman James Shelley Landon 1859-1948 late Warwicks invalided Sep 1915, GOC 33rd Division 1916 invalided, GOC 35th Division 1917 invalided

(2) 7 Oct – 29 Oct 1916 Major General Furse

Later Lieutenant General Sir William (Thomas) Furse 1865-1953 Eton late RA, GSO1 6th Division 1914, MGO 1916-20

Note:

Wanted to delay attack 12 Oct 16 for 24 or 48 hours to allow time for reconnaissance – strong protest, over-ruled

(3) 3 Dec – 15 Dec 1917 Major General Lukin

Later Major General Sir Henry Timson Lukin 1860-1925 late Bengough's Horse/Cape Mounted Riflemen

12   6 Jun – 16 Jul 1915, 17 Jun – 4 Jul 1916, 17 Nov – 6 Dec 1917

(1) 6 Jun – 16 Jul 1915 Major General Wing

Later Major General Frederick Drummond Vincent Wing 1860-1915 late RA killed in action

(2) 17 Jun – 4 Jul 1916 and 17 Nov – 6 Dec 1917 Major General Scott

Later Major General Sir Arthur Binny Scott 1862-1944 late RA, GOC Lucknow Division India 1918-1920

14   14 Jan – 15 Feb 1918 Major General Couper

Later Major General Sir Victor Arthur Couper 1859-1938 late RB

15   5 Aug 1916 – 1 Feb 1917 Major General McCracken

Later Lieutenant General Sir Frederick William Nicholas McCracken 1859-1949 late Berks, GOCinC Scottish Command 1918-1919

Notes:

Despite some unfavourable reports 'regarding his military efficiency' (Haig 4 Aug 1916) McCracken who 'was quite pleasant and amiable, but weak and lazy, and left everything to his staff' with only 'imperturbality in the worst situations' as his strong point (Major K Henderson Garwhal Rifles GSO2 HQ 15th Division)

18   9 Feb – 15 Feb 1918 Major General Lee
Later Major General Sir Richard Phillips Lee 1865-1953 late RE

19   7 May – 2 Aug 1916, 9 Dec – 15 Dec 1917 Major General Bridges
Later Lieutenant General Sir George Tom Molesworth Bridges 1871-1939 late RA/4 DG, Governor South Australia 1922-1927

20   28 Jul 1915 – 20 Jan 1916, 6 Oct – 18 Oct 1917, 29 Oct – 4 Dec 1917
(1) 28 Jul 1915 – 20 Jan 1916 Major General Davies
Later Major General Richard Hutton Davies 1862-1918 NZ committed suicide
(2) 6 Oct – 4 Dec 1917 Major General Douglas Smith
Later Major General Sir William Douglas Smith 1865-1939 late RSF, Lieutenant Governor Jersey 1920-1924
Notes:
Cavan (XIV Corps) 'Spoke in high terms of his division which had become quite a different force since his appointment' (Haig 23 Jun 1916)
'Was quite happy to crawl round trenches to see things for himself' (Major CA Milward Notts & Derby)

23   5 Sep 1915 – 29 Feb 1916, 2 Jul – 11 Aug 1916, 11 Sep – 12 Oct 1916 Major General Babington
Later Lieutenant General Sir James Melville Babington 1854-1936 late 16 L, GOC British Forces Italy 1918-1920
Note: Removal of Brigadier General Oxley late KRRC Comd 24 Bde 7 Jul 1916

24   30 Sep – 18 Oct 1917

27   27 May – 18 Sep 1915
(1) 27 May – 16 Jul 1915 Major General Snow
Later Lieutenant General Sir Thomas D'Oyly Snow 1858-1940 Eton late Somerset/R Innis Fus/Northants
Note: See 4th Division
(2) 16 Jul – 18 Sep 1915 Major General Milne
Later Field Marshal Lord (George Francis) Milne 1866-1948 late RA, CIGS 1926-1933
Note: Previously BGGS HQ III Corps

29   18 Nov – 5 Dec 1917 Major General de Lisle
Later Lieutenant General Sir Henry de Beauvoir de Lisle 1864-1955 late DLI, GOCinC Western Command 1919-1923

30   28 Jan – 10 Feb 1918 Major General Williams
Later Major General W de L Williams late R Hamps

34   23 Feb – 18 Aug 1916, 5 Jul – 30 Sep 1917
(1) 23 Feb – 22 Jul 1916 Major General Ingouville-Williams
Later Major General Edward Charles (Inky Bill) Ingouville-Williams 1861-1916 late E Kent killed in action 22 Jul 1916
Note: Comd 16 Bde when Pulteney was GOC 6th Division
(2) Jul 1916 – 30 Sep 1917 Major General Nicholson
Later Major General Sir (Cecil) Lothian Nicholson 1865-1933 late GH, GOC 55th (West Lancashire) Division 1921-1925
Note: BM 16 Bde when Pulteney was Bde Comd

35   2 Jun – 4 Oct 1917
(1) 2 Jun – 6 Jul 1917 Major General Landon
Later Major General Herman James Shelley Landon 1859-1948 late Warwicks invalided
Note: See 9th Division invalided 1915
(2) 6 Jul – 4 Oct 1917 Major General Franks
Later Major General Sir George Mackenzie Franks 1868-1958 late RA, GOC Meerut District India 1925-1928

36   3 Dec – 15 Dec 1917, 16 Dec – 29 Dec 1917 Major General Nugent
Later Major General Sir Oliver Nugent 1860-1926 late RMF/KRRC

39   7 Mar – 24 Mar 1916, 25 Jan – 29 Jan 1918
(1) 7 Mar – 24 Mar 1916 Major General Barnardiston
Later Major General Nathaniel Walter Barnardiston 1858-1919 late Middx, Head BMM Portugal 1916-1919
Note: Putty reported to him when serving in the Congo
(2) 25 Jan – 29 Jan 1918 Major General Feetham
Later Major General Edward Feetham 1861-1918 late Berks killed in action

40   2 Jun – 10 Oct 1917, 1 Nov – 15 Nov 1917
(1) 2 Jun – 24 Jul 1917 Major General Ruggles-Brise
Later Major General Harold Goodeve Ruggles-Brise 1864-1927 late Gren Gds, MS GHQ 1917-1919
(2) 24 Jul – 15 Nov 1917 Major General Ponsonby
Later Major General Sir John Ponsonby 1866-1952 Eton late Coldm Gds, GOC Madras District India 1920-1928

42   8 Apr – 19 May 1917, 2 Jun – 10 Jul 1917 Major General Mitford
Later Major General BR Mitford late E Surrey

46   Mar 1915 Major General Montagu-Stuart-Wortley
Later Major General Edward James Montagu-Stuart-Wortley 1857-1934 Eton late KRRC, GOC 65th Division Ireland 1916-1919

47   22 Aug – 14 Oct 1916, 16 Dec 1917 – 5 Jan 1918
(1) 22 Aug – 28 Sep 1916 Major General Barter
Later Major General Sir Charles St Leger Barter 1856-1931 late Madras LI
Note: Barter removed by Putty after his attack on High Wood Sep 1916
(2) Sep 1916 – 5 Jan 1918 Major General Gorringe
Later Lieutenant General Sir George Frederick (Blood Orange) Gorringe 1868-1945 late RE, GOC 10th Division Egypt 1919-1921
Note: Gorringe and Putty were bde comds in 6th Division at the same time. Gorringe commanded 18 Bde when Putty was GOC 6th Division.

48   2 Apr – 24 Jun 1915, 24 Oct 1916 – 13 May 1917
(1) 2 Apr – Jun 1915 Major General Heath
Later Major General Henry Newport Charles Heath 1860-1915 late S Staffs/KOYLI fell ill Jun died 29 Jul 1915
(2) Jun 1915 – 13 May 1917 Major General Fanshawe
Later Major General Sir Robert (Fanny) Fanshawe 1860-1946 late Ox LI, GOC 69th Division 1918-1919

50   17 Aug 1916 – 31 Mar 1917 Major General Wilkinson
Later Major General Sir Percival Spearman Wilkinson 1865-1953 late NF, Commander No 1 Area 1918-1919
Note: 'A capable and energetic commander' (Haig)

55   4 Oct – 18 Oct 1917 Major General Jeudwine
Later Lieutenant General Sir Hugh Sandham Jeudwine 1862-1942 late RA, DGTA 1923-1927

58   20 Jan – 15 Feb 1918 Major General Cator
Later Major General Albermarle Bertie Cator 1877-1932 late SG, Major General Brigade of Guards and GOC London District 1932 died in accident

59   16 Feb – 19 May 1917, 2 Jun – 10 Jul 1917, 23 – 27 Nov 1917, 25 – 31 Dec 1917
(1) 16 Feb – 8 Apr 1917 Major General Sandbach
Later Major General Arthur Edmund Sandbach 1859-1928 late RE
(2) 8 Apr – 31 Dec 1917 Major General Romer
Later General Sir (Cecil) Francis Romer 1869-1962 late RDF, AG 1933-1935
Note: Previously BGGS III Corps

61   30 Nov – 15 Dec 1917 Major General Mackenzie
Later Major General Colin John Mackenzie 1861-1956 late Seaforth, CGS Canada 1910-1913 removed, GOC 3rd Division 1914 removed

19 Bde   31 Aug 1914 – 19 Aug 1915
(1) 31 Aug – 5 Sep 1914 Brigadier General Drummond
Later Major General Laurence George Drummond 1861-1946 Eton late SG invalided
Note: Evans House Eton with Pulteney
(2) 5 Sep 1914 – 19 Aug 1915 Brigadier General Gordon
Later Brigadier General Hon Sir F Gordon late Gordons

1 Cdn   6 May – 14 May 1915, 28 Jun – 15 Jul 1915 Major General Alderson
Later Lieutenant General Sir Edwin Alfred Hervey Alderson 1859-1927 late W Kent, Inspector
of Infantry 1916-1920

2 Cav   30 Nov – 2 Dec 1917 Major General Greenly
Later Major General Walter Howarth (Bob) Greenly 1875-1955 late 12 L, Head BMM
Romania 1918-1920
Note: previously and temporarily GOC 47th Division

3 Cav   8 Jul – 14 Jul 1915 Major General Briggs
Later Lieutenant General Sir Charles James Briggs 1865-1941 late KDG, Chief BMM South
Russia 1919-1923

4 Cav   Jul – Sep 1917 Major General Kennedy
Later Major General Alfred Alexander Kennedy 1871-1926 late 3 H

Appendix E

Cambrai 1917 – III Corps Operation Order No 224

---

1. The III Corps, in conjunction with the Corps on the left, will on a date and at an hour to be communicated later attack the enemy on their front. Subsidiary attacks and feints will be carried out simultaneously by other Corps along the remainder of the Army front.

2. The III Corps will attack with the 12th Division on the right, the 20th Division in the centre and the 6th Division on the left.

   The 29th Division will be in Corps Reserve and will pass through the 20th and 6th Divisions in order to capture the heights SW of Rumilly, Nine Wood and Premy Chapel. Special instructions regarding the hour at which the 29th Division are to advance are being issued to the GOC 29th Division.

   The objectives and dividing lines between Divisions have already been issued (vide tracing "A" attached to III Corps Instruction No 1).

3. The attack will be carried out under the protection of waves of tanks. The allotment of tanks to Divisions has already been detailed (vide para. 9 of Instruction No 1).

   The attack will also be supported by:

   a) Standing artillery and smoke barrages, which open on the enemy's front line, and lift from trench to trench as the advance progresses, vide the Artillery Barrage Maps issued to all concerned;

   b) back and flank barrages of smoke and heavy artillery;

   c) machine-gun barrages.

   The tanks will advance from their assembly positions, 1000 yards distant from the enemy's front line, at Z-10 minutes followed by the infantry. The artillery and machine-gun barrages will open at Zero. The final protective barrage beyond the second objective (Brown Line) will lift at times varying from Zero+210 mins to Zero+410 mins, to enable the tanks to push on and exploit success.

4. After capture of the Brown Line, tanks will immediately exploit the success as follows:

   a) The tanks from one Company of "F" Battn, allotted to the 12th Division, will proceed immediately from Bonavis to Masnières, seize the bridges (locations given in map co-ordinates), and form a bridgehead there.

b) The tanks from a Company of "A" Battn, allotted to the 20th Division, will advance immediately to the Canal, and seize the lock and bridges at (location given in map co-ordinates), and clear the Canal bank from G.25.a (exclusive) to the Ribécourt-Marcoing Rly line exclusive (ie seize the crossings and clear the canal bank between Masnières and Marcoing).

c) The tanks from one Company of "B" Battn, allotted to the 6th Division, will occupy as soon as possible the river, canal and railway bridges at Marcoing, in (locations given in map co-ordinates).

d) The tanks from one Company of "H" Battn, on the left of the 6th Division, will push forward to Nine Wood and secure the Northern and North-eastern margins of the wood, moving one section of tanks through the "Ride", running from Premy Chapel towards Noyelles.

The above tanks will maintain their positions on their objectives until relieved by the 29th Division, or in the case of (b), until the 29th Division has passed through.

e) Simultaneously with the above, the 12th Division will extend the right flank of the Corps to about M.2.d.9.7 (1 mile north of le Quennet Farm) and secure observation into the valley of the Canal de St Quentin. The 20th Division will prolong this flank with a Brigade to the Road Junction at G.26.b.3.0 in les Rues Vertes, supporting the tanks in forming a bridgehead at Masnières, until relieved by the 29th Division. To assist in forming this flank, the 20th Division will take with them the tanks from one company of "I" Battalion. These tanks will advance and clear the Bonavis-Crèvecoeur Ridge, supported on the right by the 12th Division, and in the centre by two troops of III Corps Cavalry placed at the disposal of the 20th Division for this purpose.

The 12th Division and the troops of Corps Cavalry will establish posts along the Bonavis Spur so as to deny it to the enemy, and to prevent hostile observation from this spur of the passage of the 29th Division and the Cavalry across the Canal at Masnières. It is the intention eventually, when the Cavalry have pushed through, to establish the front of III Corps facing East along the line Bonavis-Crèvecoeur-La Belle Etoile.

f) The 20th Division will support the tanks at (b) with strong patrols followed by a Company, and the 6th Division will similarly support the tanks at (c) with strong patrols followed by Companies. Junction between the two Divisions will be effected at the cross-roads at L.22.d.30.50 (railway junction S side of Marcoing). The tanks at (d) will be supported by a Brigade of the 6th Division which will be sent forward to hold the line from Premy Chapel to L.19.b.6.4 (Corps boundary on second objective), where they connect with the 51st Division.

g) The 29th Division will be assisted by 12 special tanks in their advance to the heights SW of Rumilly, Nine Wood and Premy Chapel. No 6 MMG Battery is also placed at the disposal of the GOC 29th Division for the operations.

5. The objectives, when gained, will be consolidated, and the defence reorganised in depth. A support line of posts will be formed by the 12th, 20th and 6th Divisions approximately along the Green Dotted Line, vide tracing "A" already issued.

As the flank held by 12th Division will form the pivot for the subsequent move of the III Corps to the line Bonavis-Crèvecoeur-La Belle Etoile, the 12th Division will use every endeavour to consolidate the captured line, and to wire it as soon as possible.

6. Special parties will be told off by the 6th Division to get into touch with the 51st Division at the following points:
In the Hindenburg Line at K.36.b.1.4 (Corps boundary on support line of Hindenburg front system)
Western end of Ribécourt
In the Hindenburg Support Line at L.19.b.6.4 (Corps boundary on second objective)
Similarly, Divisions will detail special parties on their flanks to effect junction with each other on each objective at Inter-Divisional posts to be arranged between Divisions.

7. A group of Heavy Artillery is affiliated to each Division. Divisional Commanders should apply direct to their Group for any Heavy Artillery assistance they may require.
The programme for the artillery bombardment, as laid down by III Corps Artillery instructions, will not however be departed from without reference to Corps Hd Qrs.

8. Two troops of III Corps Cavalry Regt are placed at the disposal of GOC 20th Division, for the purpose detailed in para. 4(e), and one troop at the disposal of the GOC 6th Division in order to keep in touch with the 29th Division. Two troops are placed at the disposal of the APM for escort duty. The remainder of the regiment is placed under the orders of the GOC Lucknow Cavalry Bde for the mission detailed in para.10 below. The OC Corps Cavalry Regt will arrange direct with Divisions as to time and place of joining.

9. After the capture of the Red Line by 29th Division, the 5th and 2nd Cavalry Divisions will cross the Canal at Masnières and Marcoing and operate as detailed in Instruction No 1 para. 22. The 1st Cavalry Division will pass through Ribécourt and Marcoing and move Northwards.

10. In order to widen the breach by raiding Southwards the Lucknow Cavalry Brigade and one Battery of Horse Artillery have been allotted to the III Corps. This detachment will be reinforced by the Corps Cavalry Regiment (less 5 troops). The Lucknow Cavalry Bde will move forward on Z Day with the 2nd Cavalry Division to its assembly place, and on to the Canal, crossing East of or at Masnières in accordance with the local tactical situation. Detailed instructions regarding the action of this detachment will be issued separately.

11. Instructions regarding the repair of roads have already been issued.
In addition to the tasks already allotted, the 6th Division Pioneers will be responsible for making the road from Ribécourt to Marcoing passable for Cavalry. This work is most urgent and must take precedence of all other tasks. The 6th Division will be assisted in this by 12 wire-pulling tanks, which will be employed in the first instance by the IV Corps on clearing the wire from the Trescault-Ribécourt road.
The 29th Division Pioneers will be employed under the orders of the CE on the construction of a tramway from Gouzeaucourt to connect up with the German system near La Vacquerie.

12. A contact Aeroplane will fly over the Corps front at:
Zero plus 45 minutes

Zero plus 2 hrs and 15 mins
Zero plus 3 hours
Zero plus 3 hrs and 30 mins
and subsequently as ordered.

13. Watches will be synchronised by a Staff Officer from Corps Headquarters at 9 am and 12 noon on "Y" day.

14. Corps Headquarters will remain at Templeux-la-Fosse.
Divisions must be prepared to move their Headquarters forward, if the operations on Z day are successful.
The first move of Corps HQ will probably be to Sorel.

15. Acknowledge.

CG Fuller
Brigadier General
General Staff
III Corps

16.11.17
Issued by DR at 3 pm 16 Nov

Note: In addition III Corps issued the following 'Instructions' with amendments:
1.   General Scheme of the Offensive (10 Nov)
2.   Concentration and Assembly (10 Nov)
3.   Secrecy (11 Nov)
4.   Preliminary Movements (14 Nov)
5.   Issue and Distribution of Orders (12 Nov)
6.   Codes and Ciphers (14 Nov)
7 and 8.   Signal Communications (14 and 16 Nov)
9.   Third Stage of Attack (17 Nov)
10. Lucknow Cavalry Brigade (17 Nov)

Appendix F

Cambrai 1917 – III Corps Operation Order No 227

Orders for counter-attack 1 December 1917

1. The situation of III Corps this evening appears to be as follows:
    The line held runs approximately from X.13 central along the railway to R.31.d.1. 8, thence along the Northern edge of the Quentin Ridge and Gonnelieu Village to la Vacquerie, thence via R.16 central – R.11 central – R.5.a central to les Rues Vertes. Masnières is in our possession and there is no change on the left front of the Corps.
2. The Cavalry Corps (less 1st and 3rd Cavalry Divisions) will carry out an operation tomorrow morning under arrangements to be made by the Cavalry Corps with a view to capturing Gauche Wood (if not already in our hands) and Villers Hill, and Villers Guislain.
3. OC 2nd Bde Tank Corps will place all the tanks he has been able to collect tonight in W.18.c (1000 yards W of Vaucelette Farm) at the disposal of the Cavalry Corps for this attack.
4. Guards Division will simultaneously with the attack by the Cavalry Corps seize the Quentin Ridge, from Gauche Wood to Gonnelieu, and secure observation down into Twenty-two Ravine (western end of Banteux Ravine).
5. The tanks of 2nd Bde Tank Corps assembled at Queens Cross (Gouzeaucourt Wood) are at the disposal of Guards Division for the operation.
6. The artillery of 12th Division will assist in the operations of the Cavalry Corps.
7. Divisions will reorganise their defences tonight and consolidate as rapidly as possible on the remainder of the Corps front.
8. 59 Sqn RFC will place aeroplanes at the disposal of the Cavalry Corps and Guards Division as required.
9. Acknowledge.

CG FULLER
BGGS
III Corps

Issued by SDR at 10 pm 30 Nov 1917

Bibliography

Documents & Unpublished Manuscripts

RHQ Scots Guards
Balfour, C.B., Scrapbook
Cator, A.B.E., Diary 1st Battalion Scots Guards South Africa, Unpublished manuscript
Digest of Service 1899-1932
Orders Book
Pulteney, W.P., Staff Diary – Colonel Pulteney Force Unpublished
Records of Service

Imperial War Museum
Adams, H.L. Private Papers of H.L. Adams, Documents.4300 (83/50/1) Typescript (ND)
Allen, H.M. Private Papers of Lieutenant Colonel H.M. Allen, Documents 114 (PP/MCR/329)
Austin, Charles Interview, sound archive Cat No 11116
Barnardiston, N.W., Private Papers of Major General N.W. Barnardiston, Documents.14678 (67/214/1)
Boxer, H.C., Private Papers of Major HC Boxer, Documents.4891 (96/12/1)
Buckley, F.C., Private Papers of Captain F.C. Buckley Documents.14753 (67/247/1)
Collen, E.H.E., Private Papers of Lieutenant Colonel E.H.E. Collen, Documents.6607 (79/21/1 & Con. Shelf) Manuscript diary (1917)
Cordeaux, E.K., Private Papers of Colonel E.K. Cordeaux Documents.16975 (09/75/1-2)
Hanbury-Sparrow Alan H., Record of Captain A.H. Hanbury-Sparrow, Cat No 4131 (BBC Radio 4 series 1963)
Henderson, K., Private Papers of Major K Henderson Documents.10942
Horne, Harold Private Papers of Captain H. Horne, Documents.4867 (80/44/1)
Lowther, Henry Cecil, Private Papers of Major General Sir Cecil Lowther, Documents. 6388 (97/10/1)
Lynden-Bell, Arthur, Private Papers of Major General Sir Arthur Lynden-Bell, Documents. 7826 (90/1/1 & Con Shelf)
Marchant, E., Private Papers of Second Lieutenant E Marchant, Documents.12054 (DS/MISC/26)
McMurtrie, G.D.J., Private Papers of Lieutenant Colonel GDJ McMurtrie, Documents.6796 (78/23/1) Typescript (1918)

O'Rorke, F.C., Private Papers of Lieutenant Colonel F.C. O'Rorke, Documents 11985 (PP/MCR/54), Manuscript Diary (1914-1919)

Paish, F.W., Private Papers of Lieutenant FW Paish MC, Documents.5524 (96/29/1) Typescript (1977)

Rawlinson, H.S., Fourth Army Records of General Lord Rawlinson, Documents.20537 (Con Shelf), Vols 6,7 and 21

Ross, Robert, Private Papers of R Ross, Documents.8274 (99/22/1) Typescript (c1930)

Tansley, James, 'Record of Corporal James Tansley', Cat No 13682 (BBC Radio 4 series 1976)

Taylor, W.R., Private Papers of Second Lieutenant W.R. Taylor, Documents.11768 (01/60/1)

Vignoles, Walter, Private Papers of Lieutenant Colonel W.A. Vignoles, Documents.6968 (77/3/1 & Con Shelf)

Wollocombe, T.S., Private Papers of Lieutenant Colonel T.S. Wollocombe, Documents.130 (89/7/1)

Wyatt, J.D., Private Papers of Lieutenant Colonel J.D. Wyatt, Documents.4160 (83/12/1)

Liddell Hart Centre for Military Archives (Quotes by permission of the Trustees)

Barnardiston, N.W., Major General Barnardiston papers

Bartholomew, W.H., General Sir William Bartholomew papers

Broad, C.N.F. Lieutenant-General Sir Charles Broad papers

De Lisle, General Sir Henry Beauvoir De Lisle papers

Hamilton, J., Papers of Jean, Lady Hamilton

Harington, C.H. 'Tim', General Sir Charles Harington papers

Kiggell, L.E., Lieutenant General Sir Launcelot, Edward Kiggell papers

Lyttelton, N.G., General Sir Neville Lyttelton papers

McCrae, G., Colonel Sir George McCrae papers

Milne, G.F., Field Marshal Lord Milne papers

Montgomery-Massingberd, A.A., Field Marshal Sir Archibald Montgomery-Massingberd papers

Robertson, W.R., Field Marshal Sir William Robertson Papers

National Archives (Kew)

Cabinet papers, Cambrai Enquiry 1917

Cunningham, G.G., Diary of the Nandi Field Force

Edmonds, Sir J.E, Official History Correspondence, CAB 45

Foreign Office Papers (various)

GHQ, 'Visit of HM the King and Prince of Wales to France'

HQ III Corps Summary of Operations of III Corps (B638) 50 11/14 H&S 553 WO

HQ III Corps War Diaries GS (WO 95/668-678), AQ (WO 154/2-4 & WO 95/683-6), RA (WO 95/689-693), DDMS (WO 95/695-696), other staff branches and corps troops (WO 695 & 697-705)

HQ 34th Division War Diaries

Smith-Dorrien H., Papers, CAB 45/206

Thomas, H.M., 'The Action of the Artillery of 12th Division on 30 November 1917'

War Office papers 'Cambrai Enquiry', HQ 4th Army, 3rd Army War Diary 1917-18, Haig papers

War Office Expeditionary Force Tables

National Army Museum

Burn-Murdoch, J.F., Brigadier General J.F. Burn-Murdoch Diary in South African War, Accession Number NAM.2006-12-59 Council of National Museum

Milward, A.C., Major General AC Milward War Diary 1916, Accession Number NAM.1965-10-143 Council of National Army Museum

Rawlinson, H.S., Diary and Papers of General Lord Rawlinson, Accession Number NAM.1952-01-33-25 to 34 Sir Anthony Rawlinson Bart/Council of the National Museum

Other

Army Football Association records

Ashley Church Statement of Significance 2007 (St Mary the Virgin Church, Ashley)

Balfour, Charles Barrington, 'Egypt 1882', unpublished manuscript

Bonham-Carter, Charles, The Papers of General Sir Charles Bonham-Carter, BHCT 1, Churchill Archives Centre

Chamberlain, Max, 'Denigrated Regiment: 5th Victorian Mounted Rifles 1901-1902' [S.1.], unpublished manuscript

Cuthbert, Gerald, Narrative of the Advance from Bloemfontein to Pretoria with 1 SG 1900

Droogleever, Robin, 'History of 5th Victorian Mounted Rifles' (Publication in 2016)

Falvey, Jeremiah 'Sir John Arnott' (2007)

Gallant, Ros, Pulteney Family Tree

Governor-General of Canada 'Prince Arthur's Canadian Itinerary 1918', Canadian National Archives Ottawa

House of Lords Archives, misc.

Kiszely, Lady Arabella, Lord Herschell's Game Book

Lambton, W., Major General Hon Sir William Lambton Papers Courtesy of Earl of Durham

Lyttelton, N.G., General Sir Neville Lyttelton Family Papers PP5/2/12 11 Sep 1909; PP5/2/13 25 July 1910, 5 Sep 1910, 14 Sep 1910, 17 Mar 1911, 16 Sep 1911, 26 Nov 1912; PP5/30/10 26 June 1916 Queen Mary, University of London Archives

Lyttelton, Neville, Papers, letters and diary of General Sir Neville Lyttelton, Bodleian Library

Murthly Castle visitors book

Paget, Arthur P., Papers – Letters to his Wife, Vol. IV-IX and General Correspondence, British Library

Ponsonby, J War Journal and HQ Coldstream Guards

Pulteney, Rev R.T.P., Letters to agent 1870 (Ref: FS 10/55) Northamptonshire Records Office

Pulteney, W.P., and others Letters to Gerald Cuthbert, unpublished

Pulteney W.P., Letters written to Theresa, Marchioness of Londonderry (wife of 6th Marquess) by kind permission of Lady Rose Lauritzen and Deputy Keeper of Records of Northern Ireland (D4567)

Pulteney W.P., Letters written to Edith, Marchioness of Londonderry (wife of 7th Marquess) by kind permission of Lady Rose Lauritzen and Deputy Keeper of Records of Northern Ireland (D4567)

Pulteney, W.P., Reports of III Corps sent to HM King Royal Archives

Pulteney, W.P., Letter to Lord Desborough 1915 Hertfordshire County Archives

Pulteney, W.P., Letters to Ettie, Lady Desborough 1891-1920 Hertfordshire County Archives

Rawlinson H.S., The Diary and Papers of General Lord (Henry S) Rawlinson, RWLN 1/1, held at the Churchill Archives Centre
Riverhill, Sevenoaks Visitor Book
Tourin Visitor Book
Uniacke, H.C.C., Uniacke Papers Royal Artillery Archives MD/1160, Woolwich, Courtesy of the Royal Artillery Historical Trust

Published Sources

Alexander, Jack, *McCrae's Battalion* (Edinburgh: Mainstream, 2003)
Anon., *Henry Dundas Scots Guards: A Memoir* (Edinburgh: W. Blackwood & Sons, 1921)
Asquith, Earl, *Memories and Reflections 1852-1927 Vols. I & II* (London: Cassell & Co., 1928)
Bailey, Catherine. *The Secret Rooms* (New York: Viking, 2012)
Barthop, Michael, *Blood-Red Desert Sand* (London: Cassell, 2002)
Becke, A.F., *Order of Battle of Divisions Vol 1-4 (The Army Council, GHQs, Army and Corps in Vol 4) 1914-18* (London: HMSO, 1945)
Beckett, Ian, *The Army and the Curragh Incident 1914* (London: Bodley Head for Army Records Society, 1986)
Beckett, Ian, *Ypres: The First Battle, 1914* (Abingdon: Routledge, 2013)
Beesely, Lawrence, *The Loss of the Titanic* (London: William Heinemann, 1912)
Beresford, Philip & Rubinstein, William, *The Richest of the Rich* (Petersfield: Harriman House, 2007)
Blake, Robert, *The Private Papers of Douglas Haig* (London: Eyre & Spottiswoode, 1952)
Bond, Brian (ed), *Staff Officer – Diaries of Walter Guinness Lord Moyne 1914-1918* (London: Leo Cooper, 1987)
Bond, Maurice & Beamish, David, *The Gentleman Usher of the Black Rod* (London HMSO, 1981)
Boraston, J.H. & Bax, Cyril, *The Eighth Division in War 1914-1918* (London: Medici, 1926)
Bourne, John, *Who's who in World War I* (London: Routledge, 2001)
Bourne, John, *Patronage and Society in Nineteenth Century England* (London: Edward Arnold, 1986)
Brice, Beatrix, *The Battle Book of Ypres* (London: John Murray, 1927)
Bridges, Tom, *Alarms and Excursions* (London: Longman, 1938)
Brown, Ian Malcolm, *British Logistics on the Western Front 1914-1919* (Westport, Conn: Praeger, 1998)
Bruadbridge, E.U., *Fifty-Ninth Division 1915-1918* (Chesterfield: Broadbridge, 1928)
Bryant, Pete, *The Grimsby Chums* (Hull: Humberside Libraries & Arts, 1990)
Calwell, Sir Charles Edward, *Life of Sir Stanley Maude* (London: Constable, 1920)
Calwell, Sir Charles Edward, *Field Marshal Sir Henry Wilson, His Life and Diaries* (London: Cassell, 1927)
Campbell, Christy, *Band of Brigands* (London: Harper Press, 2007)
Card, Tim, *Eton Renewed* (London: John Murray, 1994)
Chamberlain, Max and Droogleever, Robin *The War with Johnny Boer* (Loftus, NSW: Military History Publications, 2003)
Charteris, John, *At GHQ* (London: Cassell & Co., 1931)

Conan Doyle, Arthur, *The British Campaign in France and Flanders* (London: Geoffrey Bles, 1928)

Conover, George S., *The Genesee Tract* (New York, 1889)

Coombs, Rose, *Before Endeavours Fade* (London: Battle of Britain Prints International, 1977)

Coop, J.O., *The Story of the 55th (West Lancashire) Division* (Liverpool: "Daily Post" Printers, 1919)

Cuthbert, Harold, *1st Battalion Scots Guards in South Africa, 1899-1902* (London: Harrison & Sons, 1904)

Davenport-Hines, Richard, *Ettie: The Intimate Life and Dauntless Spirit of Lady Desborough* (London: Weidenfeld & Nicolson © Richard Davenport-Hines, Orion, 2008)

Davson, H.M., *The History of the 35th Division in the Great War* (London: Praed, 1926)

de Courcy, Anne, *Society's Queen: the life of Edith, Marchioness of Londonderry* (London: Orion, 2004)

de la Grange, Baronne Clementine, *Open House in Flanders 1914-1918* (London: John Murray, 1929)

de Lisle, Henry de Beauvoir, *Reminiscences of Sport and War* (London: Eyre & Spottiswoode, 1939)

Dugdale, Geoffrey, *'Langemarck' and 'Cambrai': A War Narrative, 1914-1918* (Shrewsbury: Wilding, 1932)

Edmonds Sir James, et al, *History of the Great War, Military Operations: France and Belgium* (London: HMSO, 1922-1947)

Eton School Lists 1874

Everett, Henry, *History of The Somerset Light Infantry 1685-1914* (London: Methuen & Co., 1934)

Ewing, John, *The History of the 9th (Scottish) Division 1914-1919* (London: Murray, 1921)

Farndale, Martin, *History of the Royal Regiment of Artillery on the Western Front 1914-1918* (London: Royal Artillery Institution, 1986)

Farr, Don, *The Silent General, Horne of the First Army* (Solihull: Helion, 2007)

Farrar-Hockley, A.H., *The Somme* (London: Pan, 1966)

Fergusson, James, *The Curragh Incident* (London: Faber & Faber, 1964)

Fleming, N.C. *The Marquess of Londonderry: Aristocracy, Power and Politics in Britain* (London: Tauris Academic Studies, 2005)

French, Gerald, *The Kitchener-French Dispute: A Last Word* (Glasgow: William Maclellan, 1960)

French, Viscount, *1914* (London: Constable, 1919)

Gambier-Parry, Ernest, *Annals of an Eton House* (London: John Murray, 1907)

Gibbon, Frederick, *The 42nd East Lancashire Division 1914-1918* (London: Newnes, 1920)

Gibot, Jean-Luc and Gorczynski, Philippe, *Following the Tanks: Cambrai 20th November – 7th December 1917* (Arras: Philippe Gorczynski, 1998)

Gilbert, Martin, *The Somme: the Heroism and Horrors of War* (London: John Murray, 2006)

Gillon, Stair, *The Story of the 29th Division* (London and Edinburgh: Nelson, 1925)

Gleichen, Count, *The Doings of the Fifteenth Infantry Brigade: August 1914-March 1915* (Edinburgh: W. Blackwood, 1917)

Gliddon, Gerald, *The Somme 1916* (Stroud: Sutton, 1994)

Goodinge, Anthony, *The Scots Guards* (London: Cooper, 1969)

Griffith, Paddy, *Battle Tactics on the Western Front* (New Haven: Yale University Press, 1994)

Haldane, Aylmer, *A Brigade of the Old Army* (London: Arnold, 1920)

Hammond, Bryn *Cambrai 1917: the Myth of the First Great Tank Battle* (Weidenfeld & Nicholson © Bryn Hammond, Orion, 2008)

Harington, C.H., *Tim Harington Looks Back* (London, Murray, 1940)

Hart, Peter, *The Somme* (London: Cassell © Peter Hart 2006 Orion)

Harwood, B, *Chivalry and Command: 500 years of Horse Guards* (Oxford: Osprey, 2006)

Headlam, Cuthbert, *History of The Guards Division in the Great War 1915-1918* (London: Murray, 1924)

Hickey, D.E., *Rolling into Action: Memoirs of a Tank Section Commander* (Hutchinson, 1934)

Holmes, Richard, *The Little Field Marshal: Sir John French* (London: Jonathan Cape, 1981)

Holmes, Richard, *Tommy: the British Soldier on the Western Front* 1914-1918 (London: Harper Perennial, 2005)

Holohan, Wheeler, *The History of the King's Messengers* (London: Grayson & Grayson, 1935)

Holt, Major and Mrs, *Battlefield Guide to the Somme* (2008)

Home, Archibald, *The Diary of a World War 1 Cavalry Officer Brigadier General Sir Archibald Home* (Tunbridge Wells: Costello, 1985)

Inglefield, V.E., *The History of the Twentieth (Light) Division* (London: Nisbet, 1921)

Jackson, Stanley, *Rufus Isaacs First Marquess of Reading* (London: Cassell, 1936)

Jeffery, Keith, *Field Marshal Sir Henry Wilson: A Political Soldier* (Oxford: Oxford University Press, 2006)

Jenkins, Roy, *Asquith* (London: Collins, 1964)

Jones, Simon, *Underground Warfare 1914-1918* (Barnsley: Pen & Sword, 2010)

Lee, Arthur, *No Parachute: A Fighter Pilot in World War 1* (London: Jarrolds, 1968/Grub Street 2014 Extracts by permission of copyright holder)

Lee, Celia Jean, *Lady Hamilton 1861-1941: A Soldier's Wife* (London: Celia Lee, 2001)

Liddell Hart B.H., *History of the First World War* (London: Cassell, 1970)

Lloyd George, David, *War Memoirs Vol 2* (London: Odhams Press, 1937)

Londonderry, Edith, *Retrospect* (London: Frederick Muller, 1938)

Londonderry, Marquess of *Wings of Destiny* (London: Macmillan, 1943)

Lowry, Edward, *With the Guards Brigade from Bloemfontein to Koomati Poort and Back* (London: Horace Marshal, 1902)

Lowther, Henry Cecil, *From Pillar to Post* (London: Edward Arnold, 1911)

Macdonald, Lyn, *Somme* (London: Michael Joseph, 1983)

Marden, T.O., *A Short History of the 6th Division* (London: Rees, 1920)

Matson A.T., *Nandi Resistance to British Rule, 1890-1906* (Nairobi: East African Publishing House, 1972)

Maude, Alan, *The 47th (London) Division 1914-1919* (London: Amalgamated Press, 1922)

Maurice, Frederick, *The History of the Scots Guards 1642-1914* (London: Chatto & Windus 1934)

Maurice, Frederick, *The Life of General Lord Rawlinson of Trent* (London: Cassell, 1928)

Maxse, F.I., *Seymour Vandeleur* (London: William Heinemann, 1906)

McCudden, James, *Five Years in the Royal Flying Corps* (London: The Aeroplane & General Publishing Co, 1919)

Merewether, Lieutenant Colonel & Sir Frederick Smith, *The Indian Corps in France* (London: Murray, 1919)

Moore, William, *A Wood Called Bourlon: The Cover-up after Cambrai* (London: Leo Cooper, 1988)

Morton, J.W., *Diary (KRIH) of The South African War 1900-1902* (Aldershot: Gale & Polden, 1905)

Neillands, Robin, *The Great War Generals on the Western Front 1914-18* (London: Robinson, 1999)

Neillands, Robin, *The Old Contemptibles, The British Expeditionary Force, 1914* (London: John Murray, 2005)

Nicol, Graham, *Uncle George: Biography of Field Marshal Lord Milne* (Richmond: Redminster Publications, 1976)

Norman, Terry, *The Hell They Called High Wood: the Somme 1916* (Wellingborough: Patrick Stephens, 1989/Pen & Sword, 2009)

Oxford Dictionary of National Biography

Peel, Reverend Edward, *Cheam School from 1645* (Gloucester: Thornhill Press, 1974)

Petre, F.L,, Ewart, Wilfrid and Lowther, Cecil *The Scots Guards in the Great War 1914-1918* (London: Murray, 1925)

Pidgeon, Trevor, *The Tanks at Flers* (Cobham: Fairmile, 1995)

Ponsonby, Frederick, *Recollections of Three Reigns* (London: Eyre & Spottiswoode, 1951)

Powell, Geoffrey *Plumer: The Soldiers' General* (London: Leo Cooper, 1990)

Pries, Arthur, *Das RIR 40, 1914-1918* (Stalling, 1925)

Prior, Robin & Wilson, Trevor, *Command on the Western Front: The Military Career of Sir Henry Rawlinson, 1914-1918* (Oxford: Blackwell, 1992)

Prior, Robin & Wilson, Trevor, *The Somme* (New Haven, Conn: Yale University Press, 2005)

Pycroft, James, *Oxford Memories: A Retrospect After Fifty Years* (London: Bentley & Son, 1866)

Repington, C à Court, *The First World War 1914-1918 Personal Experiences Vol II* (London: Constable, 1922)

Robbins, Simon, *First World War Letters of General Lord Horne* (Stroud: History Press for the Army Records Society, 2009)

Robbins, Simon, *British Generalship on the Western Front 1914-18: Defeat into Victory* (London: Frank Cass, 2005/ Taylor & Francis)

Rowe, Michael & McBryde, William *Beyond Mr Pulteney's Bridge* (Bath: Bath Preservation Trust, 1987)

Sandilands, H.R., *The Twenty-Third Division 1914-1919* (Edinburgh and London: Blackwood, 1925)

Scott, Arthur, *History of the 12th (Eastern) Division in the Great War 1914-1918* (London: Nisbet, 1923)

Seely, Jack, *Adventure* (London: William Heinemann, 1930)

Shakespear, John, *The Thirty Fourth Division 1915-1919* (London: Witherby, 1921)

Sheffield, Gary & Bourne, John *Douglas Haig War Diaries and Letters 1914-1918* (London: Phoenix, 2006)

Sheffield, Gary, *The Somme* (London: Cassell Military, 2003)

Simkins, Peter, *Kitchener's Army: the Raising of Britain's New Armies, 1914-1916* (Manchester: Manchester University Press, 1988)

Simpson, Andy, *Directing Operations: British Corps Command on the Western Front 1914-1918* (Stroud: Spellmount, 2006)

Smith, H.R., *A Soldier's Diary: Sidelights in the Great War, 1914-1918* (Evesham: The Journal Press, 1940)

Smith-Dorrien H., *Memories of Forty-Eight Years of Service* (London: John Murray, 1925)

Snow, Dan & Pottle, Mark (eds), *Confusion in Command: Memoirs of Lieutenant General Snow, 1914-1915* (London: Pen & Sword, 2011)

Stedman, Michael, *Somme (La Boisselle): Ovillers/Contalmaison* (London: Leo Cooper, 1997)

Steinhart, Edward & Entebbe Secretariat Archives, *Conflict and Collaboration* (Princeton, NJ: Princeton University Press, 1977)

Stewart, J & Buchan, John, *The Fifteenth (Scottish) Division 1914-1919* (Edinburgh: Blackwood, 1926)

Terraine, John (ed), *General Jack's Diary 1914-1918* (London: Eyre and Spottiswoode, 1964)

Travers, Tim, *The Killing Ground: The British Army, the Western Front and the Emergence of Modern Warfare, 1900-1918* (London: Allen & Unwin, 1987/Pen & Sword 2009)

Travers, Tim, *How the War Was Won: Command and Technology in the British Army on the Western Front, 1917-1918* (London: Routledge, 1992/ Taylor & Francis)

Vandeleur, Seymour, *Campaigning in the Upper Nile and Niger* (London: Methuen, 1898)

War Office *Field Service Regulations Parts I & II* (HMSO, 1909/1912)

Whitton, F.E., *History of the 40th Division* (Aldershot: Gale & Polden, 1926)

Willan, Frank, *History of the 4th Oxfordshire Light Infantry Militia 1778-1900* (Oxford: Horace Hart, 1900)

Williams, Jeffery, *Byng of Vimy: General and Governor General* (London: Leo Cooper, 1983/Pen & Sword Books Ltd)

Williams, S.H., *Stand to Your Horses: Through the First Great War with the Lord Strathcona's Horse* (Altona: D.W. Friesen, 1961)

Winston, John Duke of Marlborough & Fane, William John, *Oxfordshire Militia: Sketch of the History of the Regiment* (Oxford: E.W. Morris Junior, 1869)

Woodward, David, *Lloyd George and his Generals* (London: Taylor & Francis, 2003)

Wyrall, Everard, *The History of the Fiftieth Division 1914-1919* (London: Humphries, 1939)

Wyrall, Everard, *The History of the Nineteenth Division 1914-1918* (London: Arnold, 1932)

Newspapers & Journals

Acadian Recorder, *Morning Chronicle* and *Morning Herald*, Nova Scotia Archives

Barley, Leslie John, 'Soldiering in Peace and War', *The Covenanter*, 1977 & 1978

Bowes, R.L., 'Waiting for "G"' *Canadian Army Journal*

Brigade of Guards Magazine, Various articles

Cork Examiner

Irish Times, Various articles

Jenkins, Stanley, *The Cork and Macroom Railway* (article)

National Rifle Association Journal, Extracts 1927, 1930, 1936 and 1971

The Times

Yea Chronicle

Index

INDEX OF PEOPLE

INDEX OF PLACES

INDEX OF FORMATIONS/UNITS

British/Dominion Brigades

British/Dominion Infantry & Mounted Infantry Units

For abbreviations see List of Abbreviations

German Formations/Units